Hayner Public Library District - Alton
0 00 30 0450013 2

P9-DNU-470

No Longer the Property of
Hayner Public Library District

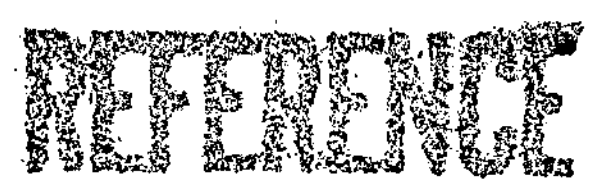
REFERENCE

New Dictionary of Scientific Biography

Published by special arrangement with the American Council of Learned Societies

The American Council of Learned Societies, organized in 1919 for the purpose of advancing the study of the humanities and of the humanistic aspects of the social sciences, is a nonprofit federation comprising thirty-three national scholarly groups. The Council represents the humanities in the United States in the International Union of Academies, provides fellowships and grants-in-aid, supports research-and-planning conferences and symposia, and sponsers special projects and scholarly publications.

MEMBER ORGANIZATIONS

American Philosophical Society, 1743
American Academy of Arts and Sciences, 1780
American Antiquarian Society, 1812
American Oriental Society, 1842
American Numismatic Society, 1858
American Philological Association, 1869
Archaeological Institute of America, 1879
Society of Biblical Literature, 1880
Modern Language Association of America, 1883
American Historical Association, 1884
American Economic Association, 1885
American Folklore Society, 1888
American Society of Church History, 1888
American Dialect Society, 1889
American Psychological Association, 1892
Association of American Law Schools, 1900
American Philosophical Association, 1900
American Schools of Oriental Research, 1900
American Anthropological Association, 1902
American Political Science Association, 1903
Bibliographical Society of America, 1904
Association of American Geographers, 1904
Hispanic Society of America, 1904
American Sociological Association, 1905
American Society of International Law, 1906
Organization of American Historians, 1907
American Academy of Religion, 1909
College Forum of the National Council of Teachers of English, 1911
Society for the Advancement of Scandinavian Study, 1911
College Art Association, 1912
National Communication Association, 1914
History of Science Society, 1924
Linguistic Society of America, 1924
Medieval Academy of America, 1925
American Association for the History of Medicine, 1925
American Musicological Society, 1934
Economic History Association, 1940
Society of Architectural Historians, 1940
Association for Asian Studies, 1941
American Society for Aesthetics, 1942
American Association for the Advancement of Slavic Studies, 1948
American Studies Association, 1950
Metaphysical Society of America, 1950
North American Conference on British Studies, 1950
American Society of Comparative Law, 1951
Renaissance Society of America, 1954
Society for Ethnomusicology, 1955
Society for French Historical Studies, 1956
International Center of Medieval Art, 1956
American Society for Legal History, 1956
American Society for Theatre Research, 1956
African Studies Association, 1957
Society for the History of Technology, 1958
Society for Cinema and Media Studies, 1959
American Comparative Literature Association, 1960
Law and Society Association, 1964
Middle East Studies Association of North America, 1966
Latin American Studies Association, 1966
Association for the Advancement of Baltic Studies, 1968
American Society for Eighteenth Century Studies, 1969
Association for Jewish Studies, 1969
Sixteenth Century Society and Conference, 1970
Society for American Music, 1975
Dictionary Society of North America, 1975
German Studies Association, 1976
American Society for Environmental History, 1976
Society for Music Theory, 1977
National Council on Public History, 1979
Society of Dance History Scholars, 1979

New Dictionary of Scientific Biography

VOLUME 3
FAIREY–HYPATIA

Noretta Koertge
EDITOR IN CHIEF

CHARLES SCRIBNER'S SONS
An imprint of Thomson Gale, a part of The Thomson Corporation

Detroit • New York • San Francisco • New Haven, Conn. • Waterville, Maine • London

HAYNER PUBLIC LIBRARY DISTRICT
ALTON, ILLINOIS

New Dictionary of Scientific Biography

Noretta Koertge

© 2008 Gale Group

Thomson and Star Logo are trademarks and Gale is a registered trademark used herein under license.

For more information, contact:
Gale Group
27500 Drake Rd.
Farmington Hills, MI 48331-3535
Or you can visit our Internet site at
http://www.gale.com

ALL RIGHTS RESERVED
No part of this work covered by the copyright herein may be reproduced or used in any form or by any means—graphic, electronic, or mechanical, including photocopying, recording, taping, Web distribution, or information storage retrieval systems—without the written permission of the publisher.

For permission to use material from the product, submit your request via the Web at http://www.gale-edit.com/permissions, or you may download our Permissions Request form and submit your request by fax or mail to:

Permissions Department
Gale Group
27500 Drake Rd.
Farmington Hills, MI 48331-3535
Permissions Hotline:
248-699-8006 or 800-877-4253, ext. 8006
Fax 248-699-8074 or 800-762-4058

Cover photographs reproduced by permission.

Since this page cannot legibly accommodate all copyright notices, the acknowledgements constitute an extension of the copyright notice.

While every effort has been made to secure permission to reprint material and to ensure the reliability of the information presented in this publication, Gale Group neither guarantees the accuracy of the data contained herein nor assumes any responsibility for errors, omissions, or discrepancies. Gale Group accepts no payment for listing; and inclusion in the publication of any organization, agency, institution, publication, service, or individual does not imply endorsement of the editors or publisher. Errors brought to the attention of the publisher and verified to the satisfaction of the publisher will be corrected in future editions.

EDITORIAL DATA PRIVACY POLICY
Does this publication contain information about you as an individual? If so, for more information about our data privacy policies, please see our Privacy Statement at http://www.gale.com.

LIBRARY OF CONGRESS CATALOGING-IN-PUBLICATION DATA

New dictionary of scientific biography / Noretta Koertge, editor in chief.
p. cm.
Includes bibliographical references and index.
ISBN 978-0-684-31320-7 (set : alk. paper)—ISBN 978-0-684-31321-4 (vol. 1 : alk. paper)—ISBN 978-0-684-31322-1 (vol. 2 : alk. paper)—ISBN 978-0-684-31323-8 (vol. 3 : alk. paper)—ISBN 978-0-684-31324-5 (vol. 4 : alk. paper)—ISBN 978-0-684-31325-2 (vol. 5 : alk. paper)—ISBN 978-0-684-31326-9 (vol. 6 : alk. paper)—ISBN 978-0-684-31327-6 (vol. 7 : alk. paper)—ISBN 978-0-684-31328-3 (vol. 8 : alk. paper)
1. Scientists—Biography—Dictionaries. I. Koertge, Noretta.

Q141.N45 2008
509.2'2—dc22
[B]

2007031384

Editorial Board

EDITOR IN CHIEF

Noretta Koertge
Indiana University, Department of History and Philosophy of Science

ADVISORY COMMITTEE

William Bechtel
James Capshew
David L. Hull
Jane Maienschein
John Norton
Eric R. Scerri
Brian Skyrms
Michael M. Sokal
Spencer Weart

SUBJECT EDITORS

William Bechtel
University of California, San Diego, Department of Philosophy and Science Studies Program
LIFE SCIENCES

Stephen Bocking
Trent University, Ontario, Environmental and Resource Studies Program
ECOLOGY

Theodore Brown
University of Illinois at Urbana-Champaign, Department of Chemistry and Beckman Institute
CHEMISTRY

Richard Burkhardt
University of Illinois at Urbana-Champaign, Department of History
ANIMAL BEHAVIOR

James H. Capshew
Indiana University at Bloomington, Department of History and Philosophy of Science
PSYCHOLOGY

Steven J. Dick
National Aeronautics and Space Administration
SPACE SCIENCE

James Fleming
Colby College, Science, Technology, and Society Program
METEOROLOGY, HYDROLOGY, OCEANOGRAPHY

Gregory A. Good
West Virginia University, Department of History
GEOLOGY AND GEOPHYSICS

Matthew Goodrum
Virginia Tech, Department of Science and Technology in Society
PALEOANTHROPOLOGY

Jeremy Gray
The Open University, United Kingdom, Department of Mathematics
MATHEMATICS AND LOGIC

Valerie Gray Hardcastle
University of Cincinnati, McMicken College of Arts and Sciences
COGNITIVE AND NEUROSCIENCE

Lillian Hoddeson
University of Illiniois at Urbana-Champaign, Department of History
PHYSICS

Editorial Board

Ernst Homburg
Universiteit Maastricht, The Netherlands, Department of History
CHEMISTRY

David L. Hull
Northwestern University, Department of Philosophy
LIFE SCIENCES

Helge Kragh
University of Aarhus, Denmark, Steno Department for Studies of Science and Science Education
COSMOLOGY

Michael S. Mahoney
Princeton University, Department of Computer Science
COMPUTER SCIENCE

Jane Maienschein
Arizona State University, School of Life Sciences, Center for Biology and Society
LIFE SCIENCES

Elizabeth Paris
Independent Scholar
PHYSICS

Carsten Reinhardt
University of Bielefeld, Germany, Institute for Science and Technology Studies
CHEMISTRY

John Rigden
Washington University in St. Louis, Department of Physics
PHYSICS

Robert Smith
University of Alberta, Department of History and Classics
ASTRONOMY AND ASTROPHYSICS

Stephen Weininger
Worcester Polytechnic Institute, Department of Chemistry and Biochemistry
CHEMISTRY

Paul Weirich
University of Missouri-Columbia, Department of Philosophy
DECISION AND GAME THEORY

CONSULTING EDITORS

Garland E. Allen
Washington University, St. Louis, Department of Biology

Domenico Bertoloni Meli
Indiana University, Center for the History of Medicine

Craig Fraser
University of Toronto, Institute for the History and Philosophy of Science and Technology

Alexander Jones
University of Toronto, Department of Classics

William Newman
Indiana University, Department of History and Philosophy of Science

Vivian Nutton
University College London, Wellcome Trust Centre for the History of Medicine

Lynn Nyhart
University of Wisconsin at Madison, Department of the History of Science

Juergen Renn
Max Planck Institute for the History of Science, Berlin

Johannes M. M. H. Thijssen
Radboud University Nijmegen, Faculty of Philosophy

ASSISTANT TO THE EDITOR IN CHIEF

Anne Mylott

Indiana University, Department of History and Philosophy of Science

F

FAIREY, JOHN

SEE **Farey, John.**

FARADAY, MICHAEL

(*b.* Newington Butts, Surrey [now London], England, 22 September 1791, *d.* Hampton Green Court, Middlesex, England, 25 August 1867), *electricity and magnetism, chemistry.* For the original article on Faraday see *DSB,* vol. 4.

Faraday's contributions to electricity and magnetism shaped nineteenth-century physics fundamentally, opened the possibility of a wider use of electric power, and laid the origin of field theory. Both for his contemporaries and for modern science studies, his experimental approach and unorthodox concepts have been challenging. At his time, his fame rested as much on his lecturing and counseling in public service as on his research.

Since the 1980s, Faraday studies have shifted their focus from Faraday's ideas, experimental discoveries, and intellectual influences toward the practice of his life, research, and religion. As a result, a new picture has emerged, and it has become clear that the degree to which Faraday's research was preshaped by philosophical ideas about the nature of matter and force had been considerably overestimated. This update article focuses on how his generation of knowledge—experimental, practical, conceptual, theoretical—was connected to, and shaped by, the other aspects of his life.

Working in the Royal Institution. Faraday's lifelong working site, the Royal Institution of Great Britain, had been founded in 1799 as a philanthropic initiative for improving the scientific education of craftsmen and practitioners, but quickly developed into a meeting point for the middle and upper class. Its finances depended largely on the income of the public lectures it offered, and hence on finding lecturers that attracted a substantial audience. In that respect, Faraday was as great a success as Humphry Davy had been before him. The Friday evening and the Christmas juvenile lecture series (founded in 1826 and 1827, respectively) were essentially his creation and much shaped by him.

Pushed by Davy, and well beyond the needs of lecturing, the Royal Institution had installed a well-equipped laboratory and a library, in a period when the very idea of such laboratories was new and just starting to be realized. The Royal Institution's facility, well apt for cutting-edge research, developed into one of the best-equipped laboratories of the period, competing with places such as the Paris École Polytechnique. Faraday thus had unrestricted access to a unique resource of experimental research, a situation that he himself strongly endorsed and of which he took significant advantage. Both the lecture hall (where he spent much time) and the apartment he shared with his wife Sarah were in the Royal Institution's building, hence he could easily switch between work and home, research and lecturing, at least as long he was not interrupted by one of the many visitors calling for information. Of course, this was not a situation without tensions. Faraday's income at the Royal Institution was certainly not adequate, given the benefits he provided for the institution. However, he lived a modest life, even at the height of his fame, and gave the surplus mostly to charity. Nevertheless, his continued (and well-paid) teaching at the Royal Mili-

Faraday

tary Academy at Woolwich for more than two decades was, among others, a deliberate step to lessen his financial dependence on one single institution with insecure financial standing. Moreover, combining living and work in one and the same house for a whole life was not necessarily a favorable arrangement. That Faraday was able to turn it into great success had also to do with the fact that his life had, besides work, also a second focus: his being part of the Sandemanian community—a life that took place outside the Royal Institution and in which, contrasted to his research and lecturing, Sarah took part equally.

To a far larger extent than hitherto realized, Faraday was active in public service. More than 10 percent of all of his correspondence deals with lighthouses alone, stemming from his work for Trinity House (from 1836 on). He was scientific adviser to the Admiralty, the Home Office, the Board of Trade, the Office of Woods and Forests, and the Board of Ordnance. These projects ranged from a gunpowder factory explosion to conservation issues of works of art. His inquiry into the devastating explosion at Haswell Colliery (1844) was a key event in the relationship of science and politics and in labor history—it is cited by Friedrich Engels for example.

The situation at the Royal Institution (which he himself had considerably shaped and stabilized), his enormous success as a public lecturer and scientific advisor, and his religious life combined to form a peculiar and very specific constellation—a constellation that gave him much inner and outer stability and relieved him to a considerable degree from the compulsion of scientific competition. This was an important element of his capacity to pursue his own ideas and conceptualizations, even through long periods of nonresponse or rejection from the academic environment.

Michael Faraday. *Michael Faraday, circa 1865.* HULTON ARCHIVE/GETTY IMAGES.

Experimenting. Faraday is most known as an experimenter. Indeed, those achievements that made him famous in his time rely on experiments, be it electromagnetic rotation (1821), the liquefaction of gases (1823), the discovery of benzene (1825), electromagnetic induction (1831), the identity of various electricities (1833), the laws of electrolysis (1834), the magneto-optical effect (1845), or diamagnetism (1845–1846). Contrasting to the older picture of Faraday's experiments being guided by speculative views on matter and force, new studies of his experimental practice by David Gooding, Friedrich Steinle, and Ryan D. Tweney have drawn quite a different picture. The core of his experimental approach was never individual, single experiments but always extended experimental series—a point that is easily eclipsed when focusing on his prominent discoveries. But these discoveries are only understandable as outcomes of those experimental series. The main experimental procedure was a systematic variation of experimental parameters, with the goal of finding constant correlations and establishing laws. Explaining a specific effect meant to him, first of all, placing it in a wider surrounding of related effects, then "deducing" one from another by building a chain of experimental phenomena, or, as he said, "putting facts closely together." Sometimes this required framing new concepts, or transferring existing ones into a totally new context, as in the case of magnetic curves.

Faraday had a laboratory assistant, the former Sergeant Charles Anderson, but it seems that in his considerations about the meaning and ordering of experimental results, and the planning of further experiments, he worked essentially alone. When other scientists visited him in the laboratory, he would show them his ready results, but not discuss ongoing research—the same holds for his well-documented and extensive correspondence.

Faraday's experimental approach was intimately linked to his practice of record keeping. He probably put down notes right in the laboratory, but edited them in clear writing afterward (typically on a daily basis), numbered each entry for later reference, and eventually bound

Faraday

these notes into books. In composing his papers for publication, he would often take directly the wording and the figures of his notebook. As the number of experiments increased greatly over the years, he started to work on indices and superindices to enable later retrieval. And even in later years he would still come back to experiments made more than a decade earlier. Such a conscious dealing with enormous amounts of experimental records was extraordinary at his time; see, for example, the contrasting case of Ampère.

Theorizing. Faraday's success as an experimentalist has long overshadowed his efforts and achievements in theorizing and conceptualizing. But his work was at least as strongly focused on understanding and ordering experimental outcomes as on obtaining new experimental effects. His approach focused more on formulating laws and on fundamental concepts than on searching for hidden entities that would provide causal explanations. More than others, he was ready to question fundamental concepts, such as electric current, electric attraction, and magnetic polarity, and to propose new concepts, such as electromagnetic rotation as an elementary effect, magnetic and electric curves (later to be renamed *lines of force*), specific capacity, dia- and paramagnetism, and of course electric and magnetic fields. In some cases he consulted other scholars (most notably William Whewell) for appropriate words in order to keep the new concepts as neutral as possible with respect to explanatory theories. Only when a firm experimental and conceptual foundation was achieved, was he ready to put real effort into the question of hidden causes, such as the theory of electrolysis or of polarization.

The concepts thus created were "empirically saturated," in the sense that Faraday formed and developed them with an ever-growing body of experimental results in mind, for which they should enable a formulation of regularities and laws. In face of new experimental evidence, he was ready to a very high degree to revise and refine those concepts again and again, with the result that in the end they found a very precise formulation, though not in mathematical language. That he was able to form such unconventional concepts at all had to do with his noncommitment to any established school of physical thinking, and with his deep feeling of the responsibility to fit his concepts to nature. At the same time, it was exactly this character of the concepts that made them appear weird for most of his contemporaries, because they did not resonate with the established body of knowledge of the period.

Ever since his first use of "magnetic curves" in 1831 for the induction law, he emphasized he was not claiming physical reality of these curves, but rather was using them

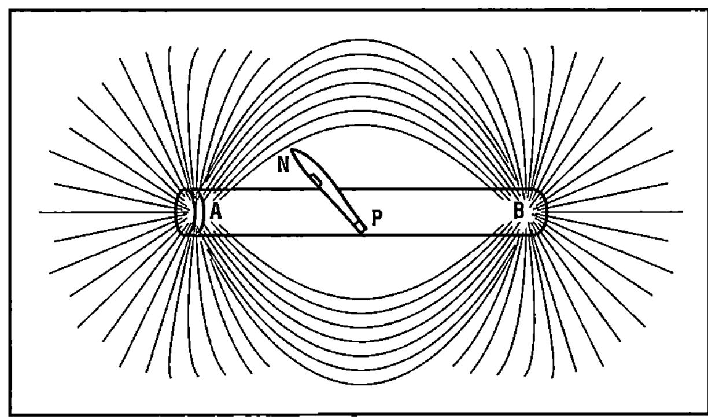

Figure 1. *To grasp the results of his numerous induction experiments (1831/32) in a law, Faraday used "magnetic curves" as a refererence frame. Despite his own success in formulating a law, the concept came to visibility only in the 1860s when Maxwell gave those "lines of force" a mathematical form.*

as a convenient tool to express the spatial distribution of magnetic force. Rather than being an "embarrassment" for Faraday, as Leslie Pearce Williams suggests in the original *DSB* article, this peculiar status of lines of force lay at the core of his approach. Faraday kept that cautious attitude for decades, even when conceiving the curves as movable (1832), introducing electric lines of force (1838), formulating diamagnetic behavior in terms of lines of force (1848), or finally developing a general theory of magnetism in terms of lines of force (1850). Only in 1851, at a stage when he oversaw a huge domain of electromagnetic effects, did he drop his reluctance and state that there probably was more to lines of force than just being descriptive tools: their successful application comprised much wider realms than any other concept of electrodynamics.

Religion. Throughout his life, and while living in the Royal Institution's building, Faraday kept apart his professional and private life. The latter was most intensely shaped by his adherence to the Sandemanian sect, a strict religious group that comprised not more than four hundred members in England and Scotland in his time. Faraday's confession of faith in 1821 was certainly one of the most important moments of his life. Like all members of that community, Faraday spent much time and effort with services, gatherings, and duties such as caring for the sick or preaching, often outside London. His important social connections were more or less completely located within the community and formed strong ties. It is indicative, for example, that while he generally refused to write support letters for anyone for positions, he deviated from this rule in the case of Sandemanian brethren. His funeral, on his own wish, and despite his wide fame, took place only within a small circle of Sandemanians.

Faraday

Both his personal faith and the Sandemanian community life gave Faraday a considerable degree of personal stability. Correspondingly, however, instabilities within the Sandemanian community (such as his temporary exclusion in 1844) affected him profoundly and made him existentially suffer, in sharp contrast to problems and lack of resonance in his scientific surroundings. Moreover, his religion provided him with a specific attitude toward researching nature. In his 1854 lecture "Mental Education," he emphasized the importance of humility in the face of God's creation. The extraordinary degree to which he kept his concepts and theoretical ideas open for revision by further experience (dubbed "Negative capability" by Elspeth Crawford), and also his persistence in keeping his unconventional ideas, can well be understood as his own way of realizing that virtue.

Impact. Faraday's impact on research in electrodynamics (and physics in general) was immense. From 1830 on, he was the one to put challenges and create the "hot topics" in electrodynamics for two and a half decades: rotation, induction, specific capacity, magneto-optical effect, diamagnetism, and lines of force. The continuing series of Faraday's papers was translated into various languages on a regular basis. However, the reception was split in a characteristic way: While his experimental results were highly praised, his conceptual approach met with silence or criticism. This had partly to do with his total lack of mathematical education in a period when physics became strongly mathematized and partly with his uneasy way of presenting his results, switching between meticulous experimental descriptions and general considerations. The largest obstacle, however, was the unconventional character of some of his new concepts. Wilhelm Weber, for example, in his 1845 *Maassbestimmungen*, mentioned Faraday as a gifted experimentalist and discoverer of the induction effect, but found there was no law of induction. Obviously he did not regard Faraday's induction law of 1832 as something to be considered seriously—it was formulated in terms of magnetic curves and hence probably too far from anything a physicist of the time could deal with.

The second half of the century saw the development of field-theory in mathematical form. It is important to note that what James Clerk Maxwell set out to mathematize was not specific effects, domains, or laws, but the *concept* of lines of force, as he took it from Faraday. The striking historical observation that Maxwell's success in mathematizing the concept provided a comprehensive theory of a vast range of electrodynamic effects, without having discussed that variety of effects in detail, can be understood just by highlighting the "empirically saturated" and highly precise character of Faraday's concepts.

A third aspect of Faraday's impact has received less attention. While Faraday never formulated anything like a methodology, his peculiar approach was quite visible and would eventually become subject of methodological considerations. The growing insight into the inadequacy of the search for the "hidden levers and screws" of nature during the last decades of the nineteenth century was in part stimulated by the complex dispute of Weberian, Neumannian, and Faraday-Maxwellian electrodynamics. A major exponent of that changing ideal of knowledge, Hermann von Helmholtz, explicitly attributed his own turn away from the search for hidden mechanisms to his reading of Faraday. Even in recent attempts to widen the understanding of experimental practice in general, Faraday figures as a prominent example and unique resource because of his peculiar productivity, the unique availability of sources that enable insight into his everyday practice, and the specific experimental approach that does not fit the standard view of experiment.

SUPPLEMENTARY BIBLIOGRAPHY

The Royal Institution of Great Britain, the Royal Society, the Guildhall Library, and the Institution of Engineering and Technology keep much archival material (manuscripts, lecture notes, and so forth), all of which has been microfilmed and stored on compact disc, available from Microform Academic, Wakefield, United Kingdom.

WORKS BY FARADAY

Faraday's Diary: Being the Various Philosophical Notes of Experimental Investigation Made by Michael Faraday during the Years 1820–1862 and Bequeathed by Him to the Royal Institution of Great Britain. Edited by Thomas Martin. London: G. Bell, 1932–1936.

Experimental Researches in Electricity. New York: Dover, 1965. Originally published 1839–1855.

Experimental Researches in Chemistry and Physics. London: Taylor & Francis, 1991. Originally published in 1859.

The Correspondence of Michael Faraday. 4 vols. Edited by Frank A. J. L. James. London: Institution of Electrical Engineers, 1991–. Complete edition, with excellent comments and introduction.

Curiosity Perfectly Satisfyed: Faraday's Travels in Europe 1813–1815. Edited by Brian Bowers and Lenore Symons. IEE History of Technology Series, 16. London: Peter Peregrinus, 1991. Faraday's notebook of the "Continental Tour."

Michael Faraday's "Chemical Notes, Hints, Suggestions and Objects of Pursuit" of 1822. Edited by Ryan D. Tweney and David Gooding. IEE History of Technology Series, 17. London: Peter Peregrinus, 1991.

OTHER SOURCES

Berman, Morris. *Social Change and Scientific Organization: The Royal Institution, 1799–1844.* Ithaca, NY: Cornell University Press, 1978.

Cantor, Geoffrey N. *Michael Faraday: Sandemanian and Scientist; A Study of Science and Religion in the Nineteenth Century.* Basingstoke, U.K.: Macmillan, 1991.

———. "The Scientist as Hero: Public Images of Michael Faraday." In *Telling Lives in Science: Essays on Scientific Biography,* edited by Michael Shortland and Richard Yeo. Cambridge, U.K.: Cambridge University Press, 1996.

Cantor, Geoffrey N., David Gooding, and Frank A. J. L. James. *Faraday.* London: Macmillan, 1991.

Caroe, Gwendy M. *The Royal Institution: An Informal History.* London: John Murray, 1985.

Cavicchi, Elizabeth. "Experimenting with Magnetism: Ways of Learning of Joann and Faraday." *American Journal of Physics* 65, no. 9 (1997): 867–882.

Crawford, Elspeth. "Learning from Experience." In *Faraday Rediscovered: Essays on the Life and Work of Michael Faraday, 1791–1867,* edited by David Gooding and Frank A. J. L. James. Basingstoke, U.K.: Macmillan; New York: Stockton, 1985.

Forgan, Sophie. "Faraday—From Servant to Savant: The Institutional Context." In *Faraday Rediscovered: Essays on the Life and Work of Michael Faraday, 1791–1867,* edited by David Gooding and Frank A. J. L. James. Basingstoke, U.K.: Macmillan; New York: Stockton, 1985.

Gooding, David. *Experiment and the Making of Meaning: Human Agency in Scientific Observation and Experiment.* Dordrecht: Kluwer, 1990.

——— and Frank A. J. L. James, eds. *Faraday Rediscovered: Essays on the Life and Work of Michael Faraday, 1791–1867.* Basingstoke, U.K.: Macmillan; New York: Stockton, 1985.

James, Frank A. J. L. "Michael Faraday and Lighthouses." In *The Golden Age: Essays in British Social and Economic History, 1850–1870,* edited by Ian Inkster with Colin Griffin, Jeff Hill, and Judith Rowbotham. Aldershot, U.K.: Ashgate, 2000.

———. "Running the Royal Institution: Faraday as an Administrator." In *The Common Purposes of Life: Science and Society at the Royal Institution of Great Britain,* edited by Frank A. J. L. James. Aldershot, U.K.: Ashgate, 2002.

——— and Margaret Ray. "Science in the Pits: Michael Faraday, Charles Lyell, and the Home Office Enquiry into the Explosion at Haswell Colliery, County Durham, in 1844." *History and Technology* 15 (1999): 213–231.

Nersessian, Nancy J. *Faraday to Einstein: Constructing Meaning in Scientific Theories.* Science and Philosophy. Dordrecht: Nijhoff, 1984.

Steinle, Friedrich. "Entering New Fields: Exploratory Uses of Experimentation." *Philosophy of Science* 64, Supplement (1997): S65–S74.

———. "The Practice of Studying Practice: Analyzing Research Records of Ampère and Faraday." In *Reworking the Bench: Research Notebooks in the History of Science,* edited by Frederic Lawrence Holmes, Jürgen Renn, and Hans-Jörg Rheinberger. Archimedes 7. Dordrecht: Kluwer, 2003.

———. *Explorative Experimente: Ampère, Faraday und die Ursprünge der Elektrodynamik.* Boethius 50. Stuttgart: Steiner, 2005.

Tweney, Ryan D. "Faraday's Notebooks: The Active Organization of Creative Science." *Physics Education* 26 (1991): 301–306.

———. "Discovering Discovery: How Faraday Found the First Metallic Colloid." *Perspectives on Science* 14, no. 1 (2006): 97–121.

Friedrich Steinle

FAREY, JOHN (*b.* Woburn, Bedfordshire, United Kingdom, 24 September 1766, *d.* London, United Kingdom, 6 January 1826), *geology, music, mathematics.* For the original article on Farey see *DSB,* vol. 4.

Farey has left a difficult legacy for those who follow him. First, he was a true polymath. His initial training was as a land surveyor. But from 1803, he pursued the entirely new profession of mineral surveyor (a term Farey invented in that decade). Farey also made significant contributions as an engineer, mathematician, musician, and geologist. Anyone trying to investigate him in the early twenty-first century should be impossibly as polymathic as he was; this has certainly not been the case in mathematics. Here, the famous, misinformed assessment of 1940, by the academic Godfrey Harold Hardy, was that "Farey is immortal [only] because he failed to understand a theorem which Haros had proved perfectly fourteen years before" (Hardy, 1940, pp. 21–22). Second, unlike Charles Darwin (to give only one famous example), Farey failed to leave any significant personal archives after his death, and thus all explorations of Farey's multiplicity of activities (and frustrations) have been made much more difficult. Another important consideration, within the worlds that Farey occupied, was that he was dependent on commissions. As he wrote in 1816, "my circumstances in life, and the state of the Times, less and less permit my indulging in any pursuits which do not make some return towards the support of my family. For several years past Mineral Surveying & Engineery have been my only dependance & source of Profit (except now and then writing a little for the periodical press and a trifle from the Smithfield Club)" (Farey, 1816). Farey had been appointed to the Smithfield Club in 1806, as paid secretary (£30 per year) and, from 1815, additionally as treasurer (£40 per year). He never enjoyed any regular salary or academic support.

Early Years and Interests. Farey was born on a farm of the fourth Duke of Bedford, tenanted by his parents, John Farey (1728–1798) and his second wife, Rachel Wright (1732–1804), who was a Wesleyan Methodist. After normal village schooling, Farey was sent in 1782 to the academy run by Robert Pullman in Halifax, Yorkshire. Farey studied drawing and surveying under this "studious man and good mathematician," who gave him "gratuitous instruction in mathematics and [natural] philosophy" and brought him to the attention of engineer John Smeaton. By 1785, Farey was based in London. This training stimulated Farey's first interest, in mathematics, which remained a hobby throughout his life. Between at least 1797 and 1811, Farey contributed many mathematical propositions and answers to journals such as the *Gentleman's Diary, Gentleman's Mathematical Companion,* and *Leybourn's Mathematical Repository.*

On 10 May 1790, Farey married Sophia Hubert (1770–1830) at St. Pancras Church, London. Both Fareys were soon also active as musicians, John as a tenor and Sophia as a soprano, in the Choral Fund, Cecilian Society, Surrey Chapel Society, and in singing oratorios at Drury Lane. John was also the first secretary and librarian to the Choral Fund, founded in 1791, "for the relief of decayed musicians, their widows and orphans" (Choral Fund, 1807). He soon became the country's expert on the theory of musical intervals, work that used his mathematical abilities. These musical interests arose directly from his mathematical work. Farey achieved a homonymous fame in mathematics in 1816, with his publication on "a curious property of vulgar fractions," soon named Farey Numbers. Using the continued fractions methods that he had established for his musical work, Farey showed the properties of such fractions when arranged in order. The fifth Farey series was, for example:

$$\frac{1}{5}\ \frac{1}{4}\ \frac{1}{3}\ \frac{2}{5}\ \frac{1}{2}\ \frac{3}{5}\ \frac{2}{3}\ \frac{3}{4}\ \frac{4}{5}$$

Such series proved to have many interesting arithmetical properties, because, if a / c and b / d are consecutive fractions in such a series, then the multiplied products $a \times d$ and $b \times c$ prove consecutive integers. They are best expressed graphically by Ford Circles. Farey, although the first to bring such properties to public attention, was not the first to recognize them, and lacking financial support, he never offered any proof. Further study of his mathematical work may reveal more.

Farey and Geology. In 1792, Farey was appointed, by Francis Russell, fifth Duke of Bedford, as land steward to Russell's extensive Bedfordshire estates. He thus returned to his birthplace and threw himself into the practice and study of agriculture. At the 1798 Woburn sheep shearing, Farey first met his future patron Sir Joseph Banks, president of the Royal Society, and showed Banks his work on improving the drainage at Woburn, which had first been planned by Joseph Elkington. Farey was encouraged by the duke to study methods of drainage. Another figure who was involved in trying to correct the drainage problems at Woburn, which Elkington had failed to master, was, from July 1801, the land and mineral surveyor and engineer William Smith, who was later called the "father of modern English geology." Farey and Smith met in October 1801; they went on tour together late in 1801 and again early in 1802, along with Farey's friend and fellow mathematician, the local Leighton Buzzard brewer and later engineer, Benjamin Bevan (1773–1833), of the Bevan Point in geometry. This was an 80 kilometer (50 mile) round trip to investigate the local strata. Smith had already realized from 1795 around Bath, Somerset, that such strata could be ordered in sequence and then identified from the fossils they often contained.

A first outcome of this connection was the support Farey and Bevan both gave to the suggestion, in April 1803, that a new society be formed to gather "scientific information." Bevan immediately supported this, and hoped it might foster relations with other existing organizations, such as the British Mineralogical Society, the London Philosophical Society, or the Royal Institution. Farey joined the debate in November 1803, writing to the *Monthly Magazine's* publisher, Richard Phillips, asking to be placed on the list of correspondents "as an enquirer in the subjects of Agriculture, Mechanics, Mineralogy, Meteorology, to which I would add, should the Society embrace those objects, Geology, Engineering, Mathematics, Music (theory of its intervals), Rural Improvements and Stewardship of Estates." That no more was heard of this society was only one result of the appalling political situation in Britain, after the Peace of Amiens had collapsed, in 1803. This is a reminder that the critical years of Farey's several careers were during Napoleonic wartime, when international scientific communications suffered badly and there were national economic difficulties that caused Farey, and Smith, real financial problems.

Farey had been studying geology before he met Smith, but he was now so impressed by both the novelty and importance of Smith's knowledge of stratification and how fossils could be used that he wrote at length to Banks, reporting on Smith's discoveries in February 1802. But on 2 March 1802, his patron the Duke of Bedford died. This proved a most "severe blow to Smith [and Farey]'s prosperity." The duke's brother, John (1766–1839), who inherited his enormous estates, dismissed Farey in June, after nearly ten years service, during which £717,800 had passed through Farey's agency in more than half a million transactions.

New Employment. Farey suddenly had to find new employment. His first thought was to take up farming, but instead he settled at 12 Crown Street, Westminster, London, earning his living as a land surveyor and as a pioneering mineral surveyor. In 1805, Farey started as a frequent, if anonymous, contributor to Abraham Rees's important *Cyclopaedia*, on "canals, geology, measures, music and trigonometrical survey." In 1806, he started another long series of publications on music, becoming an enthusiastic advocate of equal temperament tuning, using instruments on which such alternative temperaments could be demonstrated. In 1811, after a dispute with Rees about his geological contributions, he stopped writing for him, even on music, at the end of the volume I/J. Farey was replaced on geology by the German-born and Wernerian-influenced curator at the British Museum, Charles Koenig. Farey's musical work for Rees had comprised all the more theoretical and mathematical articles dealing with temperaments, tuning, and harmonics. Farey was soon active again, between 1810 and 1819, as a contributor to the rival *Edinburgh Encylopaedia*, again largely contributing on music.

In 1804, Farey and Smith together attended the Woburn sheep shearing, at which Banks opened a subscription to support the publication of Smith's planned geological map, or *Delineation of the Strata of England and Wales*. By May 1806, Banks wanted this completed, so Farey, while reporting this to Smith, threw his energies into encouraging and publicizing Smith's geological results, and demonstrating their importance, in the *Monthly Magazine* and *Philosophical Magazine*, and William Nicholson's *Journal*. Banks now commissioned Farey to prepare a stratigraphic cross section between London and Brighton. Farey's brother conveniently worked in Sussex at the time. In September 1806, Farey visited trials to find coal being made at Bexhill, Sussex, by the later railway pioneer William James and immediately realized the impossibility of their success, like those of the many other searches then being made for wartime coal in such impossible stratigraphic situations. Farey tried unsuccessfully to point out the enormous sums of money that such trials must waste. By early 1807, this enormous section was finished. His was the first detailed cross section to be prepared in England, and it correctly showed for the first time the denuded, anticlinal or "strata-ridged" (as Farey called it), structure of the Weald. Farey prepared several other stratigraphic sections across many other parts of England, but all remained unpublished in his lifetime.

Derbyshire Commissions. The year 1807 brought Farey two new commissions, in Derbyshire, to the even more peripatetic Smith's great frustration, who was hoping such commissions would come to him. Farey now also advertised his services as a "mineralogical surveyor," for, as Banks wrote to France in 1811, "we have now some Practical men well versd in stratification who undertake to examine the subterranean Geography of Gentlemens Estates in order to discover the Fossils likely to be useful for Manure, for fuel etc." [De Beer, 1960, p. 191]. The first task was to survey the county for Sir John Sinclair's Board of Agriculture. The result was Farey's best-known work, his detailed, three-volume *General View of the Agriculture and Minerals of Derbyshire* (1811–1817). This work includes a pioneering analysis of the geometry of faulting and an early discussion of English strata. The other commission, privately for Banks, was a detailed geological survey of Banks's own mineral-rich Overton estate, near Ashover. This was finished by 1812, but plans to publish it in the *Transactions of the Geological Society of London* were aborted in 1813 when it was found too minute and detailed. Many in that society still remained to be persuaded of the reliability and novelty of Smith's and Farey's methods. But enough fragments of Farey's Ashover survey have survived, in the Sutro Library, San Francisco, California, to demonstrate how extraordinarily advanced his geological field mapping skills then were. It has been rightly said of this map, "if one did not know the date, one might easily suppose by its appearance that the map was a late nineteenth-century production" (Oldroyd, 1996, p. 114).

Last Years. Farey became a leader in the new field of mineral surveying and was active all over the British Isles, preparing reports on Yorkshire alum and coal, Edinburgh water, Borrowdale graphite, North Wales slates, and coal throughout Scotland and the Welsh borders. In 1814, he raised his charges from 2 to 3 guineas per day, plus expenses. But he was never able to publish these private *Reports*, which he had gathered with this intention. They remained in manuscript and were as of 2007 mostly lost. The end of the Napoleonic Wars immediately had a devastating effect on such commissions and on sales of Smith's map published at last in 1815. Smith was rewarded with time in a debtors' prison in 1819, and, by 1824, Farey was reduced to offering himself as copyist to the Sowerbys, a family of natural history authors and publishers, at one shilling per hour.

Up to 1813, Farey had given inadvertent but vital help to the Geological Society's rival *Geological Map*, published in 1820, five years after Smith's. Farey was subsequently ostracized by this society (of which neither he, nor Smith, were ever elected members), despite W. H. Fitton's attempted mediation in 1817–1818, and so, by 1822, Farey could refer to the society as "the Anti-Smithian Association." Farey had been unjustly marginalized by the ruling elite of English geology (based at the newly founded [1807] and gentlemanly Geological Society of London) from 1811, when his writing for Rees's *Cyclopaedia* was terminated. Many of Farey's papers had now to be published under the cloak of anonymity as by "A Constant Reader." Nevertheless, Farey continued to publish to an extraordinary extent. More than 270 items have come to be identified, over an amazing range of subjects, also including astronomy (long another interest), engineering, politics, and pacifism. They range from supporting Thomas Malthus in 1804, urging that English currency be decimalized in 1817, to leading the campaign against counterfeiters of Bank of England notes (*Times*, 21 April 1820, p. 3).

Farey's many geological writings provide a fine view of the highly political battles then raging between the gentlemanly geologists of the Geological Society and the working practitioners, such as himself and Smith. Farey rightly felt that the latter had made much the most important contribution to the task of unravelling British strata. Farey died, following a stroke, at 37 Howland Street, London, where he had moved early in 1816; he was buried in St. James Church, St. Pancras. His widow, Sophia, tried in vain to sell his enormous geological collections to an uninterested British Museum in 1828, but these, like his extensive manuscript collections, afterward disappeared. Their eldest son, John Farey (1791–1851), built a reputation as one of the finest consulting engineers in England, while others of the Fareys' seven surviving children emigrated to France and the United States.

Conclusion. Farey was a man of enormous industry and of high principles, always determined to give credit where he thought it due (as to William Smith) but equally ready to deny it (as to road maker J. L. McAdam, whom he thought unoriginal). Farey was one of the first to claim that geological knowledge was of real economic importance in Britain's rapid industrialization and to demonstrate how such knowledge could and should be applied. But in such a laissez-faire and war-torn society, getting that message heard had proved a very difficult task.

BIBLIOGRAPHY

WORKS BY FAREY

Letter to Richard Phillips, November 1803. David Williams archive, Cornwall, U.K.

General View of the Agriculture and Minerals of Derbyshire. London: B. McMillan, 1811–1817.

Letter to John Baker Holroyd, May 1816. East Sussex Record Office, Lewes, U.K.

Letter to James Sowerby, May 1822. Smithsonian Institution, Washington, DC.

OTHER SOURCES

[Anonymous]. "Society for Scientific Information." *Monthly Magazine* 15 (1803): 531; 16, no. 4 (1803): 232–233.

[Anonymous]. "Rees's *Cyclopaedia*." *Philosophical Magazine* 56 (1820): 219.

Banks, R. E. R., et al., eds. *Sir Joseph Banks: A Global Perspective.* Kew, U.K.: Royal Botanic Gardens, 1994.

Choral Fund. *Laws … of the Choral Fund instituted … 1791.* London: Plummer (Library of Congress), 1807.

Conway, John H., and Richard K. Guy *The Book of Numbers.* New York: Springer, 1996.

De Beer, Gavin. *The Sciences Were Never at War.* London: Nelson, 1960.

Eyles, J. M. "William Smith, Sir Joseph Banks and the French Geologists." In *From Linnaeus to Darwin: Commentaries on the History of Biology and Geology,* edited by Alwyne Wheeler and James H. Price. London: Society for the History of Natural History, 1985.

Ford, T. D. "The First Detailed Geological Sections across England by John Farey 1806–1808." *Mercian Geologist* 2 (1967): 41–49.

Hardy, G(odfrey) H(arold). *A Mathematician's Apology.* Cambridge, U.K.: Cambridge University Press, 1940.

Kassler, Jamie Croy. *The Science of Music in Britain, 1714–1830.* New York and London: Garland Publishing, 1979.

Obituary. *Monthly Magazine,* n.s. 1, (1826): 430–431.

Oldroyd, David. *Thinking about the Earth.* London: Athlone, 1996.

Torrens, Hugh S. "Timeless Order: William Smith (1769–1839) and the Search for Raw Materials 1800–1820." In *The Age of the Earth from 4004 BC to AD 2002,* edited by Cherry L. E. Lewis and Simon J. Knell. London: Geological Society, 2001. Provides a full bibliography of his published writings as then known.

———. *The Practice of British Geology, 1750–1850.* Aldershot, U.K.: Ashgate, 2002. Chapter 6, Farey biography and bibliography.

———. "The Life and Times of Hastings Elwin or Elwyn (1777–1852)." *Geological Curator* 8 (2005): 141–168.

Vignoles, P. J. "Geological Reminiscences." *Temple Bar* 91 (1891): 551–566.

Hugh S. Torrens

FEDOROV, KONSTANTIN NIKOLAYEVICH

(*b.* Leningrad, Russia, 17 December 1927; *d.* Moscow, Russia, 21 September 1988), *physical oceanography, oceanology.*

Fedorov was a leading Soviet physical oceanographer (Russians use the term oceanologist) who took part in a number of major expeditions and contributed to the growing field of micro-oceanography and the study of oceanic fronts. He also became known to scientists outside of the Soviet Union through his leadership role in the Intergovernmental Oceanographic Commission, and his presidency of the Scientific Committee on Oceanic Research. Fedorov led much of the Russian work on satellite oceanography and used satellite images of floating ice to identify major eddy patterns in the ocean.

Background and Training. Fedorov's parents both took an interest in science and technology, and he probably inherited his gift for languages from his maternal grandfather. His father, Nikolai Fedorov, was an electrical engineer. His mother, Aleksandra Konstantinovna Fedorova-Grot, became a leading historian of physiology. She was the daughter of Iakov Karl Grot, a renowned philologist who had written the standard textbook on the Russian language prior to the Bolshevik Revolution.

Fedorov's teenage years coincided with World War II. He was evacuated to Kirov Oblast, and he planned to work in aviation. He enrolled in the Kazan Aviation Technicum in 1943, and after the war he pursued these studies closer to home at the Leningrad Aviation Instruments Technicum. During these years he took an interest in the scientific aspects of aviation, including meteorology, and soon moved to hydrometeorology. After studying oceanological engineering at the Leningrad Advanced Naval School of the Arctic for several years, in 1953 he joined the graduate program at the Shirshov Institute of Oceanology. Established in 1941, this institute was part of the USSR Academy of Sciences and had developed from Russian studies of Arctic oceanic conditions. It was named for its first director, P. P. Shirshov, who died the same year that Fedorov became a graduate student.

At the Shirshov Institute, Fedorov was able to take part in some of the Soviet Union's most important oceanographic expeditions. During the International Geophysical Year of 1957–1958, for example, Fedorov was part of the *Vityaz*'s scientific crew. In 1959, he took part in the *Akademik S. Vavilov*'s scientific cruise in the Mediterranean.

Vladimir B. Shtokman, Fedorov's mentor at the institute, had a lasting impact on Fedorov's scientific life. One of Shtokman's goals was to transform physical oceanography from a descriptive exercise to an analytical and mathematical one, to make it more of an exact discipline and a worthy subset of geophysics. Colleagues later recalled how Fedorov implored others to ask questions of the ocean, rather than just describe its properties, an attitude that perhaps came from Shtokman (later it would be reinforced by American colleague Roger Revelle, who argued along similar lines in international meetings). Shtokman trained several of Soviet oceanography's leading figures, including Fedorov, who wrote a candidate dissertation that integrated some of the theoretical ideas of ocean currents with practical applications. This work won him a prize from the academy's Presidium, and he soon won an award from the United Nations Educational, Scientific, and Cultural Organization (UNESCO) to study with oceanographers in England (1958–1959).

Years at UNESCO. Fedorov began a longer stint under UNESCO when it created the Intergovernmental Oceanographic Commission in 1960. Designed to organize and manage international scientific cooperation, the IOC tried to blend scientific expertise with intergovernmental politics. The IOC's first secretary was an American, Warren Wooster, and Fedorov became deputy secretary. Although Wooster and Fedorov had a good working relationship, the IOC's early years were marred by political sparring and competing scientific programs, particularly between American and Soviet delegations. These were tense years for the United States, the Soviet Union, and the world, with many geopolitical crises that undoubtedly strained relations between colleagues in international settings. It was a difficult period for Fedorov, whose scientific attitude about asking questions of the sea occasionally did not fit with his own delegation's proposals. Oceanographers from the United States and Britain criticized Soviet proposals as too descriptive and huge in scope, evidence that they paid more attention to size than scientific substance. Fedorov and others believed that this was a natural result of the IOC's policy of asking nations for proposals rather than asking oceanographers to agree on the scientific merits beforehand.

Fedorov became the IOC's secretary in 1963, which automatically made him the director of UNESCO's Office of Oceanography, raising his stature and responsibilities in the organization. He helped to coordinate international projects in the Indian Ocean, the Mediterranean, the tropical Atlantic, and on the Kuroshio Current in the Pacific, to name just a few. The stakes were very high for the Soviet Union, politically and scientifically, because oceanography was one of the few areas in which scientists were cooperating across national lines on specific projects. Fedorov also helped to organize the Second International Oceanographic Congress, which was held in Moscow in 1966. This was no easy task, as there were a number of political conflicts about UNESCO's role in convening or organizing such a congress with the Soviet Union as a host state, because the Soviet government refused to follow UNESCO's own standards, especially in areas of language interpretation and visas for participants. Still, Fedorov tried to ease the relationship between UNESCO and the Soviet organizers, though he could not have single-handedly erased the many political problems of the time. At the closing ceremony, Fedorov addressed his fellow scientists and said that he personally believed there were more ways to cooperate between nations than by launching large-scale surveys. Perhaps this reassured scientists in the West who criticized the Soviets' emphasis on descriptive oceanography, but it also reflected his longstanding belief that scientists should ask questions of the sea rather than only gather data.

Thermohaline Finestructures. Despite his obvious standing in international oceanographic circles, Fedorov had yet to establish his scientific reputation. In fact, he still did not have his doctorate in oceanology. But in 1965, he took part in an expedition aboard the American ship *Atlantis II,* which resulted in some collaborative work in the Indian Ocean with the eminent American physical oceanographer Henry Stommel. It was an opportune time for Fedorov to work with a leading western scientist, because the International Indian Ocean Expedition was in its final stages, and the whole project was coordinated by Fedorov's office at the IOC. This expedition brought the world's oceanographers to the Indian Ocean to do research to help the surrounding countries developing their fishing industries and scientific capabilities. Stommel was best known for his work on ocean circulation and the interaction of water masses. Together, Fedorov and Stommel began to work on the dynamics of the ocean in a different way, by focusing on much smaller water structures.

In describing the genesis of this research, Fedorov blamed the reversing thermometer, a standard oceanographic instrument invented in the 1870s by Henry (Enrico) Negretti and Joseph Warren Zambra, for contributing to the conservative ideas about the ocean's structure. Although this instrument revolutionized the study of the seas by allowing the study of temperature in deep water, it had some drawbacks. In particular, Fedorov claimed, it gave the illusion of a smooth transition to colder water at greater depths, without abrupt changes in temperature. Not only was this idea incorrect, Fedorov pointed out, but its wide acceptance among oceanographers gave a misleading impression of the rate of mixing in the ocean. Newer instruments coming into use at midcentury, especially Athelstan Spilhaus's bathythermograph, allowed for continuous or high sampling rates, and gave a different picture—the ocean consisted of distinct layers characterized by differences in temperature, salinity, and other properties. Fedorov and Stommel argued that the ocean was stratified to an extraordinary extent, with thin yet distinct thermal layers.

Fedorov built upon this work and conducted further observations when he finished his work at the IOC and could return to the Soviet Union. He used the first Soviet-manufactured STD (salinity, temperature, density) probes to continue the work begun with Stommel. This resulted finally in his doctoral dissertation, defended in 1973.

The eventual acceptance of this new view of the ocean's structure, Fedorov readily admitted, owed a great deal to the desire to achieve specific objectives. For example, the layering of the ocean disrupted the effectiveness of sound transmission underwater, so the navies in the United States and Soviet Union had every reason to try to understand these structures. Previously heterogenous masses of water were considered instrument errors, not indicators of changes in structure. Now it became a major field, sometimes called micro-oceanography, or oceanic microstructure. The very thin layers that occupied Fedorov's attention were called fine stratification, or finestructure. In 1978, Fedorov published a book emphasizing the role of this arrangement of the ocean, called thermohaline finestructure, synthesizing his own work and the contributions of other oceanographers such as Carl Eckart, Kurt Kalle, and Leslie Hugh Norman Cooper.

Space Oceanology. It was a testament to Fedorov's international reputation that in 1974, the year after he received his doctorate, he became the head of the Shirshov Institute's laboratory on mesoscale hydrophysics. He also continued to be active in international projects; for example, he went to sea aboard the *Akademik Kurchatov* as part of the Soviet Union's contribution to the U.S.-Soviet Polymode program in 1977 and 1978. This collaborative project was designed to study mesoscale dynamics at sea, particularly large (50–100 kilometers) eddies. He remained in his post at the Shirshov Institute until 1979, when he took on the chairmanship of a new unit devoted to using space satellites in oceanology: the Department of Experimental and Space Oceanology. By the early 1970s, oceanographers in several countries had begun to use satellites to take synoptic data. This term referred to observations in several different areas at once, and it was the long-standing yet unrealized dream in every international cooperative investigation. Satellite data complemented more detailed information from shipboard work (like water sampling) and provided expansive portraits of the oceans from space, using both visual information and remote measurements of wave heights. Like many leading oceanographers, Fedorov and others at the Shirshov Institute tried to make the most of the new technology, beginning the entirely new field of space oceanology.

One of the results of this reorientation towards remote sensing was Fedorov's discovery of eddy dipoles. A satellite managed by the United States National Oceanic and Atmospheric Administration (NOAA), the *Meteor 30,* provided the crucial data. Images of the Sea of Okhotsk showed ice floating in a distinct mushroom-shaped pattern. Fedorov, who viewed the ice fragments as tracers to help identify current patterns, interpreted these shapes as evidence of a special kind of whirlpool effect (oceanographers called whirlpools eddies, or ocean vortices). In a paper with Anna I. Ginzburg, Fedorov likened them to the shapes of mushrooms and naturally enough called them "mushroom-like currents." They reasoned that the water from a current, when interacting with another current moving in a different direction, might be deflected to each side, resulting in two vortices of water on the current's flanks. The vortex dipoles, or eddy dipoles, as the phenomena were called, looked like the stem of a mushroom (the current) billowing out into a mushroom cap (the twin vortices). In the Soviet Union these phenomena sometimes were called Fedorov structures.

Later Years. In the 1980s, Fedorov turned his attention more fully toward oceanic fronts and climate change. Oceanic fronts seemed to hold the key to understanding many of the ocean's major processes. His previous work on finestructure emphasized the existence of small-scale structures defined by differences in temperature and salinity (or other properties), and the boundaries separating these structures (whether small-scale or large-scale) were called fronts. Just as atmospheric fronts created dynamic and turbulent meteorological conditions, oceanic fronts contributed to the major physical processes in the oceans, albeit on a slower time scale. Fedorov made oceanic fronts a major priority for Soviet oceanographic research in the 1980s, and he published a book on the subject. He also conducted research on the effects of El Niño in the early 1980s, helping to promote study on the role of the oceans in climate change.

His final major project was his edited volume with Anna I. Ginzburg, his colleague and spouse, on the near-surface layer of the ocean. The premise of this book was to analyze the relationships between surface activities and the deeper circulatory processes in the oceans. During these years Fedorov also remained involved in international matters. Between 1976 and 1980, he was the president of the Scientific Committee for Oceanic Research (SCOR), an advisory body for the IOC that was composed of leading scientists from all over the world, and he continued his involvement with that organization in the 1980s. In 1987, he was elected a corresponding member of the Academy of Sciences of the USSR, and around the same time he became the deputy director of the Shirshov Institute. He trained many leading researchers in the Soviet Union and taught courses on finestructure and space oceanology at Moscow University in the 1970s and 1980s. Perhaps in these years he found more time to pursue his other interests, such as poetry and woodcarving, though Anna Ginzburg wrote that he really only pursued these side interests during the long hours spent at sea.

Ten years after he died in 1988, Fedorov's former colleagues organized an international symposium on oceanic fronts in his honor, drawing together scientists from over twenty countries. Perhaps this was testimony that Fedorov's involvement in international activities helped to bring global attention to his scientific work and to the marine sciences in the Soviet Union. Certainly he was one of a very few Russian oceanologists whose names and reputations were known outside the Soviet Union, and his books and articles (translated) were widely cited in the oceanographic literature. And yet his research on finestructure, fronts, and physical oceanography in general was closely linked to naval operations and therefore to the strategic interests of the Soviet Union. As an administrator in international organizations, he spent years walking the fine line between serving the interests of his nation and the interests of UNESCO, making his career a remarkable blend of science, politics, and international cooperation.

BIBLIOGRAPHY

WORKS BY FEDOROV

With Henry Stommel. "Small-Scale Structure in Temperature and Salinity near Timor and Mindanao." *Tellus* 19 (1967): 306–325.

The Thermohaline Finestructure of the Ocean. Oxford: Pergamon Press, 1978.

The Physical Nature and Structure of Oceanic Fronts. New York: Springer-Verlag, 1983.

With Anna I. Ginzburg. "'Mushroom-Like' Currents (Vortex Dipoles) in the Ocean and in a Laboratory Tank." *Annales Geophysicae* 4 (1986): 507–516.

With Anna I. Ginzburg. *The Near-Surface Layer of the Ocean.* Utrecht, Netherlands: VSP, 1992.

OTHER SOURCES

Ginzburg, Anna I., and A. Zatsepin. "Konstantin N. Fedorov (1927–1988): Contributions to Physical Oceanography and International Cooperation." Paper presented at the International Congress on the History of Oceanography, Kaliningrad, Russia, 8–12 September, 2003. Available from http://vitiaz.ru/congress/en/thesis/.

Hamblin, Jacob Darwin. *Oceanographers and the Cold War: Disciples of Marine Science.* Seattle: University of Washington Press, 2005.

"Konstantin Nikolayevich Fedorov." *Oceanology* 28, no. 6 (1988): 806–807.

Intergovernmental Oceanographic Commission. Records. UNESCO Archives, Paris, France.

Jacob Darwin Hamblin

FEIT, WALTER (*b.* Vienna, Austria, 26 October 1930; *d.* New Haven, Connecticut, 29 July 2004), *mathematics, algebra, group theory.*

Feit was an American mathematician whose main research was in the theory of finite groups and, in particular, their representations and characters. He made major contributions to the search for finite simple groups, to the theory and applications of exceptional characters, and to applications of finite group theory, particularly in Galois

Theory. His greatest contribution was joint work with John Thompson proving Burnside's Conjecture that groups of odd order are soluble.

Origins and Education. Walter Feit's parents were Paul and Esther Feit, shopkeepers in the Molkereistrasse in Vienna. After the Anschluss in March 1938 Austrian Jews were as much at risk as those in Germany, and Walter's aunt, Pauline, who lived in Miami, Florida, kept urging them to join her in the United States. The risk grew after the Krystallnacht pogrom of 9 and 10 November 1938, but their shop had survived, and they stayed. Finally they sent Walter to England on the last of the Kindertransport trains from Vienna late in August or early in September 1939. They died in a concentration camp some time during the war.

After a brief stay with another aunt, Frieda, in London, Walter settled in a refugee hostel in Oxford. In 1943 he won a scholarship to the Junior Day Department of the Oxford Technical College, a school that had been founded in 1934 in the former buildings of the City of Oxford Technical School in St. Ebbe's. This had two hundred pupils by 1940, and applications outnumbered places by five to one. After the 1944 Education Act it became a Secondary Technical School and in 1954 it moved to larger premises adjacent to the Technical College (later Oxford Brookes University) in Headington and was renamed Cheney School. He recorded his teachers as having been very encouraging, and that it was here that he became passionately interested in mathematics.

Soon after his sixteenth birthday he migrated to the United States, where he had a great many relatives, arriving in New York on 29 December 1946. He moved in with his aunt Pauline and her family in Miami and, after graduating from high school there, entered the University of Chicago in September 1947, graduating with a bachelor's and a master's degree in mathematics in June 1951. From there he moved to the University of Michigan to study for a doctorate under the supervision of Richard Brauer. After one year Brauer moved to Harvard, and Feit's formal supervision was transferred to Robert M. Thrall. He continued to work under Brauer's direction, however, and presented his thesis in the summer of 1954. He married Sidnie Dresher on his twenty-seventh birthday soon after his army service ended. They had a daughter Alexandra, an artist, and a son Paul, a mathematician.

Career. Already in 1953, a year before his Michigan doctorate was complete, Feit was appointed to an instructorship at Cornell University. Apart from drafted service in the army 1955–1956, he remained there until 1964, when he moved to Yale University, where he stayed until his retirement in 2003. At Yale he served at various times as director of undergraduate studies, director of graduate studies, and chairman of the mathematics department. His distinction was recognized by the award of the 1965 American Mathematical Society Cole Prize in Algebra, awarded to Feit and John G. Thompson jointly for their 1963 paper "Solvability of groups of odd order"; by election to the National Academy of Sciences in 1977; and to the American Academy of Arts and Sciences. He traveled all over the world attending conferences, lecturing, and serving on both national and international committees. He served as editor of many journals, and, in particular, succeeded the founding editor, Graham Higman, as editor-in-chief of the *Journal of Algebra* from 1985 to 2000.

Mathematics. Feit's early reputation was based on his work in character theory of finite groups, a subject which had been invented by Georg Frobenius in 1896, and developed by Frobenius and his student Issai Schur in Germany, by William Burnside in England, and later by Richard Brauer. Of considerable interest at the time were so-called Frobenius groups. A subgroup of a group is known as a TI subgroup if it intersects each of its conjugates (other than itself) trivially. A Frobenius group is a group with a TI subgroup that is its own normaliser, and Frobenius had shown that such a subgroup (later known as a Frobenius complement) has a normal complement (now known as the Frobenius kernel). His proof was based on the discovery that some of the characters of the group are closely related to the characters of the subgroup. In 1955, Michio Suzuki, building on work of Brauer, had generalized this work of Frobenius to define so-called "exceptional characters" of a group with a TI subgroup, and had found conditions under which restriction of characters produces an isometry to a set of characters of the subgroup. Feit found that this phenomenon could be seen also in groups that have suitably embedded Frobenius subgroups. He developed the theory of exceptional characters and combined it with the theorem proved in 1959 by John Thompson, that the Frobenius kernel is always nilpotent, to make progress with the problem of finding all the doubly transitive groups in which the stabiliser of three points is trivial. The one-point stabilisers in such groups are themselves Frobenius groups, and Feit used delicate character-theoretic arguments to prove that if the degree of the permutation group was odd then it had to be one more than a power of two. This was soon used by Suzuki to discover new groups of this kind and to complete the characterization of such groups.

At this time, the late 1950s and early 1960s, finite group theory was developing in many exciting directions. A number of significant problems were ripe for solution, and in many cases exceptional character theory was one of the main tools for the job. Feit's expertise in this area led to a number of successful collaborations, for example with

Marshall Hall and John Thompson in the characterization of groups in which the centraliser of every non-identity element is nilpotent, and with John Thompson in the characterization of finite groups having a self-centralising element of order three. What brought lasting fame far beyond the group-theoretic community, however, was the collaboration with John Thompson on groups of odd order. The proof of Burnside's conjecture that there are no simple groups of odd composite order was, and remained as of 2007, a monumental work. It was the first of the really long and intricate proofs in that area, 255 printed pages of concentrated argument. The theorem itself is of the highest importance not merely as an elegant and decisive statement about groups of odd order, but also as providing the key to the classification of the finite simple groups of composite order—all such groups must contain elements of order two, and study of their centralisers and of the normalisers of two-subgroups provides the way in. Feit's main contribution was the character theory, where he had not only to adapt known methods of exceptional character theory to the special situations that arose in the study, but also extend the general theory by the introduction of new isometries between certain sets of characters of a group and appropriate sets of characters of subgroups.

Although character theory and representation theory remained the basis of most of Feit's later work, he contributed over a wide range. He wrote on combinatorics, classifying (in joint work with Graham Higman) certain generalized polygons important in the classification of BN-pairs of small rank, and contributing to the study of balanced incomplete block designs and codes. He wrote on diophantine equations and problems of elementary number theory. He wrote extensively on the inverse Galois problem, showing that many insoluble groups could be realized as Galois groups of polynomials over the rational number field. He used his extensive knowledge of finite groups to contribute new information on the well-known problem of universal algebra that asks which lattices can occur as congruence lattices of finite algebraic systems. But although he was a mathematician who contributed throughout algebra and its applications, it is the Odd Order Theorem which will ensure that his name remains known to later generations.

BIBLIOGRAPHY

Feit wrote approximately eighty research papers in mathematics. They are listed in Mathematical Reviews. *The Feit papers are in the Archives of American Mathematics, Research and Collections division of the Center for American History, University of Texas at Austin, donated by Sidnie Feit.*

WORKS BY FEIT

Characters of Finite Groups. New York: W. A. Benjamin, 1967.

The Representation Theory of Finite Groups. Amsterdam and New York: North-Holland, 1982. Translated into Russian, 1990.

OTHER SOURCES

Scott, Leonard, Ronald Solomon, John Thompson, et al. "Walter Feit (1930–2004)." *Notices of the American Mathematical Society* 52 (2005): 728–735.

Walter Feit Biographical Information. Available at http://www.math.yale.edu/public_html/WalterFeit/WalterFeit.html.

Peter Neumann

FESTINGER, LEON (*b.* Brooklyn, New York, 8 May 1919; *d.* New York, New York, 11 February 1989), *social psychology, cognitive dissonance, groups, communication, influence, social comparison and level of aspiration.*

Festinger was recognized in 1959 with the American Psychological Association's Distinguished Scientific Contribution Award for his theory and research on social behavior as arising from a "thinking organism continually acting to bring order into his world" (Boring, Cronbach, Crutchfield, et al., 1959, p. 784). Five years earlier, Festinger was honored by *Fortune Magazine* as one of ten top young scientists in universities for his research on people using groups as a testing ground for their views and self-concepts, an experimental demonstration of the power of social determinants on beliefs and abilities. Best known for his theory of cognitive dissonance, first introduced in 1956 in the coauthored book *When Prophecy Fails,* Festinger's social psychology departed from mechanistic notions of humans, and he can well be considered as part of the vanguard of social psychologists who revamped views of cognition in line with the information and communication theory of the mid-twentieth century, and who brought these into play with individual and group dynamics. Festinger also often is regarded as at the forefront of a post–World War II remodeling of experimental social psychology, making seminal the control and manipulation of variables and finely staged laboratory situations aimed at evoking a sense of realness in human subjects. Elected to the American Academy of Sciences in 1959 and the National Academy of Sciences in 1972, Festinger was celebrated in 1980 by the Distinguished Senior Scientist Award from the Society of Experimental Social Psychology.

Early Years and Education. Born in Brooklyn, New York, Festinger was the son of Russian immigrants—Alex Festinger, an embroidery manufacturer, and Sara Solomon—who left Eastern Europe before World War I. After Boys High School, Festinger entered the College of the City of New York, and, on obtaining a BS, left in 1939 for Iowa

Festinger

City to study under German émigré Kurt Lewin, completing his MA in 1940 and his PhD in 1942, both in the Child Welfare Research Station from the University of Iowa, although his own work was not in the area of child research. As Festinger himself wryly reflected, "technically my PhD is in child psychology—although I never saw a child" (Patnoe, 1988, p. 252). Neither had one of social psychology's more recognized researchers studied social psychology, as Festinger often noted with similar irony: "I had never had a course in social psychology. My graduate education did nothing to cure that. I never had a course at Iowa in social psychology either." What drew Festinger to Iowa were Lewin's ideas, developed with his Berlin group, on "tension systems and the remembering and completion of interrupted tasks," force fields and *Umweg* situations (Festinger, 1980, p. 237). To Festinger, there was to these ideas a sense of "creativity, newness" and "importance," along with a "closeness between theory and data" (p. 237). The appeal for Festinger was thus both with Lewin's ideas and with his exquisite articulation of the relation between theory and the empirical world, an interest underlying Festinger's attraction to science: "You have very strict ground rules in science and your ideas have to check out with the empirical world" (Cohen, 1977, p. 133). Time after time, Festinger brackets together his love of science and "fascination of games," especially chess. While science absorbed his interest from early on, Festinger's entry into psychology, and social psychology in particular, was thus, as he himself acknowledged, more by fiat than design. As he took courses in one and another science, his impression of psychology grew as a science where there were "still … questions to be answered" (p. 132), a field awaiting new contributions—an irresistible draw to a young scientist and chess enthusiast.

At least two significant influences steered Festinger's interests as an undergraduate. One was Clark Hull's *Hypnosis and Suggestibility* (1933), which Festinger recalled discovering while scouting out books in various sciences in the library. He described this work as a "beautiful series of studies in which he [Hull] took what is still an obscure phenomenon and examined it" (Cohen, 1977, p. 132). Festinger himself conducted two experiments in prestige and suggestibility for his honors thesis, looking at subjects' suggestibility as a function of their tendency toward stabilizing decision estimates (1939). A second significant influence was Lewin's "conceptual framework of goal valences, goal potencies, and restraining forces," a framework used by Tamara Dembo and Sybille Escalona in their research on aspirations to attain a goal. Festinger, under the supervision of Max Hertzman, conducted a study of levels of aspiration, which they published together in 1940 in the *Journal of Experimental Psychology.*

On arriving in Iowa, however, Festinger discovered Lewin's main interest had turned to social psychology and groups, even though he continued to pursue his ideas on life spaces, forces, and tension systems. Festinger claims his "youthful penchant for rigor" led him to pursue further research on aspiration for his master's thesis and to develop a mathematical model of decision making for his dissertation. His thesis "Wish, Expectation, and Group Performance as Factors Influencing Level of Aspiration" (1940) extended his undergraduate research, a study of tensions between individual and group comparison in levels of aspiration under varying conditions of expectations, intentions, wishes, ideals, and goals. His thesis, like his undergraduate research, demonstrates the influence of Lewin's field theory concepts of need, tension, valence, force, and energy. While still conceptualized through life space and tension system, Lewin's own work had turned at this time toward the study of groups and leadership ("autocratic" and "democratic"), a shift many attributed to Lewin's experiences with anti-Semitism in Germany and "his feelings about the growing repression he saw around him" (Patnoe, 1988, p. 3). Directed by Lewin, Festinger's dissertation "An Experimental Test of a Theory of Decision" (1942) represented an effort to bridge motivation theory (a more Lewinian approach) with psychophysics for a quantitative theory of decision. Festinger also did work on statistics, and, in his own words, "even strayed to doing a study using laboratory rats" (Festinger, 1980, p. 237).

Turn to Social Psychology. It would not be until three years after completing his doctoral studies that Festinger "immersed [himself] in the field [of social psychology] with all its difficulties, vaguenesses, and challenges" (Festinger, 1980, p. 237). In the intervening years he taught statistics in the Army Specialized Training Program, granting him a deferral from service; was a research associate in psychology at the University of Iowa from 1941 to 1943; and was then once more deferred from the draft by working as a statistician for the Committee on Selection and Training of Aircraft Pilots at the University of Rochester (1943–1945). In fact, Festinger's rush to complete his doctoral studies in three years was motivated, he said, to avoid the war, claiming to be one of the "original draft dodgers" (Patnoe, 1988, p. 253).

In 1945 Festinger moved again to become an assistant professor in Lewin's newly founded Research Center for Group Dynamics at the Massachusetts Institute of Technology (MIT). On joining Lewin, along with Ronald Lippitt, Dorwin Cartwright, and Marian Radke, Festinger devoted himself to the field of social psychology.

The Research Center for Group Dynamics gathered at MIT a pioneering group of psychologists and graduate students in psychology, who simultaneously carved out the work of the center and launched their careers at the cutting-edge of the field. In addition to the faculty mentioned above, there were several outstanding graduate students—Kurt Back, Morton Deutsch, Harold Kelley, Albert Pepitone, Stanley Schachter, and John Thibaut—who would become defining figures in the field of social psychology. Festinger's social psychological research in this groundbreaking venture began with his work with Back and Schachter on a study of graduate student housing (the Westgate housing study). Many of the graduate students had interrupted their studies to serve in the war, as was the case with Schachter (with whom Festinger formed a close and lifelong friendship and colleagueship). Their study of Westgate housing offered a social ecology of group and friendship formation; people living close to or coming into frequent informal contact with one another (mail room, stairwell, etc.) often develop friendships. Close proximity or propinquity was thus found to be key to small group and/or friendship formation. Later, when the center relocated to the University of Michigan, Schachter followed up on the housing study findings in experimental laboratory work he conducted for his dissertation on deviation, rejection, and communication.

Movement between studies in situ and the laboratory became a defining signature of Festinger's early and most well-known social psychological research. As he saw it, the laboratory could limit theory and research because one has "purified the thing so that you can see whether or not what you are looking for is there." To Festinger, switching "back and forth between laboratory studies and studies in the real world," or "field studies," as he referred to them, helped to "clarify theory and get hunches and that kind of thing" (Patnoe, 1988, p. 255). There was thus a kind of feedback loop created between the "real world" and the laboratory, each serving to refine theory and research, as opposed to one site serving as the testing ground for application in the other. Two of Festinger's most definitive contributions to social psychology followed this methodological course. From the Westgate housing study came Festinger's formulation on informal communication and social comparison processes, especially what Festinger called a pressure toward uniformity, or the tendency of individuals to compare and then align opinions with those whose views are closer to one's own. But the more famous of the two real-world studies is Festinger's covert study of a small millennialist group in Oak Park, Illinois, a study serving to lay the theoretical groundwork for cognitive dissonance.

Leon Festinger. ESTATE OF FRANCIS BELLO/PHOTO RESEARCHERS, INC.

Cognitive Dissonance. The Oak Park study began while Festinger was professor of psychology at the University of Minnesota in 1951, and was published shortly after he went to Stanford University in 1955. The resulting 1956 book, *When Prophecy Fails,* recounts the undercover participation of Festinger, Schachter, Henry Riecken, and a complement of graduate students who entered the Seekers. The group's prophetess, Dorothy Martin (alias Mrs. Keech), foretold of the world ending on 21 December 1954. Festinger was interested in how the group would respond to the discrepancy between their beliefs and the failed prophecy of an apocalypse. *Cognitive dissonance* was conceptualized as a tension between opposing beliefs or between belief and behavior, with the tension functioning as a motivational force driving one to reduce the emotional or cognitive strain. His theory's counterintuitive predictions held great appeal. Groups faced with evidence that disconfirms their beliefs may find ways to use it to shore up those beliefs rather than disband previously held convictions. One year after publishing his book on failed prophecy and cognitive dissonance, Festinger presented the full scope of his theory in *A Theory of Cognitive Dissonance* (1957). Within two years of its publication, research studies on cognitive dissonance began to fill journals of experimental social psychology, and after a decade, reached three hundred "separate, published, theoretical, critical and/or research publications" (Margolis, 1969, p. 923). Fifty years after its first appearance, citation counts of works in the psychological database exceeded fifteen hundred.

But the influence of the theory of cognitive dissonance and the original study of the millennialist group has been far more extensive than numbers alone can convey. It has inspired works of fiction and stimulated research in other disciplines, including religious studies, political science, economics, sociology, legal theory, and philosophy of science. Some religious studies scholars claim this work helped to shape what is now "the standard paradigm [in the sociology of religion] for understanding failed prophecy" (Dein, 2001, p. 384), and others claim it as a "key text for understanding the logic of the 'dynamics of commitment'" of New Left groups (Gitlin, 2005). The term *cognitive dissonance* has since its conception entered into everyday conversation, and is used routinely in newspaper and popular journals as shorthand for mental tension, or conflicting beliefs, or inconsistency in belief and behavior across topics as wide-ranging as war, eating disorders, and risk and denial. Within psychology, Festinger's theory of cognitive dissonance has been heralded as "revolutionizing the way social psychologists think about human behavior" (Aronson, 1999). Popularized and part of everyday utterance, cognitive dissonance's cultural resonance has been both so vast and so deep as to prompt reference to early twenty-first-century America as an "age of dissonance."

Despite its broad appeal, Festinger's work has been dogged by controversy. Almost from its inception, cognitive dissonance was met with trenchant critique, whether for "not find[ing] a place for the description of phenomena" (Asch, 1958, p. 195), for assuming that action and cognition somehow have to be brought into line with one another (Bruner, 1957), for reducing complex social psychological phenomena to two discrepant statements (Chapanis & Chapanis, 1964), or for the evidence fitting a theory of self-perception better than cognitive dissonance (Bem, 1967). Historian of psychology Edwin G. Boring (1964) went so far as to parallel Festinger's studies of cognitive dissonance with the condition of the scientist, instancing occasion after occasion where the scientist persists and perseveres in the face of cognitive dissonance. Whereas the experimental laboratory research into cognitive dissonance was also met with forceful critical analysis of its methodological shortcomings (Chapanis & Chapanis, 1964), the original "real-world" study was, in contrast, quite remarked upon as "a far more illuminating and provocative account of it than mere natural history description would be likely to have given us" (Smith, 1957, p. 90).

The debates on cognitive dissonance are instructive on Festinger's contributions on several counts, and on developments in post–World War II psychology, especially social psychology. For that reason, reference to Festinger's revolutionary approach should be placed within the broader debate on theory and research. Festinger, along with many of his contemporaries, was seeking to rectify American psychology's slighting of cognitive phenomena in favor of behaviorism. To many, he rearticulated the relation between stimulus and response by focusing on what goes on between the two, looking at the "relation and interactions among the contents of the life space" (Heider, 1957, p. 207), and perhaps even proposing work that "lies astride the junction of general psychology, the psychology of personality, and social psychology (Bruner, 1957, p. 153). This attention to what transpires in-between inputs and outputs also revealed Lewin's influence in attention to a "psychological representation of reality in individual consciousness," relations of one person to another or group and the environment (Zukier, 1989, p. xiii). Festinger filtered Lewinian notions of life space, force fields, and tension in developing his theory of cognitive dissonance, influencing the larger shift-change in mid-twentieth-century U.S. psychology away from behaviorism, toward what some saw as a more imaginative side to human life (Gruber, Hammond, & Jessor, 1957).

Controversy also surrounded Festinger's complex experimental laboratory situations—aimed, as he argued, toward making them "real" for subjects. By "real," Festinger meant the subjects must experience powerful forces acting on them—which usually required a high degree of control, manipulation of variables, and a "great deal of subterfuge and much attention to technical detail" (Festinger, 1953, p. 153). Festinger sought to create situations that were "real and important to the subject," arguing that only then might scientific psychologists be studying what subjects are experiencing, what some call "hot" cognitions set off by motivational and/or emotional forces, rather than "cool" cognitions, regarded as the product of rational thought. Staging elaborate laboratory experiments was likened by Festinger and some of his students to the work of a playwright; in this case, art and science worked hand-in-hand to call out a "real" experience—what students of Festinger subsequently dubbed "experimental realism" (Aronson & Carlsmith, 1968). But such carefully scripted laboratory experiments involving role-playing and clever stratagem became, ironically, precisely the point of contention among scientific psychologists: some claimed their effect was to turn laboratory psychology into games whose internal rules and logic bore little to no connection to reality.

Arising out of his interest in communication and influence, especially Jamuna Prasad's 1950 study in rumors following a severe earthquake in Bihar, India, in 1934, Festinger's theory of cognitive dissonance reigned for almost a decade of experimental social psychology, and continues to spawn research in other disciplines. The research coming

Festinger

out of Festinger's collaboration with May Brodbeck, Don Martindale, Jack Brehm, and Alvin Boderman, a project funded by the Behavioral Sciences Division of the Ford Foundation, which moved from the field to the laboratory, book-ended Festinger's years of research in social psychology. Cognitive dissonance may well serve as his signature in social psychology and as a marker of ideas prevalent in post–World War II psychology. Perhaps Festinger offered the most apt description of this moment when he quoted from Fritz Heider's unpublished work: "the relationships among people and among sentiments" are predominantly concerned with "balanced, or harmonious, states," such that "if no balanced state exists, ... relations will be changed through action or cognitive reorganization" due to the tension produced by the state of imbalance. To this, Festinger added that if one "replaces the word 'balanced' with 'consonant' and 'imbalance' with 'dissonance,'" Heider's process concerning interpersonal relations and his own could be seen to be the same (Festinger, 1957, pp. 7–8). Ideas on balance and imbalance, or consonance and dissonance, marked the age and its preoccupations with homeostatic processes. Throughout Festinger's research there runs the common thread of "calculated tension between alternatives or contrary forces, which impel a change in thinking, feeling, or behavior" (Zukier, 1989, p. xvii). Although Festinger later reflected that homeostatic notions and theories may well be related to a "*Zeitgeist* or philosophy underlying assumptions ... in human beings," whereas he intended cognitive dissonance "as an explanation ... of a broad range of psychological phenomena" (Cohen, 1977, p. 141), one is nonetheless struck first by the longevity of the concept of cognitive dissonance and second by its resonance with two moments of heightened political and cultural strain in the mid-twentieth- and early-twenty-first-century United States.

Later Research Interests. After just over a decade of research on cognitive dissonance, Festinger left the field of social psychology for research in perception and eye movements. Then, in 1968, he moved back east to take a position at the New School for Social Research, where he briefly continued his research in perception before changing his field once more to archaeology and history. With forty years of experimental psychology research behind him, Festinger closed his laboratory and turned to till new fields of inquiry—anthropology, archaeology, and history—to wrestle with a larger question of what makes humans *human,* a quest of the origins of human societies and culture. Although a full explanation of his unusual intellectual trajectory is wanting, Festinger himself mused on the draw of certain questions on reaching a certain age: "Older people have too much perspective on the past and, perhaps, too little patience with the future. Very few small discoveries turn out to be important over the years; things that would have sent me jumping and shouting in my youth now left me calm and judgmental.... And even worse ... we do not seem to have been working on many of the important problems" (Festinger, 1983, p. ix). With customary dynamism, Festinger sought out colleagues in his new fields of interest, much as he drew together colleagues and students in his years of experimental research, including, during his early years, the well-remembered "Tuesday Night Meeting" or the Lewin-style *Quasselstrippe,* weekly meetings wholly given to collaborating on research (Patnoe, 1988). Building collaborative networks among psychologists and graduate students went beyond the United States as Festinger created and directed the Committee of Transnational Social Psychology, and participated in its Summer Schools at which young scholars received training and at which were held scientific colloquia. Here, Festinger also contributed to the publication of the *European Journal of Social Psychology.*

Festinger married Mary Oliver Ballou, a pianist, in 1942, and together they had three children: Richard, Kurt, and Catherine. When his first marriage ended in divorce, Festinger married his second wife, Trudy Bradley, a professor at the New York University School of Social Work. Following his 1983 publication of *The Human Legacy,* Festinger pursued questions in the history of religion, moving outside his field once more to medieval and Byzantine history. His questions "focused on differences between the Eastern and Western or Roman church and the role such differences might have played in the differential development and acceptance of material technology in these two parts of the Roman empire" (Schachter, 1994, p.106). Festinger died of cancer before publishing his last scholarly foray, leaving colleagues and others with a strong impression of Festinger as an active scholar and of the importance of stepping outside the confines of any one field or method in the study of human life.

Some of Festinger's papers are archived in the Bentley Historical Library at the University of Michigan, Ann Arbor.

BIBLIOGRAPHY

WORKS BY FESTINGER

"Experiments in Suggestibility." Honors thesis, College of the City of New York, 1939. (Leon Festinger Papers, Bentley Historical Library, University of Michigan.)

"Wish, Expectation, and Group Performance as Factors Influencing Level of Aspiration." *Journal of Abnormal and Social Psychology* 37 (1942): 184–200. Originally written as master's thesis, State University of Iowa, 1940.

"An Experimental Test of a Theory of Decision." PhD diss., State University of Iowa, 1942.

"Laboratory Experiments." In *Research Methods in the Behavioral Sciences,* edited by Leon Festinger and Daniel Katz. New York: Dryden Press, 1953.

With Henry W. Riecken and Stanley Schachter. *When Prophecy Fails.* Minneapolis: University of Minnesota Press, 1956.

A Theory of Cognitive Dissonance. Evanston, IL: Row, Peterson, 1957.

Editor. "Looking Backward." In *Retrospections on Social Psychology.* New York: Oxford University Press, 1980.

The Human Legacy. New York: Columbia University Press, 1983.

"A Personal Memory of Stanley Schachter." Leon Festinger Papers, Bentley Historical Library, University of Michigan.

OTHER SOURCES

Aronson, Elliot. "Dissonance, Hypocrisy, and the Self-Concept." In *Cognitive Dissonance,* edited by Eddie Harmon-Jones and Judson Mills, 103–126. Washington, DC: American Psychological Association, 1999.

Aronson, Elliot, and J. M. Carlsmith. "Experimentation in Social Psychology." In *The Handbook of Social Psychology: Second Edition,* edited by Gardner Lindzey and Elliot Aronson. Reading, MA: Addison-Wesley, 1968.

Asch, S. "Cacophonophobia." *Contemporary Psychology: A Journal of Reviews,* 3, no. 7 (1958): 194–195.

Bem, D. J. "Self-Perception: An Alternative Interpretation of Cognitive Dissonance Phenomena." *Journal of Experimental Social Psychology* 1 (1967): 199–218.

Boring, Edwin G. "Cognitive Dissonance: Its Use in Science." *Science* 145 (1964): 680–685.

Boring, Edwin G., L. J. Cronbach, R. S. Crutchfield, et al. "Distinguished Scientific Contribution Awards: 1959." *American Psychologist* 14, no. 12 (1959): 784–793.

Brehm, J. W. "Leon Festinger: Beyond the Obvious." In *Portraits of Pioneers in Psychology,* Vol. II, edited by Gregory A. Kimble, Michael Wertheimer, and Charlotte White. Washington, DC: American Psychological Association, 1998.

Bruner, J. "Discussion." In *Contemporary Approaches to Cognition,* edited by H. Gruber, K. R. Hammond, and R. Jessor. Cambridge, MA: Harvard University Press, 1957.

Chapanis, N. P., and A. Chapanis. "Cognitive Dissonance: Five Years Later." *Psychological Bulletin* 61, no. 1 (1964): 1–22.

Cohen, David. "Leon Festinger." In his *Psychologists on Psychology.* New York: Taplinger, 1977.

Dein, S. "What Really Happens When Prophecy Fails: The Case of Lubavitch." *Sociology of Relgion* 62, no. 3 (2001): 383–401.

Evans, Richard I. "Leon Festinger." In his *The Making of Psychology: Discussions with Creative Contributors.* New York: Alfred A. Knopf, 1996.

Gazzaniga, M. S. "Leon Festinger: Lunch with Leon." *Perspectives on Psychological Science* 1, no. 1 (2006): 88–94.

Gitlin, Todd. "Jeremy Varon: *Bringing the War Home: The Weather Underground, the Red Army Faction, and Revolutionary Violence in the Sixties and Seventies.*" *American Historical Review* 110, no. 4 (2005): 1213–1214.

Gruber, H., K. R. Hammond, and R. Jessor. Foreword. In their *Contemporary Approaches to Cognition.* Cambridge, MA: Harvard University Press, 1957.

Heider, Fritz. "Trends in Cognitive Theory." In *Contemporary Approaches to Cognition,* edited by H. Gruber, K. R. Hammond, and R. Jessor. Cambridge, MA: Harvard University Press, 1957.

Margolis, S. T. "Cognitive Dissonance: A Bibliography of Its First Decade." *Psychological Reports* 24 (1969): 923–935.

Moscovici, Serge. "Obituary: Leon Festinger." *European Journal of Social Psychology,* 19, no. 4 (1989): 263–269.

Patnoe, Shelley. "Leon Festinger." In her *A Narrative History of Experimental Social Psychology.* New York: Springer-Verlag, 1988.

Samelson, Franz. "Leon Festinger." *American National Biography* 7 (1999): 863–864.

Schachter, Stanley. "Leon Festinger." *Biographical Memoirs* 64 (1994): 99–110.

Smith, M. B. "Of Prophecy and Privacy." *Contemporary Psychology: A Journal of Reviews* 2, no. 4 (1957): 89–92.

Zukier, Henri. Introduction. In *Extending Psychological Frontiers: Selected Works of Leon Festinger,* edited by Stanley Schachter and Michael Gazzaniga. New York: Russell Sage Foundation, 1989.

Betty M. Bayer

FEYNMAN, RICHARD PHILLIPS

(*b.* New York, New York, 11 May 1918; *d.* Los Angeles, California, 15 February 1988), *physics, quantum theory, particle physics, science teaching.*

Feynman was one of the most creative and influential physicists of the twentieth century. A veteran of the Manhattan Project of World War II and a 1965 Nobel laureate in physics, he made lasting contributions across many domains, from electrodynamics and quantum theory to nuclear and particle physics, solid-state physics, and gravitation. He also became a famous public persona. Several of his popular books—including two collections of autobiographical stories, telling of his lifelong love of playing bongo drums, puzzling through scientific mysteries, and distrusting authority figures—became runaway best sellers. Over his career—cut short after a long battle with cancer—Feynman produced 125 scientific articles and books, several of which remain at the forefront of modern physics.

Early Years. Feynman grew up in Far Rockaway, in the Queens section of New York City. His father, Melville, who harbored an interest in science, helped inspire young Richard with trips to museums, nature walks, the purchase of an *Encyclopedia Britannica,* and more. Melville was in the garment business—he sold uniforms to police officers, postal workers, and the like—and he taught Richard never to take formal authority too seriously; he had, after all, seen the important figures before they acquired their fancy uniforms. Melville and his wife,

Lucille Phillips, raised their two children (Richard and his younger sister, Joan) in the tradition of reformed Judaism, although religion never played a large role in Richard Feynman's life.

Feynman raced through New York City's public schools, teaching himself algebra and soon calculus, even inventing his own idiosyncratic notation to streamline his calculations. He entered the Massachusetts Institute of Technology (MIT) in Cambridge, Massachusetts, in 1935 to begin his undergraduate studies. By his sophomore year Feynman was already enrolling in graduate-level courses in theoretical physics. He soon fell in with an equally precocious friend and study partner, Theodore (Ted) Welton. Together, Feynman and Welton dived into quantum mechanics, physicists' bizarre yet successful description of the atomic domain, and general relativity, Albert Einstein's notoriously difficult theory of gravitation. While still an undergraduate, Feynman published a brief letter to the editor of *Physical Review* with one of his professors, Manuel Vallarta, on the scattering of cosmic rays by interstellar magnetic fields. He also worked on a senior thesis with the renowned solid-state theorist John Clarke Slater, which resulted in an article of Feynman's own, "Forces in Molecules," published in *Physical Review* in 1939. This work treated the problem of molecular forces from a thoroughly quantum-mechanical point of view, arriving at a simple means of calculating the energy of a molecular system that continues to guide quantum chemists.

From MIT, Feynman went to Princeton University, in New Jersey, to pursue his PhD, starting in 1939. With the United States still trapped in the Great Depression, Feynman's father worried that his son might not be able to find a job after all his fancy schooling. Princeton also had concerns: in those days, the physics department scrutinized every applicant of Jewish background who professed a desire to study theoretical physics, fearing that the field (if not the department) already had more than its fair share—a practice that faded soon after World War II. Undaunted, Feynman began his graduate studies and immediately impressed his young mentor, John Archibald Wheeler, who had arrived at Princeton himself, as an assistant professor, only the previous year.

Together with Wheeler, Feynman explored the ins and outs of electrodynamics. Since the middle of the nineteenth century, physicists had thought about electric and magnetic forces in terms of fields—wavelike entities extended throughout space that could act on charged particles and affect their motion. Wheeler and Feynman explored a radical alternative: what if fields did not exist, and all electrodynamic interactions arose from direct forces between particles? To make their equations yield the familiar (and well-tested) results, they needed to include two different types of interactions: "retarded," which took into account the time required for an effect to propagate from one location to another, and "advanced," effects that arrived at their destination before they had been emitted. Wheeler and Feynman demonstrated that the latter, while certainly paradoxical, behaved in a mathematically self-consistent manner. In a related line of thinking, Wheeler and Feynman realized that positrons—the antimatter cousins to electrons, bearing the same mass but the opposite electric charge—could be thought of as electrons traveling backward in time. In both cases, Feynman pushed particles to the forefront, rather than fields, picturing the particles' zigzagging paths through space and time—an approach that he would continue to hone throughout his career. Feynman completed his PhD in 1942 and immediately married his high school sweetheart, Arline Greenbaum, over his parents' strenuous objections. (Arline suffered from tuberculosis.)

War Work. War was clearly on the horizon as Feynman finished his undergraduate studies in 1939; just three months after he graduated from MIT, Germany invaded Poland and World War II broke out in Europe. A college friend of his had already joined the Army Signal Corps, and Feynman thought seriously about joining, too. As Feynman later recalled, however, the army had not yet established any means by which scientifically trained people could contribute their special skills, so he elected to begin graduate studies at Princeton rather than basic training at an army boot camp. Two years later, in the midst of his studies, the Japanese attacked Pearl Harbor and the United States entered the war. The surprise attack sent American defense efforts into high gear.

For years, a small, secret group of scientists in the United States had been studying whether it might be feasible to create a weapon using nuclear fission, the process by which large atomic nuclei can be split apart, releasing large amounts of energy. (Unbeknownst to these scientists, similar groups were also studying the issue in Great Britain, Germany, the Soviet Union, and Japan.) Immediately after Pearl Harbor, this sleepy commission was transformed into what would become the largest scientific and technical project the world had ever seen: the Manhattan Project. A young physics professor at Princeton, Robert Wilson, was among the earliest recruits for the top-secret project. He, in turn, convinced many members of the department—graduate students and faculty alike—to join him in the effort to design and build nuclear bombs. When Wilson approached Feynman with a cryptic message (no one was allowed to speak openly about the secret project), asking Feynman if he would join, the latter at first refused. A few hours later, Feynman changed his mind—the thought of Adolf Hitler acquiring nuclear weapons before the Allies did was too frightening—and so by that afternoon he was hard at work trying to figure out how to separate the fissionable variant of uranium (U-235) from the much more common species (U-238). At the age of twenty-three, he had joined the war effort.

Late in 1938 the Berlin chemists Otto Hahn and Fritz Strassmann had detected fission of uranium nuclei; the surprising effect was first explained in terms of the physics of nuclear particles by Hahn's former colleague, theoretical physicist Lise Meitner, and her nephew, Otto Robert Frisch, while vacationing in Sweden. (Meitner, an Austrian Jew, had been forced to flee Berlin just weeks before, after the Nazis annexed Austria.) The vast majority of naturally occurring uranium has an atomic mass of 238 (92 protons and 146 neutrons). These common nuclei are quite stable. A rare isotope, however, of atomic mass 235 (92 protons but only 143 neutrons), is highly susceptible to fission. The question Wilson posed to Feynman (and, indeed, the question on many scientists' minds by this time) was how to separate the fissionable U-235 from the garden-variety U-238. The two types of nuclei could not be separated by chemical means; in any chemical reaction, U-235 and U-238 would behave in exactly the same way. Some physical means, exploiting the tiny mass difference, was needed. Several ideas had been advanced—some called for using powerful magnets to whip the uranium nuclei around in circles, during which time the heavier nuclei would move along slightly different paths than the lighter ones; others envisioned heating a uranium gas so that the molecules containing the lighter nuclei would drift down a chamber slightly more quickly than the heavier ones, and so on. Feynman's first assignment was to assess the theoretical feasibility of these separation procedures and to brainstorm for other possibilities.

The Manhattan Project grew quickly; by war's end, it had incorporated more than 125,000 people working at more than thirty sites throughout the United States and Canada. Central among these were huge, top-secret factory towns set up in Oak Ridge, Tennessee, and in Hanford, Washington, and a brand-new laboratory established in Los Alamos, New Mexico. Oak Ridge specialized in separating the uranium nuclei (using, in the end, both the electromagnetic and the gaseous diffusion methods). Hanford took on a different task: building enormous nuclear reactors to turn ordinary uranium nuclei (U-238) into a still heavier and more fissionable nucleus, plutonium (Pu), which contained 94 protons and 145 neutrons. The Los Alamos laboratory worked on the design and production of fission bombs.

Feynman arrived at Los Alamos early in 1943, while the laboratory was still under construction. He joined the theoretical physics division, or T-division, led by Hans Bethe. Feynman's job now was to figure out some way to calculate how neutrons would behave in various bomb configurations. In principle, the task seemed straightforward: a single starter neutron, if injected into a critical mass of fissionable material (such as uranium enriched with additional U-235), could trigger a chain reaction. The initiator neutron would split one uranium nucleus; among the detritus would be, on average, about two new neutrons released when the original nucleus split apart. Each of these newly released neutrons could split additional uranium nuclei, releasing more neutrons, and so on. Every time a nucleus split, it released energy as well as more neutrons (as Meitner and Frisch had first worked out). Simple in principle, the real mechanisms of neutron scattering, absorption, fission, and release proved remarkably difficult to calculate for any realistic design.

Feynman broke the problem into constituent parts: a given neutron had a certain probability to fly out of the region containing fissionable material altogether, without causing any nuclear reactions; it had a different probability to collide once with a nucleus and be absorbed, ending its usefulness; it had a still distinct probability of colliding and inducing fission; and so on. Moreover, the new neutrons released upon fission would come out with varying speeds and energies, which would affect their likelihood for undergoing various types of reactions later on. Feynman built up powerful calculational techniques to sum over all of these possibilities, a step-by-step accounting scheme that could help the physicists understand how neutrons would diffuse throughout a typical bomb assembly. He quickly impressed both the lab's scientific director, theoretical physicist J. Robert Oppenheimer, and the T-division leader, Bethe. By early 1944 Feynman had been promoted to be a group leader within T-division, making him the youngest group leader in all of Los Alamos.

Feynman's other main task during the war was to serve as a safety inspector for Oak Ridge. Engineers and architects at Oak Ridge had designed storage facilities for the enriched uranium. Oppenheimer deputized Feynman to inspect the Oak Ridge facilities and determine whether or not they were safe. This task, like his main job back at Los Alamos, ultimately came down to understanding how neutrons would behave in and around fissionable material. The original Oak Ridge plans looked safe until Feynman realized that any accident—a tub of enriched uranium spilling near other containers, or worse yet, a flood in one of the containment rooms, which would slow down any itinerant neutrons and make them more likely to induce fission—could lead to disastrous explosions and deadly levels of radioactivity. Although skeptical at first, the leadership at Oak Ridge heeded Feynman's warnings and redesigned their storage facilities.

Like many other scientists at Los Alamos, Feynman often chafed at the laboratory's military supervision. He delighted in sending coded messages back and forth with

Feynman

his wife, who was staying in a sanatorium for tuberculosis patients near Los Alamos, to taunt the laboratory's censors. (Arline died in July 1945, a few days before the first test detonation of a fission bomb in the so-called Trinity test.) He also learned how to crack safes, surreptitiously testing codes to a given safe's combination lock while its owner was distracted. Both activities provided Feynman a way to rebuff what he regarded as stifling military discipline at the laboratory.

Quantum Theory. As the war was ending and Allied victory looked more and more secure, physics departments across the country began jockeying to hire Feynman. In the end, he turned down several attractive offers and followed his wartime boss, Bethe, back to Bethe's home department at Cornell University in upstate New York. At Cornell, Feynman perfected his approach to quantum theory, melding several of his prewar insights with the more pragmatic, numbers-driven approach he had honed during the war.

One of his first tasks was to publish a long article, based on his dissertation, that presented a brand-new approach to quantum mechanics. Published in 1948 under the title, "Space-Time Approach to Non-relativistic Quantum Mechanics" in the journal *Reviews of Modern Physics,* his lengthy article focused on the "Lagrangian" function for a particle, a particular combination of kinetic and potential energy familiar from classical mechanics. The probability that a quantum object would travel from one location, x_1, at a time t_1, to some other location, x_2, at a later time t_2, Feynman showed, could be calculated by summing over—that is, integrating—all of the possible paths through space and time that connected these two end points. The contribution of each path to the total would be weighted by its classical Lagrangian function evaluated along that path; hence, the technique became known as path integrals. The main difference from the standard formalism lay not in outcomes, but in conceptual approach. Werner Heisenberg and Niels Bohr had argued vehemently during the 1920s that quantum mechanics spelled the end for any type of visualization of the atomic domain. Feynman countered with an intuitive approach, built around picturing the paths of particles through space and time.

His greatest success came on the heels of this path-integral approach. He returned to the problems of quantum electrodynamics (QED), physicists' quantum-mechanical description of electric and magnetic forces. QED had been developed during the late 1920s and the 1930s by many of the discipline's greatest theorists—Paul Dirac, Heisenberg, Wolfgang Pauli, Pascual Jordan, and many others. Yet as these greats had discovered, the equations of QED suffered from a dramatic sickness. When

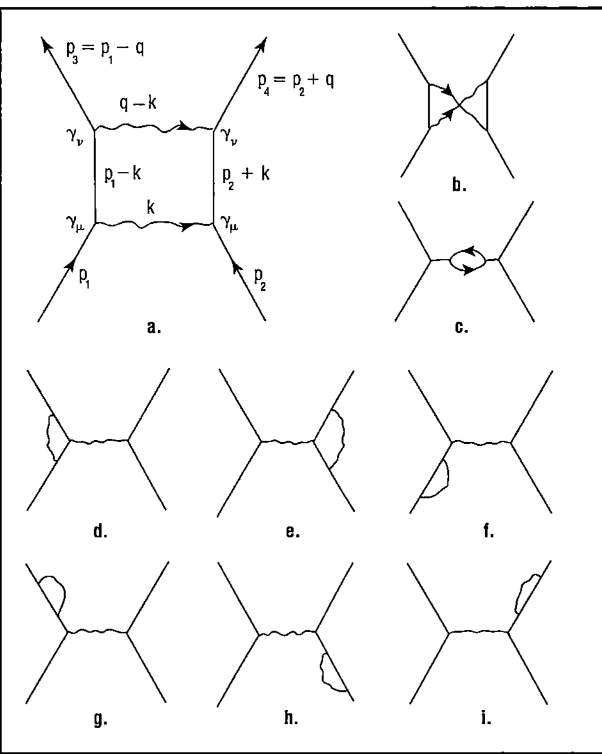

Figure 1. *Feyman diagrams as bookkeepers: Two electrons trade two photons back and forth.*

pushed beyond the lowest approximation, they routinely broke down, yielding infinity rather than any finite predictions. After the war, Feynman tackled the problem diagrammatically. He began doodling simple space-time pictures to help keep track of the morass of separate algebraic terms that littered any given QED calculation. With a more effective accounting scheme, Feynman hoped, it would be easier to assess precisely where the equations broke down and the infinities sneaked in.

He began with the problem of electron scattering: why, on the quantum-mechanical level, two objects with the same electric charge repel each other. At the lowest order of approximation, Feynman pictured the scattering as in Figure 2. An electron came in from the lower right, while a second electron approached it from lower left. At some point, the right-side electron shot out a force-carrying particle, called a photon, or quantum, of light. Having given up some of its energy and momentum to the photon, this electron would recoil backward, much like a hunter upon firing a rifle. Hence it would veer off toward the top right. A little while later, the photon would strike into the second electron. This left-side electron would absorb the photon and its momentum, getting knocked off its course and heading toward the top left.

Feynman

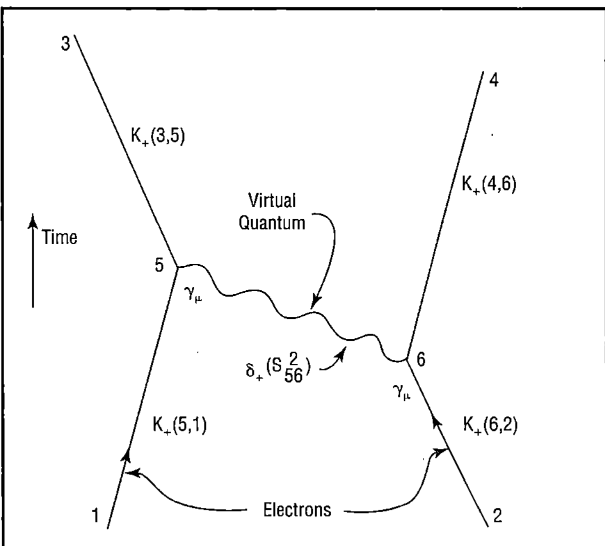

Figure 2. *The simplest Feynman diagram for electron-electron scattering.*

Feynman designed his diagram to stand in, one-for-one, for the accompanying equation. For every leg of an electron's motion, he plugged in a specific mathematical function (which gave the likelihood for an electron to travel, unperturbed, from one location to another). He plugged in a distinct function for every wavy photon line. Every "vertex," or place within a diagram at which an electron line and a photon line met, corresponded to yet a different mathematical function (giving the likelihood for an electron to emit or absorb a photon). The diagram thus functioned, for Feynman, both as a picture of a specific physical process and as a clever mnemonic or bookkeeping device, helping him wade through QED's famously complex calculational thickets.

The single-photon case had been easy enough to calculate even without Feynman's diagrams. The real payoff came when considering more complicated scenarios. Quantum mechanically, the two incoming electrons could trade any number of photons back and forth—2 photons, 3 photons, 67 photons, 9,400,083 photons—and, at least in principle, every one of these possibilities had to be included in the overall calculation. The algebra became exponentially more protracted for every additional photon in the mix. Even the next-simplest level of approximation had proven tricky without Feynman's diagrams. There were nine distinct ways the two electrons could trade just two photons back and forth. It had become frustratingly common to confuse or, worse, to omit some of these terms when working with the algebra alone. Feynman demonstrated that the various possibilities could be distinguished easily by their separate diagrams. Then their corresponding equations could be built up, piece by piece, just as the original term had been, by swapping in the appropriate mathematical expressions for every electron line, photon line, and vertex. Sure enough, when the dust settled from this extended calculation, Feynman showed that some of the infinities that had cropped up separately in several of these expressions exactly canceled each other out, leaving a finite number behind.

Feynman refined his diagrammatic approach over the course of 1947 and 1948. He first presented the new scheme at an elite, by-invitation-only conference in rural Pennsylvania in the spring of 1948—a presentation that went rather poorly. Few attendees had any idea what Feynman was doing at the blackboard, or how his strange-looking doodles fit in with the general tenets of quantum theory. Within months of the disappointing presentation, however, the younger generation of theoretical physicists began to pick up on Feynman diagrams, thanks especially to the tireless efforts of Feynman's protégé, Freeman Dyson. Dyson had learned Feynman's tricks while a graduate student at Cornell, and he quickly provided critical clarifications and powerful extensions. Dyson and Feynman each published a pair of influential articles on the new techniques in *Physical Review* during 1949.

Over the next two decades, Feynman's diagrammatic approach revolutionized nearly every branch of theoretical physics, from QED to nuclear and particle physics, solid-state theory, and even gravitation. He won the 1965 Nobel Prize in Physics for this work (sharing the award with Julian Schwinger and Shin'ichirō Tomonaga). Of all Feynman's many contributions, his diagrams have remained his greatest scientific legacy, changing the way most physicists think about the microworld.

Soon after Feynman had perfected his diagrammatic approach, the California Institute of Technology (Caltech) in Pasadena lured Feynman away from Cornell. He moved to Caltech in 1950 and remained there for the rest of his career. Two years after he moved, he married Mary Louise Bell, whom he had first met at Cornell. The relationship quickly soured, and they divorced in 1956. Among Bell's complaints: his drumming was too loud and his head was constantly lost in calculus problems, morning, noon, and night. In 1960 Feynman married Gweneth Howarth in what proved to be a far more successful relationship: they remained together until his death in 1988.

More and more during this period, the problems that Feynman worked on came from solid-state theory. He became especially interested in liquid helium. At ordinary temperatures and pressures, helium exists as a gas; but at extremely low temperatures (a few degrees above absolute zero), helium becomes a liquid—indeed, a liquid with strange properties. Liquid helium displays superfluidity, that is, it flows with no viscosity or friction at all (unlike ordinary liquids). The phenomenon had been discovered

Richard P. Feynman. *Richard Feynman accepting the Nobel Prize from King Gustaf Adolf of Sweden.* AP IMAGES.

experimentally during the 1930s, and the great Russian theorist Lev Landau had provided a successful phenomenological description during the 1940s. Feynman brought his newest tools to bear on the problem—path integrals and Feynman diagrams—to explain superfluidity on a rigorously quantum-mechanical basis. In addition to the particle-like quantum excitations that had been studied, Feynman realized that a new quantum effect also played a role: the formation of quantum vortices. Once again his intuitive, pictorial approach proved successful.

Particle Physics. By the mid-1950s, Feynman's interests had returned to his original passion: high-energy physics. Since his triumph with QED, the field had moved on to a series of new conundrums. Among them loomed the nature of nuclear forces. One type of force, dubbed the "weak force," led nuclei to decay, as in radioactivity. Although weak-force phenomena had been well studied for decades, a big shock came in the late 1950s, when experiments confirmed some theoretical speculations about the symmetries obeyed by this nuclear force. Until that time, most physicists simply assumed that the weak force obeyed parity; that is, reversing all spatial coordinates from plus (right-handed) to minus (left-handed) and vice versa would leave the underlying physics unchanged. Not so, as new experiments confirmed in 1957: the weak force violated parity. Nature was not ambidextrous after all.

Feynman had tentatively suggested as early as 1956 that the parity symmetry had been assumed but not really proven for the weak interactions. Two young theorists, Chen-Ning Yang and Tsung-Dao Lee—both working at the fabled Institute for Advanced Study in Princeton, New Jersey—picked up on Feynman's suggestion and showed that, indeed, neither experiment nor theory compelled the weak force to obey parity. Soon after parity violation had been confirmed experimentally, Feynman developed a first-principles description of the weak force, one that incorporated this basic handedness from the start.

By this time, nearly all physicists assumed that the weak force, much like the other fundamental forces, arose from the exchange of certain particles (just as the electromagnetic force arose, at the quantum-mechanical level, from the exchange of photons, as described by QED). The question remained: what types of particles carried the weak force, and what were the means by which these force-carriers coupled with other types of matter? At a conference of high-energy physicists in 1957, Feynman suggested that the weak force might arise from a particular combination of couplings: part vector coupling and part axial vector, or $V - A$. (These designations refer to the behavior of the particles' interactions under special-relativity transformations.)

Around the same time, Murray Gell-Mann—Feynman's younger colleague and friendly rival at Caltech—arrived at the same conclusion. Rather than see his two star theorists devolve into a messy priority dispute, Caltech's physics department chair, Robert Bacher, wisely suggested that Feynman and Gell-Mann publish an article together. Their paper, titled "Theory of the Fermi Interaction, arrived at *Physical Review* in September 1957, just days before another pair of theorists—the University of Rochester's Robert Marshak and his graduate student, E. C. George Sudarshan—presented a similar theory at a conference in Italy. (In fact, Marshak and Sudarshan had visited with Gell-Mann in California a few months earlier, while Feynman was vacationing in Brazil.) Feynman often considered this work to be his greatest success: for the first time, he had discovered a genuine law of nature.

With the weak force conquered, many high-energy physicists turned their attention to a distinct nuclear force, known as the "strong" force. An attractive force between nuclear particles, the strong force was assumed to bind protons and neutrons together inside atomic nuclei. By the mid-1960s, Gell-Mann (and, independently, the theorist George Zweig) had postulated that protons and neutrons themselves had inner parts; Gell-Mann dubbed them quarks. With the introduction of quarks, the nature of the strong force shifted: now it was assumed to operate directly between constituent quarks, binding them together to make stable protons and neutrons; only secondarily did it give rise to attractive forces between these composite particles.

Many physicists were skeptical of the quark idea at first—was this, they wondered, just opening up an unending series of stacked Russian dolls, one layer hiding within the next? By the late 1960s a team of experimenters from Stanford University and MIT began trying to find evidence of structure within nuclear particles. They bombarded protons with high-energy electrons provided by the new, 2-kilometer-long Stanford Linear Accelerator Center. If protons were really elementary particles, then the electrons should scatter with a characteristic pattern. If, instead, some substructure lurked within the protons, the effects of these miniscule hard scattering centers should show up in the directions along which the electrons careened after scattering.

Most theorists assumed that calculating how the electrons would scatter if protons really did possess substructure would remain simply intractable. The strong force, after all, was in fact strong, and hence most of the tricks that theorists had learned from Feynman's and others' work on weaker forces would no longer apply. With weak forces, such as QED and the weak nuclear force, theorists could break a problem down into a long series of approximations, each more complicated step ultimately contributing less, numerically, to the overall result. Not so with the strong force.

Feynman approached the problem differently. With his characteristically visual approach, he imagined how a proton would look to a high-speed electron. From the electron's point of view, the proton would be flattened like a pancake, thanks to the relativistic effect of length contraction. Moreover, if tiny particles did live inside protons—Feynman remained agnostic about Gell-Mann's quarks, referring to the sub-proton particles as simply "partons," that is, parts of a proton—then the strong forces between them would appear to act on a very slow timescale as far as the onrushing electron was concerned, owing to relativistic time dilation. So instead of seeing a horrible mess of closely packed partons teeming with the constant exchange of force-carrying particles, the electron would in effect see a handful of independent partons more or less sitting still—a far easier situation to analyze. Feynman's parton ideas helped a young Stanford theorist, James Bjorken, finalize quantitative studies of the electrons' scattering off of protons. Armed with Feynman's theoretical simplification, the experimentalists' data and Bjorken's analyses helped convince most physicists that protons and neutrons really did contain smaller particles within them. By the mid-1970s, physicists had reconciled Feynman's partons with Gell-Mann's quarks.

Feynman's other major contribution to high-energy theory concerned gravitation. Albert Einstein completed his general theory of relativity—his renowned theory of gravity—in 1915. To Einstein, gravity was nothing other than geometry: the warping of space and time accounted for how objects moved; "force" played no role at all. After a string of successes, Einstein's elegant theory had fallen from most physicists' attention by the 1930s, displaced by the new quantum theory, nuclear physics, and more. Feynman was among the handful of physicists who returned to the topic during the late 1950s. But where Einstein had banished force from his account of gravitation, Feynman put the notion of force—pictured, as he did the other physical forces, in terms of the exchange of force-carrying particles—center stage. In his reworked account of general relativity, Feynman replaced Einstein's space-time curvature with a particular set of interactions among gravitons, which traveled along a perfectly smooth, flat background space-time. Though he published little on his new approach, Feynman delivered an influential course at Caltech on the topic in 1962–1963. Soon

Feynman

mimeographed copies of his lecture notes began to circulate widely, helping to inspire a new generation of theorists to think about gravity along these particle-physics lines. Combined with his path-integral approach, Feynman's suggestive inroads led younger theorists, such as Bryce DeWitt, to make major progress on the topic of quantum gravity—the quest to combine general relativity with quantum mechanics in a self-consistent formulation.

Teaching and Service. Throughout his career, Feynman was a tremendously popular lecturer. Famously animated, he often acted out how electrons, photons, or protons would behave. During the late 1950s he was invited to teach Caltech's large introductory physics course. In one sense, the course was a flop—even Feynman admitted that he had pitched his material at too advanced a level for the incoming undergraduates. Graduate and postdoctoral students, and even his fellow faculty, on the other hand, found his "elementary" course inspiring. With the aid of two Caltech colleagues, who transcribed his lectures for publication, his "flop" turned into one of the most renowned physics textbooks of all time, *The Feynman Lectures on Physics* (3 vols., 1963–1965). In later years, Feynman frequently gave informal lectures at nearby industrial laboratories, such as Hughes Aircraft. He also offered a popular class titled "Physics X," open to anyone with questions about science.

Soon after *The Feynman Lectures*, Feynman began to publish a series of successful textbooks and popular books. *The Character of Physical Law* (1965), *Quantum Mechanics and Path Integrals*, with Albert R. Hibbs (1965), *Photon-Hadron Interactions* (1972), and *QED: The Strange Theory of Light and Matter* (1985). Each began as *The Feynman Lectures* had, with talks by Feynman as transcribed by colleagues. His most famous books, collections of autobiographical anecdotes and aphorisms—*"Surely You're Joking, Mr. Feynman!"* (1985) and *What Do YOU Care What Other People Think?* (1988)—likewise stemmed from tape-recorded, bongo-playing jam sessions with his friend, Ralph Leighton (the son of one of his Caltech colleagues).

Even as his fame grew, Feynman continued to shun the kinds of worldly, political affairs in which so many of his colleagues engaged. While many of his fellow Los Alamos veterans joined the Federation of Atomic Scientists (later renamed Federation of American Scientists) soon after the war, or the Union of Concerned Scientists twenty-five years later, Feynman famously avoided such groups. Feynman even made a bet with fellow physicist Victor Weisskopf that he would forfeit ten dollars if he ever allowed himself to become saddled with any sort of professional responsibility whatsoever.

Ironically, Feynman's fame was capped by just such a position of responsibility. In January 1986 the space shuttle *Challenger* was ripped to pieces about seventy seconds after takeoff. President Ronald Reagan convened a blue-ribbon panel to investigate the disaster, and Feynman reluctantly agreed to join. Frustrated by what he considered the bureaucratic red tape and political niceties that he thought would stymie the commission, Feynman grabbed the spotlight during televised hearings in February 1986. He had been tipped off by an insider that the accident might have stemmed from the effects of cold weather on some O-rings (rubber seals inside the shuttle's solid-rocket boosters). Waiting for just the right moment when the television cameras were focusing on him, Feynman dipped a piece of O-ring in a glass of ice water and demonstrated how quickly it lost its elasticity. Though the investigation lumbered on for several months, the O-ring explanation finally emerged as the most probable cause. Feynman's dramatic demonstration fixed him in much of the public's mind as just the kind of straight-talking, iconoclastic character whom he had described in his autobiographical sketches.

His contribution to the *Challenger* investigation proved to be his last major work. Two years later he died from kidney failure, a complication arising from his long battle with cancer. He was survived by his wife, Gweneth, and their two children, Carl and Michelle.

BIBLIOGRAPHY

The Richard P. Feynman Papers, 1933–1988, at the Institute Archives, California Institute of Technology, Pasadena, includes Feynman's unpublished correspondence, course and lecture notes, talks and presentations, and research notes. Laurie M. Brown, ed., Selected Papers of Richard Feynman, with Commentary *(River Edge, NJ: World Scientific, 2000), includes a complete bibliography of Feynman's writings.*

WORKS BY FEYNMAN

"Forces in Molecules." *Physical Review* 56 (1939): 340–343.

"Space-Time Approach to Non-relativistic Quantum Mechanics." *Reviews of Modern Physics* 20 (1948): 367–387.

"The Theory of Positrons." *Physical Review* 76 (1949): 749–759.

"Space-Time Approach to Quantum Electrodynamics." *Physical Review* 76 (1949): 769–789.

With Murray Gell-Mann. "Theory of the Fermi Interaction." *Physical Review* 109 (1958): 193–198.

With Robert Leighton and Matthew Sands. *The Feynman Lectures on Physics.* 3 vols. Reading, MA: Addison-Wesley, 1963–1965.

The Character of Physical Law. Cambridge, MA: MIT Press, 1965.

QED: The Strange Theory of Light and Matter. Princeton, NJ: Princeton University Press, 1985.

Fischer

"Surely You're Joking, Mr. Feynman!": Adventures of a Curious Character. New York: W.W. Norton, 1985.

What Do YOU Care What Other People Think?: Further Adventures of a Curious Character. New York: W.W. Norton, 1988.

Selected Papers of Richard Feynman, with Commentary. Edited by Laurie M. Brown. River Edge, NJ: World Scientific, 2000. Reprints many of Feynman's most significant scientific articles.

Perfectly Reasonable Deviations from the Beaten Track: The Letters of Richard P. Feynman. Edited by Michelle Feynman. New York: Basic Books, 2005.

OTHER SOURCES

Galison, Peter. "Feynman's War: Modelling Weapons, Modelling Nature." *Studies in History and Philosophy of Modern Physics* 29B (1998): 391–434. A detailed analysis of Feynman's wartime work and its influence on his later research.

Gleick, James. *Genius: The Life and Science of Richard Feynman.* New York: Pantheon, 1992. The best of several book-length biographies of Feynman, written by an award-winning science journalist.

Kaiser, David. *Drawing Theories Apart: The Dispersion of Feynman Diagrams in Postwar Physics.* Chicago: University of Chicago Press, 2005. A study of how Feynman's diagrammatic approach entered the physics mainstream.

Schweber, Silvan S. *QED and the Men Who Made It: Dyson, Feynman, Schwinger, and Tomonaga.* Princeton, NJ: Princeton University Press, 1994. The most thorough analysis of Feynman's research on electrodynamics and quantum theory.

Sykes, Christopher, ed. *No Ordinary Genius: The Illustrated Richard Feynman.* New York: W.W. Norton, 1994. Contains interviews and reminiscences from many of Feynman's colleagues, students, and friends.

David Kaiser

FISCHER, (LEOPOLD FRANZ) EUGEN

(*b.* Karlsruhe, Germany, 5 June 1874; *d.* Freiburg im Breisgau, 9 July 1967), *anatomy, anthropology, biological anthropology, genetics, eugenics.*

Fischer began his career as an anatomist, but dedicated his investigational effort to anthropological work that sought biological grounds for human traits and their hereditary transmission. He called his method "anthropobiology" and argued that human heredity follows Mendelian patterns. Even more important than his research work, however, were his administrative efforts. He spent 1927–1942 as the director of the Kaiser Wilhelm Institute for Anthropology, Human Heredity, and Eugenics (KWIA) in Berlin. Through this position he put significant scientific resources directly in the service of Nazi racial policy. Fischer thus demonstrates the ways in which biomedical scientists' social interests, investigational goals, and persuasive strategies drove them to participate in the complex networks through which the Nazi state and its officials generated and exploited complicity in their ideologies and crimes.

Training and Early Research. Eugen Fischer grew up in Freiburg im Breisgau, where he also studied and spent most of his career before 1927. He remained personally attached to Freiburg and southwestern Germany for the rest of his life and supported amateur archaeological work about the region. He received his doctorate of medicine in 1898 and his habilitation, in "anatomy with special consideration of anthropology," in 1900. Despite a slow process of academic promotion, his administrative skills and energetic advocacy of anthropological methods in biomedicine quickly impressed important colleagues. In 1903 he participated in the German Anthropological Society's survey of the entire population of the German Empire. This brought him into close contact with other major anthropologists, especially Felix von Luschan. Fischer's interest in eugenics and racial hygiene took concrete form in 1910, when Alfred Ploetz, the founder of the German Society for Racial Hygiene, convinced him to organize the society's Freiburg branch.

The political controversies generated by the German colonies in Africa and the Pacific led to Fischer's breakthrough as a scientific investigator. Fischer personally supported an active German colonial policy, and sought to become an expert on racial questions in the colonies. He hypothesized that a hybrid European-African population in German Southwest Africa (Namibia) should demonstrate the Mendelian hereditary patterns that had become central to biological inquiry after 1900. Financed by the Prussian Academy of Sciences, he traveled to Africa in July–October 1908. The resulting monograph, *Die Rehobother Bastards,* appeared in 1913. Fischer constructed elaborate family trees of the Rehoboth population and then classified three subpopulations ("European," "mixed," and "Hottentot") based on traits including hair form, eye color, hair color, skin color, skull shape, eye shape, and nose shape. He also argued that the Rehoboth population showed signs of "hybrid vigor," despite his expressed belief that African populations showed a lack of creativity and leadership qualities, and were therefore "inferior." Anthropologists and biologists long accepted that Fischer's work demonstrated conclusively that human traits were subject to Mendelian laws. In further works of this period, Fischer argued that human racial differences appeared through a process akin to domestication in plants and animals. He believed that Europeans had "auto-domesticated" through quasi-conscious selection for "blondness, light eye color, and light skin," and he used histological comparisons of pigmentation in brown bears and polar bears to support his

Eugen Fischer. *Fischer with anthropological photographs, c. 1938.* ARCHIV DER MAX-PLANCK-GESELLSCHAFT, BERLIN-DAHLEM

arguments against natural selection as the cause of human racial differentiation. Both of Fischer's major research claims, however, were founded on analogies drawn from unreflective acceptance of the superiority of European races. They were not supported by sophisticated statistical reasoning, and have since been discredited.

Advocacy and Administration. The Rehoboth monograph was highly regarded in its day, and made Fischer into a leading expert on the relationship between biological principles and human variation. He had thus attained sufficient status to dedicate himself to administration and advocacy of inquiry into eugenic practices, human heredity, race differences, and their political consequences. He further increased his prestige through collaborations with geneticists and eugenicists, including the American Charles B. Davenport. He also supported partisans of racial ideology such as Hans F. K. Günther. Fischer's best-

Fischer

known scientific publication, the textbook of human heredity and racial hygiene coauthored with Erwin Baur and Fritz Lenz, known as the "Baur-Fischer-Lenz," reveals how his later work contained more collaborative advocacy than new investigation. Initially published in 1921, the book went through five editions and translations into English and Swedish by 1940. Reviewers from many disciplines praised the book; it was widely cited by international geneticists and eugenicists in the 1920s and 1930s, and it became the leading textbook of heredity and eugenics in Nazi Germany. Fischer's section of the work was largely a summary of his interpretation of the historical development of human variation and the current range of human variability, with focus on the same traits that he had investigated among the Rehoboth population.

In 1918, after wartime medical service, Fischer was made full professor of anatomy and director of the Anatomical Institute in Freiburg. Nonetheless, he still sought a more prestigious position from which to expand his advocacy. In 1927 he was made professor of anthropology and founding director of the new KWIA, in Berlin. At KWIA he administered research and publication work in the three departments indicated by its name, and oversaw what he himself called "eugenic propaganda." The content of Fischer's "propaganda" changed little after the transition from the parliamentary Weimar government to the Nazi regime. He was made rector of the University of Berlin in 1933, despite some Nazi Party opposition.

Fischer's propagation of the idea of hybrid vigor among human races led some Nazi factions to denounce him in 1933 and 1934 as a "race-mixer," which ran counter to Nazi racial policy. From this experience he learned how to profile himself within the Nazi regime, and made the kind of "Faustian bargain" with the Nazi state described by Robert Jay Lifton in *The Nazi Doctors* (1986). He perceived his institute as part of a national political project and willingly modulated his advocacy and administrative work into congruence with the varied forms of Nazi racial and anti-Semitic policy. He thus transformed KWIA into the most significant source of scientific legitimation for Nazi racial policy. Fischer and his colleagues participated in the Nazi "genetic health courts" established to administer the regime's sterilization program; supported forced sterilizations on racial grounds (especially of the children of German women and French-African soldiers occupying the Ruhr area after World War I); trained race-policy bureaucrats and SS physicians; defended the Nazi regime at international scientific meetings; and gained research data from human subjects exploited and murdered in Nazi ghettos, camps, and penal institutions. Fischer retired in 1942, accepted the Nazis' highest scientific honors, and chose as his successor at KWIA his student and colleague Otmar von Verschuer. It was under Verschuer and his student Josef Mengele that many of the most flagrant violations of ethics in research on human beings in the Third Reich took place (infecting twins with virulent disease organisms, removal of body parts for analysis of phenotypic similarities and differences, etc.). While Fischer was not directly responsible for such atrocities, he laid the groundwork by putting the resources of the KWIA unfailingly in the service of the Nazi government.

After the war Fischer escaped denazification proceedings with a fine of three hundred marks. He then refrained from publication and scientific activity for some years. After 1950 he revived his work in local archaeology and actively advocated for the careers of his former students and colleagues such as Verschuer. He thus remained until his death a significant participant in the spheres of German anthropology, biology, and genetics. Fischer's career is far more than just a cautionary tale. It represents the full complexity of the cultural and political embeddedness of the German life sciences in the early twentieth century.

BIBLIOGRAPHY

Lösch, Rasse als Konstrukt, *contains a complete bibliography of publications by Fischer and KWIA, and evaluates public and private archival sources on Fischer.*

WORKS BY FISCHER

Die Rehobother Bastards und das Bastardierungsproblem beim Menschen: Anthropologische und ethnographische Studien am Rehobother Bastardvolk in Deutsch-Südwest-Afrika. Jena, Germany: Gustav Fischer, 1913. Reprint, Graz, Austria: Akademische Druck- und Verlagsanstalt, 1961.

With Erwin Baur and Fritz Lenz. *Grundriß der menschlichen Erblichkeitslehre und Rassenhygiene.* 2 vols. Munich, Germany: J.F. Lehmann, 1921. English translation, *Human Heredity,* 1 vol., translated by Eden and Cedar Paul. New York: Macmillan, 1931.

OTHER SOURCES

Berez, Thomas M., and Sheila Faith Weiss. "The Nazi Symbiosis: Politics and Human Genetics at the Kaiser Wilhelm Institute." *Endeavour* 28, no. 4 (2004): 172–177.

Gessler, Bernhard. *Eugen Fischer, 1874–1967: Leben und Werk des Freiburger Anatomen, Anthropologen und Rassenhygienikers bis 1927.* Frankfurt, Germany, and New York: Lang, 2000.

Lösch, Niels C. *Rasse als Konstrukt: Leben und Werk Eugen Fischers.* Frankfurt, Germany, and New York: Lang, 1997.

Massin, Benoit. "From Virchow to Fischer: Physical Anthropology and 'Modern Race Theories' in Wilhelmine Germany." In *Volksgeist as Method and Ethic: Essays on Boasian Ethnography and the German Anthropological Tradition,* edited by George W. Stocking Jr., 79–154. History of Anthropology, vol. 8. Madison: University of Wisconsin Press, 1996.

Proctor, Robert. *Racial Hygiene: Medicine under the Nazis.* Cambridge, MA: Harvard University Press, 1988.

Weindling, Paul J. *Health, Race, and German Politics between National Unification and Nazism, 1870–1945.* Cambridge, U.K.: Cambridge University Press, 1989.

Kevin S. Amidon

FISHER, RONALD AYLMER (*b.* London, England, 28 February 1890; *d.* Adelaide, Australia, 29 July 1962), *statistics, evolutionary genetics.* For the original article on Fisher see *DSB,* vol. 5.

Fisher's monumental influence on mathematical statistics is no greater or lesser than his influence on evolutionary genetics. Indeed, while he was at Rothamsted Experimental Station at Harpenden in Hertfordshire, England, between 1919 and 1933, Fisher not only revolutionized statistics, he helped usher in modern evolutionary theory and the historical period of evolutionary biology denoted the "evolutionary synthesis." This update deals with Fisher's contribution to evolutionary genetics, as it has only been since the mid-1980s that precisely what that contribution is has been fully understood.

The Evolutionary Synthesis. With J. B. S. Haldane and Sewall Wright, Fisher originated the field of theoretical population genetics, which synthesized the recently (1900) rediscovered principles of Mendelian heredity with Darwinian natural selection. Among the three, however, Fisher made the greatest contribution to the origins of population genetics. Fisher, of course, published much on that topic, but the three works that establish him as the dominant theorist among his contemporaries are his "The Correlation of Relatives on the Supposition of Mendelian Inheritance" in 1918; his "On the Dominance Ratio" in 1922; and the locus classicus of evolutionary genetics, *The Genetical Theory of Natural Selection,* in 1930. These three works form one long argument that defends the reconciliation of Mendelian heredity and Darwinian natural selection from the then-pervasive critics by eliminating speculative evolutionary causes or, to use William Provine's term, *constricting,* the causes correctly attributable to evolution.

In "On the Dominance Ratio," Fisher discusses, as he says, "the distribution of the frequency ratio of the allelomorphs of dimorphic factors, and the conditions under which the variance of the population may be maintained" (1922, p. 322). He saw this paper as linked to the earlier "Correlation of Relatives on the Supposition of Mendelian Inheritance." In broad brush strokes, this means that where the 1918 paper defended the principles of Mendelian heredity against the criticisms of the biometricians (and in fact showed the two schemes to be compatible), the 1922 paper continues by carrying through its mathematical methods and concepts as well as defending Darwinism's using the principles of Mendelian heredity. Specific to "On the Dominance Ratio," Fisher's aim was to respond to a set of criticisms to the effect that Darwinian natural selection cannot be the correct explanation of the modulation of genetic variation in populations because the genetics of populations are such that there is not enough variation available for selection to act upon. In his response, Fisher considered the interaction of natural selection, random survival (genetic drift), assortative mating, and dominance. During the course of the paper, Fisher eliminated from consideration what he took to be insignificant evolutionary factors, such as epistatic gene interaction and genetic drift, and argued that natural selection acted very slowly on mutations of small effect and in the context of large populations maintaining a large amount of genetic variation.

Ronald A. Fisher. *Sir Ronald Fisher lights a pipe, 5 July 1957.* HULTON ARCHIVE/GETTY IMAGES.

Analysis of Random Drift. Consider drift, or what Fisher referred to variously as random survival, steady decay, or the Hagedoorn effect. The phrase *random drift* comes from Wright's landmark paper of 1931, "Evolution in Mendelian Populations." Notwithstanding Wright's obvious contributions to the development of the concept and mathematical modeling of drift, it was Fisher who, in his 1922 paper, was the first among the architects of population genetics to explore mathematically the evolutionary consequences of drift in a Mendelian population.

In finite populations, the variation in the number of offspring between individuals may result in random fluctuations in allele frequencies. These random fluctuations affect the chances of survival of a mutant allele in a population. Fisher argued that the survival of a rare mutant depended upon chance and not selection. Indeed, he argued that such a mutation would be more likely to remain at low frequencies in a large rather than in a small population, since in a large population the mutant would have a greater probability of survival. Random fluctuations in allele frequencies also reduce a population's genetic variation. In *The Relative Value of the Processes Causing Evolution* (1921), Arund L. and Anna C. Hagedoorn argued that random survival is an important cause of the reduction of genetic variation in natural populations. Fisher argued that the Hagedoorns were mistaken. Fisher determined two key quantities for the situation in which a population is under the influence only of the steady decay of genetic variation, that is, the Hagedoorn effect: the first quantity describes the time course in generations of the Hagedoorn effect; the second describes the "half-life" in generations of the effect. Fisher determined the time course to be $4N$ (where N is population size) and the half-life to be $2.8N$. This means that the Hagedoorn effect requires $4N$ generations to reduce the genetic variation in the population to the point that all alleles are identical by descent. The "half-way" point is reached in $2.8N$ generations. (Wright demonstrated in a 1929 letter to Fisher that his, Fisher's, calculations were twice too high: the time-course in generations is $2N$ and the half-life of the Hagedoorn effect is $1.4N$. In his paper, "The Distribution of Gene Ratios for Rare Mutations" [1930], Fisher showed that the correction had only a minor effect on his argument.)

Fisher used these quantities to weight the significance of the effect of steady decay; the longer the time course, the weaker the effect. Given that the time course of the Hagedoorn effect depends on the population size, the larger the population, the weaker, or less significant, the effect. It is evident that as population size increases over 10^4, that the time course becomes considerable. Indeed, Fisher says, "As few groups contain less than 10,000 individuals between whom interbreeding takes place, the period required for the action of the Hagedoorn effect, in the entire absence of mutation, is immense" (1922, p. 330). According to Fisher, then, the Hagedoorn effect is evolutionarily insignificant and populations are large.

Fisher's insights regarding the evolutionary effects of genetic drift reflect his strong Darwinian assumptions, as he (Fisher) says: "a numerous species, with the same frequency of mutation, will maintain a higher variability than will a less numerous species: in connection with this fact we cannot fail to remember the dictum of Charles Darwin, that 'wide-ranging, much diffused and common species vary most'" (1922, p. 324).

Gene Interaction. In his 1918 paper, Fisher considered the statistical consequences of dominance, epistatic gene interaction, assortative mating, multiple alleles, and linkage on the correlations between relatives. Fisher argued that the effects of dominance and gene interaction would confuse the actual genetic similarity between relatives. He also knew that the environment could confuse such similarity. Fisher here introduced the concept of variance and the analysis of variance to the scientific literature:

> When there are two independent causes of variability capable of producing in an otherwise uniform population distributions with standard deviations σ_1 and σ_2, it is found that the distribution, when both causes act together, has a standard deviation $\sqrt{\sigma_1 + \sigma_2}$. It is therefore desirable in analyzing the causes of variability to deal with the square of the standard deviation as the measure of variability. We shall term this quantity the Variance of the normal population to which it refers, and we may now ascribe to the constituent causes fractions or percentages of the total variance which they together produce. (1918, p. 399)

Fisher then used this tool to partition the total variance into its component parts.

Fisher labeled that portion of the total variance that accurately described the correlation between relatives the "additive" genetic component of variance. The "nonadditive" genetic component included dominance, gene interaction, and linkage. Environmental effects, such as random changes in environment, comprised a third component of the total variance. In 1922, on the basis of his 1918 work, Fisher argued that the additive component of variance was important for evolution by natural selection. Indeed, he argued that, particularly in large populations ($>10^4$), nonadditive and environmental components of the total variance are negligible. He further claimed that selection would remove any factor for which the additive contribution to the total genetic variance is very high and leave those for which the contribution is low. Indeed, Fisher says, "It is therefore to be expected that the large and easily recognized factors in natural organisms will be of little adaptive importance, and that the factors affecting important adaptations will be individually of very slight effect" (1922, p. 334). Ultimately, for Fisher, evolution proceeds very slowly, with low levels of selection acting on mutations of small effect and in large populations holding considerable genetic variation.

The Genetical Theory of Natural Selection. Fisher's work discussed above and other work on, for example, the evolution of dominance and mimicry, would culminate in his book, *The Genetical Theory of Natural Selection* (1930), one of the principal texts—along with Haldane's *The Causes of Evolution* (1932) and Wright's "Evolution in Mendelian Populations" (1931) and "The Roles of Mutation ... " (1932)—completing the reconciliation of Darwinism and Mendelism and establishing the field of theoretical population genetics (and, for Fisher, its application to eugenics). *The Genetical Theory* is celebrated as the locus classicus for the reconciliation of Darwinian natural selection and Mendelian heredity. Remarkably, the book manuscript was produced by Fisher's dictating to his wife, Ruth, during the evenings. It was revised and reissued in 1958 and most recently in a variorum edition issued in 1999 (edited by J. H. Bennett).

The first seven (of twelve) chapters of *The Genetical Theory* set out Fisher's synthesis of Darwin's mechanism of natural selection and Mendelian genetics. Fisher considered the first two chapters, on the nature of inheritance and the "fundamental theorem of natural selection," the most important of the book. Indeed, these two chapters accomplish the key piece of the reconciliation. Moreover, the general argument strategy Fisher used in 1918 and 1922, of defending the principles of Mendelian heredity and defending Darwinism under the rubric of Mendelian heredity, is carried through. Fisher's aim in *The Genetical Theory* was to establish particulate inheritance against the blending theory and then demonstrate how plausibly Darwinian natural selection may be the principal cause of evolution in Mendelian populations.

Fisher's first chapter considers implications of a synthesis of natural selection with, alternatively, blending and Mendelian inheritance. He demonstrates that on the Mendelian theory, natural selection may be the main mechanism of a population's variability. The demonstration importantly resolved a persistent problem for Darwin's theory of descent with modification, one that had led biologists to abandon natural selection as an evolutionary mechanism: Darwin's acceptance of blending inheritance required him to imagine special mechanisms controlling mutation because of enormous mutation rates demanded by the blending theory. Because Mendelian heredity did not demand such enormous mutation rates, Fisher was able to eliminate these controlling mechanisms and, so, revive natural selection as an important evolutionary mechanism.

Fisher's second chapter develops, mathematically, his genetical theory of natural selection. The arguments are drawn largely from his "On the Dominance Ratio" of 1922 and "The Distribution of Gene Ratios for Rare Mutations" of 1930, the response to Wright's aforementioned correction of Fisher's 1922 paper. Three key elements may be distilled from Fisher's "heavy" mathematics in the second chapter of *The Genetical Theory.* The first is a measure of average population fitness, Fisher's Malthusian parameter—that is, the reproductive value of all genotypes at all stages of their life histories. The second is a measure of variation in fitness, which Fisher partitions into genetic and environmental components (based on his distinctions from his 1918 and 1922 papers). The third is a measure of the rate of increase in fitness, that is, the change in fitness due to natural selection. For Fisher, "*the rate of increase of fitness of any organism at any time is equal to its genetic variance in fitness at that time*" (*The Genetical Theory of Natural Selection,* 1930, p. 37; emphasis in original). This last element is Fisher's fundamental theorem of natural selection and is the centerpiece of his natural selection theory.

Understanding the Fundamental Theorem. Interestingly, inasmuch as Fisher considered his fundamental theorem the centerpiece of his evolutionary theory, it happens that the theorem is also the most obscure element of it. The theorem was thoroughly misunderstood until 1989, when Warren Ewens—in "An Interpretation and Proof of the Fundamental Theorem of Natural Selection"—rediscovered George Price's 1972 clarification and proof of it in "Fisher's 'Fundamental Theorem' Made Clear." Fisher's original statement of the theorem in 1930 suggests that mean fitness can never decrease because variances cannot be negative. Price showed that in fact the theorem does not describe the total rate of change in fitness but rather only one component of it. That part is the portion of the rate of increase that can be ascribed to natural selection. And, actually, in Fisher's ensuing discussion of the theorem, he makes this clear. The total rate of change in mean fitness is due to a variety of forces, including natural selection, environmental changes, epistatic gene interaction, dominance, and so forth. The theorem isolates the changes due to natural selection from the rest, a move suggested in Fisher's 1922 paper. The key change that Price and Ewens make in the statement of the theorem, the change that clarifies it, is to write "*additive* genetic variance" for "genetic variance" (since "genetic variance" includes both an additive and nonadditive part). With the theorem clarified and proven, Price and later Ewens argue that it is not so fundamental. Given that it is a statement about only a portion of the rate of increase in fitness, it is incomplete. The Price-Ewens interpretation of the theorem is the standard one. However, Anthony Edwards –in his 1994 paper, "The Fundamental Theorem of Natural Selection"—argues that Fisher's isolation of change in the genetic variance due to selection is biologically deep, that is, fundamental, and so the charge of incompleteness is impotent.

Fisher compared both his 1922 and 1930 explorations of the balance of evolutionary factors and the "laws" that describe them to the theory of gases and the second law of thermodynamics, respectively. The received view of these comparisons is that Fisher's interests in physics and mathematics led him to look for biological analogues. No doubt this is part of the story. However, a more plausible interpretation of the comparison comes from treating Fisher's major works of 1918, 1922, and 1930 as one long argument. If this is done, one finds that Fisher's strategy in synthesizing Darwinian natural selection with the principles of Mendelian heredity was to defend, against its critics, selection as an evolutionary mechanism under Mendelian principles. Following this argument strategy, Fisher built his genetical theory of natural selection piecemeal, or from the bottom up. That is, Fisher worked to justify the claim of his fundamental theorem by constructing plausible arguments about the precise balance of evolutionary factors. Thus, his piecemeal consideration of the interaction between dominance, gene interaction, genetic drift, mutation, selection, and so on led to his theorem. It is not, at least not primarily, the search for biological analogues to physical models and laws that underwrites the theorem.

Eugenics. The last five chapters of *The Genetical Theory* explore natural selection in human populations, particularly social selection in human fertility. According to Fisher, the decline of human civilizations is due in part to the point in economic development where an inversion in fertility of the upper classes to that of the lower classes is reached. Fisher's central observation, based upon England's 1911 census data, was that the development of economies in human societies structures the birth-rate so that it is inverted with respect to social class—low birth-rates for the upper class and high birth-rates for the lower class. Families who, for whatever reason, were not capable of producing many children rose in class because of the financial advantage of having few children. In the final chapter of *The Genetical Theory,* Fisher offers strategies for countering this effect. He proposed the abolishment of the economic advantage of small families by instituting what he called "allowances" to families with larger numbers of children, with the allowances proportional to the earnings of the father. In spite of Fisher's espousal of eugenics in this part of the book, he means the discussion to be taken as an inseparable extension of the preceding part.

No one has thought that Fisher's contribution to evolutionary genetics was less than groundbreaking. Rather, precisely what Fisher established, its nature and scope, and exactly how he did so has been less than clear. With Fisher's work on variance in 1918, his work on the balance of factors in evolution in 1922, and his fundamental theorem of natural selection in 1930, we have a unified argument setting aside pervasive anti-Darwinism, originating a new mathematical approach to the evolution of populations and establishing the very essence of natural selection. All of which are good reasons for the universal approbation of Fisher's work in evolutionary genetics.

SUPPLEMENTARY BIBLIOGRAPHY

There is a wealth of material on Fisher's contributions both to statistics and to evolutionary genetics, including unpublished correspondence. See J. H. Bennett's Natural Selection, Heredity, and Eugenics: Including Selected Correspondence of R. A. Fisher with Leonard Darwin and Others *(Oxford: Clarendon Press, 1983) and* Statistical Inference and Analysis: Selected Correspondence of R. A. Fisher *(Oxford: Clarendon Press, 1990). These works contain a bibliography of all of Fisher's publications. See also* The University of Adelaide Digital Library: R. A. Fisher Digital Archive; *available from http://digital.library.adelaide.edu.au/coll/special/fisher/.*

WORKS BY FISHER

"The Correlation of Relatives on the Supposition of Mendelian Inheritance." *Royal Society of Edinburgh* 52 (1918): 399–433.

"On the Dominance Ratio." *Proceedings of the Royal Society of Edinburgh* 42 (1922): 321–341.

"The Distribution of Gene Ratios for Rare Mutations." *Proceedings of the Royal Society of Edinburgh* 50 (1930): 205–220.

The Genetical Theory of Natural Selection. Oxford: Clarendon Press, 1930. Released in a revised, second edition in 1958 from Dover Publications. Released in a variorum edition by Oxford University Press in 1999, edited by J. H. Bennett.

OTHER SOURCES

Edwards, Anthony W. F. "The Fundamental Theorem of Natural Selection." *Biological Reviews of the Cambridge Philosophical Society* 69 (1994): 443–474.

Ewens, Warren J. "An Interpretation and Proof of the Fundamental Theorem of Natural Selection." *Theoretical Population Biology* 36 (1989): 167–180.

Gayon, Jean. *Darwinism's Struggle for Survival: Heredity and the Hypothesis of Natural Selection,* translated by Matthew Cobb. Cambridge, U.K., and New York: Cambridge University Press, 1989.

Hagedoorn, Arund L., and Anna C. Hagedoorn. *The Relative Value of the Processes Causing Evolution.* The Hague, Netherlands: M. Nijhoff, 1921.

Haldane, John B. S. *The Causes of Evolution.* London: Longmans, 1932.

Hodge, M. Jonathon S. "Biology and Philosophy (Including Ideology): A Study of Fisher and Wright." In *The Founders of Evolutionary Genetics: A Centenary Reappraisal,* edited by Sahotra Sarkar. Dordrecht, Netherlands, and Boston: Kluwer Academic Publishers, 1992.

Price, George R. "Fisher's 'Fundamental Theorem' Made Clear." *Annals of Human Genetics* 36 (1972): 129–140.

Provine, William. "Founder Effects and Genetic Revolutions in Microevolution and Speciation: A Historical Perspective." In *Genetics, Speciation, and the Founder Principle,* edited by Luther Val Giddings, Kenneth Y. Kaneshiro, and Wyatt W. Anderson. New York: Oxford University Press, 1989.

———. *The Origins of Theoretical Population Genetics.* 2nd ed. Chicago: University of Chicago Press, 2001.

Wright, Sewall. "Evolution in Mendelian Populations." *Genetics* 16 (1931): 97–159.

———. "The Roles of Mutation, Inbreeding, Crossbreeding, and Selection in Evolution." *Proceedings of the Sixth Annual Congress of Genetics* 1 (1932): 356–366.

Robert Skipper

FLEROV, GEORGIĬ NIKOLAEVICH

(*b.* Rostov-on-Don, Russia, 2 March 1913; *d.* Moscow, USSR, 19 November 1990), *nuclear physics, nuclear chemistry.*

Flerov is known for his experimental investigations of the physics of the atomic nucleus, including the discovery of the spontaneous fission of the uranium nucleus. Together with Igor V. Kurchatov, he directly participated in the development of Soviet atomic weapons. In addition, Flerov helped develop the field of the physics of heavy ions. With his coworkers, he successfully conducted experiments on the synthesis of chemical elements with atomic numbers 102–107 and discovered new physical phenomena, such as the accelerated spontaneous fission of isomeric nuclei, the delayed fission of nuclei, decay of nuclei with the emission of delayed protons, and a new class of nuclear reactions—the reactions of deep inelastic transmission of nucleons.

Scientific Path. After finishing secondary school in 1929 in his hometown, Flerov worked at a multitude of different jobs—as an unskilled worker, as an engine-house greaser, and then as an electrician. In 1931 he left Rostov-on-Don and went to Leningrad, where he took a position as an electrician at the metal-working plant named "Krasnii Putilovets" (Red Putilov). In 1933 the factory sent the young worker to study at the M. I. Kalinin Leningrad Polytechnical Institute in the engineering-physics department. During his years of study Flerov specialized in the area of thermophysics and experimental nuclear physics. In the upper courses he also studied at the Leningrad Physico-Technical Institute (LFTI). His diploma thesis, supervised by the well-known physicist Kurchatov, was a study of the interaction of slow neutrons with nuclei. Upon graduation Flerov was selected to continue work in Kurchatov's laboratory.

Spontaneous Fission of Nuclei. At the end of 1939, physicists throughout the world were surprised by news about the discovery of nuclear fission. This problem attracted Flerov's attention and, together with his colleague Lev I. Rusinov, he conducted an experiment that attempted to obtain a chain reaction of fissioning uranium nuclei. Although this experiment was not successful, it provided important results about determining the key parameters of chain reactions—the number of secondary neutrons arising from the fission of a uranium nucleus. This experiment was the first step in Flerov's major work on nuclear fission.

The next question to consider was with what probability would the naturally occurring isotopes of uranium (238, 235, 234) fission under the impact of neutrons of various energies. For these experiments Flerov and Konstantin A. Petrzhak developed a technique with extremely high sensitivity, and in 1940 they showed, for the first time, that uranium nuclei could split spontaneously. This fundamental discovery served as the basis for a whole new field of nuclear physics. In 1946 Flerov (together with Petrzhak) was awarded the State (Stalin) Prize, second class, for the discovery of the spontaneous fission of uranium.

Participation in the "Atomic Project." Soon after the German attack on the Soviet Union in the summer of 1941, Flerov volunteered to serve in the army at the front. He was sent for training at the Military-Aviation Academy, located near Leningrad, and later was evacuated to Ioshkar-Ola, where he studied the servicing of military aircraft. After completing his studies Flerov was commissioned as a lieutenant in the Ninetieth Reconnaissance Aviation Squadron of the Military-Aviation Academy of the Southwest Front. Even while on active duty in the army, Flerov took advantage of every spare moment and tried to follow the research being published on uranium. He soon noticed the disappearance of scientific articles about this topic, whereas before the war such articles appeared regularly in foreign publications. He came to the conclusion that all such work had become classified as a military project and, consequently, that foreign countries had become engaged in creating an atomic bomb. In 1941–1942, while still at the front, Flerov sent a series of letters about his suspicions to well-known scientists and government leaders, including Kurchatov, Sergei V. Kaftanov (the plenipotentiary for science at the State Defense Committee), and even Joseph Stalin himself. These letters, according to the recollections of Kaftanov, were one of the essential factors that prompted the Soviet government's decision to initiate a program for the creation of atomic weapons at such a difficult period for the country.

In December 1941 Flerov presented a talk to specialists from the USSR Academy of Sciences, which at that time had been evacuated to the city of Kazan, east of Moscow. In this presentation he emphasized the need to study nuclear chain reactions induced by fast neutrons. During the spring of 1942 Flerov sent a draft of an article to Kurchatov in which he repeated the main ideas of the talk he had given in Kazan. This article, "The Question of Using Inter-atomic Energy," proposed a scheme for the realization of atomic explosions by very rapidly joining together two hemispheres of uranium-235 in order to achieve critical mass and included a calculation of the necessary velocity for joining the two halves together. (The article remained unpublished.) Kurchatov considered this work to be spectacular. Flerov was detached from the army in June 1942 and sent to work at the Physical-Technical Institute in Kazan, where he remained during 1942–1943.

On 28 September 1942 Stalin approved the resolution of the State Defense Committee, "About the Organization of Work on Uranium," which gave the USSR Academy of Sciences the task of resuming the work on studies to realize the uses of atomic energy by the path of chain reactions of uranium nuclei that had been interrupted by the war. In February 1943 "Laboratory No. 2" was established under the direction of Kurchatov, who supervised the atomic project. The main group of the "Kurchatov team" was composed of Leningrad physicists who had graduated from the Leningrad Physico-Technical Institute—Anatoliĭ P. Alexandrov, Abram I. Alikhanov, Lev A. Artsimovich, Iuliĭ B. Khariton, Yakov B. Zeldovich, and others, including Flerov. From 1943 to 1945 Flerov was a senior scientist at Laboratory No. 2 of the USSR Academy of Sciences and from 1945 to 1949 was a section chief there.

Already in 1943 two main strategies had been outlined for the realization of the atomic project: (1) a gun variant of an atomic bomb containing uranium-235 obtained from one of the methods of isotope separation; and (2) a nuclear bomb of the implosion type using plutonium-239, an isotope that had scarcely been investigated at that time, but which held the promise of providing the material for a self-sustaining chain reaction upon of slow neutrons irradiation of uranium-238 using graphite as moderator. These two paths were proposed based on the assumption of obtaining a sufficient amount of fissionable material for an atomic bomb. Flerov's group studied the characteristic interactions of neutrons with the nuclei of heavy elements and the splitting of nuclei. The plutonium strategy won out. For a series of reasons, the gun variant (RDS-2) was inferior to a nuclear bomb of the implosion type (RDS-1), and work on the former type of bomb was ended in mid-1948. An experimental prototype RDS-1 was exploded by the United States in July 1945. The creation of the RDS-1, as is known, was based on information about the physical scheme of the American plutonium bomb.

The construction of the first atomic bombs and the necessary research for them was carried out in a special branch of Laboratory No. 2 (KB-11) in the small town of Sarov. The scientific research work of laboratory KB-11 began in the spring of 1947. In January 1948, Laboratory No. 9 was organized to measure critical masses and was headed by Flerov. This laboratory studied the transmission and reflection of fast neutrons by layers of various materials. It was important to select the optimal material for reflecting neutrons in order to minimize the critical mass of metallic plutonium-239 that was needed. At the same time, the laboratory constructed a special apparatus that provided an experimental estimation of similar critical measurements. These quite dangerous measurements of the critical mass of plutonium were carried out by a group of researchers under the direction of Flerov in June 1949 at a metallurgical plant (Cheliabinsk-40) in the Urals that prepared the metallic plutonium. On the basis of these experiments, the group of theoreticians led by Zeldovich was able to determine the necessary mass of the plutonium sphere that would satisfy the basic parameters for a nuclear explosion. The successful realization of these experiments was an important step on the path toward the testing of the first Soviet atomic bomb on 29 August 1949.

The test of the first Soviet thermonuclear bomb was conducted on 12 August 1953. Flerov's research team actively participated in conducting nuclear-physical experiments connected with developing the thermonuclear system in the years up to the test. This team studied nuclear constants that could be used for calculating and utilizing the modeling of widely varied systems.

For his work on the atomic project G. N. Flerov was awarded the State (Stalin) Prize, first class (1949) and received the title of Hero of Socialist Labor with the Order of Lenin (1949). He was also awarded the Order of the Red Banner of Labor in 1948 and 1953.

Flerov also rose in his scientific career. In 1943 he was awarded the degree of candidate of physical-mathematical sciences without the defense of a dissertation, and in 1949 he received the degree of doctor of physical-mathematical sciences. In 1953 he was elected a corresponding member of the USSR Academy of Sciences.

The Synthesis of New Elements. In the early 1950s Flerov (who from 1949 to 1957 was the head of Section No. 7 at the Laboratory of Instrumental Measurement of the Institute of Atomic Energy, USSR Academy of Sciences) decided to return to the investigation of spontaneous nuclear fission. Whereas in 1940 only uranium was known to undergo spontaneous fission, by the early 1950s a series of artificially created elements had been produced that exhibited spontaneous fission. In order for Flerov to study the properties of spontaneous fission in these new heavy nuclei, it was necessary to synthesize them. Analyzing the known methods of synthesis of transuranium elements, Flerov concluded that the best way would be to use accelerated heavy ions. His conclusion, essentially, was to irradiate the target nuclei by accelerated heavy ions and increase the atomic number of the nucleus in that way by several units in a single step. As a consequence, the question arose about how to obtain accelerated heavy ions with the needed energy and intensity.

At that time the available sources could produce ions with only a single or double charge, which would not achieve the needed energies with classical methods. Therefore Flerov decided to switch to a different method of accelerating ions—the method of peeling the electron shells by small charged ions in molecules of a residual gas by acceleration in a cyclotron. Experiments with the acceleration of heavy ions in the institute's 150-centimeter cyclotron, using short frequencies with supplementary "peeling," showed, on the one hand, the utility of using heavy ions for the synthesis of transuranium elements, and, on the other hand, the need for more intense beams of accelerated particles. This need could be satisfied only with the help of intense sources of multiply charged ions. By 1955 the first such source was created and was employed in the 150 centimeter cyclotron at the institute. Research was conducted there on the physics of heavy ions, including the synthesis and investigation of the properties of transuranium elements, such as the element with the atomic number 102.

In 1957 this work was transferred to the Ob"edinennyĭ Institut Iadernykh Issledovaniĭ (OIIaI -Joint Institute for Nuclear Research [JINR]) in Dubna, 120 kilometers from Moscow. This institute was created on the basis of an agreement signed 26 March 1956 in Moscow by representatives of the governments of eleven founding nations, with the goal of unifying their scientific and material potential for the study of the fundamental properties of matter. The scientific council of the institute included well-known physicists from Germany, Italy, the United States, and France. In 1957 Flerov proposed that a laboratory for the study of nuclear reactions be established at JINR under his supervision.

From the first days of work in his laboratory, Flerov paid special attention to modernizing its accelerators, which could produce powerful sources of multiply charged ions. The results of this work included the creation in the laboratory of a new generation of heavy ion accelerators with record sizes: a 300-centimeter cyclotron U-300, the isochronous cyclotron U-200, then the tandem cyclotrons U-300 and U-200; in the late 1970s the U-400, one of the largest isochronous cyclotrons in the world at that time, came online. These very powerful accelerators allowed the researchers to work on cutting-edge problems in the physics of heavy ions.

The research conducted in the laboratory of Flerov and his students over the course of three decades led to the synthesis of new chemical elements with the atomic numbers 102–109, the production of a large number of new nuclei at the border of nuclear stability, the discovery of new types of radioactivity, and new mechanisms of nuclear interactions.

The basis for the success of Flerov and his coworkers in their work on the synthesis of new elements was the careful employment of nuclear-physical methods for the identification of isotopes. In order to identify the newly created elements, the group developed an original method of rapid gas chromatography for separating transactinium elements (in particular, 104 and 105) from a mixture of lighter products of the reactions. One of the most important results of this work was the discovery of the high stability of extremely heavy nuclei with atomic numbers greater than 104 in regard to spontaneous fission, which opened new methods for the further development of research in this area. At the same time, workers in Flerov's laboratory decided to conduct experiments on the synthesis of hypothetical transuranium elements with very large atomic numbers and to realize the attempts to search for these elements in nature (for example, the element number 114).

In 1967 Flerov was awarded the Lenin Prize for the synthesis and investigation of transuranium elements, and in 1968 he was elected a full member of the USSR Academy of Sciences. In 1975 he was awarded the USSR State Prize for his work on nuclei close to the nucleon stability boundary.

Two other scientific groups also participated in the synthesis and investigation of elements 102–109—the Lawrence Berkeley National Laboratory (United States) and the Gesellschaft für Schwerionenforschung mbH (Association for Heavy Ion Research) in Darmstadt (Germany). Upon Flerov's initiative, an independent international commission of experts was created that recognized JINR's priority for the discovery or codiscovery of five of the eight elements from 102 through 109. The element with number 105 received the name "Dubnium."

Flerov achieved considerable success in these years with his work on the physics of nuclear fission. In 1961 Flerov's group discovered a new kind of nuclear isomerism: spontaneously fissile isomers. In these isomers, the nucleus spontaneously fissions with a probability about 10^{25} times greater than for the ground state. The new phenomenon served as the basis for the prediction of the possibility of an island of stability of super-heavy nuclei with greater than 184 neutrons and an atomic number of 110. In 1962–1963 Flerov and his collaborators discovered the phenomenon of delayed proton emission. Experiments over the course of many years confirmed that the phenomenon was a widespread property of supersaturated by protons isotopes. It has been successfully used to obtain valuable information about the structure of the nucleus.

In 1966–1967 the team discovered yet another phenomenon: the fission of nuclei from high-lying excited states formed after beta-decay (electron capture). The first observation of this phenomenon was in isotopes of americium. It has been established that such phenomena play an important role in nucleosynthesis. In 1969–1970 a new class of nuclear reaction was discovered in the Flerov laboratory—deep inelastic reactons. There has been a veritable boom in research on these new types of reactions since 1973. Researchers at Dubna, Orsay (France), and Berkeley (United States) have obtained results demonstrating that for massive ions, such as ions of argon and krypton, these nuclear reactions are the dominant nuclear processes in the collision of two nuclei. The study of the nuclei of reactions of deep inelastic scattering of nucleons is one of the main directions of nuclear physics research with heavy ions.

Practical Applications of Nuclear Physics. Flerov actively participated in the development of nuclear methods for prospecting for oil and for the most efficient use of the oil fields in the USSR. For several years after 1951 he directed a group of scientists at the Moscow Petroleum Institute (later the State Academy of Petroleum and Gas) in research that eventually developed an improved apparatus for neutron and gamma-logging of oil reservoirs. This group also developed an original impulse method of neutron-logging.

In his Laboratory of Nuclear Reactions (Laboratoriia Iadernykh Reaktsiĭ, LIaR), Flerov organized a section for applied nuclear physics, devoted to studies on polynuclear filters and on radiation aspects of materials sciences. These scientists have developed methods using heavy ion beams for analyzing the durability and other properties of construction materials for thermonuclear plants. This section also has conducted work on obtaining the shortest-lived radionuclides for biological studies and medical diagnostics. After the Chernobyl nuclear disaster of 26 April 1986, 187 workers from JINR participated in the efforts to deal with the consequences of this catastrophe. The institute not only offered its specialists but also knowledge of radiation containment and various types of apparatus and protective gear, such as gas masks and respirators with Flerov filters (nuclear membranes), which were successfully used in the zone of radiation contamination.

The scientific achievements of G. N. Flerov have been highly praised not only in his native country but also abroad. He was elected a foreign member of the Royal Danish Academy of Sciences, an honorary member of the German Academy of Sciences Leopoldina, and was awarded honorary doctorates from a variety of foreign universities. Flerov also was given awards from the governments of various countries, including Mongolia and Bulgaria.

BIBLIOGRAPHY

WORKS BY FLEROV

With L. I. Rusinov. "Opyty po deleniiu urana" [Studies on the fission of uranium]. *Izvestiia AN SSSR, Ser. fizicheskaia* 4 , no.2 (1940): 310–314.

With K. A. Petrzhak. "Spontannoe delenie urana" [The spontaneous fission of uranium]. *Doklady AN SSSR* 28, no.6 (1940): 500–501.

With S. M. Polikanov et al. "Opyty po polucheniiu 102-go elementa" [Studies on obtaining the 102nd element]. *Doklady AN SSSR* 120 , no.1 (1958): 73–75.

"Iadernye reaktsii, vyzyvaemye tiazhelymi ionami" [Nuclear reactions in heavy ions]. In *Trudy 2-oi Mezhdunarodnoĭ konferentsii po mirnomu ispol'zovaniiu atomnoĭ energii* [Proceedings of the 2nd International Conference on the Peaceful Uses of Atomic Energy], vol. 1, pp. 272–280. Moscow: Atomizdat, 1959.

With V. V. Volkov et al. *Izuchenie reaktsiĭ peredachi pri vzaimodeĭstvii tiazhelykh ionov s iadrami s pomoshch'iu zapazdyvaiushceĭ neĭtrononoĭ aktivnosti* [Investigation of the reaction transmission of the interaction of heavy ions with nuclei using delayed neutron activation]. (LIaR, 1192.) Dubna: OIIaI, 1963. Issues of the Laboratoriia Iadernykh Reaktsiĭ , LIaR (in issues in English –LNR) of his Institute (p. 8, OIIaI).

With E. D. Donets and V. A. Druin. "Spontaneous Fission and Synthesis of Far Transuranic Elements." *Journal of Nuclear Energy(London) Part A/B* 18, no. 3 (1964): 156–168.

Sintez i issledovanie svoĭstv 102-go elementa [Synthesis and investigation of the properties of the 102nd element]. (LIaR, D7-3444) Dubna: OIIaI, 1967.

With N. Martalogu et al. "Excitation Energy of Spontaneously Fissioning Isomer ^{242m} Am." *Nuclear Physics* (Amsterdam) A97, no. 2 (1967): 444–448.

Synthesis and Study of New Isotopes and Elements. (LNR, E7-4207). Dubna: JINR, 1968.

Newest Elements of the Mendeleev Periodic Table: Perspectives and Chemical Problems of the Search for Super-Heavy Elements. (LNR, E15-4651). Dubna: JINR, 1969.

With N. I. Tarantin. "Transuranovye elementy i periodicheskaia sistema D. I. Mendeleeva" [The transuranium elements and D. I. Mendeleev's periodic system]. *Voprosy istorii estestvoznaniya i tekhniki* 29, no. 4 (1969): 17–26.

With Yuri Tsolakovich Oganessian et al. *Sintez elementa 105 (Spontannoe delenie)* [Synthesis of element 105 (Spontaneous fission)]. (LIaR, P7-5164; E7-5252). Dubna: OIIaI, 1970.

With F. A. Alekseev. *Ispol'zovanie radioaktivnykh izlucheniĭ pri razvedke i razrabotke neftianykh mestorozhdeniĭ v SSSR—Doklad na IV Mezhdunarodnom neftianom kongresse v Rime* [The use of radioactive radiation in the search for and development of petroleum deposits in the USSR]. Moscow: Izd-vo AN SSSR, 1955.

Discoveries by Flerov et al., USSR State Register

With K. A. Petrzhak. "Spontannoe delenie urana. Otkrytie № 37" [The spontaneous fissioning of uranium. Discovery no. 33.] *Biulleten' izobreteniĭ i tovarnykh znakov* 8 (1965): 5.

With Yuri Tsolakovich Oganessian et al. "104- ĭ element kurchatoviĭ .Otkrytie № 37" [Kurchatovium: The 104th element. Discovery no. 37]. *Biulleten' izobreteniĭ i tovarnykh znakov* 6 (1965).

With Yuri Tsolakovich Oganessian et al. "Element 105- ĭ periodichesko ĭ sistemy D. I. Mendeleeva. Otkrytie № 114" [The 105th element in D. I. Mendeleev's periodic system. Discovery no.114]. *Biulleten'* "Otkrytiia, izobreteniia, promyshlennye obraztsy, tovarnye znaki" 32 (1972): 4.

OTHER SOURCES

"Iubilei: Akademic Georgiĭ Nikolaevich Flerov" [Anniversary: Georgiĭ Nikolaevich Flerov]. *Atomnaia energiia* 54, no. 2 (1983): 141–142.

Aleksandrov, Anatoliĭ P., et al. "Pamiati Georgiia Nikolaevicha Flerova" [In memory of Georgiĭ Nikolaevich Flerov]. *Uspekhi fizicheskikh nauk* 161 , no. 3 (1991): 173–175.

Georgiĭ Nikolaevich Flerov. K shestidesiatiletiiu so dnya rozhdeniia [Georgiĭ Nikolaevich Flerov: On his sixtieth birthday]. Dubna: OIIaI, 1973.

Goncharov, German A. "O publikatsii iskazhennykh versiĭ pisem G. N. Flerova 1941–1942 gg" [About the publication of distorted versions of G. N. Flerov's letters of 1941–1942]. *Voprosy istorii estestvoznaniia i tekhniki* 3 (2000): 35–56.

Holloway, David. *Stalin and the Bomb: The Soviet Union and Atomic Energy, 1939–1956.* New Haven, CT, and London: Yale University Press, 1994.

Kadyshevskiĭ, V. G., A. N. Sisakian, and V. M. Zhabitskiĭ, eds. *Ob"edinennomu institutu iadernykh issledovaniĭ—40 let. Khronika. Vospominaniia. Razmyshleniia* [40 years of the Joint Institute of Nuclear Research. Chronology. Reminiscences. Recollections]. Dubna: OIIaI, 1996.

Kaftanov, Sergeĭ V. "Po trevoge" [On alert]. *Khimiia i zhizn'* 3 (1985): 6–10.

Oganessian, Yuri Tsolakovich, and Pustylnik, Boris I.. "Eksperimentator s obostrennym chuvstvom novogo" [An experimentor with an acute sense of the new]. *Vestnik Rossiiskoĭ Akademii Nauk* 63, no.3 (1993): 207–212.

Sozdanie pervoi sovetskoĭ iadernoĭ bomby [The creation of the first Soviet atomic bomb]. Moscow: Energoatomizdat, 1995.

Trudy Mezhdunarodnogo simpoziuma "Nauka i obshchestvo: Istoriia sovetskogo atomnogo proekta (40-50-ye gody)" [Proceedings of the international symposium "Science and Society: The History of the Soviet Atomic Project (1940s–1950s)"]. HISAP-96. Vol. 1, Moscow, 1997; vol. 2, Moscow, 1999.

Elena Zaitseva
Nathan Brooks

FLORY, PAUL JOHN (*b.* Sterling, Illinois, 19 June 1910; *d.* Big Sur, California, 8 September 1985), *chemistry, physical chemistry of polymers, kinetics, thermodynamics.*

Once polymer chemistry had been established in the 1920s and early 1930s by Hermann Staudinger, Hermann Mark, and Wallace Hume Carothers, there was a pressing need to establish the basic underlying physiochemical principles of this new field, especially the kinetics of polymerization and the thermodynamics of polymer solutions. A start had been made by Mark and the Swiss chemist Werner Kuhn, but the physical chemistry of polymers was still in its infancy in the mid-1930s. Paul Flory met this need almost single-handedly. He had an extraordinary knack for creating simple models that could be applied to existing data with remarkable effects. This was a result of his strong intuition for how polymers behaved. He continued to apply these models over many years to new problems. He also had a great talent for explaining the physical chemistry of polymers to colleagues and other chemists who often had a nonmathematical organic chemistry background. Moving constantly between academia and industry in the first half of his career, he also assisted the transfer of knowledge and especially concepts between the two sectors. This process was assisted by Flory's association with the government-backed synthetic rubber research program in the 1940s and early 1950s, which promoted the free flow of information between different universities and firms. The net effect was the rapid development of the physical chemistry of polymers and its immediate application to industrial problems, thereby accelerating the development of plastics and synthetic rubbers, especially in the United States.

Childhood and Education. Paul John Flory was born on 19 June 1910 in Sterling, Illinois, the son of Ezra Flory, a minister in the Church of the Brethren, and Martha Flory (née Brumburgh), a former schoolteacher. The Florys were Alsatian Huguenots who had come to America from England. Sterling was a medium-sized town on the Rock River, between Chicago and the Mississippi River border with Iowa. Flory thus shared a rural midwestern background with several other American polymer chemists of his generation, including Wallace Carothers and Carl Marvel, both of whom were born within 100 miles of Sterling. Like the other members of this group, Flory took his first degree in 1931 at a small liberal arts college. In Flory's case this was Manchester College in North Manchester, Indiana, run by the Church of the Brethren, where his interest in chemistry was aroused by Professor Carl Holl. During this time, Flory shared a dorm with Roy Plunkett, another midwestern polymer chemist (from rural Ohio), who later discovered Teflon at du Pont. Again in keeping with the other Midwesterners, Flory took his master's degree in 1932 at a leading university, in his case Ohio State University in Columbus, Ohio. He then took a PhD under Professor Herrick Johnston with a dissertation on the photochemical dissociation of nitric oxide. When Flory completed his doctorate in 1934, during the Great Depression, he was fortunate to be offered a position at du Pont's Experimental Station by the director of the organic chemistry section, Arthur Tanberg.

Polymerization Kinetics: First Work. When Flory joined Carothers's group in July 1934, he had no background in polymer science, but his expertise in chemical kinetics was very valuable to Carothers, whose background was in organic chemistry. Carothers gave Flory the task of working out the relationship between the length of a polymer chain and the number of polymer molecules of that length for a condensation polymer such as a polyester. At this time it was taken for granted that the reactivity of a molecule decreased as it grew in size. Flory quickly showed that beyond a low threshold size (a few carbon atoms), the reactivity of the functional groups in a condensation polymer remained the same, regardless of the length of the chain, as long as the external conditions remained unchanged. Armed with this knowledge, he was then able to show that the number of chains of a given length decreased exponentially with increasing length.

The kinetics of addition polymerization had presented similar problems, and hitherto there had been little agreement between theory and the practical results. As with condensation polymerization, it had been assumed that the polymerization stopped when the molecule became too big to react. Flory showed that the polymerization stopped when the free radical at the end of a growing chain took an atom (usually hydrogen) from a monomer or solvent molecule (or even another chain), creating a new free radical that could start a new chain. The active site is thus transferred to another molecule, a process called "chain transfer." Using the concept of chain transfer, Flory was able to achieve good agreement between theory and practice.

While he was working at du Pont, Flory met Emily Catherine Tabor, a member of a well-established Philadelphia family; they were married in late 1936. Their marriage was very successful, and Emily was a major force behind Flory's burgeoning career. She enabled Flory to shake off his rural background and become a sophisticated international scientist. They had three children: Susan, Melinda, and Paul John Flory Jr. (known as John), who became a research scientist in genetics at the Yale University School of Medicine.

Elastic Polymers. In the space of a few years, the young chemist had revolutionized the study of polymerization kinetics at du Pont, but Carothers had in the meantime committed suicide in April 1937. Without Carothers to protect him from routine work, Flory decided to reenter the academic world, and he went to the basic science research laboratory at the University of Cincinnati in Ohio in 1938. Although the conditions there were rather rudimentary, Flory now had the freedom to develop his own ideas. He had become interested in the theory of gelation, the formation of an insoluble elastic material from a viscous polymer fluid, which occurs well before all the starting material has been used up. This process is particularly common with polymers, such as rubber or the glycerol polyesters (gyptals) used in paint, which undergo crosslinking between different chains. Flory developed a mathematical "network" theory which showed that gelation occurred at a specific "gel point." He thus showed that gelation is mathematically similar to the kinetics of explosions or nuclear chain reactions. Carothers had been interested in the kinetics of gelation but had lacked the mathematical background to explore the process properly.

With war looming, Flory returned to industry in 1940 and joined the Standard Oil Development Company (part of Standard Oil of New Jersey, now Exxon Mobil) at Linden, New Jersey. Standard Oil, as the former partner of I.G. Farben in the polymer field, was playing a leading role in the development of synthetic rubber. Flory took part in this research and applied his network theory to the swelling of rubber. He developed a statistical-mechanical model of polymer solutions that explained their thermodynamic properties, and in particular, the entropy of mixing of polymer solutions. He was disconcerted to hear Maurice Huggins, a chemist at Eastman Kodak, expound a similar theory at a conference in the summer of 1941, but when Flory offered to collaborate, Huggins encouraged the younger chemist to publish his work independently.

The rubber firm Goodyear set up a fundamental research group at its Akron, Ohio, headquarters in 1943

Flory

and invited Flory to lead it. With Norman Rabjohn, he now applied his network theory to the physical properties of rubber, relating, for instance, the degree of crosslinking to the tensile strength. Flory also began his study of the crystallization of polymers and the factors that influenced this process, a line of research that was to lead him a decade later to the study of liquid crystals.

Principles of Polymer Chemistry. The American-Dutch chemist Peter Debye—who shared a mutual interest in the gelation of rubber—invited Flory to give the Baker Lectures at Cornell University in Ithaca, New York, in 1948. As a result of this series of lectures, Flory was invited to join the chemistry faculty at Cornell. The Baker Lectures were eventually published in 1953 as *Principles of Polymer Chemistry,* which for the first time—in the United States at least—established the idea that polymer science could be studied in terms of theory rather than as a body of empirical information. This monograph was read by leading polymer chemists and students alike, and it soon became the standard work in this field, above all in industrial laboratories.

While Flory was preparing his Baker Lectures, he took up the concept of "excluded volume" in polymer solutions, which had been originally introduced by the Swiss chemist Werner Kuhn in 1934. Flory and William Krigbaum applied this concept to a statistical mechanical theory of dilute polymer solutions to show that there was a temperature at which a given polymer behaved in an "ideal" manner, acting according to theory so that its behavior could be easily analyzed. This temperature became known as the theta point or Flory temperature. Flory then used the Flory-Krigbaum theory to study the viscosity of polymer solutions and showed that several supposed complications with such solutions were not in fact relevant. With Thomas Fox, who had followed him from Goodyear, Flory showed that the increase in viscosity produced by each chain molecule was proportional to the cube of its radius. As the ratio of the intrinsic viscosity to the hydrodynamic volume was found to be constant for a wide range of polymers and solvents, Flory was able to mine existing data to study the configuration of many polymers, a task that occupied him for much of the rest of his career. With his colleagues Leo Mandelkern and Harold Scheraga, he also applied this model to the sedimentation of polymers in the ultracentrifuge. Mandelkern also collaborated with Flory on the subject of crystalline polymers, and Scheraga shared his interest in chain conformation.

In 1953 the rubber chemist Geoffrey Gee, who had just been appointed to a chair at Manchester University, invited Flory to take his sabbatical at Manchester so they could work together. Gee had previously worked at the

Paul John Flory. **EMILIO SEGRE VISUAL ARCHIVES AMERICAN INSTITUTE OF PHYSICS/PHOTO RESEARCHERS, INC.**

British Rubber Producers' Research Association (now the Malaysian Rubber Producers' Research Association), outside Hertford, England, and the two chemists shared an interest in the physical chemistry of natural rubber and the thermodynamics of polymer solutions. They were good friends and, rather exceptionally, Flory took Gee's comments on his research seriously. During this sabbatical, as a result of a personal discussion with Gee and Geoffrey Allen—then an assistant lecturer at Manchester—Flory became interested in the thermodynamics of stiff polymer chains. He later used this as a starting point for his work on the theory of liquid crystalline polymers, such as the aramid polymer Kevlar. Liquid crystals subsequently became important materials for electronic displays, but the materials used are not polymers.

The Mellon Institute and Stanford. In the mid-1950s the Mellon Institute in Pittsburgh—which had hitherto acted mainly as a research service for industry—decided to concentrate on basic and fundamental research. Paul Mellon and his board invited Flory (who was already a member of the board of trustees) to become its executive director in 1957. Flory's collaborator, Thomas Fox, became manager of polymer research and stayed on after Flory departed for Stanford University four years later. During his period at the Mellon Institute, Flory published a seminal paper, "Theory of Light Scattering by Polymer Solutions" (1958), with Arthur Bueche, carried out considerable work on elasticity with Cor Hoeve and Alberto Ciferri, and continued his research on polyelectrolytes with Thomas Orofino. However, the reform program did not go according to the agreed plan, and Flory did not see eye to eye with Paul Mellon.

Flory was already looking for an academic position in 1961 when he was offered a chair at Stanford University in California. When Fred Terman, an electrical engineer, became provost of Stanford in 1955, he was determined to turn the hitherto intellectually undistinguished but wealthy college into the equal of Harvard or Yale. He hired William S. Johnson from the University of Wisconsin as professor of chemistry in 1960. When Johnson heard that Flory was planning to leave the Mellon Institute, he invited him to visit California. Flory accepted Johnson's offer of a chair, and as a result other leading chemists, including Henry Taube and Eugene van Tamelen, also moved to Stanford. Flory subsequently became the Jackson-Wood Professor of Chemistry in 1966. The effect on the Chemistry Department was dramatic, and Stanford chemistry rose from fifteenth position in 1957 to fifth in 1964. As head of the growing department between 1969 and 1972, Flory was concerned about its lack of good laboratory facilities. A new chemistry building was eventually sanctioned by the university in 1974.

At Stanford, Flory continued his work on the configuration of polymer molecules and with Robert Jernigan developed matrix methods of describing these configurations. Flory summarized his research in this field in his classic work, *Statistical Mechanics of Chain Molecules*, in 1969. He also continued to improve the Flory-Huggins theory of mixing and his network theory of rubbers. In particular, he argued that the excluded volume effect could be ignored in the study of temperature dependence of elasticity. This simplification was controversial at the time, but it was eventually shown to be correct by the new technique of neutron scattering. This technique revealed that the size of the chains in bulk increased linearly with the chain length, consistent with a lack of excluded volume.

Later Years. Flory was awarded the Nobel Prize in 1974 for "his fundamental achievements, both theoretical and experimental, in the physical chemistry of macromolecules." While this accolade was well deserved, the award of the prize to Flory alone could also be considered controversial, as he was only one of a number of chemists who had developed the physical chemistry of polymers. By 1974 Werner Kuhn and Peter Debye had died, but Hermann Mark and Maurice Huggins were still alive, and there were other chemists of Flory's generation—including Eugene Guth and Walter Stockmayer—who had made major contributions to this field. With hindsight, it must surely be regretted that this prize for the physical chemistry of polymers was not awarded jointly to Mark.

After he retired in 1975, Flory remained an active researcher at Stanford and also became a consultant to IBM. He continued to work on liquid crystals using his model of rigid and flexible chains, and he was also interested in the structure of semicrystalline polymers. Polymers can crystallize from dilute solutions to form lamellar crystals, in which the polymer chains must be folded up. How the chains fold and reenter the crystal was a matter of controversy. Flory and Do Yoon argued that the chain formed a loop and reentered some distance away, but other polymer scientists—particularly the Anglo-Hungarian chemist Andrew Keller—insisted that the chains were folded sharply in a regular pattern with adjacent reentry. In the early twenty-first century it appears that the actual situation lies between these two extremes. Flory was still hard at work in these related fields when he died unexpectedly of a massive heart attack at his weekend home at Big Sur, California, on 8 September 1985.

Aiding Soviet Scientists. Flory was a hard-working and driven individual who was described by Johnson as "a human dynamo." He expected similar high standards from those who worked with him but also filled his students with a passion for doing science. His rather puritanical personality was balanced by his sense of humor and his loyalty to his friends. Flory had a sympathy for the underdog, and after he won the Nobel Prize, Flory and his wife put much effort into supporting scientists persecuted by the authorities in the Soviet Union—notably Andrei Sakharov, Yuri Orlov, and Anatoly (Natan) Shcharansky (the so-called SOS dissidents). He was particularly critical of the neutral stance on this issue of the American Chemical Society and the National Academy of Sciences (United States). He persuaded some nine thousand scientists to boycott scientific cooperation with the Soviet Union. At a personal level, Flory traded his agreement to give lectures in Soviet bloc countries for exit visas for persecuted scientists, including Jan Bares and Witold Brostow. He also made an unsuccessful offer to become a temporary hostage to allow Sakharov's wife, Yelena Bonner, to travel to the West for medical treatment.

BIBLIOGRAPHY

Selected Works of Paul J. Flory *(cited below) includes a bibliography of Flory's publications.*

WORKS BY FLORY

Principles of Polymer Chemistry. Ithaca, NY: Cornell University Press, 1953.

With Arthur M. Bueche. "Theory of Light Scattering by Polymer Solutions." *Journal of Polymer Science* 27 (1958): 219–229.

"Autobiography." 1974. Available from http://nobelprize.org/nobel_prizes/chemistry/laureates/1974/flory-autobio.html.

Selected Works of Paul J. Flory. Edited by Leo Mandelkern, James E. Mark, Ulrich W. Suter, et al. 3 vols. Stanford, CA: Stanford University Press, 1985. This includes an authorized biography.

Statistical Mechanics of Chain Molecules. New York: Wiley-Interscience, 1969. Reprinted with corrections, 1989.

OTHER SOURCES

Chayut, Michael. "New Sites for Scientific Change: Paul Flory's Initiation into Polymer Chemistry." *Historical Studies in the Physical and Biological Sciences* 23 (1993): 193–218.

Johnson, William S., Walter H. Stockmayer, and Henry Taube. "Paul John Flory, June 19, 1910–September 8, 1985." *Biographical Memoirs of the National Academy of Sciences* 82 (2003): 114–141.

Morris, Peter J. T. *Polymer Pioneers.* Philadelphia: Center for the History of Chemistry, 1986.

Seymour, Raymond B. "Paul J. Flory—Nobel Laureate and Polymer Scientist." In *Pioneers in Polymer Science,* edited by Raymond B. Seymour. Dordrecht, Netherlands, and Boston: Kluwer, 1989.

Peter J. T. Morris

FOLKERS, KARL AUGUST

(*b.* Decatur, Illinois, 1 September 1906; *d.* New London, Connecticut, 7 December 1997), *organic chemistry, biologically active compounds, vitamin B_{12}, mevalonic acid, coenzyme Q.*

The career of Karl Folkers sits astride one of the great transformations that took place in American economic and scientific history. During the early decades of the twentieth century, science in the United States began to make great progress, catching up in several fields with the more advanced European centers for research and professional training. This was the case with chemistry in general and organic chemistry in particular, where Germany had long been the dominant nation in conducting advanced research and training young scientists. America's new prowess in science followed the years at the turn of the century when the nation had become the world's largest industrial producer. Progress in the all-important chemical, electrical, and electro-chemical industries could only continue, however, if American businesses learned how to combine modern science with corporate entrepreneurship. Karl Folkers played an important role in both of the crucial transformations of that era—one in business and one in science.

Family. Education, and Vocation. Given his humble background, Folkers was an unlikely person to become a leader, an important contributor to either science or business. In most societies through most of human history, he would have been guided to a career like that of his father, August William Folkers, an immigrant from Germany in the 1880s. August worked in a candy store and then was a grocery clerk in a tiny community near Decatur, Illinois. Karl was the only child of August and his wife, Laura Susan (née Black), and like so many other children in the Midwest, he received a five-dollar chemistry set at Christmas one year. With help from his mother, he set up in a bedroom corner a tiny laboratory from which would spring a lifetime dedication to scientific research.

His interest in chemistry grew through high school in Decatur, which was only a few miles from the adjoining towns of Champaign-Urbana and the University of Illinois. Although his family had no money to spare, it scraped together enough to pay the low state tuition and send young Karl to the university in 1924, where he worked for his meals and spending money. He had, luckily, landed in an excellent school with a first-rate Chemistry Department, led by Roger Adams and Carl ("Speed") Marvel. Folkers concentrated on organic chemistry, and Marvel directed his senior thesis.

In the academic world of the 1920s, relationships were highly personal and relatively informal. As Karl approached graduation in 1928, Marvel simply selected him to attend graduate school at the University of Wisconsin, where he could continue his career under the direction of Homer Adkins. It was understood that if Marvel recommended him, Adkins would admit him, so Folkers applied to only one graduate program and was accepted. As Folkers later observed, "It was just that simple."

At Wisconsin, Folkers spent one unproductive year researching the impact of catalysts on ethyl alcohol and acetaldehyde, but then the work that Adkins was doing on high-pressure hydrogenation caught his imagination. His work quickly accelerated, and he made his first significant discovery, the effect under high pressure of a copper-barium catalyst on the conversion of esters to alcohols. More successful hydrogenation research followed, and by the time Folkers finished his PhD in 1931, he had published eight papers with Adkins.

As Adkins prepped his outstanding student to take a postdoctoral appointment at Harvard University (where he could work with James Conant), a glitch occurred in the old boy network. Although Folkers did not know it at the time, Conant was in line to become president of Harvard and was not accepting new postdoctoral fellows. Left adrift briefly, Folkers applied to Yale, where he could work with Treat B. Johnson. Unwilling to accept any coworker without knowing a great deal about his career and personality, Johnson first wanted a full autobiography from Folkers. Satisfied that Folkers was the sort of person who could make a strong contribution to his laboratory, Johnson accepted him for postdoctoral research. Driving an old, secondhand Model-A Ford, Folkers made the trip to New Haven, Connecticut, and approached what would become a decisive turning point in his scientific and personal life.

At Yale he met the attractive Selma Johnson, who was working in the Chemistry Department office, and after a round of dating and courtship, they were married in 1932. They would have two children, Cynthia Carol and Richard Karl, neither of whom would opt for a scientific career like their father's. At Yale, Johnson introduced Folkers to medicinal chemistry and pharmacology. Johnson was working on the chemistry of nucleic acids, synthesizing substances such as uracil. Folkers decided to follow his lead and to do so in an industrial rather than an academic setting. His choice may have been influenced by the devastating economic collapse that had hit the United States in the early 1930s. During the Great Depression, university appointments were hard to come by, even for talented, productive scientists such as Folkers.

At Merck and Co. Instead, he decided to join Randolph Major, who was turning Merck and Co. in a new direction, emphasizing innovations through research and development in medicinal chemistry. Majors had a new research facility at Merck, and he was determined to hire a cadre of top-flight scientists to work there and guide the company in new directions. Excited about the laboratory and the challenge of developing new therapies, Folkers returned to Yale to get his mentor's evaluation of the two offers he was considering. General Electric had offered him a job paying what was in those days the magnificent sum of $350 per month. Merck matched that offer, and his mentor leaned heavily toward the opportunity to do medical research. "Oh," he said, "that's going to be marvelous. That's like working on a very elegant watch." Folkers agreed.

Getting settled in Merck's Rahway, New Jersey, Laboratory of Pure Research—a name designed to distinguish the new lab from the firm's routine testing and analysis operations—Folkers spent some time floundering as he tried to focus on a promising subject. He had the opportunity to flounder because Randolph Major gave his scientists a great deal of latitude to carry forward their own projects. Major might suggest a worthwhile area of medicinal chemistry to explore, but the path of exploration itself was left to the individual to chart. That is what happened when he threw a bag of red seeds on Folkers's lab bench one day. "Here, Karl," Majors said, "See what you can do with these." Then he walked out of the room.

Folkers pushed ahead with the little red Erythrina seeds, isolating alkaloids that he could crystallize and analyze. Along the way, he was able to do some structural analysis, his forte, and to publish a series of papers on his work. The only thing that was missing was a medical discovery that would justify the time spent on the little red seeds. So too with his work on the arrow poison, curare. But in these early years in the development of what would become one of the world's leading pharmaceutical research organizations, practical results were subordinated to "pure" research. Merck was on the steep part of its organizational learning curve, trying to master the research and development techniques that had long before been mastered by the German pharmaceutical powerhouses.

Steadily adding new scientists and new capabilities, Merck and Majors soon found a niche to explore that would turn out to be interesting as well as productive. Research on vitamins was just getting underway. Merck was collaborating with Robert Williams of Bell Telephone Laboratories, who was working on thiamine (B_1), and Folkers and Stan Harris, a synthetic chemist hired from the Rockefeller Institute, began to study pyridoxine (B_6). Folkers, who favored structural analysis, and Harris made a good pair. Using ultraviolet spectra, a new technique at the time, they worked out a structural determination of the promising substance. Following carbon, hydrogen, and nitrogen microanalyses, they had an empirical formula, but they still could not be certain about the molecular structure. Library research combined with color reactions led to a successful elucidation of the structure of B_6, which they were then able to synthesize. Concerned about more than the chemistry, Folkers followed his products through testing and into development. He was interested in useful pharmaceuticals, not just elegant research.

The vitamin line of research and development continued to be productive of both good science and good products. Folkers, who had been promoted to assistant director of research in 1938, next became interested in pantothenic acid, which he was able to produce with a total synthesis. That was followed by work on biotin. In both cases, Merck's policy of being attentive to scientific progress outside the Rahway laboratory paid big dividends. Randolph Major kept in touch with pharmaceutical developments abroad as well as in the United States, and he wanted his scientists to be similarly well informed. At one point, Majors sent Folkers to Europe to go to as many universities and companies as possible and to stay as long as he felt he was being productive.

Antibiotics. By the time Folkers was drifting away from bench research and toward research administration, the global therapeutic revolution was well underway. The sulfa drugs coming out of Germany in the 1930s were an enormous breakthrough, enabling physicians to treat internal infections successfully for the first time in human history. Penicillin came next, in the early 1940s, followed by streptomycin, the first effective treatment against tuberculosis.

Folkers was on the front line in Merck's exploration of both of these important antibiotics. The penicillin research—an effort to match the molecular formula with the right structural formula—was facilitated by the specialized capabilities Folkers had been systematically building up in the laboratory. He had, for instance, acquired another one of Homer Adkins's students, Ralph Mozingo, who had set up a hydrogenation unit. Now he could also turn to a new unit in microchemistry for structural work at the micro-level. Rudimentary to later researchers, these capabilities placed the Merck laboratory on the front edge of pharmaceutical innovation in the United States. Along the way, Folkers hired the lab's first woman scientist, Dorothea Heyl, a major development for that time. As Folkers later explained, "That was really something to convince those people that you were going to hire a woman."

The research on penicillin began in the 1940s while the United States was at war— which precluded publication—but the streptomycin research took place under less restrictive conditions in peacetime. Merck's contribution to the dramatic breakthrough led by Selman Waksman and Albert Schatz was to isolate the crystalline salts of both streptomycin and streptothricin, to work out the structures of these complicated molecules, and then to mass produce the antibiotic.

These accomplishments and Merck's contribution to the development of cortisone placed Folkers and the laboratories under his direction at the front of American pharmaceutical innovation. In less than two decades, the American firm had become a leader in the world industry as well. No longer working in the shadow of the German firms, Folkers and his colleagues—including Boyd Woodruff in microbiology and Max Tishler, who led the developmental chemistry—had successfully transformed their firm from a second-tier to a top-tier position in new drug development.

As Folkers pushed ahead in research, he took on a new problem involving pernicious anemia. Working with a liver residue provided by Henry Dakin, Folkers fractionated and lyophilized the sample. While the scientific literature of that day indicated that the anti-pernicious anemia factor was a protein, Folkers had a hunch that this was not the case. He had an active substance and used it to move ahead with a project that others had tried and abandoned. Additional work in conjunction with the University of Maryland (and Mary Shorb) suggested that the newly discovered factor might be produced through fermentation. Here Folkers could call upon the substantial resources Merck had developed in its work on penicillin and streptomycin.

Vitamins. Fractionating the fermentation residues, Folkers and his team discovered vitamin B_{12}. The discovery sent reverberations through the Merck organization that reached all the way to the president, George W. Merck, and then to the public after a press conference to announce the discovery. As it turned out, B_{12} was far more important than anyone in the laboratory, including Folkers, had anticipated: it was the growth factor for all animals.

Elected to the National Academy of Sciences in 1948 and given broader research responsibilities at Merck, Folkers continued to conduct and direct research on antibiotics and vitamins. In the latter case, he reasoned (as did Randolph Major) that because vitamins were essential to life, they should be studied in the search for new therapies. Folkers was convinced that even if the search took twenty or thirty years, something important would eventually be found. Along the way, his laboratory made discoveries that were far more important to science than to the pharmaceutical industry. That was the case with mevalonic acid, a precursor in the biosynthesis of cholesterol discovered by Folkers and his colleagues in the search for vitamin B_{13} (which would ultimately have important implications for the understanding of the "development" side of research and development), but his laboratory nevertheless helped improve processes from time to time, as it did with the production of B_{12}.

Relentless on the trail of a promising new vitamin, Folkers pursued research on coenzyme Q (Q_{10}) from his Merck days to the end of his career. Coenzyme Q came from the mitochondria isolated from the heart. "Knowing that it was functional in bio-energetics was basic," Folkers said, "to the intellectual concept that it was probably vital to life itself." More than four hundred scientific papers later, the clinical results that Folkers sought had still eluded him. When he retired at Merck in 1963, the company allowed him to take the coenzyme Q research with him.

Final Years. After more than twenty-eight years of active research and science administration at Merck, Folkers decided to try a new position and a better climate. He became president and CEO of the Stanford Research Institute, a position he would hold from 1963 to 1968. David Packard, who was chairman of the institute's executive committee, and Folkers agreed that the latter could continue his own research on Q_{10} while directing the two thousand people working at the organization. Under his tenure, the institute built a new Life Sciences Building and raised additional money in support of its activities. Some difficult discussions with board members who were multimillionaire business executives left Folkers bruised, however, and ready to accept a new position in Texas.

At the University of Texas, William Shive and the university's president, Norman Hackerman, were eager to have Folkers move to Austin, and they created for him a new organization, the Institute for Biomedical Research, with which he was associated for the last three decades of his life. Here, as Ashbel Smith Professor of Chemistry and director of the institute, he was able to continue his research on Q_{10} and also explore other avenues of medical science. One involved B_6 deficiency and the role that might play in carpal tunnel syndrome, a problem of increasing significance in modern society. Folkers also pushed ahead with an analysis of peptide hormones. Using samples provided by Andrew Schally of Tulane University, Folkers and his researchers were able to determine the structure of a tripeptide from the hypothalamus and then to synthesize the hormone. Schally received the Nobel Prize in Physiology or Medicine in 1977, shared with Roger Guillemin, for this breakthrough.

Folkers also collaborated for many years with Cy Bowers of the Tulane Medical School in a study of the inhibitors of the luteinizing hormone-releasing hormone (LHRH). The hard part in this work. Folkers said, was to obtain potent inhibitory activity. As the peptide structure is changed, specificity is lost. With no ready guidelines to follow, Bowers and Folkers and a number of postdoctoral fellows pursued experiments for fifteen years designed to produce an effective antagonist and perhaps eventually an anti-tumor agent. Looking always for the ideal research group, Folkers brought together in the institute chemists, biochemists, biologists, and clinicians receptive to the research problems he and his colleagues had identified.

Asked by Leon Gortler in a 1990 interview what drove him to continue his relentless efforts to solve particular problems, Folkers replied that "one believes in something and maintains the faith until the project is solved." Faith was at the center of his life. The problem of Q_{10} was never solved but many others were. B_6 and B_{12} were high points, mountain peaks in a long, distinguished range of research accomplishments in structural and synthetic chemistry. Folkers received many awards for his accomplishments in science, including honorary degrees in the United States and abroad, the (U.S.) President's National Medal of Science (1990), and the Priestley Medal of the American Chemical Society (1986). Although Folkers's health declined after his wife died in 1992, he continued to be deeply involved in research until his death in 1997. He left behind a great tradition of collegiality in research and life, service to the health of humankind, and above all, faith in the logic and goals of modern medicinal science.

BIBLIOGRAPHY

Leon Gortler conducted a long interview with Karl Folkers; the transcript is available in the Merck Archives, Whitehouse Station, New Jersey. All of the quotations used in this essay are from this interview, and the interview file in the Merck archives contains the only complete list located of the more than 700 scientific articles that Folkers published.

WORKS BY FOLKERS

With Homer Adkins. "The Catalytic Hydrogenation of Esters to Alcohols." *Journal of the American Chemical Society* 53 (1931): 1095–1097.

With Treat B. Johnson. "Hydrogenation of Cyclic Ureides under Elevated Temperatures and Pressures I. 2-keto-1,2,3,4-tetrahydropyrimidines." *Journal of the American Chemical Society* 56 (1934): 1180–1185.

With Stanton A. Harris. "Synthesis of Vitamin B_6." *Journal of the American Chemical Society* 61 (1939): 1245–1247.

———. Synthesis of Vitamin B_6. II." *Journal of the American Chemical Society* 61 (1939): 3307–2210.

With Stanton A. Harris and Eric T. Stiller. "Structure of Vitamin B_6. II." *Journal of the American Chemical Society* 61 (1939): 1242–1244.

With Eric T. Stiller, Stanton A. Harris, Jacob Finkelstein, et al. "Pantothenic Acid. VIII. The Total Synthesis of Pure Pantothenic Acid." *Journal of the American Chemical Society* 62 (1940): 1785–1790.

With Stanton A. Harris, Donald E. Wolf, and Ralph Mozingo. "Synthetic Biotin." *Science* 97 (1943): 447–448.

With Frederick A. Kuehl Jr., Robert L. Peck, and Alphonse Walti. "Streptomyces Antibiotics. I. Crystalline Salts of Streptomycin and Streptothricin." *Science* 102 (1945): 34–35.

With Donald E. Wolf, William H. Jones, and John Valiant. "Degradation of Vitamin B_{12} to D_g-1-amino-2-propanol." *Journal of the American Chemical Society* 72 (1950): 2820.

With Edward A. Kaczka. "Vitamin B_{12}. XXII. Relation of α-ribazole Phosphate to Vitamin B_{12}." *Journal of the American Chemical Society* 75 (1953): 6317–6318.

With Donald E. Wolf, Carl H. Hoffman, Nelson R. Trenner, et al. "Coenzyme Q. I. Structure Studies on the Coenzyme Q Group." *Journal of the American Chemical Society* 80: (1958): 4752.

With Hans Sievertsson, Jaw-Kang Chang, Alexander Von Klaudy, et al. "Hypothalamic Hormones. 35. Two Syntheses of the Luteinizing Hormone Releasing hormone of the Hypothalamus." *Journal of Medicinal Chemistry* 15 (1972): 222–226.

With Robert E. Olson and Harry M. Rudney. "Biosynthesis of Ubiquinone." *Vitamins and Hormones* 40 (1983): 1–43.

With Anders Ljungqvist, Dong-Mei. Feng, William Hook, et al. "Antide and Related Antagonists of Luteinizing Hormone Release with Long Action and Oral Activity." *Proceedings of the National Academy of Science, U.S.A.* 85 (1988): 8236–8240.

With Rodney Simonsen. "Two Successful Double-blind Trials with Coenzyme Q_{10} (Vitamin Q_{10}) on Muscular Dystrophies and Neurogenic Atrophies." *Biochimica et Biophysica Acta* 1271 (24 May 1995): 281–286.

OTHER SOURCES

Olson, Robert E. "Karl August Folkers (1906–1997)." *Journal of Nutrition* 131 (2001): 2227–2230. Also available from http://jn.nutrition.org/cgi/content/full/131/9/2227.

Shive, William. "Karl August Folkers, September 1, 1906—December 9, 1997." *Biographical Memoirs of the National Academy of Sciences,* 81 (2002): 101–114. Also available from http://newton.nap.edu/html/biomems/kfolkers.html. Both Shrive and Olson provide additional references to Folkers's more than 700 scientific publications.

Louis Galambos
Jeffrey L. Sturchio

FORD, EDMUND BRISCO

(*b.* Ellislea, Dalton-in-Furness, United Kingdom, 23 April 1901; *d.* Oxford, United Kingdom, 21 January 1988), *genetics, ecological genetics, polymorphism.*

Ford was a major contributor to the development of the modern synthesis in biology. He was a tireless exponent of the view that natural selection was the preeminent factor in shaping the evolution of natural populations. He created the field of ecological genetics, which is concerned with the experimental determination of the factors contributing to the adaptation and modification of wild populations in their environments.

Life. Ford was the only child of Henry Dodsworth Ford and Gertrude Emma Bennett. Although he spoke often of his father and they shared an interest in natural history, of his mother Ford said little, and nothing is known of her ancestry. Ford grew up in rural surroundings and early on became interested in archeology and natural history. At the age of eleven, he began to collect Lepidoptera (butterflies and moths), and in 1917 began a thirteen-year study, along with his father, of the relationship between the annual fluctuation in numbers and the observed varieties of a local population of butterflies that resulted in a joint publication in 1930.

In 1920, Ford was admitted to Wadham College at Oxford, where he studied classics and zoology. There he became acquainted with Gavin de Beer, Edward Bagnall Poulton, Ray Lankester, Leonard Darwin, Julian Huxley, and Ronald A. Fisher. While still an undergraduate, he published four papers, two with Huxley and one with Fisher. After receiving his BA, he did further research to obtain a BSc in 1927. He remained at Oxford as a demonstrator and lecturer until he was appointed the first reader in genetics in 1939. He was awarded a DSc in 1943, and in 1951, with the help of grants from the Nuffield Foundation, he founded and became director of the Genetics Laboratory. In 1963, he was appointed professor of ecological genetics. He retired in 1969. After his retirement, he remained active in research. His last scientific paper appeared in 1983.

During his long career, Ford received a number of academic and scientific honors. In 1946, he was made a Fellow of the Royal Society. He received the Darwin Medal from the Royal Society in 1954. In 1958, he was made a Fellow of All Souls College in Oxford, one of the few scientists since the seventeenth century to be so honored.

To his friends and collaborators, E. B. Ford was known as "Henry." He was somewhat of an academic snob and name dropper with strong likes and dislikes. He had a lifelong interest in genealogy and heraldry and was known to recommend an entry from *Debrett's Peerage* as appropriate bedtime reading. He never married. His students remembered him as a clear and meticulous, although idiosyncratic, lecturer. A number of amusing anecdotes illustrating his idiosyncracies can be found in Bryan Clarke's biographical memoir for the Royal Society.

Background for Ford's Achievements. The background for understanding the significance of Ford's ecological research is the growing rapprochement in the 1920s and 1930s between Darwinian theory, centered on the role of natural selection in evolution, and Mendelian genetics, centered on understanding evolution in terms of the inheritance of genes.

At the beginning of the twentieth century, Mendel's laws, first published in 1865, were rediscovered and the modern science of genetics was born. Mendelian inheritance involved the transmission of discrete factors or genes from parents to offspring. It soon became the model of choice for explaining the evolution of eye color, bodily markings, and other discrete traits. The Mendelian factors, or genes, were identified as components of chromosomes and geneticists began to work out the mathematical implications of the theory in conjunction with laboratory experiments that sought to identify the particular genes associated with particular organismal traits. Darwinism, with its commitment to continuous, not discrete variation, and its commitment to gradual changes over long periods of time, appeared to be at odds with Mendelism, and during the first decade of the twentieth century, Darwinism went into decline. From 1910 to 1920, it began to become evident that the conflict between Darwinism and Mendelism was only apparent. R. A. Fisher had begun to work out the mathematical details that would show that Mendelian inheritance was compatible with and explainable in terms of the slow action of Darwinian natural selection.

Ford was a committed Darwinian even before he went to Oxford. When he was an undergraduate, biology was at the beginning stages of what came to be known as the modern synthesis. His research was devoted to promoting that integration. In the 1920s, genetics research was confined, more or less, to laboratory experiments under controlled conditions. Ecologists, by contrast, were field workers who observed and recorded the behavior of organisms in their natural environments. Ford was a field naturalist who understood the importance of genetics and who had an interest in studying the genetics of the evolution of populations in their natural environments. During his long career, Ford was a tireless and often uncompromising proponent of the importance of natural selection for the evolution of genetic diversity in natural populations.

It is an undisputed observational fact that natural populations change over time. Population numbers fluctuate from year to year, varieties appear and disappear, new stable forms emerge and replace old stable forms, new populations arise and established populations become extinct. What was controversial in the 1920s and what remained controversial at the beginning of the twenty-first century is the relative importance of the processes by means of which these changes come about. The ultimate source of variation in populations is genetic mutation. Mutations, however, occur at random with respect to the environments in which organisms find themselves and thus are as likely to be deleterious as they are to be beneficial. Natural selection, by contrast, singles out those features of organisms that are best suited for the environments they find themselves in.

If one assumes, as did Ford and his colleagues, that natural selection had been operating over long periods of time to create populations that were fine-tuned to their environments, the chances of a mutation being beneficial were correspondingly small. One might expect natural selection to drive less fit alleles to extinction. However, in certain circumstances dominant and recessive homozygotes (the AA and aa forms) are less fit than the heterozygote form (Aa). In such cases, natural selection favors the heterozygote form and the net result is a stable population including both forms of the alternative alleles. This is what is known as "balanced selection." In large populations, new varieties produced by mutation that were not as fit as others were liable to be swamped by the effects of natural selection and disappear in short order. In small populations, the chances are greater than a new variety will become fixed by chance alone. While R. A. Fisher was developing the mathematical theory of natural selection, Sewall Wright was constructing a theory that emphasized the importance of small populations and what came to known as random drift.

The task, as Ford saw it, was to demonstrate the effectiveness of natural selection in the wild as a major force in promoting and maintaining the diversity to be found in natural populations. Postulating the importance of natural selection in the wild was one thing, establishing it was another. Ford devoted himself to the development of concepts and tools that would enable researchers to establish once and for all that evolution by natural selection was not just a theory but was, in fact, the prime mover in the evolution of natural populations. This work led to the development of a new discipline that Ford called "ecological genetics." In 1959, he identified this development as his "most important contribution to the evolutionary synthesis (Mayr and Provine, 1959, p. 341)

Early Research. Ford's undergraduate work with Julian Huxley was on "rate-genes" in the sand shrimp *Gammarus chevreuxi* and culminated in five papers, two coauthored with Huxley. Their results indicated the importance of genes for controlling the timing and rate of developmental processes in different organisms.

The 1930 joint paper with his father H. D. Ford was based on thirteen years of observation and records dating back to 1881 of the population variation in a variety of butterfly found in several distinct colonies in Cumberland. The observations showed that the populations underwent a periodic fluctuation in size that was correlated with the degree of variation among types. When the population numbers were low, the variance in forms was low as well. As the population figures increased, so did the number of varieties. This increase was marked by the appearance of forms that would, under ordinary circumstances, seem to be nonviable. This was interpreted by Ford as evidence that the populations were under reduced selection pressures during the stages of population growth. At some point, the increased variation became stabilized around a number of new forms different from the variants that predominated in earlier peak populations. Ford cited this as evidence that natural selection was at work in natural populations.

In the 1930s, Ford adopted Fisher's theory of the evolution of dominance. He showed that it was possible to experimentally select for both dominant and recessive traits in natural populations.

In the 1940s, Ford, in conjunction with Fisher, perfected the mark-release-recapture method. Specimens are marked with dabs of paint or dye, released into the wild, and recaptured at various intervals. The resulting data can then be used to make estimates of population size, migration patterns, and differential death rates. The relative recapture frequencies of different varieties were construed by Ford and his colleagues as evidence of the working of natural selection in the wild.

Definition and Explanation of Polymorphism. Ford's first important theoretical result was his clarification and explanation of polymorphisms in natural populations. A polymorphism is a particular kind of variation. In 1940, Ford defined a genetic polymorphism as the coexistence of two or more forms of an organism that were distinctly different and existing at population levels that could not be attributed to chance. The condition that the forms coexist in the same locality rules out seasonal varieties and geographical varieties as examples of polymorphism. The condition that the forms are discontinuous variants rules out height differences as constituting polymorphisms. The requirement that the forms exist in proportions that cannot be explained in terms of recurrent mutation rules out rare diseases such as Huntington's chorea as constituting a distinct human polymorphism. However, the sickle-cell trait occurs in a significant enough proportion of the human population to constitute a polymorphism in Ford's sense. Similarly, Ford argued that the distinct blood groups constituted a polymorphism that was maintained by strong selective pressures. In his book *Genetics for Medical Students*, which first appeared in 1942, Ford argued that the existence of these polymorphisms had important implications for the treatment of diseases, on the one hand, and for the reality of human races, on the other.

Ford distinguished two kinds of polymorphism: balanced and transient. The balanced polymorphisms were held to be the results of balancing selective pressures. The implication was that there were strong selective pressures at work in nature—stronger than were thought to exist at the time. For example, consider the relationship between sickle cell anemia and resistance to malaria in humans. One of two alternative alleles involved in coding for hemoglobin leads to misshapen blood cells and a resulting anemia that lowers their fitness. Individuals with the normal allele do not develop anemia, but they are susceptible to contracting malaria, which also lowers their fitness. Heterozygotes are only mildly anemic but tend to be resistant to malaria. The net result is a population where the frequency of both alleles reaches an equilibrium. This is an example of what is known as "heterozygous advantage." Another kind of ploymorphism is involved in the evolution of Batesian mimicry. In Batesian mimicry, innocuous organisms mimic dangerous or unpalatable models and thereby achieve some protection from predators. Because mimicry involves the evolution of co-adapted traits, Ford argued that the genetic basis of such traits most likely is a suite of co-adapted genes that constitute a so-called "super-gene."

Ford's conception of balanced polymorphism was criticized by Muller, among others. Muller took the concept of polymorphism, as understood by Ford, to be undermined by the rejection of the concept of "heterozygous advantage." Muller's view was that natural populations did not exhibit the extensive stable diversity required by ford's concept of balanced polymorphisms. Field investigations established the fact that natural populations were more diverse than Muller and his supporters had thought. However, the explanation of that diversity remains controversial.

Transient polymorphisms, on the other hand, represented temporary coexisting forms resulting from selective pressures that, in time, would tend to eliminate one or more of the varieties. The case of the evolution of industrial melanism in the moth *Biston betularia* was held to be an example of this kind of polymorphism. Populations of these moths in nineteenth-century Britain tended to be primarily composed of a white variety. In areas of heavy industrialization with the attendant sooty atmospheres, melanic varieties began to be predominant. When pollution controls were put into effect, the white variety was reestablished as predominant.

The Peppered Moths. In 1951, Ford persuaded Henry Bernard Davis Kettlewell, a physician and amateur entomologist, to join him in the Ecological Genetics laboratory at Oxford in order to carry out field research that would further cement the role of natural selection in the wild. With Ford's encouragement, Kettlewell conducted a series of field studies that appeared to show that the evolution of melanism in the moth *Biston betularia* was due to selective predation by birds. This result was immediately hailed as the long sought-after proof positive of the result of natural selection on wild populations. As such, it appeared in numerous textbooks as an iconic illustration of the truth of Darwinian evolutionary theory.

Criticisms and Reactions. In the 1960s and 1970s, techniques using gel electrophoresis and DNA hybridization were developed that revealed an unsuspected high level of variation in natural populations at the molecular level. These techniques for measuring genetic variability, unlike the field studies of Ford that inferred genetic variability from variation in expressed traits, were more direct measures of underlying genetic variation. Using the technique of gel electrophoresis, variation in proteins could be detected by having the proteins migrate through an electrical field on a gel. The heavier the protein, the slower it moved. Because the proteins were the direct products of genes, differences in proteins were inferred to be the result of differences in the underlying genes. The results showed that there much more variation at the protein level, and by implication, at the genic level than anyone had suspected. Initially, Ford was pleased by the new molecular techniques that were revealing that polymorphisms were even more abundant at the cellular level than the ecological studies had revealed.

However, it soon became apparent that there was, in fact, too much variation at the molecular level for it all to be maintained by natural selection. This situation raised the likelihood that other factors beside selection were at work. Indeed, the vast amount of variation at the molecular level led the evolutionary biologist Motoo Kimura to propose what he called the "neutral theory of molecular evolution" that held that much of the molecular variation did not have any selective significance. The fact that such polymorphisms existed in such abundance at the molecular level gave new impetus to Ford's critics to reject his unilateral selectionist account of the evolution of the organismic polymorphisms detected in wild populations.

As a staunch defender of the important role of natural selection in evolution, Ford was at pains to reject any suggestion that the other evolutionary factors could have a comparable importance. In the 1920s and 1930s, the American geneticist Sewall Wright, one of the main architects of the modern synthesis, developed a mathematical model of what he called a "shifting balance" theory of evolution. This theory combined elements of genetic drift, or the random fixation of alleles in small populations, with natural selection. Wright suggested that some of the polymorphisms that Ford and his colleagues were discovering were, in fact, driven by the chance fixation of some variants in small populations that were then able to maintain themselves despite any overpowering by the forces of natural selection.

Ford would have none of it. He criticized Wright on the grounds that natural populations were larger than Wright's models assumed were possible for random drift to be a major factor in their evolution. He and Fisher wrote a response to Wright's criticisms in 1947 and dubbed Wright's thesis the "Sewall Wright effect." Both Ford and Fisher saw the opposition between their selectionist perspective and the alternative Wrightian view as polar opposites, *either* populations evolved through natural selection *or* by genetic drift. In fact, Wright never saw the dispute in such black and white terms; he argued that he had been misunderstood: The significance he attributed to random drift was not to be construed as a denial of the importance of natural selection. Evolution in Wright's view was a "shifting balance" of contributing factors (Wright, 1948). Subsequent studies and calculations, however, suggested that both factors were playing a role in the evolution of natural systems.

In the 1960s and 1970s, opposition to the rigid selectionism endorsed by Ford began to mount. No one doubted that natural selection played a significant role in evolution but several questions remained open. For one thing, a general consensus was building that random drift and natural selection were both contributing to the evolution of natural ecologies. The question became not whether one or the other factors were significant but rather what the relevant significance of the two factors might be.

Moreover, there was mounting concern about the tendency of Ford and other selectionists to assume, without much tangible proof, that traits that became fixed in nature, including the polymorphisms, were the result of natural selection. Ford did not necessarily think that the polymorphic banding patterns in snails or the polymorphic spotted wing patterns on butterflies and moths were themselves adaptations. Rather, the presumption was that these features were the products of genetic complexes that had *some* selective value. This view was rejected by critics such as Richard Lewontin, Motoo Kimura, and Stephen Jay Gould, among others. In their famous and controversial paper, "The Spandrels of San Marco," published in 1979, Gould and Lewontin labeled such a single-minded conviction in the efficacy of natural selection, the "adaptationist programme."

Major Work. Ford's magnum opus was his book *Ecological Genetics,* in which he summarized his life's work. First published in 1964, it went through four editions in his lifetime. His general conclusions were, first and foremost, that there were powerful natural selection forces operating in nature. Second, he felt that he had established that any effects of random drift in natural populations would be overwhelmed by the effects of selection. Third, although mutation serves as the original source of variation, living organisms are the products of evolution *controlled* not by mutation but by powerful selection. In this respect, he was a lifelong defender of what came to be labeled as panselectionism and the adaptationist program. Fourth, in light of his commitment to the significance of selective forces in the evolution of biodiversity, he held that the ecological conditions that have promoted the evolution of life on Earth have to be assumed to be special. Ford drew some cosmic conclusions from his commitment to the view that life on Earth was the product of strong selective pressures acting over huge time intervals. He argued that it was very unlikely that any similar sequence of events had or would occur elsewhere in the universe, and hence that life as humans know it on Earth is very probably unique. Fifth, he saw the primary task of ecological genetics, as he understood it, to lie in establishing that natural selection in the wild is indeed the main factor in the coevolution of organisms and their environments. Sixth, the polymorphisms responsible for Batesian mimicry in nature is to be attributed to the action of "super-genes," that is, coordinated genetic systems that have multiple effects.

Finally, the application of the polymorphism concept to human beings indicated the importance of genetics for medicine. In particular, Ford argued that the fact that human blood group polymorphisms were under balanced selection showed that there were powerful selective forces at work maintaining the differences between human populations. Ford suggested that this had significance for understanding the susceptibility of different human populations to different diseases, which he felt would contribute to the development of racial, that is, populational, medicine.

Popular Works. In addition to his scientific papers and technical works, Ford wrote a number of popular works for the general public. Among the most significant were two guides, one on butterflies (in 1945) and one on moths (in 1955), that he wrote for the New Naturalist series, a collection of works aimed at promoting an awareness and appreciation of science among the British public. Ford's two contributions were aimed at amateur collectors and entomologists but unlike most such guides, they contained a fairly heavy dose of genetics and theory.

Ford returned to the social implications of genetics in a book written for the educated layperson or specialist, *Understanding Genetics,* which appeared in 1979. There he reiterated his view that the existence of stable human polymorphisms was evidence of both the reality of human races and the significance of understanding the differences between races for the treatment of diseases. In addition, he suggested that the fact that human intelligence had a genetic basis meant that because there was genetic variation for intelligence from one individual to the next,this result could be extrapolated to conclude that the average intelligence of different races was bound to differ as well. In addition, he saw the genetic basis of variability in intelligence as a ground for what he called "hereditary social distinctions" in society.

BIBLIOGRAPHY

Research documents, correspondence, and other manuscript material relating to Ford can be found in an archive in the Bodleian Library at Oxford University.

WORKS BY FORD

With Henry Dodsworth Ford. "Fluctuation in Numbers and Its Influence on Variation in *Melitaea aurina.*" *Transactions of the Entomological Society of London* 78 (1930): 345–351.

Mendelism and Evolution. London: Methuen, 1931. 8th ed. 1965.

"Polymorphism and Taxonomy." In *The New Systematics,* edited by Julian Huxley. Oxford: Oxford University Press, 1940.

Genetics for Medical Students. London: Methuen, 1942. 7th ed., 1973.

Butterflies. New Naturalist Series. London: Collins, 1945.

Moths. New Naturalist Series. London: Collins, 1955.

Ecological Genetics. London: Methuen, 1964.

Understanding Genetics. London: Faber & Faber, 1979.

OTHER SOURCES

Cain, Arthur J., and William B. Provine. "Genes and Ecology in History." In *Genes in Ecology: The 33rd Symposium of the British Ecological Society,* edited by Robert James Berry, T. J. Crawford, and G. M. Hewitt. Oxford: Blackwell Scientific Publications, 1992.

Clarke, Bryan. "Edmund Brisco Ford." *Biographical Memoirs of Fellows of the Royal Society* 41 (1995): 147–168. Contains an extensive bibliography of Ford's publications.

Creed, Robert, ed. *Ecological Genetics and Evolution: Essays in Honour of E. B. Ford.* Oxford: Blackwell Scientific Publications, 1971.

Gould, Stephen Jay, and Richard Lewontin. "The Spandrels of San Marco and the Panglossian Paradigm: A Critique of the Adaptationist Programme." *Proceedings of the Royal Society of London, Series B, Biological Sciences,* 205 (1979): 581–598.

Mayr, Ernst, and William B. Provine. *The Evolutionary Synthesis: Perspectives on the Unification of Biology.* Cambridge, MA: Harvard University Press, 1980.

Provine, William B. *Sewall Wright and Evolutionary Biology.* Chicago: University of Chicago Press, 1986. Contains a discussion of the controversy between Ford and Sewall Wright.

Wright, Sewall. "On the Roles of Directed and Random Changes in Gene Frequency in the Genetics of Populations." *Evolution* 2 (1948): 279–294.

Michael Bradie

FORSYTHE, GEORGE ELMER

(*b.* State College, Pennsylvania, 8 January 1917, *d.* Stanford, California, 9 April 1972), *mathematics, computer science, education.*

Forsythe is considered one of founders of computer science as an academic discipline. Trained as a numerical analyst and meteorologist, he pioneered the use of digital electronic computers to solve complex mathematical equations. The Stanford University Computer Science

Department, which he formed in 1965, was exemplary, both in intellectual scope and institutional structure.

Early Life and Training. George Elmer Forsythe was born 8 January 1917 in State College, Pennsylvania, to Dr. Warren Ellsworth Forsythe, an academic physician and cofounder of the American Student Health Association (ASHA), and DeEtta Brodie Forsythe. George was raised in Ann Arbor, Michigan, where his father worked as director of the University Health Service of the University of Michigan. Evidence of his interest in computing first appeared in the seventh grade, when he attempted to use a hand-cranked desk calculator to see how digits repeated in large decimal expansions (e.g., 10000/7699). At Swarthmore College, he received a liberal arts education, earning a BA in mathematics in 1937. There he also met his future wife and lifelong intellectual collaborator, Alexandra (Sandra) Winifred Illmer. Following graduation, he and she both pursued doctorates in mathematics at Brown University in Providence, Rhode Island.

At Brown, Forsythe wrote a dissertation in numerical analysis entitled *Riesz Summabilitly Methods of Order r, for R (r) < 0, Cesaro Summability of Independent Random Variables,* under the direction of Jacob David Tamarkin and the probability theorist William Feller. While Forsythe received the support of his advisors and peers, and finished his PhD in four years, Illmer struggled in an environment that was inhospitable to female mathematicians. Ultimately, she left Brown and completed a master's degree at Smith College. Forsythe and Illmer were married in a Quaker ceremony on 14 June 1941, the same day that Forsythe received his PhD. In the fall of 1941, the Forsythes moved to California so that George could start work as an instructor for the Stanford University Department of Mathematics.

Weather, Numerical Analysis, and Computers. Forsythe's first career at Stanford was terminated by the United States' entry into World War II. During the war, he served in the U.S. Army Air Forces (USAAF) as an instructor in theoretical meteorology for a training unit based at the University of California at Los Angeles (UCLA). With the unit's head, Jörgen Holmboe, and his colleague William Gustin, he adapted the training lectures into *Dynamic Meteorology* (1945), a mathematics-oriented introductory textbook to theoretical meteorology. While working with the meteorologists, Forsythe began to develop a serious interest in employing electronic computers to solve complex applied mathematical problems. He was particularly inspired by the work of Lewis Fry Richardson, a British mathematician and meteorologist who had proposed in his 1922 *Weather Prediction by Numerical Process* that the weather might be forecast by means of a vast computation of differential equations—then far beyond human capability—provided that enough upper-air weather observations were available as input data. Pairing Richardson's proposal with the mechanical computing technology that he saw in Wallace John Eckert's 1940 *Punched Card Methods in Scientific Computation,* Forsythe came to believe that such machines could dramatically advance science and industry.

Immediately following the war, Forsythe pursued his interest in computational machines at Boeing, where he supervised the implementation of a tabulating machine set up for data processing. Sandra Forsythe also worked in private industry but left to raise the couple's two young children, future botanist Warren L. "Tuck" Forsythe (*b.* 1944) and cultural anthropologist Diana E. Forsythe (*b.* 1947). In 1948, George Forsythe returned to the UCLA campus, this time to join the short-lived but highly influential Institute for Numerical Analysis of the National Bureau of Standards. While at the institute, he published several papers on numerical analysis, some in collaboration with Feller, and organized a major effort to translate contemporary and historical Russian mathematical texts. He was also a major contributor to the institute's 1951 symposium on *Simultaneous Linear Equations and the Determination of Eigenvalues,* to which he presented a bibliographic paper, "Tentative Classification of Methods and Bibliography on Solving Systems of Linear Equations" that long served as an important reference for numerical analysts.

Most of Forsythe's energy in the early 1950s, however, was devoted to helping develop and write programs for the institute's Standards Western Automatic Computer (SWAC), an early digital electronic computer with 256 37-bit words of Williams-Kilburn tube memory, which became operational in 1950. As he became more familiar with SWAC's operation, Forsythe focused on the problem of expressing algebraic equations on computers, often collaborating in this area with his wife and the mathematician Marcia Ascher. In the mid-1950s, Forsythe began to publish the algorithms he employed to communicate algebraic equations on SWAC; these established him as one of the foremost experts on implementing higher mathematics on digital electronic computers. After the institute was incorporated by UCLA in 1954, Forsythe joined the university's faculty.

Establishing Computer Science at Stanford and the ACM. In 1957, John G. Herriot, a fellow Tamarkin student and computer enthusiast, recruited Forsythe to Stanford's Mathematics Department. At Stanford, Forsythe's initial task was to help Herriot meet the rapidly growing demand for computer courses and train graduate students in numerical analysis. There Forsythe also became vocal on the issue of how students, both inside and outside the Mathematics Department, should be educated to use computers. His widely read 1959 *American Mathematical Monthly* paper, "The Role of Numerical Analysis in an Undergraduate Program," suggested dozens of ways to incorporate computers into university courses and asserted their pedagogical value: "The automatic computer really forces that precision of thinking which is alleged to be a product of any study of mathematics" (p. 655). Meanwhile, with Sandra, he also wrote extensively on teaching computers to secondary school students; by the 1960s, Sandra had become a major authority on teaching computers to high schoolers. Her most widely read books were her *Computer Science* series (1969–1973), which included a general primer and introductions to the FORTRAN and Basic programming languages.

Despite his increased involvement with computing, Forsythe still regarded himself as a mediator between theoretical mathematics and application-oriented engineering, rather than a computer scientist per se. His 1960 textbook *Finite-Difference Methods for Partial Differential Equations* (written with Wolfgang Wasow), emphasized the role that the numerical analyst would play in bridging the gap between mathematical theory and practical application, the latter category including the use of digital electronic computers. By 1961, however, he had concluded that training in numerical analysis alone would not suffice to generate mathematicians or engineers capable of conducting meaningful work on computers within a reasonable amount of time." To provide students with "the general-purpose mental tools" he believed they needed, he founded that year the Division of Computer Science within the Mathematics Department. Though the division's offerings were at the outset hardly distinct from those of the broader department, Forsythe envisioned a curriculum that included not only more traditional mathematical training in numerical analysis and automata theory, but also offerings from experts in programming, data processing, business games, adaptive systems, information theory, information retrieval, recursive function theory, and computer linguistics.

With strong institutional support from Stanford provost Frederick Terman and dean Albert H. Bowker, who saw the establishment of computer science as resonant to their own aims of reorienting the university toward federally funded, commercially stimulating, interdisciplinary research, Forsythe imported about a dozen young computer experts of complementary strengths from diverse areas of academe and industry to fulfill his vision of a broad but nevertheless cohesive discipline of computer science. Between 1961 and 1965, he recruited, among others: John McCarthy, from the Massachusetts Institute of Technology's Mathematics Department; Niklaus Wirth, from the University of California, Berkeley's Electrical Engineering School; Edward A. Feigenbaum, from Berkeley's Business School; Gio Wiederhold, from the aeronautics industry; Bill Miller, a high-energy physicist at Argonne National Laboratories; Eugene Golub, from Lawrence Livermore Laboratories; and Donald Knuth, a mathematics graduate student at the California Institute of Technology. Under Forsythe's leadership, members of the division produced some of the most well-known computer science concepts, programming languages, and projects. These included McCarthy's and Feigenbaum's pioneering work in Artificial Intelligence (AI), Wirth's development of the programming language Pascal, and Knuth's authorship of the reference *The Art of Programming*. Collectively, they also established an exemplary culture that remained firmly grounded in mathematics while eschewing mathematicians' aversion to experimentation.

In 1961, Forsythe was also appointed director of Stanford's Computation Center, a facility that housed most of the machines used by the university's researchers. Forsythe's responsibilities included acquiring equipment, determining how various scientific projects could incorporate computers, and aggressively encouraging scientists to computerize their research agendas. The targets of his most vigorous proselytizing were life scientists, the group he believed had the farthest to travel in terms of computerizing their research but also the most to gain from computers. Beyond offering biologists the resources of the Computation Center, he led an effort in 1962 and 1963 to convince the National Institutes of Health (NIH) to grant Stanford about one million dollars toward supporting an IBM 7090 that would be used primarily by pharmacologist Keith F. Killam, Jr., neurologists Kao Ling Chow and Frank Morrell, psychologist Karl Pribram, and medical statistician Lincoln E. Moses. Ultimately the NIH turned down Forsythe's proposal on the grounds that the project was too exclusive and that biomedical researchers did not have sufficient knowledge of computers to use them nonsuperficially. Although Forsythe did not again become involved in biomedical computing endeavors, his proposal served as a model for Joshua Lederberg's successful 1965 attempt to establish a large, federally funded computing center in Stanford's Medical School.

While Forsythe was forming the Division of Computer Science and running the Computation Center, he remained a prolific contributor of both algorithms and prose to the *Communications of the Association for Computing Machinery (ACM).* In January 1964, he was appointed editor of the algorithms section of *Communications* and just six months later was elected president of the ACM, then the largest, most influential professional society within the theoretical computing and software development communities. During his two-year term as

ACM president, Forsythe used his position not only to establish computer science as a fully recognized academic discipline but also to define the discipline's priorities. Repeatedly he encouraged universities (and their sponsors) to form computer science departments along the lines of his Stanford Division: closely associated with mathematics, unhesitant to blend theory and experimentation, and attuned to the vast importance of research to the development of computer technology. From his ACM pulpit, Forsythe also called for the academic community to recognize algorithms as pieces of scientific scholarship to be refereed and edited. Although Forsythe's "scientific" approach to computing was popular within the ACM, his motion to rename the organization the Association for Computing and Information Sciences did not muster the required two-thirds of the membership's votes. Following his presidency, Forsythe initiated the Education Section of *Communications* and served as its first editor.

The Computer Science Department. By January 1965, Forsythe's Computer Science Division had garnered enough productive faculty and had drifted far enough from the Mathematics Department's immediate interests that the Stanford administration chose to accept his petition to recognize it as the Computer Science Department. Though Stanford's was not the first computer science department, it was widely recognized as one of the most important intellectual centers of the field. Under Forsythe's direction, the Computer Science Department continued the division's exemplary role in defining the priorities of computer science, but it also established a widely emulated template for how the field's departments would approach issues of research funding and collaboration with other disciplines.

Broadly, Forsythe ran Computer Science as a research institute that happened to train graduate students rather than as a traditional department. In line with Provost Terman's decision to reduce Stanford researchers' dependency on university resources, he provided department members only half-salaries, and insisted they look to federal funding agencies and private enterprise to raise the other half, as well as their research funds. Consequently, Stanford computer sciences formed longstanding and deep ties to federal agencies such as the Advanced Research Projects Agency (ARPA), the National Science Foundation (NSF), and the Office of Naval Research (ONR). Reliance on such sources provoked complaints that Stanford computer scientists would be constrained by and perhaps beholden to nonacademic forces, but the steady flow of funds into the department allowed it to expand and conduct expensive research even during times of relative poverty. Moreover, external support allowed department members to form "dukedoms," united only by teaching concerns, in which they pursued their interests largely insulated from departmental politics as well as each other's sometimes contradictory agendas. Forsythe further leveraged the department by setting up joint appointments, especially with the Engineering School, with the aim of providing computer scientists with access to pertinent research as well as more funding resources.

When he was not preoccupied with forging ties to his department's sponsors, an effort requiring hundreds of letters and memoranda each month, Forsythe continued to pursue his interest in formalizing the pedagogy of computer science. In the late 1960s, he served as editor of Prentice Hall's *Series in Automatic Computation*, a comprehensive 75-book set of computer science textbooks, monographs, and edited volumes. Among them were *Computer Solution of Linear Algebraic Systems*, which Forsythe coauthored with his student Cleve B. Moler in 1967, and *Computer Methods for Mathematical Computation*, coauthored with Moler and another student, Michael Malcolm (1977). Forsythe also remained a prolific author of algorithms and essays that attempted to stimulate computer use among a wider academic audience. Within mathematics he explored the challenges of solving quadratic and partial differential equations on computers and became active in the Society for Industrial and Applied Mathematics, to which he was elected trustee in 1971.

Around his fiftieth birthday, in 1967, Forsythe was diagnosed with terminal skin cancer. Even ill, he maintained his exceptional productivity until the last two weeks of his life in the early spring of 1972. Consequently, his apparently sudden death came as a profound shock to his colleagues. In his eulogy for Forsythe, Donald Knuth declared, "It is generally agreed that he, more than any other man, is responsible for the rapid development of computer science in the world's colleges and universities."

BIBLIOGRAPHY

The Archival Collection, George and Alexandra Forsythe Papers, 1936–1979 (Stanford University Archives, SC 098), includes forty linear feet of professional and personal correspondence, notebooks, and publications. This forty linear foot collection is split into three series. Series 1, George Forsythe Papers, 1938-1972, *includes professional and personal correspondence, publications, notebooks, and notes Forsythe took on various subjects, starting in college and continuing to just before his death. Series 2,* Alexandra Forsythe Papers, 1970-1979, *includes Alexandra Forsythe's professional and personal correspondence, lectures, and teaching materials. Series 3,* Addenda, 1936-1972, *includes the Forsythes' publications as well as annotated books, foreign language editions of their published work, and additional notes and correspondence.*

WORKS BY FORSYTHE

Riesz Summability Methods of Order r, for R (r) < 0, Cesaro Summability of Independent Random Variables. PhD diss., Brown University, 1941.

"Riesz Summability Methods of Order *r*, for *R (r)* < 0." *Duke Mathematical Journal* 8 (1941): 346–349.

With A. C. Schaeffer. "Remarks on Regularity of Methods of Summation." *Bulletin of the American Mathematical Society* 48 (1942): 863–865.

"Cesàro Summability of Random Variables." *Duke Mathematical Journal* 10 (1943): 397–428.

With Jörgen Holmboe and William Gustin. *Dynamic Meteorology.* New York: Wiley, 1945.

"Bibliographical Survey of Russian Mathematical Monographs, 1930–1951." National Bureau of Standards Report 1628, 25 March 1952 (see also: Supplement, Rep. 1628A, 25 March 1952).

"A Numerical Analyst's Fifteen-foot Shelf." *Mathematical Tables and Other Aids to Computation* 7 (1953): 221–228.

With A. I. Forsythe. "Punched-Card Experiments with Accelerated Gradient Methods for Linear Equations." *National Bureau of Standards Applied Mathematics Series* 39 (1954): 55–69.

With Marcia Ascher. "SWAC Experiments on the Use of Orthogonal Polynomials for Data Fitting." *Journal of the Association for Computing Machinery* 5 (1958): 9–21.

"Bibliography on High School Mathematics Education." *Computers and Automation* 8 (May 1959): 17–19.

"The Role of Numerical Analysis in an Undergraduate Program." *American Mathematical Monthly* 66 (1959): 651–662.

With Wolfgang Wasow. *Finite-Difference Methods for Partial Differential Equations.* New York: Wiley, 1960.

"Engineering Students Must Learn Both Computing and Mathematics." *Journal of Engineering Education* 52 (1961): 177–188.

"An Undergraduate Curriculum in Numerical Analysis." *Communications of the Association for Computing Machinery* 7 (April 1964): 214–215.

"President's Letters to the ACM Membership." *Communications of the Association for Computing Machinery* 7 (1964): 448, 507, 558, 633–634, 698; 8 (1965): 3, 143–144, 422–423, 541, 591, 727; 9 (1966): 1, 244, 325.

"Algorithms for Scientific Computation." *Communications of the Association for Computing Machinery* 9 (April 1966): 255–256.

With Cleve B. Moler. *Computer Solution of Linear Algebraic Systems.* Englewood Cliffs, NJ: Prentice-Hall, 1967.

"What to Do Till the Computer Scientist Comes." *American Mathematical Monthly* 75 (1968): 454–462. Winner of the Lester R. Ford Award, 1969.

"Solving a Quadratic Equation on a Computer." In *The Mathematical Sciences: A Collection of Essays,* edited by the National Research Council's Committee on Support of Research in the Mathematical Sciences (COSRIMS) with the collaboration of George A. W. Boehm. Cambridge, MA: MIT Press, 1969.

With Michael A. Malcolm and Cleve B. Moler. *Computer Methods for Mathematical Computation.* Englewood Cliffs, NJ: Prentice-Hall, 1977.

OTHER SOURCES

Forsythe, Diana E. *Studying Those Who Study Us: An Anthropologist in the World of Artificial Intelligence.* Stanford, CA: Stanford University Press, 2001. Includes personal accounts of George and Alexandra Forsythe's careers from the perspective of their daughter; emphasizes role of gender in shaping those careers.

Harriot, John G. "In Memory of George E. Forsythe." *Communications of the Association for Computing Machinery* 15 (1972): 719–720.

Householder, A. S. "Obituary: George E. Forsythe." *SIAM Journal on Numerical Analysis* 10–2 (April 1973).

Knuth, Donald E. "George Forsythe and the Development of Computer Science." *Communications of the Association for Computing Machinery* 15 (1972): 721–727.

McCorduck, Pamela. "An Interview with Edward Feigenbaum." The Charles Babbage Institute, OH 14, 12 June 1979.

Moler, Cleve B. "A Memory of George Forsythe." *SIGNUM Newsletter* 7 (October 1972): 8–9.

Salisbury, David, and Gio Wiederhold, "George Forsythe, His Vision and Its Effects." *Stanford News Service,* 26 November 1997. Available from http://www-db.stanford.edu/pub/voy/museum/ForsytheNews.html.

Varah, James. "The Work of George Forsythe and His Students." In *Proceedings of the ACM Conference on History of Scientific and Numeric Computation, Princeton, NJ, 13–15 May 1987,* pp. 139–150. New York: ACM Press, 1987.

———. "The Influence of George Forsythe and His Students." In *A History of Scientific Computing. ACM Press History Series,* pp. 31–40. Reading, MA: Addison-Wesley, 1990.

Joseph November

FOSSEY, DIAN (*b.* San Francisco, California, 16 January 1932; *d.* Karisoke, Rwanda, 26 December 1985), *primatology, primate conservation.*

Significantly extending and expanding the work of George Schaller, Fossey conducted long-term field studies of gorilla behavior and passionately advocated for gorilla conservation. Along with Jane Goodall and Biruté Galdikas, Fossey attracted extensive media coverage for her primate field studies and thus significantly shaped public understanding of primatology and primate conservation.

Dian Fossey and L. S. B. Leakey. Dian Fossey, daughter of George and Kitty Fossey, was passionate about wildlife throughout her childhood. She began her career in the field of primatology in 1967 through an unorthodox route. After meeting Fossey in 1963 and again in 1966, L. S. B. Leakey began to discuss with her the possibility of studying primates in the wild. During these discussions, Leakey commented that it was risky for a person to have an appendix intact when embarking on a long field study. This comment was not meant seriously. By this time, Leakey's choice of Jane Goodall, a woman without formal scientific training, for a field study of chimpanzees in Gombe, Tanzania, had already shown signs of success, and he agreed to send Fossey to the Parc des Virungas in Zaire to study mountain gorillas.

Like Goodall, Fossey embarked on her field study without a formal science degree. Fossey had failed to gain a degree in veterinary medicine from the University of California at Davis and transferred to San Jose College where she gained a BA degree in physical therapy in 1954. This initial lack of scientific training did not concern Leakey, who believed women uniquely possessed the patience required for long-term field studies and that those without formal scientific training could combine this patience with a lack of bias in terms of their observation of primate behavior.

Once Fossey arrived in Zaire in 1967, her courage and determination helped her survive. Her study of existing primatological literature and relationships with indigenous peoples taught her how to track and observe gorillas. Fossey first studied gorillas in Kabara in the Parc des Virungas, Zaire, for over six months in 1967. Following this experience, she established the Karisoke Research Center in the Parc des Volcans, Rwanda. She spent almost her entire remaining life studying gorillas in Karisoke, leaving only to gain her PhD in 1976 from Cambridge University under the guidance of ethologist Robert A. Hinde and again in 1980 to briefly teach at Cornell University. She was murdered in Karisoke in 1985.

Field Methods. As recounted in Fossey's 1983 book, *Gorillas in the Mist,* preparations for the field included reading existing primatological literature and studying Swahili. Leakey ensured financial support for the research by securing funds from the Wilkie Foundation and helped to arrange for Fossey to spend two days with Jane Goodall at the Gombe Stream Research Center where Fossey observed methods of data collection and the logistical arrangements required for long-term field research. However, by far the most significant influences on the methods adopted by Fossey were George Schaller and indigenous trackers such as Sanwekwe, Nemeye, and Rwelekana.

Schaller of the University of Wisconsin had studied gorilla behavior in Parc Albert in the Virunga Volcanoes between 1959 and 1960. This was the same site, albeit later renamed, that was used by Fossey in the initial months of her study. After a series of failed attempts to observe gorillas in other locations, Schaller selected this site due to the height and density of the vegetation which made conditions "ideal" for prolonged observation of gorilla behavior.

Together with John Emlen from the University of Wisconsin, and their wives, Schaller shattered assumptions about the impossibility of making prolonged scientific observations of gorillas in the wild by successfully observing gorilla behavior for over four hundred and fifty hours. Indigenous peoples provided instruction to Schaller and Emlen concerning how to track gorillas by observing bends in blades of grass, imprints in the soil, and scat. Once able to track gorillas, they made regular observations of certain groups. This consistent observation resulted in six groups becoming habituated, meaning their behavior was deemed essentially unaffected by the presence of the observer. Fossey identified at least some of these habituated gorilla groups as the subjects of her own field research while in Kabara in 1967.

Fossey used similar methods to Schaller in terms of tracking and observing gorillas. She also adopted Schaller's technique of identifying individuals according to sketches of their nose prints. The sheer length of Fossey's field study and her desire to be accepted by the gorillas that composed her study groups led to her application of mimicry to habituate the gorillas. Fossey would mimic vocalizations, eating, and grooming behaviors as part of her habituation of gorillas and her long-term study of their behaviors. She would, for example, make "contentment vocalizations" and also beat her chest. Although not entirely new, Fossey applied the imitation of gorilla behaviors more extensively than past researchers, who had generally restricted themselves to the imitation of vocalizations. Descriptions of this imitation method formed a central part of her popular *National Geographic* articles, ensuring that Fossey would become well known for enabling prolonged observation of gorillas by adopting their behaviors.

Her study of gorilla behavior from 1967 to 1985 also involved extensive use of indigenous peoples and indigenous knowledge. Like Schaller and others, Fossey hired local people as trackers and guides. As the length of her field study extended and her involvement in conservation developed, local people became increasingly necessary for the logistic running of the research site and patrolling of the park to deter poachers. Despite these contributions to primate conservation, it would be the role of indigenous peoples as the hunters, rather than protectors, of gorillas that would be most highlighted by the popular articles and books written by, and about, Fossey. Any form of indigenous assistance in Fossey's long-term field research is barely identifiable in her PhD dissertation and while certain individuals are mentioned for the help they provided to Fossey

Dian Fossey. *In Washington, D.C., Dian Fossey with a photo of a gorilla she studied.* AP IMAGES.

in her well-read 1983 book, *Gorillas in the Mist,* the local people in general are personified as poachers.

This negative depiction of Africa and Africans in contrast to Fossey's positive contributions to gorilla conservation is located by historian James Krasner within the context of the 1970s and 1980s, a time in which Krasner and others believe Africa continued to be commonly viewed as uncivilized. Krasner argues that, "Fossey's appeal to the reader is ... constructed along deeply conservative lines: Africa is a dark and dangerous place; gorillas are threatened because they live in Africa; white people must save the gorillas by carrying enlightened ideas about animal preservation into the darkness, thus saving the animals from the primitive natives and from themselves" (Krasner, 1997, pp. 240–241). Such discussion of representations of, and by, Fossey in popular culture reveals much about the interaction between science, the media, and the public. However, the contributions she made to the science of primatology have received less historical attention.

Intellectual Contributions. Fossey's research both built upon existing knowledge of gorilla behavior and extensively extended it. While Fossey's own research benefited from the site location and methodology of Schaller and Emlen's collaborative field study of 1959–1960, for example, Fossey's work also directly continued, and in some cases revised, the conclusions set forth in Schaller's publications. In his 1963 book, *The Mountain Gorilla,* Schaller presented basic and previously unknown information concerning gorillas in the wild. Fossey's PhD dissertation, based on her work in Parc des Virungas, Zaire, and Parc des Volcans, Rwanda, discusses Schaller's conclusions in some depth, providing answers to questions he raised concerning concepts such as immigration and emigration and particularly the ways in which females transfer between groups.

Such questions could not be answered without the kind of long-term primate field study that Fossey provided. Through close study of a number of habituated groups, Fossey identified "home groups" as those composed of individuals born into cohesive and relatively stable groups. In contrast, "transfer groups" were formed by a female joining a silverback male and were relatively unstable. It was apparently always the females, rather than the males, that would transfer to a different group. As

Fossey

demonstrated by Fossey's 1984 article, these prolonged observations of group interaction would contribute to the growing understanding of primate reproductive behavior, including the phenomenon of infanticide, which emerged during the 1980s.

Fossey's extensive observation of gorillas, including the observation of individual gorillas from birth, also provided the evidence needed to revise Schaller's age/sex classification system. Schaller had relied on captive observations, and Fossey determined that he had generally under-aged individuals. Furthermore, she extended the potential life expectancy of gorillas in the wild to sixty years, whereas Schaller had estimated that wild gorillas would live around thirty years, an assumption again based on captive studies. Schaller had also provided extensive verbal descriptions of gorilla vocalizations but made few recordings of these vocalizations because he had only limited access to a tape recorder. Fossey, however, was able to conduct a study of gorilla vocalizations with recordings made from November 1968 to December 1969. For the first time, spectrographs were made of gorilla vocalizations, and the estimated number of distinct gorilla vocalizations was reduced from the twenty-one identified by Schaller to sixteen or seventeen.

Primate Conservation. Fossey also continued Schaller's work of conducting a census of gorillas in order to track population dynamics. Working with Alexander Harcourt, Kelly Stewart, and Alan Goodall (no relation to Jane Goodall), she conducted censuses at several points during the 1970s and again in 1981. These censuses demonstrated that the gorilla population in the Parc des Volcans was drastically declining. Encroachment on gorilla habitat and poaching were central reasons for this decline, and Fossey went on to dedicate the rest of her life to protecting the gorillas of the Virunga Volcanoes.

Fossey's pursuit of what she termed "active conservation" has been seen by some as relatively distinct from her science and by others as an extension of her methodology. In the beginning, Fossey's interest in studying gorillas was motivated by her hope that through scientific research humans would learn to better protect gorillas. However, this hope faded during the course of her time in Africa and was replaced by an emphasis on conservation at the cost, some have argued, of her scientific activity. The form of conservation Fossey would come to advocate was what Donna Haraway called "anarchist direct action" (1989, p. 265). Rather than pursue education and tourism as means to improve gorilla survival in the wild, Fossey established patrols to prevent poaching and used tactics of imprisonment and physical punishment when poachers were caught. Over time, the description of these conservation activities became increasingly central in her popular publications. The death of Digit, a gorilla that Fossey was particularly attached to, at the hands of poachers came to personify the need for gorilla conservation. His beheaded body was pictured in *National Geographic* and *Gorillas in the Mist*, and Fossey honored him by forming the Digit Fund in 1978. This organization would go on to become the Dian Fossey Gorilla Fund, a conservation group that continued into the early 2000s to raise money and organize efforts to protect gorillas.

It is perhaps all too easy to emphasize Fossey's contribution to primate conservation at the expense of discussion of her intellectual contributions to the science of primatology. Mary Ann McClure has sought to characterize Fossey's conservation and science, and that of other female primatologists such as Jane Goodall, as one in which the formation of caring relationships with the primates studied formed the core of their science. Thus, rather than defining science on the basis of detachment and objectivity, McClure understands the form of primatology practiced by Fossey as one based on connection. This argument provides a refreshing perspective that contrasts with the more common interpretation of Fossey and her methods, namely that by imitating gorilla behavior and becoming intensely emotionally invested in gorilla society Fossey sought to become one of them so to speak, and, in turn abandoned the science of primatology for conservation.

Fossey's at times unorthodox methods, including her punishment of poachers and emotional connection with the gorillas she studied, and her long since unsolved murder in 1985 while in Rwanda have led to much public discussion of her private life. She has been the subject of articles in magazines from *National Geographic* to *Vogue* and of films on the small and large screen. As such, both directly and indirectly, Fossey has been a significant force in shaping popular understanding of primatology. Particularly powerful is the way in which she created a popular consciousness for the plight of wild gorillas and their need for protection. Thus, as Fossey's legacy is reflected upon, it is clear that she significantly contributed both to science and conservation. Primatology benefited from her ability to endure many years of fieldwork and in turn reveal new knowledge concerning gorilla behavior, while primate conservation gained great momentum from the combination of Fossey's bravery and ability to attract and hold the public's attention.

BIBLIOGRAPHY

WORKS BY FOSSEY

"Making Friends with Mountain Gorillas." *National Geographic* 137 (1970): 48–67.

"More Years with Mountain Gorillas." *National Geographic* 140 (1971): 574–585.

"Living with Mountain Gorillas." In *The Marvels of Animal Behavior,* edited by T. B. Allen. Washington, DC: National Geographic Society, 1972.

"Vocalizations of the Mountain Gorilla (*Gorilla gorilla beringei*)." *Animal Behaviour* 20 (1972): 36–53.

"Observation of the Home Range of One Group of Mountain Gorillas (*Gorilla gorilla beringei*)." *Animal Behaviour* 22 (1974): 568–581.

"The Behaviour of the Mountain Gorilla." PhD diss., Cambridge University, 1976.

"A Grim Struggle for Survival: The Imperiled Mountain Gorilla." *National Geographic* 159 (1981): 501–523.

Gorillas in the Mist. Boston: Houghton Mifflin Company, 1983.

"Infanticide in Mountain Gorillas (*Gorilla gorilla beringei*) with Comparative Notes on Chimpanzees." In *Infanticide: Comparative and Evolutionary Perspectives,* edited by Glenn Hausfater and Sarah Blaffer Hrdy. New York: Aldine, 1984.

"His Name Was Digit." *International Primate Protection League Newsletter* 13 (1986): 10–15.

OTHER SOURCES

Haraway, Donna. *Primate Visions: Gender, Race, and Nature in the World of Modern Science.* New York: Routledge, 1989.

Krasner, James. "'Ape Ladies' and Cultural Politics: Dian Fossey and Birutė Galdikas." In *Natural Eloquence: Women Reinscribe Science,* edited by Barbara T. Gates and Ann B. Shteir. Madison: University of Wisconsin Press, 1997.

McClure, Mary Ann. "A Passion to Connect: The Science of Jane Goodall, Dian Fossey, and Birutė Gladikas." *Research in Philosophy and Technology* 16 (1997): 49–60.

Montgomery, Sy. *Walking with the Great Apes.* Boston: Houghton Mifflin Company, 1991.

Morell, Virginia. "Called 'Trimates,' Three Bold Women Shaped Their Field." *Science* 260, no. 5106 (April 1993): 420–425.

Mowat, Farley. *Woman in the Mists.* New York: Farley Mowat Limited, 1987.

Schaller, George B. *The Mountain Gorilla: Ecology and Behavior.* Chicago: University of Chicago, 1963.

———. *The Year of the Gorilla.* Chicago: University of Chicago Press, 1964. Reprinted with a new forward. Chicago: University of Chicago Press, 1988.

Strum, Shirley C., and Linda Marie Fedigan, eds. *Primate Encounters: Models of Science, Gender and Society.* Chicago: University of Chicago Press, 2000.

Georgina M. Montgomery

FOSTER, GEORGE CAREY (*b.* Sabden, Lancashire, England, 20 October 1835; *d.* Rickmansworth, Hertfordshire, 9 February 1919), *chemistry, physics, laboratory education, electrical standards.*

A self-effacing practitioner and teacher of precision laboratory technique, George Foster achieved an early reputation in organic chemistry, especially the analysis of alkaloids. Extending his quantitative expertise to the new discipline of physics, he introduced systematic experimental training to physics undergraduates in Britain, inaugurating the first purpose-built laboratory for teaching. His skill in instrumental practice led to a significant refinement of resistance measurement techniques, and he played a leading role in the development of national electrical standards of measurement.

Early Career: Chemistry. The only son of George Foster, calico printer and justice of the peace in Lancashire and West Yorkshire, George Carey Foster was educated at private schools before enrolling at University College London (UCL) in 1853. At UCL Foster studied chemistry before graduating with a prize in 1855 and becoming assistant to Alexander Williamson at UCL's chemistry laboratory. Foster presented his first paper in 1857 to the British Association for the Advancement of Science (BAAS), proposing systematization of nomenclature in organic chemistry; although published by the *Philosophical Magazine,* it was not widely adopted. Two years later his wide-ranging survey of the constitution of formulas in organic chemistry took a more prominent place in the BAAS annual report. By then Foster was undertaking research in organic chemistry with August Kekulé at Ghent, and under his direction Foster soon published two analyses of organic acids in the *Journal of the Chemical Society* (1861 and 1862). He also studied with Adolphe Wurtz and Jules Jamin in Paris and with Robert Bunsen and Georg Quincke in Heidelberg before his return to London in 1861.

Foster produced two papers in 1865 criticizing the confusion generated by the common use of the term "oxide" to denote an acid. His most important work in chemistry was a series of three papers on alkaloid chemistry undertaken in collaboration with his London colleague Augustus Matthiessen and published by the Royal Society (1863, 1867, 1868). Their analysis of narcotine was judged by contemporaries to be "classical" in accuracy and indeed the epitome of alkaloid chemistry.

Having already been introduced to the investigation of heat, light, and electricity by Williamson as extensions of chemical knowledge, Foster was appointed professor of natural philosophy at Anderson's University in Glasgow in 1862. Soon he produced two very substantial articles on the subject of "Heat" for *Watts' Dictionary of Chemistry* (1863), and these established his expertise in the physical (vis-à-vis organic) domain of chemistry. This move to Glasgow transformed his life and career: Not only did he encounter the scheme of student-assisted laboratory research that William Thomson organized at Glasgow University, but he also met Mary Ann Frances Muir of

Foster

Carey Foster. AIP EMILIO SEGRE VISUAL ARCHIVES, BRITTLE BOOKS COLLECTION.

Greenock, whom he would marry in 1868, a marriage that produced four sons and four daughters. Meanwhile, however, Foster was called back to London in August 1865 to take up the chair of experimental physics at UCL, where he became a cherished if not greatly competent lecturer.

Experimental Physics. Foster established a students' physical laboratory at UCL in 1866 that became the model for many others to follow. In the ensuing thirty-two years his most eminent students were the distinguished physicist Oliver Lodge and the electrical physicist/engineers William Ayrton and John Ambrose Fleming. Foster's commitment to physics education extended to his editing of some important textbooks. In 1866 he revised the popular *Handbook of Natural Philosophy and Astronomy* by Dionysius Lardner, UCL's first natural philosopher. Foster also coedited the London Science Class-Books Elementary Series with Philip Magnus from 1877 to 1896. And in that latter year he worked with his fellow chemist-turned-physicist Edmund Atkinson to translate and revise Jules Joubert's *Traité élémentaire d'électricité,* publishing it in three editions of the widely read *Elementary Treatise on Electricity and Magnetism.*

In 1866 Foster joined the BAAS committee on electrical standards, frequently serving as its chairman over the next three decades. He thus came to collaborate with Thomson, Charles Wheatstone, and others in refining the science of measuring electrical resistance and current flow, especially needed for the fast-developing field of telegraphy. As the outcome of investigations on how to accomplish reproducible results in electrical standards, Foster adapted the Wheatstone bridge, which measured ratios of resistance, to a new device that measured instead small differences of resistance—a much more useful characteristic for high-precision comparative work. Subsequently known as the "Carey Foster bridge," this important innovation was first presented at the newly formed Society of Telegraph Engineers in 1871 and widely used thereafter in both physics laboratory and telegraphic work.

In recognition of his work in both chemistry and physics Foster was elected a fellow of the Royal Society in 1869, serving twice as vice president (1891–1893, 1901–1903). He was president of BAAS section A (1877) and BAAS general treasurer (1888–1904). Foster had been one of the founding members of the Society of Telegraph Engineers in 1871 (the Institution of Electrical Engineers from 1888) and served as its president in 1880–1881. Similarly he was a founding member of the Physical Society of London in 1873 (later the Institute of Physics), serving as its president from 1876 to 1878. At UCL he served as dean of the faculty of sciences from 1874, achieving BSc status for experimental physics in 1876. In conjunction with his electrical engineering colleague Ambrose Fleming he helped to design important new laboratories in 1893, the physics wing of which was renamed as the Carey Foster Laboratory after his retirement in 1898. He became the first principal of University College in 1900. Up to the time of his death from heart failure in 1919, Foster worked vigorously as the editor of the *Philosophical Magazine,* which remains a leading periodical in theoretical, experimental, and applied physics.

BIBLIOGRAPHY

WORKS BY FOSTER

"On Chemical Nomenclature, and Chiefly on the Use of the Word Acid." *Philosophical Magazine* 29 (1865): 262–269; 30 (1865): 57–59.

As editor. *Handbook of Natural Philosophy and Astronomy: Electricity, Magnetism, and Acoustics,* by Dionysius Lardner. Rev. ed. London, 1866.

With Augustus Matthiessen. "Researches into the Chemical Constitution of Narcotine and of Its Products of Decomposition, Part 2." *Philosophical Transactions of the Royal Society of London* 157 (1867): 657–668.

"On a Modified Form of 'Wheatstone's Bridge' and Methods of Measuring Small Resistances." *Proceedings of the Society of Telegraphic Engineers* 1 (1872–1873): 196–208.

Report of the [BAAS] Committee Appointed for the Purpose of Constructing and Issuing Practical Standards for Use in Electrical Measurements. London: Office of the [British] Association, 1892.

With Edmund Atkinson. *Elementary Treatise on Electricity and Magnetism Founded on Joubert's "Traité élémentaire d'électricité."* London: Longmans, 1896.

OTHER SOURCES

Bellot, H. Hale. *History of University College, London, 1826–1926.* London: University of London Press, 1929.

Brock, William. "George Carey Foster." In *Dictionary of Nineteenth-Century British Scientists,* edited by Bernard Lightman, vol. 2, pp. 718–720. Bristol: Thoemmes Continuum, 2004.

Fison, A. H. "George Carey Foster." *Journal of the Chemical Society, Transactions* 115 (1919): 412–427.

Fox, J. W. (Bill). *From Lardner to Massey: A History of Physics, Space Science and Astronomy at University College London, 1826 to 1975.* Available from http://www.phys.ucl.ac.uk/department/history/BFox1.html.

Gooday, Graeme. "Precision Measurement and the Genesis of Physics Teaching Laboratories in Victorian Britain." *British Journal for the History of Science* 23 (1990): 25–51.

———. *The Morals of Measurement: Accuracy, Irony, and Trust in Late Victorian Electrical Practice.* Cambridge, U.K.: Cambridge University Press, 2004.

Harte, Negley, and John North. *The World of University College, London, 1828–1978.* London: University College, 1978.

Lodge, Oliver. "George Carey Foster, 1835–1919." *Proceedings of the Royal Society of London* 96A (1919–20): xv–xvii.

———. *Past Years: An Autobiography.* London: Hodder and Stoughton, 1931.

Graeme J. N. Gooday

FOWLER, WILLIAM A.

(*b.* Pittsburgh, Pennsylvania, 9 August 1911; *d.* Pasadena, California, 14 March 1995), *physics, nuclear astrophysics.*

Willy Fowler, as he was universally known, shared the 1983 Nobel Prize in Physics, along with Subrahmanyan Chandrasekhar, for his role in showing that all the elements from carbon to uranium could be produced by nuclear processes in stars, starting only with the primordial hydrogen and helium produced in the Big Bang. His citation reads, "for his theoretical and experimental studies of the nuclear reactions of importance in the formation of the chemical elements in the universe." Eager to make the public feel they were a part of the enterprise, Fowler never tired of telling people, as he did at the close of his Nobel lecture, "your bodies consist for the most part of these heavy elements.... Thus it is possible to say that you and your neighbor and I, each one of us and all of us, are truly and literally a little bit of stardust."

Early Years. Fowler was one of three children of John MacLeod Fowler and Jennie Summers Watson; the family moved to Lima, Ohio, in 1913, when Willy's father, an accountant, was transferred there from Pittsburgh. The grandson of Scottish and Irish immigrants, Fowler attributed his lifelong interest in railways and steam engines to the many hours he spent as a boy hanging around the switchyards of the Pennsylvania Railroad and sheds of the Lima Locomotive Works in his hometown. He attended the public schools of Lima and after graduating from high school in 1929 entered Ohio State University, in Columbus, where he studied physics, electrical engineering, chemistry, and mathematics; spent his Sundays in the engineering laboratories; and joined a campus fraternity. In his autobiography, "From Steam to Stars to the Early Universe" (1992), Fowler later recalled waiting tables, washing dishes, stoking furnaces, and cutting and selling meat and cheese at the central market in Columbus to pay for his education.

Having set his sights on doing pure science, Fowler elected to do his bachelor's thesis in physics "Low Voltage Electron Streams" under the supervision of the physicist Willard H. Bennett, a pioneering plasma physicist and former National Research Council fellow at the California Institute of Technology (Caltech). Not only did Bennett tutor Fowler in experimental techniques in the laboratory, but he also inspired him to become a nuclear physicist, citing a long list of front-page stories about developments in physics in 1932: the discovery of the positron, the neutron, and the deuteron, as well as the discovery by the British physicists John D. Cockcroft and Ernest T. S. Walton at Cambridge University that it was possible to split atomic nuclei with artificially accelerated particles. More importantly, he pointed Fowler in the direction of Caltech, where Charles C. Lauritsen, the versatile experimental physicist and director of the W. K. Kellogg Radiation Laboratory at Caltech, had wasted little time following up on what Cockcroft and Walton had done. Lauritsen modified one of the laboratory's x-ray tubes. He had been using the tube to accelerate electrons in order to produce a beam of high-energy x-rays. Save for using an ion source instead of an electron source, Lauritsen had basically the same equipment as the English researchers. By the time Fowler finished up his bachelor's degree in engineering physics in 1933 and entered Caltech as a graduate student that fall, Lauritsen had converted one of Kellogg's high-voltage x-ray tubes into an instrument with which to accelerate ions and to split nuclei and was sending the paper announcing his discovery of artificial neutrons to *Physical Review.*

Move to Caltech. Then in the throes of the Great Depression, Caltech offered Fowler an assistantship consisting of tuition plus lodging and board in the Athenaeum, the school's faculty club, but no cash. Fowler started working in the Kellogg laboratory during his first quarter at the institute and remained associated with Kellogg until the end of his life. To earn spending money, Fowler built equipment for handling radium for one of the doctors involved in the cancer research that was also carried out in the Kellogg laboratory during the 1930s. Indeed, the laboratory led a double life for much of the 1930s. By day, Lauritsen's students, including Fowler, operated and maintained the high-potential x-ray tube used to treat cancer patients. By night, they did nuclear physics research. Hailed by Fowler as "the greatest influence in my life," Lauritsen supervised Fowler's doctoral thesis on the production of radioactive elements of carbon, nitrogen, oxygen, and other chemical elements of low atomic number. As Fowler later told an interviewer, "We were the first to come to the conclusion that the nuclear forces were charge symmetrical on the basis of experiment," adding, "That was very nice and very fundamental." Fowler received his doctorate in 1936, and for the next three years he and Lauritsen studied the excitation curves of carbon and nitrogen isotopes bombarded with protons. Fowler became a research fellow in nuclear physics in 1936, advancing to assistant professor in 1939, associate professor in 1942, professor of physics in 1946, and institute professor of physics in 1970, a chair he held until his retirement in 1982. On 24 August 1940 Fowler married Ardiane Foy Olmsted, who died in May 1988. They had two daughters. In December 1989 he married Mary Dutcher.

Research on Nuclear Resonances. The discovery of radiative capture of protons by carbon, a discovery made by Lauritsen and his graduate student Richard Crane, in 1934, became the focus of Kellogg's nuclear physics research for the rest of the decade. In radiative capture, carbon plus a proton produces nitrogen 13, plus a powerful gamma ray to take off the excess energy. The reaction is resonant in the sense that the carbon and proton must combine with exactly the right energy for it to occur. "So by studying resonances," Fowler later recalled in an interview, "you can study the excited states of nuclei and all their properties." Convinced that the excitation levels in the light nuclei were the key to understanding the structure of the nucleus, Lauritsen and his students undertook detailed measurements of nuclear reaction rates of all the light nuclei.

At the end of this decade, the theoretical physicist Hans Bethe made the seminal suggestion that the conversion of hydrogen into helium depended on the catalytic carbon-nitrogen reaction—a chain reaction involving the

William Fowler. *Fowler, at the Yerkes Observatory.* © CORBIS.

isotopes of nitrogen and carbon. This was just the first of six nuclear reactions involved in the transformation process. When Fowler read Bethe's paper on the energy production of stars in *Physical Review* in March 1939, he realized that the quantitative measurements of the group of carbon-nitrogen reactions that he had been working on in Kellogg had something to do with the operation of nuclear reactions in the Sun and other stars. Ultimately, to explain how the Sun works, the energies and capture probabilities for all these reactions would have to be measured in detail. "When Bethe came out with the carbon-nitrogen cycle, we kind of felt a proprietary interest in this group of reactions," Fowler later recalled in an interview, "because we had been working on them.... [It] all tied very closely together." By 1939 the Kellogg researchers had switched from an alternating-current high-voltage tube to a 2-million-electron-volts direct-current Van de Graaff electrostatic accelerator, capable of high-resolution work. With the new machine, Lauritsen and Fowler began to measure carefully all the effects associated with the resonance phenomena. They measured reaction rates at resonance, the width of resonances, and the resulting gamma-ray spectra. In fact, Bethe had proposed two possible solutions, the carbon-nitrogen cycle and the proton-proton chain, because not enough was known about nuclear reactions to choose between them; only by accurately measuring nuclear reaction rates could problems such as Bethe's application of nuclear physics to astronomy be solved.

Wartime Research. During World War II, Fowler shelved plans to follow up Bethe's theoretical ideas. The electrostatic accelerator was moved into a corner of the lab on the second floor of Kellogg, now retooled to work exclusively on rocket development for the Naval Bureau of Ordnance, with Lauritsen as scientific director. In January 1941, Fowler left for Washington, D.C., where he started working on photoelectric proximity fuses for bombs at the Carnegie Institution's Department of Terrestrial Magnetism. Nine months later, he returned to Caltech to serve as the rocket project's assistant director, and to carry out research and development on defense projects, particularly the design of proximity fuses for artillery shells, the type that detonates when it is near the target. In spring 1944, Fowler spent three months in the South Pacific, talking to sailors and marines who were already familiar with rocket weapons. There he learned a lot about what they liked and did not like about them. He also helped set up for the navy the Naval Ordnance Test Station at Inyokern, and was acting director of research there until 1944. Then he helped produce components of the atom bomb.

Nuclear Astrophysics. After the war, Fowler and Lauritsen resumed their work on the carbon-nitrogen cycle, and this led, in the late 1940s, to a vigorous nuclear astrophysics program at Caltech. Postwar strategies for studying thermonuclear processes in the stars included a short series of informal, weekly seminars with Mount Wilson astronomers at the director Ira Bowen's house. As a consequence of those seminars, Lauritsen and Fowler made the deliberate decision to stay in low-energy nuclear physics and focus on those nuclear reactions that take place in stars. Fowler also began a collaboration with a diverse group of scientists ranging from the cosmologist Fred Hoyle to the astronomers Margaret and Geoffrey Burbidge. In 1949 Jesse Greenstein came to Caltech to organize work in astronomy, and his interests, particularly in the abundance of the elements in stars, stimulated Caltech's nuclear physicists to pay more attention to the astronomical side of nuclear astrophysics. However, the most important step was to initiate an experimental program that would strike at the heart of Bethe's theory. In 1946 Fowler's graduate student Robert N. Hall took as his topic for a PhD thesis the determination of the rates of the reactions in the carbon-nitrogen cycle at stellar conditions. Four years later, Fowler and Hall published their first paper on the problem. Ironically, in the end Fowler and his students concluded that the carbon cycle is not the primary source of energy in the sun. However, Bethe had also suggested another process, the proton-proton chain, and measurements made in the Kellogg lab supported the latter process, in which protons combine to form helium, with the emission of large amounts of energy. To the question "What does the sun shine on?" Fowler's group answered, "It starts with the proton-proton chain." That answer marked the start of Fowler's second career, as an experimental nuclear astrophysicist.

In the early 1950s, Fowler turned his attention to the great complex of nuclear reactions that mark the later stages of stellar evolution. In 1954 he spent a sabbatical year at the Cavendish Laboratory in Cambridge, England, as a Fulbright scholar, working with Hoyle, whom Fowler once hailed as "the second great influence in my life." The prime mover behind the grand concept of nucleosynthesis in stars, in 1946 Hoyle published his first paper on the synthesis of the chemical elements from hydrogen by nuclear processes inside stars. By the time he visited Caltech in 1953, he had expanded somewhat his work on the origin of the elements from carbon to nitrogen, including the prediction that an excited state in carbon-12 existed and that a jump from helium to carbon-12 could happen in real stars. In an oral history memoir, Fowler recalls Hoyle saying that "there has to be a resonance in the reaction between beryllium-8 and the alpha particle." Moreover, Hoyle predicted where the resonance would be. Still, Fowler brushed Hoyle aside, reportedly telling him, "Go away, Hoyle, don't bother me." But, when Ward Whaling, a recent faculty addition to Kellogg, went looking for—and found—the predicted state almost at once, a light went off inside Fowler's head. Not only did he then read Hoyle's 1946 paper, but also he "saw that by studying charged-particle reactions, which we could do in Kellogg, you could go all the way up to iron. So we had a program. We had a future."

While on sabbatical in Cambridge, Fowler worked mainly with Geoffrey and Margaret Burbidge; they spent much of their time together trying to find a source of neutrons that would produce the anomalous abundances of various elements that Margaret had been finding in various types of stars. In 1956 the Burbidges and Hoyle came to Caltech and, while they were there, wrote with Fowler the classic paper "Synthesis of the Elements in Stars," published in the *Reviews of Modern Physics* (1957), in which they showed that all of the elements from carbon to uranium could be produced by nuclear processes in stars starting with the hydrogen and helium produced in the big bang. Their paper came to be known as "B^2FH" after the names of its authors.

After the theory of the origin of the chemical elements, Fowler turned his attention to the field of relativistic astrophysics, solar neutrinos, the dynamics of the expansion of the universe, supernovas, nuclear chronology, and thermonuclear reactions in stars. Fowler continued to collaborate with Hoyle; in 1965 they coauthored a book, *Nucleosynthesis in Massive Stars and Supernovae;* in 1967 Fowler gave a series of lectures on nuclear astrophysics at the American Philosophical Society in Philadelphia, which the society subsequently published. Fowler, who succeeded Lauritsen as director of the Kellogg laboratory, continued to attend Caltech's weekly astronomy seminar on Wednesdays, the physics seminar on Thursdays, and the nuclear physics seminar on Fridays until he died.

Outside the laboratory, Fowler's life included a stint in 1951 as director of Project Vista, a study project organized at Caltech to study the defense of Western Europe, including the possible use of tactical atomic weapons on the battlefield; a member of the National Science Board (1968–1974) and of the Space Science Board (1970–1973 and 1977–1980); and president of the American Physical Society (1976). Among his many other honors, Fowler received the National Medal of Science from President Gerald Ford in 1974, and the Legion d'Honneur from President François Mitterand of France in 1989. Elected to the National Academy of Sciences in 1956, he also relished his membership in the Los Angeles Live Steamers and the National Association of Railroad Passengers, a reflection of his lifelong passion for steam locomotives and steam traction engines.

BIBLIOGRAPHY

Fowler's papers occupy 94 shelf feet in the California Institute of Technology Archives in Pasadena, California. The archives also contain a 1983–1984 oral history interview in eight sessions with John Greenberg (and a supplement with Carol Bugé in 1986), and a transcript of an interview with Albert B. Christman (1969) about the history of the China Lake Naval Weapons Center.

WORKS BY FOWLER

With E. Margaret Burbidge, Geoffrey R. Burbidge, and Fred Hoyle. "Synthesis of the Elements in Stars." *Reviews of Modern Physics* 29 (1957): 547–650.

With Fred Hoyle. *Nucleosynthesis in Massive Stars and Supernovae.* Chicago: University of Chicago Press, 1965.

Nuclear Astrophysics. Philadelphia: American Philosophical Society, 1967.

"From Steam to Stars to the Early Universe." *Annual Review of Astronomy and Astrophysics* 30 (1992): 1–9.

"Experimental and Theoretical Nuclear Astrophysics: The Quest for the Origin of the Elements." In *Nobel Lectures in Physics, 1981–1990,* edited by Gösta Ekspong. Singapore: World Scientific, 1993. Text also available on the official Web site of the Nobel Foundation.

Greenberg, John. "A Conversation with William A. Fowler, Part I." *Physics in Perspective* 7, no. 1 (2005): 66–106.

———."A Conversation with William A. Fowler, Part II." *Physics in Perspective* 7, no. 2 (2005): 165–203.

OTHER SOURCES

Barnes, Charles A. "William A. Fowler." *Physics Today* 48 (1995): 116–118.

Barnes, Charles A., Donald D. Clayton, and David N. Schramm, eds. *Essays in Nuclear Astrophysics: Presented to William A. Fowler, on the Occasion of His Seventieth Birthday.* Cambridge, U.K.: Cambridge University Press, 1982. Contains a bibliography of Fowler's publications and research papers as well as twenty-three invited papers relating to Fowler's career in nuclear astrophysics.

Goodstein, Judith R. "Nuclear Reactions." In *Millikan's School: A History of the California Institute of Technology.* New York: Norton, 1991.

Hoyle, Fred. "William Alfred Fowler (1911–95)." *Nature* 374 (1995): 406.

"William A. Fowler, 83, Astrophysicist, Dies." *New York Times,* 16 March 1995.

"William A. Fowler, Nobel Laureate 1983." Special insert in *Engineering & Science* 47, no. 2 (November 1983): unpaginated.

Judith Goodstein
David Goodstein

FRANCESCA, PIERO DELLA

SEE **Piero della Francesca.**

FRANKLAND, EDWARD

(*b.* Churchtown, Lancashire, 18 January 1825, *d.* Golaa, Norway, 9 August 1899), *organic chemistry; bond; valence; synthesis; structure; industrial chemistry; organometallic chemistry; water analysis chemical education.* For the original article on Frankland see *DSB*, vol. 5.

Subsequent work on Frankland followed the discovery in the 1970s of extensive new archival material, especially a cache of more than three thousand documents, including correspondence, memoranda, lecture notes, and much else. There is also a complete collection of detailed diaries by his daughter. Three other major collections exist, one containing many portraits and photographs. All this material remains in private hands, but most has been microfilmed.

Ancestry. Until the late twentieth century, all that was known of Frankland's ancestry was that he was the illegitimate child of Margaret Frankland, daughter of a Lancashire calico printer. Her own antecedents were later explored, the Frankland line going back to the early seventeenth century in the Craven district of West Yorkshire;

her maternal line, the Dunderdales, was identified as a farming family long established in the Garstang area of Lancashire. Here, in the late eighteenth century, Frankland's maternal grandfather came as an itinerant calico printer. The identity of Frankland's father was so well concealed by the family—and never mentioned by his son—that it appeared that he was a person of substance who had his own reasons for concealment. In fact he was Edward Gorst, a lawyer who became Deputy Clerk of the Peace for Lancashire, and money was paid to preserve his secret. His own marriage later produced further family, including the politician Sir John Gorst (who was thus Frankland's half brother). These details are of much more than merely antiquarian interest; it has been argued that the circumstances of his birth, and the necessity for keeping them secret at all costs, led on the one hand to a driving ambition to prove his own worth and on the other to an acute shyness and a great reticence to give interviews or make biographical material available.

Career. While the general outlines of Frankland's career are well known, much new detail has emerged. His experience of eight schools was varied, but his great indebtedness to James Willasey, owner of a school in Lancaster (Frankland's seventh), is clear. Here he gained a new understanding of the natural world, and this was vastly increased by the services of two local doctors, the Johnsons, who provided a laboratory for young men who wanted to learn science in the evenings. Their influence was truly remarkable and extended far beyond Frankland.

Frankland depicted his first job, as a pharmaceutical apprentice, as a laborious waste of five years, and subsequent accounts have repeated that view uncritically. A revisionist view is that, for his own reasons, Frankland exaggerated his misfortunes and failed to recognize the considerable advantages he gained from the proprietor, Stephen Ross (whom he does not even name in his own embittered account). The circumstances were later clearer as to his first chemical appointment, under Lyon Playfair, and it is certain that the Johnsons played a part in securing him the job.

Frankland's year at Queenwood College (1847–1848) proved to be another formative experience in developing scientific discipline. His diary for that year was discovered and throws much light on his developing lifestyle as well as the feuds and indiscipline in a failing establishment. Following a year at Marburg, Frankland spent a similar period at Putney College before becoming the first professor of chemistry at Owens College, Manchester. The six years spent there were momentous for his development of a web of industrial consultancies (hitherto unknown). These involved much extra-university work, the acquisition of wealth (which was to become a driving force for his later life), and a deepening knowledge of all kinds of applied chemistry. Meanwhile, surviving lecture notes reveal a new breadth of coverage, depth of concern for technological chemistry, and an astonishing degree of academic professionalism.

The ambitious Frankland was not satisfied even by these opportunities and, in 1857, he moved to London, where he remained for the rest of his career. Holding a variety of posts (often in plurality), he made his mark chiefly at the Royal Institution and the Royal College of Chemistry (later part of Imperial College). Documents later discovered clarified his lecturing style and material and his relations with colleagues. They also reveal his problems of justifying the expenditure of so much time on external consultant work, which culminated in a furious dispute over his salary and his eventual resignation in 1885.

Scientific Work. In the early twenty-first century it was clear that Frankland's importance for the development of valence and structure theories had been considerably underrated. His pioneer work in organometallic chemistry was placed in a far wider context than before, and he was recognized as the effective founder of the subject, even the term *organometallic* and its modern definition being his. Frankland's invention of the term chemical *bond* also denotes a fundamentally new approach to chemistry. His extension of the concept to organic chemistry opened up the way to a new structural organic chemistry. The fact that he was rarely recognized for these singular achievements requires complex explanation, including the ambivalent role of organometallic chemistry, his use of old atomic weights and equivalents, the controversy between proponents of radicals and types, and the personal opposition of his great rival, August Kekulé.

Frankland's work in organic chemistry was further examined, and it became evident that his explorations of acetoacetic ester and related compounds gave rise not only to a powerful synthetic method but one that could lead to allocation of structures for the products. He was hailed as one of the great founders of synthetic organic chemistry. Another area of Frankland's research was water analysis. His role in its use for monitoring public water supplies has been discussed by several authors. His appointment as official analyst for London's water supply led to his dominating the scene for over twenty years, in part because the technique that he had developed was so complex that few other chemists were able to use it effectively. He introduced the concept of *previous sewage contamination* as a measure of unacceptability, and estimated this by determination of dissolved nitrogen. The discovery of his water analysis notebook revealed the astonishing extent of his consultancy, going far beyond London and extending even to the Middle East. A study in the social history of

Edward Frankland. *Edward Frankland, circa 1875.* HULTON ARCHIVE/GETTY IMAGES.

science concludes that Frankland had strong political motivations, and there is no doubt that financial ambition strongly colored his approach to this topic.

Other scientific research that came to light in fresh detail includes studies on muscular power and nutrition that became the start of measurements of what was later called the *calorific value* of foodstuffs. He produced theories of glaciers and meteorology and—more important—work on atmospheric pollution. With Joseph Lockyer he studied the spectrum of the sun and discovered a line of a previously unknown terrestrial element, naming the newcomer *helium.*

Educational Advances. Frankland's role as a leading chemical educator has long been recognized, though the magnitude of his contribution has only in the early 2000s been understood. He was the leading pioneer of popular chemical education in Victorian Britain, partly through his use of formulae showing atoms by circles and bonds by lines. Known as Frankland's Notation, it was seized upon as an effective heuristic instrument, especially with the young or those fairly new to chemistry. It was popularized in his frequent classes for mechanics and others, by his own textbook *Lecture Notes for Chemical Students* (1866), and by the ascendancy of his ideas in the Department of Science and Art examinations. It was later believed that all of this was part of a deliberate strategy by which he came to dominate the national examination system, for which he was chief examiner from 1865 to 1876. He introduced a new emphasis on theory and at least some knowledge of experiments. He was not able to persuade the authorities to introduce practical examinations until 1878. But he did run a series of courses for teachers to give training in practical work, and he published an influential book, *How to Teach Chemistry* (1875).

Scientific Institutions. For all his shyness, Frankland was much at home in the company of his fellow scientists. In the Chemical Society he was vice president and/or foreign secretary for nearly a dozen years before becoming president in 1871–1872. At just this time the chemists of Britain were beginning to agitate for professional recognition, and this was achieved in 1877 by the creation of the Institute of Chemistry. Frankland was its first president and has been considered to have been its real founder.

In addition to these two chemical bodies, the Royal Society claimed much of Frankland's spare time. Elected a Fellow of the Royal Society (FRS) in 1853, he received both its Royal and Copley medals. Frankland served for many years as the secretary of a small, informal group known as the X-Club, which had been founded by T. H. Huxley. Though not formally part of the Royal Society, all but one of its members held an FRS, and it became an active pressure group for the cause of scientific naturalism. Elected to the Royal Society Council as soon as he moved to London, Frankland might have expected the eventual accolade of presidency of the Royal Society. It was not to be, and his consolation was the post of foreign secretary when he was seventy-one. A later discovered letter about the presidency, written by Huxley, contains the pregnant phrase "Frankland won't do." Though no explanation was given, it seems that it was chiefly Frankland's trade associations that debarred him from the highest office in British science.

Personal Relations. Much of the Frankland material that emerged between 1980 and 2005 demonstrated how tortuous were some of his family relationships. His first wife, Sophie, died from consumption at Davos, where Frankland had sent her for convalescence. Letters between Sophie and her younger daughter, also named Sophie, reveal how deeply she regretted being severed from her family; Frankland rarely visited, staying only briefly, though her end was clearly near. His second marriage was far from happy, and he was often away from home. The final summers of his life were spent in Norway, writing his reminiscences with the help of Jane Lund, a secretary from the British embassy. The suggestion that she was his mistress is without foundation.

Frankland's elder son Fred was exiled to New Zealand because he failed to achieve his father's exacting academic standards. Fierce controversy raged with his other son Percy, leading to a complete rupture of family relationships, ostensibly caused by controversy about payments for water analyses. The rift was healed only just before Frankland died.

Frankland received a knighthood in the Queen's Jubilee Honours List in 1897. His KCB was awarded, not for water analysis as has been often stated, but because he (and William Crookes) had declined the honor of presidency of the British Association and to each this was a fitting consolation prize. However, the scientific community knew nothing of this and, quite rightly, rejoiced in the KCB being awarded to one of their most distinguished members. Yet Frankland's reputation remained largely unknown to generations of chemists, largely perhaps owing to his reluctance to give details of his own life. Amazingly, the Royal Society never published an obituary for its late foreign secretary, and the Chemical Society failed to honor its former president with any notice until six years after his death, and then only by an ordinary obituary rather than the usual Memorial Lecture. In the late twentieth and early twenty-first centuries, however, Frankland's achievements were recognized. The Royal Society of Chemistry now awards a Frankland Lectureship (from 1981) and a Frankland Fellowship (from 1983) for work in organometallic chemistry.

BIBLIOGRAPHY

Coley, Noel George, Gerrylynn K. Roberts, and Colin A. Russell. *Chemists by Profession.* London: Royal Institute of Chemistry/Milton Keynes, Open University Press, 1977.

Hamlin, Christopher. *A Science of Impurity: Water Analysis in Nineteenth-Century Britain.* Bristol, U.K.: Hilger, 1990.

McGrayne, Sharon Bertsch. *Prometheans in the Lab.* New York: McGraw-Hill, 2001.

Russell, Colin A. "Edward Frankland and the Cheapside Chemists of Lancaster: An Early Victorian Pharmaceutical Apprenticeship." *Annals of Science* 35 (1978): 253–273.

———. *Lancastrian Chemist: The Early Years of Sir Edward Frankland.* London: Milton Keynes, Open University Press, 1987.

———. *Edward Frankland: Chemistry, Controversy and Conspiracy in Victorian England.* Cambridge, U.K.: Cambridge University Press, 1996.

———. "The Frankland Enigma." *Chemistry in Britain* 35 (1999): 43–45.

———. "Chemical Techniques in a Pre-electronic Age: The Remarkable Apparatus of Edward Frankland." In *Instruments and Experimentation in the History of Chemistry,* edited by Frederick L. Holmes and Trevor H. Levere. Boston: MIT Press, 2000.

———. "Edward Frankland." In *New Dictionary of National Biography.* Oxford, Oxford University Press, 2004.

———, and Shirley P. Russell. "The Archives of Sir Edward Frankland: Resources, Problems, and Methods." *British Journal for the History of Science* 23 (1990): 175–185.

Seyferth, Dietmar. "Zinc Alkyls, Edward Frankland, and the Beginnings of Main-Group Organometallic Chemistry." *Organometallics* 20 (2001): 2940–2955.

Colin A. Russell

FRANKLIN, ROSALIND ELSIE

(*b.* London, United Kingdom, 25 July 1920; *d.* London, United Kingdom, 16 April 1958), *physical chemistry, x-ray crystallography.* For the original article on Franklin see *DSB,* vol. 7.

Franklin was born in London on 25 July 1920, the second of five children of Ellis Franklin and Muriel Franklin, née Waley, both from families of high standing in Anglo-Jewry. The Franklins came as Fraenkels to London from Breslau, Silesia, in 1763 and became wealthy bankers. By 1868 their financial base was a merchant bank, Keysers, which provided employment for many Franklin sons. Her novel position as an upper-class Englishwoman and a Jew shaped Rosalind Franklin's life.

Early Years. Franklin was educated in London at the academically distinguished London day school, St. Paul's Girls', where girls were encouraged to prepare for a career. Rosalind decided to specialize in science, one of her best subjects. Her family was startled because Franklin women were not expected to take paid employment. In 1938 she went to Newnham College, a women's college collect at Cambridge University. After receiving a good second-class degree in physical chemistry, she chose war-related work for the British Coal Utilisation Research Board. Her published work on the structure of coals and carbons gave her an international reputation. In 1945 she received her doctorate from Cambridge with a thesis titled "The Physical Chemistry of Solid Organic Colloids with Special Reference to Coal and Related Materials."

From 1947 until the end of 1950, Franklin worked in Paris at the Laboratoire central des services chimiques de l'état, becoming skilled at the x-ray diffraction of disordered crystalline material such as coal. At the end of 1950, at the age of thirty, she accepted an appointment at King's College London (KCL), associated with the University of London. On 4 December 1950, John Turton Randall, head of biophysics at KCL, wrote her a letter that changed

Franklin

completely the direction of her planned research. Randall said it now seemed more important for her "to investigate the structure of certain biological fibers in which we are interested. This means that as far as the experimental x-ray effort is concerned there will be at the moment only yourself and [graduate student Raymond] Gosling" (Olby, 1974, p. 346).

Randall did not explain that Dr. Maurice Wilkins, his deputy, had published important papers on the deoxyribonucleic acid, DNA, and considered the DNA project "his." As Randall never showed Wilkins his letter, Wilkins thought that Franklin was coming to join his team. Yet Franklin sensed trouble. From Paris she wrote in a letter to her brother, "I far prefer here the place, the people, the life and the climate. I feel—and felt even before I came to France—far more European than English" (Maddox, 2002, p. 115).

In fact, however, returning to England was a good career move, taking Franklin into the new hybrid field of biophysics, where Britain was far more advanced than France. However, when Franklin arrived at KCL in January 1951 she hated it instantly. In the London of King George VI, Franklin's quick, clipped voice carried a class label. According to Dr. Jean Hanson, the senior biologist at King's College's Biophysics Unit, "Just the way she spoke … there were people at that time who sneered at the upper-class way of speaking, and really *hated* it" (Maddox, 2002, p. 127). More alienating for Franklin was King's College's ecclesiastical atmosphere. Theology was its biggest department, with four hundred students training for the Anglican priesthood. When she was informed that women were not allowed in the college's senior common room, where some of the staff ate lunch, she was angry. As she wrote to her American friend, Anne Sayre, on 1 March 1952, "King's has neither foreigners nor Jews" (Maddox, 2002, p. 172). She was wrong, but her words show that she felt like an outsider.

DNA Crystallography. Franklin's work went well. In making x-ray photographs of crystalline fibers of DNA, she was assisted by her graduate student, the amiable Raymond Gosling, and by the excellent samples of DNA fibers prepared by Professor Rudolf Signer of the University of Berne, in Switzerland, which were obtained for King's College by Wilkins, who was away when she arrived. The only researcher working at high humidity, she took sharp, clear pictures that revealed two forms of DNA. When hydrated to absorb water, the fiber became longer and thinner. When placed over a drying agent, it changed back. This transformation explained why earlier attempts—made by Wilkins, among others—to understand DNA's structure had been unsuccessful, as they had been looking at a blur of the two forms.

Franklin and Gosling called the longer, heavily hydrated DNA the "B" form; they called the other, shorter and drier, the "A" form. This discovery was indebted to Franklin's expertise, for she had ordered special equipment from Paris, designed a tilting camera, pulled exceptionally thin DNA fibers, and perfected her technique for orienting the fibers in front of the camera's beam.

Franklin did not share her findings with Wilkins because she was shocked by his ignorance of what she felt were simple hydration techniques. Trouble between them began in the summer of 1951. When he offered an adverse opinion on some of her results, she was outraged.

This was the type of dispute some could settle over a drink at the pub. But Franklin and Wilkins were temperamental opposites, she quick speaking and combative; he shy, tentative, and evasive. He thought she had been brought in to help his team with x-ray crystallography. She thought she had the x-ray work to herself. Finally, Randall intervened and gave Franklin all the Signer DNA and told her to concentrate on the A form.

Consequently, Wilkins felt shut out of his own project. On frequent visits to Cambridge, he talked with his old friend, Francis Crick, at the Cavendish Laboratory. Crick, although working on horse hemoglobin, was interested in DNA. So was the American, James Watson, who heard Wilkins pour out his troubles with "Rosie." In November 1951, after Watson had heard Franklin describe her work at a King's College seminar, he and Crick constructed a model of a possible structure for DNA. When Franklin and others from King's came to inspect it, they knew at a glance that it was wrong. Embarrassed, Sir Lawrence Bragg, head of the Cavendish Laboratory, which was not supposed to be working on DNA, ordered Watson and Crick to drop it immediately.

Continuing her systematic x-ray investigation of the Signer DNA fibers, Franklin calculated the dimensions of the unit cell of the molecule and the location of its phosphates—on the outside. In early 1952 she reported that her evidence suggested "a helical structure (which must be very closely packed) containing probably 2, 3 or 4 co-axial nucleic acid chains per helical unit" (Report to Turner-Newall, in Franklin Archives).

Over 1 and 2 May 1952, Franklin and Gosling got an exceptionally clear picture of the B form of DNA, showing a stark "X" that suggested a helix. She worked out the distance between turns of the helix and the number of base pairs within it. Numbering the photograph 51, she put it aside, to return (as agreed with Randall) to the A form.

In mid-December 1952 the unpublished results of her x-ray work were included in a report prepared for the visiting biophysics committee of the Medical Research Council (MRC), the government agency financing both

Franklin

Rosalind Elsie Franklin. PHOTO RESEARCHERS, INC.

Randall's research unit at King's and Bragg's at the Cavendish Laboratory. Franklin's summary gave the full dimensions of the DNA unit cell, its density, and her claim to have established "with certainty" that the crystal fell into the C2 space group that crystallogrphers call "face-centered monoclinic."

Move to Birbeck. In January 1953 Franklin announced that she was leaving KCL in March, having negotiated the transfer of her Turner and Newall Fellowship to Birkbeck College, a secular institution within the University of London. She was giving up DNA work for as-yet-unspecified research. "I may be moving from a palace to the slums," she wrote to a friend on 10 March 1953, "but I'm sure I will be happier" (Maddox, 2002, p. 205). Her new boss, J. Desmond Bernal, a well-known physicist and a Communist, was a brilliant crystallographer.

At King's College, Ray Gosling, about to lose Franklin as his thesis adviser, gave the photographs he and Franklin had taken to Maurice Wilkins. On 30 January 1953, Watson came into Franklin's room at King's and offered to show her the pre-publication paper of Linus Pauling of the California Institute of Technology in Pasadena, claiming to have solved the structure of DNA. The paper, given to Watson by Pauling's son Peter, showed that Pauling had made a fundamental chemical mistake in placing the phosphates in the center where they could not be ionized. He also proposed a triple-strand helix.

Franklin countered with her own evidence against a helical structure. Watson then went into Wilkins's lab where Wilkins, defending the helical theory, showed Watson Photo 51 of Franklin and Gosling. One look told Watson that the DNA molecule has the form of a helix. He then persuaded Crick to try another model.

At the Cavendish Laboratory, Watson and Crick asked their colleague, Max Perutz, a member of the MRC's biophysics committee, to show them a copy of the MRC report. When Crick saw Franklin's evidence that the molecule belonged to the "monoclinic C2" space group, he knew instantly that the DNA's two chains of nucleic acid must be anti-parallel.

Then Watson spotted that the two chains of DNA were linked by pairs of bases that always occurred in the same combinations. When the chains came apart, these bases would seek each other out and, therefore, copy themselves. By the end of February 1953 Watson and Crick had completed their now-celebrated model, with its twisting coils of paired atoms.

Meanwhile, Franklin's notebooks show that at the end of February 1953, she took out Photo 51 and concluded that both the A and the B forms of DNA were two-chain helices. Her work was ready for publication just as Crick and Watson began trying to publish their discovery quickly, and to find a way to acknowledge the embarrassing fact that all the experimental work behind it had been done at King's College. Wilkins got Watson and Crick to agree that there should be a second paper in *Nature*, written by himself (Wilkins), Alec Stokes, and Herbert Wilson, describing the DNA research of the three of them. Wilkins then learned that Franklin and Gosling had finished writing their own paper.

On 17 March 1953 Franklin adapted this paper in order for it to accompany the Watson-Crick paper, making three papers in *Nature*. She inserted the words, "Thus our general ideas are consistent with the model proposed by Crick and Watson." So they should have been added, as the Watson-Crick model was in large part derived from her work. Photo 51 of the B form of DNA appeared as an illustration to the Franklin-Gosling paper, "Molecular Configuration in Sodium Thymonucleate," published in *Nature* on 25 April 1953, with no suggestion that Watson had seen it.

Franklin had no sense of having been exploited. Nor did she accept Watson and Crick's ideas as more than a hypothesis. In the second of her two papers that appeared in *Acta Crystallographica* in September 1953, she wrote of "the Watson-Crick model" that "discrepancies prevent us from accepting it in detail" (Maddox, 2002, p. 223).

Franklin

Work on TMV. At Birkbeck College, Franklin formed her own team of dedicated disciples (including the subsequent Nobel laureate, Sir Aaron Klug) and published seventeen papers on the tobacco mosaic virus, TMV.

Starting in 1954, Franklin's earlier carbon work brought her several welcome invitations to conferences in the United States. In August 1956 she was diagnosed in London with ovarian cancer. She died in April 1958. That year Bernal wrote of her in *Nature* that "her photographs are among the most beautiful x-ray photographs of any substance ever taken" (1958, p. 154). In 1962 Watson, Crick, and Wilkins got the Nobel Prize. Only Wilkins mentioned, very briefly, Franklin's part.

Franklin had come very close to getting the answer to the structure of DNA. That her draft manuscript of 17 March 1953, proving how close she was, should not have come to light until many years later—reported in an article, "Corrigendum," by Klug, for *Nature* (1968)—is one of the many ways in which fortune did her no favors. In the late twentieth and early twenty-first centuries she became an icon of the oppressed female scientist. Ironically, posterity would not have known of her part in discovering DNA's structure had Watson not revealed it, however unflatteringly, in his 1968 book, *The Double Helix.*

SUPPLEMENTARY BIBLIOGRAPHY

Rosalind Franklin's papers are held in the Churchill College Archives, Cambridge University, England.

WORKS BY FRANKLIN

"The Physical Chemistry of Solid Organic Colloids with Special Reference to Coal and Related Materials." PhD diss., Cambridge University, Cambridge, UK, 1945.

"A Note on the True Density, Chemical Composition, and Structure of Coals and Carbonized Coals." *Fuel* 27 (1948): 46–49.

"Influence of the Bonding Electrons on the Scattering of X-Rays by Carbon." *Nature* 165 (14 January 1950): 71–72.

"Crystallite Growth in Graphitizing and Non-graphitizing Carbons." *Proceedings of the Royal Society* 209 (1951): 196–218.

With R. G. Gosling. "Molecular Configuration in Sodium Thymonucleate." *Nature* 171 (25 April 1953): 740–741.

With R. G. Gosling. "Evidence for 2-Chain Helix in Crystalline Structure of Sodium Deoxyribonucleate." *Nature* 172 (25 July 1953): 156–157.

With R. G. Gosling. "The Structure of Sodium Thymonucleates Fibres. I. The Influence of Water Content." *Acta Crystallographica* 6 (10 September 1953): 673–677.

With R. G. Gosling. "The Structure of Sodium Thymonucleate Fibres. II. The Cylindrically Symmetrical Patterson Function." *Acta Crystallographica* 6 (10 September 1953): 678–685.

"Structure of Tobacco Mosaic Virus." *Nature* 175 (26 February 1955): 379–381.

With K. C. Holmes. "The Helical Arrangement of the Protein Sub-units in Tobacco Mosaic Virus." *Biochimica et Biophysica Acta* 21 (1956): 405–406.

With A. Klug. "The Nature of the Helical Groove on the Tobacco Mosaic Virus Particle." *Biochimica et Biophysica Acta* 19 (1956): 403–416.

"Location of the Ribonucleic Acid in the Tobacco Mosaic Virus Particle." *Nature* 177 (1956): 928–930.

With A. Klug and J. T. Finch. "Structure of Turnip Yellow Mosaic Virus: X-ray Diffraction Studies." *Biochimica et Biophysica Acta* 25 (1957): 242–252.

With A. Klug, J. T. Finch, and K. C. Holmes. "On the Structure of Some Ribonucleoprotein Particles." *Transactions of the Faraday Society* 25 (1958): 197–198.

With A. Klug. "Order-disorder Transitions in the Structures Containing Helical Molecules." *Discussions of the Faraday Society* 25 (1958): 104–110.

With K. C. Holmes. "The Radial Density Distribution in Some Strains of Tobacco Mosaic Virus." *Virology* 6 (1958): 328–336.

With A. Klug. "The Structure of RNA in Tobacco Mosaic Virus and in Some Other Ribonucleoproteins." *Transactions of the Faraday Society* 55 (1959): 494–495.

OTHER SOURCES

Bernal, J. D. "Dr. Rosalind E. Franklin." *Nature* 182 (19 July 1958): 154.

Elkin, Lynne Osman. "Rosalind Franklin and the Double Helix." *Physics Today* 56 (March 2003): 42–48.

Franklin, Arthur E. *Records of the Franklin Family and Collaterals.* 2nd ed. London: Routledge, 1935.

Glassman, Gary. *The Secret of Photo 51.* WGBH-Noval, PBS. 22 April 2003.

Glynn, Jenifer. "Rosalind Franklin 1920–1958." In *Cambridge Women: Twelve Portraits,* edited by Edward Shils and Carmen Blacker. Cambridge, UK: Cambridge University Press, 1996.

Harris, Peter. "On Charcoal." *Interdisciplinary Science Reviews* 24 (1999): 301–306.

———. "Rosalind Franklin's Work on Coal, Carbon, and Graphite." *Interdisciplinary Science Reviews* 26 (2001): 204–209.

Hubbard, Ruth. "The Double Helix: A Study of Science in Context." In *The Politics of Women's Biology.* New Brunswick, NJ, and London: Rutgers University Press, 1990.

Klug, Aaron. "Rosalind Franklin and the Discovery of the Structure of DNA." *Nature* 219 (24 August 1968): 808–810, 843–844, 879–880.

———. "Corrigendum." *Nature* 219 (14 September 1968): 1192.

———. "Rosalind Franklin and the Double Helix." *Nature* 248 (26 April 1974): 787–788.

———. "The Tobacco Mosaic Virus Particle: Structure and Assembly." *Philosophical Transactions: Biological Sciences* 354 (29 March 1999): 531–535.

Maddox, Brenda. *Rosalind Franklin: The Dark Lady of DNA.* New York: HarperCollins, 2002.

Nicholson, W. *Life Story.* BBC2 Horizon Programme. 27 April 1987.

Olby, Robert. *The Path to the Double Helix.* London: Macmillan, 1974.

Sayre, Anne. *Rosalind Franklin and DNA .* New York: Norton, 1975.

Watson, James D. *The Double Helix: A Personal Account of the Discovery of the Structure of DNA.* New York: Atheneum, 1968.

Wilkins, Maurice. *The Third Man of the Double Helix: The Autobiography of Maurice Wilkins.* Oxford: Oxford University Press, 2003.

Brenda Maddox

FREGE, FRIEDRICH LUDWIG GOTTLOB

FREGE, FRIEDRICH LUDWIG GOTTLOB (*b.* Wismar, Germany, 8 November 1848; *d.* Bad Kleinen, Germany, 26 July 1925), *mathematics, logic, foundations of mathematics.* For the original article on Frege see *DSB,* vol. 5.

Although a mathematician, Gottlob Frege is regarded as one of the founding fathers of modern (analytical) philosophy. With his *Begriffsschrift* (concept script) of 1879 he created modern mathematical logic. He used it as a linguistic tool for a program of founding mathematical concepts exclusively on logical concepts (logicism). Frege was involved in controversies with representatives of the algebraic tradition in logic concerning the power of the different systems of symbolic logic, and with David Hilbert on the nature of mathematical axiom systems.

Frege in Jena. Frege spent most of his academic life at the University of Jena, except for five semesters of studies in Göttingen (1871–1873). He took courses in mathematics, physics, chemistry, and philosophy. Among his most important teachers in Jena were Karl Snell, who followed Jakob Friedrich Fries as chair of mathematics and physics, and Ernst Carl Abbe, at that time privatdozent for mathematics. Abbe became Frege's mentor. He encouraged Frege to transfer to Göttingen in order to complete his university studies and later supported him in his career.

Back in Jena, Frege applied for the post of a privatdozent for mathematics, submitting as *Habilitationsschrift* "Methods of Calculation Based on an Extension of the Concept of Quality," which contributed to the theory of functional equations, in particular iteration theory. Abbe initiated Frege's promotion to außerordentlicher Professor (roughly equivalent to associate professor or reader) of mathematics in 1879. This early promotion was possible because Frege had published his first monograph, *Begriffsschrift,* in January of that year. In 1866 Abbe had become a scientific consultant for improving the construction of microscopes built by the Carl Zeiss optics industry. In 1875 he became an associate and limited partner of Zeiss. Abbe set up the Carl Zeiss Foundation (1889) by first establishing a fund for scientific purposes (Ministerialfond für wissenschaftliche Zwecke) in 1886, supporting teaching and research in mathematics and sciences at the University of Jena. Abbe's foundation also made an improvement in Frege's remuneration possible, and later financially supported his promotion to *ordentlicher Honararprofessor* (a payroll professorship in honor of the person) in 1896.

In 1907 Frege was awarded the prestigious title of *Hofrat.* His growing reputation is indicated by Ludwig Wittgenstein's visit in 1911 (further visits took place in 1912 and 1913). In summer semester 1913 Rudolf Carnap attended Frege's course Begriffsschrift II, and another course, Logic in Mathematics, in 1914. In 1918 Frege retired after having been on sick leave for a year. He moved to Bad Kleinen, a resort near Wismar. On the initiative of Heinrich Scholz, Frege's *Nachlass* (literary estate) was transferred in 1935 to Münster, where it was purportedly destroyed during a bomb raid on Münster on 25 March 1945.

Logic. Frege's publication of the *Begriffsschrift* is regarded in the early twenty-first century as "the single most important event in the development of modern logic" (Thiel and Beaney, p. 26). In this work, Frege created the first strict logical calculus in the modern sense, based on precise definitions of expressions and deduction rules arriving for the first time at an axiomatic development of classical quantification theory. Frege replaced the traditional analysis of elementary statements into subject and predicate with an analysis of a proposition into function and argument, which could be used to express the generality of a statement (and with this also existence statements) by bound variables and quantifiers.

It can be assumed that Frege took over the term *Begriffsschrift* from Friedrich Adolf Trendelenburg's characterization of Gottfried Wilhelm Leibniz's general characteristics (1854). The term had, however, already been used by Wilhelm von Humboldt in a treatise (1824) on the letter script and its influence on the construction of language.

In a lengthy review of the *Begriffsschrift* (1880), Ernst Schröder accused Frege of ignoring George Boole's algebra of logic, first presented in *The Mathematical Analysis of Logic* (1847). Frege answered in articles (published only posthumously) by comparing Boole's calculatory logic

Frege

with his own, where he determined quantification theory as the main point of deviation (Frege, 1880–1881, 1882). It is indeed historically true that the Booleans had no quantification theory at that time, but this cannot be regarded as an essential difference between these variations of symbolic logic on a systematic level, because in 1883 the U.S. logician Charles S. Peirce and his student Oscar Howard Mitchell developed an almost equivalent quantification theory within the algebra of logic. The essential difference between the algebra of logic and Frege's mathematical logic can thus be seen in different interpretations of the judgment. Another essential difference can be seen in the fact that Frege aimed at giving a logical structure of judgeable contents, which implied an inherent semantics. The Booleans, in contrast, were interested in logical structures themselves, which could be applied in different domains. Their systems allowed various interpretations. This required a supplementary external semantics.

Logicism. Frege's work was above all devoted to investigations on the nature of number. It was, thus, essentially philosophical. There is evidence that he was influenced by the philosophy of his contemporaries, especially by neo-Kantian approaches. These influences found their way into Frege's philosophy of mathematics with its metaphysical qualities.

Contrary to Immanuel Kant, who regarded mathematical (arithmetical and geometrical) propositions as examples for synthetic a priori propositions, that is, propositions that are not empirical, but enlarging knowledge, Frege wanted to prove that arithmetic could completely be founded on logic, that is, that each arithmetical concept, in particular the concept of number, could be derived from logical concepts. Arithmetic was, thus, analytical.

The logicist program is only sketched in the *Begriffsschrift,* where Frege gave purely logical definitions of equinumerousity and the successor relation. In his next book, the *Grundlagen der Arithmetik* (1884). Frege formulated the classical logicistic definition of number, according to which the number n is defined as the extension of the concept "equinumerous to the concept F_n" with F_n standing for a concept with exactly n objects falling under it. The series of F_ns starts with $F_0 = \neg x = x$. F_{n+1} can be reconstructed recursively from F_n. The number 0 is defined as the extension of the concept "equinumerous to the concept 'different from itself,'" and the number 1 as the extension of the concept "equinumerous to the concept 'equals 0.'" The purely logical foundation of mathematics should not only disprove the Kantian paradigm, but also refute empiricist approaches to mathematics such as the one advocated by John Stuart Mill, and with this psychological interpretations of numbers as mental constructions. Frege pointedly expressed this criticism of psychologism in his harsh review of Edmund Husserl's *Philosophie der Arithmetik* in 1894, as a result of which Husserl was brought to revise the foundational program of phenomenology and convert to antipsychologism.

Frege elaborated the logicistic program in the two volumes of the *Grundgesetze der Arithmetik* (1893/1903). In this last of his monographs Frege also presented the mature version of his ontology, developed earlier in the three papers "Function and Concept" (1891), "On *Sinn* und *Bedeutung*" (1892), and "Concept and Object" (1892), all three currently regarded as classic texts of analytical philosophy. There he further elaborated his earlier distinction between concept and object. In particular he introduced in the *Grundgesetze* value-ranges considered as a special kind of objects. The identity criterion is given in Basic Law V, according to which the value-ranges of two functions are identical if the functions coincide in their values for every argument, with this giving the modern abstraction schema. In terms of concepts the law says that whatever falls under the concept F falls under the concept G and vice versa, if and only if the concepts F and G have the same extension.

Frege's conception of logicism failed, as Frege himself diagnosed, because of Basic Law V. Frege suggested an ad hoc solution forbidding that the extension of a concept may fall under the concept itself. This solution was proved to be insufficient by Stanisław Leśniewski (1939, unpublished) and Willard Van Orman Quine in 1955, but it indicates that the logical form of Basic Law V may be innocent of the emergence of the paradox and that the formation rules for function names may be too liberal in allowing impredicative function names.

In his latest publications Frege gave up logicism. He abandoned the talk of extensions of concepts and value-ranges, and the idea of numbers as logical objects, although he still held that they are objects of some other kind, based on the source of "geometrische Erkenntnisquelle," that is, pure intuition.

Frege's logicist program was later revived by the proponents of Frege-arithmetic and neologicism. In some of these directions Basic Law V is replaced by Hume's principle, according to which two concepts F and G have the same number if and only if they are equinumerous, that is, if there is a one-to-one correspondence between the F's and G's.

The Nature of Axiomatics. After the failure of his logicistic program, Frege focused his research on geometry as the foundational discipline of mathematics. He kept the traditional understanding of geometry as an intuitive discipline, thereby opposing David Hilbert's new formalistic approach to geometry that came along with a new kind of

Frege

axiomatics. Frege's opposition had its prehistory in his criticism of the older arithmetical formalism presented in a paper "Über formale Theorien der Arithmetik" (1885), taken up again in papers against his Jena colleague in mathematics, Carl Johannes Thomae (1906/1908). In these papers Frege opposes the understanding of arithmetic as a purely formal game with calculations bare of any contents. The older formalism regards arithmetic as a game like chess. It starts from certain initial formulas, then derives new formulas using a fixed set of transformation rules. But, neither the initial formulas nor the transition rules are justified, so the derived formulas are not justified either. Therefore, Frege concludes, these approaches could not provide any contribution to the foundations of arithmetic.

Hilbert overcame the traditional conception of axiomatics according to the model of Euclid's *Elements* by giving an example. In his *Grundlagen der Geometrie* of 1899 he gave an axiomatic presentation of Euclidean geometry. Hilbert's system proceeds from "thought things" in the Kantian sense, products of the human mind, but empty concepts because of lacking any element of (empirical) intuition. The geometrical concepts were not directly defined, but implicitly gained as concepts obeying the features set by some group of axioms, and justified by proving the independence of the axioms from one another, the completeness of the system, and its consistency. The formalistic approach aims at a theory of structures. This is pointedly expressed in Hilbert's letter to Frege of 29 December 1899, in which Hilbert claimed that every theory is only a half-timbering or schema of concepts and implications with arbitrary basic elements. If instead of the system of points some system love, law, chimney sweep is thought, and if all axioms are regarded as relations between these elements, then all theorems, for example Pythagoras's theorem, would be valid for them.

In a letter sent two days earlier, Frege had correctly criticized Hilbert's use of implicit definitions arguing that he had blurred the differences between axioms and definitions. It became clear that Frege stuck to the traditional (Aristotelian) understanding of axioms in geometry, calling axioms sentences that are true but not proved, because they have emerged from a source of knowledge completely different from the logical, a source that can be called spatial intuition. From the truth of the axioms follows that they do not contradict each other, so no consistency of proof was needed. Hilbert answered that if the arbitrarily set axioms do not contradict each other with all their implications, then they are true and the defined objects exist. For Hilbert consistency (logical possibility) is, thus, the criterion of truth and existence.

Hilbert rejected Frege's suggestion to publish the exchange of letters, so Frege took up his criticism in a series of papers published in 1903 and 1906 on the foundations of geometry, where he argued for his antiformalistic position. He demanded that after having defined the concept "point," it should be possible to determine whether a certain object, for example, his pocket watch, was a point or not.

The two controversies mentioned show that Frege followed that traditional understanding of philosophy as all-embracing fundamental discipline that formed, along with logic, logical ontology, and epistemology the foundation for mathematics and sciences. He did not share the pragmatic attitude of some influential contemporaries in mathematics and sciences (like Hilbert) to keep philosophy away from their mathematical and scientific practice by simply fading out philosophical problems. Nevertheless, Frege opened the way for directions like philosophy of science, which aimed at bridging the gap between philosophy on the one hand and mathematics and science on the other, and which became successful in the twentieth century. His influence on Bertrand Russell's logicism, codified in *Principia Mathematica,* Russell's joint work with Alfred North Whitehead (1910/13), is well known. Through Carnap, Frege gained influence on logic and foundational research in the neopositivist movement of the Vienna Circle, which constituted the context of Kurt Gödel's shaping of modern logic and foundational studies.

SUPPLEMENTARY BIBLIOGRAPHY

WORKS BY FREGE

"Methods of Calculation Based on an Extension of the Concept of Quantity" (1874). In McGuiness, *Collected Papers on Mathematics, Logic, and Philosophy,* 56–92.

Begriffsschrift, eine der arithmetischen nachgebildete Formelsprache des reinen Denkens. Halle, Germany: L. Nebert, 1879. In *Conceptual Notation and Related Articles,* translated and edited with a biography and introduction by Terence Ward Bynum, 101–203. Oxford: Oxford University Press, 1972.

"Boole's Logical Calculus and the Concept-Script." (1880–1881). In Hermes et al., *Posthumous Writings,* 9–46.

"Boole's Logical Formula-Language and My Concept-Script." (1882). In Hermes et al., *Posthumous Writings,* 47–52.

Die Grundlagen der Arithmetik, eine logisch mathematische Untersuchung über den Begriff der Zahl. Breslau, Germany: W. Koebner, 1884. Translated by John L. Austin as *The Foundations of Arithmetic.* 2nd ed. Oxford: Blackwell, 1953.

"On Formal Theories of Arithmetic" (1885). In McGuiness, *Collected Papers on Mathematics, Logic, and Philosophy,* 112–121.

"Function and Concept" (1891). In Beany, *The Frege Reader,* 130–148.

"On *Sinn* und *Bedeutung*" (1892). In Beany, *The Frege Reader,* 151–171.

"On Concept and Object." (1892). In Beany, *The Frege Reader,* 181–193.

Frege

"Grundgesetze der Arithmetik." 2 Vols. Jena: H. Pohle, 1893 (Vol. 1); 1903 (Vol. 2).

Review of E. H. Husserl, *Philosophie der Arithmatik* I. (1894). In McGuiness, *Collected Papers on Mathematics, Logic, and Philosophy,* 195–209.

"On the Foundations of Geometry. First Series." (1903). In McGuiness, *Collected Papers on Mathematics, Logic, and Philosophy,* 273–284.

"On the Foundations of Geometry. Second Series." (1906). In McGuiness, *Collected Papers on Mathematics, Logic, and Philosophy,* 293–340./bibcit.composed>

"Reply to Mr. Thomae's Holiday *Causerie.*" (1906). In McGuiness, *Collected Papers on Mathematics, Logic, and Philosophy,* 341–345.

"Renewed Proof of the Impossiblity of Mr. Thomae's Formal Arithmetic." (1908). In McGuiness, *Collected Papers on Mathematics, Logic, and Philosophy,* 346–350.

Posthumous Writings. Edited by Hans Hermes, Friedrich Kambartel, and Friedrich Kaulbach, with the assistance of Gottfried Gabriel and Walburga Rödding. Translated by Peter Long and Roger White, with the assistance of Raymond Hargreaves. Chicago: University of Chicago Press, 1979.

Philosophical and Mathematical Correspondence. Edited by Gottfried Gabriel, et al. Abridged for the English edition by Brian McGuinness. Translated by Hans Kaal. Chicago: University of Chicago Press, 1980.

Collected Papers on Mathematics, Logic, and Philosophy. Edited by Brian McGuinness. Translated by Max Black et al. Oxford: Blackwell, 1984.

Kleine Schriften. 2nd ed. Edited by Ignacio Angelelli. Hildesheim, Germany: G. Olms, 1990. Collection of Frege's published papers and reviews, together with some letters and notes on Frege's works by H. Scholz and E. Husserl.

"Diary: Written by Professor Dr. Gottlob Frege in the Time from 10 March to 9 April 1924." Edited by Gottfried Gabriel and Wolfgang Kienzler. *Inquiry* 39 (1996): 303–342.

The Frege Reader. Edited by Michael Beaney. Oxford: Blackwell, 1997. The volume brings together all of Frege's seminal writings, substantial parts of his three books, and selections from his posthumous writings and correspondence.

Frege's Lectures on Logic: Carnap's Student Notes, 1910–1914. Translated and edited by Erich H. Reck and Steve Awodey. Chicago: Open Court, 2004. Gives evidence for Frege's late positions in logic and foundations. With an introductory essay by Gottfried Gabriel and a paper by the editors on Frege's influence on the development of logic.

OTHER SOURCES

Beaney, Michael. *Frege: Making Sense.* London: Duckworth, 1996. Frege's concept of sense within his philosophy as a whole.

Beaney, Michael, and Erich H. Reck, eds. *Gottlob Frege: Critical Assessments of Leading Philosophers.* 4 vols. London: Routledge, 2005. Comprehensive collection of papers on Frege.

Brady, Geraldine. *From Peirce to Skolem: A Neglected Chapter in the History of Logic.* Amsterdam: Elsevier, 2000. Stresses the significance of the algebraic tradition for the development of logic.

Demopoulos, William, ed. *Frege's Philosophy of Mathematics.* Cambridge, MA: Harvard University Press, 1995.

Dummett, Michael. *Frege: Philosophy of Language.* 2nd ed. London: Duckworth, 1981.

———. *Frege and Other Philosophers.* Oxford: Clarendon Press; 1991.

———. *Frege: Philosophy of Mathematics.* Cambridge, MA: Harvard University Press, 1991.

Gabriel, Gottfried, and Uwe Dathe, eds. *Gottlob Frege: Werk und Wirkung; Mit den unveröffentlichten Vorschlägen für ein Wahlgesetz von Gottlob Frege.* Paderborn, Germany: Mentis, 2000.

Grattan-Guinness, Ivor. *The Search for Mathematical Roots, 1870–1940: Logics, Set Theories, and the Foundations of Mathematics from Cantor through Russell to Gödel.* Princeton, NJ: Princeton University Press, 2000. See pp. 177–199. Frege's role within the development of research in logic and the foundations of mathematics.

Gronau, Detlef. "Gottlob Frege's Beiträge zur Iterationstheorie und zur Theorie der Funktionalgleichungen." In *Gottlob Frege: Werk und Wirkung; Mit den unveröffentlichten Vorschlägen für ein Wahlgesetz von Gottlob Frege,* edited by Gottfried Gabriel and Uwe Dathe, 151–169. Paderborn, Germany: Mentis, 2000.

Hale, Bob, and Crispin Wright. *The Reason's Proper Study: Essays towards a Neo-Fregean Philosophy of Mathematics.* Oxford: Clarendon Press, 2001. Collection of papers neo-Fregeanism and Frege arithmetic.

Kreiser, Lothar. *Gottlob Frege: Leben—Werk—Zeit.* Hamburg, Germany: Meiner, 2001. Full-scale biography of Frege.

Newen, Albert, Ulrich Nortmann, and Rainer Stuhlmann-Laeisz, eds. *Building on Frege: New Essays on Sense, Content, and Concept.* Stanford, CA: CSLI Publications, 2001. Collection of essays on Frege's significance and heritage.

Quine, Willard Van Orman. "On Frege's Way Out." *Mind,* n.s., 64 (1955): 145–159. Proof that Frege's solution of Russell's paradox was not feasible.

Schirn, Matthias, ed. *Frege: Importance and Legacy.* Berlin: de Gruyter, 1996. Collection of essays on Frege's significance and heritage.

Schröder, Ernst. "Review of Frege, 1879." *Zeitschrift für Mathematik und Physik. Historisch-litterarische Abteilung* 25 (1880): 81–94.

Sluga, Hans D. *Gottlob Frege.* London: Routledge and Kegan Paul, 1980.

Sullivan, Peter M. "Frege's Logic." In *Handbook of the History of Logic,* vol. 3, edited by Dov M. Gabbay and John Woods, 659–750. Amsterdam: Elsevier North Holland, 2004.

Thiel, Christian. "Zur Inkonsistenz der Fregeschen Mengenlehre." In *Frege und die moderne Grundlagenforschung: Symposium, gehalten in Bad Homburg im Dezember 1973,* edited by Christian Thiel, 134–159. Meisenheim am Glan, Germany: Verlag Anton Hain, 1975.

———. "'Not Arbitrarily and Out of a Craze for Novelty': The Begriffsschrift 1879 and 1893." In *Gottlob Frege: Critical Assessments of Leading Philosophers,* 4 vols., edited by Michael

Freud

Beaney and Erich H. Reck, vol. 2, 13–28. London: Routledge, 2005. Surveys the nature of Frege's logical notation and its development.

Thiel, Christian, and Michael Beaney. "Frege's Life and Work: Chronology and Bibliography." In *Gottlob Frege: Critical Assessments of Leading Philosophers,* 4 vols., edited by Michael Beaney and Erich H. Reck, vol. 1, 23–39. London: Routledge, 2005. Brief chronology on the basis of information now available, and comprehensive bibliography.

Weiner, Joan. *Frege Explained: From Arithmetic to Analytic Philosophy.* Chicago: Open Court, 2004. Compact explanation of Frege's work.

Volker Peckhaus

FREUD, SIGMUND (*b.* Freiburg, Moravia, 6 May 1856; *d.* London, 23 September 1939), *psychoanalysis, psychiatry, psychotherapy.* For the original article on Freud see *DSB,* vol. 6.

Over the nearly forty years since the original Freud article in the *DSB,* Sigmund Freud's biography, his standing, and his influence on twentieth-century thought have been examined in many thousands of books and papers. This article will deal with the more salient developments under three different categories: personal and biobibliographical; scientific, medical, and philosophical; and cultural, institutional, and ethical.

Personal and Biobibliographical. The materials available publicly for the study of Freud's life and work have expanded enormously, principally through the publication of a major series of correspondences with Freud's early followers (Wilhelm Fliess, Carl Gustav Jung, Ernest Jones, Sándor Ferenczi, Karl Abraham, Eugen Bleuler, Ludwig Binswanger, and many others). The archival labors of Kurt Eissler (who founded Sigmund Freud Archives in the 1950s, recorded interviews with many who had known Freud, and amassed a very large number of documents pertaining to Freud) and of Gerhard Fichtner (who has produced reliable databases of Freud's work and correspondences) have ensured that the wealth of materials relating to Freud rival those of any other major scientific figure (Falzeder 2007). However, some of this material, since deposited at the Library of Congress in Washington, DC, was closed to scholars for many years; this policy, like so many other features of Freud's life and work, became a matter of intense controversy, documented in Janet Malcolm's fine journalistic account of the politics and personal antagonisms surrounding Freud scholarship (1984).

Freud's life was celebrated in a quasi-Victorian fashion by the publication in the 1950s of Ernest Jones's three-volume biography, subsequently criticized for its hagiographical tendencies but never surpassed as a systematically researched and organized source of biographical information. Three major biographies have since been published—by Freud's doctor Max Schur (1972), Ronald Clark (1980), and Peter Gay (1988)—each with strengths not to be found in Jones, each able to make use of important new material available through archival research and the rapid growth in historical scholarship on Freud, Vienna, and the psychoanalytic movement. In addition, the wave of critical biographical studies of Freud that began in the 1970s sought in his private life (both personal and scientific) and the intimate politics of the psychoanalytic movement the hidden secret that would explain the origins of his thought, his life, his science, and his role in the development of the psychoanalytic profession.

Following on his study of the tense relationship between Freud and a talented Viennese follower, Victor Tausk (1969), Paul Roazen's study of *Freud and his Followers* (1974) provided materials for an alternative account of the politics of the growth of psychoanalysis in Freud's lifetime, centered on a portrait of Freud as an authoritarian, even despotic, and certainly often ruthless leader of his "horde" of followers. In parallel, the researches of Peter Swales on Freud's life and relationship to his family and patients in the 1890s portrayed Freud's self-presentation, so important to his account of the development of clinical discoveries, as at best only partial and at worst as fraudulent (Swales, 1983, 1986a, 1986b, 1988, 1989 [1982]).

Equally heterodox and equally headline-catching was the claim of Jeffrey Masson that Freud had, out of intellectual cowardice, reneged on his early etiological claim that the sexual abuse of children was the necessary condition for adult neurosis, and thereby broken faith with his patients: The central position of fantasy and infantile sexuality within psychoanalytic theory was thus, according to Masson, a result of this moral failing, transposed into an equivocal psychological doctrine (Masson, 1984). Importantly for the plausibility of Masson's revisionist history among a wide audience was the coincidence of his claims with the gathering movement among feminists, clinicians, and social workers throughout the Western world in the early 1980s asserting that the sexual abuse of children, in particular female children, was endemic, consistently underreported, and a major psychopolitical scandal of the twentieth century (Hacking, 1991, 1995). This episode was symptomatic of the way in which revisionist biographical theses concerning Freud and his work could so easily take on larger cultural and medico-scientific resonance (Crews, 1995). Contemporary scientific and political

Sigmund Freud. Sigmund Freud at his desk in London, 1938. HULTON ARCHIVE/GETTY IMAGES.

debates—what was the extent of sexual relations between children and adults? How reliable are procedures for reviving memories of early childhood?—became intimately entangled with biographical claims about Freud. The culmination of the critical and negative attention to Freud's person was Frederick Crews's scintillatingly vicious article attacking Freud's scientific and moral character, "The Unknown Freud" (1993; see Crews, 1995).

Scientific, Medical, Philosophical. If Jones's biography had set a standard for factual comprehensiveness and James Strachey's 24-volume *Standard Edition* (1953–1974) of Freud in English an unmatchable standard of editorial, philological, and accuracy of translation, furnishing the English language and a series of non-English editions with a literal model, two other works opened up new avenues for serious research on Freud's ideas: firstly *Vocabulaire de la Psychanalyse* (Laplanche and Pontalis, 1967; English translation 1973), a philologically rigorous and philosophically astute conceptual analysis of the key terms in Freud's scientific work; secondly, Henri Ellenberger's *The Discovery of the Unconscious* (1970), which placed Freud's conception alongside that of Jung, Alfred Adler, and Pierre Janet in a comprehensively researched broader context of a psychodynamic psychiatry that had its roots in the Mesmerism, hypnotism, and German Romantic psychiatry, not to speak of studies of the occult and spiritualism, of the long century preceding Freud's invention of psychoanalysis. Both the quantity and meticulousness of Ellenberger's scholarship set a standard that is still rarely met.

Yet both these works were fruits of conventional intellectual history or conceptual analysis. It was increasingly realized that there were many competing visions of Freud's significance and that these also gave rise to different histories. Through situating Freud in the cultural context of fin-de-siècle Vienna, Carl Schorske gave him the status of an exemplary frustrated political intellectual turning inwards to a science of the interior (1980). Freud's Jewishness fuelled a considerable number of important studies of the culture of Viennese Jewry (Beller, 1989), of anti-Semitism (Gilman, 1993), of the question of psychoanalysis as a Jewish science (Yerushalmi, 1991). The eruption of political movements in which sexuality and the new historical category of gender played an important part was linked to the social history of sexuality and sexology. The impact on the history of Freud's theories of sexuality was greatest following Michel Foucault's three volume study *The History of Sexuality* (1976), but Stephen Kern (1973) and K. Codell Carter (1980, 1983) and, without influence from Foucault, Gay's studies of nineteenth-century bourgeois sexuality (1985) provided an entirely new context for Freud's theories of sexuality. So, too, did Arnold I. Davidson (1988), who reconceived entirely the significance of Freud's novel "scientific" conception of sexuality with its subversion of the difference between normal and pathological. But the strongest force affecting this aspect of Freud's work was the rise of feminism and the scholarship that sometimes presented Freud as the principal enemy of the liberation of women's inner lives from male domination, sometimes as an ally whose inquiry into those inner lives had revealed the complex forces ruling women for the first time (Appignanesi and Forrester, 1992).

Ellenberger's monumental study was only part of a transformation of the historiography of psychiatry that had profound effects on the portrait of Freud. Foucault in particular demolished the historiography of psychiatry that had portrayed it as the march of enlightened, humanitarian progress culminating in the psychological theories of madness espoused by Freudians. Instead Foucault substituted a history of confinement, of the exclusion of madness and the installation of chains of discipline rather than steel, in which Freud represented the figure of the moral master, the epitome of magical therapeutic power framed by the new institutions, both built of brick and of newly invented therapeutic relationships. The way was prepared for the later historiography of psychiatry, best achieved by Edward Shorter's *A History of Psychiatry* (1997), in which Freud represented an interlude between more truly scientific hereditary-genetic, biological-physical, and pharmacological theories of madness that achieved victory in the late twentieth century. Freud's historical significance for psychiatry now became as inventor of a low-capital-intensive, quasi-scientific practice of talk therapy, easily marketable in middle-class, urban environments, preparatory for the more disguised high-capital-intensive, low-cost delivery of psychopharmacological drugs that would sit uneasily side by side with the still indispensable talk therapies. More specifically on Freud's relationship with psychiatry, Albrecht Hirschmüller, in addition to providing the definitive study of the science, medical practice, and life of Freud's mentor and collaborator, Josef Breuer (1989 [1978]), also documented and analyzed major new sources on Freud's early psychiatric experience and thought (1991).

Applying the sophistication of the professional history of science, Frank J. Sulloway's *Freud: Biologist of the Mind* (1979), a major study of the biological roots of Freud's work, examined its sources within Darwinian and Lamarckian evolutionary biology, German developmental biology, and the specific influence of the exotic theories of Freud's closest scientific colleague in the formative years, Fliess. Even Sulloway's balanced scholarship became entangled with his less persuasive theses concerning the construction by Freud of "myths" about his own history combined with Sulloway's internally contradictory thesis that "psychoanalysis" was "really" biology in disguise. The influence of Charles Darwin on Freud, of John Hughlings Jackson and aphasia studies, of Jean-Martin Charcot and the golden era of hysteria in the late nineteenth century, of Freud's early work on cocaine and its persistent influence on his life and work, of the rise and fall of hypnotism as therapy and as model of human relationships were all comprehensively documented.

Within the philosophy of science, a major study (Grünbaum, 1984) challenged both the Popperian claim that psychoanalysis was not scientific because it was irrefutable, and the claim (as represented by Jürgen Habermas, 1971, and Paul Ricoeur, 1970) that psychoanalysis was not a straightforward natural science, on a par with botany or biochemistry, but a hermeneutic discipline, founded in philosophy and practices of the interpretation of language. Adolf Grünbaum insisted that psychoanalysis did conform to the hypothetico-deductive model of the natural sciences and had generated testable hypotheses, but its principal method of gathering data was irredeemably unreliable and, where trustworthy data had become available, its principal claims had not been confirmed. Some defenders of Freud pointed out that his claims were not scientific in a conventional sense, but rather plausible and effective extensions of everyday psychological explanations and redescriptions—a curious extension and reversal of Ludwig Wittgenstein's critical claim that psychoanalysis offered only redescription and not conventional, experimentally founded explanations. Analytic philosophers returned to and reexamined Freud's concepts of the unconscious and explanations of irrational action within the philosophy of mind, where resonances with other contemporary preoccupations—with Jean-Paul Sartre's account of bad faith, with neuropsychological conceptions of the unconscious—were continually rediscovered.

The reevaluation of Freud as more of an interpreter of the significant world of language and symbol, hence a "social" scientist, maybe even an "artist," gathered strength as his standing increased in the academic humanities and touched even the question of the appropriate way of translating his work (Bettelheim, 1982; Bourguignon et al, 1989; Ornston,1992). The strongest, but by no means the only, thread of this reevaluation owed much to the impetus of Jacques Lacan's "return to Freud" and to the acceptance of Freud in French intellectual life as an unmatched innovator in the "human sciences"; many of these reinterpretations, such as Jacques Derrida's (1980), portrayed Freud as an unchallengeable explorer of a new philosophy of the human, of the "subject," as much in the tradition of Michel de Montaigne, Immanuel Kant, and Martin Heidegger as of the empirical sciences (Forrester, 1980, 1990; Spence, 1982).

Cultural, Institutional, and Ethical. A major source of reevaluation of Freud as a scientific figure stems from a feedback loop generated by the influence of his own theories. Philip Rieff's classic *Freud: The Mind of the Moralist* (1959) had portrayed Freud as a unique kind of scientist, whose work—whose message—was simultaneously a morality (in truth, an anti-morality) for the twentieth century, a medico-scientific antidote to the religion-infused ethical ideals of the European past. This new figure of "psychological man" was expressed in Freud's theories and disseminated by the practice of therapy, but also in the autobiographical elements of Freud's writings—and then in the contest over the facts of Freud's life. Peter Gay's supremely well-researched *Freud* (1988) had as its subtitle: *A Life for Our Time.* The Freud portrayed by Gay, with his stoicism, generosity, intellectual honesty and imaginativeness, also serves as an underpinning of the value and even the truth of psychoanalysis. With a similar evaluation of its crucial character, critics of psychoanalysis over of the last two decades have chosen Freud's actual person as the primary target. In this way the battle over Freud's biography is also a battle over the moral values embodied in Freud's work.

Among the several fundamental additions to Freud's biography in recent decades, there has been serious attention paid to the fact that he was a major intellectual entrepreneur, whose "movement," institutional inventions and profession became enduring cultural and economic monuments. The Psychoanalytic Societies, based in major cities, bound together by the International Psychoanalytic Association from 1910 on, led by close disciples bonded to Freud through his extensive correspondence and then by the Secret Committee (Grosskurth, 1991), were independent of universities and medical schools—autonomous in a free market discovered (invented?) by Freud and the other founders of psychotherapy. The products of these institutions—as cultural figure, the "shrink" (Gabbard and Gabbard, 1987), the "therapist" (MacIntyre, 1981)—offered simultaneously a cure and a lifestyle, even a path through life; the market they created and served was analyzed by Ernest Gellner (1985) as a secular pseudoscientific religion, obliged to fulfill this function, and offering its clinical pastoral, because of the wholesale failure of religion in the West.

The upshot of these radical revisions is that for some, Freud is a discredited scientist and progenitor of a parasitic profession; for others, a hybrid figure, philosopher, writer of genius, exemplar of an ethic beyond the illusions of political or religious ideals and repressive moral codes. For some he is still a great pioneer scientist.

SUPPLEMENTARY BIBLIOGRAPHY

Appignanesi, Lisa, and John Forrester. *Freud's Women.* London: Weidenfeld & Nicolson, 1992.

Beller, Steven. *Vienna and the Jews, 1867–1938: A Cultural History.* Cambridge, U.K.: Cambridge University Press, 1989.

Bettelheim, Bruno. *Freud and Man's Soul.* New York: Knopf, 1982.

Bourguignon, André; Pierre Cotet; Jean Laplanche; and François Robert. *Traduire Freud.* Paris: Presses Universitaires de France, 1989.

Byck, Robert, ed. *Cocaine Papers.* New York: Stonehill, 1974.

Carter, K. Codell. "Germ Theory, Hysteria, and Freud's Early Work in Psychopathology." *Medical History* 24 (1980): 259–274.

———. "Infantile Hysteria and Infantile Sexuality in Late Nineteenth-Century German-Language Medical Literature." *Medical History 27* (1983): 186–196.

Clark, Ronald. *Freud, The Man and the Cause.* New York: Random House, 1980.

Crews, Frederick. *The Memory Wars: Freud's Legacy in Dispute.* New York: New York Review of Books, 1995.

Davidson, Arnold I. "How to Do the History of Psychoanalysis: A Reading of Freud's *Three Essays on the Theory of Sexuality.*" In *The Trial(s) of Psychoanalysis,* edited by Françoise Meltzer. Chicago: University of Chicago Press, 1988.

Derrida, Jacques. *The Post Card: From Socrates to Freud and Beyond,* trans. Alan Bass. Chicago: Chicago University Press, 1987 [1980].

Didi-Huberman, George. *Invention de l'Hystérie: Charcot et l'iconographie photographique de la Salpêtrière.* Paris: Macula, 1982.

Ellenberger, Henri. *The Discovery of the Unconscious: The History and Evolution of Dynamic Psychiatry.* New York: Basic Books, 1970.

Falzeder, Ernst. "Is There Still an Unknown Freud? A Note on the Publications of Freud's Texts and on Unpublished Documents." *Psychoanalysis and History* 9, no. 2 (2007): 201–232.

Forrester, John. *Language and the Origins of Psychoanalysis.* London: Macmillan, 1980.

———. *The Seductions of Psychoanalysis: Freud, Lacan, and Derrida.* Cambridge, U.K.: Cambridge University Press, 1990.

Gabbard, Krin, and Glen O. Gabbard. *Psychiatry and the Cinema.* Chicago: The University of Chicago Press, 1987.

Gay, Peter. *The Bourgeois Experience: Victoria to Freud,* Vol. 1, *Education of the Senses.* New York: Oxford University Press, 1984.

———. *Freud: A Life for Our Time.* New York: Norton, 1988.

Gellner, Ernest. *The Psychoanalytic Movement: The Cunning of Unreason.* London: Granada, 1985.

Gilman, Sander L. *Freud, Race, and Gender.* Princeton, NJ: Princeton University Press, 1993.

Greenberg, Valerie D. *Freud and His Aphasia Book: Language and the Sources of Psychoanalysis.* Ithaca, NY: Cornell University Press, 1997.

Grünbaum, Adolf. *The Foundations of Psychoanalysis.* Berkeley: University of California Press, 1984.

Grosskurth, Phyllis. *The Secret Ring: Freud's Inner Circle and the Politics of Psychoanalysis.* Reading, MA: Addison Wesley, 1991.

Habermas, Jürgen. *Knowledge and Human Interests,* translated by Jeremy J. Shapiro. Boston: Beacon, 1971 [1968].

Hacking, Ian. "The Making and Molding of Child Abuse." *Critical Inquiry* 17 (1991): 253–288.

———. *Rewriting the Soul: Multiple Personality and the Sciences of Memory.* Princeton, NJ: Princeton University Press, 1995.

Hirschmüller, Albrecht. *The Life and Work of Josef Breuer: Physiology and Psychoanalysis.* New York: New York University Press, 1989 [1978].

———. *Freuds Begegnung mit der Psychiatrie. Von der Hirnmythologie zur Neurosenlehre.* Tübingen: Edition Diskord, 1991.

Kern, Stephen. "Freud and the Discovery of Child Sexuality." *History of Childhood Quarterly: The Journal of Psychohistory* 1 (1973): 117–141.

Laplanche, Jean, and J.B. Pontalis. *The Language of Psychoanalysis.* Translated by Donald Nicholson-Smith. London: Hogarth Press, 1973 [1967].

MacIntyre, Alasdair. *After Virtue.* Notre Dame, IN: University of Notre Dame Press, 1981.

Malcolm, Janet. *In the Freud Archives.* London: Jonathan Cape, 1984.

Masson, Jeffrey M. *The Assault on Truth: Freud's Suppression of the Seduction Theory.* London: Faber & Faber, 1984.

Micale, Mark S. *Approaching Hysteria: Disease and its Interpretations.* Princeton, NJ: Princeton University Press, 1995.

Ornston, Darius Gray, Jr., ed. *Translating Freud.* New Haven, CT: Yale University Press, 1992.

Ricoeur, Paul. *Freud and Philosophy: An Essay on Interpretation.* Translated by Denis Savage. New Haven, CT: Yale University Press, 1970.

Rieff, Philip. *Freud: The Mind of the Moralist.* New York: Viking, 1959.

Roazen, Paul. *Brother Animal: The Story of Freud and Tausk.* New York: Knopf, 1969.

———. *Freud and his Followers.* New York: Knopf, 1974.

Ritvo, Lucille B. *Darwin's Influence on Freud: A Tale of Two Sciences.* New Haven, CT: Yale University Press, 1990.

Schorske, Carl. *Fin-de-siècle Vienna: Politics and Culture.* New York: Knopf, 1980.

Schur, Max. *Freud: Living and Dying.* London: Hogarth Press, 1972.

Spence, Donald. *Narrative Truth and Historical Truth.* New York: Norton, 1982.

Swales, Peter. "Freud, Martha Bernays and the Language of Flowers, Masturbation, Cocaine, and the Inflation of Fantasy." Privately printed, 1983.

———. "Freud, Breuer and the Blessed Virgin." Privately printed, 1986a.

———. "Freud, His Teacher, and the Birth of Psychoanalysis." In *Freud: Appraisals and Reappraisals: Contributions to Freud Studies,* Vol. 1, edited by Paul E. Stepansky, pp. 3–82. NJ: The Analytic Press, 1986b.

———. "Freud, Katharina, and the First 'Wild Analysis'." In *Freud: Appraisals and Reappraisals: Contributions to Freud Studies,* Vol. 3, edited by Paul E. Stepansky, pp. 79–164. Hillsdale, NJ: The Analytic Press, 1988.

———. "Freud, Fliess and Fratricide: The Role of Fliess in Freud's Conception of Paranoia." In *Sigmund Freud. Critical Assessments,* Vol. 1: *Freud and the Origins of Psychoanalysis,* edited by Laurence Spurling, pp. 302–329. London and New York: Routledge, 1989 [1982].

Yerushalmi, Yosef Hayim. *Freud's Moses: Judaism Terminable and Interminable.* New Haven, CT: Yale University Press, 1991.

John Forrester

FRIEDMAN, HERBERT (*b.* Brooklyn, New York, 21 June 1916; *d.* Arlington, Virginia, 9 September 2000), *solid-state physics, x-ray diagnostics and radiation detection, solar physics, astrophysics, space science.*

Friedman was the first to develop and apply reliable electronic detection devices to the study of the high-energy radiation from the Sun by carrying them into space on a succession of sounding rockets and satellites. His team pioneered x-ray solar astronomy from rockets and became the first to detect x-ray emission from the Sun and were among the first to explore nonsolar x-ray sources in the night sky. He is remembered as one of the founders of x-ray astronomy.

Early Life and Training. Friedman was the second of three children of fine-art framer and dealer Samuel Friedman and Rebecca Seligson and grew up near his birthplace in Brooklyn, New York. His family was of modest means, but even during the Great Depression insisted that Herb get a college education. He therefore entered Brooklyn College choosing art initially, partly because his father had at one time encouraged him to seek out an apprenticeship to an Israeli artist. He spent two years in the major, finally becoming disillusioned about a career, and switched to physics partly because of a fine teacher. This change was acceptable to his family, for whom Albert Einstein was, as

Friedman recalls "a folk figure, a hero figure" (Friedman oral history, 2 September 1983, NASM, p. 5).

He came under the direction of the physicist Bernhard Kurrelmeyer, a specialist in photoelectricity, photoconductivity, and secondary emission phenomena, and who was married to the Columbia University physics professor Lucy Julia Hayner. Friedman graduated in physics in 1936 after spending considerable time in Kurrelmeyer's laboratory, who then directed him to a student instructorship at the Johns Hopkins University, Kurrelmeyer's alma mater.

Friedman continued to specialize in laboratory physics, working at first for James Franck, head of the Physics Department and corecipient of the 1925 Nobel Prize in Physics. Franck soon left for the University of Chicago, so Friedman found a place in x-ray spectroscopist Joyce Alvin Bearden's laboratory and learned how to interpret the detailed signatures of x-ray absorption edges (found at spectral series limits) to determine the binding energies of the electrons in metals and hence explore their structure. Friedman's task was to develop an improved detector, based upon the classic Geiger counter design, but using thin metallic entrance windows that would admit soft x-rays and then get them to discharge inside an argon gas–filled chamber, producing an electric current that could be measured. Friedman's photoelectric amplifier circuits consisted of cylindrical metal chambers with a thin wire running on the axis, insulated from the chamber walls. The chambers would be evacuated and then filled with a halogen, typically argon, using alcohol as a quenching agent. An entrance window at the end of the cylinder held a variety of thin metallic windows to admit x-radiation and isolate the tube from other radiations. Its composition and thickness determined the energy threshold desired. After just a few weeks of building and testing these tubes, Friedman found them to be reliable and highly linear detectors of soft x-rays. The metallic windows permitted almost one atmosphere of pressure, which simplified manufacture and ensured high sensitivity.

Employing Bearden's large double-crystal x-ray spectrometer and his improved detector, Friedman contributed to a better understanding of the nature of a group of metals (from iron to germanium) on the periodic chart known as the transition metals, elements whose second outer atomic levels are not completely filled with electrons. He was able to relate his observations to new theories of the metallic solid state, and received his PhD for this work in 1940. With Bearden he applied his techniques and new detectors to a number of metallic alloys.

At graduation, Friedman hoped to get an industry job and interviewed at both General Electric and at Bell Laboratories, but even though the scientists there were receptive, he never got beyond the personnel offices. So he stayed at Johns Hopkins for another year as an instructor performing contract research under Bearden on electrolytic polishing. Meanwhile the senior Johns Hopkins spectroscopic physicist August Herman Pfund steered Friedman into the civil service sector, where anti-Semitism was less entrenched, and soon found him a job at the Naval Research Laboratory (NRL), which had strong Johns Hopkins connections. Finally permanently employed, Friedman was ready to marry, asking Gertrude Miller, who had been an instructor at Brooklyn College, to be his wife. They raised two sons.

The NRL. Friedman, "elated to get a job," (Friedman oral history, 2 September 1983, NASM, p. 16) started to work in the Metallurgy Department under Richard Canfield, hoping to apply his thesis knowledge, essentially his expertise at the forefront of the study of the solid state, to stress-analysis problems such as low expansion alloys and high tensile strength alloys that would be useful for things like turbine blades. Canfield soon left, however, and though Friedman worked among Johns Hopkins graduates and found the general atmosphere at the NRL stimulating, he felt he was being constrained to less exciting areas of testing, although he still managed to apply his expertise, developing nondestructive testing techniques using sensors in different sensitivity ranges from Geiger counters and proportional counters to ion chambers.

During his first year in Metallurgy, Friedman responded to wartime orders to develop new and more efficient techniques to manufacture oscillator plates using quartz crystalline plates, an essential ingredient in radio communications gear. The problem was to find a way to orient raw crystals in a cutting machine quickly and accurately. He immediately knew from his x-ray spectroscopy experience that one could rapidly determine crystalline orientation using x-ray diffraction, and it would be far quicker to employ a photoelectric detector than the usual photographic methods. One could orient the crystal in real time, controlling the process by monitoring the Bragg reflections from the crystals, and make the cut then and there. Friedman was able to create a prototype device literally overnight, which impressed the Signal Corps and industry inspectors and led to the immediate production, under Friedman's direction at NRL, of some two hundred proportional counters for use in industry. In 1945 Friedman was recognized for this work by the U.S. Navy's Distinguished Civilian Service Award.

But more important, this early achievement gave Friedman increased leverage to apply his techniques and detectors to a wide range of uses. Industry provided him with better facilities at NRL, and so he set about various projects converting all types of detection devices, diagnostic systems, and maintenance procedures that heretofore used photography or mechanical methods, to employ his high-energy x-ray detectors. He developed electronic analogues for a wide variety of applications including a diffractometer that used x-ray diffraction patterns to improve an antifouling ship-bottom paint formula that would resist the growth of barnacles. With the diffractometer he found that he could discriminate between different copper paint alloys that had very different resistances to barnacles. He also found that his techniques could be used to maintain the consistency of pigments and to determine the minimum amount of silver required to create an efficient electrical contact.

Friedman applied his improved x-ray detectors to a very broad range of applications. His laboratory notebooks during this time attest to his constant search for new uses, from the examination of thin films, x-ray fluorescence analysis, radiation exposure surveys, and ultimately, in the late 1940s, an extensive radiation monitoring system that detected Soviet nuclear tests in 1949.

By the end of the war Friedman was head of an electron-optics branch in the Optics Division of NRL, working directly under Edward O. Hulburt. He made the transition in 1942 when Hulburt set up the new branch, mainly to accommodate Friedman and to grab a new electron microscope that had been slated for the Chemistry Division. The Chemistry Division had balked at taking in Friedman, so Friedman, disgruntled, was well along looking for another job at the National Bureau of Standards when Hulburt made his move. Hulburt acted quickly and effectively setting up the new branch and Friedman spent the rest of the war years developing techniques in x-ray analysis and diagnostics. After the war he continued in radiation detection ranging from electronic aircraft fuel tank gauges to long-range nuclear bomb detection. He directed the development of the navy's "Project Rainbarrel," a network of detectors at air weather stations that sensed trace radioactivity in rainwater. When increased radiation was detected, aluminum hydroxide–doped water samples were collected and rushed back to the NRL for precise determination of the spectral signature of the Russian tests.

Research with Rockets. Early in 1946, Friedman and other members of Hulburt's Optics Division became aware of the possibility of performing research with captured German V-2 rockets. Friedman, however, remained in x-ray analysis, but in July 1947 he was alerted to the fact that his Rainbarrel system had recorded radiation that was linked to a giant solar flare. This was a fascinating coincidence, merely a sidelight at the time, but it sparked an interest in solar phenomena. He had already studied natural radiation sources to calibrate Rainbarrel, but now knew that the Sun could be an x-ray emitter as well. Eventually, Hulburt drew Friedman into the rocket sonde work by 1949. By then, one of the branches led by Richard Tousey had been successful obtaining photographic ultraviolet spectra, but they had still not penetrated down to the high-energy region of the solar spectrum, especially where the source of ionizing radiation in Earth's upper atmosphere was thought to lurk. Doing this was critical to the navy's mission because it was thought to be the natural agent governing long-range radio communications.

Once again, Friedman had the ideal detector system. Not only could it reach the extreme-ultraviolet and x-ray regions easily, but it was electronic and so could send its information back to Earth by radio. So Friedman formed a small group within his electron optics branch to build and fly banks of counters on V-2 rockets and soon provided the first observations that led to a detailed understanding of the relative importance of solar ultraviolet and x-ray radiation as ionizing agents upon different layers in Earth's atmosphere. This new application was especially appealing to Friedman as it was for members of his group, especially Edward Taylor Byram, who had a specific interest in astronomy. The evident success of their first 1949 flight convinced Friedman to move heavily into space research. He recalled not being able to resist it, "because it was just too rich, too exciting" (Friedman oral history, 2 September 1983, NASM, p. 60). He had gained more than enough equity in the navy to pursue this professionally risky work, he felt, and Hulburt was very supportive. Although he recalled this as a watershed time in his life, breaking away from solid-state physics and moving into geophysical and astrophysical areas, in fact much of his electron-optics group remained in the original problem area for some time.

After the V-2s ran out, Friedman's rocket team continued flying detectors on the navy's Viking rocket as well as on Aerobees and even smaller balloon/rocket combinations called Rockoons. They performed a wide range of solar observations in the far ultraviolet through the hard x-ray region. In 1952, from an especially ambitious array of detectors they built and flew on a Viking, they obtained data that confirmed the type of radiation that created Earth's ionospheric E layer. The economical Rockoons became their favored transport system, however, because these vehicles could be launched from shipboard to anywhere over a great range of latitude to study provide geophysical information.

Friedman became a major contributor to x-ray detector and instrumentation development for space research during the late 1950s and 1960s. His team was literally the only one working in the field before *Sputnik,* and was by far the largest. Among many accomplishments, they found that solar flares emit hard, or extreme high-energy, x-radiation that can produce radio blackouts, and they also used a total solar eclipse to study the spatial structure of x-radiation in the solar corona. They were also the first to successfully image the Sun in x-rays, using a simple pinhole camera design. Starting in 1955, members of his group started performing nighttime stellar ultraviolet observations from Aerobee rockets. In 1958, Friedman became superintendent of a new atmospheric and astrophysics division at the NRL.

Friedman was always dedicated to mentoring and training, and constantly invited graduates and postdoctoral students to assist his team at the NRL. Under his guidance his core team for rocketry, Byram, Talbot Chubb, and Robert Kreplin, guided numerous students. In 1962, Friedman secured funding from the National Science Foundation to establish the E. O. Hulburt Center for Space Research at the NRL, which provided a formal means of mentoring younger professional workers interested in learning the art and craft of the space sciences. In another reorganization in 1963 he was designated superintendent of a new Space Science Division and made chief scientist in the E. O. Hulburt Center for Space Research. He held these positions concurrently until his retirement in 1980.

The Satellite Era. The seniority and equity Friedman enjoyed by the time *Sputnik* flew and the National Aeronautics and Space Administration (NASA) was formed led him to remain within the navy. NASA had invited him to take the position of chief physicist at the Goddard Space Flight Center, to make the move along with many of his NRL colleagues, but, as he implied in an interview, he was not interested in moving from one administrative position that allowed him to continue research, to another where the personal research option was unknown or unlikely. At least, thinking about those among his colleagues who did leave for NASA, such as Homer Newell, he rationalized their decisions as being promoted by the chance to move up the administrative ladder. He was as far as he wanted to go on that ladder.

Friedman and his staff not only set the stage for scientific research with sounding rockets and then satellites in the 1960s, but they provided a means through which a broader population of workers might gain needed hands-on experience in the complex and demanding technical and organizational enterprise, carrying this experience back into the academic world. Friedman's team was unparalleled in its ability to devise counters that worked reliably and consistently in the very hostile environment of the payload of a rocket or satellite. They developed both dispersive and nondispersive systems for a wide range of applications, flying them on balloons, sounding rockets, and many navy and NASA satellite missions.

Friedman's group instrumented the navy's Solar Radiation Satellite (SOLRAD) series that, first launched in 1960, was dedicated to long-term monitoring of the high-energy radiation from the Sun and could detect local sources of high-energy radiation as well. About a year after the first launch Friedman recalled, he was asked by the President's Science Advisory Committee (PSAC) to examine SOLRAD monitoring records to see if any anomalous radiation had been detected, as well as to discuss with them the feasibility of monitoring for nuclear tests using satellites. SOLRAD had apparently detected nonsolar sources as "noise," but their origins remained undetermined and were probably celestial. Nevertheless, SOLRAD showed that it was feasible, which led to the VELA (Spanish for "vigil") program based at Los Alamos, a program he would have been happy to acquire for the navy.

The great challenge for Friedman in the late 1950s and early 1960s was to adapt his detectors for night operations and to detect nonsolar diffuse and discrete x-ray sources. His team increased collecting aperture and gas volume in the detectors and added small collimators and telescopic devices to try and detect and then isolate spatially the discrete sources. Initial broadband nondispersive studies yielded confusing results at first that could not be reproduced, but Friedman believed they were detecting emissions from diffuse sources within the Milky Way. Meanwhile, in 1962, another x-ray group that grew out of cosmic-ray physics, led by Bruno Rossi and Riccardo Giacconi from American Science and Engineering and the Massachusetts Institute of Technology (MIT), succeeded in detecting the first nonsolar x-ray source, in the constellation of Scorpius, so dubbed Sco X-1.

In rapid response, Friedman flew an instrument with a better collimating system that pinned down the position of the source, and then went on to find other point sources, confirming as well the existence of a diffuse x-ray background. In 1963 they confirmed that the Crab Nebula in Taurus was a strong emitter of x-rays, and then in 1964, again using a naturally occurring celestial occultation, the passage of the lunar limb over the source on 7 July, they further localized the x-ray source and determined its structure and size. During the five-minute data-gathering window offered by the Moon and rocket flight trajectory, they thought the source would disappear quickly, but it dimmed gradually, which told them that the x-rays were coming from an extended source, the nebula itself in a volume at least one light year in extent, and not from the suspected central neutron star. And then in 1966, in a highly cited paper resulting from an Aerobee flight in 1965, Friedman's group was the first to announce x-ray emission from an extragalactic source, the giant elliptical galaxy M[essier] 87.

Friedman

NASA frequently consulted Friedman for long-range planning in x-ray astronomy. In the mid-1960s he suggested the possibility of using surplus Apollo-era hardware to create a huge crewed x-ray telescope in orbit as well as an "x-ray fence" on the Moon using the horizon as an occulting disk. His largest-scale endeavor was as a principal investigator in the High Energy Astrophysics Observatory (HEAO) mission series, which NASA began conceptualizing in the early 1960s. This was originally envisioned as a huge Titan launch platform carrying a wealth of instrumentation, equivalent to or greater than what could be carried aloft by high-altitude balloons and aircraft. Friedman was among those lobbying for this capability since the early 1960s. By 1970 the HEAO program was funded, and after various setbacks, its scope diminished by 1974. Friedman's instrumentation survived severe cost-cutting measures and finally his bank of seven traylike thin-window collimated x-ray proportional counters, the NRL's Large Area Sky Survey Experiment, flew on the first HEAO (A-1) launched in August 1977. In seventeen months of observations, in almost three full scans of the sky, it produced a sensitive map of the x-ray sky that added some 1,500 new sources beyond those already known from sounding rocket studies and from the Uhuru satellite, launched in 1970. HEAO A-1 data included spectrum, intensity, and time variations of sources in the 0.25 to 25 KeV energy range. These observations were accumulated into a vast databank on galactic and extragalactic sources that Friedman's team, among others, mined for decades, resulting in scores of professional papers.

In the 1970s Friedman remained active in research and administration, but also began to write for the popular market. He had long been an active voice in scientific Washington, lending his expertise to policy issues through numerous venues including Richard Nixon's PSAC, the Atomic Energy Commission, and the Space Science Board of the National Academy of Sciences. He received many honors and academic distinctions, and in 1968 won the National Medal of Science followed by the Wolf Foundation Prize in Physics in 1987 for cofounding x-ray astronomy. Herbert Friedman died of cancer at his home in Arlington, Virginia.

BIBLIOGRAPHY

Oral and video histories with Herbert Friedman and his team members are housed at the American Institute of Physics Center for History of Physics, at the National Air and Space Museum (NASM), and at the Smithsonian Institution Archives. His papers are housed at the NRL and at the American Philosophical Society.

WORKS BY FRIEDMAN

"The X-ray K Absorption Edges of the Elements Iron to Germanium." PhD diss., Johns Hopkins University, 1940.

With S. W. Lichtman and Edward Taylor Byram. "Photon Counter Measurements of Solar X-rays and Extreme Ultraviolet Light." *Physical Review* 83 (1951): 1025–1030.

With Edward Taylor Byram, Talbot Chubb, and J. Kupperian. "Far Ultraviolet Radiation in the Night Sky." In *The Threshold of Space: The Proceedings of the Conference on Chemical Aeronomy,* edited by M. Zelikoff. New York: Pergamon Press, 1957.

With Talbot Chubb and J. Kupperian. "A Lyman Alpha Experiment for the Vanguard Satellite." In *Scientific Uses of Earth Satellites,* edited by James A. Van Allen. 2nd rev. ed. Ann Arbor: University of Michigan Press, 1958.

"X-ray and Ultraviolet Radiation Measurements from Rockets." In *Space Astrophysics,* edited by William Liller. New York: McGraw-Hill, 1961.

With S. Bowyer, Edward Taylor Byram, and Talbot Chubb. "Lunar Occultation of X-ray Emission from the Crab Nebula." *Science,* n.s., 146 (13 November 1964): 912–917.

———. "Cosmic X-ray Sources." *Science,* n.s., 147 (22 January 1965): 394–398.

With Edward Taylor Byram and Talbot Chubb. "Cosmic X-ray Sources, Galactic and Extragalactic." *Science,* n.s., 152 (1 April 1966): 66–71.

With Edward Taylor Byram. "X-rays from Sources 3C 273 and M 87." *Science,* n.s., 158 (October 1967): 257–259.

With Edward Taylor Byram and Talbot Chubb. "Distribution and Variability of Cosmic X-ray Sources." *Science,* n.s., 156 (April 1967): 374–378.

With A. Davidsen, S. Shulman, G. Fritz, et al. "Observations of the Soft X-ray Background." *Astrophysical Journal* 177 (November 1972): 629–642.

The Amazing Universe. Washington, DC: National Geographic Society, 1975.

With R. Lucke, D. Yentis, G. Fritz, et al. "Discovery of X-ray Pulsations in SMC X-1." *Astrophysical Journal* 206, pt. 2 (15 May 1976): L25–L28.

Reminiscences of 30 Years of Space Research. NRL Report 8113. Washington, DC: Department of Defense, Navy Research Laboratory, 1977.

With M. P. Ulmer, et al. "A Search for Extended Halos of Hot Gas in the Perseus, Virgo, and Coma Clusters." *Astrophysical Journal,* 236, pt. 1 (15 February 1980): 58–62.

With Kent S. Wood. "The HEAO A-1 X-ray Source Catalog." *Astrophysical Journal Supplement* 56 (December 1984): 507–649.

Sun and Earth. San Francisco: Scientific American Books, 1986.

The Astronomer's Universe: Stars, Galaxies, and Cosmos. New York: W.W. Norton, 1990. Revised and updated, 1998.

OTHER SOURCES

DeVorkin, David. *Science with a Vengeance: How the Military Created the US Space Sciences after World War II.* New York: Springer-Verlag, 1992.

———. "Where Did X-ray Astronomy Come From?" *Rittenhouse* 10 (1996): 33–42.

Gursky, Herbert. "Herbert Friedman, 1916–2000." *Bulletin of the American Astronomical Society* 32 (2000): 1665–1666.

Gursky, Herbert, and Frank Press. "Herbert Friedman." *Proceedings of the American Philosophical Society* 146, no. 2 (2002): 195–203.

Hirsh, Richard F. *Glimpsing an Invisible Universe: The Emergence of X-ray Astronomy.* New York: Cambridge University Press, 1983.

Tucker, Wallace, and Riccardo Giacconi. *The X-ray Universe.* Cambridge, MA: Harvard University Press, 1985.

David DeVorkin

FUJITA, TETSUYA THEODORE (*b.* Kyushu, Japan, 23 October 1920; *d.* Chicago, Illinois, 19 November 1988), *meteorology.*

Tetsuya "Ted" Fujita was one of the world's most famous and successful storm investigators. His contributions to the field are numerous, but he is most remembered for his invention of the Fujita (F) scale for tornadoes and his extensive studies on microbursts. His identification of downbursts revolutionized the understanding and full impact of strong straight-line thunderstorm winds. Fujita was also a forensic mesometeorologist, photographer, and a scientific cartographer. Among his talents were photography and photogrammetry (still movie, satellite, video), technical illustration and scientific cartography, classical simple measurements (depth of snow, his own blood pressure), mesoscale analysis, reconstruction of surface wind fields from damage patterns on a wide range of scales, inferring storm dynamics from imagery and estimated surface winds (tropical storms, thunderstorms, and downbursts) and the climatology of tornadoes.

Early Years in Japan. Tetsuya Fujita was born in Sone Town, now part of South Korea, on the island of Kyūshū, Japan, on 23 October 1920, the eldest child of Tomojiro and Yoshie Fujita. He developed an interest in mapping early in his life; Japanese prewar topographic maps had many blank areas due to military secrecy, including many near his home, and he began mapping these areas. Fujita earned a bachelor's degree in mechanical engineering in 1943 from Meiji College of Technology. He later recalled that his father's last words saved his life. Fujita had wanted to attend Hiroshima College, but his father insisted that he attend Meiji College. Had he attended Hiroshima College, he might have been killed by the first atomic bomb dropped by U.S. forces near the end of World War II.

In 1945 Fujita was teaching physics at Meiji College. In September of that year, the Japanese government sent him to survey the destruction at both Hiroshima and Nagasaki to determine the number of bombs and the height of their detonation by using the starburst method, which matches the pattern of knocked-down trees and other structures to the starburst shape. He observed the shock-wave effects on trees and structures in these areas. In April 1946 he surveyed a volcanic eruption at Sakurajima, and in 1947 he conducted studies of downflows in thunderstorms using data from Seburiyama.

Fujita conducted his first tornado survey—of the Enoura tornado near Saga in Kyūshū—on 26 September 1948. He gave briefings on his findings from this survey and soon realized that they should be published, and the experience motivated his interested in weather. In August 1950, he sent copies of his papers on his findings from this tornado survey to Horace Byers, chairman of the Department of Meteorology at the University of Chicago. Byers had just completed an extensive U.S. government–sponsored study of thunderstorms, and he was impressed by Fujita's work. In May 1951 Shigekata Shono sponsored Fujita's research through the University of Tokyo. In August 1952 Fujita completed his doctoral dissertation, and he formally received his degree in 1953 from the Kyūshū Institute of Technology with a dissertation on "Analytical Study of Typhoons." His doctoral thesis was a study of the damage from several typhoons that struck Kyūshū Island in three consecutive years.

Early Years at the University of Chicago. In 1953 Byers invited Fujita to a two-year research appointment at the Department of Meteorology at the University of Chicago. He arrived in Chicago on 13 August 1953. In 1955 Byers suggested that he stay and become a permanent member of the department. Fujita returned to Japan to obtain an immigrant visa and returned to the United States with his family in July 1956 (he had married Tatsuko Hatano in 1948). His official title at this time at the University of Chicago was research professor and senior meteorologist.

Thunderstorm research is another topic that highlights Fujita's career. He wanted to see them from above, from the side, and from below. His interest in thunderstorms led to the application of his microanalysis techniques to barograph traces in order to correlate tornado formation with pressure jump lines. This was the introduction of mesoanalysis (study of features on a horizontal scale of 10–100 km). During this time he coauthored the landmark paper "Mesoanalysis," which was published in 1956 as U.S. Weather Bureau research paper number 39. He began his research in the old building of the Department of Meteorology, where he established the Severe

Local Storms Project (SLSP). The mesoanalysis of thunderstorms resulted in Fujita's primary focus on tornadoes during the twenty-year period from the 1950s to the mid-1970s.

Research Leading to the Fujita Scale. Although Fujita surveyed his first tornado damage in 1948, his study of the 20 June 1957 tornado in Fargo, North Dakota, placed him in the forefront of tornado research. His detailed description of this outbreak, published in 1960, has become a classic in the field of storm study below the continental scale of synoptic meteorology and beyond the resolution of numerical models. He coined the terms *wall cloud* and *tail cloud* during this study. SLSP became the Meteorology Research Project (MRP) in 1961 and moved into a location next to the old weather service offices. In 1962 Fujita was promoted to associate professor and subsequently to full professor in 1965. In 1964 the MRP was changed to the Satellite and Mesometeorology Research Project (SMRP). In the 1960s Fujita analyzed the Palm Sunday outbreak of 11 April 1965, constructing maps from thousands of aerial photographs of storm damage, and he concluded that certain tornadoes must contain more than one vortex and propagate as "families."

In 1968 Fujita and his wife divorced, and he also became a U.S. citizen. At this time he added the middle name Theodore (Ted) to his name. In 1969 he was remarried to Sumiko Yanamoto of Tottori, Japan.

Among Fujita's many interests, tropical cyclones were a lifelong passion, dating back to his doctoral thesis in 1952. Fujita did his first major study of a hurricane in 1949 with Typhoon Della and later he conducted his first hurricane survey on Hurricane Camille in August 1969. He was able to display concepts in his damage surveys that were easy to visualize, even for a layperson. His multicolor damage survey maps of hurricanes and tornado outbreaks remain classics. Fujita's last hurricane survey work concerned Hurricane Andrew and Typhoons Omar and Iniki in 1992.

In 1971 Fujita, along with Alan Pearson of the National Severe Storms Forecast Center, proposed what became known as the Fujita scale for tornado intensity, which classifies tornadoes based on their wind speed and resultant damage. Fujita recognized that estimates of wind speed associated with described damage would be demanded, so he provided a wind speed range for each scale value. The wind speed range extends from that of a violent hurricane to sonic speed. The Fujita scale and extensive documentation of tornado damage are two of his most important legacies. Later in 1971, he proposed the concept of "suction spots" or "suction vortices" embedded within tornadoes to explain the details of damage patterns observed. He was instrumental in developing the concept of multiple vortex tornadoes (families of tornadoes), which feature multiple small funnels (suction vortices) rotating within a larger parent thunderstorm cloud. Fujita's work established that most powerful tornadoes were composed of multiple vortices. He based this conclusion on swaths in the debris patterns left by the tornadoes.

On 3 and 4 April 1974, an outbreak of tornadoes occurred in the central United States, killing 315 and injuring 5,484. The SMRP group conducted extensive aerial damage surveys of this "super outbreak" of approximately 148 tornadoes that occurred in eleven southern and midwestern states. He was able to map the entire path in Fujita scale intensity contours.

Fujita and his colleagues flew over more than three hundred tornado damage swaths from 1965 to 1991. He had an ability to sort out damage indicators on the ground and come up with plausible flow patterns. Fujita also had a unique ability to present his analysis in a clear, concise graphical form. He was often called "Mr. Tornado" by his associates and by the media. Even though he was well known for his tornado research, he did not actually see his first tornado until 12 June 1982, when he witnessed several small tornadoes near Stapleton Airport in Denver, Colorado, as part of a National Center for Atmospheric Research downburst study.

Discovery of Microbursts (1975). During the mid-1970s Fujita shifted his primary focus from tornadoes to microbursts and downbursts, with an emphasis on aviation safety. This shift was due to the crash of Eastern Airlines Flight 66 on 24 June 1975 at New York's Kennedy Airport, and it launched his socially most significant work, that of the identification and prediction of microbursts (small downbursts). He defined a downburst as a strong downdraft that induces an outburst of damaging winds on or near the ground. The downbursts were later categorized into microbursts and macrobursts according to their scale of damaging winds.

The crash of Flight 66 was one of the worst airline disasters in the United States at the time, killing 122 people. Fujita extensively analyzed the data from Flight 66. He reviewed the radio communications prior to the crash, noting that the pilots had reported high winds on the runway. He analyzed weather conditions, satellite images, radar scans, and weather maps that displayed observations over large areas. In March 1976 he published the results of his study and explained the cause of the crash of Flight 66 as a microburst. At the time, many meteorologists found it difficult to believe that a small-sized downdraft would be capable of generating an outburst of 150 mile per hour winds on or near the ground, focused on a relatively small area of about one-quarter of a mile in diameter. Some

Fujita

claimed that he was mistaking the wind for the gust front of a squall line thunderstorm.

Fujita continued to collect data on microbursts. The first major breakthrough came on 29 May 1978, when Fujita and his colleagues observed their first microburst on a Doppler radarscope near Yorkville, Illinois. Three Doppler radars, deployed in a triangle near Chicago, detected fifty downbursts in forty-two days in the summer of 1978. Microbursts were subsequently identified all over the world, and airplane pilots were trained regarding how to react to them. This information was also used for training meteorologists and ultimately reduced the number of aircraft disasters due to downbursts (small localized downdrafts of air that spreads at the ground). Fujita investigated additional aircraft accidents and launched a series of experiments and major field projects (Northern Illinois Research on Downburst [NIMROD] in 1978, Joint Airport Wind Shear [JAWS] in 1982, and Microburst and Severe Thunderstorm Project [MIST]) in 1986 to definitively identify the microbursts, whose existence had been doubted by many. These studies enabled him to further his studies on wind shear (change in wind direction and speed) phenomena, which were crucial to the understanding of downbursts and microbursts.

By this time, the downbursts and microbursts were studied as a unique phenomenon generated by events such as dry air intrusion. The Joint Airport Weather Studies Project at Stapleton Airport in Denver led to research that was instrumental in understanding the structure and cause of microbursts. Microburst accidents were responsible for killing more than five hundred airline passengers at U.S. airports alone. It was during these investigations that Fujita coined the terms *wet* and *dry microbursts,* indicating whether rain had occurred at the surface during the event. Fujita's work eventually led to the installation of Doppler radars at airports to improve the detection and warning of these events. A mere ten years after Fujita's discovery of the microburst in 1976, practical lifesaving solutions were in place.

Other Career Highlights. Fujita was also a pioneer in the remote sensing of atmospheric motion. When meteorological satellites were introduced, he developed techniques for the precise analysis of satellite measurements (sequences of images, first from polar orbiting platforms and then from geostationary platforms). After his initial work, the ability to track clouds and relate them to flow patterns in the atmosphere was transferred into routine operations at the national forecast centers. The diversity and large number of Fujita's ideas may have affected his ability to formally publish much of his work.

In 1988 SMRP was renamed the Wind Research Laboratory (WRL) to better reflect the wide variety of phe-

Ted Fujita. *Working with a tornado simulator at the University of Chicago in 1979.* © BETTMANN/CORBIS.

nomena that was studied. This facility included the famous "tornado machine," the first of its kind to simulate a tornado. This machine was dismantled in the 1990s, and no record of it appears to remain; at the time, no institution was interested in preserving the apparatus.

Fujita retired in September 1990. During his academic career, he mentored a group of students who became leaders in many areas of meteorology, including Roger Wakimoto and Greg Forbes. In 1991 Fujita produced a small booklet with photographs of the WRL. He wrote his *Memoirs of an Effort to Unlock the Mysteries of Severe Storms* in 1992. In his last years, he concentrated on the study of storm tracks and the El Niño phenomenon. His health started to deteriorate as a result of several illnesses in 1995, and after the summer of 1996 he was unable to work at the office, but continued his work from home until his condition worsened in August 1998. Fujita suffered from diabetes and often had severe pains in his legs; because he never complained about his health, no one outside his family was aware of his chronic condition. During this period, even when he was confined to bed, he continued his research, greatly assisted by James Partacz and Duane Stiegler, and he maintained contacts with the research community. Stiegler recalls that Fujita did not trust computers to conduct his analyses, preferring to do it himself, saying that the computer did not understand these things. His ability to simplify concepts of severe storms was very important in terms of public education. He passed away in his sleep at home in the early morning of 19 November 1998 at age seventy-eight. The WRL was formally closed on 1 October 1999.

The American Meteorological Society held a memorial symposium and dinner at their eightieth annual meeting in Long Beach, California, in January 2000, organized by Fujita's former students Forbes and Wakimoto. The proceedings of this volume were published in the January 2001 issue of the *Bulletin of the American Meteorological Society.* Fujita was one of the great severe storms researchers of the twentieth century. His research on severe thunderstorms, tornadoes, hurricanes, and typhoons provided invaluable information and added to our understanding of these phenomena. Fujita's achievements were fundamental in terms of severe storm meteorology, and he was arguably one of the greatest contributors to mesometeorology and wind science. During his life, he had great insight into the nature and cause of damaging convective storms. His contributions include terminology, damage surveys, the Fujita scale, and downbursts.

BIBLIOGRAPHY

WORKS BY FUJITA

"Mesoanalysis: An Important Scale in the Analysis of Weather Data." U.S. Department of Commerce, Weather Bureau, Research Paper 39 (1956).

"Recent Studies in Mesometeorology." *Journal of the Meteorological Society of Japan,* 75th Anniversary Volume (1957): 256–261.

"A Detailed Analysis of the Fargo Tornadoes of June 20, 1957." University of Chicago, Department of Meteorology, Severe Local Storms Project, Technical Report no. 5, U.S. Weather Bureau (1959).

"Tornadoes and Downbursts in the Context of Generalized Planetary Scales." *Journal of Atmospheric Science* 38 (1978): 1511–1534.

"The Downburst: Mircroburst and Macroburst." SMRP Research Paper 210, University of Chicago (1985).

Memoirs of an Effort to Unlock the Mysteries of Severe Storms. Chicago: Wind Research Laboratory, University of Chicago, 1992.

OTHER SOURCES

Cox, John D. *Storm Watchers.* Hoboken, NJ: John Wiley & Sons, 2002.

Forbes, Greg, and Roger Wakimoto. "Tetsuya Theodore Fujita: Meteorological Detective and Illustrator." Available from http://www.stormtrack.org/library.

Fujita, Kazuya. "Tetsuya Theodore Fujita (1920–1998): Biographic Notes." Produced for the Weather Classroom at University of California, Los Angeles; available from http://www.msu.edu/~fujita/tornado/ttfujita/biogrpahy.html. The author is the son of Tetsuya Fujita.

Fujita, Kazuya, James W. Partacz, Duane J. Steigler, and Robert F. Abbey Jr. *A Bibliography of the Publications and Research Reports of Tetsuya T. Fujita (1920–1998).* SMRP Research Paper 252. University of Chicago (2000).

McDonald, James R. "Theodore Fujita: His Contribution to Tornado Knowledge through Damage Documentation and the Fujita Scale." *Bulletin of the American Meteorological Society* 82, no. 1 (2001): 63–72.

Menzel, W. Paul. "Cloud Tracking with Satellite Imagery: From the Pioneering Work of Ted Fujita to the Present." *Bulletin of the American Meteorological Society* 82, no. 1 (2001): 3347.

Snow, John T., and Theresa A. Leyton. "Reflections on Ted Fujita: The Relevance of His Many Contributions to Today's Wind Science." Invited Keynote address, 11th International Conference of Wind Engineering, Lubbock, Texas, 3 June 2003.

Wakimoto, Roger. "A Tribute to the Works of T. Theodore Fujita." *Bulletin of the American Meteorological Society* 82, no. 1 (2001): 911.

Sepideh Yalda

FUKUI, KEN'ICHI

(*b.* Nara, Japan, 4 October 1918; *d.* Kyoto, Japan, 9 January 1998), *physical organic chemistry, chemical theory.*

One of the great theoretical chemists of the twentieth century, Ken'ichi Fukui was Japan's first recipient of the Nobel Prize in Chemistry for his theory of chemical reactions. Solidly based in quantam mechanics, Fukui's work and that of Roald Hoffmann, with whom he shared the award, enhanced the ability of chemists to predict the course of chemical reactions. Significant applications followed in medicine and pharmacology.

Family Background. Ken'ichi Fukui was born in Nara, Japan on 4 October 1918. He was one of three brothers. His family, though not wealthy, was solidly middle class and well educated for the time. Both parents were formative influences on the chemist's life. Fukui's father, Ryokichi, was a graduate of the Tokyo institution that became Hitotsubashi University. Working in management for much of his career, Ryokichi Fukui at one point worked for a British export-import firm and spent a year in Europe during the mid-1920s. Ryokichi had a good command of English and was an ardent reader of *National Geographic* magazine. Ken'ichi Fukui often said that this publication was a significant influence on what ultimately became his deep interest in science because of its many articles on insects, plants, and other natural phenomena. The chemist's mother, Chie Sugisawa Fukui, graduated from high school—the Nara High School for Women—at a time when few Japanese women did so. Never inclined to push her children in a particular direction, her approach was rather to introduce books and subjects to Fukui and his brothers and encourage them to cultivate their own interests. From his mother Fukui acquired a deep interest in the literary works of Natsume Soseki, Japan's greatest writer of the early twentieth century and coincidentally an intellectual with a considerable interest in science.

Education. Fukui's path into chemistry was by no means predictable. He was not a dedicated student but preferred hiking, fishing, the martial art of Kendo, and the board game of Go to classroom work. Chemistry in particular struck him as boring because it appeared to be based on endless memorization. But he did well in mathematics with very little studying, was active in the biology club, and as a middle school student discovered the writings of the French entomologist and chemist Jean Henri Fabre (1823–1915). It seems to have been the life and work of Fabre that ultimately led Fukui to chemistry. He was impressed as a youth with the natural world of plants and animals described by Fabre, in which he himself was actually living. And Fukui found Fabre's development of alizarine dye, plus his courage to go ahead after commercial failure in its production, both intellectually stimulating and morally inspiring.

Given Fukui's talent for mathematics and his general love of nature, the most likely course might have been for him to enroll in the Faculty of Science at Kyoto University, where he ultimately matriculated. Instead, Fukui enrolled in the university's faculty of engineering on the advice of his father's cousin, Gen'itsu Kita, an engineering professor who had studied at the Massachusetts Institute of Technology and the Pasteur Institute. Fukui's enrollment in engineering proved a fateful decision. Overwhelmingly practical in its pedagogical and research orientation, the faculty of engineering seemed an inhospitable environment with its emphasis on ceramics, synthetic textiles, synthetic rubber, resins, petroleum chemistry and other applied subjects. However, Kita recommended it on the basis of Fukui's mathematical talent and general orientation; and his emphasis on pursuing "basic studies"—which Kita never defined—and building on basic knowledge would in fact serve Fukui well.

A graduation thesis project in late 1940 under the direction of a new assistant professor, Haruo Shingu, proved to be the first step in arousing Fukui's interest in a line of work that would sustain his entire career. Shingu assigned Fukui to study the Schaarschmidt reaction in hydrocarbon chemistry. Alfred Schaarschmidt had described the reaction patterns of hydrogen atoms attached to various carbon chains; and Fukui had to analyze the iso-paraffin in a hydrocarbon mixture by conducting various experiments. These tests were designed to ascertain slight differences in how the carbon atoms and hydrogen atoms in various paraffin hydrocarbons combine with each other and how the nature of these reactions differ from those involving antimony pentachloride. What he observed was that even when the chemical structures of two hydrocarbon compounds were very similar, they showed very different reaction patterns compared to the antimony pentachloride. He became interested in subtle differences in the reactivity of hydrocarbons like paraffin, benzene, or naphthalene. This work, in fact, elicited his long-term interest in the chemical reactions of pure hydrocarbon molecules. These investigations in the faculty of engineering prepared him well, in crucial respects, for the work in chemical reaction theory that led to his Nobel Prize.

But an engineering education was not sufficient by itself. Although he ably performed such chemical experiments, Fukui did not particularly enjoy this aspect of chemistry. He was interested, as always, in mathematics and even as an undergraduate spent considerable time attending physics lectures and consulting the library of the nearby faculty of science. Both were open to engineering students, and there Fukui found the *Handbuch der Physik,* works by Richard Courant and David Hilbert, and various texts on quantum mechanics that he considered essential to his education. On one occasion he wrote that he had agreed, following the advice of Gen'itsu Kita, to study applied chemistry on the presumption that it would gradually become a more theoretically and mathematically based field of study. In the spring of 1941, Fukui completed his undergraduate degree and began graduate study in the Department of Fuel Chemistry under the direction of Shinjiro Kodama.

Kodama was a protégé of Kita, who had studied in Germany during the late 1920s and who saw the future of chemistry much as Kita had done. At Kyoto Kodama was at first professor of hydrocarbon physical chemistry, then professor of high temperature chemistry. The combination of applied studies with the emphasis on theory under Kodama's direction was ideal for Fukui. Often leaving Fukui to his own devices, Kodama lent him books on quantum mechanics, physics, and electromagnetism that were otherwise difficult to obtain in Japan. And in the late summer of 1941 when Fukui became subject to the military draft, Kodama arranged for him to work part time at the Imperial Army Fuels Research Laboratory at Fuchu near Tokyo.

Early Career. What might well have been a hardship assignment became a significant opportunity. The Fuchu laboratory held an extensive collection of books on subjects of interest to Fukui, such as Ralph Howard Fowler's textbook on statistical mechanics and texts on quantum mechanics and hydrocarbon chemistry. Moreover, his assignment and that of his team played to his strengths and interests. Their task was to find a technique for raising the octane level of ordinary gasoline (or a substitute) so as to render it suitable for use in airplanes. Branched chain hydrocarbons such as 2,2,4-trimpthylpentance were not available in Japan. Instead the Fukui group fermented sugar to obtain butyl alcohol, which was then used as a substitute for the trimethylpentane. Although their fuel additive actually worked in airplanes, it was never produced in volume; nonetheless, in 1944 Fukui and his team received an Order of Technical Merit from the army.

Although Fukui had formally launched his academic career in 1943 when the university made him a lecturer in the Department of Fuel Chemistry, it was his 1945 appointment as an assistant professor—together with the end of the war—that enabled him to pursue his academic interests full time. Interested in chemical reaction engineering, Kodama had been trying to produce polyethylene, a synthetic polymer, by high pressurization technology. When this senior colleague left the university for private industry, Fukui took over the project and produced one of his first publications. He also took up another of Kodama's lines of inquiry—what temperature distributions or reaction conditions were most efficacious for producing chemical reactions in chemical factories—and made it the subject of his doctoral dissertation. Fukui received his doctoral degree, the DScEngr, in June 1948.

Chemical Reaction Theory. Fukui's career took a major turn in 1951. In that year he was advanced to the rank of full professor at the age of thirty-three. Because of the power inherent in the senior occupant of a university chair in the Japanese system, he was able—while continuing to teach various applied subjects—to gradually shift the focus of his laboratory away from applied research and more toward chemical theory. Not coincidentally, 1951 was also the year in which he began to formulate his path-breaking theory of chemical reactions. When Fukui began this work, the reigning paradigm was the so-called electronic theory of organic chemistry associated with the English chemists Robert Robinson and Christopher Keld Ingold. First published in 1926, this theory held that a chemical reaction could easily occur in one of two situations: in response to a positively charged electrophilic reagent at a site where the electron density is high, or in response to a negatively charged nucleophilic reagent at a site of low electron density. Fukui accepted electrons as the crucial element in chemical reactions but considered the Robinson-Ingold formulation inadequate at worst and inelegant at best. Moreover, it was not based on quantum mechanics, an approach to theorizing that Robinson in particular had largely disdained. Because of his own extensive investigations of hydrocarbons both in Kyoto's Department of Fuel Chemistry and at the army's laboratory in Fuchu, Fukui realized that this formulation simply did not work for many hydrocarbon chemical reactions. On the contrary, his own experiments had shown that aromatic hydrocarbons such as naphthalene could undergo reactions at the same site, both in the presence of reagents which accept electrons and in the presence of reagents that contribute them.

Fukui was strongly influenced in his theoretical work by the investigations of Robert S. Mulliken, who had earlier adopted Erwin Schrödinger's view of the electron as a wave that spread out in so-called orbitals over the atoms in a chemical bond. Both chemists defined an orbital not as a physical entity or path, but rather as a mathematical function referring to the movements of electrons within an atom or molecule. Mulliken's analyses were not directed to the rearrangement of chemical bonds in chemical reactions, as were Fukui's. Nonetheless, the University of Chicago chemist's focus on electric charge transference between molecules did involve the delocalization of electrons in such encounters. For this reason his work provided a valuable context for Fukui's discussion.

This was the perspective from which Fukui developed his frontier orbitals theory of chemical reactions. Using quantum mechanics he began by investigating naphthalene, largely because of its more or less regular shape. He did not focus on all the orbitals of its electrons but only the orbital with the highest energy level. From this initial inquiry he then investigated anthracene, pyrene, perylene, and other aromatic hydrocarbons one by one, but found the inquiry tedious and time-consuming because of the irregular shapes of their molecules. Teijiro Yonezawa, a special research student at the time but later professor of molecular engineering at Kyoto, cooperated with the task. Haruo Shingu, who had been the first to interest Fukui in hydrocarbon chemistry back in 1940, was also involved in the project. Late in 1951 they submitted their first major paper from the new project to the *Journal of Chemical Physics,* published by the American Institute of Physics. After minor revisions it appeared in the journal's April 1952 issue.

This 1952 paper did not attempt to offer a complete explanation of the new theory; in fact, even the theoretical nomenclature was evolving. The principal focus in 1952 was on the molecule that contributes electrons in a chemical reaction. The argument was that when two molecules exert a mutual influence on each other, the

Fukui

molecule contributing electrons gives a high-energy—so-called frontier—electron to the other molecule. In a subsequent 1954 article published in the same journal, the focus was on the molecule that receives the electron or electrons. In this case, reception took place in the unoccupied orbital of the lowest energy. With respect to the location of the reaction, Fukui and his colleagues argued that this occurs at a specific site within the expanse of the unoccupied orbital. This orbital became known as the lowest unoccupied molecular orbital (LUMO), while its occupied counterpart came to be known as the highest occupied molecular orbital (HOMO). Over the decade of the 1950s, Fukui and his colleagues demonstrated that the site and rate of a chemical reaction depends on the geometries and relative energies of the HOMO of one reactant and the LUMO of the other.

Reception of the Frontier Orbitals Theory. Presenting a theory was one thing, winning wide acceptance another. One early source of support was Mulliken himself. In 1953 Tokyo University hosted Japan's first big international scientific meeting after World War II, the International Symposium on Molecular Structure and Spectroscopy. Mulliken attended the meeting and referred approvingly to Fukui's 1952 paper. Fukui was also present and made other valuable contacts, including Per-Olov Löwdin of the University of Uppsala. In general, the meeting, together with Mulliken's lecture and endorsement of Fukui's approach, gave a significant boost to the frontier orbitals theory of chemical reactions. But there was still considerable opposition. Robinson was a Nobel laureate, and many chemists were reluctant to accept a theory of chemical reactions so thoroughly derived from physics and quantum mechanics. Did the new theory account for an experimentally verified, regularity of chemical reactions known as the Hammett rule? Fukui was able to show that it did so; moreover, he and his collaborators demonstrated through the course of the 1950s that the frontier orbitals approach explained all of the reactions explicable by the electronic theory as well as the hydrocarbon reactions that Robinson's theory could not explain.

In the 1960s Fukui's work slowly gained wider recognition both in Japan and the rest of the world. In 1962 he received the Japan Academy Prize for "research on chemical reactions and the electron states of conjugate compounds," and in 1964 he was invited to a major meeting of chemists in Florida organized by Löwdin. There he met Roald Hoffmann, with whom he would later share the Nobel Prize. As a junior fellow at Harvard University, Hoffmann and the senior chemist and Nobel laureate Robert B. Woodward published, in 1965, what came to be called the Woodward-Hoffmann Rule. Their observations linked experimental results with the phenomenon of orbitals, highlighting the importance of orbital symmetry control in chemical reactions. Together with another 1965 paper by Hoffmann on stereo-selectivity, their work called additional attention to Fukui's investigations on the importance of frontier orbital electrons in chemical reactions.

In 1970 Fukui spent six months as a visiting scholar at the Illinois Institute of Technology in Chicago with support from the U.S. National Science Foundation. During this period he wrote two major papers on chemical reaction theory. One dealt with the concept of orbital symmetry control developed by Hoffmann and Woodward as a way to demonstrate the greater breadth of the frontier orbitals theory as compared to the older electronic theory. His other paper applied perturbation theory to some original qualitative notions, showing that as perturbations distort the HOMO of one reactant and the LUMO of the other, they affect the energetics of various reaction pathways. By lecturing during this period at a number of American research universities while visiting corporate laboratories, Fukui gradually became better known in the United States. In 1981 he was named a member of the National Academy of Sciences.

Other awards followed, including the Order of Cultural Merit from Japan (1981), membership in the Pontifical Academy of Sciences in Rome (1985), and the 1981 Nobel Prize for Chemistry, together with Hoffmann. Following his retirement from Kyoto University, Fukui was named director of the Institute for Fundamental Chemistry in Kyoto, created with funds from the Kao Soap Corporation. As Japan's first Nobel laureate in chemistry, Fukui attracted a great deal of public attention and was named chair of a committee to organize the twelve-hundredth anniversary celebration of Kyoto's founding. On 9 January 1998 Fukui died in Kyoto of peritoneal cancer, survived by his wife Tomoe Horie Fukui, whom he married in 1947, and their two grown children.

BIBLIOGRAPHY

WORKS BY FUKUI

With Teijiro Yonezawa and Haruo Shingu. "A Molecular Orbital Theory of Reactivity in Aromatic Hydrocarbons." *Journal of Chemical Physics* 20 (1952): 722–725.

With Teijiro Yonezawa, Chikayoshi Nagata, et al. "Molecular Orbital Theory of Orientation in Aromatic, Heteroaromatic and Other Conjugated Molecules." *Journal of Chemical Physics* 22 (1954): 1433–1442.

With Chikayoshi Nagata, Teijiro Yonezawa, et al. "Novel Perturbation Theory in Simple LCAO Treatment of Conjugated Molecules—Method of Perturbed Secular Determinant." *Journal of Chemical Physics* 31 (1959): 287–293.

With T. Teijiro Yonezawa and Chikayoshi Nagata. "Reply to the Comments on the 'Frontier Electron Theory.'" *Journal of Chemical Physics* 31 (1959): 550–551.

Hiroshi Fujimoto, Shigeki Kato, et al. "Orbital Symmetry Control in the Interaction of Three Systems." *Bulletin of the Chemical Society of Japan* 46 (1973): 1071–1076.

Hiroshi Fujimoto, Morio Miyagi, et al. "On the MO Perturbation Theory of Molecular Rearrangements." *Bulletin of the Chemical Society of Japan* 46 (1973): 1357–1361.

"A Simple Quantum-Theoretical Interpretation of the Chemical Reactivity of Organic Compounds." In *Molecular Orbitals in Chemistry, Physics, and Biology: A Tribute to Robert S. Mulliken,* edited by Per-Olov Löwdin and Bernard Pullman, 513–537. New York: Academic Press, 1964.

Kagaku to Watakushi: Noberusho Kagakusha Fukui Ken'ichi. Edited by Yamabe Tokio. Kyoto, Japan: Kagaku Dojin, 1982.

Gakumon no Sozo. Tokyo: Kosei Shuppansha, 1984.

Fukui

OTHER SOURCES

Bartholomew, James. "Fukui Ken'ichi." In *The Oxford Companion to the History of Modern Science,* edited by John Heilbron. Oxford and New York: Oxford University Press, 2003, pp. 316–317.

Buckingham, A. D. and H. Nakatsuji. "Kenichi Fukui." In *Biographical Memoirs of Fellows of the Royal Society,* vol. 47, edited by the Royal Society, 225–237. London: Royal Society, 2001.

Davis, Scott. "Kenichi Fukui, 1981." In *The Nobel Prize Winners: Chemistry,* vol. 3, edited by Frank N. Magill, 1061–1066. Pasadena, CA: Salem Press, 1990.

Hoffmann, Roald. "Obituary: Kenichi Fukui (1918–98)." *Nature* 391 (1998): 750.

James R. Bartholomew

G

GALEN (GALÊNOS) (*b.* Pergamum, September 129; *d.* c. 216, Rome), *medicine, biology, physiology, anatomy, psychology, logic, philosophy.* For the original article on Galen see *DSB,* vol. 5.

Galen was one of the most important and influential medical practitioners and theorists of antiquity. His synthetic but innovative general accounts of anatomy, physiology, pathology, and therapeutics dominated medicine in late antiquity, and, by way of the Arabic world, were reintroduced into the West in Latin translation from the twelfth century, where they rapidly became canonical. His anatomy was not superseded until the publication of Vesalius's *De Humani Corporus Fabrica* (1543); his physiological and therapeutic views remained influential until the nineteenth century.

The very size of Galen's surviving corpus, and the fact that much of it as of 2007 has yet to be properly edited according to modern critical methods, has held back the development of Galenic scholarship. But this situation is gradually being remedied, and the thirty-five years that have elapsed since the appearance of the previous *DSB* have witnessed a resurgence and quickening of Galenic studies. New texts of Galen, now generally equipped with detailed commentaries and a translation into a modern language, have been appearing with increasing frequency from the *Corpus Medicorum Graecorum*; a number of individual translations of important texts have appeared in English and other languages (see bibliography for some examples); and three volumes have now appeared in the ambitious project Les Belles Lettres has undertaken to produce substantial new editions and French translations of Galen's work. In addition, a series of international conferences have begun to open up new avenues of exploration in Galenic studies; his contributions to philosophy, in particular, have benefited from substantial and sympathetic detailed treatments. That he was honoured in 2007 with a volume in the *Cambridge Companion* series is a testament to the revival of his scholarly fortunes.

Life and Work. Galen (sometimes still mistakenly referred to as Claudius Galen) was born in September 129 C.E. in Pergamum, a rich and thriving Greek city on what is now the west coast of Asian Turkey. His father was a successful architect of broad intellectual interests, and Galen was given a fine education, studying philosophy as a teenager with leading representatives of the major schools—Platonist, Aristotelian, Stoic and Epicurean, before his father, moved by a dream, decided to turn his son toward a career in medicine. On his father's death in 149, Galen traveled for several years in search of the best doctors and teachers of his time, to Smyrna, Corinth, and finally Alexandria. He returned to Pergamum in 157, where, as a result (as he relates in *On Recognizing the Best Physician,* Kühn, 1965, vol. IX, pp. 4–7) of his superior knowledge and competence in a public display of animal dissection and surgery, he won the position of physician to the gladiatorial school, a post he held for four years. He then set off once more, this time for Rome, after a further period of travel, observation, and collection of *materia medica* in the eastern Mediterranean that took him as far afield as the Dead Sea.

Arriving in Rome in 162, Galen immediately (on his own account) began to make a name for himself in the cut-throat world of upper-class medical practice, as a result of his skill in prognosis and treatment, and his spectacular public demonstrations in functional anatomy. His

Galen

work *On Prognosis,* written perhaps fifteen years later, paints a vivid, if undeniably self-interested, picture of his meteoric rise in Roman society, culminating with his appointment in 169, after a brief return to his native city, as one of the imperial physicians to the philosopher-emperor Marcus Aurelius (r. 161–180), with special responsibilities for the latter's son Commodus. There is less information available about Galen's later years, but it is clear that he remained within the imperial orbit until his death, which probably took place around 216 (a very late tradition which has him dying at the age of seventy—that is, in 199—has been definitively exploded, although it is still often recycled in popular histories). His working life covered almost seventy years, and there are literary remains from all of it, although what survives intact of Galen's work probably amounts to no more than a third of his total, voluminous output. Even so, millions of words survive, more—much more—than from any other ancient author. He himself stated that he dictated to relays of slaves, often working on several texts at once.

Scholars know more than otherwise might have been even about his lost output, because Galen wrote two texts, *On My Own Books* and *The Order of My Own Books,* motivated by the need to expose forgeries that were circulating under his name during his lifetime (and several such spurious works are to be found in the Galenic canon), and in order to recommend an order of study for the genuine works. These are late treatises, but are not complete. Obviously they do not refer to works composed later; but in one case at least (*On Prognosis*) where the work was written earlier, the autobibliographies contain no mention of it, presumably because Galen himself supposed no genuine copy still to be extant. He had lost most of his own library in the fire that destroyed the Temple of Peace (which served as a public depository and intellectuals' meeting place) in 192. The first surviving work from his hand is a school exercise, *On Medical Experience,* composed when he was about twenty; his last work, *On My Own Opinions,* a summary of his views on philosophy and science, may even have been composed on his deathbed. In the interim, he wrote voluminously on anatomy, physiology, therapeutics, pharmacology, diagnosis and prognosis, and the pulse, as well as composing numerous polemics against other doctors, and commentaries on the Hippocratic texts (which he regarded as being the basic source of medical wisdom: the surviving commentaries—and many are lost—run to thousands of pages, about 20 percent of his total surviving oeuvre); he also wrote on grammar, logic, and scientific demonstration, and other topics in philosophy. In what follows, this author will seek to sketch the outlines of his achievement.

Galen and the Medical Schools. Galen distinguishes the medical practitioners of his own and earlier times into three general classes or "sects": Dogmatists (or Rationalists), Empiricists, and Methodists. The distinction is not Galen's own (it occurs a century earlier in the medical encyclopedia of Celsus); but Galen makes it canonical, and it is to Galen that scholars owe most of their knowledge of them (he wrote a short treatise *On Sects for Beginners,* but he scatters remarks, usually of an uncomplimentary nature, on the schools and their adherents throughout his works. It is a rough and ready taxonomy (the Dogmatist category in particular is a very broad one), but for all that, it is a serviceable one. Roughly, Dogmatic doctors are those who believe that sound medical practice must be founded on etiology, accounts of the fundamental structure of things and how they work that serve to explain how organisms function properly, what accounts for their failure to do so, and how such failures can be countered and repaired. But as their various opponents, in particular the Empiricists, were not slow to point out, there was no agreement at all among the various Dogmatic schools as to the facts of physiology and pathology.

In the face of this dispute, Empiricists declared such attempts to determine the hidden, fundamental structures of things both hopeless and unnecessary (thus they dismiss anatomy as of little importance; see *Anatomical Procedures,* Kühn, 1965, vol. II, pp. 282–85). The Empiricists argued that perfectly successful medical practice could be founded simply on the observation and categorization of the regular conjunctions of suitable observable phenomena: If one sees that diarrhea is stayed by the ingestion of pomegranates on a sufficiently large number of occasions, then one may conclude that pomegranates cure diarrhea; one does not need to know *how* they do. Empiricists rely on personal experience, and on the reports of others, to build up their empirical connections, while some of them also allowed a certain type of analogical reasoning at least to suggest candidates for therapy. But officially they insist that all medical knowledge is the result of random successes subsequently repeated and tested.

Methodists held that there were only three basic disease types: the pores of the body might be too loose, too constricted, or a mixture of the two (in different places of course). To the moderately trained eye, the existence of these conditions was evident; treatment simply consisted in seeking to counteract them. Thus no causal theory, or indeed developed physiology, was required of the practitioner. Methodism was developed in the first century CE by Thessalus of Tralles, who promised to teach it all in six months, a claim that Galen dismisses contemptuously on several occasions. For Galen, medical competence could only be won by years of study and effort, and only by someone versed not only in the best medical theory, but also in all aspects of philosophy. Indeed, he wrote a short treatise, *The Best Doctor Is Also a Philosopher* devoted to

Galen

establishing this premise. A properly competent doctor must understand the basics of physical science (in Galen's view the canonical four-element and quality theory: all substances are composed of the elements earth, water, air, and fire, which in turn exhibit pairs of the qualities, cold/dry, cold/wet, warm/wet, and warm/dry, respectively), because the majority of illnesses consist in damage to the body's natural functions that result from an imbalance in the qualities. The doctor needs to be able to recognize the signs of specific imbalances, and to treat them (allopathically, "opposites cure opposites" is for Galen an a priori Hippocratic truth). Galen outlines his physics (which involves an attack on monisms and atomism) in *Elements According to Hippocrates*, whose title indicates one of Galen's particular intellectual debts, and in *On Temperaments*. The doctor also needs to understand logic, in order to avoid the traps of the "sophists," and to distinguish demonstrative arguments from those that are merely probable (or worse). Finally, he should be versed in ethics: He should value knowledge for its own sake and realize that the good life consists not in the pursuit of pleasure, fame or riches, but in the service of mankind.

Much of attitude is self-serving, but contempt and disgust at the venality and incompetence of his medical opponents is a constant refrain throughout Galen's work, and there can be no doubt either of Galen's own vast learning. He himself, he says, belongs to no school, preferring the truth to sectarian affiliation. Although by temperament he is a Dogmatist (because he believes that comprehensive medical practice is to be founded on a causal secure understanding of physics and physiology), early in his career he noted the apparently intractable nature of their disagreements. In fact, he says, it might have made him a skeptic had he not been aware of the demonstrative certainty of geometry. Thus he is in some ways sympathetic to the charge made by the Empiricists that the Dogmatists cannot securely found their own theories, but he ascribes this to the Dogmatists' own shortcomings rather than to any intrinsic impossibility in the enterprise. Again what is needed is a thorough grounding in demonstrative theory, and serious intellectual application. For this reason, he is not as hostile to the Empiricists as he is to the Methodists. Within limits, he allows, Empiricists can become reasonable practitioners. They observe the same phenomenal regularities that allow someone like Galen to deduce the hidden, internal states of the body, but instead of doing so and then working out the appropriate therapy, they simply infer therapies directly from them on the basis of experience alone. This means that Empiricists are at a loss when confronted with unfamiliar concatenations of symptoms, and have to trust to luck and improvisation. At the same time, the Empiricists' emphasis on empirical testing is perfectly justified, and a corrective to the excessively aprioristic attitude of

Galen. AP IMAGES.

some of the Dogmatists. In fact, Galen sets out to elaborate (largely successfully) a new scientific epistemology that seeks to unite theoretical and practical considerations in a fruitful synthesis. Proper medical science requires a theoretical underpinning, and its practical suggestions should all be undergirded by a true causal theory, as the Dogmatists insist; yet those suggestions, and hence the theory that delivers them, should also be subjected to constant and rigorous empirical testing, in the manner of the Empiricists. It is for this reason that he consistently abjures certain metaphysical and cosmological questions, such as whether there is more than one cosmos, and whether a void exists outside it, or what the nature of the human soul is and whether it is immortal, as being unanswerably pointless.

Anatomy and Physiology. In order to be able to preserve health and cure disease, the fully armed doctor needs to understand the structures and proper functioning of the body and its parts. This (*pace* both Empiricists and Methodists) requires extended and difficult study. This is not just a matter of distinguishing and mapping the various structures of the body; it also involves determining their functional interrelations, of seeing why things are where they are and doing what they do, and this in a particularly strong sense, for Galen is committed to a strong version of biological teleology. One can only understand the body and its workings, he thinks, on the assumption that it is the product of intelligent and benevolent design. The view of the atomists (and other mechanists) to the effect that the structures of animals' bodies (and indeed every structure) are simply the outcome of the interplay of random physical forces is simply, he thinks, rationally unsustainable when one has a sufficiently clear and detailed understanding of the complexity of those systems and their degree of functional interrelatedness. The establishment of this teleological anatomy is the object of *On the Utility of the Parts*, a long treatise that Galen himself describes as a hymn to purposive nature, which he personifies using the Platonic designation of the "Demiurge." The whole of the first book is devoted to a discussion of the human hand (although Galen's treatment is vitiated by the fact that he was forced to rely on dissections of apes, and his over-confidence in interspecies homology). Galen is particularly impressed by the fact that nature has supplied only as many tendons as are required to move the fingers and thumb in the appropriate directions, and he heartily endorses Aristotle's claim (against Anaxagoras) that humans have hands because they are intelligent rather than the other way round. In effect, while the general tenor of his teleology is Platonic (he believes that the complexity of animals' structures entail that they were intelligently designed, although as he regularly says, he has no idea of the precise mechanisms by which such a design are realized: see *On the Formation of the Foetus*, Kühn, 1965, vol. IV, pp. 652–702), the fine detail of his teleological analysis owes a great debt (which he acknowledges) to Aristotle.

But whereas Aristotle was prepared to allow that certain structures lack functions, being the necessary "residual" causal consequences of others which were purposive, Galen is far less willing to water down the teleology in this way; thus, in *On the Natural Faculties*, a treatise in which he argues that the body's organs must be supposed to dispose of specific faculties for attracting, retaining, metabolizing, and eliminating what is appropriate (and in the last case inappropriate) to them, he contends that, first appearances notwithstanding, the gall bladder, spleen, and omentum all fulfill important roles in the overall economy of the animal. For Galen, nature does nothing in vain, and with a vengeance. This commitment in turn provides him with a powerful heuristic: If at first no function is discernible in some structure, look more closely until you find one (and, as far as it goes, this is a reasonable heuristic, even if Galen is wrong to suppose that there can be no functionless structures). Nature also strives to produce economical design solutions: In the last book of *On the Utility of the Parts*, Galen marvels at the structural economy of the elephant's trunk (he had dissected one of the emperor's beasts), which it can use as a hand, but also as a kind of snorkel when fording deep rivers, in order to allow for which nature has providentially extended the nasal passage along its entire length.

For Galen, widespread experience and regular practice in dissection (and vivisection) was absolutely essential in order for the aspirant doctor to form a proper understanding of the structural arrangements of animal (and by extension human) bodies. Galen himself reports dissecting goats, pigs, bears, horses, and cattle (as well as elephants and apes), and recommends that the student take any opportunity to examine human skeletons they happen to come across, if they are not lucky enough to be able to visit Alexandria, which is the only place where medical training involved actual human skeletons. With application and ability, the doctor can come to an understanding, by means of dissection and vivisection, of how the various parts of the body work, and of what they contribute to the overall functioning of the animal; only then will he be in a position properly to understand, and hence to treat, diseases, since diseases are, by definition, physical conditions ("dispositions") which serve to impair the proper functioning of the parts of the body. The individual parts themselves are attributed the appropriate mixture of the natural "faculties" required in order to perform their function. In turn, these faculties make use of, but are not reducible to, the simple potentialities of the elements and qualities. Such "explanations," as Galen was well aware, risk vacuity, and he is clear that such talk of faculties and potentialities is useful only up to a point. But for all that, it is useful to know what things do, and (if they do) that they do them per se, as a result of their own structure. And that is what one needs to know in order to become a successful theoretician and practitioner of medicine.

Conclusions: Galen's System. In this brief survey, it is not possible to do full justice to the range and diversity of Galen's achievement. In particular, his contributions to pharmacology, largely contained in three vast theoretical and practical compendia, *On the Composition of Simple Drugs*, *On the Composition of Drugs According to Places*, and *On the Composition of Drugs According to Type*, in which Galen not only records (critically) a vast amount of existing drug lore, but also seeks to classify drugs and their efficaciousness according to his fundamental physical categories (drugs work in virtue of their particular mixtures of the fundamental qualities of hot, cold, wet, and dry), have not been surveyed here.

Galen's systematization of pulse-doctrine, contained in four major treatises (*Differences of Pulses*, *Diagnosis by Pulses*, *Causes of Pulses*, and *Prognosis by Pulses*), and two summary ones (*Pulses for Beginners* and the possibly spurious *Synopsis Concerning the Pulse*), is also beyond the scope of this article. Here as usual he built upon his predecessors (all the while trumpeting his own innovations and excoriating their mistakes), but in this case, uniquely, he was prepared to allow that the great Hippocrates had fallen short and had not realized the immense diagnostic importance of the pulse. Accordingly, Galen produces an extremely detailed taxonomy of pulse types, where the variables included speed, vigorousness, depth, and regularity, which could be used (along with other diagnostic and prognostic signs) to determine the internal conditions of the patient's system; the pulse is highly responsive, in Galen's view, to internal imbalances, and hence serves as an invaluable tool for distinguishing them—although here, as elsewhere, Galen emphasized that the doctor also needed to know the particular patient's normal sphygmology, because every individual's natural condition was idiosyncratic, an English term which in fact derives from Galen's term for the "particular admixture" of the patient's body. Moreover, the normal ranges differ with age, gender, and location. Doctors in the Islamic tradition still make use of the Galenic classifications of pulse.

Equally exhaustive was Galen's classification of types of disease and distemper (*Differences of Diseases, Causes of Diseases, Differences of Fevers, Opportune Moments in Disease, On Crises, On Critical Days,* as well as a number of short treatises on particular types of illness), and of symptoms (*Differences of Symptoms, Causes of Symptoms,* and *On Affected Parts*). In Galen's view, once the doctor understood the physical basis of human physiology, and what sorts of things could go wrong with it, and once he was armed with a reasonably sure set of diagnostic and prognostic tools for determining the precise natures of the distempers involved, then the appropriate therapy (in general terms) followed as a matter of the logic of allopathy: an individual or part that was too hot or dry needed cooling and moistening, and so on. For all that, particular clinical decisions still required long experience and precise skills, as well as the application of logical reasoning (whether to employ drugs or other remedies; whether the patient's constitution was capable of withstanding a particular treatment or not); and so it is no surprise that his masterpiece of therapeutics, *On the Method of Healing,* should have occupied more than a thousand pages (he also wrote a shorter compendium: *Therapeutics to Glaucon*).

Galen's system was thoroughgoing and comprehensive; it offered a rationally constructed account (indeed one which Galen supposed—or at least pretended to suppose—was securely founded on logical demonstration) that made sense of the body and its ills within the context of general, if traditional, physics. It was learned, stressing both theoretical understanding and historical engagement, and Galen never wavers in his view that all wisdom is owed ultimately to Hippocrates and Plato. He wrote a massive work, *On the Doctrines of Hippocrates and Plato,* dedicated to proving that, on all major points of method and substance, the two great masters of old were both correct, and in agreement with one another (thus he thinks that Plato's view of the tripartition, and trilocation, of the soul can be given an empirical demonstration using the discoveries and methods of later dissective and vivisective anatomy). But his system was also rooted methodologically (at least in theory) in empirical observation and (occasionally) experiment, and here he owes (avowedly) a debt to Aristotle and the later scientific tradition. Galen insisted continually that the deliverances of theory, physiological, pathological, prognostic, and therapeutic, should be subject to empirical testing. Moreover, this methodology is, as far as it goes, an admirable one. Galen had neither the instruments nor the conceptual machinery to carry it through into a fully scientific medical theory. Yet, in the former case at least, he was aware of the deficiency. Lacking reliable thermometers, determinations of heat and cold are always going to be approximative. Still the ideal was an admirable one, and one which, albeit in an ossified, scholastic form that Galen himself would have found most uncongenial, was to dominate Islamic and medieval medicine for a millennium and a half, and was to have its reverberations felt much later still than that (for example, in the practice of therapeutic phlobotomy, on which Galen wrote three short treatises). Indeed, its faint echoes may still be detected in a not entirely superseded medical, and psychological, terminology.

SUPPLEMENTARY BIBLIOGRAPHY

WORKS BY GALEN

Marquardt, J., I. Mueller, and G. Helmreich, eds. *Claudii Galeni Pergameni Scripta Minora.* 3 vols. Leipzig: Teubner, 1884–1893. Contains critical editions (but no translation) of short works.

Brock, Arthur J., trans. *Galen on the Natural Faculties.* London: William Heinemann, 1916.

Singer, Charles, trans. *Galen on Anatomical Procedures.* Oxford, U.K.: Oxford University Press, 1956. What survives in Greek of Galen's major anatomical treatise, *On Anatomical Procedures.*

Duckworth, W. L. H., trans.; M. C. Lyons and B. Towers, eds. *Galen on Anatomical Procedures: The Later Books.* Cambridge, U.K.: Cambridge University Press, 1962. Translation of Arabic version of *On Anatomical Procedures.*

Kühn, C. G., ed. *Galeni Opera Omnia,* 20 vols. Leipzig: Georg Olms, 1821–1833. Reprint, Hildesheim, 1965. The most comprehensive edition of Galen's works, it is incomplete, and in many ways inadequate. The process of producing proper modern critical editions continues, in particular in the series *Corpus Medicorum Graecorum,* published by Akademie Verlag.

May, Margaret Tallmadge, trans. *Galen on the Usefulness of the Parts of the Body.* Ithaca, NY: Cornell University Press, 1968. Includes Galen's great work of teleological anatomy, *On the Utility of the Parts.*

Siegel, Rudolph E., trans. *Galen on the Affected Parts.* Basel: S. Karger, 1976.

De Lacy, Phillip, ed., trans., and commentary. *On the Doctrines of Hippocrates and Plato.* 3 vols. Berlin: Akademie Verlag, 1978–84.

Nutton, Vivian, ed., trans., and commentary. *On Prognosis.* Berlin: Akademie Verlag, 1979.

Walzer, Richard, and Michael Frede, trans. *Three Treatises on the Nature of Science: Galen.* Indianapolis: Hackett, 1985. Includes three important methodological treatises, one of which, *On Medical Experience*, survives mostly in Arabic, and was translated by Walzer in 1944.

Brain, Peter, trans. and commentary. *Galen on Bloodletting.* Cambridge, U.K.: Cambridge University Press, 1986. Includes Galen's three treatises on bloodletting.

Hankinson, R. J., trans. and commentary. *Galen on the Therapeutic Method Books I and II.* Oxford: Clarendon Press, 1991. Includes first two methodological books of *The Method of Healing.*

De Lacy, Phillip, ed., trans., and commentary. *On Semen.* Berlin: Akademie Verlag, 1992.

De Lacy, Phillip, ed., trans., and commentary. *On the Elements According to Hippocrates.* Berlin: Akademie Verlag, 1996.

Singer, P. N., trans., with introduction and notes. *Selected Works.* Oxford: Oxford University Press, 1997. Good English translations of several important texts.

Nutton, Vivian, ed., trans., and commentary. *On My Own Opinions.* Berlin: Akademie Verlag, 1999.

Grant, Mark, trans. *Galen on Food and Diet.* London: Routledge, 2000. Includes important texts on diet and regimen; covers more ground than the Powell volume.

Powell, Owen, trans. *On the Properties of Foodstuffs.* Cambridge, U.K.: Cambridge University Press, 2003. Includes important texts on diet and regimen; more reliable and easier to use than Grant volume.

Johnston, Ian, trans. *Galen On Diseases and Symptoms.* Cambridge, U.K.: Cambridge University Press, 2006. Includes several important works in nosology.

Boudon-Millot, Veronique, trans. *Galien.* Vol. I. Paris: Les Belles Lettres, 2007. Includes new material from a previously unknown Greek codex.

OTHER SOURCES

Boudon-Millot, Veronique, and Antoine Pietrobelli. "Galien ressuscité: Edition princeps du texte grec du *De propriis placitis.*" *Revue des Études Grecques* 118 (2005): 168–213. Includes new material from a previously unknown Greek codex.

Hankinson, R. J., ed. *The Cambridge Companion to Galen.* Cambridge, U.K.: Cambridge University Press, 2007. A work covering many aspects of Galen's achievement, by several hands.

Nutton, Vivian. *Ancient Medicine.* London: Routledge, 2004. Offers a magisterial general survey, with fine chapters on Galen and his achievement.

Rocca, Julius. *Galen on the Brain.* Leiden: Brill, 2003. A fascinating modern reconstruction and analysis of Galen's dissective experiments.

Siegel, Rudolph E. *Galen's System of Medicine and Physiology.* Basel: Karger, 1968.

———. *Galen on Sense Perception.* Basel: Karger, 1970.

———. *Galen on Psychology, Psychopathology, and Function and Diseases of the Nervous System.* Basel: Karger, 1973.

Smith, Wesley D. *The Hippocratic Tradition.* Ithaca, NY: Cornell University Press, 1979. Deals with Galen's debt to (and construction of) Hippocrates.

R. J. Hankinson

GALILEI, GALILEO (*b.* Pisa, Italy, 15 February 1564; *d.* Arcetri, Italy, 8 January 1642), *physics, astronomy, philosophy of science.* For the original article on Galileo see *DSB,* vol. 5.

Since the publication of Stillman Drake's *DSB* entry on Galileo in 1972, Galilean studies have come a long way. New translations have made Galileo's works accessible to a large, multinational reading public. New critical editions of his texts, in many cases complemented by a sophisticated apparatus and explanatory comments, have helped to provide a more profound appraisal of his splendid prose. Above all, a host of studies on nearly every aspect of Galileo's life and accomplishments have deepened scholars' understanding of his eminent intellectual legacy. As a rough indication as of 2007 of the number of studies on Galileo published after Drake's *DSB* article, suffice it to say that the *International Galilean Bibliography* (edited by the Institute and Museum of History of Science in Florence) counts more than 6,100 post-1972 records.

Thanks to this vast number of studies scholars are in a position to assess from a sounder historical standpoint the many facets of Galileo's achievements. Even though the results of these studies do not significantly affect the excellent outline provided by Drake, subsequent works have added pieces of information that deserve to be taken into account in order to achieve a more comprehensive appraisal of Galileo's accomplishments.

Editions. A noteworthy feature of Galilean studies since the 1970s is the publication of new, often outstanding editions of Galileo's works. Of special value are the *Sidereus nuncius* edited by Isabelle Pantin (with French translation and very detailed notes) and the critical editions of the *Dialogue on the Two Chief Systems,* the *Discourse on the Comets,* and *The Assayer* prepared by Ottavio Besomi and Mario Helbing. All these editions couple philological exactitude with extensive and accurate commentaries. Of great interest for Galilean scholars is the edition of the proceedings of Galileo's trial by Father

Sergio Pagano, which adds to the known documentation some materials not included in the Edizione Nazionale (National Edition) of Galileo's works.

Readers in English have increased opportunities to read Galileo's texts thanks to improved or fresh translations. In 1974 Stillman Drake replaced the old version of the *Two New Sciences* by Henry Crew and Alfonso De Salvio (first issued in 1914) with a subsequent, more careful one. Further, in 1977 William Wallace translated from the Latin *Galileo's Early Notebooks* (the so-called *Juvenilia*), and in 1989 Albert Van Helden edited a remarkable English *Sidereus nuncius* (*The Sidereal Messenger*). In the same year, Maurice Finocchiaro translated the most relevant documents pertaining to the "Galileo affair," comprising the theological letters to Benedetto Castelli, Piero Dini, and Grand Duchess Cristina, as well as the *Discourse on the Tides* (1616) and the *Reply to Francesco Ingoli* (1624). Eight years later, in 1997, Finocchiaro also published a large collection of excerpts from Galileo's *Dialogue*, which he complemented with explanatory notes.

Editorial work has also been actively engaged with Galileo's unpublished texts. This has been the case notably with the logical notes of Manuscript 27 of the Galilean Collection in the National Library of Florence, which were integrally edited by William F. Edwards and William Wallace in 1988 under the title *Tractatio de praecognitionibus et praecognitis and Tractatio de demonstratione.* Wallace also provided an English translation of these treatises, emphasizing their importance for the development of Galileo's scientific methodology.

Another remarkable edition concerns the Galilean Manuscript 72, whose contents show the evolution of Galileo's thought on mechanics from his early years in Padua to the printing of *Two New Sciences* in 1638. Under the title *Galileo Galilei's Notes on Motion*, the Central National Library (Florence), the Institute and Museum of History of Science (Florence), and the Max Planck Institute for the History of Science (Berlin) have carried out an innovative project, publishing on the Internet an electronic reproduction (accompanied by transcriptions and apparatus) of this manuscript. The Institute and Museum of History of Science in Florence has also edited a Web archive, *Galileothek@*, which offers texts of all of Galileo's works as well as images, bibliographical records, lexicographical and thematic indexes, sections devoted to experiments, and a detailed Galilean chronology, along with powerful tools for searching and navigating through the various repositories.

Finally, it should be added that a project of updating the masterful twenty-volume National Edition of Galileo's *Works* (*Opere*), edited by Antonio Favaro and published between 1890 and 1909, was initiated in 2006. This project, anticipated to be completed by 2010, includes the publication of several volumes devoted to all those Galilean materials (works, letters, documents) that were unknown to Favaro and accordingly were not included in his edition.

Jesuit Sources. One of the most interesting debates surrounding Galileo concerns the sources of the above-mentioned notes on logic (Galilean Manuscript 27) and of the treatises edited by Favaro under the title *Juvenilia.* A few scholars (Alistair Crombie, Adriano Carugo, and William Wallace) have argued that these texts are based on works of Jesuit authors. As the specific sources of Galileo's *Juvenilia* they name Franciscus Toletus's commentaries (1573 and 1575) on Aristotle's *Physics* and *De generatione et corruptione,* Benedictus Pererius's textbook *De communibus omnium rerum naturalium principiis et affectionibus* (1576), and the commentary on Sacrobosco's *Sphere* by the distinguished Jesuit astronomer Christopher Clavius (1581). More controversial is the identification of the precise texts said to have inspired the notes on logic of Galileo's Manuscript 27. Crombie and Carugo held that Galileo relied on a printed book (Ludovico Carbone's *Additamenta ad commentaria D. Francisci Toleti in Logicam,* 1597), while Wallace has maintained that the real source of these Galilean comments on Aristotle's *Posterior Analytics* was a manuscript *reportatio* of the logic course offered at the Collegio Romano by the Jesuit professor Paolo Della Valle during the academic year 1587–1588. Though no copy of this manuscript is extant, Wallace holds that its contents were plagiarized by Ludovico Carbone, a circumstance that would account for the resemblances between Galileo's Manuscript 27 and Carbone's *Additamenta.*

On these grounds, Wallace has emphasized the crucial role played by Aristotelian logic and methodology for Galileo's achievements, adding that the alleged strong epistemological continuity perceptible in Galileo's scientific evolution is the result of his unwavering reliance on the Aristotelian demonstrative method he learned from the Jesuit commentaries. Wallace's conclusion is in fact quite bold, arguing that "Galileo's methodology was already spelled out in the treatises he appropriated from the Collegio Romano" (1992, p. xvi). Although it is not possible to provide here a detailed survey of Wallace's arguments, it must be observed that, apart from its pronounced conjectural character—there is no compelling evidence of Galileo's use of the Collegio Romano's materials—Wallace's reconstruction obscures Galileo's vehement anti-Aristotelian polemic, which actually forms a substantial part of his accomplishments.

As antidote to such a "pan-logical" view of Galileo's epistemology, one should also bear in mind what Galileo claims in the "Second Day" of the *Two New Sciences*: "It

Galilei

seems to me that logic teaches how to know whether or not reasonings and demonstrations already discovered are conclusive, but I do not believe that it teaches how to find conclusive reasonings and demonstrations" (Drake trans., 2nd edition, 1989, p. 133).

Galilean Manuscript 72. As a central contribution to modern science, Galileo's theory of motion has always attracted much scholarly attention. In the last decades of the twentieth century a more precise assessment of the development of Galileo's views on this matter became possible thanks to more careful studies of the scraps of Manuscript 72.

It is known that Galileo had planned to write a treatise on motion prior to his discoveries with the telescope in the 1609–1610 period. In May 1610 he wrote to the secretary of the Grand Duke of Tuscany, Belisario Vinta, that he was about to bring to completion "three books on local motion, an entirely new science, no one else, ancient or modern, having discovered some of the very many admirable properties that I demonstrate to exist in natural and forced motions" (*Opere*, Edizione Nazionale a cura di A. Favaro, Florence: Giunti Barbera, 1890–1909, repr. 1968, X, pp. 351–52). However, because Galileo embarked on different scientific pursuits and became involved in a number of scientific disputes, he was unable to bring out his "new science of motion" before 1638, when he published the *Two New Sciences*. Manuscript 72 constitutes a kind of filing cabinet in which Galileo saved the drafts of the theorems that he was to include in his *Two New Sciences*, along with numerous textual fragments, drawings, and calculations related to his mechanical research. Because they cover a period of nearly forty years, the materials of the codex are of the utmost importance for a more precise appraisal of Galileo's route to his final theory of motion. For this reason, Galileo scholarship has paid increasing attention to Manuscript 72.

A remarkable result of these studies concerns clues in Manuscript 72 that indicate Galileo carried out an extensive experimental program. Several diagrams and calculations contained in the codex seem to provide evidence that, since the earliest years of the seventeenth century, Galileo performed experiments by rolling balls down planes inclined at small angles to the horizontal and by studying the swings of pendulums of different lengths. Although scholars have proposed different interpretations and chronologies of its contents, consensus exists that several folios of Manuscript 72 record experimental data. This evidence strongly reinforces the thesis that an important part of Galileo's accomplishments in mechanics was rooted in experimentation.

Thus, while in his entry for the *DSB* in 1972 Drake wrote that "the role of experiment in Galileo's physics was limited to the testing of preconceived mathematical rules and did not extend to the systematic search for such rules" (p. 247), seven years later, in 1979, he argued that the contents of Manuscript 72 bear out the conclusion that "Galileo found the law of free fall by experiment, or rather by the making of very careful measurements" (1979, p. x).

Nevertheless, it is still difficult to ascertain whether Galileo resorted to experiments merely to confirm the results he had already obtained via mathematical reasoning or whether the experimentation itself played a role in obtaining the results. At any rate, relying on careful survey of the contents of Manuscript 72, one can confidently assume that experimental practice was an essential constitutive element of Galileo's "new science of motion."

Atomism and the Eucharist. In section 48 of *The Assayer* (1623), Galileo set forth a theory of knowledge based on a sharp distinction between "objective" and "subjective" qualities. According to this view, whereas features such as shape, size, position, motion, and number are qualities intrinsic to real things, impressions such as colors, tastes, smells, or tactile properties do not exist in the objects themselves but only in the sentient subject experiencing them. For this reason, sensible qualities were characterized by Galileo as "mere names," qualities that "reside only in the consciousness" and that would be "wiped away and annihilated" once human sensibility is removed. Behind sensible qualities are the true components of the real world, atoms, whose impinging on the sense organs produces sensory impressions. Hence, for example, the sensation of heat stems from the motion of a "multitude of minute particles" that penetrate human bodies; "their touch as felt by us when they pass through our substance is the sensation we call 'heat.'" (trans. in Drake, *Discoveries and Opinions of Galileo*, New York: Anchor Books, 1957, p. 277). Galileo's stance was clearly rooted in the tradition of ancient atomism, whose most distinguished representatives, such as Democritus and Lucretius, had already stated similar views.

Two documents discovered in the Archives of the Congregation for the Doctrine of the Faith (formerly Holy Office) show that Galileo's atomistic theory was brought to the attention of the Inquisitorial authorities, most likely before the trial of 1633. The first document was found in 1982 by Pietro Redondi and is usually referred to as "G3," from the code appearing on the top of its first page. G3 is a denunciation of the atomism of *The Assayer*. The anonymous author protested that Galileo's interpretation of sensible qualities clashed with the Catholic doctrine of the Eucharist, according to which, after consecration in the Mass, bread and wine become the body and blood of Jesus Christ. This transformation is understood as transubstantiation because it concerns the

Galileo Galilei. SCIENCE PHOTO LIBRARY/PHOTO RESEARCHERS, INC.

substances of bread and wine, whereas their "accidents," or apparent qualities (color, odor, exterior shape), remain unchanged by virtue of a divine miracle. The author of G3 remarked that, according to the terms of Galileo's argument, it would be impossible to separate the accidental properties of bread and wine from their own substances. Indeed, because those accidental properties are regarded as "mere names" and as nonexistent outside

Galilei

human sensory perception, on the basis of Galileo's theory one would be obliged to conclude that "in the Sacrament there are substantial elements of the bread and the wine, which is an error condemned by the Sacred Council of Trent."

Redondi dated G3 to 1624 and attributed it to Orazio Grassi, the Jesuit mathematician against whom Galileo had written *The Assayer.* Redondi also connected the document to the trial of 1633, suggesting that the charge of Copernicanism that motivated the trial was a stratagem devised by Pope Urban VIII (a former friend of Galileo) in order to avoid having the scientist face the more serious accusation of Eucharistic heresy.

Redondi's ascription of G3 to Grassi has been proved to be mistaken, and his thesis concerning the "true" (although disguised) reasons of the trial has been generally rejected by scholars. Nevertheless, Redondi's book triggered a fresh wave of interest in the Galileo affair and renewed investigations into its cultural and political context.

Another document, similar to G3, was discovered by Mariano Artigas in 1999 and has been carefully studied by Artigas himself along with Rafael Martinez and William Shea. This document is placed in the same volume as G3, the volume EE of the collection "Acta et Documenta," where it occupies sheet 291. For this reason it has been called "EE 291."

Like G3, EE 291 is anonymous (it is in Latin while the former is in Italian), and it equally develops a criticism of the theory of sensible qualities expounded in *The Assayer,* which it deems incompatible with the doctrine of the Eucharist. The author of this document has been identified as the Jesuit Melchior Inchofer, who probably was a member of the commission appointed by the pope in the summer of 1632 to examine Galileo's *Dialogue.* Inchofer, a firm opponent of Copernicanism, could have written EE 291 in order to worsen Galileo's position by adding a further charge against him. Thus, the discoveries of G3 and EE 291, besides providing valuable pieces of information on previously unknown episodes of Galileo's life, also opened a new chapter of investigation concerning the difficult relationship between atomism and Eucharistic doctrine.

The Role of Patronage. It is well known that Galileo spent a great part of his mature life, from 1610 until his death in 1642, at the Medici court as mathematician and philosopher of the Grand Duke of Tuscany. Furthermore, even before his return to Florence from Padua (in the autumn of 1610), Galileo had to deal with several patrons in order to promote his career and to obtain academic positions. Indeed, the practice of relying on the support of influential patrons was quite normal at the time. As Richard S. Westfall remarked: "Patronage was perhaps the most pervasive institution of preindustrial society" (1985, p. 29); hence: "the system of patronage [...] was a feature of 17th century life as distinctive as scientific technology is in the 20th century" (1984, p. 200).

For this reason, the last decades have witnessed a growing interest in re-interpreting Galileo's life and achievement in the light of the patronage culture. Richard S. Westfall focused on the role played by patronage in Galileo's relationship with the Accademia dei Lincei (1984) and the Jesuit order (1988) as well as in the controversial episode of the discovery of the phases of Venus (1985), while Frederick Hammond provided a fascinating outline of the connection between Pope Barberini's system of patronage and the Galileo affair.

But the most comprehensive study on this matter is certainly Mario Biagioli's seminal book, *Galileo Courtier.* Biagioli argues that "Galileo's courtly role was integral to his science" (1993, p. 1), because "the court contributed to the cognitive legitimation of the new science by providing venues for the social legitimation of its practitioners" (1993, p. 2). Actually, courtly patronage being "the social world of Galileo's science" (1993, p. 4), the latter was involved in a process of self-fashioning, aimed to work out a fresh social and intellectual image, best fitted to courtly codes and rules. In this process, Galileo "used the resources he perceived in the surrounding environment to construct a new socio-professional identity for himself, to put forward a new natural philosophy, and to develop a courtly audience for it" (1993, p. 5). In short, Biagioli views Galileo "not only as a rational manipulator of the patronage machinery but also as somebody whose discourse, motivations, and intellectual choices were informed by the patronage culture in which he operated throughout his life" (1993, p. 4).

Biagioli's detailed account (based on detailed documentation from primary and secondary sources) mainly concerns Galileo's experience at the Medici court, spanning from 1610 to just after the 1633 trial. The core of his interpretation relies on the assumption that the social legitimation Galileo acquired in the courtly *milieu* assured the cognitive legitimation of his theories.

While innovative and appealing, Biagioli's historiographical proposal runs the strong risk of being sometimes unreliable and implausible. For example, Biagioli views Galileo's Copernican commitment as an outcome of a strategy based on the logic of patronage. As he puts it: "Copernicanism was the 'natural' choice for someone such as Galileo who aspired to a higher socioprofessional status, while the court was the social space that could best legitimize such an unusual socioprofessional identity" (1993, p. 226). Hence, "the increasing commitment to Copernican astronomy that Galileo developed in those years [i. e.

after 1609–1610] may have resulted also from the patronage dynamics that pushed him to defend his discoveries and produce even more of them" (1993, p. 91).

This seems an oversimplified account of the motivations that drove Galileo to embrace the Copernican theory, because it completely ignores the theoretical reasons behind his choice, which were rooted in the interplay between astronomical arguments and the principles of Galileo's "new science of motion." Indeed, by reducing the cognitive acceptance of science to its social legitimation, Biagioli tends to obscure the autonomy of scientific debate. Consequently, he often disregards the multifaceted complexity of history, failing to recognize that ideas follow often their own paths, connected to, but not always dependent on, social features.

The Galileo Affair Revisited. On 10 November 1979, on the occasion of the one hundredth anniversary of the birth of Albert Einstein, before a plenary session of the Pontifical Academy of Sciences, Pope John Paul II delivered an address on the "deep harmony that unites the truths of science with the truth of faith" (*L'Osservatore Romano*, English week edition, November 26, 1979, pp. 9–10). In his speech John Paul II dealt with the trial and condemnation of Galileo, frankly admitting that the scientist "had to suffer a great deal at the hands of men and organs of the Church." John Paul II expressed the hope that "theologians, scholars and historians, animated by a spirit of sincere collaboration, will study the Galileo case more deeply and, in loyal recognition of wrongs from whatever side they come, will dispel the mistrust that still opposes, in many minds, a fruitful concord between science and faith."

As a consequence of this wish, in July 1981, the Vatican constituted a study commission divided into various sections (exegetical, cultural, scientific-epistemological, and historical-juridical). The commission met several times, held a few conferences, and issued a significant number of publications. Its work was declared to be concluded on 31 October 1992, at an audience given by the pope at a plenary session of the Pontifical Academy. On that occasion the pope underlined Galileo's mistake in not presenting the Copernican system as a hypothesis, because "it had not been confirmed by irrefutable proofs" (trans. in Fantoli, 2003, p. 370). Yet John Paul II acknowledged that Galileo's views on scriptural interpretation were sounder than those put forth by the theologians of his epoch. The pope also claimed that the Galileo affair resulted from a "tragic mutual incomprehension" that would have poisoned the subsequent relationship between faith and science, creating the myth of the Church's opposition to the free search for truth. He concluded that "the clarifications furnished by recent historical studies enable us to state that this sad misunderstanding now belongs to the past."

John Paul II's words were of the highest importance, marking a break with the Church's long-held attitude toward Galileo by honestly recognizing the errors committed by the Catholic Church. Nevertheless, some of the arguments put forth by John Paul II suggested a defensive strategy not consonant with that "loyal recognition of wrongs from whatever side they come." It is misleading to blame Galileo for his refusal to consider Copernicanism as a hypothesis while emphasizing his alleged inability to provide definitive evidence in support of the Copernican theory. Indeed, Galileo did not regard Copernicanism as a purely mathematical expedient to predict celestial events. According to his view, in fact, a system of the world should account for the true structure of the universe. At the same time, Galileo was firmly convinced of having good reasons in support of Copernicanism, because observations and theoretical explanations (not only his mistaken theory of tides, but also his new science of motion) confirmed to him that the arguments for the Earth's motion were much stronger than those against it.

Still, it must be remembered that Galileo was not condemned for the inadequacy of his scientific or epistemological position but for exegetical considerations pertaining to the clash between heliocentrism and several passages of the Bible. The epistemological concerns raised by John Paul II were never addressed by the Roman inquisitors, who only focused on the theological consequences of Galileo's Copernicanism.

In conclusion, the Galileo affair is by no means a closed question and continues to be a promising field for historical investigation. Many of its most obscure facets are as of 2007 still in need of clarification, and it also deserves to be carefully and constantly pondered for its worth as a significant memento. As Annibale Fantoli has observed, the Galileo affair "remains, and should remain, 'open', as a severe lesson of humility to the Church at all levels and as a warning, no less rigorous, not to wish to repeat in the present or in the future errors similar to those which have brought about [such a] heavy burden" (2003, p. 373).

SUPPLEMENTARY BIBLIOGRAPHY

The most useful and complete bibliographical resource in the field of Galilean studies is the International Galilean Bibliography, *edited by the Institute and Museum of History of Science in Florence. Covering the entire reception of Galilean work, it lists more than 17,000 records. Available from http://www.imss.fi.it/biblio/ebibgali.html.*

WORKS BY GALILEO

Galileo's Early Notebooks: The Physical Questions. Translated from the Latin with historical and paleographical commentary by

William A. Wallace. Notre Dame, IN: University of Notre Dame Press, 1977.

I documenti del processo di Galileo Galilei. A cura di Sergio M. Pagano. Vatican City: Pontificia Academia Scientiarum, 1984.

Tractatio de praecognitionibus et praecognitis and Tractatio de demonstratione. Transcribed from the Latin autograph by William F. Edwards, with an introduction, notes, and commentary by William A. Wallace. Padua: Antenore, 1988.

The Galileo Affair: A Documentary History. Edited and translated with an introduction and notes by Maurice A. Finocchiaro. Berkeley: University of California Press, 1989.

Sidereus nuncius, or, The Sidereal Messenger. Translated with introduction, conclusions, and notes by Albert Van Helden. Chicago: University of Chicago Press, 1989.

Two New Sciences Including Centers of Gravity and Force of Percussion. Translated with introduction and notes by Stillman Drake. Madison: University of Wisconsin Press, 1974; 2nd ed., Toronto: Wall & Thompson, 1989.

Discorsi e dimostrazioni matematiche intorno a due nuove scienze, attinenti alla meccanica ed i movimenti locali. A cura di Enrico Giusti. Turin, Italy: Einaudi, 1990.

Galileo's Logical Treatises: A Translation, with Notes and Commentary, of His Appropriated Latin Questions on Aristotle's Posterior Analytics. By William A. Wallace. Dordrecht-Boston: Kluwer, 1992.

Sidereus nuncius/Le messager céleste. Texte, traduction et notes établis par Isabelle Pantin. Paris: Les Belles Lettres, 1992.

Galileo on World Systems: A New Abridged Translation and Guide. By Maurice A. Finocchiaro. Berkeley: University of California Press, 1997.

Dialogo sopra i due massimi sistemi del mondo tolemaico e copernicano. Edizione critica e commentata a cura di Ottavio Besomi e Mario Helbing. Padua: Antenore, 1998.

Discorso delle comete. Edizione critica e commentata a cura di Ottavio Besomi e Mario Helbing. Padua: Antenore, 2002.

Le mecaniche. Edizione critica e saggio introduttivo di Romano Gatto. Florence: Olschki, 2002.

Il Saggiatore. Edizione critica e commentata a cura di Ottavio Besomi e Mario Helbing. Padua: Antenore, 2005.

Galileo Galilei's Notes on Motion. Electronic representation of Galilean Manuscript 72. Available from http://www.mpiwg-berlin.mpg.de.

OTHER SOURCES

Artigas, Mariano, Rafael Martinez, and William R. Shea. "New Light on the Galileo Affair?" In *The Church and Galileo,* edited by Ernan McMullin. Notre Dame, IN: University of Notre Dame Press, 2005.

Beretta, Francesco. "Le procès de Galilée et les archives du Saint-Office: Aspects judiciaires et théologiques d'une condamnation célèbre." *Revue des sciences philosophiques et théologiques* 88 (1999): 441–490.

———. "The Documents of Galileo's Trial: Recent Hypotheses and Historical Criticism." In *The Church and Galileo,* edited by Ernan McMullin. Notre Dame, IN: University of Notre Dame Press, 2005.

Biagioli, Mario. *Galileo Courtier: The Practice of Science in the Culture of Absolutism.* Chicago: University of Chicago Press, 1993.

———. *Galileo's Instruments of Credit: Telescopes, Images, Secrecy.* Chicago: University of Chicago Press, 2006.

Blackwell, Richard J. *Galileo, Bellarmine, and the Bible.* Notre Dame, IN: University of Notre Dame Press, 1991.

Bucciantini, Massimo. *Contro Galileo: Alle origini dell'affaire.* Florence: Olschki, 1995.

———. *Galileo e Keplero: Filosofia, cosmologia e teologia nell'età della Controriforma.* Turin, Italy: Einaudi, 2003.

Camerota, Michele, and Mario Helbing. "Galileo and Pisan Aristotelianism: Galileo's *De motu antiquiora* and the *Quaestiones de motu elementorum* of the Pisan Professors." *Early Science and Medicine* 5 (2000): 319–365.

Camerota, Michele. *Galileo Galilei e la cultura scientifica nell'età della Controriforma.* Rome: Salerno, 2004.

Carugo, Adriano, and Alistair C. Crombie. "The Jesuits and Galileo's Ideas of Science and of Nature." *Annali dell'Istituto e Museo di Storia della Scienza di Firenze* 8, no. 2 (1983): 3–67.

Clavelin, Maurice. *Galilée copernicien: Le premier combat (1610–1616).* Paris: Albin Michel, 2004.

Coyne, George V., SJ. "The Church's Most Recent Attempt to Dispel the Galileo Myth." In *The Church and Galileo,* edited by Ernan McMullin. Notre Dame, IN: University of Notre Dame Press, 2005.

Drake, Stillman. *Galileo at Work: His Scientific Biography.* Chicago: University of Chicago Press, 1978.

———. *Galileo's Notes on Motion.* Florence: Istituto e Museo di Storia della Scienza, 1979.

———. *Essays on Galileo and the History and Philosophy of Science.* Selected and introduced by Noel M. Swerdlow and Trevor H. Levere. 3 vols. Toronto: University of Toronto Press, 1999.

Fantoli, Annibale. *Galileo, for Copernicanism and for the Church.* 3rd rev. and enl. ed. Translated by George V. Coyne. Vatican City: Vatican Observatory Publications, 2003.

Feldhay, Rivka. *Galileo and the Church: Political Inquisition or Critical Dialogue?* Cambridge, U.K.: Cambridge University Press, 1995.

Finocchiaro, Maurice A. *Retrying Galileo, 1633–1992.* Berkeley: University of California Press, 2005.

Galilaeana: Journal of Galilean Studies. 2004– . Promoted by the Institute and Museum of History of Science in Florence and edited by Massimo Bucciantini and Michele Camerota. Published annually and specifically devoted to investigating all aspects of the life, work, scientific findings, and fortunes of Galileo Galilei.

Galluzzi, Paolo. *Momento: Studi galileiani.* Rome: Edizioni dell'Ateneo & Bizzarri, 1979.

———, ed. *Novità celesti e crisi del sapere.* Florence: Giunti Barbera, 1984.

Hammond, Frederick. "The Artistic Patronage of the Barberini and the Galileo Affair." In *Music and Science in the Age of Galileo,* edited by Victor Coelho. Dordrecht and Boston: Kluwer, 1992

Machamer, Peter, ed. *The Cambridge Companion to Galileo.* Cambridge, U.K.: Cambridge University Press, 1998.

McMullin, Ernan, ed. *The Church and Galileo.* Notre Dame, IN: University of Notre Dame Press, 2005.

Montesinos, José, and Carlos Solís, eds. *Largo campo di filosofare: Eurosymposium Galileo 2001.* La Orotava, Spain: Fundación Canaria Orotava de Historia de la Ciencia, 2001.

Naylor, Ronald H. "Galileo's Theory of Motion: Processes of Conceptual Change in the Period 1604–1610." *Annals of Science* 34 (1977): 365–392.

———. "Galileo's Theory of Projectile Motion." *Isis* 71 (1980): 550–570.

Palmerino, Carla Rita, and J. M. M. H. Thijssen, eds. *The Reception of Galilean Science of Motion in Seventeenth-Century Europe.* Dordrecht and Boston: Kluwer, 2004.

Pesce, Mauro. *L'ermeneutica biblica di Galileo e le due strade della teologia cristiana.* Rome: Edizioni di Storia e Letteratura, 2005.

Redondi, Pietro. *Galileo: Heretic.* Translated by Raymond Rosenthal. Princeton, NJ: Princeton University Press, 1987.

Renn, Jürgen. "Proofs and Paradoxes: Free Fall and Projectile Motion in Galileo's Physics." In *Exploring the Limits of Preclassical Mechanics,* edited by Peter Damerow et al. New York and Berlin: Springer, 1992.

Renn, Jürgen, ed. *Galileo in Context.* Cambridge, U.K.: Cambridge University Press, 2001.

Shea, William R., and Mariano Artigas. *Galileo in Rome: The Rise and Fall of a Troublesome Genius.* Oxford: Oxford University Press, 2003.

Stabile, Giorgio. "Linguaggio della natura e linguaggio della Scrittura in Galilei: Dalla *Istoria* sulle macchie solari alle lettere copernicane." *Nuncius* 9 (1994): 37–64.

Wallace, William A. "Galileo and the Accademia dei Lincei." In *Novità celesti e crisi del sapere,* edited by Paolo Galuzzi. Florence: Giunti Barbera, 1984.

———. *Galileo and His Sources: The Heritage of the Collegio Romano in Galileo's Science.* Princeton, NJ: Princeton University Press, 1984.

———. *Galileo's Logic of Discovery and Proof: The Background, Content, and Use of His Appropriated Treatises on Aristotle's Posterior Analytics.* Dordrecht and Boston: Kluwer, 1992.

———, ed. *Reinterpreting Galileo.* Washington, DC: Catholic University of America Press, 1986.

Westfall, Richard S. "Science and Patronage: Galileo and the Telescope." *Isis* 76 (1985): 11–30.

———. "Galileo and the Jesuits." In *Metaphysics and Philosophy of Science in the Seventeenth and Eighteenth Centuries: Essays in Honour of Gerd Buchdahl,* edited by Roger S. Woolhouse. Dordrecht and Boston: Kluwer, 1988.

Wisan, Winifred L. "The New Science of Motion: A Study of Galileo's *De motu locali.*" *Archive for the History of Exact Sciences* 13 (1974): 103–306.

Michele Camerota

GARROD, DOROTHY ANNIE ELIZABETH

(*b.* Oxford, United Kingdom, 5 May 1892; *d.* Cambridge, United Kingdom, 18 December 1968), *paleoanthropology, prehistoric archaeology.*

Garrod was the pioneer excavator of the famous Mount Carmel caves, where a long sequence of prehistoric cultures and human fossils was discovered. The fossils and their archaeological context continue to play a major role in the study of human evolution, even after additional modern excavations were carried out in these caves. Most prominent are et-Tabun and es-Skhul where a Neanderthal skeleton and a host of archaic modern humans were uncovered. Her discovery and definition of the Natufian culture, first in Shukbah cave and later in el-Wad cave and terrace, became one of the cornerstones for understanding the transition from foraging to farming in the Fertile Crescent. Dorothy Garrod's academic career followed a stellar trajectory: she became the Disney Professor of Archaeology in the University of Cambridge and the first woman to hold a chair in either of the United Kingdom's ancient universities.

Early Years. Dorothy Annie Elizabeth Garrod was born in 1892 into a late-Victorian English upper-middle-class family, the only daughter with three brothers. Her grandfather Sir Alfred Garrod was a physician, and her father Sir Archibald Garrod was both a physician and a biochemist, while her uncle Alfred Garrod was a physiologist and zoologist. All were Fellows of the Royal Society. On her mother's side, the grandfather Sir Thomas Smith was a distinguished surgeon. Dorothy and her three brothers were expected to carry on the family scientific tradition. In the year of her birth higher education for women was slowly gaining ground as five women's colleges were already functioning at Oxford and Cambridge. Until she was nine years old Dorothy was taught at the family home at Merton in Suffolk by a series of governesses. For an East Anglian family, Cambridge was the natural choice for higher education, and in 1913 she entered Newnham College to study history and classics, as no degree course in archaeology yet existed at either Oxford or Cambridge.

When Dorothy Garrod arrived at Newnham young female students were still denied full membership in the university. Women admitted since 1881 could take only the honors examination for the bachelor of arts degree, called the Tripos at Cambridge, but it would take some twenty years before they were included in the official lists of results, and a further two decades before they were admitted to take degrees (in 1921). Full admission came only in 1948. In this reactionary practice Cambridge and Oxford lagged behind London and some provincial universities where, since the late nineteenth century, women could be full university members.

Garrod

In 1914, her second year at Newnham, World War I broke out and turned her ordered, secure future upside down, as it would for so many of her generation. In 1916 her brother Thomas, twenty-one years old, died of wounds while serving in France. The next year her eldest brother, Alfred Noel, already a qualified doctor aged twenty-nine, was also killed in France while serving with the Royal Army Medical Corps. Basil, the youngest, died just before demobilization in 1919, in the influenza pandemic, which caused more death than the guns of the entire war.

Garrod left Newnham in 1916 with a second-class degree, determined also to play her part in the Great War. She served briefly in the Ministry of Munitions, then followed her brothers to France with the Catholic Women's League, although she did not convert to the faith until 1917. She was demobilized in Germany in 1919 and in her grief she pledged that for her bereaved parents' sake her future life should compensate in achievement for her lost brothers.

She joined her parents in Malta where her father was now head of War Hospitals and it was his inspired suggestion that she should occupy her time and her mind among the island's spectacular prehistoric antiquities. When Archibald Garrod returned to England in 1921 as Regius Professor of Medicine at Oxford, Dorothy registered for the university diploma course in anthropology under the direction of Robert Ranulph Marett. Inspired by him she determined to become a prehistorian specializing in the Old Stone Age, and gained her diploma with distinction in 1921. Among her contemporaries at Oxford was Francis Turville-Petre, who left and went to Palestine and was the first, in 1925, to conduct excavation in the country that beginning in 1918 was under British rule for the ensuing thirty years.

Garrod visited the French painted caves and at Count H. Bégouën's house she met the Abbé Henri Breuil who agreed to take her as his student for two years at the Institut de Paléontologie Humaine in Paris. There she studied the extensive collections of Victor Commont from the Somme gravels, where in the mid-nineteenth century Jacques Boucher de Perthes first identified the flint handaxes (which are shaped bifacially and often have a pointed tip) as the Lower Paleolithic Abbevillian, Chellean, and Acheulean cultures. While working in the institute basement she discovered shared experiences with the paleontologist Pierre Teilhard de Chardin, a Jesuit priest. Garrod was now finding her Catholic faith hard to reconcile with her new knowledge of human prehistory. Her intellectual honesty obliged her to admit to Breuil that the Somme gravels left her baffled. It also caused her to withdraw from the church. Teilhard de Chardin, twelve years her senior, had reasoned his way through the conundrum to his own satisfaction and his philosophy of evolution showed her a way back to her faith.

In the summer of 1921 she participated in an excavation with Louis Didon at Abri Labattut, near Périgueux, in southwestern France. At their hotel she met the American anthropologist George Grant MacCurdy from Yale University, the founder of the American School of Prehistoric Research. His friendship with Garrod would have profound consequences both for her future and her excavations in Mount Carmel. Garrod continued to gain field experience by working on other French digs such as La Quina. After returning to England and studying local collections from Upper Paleolithic sites dispersed in various museums, she completed and published her book *The Upper Palaeolithic Age in Britain* (1926). The book was published by the Clarendon Press of Oxford University and Garrod gained a BSc from the university as a result of that research.

Excavations in Gibraltar and the "Glozel Affair." The publication of her book established Garrod as a significant figure in British prehistoric archaeology, and as a result Breuil proposed that she should dig the Devil's Tower rock shelter, which he had discovered in Gibraltar, just 350 meters from Forbes Quarry, where the first Neanderthal skull in Europe had been found in 1848, although it was not recognized as such until 1907. Garrod's excavations from 1925 to 1926 unearthed a Late Mousterian industry as well as the frontal bone and left parietal of a human skull similar to the juvenile Neanderthal from La Quina.

In 1927 Garrod was invited to be a member of an international commission of inquiry into the "Glozel affair." This was supposedly a discovery made by a farmer with an interest in archaeology of a collection of inscribed clay tablets, Bronze Age pottery, and Paleolithic animal engravings and tools, which he claimed was evidence of an ancient indigenous "Glozelian" civilization. French scholars had divided opinions and several, including the Abbé Breuil, were not persuaded of their originality. Garrod, trying to keep an open mind, and her fellow male commissioners were invited to dig at the site for three days. Glozelian objects conveniently appeared on the second and third days. Garrod, while checking their trench for evidence of suspected interference, was even accused by a local amateur archaeologist of manufacturing evidence herself to discredit the site. Despite the commission's verdict of fraud and a police raid that found unfinished objects on the Fradin farm, the Glozel affair has proved curiously persistent. Dating by thermoluminescence in the 1970s produced confusing results and revived the controversy, and even after her death accusations against Garrod were repeated.

Garrod

Dorothy Annie Elizabeth Garrod. CORBIS.

Excavations in Mt. Carmel. A fragmentary human skull found in 1925 by Francis Turville-Petre in Zuttiyeh cave in Wadi Amud, near the sea of Galillee in Palestine, convinced MacCurdy of the archaeological importance of the Levant. While visiting Oxford in 1927, his friend Sir John Linton Myres, chair of the Council of the British School of Archaeology in Jerusalem, proposed that Garrod be admitted to the British School as a student to continue research in Palestine. The years between the two world wars had been the formative period in archaeology in Palestine, with research ranging from the Stone Age to the Islamic period as a result of the establishment of the Department of Antiquities, the British School of Archaeology, the Hebrew University, and the presence in Jerusalem of the French École Biblique.

Garrod arrived in Palestine in 1928 and was informed by the Jesuit Père Alexis Mallon about the cave of Shukbah in the Wadi en-Natuf. But before she started there she went on a survey to Iraq where, in the Sulaymaniyah area, she found the Zarzi cave, which she later excavated. Back in Palestine the same year she dug in Shukbah cave where she identified above Mousterian and sterile deposits a layer containing a Mesolithic industry that she named Natufian. The assemblage of stone tools—consisting of sickle blades for harvesting, lunates (known as parts of hunting tools), and perforators for drilling holes in various materials, as well as mortars and pestles employed in food preparation—led her to suggest that the producers of the Natufian were the first farmers. Her interpretation of the Natufian subsistence activities has been alternately rejected and adopted several times since 1928.

Returning to Zarzi later in 1928, she found that the cave contained three identifiable layers: Layer A was a mixture of pottery fragments and flint implements; layer B produced a microlithic Upper Paleolithic industry with notched blades, scrapers, and geometric types, known today as a Late Pleistocene Zarzian culture. In the other two Hazar Merd caves (located 8 kilometers from Zarzi), she found both the Zarzian and evidence for Mousterian occupations, later compared by American archaeologist Ralph Solecki (the excavator of Shanidar cave in the 1950s) to his layer D, the level of the Neanderthal burials now roughly dated to 60,000 years.

In 1927 the British Mandatory government decided that Haifa should become the main port of Palestine, and the construction of a port would require massive quantities of good quality stone. The plan was to open a quarry in the cliffs of Wadi el Mughara in Mount Carmel. However, following a survey by the local inspector, Charles Lambert (a numismatist working for the Department of Antiquities in Jerusalem) was sent to test el-Wad cave, one of several along the Wadi. His trial trenches uncovered rich Natufian deposits including art objects. Following publication in the *Illustrated London News,* the sites were saved by a decision taken in London, and Garrod was invited to excavate three caves.

The excavations in el-Wad, es-Skhul, and et-Tabun caves were conducted during many months from 1929 through 1934. Each of the sites provided a wealth of information on past prehistoric cultures and after more than seven decades, most of it is still relevant for understanding the prehistory of the Levant. In el-Wad cave and terrace Garrod exposed thick Natufian deposits along with a cemetery containing numerous burials. Several skeletons bore body decorations. The rich stone tool assemblages contained sickle blades and lunates shaped in two major types—with Helwan (or bifacial) and abrupt retouch, bone tools, beads and pendants made of bones, teeth, and marine shells (with a dominance of *Dentalium* sp.). She subdivided the deposits into two periods, Early and Late Natufian, and this basic rough subdivision still holds in the twenty-first century.

The underlying layers were a Late Upper Paleolithic industry called Atlitian, and two layers of Levantine Aurignacian, which is similar to the classical Aurignacian of western Europe, with some bone and antler tools, pendants made of teeth as well as nosed and carinate scrapers and the special el-Wad point (formerly known as the Font Yves point and shown to have been used as a spear point or arrowhead).

Garrod

The layers beneath contain the stone tool assemblage of what she thought were the earliest Upper Paleolithic industry. This was later designated as a "Transitional Industry" with blades and scrapers and a few Emireh points (triangular flakes or Levallois points with basal bifacial retouch that were used as spear points). The interpretation in her time was that this archaeological entity expressed the technological and cultural transition from the Mousterian (Middle Paleolithic) to the new era of the Upper Paleolithic.

The excavation in Tabun cave produced a very long sequence, some 23 meters deep, still one of the deepest prehistoric caves in the world. The chimney of this karstic cave (formed by the dissolution of the limestone by water in the geological past) was also filled with archaeological deposits, mainly attributed to the late Mousterian. The first layer (B) inside the cave contained some rockfall that entered the chimney and a rich Late Mousterian industry with well-shaped Levallois points. Layer C was characterized by numerous superpositioned hearths resulting from using wood as the main combustible. The lithic industry was dominated by flakes often produced from uni- and bidirectional cores, and rare points. The layer below this, layer D, demonstrated an additional change with a proliferation of Levallois blades.

The early part of the sequence contained rich and thick deposits of the Acheulo-Yabrudian layer E (containing numerous thick flake scrapers and small bifaces with a proliferation of blades in a couple of horizons later named Amudian). Underlying this was layer F with typical Late or Upper Acheulean bifaces and at the base an older flake-dominated industry attributed to the Clactonian/Tayacian.

One of the most striking discoveries was the skeleton of a woman, considered to be a Neanderthal, in an unclear stratigraphic position according to Garrod's own observations. It could have been a grave dug down from layer B, or a burial attributed to layer C. A human jaw found at the base of layer C was compared and found to be similar to the human relics from Skhul, where all were considered archaic modern humans similar to the skeletons discovered during the early 1930s by René Neuville and Moshe Stekelis in Qafzeh cave, near Nazareth.

The excavations at Skhul cave, essentially conducted by Theodore D. McCown (with Garrod's assistance), uncovered a deposit about 2 meters thick containing several burials, associated with a Mousterian lithic industry that resembled the assemblage of layer C at Tabun. The human type was first identified as being different from the woman from Tabun, however, later all the human remains were incorporated by McCown and Sir Arthur Keith under the term *Paleanthropus palestinensis*, as a particular population that existed in the Levant.

In addition, Dorothea Bate, a close colleague of Garrod and a respected paleontologist who studied the fauna from these sites, recognized a change that she labeled a "faunal break" between layer B and layers C–D in Tabun. She attributed this break to the shift from interglacial to glacial conditions in the Near East. Only with the proliferation of paleoclimatic information, and the current thermoluminescence and electronic spin resonance dating for many of the cave sites in this region, has it been possible to support her proposal.

Professor in Cambridge and Excavations in Lebanon. Publication of *The Stone Age of Mount Carmel* (1937–1939) on the Mount Carmel excavations, brief periods of fieldwork in Anatolia and Bulgaria, and the outbreak of World War II (in which she served, with other archaeologists, in the interpretation of aerial photographs of occupied Europe), then her unexpected election as Disney Professor of Archaeology at Cambridge University, all combined to keep Garrod from any major participation in field archaeology for over twenty years. Among her achievements during her tenure as Disney Professor of Archaeology (1939–1952) was to advance the study of prehistory at Cambridge University, ensuring that archaeology and anthropology was recognized as a full degree course. Nevertheless, retirement enabled her to plan a return to the Levant to attempt a resolution of the chronological sequence of the Late Lower and entire Middle Paleolithic periods in this region.

In 1958 Garrod and British archaeologist Diana Kirkbride began digging the Abri Zumoffen on the 15-meter shoreline at Adlun, and in the large Mugharet el-Bezez cave. At this time, prior to the introduction of new dating techniques such as thermoluminescence and electron spin resonance, correlations with raised Mediterranean beaches seemed the safest chronological model.

Abri Zumoffen contained mainly the Amudian industry (as Garrod had defined it in her reanalysis of Tabun cave layer E) while Bezez cave preserved both an Acheulo-Yabrudian assemblage as well as a Mousterian of the Tabun D-type. Between two seasons Garrod and her colleague Germaine Henri-Martin studied the cave of Ras el-Kelb where the brecciated deposits were the remainders of the site that was partially destroyed by building the coastal railway. Garrod observed that the Mousterian stone implements from this site resembled those of Tabun layer C and the layers accumulated on the 6-meter beach above sea level could be attributed to the last interglacial.

Last Years. In 1962 Garrod delivered the Huxley Lecture in London, presenting her model of the evolution of the Middle Paleolithic of the Levant. She continued the excavations at Bezez cave with great effort as her health deteriorated, but in 1966 she broke her femur in a fall in her French garden. Extended periods in France and London now began. Nevertheless, an interim report on the Bezez was completed and by 1968 she was in London working on the final report. The Society of Antiquaries awarded her their Gold Medal that spring. In summer 1968 her health continued to decline and wanting the comfort of her faith and of her friends, she was moved to a Catholic nursing home in Cambridge and died there on 18 December 1968, aged seventy-six.

In retrospect, Dorothy Garrod was one of the pioneers of prehistoric research in the Levant and her publications not only outlined the main phases of the cultural evolution of the region, including major transitions, but also determined some of the questions with which later generations are dealing. The results of her Tabun stratigraphy (extended by the ensuing excavations conducted by Arthur Jelinek and Avraham Ronen from 1968 onward) facilitated the formulation of the sequence of Middle Paleolithic entities, called today Tabun B-type, C-type, and D-type, with the understanding that within each there is a technological and typological variability, as shown by additional excavated sites. However, the geochronology of the layers at Tabun cave was found to be much older. The Acheulo-Yabrudian beginning much earlier, about 450,000 years ago, with the Middle Paleolithic beginning about 250,000 to 220,000 years ago and ending with the onset of the Upper Paleolithic around 47,000 to 45,000 years ago.

Garrod's contributions to the later periods were mainly in defining Upper Paleolithic cultures and phases (with René Neuville) and reconstituting the excavated assemblage of Emireh cave (dug by Francis Turville-Petre) as the characteristic "Traditional Industry." This meant that the makers of these stone tool assemblages were most probably modern humans. An additional important contribution was the definition of the Natufian culture, which dates to the end of the Pleistocene, and its main chronological subdivision. This is now the best-known culture of a complex society of foragers whose descendants were the first real Neolithic farmers in the Levant. The issue of whether the Natufians were the first cereal cultivators is still hotly debated. Other sites provide the needed detailed information, but the intuitive proposal of Garrod is still with us. In sum, after more than seventy-five years, a major part of her field observations and written contributions are still serving the prehistorians of the region.

BIBLIOGRAPHY

WORKS BY GARROD

The Upper Palaeolithic Age in Britain. Oxford: Clarendon Press, 1926.

With Dorothea M. Bate, Theodore McCown, and Arthur Keith. *The Stone Age of Mount Carmel.* 2 vols. Oxford: Clarendon Press, 1937–1939.

"The Upper Palaeolithic in the Light of Recent Discovery." *Proceedings of the Prehistoric Society* 4 (1938): 1–26. An early review that should be compared to the next one.

"The Relations between South-West Asia and Europe in the Later Palaeolithic Age." *Journal of World History* 1 (1953): 13–38.

"The Mugharet el Emireh in Lower Galilee: Type Station of the Emiran Industry." *Journal of the Royal Anthropological Institute* 85 (1955): 141–162.

"Notes sur le Paléolithique supérieur du Moyen Orient." *Bulletin de la Société Préhistorique Française* 54 (1957): 439–446.

The Natufian Culture: The Life and Economy of a Mesolithic People in the Near East. London: British Academy, 1958.

"The Middle Palaeolithic of the Near East and the Problem of Mount Carmel." *Journal of the Royal Anthropological Institute* 92 (1962): 232–259.

With Grahame Clark. *Primitive Man in Egypt, Western Asia and Europe: In Palaeolithic Times.* Cambridge, U.K.: Cambridge University Press, 1965.

OTHER SOURCES

Bar-Yosef, Ofer. "The Chronology of the Middle Paleolithic of the Levant." In *Neandertals and Modern Humans in Western Asia,* edited by Takeru Akazawa, Kenichi Aoki, and Ofer Bar-Yosef. New York: Plenum Press, 1998.

———. "Natufian: A Complex Society of Foragers." In *Beyond Foraging and Collecting: Evolutionary Change in Hunter-Gatherer Settlement Systems,* edited by Ben Fitzhugh and Junko Habu. New York: Kluwer Academic, 2002.

Bar-Yosef, Ofer, and Jane Callander. "Dorothy Annie Elizabeth Garrod 1892–1968." In *Breaking Ground: Pioneer Women Archaeologists,* edited by G. M. Cohen and M. S. Jukowsky. Ann Arbor: University of Michigan Press, 2004.

Davies, William, and Ruth Charles, eds. *Dorothy Garrod and the Progress of the Palaeolithic: Studies in the Prehistoric Archaeology of the Near East and Europe.* Oxford: Oxbow Books, 1999.

Gorring-Morris, N., and A. Belfer-Cohen. *More than Meets the Eye: Studies on Upper Palaeolithic Diversity in the Near East.* Oxford: Oxbow Books, 2003.

Jelinek, A. J. "The Tabun Cave and Paleolithic Man in the Levant." *Science* 216 (1982): 1369–1375.

Kozlowski, Janusz K. *Excavation in the Bacho Kiro Cave (Bulgaria): Final Report.* Translated by Stephen and Ewa Lee. Warsaw: Panstwowe Wydawnictwo Naukowe, 1982.

Mercier, N., H. Valladas, G. Valladas, et al. "TL Dates of Burnt Flints from Jelinek's Excavations at Tabun and Their Implications." *Journal of Archaeological Science* 22 (1995): 495–510.

Roe, Derek A. *Adlun in the Stone Age: The Excavations of D. A. E. Garrod in the Lebanon, 1958–1963.* Oxford: British Archaeological Reports, 1983.

Smith, Pamela J. "Dorothy Garrod, First Woman Professor at Cambridge." *Antiquity* 74, no. 283 (2000): 131–136.

Wahida, G. A. "The Zarzian Industry of the Zagros Mountains." In *Dorothy Garrod and the Progress of the Palaeolithic,* edited by William Davies and Ruth Charles. Oxford: Oxbow Books, 1999, pp. 181–208.

Ofer Bar-Yosef
Jane Callander

GARZONI, LEONARDO S. J. (*b.* Venice, Italy, 1543, *d.* Venice, 10 March 1592), *magnetism.*

The little data researchers have on Garzoni's life are the brief notices registered on official documents of the Society of Jesus. From these sources it is known that Garzoni was born into a patrician family and that he began his philosophical studies before 1565. Around 1565, he joined a congregation near the Jesuits' College in Brescia and entered the Society of Jesus in 1567 or 1568. In 1568, he lectured in logic in Parma, and in 1573, he was a third-year student in theology in Padua. On 9 June 1579, he took his four vows in Brescia and from 1579 lived, as a confessor, in Venice. After a stay in Verona (around 1588) he came back to Venice, where he died.

Garzoni's only extant work, the *Due trattati sopra la natura, e le qualità della calamita,* is the first known example of a modern treatment of magnetic phenomena. Written in years near 1580 and never published, the treatise was widely disseminated immediately after Garzoni's death. In particular, Garzoni is referred to as an expert in magnetism by Niccolò Cabeo, whose *Philosophia Magnetica* (1629) is simply a readjustment of Garzoni's work. More interestingly, Garzoni's treatise was known also to Giovan Battista Della Porta and William Gilbert. Even if the Jesuit is never mentioned, both Della Porta's *Magia Naturalis* (1589) and Gilbert's *De Magnete* (1600) show a heavy dependence on Garzoni's treatise. In the case of Della Porta, there was blatant plagiarism, as has already been remarked upon by Niccolò Cabeo (*Philosophia Magnetica,* Praefatio ad lectorem) and Niccolò Zucchi (*Philosophia magnetica* ..., fols. 62v–63r).

The *Due trattati sopra la natura, e le qualità della calamita* is composed of two parts, or treatises. In the first treatise, consisting of seventeen chapters, Garzoni works out the details of his theory of magnetism. The second treatise is divided into two sections. The first section contains a description of a number of experiments, presented as ninety conclusions or doubts, and thirty-nine corollaries. The second section contains the theoretical interpretation of the experiments.

After a few short remarks about the crucial role of experiments in a scientific investigation, Garzoni outlines the aims and contents of the work: The author's goal is to explain the two principal magnetic effects displayed by the lodestone, namely, its tendency to the poles and its interaction with other lodestones, or with iron. In fact, Garzoni says, the cause of every magnetic effect can be understood once the common cause of both the motion that aligns the stone in the direction of the poles and the motion that aligns two stones relative to each other is understood. Garzoni's theory can be summarized as follows. First, the author ascertains that the motion toward the poles is a natural one, ascribes it to an internal mover—namely, the substantial form of the lodestone—and says that, in order to carry out the motion, the form needs an appropriate instrument, which he calls the "quality of two faces." The lodestone naturally possesses the quality, or verticity, while iron can acquire it from the stone, thus becoming magnetized. Iron naturally possesses a similar quality, or "quality of one face," by which means it is disposed to receive verticity from a lodestone. Once magnetized, iron behaves exactly like a lodestone. Of particular interest are the chapters devoted to the description of the way verticity moves the lodestone and the way it alters surrounding bodies, virtually propagating itself outside the stone, in the so-called sphere of activity. To explain the different ways in which the quality exists in the stone, in the medium and in the iron, Garzoni draws a comparison with light, in line with the medieval tradition of the perspectivists. Other interesting features arise out of the explanation of the double nature of magnetic quality, and out of the problem of the location of the (celestial) magnetic poles.

In the second treatise, entirely devoted to the experiment, Garzoni lists a number of magnetic phenomena. The first experimental result listed is the one showing the proper alignment of the lodestone to the poles. Some observations about the interaction between lodestones follow, and Garzoni then considers the interaction between the lodestone and iron. A long series of experiments devoted to the transmission of the magnetic virtue is discussed. The observations are very carefully managed. Garzoni then considers the diffusion of the magnetic virtue inside the stone, outside it, and inside iron. These results are obtained by magnetizing bodies of different shapes and sizes. In particular, Garzoni considers the behavior of magnetized iron dust. The behavior of iron placed in the sphere of action of one or more lodestones is subsequently investigated. In this case, the experiments are also managed with bodies of different shape and size.

In subsequent experiments, Garzoni studies the external diffusion of magnetic virtue by displacing a magnetic needle within the sphere of action. At every point, the direction of the needle gives the direction of the magnetic virtue: In fact, the virtue of the needle is far lower than the virtue of the lodestone, so that the action of the needle on the stone is negligible. The configuration that Garzoni obtains coincides with the one theorized in the first treatise, where the accompanying diagrams look remarkably modern in their outline of the lines of propagation of verticity. Garzoni then studies the behavior of two magnetized needles. Given that, in this case, the action is not negligible, the effects are very different from those recorded before, unless one of the needles is considerably smaller (or weaker) than the other. In this case, one observes the same results as when using a needle and a lodestone. Then Garzoni investigates the action of nonmagnetized iron, the properties of the quality of one face, and the alteration of the quality of one and two faces. Finally, he quickly mentions spontaneous magnetization. The first section of the second treatise ends with two marginal observations about the loss of verticity.

BIBLIOGRAPHY

WORKS BY GARZONI

Trattati della calamita, a cura di M. Ugaglia. Milano: Franco Angeli, 2005. Edition and analysis of the only extant manuscript (Milan, Biblioteca Ambrosiana, S 82 SUP) of Garzoni's treatise.

OTHER SOURCES

Baldini, Ugo. *Legem impone subactis: Studi su filosofia e scienza dei gesuiti in Italia 1540–1632.* Roma: Bulzoni, 1992. The book contains the first mention of the surviving copy of Garzoni's treatise, together with a discussion of Garzoni's role within the Society of Jesus.

Bertelli, Timoteo. "Sopra Pietro Peregrino di Maricourt e la sua epistola de magnete. Memoria Prima." *Bullettino di Bibliografia e di Storia delle scienze matematiche e fisiche* I (1868): 1–32.

———. "Sulla Epistola di Pietro Peregrino di Maricourt e sopra alcuni trovati e teorie magnetiche del secolo XIII. Memoria Seconda." *Bullettino di Bibliografia e di Storia delle scienze matematiche e fisiche* I (1868): 65–139 and 319–420. Rome: *Bibliotheca Scriptorum Societatis Jesu,* 1676. The two contributions contain an attempt to reconstruct the contents of the not yet uncovered treatise and to assess its role in the history of magnetism.

Cabeo, Niccolò. *Philosophia Magnetica in qua magnetis natura penitus explicatur.* Ferrariae, 1629.

Petrus Peregrinus de Maricourt. *Opera,* edited by Loris Sturlese and Ron B. Thomson. Pisa: Scuola Normale Superiore, 1995. It contains the *Epistula de magnete* (1269), the only organic treatment of magnetism circulating before Garzoni's time (and well known to Garzoni).

Ugaglia, Monica. "The Science of Magnetism before Gilbert: Leonardo Garzoni's Treatise on the Loadstone." *Annals of Science* 63 (2006): 59–84.

Zucchi, Niccolò. *Philosophia magnetica per principia propria proposita et ad prima in suo genere promota.* Rome: Biblioteca Nazionale Vittorio Emanuele II, Fondo Gesuitico 1323.

Monica Ugaglia

GASSENDI, PIERRE

(*b.* Champtercier, France, 22 January 1592; *d.* Paris, France, 24 October 1655), *natural philosophy, atomism, astronomy, optics, mechanics.* For the original article on Gassendi see *DSB,* vol. 5.

Since 1972, when Bernard Rochot wrote his entry for the *DSB,* Gassendi has been the object of increasing scholarly attention, and new light has been shed on virtually all aspects of his multifaceted philosophical and scientific activity. Besides adding some factual information to Rochot's biographical account, the present postscript aims at providing a reassessment of four crucial issues, namely:

1. the relation between Gassendi's epistemological convictions and his scientific practice;
2. the nonreductionist character of Gassendi's matter theory, in which a crucial role is played by seminal virtues and organizing principles;
3. Gassendi's engagement in defense of Galileo Galilei's theory of motion, of which he fully understood the cosmological implications;
4. and, finally, Gassendi's problematic attempts to derive the Galilean law of free fall from a physical explanation of gravity and to reconcile the principle of inertia with the laws governing the motion of atoms.

Early Intellectual Life. Second child of Antoine Gassend and Françoise Fabry, Pierre begun his schooling at Digne, and in 1602 was sent to Aix-en-Provence, where he studied philosophy under Father Philibert Fesaye and theology under Professor Raphaelis. In 1613, he was appointed principal of the College of Digne and professor of rhetoric. One year later he obtained the doctorate in theology at Avignon and was elected canon of the Cathedral of Digne. Ordained a priest in 1616, he became a professor of philosophy at Aix in 1617. In 1618 he started his astronomical observations under the guidance of Joseph Gaultier. The first entry in Gassendi's astronomical diary records the observation of the comets made in Gaultier's company in November 1618.

When, in 1621, the Jesuits took over teaching at Aix, Gassendi decided to return to Digne. His trips to Paris (1624, 1628, 1629, 1631) were marked by some important encounters: Marin Mersenne introduced him into his circle; the brothers Pierre and Jacques Dupuy, wardens of the king's library, admitted him into their academy; with Elia Diodati, Gabriel Naudé and François de La Mothe Le Vayer he was to form the so-called *Tétrade;* with Ismael Bouillau he discussed astronomical matters; and with François Luiller he traveled through the Low Countries between 1628 and 1629.

However, the most important figure in Gassendi's early intellectual life was certainly his first mentor, Nicolas Fabri de Peiresc, counselor to the Parliament of Provence and owner of an impressive library and of a collection of instruments. Peiresc offered Gassendi material and intellectual support, and the two shared an interest in humanism, philology, numismatics, cartography, astronomy, optics, and physiology.

Peiresc was always the first to be informed about the evolution of Gassendi's Epicurean project. In 1626, Gassendi announced to Pieresc his intention to write an apology of Epicurus; and in 1631 he communicated his decision to extend his project beyond the field of ethics to include all of Epicurus's philosophy (*De vita et doctrina Epicuri*). In the course of 1634, Gassendi sent to Peiresc eight manuscript quires (*cahiers*) containing the fruit of his work. These *cahiers*, which contained an apology *De vita et moribus Epicuri* (an updated version of which was published in 1647) and a preface *De philosophia Epicuri universe*, are now lost, but a manuscript containing a copy of the preface resurfaced at the British Library.

Several interests and engagements interfered with the elaboration of the Epicurean project. In 1629 Gassendi wrote an astronomical treatise, the *Parhelia;* in 1630 he published the *Epistolica exercitatio*, an attack against Robert Fludd written at Mersenne's request; in 1631, he observed the transit of Mercury; in 1634, he composed the *De veritate* against Herbert de Cherbury and the first letter *De apparente magnitudine solis humilis et sublimis* (published in 1636).

Contrary to what has sometimes been maintained, the *Exercitatio* of 1630 was not intended as an attack against alchemy as such, but rather against the synthesis of alchemy, kabbalah, and religion operated by Fludd. In the *Exercitatio* a distinction is drawn between "false alchemy" and "real alchemy." While rejecting Fludd's interpretation of Genesis in alchemical terms, and his identification of God with the Platonic world soul, Gassendi recognized the importance of alchemy for natural philosophy, and even expressed the conviction that the transmutation of metals would become possible, if the seeds of gold were discovered. In the *Exercitatio* one also finds the hypothesis, which reappears in the *Syntagma,* that the generation and transformation of metals resemble biological processes, as they are brought about by seminal powers.

Both the *Exercitatio* against Fludd and *De veritate* against Herbert de Cherbury echo the epistemological stance already taken in Gassendi's *Exercitationes* of 1624. In all these works Gassendi chastises the ambition of arriving at universal truths by means of a purely intellectual act (be this the *intellectus principiorum* of the scholastics or the *instinctus naturalis* of Herbert de Cherbury) and opposes to the dogmatic ideal of a *scientia per causas* his own model of a *philosophia aperta et sensibilis,* based on a direct reading of the book of nature. When, in March 1634, Gassendi left Digne for an extended sojourn at Peiresc's villa at Aix-en-Provence, the two men engaged in an intense scientific activity that perfectly conformed to Gassendi's ideal of a descriptive-cumulative science. Between 1634 and 1636, they undertook studies of meteorological phenomena as well as geological investigations concerning the nature of stones, minerals and fossils, the formation of caverns, and the circulation of waters; they planned to produce a lunar atlas, for which Claude Mellan began to make the engravings; most importantly, Gassendi followed Peiresc in his numerous microscopic observations and in his study of the physiology of vision.

Peiresc had acquired a Drebbel microscope as early as 1623, and he used the instrument to test recent anatomical and physiological discoveries, including William Harvey's discovery of the circulation of blood and Gaspare Aselli's discovery of the lactic vessels. Interestingly the two findings appeared to be incompatible with one another, for Aselli believed, in accordance to Galen's view, that these vessels transported intestinal lymphatic material to the liver, the organ in which blood was produced. Gassendi himself found it difficult to dismiss Galen's authority. While in 1629 he thought that Harvey's theory of the continuous circulation of blood was probable and well-founded, in the *Syntagma* he would eventually endorse some of Jean Riolan's and Guy Patin's objections. The anatomical observations conducted with Peiresc were to be invoked in the *Disquisitio metaphysica* and in the *Syntagma* as a proof of the existence of final causes in the biological realm. Peiresc and Gassendi also anatomized the eyes of many different animals, seeking a physiological, rather than psychological, explanation of the problem of retinal inversion. After being inverted by the convex crystalline, the image was reinverted by the concave retina and reflected back into the vitreous humor.

The Microscope and the Atoms. If Peiresc's enthusiasm for the microscope had been essentially directed toward its descriptive capacity, Gassendi appreciated it mostly for its analytic potential, viewing it as an ally in the rehabilitation of atomism. Waiting for the day that microscopes would become so powerful as to make atoms visible, Gassendi used the available instruments to collect empirical evidence in favor of his theory of matter. This evidence was, however, somewhat ambivalent. If applied to little organisms, the microscope revealed an immense variety of different forms underneath a seemingly homogeneous surface: the fact that an insect no bigger than a dot, when put under a magnifying lens, displayed a great variety of organs, appeared as an illustration that innumerable atomic shapes could combine to form compound bodies. The microscopic observation of salts and minerals suggested instead that nature repeated its basic patterns from the macroscopic world down to the atom. In 1636, after a visit to saline springs, Gassendi wrote to Peiresc that the microscopic observation of salts seemed to validate the principles of Epicurean philosophy: the fact that these cubic, hexahedral, or octahedral solids were made out of components of the same shape allowed for the conclusion that this shape was preserved up to the level of atoms. His observation of salts, moreover, further strengthened Gassendi's belief in the existence of seminal virtues in charge of organizing the corpuscles according to pre-established patterns.

Since his visit to the chemist Jan Baptista van Helmont, in 1629, Gassendi had begun to embed ideas of Paracelsian extraction within his Epicurean program, a task rendered easier by Lucretius's use of the expression "seeds of things" (*semina rerum*) to designate atoms. Of particular influence on Gassendi's treatment of so-called natural *res mixtae* (animals, plants, and fossils) was the Paracelsian synthesis provided in Petrus Severinus's *Idea medicinae* (1571). In the *Syntagma,* Gassendi explains that growth and internal organization of all beings, from metals and crystals upward, are due to seminal forces which are not immaterial principles, but rather physical agents composed of very active corpuscles endowed by God with a program. But how exactly the "divine and incomparable Architect" has set up the "occult internal economy" that leads to the formation of the seeds responsible for the generation of living forms remains unknown, as Gassendi professes in his *Syntagma.*

However, he explicitly adopts Severinus's term *mechanical spirits* to account for this process. There is, from the historians' point of view, some irony in this seemingly oxymoronic expression. It has often and convincingly been argued that Gassendi's atomism was not of a mechanical sort, if by "mechanical" we understand the Cartesian program of reducing all upper-level phenomena to the structure of, or collisions by, material corpuscles. But before Robert Boyle popularized the term *mechanical philosophy,* this predicate had a wide variety of meanings. In fact, when invoking Severinus's "mechanical spirits," Gassendi meant intelligent agents, which had nothing in common with René Descartes's inert chunks of matter.

Astronomical Observations and Optical Puzzles. A further influence on Gassendi's matter theory was astronomy and in particular the observations he carried out in the 1630s. In his *Admonitio* of 1629, Johannes Kepler had predicted a solar transit of Mercury for 7 November 1631, explaining how the shadow of the planet on the solar disk could be used to calculate its apparent size. Gassendi, who was in Paris at the time, was the only person to observe the phenomenon predicted by Kepler. Using a telescope, he

Pierre Gassendi. *Copper engraving of Pierre Gassendi.* © CORBIS.

projected the image of the sun on a paper screen, and on 7 November he saw a tiny shadow appear on the solar disk. As he explained in the *Mercurius in Sole visus,* the smallness of the apparent size of Mercury seemed to indicate that the solar system was much bigger than so far believed. The observation of the transit of Mercury triggered Gassendi's interest in optical questions. Between 1636 and 1641 he performed various experiments to measure the shadows cast by a larger or smaller apparent sun. In his letters *De apparente magnitudine solis humilis et sublimis,* Gassendi invoked the corpuscular composition of light rays and atmosphere to account for some curious optical phenomena. He explained that when the sun is at the horizon more light rays are absorbed by the atmosphere than when it is at the zenith, so that less luminosity reaches the eye. This provokes a dilation of the pupil, which makes the sun appear larger. The optical experiments further reinforced Gassendi's conviction that natural philosophy cannot rely exclusively on mathematical reasoning, which is often misleading: that the midday sun produces the smallest shadows contradicts the principles of geometrical optics, which would require that the shadow cast by the greater apparent sun (i.e., the horizon sun) be smaller than the one cast by the smaller apparent sun (i.e., the sun at the zenith).

Atoms, Mechanics, and Cosmology. When Peiresc died, on 24 June 1637, Gassendi was so devastated that he interrupted his scholarly activity as well as his epistolary contacts for nearly two years. In 1638, however, he encountered the new governor of Provence, Louis de Valois, who was to become his new protector. The two men entertained a very dense correspondence. Besides keeping de Valois informed about the advancement of his research, Gassendi devised for him a philosophy course, articulated in fifty-nine letters written between October 1641 and November 1642. The course followed the contents and the structure of the *De vita et doctrina Epicuri.* Gassendi started with an apology for Epicurus, continued with a historical analysis of various philosophical traditions, then offered a history of dialectics, and finally engaged in a reconstruction of Epicurus's thought, notably of his canonics and physics. The letters reveal how different Gassendi's relation with de Valois was from that with Peiresc. He treated the new mentor with the respect due to a prince and the benevolence due to an eager, but not particularly talented student.

In October 1640, de Valois witnessed a spectacular event of which he was also the sponsor: Gassendi left the port of Marseille on a galley to perform an experiment imagined by Galileo in the *Dialogo.* Gassendi verified that a ball dropped from the top of the mast landed at its foot no matter whether the ship was at rest or sailing at high speed. The experiment had important cosmological implications, for it falsified one of the crucial arguments against the daily motion of Earth. In the year of Galileo's death, 1642, Gassendi published the *Epistolae duae de motu impresso a motore translato,* in which he provided a physicomathematical analysis of this experiment, as well as an examination of its cosmological implications. One of the major conceptual novelties introduced there was the identification of gravity with the attractive force of Earth. According to Alexandre Koyré's interpretation, which many scholars have endorsed, the recognition of the external nature of gravity allowed Gassendi to publish the first correct statement of the principle of rectilinear inertia. This judgment is, however, overly generous. True, in the *Epistolae* and in the *Syntagma,* Gassendi does state that in an imaginary void space a stone set in motion would persist in a state of uniform rectilinear motion. But when talking about the behavior of bodies in the real world, he does not hesitate to describe uniform circular motion (e.g., of planets, or of a ball rolling on Earth's surface) as maximally natural. Also, contrary to Galileo, he does not have the slightest notion of a centrifugal force. Moreover, as Koyré himself recognized, the principle of inertia is incompatible with Gassendi's laws of microscopic dynamics. Far from being indifferent to motion and rest, Gassendi's atoms are endowed with an innate tendency to move at maximum speed, so that the variety of motions of macroscopic bodies must be explained as the result of the clashes among the underlying atoms. Rather than in the formulation of some principle of inertia, the importance of Gassendi's *Epistolae* resides in the emphasis that Gassendi places on the relation between Galileo's new science of motion and Copernican cosmology.

Gassendi's attempt to derive Galileo's law of natural acceleration from a causal analysis of free fall is also interesting, although ultimately unsuccessful. Contrary to Descartes, who considered Galileo's theory of motion a mathematical abstraction, incompatible with any mechanistic explanation of gravity, Gassendi stubbornly tried to devise a causal account of free fall that could be reconciled with the odd-number law. In the *Epistolae de motu* he described falling bodies as being subjected to the joint action of two forces. The first, which he calls the *vis attrahens,* is the force of the earth, which emits chains of magnetic particles capable of reaching distant bodies and carrying them back. The second, which he calls *vis impellens,* is the force of the air, which rushes upward to fill the space evacuated by the falling body and thereby produces an additional pressure from behind.

In the course of his polemics with the Jesuit Pierre Le Cazre, which led to the publication of the *Epistolae de proportione qua gravia decidentia accelerantur* (1646), Gassendi came to the conclusion that the *vis attrahens* was by itself capable of bringing about an acceleration according to Galileo's odd-number law. But the relation Gassendi establishes between causal explanation and mathematical analysis of fall appears forced and artificial. For in no way can he account for the fact that a force acting through contact, by means of discrete pushes, will bring about a continuous acceleration. In the *Syntagma* Gassendi reconfirms his support for Galileo's theory of motion, without, however, subscribing to its mathematical foundation. He denies that physical magnitudes can be made out of mathematical points, and postulates the composition of space and time out of extended *minima.*

In the *Epistolae* and the *Syntagma,* Gassendi stressed the conjectural character of his explanation of gravity. He claimed to be certain about the general mode of action of *vis attrahens,* which can operate only through contact, but admitted his ignorance concerning the particular configuration of the magnetic chains. Yet, the conjectural science proposed here was no longer the *scientia experimentalis* described in the *Exercitationes,* which denied to the human mind any access to the causes of things. In the *Disquisitio metaphysica* of 1641, Gassendi endorsed a conception of the scope of science that perfectly conformed to his new scientific practice. He declared science to be something more than a simple collection of sensible data and admitted the legitimacy of a process of inference that enabled the mind to proceed from known effects to possible causes.

In the *Epistolae de motu,* Gassendi even dared to expound Galileo's proof of Earth's motion based on the tidal phenomenon. Although he presented it as a faithful summary of someone else's theory, he surreptitiously modified it so as to render it more compatible with the observed phenomena. Interestingly enough, a revised version of Galileo's tidal theory is also found in the *Syntagma,* although Gassendi there officially adheres to Tycho Brahe's cosmological system. To be sure, this adhesion represents a last-minute act of obedience to the Catholic Church. If one looks at the various drafts of the work, one sees that in 1642 (Ms. Tours 709) Gassendi presented Ptolemy's and Copernicus's as the only two possible world systems, and that in 1643 (Ms. Tours 710) he summarized Tycho's proposal in merely ten lines. From the published version of the *Syntagma,* where attention is given to the Ptolemaic, Tychonic, and Copernican systems, it is still evident that Gassendi's preference is for the latter, which is described as the most simple and elegant. But in two passages that were added to the manuscript at a late stage, the Tychonic cosmos is declared to be the only one capable of saving the phenomena while being compatible with sacred scriptures.

If in matters of cosmology Gassendi was ready to advocate the compromise favored by the church, he fought until the end of his life to demonstrate the compatibility between atomism and the Catholic faith. In a moment in which Jesuit natural philosophers were obliged to subscribe to the traditional Peripatetic theory of substance and accident as the only one that could explain the real presence of Christ in the Eucharist, Gassendi did not hesitate to get rid of substantial and accidental forms. To the Jesuit Le Cazre, who reminded him of the dangers that atomism posed to religion, Gassendi answered that transubstantiation was a "supernatural process" that should and could not be explained in physical terms.

With extraordinary erudition and seemingly orthodox piety, Gassendi argued that Epicurus was, just like Aristotle, a pagan philosopher in need of mending. Epicurus had to be corrected in some crucial points, notably with respect to

1. the creation and dissolution of the world and on the eternity of atoms;
2. the infinite plurality of worlds;
3. the blindness of causal necessity;
4. the use of parts in living organisms; and
5. the material and atomistic constitution of the soul.

But the fruits that could be obtained from a converted Epicurus were immensely more palatable than those gained from the Christianized Aristotle.

SUPPLEMENTARY BIBLIOGRAPHY

WORKS BY GASSENDI

The Selected Works of Pierre Gassendi. Edited and translated by Craig Brush. Texts in Early Modern Philosophy. New York: Johnson Reprints, 1972.

Institutio Logica (1658). A Critical Edition with Translation and Introduction. Edited and translated by Howard Jones. Assen, Netherlands: Van Gorcum, 1981.

Descartes and His Contemporaries: Meditations, Objections, and Replies. Edited and translated by Marjorie Grene and Roger Ariew. Chicago: University of Chicago Press, 1995.

Pierre Gassendi (1592–1655): Lettres Latines. Edited and translated into French by Sylvie Taussig. Turnhout, Belgium: Brepols, 2004.

OTHER SOURCES

Alberti, Antonina. *Sensazione e realtà. Epicuro e Gassendi.* Florence, Italy: Olschki, 1988.

Ariotti, Pietro. "From the Top to the Foot of a Mast on a Moving Ship." *Annals of Science* 28 (1972): 191–203.

Beaulieu, Armand. "L'enigmatique Gassendi: Prevot et savant." *La vie des sciences* 9 (1992): 205–229.

Bernier et les gassendistes. Special issue of *Corpus,* edited by Sylvia Murr, 20–21 (1992): 47–64.

Brundell, Barry. *Pierre Gassendi: From Aristotelianism to a New Natural Philosophy.* Dordrecht, Netherlands: Reidel, 1987. The book describes Gassendi's commitment to empiricism, Copernicanism, and Epicurean physics as being subordinated to the overall project of overthrowing Aristotle's metaphysics and natural philosophy.

Clark, Joseph T. "Pierre Gassendi and the Physics of Galileo." *Isis* 54 (1963): 352–370.

Clericuzio, Antonio. *Elements, Principles and Corpuscles. A Study of Atomism and Chemistry in the Seventeenth Century.* Dordrecht, Netherlands: Kluwer, 2000. The chapter on Pierre Gassendi (pp. 63–74) investigates the connection of atomism and chemistry in Gassendi's thought.

Debus, Alan G. "Pierre Gassendi and His Scientific Expedition of 1640." *Archives internationales d'histoire des sciences* 63 (1963): 133–134.

Descartes versus Gassendi. Special issue of *Perspectives on Science,* edited by Roger Ariew, 3 (1995): 425–581.

Detel, Wolfgang. "War Gassendi ein Empirist?" *Studia leibnitiana* 6 (1974): 178–221.

———. *Scientia Rerum Natura Occultarum: Methodologische Studien zur Physik Pierre Gassendis.* Berlin: De Gruyter, 1978.

———. "Scepticism and Scientific Method: The Case of Gassendi." In *Wissensideale und Wissenskulturen in der frühen Neuzeit; Ideals and Cultures of Knowledge in Early Modern*

Europe, edited by Wolfgang Detel and Claus Zittel. Berlin: Akademie Verlag, 2002.

Dumont, Simone, Jean Meeus, and Marcel Anstett. "Passage de Mercure devant le Soleil, observé par Gassendi (1592–1655), le 7 novembre 1631." *L'Astronomie* 106, no. 4 (1992): 5–7.

Festa, Egidio. "Gassendi interprete di Cavalieri." *Giornale critico della filosofia italiana* 71 (1992): 289–300.

Fisher, Saul. *Pierre Gassendi's Philosophy and Science.* Leiden, Netherlands: Brill, 2005.

Galluzzi, Paolo. "Gassendi and *l'Affaire Galilée* of the Laws of Motion." In *Galileo in Context,* edited by Jürgen Renn. Cambridge, U.K.: Cambridge University Press, 2001.

Gregory, Tullio. "Pierre Gassendi dans le quatrième centenarie de sa naissance." *Archives Internationales d'Histoire des Sciences* 42 (1992): 203–226.

Hirai, Hiro. *Le concept de semence dans les théories de la matière à la Renaissance. De Marsile Ficin à Pierre Gassendi.* Turnhout, Belgium: Brepols, 2005. The concluding chapter (pp. 463–491) traces notably Gassendi's debt to Petrus Severinus for the notion of seminal forces.

Jones, Howard. *Pierre Gassendi (1592–1655): An Intellectual Biography.* Nieuwkoop, Netherlands: B. de Graaf, 1981.

Joy, Lynn Sumida. *Gassendi the Atomist: Advocate of History in an Age of Science.* Cambridge, U.K.: Cambridge University Press, 1987. Joy argues that Gassendi's atomistic natural philosophy was influenced and shaped by his historical researches.

Lennon, Thomas L. *The Battle of Gods and Giants: The Legacies of Descartes and Gassendi, 1655–1715.* Princeton, NJ: Princeton University Press, 1993.

Lüthy, Christoph. *Matter and Microscopes in the Seventeenth Century.* PhD thesis, Harvard University, 1995. Describes (pp. 255–291) Gassendi's microscopic research and its impact on his atomism.

Lüthy, Christoph, John E. Murdoch, and William R. Newman, eds. *Late Medieval and Early Modern Corpuscular Matter Theories.* Leiden, Netherlands: Brill, 2001. Contains the following chapters on Gassendi: Clericuzio, Antonio. "Gassendi, Charleton and Boyle on Matter and Motion," pp. 467–482; Osler, Margaret. "How Mechanical Was the Mechanical Philosophy? Non-Epicurean Aspects of Gassendi's Philosophy of Nature," pp. 423–439; Palmerino, Carla Rita. "Galileo's and Gassendi's Solutions to the *Rota Aristotelis* Paradox: A Bridge between Matter and Motion Theories," pp. 381–422.

Mazauric, Simone. *Gassendi, Pascal, et la querelle du vide.* Paris: Presses universitaires de France, 1998.

Messeri, Marco. *Causa e Spiegazione: la Fisica di Pierre Gassendi.* Milan, Italy: F. Angeli, 1985. Follows the parallel evolution of Gassendi's epistemology and natural philosophy, through an analysis of his concepts of causality and explanation.

Murr, Sylvia, ed. *Gassendi et L'Europe (1592–1792). Actes du colloque international de Paris, "Gassendi et sa postérité (1592–1792)," Sorbonne, 6–10 Octobre 1992.* Paris: J. Vrin, 1997.

Osler, Margaret J. *Divine Will and the Mechanical Philosophy: Gassendi and Descartes on Contingency and Necessity in the Created World.* Cambridge, U.K.: Cambridge University Press, 1994. Osler argues that Gassendi's probabilistic epistemology and his empiricist approach to science were deeply influenced by his voluntaristic theology.

Palmerino, Carla Rita. "Pierre Gassendi's *De philosophia Epicuri universe* Rediscovered. New Perspectives on the Genesis of the *Syntagma philosophicum.*" *Nuncius* 14 (1999): 131–162.

———. "Gassendi's Reinterpretation of the Galilean Theory of Tides." *Perspectives on Science* 12 (2004): 212–237.

———. "Galileo's Theories of Free Fall and Projectile Motion as Interpreted by Pierre Gassendi." In *The Reception of the Galilean Science of Motion in Seventeenth-Century Europe,* edited by C. R. Palmerino and J. M. M. H. Thijssen, 137–164. Boston Studies in the Philosophy of Science, 239. Dordrecht, Netherlands: Kluwer, 2004.

Pancheri, Lillian U. "The Magnet, the Oyster, and the Ape, or Pierre Gassendi and the Principle of Plenitude." *Modern Schoolman* 53 (1976): 141–150.

Pav, Peter Anton. "Gassendi's Statement of the Principle of Inertia." *Isis* 57 (1966): 24–34.

Popkin, Richard. *The History of Scepticism: From Savonarola to Bayle.* Rev. ed. Oxford: Oxford University Press, 2003.

Sarasohn, Lisa T. "Motion and Morality: Pierre Gassendi, Thomas Hobbes, and the Mechanical World View." *Journal of the History of Ideas* 46 (1985): 363–379.

———. "French Reaction to the Condemnation of Galileo, 1632–1642." *Catholic Historical Review* 74 (1988): 34–54.

———. *Gassendi's Ethics: Freedom in a Mechanistic Universe.* Ithaca, NY: Cornell University Press, 1996. Examines how Gassendi made Epicurean ethics consonant with the new science and with the Christian notions of provindence and free will.

Société Scientifique et Littéraire des Alpes de Haute-Provence, ed. *Quadricentenaire de la naissance de Pierre Gassendi, 1592–1992. Actes du Colloque International, Digne-les-Bains, 18–21 Mai 1992.* 2 vols. Digne-les-Bains, France, 1994.

Taussig, Sylvie. *Pierre Gassendi (1592–1655). Introduction à la vie savante.* Turnhout, Belgium: Brepols, 2003.

Turner, Anthony, and Nadine Gomez, eds. *Pierre Gassendi, explorateur des sciences. Catalogue de l'exposition, quatrième centenaire de la naissance de Pierre Gassendi.* Digne-les-Bains, France: Musée de Digne, 1992.

van Helden, Albert. "Saturn and His Anses." *Journal for the History of Astronomy* 5 (1974): 105–121.

———. "The Importance of the Transit of Mercury of 1631." *Journal for the History of Astronomy* 7 (1976): 1–10.

Carla Rita Palmerino

GEBER IBN HAYYĀN

SEE **Jābir ibn Hayyān**.

GEOFFROY SAINT-HILAIRE, ÉTIENNE

(*b.* Etampes, France, 15 April 1772; *d.* Paris, France, 19 June 1844), *zoology.* For the original article on Étienne Geoffroy Saint-Hilaire see *DSB,* vol. 11.

Geoffroy was a French zoologist who was appointed in 1793, at the age of twenty-one, professor of zoology in charge of Mammals and Birds at the National Museum of Natural History. Founder and director of the Menagerie of this establishment and member of the Academy of Science, he was also made the first professor of zoology at the Faculty of Science in Paris, after the reformation of the University by Napoleon in 1808. He is, with Jean-Baptiste Lamarck, who preceded him in this theory, one of the most important contributors to the development of the theory of transformism during the nineteenth century. He was the father of Isidore Geoffroy Saint-Hilaire, a prominent leader of the young naturalists who were to spread transformism in France during the second half of the nineteenth century.

The Unity of Plan in the Animal World. While classifying the collections of mammals and birds under his management in the National Museum of Natural History, Geoffroy discovered that the same elements of the skeletons were constantly repetitive, "and in the same respective places," as he claimed in the *Principes de philosophie zoologique* (1830, p. 84). It was from these observations that he developed his zoological classification, which he based on the "unity of plan" in the animal world, itself founded upon the principle of the stability of organic connections: The various parts of an organ can be modified, but they always remain in the same invariable order. For example, again in the *Principes,* Geoffroy remarks that for "the anterior part" of vertebrate animals, it is easy to recognize "four sections: the shoulder, the arm, the forearm, and a terminal section, forming the hand of a man, the claw of a cat, the wing of a bat" (p. 9).

Geoffroy knew he was introducing a new element into zoological science with his principle of connections, "a doctrine which was his own," he assured in his *Philosophie anatomique* (1818, p. 405). "It was a conclusive and decisive fact, found in natural philosophy, that animals are the results of the same composition systems and the same connection of organic parts in the same invariable order." There was, therefore, a self-imposed "law of Nature" (p. 19).

While limiting his comparative studies to vertebrates, the application of his principle of unity evoked little criticism. The criticism began when, in 1818–1820, he wrote a series of articles in his *Philosophie anatomique* in an attempt to show that molluscs and insects were formed on the same plan as vertebrates. According to his "Premier Mémoire," each part of the insects corresponded "to each of the bones of a skeleton of the superior classes" (1819, p. 340). "In detail," he stated, "each part of the insects was also found in vertebrate animals" (p. 347). Also, "beings said and believed until then to be without vertebra would have to be classed, according to our natural series, amongst vertebrate animals" ("Troisième Mémoire," 1820, p. 166).

Étienne Geoffroy Saint-Hilaire. HULTON ARCHIVE/GETTY IMAGES.

These affirmations provoked fierce reaction from Georges Cuvier. "Your theory of the skeleton of insects is totally illogical from the beginning to the end," he told his old friend (cited in the "Second Mémoire," 1820, p. 34). This difference of opinion obviously raised fierce controversy, and it was the famous debate of 1830, at the Collège de France, that was to attract the attention of Johann Wolfgang von Goethe. Cuvier won his argument against Geoffroy by easily showing that "many animals had no trace whatsoever" of the organs Geoffroy wanted to be recognized.

Up to the end of his life, Geoffroy was to continue his profound interest in wide speculative theories, which has led certain commentators to portray him as a brilliant visionary! Even so, he eventually had to admit that his unity of plan, its basic principle of connections, were to lead the latter into deadlock and the former into a contradiction of facts. His intellectual interests were to lead him in a different direction and to show him a new path and another conception of nature: In 1821 he turned to embryology, teratology, and soon after, paleontology.

Embryology. After comparing the skulls of fishes and mammals, Geoffroy came to the conclusion that "the fishes, at their first age," were "in the same conditions of development as mammal foetuses" (1807, p. 344). But, unaware of this work, the German anatomist Johann Friedrich Meckel began developing embryology; Geoffroy, rather exaggeratedly, claimed this work to be partly his own. Through the development of the field of embryology, the principle of the unity of plan received new confirmation: In an 1822 work, Geoffroy claimed that, for the degree of organization, "the animals of the lower ranks" correspond to divers ages of the fetus of high vertebrates (pp. 104–105). Reptiles and fishes make the "links."

Geoffroy thus addressed an entirely new concept: the development from the simple to the complex according to a linear scale. In his *Recherches sur de grands Sauriens* (1831), he proposed a new explanation of the world: "try to find out about the succession of the differential facts of the evolution of a being which has gone through all its phases of life and you have shortened, in some way, the view of the evolution of the terrestrial globe, a succession of differential facts engendered from each other" (p. 81).

Geoffroy considered that to understand the animal world and its unity, it was no longer simply a question of the organs being always "the same, of the same number and with the same connections," but "the succession of differential facts" in the development of a being. Geoffroy offered the same theory for the development of the individual and for the development of the animal series, consequently a "historical" development: each stage of the series "corresponds to one of the ages a bud must go through in order to produce its branch and its fruits as an entirety" (1830, p. 115).

Teratology. Embryology gave Geoffroy another opportunity to develop his explanation of the unity of the animal world. This science was to provide a certain number of deviant forms—"monstrosities"—and through them Geoffroy explained the diversity of the animal world. If "the formation of an organ is stopped, the afflux of the fluids feeding it benefits other organs," and creates a totally different being. Hence, monstrosities become ordinary species, subjected to the same laws. His son, Isidore, was to develop this theory in more detail.

Paleontology. In 1825, with the Saurians of Normandy, Etienne Geoffroy Saint-Hilaire became interested in fossils. These ancient beings confirmed the unity principles.

The new paleontologist was clever enough to foresee the real descendant links between these species of the past and the species of the present. He discovered that their "organic system" was "close to that of mammals, linking what was previously thought to be separate" (1825, p. 39). In shortening the distance between reptiles and mammals, in a progressive series, the fossil sequences explained how certain elements of higher living forms, those of his current world, were formed. This led him to affirm that after generations and without interruption, "the living animals of today originate from animals lost in the antediluvian world" (p. 74). Hence, it is possible to establish a direct link of descendants between "the crocodiles of today" and "the antediluvian species found in fossil forms on our territory" (1825, p. 159).

The evolution of the thought of Geoffroy became clear. It went from an ideal to a real link, following the connection between embryonic development and degrees of zoological classification, which introduced the idea of a progressive scale (something he had first refused to admit). In his "Considérations sur des Ossemens fossils" (1833a), Geoffroy acknowledged that the "scale of beings" of "higher and lower classes" showed the stages of life's progression through a greater complexity of organization. This progressive series can be found in successive historic forms in the animal world. Although he knew that the sequences he proposed were far from perfect, he wanted to establish a law of the succession of beings: "a sort of chronology could be tried … certain degrees of organization could fix the ages of the antediluvian world" (1828, p. 215).

Transformism. The importance of paleontology is well understood, and through his work in this field Geoffroy is classed as a true transformist. It seemed more than obvious to him that "present races result from the same, continually successive and progressive, creation, and that they are descendants of a continual line of now lost, ancient races" (1833b, p. 220).

Man also has his role to play, as Geoffroy says in *Fragments biographiques* (1838): He taught his students that the monkey itself, the monkey type is, under the point of view of the organic structure, already very close to the human (Course of the natural history of the mammals, 7th lesson, p. 4). He goes further, affirming that the troglodyte presents the entrance to the human and the monkey another organic condition that forms a ring between these two terms.

Étienne Geoffroy Saint-Hilaire began with speculative transformism, and eventually reached veritable, truthful transformism.

SUPPLEMENTARY BIBLIOGRAPHY

WORKS BY GEOFFROY SAINT-HILAIRE

"Considérations sur les pièces de la tête osseuse des animaux vertébrés, et particulièrement sur celle du crâne des oiseaux."

Annales du Muséum d'Histoire naturelle, Vol. 10. Paris: Bailliere, 1807.

"Des organes respiratoires sous le rapport de la détermination et de l'identité de leurs pièces osseuses." In *Philosophie anatomique,* Vol. 1. Paris: Bailliere, 1818.

"Mémoires sur l'Organisation des Insectes, Premier Mémoire." *Journal complémentaire du Dictionnaire des Sciences médicales* 5 (1819): 340–351.

"Second Mémoire." *Journal complémentaire du Dictionnaire des Sciences médicales* 6 (1820): 31–35.

"Troisième Mémoire." *Journal complémentaire du Dictionnaire des Sciences médicales* 6 (1820): 138–168.

"Considérations générales sur la Vertèbre." In *Mémoires du Muséum d'Histoire naturelle,* Vol. 9. Paris: Bailliere, 1822.

"Des monstruosités humaines." In *Philosophie anatomique,* Vol. 2. Paris: Bailliere, 1822.

"Recherches sur l'organisation des Gavials." In *Mémoires du Muséum d'Histoire naturelle,* Vol. 12. Paris: Bailliere, 1825.

"Mémoire où l'on se propose de rechercher dans quels rapports de structure organique et de parenté sont entre eux les animaux des âges historiques et vivant actuellement, et les espèces antédiluviennes et perdues." In *Mémoires du Muséum d'Histoire naturelle,* Vol. 17. Paris: Bailliere, 1828.

Cours de l'histoire naturelle des Mammifères. Paris: Didier, 1829.

Principes de philosophie zoologique. Paris: Pichon et Didier, 1830.

Recherches sur de grands Sauriens: trouvés à l'état fossile. Paris: Firmin Didier, 1831.

"Considérations sur des Ossemens fossiles la plupart inconnus, trouvés et observés dans les bassins de l'Auvergne." *Revue encyclopédique* 59 (1833a): 75–95.

"Rapport lu à l'Académie des Sciences sur le livre de M. Buchez: Introduction à la Science de l'Histoire." *Revue encyclopédique* 59 (1833b): 210–221.

Fragments biographiques, précédés d'études sur la vie, les ouvrages et la doctrine de Buffon, 1838.

OTHER SOURCES

Appel, Toby B. *The Cuvier Geoffroy Debate: French Biology in the Decades before Darwin.* New York: Oxford University Press, 1987.

Cahn, Theophile. *La Vie et l'Oeuvre d'Etienne Geoffroy Saint-Hilaire.* Paris: Presses Universitaires de France, 1962.

"Etienne Geoffroy Saint-Hilaire." *Histoire et Nature* 3 (1973). Special edition of journal; includes "Catalogue des manuscrits d'Etienne Geoffroy Saint-Hilaire conservés aux Archives de l'Académie des sciences de l'Institut de France."

Fischer, Jean-Louis. "Le concept expérimental dans l'œuvre tératologique d'Etienne Geoffroy Saint- Hilaire." *Revue d'histoire des sciences* 25 (4, 1972): 347–364.

———. "Etienne Geoffrey Saint-Hilaire (1772–1844) face au déterminisme du sexe." *History and Philosophy of the Life Sciences* (1, 1979): 261–283.

———. "L'anatomie transcendante et le concept de 'récapitulation' chez Etienne Geoffroy Saint-Hilaire." In *Histoire du concept de récapitulation,* edited by Paul Mengal. Paris: Masson, 1993.

———. "Les manuscrits égyptiens d'Etienne Geoffroy Saint-Hilaire." In *L'expédition d'Egypte, une entreprise des Lumières, 1798–1801,* edited by Patrice Bret. Paris: Académie des Sciences, éditions TEC et DOC, 1999.

Geoffroy Saint-Hilaire, Isidore. *Vie, Travaux et Doctrine scientifique d'Etienne Geoffroy Saint-Hilaire.* Paris: Bertrand, 1847.

Le Guyader, Hervé. *Geoffroy Saint-Hilaire: A Visionary Naturalist.* Translated by Marjorie Grene. Chicago: University of Chicago Press, 2004. Originally published as *Geoffroy Saint-Hilaire: Un naturaliste visionnaire.* Paris: Belin, 1998.

Goulven Laurent

GEOFFROY SAINT-HILAIRE, ISIDORE

(*b.* Paris, France, 16 December 1805; *d.* Paris, 10 November 1861), *zoology, acclimatization, zookeeping, natural history, teratology, transformism, evolution, Étienne Geoffroy Saint-Hilaire, Muséum National d'Histoire Naturelle, animal studies.* For the original article on Geoffroy Saint-Hilaire see *DSB,* vol 5.

Isidore Geoffroy Saint-Hilaire awaits a biographer. But Goulven Laurent (1987) and Michael A. Osborne (1994) have addressed his tranformist theories, anthropology, animal domestication studies, teratological investigations (studying serious deviations from the normal type), and influence. These authors rely on manuscript and printed sources, and both interpret Geoffroy Saint-Hilaire as refining aspects of his father's scientific legacy, including the thesis of the unity of organic composition, battling diverse propositions of Cuvierian science, and adding new and synthetic, if not original, theories to midcentury science.

Evolution and Transformism. Yvette Conry's 1974 study of the nonreception of Darwinism in France, and more recent analyses of the nuances of transformism and Lamarckian ideas, focused attention on the construction and fate of French transformism and its relationship with evolutionism. Much scholarship since the 1970s evaluates Geoffroy Saint-Hilaire's contributions with reference to these ideas. Geoffroy Saint-Hilaire, who died in 1861, did not comment extensively on Charles Darwin. Yet posthumous sources make clear his reservations about Darwin's evolutionary theory, and like so many others he could not accept natural selection as a sufficient engine of biological diversity. If historians and philosophers have tended to treat Geoffroy Saint-Hilaire's career in light of his relationship to transformism and evolution, and the ideas of his father, the naturalist Étienne Geoffroy Saint-Hilaire, it is now clear that he contributed to several fields of biological, agricultural, and anthropological endeavor.

For example, Laurent presents Geoffroy Saint-Hilaire as a cautious zoologist, elegant spokesman for geological gradualism, collector of precise observations from nearly all domains of natural history, and the creator of a limited variability of type theory. Laurent likens this theory to a kind of Trojan horse, an ostensibly conservative view of the malleability of organic form that facilitated acceptance of the fully evolutionary scheme of Darwin and varieties of Lamarckian and neo-Lamarckian transformism. Simply put, the limited variability of type viewed the organism as anchored by a specific type, an idealized rather than real form, which constituted a fixed point around which the oscillations of nature played.

Cédric Grimoult also comments on Geoffroy Saint-Hilaire's role in the acceptance of transformism and evolution in France. Writing mainly from a philosophical perspective, Grimoult (1998) sees Geoffroy Saint-Hilaire as chiefly a rehabilitator of his father's ideas. Grimoult also argues that Geoffroy Saint-Hilaire's limited variability of type theory was used after 1860 to reject a full-blown transformism and contests Laurent's interpretation of the limited variability of type theory leading French scientists to adopt firmer evolutionary views. Regardless of how the theory of limited variability of type functioned within the panorama of French science, it was clearly Geoffroy Saint-Hilaire's construction and was bolstered by much empirical evidence including animal hybridization experiments undertaken at the menagerie of the Muséum National d'Histoire Naturelle. It was also supported by exhaustive taxonomic work on teratological anomalies and comparisons with lesser morphological variations. As such, the theory constituted a kind of middle ground between what Geoffroy Saint-Hilaire saw as the excesses of his father's ideas and those of Jean-Baptiste Lamarck (1744–1829) on the one hand, and the antitransformism and comparative anatomy of Georges Cuvier (1769–1832) and his disciples, on the other.

Place in Natural History. In both *Nature, the Exotic, and the Science of French Colonialism* and "Zoos in the Family: The Geoffroy Saint-Hilaire Clan and the Three Zoos of Paris," Osborne evaluates Geoffroy Saint-Hilaire's career against his natural historical activities, zookeeping, anthropology, and activities in scientific societies and institutions. He places Geoffroy Saint-Hilaire in the tradition of applied natural history, an activity whose proximate lineage stemmed from work on imported merino sheep by Louis-Jean-Marie Daubenton (1716–1800), who collaborated with Georges-Louis Leclerc, Comte de Buffon (1707–1788). Unlike Darwin, who viewed the organic world as one of competition and stress, Geoffroy Saint-Hilaire inclined toward views popularized by Alexander von Humboldt (1769–1859) and wrote of organisms as existing in a harmonious relationship with their surrounding environment. This was an interest of long standing, extant since the early 1830s when he gave a course at the Athénée Royal de Paris on the internal and external harmonies of animals. This manner of thinking persisted into his scientific maturity, when he frequently wrote that once organisms were transplanted to new environments they underwent a process of acclimatization and established a new set of harmonies with their surroundings. The limited variability of type theory sprang from observations and experiments on Egyptian geese, llamas, and other live animals at the museum's menagerie and from descriptive teratology. Geoffroy Saint-Hilaire was clearly uncomfortable with several aspects of Lamarckian transformism, including the emphasis on gradual organic change and the latter's notion of an organism possessing an internal drive to perfection. His research program on the variability of animal form stressed the direct environmental influences of heat, light, soil composition, and humidity, as well as diet. Humans, by moving organisms from one climatic zone to another, merely mediated or in some ways temporarily managed natural environmental forces.

Osborne and Laurent identify several quotations from Geoffroy Saint-Hilaire on generic and specific level variations seemingly induced by environmental agency, and it is true that his theory of organisms establishing harmonies with their surroundings strongly implied that acclimatization provoked deep functional and sometimes anatomical changes within those organisms. Logically then, provided that environmental and geological changes were somewhat gradual, the functional and anatomical characteristics of organisms would change in concert with the altered ambient environment. When taken out of context, these ideas, combined with comments from the 1830s on the transmissibility of minor anomalies such as albinism and polydactylism, can be read as endorsing a strong transformist program provided past terrestrial environments differed substantially from what is now the case. In some instances, however, passages mentioning environmentally induced variations seem more directed at taxonomic practice, specifically the definition of taxonomic characters, and at the considerable challenges of establishing a natural system of classification. Additionally, he often wrote of the limited variability of type theory as a hypothesis, the most likely explanation for the diversity of nature and one that current scientific practices had failed to refute. The true extent of Geoffroy Saint-Hilaire's transformism may well remain enigmatic, as he died prior to giving his own account of geological history.

Anthropology and Ethnology. A founding member of the Société d'Anthropologie de Paris, Geoffroy Saint-Hilaire's views on the science of man diverged from those of the French anthropologist Paul Broca (1824–1880). A monogenist and early supporter of the work of Jacques Boucher de Crèvecoeur Perthes (1788–1868), who adopted actualist geological views and opposed Cuvier's thesis on the nonexistence of fossilized human bones, Geoffroy Saint-Hilaire was interested in anthropometry but called for historical, functional, and anatomical studies of humanity. In 1854 he was likely the first to employ the term *ethnology* in its modern sense, and his concepts influenced subsequent work. Positing the existence of ethnological laws, he called for the scientific study of the human family to include investigation of instinct, behavior, diet, and ethnological variations between the tribes of humanity. His vision of ethnology was ecumenical in approach but in some ways privileged general natural historians and zoologists, such as himself, in calling for the reconstruction of past human migrations by attending to the animal species domesticated by ancient peoples. In so doing he distanced himself from the emergent and methodologically more narrow physical anthropology of Broca and others.

Domestication and Zootechny. Jean-Pierre Digard (1990), Claude Blanckaert (1992), and Osborne (1994) signal Isidore Geoffroy Saint-Hilaire's role as a pioneer theoretician of animal domestication and practitioner of zootechny (the scientific practice of maintaining and improving animals under domestication). Access to and later direction of the museum's menagerie most certainly enabled these activities. His sometime rival, Cuvier, had also studied animal behavior in the same venue. Digard praises Geoffroy Saint-Hilaire for identifying the key theoretical problems of domestication, acclimatization, and naturalization, and also investigating animal intelligence and humanity's diverse relationships with domesticated animals. He regards contemporary zootechny as working largely within a paradigm established by Geoffroy Saint-Hilaire.

Blanckaert's investigation of the social mission of zootechny provides a rich portrait of Geoffroy Saint-Hilaire's activities. Like his friend the engineer and philosopher Jean Reynaud, he too harbored passionate concern for the social and material betterment of the laboring and impoverished classes. An advocate of social efficiency and dietary cosmopolitanism, he spoke against dietary prejudices and supported hippophagia (the consumption of horse meat) for a variety of reasons including advancement of a republican social agenda linked to hygienist intentions, and an ethical conviction that it was better to kill horses cleanly and quickly after accidents or at the end of their useful lives, than to let them linger without proper care while awaiting the rendering works. All members of his family, including his mother, his sister Stéphanie Geoffroy Saint-Hilaire, and his son Albert, supported the activities of the Société Protectrice des Animaux.

Teratology. The two thousand or so published pages of Geoffroy Saint-Hilaire's work on teratology, though informed by an epigenetic view of embryogenesis and his father's embryological investigations and ideas on arrested development, are highly descriptive. While demonstrating the immense variations possible on a single morphological plan, the studies were largely devoid of physiological considerations, except as they related to the taxonomy and morphology of anomalies. According to Patrick Tort (1982) Geoffroy Saint-Hilaire was a transformist zoologist at least since 1836, and the taxonomy of teratological anatomy published prior to that date proffered evidence confirming existence of a uniform material plan for all living creatures. In seeking a natural taxonomic system for anatomical anomalies, Geoffroy Saint-Hilaire classified anomalous characters by scales of complexity and severity. Anomalies of complexity, for example, included cases of the reversal of internal organs, a condition that might still allow the organism to function normally, or nearly so. Anomalies of severity, in contrast, compromised physiological function in greater or lesser degree. The two scales, however, were not entirely compatible and he eventually emphasized severity over complexity by reference to the embryogenetic research of his father's disciple, Antoine Étienne Reynaud Augustin Serres (1786–1868). Tort also proposes that Geoffroy Saint-Hilaire regarded genealogy as the proper basis of the classificatory enterprise and elaborated a kind of philosophical evolutionism quite similar to Darwin's views.

Geoffroy Saint-Hilaire's ideas, although in some cases not his transformism, provoked further research on the habits and diets of economically useful exotic animals, animal and environment relationships, and human and animal relationships. His concepts also inspired creation of one of the Second Empire's largest scientific societies, the Société Zoologique d'Acclimatation, of which he served as the first president, and several similar societies throughout the world. He was instrumental as well in the history or planning of all three Parisian zoos, especially the museum's menagerie, and the Jardin Zoologique d'Acclimatation, which showcased his ideas.

SUPPLEMENTARY BIBLIOGRAPHY

WORK BY GEOFFROY SAINT-HILAIRE

Acclimatation et domestication des animaux utiles. Paris: La Maison Rustique/Flammarion, 1986. Reprint of 1861 edition.

OTHER SOURCES

Aragón Albillos, Santiago. "Le rayonnement international de la Société zoologique d'acclimatation: Participation de l'Espagne entre 1854 et 1861." *Revue d'Histoire des Sciences* 58 (2005): 169–206.

———. *El zoológico del Museo de ciencias naturales de Madrid: Mariano de la Paz Graells (1809–1898), la Sociedad de aclimatación y los animals útiles.* Madrid: Museo Nacional de Ciencias Naturales, 2005.

Blanckaert, Claude. "Les animaux 'utiles' chez Isidore Geoffroy Saint-Hilaire: La mission sociale de la zootechnie." *Revue de Synthèse* 113, nos. 3–4 (1992): 347–382.

Burkhardt, Richard W. *The Spirit of System: Lamarck and Evolutionary Biology; Now with "Lamarck in 1995."* Cambridge, MA: Harvard University Press, 1995.

Conry, Yvette. *L'introduction du darwinisme en France au XIXe siècle.* Paris: Vrin, 1974.

Corsi, Pietro. *The Age of Lamarck: Evolutionary Theories in France, 1790–1830.* Berkeley: University of California Press, 1988.

Digard, Jean-Pierre. *L'homme et les animaux domestiques: Anthropologie d'une passion.* Paris: Fayard, 1990.

Ducros, Albert, and Jacqueline Ducros. "De la découverte des grands singes à la paléo-éthologie humaine." *Bulletins et Mémoires de la Société d'anthropologie de Paris,* n.s., 1, nos. 3–4 (1989): 301–320.

Grimoult, Cédric. *Évolutionnisme et fixisme en France: Histoire d'un combat; 1800–1882.* Paris: CNRS Éditions, 1998.

———. *L'évolution biologique en France: Une révolution scientifique, politique et culturelle.* Geneva: Droz, 2001.

———. *Histoire de l'histoire des sciences: Historiographie de l'évolutionnisme dans le monde francophone.* Geneva: Droz, 2003.

Laurent, Goulven. *Paléontologie et évolution en France de 1800 à 1860: Une histoire des idées de Cuvier et Lamarck à Darwin.* Paris: Éditions du Comité des travaux historiques et scientifiques, 1987.

Osborne, Michael A. *Nature, the Exotic, and the Science of French Colonialism.* Bloomington: Indiana University Press, 1994.

———. "Zoos in the Family: The Geoffroy Saint-Hilaire Clan and the Three Zoos of Paris." In *New Worlds, New Animals: From Menagerie to Zoological Park in the Nineteenth Century,* edited by Robert J. Hoage and William Deiss, 33–42. Baltimore, MD: Johns Hopkins University Press, 1996.

———. "Acclimatizing the World: A History of the Paradigmatic Colonial Science." *Osiris* 15 (2000): 135–151.

Schurig, Volker. "Die Eingliederung des Begriffs 'Ethologie' in das System der Biowissenschaften im 19. Jahrhundert." *Sudhoffs Archiv für Geschichte der Medizin und der Naturwissenschaften* 68 (1984): 94–104.

Tort, Patrick. "La logique du déviant (Isidore Geoffroy Saint-Hilaire et la classification des monstres)." *Revue des Sciences Humaines* 59, no. 188 (1982): 7–32.

Michael A. Osborne

GIBSON, ELEANOR JACK

(*b.* Peoria, Illinois, 7 December 1910; *d.* Columbia, South Carolina, 30 December 2002), *psychology, perceptual learning and development.*

Gibson was one of the most prominent experimental psychologists of the twentieth century, contributing profound conceptual and empirical insights about the nature and development of perception and action. Her theory of perceptual learning, including the ideas that differentiation is an essential form of learning and that learning brings about changes in what is perceived, led to new understanding of perceptual development in human infants and children and of basic processes in reading. She was elected to the National Academy of Sciences, and, in 1992, was awarded the National Medal of Science, the highest scientific honor in the United States.

The Early Years. Eleanor Grier Jack received her bachelor's degree from Smith College, a well-known women's college, in 1931. She described Smith as "a place where women were not only permitted but encouraged to be scholars, even scientists" (Gibson, 1980, p. 240). Kurt Koffka, the famous Gestalt psychologist, was a member of the faculty, but a far more profound influence on her was that of James J. Gibson who became a junior faculty member as she became a psychology major. Their marriage in 1932 marked the formal beginning of a close personal and intellectual colleagueship that continued until his death in 1979.

After obtaining her master's degree from Smith (1933), Gibson (known to her colleagues and friends as "Jackie") went to Yale intending to pursue a PhD studying animal behavior with Robert Yerkes. However, at their first meeting Yerkes informed her that he did not permit women to work in his laboratory. Manifesting a different attitude, Clark Hull, a renowned S-R (stimulus–response) learning theory psychologist, welcomed her as an advisee. She completed her dissertation under his direction on principles of conditioning applied to verbal learning. Gibson first began to clarify the concepts of generalization and especially differentiation, fundamental in all of her subsequent work, in her dissertation. She worked out a detailed theoretical analysis of how generalization and differentiation might influence performance in traditional paired associate learning tasks. This was followed by a systematic series of experiments testing multiple specific hypotheses from that theoretical analysis (Gibson, 1939; 1940; 1941; 1942). The elegance of this programmatic research, with rigorous empirical work closely tied to the theoretical analyses from which it derived, characterized her science throughout her career.

Even before completing her dissertation, Gibson returned to Smith College and full-time teaching. The Gibsons' first child, a son, was born in 1940, and their daughter was born in 1943. World War II interrupted the Gibsons' academic careers: They spent the war years in Texas and California, where James Gibson conducted

Gibson

research on aircraft recognition and space perception for the Army Air Forces Aviation Psychology Program. After the war, they returned to Smith and both resumed their academic lives, but in 1949 they moved to Cornell University, where they remained for the rest of their careers.

The Cornell Years and the Study of Perceptual Learning. Cornell, unlike Smith, had a nepotism rule that precluded close relatives from serving on the faculty. Thus Eleanor Gibson was given the title research associate, a small office, and the obligation to support herself and her research as best she could. She found a way to act on her conviction of the importance of a comparative approach to understanding learning and development, a conviction that had taken her to Yale in the first place. She began to study conditioning and maternal-infant interaction with a new species, young goats. In the course of this work she made an observation that foreshadowed some of her most well known subsequent research. Newborn kids, genetically related to mountain dwellers but never having experienced a drop-off, would stand motionless on a small platform several feet above the ground. Students of psychology the world over now learn about the elegant systematic "visual cliff" studies of the sensitivity of the young of many species to information concerning a drop-off.

Gibson and Richard Walk, a faculty colleague at Cornell, devised an apparatus for studying the development of depth discrimination, a visual (or virtual) cliff. The apparatus consisted of a rectangular sheet of glass supported parallel to the floor and some distance above it. A textured pattern is fixed directly to the underside of one-half of the glass (the "near" or "shallow" side of the cliff), and the same textured pattern covers the floor below visible through the other half of the glass (the "far" or "deep" side of the cliff). A slightly raised platform bisects the glass, separating the two sides of the cliff. An animal, or a young human, is placed on the platform and its exploratory behavior and descent to one side or the other of the cliff are observed. Using this simple situation, Gibson and Walk studied depth discrimination in a variety of species and found that, for the most part, animals and humans discriminate the optically deep drop-off from the shallow one at least by the time they can locomote (Walk and Gibson, 1961). For example, human infants who are crawling will readily cross the shallow side to reach their parents who are holding out an attractive toy. The same infants, when encouraged in the same way by their parents to crawl over the deep side, rarely will do so, despite the fact that their tactile contact with the glass surface provides information that it is a suitable surface of support for locomotion.

An important feature of the visual cliff situation is that it uses a natural response of the creatures being observed—that is, locomoting over surfaces. The use of naturally occurring behaviors, for example exploratory behaviors, to study the development of perception characterized most of Gibson's research, especially her research with human infants.

The visual cliff studies followed a series of experiments on the effects of early experience on rats' discrimination of two-dimensional shapes. In these experiments rats were raised with geometric forms hanging on the sides of their cages, and their subsequent discrimination of similar forms was assessed (Gibson and Walk, 1956). The question of interest was whether perceptual learning would occur without differential reinforcement of particular responses.

This is the same question that Gibson first began to investigate in her dissertation experiments in the context of verbal learning. Previous theorists had argued that improvement in perceptual discrimination is brought about by the reinforced learning of some kind of responses attached to the items to be discriminated. This is a kind of "enrichment" process that renders the items more distinctive than they once were. Gibson argued that to associate or attach new responses to two similar items logically requires that the items must be distinguishable in the first place. Gibson and her husband published an important paper titled "Perceptual Learning: Differentiation or Enrichment?" in which they articulated a "specificity" theory of the nature of perceptual learning (1955). Departing radically from then-current theories of perceptual learning, they argued that the information available to the sensory systems to support perceiving is rich, and fully specifies its sources in the environment. Perceptual learning involves improvement in discrimination rather than association or inference-making. Through such learning, perception changes, becoming into ever-closer correspondence with the environment. There are many examples of such learning by adults, such as skilled wine tasters, birders, and interpreters of radiological images (such as x-rays and scans). This kind of learning is especially important in understanding development as children, in the normal course of growing up, increasingly distinguish among the features of the worlds in which they function.

During the early 1960s Gibson's research was concentrated on perceptual development and learning in the context of children's acquisition of reading skill. Her empirical investigations ranged from questions about the processes of learning to discriminate among letters to questions about extracting the structure of the written language. The focus of this work was on development: how perception develops during childhood, what perceptual learning is, and how it comes about. During this period she wrote a monograph, *Principles of Perceptual Learning and Development* (1969), in which she presented extant theories of perceptual learning, organized the very large experimental literature on perceptual learning and development, and first laid out in detail her own new theory of perceptual development.

The theory was summarized in terms of three trends in perceptual development. The first is a trend toward increasing specificity of discrimination. Perceptual learning involves a gradual, progressive increase in the specificity of discrimination to what she then called "stimulus information." Perceiving becomes in closer correspondence to the properties of things and events in the world.

The second trend she described as the optimization of attention. This trend refers to changes in the nature of the exploratory activity that underlies perceptual learning. Such activity becomes more active and more systematic and less captured by the immediate features of the objects of perception. The third trend is toward an increasing economy of perceiving, including processing of larger units of stimulus structure—so-called higher order structure.

After more research on reading, she wrote another book with her research colleague Harry Levin, *The Psychology of Reading* (1975). In this book they elaborated and extended the principles of perceptual learning to include processes of children's progression toward becoming skilled readers.

A Laboratory of her Own. Sixteen years after she arrived at Cornell and after she had begun to receive many academic and professional honors, Gibson was appointed a full professor, and shortly thereafter was awarded an endowed professorship. She now had her own laboratory, the Eleanor J. Gibson Laboratory of Developmental Psychology, and she turned to new questions about the development of perception during infancy.

She began to investigate the development of perception of invariants during infancy. For example, using habituation methods, she discovered that young infants detect invariant information for the rigidity or elasticity of moving objects. It had been found that repeated viewing of a display (habituation) changes infants' preference for looking at that display. Gibson presented repeatedly to infants an object undergoing three rigid motions: rotation in a frontal plane, rotation around the vertical axis, and rotation around the horizontal axis. Then, the infants would be shown an object undergoing a fourth rigid motion, displacement to and fro on the Z axis (so-called looming), as well as the object undergoing a deforming motion. The infants would generalize habituation to the object in rigid motion, and visually discriminate between it and the deforming apparently elastic object (Gibson, Owsley, and Johnston, 1978).

The research on the development of the perception of invariants led quite directly to new research on the development of the perception of affordances in young infants. The concept of affordances was introduced widely in James Gibson's last book, *The Ecological Approach to Visual Perception* (1979)—published shortly before his death—although the concept had been evolving for many years. Affordances are features of the world that provide possibilities for action for creatures with specific capabilities. Eleanor Gibson's first paper on the implications of the affordance concept for a theory of development was titled "The Concept of Affordances in Development: The Renascence of Functionalism" (1982) and the title captures well her point of view. It is first of all a functional view, emphasizing the relation of the perceiver and the environment. For example, she argued that perceptual development and motor development, or the development of action systems, are bound up together. This view is reflected in a conceptual analysis of the development of mobility in infants and young children (Gibson and Schmuckler, 1989).

In that analysis Gibson suggested that three essential components in a child's mobility are guiding or steering their movement, choosing a traversable surface for locomotion, and maintaining balance (when walking). She and her students investigated all three of these components. Illustrative of the research on surface traversibility was a series of experiments in which infants (about eleven months of age) and toddlers (about fourteen months of age) were presented with two surfaces over which they might locomote (Gibson, Riccio, Schmuckler, et al., 1987). One was a rigid surface and the second was a waterbed surface covered in the same pattern as the first. The infants were all locomoting by crawling and the toddlers were all walking. The question of interest was whether the children would differentiate the two surfaces of support in relation to their own locomotion capabilities. Encouraged by their mothers, the toddlers readily locomoted over the rigid surface but not over the waterbed surface. If they did cross the latter surface, they crawled over it. The younger, crawling infants readily locomoted over both surfaces to reach their mothers. Thus, the children detected the affordances of the surfaces for supporting locomotion relative to their own mode of locomotion.

In addition to stressing the functional nature of the perceiver and the environment, Gibson's view of perceptual development stressed the importance of exploratory activity in learning about affordances. Babies as young as one month were found to acquire information about objects' substances by exploring them in their mouths (Gibson and Walker, 1984). In this experiment, the infants' mothers encouraged them to mouth either a hard object or a spongy object. They inserted the objects in the babies' mouths in such a way as to conceal the objects from the babies' view. After a period of mouthing, the objects were removed and the babies watched a rigid object in motion and a spongy object in motion. The babies showed preferential looking (i.e., looked longer) to the object of novel substance—that is, a different substance than the object they had mouthed. Thus, what they had learned about the objects' substances by mouthing them was reflected in their preferential looking. This learning by exploring is similar to the learning demonstrated by the older babies described above who learned about objects' substances by watching them move in ways that specified their rigidity or elasticity. Moreover, in this case the infants demonstrated a rather remarkable capacity to detect the correspondence of haptic (active tactual) and visual information about object substance.

The examples just described illustrate Gibson's idea that differentiation is a fundamental process of perceptual learning. She disliked reductionism and was not interested in uncovering mechanisms of change at the physiological or neural level. Instead, she advocated the description of learning processes at the behavioral level. Differentiation as perceptual learning is a concept analogous at the behavioral level to the biological differentiation process where it refers to cell division and reorganization during embryonic development. For perceptual development, differentiation refers to discerning finer distinctions, finer discrimination of specific features, as well as abstracting higher order structure in the information available to the sensory systems. A previously mentioned illustrative example of perceptual learning in adults is learning to "read" radiological images. One learns to perceive more distinctions among the subtle shadings and also to discover or identify the structural patterns in the display. Perceptual development and learning in infants and young children is characterized by progressive increase in discrimination and detection of the meaningful properties of the environment, the affordances.

Gibson argued that exploratory behavior plays a fundamental role in perceptual learning and development, a point of view she elaborated on in a review essay titled "Exploratory Behavior in the Development of Perceiving, Acting, and the Acquiring of Knowledge" (1988). She summed up her argument by asking a rhetorical question, whether evolution has prepared infants to learn by providing "representations of the world, and rules for how to act?" Her answer: "I doubt that very much. But I think evolution has provided (them) with action systems and sensory systems that equip (them) to discover what the world is all about" (p. 37).

The Ecological Approach to Perceptual Learning and Development. Gibson's approach to understanding perceptual development, like that of James Gibson for understanding perception, came to be called an "ecological" approach, emphasizing the reciprocity and complementarity of the animal (including humans) and the environment in which it lives and behaves. Beginning in about 1980 and continuing through the early years of the twenty-first century, the study of human development had a heavy emphasis on the period of infancy. This was also true of the study of development from an ecological perspective as Gibson and her colleagues, many of them former students, produced much new knowledge about the development of perception and action during infancy. The publication of a new book with Anne Pick, *An Ecological Approach to Perceptual Learning and Development* (2000), presented the theoretical formulation as it had evolved and incorporated much of the most recent research on perceptual development in infancy as it pertains to the theory.

The book is organized around three general modes of behavior that emerge during infancy and underlie and affect all subsequent complex activities. These are (1) early social interaction and communication, (2) the emergence of reaching and knowledge of objects, and (3) locomotion, getting around in the environment. With respect to each of these developing modes of behavior, Gibson stressed that learning changes the relations of a developing baby with the environment.

The first mode of behavior addressed in Gibson and Pick's 2000 work is communication and social interaction. Although human newborns are completely dependent on adult caregivers, they begin life as active perceivers of their caregivers' faces and voices. From the start infants participate in rudimentary face-to-face interactions, thus providing opportunities for learning from others. Caregivers' affective expressiveness toward infants has obvious important significance as it may foretell comfort and soothing or distress or avoidance. Perceiving affect in others directed to oneself is thus an important achievement, and infants begin to develop sensitivity to facial and vocal expressions during their first months of life. In addition to facial/gestural patterns, infants come to detect information for affective meaning in the intonation, rhythm, and stress patterns of others' speech.

The second mode of behavior addressed is the emergence of goal-directed reaching. Inanimate objects become accessible for exploration by the middle of the first year as infants gain motor and postural control necessary for reaching, grasping, and manipulating. Exploration by mouthing continues, however, as evidenced by the well-known proclivity of infants to transport objects of appropriate size and substance quickly and directly to their mouths. Exploratory behaviors—banging, throwing, squeezing, mouthing, shaking, and so on—are the means by which infants discover the affordances of objects. Especially important in such exploratory activities is multi-modal exploration, integrated exploration by more than one sensory modality. Important examples are visual and manual exploration, actively looking at and manipulating objects, examining them and bringing them up close for further scrutiny, mouthing and manipulating, and banging or shaking objects to learn about the sounds they make. Exploratory actions become increasingly differentiated in relation to objects' specific properties.

The component abilities of goal-directed reaching develop earlier in infancy, including visually tracking moving objects, and gaining visual and motor control of arm movements. The development of such component skills of functional reaching demonstrate how exploratory actions are the means for linking perceptual information with motor control.

The third mode of behavior addressed by Gibson and Pick (2000) is learning to locomote. Human infants become capable of active self-locomotion typically sometime during the latter months of their first year. Gibson emphasized that active self-locomotion emerges gradually, from rolling over, to changing posture to sitting, to crawling, cruising, and eventually bipedal locomotion, usually more or less in that order. The achievements of postural stability, orientation to the environment, and balance underlie the development of each new phase of locomotion. The research with crawling and walking babies locomoting over rigid and pliable surfaces described earlier highlights the role of perceptual exploration in guiding locomotion as new action systems gradually become available.

Persistence of Perceptual Learning in Cognitive Development. Gibson's research during her last decades as well as her theorizing was concentrated on development during infancy. Her discoveries countered a view prevalent at the time that in the course of development beyond infancy, perceiving becomes overridden by knowledge acquired by "higher" cognitive processes. Further, Gibson's own earlier research—for example, on reading—attests that perceptual learning is fundamental for later achievements of language, conceptualization, and thinking.

What characterized Gibson's approach to her science? First, beginning with her dissertation, her experimental investigations were always theoretically motivated. This meant that not only were the immediate empirical results informative, but also that the theoretical and conceptual analysis that was the context for the problem yielded new understanding and questions. Second, her experimental questions were posed clearly and distinctly, permitting the use of straightforward and rigorous methods to answer them. The research in which she discovered that young infants perceive objects' substance (solid or elastic) from kinetic information as they move in particular ways illustrates this characteristic of her research.

Finally, she devised elegantly simple tasks and situations to investigate her experimental questions. The visual cliff is perhaps the most well-known example of this characteristic of her science. She was a consummate experimenter. In a memorial tribute, Elizabeth Spelke, a student of Gibson's and herself an eminent scientist, wrote that at Gibson's death at the age of ninety-two, "we lost the greatest experimental psychologist of the twentieth century. Twenty-first century psychology will be built on the comparative, developmental, and experimental foundations that Eleanor J. Gibson gave us" (2003, p. 26).

BIBLIOGRAPHY

WORKS BY GIBSON

"Sensory Generalization with Voluntary Reactions." *Journal of Experimental Psychology* 24 (1939): 237–253.

"A Systematic Application of the Concepts of Generalization and Differentiation to Verbal Learning." *Psychological Review* 47 (1940): 196–229.

"Retroactive Inhibition as a Function of Degree of Generalization Between Tasks." *Journal of Experimental Psychology* 28 (1941): 93–115.

"Intra-list Generalization as a Factor in Verbal Learning." *Journal of Experimental Psychology* 30 (1942): 185–200.

With James J. Gibson. "Perceptual Learning: Differentiation or Enrichment?" *Psychological Review* 62 (1955): 32–41.

With Richard D. Walk. "The Effect of Prolonged Exposure to Visually Presented Patterns on Learning to Discriminate Them." *Journal of Comparative and Physiological Psychology* 49 (1956): 239–242.

With Richard D. Walk. "A Comparative and Analytical Study of Visual Depth Perception." *Psychological Monographs* 75, no. 15 (1961).

Principles of Perceptual Learning and Development. New York: Appleton-Century-Crofts, 1969.

With Harry Levin. *The Psychology of Reading.* Cambridge, MA: MIT Press, 1975.

With Cynthia J. Owsley and J. Johnston. "Perception of Invariants by Five-Month-Old Infants: Differentiation of Two Types of Motion." *Developmental Psychology* 14 (1978): 407–415.

"Eleanor J. Gibson." In *A History of Psychology in Autobiography,* Vol. VII, edited by Gardner Lindzey. San Francisco: W. H. Freeman, 1980.

"The Concept of Affordances in Perceptual Development: The Renascence of Functionalism." In *The Minnesota Symposia on Child Psychology,* Vol. 15: *The Concept of Development,* edited by W. Andrew Collins. Hillsdale, NJ: Erlbaum, 1982.

With Arlene S. Walker. "Development of Knowledge of Visual-Tactual Affordances of Substances." *Child Development* 55 (1984): 453–460.

With Gary Riccio, Mark A. Schmuckler, Thomas A. Stoffregen, et al. "Detection of the Traversability of Surfaces by Crawling and Walking Infants." *Journal of Experimental Psychology: Human Perception and Performance* 13 (1987): 533–544.

"Exploratory Behavior in the Development of Perceiving, Acting, and the Acquiring of Knowledge." *Annual Review of Psychology* 39 (1988): 1–41.

With Mark A. Schmuckler. "Going Somewhere: An Ecological and Experimental Approach to Development of Mobility." *Ecological Psychology* 1 (1989): 3–25.

An Odyssey in Learning and Perception. Cambridge, MA: MIT Press, 1991.

With Ann D. Pick. *An Ecological Approach to Perceptual Learning and Development.* New York: Oxford University Press, 2000.

Perceiving the Affordances: A Portrait of Two Psychologists. Mahwah, NJ: Lawrence Erlbaum, 2002.

OTHER SOURCES

Spelke, Elizabeth. "In Appreciation: Eleanor Gibson." *Observer* 16 (2003): 25–26.

Anne D. Pick
Herbert L. Pick Jr.

GIBSON, JAMES JEROME (*b.* McConnelsville, Ohio, 27 January 1904; *d.* Ithaca, New York, 11 December 1979), *psychology, perception, vision, ecological psychology, perception-action, epistemology.*

Gibson was an innovative twentieth-century experimental psychologist whose work focused primarily on visual perception of the everyday world. His research and theoretical contributions over five decades culminated in a highly original perspective, the ecological approach to perceiving. This approach is unique in providing theoretical grounds and empirical support for the epistemological position of direct realism, which is the view that individuals perceive the environment directly. As such, it offers an alternative to the long-dominant claim that perception of the environment is mediated by subjective, mental processes (indirect realism).

Gibson's first book, *The Perception of the Visual World* (1950), was highly acclaimed and influential because of the compelling case it made for the presence of higher-order structures in patterns of visual stimulation. Recognition of these structural patterns offered some novel solutions to several long-standing perceptual problems. This book anticipated the later ecological approach in several ways, but because of its psychophysical framework, it remained tied to standard formulations of perceiving. With the publication of his later two books, *The Senses Considered as Perceptual Systems* (1966) and *The Ecological Approach to Visual Perception* (1979), Gibson fully broke from traditional approaches and offered his radical and original reformulation of perception from an ecological perspective.

Among the notable concepts that Gibson developed in formulating the ecological approach were perceptual systems and affordances. The concept of perceptual systems portrays perceiving as a process of exploration and detection of structure from a rich array of stimulus information. Such a view is a departure from standard accounts, which take perception as beginning with the imposition of stimulation on the receptor surfaces of a passive perceiver. In the case of vision, for example, visual perception is conventionally taken to be initiated by stimulation falling on the retinal receptors; whereas vision from the viewpoint of perceptual systems recognizes the essential role of the individual's self-directed movements in revealing environmental structure. The concept of affordance refers to the perceived functional meaning of an environmental feature for an individual. Affordances of an environment are specified by stimulus information taken relative to an individual; as a consequence, this concept locates the meaning of environmental features in the individual-environment relationship rather than as a subjective quality imposed on the environment by an individual mind.

Education and Early Career. Gibson received a bachelor's degree from Princeton University in 1925, where he majored in philosophy. He took his first course in experimental psychology during his senior year from H. S. Langfeld, formerly of the William James–inspired Harvard Psychology Department, who had previously studied with the experimental phenomenologist Carl Stumpf. After graduation Gibson returned to Princeton as one of Langfeld's graduate assistants and completed his doctoral dissertation under him. The dominant intellectual influence on Gibson during his graduate studies was the philosophical behaviorist E. B. Holt, who had been a student of William James and later became a central figure among the New Realist philosophers. Holt's writings fused the nondualistic metaphysics of James's philosophy of radical empiricism with a behavioristic focus on action. Holt's distinctive brand of behaviorism was molar in level of analysis (which considers the organism as a functioning whole rather than reducing it to a set of microaction, or S-R, units), purposive in motivational character (which assumes an intentional, goal-directed organism rather than one that must be prodded into action by an extrinsic stimulus), and distal in identification of the effective stimulus for action (which seeks the effective stimulus for perception and action in the environment rather than at the receptors). All of these qualities would characterize Gibson's later perceptual theory.

Gibson

Gibson's first academic appointment was at Smith College beginning in the fall of 1928. Over the ensuing fifteen years, Gibson taught courses in experimental psychology and social psychology, and published numerous research papers with his students. A significant influence on Gibson at Smith was his faculty colleague, the émigré Gestalt psychologist Kurt Koffka. Although Gibson's behaviorist leanings initially set him somewhat at odds with Koffka theoretically, the European experimental phenomenology that Gibson had picked up from Langfeld gave them some common ground. A phenomenological strain runs through much of Gibson's subsequent work to good effect. Moreover, Koffka's focus on organization in perceptual experience heightened Gibson's sensitivity to higher-order relations in patterns of sensory stimulation. Two other influential colleagues at Smith were Fritz Heider, whose writings on the role of the medium in perceiving had a profound impact on Gibson at a later point in his career, and his wife, Eleanor Jack Gibson, who became an equally distinguished psychologist with her primary interests in perceptual learning and development. Although the Gibsons rarely collaborated in a formal manner in their writing or research, they were lifelong intellectual partners, and their research programs were mutually supportive and mutually influential.

One of James Gibson's most important publications during the Smith years was a report on his research of perceptual adaptation to curved lines. Gibson discovered that prolonged visual inspection of a curved line resulted in experiencing the line as straight, and that subsequent examination of straight lines revealed an aftereffect of apparent curvature in the opposite direction. These findings are significant for indicating that a seemingly basic stimulus attribute such as linearity/curvilinearity is not merely an elementary sensation imposed on sensory receptors, but instead is a product of ongoing perceiver-environment relations. This early expression of the dynamic relationship between perceiver and environment became more fully developed over subsequent decades.

Perceiving from a Moving Point of Observation. During the years of World War II, Gibson worked in the psychological research unit of the U.S. Army Air Forces. This period was an especially rich one in the development of his thinking. Gibson's primary responsibility was formulating selection procedures for prospective pilots; in the course of doing so, he was struck by how inadequate standard measures of perceptual abilities were for this purpose. He realized that their inadequacy stemmed in large measure from a reliance on static visual displays; whereas when pilots operate aircraft, they perceive themselves and the plane moving relative to ground surfaces, especially during takeoff and approach. This realization led, first, to Gibson's innovative use of dynamic displays (motion pictures) for presenting test materials; and second, it transformed his ideas about the nature of perceiving more broadly.

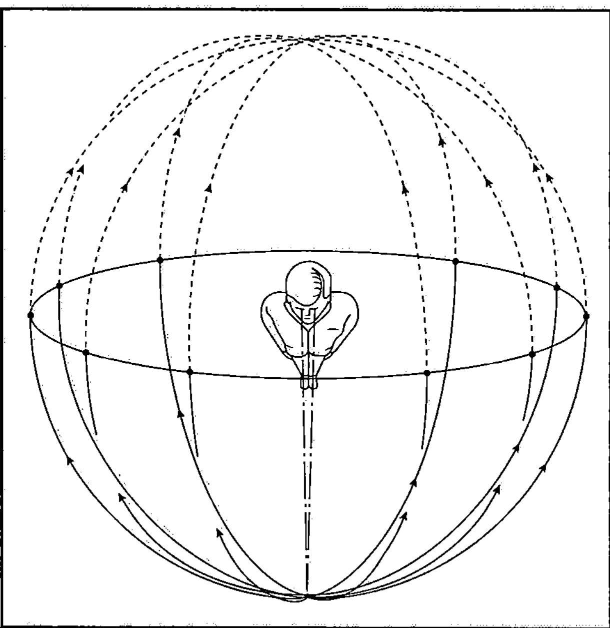

Figure 1. Self-movement generates optical streaming in the visual field.

In particular, Gibson's use of dynamic displays, as well as his attention to everyday experience, revealed that moving through the environment generates an optical streaming as surfaces appear to flow around the perceiver. This optical flow, produced as it is by self-generated movement, specifies the self moving through the environment. Further, the point of outflow from which these streaming patterns appear to originate specifies the direction of heading when locomoting. In later work, Gibson proposed that animals guide their locomotion by maintaining this point of outflow on the intended target and control their speed with reference to the rate of flow. In this way, directed movement toward some object is a dynamic relationship between environmental features and self-produced patterns in the optic flow. Such a relational account runs counter to the long-held view that perception of one's own movement is based solely on motor feedback (motor kinesthesis) from the limbs and joints.

Further, in the process of utilizing dynamic displays to develop observers' skills for identifying aircraft, Gibson became sensitized to the critical, and often overlooked, distinction between form perception, which involves static two-dimensional displays, and object perception, which involves solid objects perceived when the object, the perceiver, or both, are in motion. This work created the foundation for Gibson's later insight that the perceptual

Gibson

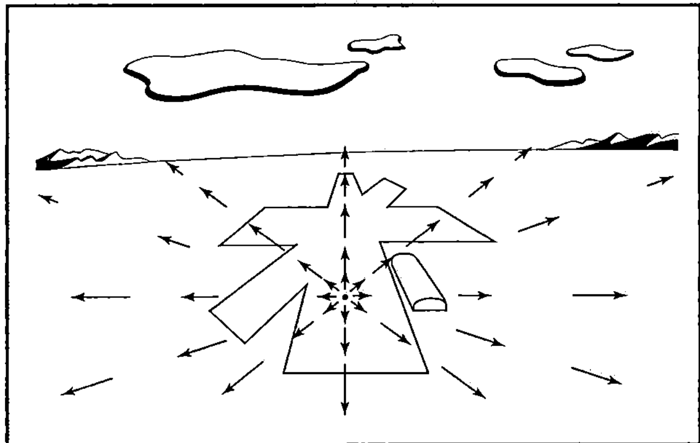

Figure 2. An optical flow field: Point of outflow specifies direction of heading.

information specifying object shape is invariant structure under transformation. It also led to Gibson's separation and parallel studies of, on the one hand, environmental perception and, on the other hand, picture perception—topics that are often conflated in standard accounts of perceiving.

Texture Gradients, Ecological Optics, and Perceptual Systems. Returning to Smith College after the war, Gibson began writing *The Perception of the Visual World*, which explored the preceding decade's research and its implications. Its central claim that visual stimulation carries higher-order structures corresponding to the perceived environment offered some original solutions to several perennial problems in perceptual theory, perhaps most notably the problem of object size constancy.

Because an object's projected size on the two-dimensional retinal surface varies inversely with its distance from the perceiver, it has been a long-standing puzzle why object size appears to be relatively constant independent of its distance. Such perceived size constancy has been explained traditionally by proposing that perceivers supplement impressions of apparent size with distance cues to compensate for variations in projections on the retina. According to this account, then, perception of object size is mediated by inference-like processes. From that supposition it follows that experience of the object, and by extension of much of the environment, is indirect. Gibson pointed out, however, that this way of framing the problem fails to appreciate that in a terrestrial environment objects typically rest on textured ground surfaces, that surface textures tend to be stochastically regular, and as a result, texture density increases as the surface extends away from the perceiver. When these conditions obtain, which they normally do, objects of equal size located at different distances from a perceiver occlude equal portions

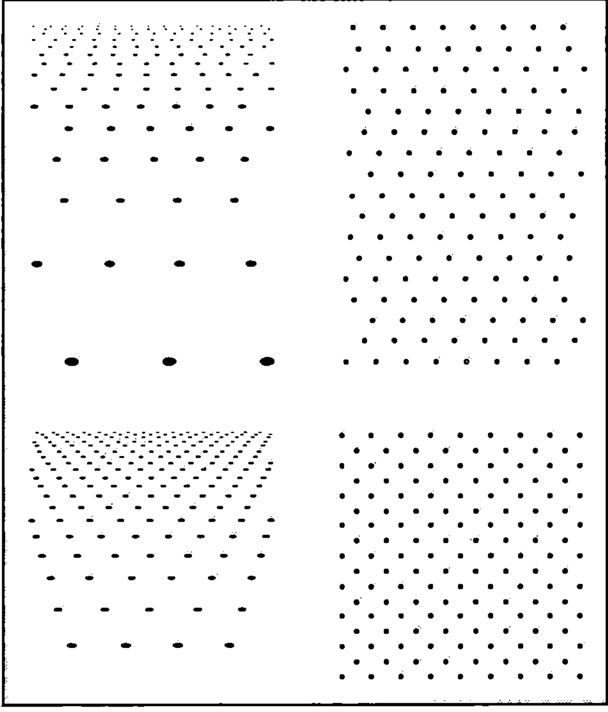

Figure 3. Texture gradients correspond to depth and degree of surface slant.

of the gradient of surface texture. Likewise, the ratio of object size to background texture remains relatively constant as an object is positioned at successively greater or closer distances from a perceiver. The presence of this higher order structure—an object-ground surface invariant—in the visual field raises the possibility that relative object size can be directly perceived in patterns of visual stimulation.

Over the decades of the 1950s and 1960s Gibson investigated the perception of surface and object properties, and this experimental work deepened his theoretical analysis of visual perception. To mention but three critical advances during this period: First, in collaboration with Eleanor J. Gibson, he offered an original account of perceptual learning. The Gibsons proposed that perceptual learning is a process of differentiating structure present in the stimulus array. In the course of detecting as yet unrecognized structure in available sensory information, perceivers discern in an ongoing process more about the environment in an unmediated fashion. Second, separate investigations by the Gibsons began to reveal that meaningful properties of the environment are available to be perceived in the available stimulus information. The earliest evidence for this possibility was shown in E. J. Gibson and R. D. Walk's classic "visual cliff" experiments, in which it was found that newly crawling infants are sensitive to depth at an edge. The visual information specifying

Gibson

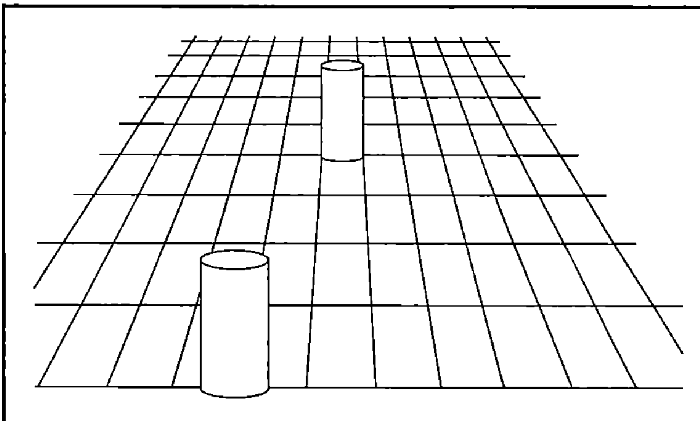

Figure 4. Relative size constancy specified by object-ground surface relationship.

depth at an edge is the shearing of the texture of a lower surface at the edge of the upper surface, with this shearing effect being produced by movements of the infant situated on the upper surface. Such dynamically generated information is perceived as affording the possibility of falling. Similarly, William Schiff, James Caviness, and James Gibson demonstrated that immature animals perceive an expanding form in the visual field as a looming surface that affords impending collision. Both of these studies demonstrate that features of the environment with functionally significant meaning are available to be perceived in the stimulus array, and also that self-motion and motion of objects are critical facets of the process of detecting visual information and the functionally meaningful properties that such information specifies. Third, Gibson, George Kaplan, Horace Reynolds, and Kirk Wheeler showed that when the texture of one surface is continuously deleted at the moving edge of another surface, the first is perceived as being covered up by the second, and significantly, it is perceived as existing although temporarily out of sight. This discovery of the effect of occluding edges affirmed that when perception is considered as a process that occurs over time, the environment is perceived in an extended fashion beyond what can be seen in a discrete slice in time.

These research findings converged to mark an important shift in Gibson's thinking. His earlier work on the psychophysical correspondence between higher-order patterns of stimulation and retinal projections carried with it an implicit assumption that stimulation is imposed on receptor surfaces. Gibson came to reject the stimulus-response mode of thinking that characterized these writings, and he began to reformulate a new approach to perceiving. This reconceptualization required two critical and innovative steps. First, drawing on Heider's distinction between object and medium, Gibson began to develop the program of ecological optics, which considers

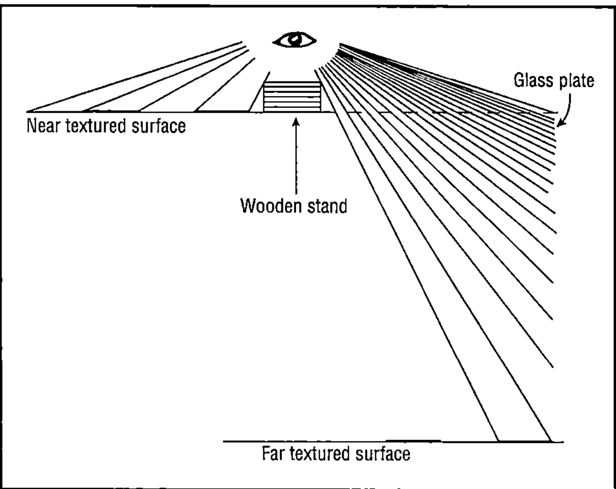

Figure 5. Texture density differences on either side of the visual cliff.

how stimulus information that specifies object properties could be conveyed in reflected light, and accordingly, is available to be perceived directly. Second, Gibson rejected the idea that perceiving is based on the passive imposition of stimulation on the sensory receptors, and instead proposed that perceiving is an activity of an embodied agent whose exploratory actions play an essential role in revealing structure in the stimulus array. Jointly, ecological optics and perceptual systems become the platform for the ecological approach to perceiving, each serving as complementary facets of a dynamic system of animal-environment reciprocity. These innovations were initially presented in Gibson's groundbreaking book, *The Senses Considered as Perceptual Systems.*

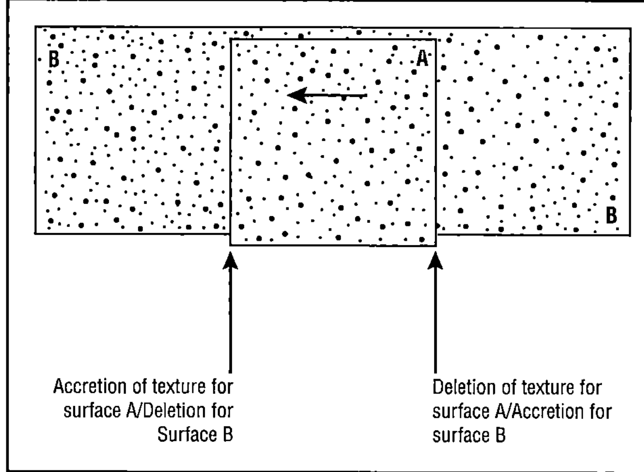

Figure 6. Deletion and accretion of optical texture at the leading edge and trailing edge of an occluding surface, respectively.

An Ecological Approach to Perceiving. Gibson's analysis of stimulus information was more fully elaborated and his treatment of perceiving was further refined in his last major work, *The Ecological Approach to Visual Perception.* A distinctive feature of this book as compared to standard treatments of perception is that the perceiver is not considered until midway through the work. Fully the first half of the book is a detailed discussion of properties of the environment considered from the standpoint of a terrestrial animal, followed by an extensive consideration of ecological optics and stimulus information. This is as it should be for an ecological approach to perceiving: examination of the "econiche" in relation to which perceiving has evolved and continues to operate is the essential first step in developing an understanding of perceiving considered as a functional activity. When Gibson turns to consider the perceiver, emphasis is on perceiving as a functional activity of an embodied agent, and here the previously developed concept of perceptual systems plays an essential role.

An especially significant feature of this book is Gibson's explication of his influential concept of affordances. Gibson proposed that what is perceived in the process of detecting stimulus information are the affordances of the environment, which are its functionally meaningful properties taken with reference to an individual. For example, an object affords "sitting-on" for an individual if it is perceived at an appropriate height relative to leg length, and if its structure and composition appear to support that person's weight. As such, affordances are mutually constituted by characteristics of the environment and the perceiver; and this concept locates functionally significant meanings in the dynamic perceiver-environment relationship.

The concept of affordance has generated much interest in psychology and philosophy because it offers a fresh way of approaching the challenging issue of perceived meaning. Standard approaches would have it that meaning results from the individual interpreting equivocal sensory input. What is troubling about this explanation is that it places all meanings within individual minds, and in doing so, it puts out of reach a psychologically meaningful ground for an individual's actions as well as a common ground for individuals' shared social existence. In contrast, affordances are relational properties of perceiver and environment, and hence directly perceivable. And because all individuals engage the environment as embodied agents, properties of the environment perceived relationally can have similar functional meanings across individuals. In short, the picture that emerges is of an environment rich with potential meaning for perceivers. Affordances, understood within the relational framework of ecological optics and perceptual systems, provide psychology and the philosophy of mind with something previously unattainable given their historical roots in mind-world dualism, namely, grounds for a realist account of knowing.

Style of Thinking. A reviewer of *The Ecological Approach to Visual Perception* posthumously referred to Gibson as "the Seer of Ithaca." That description is very astute, and not only because of Gibson's groundbreaking theoretical work and his highly original concepts. What may be most remarkable about Gibson was an ability throughout his career to identify problems in the domain of visual perception that others failed to see. His prescience was due, in large measure, to his stance toward the phenomena of vision. Gibson identified himself as a behaviorist and functionalist in the James-Holt tradition, which led him to adopt a Darwinian perspective in a more thoroughgoing manner than most perceptual researchers tend to do. This stance is evident in his attention to the environment and to the active nature of perceiving. Furthermore, he was spurred by his contact with psychologists of a phenomenological inclination to observe the way things look. Gibson's primary concern throughout most of his career, and prompted by his early contact with Koffka, was "how do we see the world as we do?" This question led him to place at the center of his investigations of visual perception a consideration of how the environment is experienced by an individual. This functional and phenomenological attitude kept bringing Gibson back to perceptual phenomena that needed to be explained. Attention to the way things look reveals that visual experience is dynamic, not static; that the environment is experienced continuously over time, not in discrete moments; that perceivers are actively engaged in detecting information, not passively receiving sensory stimulation; and that the environment is made up of perceptually meaningful features, not merely congeries of forms, angles, and edges. Recognition of these fundamental features of visual experience transforms how perceiving is conceptualized and how it needs to be studied.

Gibson was a model scientist. He thought deeply about central problems in the field of perception, carefully developed and then refined the concepts that lay at the heart of his work, and designed rigorous, elegant experiments. There is an economy in Gibson's research and in his writing that reflects an exceptional degree of deliberation and thoughtfulness in the formulation of his ideas. Gibson relished a vigorous debate that challenged him to better articulate his position, and he would press his case doggedly. But he demonstrated over the course of his career that he was prepared to give up a position when it proved inadequate to problems at hand and in the face of better formulations. Gibson exhibited a remarkable combination of steadfast commitment to a theoretical framework and a willingness to start fresh when that was called for. In this regard, he implored his students and readers to reject "the dead hand of habit" when thinking about perception, and about psychological issues more generally. The consummate scientist, he urged his students and readers to look for themselves.

BIBLIOGRAPHY

WORKS BY GIBSON

"Adaptation, After-Effect and Contrast in the Perception of Curved Lines." *Journal of Experimental Psychology* 16 (1933): 1–31.

Motion Picture Testing and Research. Aviation Psychology Research Reports, no. 7. Washington, DC, 1948.

The Perception of the Visual World. Boston: Houghton-Mifflin, 1950.

With Paul Olum and Frank Rosenblatt. "Parallax and Perspective during Airplane Landing." *American Journal of Psychology* 68 (1955): 372–385.

With Eleanor J. Gibson. "Perceptual Learning: Differentiation or Enrichment?" *Psychological Review* 62 (1955): 32–41.

"Visually Controlled Locomotion and Visual Orientation in Animals and Men." *British Journal of Psychology* 49 (1958): 182–194.

"The Concept of the Stimulus in Psychology." *American Psychologist* 16 (1960): 694–703.

With William Schiff and James Caviness. "Persistent Fear Responses in Rhesus Monkeys to the Optical Stimulus of 'Looming.'" *Science* 136 (1962): 982–983.

The Senses Considered as Perceptual Systems. Boston: Houghton-Mifflin, 1966.

"James J. Gibson." In *A History of Psychology in Autobiography*, vol. 5, edited by E. G. Boring and G. Lindzey. New York: Appleton-Century-Crofts, 1967.

"New Reasons for Realism." *Synthese* 17 (1967): 162–172.

With George Kaplan, Horace Reynolds, and Kirk Wheeler. "The Change from Visible to Invisible: A Study of Optical Transitions." *Perception & Psychophysics* 5 (1969): 113–116.

"The Information Available in Pictures." *Leonardo* 4 (1971): 27–35.

The Ecological Approach to Visual Perception. Boston: Houghton-Mifflin, 1979.

Reasons for Realism: Selected Essays of James J. Gibson. Edited by E. S. Reed and R. Jones. Hillsdale, NJ: Lawrence Erlbaum Associates, 1982. A full listing of Gibson's works.

OTHER SOURCES

Gibson, Eleanor J. *Principles of Perceptual Learning and Development.* New York: Appleton-Century-Crofts, 1969.

———. *Perceiving the Affordances: A Portrait of Two Psychologists.* Mahwah, NJ: Lawrence Erlbaum Associates, 2002.

———, and Richard Walk. "The 'Visual Cliff.'" *Scientific American* 202 (1960): 64–71.

Heft, Harry. *Ecological Psychology in Context: James Gibson, Roger Barker, and the Legacy of William James's Radical Empiricism.* Mahwah, NJ: Lawrence Erlbaum Associates, 2001.

Reed, Edward S. *James J. Gibson and the Psychology of Perception.* New Haven, CT: Yale University Press, 1988.

Harry Heft

GÖDEL, KURT FRIEDRICH

(*b.* Brünn, Moravia [now Brno, Czech Republic], 28 April 1906; *d.* Princeton, New Jersey, 14 January 1978), *mathematical logic, set theory, general relativity, philosophy of mathematics, philosophy of space and time.* For the original article on Gödel see *DSB*, vol. 17, Supplement II.

The year 2006 marked the centenary of Gödel's birth. With the fifth and final volume of *Kurt Gödel: Collected Works*—which made available many of his previously unpublished writings—having been published in 2003, renewed attention has been paid worldwide to the great debt logic and set theory owe to Gödel. The appearance of this new material, as well as the publication by Hao Wang of his account of his conversations with Gödel (1996), has caused philosophers to reassess the significance of Gödel's contributions to much less settled debates. His strictly formal achievements have, to no one's surprise, stood the test of time. What remains striking is the continued inability of all takers to resolve, in a manner that is universally acceptable, the greatest formal challenge left unresolved by Gödel—namely, Georg Cantor's continuum hypotheis (CH), after Paul Cohen proved its independence from the axioms of set theory. In this, Gödel's problematic legacy strangely resembles that of his close friend and associate at the Institute for Advanced Study, Albert Einstein, for whom the previous year, 2005, marked the centenary of his own "miraculous year." Einstein's unclimbed peak, the unification of relativity theory with quantum mechanics, continues to beckon, yet remains a goal more than an achievement.

Continuing Research. To be sure, there are contenders for Gödel's prize, such as W. Hugh Woodin, whose research program, following Gödel's lead, looks for new, large cardinal axioms for set theory that will settle CH. For Woodin, the independence results showed only that CH is a difficult problem (Woodin, 2001). Yet there is far from universal agreement among set theorists concerning Woodin's approach. Solomon Feferman, for example, a prominent skeptic, has written, "my personal attitude concerning the 'actual' existence of various kinds of large cardinals … is that *it is all pie in the sky*" (Feferman, 1996, p. 20; emphasis in the original). Indeed, Feferman has raised questions about what relevance Gödel's incompleteness theorems have for mainstream mathematics—in particular, whether there are "natural arithmetical statements

Gödel

which have resisted attack so far ... because they are not decided by systems that formalize a significant part of mathematical practice" (2006, p. 437). It is suggestive, he argues, that to date none has been found. (However, here one should also bear in mind Harvey Friedman's research program, as represented, for example, in Friedman [2000], discussed by Feferman.)

There are, of course, also contenders for Einstein's prize, such as string theory. Yet, in spite of its impressive development in recent years, string theory remains, to a considerable extent, an IOU. The prize, most would agree, is not yet in sight. The parallel between Gödel and Einstein goes further. Cosmologists have to a considerable extent appreciated the significance of Gödel's discovery of new cosmological solutions—the so-called rotating or Gödel universes—to the field equations of general relativity, which possess striking properties, such as the possibility of time travel, threatening the very idea of time and causality. Indeed, one cosmologist, Stephen Hawking, proposed a "Chronology Protection Conjecture" (Hawking, 1992) that would rule out world models such as Gödel's as unphysical. Philosophers, by contrast, were only in the late 1990s beginning to catch on to the significance, from a philosophical point of view, of what Gödel dug up in Einstein's backyard. The posthumous publication of Gödel's "Some Observations about the Relationship between Theory of Relativity and Kantian Philosophy" (Gödel, 1995) accelerated debate over the logic and cogency of Gödel's argument that relativity theory implies the ideality of time.

The same is true of Gödel's ontological argument for the existence of God. Indeed, what is striking is that both are "modal" arguments, from possibility to actuality. Gödel moved from the provable nonexistence of time in a merely possible Gödel universe to its nonexistence in the actual world. The ontological argument, in turn, purports to derive from the mere possibility of a necessary being, like God, his actual existence. Surprisingly, the rebirth in the late twentieth century of modal logic and metaphysics did little on its own to change the climate in regard to reassessing Gödel's modal arguments. The posthumous publication, however, of his formal, Leibnizian version of the ontological argument has given rise to a lively discussion, beginning with Jordan Howard Sobel's reformulation and critique. Interestingly, just as Gödel's hero, Gottfried Wilhelm Leibniz (1646–1716), had maintained, the crucial step appears to be the very first one, proclaiming the possibility of the existence of God. Even those like C. Anthony Anderson who have attempted to repair and improve Gödel's own formulation in the light of Sobel's criticism, believe that this premise can in effect only be taken on faith. Even if this were true, however, the amended argument would still have the very interesting consequence that only "super atheism" is consistent—

Kurt Friedrich Gödel. *Kurt Friedrich Gödel, circa 1935.* TIME LIFE PICTURES/GETTY IMAGES.

namely, the view that the existence of God is not even possible. (See Fitting [2002] for an extensive study of modal arguments like Gödel's.)

Philosophical Development. More generally, what has begun to receive the attention it deserves is Gödel's overall philosophical development, culminating, after 1959, in a turn to the German "idealist" philosopher Edmund Husserl (1859–1938), a figure conspicuously absent from the mainstream of analytical philosophy in which Gödel found himself (uncomfortably) situated. Mark van Atten and Juliette Kennedy's monograph (2003)—building on seminal work by Robert Tragesser—has gone a long way toward putting philosophers on the right track in coming to terms with the kind of philosopher Gödel aspired to be. New light, for example, has been shed on why Gödel turned to Husserl's later, more "subjective" or "idealistic" philosophy, as well as on Gödel's (in)famous defense of mathematical Platonism and on the idea of mathematical intuition. Charles Parsons, to be sure, has made important contributions to these subjects, but to a considerable extent they have proceeded from a Kantian point of view not shared by Gödel. In turn, John Dawson's exhaustive biography (1997) does not contain much by way of insights into Gödel's philosophical enterprise, either on its own or as it relates to his formal achievements. Bernd Buldt's review essay (1995) of Dawson's and other recent accounts of Gödel's life and work provides a balanced assessment of the strengths and weaknesses of the competing monographs. (For an account focusing on the formal and philosophical consequences of Gödel's relationship with Einstein, see Yourgrau [2005].)

In sum, in the early 2000s historians were for the first time in a proper position to begin to assess the significance of the full spectrum of Gödel's contributions, formal and philosophical, to logic and set theory and also to physics, as well as to the philosophy of these and other disciplines, and more generally, to the question of the relationship of philosophy to mathematics and science. Perhaps in the near future they will be able to take the true measure of a mind the like of which is seen once a millennium.

SUPPLEMENTARY BIBLIOGRAPHY

WORKS BY GÖDEL

"Some Observations about the Relationship between Theory of Relativity and Kantian Philosophy." In *Collected Works,* edited by Solomon Feferman et al., vol. 3, 230–259. New York: Oxford University Press, 1995.

Collected Works. 5 vols. Edited by Solomon Feferman et al. New York: Oxford University Press, 1986–2003.

OTHER SOURCES

Anderson, C. Anthony. "Some Emendations of Gödel's Ontological Argument." *Faith and Philosophy* 7 (1990): 291–303.

———, and Michael Gettings. "Gödel's Ontological Argument Revisited." In *Gödel '96: Logical Foundations of Mathematics, Computer Science, and Physics; Kurt Gödel's Legacy,* edited by Petr Hajek, 167–172. Berlin: Springer, 1996.

Atten, Mark van, and Juliette Kennedy. "On the Philosophical Development of Kurt Gödel." *Bulletin of Symbolic Logic* 9, no. 4 (December 2003): 425–476.

Buldt, Bernd. "Stories of Genius: Recent Accounts of Kurt Gödel's Life." In *Europolis 5: Kurt Gödel und die Mathematische Logik.* Linz: Linzer Universitätsverlag, 1995.

Dawson, John. *Logical Dilemmas: The Life and Work of Kurt Gödel.* Wellesley, MA: Peters, 1997.

Earman, John. "Appendix: Gödel on the Ideality of Time." In his *Bangs, Crunches, Whimpers, and Shrieks: Singularities and Acausalities in Relativistic Spacetimes,* 194–200. New York: Oxford University Press, 1995.

Ellis, G. F. R. "Contributions of K. Gödel to Relativity and Cosmology." In *Gödel '96: Logical Foundations of Mathematics, Computer Science, and Physics; Kurt Gödel's Legacy,* edited by Petr Hajek, 34–49. Berlin: Springer, 1996.

Feferman, Solomon. "Gödel's Program for New Axioms: Why, Where, How, and What?" In *Gödel '96: Logical Foundations of Mathematics, Computer Science, and Physics; Kurt Gödel's Legacy,* edited by Petr Hajek, 3–22. Berlin: Springer, 1996.

———. "The Impact of the Incompleteness Theorems on Mathematics." *Notices of the American Mathematical Society* 53, no. 4 (April 2006): 434–439.

Fitting, Melvin. *Types, Tableaus, and Gödel's God.* Dordrecht, Netherlands: Kluwer Academic, 2002.

Friedman, Harvey. "Normal Mathematics Will Need New Axioms." *Bulletin of Symbolic Logic* 6, no. 4 (2000): 434–446.

Hajek, Petr, ed. *Gödel '96: Logical Foundations of Mathematics, Computer Science, and Physics; Kurt Gödel's Legacy.* Berlin: Springer, 1996.

Hawking, Stephen. "Chronology Protection Conjecture." *Physical Review* D46 (1992): 603–611.

Kennedy, Juliette, and Mark van Atten. "Gödel's Modernism: On Set Theoretic Incompleteness." *Graduate Faculty Philosophy Journal* 25, no. 2 (2004): 289–349.

Köhler, Eckehart, Bernd Buldt, et al., eds. *Kurt Gödel: Warheit und Beweisbarkeit.* Vienna: Öbv & Hpt, 2002.

Parsons, Charles. "Platonism and Mathematical Intuition in Kurt Gödel's Thought." *Bulletin of Symbolic Logic* 1, no. 1 (March 1995): 44–74.

Sobel, Jordan Howard. "Gödel's Ontological Proof." In *On Being and Saying: Essays for Richard Cartwright,* edited by Judith Jarvis Thomson, 241–261. Cambridge, MA: MIT Press, 1987.

Takeuti, Gaisi. *Memoirs of a Proof Theorist: Gödel and Other Logicians.* Translated by Mariko Yasugi and Nicholas Passell. River Edge, NJ: World Scientific, 2003.

Tragesser, Robert. *Phenomenology and Logic.* Ithaca, NY: Cornell University Press, 1977.

Wang, Hao. *Reflections on Kurt Gödel.* Cambridge, MA: MIT Press, 1987.

———. *A Logical Journey: From Gödel to Philosophy.* Cambridge, MA: MIT Press, 1996.

Woodin, W. Hugh. "The Continuum Hypothesis I." *Notices of the American Mathematical Society* 48, no. 6 (2001): 567–576.

———. "The Continuum Hypothesis II." *Notices of the American Mathematical Society* 48, no. 7 (2001): 681–690.

Yourgrau, Palle. "Kurt Gödel." In *Encyclopedia of Philosophy: Supplement,* edited by Donald Borchert, 220–222. New York: Macmillan, 1996.

———. *Gödel Meets Einstein: Time Travel in the Gödel Universe.* Chicago: Open Court, 1999.

———. *A World without Time: The Forgotten Legacy of Gödel and Einstein.* New York: Basic, 2005.

Palle Yourgrau

GOETHE, JOHANN WOLFGANG VON

(*b.* Frankfurt am Main, Germany, 28 August 1749; *d.* Weimar, Germany, 22 March 1832), *color theory, morphology, zoology, botany, geology, history and philosophy of science, scientific administration.* For the original article on Goethe, see *DSB,* vol. 5.

Since George Wells's entry in the original *DSB,* Nicholas Boyle's multivolume biography (only part of which has been published) has refashioned scholars' understanding of the processes by which Goethe shaped his thought and work. Goethe was able to absorb the most diverse intellectual influences without compromising the individuality and integrity of his vision because he knew (at first instinctively, then consciously) how to trace the threads of law-governed activity in personal, social, and natural phenomena. After accepting the invitation of Duke Carl August of Saxe-Weimar to join his court (1775), he rapidly ascended from the role of court poet and intellectual to become the duke's most trusted advisor and minister. Responsibility for ducal parks, roads, and the duchy's silver mines caused him (shortly before 1780) to study botany, mineralogy, and geology, while his amateur's passion for painting and drawing led him to anatomical studies. In all his scientific endeavors he strove to acquire experimental, observational, and theoretical comprehensiveness and drew on every professional resource, human and institutional, within his reach. This included the faculty and collections of the duchy's university in nearby Jena, where in the 1780s he began building up the scientific faculty and its commitment to research.

From the beginning of his independent scientific efforts Goethe was attentive to method. In his botanical and zoological research he developed ways to articulate, sequence, ramify, and ultimately reunify the results of observation and experiment so that researchers might more easily recognize the typical stages and forms that appear in the phenomena. He articulated a conception of science conducted on multiple levels: a basis in accurately observed experience, followed by coordination, comparison, and organization of the phenomena, and finally by the use of hypotheses to relate the phenomena to more distant fields. In the mid-1790s, as he began to reconceive his botanical and zoological work as part of a more encompassing science of living forms, he proposed a plan that would draw together researchers in natural history, general physics, anatomy, chemistry, zoology, physiology, and morphology. Within a few years he was plotting an even more extensively multidisciplinary project for studying color. The circle of scientists, naturalists, philosophers, and distinguished visitors who assembled in Jena and Weimar gave him hope that a new era of comprehensive approaches to nature was dawning. But by the early years of the new century many had left, driven off by the fear of persecution for heterodoxy (after the Jena controversy over Johann Gottlieb Fichte's putative atheism) or the advance of Napoléon Bonaparte's army.

Studies since the 1970s have compelled a reassessment of two much-discussed historical issues. With respect to evolution, recent studies have shown that Goethe's approach strongly supported the gradual change and emergence of species and that his morphology directly and indirectly influenced Charles Darwin. Although the older historiography regarding his color science (*Farbenlehre*) was dominated by the notion that Goethe's poetic sensibility did not allow him to appreciate modern science, it has become clear that he was in fact inclined to accept the theory of the differential refrangibility of white light according to color. Defective explanations in German physics manuals probably gave him false expectations, however. In any case, he arrived at serious objections to the theory's omissions and phenomenological misrepresentations by undertaking a comprehensive experimental investigation of prismatic phenomena, which led to two publications, under the title *Contributions to Optics,* with prism and display cards included. At the same time his investigation into contrast colors led him to recognize that there were profound physiological issues involved in color perception. As he investigated past optics and color science to understand better the rise of Isaac Newton's theory, he began to grasp the complex historical character of science and scientific change. Immanuel Kant's first and third *Critiques* and discussions with Friedrich von Schiller made him progressively more aware of phenomenological, methodological-conceptual, and historical issues.

After nearly two decades, this research, which Goethe considered to be more important than his literary production, culminated in the tripartite *Zur Farbenlehre* (1810). It consisted of a didactic part (a detailed presentation of the chief phenomena of color according to physiological, physical, and chemical causes, along with a discussion of major topics for future, multidisciplinary studies of color), a polemical part (an analysis and deconstruction of the methods and experiments of Newton's *Opticks*), and a history (from antiquity to the early 1800s, with an approach that took both internalist and externalist perspectives and developed a quasi-Kantian theory of scientific change based on *Vorstellungsarten,* typical ways of conceiving and portraying phenomena).

Although he was a source of inspiration to *Naturphilosophie* and Romantic science, Goethe maintained a certain independence with respect to both. After *Zur Farbenlehre* he only occasionally did new scientific work. He edited and published some of his earlier scientific manuscripts and commented on developments in the contemporary sciences. He updated the *Farbenlehre* to incorporate interference colors (in the course of which he developed a qualified enthusiasm for the wave theory of light), encouraged younger researchers who showed an affinity to his own approaches (such as Arthur Schopenhauer, Johannes Peter Müller, and Jan Purkyn), and made a (disputed) claim to have anticipated Lorenz Oken's theory of the vertebral construction of the skull. In the last year of his life he published a commentary on the Parisian dispute between Georges Cuvier and Étienne Geoffroy Saint-Hilaire over the principles of animal morphology. Though his sympathy lay with the latter, he tried to work

Johann Wolfgang Goethe. AP IMAGES.

out conceptual and empirical common ground that would capitalize on the strengths of both men's approaches.

Much of this late work was undertaken in the hope of preserving and cultivating the legacy of his research and methods. Nineteenth-century scientists, more taken by positivism and mathematization, resisted these efforts. Despite a not inconsiderable influence on later work in morphology and in the physiology of color perception, Goethean scientific practice never achieved mainstream recognition.

SUPPLEMENTARY BIBLIOGRAPHY

The editions of Goethe, in the original German and in translation, are legion, and the secondary literature is vast. There are many hundreds of books and thousands of articles about his scientific writings alone. The selection listed here is intended to help the reader acquire only an introductory orientation in Goethe's scientific work and in the historical and philosophical issues that work raises.

WORKS BY GOETHE

Scientific Studies. Edited and translated by Douglas Miller. Goethe Edition 12. New York: Suhrkamp, 1988. Includes new translations of the most frequently cited scientific and methodological essays, along with a brief selection from *Zur Farbenlehre.*

Goethe in the History of Science. Edited by Frederick Amrine. Vols. 29–30 of *Studies in Modern German Literature.* New York: Lang, 1996. The most complete bibliography of Goethe's scientific writings and the scholarship about them, from 1776 to 1990.

Goethe in English: A Bibliography of the Translations in the Twentieth Century. Edited by Derek Glass. Modern Humanities Research Association bibliographies 2. Leeds, U.K.: Maney, 2005.

OTHER SOURCES

Amrine, Frederick, Francis J. Zucker, and Harvey Wheeler, eds. *Goethe and the Sciences: A Reappraisal.* Boston Studies in the Philosophy of Science 97. Boston: Reidel, 1987. A collection of articles surveying, and revising the conception of, Goethe's entire scientific production.

Boyle, Nicholas. *Goethe: The Poet and the Age.* 2 vols. Oxford: Clarendon Press; New York: Oxford University Press, 1991–2000. The standard biography in any language, through 1803, with a third volume in preparation.

Cornell, John F. "Faustian Phenomena: Teleology in Goethe's Interpretation of Plants and Animals." *Journal of Medicine and Philosophy* 15 (1990): 481–492. Explains the kind of developmental, evolutionary theory compatible with, and perhaps intended by, Goethe's morphological science.

Engelhardt, Wolf von. *Goethe im Gespräch mit der Erde: Landschaft, Gesteine, Mineralien und Erdgeschichte in seinem Leben und Werk.* Weimar, Germany: Böhlau, 2003. An overview of Goethe's geological and mineralogical interests, by one of the editors of the geological writings in the Leopoldina edition of his scientific works.

Krätz, Otto. *Goethe und die Naturwissenschaften,* 2nd ed. Munich, Germany: Callwey, 1998. First edition published 1992. A brief, accurate account of Goethe's scientific studies.

Kuhn, Dorothea. *Empirische und ideelle Wirklichkeit: Studien über Goethes Kritik des französischen Akademiestreites.* Neue Hefte zur Morphologie 5. Graz, Austria: Böhlau, 1967. An account of Goethe's intervention in the Cuvier-Geoffroy controversy, by one of the editors of the Leopoldina edition of Goethe's scientific writings.

Mandelkow, Karl Robert. *Goethe im Urteil seiner Kritiker: Dokumente zur Wirkungsgeschichte Goethes in Deutschland.* 4 vols. Munich, Germany: Beck, 1975–1984. A survey of the reception and criticism of Goethe's works from 1773 to 1982.

Nicolai, Heinz, and Hans Henning, eds. "Goethe-Bibliographie." *Goethe* 14/15–33 (1952/53–1971) and *Goethe-Jahrbuch* 89ff. (1972ff.). The authoritative annual update of Goethe bibliography (both primary and secondary literature).

Richards, Robert J. *The Romantic Conception of Life: Science and Philosophy in the Age of Goethe.* Chicago: University of Chicago Press, 2002. Explains in authoritative detail the scientific influence of German Idealism and Romanticism on nineteenth-century biology, with nearly a third of the work (pp. 325–508) specifically devoted to Goethe.

Seamon, David, and Arthur Zajonc, eds. *Goethe's Way of Science: A Phenomenology of Nature.* Albany: State University of New York Press, 1998. Presents Goethe's phenomenological approach to science.

Sepper, Dennis L. *Goethe contra Newton: Polemics and the Project for a New Science of Color.* Cambridge, U.K.: Cambridge University Press, 1988. Explains the scientific background of the *Farbenlehre,* its critique of Newton's color theory, and its anticipations of trends in later history and philosophy of science.

Tantillo, Astrida Orle. *The Will to Create: Goethe's Philosophy of Nature.* Pittsburgh: University of Pittsburgh Press, 2002. A deft combination of conceptual analysis and historical explanation.

Dennis Sepper

GOLD, THOMAS

(*b.* Vienna, Austria, 22 May 1920; *d.* Ithaca, New York, 22 June 2004), *cosmology, astrophysics, geophysics, space science, physiology of hearing.*

Gold, together with Fred Hoyle and Hermann Bondi, originated the steady state model of the universe, in competition with the previously existing and eventually dominant evolutionary (or big bang) model. He also contributed important ideas to our understanding of pulsars (rotating, magnetized neutron stars left from supernova explosions), the physics of astronomical dust, solar flares and energetic particles, interstellar gas, and the operation of the cochlea in human hearing.

Early Years. Industrialist Maximillian Gold (of Jewish heritage) moved with his wife, Josephine, daughter Elizabeth, and son Thomas from Vienna to Berlin shortly after Adolf Hitler's 1933 rise to power, being protected initially by their foreign citizenship. They soon decided, however, that it would be wiser to move on to London, sending Tommy (as most of his friends called him) or Tom (as he called himself in later life) to boarding school in Zuoz, Switzerland. His skill in downhill skiing dated from that period, with comparable fondness for water skiing developing later. Elizabeth eventually settled permanently in Switzerland and died there.

Returning to England in 1938, Gold enrolled at Trinity College, Cambridge, to read mechanical sciences (BA 1942, MA 1946). In 1940 the British government,

Gold

concerned about possible fifth columnists, interned Gold and many other Austrian and German émigrés as enemy aliens. After a brief stay in a camp in Bury St. Edmunds, Gold was sent to Canada, and it took fifteen months before he was declared a friendly alien and sent back to Britain to take up war work. By remarkable coincidence, in the same camp was Hermann Bondi, a fellow Viennese Jew, also a student at Trinity, though they had not previously met. The slightly more senior camp resident Max Perutz organized an informal "school," at which the young students could teach each other. Bondi's extraordinary mathematical skills and Gold's outstanding physical insights soon became obvious and complementary.

After Bondi was liberated in 1942, he and Fred Hoyle, who had recently completed a Cambridge degree in applied mathematics, were established in a cottage in Dunsfold, Surrey, to work on radar devices and anti-U-boat warfare. Gold soon joined them, and many of their leisure hours were spent discussing a wide range of scientific issues, including cosmology (the large-scale structure of the universe). The three remained collaborators for many years.

Gold returned to Cambridge in 1946, holding a one-year research grant at the Cavendish Laboratory of Physics, a two-year Medical Research Council Grant at the Zoological Laboratory (1947–1949), and a demonstrator (teaching) position back at Cavendish from 1949 to 1952. He became a British subject in February 1947. During this period, he worked first with R. J. Pumphrey on how resonance and feedback in the cochlea permit much better pitch discrimination by the human ear than would initially seem possible. The resulting papers were largely ignored at the time but were cited quite frequently in the 1990s, when it became clear that the ear must be an active organ during the hearing process. Gold never completed a PhD (nor did Hoyle), but he received an honorary Cambridge DSc in 1969.

Steady State Cosmology. In 1948 came a pair of papers, one by Bondi and Gold and a more mathematical one by Hoyle, putting forward the idea of a steady state universe. This incorporated the observed fact of the expansion of the universe (a discovery of Edwin Hubble), but, instead of the expansion resulting in an ever-decreasing density of matter, new matter appeared and formed new galaxies. Thus, on average, a steady state universe looks the same to observers at all times, as well as at all places (as also in evolutionary cosmologies). The authors' motivations were at least twofold. The first, and to them philosophically the more important, was to place the process of creation in the present time and in nearby places, where it might be studied scientifically. Second, the steady state model overcame some practical problems with evolutionary models, particularly an apparent age discrepancy in which the universe seemed to be younger than the Sun and many other stars. A steady state universe has both an infinite past and an infinite future, while evolutionary models have finite age.

Thomas Gold. SPL / PHOTO RESEARCHERS, INC.

Steady state was of enormous importance in the history of astronomy, because it turned cosmology into a serious, observational part of science, by making predictions different from those of an evolutionary universe, for which Hoyle coined the name *big bang.* The predictions included numbers, sizes, colors, and brightnesses of galaxies at large distances compared to those near us. A number of astronomers, both optical and in the new community of radio observers, turned their attention to testing the predictions, sometimes with a explicit goal of "disproving steady state." Observations gradually accumulated and, in due course, showed that in fact the universe has changed a great deal with time. It was hot and dense long ago ("standard hot big bang"), and galaxies were once young, blue, and bright while they formed their first generations of stars.

The apparent difficulties with big bang models faded with better estimates of the cosmic expansion rate (first from Walter Baade, and later from Allan R. Sandage and others), and direct supporting evidence for the hot, dense past came with the 1965 discovery of the cosmic microwave background radiation by Arno Penzias and Robert Wilson (shared Nobel Prize in Physics, 1978). That radiation was once gamma rays about 15 billion years ago, then x-rays, ultraviolet, visible light, and infrared, and, with the continuing expansion of the universe, the photons have now been redshifted (dragged to longer wavelengths) until they are microwaves with a temperature of 2.7 K. Thus the number of professional astronomers and cosmologists who took steady state seriously declined from many to few to, after the mid-1970s, almost none except the original proposers and a handful of their coworkers. A recent variant, called quasi-steady-state, clings to precarious life in occasional journal publications and conference talks. Gold's last published cosmology paper appeared in 1973, but both public lectures and private conversion made clear that he continued to regard steady state as closer to the truth than a universe with a finite past.

Later Career. Gold was appointed chief assistant at Greenwich Observatory in 1952, under Harold Spencer Jones (Astronomer Royal, 1933–1955). In 1957, he accepted a professorship of astronomy at Harvard University, becoming the Robert Wheeler Willson Professor of Applied Astronomy there in 1958. Cornell University appointed him professor of astronomy, chair of the (then very small) department, and founding director of the Center for Radio Physics and Space Research, all in 1959. He remained chairman until 1968 and director until 1981, building these institutions up into major ones by means of both new appointments (including Yervant Terzian, who eventually took over the chairmanship) and collaborations with people in other departments (Edwin E. Salpeter in nuclear physics, Marshall Cohen in electrical engineering, and Gordon Pettengill in earth and planetary sciences, among others). The center built and operated what is still the world's largest single radar and radio astronomy dish at Arecibo, in Puerto Rico, as part of the National Astronomy and Ionospheric Center. The name reflects that the 1,000-foot dish had originally been intended for ionospherics—studies of the upper, ionized layers of Earth's atmosphere. But Gold and his colleagues made it, in addition, a unique facility for radar and radio astronomy.

He held the John L. Wetherill Chair from 1971 until his statutory retirement in 1985, after which he briefly returned to Cambridge and an honorary fellowship at Trinity, his old college. The family returned soon to Ithaca, and Gold remained active in astronomy for more than a decade beyond his retirement. He became a U.S. citizen in about 1964.

Among the honors accorded Gold were memberships in the U.S. National Academy of Sciences and the Royal Society (London), lectureships and visiting professorships in Bonn, Copenhagen, and Toronto, and both the Gold Medal and the George Darwin Lectureship of the Royal Astronomical Society (London). Close colleagues were of the opinion that these honors would have been even more numerous if Gold had not spent quite such a large fraction of his time in both scientific and political semi-opposition to most of the astronomical and geophysical communities. He started writing, for instance, on science that could be done from space in 1954, but slowly evolved into a serious opponent of a human presence in space for scientific purposes, testifying before the U.S. Congress and elsewhere against Skylab, the shuttle, and the international space station.

One can count twenty or more ideas that came first or most vigorously from Gold. "Right" and "wrong" is too simple a classification; indeed for some the votes are not all yet in. But "controversial" applies to most, and one of his own summaries of his intellectual career is titled "Controversial Topics."

Controversies and Prescience: Cambridge and the United States. Gold's later years at Cambridge coincided with the rise of radio astronomy there and elsewhere, and several of the controversies arose from that concatenation. Martin Ryle, head of the Cavendish radio astronomy group, had called the sources they were discovering "radio stars," implying a location within the Milky Way. Gold said and wrote in 1951 that the sources must be outside our galaxy, associated with other, perhaps very distant, galaxies. Identification of the sources with visible objects showed this to be correct. But it then became possible to use counts of the sources as a cosmological test. It was one that, when the smoke had cleared, had ruled out steady state from about 1955 onward, though not quite so firmly as Ryle had originally claimed. John Bolton produced the most reliable counts, showing that a larger fraction of galaxies had been radio sources in the past than now.

Gold's contributions to understanding of magnetic phenomena on cosmic scales began in Cambridge. He wrote on the connection between Earth's rotation and its magnetic field in 1949 and, in 1959, coined the name *magnetosphere* to describe the region of space where effects of that field dominate those of the solar wind. He and Bondi wrote in 1950 on the processes that generate magnetic fields in Earth and elsewhere, and Gold's 1955 paper on turbulence in interstellar gas introduced the idea of magnetohydrodynamic shock waves, now recognized in a variety of laboratory and astronomical contexts. In partial collaboration with Hoyle, Gold put forward the ideas that both solar flares and the heating of the solar corona derive their energy from magnetic fields tangled by solar rotation and photospheric motions and that the energy can be

Thomas Gold. *Thomas Gold, at a summer school for outstanding high school students in Australia in the early 1970s, explaining how certain observations of pulsars can be used to study the magnetic field of the Milky Way Galaxy.* COURTESY OF CARVEL GOLD, CORNELL UNIVERSITY.

released very quickly by reconnection of magnetic field lines, which squeeze electric currents and so accelerate particles (1956–1960).

By contrast, when the polarization of starlight was discovered in 1949 by John Scoville Hall and William Hiltner at Yerkes Observatory, it was Leverett Davis and Jesse Greenstein at the California Institute of Technology who came forward with a magnetic model, in which the polarization was due to scattering by interstellar dust grains aligned with a galactic magnetic field (later shown to exist and to be responsible for radio emission from the galactic plane). Gold, however, put forward a nonmagnetic model, in which grains were set spinning by collisions with gas molecules and aligned by gas streaming in the plane. Modern thought requires both processes: collisions set grains spinning, but they are magnetically aligned.

In the days before mantle convection, plate tectonics, and continental drift were accepted as the cause of particular regions of Earth's crust having been at very different magnetic and geographical latitudes in the past, Gold pointed out that Earth's rotation axis could shift by large amounts relative to the surface without violating conservation of angular momentum. (The standard analogy is a cat or a diver twisting over in midair to come down right side up.) It has since been shown, partly by Gold, that Earth's rotation axis is stabilized against large shifts of this sort by the Moon, but that Mars is subject to them.

Most incendiary of all was the outcome of Gold's thinking about likely conditions on the lunar surface. He considered the accumulation of micrometeorites, sputtering of rock when it was repeatedly heated and cooled by large amounts (as happens on the airless and slowly rotating moon), and the effects of direct exposure to ultraviolet and x-ray radiation from the Sun, and concluded that there would be a surface dust layer, probably very thick and hazardous to both manned and unmanned landers. Also important in his 1955 and later papers on this topic was an electrostatic mechanism of dust transport, so that all surfaces would be covered. When the Lunar Surveyors and Apollo landers got to the Moon, dust there certainly was enough to take clear footprints and cling (electrostatically and annoyingly) to everything, but it did not have the quicksandlike properties that Gold was generally thought to have predicted. Indeed after the return of the first lunar seismic data, recording the patterns of small quakes caused by meteorite impacts, he concluded in

1969 that the Moon responded as one would expect from a deep but highly compressed layer of powder. Another contemporary reaction to the very short lunar ring down-time was that lunar rocks must have some of the acoustic properties of green cheese.

After moving to the United States, Gold continued to put forward new ideas in connection with still other astronomical and planetary phenomena, some of them well in advance of their time. These included:

1. the 1961 proposal that interstellar gas would be dominated by molecular hydrogen and a 1963 collaboration with Robert Gould and Edwin Salpeter to explain its formation on dust grain surfaces (the molecular component is now thought to be only slightly less massive than the cool, atomic hydrogen phase);
2. analyses of the rotation of Mercury (1965, with Stanton Peale), the rotation period being two-thirds of the orbit period, and of Venus (1969, with Steven Soter), the solid planet rotation being phase-locked to passages by Earth, but the atmosphere rotating much faster, and of structure in the rings of Uranus (1977, with Stanley Dermott), again resonance phenomena;
3. a maser interpretation for the newly discovered bright emission by OH molecules (1966, with Francis Perkins and Salpeter); and
4. the possibility of operating two or more radio telescopes as an interferometer, even without any connection between them, provided only that each was equipped with a clock sufficiently accurate to record phases as well as amplitudes of the waves received by each.

All of these ideas are today part of mainstream astronomy, and indeed Very Long Baseline Interferometry, using accurate clocks rather than delay lines, now spans the diameter of Earth and even small steps into space.

Pulsars and Beyond. Reading these many papers one is struck by how rarely Gold provided numerical estimates or calculations for the phenomena he was proposing. This is true also for the best-known and most-cited of his Cornell papers. The discovery of pulsars was announced by a group of Cambridge (U.K.) radio astronomers in March 1968. Gold's explanation of them, as neutron stars rotating at the pulsation periods (then 0.25 to 1.33 seconds) and radiating from the analog of sunspots as a result of strong magnetic fields, appeared within a few months. It was, however, left for others to calculate how strong the fields would have to be and what one would expect them to be if a neutron star was the remnant core of a massive normal star with an initial field of hundreds or thousands of gauss, as commonly observed. This history has two curious side branches. First, just down the hall from Gold at the time was the office of Franco Pacini (later director of Arcetri Observatory in Florence), who had been thinking about what neutron stars should be like (rapidly rotating and strongly magnetic) and attempting to associate them with supernova remnants before the discovery of pulsars. Second, it was the Arecibo radio telescope (operating in the receiver mode that Gold had insisted upon a decade before) that collected data on the pulsar in the Crab Nebula supernova remnant showing conclusively that Gold and Pacini were on the right track and permitting accurate measurements of neutron star magnetic fields and ages.

In three additional areas, Gold put forward ideas over a number of years without the scientific issues ever being fully resolved. First (from 1958 to 2003) is the question of the direction of the flow of time ("arrow of time"). There seem to be three separate arrows, all pointing in the same direction. One comes from the expansion of the universe, one from thermodynamics (the cream never unstirs itself from the coffee), and one from the behavior of light (which could, according to Maxwell's equations, go backward in time, but never seems to). Gold suspected that the cosmic expansion drove the other two and, as a result, if the universe should eventually recontract, all of physics would be reversed. A big bang universe could indeed recontract (though apparently ours will not); a steady state universe cannot, an additional argument in its favor in Gold's mind.

Second (1974–1997) was consideration of the possibility of life elsewhere in the universe and ways we might communicate with it. Gold was a member of the optimistic school, thinking even that life might have first reached Earth from elsewhere. He supported the radio search efforts by his Cornell colleague Frank Drake (long director of Arecibo and originator of an eponymous equation to estimate the frequency of inhabited planets). Gold even suggested, perhaps tongue in cheek, that the interstellar masers might be the broadcast stations of other civilizations.

Third, relatively late in his career (1977–1997), Gold adopted a view, already fairly common in the Russian geophysical community, that there were very large quantities of methane (pronounced, of course, with the long British "e") that had been trapped inside Earth since the time of its formation, and that this gas was gradually leaking out and being partially transformed into petroleum by bacteria living very deep inside the crust. This, if true, would of course make an enormous difference to the total amount of oil and gas available for future use. At Gold's urging, a couple of very deep boreholes were drilled in Sweden at

Gold

promising sites. These found, if not upward-flowing gas and oil, at least petrologic signatures that Gold believed were indicative of the processes he had in mind. In addition, viable bacteria have been found in many inhospitable places on Earth, around undersea vents, in deep rock fissures, and under ice sheets. The geophysical community as a whole has, however, noted specific biological signatures in most petroleum, decided that the required processes almost certainly do not occur, and opted not to count on or look for nonfossil fuels of this sort.

Folklore. The extreme breadth of Gold's astronomical concerns is revealed by his membership in commissions of the International Astronomical Union. There is a formal upper limit of three per person. He belonged to five, dealing with physical study of planets and satellites, radio astronomy, science from space, cosmology, and high-energy astrophysics. Like most charismatic scientists, he was accompanied by a small cloud of "Gold stories" and famous quotes. Among those vouched for by more than one source was the belief that "all positive quantities are correlated," that is, people who are very good at one thing are likely to be pretty good at other things, and also rather healthier and better looking than the general run of humanity. But he also could always see ways to make things better, for instance, improving Olympic swimming records by designing suits in the shape of "the minimum circumscribed porpoise." Gold maintained an emotional identification with Austria throughout his life, describing Franz Josef as "almost my emperor" and quoting him in the face of difficult decisions in the form, "I will have the matter thought about."

BIBLIOGRAPHY

Gold was interviewed by Spencer Weart, as part of the "Sources for History of Modern Astrophysics" project; transcript available at Center for History of Physics, American Institute of Physics.

WORKS BY GOLD

With R. J. Pumphrey. "Hearing. I. The Cochlea as a Frequency Analyzer." *Proceedings of the Royal Society,* series B, 135 (1948): 462–491. Closely related to the thesis for which he was awarded the Trinity College fellowship.

With Hermann Bondi. "The Steady-State Theory of the Expanding Universe." *Monthly Notices of the Royal Astronomical Society* 108 (1948): 252–270. The first explication of steady state cosmology. The complementary paper by Fred Hoyle appears in the same volume.

"Rotation and Terrestrial Magnetism." *Nature* 163 (1949): 513–515.

With Hermann Bondi. "On the Generation of Magnetism by Fluid Motion." *Monthly Notices of the Royal Astronomical Society* 110 (1950): 607–611. How astrophysical fluids can carry the currents needed to sustain large-scale magnetic fields.

"The Origin of Cosmic Radio Noise." In *Proceedings,* Conference on Dynamics of Ionized Media, University College London, March 1951, edited by R. L. F. Boyd. London, 1951. Radio sources as extragalactic rather than stars in the Milky Way.

"Polarization of Starlight." *Nature* 169 (1952): 322. A nonmagnetic mechanism for aligning spinning dust grains with the galactic plane.

"Suggestions for Rocket Astronomy." In *Rocket Research of the Upper Atmosphere.* London: Pergamon Press, 1954. Early enthusiasm for science from space.

"Instability of the Earth's Axis of Rotation." *Nature* 175 (1955): 526–529. Major axis shifts as the explanation for changes in continent locations in climate and magnetic zones.

"The Lunar Surface." *Monthly Notices of the Royal Astronomical Society* 115 (1955): 585–604. Prediction of a significant, possibly dangerous, dust layer based on likely physical processes.

"Turbulence in the Interstellar Gas." In *Gas Dynamics of Cosmic Clouds.* Amsterdam: North Holland Publishing, 1955. The introduction of magnetohydrodynamic shocks.

"The Arrow of Time." In *Structure and Evolution of the Universe (Proceedings of the Solvay Conference),* Institut International de Physique Solvay, University of Brussels, 9–13 June 1958. Brussels: R. Stoops, 1958.

"Motions in the Magnetosphere of the Earth." *Journal of Geophysical Research* 64 (1959): 1219–1224. The coining of the name.

With Fred Hoyle. "On the Origin of Solar Flares." *Monthly Notices of the Royal Astronomical Society* 120 (1960): 89–105. Magnetic fields as the energy source and how the energy is released.

"The Problem of the Abundance of the Hydrogen Molecule." *Memoirs de la Société Royale des Sciences de Liège* 20 (1961): 476. The possibility that most interstellar material might be molecular, long before this could be measured.

"The Arrow of Time." *American Journal of Physics* 30 (1962): 403–410. The 21st Richtmyer Memorial Lecture for the American Association of Physics Teachers.

With Robert J. Gould and Edwin E. Salpeter. "The Interstellar Abundance of the Hydrogen Molecule: II. Galactic Abundance and Distribution." *Astrophysical Journal* 138 (1963): 408–425. How such molecules might form.

"Magnetic Energy Shedding in the Solar Atmosphere." In *AAS-NASA Symposium on the Physics of Solar Flares,* edited by Wilmot N. Hess. Washington, DC: National Aeronautics and Space Administration, Scientific and Technical Information Division, 1964. Coronal heating by magnetic reconnection.

"Rotation of the Planet Mercury." *Nature* 206 (1965): 1240–1241. The period is a 2:3 resonance with the orbit, rather than equal to it, which was an Arecibo radar discovery and required analysis, provided here.

"Long Term Stability of the Earth Moon System." In *The Earth-Moon System,* edited by B. G. Marsden and A. G. W. Cameron. New York: Plenum Press, 1966. Why major axis shifts do not actually occur.

With Francis Perkins and Edwin E. Salpeter. "Maser Action in Interstellar OH." *Astrophysical Journal* 145 (1966): 361–365.

"Radio Method for the Precise Measurement of the Rotation Period of the Earth." *Science*, n.s., 157 (1967): 302–304. Suggests the possibility of radio interferometry with phase information preserved by very accurate time keeping.

"Rotating Neutron Stars as the Origin of the Pulsating Radio Sources." *Nature* 218 (1968): 731–732. The pulsar model that has been his most cited paper.

With Steven Soter. "Apollo 12 Seismic Signal: Indication of a Deep Layer of Powder." *Science*, n.s., 169 (1970): 1071–1075.

With Steven Soter. "Atmospheric Tides and the 4-Day Circulation on Venus." *Icarus* 14 (1971): 16–20. An attempt to understand why the atmosphere rotates so much faster than the solid surface, an effect not previously seen anywhere in the solar system.

"The Evidence for the Existence of Other Solar Systems and the Question of Life on Them." In *Communication with Extraterrestrial Intelligence (CETI)*, edited by Carl Sagan. Cambridge, MA: MIT Press, 1973.

"The Skylab: Is It Really Necessary?" *Ithaca Journal*, 11 May 1973.

"The Skylab: Is It Worth the Risk and the Expense?" *Bulletin of the Atomic Scientists* 30 (February 1974): 4–8. Increasing opposition to manned missions.

With Stanley F. Dermott. "The Rings of Uranus: Theory." *Nature* 267 (1977): 590–593. Another sort of resonance, with the Uranian moons.

"Don't Send People into Space Unnecessarily." *New York Times*, 28 September 1987.

Power from the Earth: Deep Earth Gas—Energy for the Future. London: Dent, 1987. The possibility of large quantities of methane trapped inside Earth from its formation epoch.

"An Unexplored Habitat for Life in the Universe?" *American Scientist* 85 (1997): 408–411.

OTHER SOURCES

Cole, Simon A. "Which Came First, the Fossil or the Fuel?" *Social Studies of Science* 26 (1996): 733–766. A well-known paper on Gold's "abiogenic" theory of oil/gas.

Hoyle, Fred. "A New Model for the Expanding Universe." *Monthly Notices of the Royal Astronomical Society* 108 (1948): 372–382. Complements Bondi and Gold's paper in the same volume.

Kragh, Helge. *Cosmology and Controversy.* Princeton, NJ: Princeton University Press, 1996. The definitive study of the rise and fall of steady state cosmology.

Salpeter, Edwin E. "Thomas (Tommy) Gold." *Proceedings of the American Philosophical Society* 150, no. 3 (2006): 479–486.

Terzian, Y., and E. M. Bilson, eds. *Cosmology and Astrophysics: Essays in Honor of Thomas Gold.* Ithaca, NY: Cornell University Press, 1982.

Virginia Trimble

GOLDBERG, LEO (*b.* Brooklyn, New York, 26 January 1913; *d.* Tucson, Arizona, 1 November 1987), *solar physics, space astronomy.*

Goldberg was an American solar physicist whose research and organizational efforts helped pioneer efforts to study the Sun from outer space. He played a prominent role in building up the Department of Astronomy at the University of Michigan (1946–1960) before moving to Harvard University. He served as director of the Harvard College Observatory from 1966 to 1971. His final post before retirement was director of the Kitt Peak National Observatory near Tucson, Arizona, from 1971 to 1977. In addition to his research in solar physics, Goldberg was influential in reshaping the institutional and instrumental landscape of astronomy in the United States after World War II. He contributed to the formation of national observatory facilities for both radio as well as optical astronomy and advocated space-based astronomical research.

Childhood and Education. Goldberg's parents emigrated to the United States from eastern Poland before World War I broke out. They settled in Brooklyn and worked in that city's garment industry. They were strongly orthodox and Leo, a middle child, attended a Jewish parochial school in Brooklyn. His family was poor; a colleague once recalled that Goldberg was the quintessential Horatio Alger character. In 1922 disaster struck the family when a tenement fire killed Leo's mother and younger brother. His father soon remarried and in 1925 moved Leo and his older brother to New Bedford, Massachusetts.

Goldberg earned his undergraduate degree from Harvard in 1934, attending that school on a scholarship. He initially planned on becoming an engineer but later switched to astronomy. This was somewhat risky given Goldberg's precarious personal finances and the relative dearth of professional opportunities for those choosing a career in astronomy at this time.

Goldberg remained at Harvard for his graduate work. His advisor there was Donald H. Menzel, an early practitioner of theoretical astrophysics in the United States who had come to Harvard from Lick Observatory in 1932. For his dissertation research Goldberg studied the intensities of lines in the helium spectrum, an important part of interpreting spectra from the Sun and other stars. In 1938, after the completion of his doctorate, Harvard awarded Goldberg a special postdoctoral fellowship. He later discovered it was a gift from a professor whose son Goldberg had tutored a few years earlier. This fellowship enabled Goldberg to continue his research and visit the renowned California observatories at Mount Wilson and Lick.

The University of Michigan. Goldberg remained at Harvard until 1941 when, with Menzel's help, he landed a more secure post at the McMath-Hulbert Observatory, a small observatory near Detroit, Michigan. It was founded in the 1920s by Robert R. McMath, a young Detroit businessman who began making astronomical observations with a prominent Michigan judge, Henry S. Hulbert. During the 1930s the observatory gained fame for its motion pictures of solar activity and, in 1932, it became part of the University of Michigan.

Soon after Goldberg arrived in Michigan, the United States entered World War II. Goldberg was determined to contribute to war-related research. He considered returning to Cambridge to work in the Massachusetts Institute of Technology's Radiation Laboratory on radar, but he decided to remain at the McMath-Hulbert Observatory. McMath's Washington contacts helped bring research contracts from Vannevar Bush's National Defense Research Committee to the observatory. Goldberg spent the war as a consultant to the U.S. Navy's Bureau of Ordnance, researching antiaircraft applications and bombsight designs. In 1943 he met and married Charlotte Wyman, a local schoolteacher. They had two sons, Edward and David, and a daughter, Suzanne.

After the war Goldberg was eager to leave the confines of the McMath-Hulbert Observatory for a major university position. He considered an offer from Lyman Spitzer to join Yale University, where he could carry out astronomical research with captured German rocket technology. However, the University of Michigan proposed that Goldberg chair its astronomy department and he began his tenure there in November 1946.

Goldberg's main challenge was to rebuild an astronomy department much depleted during the war and which lacked major optical telescope facilities. The best and most modern equipment was still located at the McMath-Hulbert Observatory, nearly 60 miles away; this included a recently completed twenty-four-inch telescope and extensive solar observing facilities. In the late 1940s, before funding from the Office of Naval Research and the National Science Foundation (NSF) became widely available to Goldberg's program, Judge Hulbert and local philanthropic funds supported the rejuvenation of the Michigan astronomy program and helped attract new staff and students.

Goldberg raised his department's international profile by organizing a series of summer schools in astrophysics. Astronomers and students hailed a symposium held in 1953 as a watershed for astrophysics and astronomy. Important scientists such as Walter Baade and George Gamow spoke on some of the most important and controversial topics in astronomical research. The meetings Goldberg organized helped the field regain some of the momentum lost during the war.

While at Michigan, Goldberg continued his research on the physics of the Sun, especially the elemental abundances of the solar atmosphere. His work built on earlier studies such as those of Henry Norris Russell and took into account the variation of the Sun's atmosphere with distance from its center. He was especially eager to exploit the scientific possibilities of rocketborne observing. As he wrote his former mentor Menzel in 1945, studying the spectra of the Sun from above Earth's atmosphere would be worth "shaving my head and working in a cell for the next ten or fifteen years." Nevertheless, Goldberg, like many pioneers in space-based astronomy, was frustrated by the effort required to secure even the most basic results from early rocketborne instruments. In the late 1940s most astronomers, unlike Goldberg, considered rocket-based astronomy unrealistic and outside the mainstream of scientific research.

Goldberg and National Facilities. In the 1950s Goldberg became increasingly vocal about the need for the United States to fund and build national observatories for traditional optical astronomy as well as the emerging field of radio astronomy. Part of his activism was motivated by his participation on several national panels, which debated how and to what extent the NSF should support astronomy. While Goldberg did not believe federal sources should provide all funding for astronomy, he was more enterprising than many of his colleagues in pursuing government support for research. He had already seen the benefits of this approach. By the mid-1950s his astronomy department at the University of Michigan had half of its faculty salaries paid by federal funding, the highest proportion of any program in the United States.

In 1953 Goldberg attended a national meeting on observational facilities held at Flagstaff, Arizona. Goldberg told his colleagues that the NSF should think big and beyond parochial needs. One colleague remembered Goldberg saying, "What this country needs is a truly National Observatory to which every astronomer with ability and a first-class problem can come on leave from his university" (Irwin, 1955, p. 107). Significantly, Goldberg proposed that this national, publicly funded facility rival the size of the large private telescopes at Lick and Palomar.

Goldberg's motivation in promoting national observatories rested on two premises. In the 1950s, especially before the Soviet launch of *Sputnik*, the NSF's budget allocation was relatively small. Goldberg saw the building of national facilities for astronomy as one way the NSF could strengthen its research portfolio and infrastructure. He also believed that national facilities available to scientists on a peer-reviewed basis would be beneficial to the entire astronomy community.

Goldberg's lobbying helped bring about the formation of the Association of Universities for Research in Astronomy, Inc. (AURA) in March 1957. Seven universities—California, Chicago, Harvard, Indiana, Michigan, Ohio State, and Wisconsin—were AURA's original members. Astronomers and engineers soon broke ground for the first telescopes at what became Kitt Peak National Observatory in Arizona. Its facilities enabled American astronomers without access to privately owned observatories like Palomar to carry out observing programs. AURA also later established the Cerro Tololo Interamerican Observatory in Chile, which gave U.S. and Chilean astronomers access to southern hemisphere skies. Goldberg also played a role in the formation of the National Radio Astronomy Observatory (NRAO) located in Green Bank, West Virginia. He was later offered the directorship of NRAO but chose instead to remain at Michigan.

As an active member of the International Astronomical Union (IAU), Goldberg served as a delegate to international meetings in 1958 and 1961. He also served as vice president (1958–1964) and president (1973–1976) of the IAU. Goldberg's leadership in the IAU at times required him to balance science goals with national and international politics. For example, in 1958 the U.S. State Department asked Goldberg and Otto Struve to invite Taiwan to the 1961 IAU meeting planned for Berkeley, California, and to exclude scientists from the People's Republic of China. At this time Taiwan, unlike the People's Republic of China, had no astronomy program to speak of, nor was it an IAU member. The State Department's move placed Goldberg in a difficult situation in which he wanted to avoid alienating researchers from mainland China and violating norms of scientific internationalism by not including Taiwan. Goldberg, with support from the National Academy of Sciences, negotiated a solution that brought about Taiwan's acceptance into the IAU in 1959 and the eventual establishment of astronomy as a research field in that country. However, the People's Republic of China broke its ties with the IAU, an event that Goldberg regretted. Nevertheless, colleagues later credited Goldberg with skillfully defusing what could have threatened the viability of the IAU as an international organization.

Goldberg also played a role in IAU negotiations concerning Project West Ford, a 1961 military experiment in which thousands of copper filaments were launched into space to see if they might serve as a communications aid. At the time West Ford was controversial among astronomers and other space scientists who feared the experiment, which ultimately failed, would interfere with research observations. Like the "two China" problem Goldberg confronted earlier, West Ford required that he find a compromise between his state and professional responsibilities.

Back to Harvard. In 1960 Goldberg accepted an offer from Harvard University's Astronomy Department and returned to Cambridge, where he also had an appointment with the Smithsonian Astrophysical Observatory (SAO). His move back east was in part precipitated by unhappiness with what he saw as Michigan's reluctance to enter the emerging field of space-based astronomy.

For decades Goldberg had been interested in the elemental abundances of the solar atmosphere and the application of laboratory-based atomic physics to astrophysical problems. Goldberg was also motivated by the launches of the first Soviet and American satellites and became a spirited advocate of the scientific possibilities offered by space-based astronomy. While at Harvard he became increasingly active in helping develop the series of Orbiting Solar Observatories (OSO), which the National Aeronautics and Space Administration (NASA) launched in the 1960s and 1970s. In March 1962 NASA launched the OSO-I spacecraft. While in operation, OSO-I monitored the Sun for solar flare activity and also scanned the sky for gamma-ray sources.

The next two satellites in the OSO series failed. However, success was achieved again in October 1967 with OSO-IV. Goldberg and other scientists took advantage of these platforms to make observations of the Sun at x-ray and ultraviolet wavelengths. While at Harvard, Goldberg also worked with Richard Tousey (Naval Research Laboratory), Gordon Newkirk (High Altitude Observatory), and Riccardo Giacconi (American Science and Engineering) on what became the Apollo Telescope Mount, which NASA flew on its 1973 Skylab mission. Skylab turned out to be an excellent solar observatory, due in part to the contributions of Goldberg and other scientists to its design.

During the 1960s Goldberg wrote or cowrote several scientific papers that helped cement his scientific reputation. For example, he and two colleagues from the University of Michigan presented several years of research in a frequently cited 1960 paper, which derived abundances for forty-two elements found in solar spectra. In 1967 Goldberg wrote a review article that gave results from a series of space-based observations of the Sun made at ultraviolet and x-ray wavelengths. Goldberg also noted the rapid progress, enabled in large part by the innovative instrumentation he advocated, scientists had made in improving spectroscopic resolution as well as advances in studying solar emission of x-rays. Finally, in 1968 Goldberg and several colleagues published data from the OSO-IV mission. The observatory featured an ultraviolet spectroheliograph, a device that could photograph the Sun at a variety of wavelengths between 300 and 1,400 angstroms. This instrument and the data it produced provided scientists with a more complete and complex

Goldberg

picture of the Sun's atmosphere and its three-dimensional structure.

Goldberg's work on the OSO series impressed officials at NASA, and in 1966 NASA offered him the directorship of the Goddard Space Flight Center in Greenbelt, Maryland. He opted to remain at Harvard where he became director of the Harvard College Observatory (HCO) that same year. One of the activities that consumed Goldberg's time at Harvard was expanding HCO's financial support from donors as well as its facilities. His efforts resulted in additional laboratory space as HCO staff undertook more intensive research in experimental and theoretical astrophysics.

As director of the HCO, Goldberg experienced a difficult administrative relationship between his organization and the SAO. Fred L. Whipple, the SAO's director, and Donald Menzel, the HCO's previous director, had established interinstitutional cooperation, which served both organizations for some time. Eventually, the rapid growth of the SAO and Goldberg's efforts to expand activities of the HCO created difficulties. These were exacerbated by the fact that Whipple sat on the HCO council while Goldberg had no corresponding influence over SAO activities or appointments. Displeased by this situation, in 1971, when AURA offered Goldberg the opportunity to direct the Kitt Peak National Observatory (KPNO), he accepted it.

Kitt Peak and After. When Goldberg arrived at the KPNO in September 1971, the national observatory was in a crucial period of transition. For almost fifteen years KPNO had pursued an aggressive program of telescope construction. By 1970 the observatory operated several small-to-moderate size telescopes, and its 4-meter instrument was nearing completion. In Chile, engineers and astronomers were finishing another 4-meter telescope for AURA at its Cerro Tololo facility. As these new telescopes entered service, many scientists expected the national observatories to switch from building facilities to operating them efficiently, serving the user community, and, perhaps, doing frontier research rivaling the work done at places such as Palomar and Lick.

Goldberg, however, believed that not pursuing future projects would lead to poor morale and eventual decline at the observatory. He encouraged a small group of telescope engineers and astronomers to consider what large optical telescopes of the future might look like. From 1974 to 1980, staff at the KPNO proposed a diverse array of telescope designs that would feature light collecting areas as large as 15 or 25 meters. These telescope projects, Goldberg believed, represented an opportunity for the future expansion of the national observatory and U.S. astronomy in general. While not realized in his lifetime, Goldberg's plans for national observing facilities with greater light collecting power eventually contributed to the building of the Gemini Observatories in Hawaii and Chile in the 1990s.

Not all astronomers agreed with Goldberg's management decisions, including his efforts to recruit top-notch staff and build innovative instrumentation. Goldberg soon found himself forced to choose between providing service facilities to visiting astronomers or devoting resources to build up the quality of his observatory's staff and instruments. This was a difficult balance to strike due to budget limitations as well as a general lack of consensus among astronomers as to the national observatory's mission.

These debates brought Goldberg into conflict with AURA's board and its chairman (his former classmate) Jesse L. Greenstein. The showdown between Greenstein and Goldberg was more than just a philosophical disagreement over what was best for science. At its core was a larger question of who would dominate and control astronomical research: elite universities and a relatively few autonomous observers or large national facilities serving a broader community of scientists. Their different visions of how science should be practiced and managed became sources of tension between Goldberg and Greenstein. Finally, in 1977, Goldberg stepped down as Kitt Peak's director.

Goldberg remained at the KPNO as a research scientist. He also held a series of visiting appointments including the Martin-Marietta Chair of Space History at the National Air and Space Museum. In his lifetime, Goldberg received a number of honors including election to the National Academy of Sciences in 1958 and the Distinguished Service Medal from NASA in 1973, the same year that he gave the Henry Norris Russell lecture for the American Astronomical Society. After his divorce, Goldberg married astronomer Beverly T. Lynds in January 1987, less than a year before his death from cancer.

BIBLIOGRAPHY

Many of the quotes used here are drawn from Goldberg's correspondence and papers, which are in the Harvard University Archives. Further information may be found in oral history interviews with Goldberg (including a full-length biographical interview dated 16 May 1978 by Spencer R. Weart). These interviews are in the collections of the Niels Bohr Library at the American Institute of Physics in College Park, Maryland.

WORKS BY GOLDBERG

With Edith A. Müller and Lawrence H. Aller. "The Abundances of the Elements in the Solar Atmosphere." *Astrophysical Journal Supplement* 5 (1960): 1–137.

"Ultraviolet and X-Rays from the Sun." *Annual Review of Astronomy and Astrophysics* 5 (1967): 279–324.

With Robert W. Noyes, William H. Parkinson, Edmond M. Reeves, et al. "Ultraviolet Solar Images from Space." *Science* n.s. 162 (1968): 95–99.

OTHER SOURCES

Aller, Lawrence H. "Leo Goldberg, January 26, 1913–November 1, 1987." In *Biographical Memoirs,* vol. 72. Washington, DC: National Academy of Sciences, 1994. Provides basic biographical information from a former colleague.

DeVorkin, David H. *Science with a Vengeance: How the Military Created the US Space Sciences after World War II.* New York: Springer Verlag, 1992. Presents early rocket-based research programs including those in solar physics.

Doel, Ronald E., Dieter Hoffmann, and Nikolai Krementsov. "National States and International Science: A Comparative History of International Science Congresses in Hitler's Germany, Stalin's Russia, and Cold War United States." *Osiris,* n.s., 20 (2005): 49–76. Discusses, in part, Goldberg's involvement with the IAU regarding the question of China and Taiwan.

Edmondson, Frank K. "AURA and KPNO: The Evolution of an Idea, 1952–58." *Journal for the History of Astronomy* 22 (1991): 68–86. Discusses the development of a national observatory for optical astronomy.

Hufbauer, Karl. *Exploring the Sun: Solar Science since Galileo.* Baltimore, MD: Johns Hopkins University Press, 1991. Provides information on modern programs of solar physics including Goldberg's work on the OSO series.

Irwin, John B. *Proceedings of the NSF Astronomical Photoelectric Conference.* Bloomington: Indiana University Press, 1955.

Levin, Tanya J. "Contaminating Space: Project West Ford and Scientific Communities, 1958–1965." MA thesis, University of Alaska, Fairbanks, 2000. Described Project West Ford and Goldberg's involvement.

McCray, W. Patrick. "The Contentious Role of a National Observatory." *Physics Today* 56, no. 10 (2003): 55–61.

———. *Giant Telescopes: Astronomical Ambition and the Promise of Technology.* Cambridge, MA: Harvard University Press, 2004. Both works by McCray discuss Goldberg's activities in promoting national observatory facilities in the United States as well as his conflicts with his former classmate Jesse L. Greenstein.

Needell, Allan. "Lloyd Berkner, Merle Tuve, and the Federal Role in Radio Astronomy." *Osiris,* n.s., 3 (1987): 261–288. Describes the debate over radio astronomy facilities that Goldberg took part in.

W. Patrick McCray

GOLDMAN-RAKIC, PATRICIA SHOER

(*b.* Salem, Massachusetts, 22 April 1937; *d.* New Haven, Connecticut, 31 July 2003), *neuroscience, prefrontal cortex, schizophrenia, brain anatomy and physiology.*

Goldman-Rakic defied tradition and became one of the first female tenured neuroscientists, first at the National Institute of Mental Health and then later at Yale University. Known especially for her work on the anatomy and physiology of the prefrontal cortex, she was the first to see the prefrontal cortex as the locus of short-term memory. Goldman-Rakic described this memory system as the "blackboard of the mind." The driving issue for her was to determine how the brain represents information in short-term memory and how this information is accessed. Her work also provided anatomical and physiological bridges between the neurotransmitter dopamine and psychiatric ailments connected to disrupted cognition, such as schizophrenia and Alzheimer's. She was one of the earliest to demonstrate connections between what the brain is doing and how things seem in the mind.

Childhood. Patricia Shoer Goldman-Rakic, known to family, friends, and colleagues as Pat, was born on 22 April 1937 in Salem, Massachusetts. Her father, Irving Shoer, was the son of Latvian immigrants; her mother, Jennie Pearl, was a Russian immigrant herself. Soon after Goldman-Rakic was born, her family moved to Peabody, Massachusetts, where she remained until she left to attend college. Goldman-Rakic grew up with her twin sister Ruth and younger sister Linda; all three graduated from Peabody High School, each winning the George Peabody Medal, and each eventually earned a doctorate in the sciences. During her youth, Goldman-Rakic never expected to become a scientist. As a teenager, she played piano for a dance studio in the afternoons and waited tables at a local restaurant in the evenings. She also studied violin and even mastered the art of calligraphy.

Goldman-Rakic earned a bachelor's degree in experimental psychology at Vassar College, graduating summa cum laude in 1959. She then went to graduate school in psychology at the University of California, Los Angeles (UCLA), and completed her PhD in 1963 under the mentorship of developmental psychologist Wendell Jeffrey. Goldman-Rakic's dissertation concerned the effects of stress on the cognitive development of rats. That research marks the beginning of her lifelong interest in the connections between brain development and behavior, with the rest of her career focused almost exclusively on the frontal lobes.

National Institute of Mental Health. Hired as a staff member at the National Institute of Mental Health (NIMH) in 1965, Goldman-Rakic started research on the frontal lobe under the tutorship of and in collaboration with Enger "Hal" Rosvold, who established the first laboratory at NIMH for the study of higher cortical function and complex behavior. There she investigated the

Goldman-Rakic

associative cortex of the frontal lobe, also known as prefrontal cortex, in monkeys. She and Rosvold showed that lesions in certain areas of prefrontal cortex, such as the sulcus principalis, caused difficulties in short-term memory. In particular, monkeys with these deficits could not perform delayed-response tasks, a psychological research protocol used in the early twentieth century to study retention in primates and younger children. Goldman-Rakic saw that this task could also be used to examine the biological substrates of short-term memory.

Goldman-Rakic would show an animal a bit of food and then hide the food in one of two containers. Then, for a varying period, she would prevent the animal from seeing the containers. Once the animal could see the containers again, she would note whether it would look at the container that contained the hidden food. It turns out that rhesus monkeys have difficulties with this task if their prefrontal cortex is lesioned, even though they can perform the task normally if they are allowed to see the containers for the duration of the experiment. That is, lesioning the prefrontal cortex in rhesus monkeys appears to impair their short-term memory systems.

At the NIMH, she also studied the effects of early (pre- and postnatal) lesions of the prefrontal cortex on development and behavior. She was one of the first researchers to document and measure functional plasticity in the cortex. In particular, she showed that monkeys performed remarkably well when their prefrontal cortices are damaged early in life, but detrimental cognitive abnormalities appear when the lesion occurs in postadolescence.

It is noteworthy that Goldman-Rakic was not promoted to a tenure track position at the NIMH until 1975—eight years after she joined the program. Eventually, in the years before she left, she was named chief of the Section on Developmental Neurobiology. Her career was not without its challenges, not the least of which was being a woman in what was then a man's career. Throughout her professional life, Goldman-Rakic worked tirelessly as a mentor to female graduate students and young faculty. It is not mere chance that at the time of her death, more than 50 percent of all new neuroscience PhDs worldwide were women.

Massachusetts Institute of Technology. In 1974 the Massachusetts Institute of Technology (MIT) hired Goldman-Rakic as a visiting scientist. There she worked closely with Walle Natua, an authority on central nervous system anatomy. Natua and Goldman-Rakic investigated the internal connections of the prefrontal cortex and its connections with the caudate nucleus. Together, they made an important discovery: the axons—the ends of neurons—were distributed in a regular pattern. In the prefrontal cortex in particular, the terminal arbors were arranged in a regular fashion. Cross-sections of cortex revealed that columns of axonal ends spanned the entire gray matter, interrupted by columns of space that presumably contained the terminals of other areas.

These discoveries strongly influenced her later research. Finding columns in prefrontal cortex told her that these areas were functionally specialized in some way, just as previously discovered columns in primary sensory cortex had indicated functional specialization. The Nobel Prize–winning studies of David Hubel and Torsten Wiesel established that the neurons in brain regions that processed sensory inputs were grouped vertically in columns and that these columns were differentiated in terms of their function. Scientists assumed that these columns were therefore a basic unit of information processing. Goldman-Rakic had isolated similar structural components in the frontal cortex.

Also in 1974, Goldman-Rakic met her future husband, Pasko Rakic, who then was on the faculty at Harvard. They began a personal and professional collaboration that would change the course of contemporary neuroscience. They married in 1979 and moved as a couple to Yale University, where he headed the newly created Section of Neurology; she joined the Section of Neuroanatomy. Together, they built those units into one of the premier departments of neurobiology in the world. By all accounts, theirs was a strong, happy, and successful marriage, one in which they each viewed the other as a friend, colleague, and supporter. They had no children.

Yale University. At Yale, Goldman-Rakic continued the anatomical and histochemical studies of prefrontal cortex that she started at NIMH, though she was now more focused on the cognitive and behavioral contexts of memory. She launched a series of experiments that traced cortico-cortical connections using just about every axon-tracing technique available, eventually characterizing the three-dimensional structure of individual prefrontal cortical cells and the thousands of connections each cell makes to other cells. As cognitive scientists and other brain researchers around her were proposing parallel processing as the model of cognition in the brain as a theoretical possibility, she continued her detailed study of the connections between areas of frontal cortex, with the goal of outlining the actual parallel processes there.

One of her most important discoveries was the alternating columns of the sulcus principalis, which confirmed her previous work with Nauta. Many believed that the alternating inputs into the prefrontal cortex indicated that this area integrated information; Goldman-Rakic, however, remained committed to the idea of cortical modularity, that the cortex was divided into discrete areas, each of which handled a different processing job. Her laboratory produced a large body of evidence illustrating that the organizational structure of the neocortex was conserved across different areas, extending from the primary sensory systems to the frontal lobes. In all regions, parallel streams of information flowed next to one another.

At the same time, Goldman-Rakic, in collaboration with Pasko Rakic and Jean-Pierre Bourgeois and others, ran detailed studies of neurochemical development. They discovered that all areas of the cerebral cortex, including primary sensory, motor, and associative regions, develop at the same rate. That is, synapses grow and proliferate at the same speed in all cortical areas. This evidence for concurrent synaptogenesis belied earlier theories of brain development, which tied neural cell growth to myelination schedules.

Additionally, with Gallager, Kostovic, Levitt, Lidow, Mrzljak, and others, she demonstrated the presence of several neurotransmitters in the prefrontal cortex, including gamma-aminobutyric acid, acetylcholine, serotonin, and, most importantly, dopamine. She and her colleagues worked to discover what each of them was doing functionally in the prefrontal cortex, especially as their activities pertained to memory. In particular, she showed that dopamine and its receptors were crucially important to the development and maintenance of short-term memory, again by using the delayed response task paradigm. She also tied a decrease in dopaminergic activity to schizophrenia, Parkinson's disease, Alzheimer's dementia, and general aging.

The reasons Goldman-Rakic linked schizophrenia to the prefrontal cortex were threefold; each of these also shaped psychiatrists' understanding of how the disease fundamentally operated. First, Goldman-Rakic saw schizophrenics as having difficulties with integrating reasoning and behavior across time, which, according to her, demonstrated failures in short-term memory. This interpretation of schizophrenic behavior was a relatively new one in psychiatry when Goldman-Rakic first advanced it. Second, many antipsychotic medications that help schizophrenics target dopamine interactions. Prior to Goldman-Rakic's work, antipsychotic medications were often dispensed without any deep understanding of exactly what they were doing in the brain. Third, Goldman-Rakic learned that the prefrontal cortex of schizophrenics is structurally abnormal. This last fact she discovered through careful study of the prefrontal cortex of autopsies of patients diagnosed with schizophrenia. She later connected those data to brain imaging studies taken of live schizophrenia patients.

In addition to helping psychiatrists understand schizophrenia, Goldman-Rakic's analysis of dopamine receptors in the prefrontal cortex have also pointed to new treatments for schizophrenia and Parkinson's disease. She and her colleagues identified the hitherto unknown protein calcyon in the brain, which pharmaceutical developers are trying to target to improve the signaling in cells that are otherwise desensitized to dopamine. Near the time of her death, she was working on understanding how abusing amphetamines, even for short periods, in childhood or early adulthood can lead to long-lasting cognitive difficulties.

Goldman-Rakic's Legacy. Goldman-Rakic is perhaps best known for her role in connecting the prefrontal cortex to short-term memory. Though she used multidisciplinary techniques in her research, this connection is best highlighted through her single-celled microelectrode recordings of neuronal firing patterns in the prefrontal cortex of monkeys performing a delayed-response task in the late 1980s. She and her colleagues showed that neurons fired more and more rapidly during the delay or memory portion of the task. While similar firing patterns had been documented before in the prefrontal cortex, what stood out about Goldman-Rakic's cells was their finely tuned sensitivity to location. Thus, she was able to show that the memory in the prefrontal cortex could be mapped modularly and was arranged in columns. This contradicted the prevailing views of the times, which held that memory was a single process located in a single place in the brain.

At about the same time, Goldman-Rakic began to use the term *working memory* (as well as *representational memory*) to refer to the presumed function of these cells. Psychologists had used the term *working memory* for years to describe the short-term retention of information during cognitive problem solving. Goldman-Rakic used the delayed-response task as a way to operationalize the idea of working memory and suggested that the cells she had recorded were the neural underpinnings for this psychological concept. Later, using the data from additional microelectrode recordings, she argued that the prefrontal cortex contained segregated processing streams for memories of the different modalities of information (e.g., visual memory vs. spatial memory).

In addition to her work on memory, Goldman-Rakic also is well known for her work on the plasticity of the prefrontal cortex. She found that brains could change fairly easily early in development, compensating for injuries and sparing critical functions—processes that cannot occur later in life. This realization stimulated her to study the ontogenetic development of prefrontal cortex, using radioactive tracers to follow individual cellular activities. She uncovered many influences on brain development, including gender and age.

Over the course of her career, she published—either as sole author or as a coauthor—more than 250 articles, many of which are considered seminal in the early twenty-first century. In 1991 she and Pasko Rakic founded the journal *Cerebral Cortex.* As the chief coeditors, they made that journal into the premier publication for basic cortical research.

Patricia Goldman-Rakic received numerous honors and awards. She was elected president of the Society for Neuroscience in 1989; she was elected to the National Academy of Sciences (U.S.) in 1990, the American Academy of Arts and Sciences in 1991, and the Institute of Medicine of the National Academy of Sciences in 1994. She received France's Fyssen Prize in Neuroscience in 1990, the Merit Award of NIMH in 1990, the Lieber Award for the National Alliance for Research on Schizophrenia and Depression in 1991, the Karl Lashley Award of the American Philosophical Society in 1996, the Ralph Gerard Award of the Society for Neuroscience in 2002, and the Gold Medal for Distinguished Scientific Contributions from the American Psychological Association. She was awarded a *doctor honoris causa* from the University of Utrecht in 2000 and an honorary degree from St. Andrews College of the University of Edinburgh in 2003, just a few months before her death.

Goldman-Rakic died at the age of sixty-six on 31 July 2003 from injuries sustained when a car struck her as she was crossing a street in Hamden, Connecticut. At the time of her death, she held appointments at Yale as professor in the Departments of Neurobiology, Psychiatry, Neurology, and Psychology. She was struck down at the pinnacle of her career and died one of the most innovative and dedicated neuroscientists in the modern era of brain research.

BIBLIOGRAPHY

WORKS BY GOLDMAN-RAKIC

With Howard T. Crawford, Linton P. Stokes, Thelma W. Galkin, et al. "Sex-Dependent Behavioral Effects of Cerebral Cortical Lesions in the Developing Rhesus Monkey." *Science* 186 (1974): 540–542.

"Neuronal Plasticity in Primate Telencephalon: Anomalous Projections Induced by Prenatal Removal of Frontal Cortex." *Science* 202 (1978): 768–776.

With Thelma W. Galkin. "Prenatal Removal of Frontal Association Cortex in the Fetal Rhesus Monkey: Anatomical and Functional Consequences in Postnatal Life." *Brain Research* 152 (1978): 451–485.

"Contralateral Projections to the Dorsal Thalamus from Frontal Association Cortex in the Rhesus Monkey." *Brain Research* 166 (1979): 166–171.

With Lynn D. Selemon and Michael L. Schwartz. "Dual Pathways Connecting the Dorsolateral Prefrontal Cortex with the Hippocampal Formation in the Rhesus Monkey." *Neuroscience* 12 (1984): 719–743.

"Circuitry of Primate Prefrontal Cortex and Regulation of Behavior by Representational Memory." In *Handbook of Physiology: The Nervous System: Higher Functions of the Brain,* edited by Vernon B. Montcastle, Fred Plum, and Stephen R. Geiger, 373–417. Bethesda, MD: American Physiological Society, 1987.

"Topography of Cognition: Parallel Distributed Networks in Primate Association Cortex." *Annual Review of Neuroscience* 11 (1988): 137–156.

With Shintaro Funahashi and Charles J. Bruce. "Mnemonic Coding of Visual Space in the Monkey's Dorsolateral Prefrontal Cortex." *Journal of Neurophysiology* 61 (1989): 331–349.

"Cortical Localization of Working Memory." In *Brain Organization and Memory: Cells, Systems, and Circuits,* edited by James L. McGaugh, Norman M. Weinberger, and Gary Lynch, 285–298. New York: Oxford University Press, 1990.

With Michael S. Lidow and D. W. Gallager. "Overlap of Dopaminergic, Adrenergic, and Serotonergic Receptors and Complementarity of Their Subtypes in Primate Prefrontal Cortex." *Journal of Neuroscience* 10 (1990): 2125–2138.

"Regional and Cellular Fractionation of Working Memory." *Proceedings of the National Academy of Sciences of the United States of America* 93 (1996): 13473–13480.

With Amy F. Arnsten. "Noise Stress Impairs Prefrontal Cortical Cognitive Function in Monkeys: Evidence for Hyperdopaminergic Mechanism." *Archives of General Psychiatry* 55 (1998): 362–628.

With Srinivas G. Rao and Graham V. Williams. "Isodirectional Tuning of Adjacent Interneurons and Pyramidal Cells during Working Memory: Evidence for Microcolumnar Organization in PFC." *Journal of Neurophysiology* 81 (1999): 1903–1916.

OTHER SOURCES

Aghajanian, George, Benjamin S. Bunney, and Philip S. Holzman. "Patricia Goldman-Rakic, 1937–2003." *Neuropsychopharmacology* 28 (2003) 2218–2220.

"Award for Distinguished Scientific Contributions: Patricia S. Goldman-Rakic." *American Psychologist* 47, no. 4 (1992): 471–473.

Fuster, Joaquín. M. "Patricia Shoer Goldman-Rakic (1937–2003)." *American Psychologist* 59, no. 6 (2004): 559–560.

Jonides, John. "In Memory of Patricia Goldman-Rakic." *Cognitive, Affective and Behavioral Neuroscience* 4, no. 4 (2004): 407–408.

Nestler, Eric J. "Obituary: Patricia S. Goldman-Rakic (1937–2003)." *Nature* 425, no. 6957 (2003): 471.

Valerie Gray Hardcastle

GOODMAN, NELSON HENRY

(*b.* Somerville, Massachusetts, 7 August 1906; *d.* Needham, Massachusetts, 25 November 1998), *theory of induction and confirmation, logic, scientific methodology, aesthetics, metaphysics.*

Goodman

Goodman is most famous for his discovery of the new riddle of induction and its consequences for the theory of induction. His famous grue-bleen example shows that contextual and pragmatic factors are crucial for the validity of inductive and counterfactual arguments, because their compellingness varies with the selection of predicates and rules for their application by competent judges. Goodman's second groundbreaking methodological contribution to the inductive sciences is the proposal to model inductive and counterfactual inferences as the partly informal process of producing a coherent whole in "reflective equilibrium." Goodman's work decisively shifted the attention of theorists of induction away from mathematical formalisms (like the probability calculus) toward the pragmatic conditions of nondeductive reasoning.

Biographical Sketch, Wider Influence. Goodman was educated at Harvard University (BSc 1928), and obtained his PhD there in 1941 with a groundbreaking dissertation that was later published as *A Study of Qualities.* From 1929 to 1941 he was director of the Walker-Goodman Art Gallery (Boston), and he performed military service from 1942 to 1945. Goodman taught at Tufts College, the University of Pennsylvania, and Brandeis University before becoming professor of philosophy at Harvard University (1968–1977). Goodman's work displays a remarkable unity of thought, starting out from the early nominalist constructionism in his *The Structure of Appearance* (1951), through the studies in general symbol theory in his *Languages of Art* (1968; largely focused on aesthetics), until the late metaphysics of "worldmaking" in *Ways of Worldmaking* (1978), which propounds a radically pluralist form of constructivism ("irrealism"). Whereas the latter aspects of his work in aesthetics and metaphysics earned him wide popularity even outside philosophical circles, it is often overlooked that they are firmly rooted in his earlier studies of foundational problems in the methodology of the inductive sciences. Most famous among these are his new riddle of induction and his study of counterfactual conditionals.

The Problem of Projectibility. In *Fact, Fiction, and Forecast* (1955, chaps. 1 and 3), Goodman elaborated earlier reflections on the conditions for evaluating inductive inferences and counterfactual conditionals. Regarding the former, he discovered the new riddle of induction by making the following observation. Suppose all emeralds examined so far have been found green, and that there are still some to be discovered, and consider the question whether our knowledge is evidence for the hypothesis that the next, or all emeralds without regard to when they were found, are green. We usually think that it is, tacitly relying on an inference licensing principle like (U): "Whenever some Fs have been observed to be Gs in n% of the cases, then inferring that n% of the remaining Fs are G is admissible."

Goodman's new riddle showed that such general principles allow too many hypotheses to be equally well supported by the evidence. To show this, he stipulated that something is grue if it either has been observed until some time *t* and been found green, or blue otherwise. Clearly, the principle licenses reasoning from the evidential fact that (by definition) all emeralds observed so far were (since green before *t*) grue, to the conclusion that the remaining emeralds are grue as well. However, accepting this generalization commits us to expecting emeralds observed after *t* to be (grue, hence) blue, whereas the original hypothesis commits us to expecting the same emeralds to be green. If the evidence is described in these terms, it seems that our knowledge about green emeralds supports something equivalent to the hypothesis that not all emeralds are green just as much as it supports the rival thesis that all emeralds are green, when the evidence is described in familiar terms. It just seems obvious that the grue hypothesis is not supported at all by our knowledge, but given the example, it becomes unclear why we ought to think this.

The new riddle of induction is to say why some regularities work (i.e., are lawlike or confirmable by their instances) while other, formally analogous ones do not. Goodman's answer was to connect inductive validity and the acceptance of predicate systems. Predicates are expressions for the attribution of properties to particular objects, and predicate systems are sets of predicates that are interrelated in systematic ways. For example, color terms are predicates that are true of objects if they have a certain color. Color terms become a system by rules such as "If a given color predicate applies to a uniformly colored object, then no other color predicate applies to it," which regulate the application of all color terms by relating them to one another in this way, predicate systems afford classifications of objects. Goodman's "grue" calls attention to the fact that our expectations of inductive validity may vary with the ways we classify objects, and so with the kinds of systems of predicates that we apply to a given range of particulars. He calls predicate systems that yield descriptions of experiential input and permit inductive inferences regarding generalizations in ways analogous to principle (U) projectible and comes to the following result: normal inductive methods (i.e., those that allow learning from experience or supporting generalizations by instances) yield adequate results only when the evidence and hypotheses are formulated in projectible predicates. By thus underscoring the inseparability of conceptualization and generalization, Goodman's new riddle challenges methodologists who wish to formulate purely general rules of inductive inference to say what it takes for a given predicate within a given set of alternatives (and empirical

Goodman

statements) to be projectible. Without a general answer to this question, unconstrained inductive methods that allow the projection of any regularity from given evidence will always also allow the projection of grue-like regularities. The concomitant incoherencies, however, make it difficult to avoid that such methods will ultimately license any arbitrary hypothesis on any given evidence.

The main difficulty for finding a general and informative account of projectibility is that it concerns nonformal properties of predicates, but also cannot project traits of known successful predicates to a larger class of predicates, since this assumes the legitimacy of the very kind of inference it is supposed to ground. Goodman himself therefore did not believe that there is a general, noncircular account of projectibility. While this leaves dim hopes for a global "justification" of all inductive inferences, Goodman did believe that our judgments answer to shared local standards of inductive correctness. According to him, the required projectibility verdicts are reached locally in pragmatic procedures that terminate in reflective equilibrium (see below).

Another case of projection studied by Goodman comes to light in the analysis of the truth conditions of counterfactual conditionals (CCs), that is, hypothetical statements of the type "If it had been the case that A, then it would have been the case that B." The importance of analyzing CCs stems from their indispensability, among others, for causal analysis, for resolving decision-theoretic problems (common knowledge), and for modeling reasoning within artificial intelligence research. Just as in prediction we attempt to extrapolate from known to unknown cases, in CCs we attempt to extrapolate from known circumstances to hypothetical ones. Goodman's analysis displayed the partial dependency of such extrapolations on our conceptual commitments. His example was "If match *m* had been struck, then *m* would have lighted"; another was "Had Julius Caesar been in command in Korea, he would have used only nuclear bombs." The first step in his analysis is to regard sentences like these as being of the form "if A, then B," or as ordinary implications.

According to most standard semantics, the truth value (i.e., "true" or "false") of a given sentence is determined by the truth values of its truth-evaluable parts and the way they are put together. This is often expressed by saying that the truth value of the whole is a function of the truth values of its parts and the way in which connectives like "and" or "if-then" combine them. In particular, the rule for a material conditional of the form "if A, then B" is that it is false only when the if-part ("antecedent") is true and the then-part ("consequent") is false. This rule captures an intuitive rule of inference. Suppose we hypothesize that if it rains, then the streets are wet, and suppose that we know that it just rained where we are standing. Were the hypothesis true, we could regard our knowledge of the rain and the hypothesis as sufficient for inferring that the streets are wet. However, were the streets not wet although it rained, we would, without further information, first regard the hypothesis as false.

This rule about the material conditional likewise entails (somewhat less intuitively) that an implication is always true if its antecedent is false. Given these standard semantic assumptions, however, CCs quickly lead to perplexities.

The reason for this is that, usually, at least the antecedent of a CC is a known falsehood (whence the name "counterfactual"). Thus, according to standard semantics, all counterfactual conditionals should be true if their truth were determined by the ordinary truth-function for if-then statements mentioned above and the truth-value of the component statements alone. However, some CCs with a given antecedent are clearly false, and some are in conflict with others: consider "If match *m* had been struck, my grandmother would have been a schoolbus" or "If Julius Caesar had been in command in Korea, he would have used only catapults."

Goodman observed that typical CCs can be determined as true or false only with additional (extralogical) facts and assumptions. The needed information concerns (a) particular facts (e.g., background conditions such as that the match was dry, surrounded by sufficient oxygen, struck strongly enough, that Julius Caesar was a Roman emperor), and (b) actual regularities that are supposed to hold between what is described in the antecedent and the consequent, respectively (e.g., all matches struck under the right conditions light, no Roman emperor could use nuclear arms). To yield an interpretation, this additional information has to be (C1) compatible with the antecedent, and (C2) relevant in the sense that with it the antecedent entails the consequent when neither the antecedent nor the additional information alone *would have*. Goodman called such information sets *cotenable* with the antecedent. Since any false statement we posit as antecedent in a CC is in conflict with some truths we know, the cotenable set has to suspend some of what we know. Conversely, such a selection amounts to a decision in which particular facts and which actual regularities applying to the case we are to hold fixed in the hypothetical situation.

Goodman aptly called the regularities that we single out as fixed in a given case lawlike because in effect, they are then not only generalizations about, for example, all known matches under given conditions, but also about what a match is to be like under similar conditions. The problem is to say in a general and informative way on what basis some of the grammatically general statements applying to the antecedent are to be selected as lawlike

Goodman

while others are not. Again, Goodman's analysis undermines hopes for the project of modeling such judgments in a formal mechanism because cotenability judgments themselves depend on judging what would have followed from an information set, that is, other CCs (see the italicized part of C2). Judging CCs as true at all also (via C1) clearly requires attention to our acceptance of whole systems of other CCs. Goodman's analysis thus shows how, by fusing empirical {(a) and (b)} and conceptual {(C1) and (C2)} information, cotenability judgments implicitly articulate our priorities regarding predicate systems. This is most obvious from the fact that typically, factual knowledge alone determines no unique selection of additional information for any given antecedent. The same if-part in most cases makes reference to several mutually incompatible sets of facts and regularities that, for all we know, support the consequent.

The pair of Caesar conditionals illustrates this. Logic, known regularities, and the facts of the matter require only suspending at least one part of our knowledge about Caesar to facilitate the antecedent. While it is open whether we stress that Caesar was a Roman or his brutality to infer either of the (incompatible) consequents, it is clear that applying one of the regularity sets to Caesar excludes applying the other. That is, under invariant cognitive conditions, the same regularity statement can appear, for the same antecedent, either as a law or as capable of being false in a hypothetical situation ("accidental"). How it ultimately appears clearly depends on pragmatic factors like our attitude to other CCs, our interests, and the question we wish to answer. Goodman's answer to the obvious question how rational agreement on CCs (and the lawlikeness of generalizations sustaining them) is possible was that, given our competence in using the language, our empirical and theoretical knowledge, and the available alternatives, some information sets simply are implausible. Once again, having no formal mechanism or global solution does not exclude having good arguments that can locally show why some selections are more reasonable than others.

Reflective Equilibrium. In both cases of projectibility judgments, Goodman pointed to an apparent circularity. In both cases he took certain exemplary cases (grue, Caesar, the match) as a standard to correct and refine general principles like (U) or the general constraints on cotenability (C1) and (C2). Thus (U) is rejected as an unconditional general principle because it licenses "grue" and "green" on the same evidence. But at the same time, the inference to the greenness of the next or all emeralds on the given evidence is regulated by (U) if the familiar predicates are used. The circle is that we cannot judge the adequacy of a fundamental rule without any reference to accepted particular inferences, but we also cannot reasonably accept the relevant particular inferences as good standards without the advantage of any application of a roughly equivalent rule. According to Goodman, this is a "virtuous" circle; in fact, it might be better described as the claim that judgments in inductive and counterfactual contexts are not reducible to mechanical decision methods. Goodman consequently proposed that justifying inductive and counterfactual inferences should be modeled as the process of producing a coherent whole of aligned empirical, normative, and theoretical beliefs together with judgments of particular cases, aimed at reaching a "reflective equilibrium," as opposed to mechanical, "judgment-free" models of inductive practices, the results of such scientific deliberations are not predictable on the basis of given formal patterns of inference alone. Such models do not admit standpoint-free, judgment-free ways to justify particular results of good inductive or counterfactual reasoning, independent of actual conditions of being competent in making inductive and counterfactual judgments in general. Since the latter are open ended, mechanical models are inadequate.

Nonetheless, Goodman was not a methodological nihilist or relativist. Scientific practice is rife with cases where it is more reasonable to discount data as abnormal, biased, or incomplete. In such cases, theoretical knowledge and methodological rules decide against experience. Conversely, Goodman's analysis showed how persistent anomalies of such kinds can come to be taken as symptoms of defective conceptual systems or methodological inadequacies. According to Goodman, we always take some inductive judgments for granted when assessing others, just as we take some results of inductive reasoning (considered judgments) for granted when judging the adequacy of a rule with regard to other results, or when, in unproblematic cases, we apparently just apply the rule to the next case. In this way responding to changes in empirical information can consist in revising theoretical hypotheses, experimental results, or methodological rules whenever there is enough "firm ground" from the remnant established knowledge. Which way is most reasonable in each case will depend on the available alternatives, theoretical expertise, and experimental creativity, and is thus not unconstrained or arbitrary. But knowing which way is most reasonable will in any case involve the deliberative and open-ended activity of going back and forth between all these poles until the whole system of beliefs is reasonably balanced. In a classical quote, Goodman's *Fact, Fiction, and Forecast* puts it thus: "The process of justification is the delicate one of making mutual adjustments between rules and accepted inferences; and in the agreement achieved lies the only justification needed for either."

It is important not to confuse Goodman's methodological point that this is how we can come to evaluate evidence and principles with the different, metaphysical doctrine that empirical correctness depends on the coherence produced by such mutual adjustments. The latter view can lead to an epistemological relativism Goodman never endorsed. The famous Harvard political philosopher John Rawls (1971) coined the term *reflective equilibrium* for the coherent outcome of such justificatory procedures. Under this name, the underlying model of reasoning and justification has become central for decision and game theorists and methodologists, as well as ethicists and political theorists.

BIBLIOGRAPHY

WORKS BY GOODMAN

"A Study of Qualities: An Essay in Elementary Constructional Theory." PhD diss., Harvard University, 1941. Reprinted as *A Study of Qualities.* New York: Garland, 1990.

"A Query on Confirmation." *Journal of Philosophy* 43 (1946): 383–385.

"On Infirmities of Confirmation-Theory." *Philosophy and Phenomenological Research* 8 (1947): 149–151. First important texts concerning confirmation theory.

"The Problem of Counterfactual Conditionals." *Journal of Philosophy* 44 (1947): 113–120. Classical discussion of counterfactuals. Reprinted in his *Fact, Fiction, and Forecast.*

The Structure of Appearance. Cambridge, MA: Harvard University Press, 1951. 3rd ed., Boston: Reidel, 1977.

Fact, Fiction, and Forecast. Cambridge, MA: Harvard University Press, 1955. 4th ed., 1983. His pathbreaking book; chapter 1 discusses counterfactual conditionals and chapter 3 discusses the new riddle of induction.

Languages of Art. Indianapolis: Bobbs-Merrill, 1968.

Problems and Projects. Indianapolis: Bobbs-Merrill, 1972.

Ways of Worldmaking. Indianapolis: Hackett, 1978.

Of Mind and Other Matters. Cambridge, MA: Harvard University Press, 1983.

With Catherine Z. Elgin. *Reconceptions in Philosophy and other Arts and Sciences.* Indianapolis: Hackett, 1988.

OTHER SOURCES

Berka, Sigrid. "An International Bibliography of Works by and Selected Works about Nelson Goodman." *Journal of Aesthetic Education* 25, no. 1 (1991): 99–112. Full bibliography until 1991. Updated bibliography available from http://www.hcrc.ed.ac.uk/~john/GoodmanBib.html.

Douglas, Mary, and David Hull, eds. *How Classification Works: Nelson Goodman among the Social Sciences.* Edinburgh: Edinburgh University Press, 1992.

Elgin, Catherine Z., ed. *The Philosophy of Nelson Goodman: Selected Essays.* 4 vols. New York: Garland, 1997.

"General Topic: Languages of Art." Spec. issue, *Monist* 58, no. 2 (1974): 175–318. Edited by Monroe C. Beardsley; includes replies by Goodman.

McCormick, Peter J., ed. *Starmaking: Realism, Anti-realism, and Irrealism.* Cambridge, MA: MIT Press, 1996.

"The Philosophy of Nelson Goodman," parts 1 and 2. Spec. issue, *Erkenntnis* 12, no. 1/2 (1978): 3–291. Edited by Carl G. Hempel, Wolfgang Stegmüller, and Wihelm K. Essler.

Rudner, Richard S., and Israel Scheffler, eds. *Logic and Art: Essays in Honor of Nelson Goodman.* Indianapolis: Bobbs-Merrill, 1972.

Stalker, Douglas, ed. *Grue!* Chicago: Open Court, 1994.

Axel Mueller

GORENSTEIN, DANIEL

(*b.* Boston, Massachusetts, 1 January 1923; *d.* Martha's Vineyard, Massachusetts, 26 August 1992), *mathematics, algebra, group theory.*

Gorenstein was an American mathematician whose main research was in the theory of finite groups, where he focused single-mindedly on the search for simple groups. Besides contributing major theorems himself, he mapped out the path that would lead to the goal of a complete classification, and became the informal leader of a disseminated team which achieved that goal.

Private Life. Born and bred in Boston, Daniel Gorenstein attended the Boston Latin School, from which he entered Harvard College, earning his AB in 1943 and PhD in 1950. His doctoral advisor was Oscar Zariski and his thesis was on a problem in algebraic geometry and its foundations in commutative algebra, a subject that he did not pursue after his first published paper. He married Helen Brav in 1947; they had four children, three girls and a boy. In his obituary of Gorenstein (*The Independent,* London 1992), Michael Collins wrote "He was a short stocky man, who applied the same muscular techniques to his mathematics as to his tennis," and "Gorenstein both worked hard and played hard. [...] Research was over by lunchtime. Living in Portland Place [London] in 1972–73 must have been ideal, for he could then devote the rest of the day to seminars and to visits to art galleries, museums, restaurants and the theatre. He collected modern art, with a good eye for artists yet to be recognised, and for the value of the works of those who were."

Career. Soon after he achieved his doctorate Gorenstein became assistant professor at Clark University in Worcester, Massachusetts. He remained there until 1964, when he became professor at Northeastern University in Boston. In 1969 he moved to Rutgers University, New Brunswick, New Jersey, where he remained for the rest of his life, serving as chairman of the mathematics department from 1975 to 1981 and director of DIMACS, the NSF Center for Discrete Mathematics and Computer

Science, from 1989 until his death. In addition, he held visiting positions in other parts of the world: Cornell University, 1958–1959; Princeton Institute for Advanced Study, 1968–1969; London and the Weizmann Institute, 1972–1973 as Guggenheim Fellow and Fulbright Research Scholar; and California Institute of Technology, 1978. He served at various times also as consultant to the MIT Lincoln Laboratory and to the Institute for Defense Analysis. His distinction was recognized by election to the National Academy of Sciences and to the American Academy of Arts and Sciences in 1987, by the award of the 1989 Steele Prize for Expository Writing by the American Mathematical Society, and by countless invitations to deliver lectures at prestigious national and international mathematical meetings.

Mathematics. For a mathematician Gorenstein was unusually slow to establish himself. He published one paper arising out of his doctoral research in algebraic geometry. Its influence is still visible in the term *Gorenstein ring*, but he left the area and moved on to coding theory and finite group theory. In the former he wrote two papers jointly with colleagues from the Lincoln Laboratory, one of which, on generalized BCH codes published in 1961, introduced a significant decoding algorithm and was reissued thirteen years later in a collection titled *Key Papers in the Development of Coding Theory*, edited by Elwyn Berlekamp. In finite group theory his first dozen papers contain respectable but generally inconsequential contributions. In his late thirties, however, inspired by what he heard and by the colleagues he met at the 1960–1961 group-theory year at the University of Chicago, his attention became focused on the search for finite simple groups. His first major contribution was joint work with John H. Walter of the University of Illinois, classifying the simple groups whose Sylow 2-subgroups are dihedral. Their four papers on the subject come to more than 200 pages in print, not as long as the paper by Walter Feit and John G. Thompson on groups of odd order, but nevertheless an indication of what was to come. These papers made a major impact, important not only for the theorems they contain but for the development of local methods, in particular the so-called signalizer-functor theory, that exploited ideas introduced by Philip Hall and Graham Higman in 1956 and by John G. Thompson in 1959 and 1962. Further huge projects followed: For example, with J. L. Alperin and Richard Brauer he classified the simple groups in which the Sylow 2-subgroups are quasi-dihedral or wreathed (261 pages); with Koichiro Harada he classified the simple groups in which every 2-subgroup can be generated by four elements (464 pages), a work which comprehensively dealt with all small Sylow 2-subgroups. His contributions in this area were many and varied, classifying simple groups either by the structure of their Sylow 2-subgroups or by the structure of the centralisers of their elements of order 2.

Significant though this research was, it was not his most important contribution. Although he had made himself a master, he was not uniquely qualified for the technical work; others could have done it. What made him unique were his vision and his leadership. Some time late in the 1960s he began to formulate a strategy for the classification of the finite simple groups. This was gradually refined and formulated, expounded in lectures in 1972 first in Chicago, then in London and at the Weizmann Institute in Israel, and published in a paper in the *Israel Journal of Mathematics* in 1974. There were many who doubted. But in the end his imagination proved correct. Although much of the technical work was done by many others, among whom Michael Aschbacher was foremost, it was Gorenstein ("The Godfather") who had the personality and the ability to see the whole picture, to inspire and direct, to keep an army of research workers in many parts of the world working individually but together to ensure that none of the many cases was forgotten. The conclusion of the project was announced with a mixture of triumph and diffidence in 1980. Triumph because it did seem that methods adequate to solve the problem had been developed, that all the theorems had been proved, that no cases had been overlooked. Diffidence because all involved knew that some papers were yet to be published, and that the published papers, lengthy and technical as they were, were bound to contain mistakes. Indeed, as emerged later, one significant piece of the structure was missing and had to be supplied in a two-volume work on quasi-thin groups by Aschbacher and Stephen Smith.

At this point Gorenstein recognized that his task was only half done. He wrote books and papers surveying the work and explaining the classification. It was for this that he was awarded the Steele Prize for Mathematical Exposition. In his response to the Steele Prize citation he wrote:

> Simultaneously with this burgeoning research effort, finite simple group theory was establishing a well-deserved reputation for inaccessibility because of the inordinate lengths of the papers pouring out. [...] Although there was admiration within the mathematical community for the achievements, there was also a growing feeling that finite group theorists were off on the wrong track. No mathematical theorem could require the number of pages these fellows were taking!
>
> The view from the inside was quite different: all the moves we were making seemed to be forced. It was not perversity on our part, but the intrinsic nature of the problem that seemed to be controlling the directions of our efforts and shaping the techniques being developed.

> Thus in writing about the classification for the general mathematical audience, I had a dual motivation: on the one hand, to convey the nature of the solution as it was unfolding, both the methods involved and the striking results themselves, and, on the other, to attempt to convince the larger community that the internal inductive approach we were taking to the classification was, despite its resulting length, the only viable one for establishing the desired theorem. (American Mathematical Society, p. 833)

Just as important as his expository writing, however, was Gorenstein's instigation of the project to produce a "new generation" proof of the classification. The idea was to produce a shorter, self-contained, properly structured proof, with all the gaps filled and all the slips and errors removed. He recruited Richard Lyons of Rutgers University and Ronald Solomon of Ohio State University and they began the project together. Much of the work was written at the time of his death but much was still to be done, and the first of a projected eleven volumes (six of which had been published by December 2006), did not appear until two years later. But the volumes carry his name as coauthor, a fitting tribute to his vision and his huge contribution to mathematics.

BIBLIOGRAPHY

Gorenstein's writings are listed by Mathematical Reviews. *In addition to his books, there are approximately seventy research articles, most of them on simple groups.*

WORKS BY GORENSTEIN

Finite Groups, 2nd ed. New York: Chelsea Publishing, 1980. (Orig. New York: Harper & Row, 1968.)

As editor. *Reviews on Finite Groups: As Printed in Mathematical Reviews*, 1940 through 1970, Volumes 1–40 Inclusive. Providence, RI: American Mathematical Society, 1974.

Finite Simple Groups: An Introduction to Their Classification. New York: Plenum, 1982. Russian translation by V. I. Loginov. *Konechnye prostye gruppy.* Moscow: Mir, 1985.

The Classification of Finite Simple Groups. Vol. 1, *Groups of Noncharacteristic 2 Type.* New York: Plenum, 1983.

With Richard Lyons and Ronald Solomon. *The Classification of the Finite Simple* Groups, vols. 1–6. Providence, RI: American Mathematical Society, 1994–2006. (Eleven volumes are planned.)

OTHER SOURCES

American Mathematical Society. "Citation for the 1989 Steele Prize for Expository Writing." *Notices of the American Mathematical Society* 36 (1989): 831–833.

Aschbacher, Michael. "Daniel Gorenstein, 1932–1992." *Notices of the American Mathematical Society* 39 (1992): 1190. Obituary.

Collins, Michael. "Professor Daniel Gorenstein." *The Independent* (London), 9 September 1992. Obituary.

Peter Neumann

GORJANOVIĆ-KRAMBERGER, DRAGUTIN (KARL)

(b. Zagreb, Croatia, 25 October 1856, *d.* Zagreb, Austro-Hungarian Empire, in present-day Croatia, 24 December 1936), *paleontology, geology, cartography.*

Gorjanović-Kramberger is best known for his discovery and descriptions of the Neandertal remains from the Hušnjakova rock shelter at Krapina in northwestern Croatia. The richness of human fossils, tools, and vertebrate fauna at Krapina made Gorjanović-Kramberger's descriptions critical for understanding Neandertal's place in human evolution. His careful excavation of the site, preservation of most of the material recovered from the excavations, application of modern techniques such the use of trace elements in relative dating and radiography, and documentation of evidence for cannibalism put him and the Krapina fossils in the vanguard of paleoanthropological research at the turn of the twentieth century. He also made important contributions in cartography and the evolution of neogene fish and reptiles. Of German heritage in the Austro-Hungarian Empire, in 1882 he dropped "Karl" from his name and added "Gorjanović" to reflect Croatian solidarity and generally signed his scientific papers Dragutin Gorjanović-Kramberger afterward.

Early Life. His father, Matija Kramberger, was a cobbler and innkeeper, and his mother, Terezija Dušek (née Vrbanović), was a widow who had three children from an earlier marriage. Gorjanović-Kramberger became interested in natural history as a boy and frequently visited the natural history collection of Slavoljub Wormastiny, a pharmacist and taxidermist who worked for the National Museum in Zagreb. He began to collect fossils found by workers at the nearby quarry at Dolje and thus originated his interest in paleontology. He studied geology and paleontology for a few years at Zurich University and later at Munich University, where he met Karl Alfred von Zittel. At the time von Zittel was the leading vertebrate paleontologist in Europe, author of the five-volume *Handbuch der Palaeontologie* (1880–1893), and he greatly influenced Gorjanović-Kramberger's thinking about morphological variation and taxonomy. Munich could not offer an advanced degree, so Gorjanović-Kramberger transferred to the Universität Tübingen; in 1879, at the age of twenty-three, he received his doctorate in natural sciences. Gorjanović-Kramberger's doctoral research focused on fossil fish from the Carpathian Basin, but he was interested in the evolution of lizards as well and was broadly trained in the fundamentals of geology and cartography. These skills would become especially useful in 1899.

For his entire career, Gorjanović-Kramberger was located at the Croatian National Museum in Zagreb, starting as curator of the geology department in 1880 and later becoming director of the Department of Geology and Paleontology in 1893. He also accepted a position as assistant professor of vertebrate paleontology at the University of Zagreb in 1884, where he became a full professor in 1896. He was also involved in establishing the Croatian Natural History Society as well as the Mountain Climbing Society, and in 1892 he was appointed an associate member of the Academy of Arts and Sciences. During this time Gorjanović-Kramberger met Emilija Burijan, a young Croatian woman of Czech descent, and the two were married in 1881. He quickly began conducting fieldwork and published on a variety of topics from the geological mapping of Croatia to the identification of natural resource localities to mollusks, though Miocene fish and Cretaceous lizards remained his primary academic interest. His highly respected reputation in Central European paleontology is reflected in the two plant and eleven animal species named after him (e.g., *Apogon krambergeri*).

The Krapina Neandertals. Gorjanović-Kramberger's paleontological research focus took a new turn in 1899 when he found the first Neandertal tooth at Krapina. Extinct mammals had been recovered from Krapina and sent to the National Museum several years earlier and as a result Gorjanović-Kramberger began a search of a rock shelter on Hušnjak Hill, located on the outskirts of town. Fieldwork from 1899–1905 at the site by Gorjanović-Kramberger and his associates, including Stjepan Osterman, who was a student at the University of Zagreb, led to the recovery of about 900 Neandertal bones representing most skeletal elements, almost 200 isolated human teeth, 1,191 tools, and approximately 3,000 remains from more than 40 taxa of extinct animals. Modern geological divisions of the Pleistocene had yet to be introduced, explaining why Gorjanović-Kramberger placed the remains in what was referred to at the time as the "diluvium." Later, when glacial periods were formally identified, he assigned the material in the Riss/Würm interstadial. Subsequent absolute dating by electron spin resonance (ESR) confirmed this and established an antiquity for the hominids of 120,000–130,000 years ago, in what came to be called the Oxygen Isotope Stage (OIS) 5e.

Compared to other early-twentieth-century human paleontologists, Gorjanović-Kramberger used advanced techniques and practiced many procedures well before their time. He mapped a detailed stratigraphic profile, excavated following natural levels, saved every Neandertal fossil he encountered, numbered each fossil and recorded directly on it the level of derivation, kept most of the faunal remains and all the stone tools, and allowed qualified scientists to see *his* fossils before they were fully published. He was the first to use the new field of radiology for documenting Neandertal morphology and published the first radiograph image of a hominid fossil in 1902. He conducted trace element (fluorine) analysis to confirm the contemporaneity of fossil mammals and the Neandertals, and published multiple, high-quality photographs of the fossils. He was first to provide evidence for cannibalism in the human fossil record based on burned specimens, cut marks, and other bone damage, using this as a way of authenticating the fossils' antiquity.

Gorjanović-Kramberger delivered an early paper on his work to the Croatian Academy of Arts and Sciences in December 1899, where he compared the Krapina fossils with the Neandertal jaw found at La Naulette, in Belgium, in 1866 and with the juvenile Neandertal jaw found at Šipka, in Moravia, in 1880. The German anatomist Hermann Klaatsch, a professor at the University of Heidelberg, was one of the first scientists to visit Gorjanović-Kramberger and to inspect the Krapina fossils and offer his interpretation of their significance. Gorjanović-Kramberger's own views about the Krapina fossils were influenced by his meeting the German anatomist Gustav Schwalbe at the Anthropological Congress held in Kassel in 1903. Schwalbe, an early supporter of the idea that Neandertals were ancestral to modern humans. His perspective greatly influenced Gorjanović-Kramberger's conclusion that the Krapina fossils were Neandertals, or in Schwalbe's terminology, *Homo primigenius.* Gorjanović-Kramberger eventually produced eighty-four single authored publications on Krapina, and while his ideas were especially influential with German scholars, it took some time for the importance of his work to be recognized.

In 1906 Gorjanović-Kramberger published a lengthy monograph on the fossils, *Der diluviale Mensch von Krapina in Kroatien* (Diluvial man from Krapina in Croatia), which contained a detailed analysis of the Neandertal fossils, along with discussions of the geology, stratigraphy, animal fossils, and archaeology of the site. He promoted the view that the Neandertals were the direct ancestors of modern humans and that they marked a transitional phase between apes and humans. He explained the robust anatomy of the Neandertals—which had been considered the result of various pathologies by the German anthropologist and anatomist Rudolf Virchow—as being caused by the harsh environment within which the Neandertals lived, as well as the crudeness of the tools they used. Moreover, Gorjanović-Kramberger identified evidence in the bones of numerous injuries, which indicated to him the dangerous and difficult conditions of Neandertal life. In addition to his many publications, Gorjanović-Kramberger also traveled to Vienna, Strasbourg, Budapest, Munich, and other German cities to lecture on his discoveries, but perhaps due to language barriers he did not lecture in France, England, or the United States.

In the early twenty-first century, Gorjanović-Kramberger is widely recognized as one of Europe's first paleoanthropologists in his effective incorporation of archaeology and biological aspects of human evolution. While referring to the Krapina fossils as *Homo primigenius*—the name given to the original Neandertal specimen by German anatomist Hermann Schaaffhausen and widely used by German scientists in the nineteenth century—Gorjanović-Kramberger always contended that Neandertals possessed considerable morphological variation and were on the line leading to modern humans. The influential American physical anthropologist at the Smithsonian Institution, Aleš Hrdlička, wrote some of the first descriptions in English about the Krapina remains in 1914 (and in more detail in 1930) and the German anatomist Franz Weidenreich dedicated his classic monograph on the Zhoukoudian Peking Man teeth to Gorjanović-Kramberger in 1937, a year after his death. But it was not until the reanalysis of the specimens and the resulting publications of American paleoanthropologists Fred H. Smith and Milford H. Wolpoff in the 1970s that Krapina became widely known among American and British paleoanthropologists. As of 2007, almost any analysis of Neandertal anatomy or evolution includes Krapina as a starting or comparative point, because of the meticulous collection of the hundreds of Neandertal bones and teeth by Gorjanović-Kramberger. In 2006, along with Nikola Tesla, a Croatian birth cohort of 1856, the United Nations Educational, Cultural, and Scientific Organization (UNESCO) recognized Gorjanović-Kramberger's contributions to science on the sesquicentennial of his birthday.

Other Achievements. While the Krapina Neandertals occupied much of his time after 1899, of his 242 publications, those about Krapina constitute only a third of the total. Other research involved Croatian cartography and surveying projects especially designed at recovering natural resources, and he wrote on diverse topics from water supplies to earthquakes to fossil whales. In 1909 Gorjanović-Kramberger helped to create the Geological Survey of Croatia, and in 1911 he founded the journal *Vijesti geoloskog povjerenstva* (Geological Survey News), which he edited from 1911 to the final year of its publication in 1916. Outside paleoanthropology, Gorjanović-Kramberger is most recognized for his contributions to the evolution and taxonomy of fossil mollusks, fish, and lizards. These include his naming the genus *Aigialosaurus* and the evolutionary sequences of fish and invertebrates. In recognition of his scientific achievements, Emperor Franz Josef of the Austro-Hungarian Empire named Gorjanović-Kramberger a Court Counselor and awarded him the coveted Golden Chain Award in 1907. He retired from his professorship at the University of Zagreb and as director of the National Museum in 1924. In his lifetime, Gorjanović-Kramberger was also famous for these contributions in nonhuman paleontology, but he will be remembered for his methodical, far-sighted work about the Krapina Neandertals.

BIBLIOGRAPHY

WORKS BY GORJANOVIĆ-KRAMBERGER

"Der paläolithische Mensch und seine Zeitgenossen aus dem Diluvium von Krapina in Croatien." *Mittheilungen der Anthropologischen Gesellschaft in Wien* 29 (1899): 65–68.

"Der diluviale Mensch aus Krapina in Kroatien." *Mittheilungen der Anthropologischen Gesellschaft in Wien* 30 (1900): 203.

"Der paläolithische Mensch und seine Zeitgnossen aus dem Diluvium von Krapina in Kroatien." *Mittheilungen der Anthropologischen Gesellschaft in Wien* 31 (1901): 164–197.

"Der paläolithische Mensch und seine Zeitgenossen aus dem Diluvium von Krapina in Kroatien (Nachtrag, als zweiter Theil)." *Mittheilungen der Anthropologischen Gesellschaft in Wien* 32 (1902): 189–216.

"Der paläolithische Mensch und seine Zeitgnossen aus dem Diluvium von Krapina in Kroatien. Zweiter Nachtrag (als dritter Teil)." *Mittheilungen der Anthropologischen Gesellschaft in Wien* 34 (1904): 187–199.

"Der paläolithische Mensch und seine Zeitgnossen aus dem Diluvium von Krapina in Kroatien. Dritter Nachtrag (als vierter Teil)." *Mittheilungen der Anthropologischen Gesellschaft in Wien* 35 (1905): 197–229.

Der diluviale Mensch von Krapina in Kroatien. Ein Beitrag zur Paläoanthropologie. Wiesbaden: Kreidel, 1906.

"Die Kronenund Wurzelnder Mahlzähnedes *Homo primigenius* und ihre genetische Bedeutung." *Anatomischer Anzeiger* 31 (1907): 97–134.

Fosilni proboscidi Hrvatske i Slavonije. (*De proboscidibus fossilibus Croatiæ et Slavoniæ*). Zagreb: Knjizara Jugoslavenske akademije, 1912.

"Život i kultura diluvijalnoga čovjeka iz Krapine u Hrvatskoj (*Homo diluvialis* e Krapina, Croatia, vita et cultura)." *Djela Jugoslavenske akademije znanosti i umjetnosti* 23 (1913): 1–54.

Pračovek iz Krapine. Zagreb: Hrvatski prirodoslovno društvo, 1918.

OTHER SOURCES

Frayer, David W. *The Krapina Neandertals: A Comprehensive, Centennial, Illustrated Bibliography.* Zagreb: Croatian Natural History Museum, 2006.

Henke, Winfried. "Gorjanović-Kramberger's Research on Krapina: Its Impact on Paleoanthropology in Germany." *Periodicum biologorum* 108 (2006): 239–252.

Hrdlička, Aleš. "The Most Ancient Skeletal Remains of Man." *Annual Report of the Smithsonian Institution* (1913), 491–552.

———. *The Skeletal Remains of Early Man.* Vol. 83, Miscellaneous Collections. Washington, DC: 1930.

Kochansky-Devidé, Vanda. "Prof. Dr. Gorjanović als Paläontologe. Poseban otisak iz knjige." In *Krapina, 1899-1969,* edited by Mirko Malez, 5–11. Zagreb: Jugoslavenska akademija znanosti i umjetnosti, 1970.

———. "Dragutin Gorjanović-Kramberger als Anthropologe." In *Krapinski Pračovjek i evolucijy Hominida,* 53–59. Zagreb: Jugoslavenska akademija znanosti i umjetnosti, 1978.

———, and Mirko Malez. "Bibliografija Gorjanovićevih radova i članaka o Gorjanoviću." *Geološki vjesnik* 10 (1957): 17–29.

Kricun, Morrie, Janet Monge, Alan Mann, et al. *The Krapina Hominids: A Radiographic Atlas of the Skeletal Collection.* Zagreb: Croatian Natural History Museum, 1999.

Malez, Mirko. *Dragutin Gorjanović-Kramberger (1856–1936).* Zagreb: Jugoslavenska akademija znanosti i umjetnosti, 1987.

Radovčić, Jakov. *Dragutin Gorjanović-Kramberger i krapinski pračovjek: počeci suvremene paleoantropologije* (Dragutin Gorjanović-Kramberger and Krapina Early Man: The Foundations of Modern Paleoanthropology). Zagreb : Hrvatski prirodoslovni muzej, 1988.

———, Fred H. Smith, Erik Trinkaus, et al. *The Krapina Hominids: An Illustrated Catalog of the Skeletal Collection.* Zagreb: Mladost Press and the Croatian Natural History Museum, 1988.

Rink, Jack, Henry P. Schwarcz, Fred H. Smith, et al. "ESR Dates for Krapina Hominids." *Nature* 378 (1995): 24.

Smith, Fred. "The Neandertal Remains from Krapina: A Descriptive and Comparative Study." *University of Tennessee Department of Anthropology Reports of Investigations* 15 (1976): 1–359.

———. "Gorjanović-Kramberger, Dragutin (Karl) (1856–1936)." In *History of Physical Anthropology: An Encyclopedia,* edited by Frank Spencer. New York: Garland, 1997.

———. "Krapina." In *History of Physical Anthropology: An Encyclopedia,* edited by Frank Spencer. New York: Garland, 1997.

Trinkaus, Eric, and Pat Shipman. *The Neandertals: Changing the Image of Mankind.* New York: Knopf, 1993.

Weidenreich, Franz. "The Dentition of *Sinanthropus pekinensis*: A Comparative Odontography of the Hominids." In *Palaeontologia Sinica, New Series D,* No.1, Whole Series No. 101, 1937.

Wolpoff, Milford H. "The Krapina Dental Remains." *American Journal of Physical Anthropology* 50 (1979): 67–114.

———, Jakov Radovčić, Fred H. Smith, et al. *The Krapina Neandertals: An Illustrated Catalog of the Skeletal Collection.* Zagreb: Croatian Natural History Museum, 1988.

David W. Frayer
Jakov Radovčić

GORLAEUS (VAN GOORLE, VAN GOOIRLE), DAVID

(*b.* Utrecht, Netherlands, 15 January 1591; *d.* Cornjum, Netherlands, 27 April 1612), *natural philosophy, matter theory.*

Gorlaeus is counted among the founders of modern atomism, which he proposed as an alternative to Aristotelian matter theory. Because of his notion of atomic compounds, he is also regarded as a contributor to the evolution of chemistry.

Gorlaeus's Identity. Given his latter-day reputation, Gorlaeus's biography is rather surprising: He died very young, at age 21, as a student of theology. In fact, his scientific reputation is entirely posthumous, and moreover started with a certain delay. The two manuscripts he composed in Leiden in 1611, the voluminous *Exercitationes philosophicae* and the succinct *Idea physicae,* were published in 1620 and 1651, respectively.

From the correspondence of his father, David Gorlaeus Sr., it appears that alchemical interests were being cultivated in his family. Still, the interests of the younger Gorlaeus in natural philosophy had above all philosophical and theological sources. As for philosophy, as an undergraduate student at Franeker between 1606 and 1610, Gorlaeus followed the comparatively innovative natural science course of Henricus de Veno, who incorporated recent developments in the fields of astronomy, meteorology, and natural philosophy into his otherwise Aristotelian framework. By 1610, Gorlaeus had furthermore come under the influence of Julius Caesar Scaliger's *Exercitationes exotericae* (1557), which explained a range of natural phenomena in terms of corpuscles and interstitial voids. Scaliger figures as the only recent author in Gorlaeus's two books and is quoted with great frequency.

Whereas Scaliger depicted himself as an Aristotelian and anti-atomist, Gorlaeus's strongly anti-Aristotelian physics relied fully on the interaction of atoms. In order to understand why a theology student should have ended up developing such a system, one must consider his circumstances in 1611. A crisis pitting two currents of Calvinism against each other was just then reaching its acme at Leiden University's theological faculty, where Gorlaeus had recently enrolled. The point of departure for the conflict had been the non-orthodox view of one of the professors, Jacob Arminius, that the election of the faithful to heaven was not predestined by God since eternity, a view that was combated by his colleague Franciscus Gomarus. The so-called Arminian conflict, which quickly turned into a national and indeed international affair, had strong political overtones, but conceptually revolved around such philosophical concepts as the nature of divine and human causality, time and eternity, place and ubiquity, and determinism and free will. When Arminius died in 1609, Conrad Vorstius was chosen to succeed him, but upon his arrival at Leiden in 1611 was expelled speedily on charges of heresy. Some of the alleged heresies, which King James I of England stooped to rebut in person, were said to reside in his physicalist understanding of God, an understanding that had been inspired, it was charged, by the metaphysics of the German professor of medicine Nicolaus Taurellus. The point is that Gorlaeus, who was a partisan of the Arminian cause, quickly acquainted himself with the writings of both Vorstius and Taurellus, and his atomism can be understood as a radicalization of the ontology he had found particularly in Taurellus's metaphysics.

Gorlaeus's System. Gorlaeus's atomism, which took center stage in his *Idea physicae*, is however more fully embedded in the *Exercitationes philosophicae.* There, philosophy is defined as "the naked knowledge of entities" and thus identified with ontology. Each discipline, wrote Gorlaeus, tackles one type of entity, whereby physics deals with natural entities. His ontology distinguishes between self-subsisting entities (*entia per se*), which are defined as numerically unique, fully existing, unchanging, and indivisible, and the accidental compositions (*entia per accidens*) that are brought about when several *entia per se* gather. This view of reality is essentially atomistic, although primarily in a metaphysical sense. By denying universals and allowing only for individuals, it is also heavily indebted to medieval nominalism. The only self-subsisting entities are God, angels, souls, and physical atoms, whereas all other entities, including humans, are transitory composites. Gorlaeus's definition of man as an "accidental being," which he took from Taurellus, was to be used in a 1641 university disputation by René Descartes's friend Henricus Regius and triggered the first conflict between Descartes and the Aristotelian university establishment. Since that episode Gorlaeus has, somewhat misleadingly, been seen as a forerunner of Cartesianism.

Although his atomism is primarily metaphysical, Gorlaeus spent much time and effort to apply it to the realms of physics and chemistry. Rejecting Aristotle's concept of place, he maintained that atoms move in an absolute space, which does not necessarily have to be filled. Possessing quantity, atoms are furthermore extended, and they come in two types, namely dry (as earth atoms) and wet (as water atoms). All natural bodies can be resolved into these two types of atoms. Fire is explained in terms of the friction of closely packed atoms, while air is defined as a real, but non-elementary substance, which fills all voids and which is capable of transmitting celestial heat, but not of combining into compounds. When bodies rarefy, this is due to the entrance of air between the atoms; air itself cannot be rarefied or condensed. The emergent physical and chemical properties of higher-level compounds are due to the mixing of the elementary qualities of wet and dry with the so-called "real accidents" of warm and cold, which are communicated to the elementary atoms from the ambient air. Within this framework, Gorlaeus explained the most common physical and chemical properties of substances as a "temperament" created by the interacting atoms under the influence of ambient heat or cold. Although he demonstrated a certain ingenuity in this enterprise, he was yet forced to introduce additional elements such as heaviness, which is a divinely "impressed downward force." Divine providence is also responsible for the aggregation of atoms into the more complex bodies.

Although never truly influential, Gorlaeus's views were received in Arminian circles, both in the Low Countries and in England, where the implications of his "composite ontology" for both the explanation of the relationship between the divinity and mankind and the behavior of natural bodies was appreciated. His *Idea physicae*, which from a scientific point of view is more straightforward and forceful, had the misfortune of being published too late, and worse yet, in the heyday of Cartesianism. The small number of extant copies testifies to its low circulation.

BIBLIOGRAPHY

WORKS BY GORLAEUS

Exercitationes philosophicae quibus universa fere discutitur philosophia theoretica et plurima ac praecipua Peripateticorum dogmata evertuntur. Leiden, Netherlands: In Bibliopolio Commeliano sumptibus viduae Iannis Comelini, 1620.

Idea physicae, cui adjuncta est Epistola cujusdam Anonymi de terrae motu. Utrecht, Netherlands: Johannes a Waesberge, 1651.

OTHER SOURCES

Gregory, Tullio. "Studi sull'atomismo del Seicento. II. David van Goorle e Daniel Sennert," *Giornale critico della filosofia italiana* 45 (1966): 44–63. Provides a good analysis of Gorlaeus's nominalism.

Jaeger, F. M. "Over David van Goorle als atomist, en over het geslacht van Goorle in Noord-Nederland," *Oud-Holland* 36 (1918): 205–242. Discovered the main biographical data of the life of Gorlaeus and of his family.

Lasswitz, Kurd. *Geschichte der Atomistik vom Mittelalter bis Newton.* 2 vols. Hamburg: Leopold Voss, 1890, repr. Hildesheim: Georg Olms, 1984, vol. I, 333–335; 455–463. Still a valid summary of Gorlaeus's atomism.

Lüthy, Christoph. "David Gorlaeus' Atomism, or: The Marriage of Protestant Metaphysics with Italian Natural Philosophy." In *Late Medieval and Early Modern Corpuscular Matter Theories*, edited by Christoph Lüthy, John E. Murdoch, and William R. Newman, 245–290. Leiden, Netherlands: Brill, 2001. Analyzes Gorlaeus's philosophy through the lens of his education and the Arminian crisis.

———, and Leen Spruit. "The Doctrine, Life, and Roman Trial of the Frisian Philosopher Henricus de Veno (1574?–1613)." *Renaissance Quarterly* 56 (2003): 1112–1151. Describes life and doctrine of Gorlaeus's teacher and the roots of Gorlaeus's own mixture of Italian natural philosophy and Protestant metaphysics.

Verbeek, Theo. "*Ens per accidens*. Le origini della *Querelle* di Utrecht." *Giornale critico della filosofia italiana*, sixth series, 71 (1992): 276–288. Retraces the role of Gorlaeus's most famous thesis in the Cartesian controversies of 1641 to 1642.

Christoph Lüthy

GOULD, STEPHEN JAY

(*b.* New York City, New York, 10 September 1941; *d.* New York City, 20 May 2002), *geology, paleontology, evolutionary biology, history and philosophy of science, popular publications.*

In 1977, Gould published his *Ontogeny and Phylogeny* as a practice run for writing his magnum opus *The Structure of Evolutionary Theory* (2002). As it turned out, he did not publish this projected work until a couple of months before he died. Quite early in his professional life Gould had introduced all of the topics for which he would eventually become famous. For example, he argued for punctuated equilibria, the use of stochastic models in paleontology, species selection, macroevolution, and hierarchical structure, while opposing Panglossian adaptationism, sociobiology, genetic determinism, and evolutionary psychology. He combined these scientific issues with his views on history and philosophy of science, rejecting determinism and inductivism while adopting pluralism. Gould not only integrated these technical subjects into a coherent system but also between 1972 and 2001 he published three hundred popular articles in *Natural History.*

In the best Horatio Alger tradition, Gould, a third-generation descendant of Jewish immigrants, ended up at Harvard University, one of the most prestigious universities in the world. He dedicated one of his last collections of essays to his maternal grandparents, Grammy and Papa Joe. He had a penchant for baseball that stemmed from his childhood years. His wife at his death was Rhonda Roland Shearer. He had two sons, Jesse and Elton, from a previous marriage.

A feature of Gould's career was his rapid rise in rank. He received a BA in geology and philosophy from Antioch College in 1963 and a doctorate from Columbia University in 1967, although he did most of his work at the American Museum of Natural History. In that same year he joined the faculty of Harvard University as an assistant professor. Four years later in 1971, he was promoted to associate professor with tenure and in only two additional years became a full professor.

Punctuated Equilibria. Gould's early work on land snails in Bermuda, evolutionary patterns in pelycosaurian reptiles as well as allometry, was solid but hardly revolutionary. Then in 1972 all that changed when Gould published a paper with Niles Eldredge, arguing that evolutionary biologists should replace phyletic gradualism, the traditional view in paleontology at the time, with a radically new view—punctuated equilibria. From before Charles Darwin everyone acknowledged that gaps exist in the fossil record. Advocates of phyletic gradualism explained a large percentage of these gaps as being due to the imperfection of the fossil record; they assumed that phyletic change is gradual. Eldredge and Gould disagreed: they argued that phylogeny is primarily a matter of stasis, punctuated with periods of rapid change. The fossil record is not as imperfect as previous paleontologists had thought. A large percentage of the apparent gaps are actually real. Like it or not, stasis is data.

The paper by Eldredge and Gould was unusual in several respects. It began with a history of phyletic gradualism, explaining how generations of their fellow paleontologists could be so wrong for so long. One reason was the inductivist philosophy of science that so many practicing paleontologists professed at the time. According to Eldredge and Gould (1972, p. 85), science does not proceed by a steady accumulation of facts but facts viewed from a theoretical perspective. Scientists do not encounter facts as objectively given "data" but as seen through the light of theory, and theories in turn act as "party lines" that dictate what they see. Adherents of phyletic gradualism view their data through the eyes of their theory, while Eldredge and Gould quite naturally view their data through their own theory (1972, p. 98). The preceding statements can be given a radical interpretation, as if scientists can never free themselves from their preconceptions, but it can also be interpreted quite conservatively. People are all biased in some respect or other on a whole range of issues. Luckily, different people tend to possess difference biases. Science is the most successful method thus far developed to reconcile these differences. Eldredge and Gould adopted the more conservative view.

From here on, the paper takes on a more conventional character. Eldredge and Gould do their best to show that very little in the way of evidence supports the phyletic gradualist view. Of course, even less evidence exists for the prevalence of punctuated equilibria. However, they do argue that their theory is more in accord with Ernst Mayr's biospecies than is phyletic gradualism. According to Mayr, new species arise in small populations at the periphery of species—a phenomenon termed allopatric speciation. This process allows change to occur rapidly. What is the mechanism for stasis? Eldredge and Gould argue that just as organisms are homeostatic systems, species themselves incorporate homeostatic mechanisms

Stephen Jay Gould. *Stephen Jay Gould next to a drawer filled with fossils at Harvard University.* STEVE HANSEN/TIME LIFE PICTURES /GETTY IMAGES.

but to a lesser degree. Finally, they present two detailed examples of allopatric speciation that fit better with punctuated equilibria than they do with phyletic gradualism.

Reinvigorating Paleontology. While Eldredge and Gould were busy ushering in a new view of the fossil record, Gould joined with David Raup, Thomas Schopf, Jack Sepkoski, and Dan Simberloff in an effort to make paleontology more lawful (nomothetic) and quantitative. In particular they introduced stochastic (probabilistic) models of phylogeny that they hoped would help them discover the laws governing the evolutionary process. For example, clades (all the taxa descended from one ancestor) can be characterized by their shape. Bottom-heavy clades expand, forming many species, early in their history and then peter out with few or no species. Top-heavy clades start off quite small but then gradually expand. Raup and Gould (1974) discovered patterns in these clades; for instance, an increase in bottom-heavy clades as one goes back in history. This pattern might be due to some regularity in nature or possibly just an artifact of how systematists classify organisms.

During this same period Gould and Eldredge joined with Steven Stanley (1975, 1979) to advocate species selection. A common view at the time was that selection occurs primarily (or exclusively) at the level of genes: genes are what replicate from generation to generation. Others argued that organisms are the primary focus of selection: organisms interact with their environments in ways that favor reproduction of some organisms rather than others. Gould, Eldredge, and Stanley argued that "selection" in this sense can occur at higher levels of organization than anyone had previously thought, possibly even at the level of entire species, resulting in macroevolution. Still others argued for a hierarchical view. Selection wanders up and down the biological hierarchy from genes and organisms to entire species. One thing common among genes and organisms is that they are individuals. If species can be selected, then it seems only right that species themselves must be construed as individuals—a position being urged at the time by Michael Ghiselin (1974) and David Hull (1976), a position that Gould himself eventually came to adopt.

In 1973 Gould started publishing short essays in *Natural History,* culminating in his first collection of these more popular pieces, *Ever since Darwin* (1977b). These papers dealt with a variety of topics including those that he discussed in much greater detail in his *Ontogeny and Phylogeny* (1977c): topics such as allometry, heterochrony, orthogenesis, neoteny, ontogeny, paedomorphosis, parthenogenesis, and recapitulation. Gould was well aware that these ideas were currently out of favor among biologists, especially in the English-speaking world. These terms still retain an air of belonging to "suspect" science, but Gould continued to pursue them both in his popular works and more extensively in his *Ontogeny and Phylogeny.* As it turned out, Gould was more than a little prescient in emphasizing the role of development in evolution, as the rise of evo-devo clearly indicates.

The Spandrels of San Marco. The year 1977 was a banner year for Gould: he published two books as well as several important papers, including his punctuation paper with Eldredge. Two years later he published an even more controversial paper with Richard Lewontin: "The Spandrels of San Marco and the Panglossian Paradigm: A Critique of the Adaptationist Programme" (1979). In his paper with Eldredge, Gould argued against one of the most cherished beliefs held by paleontologists, a belief that evolutionary change is largely gradual and continuous. In his later paper with Lewontin, he took on two equally cherished beliefs: that nearly all characteristics of living creatures are adaptations and that natural selection is the major mechanism producing these adaptations.

In his early years, Gould shared in these widely held beliefs. However, as the years went by, he decided that complex structures can arise in the absence of selection and that not all of these structures are adaptations. The two metaphors that Lewontin and Gould used to illustrate these positions were the Panglossian paradigm and the spandrels of San Marco. Voltaire's Dr. Pangloss was famous for finding the world in which we live to be the best of all possible worlds, even in the face of a massive earthquake that all but destroyed Lisbon.

The adaptationist program has Panglossian echoes. Spandrels also suggest a criticism of the prevailing emphasis on adaptation. The arches in cathedrals such as San Marco clearly perform a function: They hold up the ceiling. The spandrels do not: They simply fill in the empty spaces between the arches. The same situation may well prevail in the living world. Many characteristics that seem to be adaptations may well be nothing but "spandrels" or "exaptations," as they were later termed by Gould and Elizabeth Vrba (1982). These distinctions led Vrba and Gould (1986) to replace species selection with species sorting. Species do not have what it takes to be selected, but they can be sorted. The distinction is between changes due to a variety of causal mechanisms and mere sorting—simple, descriptive observations about differential reproductive success.

During the rest of their careers Gould and Eldredge defended, expanded, and corrected their original views. In 1977 they wrote a response to their critics, ratcheting up their claims about the frequency of punctuational change. It "dominates the history of life," while phyletic gradualism is "very rare and too slow, in any case, to produce the major events of evolution" (p. 115). Early on Gould and Eldredge thought that their punctuational model of evolution was quite radical, but five years later they could not understand what all the hubbub was about. It was "scarcely a revolutionary proposal" (p. 117). For the rest of their rebuttal, Gould and Eldredge evaluated the evidence that had been generated over the past decade both pro and con.

Paleontologists were convinced that they made the decisions that they did on the basis of reason, argument, and evidence, but once again Gould and Eldredge argued that their fellow "paleontologists have worn blinders that permit them to accumulate cases in one category only" (1977, p. 116). Testing such claims is quite difficult. Even so, Gould took on a series of examples drawn from the study of human beings. They should provide the clearest examples of the influence of society on science. If scientists can retain their objectivity in studying the human species, then it is likely that they can achieve this end when studying other species as well. Of course, if society plays a significant role in the study of human beings, it does not follow that researchers are equally biased when it comes to other areas of science.

In 1978 Gould published a paper detailing the unconscious bias that influenced the conclusions that Samuel George Morton drew about racial differences in human beings from his study of their cranial capacities. Needless to say, Caucasoids had the largest capacity, Negroids the smallest. When Gould ran these same experiments, using Morton's own skulls, he discovered that all races have approximately the same capacities. In his *The Mismeasure of Man* (1981), Gould expanded his study to include the works of Paul Broca, Cesare Lombroso, and Alfred Binet, as well as Sir Cyril Burt and Arthur Jensen. He found little in the way of outright fraud or conscious manipulation in this research. Instead, he used these studies to show how socially embedded science actually is. In response other scientists ran Morton's experiment yet again and came up with different results, but that is science.

Replaying the Tape of Life. Gould had two reasons for writing his *Wonderful Life* (1989). First, the discovery of unbelievably weird species right after the Cambrian explosion in the Burgess Shale in British Columbia was too good to pass up. Second, he proposed to use this study to illustrate the nature of history. Immediately after the Cambrian explosion (570 million years ago), a large number of organisms evolved that embodied a range of anatomical design that has never been equaled since. However, this original stock of organisms was soon decimated, leaving only a relatively few groups to give rise to the next flora and fauna. Out of twenty-five basic plans, only four led to successful groups.

Gould could not see how the history of life, in particular this episode, could ever have been predicted. Contingency played too significant of a role. Will human beings eventually lose their little toe? There is no way of knowing. If one were to rewind the tape of life and play it back again, what is the likelihood that it would be anything like the one that did occur? Only if one adopts a Laplacian epistemology is any such prediction possible. In any real world, it would be impossible. Paleontology might become more quantitative and nomothetic than it is now, but there are limits.

Science and Society. Both scientists and nonscientists alike complain about how little the general public understands about science, but they are equally uneasy when a professional scientist publishes popular works. Gould was as good a popularizer as we are likely to get. Yet his fellow scientists were put off by all the attention he received in the popular press—interviews with *Mainliner* (1981), *Newsweek* (1982), the *New York Times Magazine* (1983), *People* (1986), and *Time* (1990). His photograph actually appeared on the cover of *Newsweek*. Gould's fellow scientists also did not like what they took to be his deliberate intrusion of politics into science. Gould, Lewontin, and Richard Levins, three of the most important evolutionary biologists at the time, took the lead in protesting the Vietnam War in ways that their fellow-scientists found unseemly.

Just as the Vietnam War ground to a close, another controversy arose when an equally influential evolutionary biologist, Edward O. Wilson, published his *Sociobiology: The New Synthesis* (1975). Science for the People, an informally organized group of scientists based at Harvard University, attacked Wilson's book for its perceived promotion of racism, sexism, and a host of other social ills. The ensuing dispute led to a sharp split among scientists. Many scientists opposed the same panoply of social ills as did members of Science for the People but objected to the polemical tactics used by this group. They did not think Wilson was a capitalist running dog. Numerous scientists became part of the sociobiology research program, which later transmuted into evolutionary psychology.

Gould opposed both sociobiology and evolutionary psychology, finding them too heavily weighted toward the role of genes in development. Chief among Gould's critics were Dan Dennett, John Maynard Smith, Richard Dawkins, and Steven Pinker. One problem with these disputes was the ease with which all sides could elide from genes being the primary units of replication in natural selection to their being the primary units of selection.

Science, Religion, and the Humanities. In 1981 creationism raised its head again, and Gould was called upon to testify at the Arkansas trial, but this time Gould's advocacy won the unequivocal approval of his peers. Many of Gould's fellow scientists were put off by his activism with respect to the Vietnam War and sociobiology. Opposition was greatly reduced when it came to creationism. Here was a social cause that touched scientists directly. Very few scientists thought that school boards should be able to force biology teachers to include Bible stories in their biology courses.

If nothing else, the resurgence of creationism led Gould to think seriously about the relation between science, religion, and later the humanities. Creationists were clearly intruding into the proper domain of science, but then sociobiologists and evolutionary psychologists seemed to be encroaching on intellectual territories that traditionally were the province of religion and the humanities. Gould's solution to this problem was to postulate nonoverlapping magisteria—intellectual domains where "one form of teaching holds the appropriate tools for meaningful discourse and resolution" (1999, p. 5; see also 2003, pp. 87, 156a).

For example, according to Gould, science deals exclusively with empirical facts and scientific theories, while religion deals with ultimate meaning and moral values. The boundaries between the humanities on the one hand and science and religion on the other hand turn out to be quite problematic. At one time, all areas of knowledge were termed "philosophy," but gradually all sorts of disciplines peeled off, stripping the humanities to bare bones, primarily to those areas of enquiry that deal with human beings. As science grew in stature, the humanities tended to be left behind, but in universities and colleges at least half of the departments deal with one species and one species only—*Homo sapiens*. According to Gould, the humanities can help scientists learn how to communicate more successfully and set out the boundaries that separate science, religion, and the humanities but that is about all.

Gould insists that these three magisteria are nonoverlapping. Disputes certainly arise within each of these magisteria, but they can be dealt with and must be dealt with using the tools inherent in each. For example, evidence can help to decide if the Permian mass extinction was caused by a comet hitting Earth. Poring over the Bible, the Koran, or the Constitution of the United States of America is beside the point. Biologists can discover the limits of kin selection but have no special training in deciding how morally wrong or right nepotism might be. Humanists tend to concentrate on language—the various meanings that terms take, including those terms that occur in science. Scientists surely analyze the language that they use, but they are not especially trained in this skill. People are generally social and moral beings, but again few have received special training in the humanities or theology. Social scientists quite obviously study human beings as social beings, but other scientists remain largely ignorant of this work.

In his *Rocks of Ages* (1999) Gould made a persuasive case for science and religion forming separate and distinct magisteria. In his *The Hedgehog, the Fox, and the Magister's Pox* (2003), he found it harder to treat the humanities as a single, coherent magisterium and to distinguish the humanities from the other two magisteria. Problems arise when those scholars working in one magisterium invade the territory of another, and these incursions are quite common. At least some creationists think that the creation stories told in the Bible trump anything that scientists can find out about the big bang, the origin of life on Earth, and the evolution of species. But then at least some sociobiologists think that they are in a position to decide which acts are morally wrong and which right, and at least some postmodernist philosophers think that they can deconstruct AIDS, because after all it is nothing but a social construct. Setting out the boundaries of these three magisteria is difficult enough. Convincing people to respect them is even more difficult, but this is the solution that Gould proposes.

The Essence of Darwinism. The main goal of Gould's *The Structure of Evolutionary Theory* (2002) was to bring together all of the views that he had promulgated throughout his career under one cover. Another goal was to set out the essence of Darwinism, both Darwin's Darwinism and his own Darwinism, convinced that they were one and the same, and to justify this endeavor. In the past his efforts on this score had gotten him in trouble.

When professionals argue among themselves, they frequently use modes of expression quite different from those that they use when writing for a more general audience. For example, Gould details how Ernst Mayr's version of the synthetic theory of evolution beguiled him when he was a graduate student, but in the interim he had been forced to admit that "if Mayr's characterization of the synthetic theory is accurate, then that theory, as a general proposition, is effectively dead, despite its persistence as text-book orthodoxy"(1980b, p. 120). Creationists certainly made considerable mileage out of this hyperbole. In their internal disputes scientists frequently overstate their case.

Later Gould argued that Darwinism can best be defined as "embodying two central claims and a variety of peripheral and supporting statements more or less strongly tied to the central postulates" (1982, p. 380). These two central postulates are that natural selection is a creative force and that the locus of evolutionary change is selection on individual organisms. But Gould is forced to admit that he overstated both of these central claims. For example, natural selection is a creative force, but it is not as efficacious as Darwin had thought, and organisms are the main locus of selection, but they are not the sole locus. In his own hierarchical theory of evolution, entities at various levels of organization can be selected. Although in this respect Gould departs from Darwin, he still maintains that his theory captures "the fundamental feature of Darwin's vision" (1982, p. 381).

The main cause for the terminological dispute about which versions of evolutionary theory are or are not Darwinian is treating scientific theories as if they are essential natural kinds, as if every scientific theory can be characterized in terms of a set of postulates that this theory and only this theory incorporates. One way around this dilemma is to treat Darwinism at any one time as a cluster concept and through time as a historical entity, and this is the tack that Gould takes. Biological species are individuals that have a beginning and ending in time, split, merge, and go extinct. The same can be said for Darwinism. It too is an individual that has a beginning in time. It too splits and merges, but so far has yet to go extinct. The failure of so many evolutionary biologists to ignore all this change and to concentrate on one version of evolutionary theory and one version only has resulted in the hardening of this theory (1982, p. 383; 2002, p. 46).

When Gould adopted the view that biological species are best viewed as historical entities, he was willing to go the "whole orang." Gould is willing to accept the position that particular species lack an essence (i.e., a set of characteristics that all and only the organisms belonging to this species possess). In particular, the human species has no essence. "We are a thing, an item of history, not an embodiment of general principles … *Homo sapiens* is an entity, not a tendency" (1989, p. 319–320). However, he was not able to apply this perspective in its entirety to scientific theories such as Darwinism. He began his magnum opus with a subheading, "Theories Need Both Essences and Histories" (Gould, 2002, p. 1). Some biological species may exhibit both essences and histories, but they need not. Genealogy alone will do. Gould insists that scientific theories must exhibit both essences and histories. Each theory must be treated as if it can be characterized in terms of one set of basic postulates and one set only. Scientists are willing to go along with this position just so long as their version of the essence of a particular theory is the correct version. For instance, they agree with each other that there is an essence to Darwinism, but they disagree about what this essence is. Gould himself is commonly thought of as rejecting Darwin's theory or at least Mayr's version of it.

Gould's influence outside of science has been unequaled. He had the knack for explaining scientific ideas in ways that captured the imagination of the general public. More than one student decided on adopting a life in science from reading Gould's writings. His professional publications were taken seriously by his colleagues even if they were not universally adopted. His open advocacy of his political views worked against him. For most scientists, science comes first and almost nothing comes in second.

BIBLIOGRAPHY

WORKS BY GOULD

With Niles Eldredge. "Punctuated Equilibria: An Alternative to Phyletic Gradualism." In *Models in Paleobiology,* edited by Thomas J. M. Schopf. San Francisco: Freeman, Cooper, 1972.

With David Raup. "Stochastic Simulation and Evolution of Morphology: Towards a Nomothetic Paleontology." *Systematic Zoology* 23 (1974): 305–322.

"Eternal Metaphors of Paleontology." In *Patterns of Evolution: As Illustrated by the Fossil Record.* edited by Anthony Hallam. New York: Elsevier Scientific Publishing, 1977a.

Ever since Darwin: Reflections in Natural History. New York: W. W. Norton, 1977b. Gould's first collected *Natural History* articles.

Ontogeny and Phylogeny. Cambridge, MA: Belknap Press of Harvard University, 1977c. Gould's exposition of a biological worldview that was far from popular at the time.

With Niles Eldredge. "Punctuated Equilibria: The Tempo and Mode of Evolution Reconsidered." *Paleobiology* 3 (1977): 115–151.

With David M. Raup, J. John Sepkoski Jr., Thomas K. M. Schopf, et al. "The Shape of Evolution: A Comparison of Real and Random Clades." *Paleobiology* 3 (1977): 23–40. Attempts by a group of biologists to find regularities in evolution.

"Morton's Ranking of Races by Cranial Capacity: Unconscious Manipulation of Data May Be a Scientific Norm." *Science* 200 (1978): 503–509. An illustration of how firmly social influences are embedded in science.

With Richard Lewontin. "The Spandrels of San Marco and the Panglossian Paradigm: A Critique of the Adaptationist Programme." *Proceedings of the Royal Society London,* series B, 205 (1979): 581–598. One of the most cited papers in the philosophy of biology.

"The Promise of Paleobiology as a Nomothetic, Evolutionary Discipline." *Paleobiology* 6 (1980a): 96–118.

"Is a New and General Theory of Evolution Emerging?" *Paleobiology* 6 (1980b): 119–130.

The Mismeasure of Man. New York: W. W. Norton, 1981. An expansion of Gould's 1978 paper.

"Darwinism and the Expansion of Evolutionary Theory." *Science* (1982): 380–387.

With Elizabeth Vrba. "Exaptation—A Missing Term in the Science of Form." *Paleobiology* 8 (1982): 4–15.

With Elizabeth Vrba. "The Hierarchical Expansion of Sorting and Selection: Sorting and Selection Cannot Be Equated." *Paleobiology* 12 (1986): 217–228.

With Norman L. Gilinsky and Rebecca Z. German. "Asymmetry of Lineages and the Direction of Evolutionary Time." *Science* 236 (1987): 1436–1441. An attempt to find regularities in evolution.

Wonderful Life: The Burgess Shale and the Nature of History. New York: W. W. Norton, 1989. The role of history in science.

"The Confusion over Evolution." Review of *The Ant and the Peacock: Altruism and Sexual Selection from Darwin to Today,* by Helena Cronin; *The Miner's Canary,* by Niles Eldredge; and *On Methuselah's Trail: Living Fossils and the Great Extinctions,* by Peter Douglas Ward. *New York Review of Books,* 19 November 1992.

"Confusion over Evolution: An Exchange." *New York Review of Books,* 14 January 1993. The beginning of a series of exchanges between Gould and his critics—John Maynard Smith, Daniel Dennett, Richard Dawkins, and Steven Pinker.

"Darwinian Fundamentalism." *New York Review of Books,* 12 June 1997a.

"Evolution: The Pleasures of Pluralism." *New York Review of Books,* 26 June 1997b.

"Darwinian Fundamentalism: An Exchange." *New York Review of Books,* 14 August 1997c.

Rocks of Ages: Science and Religion in the Fullness of Life. New York: Ballantine Books, 1999. Gould's attempt to reconcile religion and science.

"Deconstructing the 'Science Wars' by Reconstructing an Old Mold." *Science* 287 (2000): 253–261.

The Structure of Evolutionary Theory. Cambridge, MA: Belknap Press of Harvard University Press, 2002. Gould's magnum opus.

The Hedgehog, the Fox, and the Magister's Pox: Mending and Minding the Misconceived Gap between Science and the Humanities. New York: Harmony Books, 2003.

OTHER SOURCES

Adler, Jerry. "Evolution's Revolutionary." *Newsweek,* 3 June 2002.

———, and John Carey. "Enigmas of Evolution: How a Remarkable Paleontologist Named Stephen Jay Gould Evolved from Charles Darwin." *Newsweek,* 29 March 1982.

Alcock, John. "Darwinian Fundamentalism: An Exchange." *New York Review of Books,* 14 August 1997.

———. Unpunctuated Equilibrium in the Natural History Essays of Stephen Jay Gould." *Evolution and Human Behavior* 19 (1998): 321–336.

Ghiselin, Michael. "A Radical Solution to the Species Problem." *Systematic Zoology* 23 (1974): 536–544. Ghiselin recommends treating species as individuals rather than as kinds.

Gleick, James. "Breaking Tradition with Darwin." *New York Times Magazine,* 23 November 1983.

Green, Michelle. "Stephen Jay Gould: Driven by a Hunger to Learn and to Write What He Knows, an Outspoken Scientist Fights Back from Life-Threatening Illness." *People,* 2 June 1986.

Hull, David L. "Are Species Really Individuals?" *Systematic Zoology* 25 (1976): 174–191. Hull shows how treating species as individuals fits in well with Gould's views on species.

———. "A Career in the Glare of Public Acclaim." *Bioscience* 52 (2002): 837–842.

———. "A Final Call for Peace." Review of *The Hedgehog, the Fox, and the Magister's Pox: Mending and Minding the Misconceived Gap between Science and the Humanities,* by S. J. Gould. *Nature* 422 (2003): 810–811.

Levy, Daniel S. "Evolution, Extinction and the Movies." *Time,* 14 May 1990.

Maynard Smith, John. "Confusion over Evolution: An Exchange." *New York Review of Books,* 14 January 1993.

Ridley, Mark. "The Evolution Revolution." Review of *The Structure of Evolutionary Theory,* by S. J. Gould. *New York Times Book Review,* 17 March 2002.

Roberts, David. "The Eloquent Champion of Evolution: Stephen Jay Gould Uses Wit, Verve and the Incongruous Analogy in His Prizewinning Writing on the Mysteries of Science." *Mainliner* (October 1981): 81–82, 100–104.

Selzer, Jack, ed. *Understanding Scientific Prose.* Madison: University of Wisconsin Press, 1993. Postmodernists interpret the "The Spandrels of San Marco and the Panglossian Paradigm."

Stanley, Steven. "A Theory of Evolution above the Species Level." *Proceedings of the National Academy of Sciences of the United States of America* 72 (1975): 646–650.

———. *Macroevolution: Pattern and Process.* San Francisco: W. H. Freeman, 1979.

Wilson, E. O. *Sociobiology: The New Synthesis.* Cambridge, MA: Harvard University Press, 1975. The book that gave rise to the controversy over sociobiology.

Yoon, Carol Kaesuk. "Stephen Jay Gould, 60, Is Dead: Enlivened Evolutionary Theory." *New York Times,* 21 May 2002. Excellent overview of his ideas and major life events.

David L. Hull

GRAFF, MARIA SYBILLA MERIAN

SEE **Merian, Maria Sybilla.**

GREAVES, JOHN

(*b.* Colmore, Hampshire, England, 1602; *d.* London, England, 8 October 1652), *observational astronomy, historical astronomy, mensuration, textual scholarship.*

Greaves, an observational astronomer and orientalist, was one of the leading English figures of the middle of the seventeenth-century effort to recover learning and scholarship from eastern sources.

Early Years and Education. John Greaves was the eldest of four talented sons of the Reverend John Greaves, an Oxford graduate. All pursued professional and academic careers. The younger John Greaves matriculated at Balliol College, Oxford, on 12 December 1617 and was admitted to the BA from St Mary Hall on 6 July 1621. In 1624, he came first in the fellowship examinations at Merton College, where he remained for nearly the whole of his career. He proceeded to the MA on 25 June 1628. He was never ordained.

Like his close friend and mentor, John Bainbridge (1582–1643), and other contemporary English astronomers, Greaves left no evidence to explain whence his interest in astronomy and mathematics arose. It would have been nourished at Merton, where the late warden, Sir Henry Savile (1549–1622), had endowed chairs in astronomy and geometry. As early as 1629, Greaves was recording astronomical observations in Oxford, perhaps made with Bainbridge, the first Savilian professor of astronomy at Oxford and a fellow of Merton. At Merton, Greaves became acquainted also with Peter Turner (1586–1651/1652), then the professor of geometry at Gresham College in London, and this connection seems a plausible partial explanation for Greaves's election to the same position on 22 February 1630/1631 as Turner's immediate successor, when Turner came to Oxford as the second Savilian professor of geometry. The letters of support Greaves received for this position, including one from Bainbridge, testified to his competence in mathematics as shown for some years in "private conferences" and "daily conversation." He remained a member of this close Oxford circle throughout his life, and it was in part through this Oxford circle that he arranged his extensive travels and determined their purposes.

Travels. There is, similarly, little evidence of when Greaves began to study the oriental languages, but in 1633, when he undertook his first visit overseas, he went to Leiden and enrolled as a student, almost certainly studying Arabic with Jacobus Golius (1596–1667), a leading scholar of the language. He later acquired a knowledge of Persian and possibly Turkish.

This was the first of three long trips abroad. In 1635, on his second trip, he traveled to Paris, Padua, Rome, and Leiden again, and returned to Oxford by late 1636. This first sojourn in Rome and Greaves's concern with mensuration led to his publication, more than ten years later, of *A Discourse on the Roman Foot and the Denarius* (1647).

Greaves

In 1637, at first in the company of Edward Pococke (1604–1691), the first professor of Arabic at Oxford, and later on his own, Greaves traveled to Leghorn, Rome, Constantinople, Rhodes, Alexandria, Cairo, various cities in Italy, and in 1640, back to Oxford. During their absence, Greaves's brother Thomas was deputed to take Pococke's place at Oxford, and his brother Nicholas evidently delivered the Gresham geometry lectures in London.

This third tour, funded in part by himself with an allowance from his mother, was under the patronage of William Laud (1573–1644/1645), archbishop of Canterbury and chancellor of Oxford (and founder of the university's chair in Arabic), and with difficulty Greaves collected Arabic books and a very large number of Arabic and other manuscripts that he sent to Archbishop Laud and Oxford. One of these was evidently a very fine Arabic copy of Ptolemy's *Almagest,* which unfortunately seems to have vanished some time after its arrival in England.

Astronomical Work. Continuing his practice begun in Oxford, Greaves made precise astronomical observations all the while that he traveled. In particular, he repeatedly made precise observations of latitude, which he compared with existing records, in an attempt to check the reliability of the long-established sources. In Rhodes, for example, he compared his observations with the latitude given by Ptolemy. In addition, he attempted to arrange for simultaneous eclipse observations in order to improve determinations of differences in longitude. His instruments, which he sometimes describes, had nontelescopic sights but permitted a high level of precision. He did not publish this work.

He combined his visits to Cairo with visits to Saqqara, and he made very precise measurements of the Great Pyramid, which, although it was original work, was not quite as original as he portrayed it, as other Europeans had measured its dimensions and spaces in the preceding century. Ten years later, he published the results of his investigations of the structure, the *Pyramidographia* (1646). He reported on his systematic measurements, inside and out, and provided an organized conspectus of scholarly accounts of the pyramids from antiquity to his own time. The book contains hardly any speculation, and Greaves therefore cannot be recruited into the later occult tradition of "pyramidology."

Greaves wrote next to nothing on planetary theory, or indeed on any theoretical considerations. He did own a copy of the first edition of Nicolaus Copernicus's *De Revolutionibus* (1543), which he annotated extensively. His notes refer primarily to chronology and spherical astronomy, with one elaboration on Chapter 11 and its "triple motion of the earth." Other notes that he wrote into the book, however, refer to matters entirely apart from Copernicus and astronomy, such as experiments with mercury and someone else's eastern travels.

Last Years and Publications. Greaves was embroiled in the Oxford politics that followed from the turmoil of the civil wars in the 1640s. He evidently tried to negotiate a passage between the factions, but he failed; his close association with Archbishop Laud, though not explicitly noted by the Parliamentary Visitors, could not have helped. On 14 November 1643, shortly after Bainbridge's death, he succeeded his friend as Savilian Professor of Astronomy (and his brother Edward succeeded Bainbridge as senior reader of the Linacre lecture in physic (the term *physic* covered the modern fields of medicine and psychology), but he was also removed one day later from his position as Gresham professor, ostensibly for nonattendance at his lectures, but possibly for being too supportive of King Charles. In 1648, he was ejected from the professorship of astronomy and obliged to leave Merton College. After arranging that Seth Ward (1617–1688/1689) be appointed professor of astronomy in his place, he retired with his books and papers to London, where he married.

Greaves had published very little up to this point, but beginning in the years of Oxford turmoil and through the few years in London remaining to him, he published a number of bilingual editions of astronomical and geographical texts, in Latin and Arabic, and Latin and Persian. Among these were several texts derived from tables of Ulugh Beg (1394–1449), and extracts from Abu'l-Fida' (1273–1331) and Nasir al-Din al-Tusi (1201–1274). He also published the first English grammar of Persian, as well as the two English books cited earlier, and he was preparing more texts for publication at the time of his sudden death in London, on 8 October 1652. Some were subsequently seen through the press, along with such miscellaneous pieces as his observations on "The Manner of Hatching Chicken at Cairo," and "An Account of Some Experiments for Trying the Force of Great Guns," which dates from his last years in London. The Bodleian Library at Oxford owes a large part of its early collection of Arabic and Persian texts to Greaves.

Greaves's astronomical research bears a strong resemblance to the modern field of historical astronomy, which is historical research—frequently, as it happens, in oriental sources—on early astronomical observations. In contrast to the modern field, however, which has the explicit purpose of recovering data in order to establish a long observational baseline, Greaves's textual researches have no explicit purpose, except in the field of chronology, though he may have expected the knowledge contained in the old texts to be of contemporary value. Greaves's career is not easily categorized. One modern historian attempts the description "scientific-antiquarian," which serves to indicate similarities with some contemporaries, but does not really summarize his life's work. He more nearly resembles a textual scholar than an astronomer. As an astronomer, however, he was an observer and measurer, not a theoretician.

BIBLIOGRAPHY

The fullest bibliography of Greaves's work appears at the end of the life of Greaves given by John Ward, cited below. Ward's bibliography includes eighteen works published before and after his death, and a number of unpublished books, textual editions, and collections of papers.

WORKS BY GREAVES

Miscellaneous Works of Mr. John Greaves, Professor of Astronomy in the University of Oxford. Edited by Thomas Birch. 2 vols. London: J. Brindley and C. Corbett, 1737. Contains the principal works in English, including the two cited above, as well as some correspondence and short Latin pieces.

OTHER SOURCES

Birch, Thomas. "An Historical and Critical Account of the Life and Writings of Mr. John Greaves." In *Miscellaneous Works of Mr. John Greaves, Professor of Astronomy in the University of Oxford,* vol. 1: pp. i–lxxii. London: J. Brindley and C. Corbett, 1737. This and the entry on Greaves by John Ward, below, are the best early lives of Greaves.

Highland, J. R. L., ed. *Registrum Annalium Collegii Mertonensis, 1603–1660.* Oxford: Oxfordshire Historical Society, 2006.

Mercier, Raymond. "English Orientalists and Mathematical Astronomy." In *The "Arabick" Interest of the Natural Philosophers in Seventeenth-Century England,* edited by Gül A. Russell, 158–214. Leiden, Netherlands, and New York: E.J. Brill, 1994.

Quarrie, Paul, ed. *The Library of the Earls of Macclesfield Removed from Shirburn Castle, Science D–H: London 4 November 2004.* London: Sotheby's, 2004, pp. 304–309. This is an auction catalog; it provides the fullest description of Greaves's copy of Copernicus, which remains in private hands.

Shalev, Zur. "John Greaves and the Great Pyramid." *Journal of the History of Ideas* 63 (2002): 555–575.

———. "The Travel Notebooks of John Greaves." *Intersections: Yearbook for Early Modern Studies* 5 (2005): 77–102.

Toomer, Gerald J. *Eastern Wisdome and Learning: The Study of Arabic in Seventeenth-Century England.* Oxford: Clarendon Press, 1996. Greaves is discussed passim, but especially pp. 127–179. This is the best biographical reference for Greaves.

Ward, John. *The Lives of the Professors of Gresham College.* London: J. Moore, 1740, pp. 135–153.

Wood, Anthony à. *Athenae Oxonienses: An Exact History of All the Writers and Bishops Who Have Had Their Education in the University of Oxford,* edited by Philip Bliss. London, 1817. Vol. 3, columns 324–328. The earliest life of Greaves, first published in 1691–1692.

Adam Jared Apt

GREEN, DAVID EZRA

(*b.* Brooklyn, New York, 5 August 1910; *d.* Madison, Wisconsin, 8 July 1983), *biochemistry, enzymology.*

Green was a biochemist who, early in his career, made substantial contributions to the identification and characterization of soluble enzymes responsible for biological activities. Later in his career he established a laboratory that made major discoveries about complex cellular oxidation systems. As time advanced, Green became ever more theoretical and speculative in his own work, while supporting postdoctoral fellows who made important empirical discoveries in biochemistry.

Early Life and Education. Green's parents were Hyman Levy Green, a garment manufacturer (he later managed the Harwood Factory in Marion, Virginia), and Rose Marrow Green. David Green was born on 5 August 1910 in Brooklyn, New York, where he attended public grade and high schools in Brooklyn. He initially intended to prepare for medical school and pursued a premedical curriculum for two years at New York University (NYU), beginning in 1928. Having been offered a student assistantship in the Biology Department, however, he shifted his efforts toward basic research. He was awarded a bachelor's degree in biology in 1931 and a master's degree the following year, both at NYU. Green spent the summers of 1930, 1931, and 1932 at the Marine Biological Laboratory at Woods Hole, Massachusetts, working with NYU professor Robert Chambers and Leonor Michaelis. Michaelis in particular helped inspire Green's subsequent interest in biological oxidations.

After completing his master's degree, Green went to Cambridge University in England, where Frederick Gowland Hopkins directed a world-renowned center of biochemical research that employed Malcolm Dixon, David Keilin, Joseph and Dorothy Needham, Judah Quastel, and Marjorie Stephenson, among others. Together, they pioneered in the quest to identify the enzymes responsible for a host of physiological processes. In his initial year, working in the laboratory of Dixon, he conducted research on the reduction potentials of three metabolites: cysteine, glutathione, and glycylcysteine. This research resulted in his first paper, "The Reduction Potentials of Cysteine, Glutathione, and Glycylcysteine," published in *Biochemical Journal* in 1933. It became the basis for his PhD, awarded the following year. Green remained at Cambridge for the rest of the decade, first as a Beit Memorial Fellow and later a Senior Beit Fellow, pursuing an ambitious agenda of research on soluble oxidative enzymes that culminated in thirty-two papers in peer-reviewed journals.

During his years at Cambridge University, Green met Doris Cribb, director of the design department at the

Cambridge School of Art, whom he married on 16 April 1936. Their first daughter, Rowena, who became a distinguished biochemist herself, was born while the two lived in Cambridge.

At Harvard and Columbia. Although Green would have preferred to remain in England, the United States recalled all U.S. citizens living in Europe following the British defeat at Dunkirk in 1940. Green then had to scramble to find a suitable position in the United States, a challenge because enzymology had yet to develop as a major specialization in the United States. Initially, he accepted a position at Harvard Medical School in Cambridge, Massachusetts, as a research fellow in biochemistry. Despite Harvard's overall prominence, the facilities available to Green were far inferior to those to which he was accustomed at Cambridge University, lacking a cold room, a centrifuge, and a Warburg constant volume respirometer system, equipment that had been crucial in his earlier research. Green, though, was able to procure a grant from the Ella Sachs Ploetz Foundation, enabling him to establish a small laboratory and to continue his research. During his year at Harvard he isolated a yeast flavoprotein ("A Flavoprotein from Yeast," 1941) and purified potato starch phosphorylase ("Starch Phosphorylase of Potato," 1942), results which he published in the *Journal of Biological Chemistry*.

Green's focus was not only on obtaining new results himself but on giving focus to the field of enzymology. Part of his effort was directed to writing *Mechanisms of Biological Oxidation*, published in 1940, in which he attempted to synthesize what was then known about enzyme systems figuring in biological oxidations. He also contributed an essay, "Enzymes and Trace Substances" (1941), to the first volume of the new annual series *Advances in Enzymology*, in which he proposed the thesis that any substance required in trace amounts in the diet must be part of an enzyme. This book and paper proved extremely influential in enticing researchers, especially in the United States, into the field of enzymology.

In 1941 Green was appointed instructor in biochemistry in the College of Physicians and Surgeons at Columbia University, where he remained until 1948. Green's modest two-room laboratory became a focus of interactions with many of the major emerging biochemists in the United States, including Fritz Lipmann, Herman Kalckar, David Nachmanson, Severo Ochoa, and Efraim Racker. During this period Green organized the Enzyme Club, which held monthly meetings at the faculty club at Columbia University. These gatherings provided a stimulating forum for investigators drawn to the study of enzymes and the prospects for explaining biological reactions in terms of enzymes.

While at Columbia, Green not only pursued research on the enzymes involved in the oxidation of amino acids, the mechanism of pyruvic acid oxidation, and transamination, but also participated in the development of a new instrument, an ultrasonic device to disintegrate bacteria, and pioneered in the application of the Waring blender to extract enzymes from tissues and the battery-driven Beckman DU spectrophotometer. Green's focus during this period turned increasingly to the recently characterized phenomenon of oxidative phosphorylation, and especially to the complex of reactions involved in the complete oxidation of pyruvic acid to carbon dioxide and water. In the 1930s David Keilin, a member of the research group at Cambridge University, had identified cytochromes as reversibly oxidizable components of living cells and had begun to ascertain how they were sequenced to constitute an electron transport chain. When he and Edward Hartree had tried to isolate the enzymes during the 1940s, they found that any preparation which retained the capacity to carry out oxidative phosphorylation retained cell particulates. They interpreted this finding, which many biochemists regarded as a nuisance, as showing that the respiratory reactions were somehow linked to the physical-chemical structure of the cell.

Cyclophorase Proposal. Green set out to study the complete oxidation of pyruvic acid to carbon dioxide and water employing a preparation from rabbit kidney. The preparation was complex, requiring homogenation with potassium chloride using alkali to neutralize the acid that formed, followed by multiple resuspensions in saline and centrifugation. His first goal was to isolate, through fractionation of the preparation, the enzyme responsible for catalyzing pyruvic to acetic acid. But any preparation that reacted with pyruvic acid performed the entire set of reactions resulting in carbon dioxide and water. From these studies, Green became convinced that the insoluble character of the enzymes pointed to the fact that they were bound into a unit, which he designated the "cyclophorase system." By referring to a cyclophorase *system*, he meant to contrast the enzymes involved in aerobic respiration with those involved in other biochemical processes such as glycolysis, purine synthesis, and the pentose and urea cycles. In those cases the enzymes can be isolated and an operative system reconstituted from the isolated components. He explained the term *cyclophorase* as "literally meaning the system of enzymes carrying through the (citric acid) cycle" (Green, 1951b, p. 17). Green acknowledged that the ending "ase" is usually applied to individual enzymes, but cited precedent for his extension to a "team of enzymes": "Keilin and his school have been referring for more than two decades to the succinic oxidase and cytochrome oxidase systems. Neither the one nor the other represents a single enzyme. They represent a considerable group of enzymes all of which are associated with the same particulate elements" (Green, 1951b, pp. 17–18).

Green conceptualized the cyclophorase system as involving a precise physical arrangement that would facilitate cooperative action between spatially proximal enzymes. He also maintained that this arrangement would enable the components to behave in ways they could not otherwise: "The chemical organization by which the many constituent enzymes are integrated confers properties on the various enzymes which they may not necessarily enjoy when separated from the complex and isolated as single enzymes" (Green, 1951b, p. 18). At the time, Green claimed that the cyclophorase system represented a newly discovered constituent of the cell.

Most biochemists reacted to Green's cyclophorase proposal with extreme skepticism. In part this was due to Green's introduction of a new name and his often-poetical accounts of the proposed system, whereas many found the particulate nature of any preparation capable of performing oxidative phosphorylation as a challenge to be overcome. In part this negative response was also due to the fact that whereas Green had been a master in the techniques required to isolate and study single enzymes, his procedures for preparing the cyclophorase system were regarded as less precise. Green himself made efforts to relate his proposal to the research of other biochemists. At the same time as he was first formulating his cyclophorase proposal, a group of researchers at the Rockefeller Institute was analyzing the chemical composition of the four fractions that Albert Claude had isolated from mammalian liver cells through centrifugation. The team, led by George Hogeboom, determined that most of the capacity to oxidize cytochrome *c* and succinic acid was due to what Claude had termed the large granule fraction and which the team now determined to originate from mitochondria. Claude himself designated the mitochondrion as the power plant of the cell, and soon other researchers, such as Albert Lehninger, localized other oxidative systems, like that responsible for fatty acid metabolism in the mitochondrion, as well. Although at first resistant to the claim that these oxidative systems were localized in a known cell organelle, Green eventually linked his cyclophorase system with the mitochondrion, crediting John W. Harman, who was working with him, with establishing in 1950 the proportionality of cyclophorase activity and the presence and number of mitochondria. He continued to insist, however, in using the term *cyclophorase system* "for the functional attributes of the same entity" (Green, 1951b, p. 19, n. 2). Green failed, however, to convince other biochemists to adopt the term *cyclophorase,* and many remained extremely skeptical of his emphasis on systems or teams of enzymes.

Green was not dissuaded, and he began to propose an even more elaborate scheme in which the cyclophorase system not only linked together the enzymes, but also bound them to the coenzymes that figured in the reactions. Washing the preparation would remove the coenzymes and, as well, most of the NAD, NADP, FAD, and ATP in the cell that was normally bound in the cyclophorase system. Green proposed further that a coenzyme was bound as a prosthetic group to the protein component of an enzyme, which he referred to as the apoenzyme, and that when the two were split, the enzyme was modified. Green suggested that such an arrangement was most efficient because it required only one coenzyme molecule per enzyme molecule, whereas if they were dissociated and relied on random processes such as diffusion to encounter each other, many times more coenzyme molecules would be required. Green, however, noted a serious problem posed by binding of the coenzyme to the enzyme:

> Pyridinenucleotide must be capable not only of being reducible by the substrate of the oxidase with which the former is combined but also in its reduced form has to interact with the flavin prosthetic group of diaphorase—the enzyme that catalyzes the oxidation of dihydropyridinenucleotide by one of the cytochrome components. When the pyridinenucleotide is free as in the case of the classical, soluble systems, this sequence of reactions poses no difficulty. The co-enzyme is free to shuttle back and forth.... In the cyclophorase system with bound pyridinenucleotide, the extent of shifting back and form is severely limited. Some mechanism must be invoked to explain how a coenzyme fixed in a rigid structure would be capable of interacting with a variety of systems. (Green, 1951b, p. 429)

Establishing the Enzyme Institute. While Green had found little knowledge or interest in enzymes at Harvard and only emerging interest in New York, there was a location in the United States where appreciation and empirical study of enzyme systems was well advanced. This was the University of Wisconsin, where Conrad Elvehjem had carried out pioneering work identifying precursors of respiratory coenzymes such as nicotinic acid with vitamin B_3, crucial for preventing black tongue in dogs and pellagra in humans. Wisconsin had also recruited a substantial number of already well-established researchers investigating enzymes, including Van R. Potter, who was studying respiratory enzyme systems in cancer cells; Perry Wilson, who was studying processes of nitrogen fixation; and many promising investigators in the early stages of their careers. As the University of Wisconsin developed plans for a new enzyme institute, they initiated efforts to recruit Green.

Green

The idea of establishing a postdoctoral research training center in enzymology in the United States appears to have emerged first at the Conference on Intracellular Enzymes of Normal and Malignant Tissues in Hershey, Pennsylvania, in the fall of 1945, a conference devoted to basic research concerning cancer. Major pioneering work in enzyme chemistry had been carried out by Otto Warburg, Otto Meyerhof, and Gustav Embden at research centers in Germany that had been closed by World War II. Hopkins's laboratory at Cambridge University was the premier site for enzyme research in the English-speaking world, but it too had been severely impacted by the demands of the war. Recognizing the demise of the major training centers in Europe, Charles Glen King, scientific director of the Nutrition Foundation, approached Harry M. Miller of the Rockefeller Foundation, who in turn presented the idea of developing a center in the United States to Warren Weaver, director of the natural sciences at the Rockefeller Foundation. King identified the University of Wisconsin as offering the best foundation for establishing an institute for studying enzymes, noting the presence there of Elvehjem and Potter. In addition, beginning in 1938 the university had published a handbook on respiratory enzymes and another on methods of enzyme research; it had also hosted an international symposium on enzymes. The idea fell on very sympathetic ears as Weaver had just completed an assessment in which outside reviewers had examined the Rockefeller Foundation's activities in the natural sciences and had targeted enzyme chemistry as a potent field for future investment. Weaver asked King for names of leaders in the field of enzymology, and Green was one of the eight King supplied. Weaver also approached the University of Wisconsin, and by September 1946 a task force appointed by the university president had developed plans for an institute.

In the end, the university went forward with its plans for what became the Enzyme Institute with only modest support for equipment from the Rockefeller Foundation, and Green was recruited to head the first of what was envisaged as several research teams. His team focused on the separation and identification of enzymes. A second team, headed by Henry Lardy, already an assistant professor of biochemistry at the university, was established a couple years later.

Research at Wisconsin. Green arrived in Madison in early 1948, before the new facilities for the institute were finished. He resumed his research and assembled a team of investigators in an abandoned building on the engineering campus. Green restricted his team to postdoctoral fellows and visiting researchers and so was not engaged in either undergraduate or graduate training at Wisconsin. Focusing on his proposed cyclophorase system he, together with his new collaborators, attempted to render the preparations more soluble so as to separate individual components of the enzyme systems. This involved varying the pH and salt concentrations of the preparations as well as modifying the centrifugation regime.

In addition to the oxidation of pyruvic acid, Green began to focus on fatty acid metabolism. None of the preparations the team members developed was sufficiently active to merit further purification, but Henry Drysdale, a student in Lardy's group, had found he could increase fatty acid metabolism in extracts from rat livers by beginning with an acetone powder of rat liver. Finding rat liver to be an unsuitable source for his fractionation studies, Green applied the acetone powder approach to liver, kidney, and heart tissues from pigs and cows that he obtained from local Oscar Meyer slaughterhouses. To assay for reactions involved in the oxidation of fatty acids, Green used triphenyl-tetrazolium as the final acceptor and developed an approach in which he measured the quantities of acyl-CoA (activated fatty acid) formed, the generation of a double bond in the fatty acid chain, the hydration of the double bond, the oxidation of hydroxyl-acyl-CoA to form keto-acyl-CoA, and the separation of keto-acyl-CoA into two acyl-CoA derivatives. Green determined that the preparation also had to contain malate dehydrogenase, oxaloacetate-condensing enzyme, diaphorase, CoA, ATP, NAD, and a dye such as pyocyanin. Procuring sufficient CoA (coenzyme A, only recently discovered by Fritz Lipmann in 1945), was one of the major challenges confronting this project, since it was generally available only in minute quantities extracted from bacteria. In his laboratory, Helmut Beinert developed a procedure for procuring CoA that relied on glutathione with mercuric ions. Green organized a team of technicians to produce large quantities until he persuaded Pabst Laboratories to adopt his method in exchange for providing him a continual supply of CoA. With this assay system in place, Green and his collaborators succeeded in rapid order in identifying the enzymes required for fatty acid metabolism and presented their results at a meeting of the American Society of Biological Chemists in Chicago during 1953.

After his work on fatty acid oxidation, Green returned to the cyclophorase system. Accepting the identification of the cyclophorase system with the mitochondrion, he now set out to describe the components of that system. His strategy was to decompose the mitochondrion into subunits until he could carry out each reaction individually in a purified preparation. To do this Green, together with Fred Crane, developed a "factory" for the production of mitochondria from cow and pig heart and liver so as to have an abundance of material on which to conduct his studies. These preparations routinely damaged mitochondria, resulting in two classes of submitochondrial particles that were localized in what he referred to as "light" and "heavy" fractions. The main difference between the particles was that in oxidizing succinate, the light fraction lacked the capacity to synthesize ATP, while the heavy fraction retained that capacity. Both fractions, though, phosphorylated ATP when other citric acid cycle substrates were supplied. Green further divided the light fraction (after treating it with 15 percent alcohol) into subfractions, one of which carried out electron transport but not oxidative phosphorylation. (He referred to these as "electron transport particles," or ETP.) Another fraction supported phosphorylation when oxidizing compounds other than succinate. (He termed these "phosphorylating electron transport particles," or PETP.)

To understand the genesis of these particles, Green collaborated with electron microscopist Hans Ris, also at the University of Wisconsin. A few years before this another electron microscopist, George Palade, had discovered not only that the mitochondrion was enclosed by two layers of membrane, but that there were repeated infoldings of the inner membrane, creating was Palade labeled "cristae mitochondriales," which projected into the interior of the mitochondrion. The micrographs of Green's fractionated particles revealed open fragments of what were identified as mitochondrial cristae in the PETP and less functional closed fragments of cristae in the ETP particles. The researchers viewed these results as supporting Palade's suggestion that the processes of oxidative phosphorylation were localized in the cristae.

Contributions of Collaborators. Many biochemists became increasingly skeptical of Green's research during this period. His techniques for subfractionating mitochondria appeared to many as unprincipled and as generating artifacts. His theoretical interpretations, which continued to emphasize complexes of enzymes interacting, struck many as purely speculative. But while his own credibility was diminished, Green succeeded in attracting a large cadre of young researchers to the Enzyme Institute who generated results that were highly respected. For example, he assigned David Gibson and Salih Wakil to follow up his research on the oxidation of fatty acids. In particular, they set out to show experimentally that, as was widely believed, the synthesis of fatty acids involved reversing the steps in fatty acid oxidation. They developed a preparation composed of three fractions from pigeon liver extracts that would convert labeled acetate into long-chain fatty acids when ATP, isocitrate, NADPH, and Mn were supplied. Wakil identified two protein fractions, one of which, acetyl-CoA carboxylase, in the presence of acetyl-CoA, ATP, and Mn^{++}, produced malonyl-CoA, which could then be made into fatty acids by the second protein fraction. Acetyl-CoA carboxylase was determined by other researchers at Wisconsin to contain the vitamin biotin.

Another major contribution by researchers in Green's laboratory was the discovery of coenzyme Q by Fred Crane, Youssef Hatefi, Robert L. Lester, and Carl Widmer. These researchers found a lipid-soluble but water-insoluble factor that was required for the electron transfer from dehydrogenases to the electron transport system which had the properties of a quinone. (It was later found to be identical to ubiquinone, discovered by Richard A. Morton in 1955 and named "ubiquinone" because of its ubiquity.) After Crane left for a faculty position elsewhere, Hatefi collaborated with Daniel Ziegler in developing subfractions of mitochondria that would carry out the reactions of different parts of the electron transport chain. They were led to characterize four complexes of cytochromes and other constituents:

1. an NADH-ubiquinone reductase complex that included FMN and nonheme iron;
2. a succinate-ubiquinone reductase complex that included FAD and nonheme iron;
3. a ubiquinol-cytochrome *c* reductase complex that included cytochromes *b* and c_1, and a nonheme iron protein; and
4. a cytochrome *c* oxidase complex that included cytochrome *a* and copper.

Thereafter, four of Green's collaborators—Hatefi, A. G. Haavik, L. R. Fowler, and David E. Griffiths (1962)—succeeded in reconstituting two systems: one capable of oxidizing NADH to carbon dioxide and water by combining complexes 1, 3, 4, and another capable of oxidizing succinate to carbon dioxide and water by combining complexes 2, 3, and 4. Both reconstitutions revealed particulate structures, suggesting that the respiratory chain was formed into a fixed assembly electron transfer system (one in which the molecules were in advantageous spatial relations for passing electrons sequentially from molecule to molecule).

At this point Green sought out another collaboration with an electron microscopist, this time Humberto Fernández-Morán at the University of Chicago. He had developed a technique for negative staining specimens with substances such as phosphotungstate or uranyl acetate that are electron dense but chemically inert. These substances do not react with membrane material, which then appears light against the dark background created by the electron dense material. With this technique, in 1964 Fernández-Morán discovered small particles (70–90 Å in size) located on stalks about 50 Å in length projecting from the cristae into the inner mitochondrial milieu. While small, these particles are numerous (between ten thousand to one hundred thousand per mitochondrion). When he applied the negative stains without prior

Green

fixation, mitochondria swelled and burst, extruding membranous material in the form of sheets, tubules, or ribbons that were studded with small spherical knobs about 90Å in diameter.

Green seized upon Fernández-Morán's discovery, naming the knobs "inner membrane spheres" and proposing that they constituted the complete system of enzymes for electron transport. Albert Lehninger, however, calculated that the weight of the respiratory assembly was between one and two orders of magnitude greater than that of these particles. Green was not fully dissuaded and proposed instead that the four different complexes of enzymes Hatefi and Ziegler had identified as involved in electron transport were distributed over the base membrane (complexes 1 and 2), the stalk (complex 3), and the spheres (complex 4) respectively. Although much of their analysis focused on the relative sizes of the stalk and spheres and the minimum sizes, based on molecular weight, of the enzyme complexes, ultimately the investigators appealed to "biochemical considerations" to defend this localization: "Complexes I and II must interact with DPNH and succinate, respectively, both of which are localized in the interior of the crista, whereas complex IV must interact with molecular oxygen which would be more readily available in the solution outside the crista rather than in its interior" (Green, Fernández-Morán et al., 1964, p. 95). Green's speculations about the organization of complexes, however, was cut short by the determination by Efraim Racker and his colleagues that the spheres contained ATPase, not complexes of the electron transport chain.

Later Work and Recognition. Although Green's early successes were built on his skill in isolating and characterizing individual enzymes, he exhibited far less technical skill in his subsequent work on complex systems of nonsoluble enzymes. Rather, he often seized upon a result and attempted to synthesize a theoretical account of possible biochemical mechanisms in living systems. In the process, he often presented his theoretical ideas in more popular forums such as *Scientific American* and monographs, thereby prompting even more skeptical responses from his peers in biochemistry. Even as his peers questioned his turn to speculative theorizing and model building, though, he succeeded in recruiting talented young researchers to his laboratory who rewarded him with a continued record of important empirical results.

Green received a number of prominent awards and honors during his life. He was most proud of being selected first as a Junior Beit Fellow and then as a Senior Beit Fellow while at Cambridge University. In 1946 he was the first recipient of the Paul-Lewis Award in Enzyme Chemistry of the Division of Biological Chemistry of the American Chemical Society, and in 1962 he was elected to the National Academy of Sciences. During the latter years of his career Green became less engaged in conducting his own experiments while still overseeing a productive laboratory. In his last years he suffered from lymphoma, and he died in Madison on 8 July 1983.

BIBLIOGRAPHY

The Rockefeller Foundation Archives Center has archival material on the establishment of the Enzyme Institute at the University of Wisconsin and on David Green's role in it. The institute itself has a complete compilation of Green's papers. The obituary by Beinert, Stumpf, and Wakil (2003) in Biographical Memoirs *(cited below) includes a complete listing of his publications.*

WORKS BY GREEN

"The Reduction Potentials of Cysteine, Glutathione and Glycylcysteine." *Biochemical Journal* 27 (1933): 678–689.

"Reconstruction of the Chemical Events in Living Cells." In *Perspectives in Biochemistry,* edited by Joseph Needham and David E. Green. Cambridge, U.K.: Cambridge University Press, 1937.

Mechanisms of Biological Oxidations. Cambridge, U.K.: Cambridge University Press, 1940.

"Enzymes and Trace Substances." In *Advances in Enzymology,* edited by F. F. Nord and C. H. Werkman. Vol. 1. New York: Interscience, 1941.

With Eugene Knox and Paul K. Stumpf. "A Flavoprotein from Yeast." *Journal of Biological Chemistry* 138 (1941): 775–782.

With Paul K. Stumpf. "Starch Phosphorylase of Potato." *Journal of Biological Chemistry* 142 (1942): 355–366.

With William F. Loomis and V. H. Auerbach. "Studies on the Cyclophorase System I." *Journal of Biological Chemistry* 172 (1948): 389–402.

"Enzymes in Teams." *Scientific American* 181 (1949): 48–50.

"The Cyclophorase System of Enzymes." *Biological Reviews* 26 (1951a): 410–455.

"The Cyclophorase System." In *Enzymes and Enzyme Systems,* edited by John T. Edsall. Cambridge, MA: Harvard University Press, 1951b.

With Helmut Beinert. "Biological Oxidations." *Annual Review of Biochemistry* 24 (1955): 1–44.

"Studies in Organized Enzyme Systems." *Harvey Lectures* 53 (1957–1958): 177–227.

"Biological Oxidation." *Scientific American* 199, no. 1 (1958): 56–62.

With Daniel M. Ziegler, Anthony W. Linnane, C. M. S. Dass, et al. "Studies on the Electron Transport System: Correlation of the Morphology and Enzymic Properties of Mitochondrial and Sub-mitochondrial particles." *Biochimica et Biophysica Acta* 28 (1958): 524–539.

"Electron Transport and Oxidative Phosphorylation." *Advances in Enzymology* 21 (1959): 73–129.

With J. Jarnefelt. "Enzymes and Biological Organization." *Perspectives in Biology and Medicine* 2 (1959): 163–184.

With Youssef Hatefi. "The Mitochondrion and Biochemical Machines." *Science* 133 (1961): 13–19.

"Structure and Function of Subcellular Particles." *Comparative Biochemistry and Physiology* 4 (1962): 81–122.

"The Mitochondrion." *Scientific American* 210 (1964): 63–74.

With Humberto Fernández-Morán, T. Oda, and P. V. Blair. "A Macromolecular Repeating Unit of Mitochondrial Structure and Function: Correlated Electron Microscopic and Biochemical Studies of Isolated Mitochondria and Submitochondrial Particles of Beef Heart Muscle." *Journal of Cell Biology* 22 (1964): 63–100.

"The Mitochondrial Electron-Transfer System." In *Comprehensive Biochemistry*, edited by Marcel Florkin and Elmer H. Stotz. Vol. 14. Amsterdam: Elsevier, 1966.

With Harold Baum. *Energy and the Mitochondrion.* New York: Academic, 1970.

OTHER SOURCES

Beinert, Helmut, and Paul K. Stumpf. "David Green Obituary." *Trends in Biochemical Sciences* 8 (1983): 434–436.

———, Paul K. Stumpf, and Salih J. Wakil. "David Ezra Green, 1910–1983." *Biographical Memoirs* 84 (2003): 112–145.

Huennekens, Frank M. "David E. Green: A Personal Recollection." *Journal of Bioenergetics and Biomembranes* 16 (1984): 315–319.

———. "Enzyme Institute Days." In *The Molecular Biology of Membranes*, edited by S. Fleischer, Youssef Hatefi, David H. MacLenna, and Alexander Tzagoloff. New York: Plenum Press, 1978.

"Impressions of David E. Green by His Colleagues." In *The Molecular Biology of Membranes*, edited by S. Fleischer, Youssef Hatefi, David H. MacLenna, and Alexander Tzagoloff. New York: Plenum Press, 1978.

William Bechtel

GREENSTEIN, JESSE LEONARD

(*b.* Brooklyn, New York, 15 October 1909; *d.* Arcadia, California, 21 October 2002), *astronomy, astrophysics.*

Greenstein was an American astronomer and astrophysicist noted for his research on stellar abundances and white dwarfs, his role in helping discover quasi-stellar objects (quasars), and his directorship of the astronomy program at the California Institute of Technology (Caltech) from 1948 until 1973. He was also one of the major leaders of the post–World War II astronomy community, both internationally and in the United States, and helped shape the organization of astronomy in the United States.

Early Life and Education. Greenstein was born in 1909, the grandson of Russian émigrés. His family of cultured, wealthy, and nonobservant Jews ran a furniture-making business. Greenstein's early years were pleasant, lacking—as he once put it—the "oft-quoted advantage of an impoverished and embittered childhood." Greenstein developed an interest in science at a young age after his grandfather gave him a small brass telescope. As a teen he did elementary spectroscopy experiments, built crystal radio sets in his parents' basement, and displayed enthusiasm for chemistry. His scientific career would eventually combine elements of all of these childhood hobbies.

After attending the Horace Mann School for Boys, Greenstein entered Harvard University at age fifteen, where he took courses in both astronomy and physics. Education in astronomy at Harvard at this time was still based on the positions and motions of celestial bodies and Greenstein learned about traditional topics such as celestial mechanics. He was also exposed to more modern topics in stellar astronomy and astrophysics and took courses in the relatively new field of quantum mechanics. During his undergraduate time at Harvard Greenstein met Naomi Kitay, whom he later married in 1934.

Greenstein received his AB in 1929, after which Oxford University offered him a postgraduate position. However, the Great Depression hit Greenstein's family hard and he was forced to postpone formal training in astronomy. For several years he worked for his family in the real estate business, but kept active in research by volunteering for Isidor I. Rabi, a future Nobel Prize winner, at Columbia University. By 1934, his family's finances had recovered and Greenstein returned to Harvard.

During Greenstein's absence, the school had added new faculty such as Donald Howard Menzel, Fred Lawrence Whipple, and Bart Bok. These scientists helped modernize Harvard's research and teaching profile in astronomy. Greenstein quickly completed his PhD and graduated in 1937. His dissertation research harkened back to an interest he had nurtured from his undergraduate years: the influence of interstellar dust on the color and magnitude of certain classes of stars. Greenstein, along with Whipple, had also taken notice of Karl Jansky's discovery of cosmic static coming from the central galactic bulge. While their explanation of the phenomenon—that it might be due to thermal emission from dust clouds at the galactic center—was incomplete and overly simplified, Greenstein's work marked his early interest in the nascent field of radio astronomy.

Yerkes Observatory. After completing his PhD, Greenstein obtained a prestigious National Research Council Fellowship for 1937 to 1939. Permitted to choose where he wished to spend his time, Greenstein picked Yerkes Observatory. Located in Williams Bay, Wisconsin, and operated by the University of Chicago, Yerkes was one of the world's premiere institutions for astronomy at this time. Astronomers at Yerkes had access to several large telescopes including the world's largest refractor and an 82-inch instrument (in 1939, the world's second-largest reflecting telescope) that was nearing completion at McDonald Observatory near Austin, Texas. Greenstein thrived at Yerkes, doing both theoretical research and nighttime observing. He also learned the craft of spectroscopy and benefited from his association with prominent scientists at Yerkes such as Gerard Kuiper and William W. Morgan. Greenstein also became friends with Louis Henyey, another Yerkes scientist. The two men built a specially designed spectrograph for the observatory's 40-inch refractor and coauthored several papers together. Finally, at McDonald Observatory, Greenstein was introduced to the research possibilities enabled by access to large optical telescopes.

After his fellowship ended, Yerkes Observatory invited Greenstein to remain as an instructor. As he later described it, 1939 "effectively ended my youth" when he turned thirty and World War II broke out. His research interests shifted too. For example, he used instruments at Yerkes and McDonald to obtain spectra of Upsilon Sagittari, a star with unusual elemental abundances. These studies encouraged Greenstein to devote more attention to the relative elemental composition of stars and their development over time, a project that he pursued more intently in the 1950s and 1960s.

Following the entry of the United States into World War II, Greenstein participated in war-related research brought to Yerkes by director Otto Struve. In mid-1942 he and Henyey formed a group to study new designs for optical systems. One of the more innovative devices Greenstein helped the Yerkes optical bureau produce was an all-sky camera that could photograph a large swath of the sky at one time.

After the war, Greenstein resumed his research at Yerkes. In addition to more traditional astronomical research, he continued to experiment with optical design and the possibilities of making observations with radio telescopes. Greenstein also used captured V-2 rockets as a tool to make astronomical observations from high in the atmosphere. In 1946, Greenstein designed a spectrograph that could make measurements in both the ultraviolet and visible light regions. With funding from the Johns Hopkins University's Applied Physics Laboratory, his experiment was launched at White Sands, New Mexico, on the inauspicious date of 1 April 1947. Disappointment soon followed when Greenstein developed the film and found it unexposed. Consequently, Greenstein maintained a preference for ground-based observing throughout his career, preferring to avoid the complexity and risk of relying on space- or rocketborne instruments.

Greenstein Moves to Caltech. By 1948, Greenstein's research had brought him substantial recognition in the astronomy community and he received numerous offers from institutions eager to lure him from Yerkes. He ultimately decided to accept an offer from Caltech president Lee A. DuBridge to lead that school's astronomy program, and Greenstein arrived in Pasadena in June 1948, the same month the famous 200-inch telescope on Palomar Mountain was dedicated. Greenstein was a logical choice for Caltech as his background combined theoretical research and observing experience with big telescopes. The scientists Greenstein eventually recruited to Caltech's astronomy program enjoyed access not only to Palomar (which Caltech operated jointly with the Carnegie Institution of Washington) but also telescopes on Mount Wilson and, in time, major radio astronomy facilities that Greenstein helped shepherd into existence.

Greenstein had a big task ahead of him as he built up and promoted Caltech's astronomy program. While the Carnegie Observatory's staff was large and included luminaries such as Edwin Hubble and Walter Baade, Caltech had only one other astronomer when Greenstein arrived—Fritz Zwicky, a brilliant and sometimes volatile Swiss scientist. Most of Caltech's early teaching and administrative duties fell to Greenstein, and his program began with only a handful of graduate students who signed up for his yearlong courses on stellar evolution and star interiors.

Greenstein staffed Caltech's astronomy program with scientists who could combine expertise in theoretical astrophysics with observations made on the world's biggest telescopes. Greenstein also brought famous visitors such as Fred Hoyle and Jan Oort to Caltech to do research and teach his students. The strong linkage of physics with astronomy at the school meant that new areas of research and expertise were incorporated into Caltech's program of traditional optical observing. As he described it in his memoir, he succeeded in converting physicists and engineers into "hyphenated-astronomers" who applied skills from other fields to astrophysical research. With the support of Caltech president DuBridge, Greenstein actively lobbied for his department's participation in the newly emerging field of radio astronomy. His efforts bore fruit when Caltech's Owens Valley Radio Observatory was dedicated in 1958.

Research Activities. Throughout his career, Greenstein frequently entered new areas of investigation, published several papers, and moved to another topic that caught his attention. His primary field of interest was the physics of astronomical objects, a topic that allowed him to combine his talents as a theoretician and observer. Greenstein's ample share of telescope observing time helped him pursue diverse

Jesse Leonard Greenstein. *Jesse Leonard Greenstein with the Greenstein-Henyey camera.*
COURTESY OF THE ARCHIVES, CALIFORNIA INSTITUTE OF TECHNOLOGY.

research interests while skimming the scientific cream: "We had a big telescope, we could work on faint objects," he said once in an interview. "You can't resist the fact that you've got an unbeatable gadget that nobody else has."

Greenstein was an especially active user of the 200-inch telescope on Palomar for spectroscopic observations. One of Greenstein's research goals was to use the telescope and its accompanying instruments as tools to probe the chemical composition of stars. During the 1950s, astronomers were keenly interested in understanding how nuclear reactions inside stars formed elements heavier than helium. Greenstein's study of the relative abundance of certain elements and isotopes was enlightened by his association with physicists at Caltech's Kellogg Laboratory (including William A. Fowler, who later won a Nobel Prize for his work on the formation of chemical elements in the universe) who were interested in the stellar creation of chemical elements. In 1956 he and Fowler coauthored a paper describing element-building reactions in stars.

Building on his long-standing interest in stellar compositions, in 1957 Greenstein began his Abundance Project, which he ran for the next thirteen years with support from the Air Force Office of Scientific Research. In addition to the project's scientific results, the project served a pedagogical function by helping train a cohort of astronomy students, many of whom went on to have notable careers themselves. One of Greenstein's notable papers from this period, written in 1959 with George Wallerstein and H. Lawrence Helfer, showed that the metal abundances in globular cluster giant stars were as much as a factor of a hundred below that of the Sun. Research such as this helped advance scientists' knowledge of stellar abundances as a function of time and, more broadly, improved understanding of galactic chemical evolution.

Another long-term research program Greenstein undertook, after learning more about nuclear physics from Hoyle and Fowler, was the study of white dwarfs. Greenstein was drawn to this research for several reasons, not least because, as he put it, they were extraordinary celestial objects with "all the romance astronomy should have." These objects form when nuclear burning at a star's interior stops and its core begins to collapse and contract under its own gravity. Eventually the star becomes extremely dense with all the star's material compressed such that the electrons cannot be packed any closer together. Besides being astronomically interesting, white dwarfs offered scientists an opportunity to measure the behavior of matter under extreme conditions that cannot be duplicated elsewhere. He was especially interested in studying their magnetic fields and luminosities. By the mid-1950s Greenstein had discovered over five hundred new white dwarfs and had contributed to astrophysicists' better understanding of them.

In 1963 Greenstein and Maarten Schmidt (another Caltech astronomer) reported their observations of two quasi-stellar radio sources or quasars. While radio and optical astronomers had previously observed the two objects, innocuously named 3C 48 and 3C 273, Greenstein and Schmidt were the first to ascertain their cosmological significance. After reinterpreting the spectra Schmidt took at the prime focus of the 200-inch telescope, the two Caltech astronomers realized that the position of the spectral lines implied that 3C 48 was redshifted by 37 percent. This placed it more than five billion light-years from Earth, making it one of the most distant objects observed up to then. Their discovery made the cover of *Time* magazine in 1966 and helped reveal a universe that was far stranger and more violent than astronomers had suspected. Astronomers eventually identified thousands more quasars, work that helped open up a valuable new area of astronomical research with far-reaching implications for cosmology.

Greenstein's Scientific Leadership. After Greenstein moved to Caltech, he became increasingly active as a leader of the science community and soon exerted influence over the priorities and funding for astronomical research. Greenstein began his service in this area as a member of the panel that helped oversee awards to astronomers from the Office of Naval Research, an important postwar patron for basic science. In 1952, after President Harry S. Truman signed the law creating the National Science Foundation (NSF), the new agency asked Greenstein to chair its advisory panel for astronomy. In 1954 he also served as secretary of a group that held a conference on organizing research in radio astronomy. This gathering helped create momentum that eventually resulted in the creation of the National Radio Astronomy Observatory in November 1956, which was funded by the NSF and managed by Associated Universities, Inc.

Greenstein contributed to defense-related research during the Cold War. For example, he consulted with the military on reconnaissance and optics-related topics including those for the U-2 spy plane. He was also a participant in Project Vista, a top secret "summer study" done at Caltech in 1951. The purpose of Project Vista was to determine how existing technologies as well as ones soon to be available (tactical nuclear weapons in particular) could repel a hypothetical Soviet invasion of Europe. Greenstein's group explored how tools and expertise for astronomical research could be applied to aerial photography, infrared detection of troops and tanks, and the use of night-vision equipment.

In July 1969 the National Academy of Sciences (NAS) asked Greenstein to take responsibility for astronomy's second "decadal survey." These reports describe the field's health, summarize important scientific advances of the past decade, and set research goals for the next ten years. More importantly, through a process of debate and negotiation closed to the public and the general astronomy community, the decadal survey committees present a prioritized list of instruments and facilities that should receive federal funding.

The survey Greenstein led differed from the earlier effort chaired by Albert E. Whitford in two important respects. First, it considered astronomy practiced from the ground, funded mainly by the NSF, along with space-based research supported by the National Aeronautics and Space Administration (NASA), which the Whitford report did not address. All techniques of observation would be examined. Second, Greenstein and his committee had a strong mandate from the NAS as well as the Office of Management and Budget to make recommendations for what should be funded first. "It was no longer possible to send a shopping list to the government." Greenstein recalled, "They wanted priorities."

Greenstein, as head of Caltech's astronomy program, epitomized one style of astronomy—ground-based observing dominated by unparalleled access to large private telescopes in the West. By 1970 Greenstein was concerned about what he perceived as a disproportion between the federal support for astronomy at private institutions such as Caltech and that given to the national centers for optical and radio astronomy. Greenstein favored, as he phrased it in a 1963 letter to physicist Geoffrey R. Burbidge, "the benevolent dictatorship of the elite." Nevertheless, the other members of Greenstein's committee selected the Very Large Array as their number one funding priority. This was planned as a national facility for radio astronomy in Socorro, New Mexico, and estimated to cost at least sixty million dollars. While this recommendation was personally difficult for Greenstein to support, he wrote the committee's final report and presented its recommendations to astronomy's patrons throughout the 1970s.

Greenstein's final major leadership role came in 1974 when the Association of Universities for Research in Astronomy, Inc. (AURA), a university consortium that managed the nation's optical astronomy facilities, asked Greenstein to chair its board. Greenstein agreed although the task brought him additional conflict, especially with former Harvard classmate Leo Goldberg, over issues related to AURA's mission and future growth.

Honors and Retirement. During his career Greenstein received many honors and awards. These included election to the National Academy of Sciences in 1957, the Bruce Medal of the Astronomical Society of the Pacific in 1971, the NASA Distinguished Service Medal in 1974, and the Gold Medal of the Royal Astronomical Society in 1975. He also served on the Board of Overseers for Harvard University from 1965 to 1971 and received the title of Lee A. DuBridge Professor of Astrophysics at Caltech in 1971. Greenstein stepped down as head of Caltech's astronomy program in 1972 and retired from Caltech's faculty in 1980. Greenstein's wife Naomi died in 2002 after sixty-eight years of marriage. Jesse Greenstein died later the same year, leaving behind two sons, Peter and George, the latter also an astronomer.

BIBLIOGRAPHY

All of the unattributed quotes used here are drawn from Greenstein's correspondence and papers, which are in the Caltech Institute Archives, as well as his 1984 memoir. Further information may be found in oral history interviews Greenstein did, including those in the collections of the Niels Bohr Library at the American Institute of Physics in College Park, Maryland, and the Caltech Archives in Pasadena.

WORKS BY GREENSTEIN

With William A. Fowler. "Element Building Reactions in Stars." *Proceedings of the National Academy of Sciences of the United States of America* 42 (1956): 173–180.

With H. Lawrence Helfer and George Wallerstein. "Abundances in Some Population II K Giants." *Astrophysical Journal* 129, no. 5 (1959): 700–719.

With Maarten Schmidt. "The Quasi-Stellar Radio Sources 3C48 and 3C273." *Astrophysical Journal* 140, no. 1 (1964): 134.

Astronomy and Astrophysics for the 1970s. 2 vols. Washington, DC: National Academy of Sciences, 1972–1973. The report was written by the NRC Astronomy Survey Committee, which Greenstein chaired.

Interview with Spencer Weart, 7 April and 21 July 1977, oral history interview, Niels Bohr Library at the American Institute of Physics, College Park, MD.

"An Astronomical Life." *Annual Reviews of Astronomy and Astrophysics* 22 (1984): 1–35. Greenstein's own autobiographical recollections.

OTHER SOURCES

DeVorkin, David. "The Maintenance of a Scientific Institution: Otto Struve, the Yerkes Observatory, and Its Optical Bureau during the Second World War." *Minerva* 18, no. 4 (1981): 595–623. Discusses optics research Greenstein did at Yerkes.

———. *Science with a Vengeance: How the Military Created the US Space Sciences after World War II.* New York: Springer Verlag, 1992. Details early efforts, including those of Greenstein, to make astronomical observations with rocketborne instruments.

Edmondson, Frank K. *AURA and Its US National Observatories.* Cambridge, U.K.: Cambridge University Press, 1997.

Kraft, Robert P. "Jesse Leonard Greenstein." *Biographical Memoirs,* vol. 86. Washington, DC: National Academy of Sciences, 2005. A biography of Greenstein by a former colleague.

McCray, W. Patrick. "The Contentious Role of a National Observatory." *Physics Today* 56, no. 10 (2003): 55–61.

———. *Giant Telescopes: Astronomical Ambition and the Promise of Technology.* Cambridge, MA: Harvard University Press, 2004. Both works by McCray discuss Greenstein's experiences at Caltech.

W. Patrick McCray

GRIFFIN, DONALD REDFIELD *(b.* Southampton, New York, 3 August 1915; *d.* Lexington, Massachusetts, 7 November 2003), *zoologist, ethologist, cognitive ethologist, animal behavior, animal mind and consciousness.*

Behavior scientist Griffin enjoyed a scientific career of startling discoveries about animal behavior made by himself and other scientists. Early on he studied how birds and bats migrate. During the last thirty years of his life he immersed himself in the investigation of animal mind, spearheading inquiry into what was considered, during most of his career, to be an unacceptable or marginal topic within behavioral science—conscious awareness in the animal world.

Overview. Griffin was the only child of Mary Whitney Redfield Griffin and Henry Farrand Griffin. His mother kindled his interests early on by reading him Ernest Thompson Seton stories and the color-illustrated *Mammals of North America.* His father, a journalist and graduate of Yale, eventually turned amateur historian and wrote two historical novels. Griffin's uncle Alfred C. Redfield, who encouraged his boyhood nature interests, was a founding scientist of the Woods Hole Oceanographic Institution. Griffin's beloved wife, Jocelyn Crane Griffin, was an internationally recognized ethologist, who during her retirement earned a PhD in art history and studied human gestures in art. She died in 1998. Donald and Jocelyn Griffin were survived by their three children.

Griffin's fascination with natural history and animals had roots in his childhood and adolescence, from his mother reading him animal stories to his roaming the countryside observing and trapping critters. He entered the field that came to be known as ethology in the 1930s, when the scientific study of naturally occurring behavior was beginning to emerge with the pioneering work of European scientists Konrad Lorenz and Nikolaas (Niko) Tinbergen (Burkhardt, 2005). Griffin dedicated himself to the study of animal behavior at a time when scientists were urged to put aside such "naive" interests, and devote themselves to respectable areas within the life sciences (such as physiology). Griffin's commitment to learning about animal life remained steadfast in the face of institutional discouragement throughout his career.

By dint of determination and creative research, his career as a student of animal behavior from the 1930s to the end of his life in 2003 was enormously successful. He received his bachelor's, master's, and doctoral degrees from Harvard University between 1934 and 1942. After holding a faculty position in zoology at Cornell University until 1953, he returned to Harvard where he worked until 1965. He subsequently joined Rockefeller University until he retired in 1986. Griffin spent his last years affiliated with Harvard University's Concord Field Station, in Lexington, Massachusetts, where he continued his lively writing and research career to the end of his life. He was a member of the National Academy of Sciences, American Academy of Arts and Sciences, Animal Behavior Society, and American Philosophical Society.

Griffin's career can be divided into two phases. The first spanned to the mid-1970s, and was dedicated to ethological studies of animal behavior both in the field and in experimental settings. His research focused especially on the navigation behaviors of bats and birds. The second phase of his scientific life was devoted to the question of animal mind and to the work of building the subdiscipline of cognitive ethology. Considering his career as a whole, it is possible to discern how his behavioral research prepared him to inquire into the role of consciousness in animal life. In an autobiographical account, Griffin himself acknowledged how behavioral discoveries primed him to turn to the question of animal consciousness (1998a).

Research on Navigation. As a field and experimental scientist Griffin is renowned as codiscoverer of bat echolocation (Griffin and Galambos, 1941). His early work demonstrated that bats are able to avoid obstacles by emitting high frequency signals, which allow them to see their environs through the echoes bouncing back to them. At the time of Griffin's research on echolocation, in the 1940s and 1950s, no one suspected that bats also use this detection system to catch flying insects; indeed, the idea that they might echolocate moving targets was deemed improbable. It took Griffin several years of working with different experimental designs, but he eventually showed conclusively that bats use their bioradar to catch flying prey.

Griffin researched diverse aspects of bats' complex perceptual apparatus. He showed that bats can evade wires of 1 millimeter diameter or less, that they avoid such wires even in the presence of jamming sounds by modifying their flying pattern, and that they learn to distinguish between different sorts of objects (especially edible versus inedible), even if those objects return echoes of similar wavelength. He also found that echolocation is not used in a monolithic fashion, for bats will not deploy their radar detection abilities in known territory—relying instead on their familiarity with the surroundings. This was demonstrated by experiments in which bats steer clear of a previously present obstacle that has been removed, and run into obstacles newly erected on familiar routes. Griffin's field and experimental studies of bats are presented in his elaborate 1958 work, *Listening in the Dark,* for which he received the Daniel Giraud Elliot Medal of the National Academy of Sciences in 1961.

From his comprehensive study of the perceptual modality of a single animal, Griffin gleaned two crucial insights: one, that echolocation is a versatile mode of perception—used (or not) by bats in different contexts and for different purposes; and two, that scientists, like most people, have consistently underestimated animal capacities. These insights disposed Griffin favorably to the possibility that animal mind, in the sense of conscious awareness, may be an active and efficient modality for animals to navigate a complex world. The use of echolocation by bats as a versatile tool also prepared him to argue that, though animal consciousness may seem implausible to many, inquiry into the question is justified by amazing discoveries about animals that would remain unknown without suspension of disbelief and dogged research.

Griffin also studied bird navigation, designing experiments to see whether and how birds find their way back

Donald Redfield Griffin. © ED QUINN/CORBIS.

home after they are experimentally relocated in distant places. He pioneered the method of following birds in light airplanes to observe their homing patterns. He found that some species make their way home via indirect routes (suggesting that they search for familiar territory), while others immediately orient homeward often with great accuracy. Griffin researched bird navigation at a time when, as he put it, "the possibility that birds might distinguish Polaris from other stars was … outlandish" (1998a, p. 79). His work contributed to highlighting the sophistication of bird navigation.

In 1948 a startling discovery in the history of behavioral science made a huge impression on Griffin: Karl von Frisch's announcement that honeybees use a symbolic system to communicate about the distance and direction of food sources. On hearing about this discovery, at first Griffin was incredulous. In his characteristic scientific style he immediately set out to repeat some of von Frisch's experiments and confirmed for himself the efficacy of the honeybees' symbolic code—known in the behavioral literature as their "dance language." Though it was not until some thirty years later that Griffin would openly broach the question of animal awareness, the discovery of the dance language played a significant role in turning him in that direction. For Griffin the use of symbolism by a group of insects underscored, once again, how profoundly animal abilities are underestimated; it reinforced his intuition that an indefinite number of astounding facts about animal life remain to be uncovered; and lastly, the dance language suggested the possibility that honeybees use it to consciously share, and follow up on, information about their surroundings. Griffin became so excited with von Frisch's breakthrough that he arranged an American lecture tour for the German scientist and his wife, and also negotiated with Cornell University Press to publish a translation of von Frisch's manuscript *Bees: Their Vision, Chemical Senses, and Language* (1950).

Cognitive Ethology. Griffin's work in ethology spanned the decades of its creation and establishment as a legitimate scientific field. Exciting discoveries about animal behavior, as well as firsthand experience of seeing ethology battle for acceptance as a worthy arena of scientific inquiry, seasoned Griffin to lead the founding of cognitive ethology, the subdiscipline he introduced with his first book on animal mind in 1976—*The Question of Animal Awareness: Evolutionary Continuity of Mental Experience.*

Ethology had by this time come of age as a lively research field—also recognized more broadly with the Nobel Prize awarded to Lorenz, Tinbergen, and von Frisch in 1973. The question of consciousness, however, remained a proscribed topic within ethological science; behavioral scientists were actively discouraged from inquiring into animals' conscious mental lives. The reception of *The Question of Animal Awareness* showed that Griffin had broached an idea whose time had come. Whatever the perceived shortcomings of his first book on animal mind, many reviewers hailed it as refreshing, important, exciting, and stimulating (Friedman, 1977; Dawkins, 1977; Hilgard, 1978; Sarles, 1978). While some twentieth-century scientists, in both zoology and psychology, had previously wrestled with questions about "the complexities of the animal mind" and with "the evolutionary continuity of mental experience"—as certain critical reviewers reprimanded Griffin (Mason, 1976; Humphrey, 1977), no scientist had yet suggested establishing animal *conscious awareness* as a question for science.

It was extremely fortunate for the fate of cognitive ethology that its creator was a highly regarded, successful scientist who had proved his mettle with nearly half a century of productive research. In her review article of *The Question of Animal Awareness,* for example, Caryl Haskins noted that "no one is more eminently fitted to speak strongly on the matter than Donald Griffin" (1978, p.

383). William Mason as well, despite his critical commentary, began his review by noting Griffin's eminence in the field of animal navigation and orientation (1976, p. 930). Reviewers agreed that the book was too short and limited in scope for its subject matter—with much of its focus on the natural language of honeybees and experimentally taught languages to chimpanzees. One reviewer offered that he "would have preferred a more leisurely book, one argued more closely, more widely and more deeply to reflect the author's marvelous scientific intellect" (Hailman, 1978, p. 615; see also Beer, 1977). In his next books on the topic, Griffin took the criticisms to heart.

After *The Question of Animal Awareness,* Griffin went on to publish two more books on the animal mind: *Animal Thinking* with Harvard University in 1984 and *Animal Minds* with the University of Chicago Press in 1992 (revised and expanded in 2001). In *Animal Thinking* he updated and extended evidence of conscious awareness, by including the examination not only of animal communication (the focus of his 1976 work), but also of complex behaviors such as foraging, predator-prey interaction, artifact construction, and tool use. The variety and number of animals he considered in his second book also broadened considerably. While reviewers of *Animal Thinking* continued to perceive Griffin as "challenging conventional wisdom," "heretical," and "iconoclastic" (Dunbar, 1984; Graham, 1984; Herman, 1985), they also recognized that his inclusion of new lines of evidence and a richer database promised to make a greater impact on the field (Beer, 1984). Griffin himself closed his 1984 book with the assessment that changing the scientific community's beliefs about animal consciousness "will require an accumulation of extensive and mutually reinforcing evidence, far beyond evidence now available" (1984, p. 209). Marshaling this evidence was the task he set himself in writing his magnum opus. His 1992 (revised, 2001) *Animal Minds* was meticulously compiled, lucidly argued, and written for a broad audience of scientists, other academics, and a lay public.

Animal Minds. In the span of three decades and three books, Griffin's thinking on animal mind evolved profoundly both qualitatively and quantitatively. No one has gone so far as Griffin in classifying behavioral indicators of mental experience, and collecting a comprehensive dataset of animal behaviors under those headings. In his third and last book on the topic, Griffin brought together a rich collection of findings from ethological and psychological research, an extensive database of behaviors—ranging from the insightful to the commonplace—suggestive of conscious awareness. "If nothing else, but is much more," ethologist Marc Bekoff wrote in his review, "*Animal Minds* is a fine natural history of the behavior of a wide variety of organisms; it is a comprehensive and comparative review of evidence, including anecdotes, data from rigorous observations, and experimental findings that suggest animal consciousness" (1993, p. 166).

The book's central strategy consists of a systematic consideration of behavioral evidence amassing since Charles Darwin's work on animal mind (1871, 1872). Indeed, Griffin's strategy in *Animal Minds* recalls the approach of *On the Origin of Species,* in which Darwin assembled a variety of evidence for the purposes of making "one long argument" for evolution by common descent (1859). Griffin compiled an enormous amount of behavioral data suggestive of conscious thinking and feeling in the animal world. His project is also analogous to Darwin's in challenging the human predilection to assign ourselves special origins and/or distinguishing qualities. While the idea that the human species was specially created has been largely discredited, the view that conscious awareness is the privileged possession of our species continues to have purchase, in one form or another.

In *Animal Minds,* Griffin organized the empirical evidence in terms of broad categories of naturally occurring and experimentally studied behaviors suggesting conscious awareness: finding food, predation, constructing artifacts, tools and devices, category learning, communication, and deception. Under these headings, Griffin gathered a gamut of behavioral examples. Herons' practice of baiting fish, raptors drowning their prey, ingenious cooperative hunting in several species, injury-feigning by birds as a distracting tactic, experimental evidence of concept formation in pigeons, the honeyguide bird guiding people to bee hives, the experimental demonstration of some animals' simple numerical competence, ravens' solution of piecemeal hauling of a string on which food is suspended, the semantic information communicated by vervet alarm calls, the linguistic feats of honeybees, apes, and African parrots: these examples are but a fraction of the complex behaviors, suggesting the action of mind, that Griffin discusses.

His point of amassing example after example is to suggest that the accumulating knowledge from field and experimental psychology studies belies the received zeitgeist of animals as sleepwalkers, and encourages an understanding of nonhumans as wide-awake to their lived experience. "A conscious organism," Griffin maintained, "is clearly different in an important way from one that lacks any subjective mental experience. The former thinks and feels to a greater or lesser degree, while the latter is limited to existing and reacting" (2001, p. 253).

The perennial difficulty that Griffin faced in making the case for conscious awareness was that the (hypothetical or real) skeptic might redescribe the same behaviors as unconscious reactions. An example may illustrate this interpretive parallax: in autumn, a bird known as the

Griffin

Clark's nutcracker stores seeds underground and in crevices that it retrieves and feeds on during the winter. Experimental research has shown that this species relies on landmarks for caching its seeds and subsequently finding them. In his narrative, Griffin noted two divergent interpretations: the behavior might be understood as involving simple conscious thinking on the bird's part; or it might be regarded as the outcome of unconscious memory mechanics (2001, p. 60).

Griffin often simply highlighted such contrasting interpretations/images of a behavior—as mindful versus mindless—and then entreated the reader to consider the plausibility, or at least the possibility, of the former over the latter. In juxtaposing images of animals as aware creatures versus robots, Griffin might be seen as problematizing what philosopher Ludwig Wittgenstein referred to (for different purposes than the subject matter in consideration) as *pictures* (1953). *Pictures* in Wittgenstein's sense conjure the concept-ladeness or assumption-ladeness of perception. Such perception, tinted by preconceived notions, is vividly exemplified in how people see and understand animal action. Griffin's descriptions sometimes appear tacitly aimed at shifting the reader-observer from an automaton picture of animal behavior to a mindful one of how and why animals act as they do. His overt tactic was to argue that the accruing behavioral evidence has begun to weigh in favor of consciousness over mechanistic conceptions.

In his investigations into animal mind, Griffin never wavered from his interest in subjective conscious experience—as opposed to framing his approach in terms of the study of "animal cognition." The subtitle added to the 2001 edition of *Animal Minds—Beyond Cognition to Consciousness*—underscores this focus (see also Griffin, 1998b). "Cognition" can be framed with a raft of computer metaphors such as information processing, input-output schemata, neuronal maps and representations, memory storage, and the like—a mechanistic vocabulary that either suggests that mental processes are carried out unconsciously or elides the question of consciousness altogether.

Whereas Griffin engaged philosophy of mind literature (much of which abounds with computer jargon), he was interested in animal mind in the phenomenological, quasi-commonsense view of the wide-awake, aware experience of living. He applauded the fact that the reign of behaviorism was supplanted in the 1960s by the cognitive turn—in which inner representations finally became plausible phenomena for inquiry. But he also repeatedly highlighted the fact that within cognitive science "animals are granted only *un*conscious cognition" (1997).

Animal Consciousness. Griffin was thus tuned to phenomena of awareness, which, with refreshing straightforwardness, he identified as the quest for what animals think and feel. Griffin wrestled with definitions of such terms as *mind, consciousness, conscious, awareness, thinking,* and the like, but in the end opted for using their down-to-earth meanings. "We all know what consciousness experiences are," he wrote, and went on to identify the key question as "whether other species have any conscious experiences, and if so what these are like to the animals themselves" (2000, p. 889). But while using human conscious experience as the rough-and-ready yardstick of the meaning of "consciousness," Griffin also acknowledged that animal conscious states are likely to be qualitatively different from humans'. Perhaps endeavoring to preempt the charge that he was humanizing animals, Griffin often insisted that human mind and animal mind must differ profoundly—and that his interest was in uncovering "the simplest thoughts and feelings" of animals, not in overattributing mental abilities. He admitted that human language underskirts the vast scope of the human species' thinking ability. Griffin did not completely rule out "more complex forms of consciousness [in animals] such as introspective metacognition or thinking about thoughts," but thought such topics of investigation "best left for future inquiries" (1997).

In making the case that a subdiscipline devoted to animal consciousness is a worthwhile endeavor, Griffin had a multilevel approach. As noted, he systematized large amounts of evidence from the corpus of behavioral, biological, and psychological knowledge. But besides considering the empirical evidence in toto and afresh, Griffin also contested the institutional barriers and background-assumption roadblocks to exploring the question of animal mind. He exposed the institutional resistance, historically entrenched in the behavioral sciences, to the investigation of animal consciousness, and deconstructed the ingrained assumptions that blocked the consideration of animal mind within science.

Griffin's inquiry into animal mind thus involved scrutinizing the attitude of the scientific community toward the question itself. Throughout his work, he consistently highlighted the institutional resistance to the idea of nonhuman consciousness, and criticized such closure to inquiry as contrary to the spirit of science. Griffin called the twentieth-century doctrine that entreated scientists to focus solely on observable behavior, without any reference to the mental experience, as "inclusive behaviorism." He regarded most behavioral scientists as "inclusive behaviorists" for excising phenomena of animal awareness as either epistemologically inaccessible or empirically nonexistent. Griffin also challenged cognitive scientists for rendering conscious thoughts or feelings superfluous by framing cognition as "information-

Griffin

processing" (2001, pp. 263–264)—a mechanistic conceptualization that served to avoid grappling with the question of consciousness. By shunning conscious awareness in animal life in different ways, behavioral scientists of all stripes (psychologists, ethologists, behavioral ecologists, and cognitive scientists) have contributed to perpetuating the received zeitgeist of animals as nonconscious beings.

Reaction of the Scientific Community. To promote the emergent field of cognitive ethology, Griffin was compelled to face resistance to change. He highlighted inhibitions to engaging the topic of animal mind, noting how behavioral scientists have been indoctrinated to regard a fascination with animal consciousness as a kind of tender-mindedness. (Indeed, one reviewer called Griffin a "sentimental softy" for proposing that animals are consciously aware [Cronin, 1992].) He exposed many other mechanisms by which a scientific discourse about animal consciousness has been preempted and silenced: by students being trained that it is unscientific to raise questions about animal awareness, and discouraged or ridiculed whenever they do so; by field and experimental scientists avoiding to report evidence suggestive of conscious thinking; by scientific journals being reluctant to publish such evidence; and by a general filtering out and censoring of observations relating to animal consciousness. Griffin used words such as *taboo* and *brainwashing* to characterize how animal awareness has been handled by the scientific community; he called the avoidance of mind "mentophobia"—diagnosing it as the vestige of the long reign of behaviorism in the life sciences (2001, pp. 34–36).

Another barrier to the study of mind that Griffin noted is the "fear of anthropomorphism" in behavioral science—the concern of attributing to animals specifically human traits. He challenged the notion that ascribing consciousness to animals is a form of anthropomorphism by pointing out that this "merely reiterates a prejudgment that consciousness is uniquely human" (1997). The assumption that the attribution of mind to animals reflects the error of anthropomorphism begs two important questions: whether mind is a privileged human possession, and whether empathy (that is, some form of critical anthropomorphism) may not be useful, or even necessary, in discerning the presence of mind in others. Griffin also realized that the accusation of anthropomorphism is a whitewash over diverse mental ascriptions of extremely different levels of plausibility. Referring to Clever Hans, the famous turn-of-the-twentieth-century horse claimed to know mathematics, Griffin highlighted the crass generalizations encouraged by the charge of anthropomorphism: "We were in fact brainwashed into equating the belief that a horse can carry out a long division with the suggestion that a rabbit consciously anticipates escaping from a fox by plunging into its burrow" (1992, p. 24).

Beyond criticizing the inhibitions of the scientific community toward the question of animal mind, Griffin also unpacked widespread assumptions that blocked inquiry. One key assumption he challenged, in all his works, is the long-standing idea of a "Rubicon" separating animal and human mentality. While the assumption of a radical disparity is far less common in the early twenty-first century than it was in the 1970s, the belief that only humans possess mind in the sense of complex thoughts, reasons, deliberations, or intentions that accompany, or underlie, action continues to hold sway. Griffin contended that such an exemptionalist belief is out of synch with the knowledge of evolutionary continuity bequeathed by the Darwinian worldview—a continuity that only "conceit" would keep scientists from extending to the realm of consciousness.

A second entrenched assumption that Griffin scrutinized is the belief that if an animal's behavior is genetic or learned, it is executed automatically. In countering this assumption Griffin raised two points. Firstly he argued that there is no compelling evidence that an instinctive or learned behavior cannot also be consciously executed; a bird, for example, may inherit its nest-building pattern, but this does not mean that while constructing its nest the bird is unaware of what it is doing—that it is being run by its "genetic program" like a virtual sleepwalker. Secondly Griffin insisted that instinctive and learned behaviors are rarely as invariant, or as rigidly expressed, as the language of "programming" suggests. The hunting behavior of certain predatory spiders, for example, while inherited (that is, "genetically programmed"), is not a stereotyped pattern, but rather a set of tactics subtly adjusted to the particular prey hunted and its responses. Griffin shrewdly pointed out about this case that "if monkeys did what these spiders do, we would be strongly tempted to conclude that they were acting intentionally" (2001, p. 63).

Behavioral scientist Colin Beer rightly pointed out that "Griffin takes the whole animal kingdom as his province," and is "an advocate of equal rights to cognitive consideration for all animals" (1984, p. 31). Griffin's extensive inclusion of invertebrate examples was noted by most commentators—one reviewer called it "the strength and challenge" of his work (Norris, 1985). Indeed, a third pervasive assumption Griffin contested is the prejudice against conscious awareness among so-called lower animals, especially invertebrates. He repeatedly exposed how deep-seated assumptions of an obsolete (but diehard) phylogenetic scale of mentality in the animal kingdom—from mindless automatism to self-conscious agency—inform scientific judgments about animal behavior (2001, pp. 262–263).

Griffin noted that the complexity and variability of behaviors in a wide range of animals, including insects and other invertebrates, belie human prejudgments. For example, he discussed the behavior of the assassin bug, an insect that camouflages itself by gluing pieces of termite nest to its body, thereby luring in termites that it kills and consumes. In reporting the assassin bug's predatory tactics, Griffin brings up the analogy of "chimpanzees fashion[ing] sticks to probe termites." But when scientists discover "assassin bugs carrying out an almost equally elaborate feeding behavior," he goes on to ask, "must we assume that the insect is only a genetically programmed robot incapable of understanding what it does?" (1984, p. 124). Thus he both exposes human preconceptions about invertebrates and highlights the intentionality of the insect's behavior.

Griffin devoted extensive attention to describing the honeybee dance language, which he called a "sort of geometrical symbolism" (2001, p. 195). His elaborate account highlights that the dance is a communicative tool used only when there is need in the hive and strictly in the presence of an audience. Honeybees deploy the dance for a variety purposes: for nectar by indicating the location of flower patches, but also for water when the hive is overheating, pollen when supplies in the colony diminish, and, in its most enterprising use, for the purposes of identifying the whereabouts of potential cavities when the swarm needs to relocate. After underscoring the multiple uses of this direction-giving language, Griffin argued that the honeybees do not dance mechanically. Its versatility suggests it is more likely a tool employed by mindful actors than a rigid program executed by quasi-automata (2001, pp. 190–211; see Crist, 2004).

A fourth received assumption that Griffin found questionable if not fallacious is that accounts of behavior in terms of mental experience violate the law of parsimony. He sums up this view by quoting behavioral scientist David Premack: "What need is there for mind when there are contingencies and reinforcement?" (Premack quoted in Griffin, 2001, p. 144). On the contrary, Griffin argued, having direct awareness of what needs to be done, or of how to accomplish a task, would confer an adaptive advantage in an animal's life, while blindly following a fixed genetic or learned program can be inefficient in a world that presents unpredictable challenges, and in which doing the wrong thing can be fatal (2000, p. 891). Natural selection would likely favor an aptitude for conscious thinking about alternative courses, given the survival value of such an aptitude in a changeable and dangerous world.

Behavioral versatility is especially difficult to account for in a parsimonious manner, when the metaphor of "programming" is reified and projected onto the reality of animal lives. Certain ground-nesting birds, for example, exhibit markedly distinct behaviors in the presence of a lurking predator versus an approaching grazer. Positing the bird's conscious awareness of its experience offers a more straightforward account of why it will respond one way to a fox and another way to a cow, than adding "special subprograms" to account for its versatile modulation of behavior protective of its eggs or chicks (2001, p. 112). Similarly, after detailing the intricate maneuvers of pike and minnows (predator and prey fish, respectively), Griffin noted that the scientist "can postulate a complex network of instinctive reflexes for the observed behaviors, complete with random noise generators at strategic points to explain unpredictable sequences." Highlighting the ad hoc nature of such schemes, he submitted that "it becomes increasingly plausible, and more parsimonious, to infer that both pike and minnows think consciously in simple terms about their all-important efforts to catch elusive food or to escape from a threatening predator" (2001, p. 66). Recognizing mindfulness in the behavior of predators and their prey is a more economical way of understanding their flexible maneuvers than postulating a complex series of stimulus-response connections to render the same phenomena.

Lastly, Griffin faced a fifth obstructing assumption about animal mind, perhaps the most difficult to crack: that the study of conscious mental states is moot because they are fundamentally inaccessible. The view that mental states are private and unattainable, if indeed existent at all, is a shared premise of inclusive behaviorism. As an example, Griffin cited cognitive scientist Edward Wasserman, who steered clear of subjective experience in animals despite his extensive work on pigeon cognition. "No statement concerning consciousness in animals is open to verification and experiment. Isn't it time we set aside such tantalizing but unanswerable questions?" (Wasserman, quoted in Griffin, 2001, p. 147).

Regarding the inaccessibility of mind, Griffin noted that while people can claim the same about their fellow humans, they are not hampered in drawing conclusions about one another's inner states on the basis of their behavior. "We routinely make valid (if not totally perfect) inferences about the conscious experiences of our human companions," he noted, and immediately identified the challenge as developing "ways to make reasonably plausible inferences about private experiences of other species" (1997). Griffin thus did not question the idea of mind as a "private realm." He called for extending the circle of analogy from one's own experience, beyond our fellow humans, to other species; and he deplored that the privacy of animals minds should lead to hopeless pessimism and the abandonment of all investigation.

Griffin

But in descriptions of behaviors redolent with intentionality and mindfulness, Griffin implicitly challenged the doctrine of the "privacy of mind." When the observer is receptive to a view of animals as mindful, then their intentionality is witnessed as an observable aspect of their actions—a bending upon a task, a lone or concerted effort toward a particular end, and a persistence, deliberateness, or texture of presence in the expression of behavior. In his thick descriptions, for example, of how different insects, birds, and beavers build their nests (2001, pp. 85–112), Griffin's tacitly conveyed message is that mind is visible to the patient, open-minded, careful investigator. But in his explicit conclusions Griffin usually maintained that the behaviors he described were highly "suggestive" of conscious awareness—but did not constitute foolproof evidence. Thus he remained party to the entrenched western philosophical and scientific paradigm of mind (challenged by late Wittgensteinian and phenomenological traditions) as a purely inner realm that behavior hints at only obliquely (see Crist, 1999).

While complying with the idea that thinking and feeling are not directly accessible phenomena, Griffin was bent on offering empirical approaches that might render animal consciousness more plausibly transparent. He offered three criteria, or lines of evidence, for the discernment of conscious awareness: one, the versatility of animal behavior—the ability to modulate behavioral repertoires in the face of challenging conditions; two, similarities in brain neuronal function between animals and humans; and three, the complex communicative skills of many species (1999).

Of these lines of argumentation, his most compelling insight for empirical access to animal consciousness involved the documentation of what he called "versatility," which Griffin viewed as a powerful indicator of intelligent adaptation to the peculiarities at hand. Versatility may indeed be regarded as subsuming Griffin's third criterion for mind (that of complex communicative skills) for versatility may be broadly defined as the capacity of animals to engage in nuanced conversation with their environments. For Griffin, an animal's ability to adapt or tweak its behaviors indicates a deliberateness and reasonableness underlying its relationship with the world. At the very least, flexibility in response to environmental modulations belies a picture of behaviors (inherited or conditioned) as rigidly expressed.

It is difficult to read descriptions of raptors drowning their struggling prey without a sense that such an act is mindful of the desired and anticipated consequence (2001, pp. 66–67). Yet routine behaviors, as well, such as nest-repair among birds, are carried out in a reasonable as opposed to stereotyped fashion, suggesting that versatility may be a ubiquitous aspect of animal life, not simply a feature of clever behaviors (2001, p. 91). Beavers modify their dam and lodge building styles according to local conditions and materials, suggesting flexible behavior and a sensible use of resources, rather than "the thoughtless unfolding of a genetically determined program" (2001, p. 112). Moreover, animals can sometimes apply a previously well-developed type of action to a new situation—such as the famous tits who, utilizing their skill of stripping off the bark of trees, learned to open milk bottles (2001, p. 53).

"To what extent," Griffin wondered, "does the novelty in applying well-established actions to new situations indicate conscious thinking?" (2001, p. 54). While he posed this as a tantalizing question, he did his utmost to compile such novel applications of behaviors showing versatility to be pervasive in the animal world. The importance of this project cannot be underestimated: no other behavioral scientist has gathered such extensive empirical material to show that the ways of animals are rarely, if ever, rigid patterns of acting. His encyclopedic vista of behavioral data documenting versatility—from subtle to innovative modulations of behavior in response to circumstances—would alone earn him the title of founder of cognitive ethology.

Griffin's interest in considering animals as mindful creatures with a subjective point of view was not limited to insightful behaviors, nor to animals' performance under unprecedented conditions, but extended to their everyday life as well. An example is Griffin's description of the interactions between tommies (a type of gazelle) and their predators on the African plains. His description provided a commonplace, yet more subtle, way of seeing mind: in the watchful behavior of the tommies that intermittently monitor the movement and position of predators, such that in the herd there is at least one gazelle always watching; in their alert posture, and soft snort or stomp on the ground, warning others if something suspicious or unusual occurs; and in the variation of the speed of their gait, according to the type of predator attacking, its approaching speed, and initial distance from the herd.

Furthermore, the futile attempts of female tommies to distract hyenas chasing their fawns, and the frantic efforts of tommies, just before capture, to escape by rapid change of direction, have no statistical survival value, and thus cannot be convincingly explained as adaptive behaviors that have been forged by natural selection. "But when we broaden our horizons," Griffin submitted, "by considering what life may be like to the animals themselves, it is not surprising to find that they make strenuous efforts to avoid being killed, or having their offspring killed, even when such efforts have little or no chance of success. This is an example of how our theoretical concepts can be broadened by considering how life may seem to the animals themselves" (2001, p. 70). Griffin thus called attention to how

Griffin

the inclusion of animals' experiential perspective can elucidate and enrich one's perception of their behaviors.

It is admirable that Griffin never compromised his interest in consciousness, despite its being a non sequitur for many of his colleagues; nor did he shrink from the challenging endeavor of finding scientific venues to peer into the subjective experience of animals, despite the insistence of some that it is a "hopeless enterprise" (Galef, 1993). Griffin's pioneering spirit was rewarded toward the end of his life, when he witnessed "a marked departure" within science from erstwhile inhibitions to consider questions about animal consciousness (2000, p. 889). From his inception of the field of cognitive ethology in the late 1970s to the turn of the twentieth-first century, he saw the expansion of an arena of scientific inquiry that was once "forbidden territory" (2000, p. 891). As behavioral scientist James Gould put it in his eloquent obituary in *Animal Cognition,* because of Griffin's masterful work the view "that animals are not robots, but ... part of the mental continuum Darwin felt was obvious, has moved from the lunatic fringe to what may be described as the default assumption: the burden of proof has shifted" (2004, p. 4).

Griffin was the forerunner of an altogether new way of thinking about animal life. It remains for the future to witness whether his work and discipline building will topple the deeply lodged skepticism, in science and western discourses more generally, toward the existence or accessibility of animal conscious awareness. For many agnostics in particular, the important issue is whether explanations relying on consciousness are more useful than behaviorist renditions or accounts invoking the forging of behaviors by natural selection (Baenninger, 1994). Yet what is at stake with the question of animal consciousness is more complex than the relative efficacy of explanatory schemes.

During the hottest hours of the day, the Egyptian plover wets its belly feathers in the river before returning to settle on, and thereby cool, its eggs or young (Griffin, 2001, pp. 121–123). This behavior may be regarded as mechanically executed or as mindfully enacted; in either case, it is clearly adaptive and shaped by natural selection. Does it matter if the parent plovers, as Griffin suggests, may be thinking about keeping their eggs and young cool when they wet their feathers? Does it matter, in other words, whether animals really mean what they do?

There are at least two ways in which Griffin's raising this question of consciousness matters deeply. Firstly, in challenging restrictive injunctions against mindfulness, he opened new horizons of researching, thinking about, and seeing animal life. His work has thus brought greater freedom of thought and expanded realms of knowledge, both to students of behavioral science and to a broader public that scientific knowledge eventually reaches. Secondly, by encouraging a shift toward regarding animals as conscious beings with experiential viewpoints, Griffin also beckoned a change in how humans perceive animals and, therefore, how humans relate to them and to their habitats. The more widely consciousness is viewed as a realistic feature of the animal world, the more awe and respect animals and their homes will be perceived as due.

BIBLIOGRAPHY

WORKS BY GRIFFIN

With Robert Galambos. "The Sensory Basis of Obstacle Avoidance by Flying Bats." *Journal of Experimental Zoology* 86 (1941): 481–506.

"The Sensory Basis of Bird Navigation." *Quarterly Review of Biology* 19, no. 1 (1944): 15–31.

"Bat Sounds under Natural Conditions, with Evidence for the Echolocation of Insect Prey." *Journal of Experimental Zoology* 123 (1953): 435–466.

Listening in the Dark: The Acoustic Orientation of Bats and Men. New Haven, CT: Yale University Press, 1958. Reprint, Ithaca, NY: Comstock, 1986.

With Frederic A. Webster and Charles R. Michael. "The Echolocation of Flying Insects by Bats." *Animal Behaviour* 8, no. 3 (1960): 141–154.

The Question of Animal Awareness: Evolutionary Continuity of Mental Experience. New York: Rockefeller University Press, 1976. Rev. ed., New York: Rockefeller University Press, 1981.

Animal Thinking. Cambridge, MA: Harvard University Press, 1984.

Animal Minds. Chicago: Chicago University Press, 1992.

"Adaptiveness of Perceptual Consciousness." Poster at June 1997 meeting of *Animal Behavior Society.*

"Donald R. Griffin." In *History of Neuroscience in Autobiography,* Volume II, edited by Larry R. Squire. Washington, DC: Society for Neuroscience, 1998a.

"From Cognition to Consciousness." *Animal Cognition* 1, no. 1 (1998b): 3–16.

"Mind, Animal." In *Elsevier's Encyclopedia of Neuroscience,* 2nd ed., edited by George Adelman and Barry H. Smith. New York: Elsevier, 1999.

"Scientific Approaches to Animal Consciousness." *American Zoologist* 40, no. 6 (2000): 889–892.

Animal Minds: Beyond Cognition to Consciousness. Rev. ed. Chicago: Chicago University Press, 2001.

OTHER SOURCES

Baenninger, Ronald. "A Retreat before the Canon of Parsimony." *Contemporary Psychology* 39, no. 8 (1994). Review of *Animal Minds.*

Beer, Colin. "Review: *Animal Awareness.*" *BioScience* 27, no. 5 (1977): 360–361.

———. "In Search of Solomon's Ring: New Light on Animal Ways." *Natural History* 6 (1984): 30–31.

Bekoff, Marc. Review of *Animal Minds. Ethology* 95 (1993): 166–176.

Burkhardt, Richard W., Jr. *Patterns of Behavior: Konrad Lorenz, Niko Tinbergen, and the Founding of Ethology.* Chicago: Chicago University Press, 2005.

Crist, Eileen. *Images of Animals: Anthropomorphism and Animal Mind.* Philadelphia: Temple University Press, 1999.

———. "Can an Insect Speak? The Case of the Honey Bee Dance Language." *Social Studies of Science* 34, no. 1 (2004): 7–43.

Cronin, Helena. Review of *Animal Minds. New York Times Book Review,* 1 November 1992.

Darwin, Charles. *On the Origin of Species.* Cambridge, MA: Harvard University Press, 1859. Reprint, 1964.

———. *The Descent of Man and Selection in Relation to Sex.* Princeton, NJ: Princeton University Press, 1871. Reprint, 1981.

———. *The Expression of Emotions in Man and Animals.* Chicago: Chicago University Press, 1872. Reprint, 1965.

Dawkins, Marian. Review of *The Question of Animal Awareness. Ibis* 119 (1977): 253.

Dunbar, Robin. "The Awareness of Animals." *New Scientist* (18 October 1984). Review of *Animal Thinking.*

Friedman, Herbert. Review of *The Question of Animal Awareness. Journal of Wildlife Management* 41, no. 2 (1977): 332.

Frisch, Karl von. *Bees: Their Vision, Chemical Senses, and Language.* Ithaca, NY: Cornell University Press, 1950.

Galef, Bennett. Review of *Animal Minds. Animal Behaviour* 49, no. 4 (1993): 1133–1134.

Gould, James L. "Thinking about Thinking: How Donald Griffin (1915–2003) Remade Animal Behavior." *Animal Cognition* 7 (2004): 1–4.

Graham, Frank. "Mentioning the Unmentionable." *Audubon* 86, no. 3 (1984): 138–140. Review of *Animal Thinking.*

Hailman, Jack. Review of *The Question of Animal Awareness. Auk* 95 (1978): 614–615.

Haskins, Caryl. Review of *The Question of Animal Awareness* by Donald R. Griffin. Review "The Evolving Mind." *Semiotica* 23, no. 3/4 (1978): 381–385.

Herman, Louis M. "Raising Consciousness." *Contemporary Psychology* 30, no. 4 (1985): 266–268. Review of *Animal Thinking.*

Hilgard, Ernest. Review of *The Question of Animal Awareness. Journal of Psycholinguistic Research* 7, no. 3 (1978): 243–248.

Humphrey, Nicholas K. Review of *The Question of Animal Awareness. Animal Behaviour* 25 (1977): 521–522.

Mason, William A. "Windows on Other Minds." Review of *The Question of Animal Awareness. Science* 194 (1976): 930-931.

Norris, Kenneth. Review of *Animal Thinking. Quarterly Review of Biology* 60, no. 3 (1985): 393–394.

Sarles, Harvey. Review of *The Question of Animal Awareness. Physical Anthropology* 80 (1978): 164–165.

Wittgenstein, Ludwig. *Philosophical Investigations,* translated by G. E. M. Anscombe. Oxford: Basil Blackwell, 1953.

Eileen Crist

GROBSTEIN, CLIFFORD (*b.* New York, New York, 20 July 1916; *d.* La Jolla, California, 6 September 1998), *ethics, developmental biology, stem cell biology, public policy.*

Grobstein was one of the preeminent scientists of the twentieth century, influencing the now blossoming field of developmental biology, pioneering in the area of biological and medical education, and contributing materially to the controversies and ethical underpinnings surrounding fetal research and manipulation. The studies he initiated on tissue interactions in development influenced a whole generation of researches in developmental biology and oncology. In his later years, as he assumed advisory positions on committees of the National Institutes of Health, the National Science Foundation, and the National Academy of Sciences, he demonstrated a unique ability to communicate difficult concepts in simple but eloquent language, thereby influencing the establishment of bioethical guidelines for fetal research, guidelines that are still contemporary in the current context of human embryonic research and stem cell biology.

Education. Clifford Grobstein was the son of Aaron and Birdie Grobstein. His siblings included a brother, Richard, and a sister, Fern. Grobstein received his early training in New York City at what became the Bronx High School of Science, one of the exciting new educational ventures of Fiorello H. LaGuardia that predated the magnet schools of later decades. The Bronx High School of Science selected students from the greater New York area and provided the springboard for numerous scientific careers. After high school, Grobstein attended City College in New York. Just as the Bronx High School of Science gave a start to many young prospective scientists, City College was almost unique in providing a free or near-free opportunity to further the careers of promising students regardless of income, sex, or religious orientation. Grobstein continued his scientific training by pursuing a doctorate in zoology at the University of California at Los Angeles (UCLA), receiving a PhD in 1940. The doctoral research focused on endocrine influences on anal fin regeneration in fish, work that greatly influenced many of the subsequent studies in developmental biology carried out first on fish and then on mice.

Professional Appointments. Following completion of his formal scientific training, Grobstein assumed an academic appointment at Oregon State University where he continued to study tissue interactions and regulation of appendage differentiation in fish (1940–1942). However, World War II interrupted his scientific career: He served in the U.S. Army Air Force for three years (1943–1946). On returning from military service, he accepted a research appointment in the Biology Division of the National Cancer Institute (NCI) in Bethesda, Maryland, and it was here that his seminal studies in developmental biology led to his preeminence in that field. In 1957 he left the NCI to accept a professorship at Stanford University. In the mid-1960s, however, he was recruited by the University of California System to head the Department of Biology at the newly formed University of California at San Diego (UCSD). Here he moved rapidly from chair of the biology department to a deanship of the medical school, the vice chancellor for health sciences and finally the position of vice chancellor for special programs, a position he held until his retirement as a result of progressive illness.

Contributions to the Field of Developmental Biology. The early work on fish embryos had introduced Grobstein to the field of embryology (which was renamed "developmental biology"). He resumed his own research program on his return from military service in 1946, at which time he received an appointment as a researcher in the Biology Division of the NCI in Bethesda, Maryland. Grobstein first established a fish colony to continue to study fish development, but, surrounded by mammalian biologists, he soon recognized both the advantages and the challenges provided by changing to the mouse. The Biology Division at NCI included the chair, Walter Heston, an expert on mouse genetics; Wilton Earle, a pioneer in the area of tissue culture; and Glenn Algire, a leader in the field of experimental oncology, who studied the interactions of tumor cells with their tissue environment in vivo through the use of diffusion chambers. The influence of these three scientists can readily be seen in the work carried out by Grobstein, which included in vivo transplantation studies of early mouse embryos, the study of cell and tissue interactions during morphogenesis of embryonic mouse organ rudiments in vitro, and the adaptation of diffusion chamber technology to permit analysis of tissue interactions across diffusible membranes in tissue culture.

The number of scientists with whom Grobstein collaborated in these research studies were relatively few, but each in turn became prominent over the subsequent years. Among the first was Edgar Zwilling, with whom Grobstein described the role of tissue mass in controlling the growth and differentiation of early chick and mouse rudiments. They initiated work on separating different tissues of early embryonic rudiments, work that led Zwilling to the seminal studies of tissue interactions during chick embryonic limb development. A second visitor to the NCI laboratory of Grobstein was Julius S. Youngner, whose work with Grobstein on kidney cell differentiation led to Youngner's subsequent establishment in Pittsburgh of the kidney cell culture system that was of key importance in the development of the polio vaccine by Jonas Salk. Howard Holtzer, over a three-month visit to Bethesda, collaborated with Grobstein and his longtime assistant, George Parker, in establishing the in vitro system for studying somite development into cartilage, a system that Holtzer and his student Jay Lash later employed over a lifetime of research at the University of Pennsylvania. Robert Auerbach, the only junior fellow to work with Grobstein at the NCI (1955–1957), applied the cell dissociation and reaggregation systems introduced a decade earlier for amphibian systems by Johannes Holtfreter, and stimulated by Aaron Moscona's description of trypsinization protocols, led to the recognition that self-organization of tissues and organs developed gradually during organ differentiation. Auerbach, in his subsequent studies on thymus differentiation and angiogenesis and along with his students, Veerappan Muthukkaruppan, Joseph Taderera, and Jane Barker, extended Grobstein's influence into the areas of lens, lung, and yolk sac differentiation in mice.

Perhaps most important was Grobstein's work describing the role of cell contact and extracellular matrix in the regulation of tissue interactions. The major ideas were described best in the symposium paper presented at the Growth Society (later named the Society for Developmental Biology) meeting in 1954 (published in 1955). In this paper Grobstein described the results obtained when ultrathin millipore filters were interposed between epithelium and mesenchyme from mouse embryonic organ rudiments. This first use of millipore filters led to an explosion of studies, first with millipore and then Nuclepore filters (later called transwell assays) in the investigation of cell interactions and cell migration.

In a 2004 series of articles celebrating the centennial of the *Journal of Experimental Zoology*, Grobstein's work at the NCI was placed in contemporary perspective:

> Grobstein had made the transition from fish to mouse in 1951. Half a century later we are now making the transition back from mouse to fish (and beyond). Grobstein's keen insight into the mechanisms governing differentiation is as contemporary now as it was at the time. The questions that Grobstein defined so long ago are still largely unanswered. Will genomics and proteomics, site-specific mutagenesis and gene knockouts, multi-proton microscopy and high-speed cell sorting, cloned growth factors and signaling cascades provide the answers Grobstein was eager to find? Are we entitled to be optimistic or will another half century be needed before we truly understand the nature of inductive interactions during development? (Auerbach, 2004, p. 116)

Grobstein continued the research studies initiated at the National Institutes of Health (NIH) on his move from the NIH to Stanford University in 1957. Stanford hoped to bring together three of the most prominent figures in biology—Arthur Kornberg, Joshua Lederberg, and Grobstein, who, together, were hoping to make major inroads into the key problem of developmental biology, the role of DNA and genetics as regulators of cell differentiation during embryogenesis. That, in fact, they did not fully succeed is a stark reminder that cell differentiation is a complex, elusive process requiring more than three brilliant minds to unravel.

At Stanford, Grobstein's most notable professional collaborators included Norman Wessels and William Rutter, whose work on pancreas development have become classic examples of epithelial-mesenchymal interactions leading to functional differentiation. Their work has become important for the interpretation of the late-twentieth-, early-twenty-first-century work of Douglas Hanahan and Judah Folkman on the progression of angiogenesis during the development of pancreatic cancer. Frances Kallman was a major contributor to the work of Grobstein during this period, as were a number of undergraduate and graduate students. However, even at Stanford, Grobstein had begun to move from experimental studies into the area of bioethics, and this move was reflected in the transition of one of his undergraduate students, Michael Flower, from studies of embryonic induction begun at Stanford as an undergraduate, continued during Flower's doctoral studies at Wisconsin, and by his subsequent long-term collaboration with Grobstein in the study of ethical considerations in the area of developmental biology.

Contributions in the Area of Bioethics and Public Policy. In 1976 Grobstein became identified with various ethical and safety questions relating to biological research. A meeting in Asilomar in 1975, following a prior Gordon Conference, was convened to discuss guidelines that might be proposed for the then emerging recombinant DNA technology. A 1976 publication by Grobstein in *Science* provided significant new insight into the problems associated with regulating DNA research—problems that, in a way, were still current even thirty years later. From this early beginning of his emergence as an intellectual leader in the area of research ethics and responsibilities, Grobstein could be viewed both as a proponent of and a restraining influence in the area of fetal research. In his 1976 paper, Grobstein's vision is clear:

> [We] should be dominated not by fears but by fundamental and positive objectives (i) to continue expansion of the understanding of genetic phenomena, (ii) to minimize foreseeable hazards, whether to health, essential human relations, or biotic environment; (iii) to consider the priorities to be assigned to realization of positive social benefits from growing genetic engineering capability; (iv) to give "due process" to deeply held values whose accommodation may require time and special attention, and to provide opportunity for "informed consent" or other reaction from the several publics that may otherwise see themselves involuntarily placed at risk. (Grobstein, 1976, p. 1134)

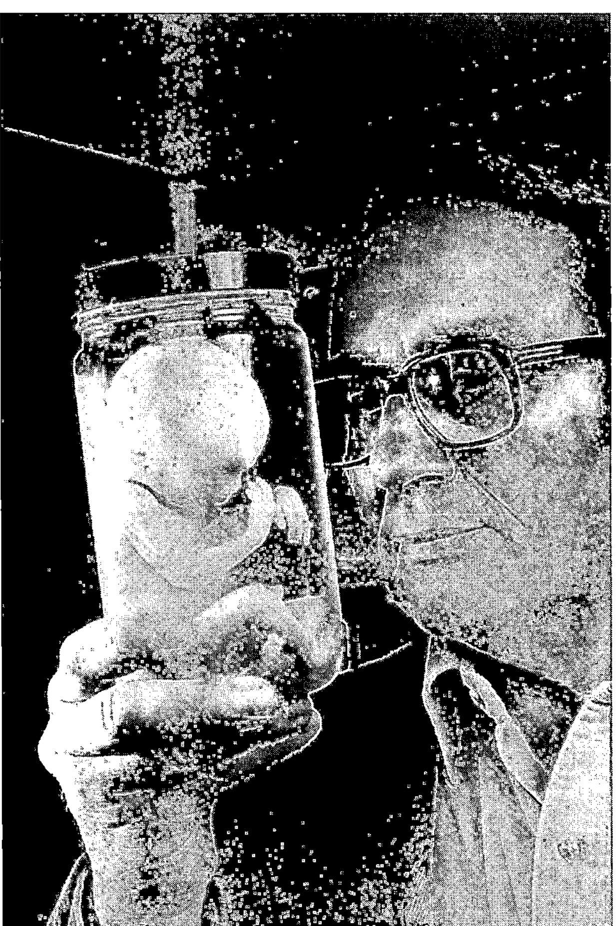

Clifford Grobstein. *Biologist Clifford Grobstein examines a human fetus from about 18 weeks after conception.* © ROGER RESSMEYER/CORBIS.

These words are as apt at the beginning of the twenty-first century when applied to the areas of genetic engineering and stem cell research as they were when DNA manipulations were first begun.

Grobstein's views on in vitro fertilization (the first child following in vitro fertilization was born in July 1978) became widely discussed in the popular press after the appearance of his *Scientific American* article, "External Human Fertilization," in 1979. His discussions ranged from questions such as when does the human embryo become more than groups of cell, tissues, and organs, to ethical and legal questions such as storage of frozen human embryos. More importantly, perhaps, was a paper by Grobstein, Flower, and John Mendeloff, published in

Science in 1983 after five years of this new in vitro technology; that paper became the foundation for much of the legislation and policy determinations up to the beginning of the twenty-first century, when stem cells became the focus of national ethical, legal, and political attention. A further expansion of Grobstein's discussion of embryo storage was published in collaboration with Flower and Mendeloff, appearing in the *New England Journal of Medicine* in 1985. Grobstein's *From Chance to Purpose: An Appraisal of External Human Fertilization* (1981) was chosen as the "Best Publication of the Year" by the Association of American Publishers.

The essence of Grobstein's approach to ethics and public policy has been described by Michael Flower:

> Cliff was especially convinced ... that it was important to sketch out and direct to the appropriate audiences the specific public policy implications that were consistent with what developmental and molecular biologists could tell us about blastocysts, embryos, fetuses, genome structure, and gene expression mechanisms. He didn't hesitate to say what directions for policy-making the science was and was not consistent with. (Personal written communication to the author)

Contributions to Education in Biology and Medicine. Although not as visible as Grobstein's forays into bioethics and public policy, Grobstein's contributions to biology education were equally influential. His book *The Strategy of Life* (1965) showed his interest in the organization of biological systems, and presaged his proposal—outlined in two publications in 1966—of a major reorganization of biology curricula in secondary school and college programs. His ideas were incorporated into the revolution in high school biology teaching seen in the incorporation of the Biological Sciences Curriculum Study (BSCS) series of course outlines initially sponsored by the National Science Foundation.

Grobstein's influence in medical education, already seen in the changes initiated at Stanford University during his tenure there, was exerted forcefully and convincingly in the development of the medical curriculum at UCSD. Grobstein had the opportunity to be at UCSD as the first class of medical students was enrolled and the medical curriculum was established. The curriculum evolved under his influence as he became increasingly influential during his transition from the chair of biology to dean of the medical school and to vice chancellorship. His role in medical education was well described by Norman Wessells:

> Just as Grobstein in the early 1960s had helped formulate and advance the levels-of-organization debate in the life sciences, he used his decanal pulpit to stimulate thinking about medical education. Beginning in 1970, a series of five papers published in such places as *The Journal of Medical Education* and *The British Journal of Medical Education* focused on the two-cultures issue, and more specifically on research, teaching, and curriculum in clinical and basic science departments of medical schools. Those were days when new medical schools were being started in the United States and when both new and old ones were being impacted by the early stages of the revolution in biomedical knowledge that continues ever faster today. Cliff used the UCSD Medical School as example, but really tried to help medical school faculty to think about what kinds of training could best help graduate physicians remain current during their careers as biomedical knowledge expands at unprecedented rates. (Wessells, 2000, Internet page)

An "In Memoriam" article published by the University of California in 2001 captures the essence of Grobstein's contribution to biology education:

> As an academic and scientific leader, Cliff Grobstein helped to reshape the biological community through his strong advocacy of a multilevel research approach involving different disciplines and simultaneous studies at the molecular, cellular and supracellular levels. This was a timely role for him in the 1960s.... In the decades that followed, Cliff's vision became a reality as cell biologists, biochemists, geneticists, molecular biologists, physical and organic chemists, physicists and scientists from other backgrounds all brought to bear their particular insight to the solution of a number of complex phenomena in cell and developmental biology. (*University of California: In Memoriam, 2001*, available from http://oac.cdlib.org/texts/)

Personal Life. Grobstein's children, Paul and Joan, were born while Grobstein and his wife Rose Gruyer, a social worker, lived in Bethesda and subsequently at Stanford. Paul Grobstein has become a distinguished neurobiologist and chair of biology at Bryn Mawr. Joan Grobstein is a practicing physician in Philadelphia, specializing in neonatal and perinatal medicine. A second marriage coincided with Grobstein's acceptance of the biology professorship at UCSD. His second wife, Ruth Hirsch Beloff, was a well-known radiologist who later became founder and interim director of the Ida M. and Cecil H. Green Cancer Center at the Scripps Clinic in La Jolla, California. For thirty-two years, Ruth Grobstein was a collaborator, critic, and supporter of Clifford Grobstein, and she and her children protected Grobstein as his manifestations of Alzheimer's disease became increasingly debilitating. In 2005, Ruth Grobstein published the widely acclaimed

The Breast Cancer Book: What You Need to Know to Make Informed Decisions (Yale University Press).

During the course of his career, Grobstein held research appointments at the NCI, professorships at Stanford University and UCSD, as well as chairmanship of the biology department, deanship in the medical school, and vice chancellorship for university relations and special programs at UCSD. Recognition of his status and achievement was shown by his election to the National Academy of Sciences, the Institute of Medicine, and the American Academy of Arts and Sciences. He received many awards including a "best book" award from the Association of American Publishers and the Brachet Medal of the Belgium Royal Society. His public service included leadership positions in numerous governmental policy committees, panels convened by the National Science Foundation and the National Institutes of Health, and study groups sponsored by the National Academy of Sciences.

Grobstein was one of the preeminent scientists of the twentieth century. Aside from being a brilliant experimentalist, he was a superb teacher and a warm person who cherished his role as a mentor and friend to young students. It was through the combination of his breadth of knowledge, his ability to express himself clearly, and the strength of his personality that he was able to communicate not only with students and colleagues but with a wider audience, thereby influencing science education and public policy.

BIBLIOGRAPHY

WORKS BY GROBSTEIN

"Inductive Epithelio-Mesenchymal Interaction in Cultured Organ Rudiments of the Mouse." *Science* 118 (1953): 52–55.

"Morphogenetic Interaction between Embryonic Mouse Tissues Separated by a Membrane Filter." *Nature* 172 (1953): 869–871.

"Tissue Interaction in the Morphogenesis of Mouse Embryonic Rudiments In Vitro." In *Aspects of Synthesis and Order in Growth,* edited by Dorothea Rudnick. Princeton, NJ: Princeton University Press, 1954.

With Robert Auerbach. "Inductive Interaction of Embryonic Tissues after Dissociation and Reaggregation." *Experimental Cell Research 15* (1958): 384–397.

"Levels and Ontogeny." *American Scientist* 50 (1959): 46–58.

"Cytodifferentiation and Its Control." *Science* 143 (1964): 643–650.

With William J. Rutter and Norman K. Wessells. "Control of Specific Synthesis in the Developing Pancreas." *National Cancer Institute Monograph* 13 (1964): 51–65.

The Strategy of Life. San Francisco: W.H. Freeman, 1965.

"New Patterns in the Organization of Biology." *American Zoologist* 6 (1966): 621–626.

"Recombinant DNA Research: Beyond the NIH Guidelines." *Science* 194 (1976): 1133–1135.

A Double Image of the Double Helix: The Recombinant-DNA Debate. San Francisco: W.H. Freeman, 1979.

From Chance to Purpose: An Appraisal of External Human Fertilization. Reading, MA: Addison-Wesley, 1981.

With Michael Flower and John Mendeloff. "External Human Fertilization: An Evaluation of Policy." *Science* 222 (1983): 127–133.

With Michael Flower and John Mendeloff. "Frozen Embryos: Policy Issues." *New England Journal of Medicine* 312, no. 24 (1985): 1584–1588.

Science and the Unborn: Choosing Human Futures. New York: Basic Books, 1988.

OTHER SOURCES

Auerbach, Robert. "From Fish to Mouse: Clifford Grobstein's Work at the National Cancer Institute, 1951–1957." *Journal of Experimental Zoology* 301A, no. 2 (2004): 115–117.

Flower, Michael. Personal communication.

Helinski, Donald R., Daniel Steinberg, and Norman K. Wessells. "Clifford Grobstein, Biology: San Diego." *California Digital Library* (2001): 1–3.

Nanney, David L. "Biology Texts." In *Tilting at Windmills: Educational Misadventures in the Big Ten.* Available from http://www.life.uiuc.edu/nanney/autobiography/index.html.

Wessells, Norman K. "Clifford Grobstein, 1916–1998." *National Academy of Sciences Biographical Memoirs* 78 (2000): 65–93. Available from http://books.nap.edu/html/biomems/cgrobstein.html.

Robert Auerbach

GROSSMANN, MARCEL (*b.* Budapest, Hungary, 9 April 1878; *d.* Zurich, Switzerland, 7 September 1936), *mathematics.* For the original article on Grossmann see *DSB*, vol. 5.

Grossmann's main achievements concerned geometry, but he was also deeply engaged in mathematical education, and even interested in politics. He was one of Einstein's most important student friends, contributing to Einstein's understanding of tensor calculus, a necessary requirement for relativity theory.

Life Overview. The Grossmann family was originally from Höngg, Switzerland. Marcel Grossmann was the son of the merchant Jules Grossmann and Katharina Henriette Grossman (nee Lichtenhahn). Marcel was born in Budapest, where his family lived until he was fifteen years old. Then his family moved to Switzerland and Grossmann attended high school in Basel. After his examinations in 1896, he began to study at the Eidgenössische

Technische Hochschule (ETH) in Zurich. His main professors in geometry had been Wilhelm Fiedler and Carl Friedrich Geiser; Geiser had organized the first International Mathematical Congress in 1897 in Zurich. Grossmann's fellow students in class of Section VIa (for teachers of mathematic and physics) were Louis Kollros, Jakob Ehrat, Louis-Gustave Du Pasquier, Mileva Maric, and Albert Einstein. Grossmann graduated in 1900, and immediately afterward became assistant to Fiedler. One year later he was professor of mathematics at the cantonal school in Frauenfeld; in 1903 he married Anna Keller.

In 1902 Grossmann earned his doctorate with a thesis "Über die metrischen Eigenschaften Kollinearer Gebilde" (Frauenfeld, 1902), where he presented major constructions within hyperbolic and elliptic geometry; he quoted especially Fiedler, Jakob Steiner, and Heinrich Liebmann; and textbooks of Felix Klein, George Salmon, and Fiedler, and Alfred Clebsch Ferdinand von Lindemann. Grossmann received his degree from the university of Zurich, because the ETH was not yet able to accept mathematical dissertations.

In the following years Grossmann published many articles and textbooks on geometry, some of the latter in several editions. His main fields were analytical, descriptive, projective, and non-Euclidean geometry. Four students wrote doctoral theses under his auspices

In 1905 Grossman moved to the Oberrealschule in Basel and became privatdocent at the university. In 1907 Grossmann was appointed professor of descriptive geometry at the ETH, a position which he held until 1927. He had to retire prematurely, because he fell ill; he died nine years later in 1936. He was succeeded by his former assistant Walter Saxer.

Grossmann was also interested in organization, and together with others in 1910 he founded the Swiss Mathematical Society. He served as its president during the years 1916 and 1917. In 1911 Grossmann published an important Report concerning lecturing on mathematics; Grossmann was deeply involved with pedagogical problems and published numerous papers to ameliorate instruction. During World War I, Grossmann worked for a better unification of the French and German parts of Switzerland, becoming co-editor of an important newspaper, the *Neue Schweizer Zeitung*.

Marcel Grossmann. SPL / PHOTO RESEARCHERS, INC.

Grossmann's Relationship with Einstein. Grossmann and Einstein had been fellow students at the ETH. They had attended Geiser's lectures on differential geometry, which played a crucial role in Einstein's later work: "Professor Geiser's lectures on differential geometry, true masterpieces of the pedagogical art, fascinated me and later were very helpful to me in the search for general relativity" (Einstein, 1955). Grossmann's lecture notes are preserved in the archive of the ETH. Einstein was unable to find an academic position after graduation. He wrote, "The greatest thing that Marcel Grossmann did for me as a friend was this: About a year after the end of our studies, with his father's help he recommended me to the Director (Friedrich Haller) of the Swiss Patent Office, which was then still called 'The Office for Intellectual Property.' After a thorough oral examination, Herr Haller hired me" (Einstein, 1955). True to his earlier promise, in 1905 Einstein dedicated his dissertation, "Eine neue Bestimmung der Moleküldimensionen," to "my friend Marcel Grossmann."

In 1912, when Einstein moved from Prague back to Zurich, he was already aware of the analogy between the non-flat space-time he was introducing in his new theory of gravitation, and Gauss's surface theory, a full account of which Geiser had presented. The problem was to find a four-dimensional version of Carl Friedrich Gauss's theory. "With this problem in mind, I visited my old student friend Marcel Grossmann, who in the meantime had become Professor of Mathematics at the Swiss Polytechnic. He caught fire immediately, even though as a true mathematician he took a somewhat skeptical attitude to physics. … [H]e was indeed quite ready to collaborate on the problem with me, but with the limitation that he would take no responsibility for any claims and interpretations of a physical nature. He reviewed the literature and soon discovered that the mathematical problem had already been solved, in particular by Riemann, Ricci and Levi-Cività" (Einstein, 1955). Gregorio Ricci-Curbastro and Tullio Levi-Cività had developed a useful formalism, the absolute differential calculus (tensor calculus), which Einstein and Grossmann adopted. On 9 September 1913 the two presented their first lectures on this subject. These were published in the same year in the *Vierteljahrsschrift der Naturforschenden Gesellschaft in Zürich,* vol. 58, under the titles: "Physikalische Grundlagen einer Gravitationstheorie" (pp. 284–290) and "Mathematische Begriffsbildungen zur Gravitationstheorie" (pp. 291–297). Shortly afterward, their paper "Entwurf einer verallgemeinerten Relativitätstheorie und einer Theorie der Gravitation" followed, the first mathematical part by Grossmann and the second physical part by Einstein (*Zeitschrift für Mathematik und Physik* 62, 1913–1914, pp. 225–261). In 1915 they published their last joint paper, "Kovarianzeigenschaften der Feldgleichungen" (*Zeitschrift für Mathematik und Physik* 63, 1915, pp. 215–225).

In 1914 Einstein moved to Berlin and continued to work alone on general relativity until its definitive formulation at the end of 1915. Einstein praised Grossmann's contribution with warm words in his main publication on the general relativity theory in 1916: "Grossmann supported me through his help, not only in sparing me the study of the relevant mathematical literature, but also in the search for the gravitational field equations" (Einstein, 1995, vol. 6, p. 284).

Near the end of his life, Einstein paid a final tribute to his long-departed friend:

> In these student years I developed a true friendship with a fellow student, Marcel Grossmann. Once a week as a special treat, I went with him to the Cafe Metropol on the Limmatquai; our discussions concerned not only our studies, but ranged far beyond over all the topics that could interest young people who kept their eyes wide open. Not such a vagabond and off-beat character as I, he was anchored in the Swiss milieu without thereby losing any of his inner independence. In addition, he possessed in full measure just those gifts that I lacked: the ability to grasp things quickly and a sense of order in everything. He not only attended all the lectures that we were supposed to, but his notes on them were worked out in such excellent fashion, that his notebooks could very well have been published. In preparation for examinations, he lent these notebooks to me and they served as a life preserver; I would rather not speculate on what would have happened to me without them. (Einstein, 1955)

SUPPLEMENTARY BIBLIOGRAPHY

WORKS BY GROSSMAN

Die fundamentalen Konstruktionen der nichteuklidischen Geometrie. Programm der Thurgauischen Kantonsschule vom Jahre 1903/04.

Analytische Geometrie. Basel: Helbling & Lichtenhahn 1906.

Einführung in die Darstellende Geometrie. Leitfaden für den Unterricht an höheren Lehranstalten. Basel: Helbling & Lichtenhann, 1906; 2nd ed. 1912; 3rd ed. 1917.

Der *mathematische Unterricht an der Eidgenössischen Technischen Hochschule.* Basel und Genf: Georg & Co., 1911.

Darstellende Geometrie. Leipzig: B.G. Teubner, 1915; 2nd ed., 1921; 3rd ed., 1932.

Elemente der darstellenden Geometrie. Leipzig: B. G. Teubner, 1917.

Darstellende Geometrie für Maschineningenieure. Berlin: Springer Verlag, 1927.

OTHER SOURCES

Einstein, Albert. "Erinnerungen—Souvenirs." *Schweizerische Hochschulzeitung* 28 (1955): 145–153. Reprinted as "Autobiograpische Skizze." In *Helle Zeit–Dunkle Zeit,* edited by Carl Seelig. Zurich: Europa, 1956.

———."Einstein on Gravitation and Relativity: The Collaboration with Marcel Grossman." In *The Collected Papers of Albert Einstein,* Vol. 4. Princeton, NJ: Princeton University Press, 1995.

Kollros, L. "Prof. Dr. Marcel Grossmann." *Verhandlungen der Schweizerischen naturforschenden Gesellschaft* 118 (1937): 325–329.

Reich, Karin. "Einsteins und Großmanns Zusammenarbeit." *Die Entwicklung des Tensorkalküls.* Basel: Birkhäuser, 1994.

Saxer, Walter. "Marcel Grossmann." *Vierteljahrsschrift der Naturforschenden Gesellschaft in Zürich* 81 (1936): 322–326.

Karin Reich

GÜRSEY, FEZA (*b.* Istanbul, Turkey, 7 April 1921; *d.* New Haven, Connecticut, 13 April 1992), *theoretical physics, nonlinear chiral Lagrangians, SU(6) symmetry, conformal invariance in field theory, exceptional groups, gauge theories.*

Gürsey's work in theories of elementary particles and general relativity is characterized by his skill in discovering symmetries in physical systems and his ability to express them mathematically through group theoretical methods, an approach pioneered by Hermann Weyl and Eugene Wigner in the 1930s. As specific examples, one may cite the nonlinear chiral sigma model, his proposal (with Luigi Radicati) for classifying hadrons into representations of the SU(6) algebra, the de Sitter and the conformal groups in relativity, and grand unified theories based on exceptional Lie groups.

Youth and Education. Feza Gürsey's father, Reşit Gürsey, was a military doctor of wide-ranging intellectual and scientific interests, in pursuit of which he traveled to Vienna in the 1920s to learn about quantum mechanics. His mother, Remziye Hisar, received a PhD in chemistry at the Sorbonne in the same decade, when it was highly unusual for European women to do so, let alone women from more traditionally conservative societies. The parents had met in post–World War I revolution- and war-torn Baku, Azerbaijan, having independently arrived there from Istanbul. After receiving his primary education in Paris and secondary education at the elite Galatasaray Lycée in Istanbul, Feza Gürsey obtained his degree in physics-mathematics from the Science Faculty of Istanbul University in 1944. He worked briefly as an assistant at Istanbul University before receiving a Turkish Ministry of Education scholarship to do a PhD in physics at Imperial College, London. His 1950 study of the statistical mechanical analysis of a one-dimensional classical rectilinear assembly of interacting particles became relevant in the 1990s to the study of carbon nanotubes. He returned to Istanbul University as an assistant after spending 1950–1951 as a postdoctoral fellow at Cambridge University, England, and married Suha Pamir, also an assistant in the Istanbul University physics department, in 1952.

Istanbul, Brookhaven, Princeton, and Columbia. Between 1951 and 1956 in Istanbul, Gürsey published papers on the conformal group, quaternions, the classical spinning electron and the Dirac equation, and a conformally invariant version of Heisenberg's nonlinear spinor theory. The conformal group includes scale transformations and inversions of spacetime coordinates in addition to the rotations and Lorentz transformations from one inertial frame to another that define the Lorentz group; it is relevant for physical systems without a built-in mass or length scale. These subjects were by no means mainstream research topics for the newly developing area of particle physics, which was at that time focused on identifying new unstable particles found in cosmic rays or accelerators and understanding their interactions. The significance of the conformal group was widely appreciated much later, first upon the observation of scale invariance in deep-inelastic electron or neutrino-nucleon scattering experiments in the 1970s, and then in the 1980s, when conformal symmetry was shown to be sufficient for a providing a complete solution of two dimensional field-theoretic problems. Gürsey, with his student Sophocles Orfanidis, also anticipated the latter results in a pioneering paper in 1973. John Wheeler once wrote, "Gürsey, as a largely self-educated physicist, has a most valuable independence of point of view and originality" (read by Yale Prof. Vernon Hugues at the Feza Gürsey memorial service, 20 May 1992). In the light of Gürsey's later work, it appears that a good part of this self-education took place in the 1951–1956 Istanbul period.

In 1957, Gürsey caught the attention of Wolfgang Pauli by a paper suggesting that the SU(2) isospin symmetry of hadrons, the strongly interacting particles, might emerge from mixing half-integer spin particles with their antiparticles. Pauli had originally introduced such a mixing, which came to be called the Pauli-Gürsey transformation, while examining the theory of beta-decay proposed by Enrico Fermi. Pauli and Werner Heisenberg attempted to incorporate this mechanism of symmetry generation into Heisenberg's theory of a fundamental spinor field with a non-linear self-interaction, but the idea proved unfruitful in that context. However, generalized currents capable of simultaneously creating or destroying a pair of spin-1/2 particles, which is an essential feature of Pauli-Gürsey symmetry, were seen to be inevitable in the context of grand unified theories of strong, weak and electromagnetic interactions introduced by Howard Georgi and Sheldon Glashow and by Jogesh Pati and Abdus Salam in 1974.

From 1957 to 1961, Gürsey worked at the Brookhaven National Laboratory, the Institute for Advanced Study, Princeton, and Columbia University, meeting and collaborating with J. Robert Oppenheimer, Eugene Wigner and Tsung Dao Lee. His 1959 nonlinear sigma model is based on a proton-neutron isospin SU(2) doublet interacting with pions, particles which were at the time believed to be the main carriers of the strong force. The nucleon doublet is initially massless, and can thus generate two independent SU(2) symmetries through left and right-handed currents. The pions and their interactions with the nucleons are brought in via a nonlinear representation of this $SU(2)_L \times SU(2)_R$ *chiral,* or handed symmetry. The nonlinear interaction gives masses to the nucleons, but keeps the pions massless as required by the observed (partial) conservation of the weak pseudovector current. The model, while never claiming to be a fundamental theory of hadrons, introduced several important ideas: the first explicit example of a spontaneously broken symmetry, and the attendant appearance of massless bosons perhaps being the most important. Shortly afterward it was realized by Yoichiro Nambu, Jeffrey Goldstone, and others that massless bosons would always accompany spontaneous symmetry breakdown when a system randomly settles into one of its many possible lowest energy states.

Middle East Technical University, Ankara. In 1961, Gürsey left Columbia University to take up a professorship at the newly founded Middle East Technical University in Ankara, Turkey, where he worked until 1969, except for brief visits to the Institute for Advanced Study at Princeton, the Brookhaven National Laboratory, and Yale University. He initially returned to General Relativity, reformulating the theory so that an overall factor in the metric of the universe serves as a cosmological scalar field and gives rise to effects expected from Mach's principle. The novel scalar-field energy-momentum tensor introduced by Gürsey in this work was rediscovered about a decade later in studies of scale invariance. His work on spin-1/2 particles in de Sitter space also dates from this period; de Sitter space has attracted general interest since 1981, first upon Alan Guth's proposal of an rapidly inflating early universe scenario, and later with observations that the expansion of the universe is accelerating.

Gürsey's best-known work from this period is his identification of hadronic SU(6) symmetry in a paper he wrote with Luigi Radicati while visiting the Brookhaven National Laboratory in 1964. The idea that all hadrons are made up of hypothetical u, d, and s quarks had been introduced earlier by Murray Gell-Mann and George Zweig. Gürsey and Radicati proposed to extend the resulting SU(3) symmetry to SU(6) by considering the spin up and down states of each quark as separate particles. The surprising ability of SU(6) to explain and correlate a large mass of data strengthened the view that quarks were real physical constituents of hadrons, and not just mathematically useful but fictitious constructs. The success of SU(6), however, pointed to deeper problems. For example, the three-quark wavefunction for a proton or neutron seemed to be in conflict with the sacrosanct Pauli exclusion principle. Furthermore, confining the quarks to the volume of a proton would be expected to give them relativistic energies, at which only the total angular momentum of a quark would be conserved, while its spin by itself would not be. However, attempts to formulate a relativistic generalization of SU(6) not only failed to improve agreement with experiments, but also were proven to be forbidden on seemingly unassailable theoretical grounds, a situation reminiscent of aerodynamics proofs that the bumblebee should not be able to fly. The justification for SU(6) came ten years later when the field theory of strong interactions between quarks was formulated. The theory that has since become commonly known as Quantum Chromodynamics, or QCD for short, solves the Pauli exclusion problem by introducing a new degree of freedom called *color* for each quark. It also has the feature that the quark-quark interaction weakens as quarks get closer, explaining the separate conservation of spin and the success of SU(6).

Yale University. In 1969 Gürsey took up a professorship at Yale, filling the position of Gregory Breit who retired. He was appointed to the J. Willard Gibbs chair in 1977, holding the position until his own retirement in 1991. In this period, while continuing to work on non-linear chiral models, conformal symmetry and general relativity (in particular, on Kerr-Schild type metrics), he renewed his interest in quaternionic and octonionic structures, and suggested possible uses for them in physics. Pascual Jordan, John von Neumann, and Eugene Wigner, together with Abraham Albert, had already in the 1930s examined algebras of 3x3 real, complex, quaternionic and octonionic matrices subject to a non-commutative symmetric Jordan product. Their hope was to find alternative formulations of quantum mechanics through such Jordan algebras. From 1973 onwards Gürsey drew attention to the close links between the Exceptional Lie groups (F_4, E_6, E_7, E_8) and Jordan algebras, and proposed models of Grand Unified Theories (GUTs) based on E_6 and E_7. In the following three decades, evidence accumulated that if some version of superstring/M-Theory succeeds as a quantum theory of all known interactions, octonions and Exceptional groups will figure prominently in it. From the phenomenological point of view, the most promising GUT groups are SU(5), SO(10) and E_6, where the first two may be also regarded as the exceptional groups E_4 and E_5. One version of string theory, which aims also to include gravitation, naturally leads to the gauge group E_8xE_8. The E-series also appears in the reduction of eleven dimensional supergravity to lower dimensions. Among the many other suggestive connections between octonions and eleven dimensional superstring/M-Theory, one may mention that seven dimensions have to be compactified into a manifold of G_2 holonomy in the reduction to four spacetime dimensions. The smallest exceptional group G_2 happens to be the automorphism group of octonion multiplications.

Feza Gürsey was given the Science Award of the Scientific and Technological Research Council of Turkey (TUBITAK) in 1969, the J. R. Oppenheimer Prize (with Sheldon Glashow) and the A. Cressey Morrison Prize (with Robert Griffiths) in Natural Sciences in 1977, the Albert Einstein Award in 1979, the College de France Award in 1981, the title of Commendatore by the Italian government in 1984, and the Wigner Medal of the Group Theory and Fundamental Physics Foundation in 1986. The Wigner Medal has been awarded biennially since 1977 at the International Colloquium on Group Theoretical Methods in Physics, a conference series Gürsey himself started in 1962 in Istanbul. He died in New Haven, Connecticut, on 13 April 1992. In recognition of his leading role in starting a school of theoretical physics in Turkey through the students he trained, TUBITAK, jointly with Boğaziçi University, established the Feza Gürsey Institute for research in theoretical physics and mathematics in 1996.

BIBLIOGRAPHY

WORKS BY GÜRSEY

"Classical Statistical Mechanics of a Rectilinear Assembly." *Proceedings of the Cambridge Philosophical Society* 46 (1950): 182–194.

"On the Symmetries of Strong and Weak Interactions." *Nuovo Cimento* 16 (1960): 230–240.

"Reformulation of General Relativity in Accordance with Mach's Principle." *Annals of Physics* 24 (1963): 211–242.

"Introduction to Group Theory." In *Relativity, Groups and Topology*, edited by C. DeWitt and Bryce DeWitt. New York: Gordon and Breach, 1964. Lectures delivered at Les Houches during the 1963 session of the Summer School of Theoretical Physics, University of Grenoble.

"Introduction to the de Sitter Group." In *Group Theoretical Concepts and Methods in Elementary Particle Physics; Lectures*, edited by Feza Gürsey. New York: Gordon and Breach, 1964. Proceedings of the Istanbul Summer School of 1962.

With Luigi Radicati. "Spin and Unitary Spin Independence of Strong Interactions." *Physics Review Letters* 13 (1964): 299–301.

With Sophocles Orfanidis. "Conformal Invariance and Field Theory in Two Dimensions." *Physics Review* D7 (1973): 2414–2437.

With Pierre Ramond and Pierre Sikivie. "A Universal Gauge Theory Model Based on E_6." *Physics Letters* 60B (1976): 177–180.

With Hsiung Chia Tze. "Complex and Quaternionic Analyticity in Chiral and Gauge Theories I." *Annals of Physics* (1980): 128: 29–130.

With Yoram Alhassid and Francesco Iachello. "Group Theory Approach to Scattering." *Annals of Physics* 148 (1983): 346–380.

With B. S. Balakrishna and Kameshwar Wali. "Noncommutative Geometry and Higgs Mechanism in the Standard Model." *Physics Letters* B254 (1991) 430–434.

With Chia-Hsiung Tze. *On the Role of Division, Jordan and Related Algebras in Particle Physics.* Singapore: World Scientific, 1996.

OTHER SOURCE

Bars, Itzhak, Alan Chodos, and Chia-Hsiung Tze, eds. *Symmetries in Particle Physics.* New York and London: Plenum Press, 1984.

Cihan Saclioglu

GUTOWSKY, HERBERT SANDER

(*b.* Bridgman, Michigan, 8 November 1919; *d.* Urbana, Illinois, 13 January 2000), *chemistry, chemical physics, organic chemistry, nuclear magnetic resonance, molecular spectroscopy.*

Gutowsky contributed decisively to the introduction of nuclear magnetic resonance (NMR) into chemistry. In the early 1950s he participated in research that enabled more powerful elucidation of molecular structure and dynamics and in which NMR was probably the most instrumental technique. Throughout his lifetime he was active in molecular spectroscopy, delving into the phenomenology of new effects and designing novel methodologies.

Early Life and Education. Gutowsky was the second youngest of seven children of German immigrants to the United States, Otto Gutowsky and Hattie Meyer, who owned a farm near Bridgman, Michigan. During the first years of the Great Depression, the Gutowskys sold their property and moved to Hammond, Indiana, where they bought a gasoline station. While in high school, Gutowsky supported himself by delivering newspapers. Inspired and financially supported by his older brothers, Gutowsky chose to study the sciences and entered Indiana University at Bloomington. Fascinated by astronomy, and particularly by the teaching of Frank Kelley Edmondson, he received an undergraduate assistantship. Though greatly impressed by the enthusiasm and intellectual atmosphere in astronomy, he was aware that the economic prospects of a career in chemistry were much better, which persuaded him to opt for a major in that field. In 1940 he graduated with honors. In Gutowsky's senior year at Indiana, a tutorial on Linus Pauling's theory of the chemical bond taught by Fred Stitt, a former PhD student of Pauling, had a great and lasting influence on him.

For graduate studies, Gutowsky went to the University of California at Berkeley, where he considered himself a misfit because of his incongruous social background. His research, undertaken with Willard F. Libby in the field of isotope separation, was not successful. In the summer of 1941, as a member of the Army Reserve Officer Training Corps that he had joined at Indiana, he applied for active duty. He spent the next four years working for the Los Angeles subbranch of the San Francisco District of the U.S. Army Chemical Warfare Service. He was responsible for the subcontracting and the supervising of small companies that produced chemical weapons. He left the Chemical Warfare Service with the rank of captain in 1945.

During the war he contracted diabetes (which eventually led to his discharge for medical reasons), and for treatment he occasionally returned to Berkeley. There a young faculty member, the chemical physicist Kenneth S. Pitzer, accepted him as a master's student. Gutowsky's studies, on electron deficient molecules, were completed in February 1946. He had investigated the bond types of molecules that have fewer valence electrons than normally required to fill their orbitals. These were compounds whose bonds were not formed by the usual sharing of electrons, but nevertheless were neither ionic nor metal-like. Using the group of aluminum alkyls, Gutowsky and Pitzer observed and explained dimerization: the combination of two identical molecules to form a single one. This was based on the classical method of freezing point lowering, though they also employed spectroscopic evidence available from other research groups. Pitzer, in his general vision of quantum chemistry, emphasized the importance of observable quantities that could be related to the core of a theory based on mathematical equations. Thus, with his master's thesis Gutowsky undertook the type of study that would remain with him during his entire career: elucidating the electronic structures of molecules with instrumental techniques by making use of advanced theories of the chemical bond.

Having lived in the Midwest and in California, Gutowsky chose for further graduate studies one of the foremost scientific institutions, Harvard University, in Cambridge, Massachusetts. There, pragmatic philosophy had a great impact on science, as so influentially advocated in the interwar years by the operationalism of the physicist Percy W. Bridgman. Bridgman defined the objects of physical inquiry by the operations needed to measure them. This approach was shared by the chemical physicist E. Bright Wilson, formerly Pitzer's laboratory section instructor at the California Institute of Technology and the coauthor, with Pauling, of a textbook, *Introduction to Quantum Mechanics* (1935). Wilson explicitly based the criteria for success of scientific theories on their ability to generate explanatory models and afford hypotheses that could be experimentally studied. Foremost, he stressed the scientist's obligation to achieve control over the effects studied as completely as possible; this was most often achieved with the help of sophisticated instrumentation. Though he was not accepted as Wilson's graduate student, Gutowsky followed this style of molecular spectroscopy during his entire career. His PhD supervisor, the physical chemist George B. Kistiakowsky, who had taken part in the Manhattan Project at Los Alamos, New Mexico, and later became science advisor to Presidents Dwight D. Eisenhower, John F. Kennedy, and Lyndon B. Johnson, gave Gutowsky a quite unrealistic problem with his first assignment—the structure of the methyl radical—a problem that remained an unsolved riddle for many years to come. However, this project did provide Gutowsky with the opportunity to become familiar with the operational modes of an infrared spectrometer and introduced him to the problem sets and methods of molecular spectroscopy.

Nuclear Magnetic Resonance Spectroscopy. Under pressure to find a suitable subject to complete his PhD thesis, Gutowsky stumbled onto an exciting and novel technique for elucidating molecular structures whose origins lay in war-related radar research and nuclear physics, namely, nuclear magnetic resonance (NMR). It had just been independently developed by Edward M. Purcell, Henry C. Torrey, and Robert V. Pound at Harvard and the Massachusetts Institute of Technology (MIT), both in Cambridge, and by Felix Bloch, William Hansen, and Martin Packard at Stanford University in California. The NMR spectrometer basically consisted of a radiofrequency (rf) generator, a magnet, and an rf detector. NMR is based on nuclear spin, a quantum mechanical effect best visualized as a rotation of the nucleus. Together with the nuclear charge, the spin imparts a magnetic moment to the nucleus. Placed inside a strong magnetic field, some of the nuclei precess in the direction of the magnetic field with a certain frequency, depending on the particular type of nucleus and the strength of the magnetic field applied. In the case of hydrogen, the spin of the protons can have two values, +½ and -½, corresponding to the existence of two energy levels. If a weaker electromagnetic field is irradiated perpendicular to the direction of the strong magnetic field, and if the frequency of the electromagnetic radiation matches the difference of the energy levels, absorption or emission of radiation occurs: the nuclei are in resonance.

Purcell and Bloch designed NMR as a high-precision technique for the measurement of nuclear magnetic moments, and thus they firmly embedded the technique in nuclear physics. In addition, NMR almost instantly became an important method in molecular spectroscopy, making use of the now reliably and precisely accessible radio frequency range of the electromagnetic spectrum. In particular, the group around Purcell studied the structures and dynamics of solids and, through a contact provided by Kistiakowsky, Gutowsky in late 1947 cooperated with Purcell's graduate student, George Pake. Pake had just developed an NMR method for studying the relative positions of protons in the crystalline water of solid gypsum that supplemented x-ray measurements. Gutowsky and Pake were supposed to tackle the structure of diborane (B_2H_6), one of the electron deficient molecules that Gutowsky had become familiar with during work for his master's thesis at Berkeley, and a classic problem since Robert S. Mulliken applied a theoretical treatment in 1935. Chemists were unable to decide between two possible structures: a bridge structure, in which two of the six hydrogen atoms are located between the two boron atoms, and an ethane-like structure, with all hydrogen atoms being equivalent. Unfortunately, Gutowsky and Pake's experiments did not lead to interpretable results, and in 1948 and 1950, respectively, the rival techniques of infrared spectroscopy and microwave spectroscopy settled the question in favor of the bridge structure.

However, in need of interpretable data, Gutowsky and Pake extended their project beyond diborane by

Gutowsky

investigating structurally related compounds. Here, they made the surprising observation that the broad lines being studied in investigations of solids showed characteristic peaks. (The broadening of the resonance lines was caused by dipolar interactions of the nuclei in a rigid lattice.) Their conclusion was that molecular motions in "plastic" solids narrowed the broad lines. Thus, in searching for a method to study static molecular structures, they additionally found a technique suitable for investigating molecular dynamics, in particular rotational motions in solids. This was a topic of great interest to the chemical physics community of that time, and although their method soon was superseded by the quite different NMR technique of Nicolaas Bloembergen, Purcell, and Pound, it showed the general feasibility of NMR for studying such topics.

During the time that he worked with Pake, Gutowsky was not permitted to tune the instrument. His tasks were those deemed suitable for a chemist: the synthesis of the sample compounds and the design of the cryostat employed to study compounds that were not solids at room temperature. Significantly, throughout his life, Gutowsky felt that chemists were inferior to theoretical physicists, as they were dealing with less fundamental laws in science. Nevertheless, chemists had different research agendas, and they looked for different answers than those sought by physicists. For this reason it was important that chemists become independent of their colleagues in physics with regard to the uses of physical instrumentation. They could achieve this independence only by securing control of the instrument and by being able to interpret the results in chemical, and not only physical, terms.

The Chemical Shift. It was his own professional independence that Gutowsky set out to achieve when, in September 1948, he joined the faculty of the Department of Chemistry of the University of Illinois at Urbana. Initially, however, he had to acquiesce to dependence on others, albeit of a different kind than at Harvard. The reason that he had been hired was not his promise in NMR-related matters, but his experience in infrared spectroscopy. At Urbana, Roger Adams, head of one of the most successful American groups in organic chemistry, clearly recognized the importance of the new spectroscopic methods for research on structures of organic molecules. During the war, organic chemists at the University of Illinois had become used to the benefits of a Perkin-Elmer infrared spectrometer. Gutowsky replaced the spectroscopist in charge of the spectrometer and was assigned to managing a service laboratory for the organic chemists, assisted by a technician. This work made Gutowsky familiar with the needs and expectations of organic chemists. Furthermore, infrared spectroscopy provided a model that could be emulated for the future development of NMR.

In Urbana, Gutowsky planned to build up a research program based on structural studies of solids along the same lines as at Harvard. For that purpose he constructed his own NMR spectrometer, with funds provided first by the Graduate Research Board of the University of Illinois and then by the Research Corporation, a nationwide foundation for the support of basic research. In the late 1940s, the construction of such a high-technology instrument was not an easy task for a young instructor in chemistry. Indeed, after the magnet had been installed in October 1949, it took Gutowsky several months to get the instrument working. In general, problems with the electronic equipment hampered progress, making broad-line studies of solids impossible at first. But in March 1950, the discovery of chemical shifts in NMR spectral lines—independently by Walter Knight at Brookhaven Laboratory, William C. Dickinson of the MIT Research Laboratory of Electronics, and Warren Proctor and Fu Chun Yu in Bloch's group at Stanford—directed Gutowsky's research in an unexpected and very fruitful direction: NMR studies of molecules in liquids. The discovery of the chemical shift threatened to disturb the precision measurements of nuclear moments underway in several physics laboratories because it demonstrated that the resonance frequencies of the nuclei under scrutiny depended on the electronic environment of the atoms in the molecule. For the physicists this was an unpleasant surprise. For the chemists it was exactly what they needed to use NMR as a probe for the structures of molecules. It proved to be the beginning of a stellar rise of NMR in organic chemistry and other areas of the chemical sciences and technologies.

Gutowsky, together with his first graduate student, Charles J. Hoffman, extended the validity of the chemical shift measurements by observing the shift with protons. In addition, Gutowsky and Hoffman made suggestions for the refinement of the quantum physical theory of the chemical shift, originally provided by the Harvard physicist Norman Ramsey. In correlating the chemical shift data of fluorine compounds with the electronegativity of the atoms bound to fluorine in the respective molecules, Gutowsky and Hoffman laid the empirical groundwork for an important simplification of Ramsey's formula, achieved in 1953 by Apollo Saika in Gutowsky's group and his Illinois colleague, the physicist Charles P. Slichter.

In 1951 Gutowsky and his group embarked on a research project that firmly embedded NMR in one of the most prestigious and progressive areas in chemistry of the time, physical organic chemistry. Meanwhile, a group of three graduate students in the laboratory, David McCall, Bruce McGarvey, and Leon (Lee) H. Meyer, together with

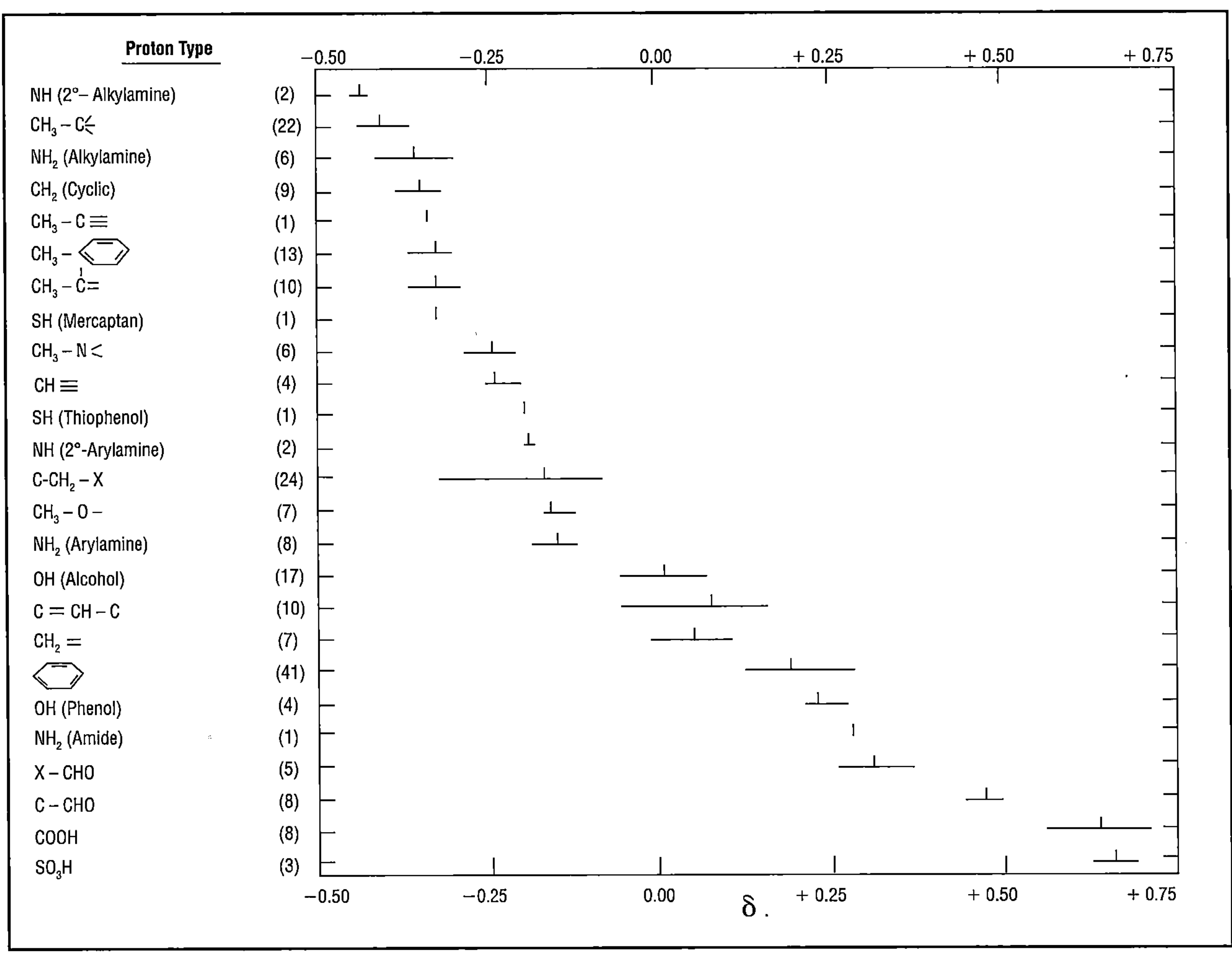

Figure 1. *Chart showing the chemical shifts (ä) related to atomic groupings in organic compounds. In following the model of similar graphs applied in infrared spectroscopy, Gutowsky made clear the usefulness of NMR for research in organic chemistry.*

the assistant in electronics, Robert McClure, constituted the group that made decisive observations and interpretations for the foundations of chemical NMR. The first of their joint projects considered the relation of chemical shift data in fluorine-substituted benzene compounds with resonance and inductive effects. The resonance effect explains the variations of the distribution of electrons in molecules by means of their delocalization; the inductive effect accounts for the ability of the substituents to attract or repel the localized bonding electrons. Both effects were used very successfully for explaining the courses of chemical reactions. In general, Gutowsky speculated about the origins of the chemical shift in terms of bond hybridizations, inspired by the theoretical contributions of Pauling and Mulliken. Moreover, Gutowsky extensively applied the technique of correlation analysis, following the ruling that a linear correlation of two parameters enabled insights into the nature of both. In 1951, and related to such a correlation, Gutowsky defined the chemical shift parameter δ, which is still in use in the early twenty-first century.

Even though by 1952 Gutowsky, his coworkers, and other scientists had successfully established NMR in the fields of chemical physics and physical organic chemistry, the majority of organic chemists working on syntheses were still unaware of the potential of the method. In the course of a study of 220 organic compounds, Meyer, Saika, and Gutowsky recognized that the chemical shift data of protons embedded in functional groups, that is, characteristic atomic groupings in a molecule, were distinctive enough to enable identification of the functional groups. Thus, just as in infrared spectroscopy, NMR could be applied as a fingerprint technique. Also, with regard to the presentation of his results, Gutowsky chose infrared spectroscopy as his model. Figure 1 shows a chart relating the chemical shift data to functional groups. It

Gutowsky

was designed after the famous Colthup chart that was a standard tool in the interpretation of infrared spectra.

In 1953 the manufacturer of NMR spectrometers, Varian Associates of Palo Alto, California, asked Gutowsky for permission to reprint the chart in its *Technical Information Bulletin.* Varian Associates, founded in 1948 by the brothers Sigurd and Russell Varian, among others, was closely allied to Stanford's Department of Physics, where Felix Bloch had coinvented NMR in 1946. Varian Associates had secured the patents of Bloch and employed him as a consultant. Many of Bloch's coworkers (among them Packard) entered the firm, which was the first company to manufacture NMR spectrometers and until the early 1970s dominated the market. Members of Bloch's team and scientists of Varian Associates crucially contributed to technical improvements and to scientific breakthroughs, among them the chemical shift and the second chemically relevant phenomenon in NMR, the so-called spin-spin coupling.

Spin-Spin Coupling. In a memorandum for a chemistry course that he held in 1949, Gutowsky noted that "'errors' sometimes are more important than preconceptions as to what is to be obtained in a given experiment" (Reinhardt, 2006, p. 71). This is exactly what happened in his own laboratory a year later, when Hoffman and McClure observed unexplainable double resonance lines during experiments with phosphorustrifluoride. At first they regarded the phenomenon as accidental, due to an impurity. Later they simply set it aside as an anomaly. Gutowsky did not become aware that this could be a new effect until Proctor and Yu of Bloch's group reported multiplets that were inexplicable by the chemical shift alone. He assigned McCall to undertake an experimental characterization with pure compounds containing different numbers of phosphorus and fluorine atoms. Soon it became clear that the effect was associated with the nuclear magnetic moments, though it was not caused by an already-known mechanism. At the same time, observations of Erwin L. Hahn, employing his spin-echo NMR method while he was still at the Department of Physics at the University of Illinois at Urbana, led to similar conclusions. In due course four teams—Gutowsky's and Slichter's at Urbana and Packard's and Hahn's at Stanford (Hahn being then in Bloch's unit)—in close cooperation established the spin-spin coupling constant as a novel parameter in NMR. The accepted theoretical interpretation, however, originated with Ramsey and Purcell at Harvard, who attributed the splitting of the spectral lines to a coupling mechanism of the nuclei via the spins of the bonding electrons. Characteristically, as had been the case with the chemical shift, Gutowsky's description of the new effect explicitly included its use as a means for unraveling molecular structure, while Ramsey's more exact and refined treatment did not account for this possibility.

In the following decades, spin-spin couplings opened several avenues for the study of molecular structure. With refined equipment, couplings between nuclei separated by several bonds could be measured, and it became possible to detect their relative orientation in space. While at the University of Illinois in the late 1950s, and partially in cooperation with members of Gutowsky's group, Martin Karplus set up a mathematical equation that related the dihedral angle between bonds to the spin-spin coupling constants measured. In Gutowsky's group, Cynthia Jameson later on decisively contributed to this topic. This work was the basis for using NMR in the unraveling of the stereochemistry of molecules. In general, however, the exact assignment of the peaks—considerably complicated by the overlay of chemical shifts and spin-spin couplings in the spectrum of a large molecule—could be a time-consuming endeavor, and several partially computer-based interpretational methods were developed for this purpose. Gutowsky contributed here, making use of the available computing power of the ILLIAC, an early supercomputer built at the University of Illinois.

An issue of great concern to the scientists involved in the discovery of the spin-spin coupling was the disappearance of splittings due to various chemical and physical effects. One such effect was chemical exchange, a term that refers here to both exchange of atomic groupings and to internal rotations of the molecules. The first systems that Gutowsky investigated in this area were acids in aqueous solutions. By observing the concentration-dependence of the proton chemical shift between the water molecules, the hydronium ions, and the undissociated acid, Gutowsky and Saika postulated the collapse of the multiplet observed into a single line, when the exchange rate increased. But they could not experimentally verify their hypothesis. Later, Gutowsky ascribed this neglect to the shortage of molecular systems showing an exchange rate at the appropriate time range and to the lack of mathematical sophistication among the chemists who observed such exchanges. Only in 1955, when William D. Phillips of Du Pont reported on restricted rotation of amides, did Gutowsky, with his graduate student, Charles H. Holm, go back to the topic. They examined intramolecular rotational rates and determined the energy barriers between the different conformational forms of the molecules. Their study, although it needed considerable refinement in both theoretical and instrumental respects, opened a whole new area for NMR studies of dynamics of molecules, and it subsequently was often cited. In the 1960s Gutowsky—together with Adam Allerhand—questioned the accuracy of existing methods for studying chemical exchange and made proposals for basing the experimental values on a more secure footing. Although their plea was

Gutowsky

largely ignored in the chemical community, it was a sign of Gutowsky's ongoing commitment to improving the methods available to the scientific community and an example of his quest for experimental rigor.

Until the late 1960s, Gutowsky's research program comprised all important areas of NMR and also occasionally included the related technique of electron spin resonance. The program's aim was to obtain insights into the complex phenomenology of NMR spectra through the development of novel methods that could be of use in chemistry. Its range stretched from theoretical aspects to applications in organic chemistry and biochemistry. Its core was the experimental approach of molecular spectroscopy using self-built instrumentation. In the 1960s Gutowsky's contributions tended to be pushed aside by the waves of organic chemists entering the field with commercially available instruments. An equally important cause for his diminished activity was the administrative roles that he pursued. In the 1970s, a collaboration with his Illinois colleague, Eric Oldfield, enabled Gutowsky to contribute to recent NMR applications in biochemical research, although even then most of his time was consumed by managerial duties.

Administrative Work. For Gutowsky, career steps closely followed scientific achievements. In 1951, he was promoted to assistant professor; in 1955 he became associate professor and in 1956 full professor of physical chemistry. The latter came with headship of the division of physical chemistry, lasting until 1962. The Department of Chemistry and Chemical Engineering at the University of Illinois was unusual for the times in comprising six divisions: organic chemistry, physical chemistry, inorganic chemistry, analytical chemistry, chemical engineering, and biochemistry. The fact that biochemistry and chemical engineering still belonged to chemistry was attributed in many respects to the strong leadership of Roger Adams, under whom organic chemistry was by far the dominant subdiscipline. When, in 1967, Gutowsky accepted the position of head of the department, he realized that in the long run, this organizational arrangement had to be changed. In 1970 he oversaw the reorganization of the department into a school of chemical sciences with three separate departments. As director of the school and head of chemistry department, Gutowsky until 1983 mainly pursued administrative functions.

In his very first year as department head, Gutowsky faced demonstrations against the presence of Dow Chemical employees on campus. Dow was heavily criticized because of its production of napalm during the Vietnam War, but Gutowsky diplomatically prevented the outbreak of violence. Next to local responsibilities, issues of national importance in the area of education were at the forefront of Gutowsky's agenda. By the mid-1960s he was a member of the committee that prepared the so-called Westheimer Report on the state of the chemical sciences in the United States, named after the committee chairman, Frank Westheimer. The report was comprehensive, influencing science policy in general and serving as a model for similar reports in the related sciences. In a 1972 letter to the journal *Science,* Gutowsky challenged the use of quota to improve the access of women to university positions. Characteristically, even regarding societal matters, he used quantitative methods, in this case related to his assumption that a shortage of both highly trained and mobile female scientists existed. He was chairman of the American Chemical Society's Committee on Professional Training, and in his function as advisor to the National Science Foundation in 1973, he called for a reversal in the U.S. educational system of cutbacks in the 1970s after the major expansion in the 1960s. In times of heightened ecological awareness, his contribution toward dealing with environmental threats was directing a National Research Council study on the impact of halocarbons on the ozone layer. The ecological crisis never lost his attention.

Gutowsky used NMR as a method for the design and control of novel effects, and he was convinced that NMR enabled scientists to understand natural phenomena better. Nevertheless, the enormous resources that a technology-centered society was spending on scientific research caused him to question the future of the scientific enterprise:

> One of my pet sayings is that research is oversupported. That it's a natural resource we are mining, taking it out at such a rage that there won't be any left for our grandchildren. We should leave some natural discoveries for the future. I tried that one on my colleagues at academy meetings designed to get more money out of the government. That was after Frank Westheimer made a pitch for 15 percent increase per year for ever and ever. I was teaching physical chemistry then and I amused myself and the class by computing how long it would be before the national budget would be totally spent. I think more undergraduate students carried away this lesson than anything else I ever taught. (Reinhardt, 2006, p. 82)

In 1983, after his resignation as director, he embarked on a new research field, pulsed microwave spectroscopy. For this, he took over the equipment of his recently deceased colleague, William H. Flygare. At first, Gutowsky regarded this task as a means for enabling Flygare's students to finish their projects. But pulsed microwave spectroscopy became Gutowsky's main scientific occupation for more than a decade. His work on weakly bound clusters of atoms and molecules resulted in more than fifty publications, with Tryggvi Emilsson being

Gutowsky

his most important coworker during this period. Here, he was able to retain his peculiar style of scientific work: investigating the effects of radiation on molecules, undertaken with self-built equipment in a relatively small group. For his NMR work, he received many honors, among them the National Medal of Science in 1976 and the 1984 Wolf Prize in Chemistry.

In 1949 Gutowsky married Barbara J. Stuart, a Radcliffe graduate. They had three children: Daniel K., Robb E., and Christopher C. Gutowsky. Divorced in 1981, the following year he married Virginia A. Warner, a psychologist, elementary school teacher, and violinist. For recreation, Gutowsky loved to work in his rose garden, occasionally breeding new varieties. Although Gutowsky officially retired in 1990, he continued working until the late 1990s. He died of myocardial infarction at Carle Foundation Hospital.

BIBLIOGRAPHY

WORKS BY GUTOWSKY

With George B. Kistiakowsky and George E. Pake. "Structural Investigations by Means of Nuclear Magnetism, I. Rigid Crystal Lattices." *Journal of Chemical Physics* 17 (1949): 972–981.

With George E. Pake. "Structural Investigations by Means of Nuclear Magnetism, II. Hindered Rotation in Solids." *Journal of Chemical Physics* 18 (1950): 162–170.

With Charles J. Hoffman. "Nuclear Magnetic Shielding in Fluorine and Hydrogen Compounds." *Journal of Chemical Physics* 19 (1951): 1259–1267.

With David W. McCall. "Nuclear Magnetic Resonance Fine Structure in Liquids." *Physical Review* 82 (1951): 748–749.

With David W. McCall and Charles P. Slichter. "Coupling among Nuclear Magnetic Dipoles in Molecules." *Physical Review* 84 (1951): 589–590.

With Leon H. Meyer and Apollo Saika. "Electron Distribution in Molecules III. The Proton Magnetic Spectra of Simple Organic Groups." *Journal of the American Chemical Society* 75 (1953): 4567–4573.

"Nuclear Magnetic Resonance." *Annual Review of Physical Chemistry* 5 (1954): 333–356. A review that covers most of the early NMR work in its scientific context.

With Charles H. Holm. "Rate Processes and Nuclear Magnetic Resonance Spectra II. Hindered Internal Rotation of Amides." *Journal of Chemical Physics* 25 (1956): 1228–1234.

With Martin Karplus and David M. Grant. "Angular Dependence of Electron-Coupled Interactions in CH_2 Groups." *Journal of Chemical Physics* 31 (1959): 1278–1289.

"Chemical Aspects of Nuclear Magnetic Resonance." *Journal of Magnetic Resonance* 17 (1975): 281–294. A historical address on the occasion of receiving the 1974 award of the International Society of Magnetic Resonance.

With Jiri Jonas. "NMR—An Evergreen." *Annual Review of Physical Chemistry* 31 (1980): 1–27.

"The Coupling of Chemical and Nuclear Magnetic Phenomena." In *Encyclopedia of Nuclear Magnetic Resonance,* edited by David M. Grant and Robin K. Harris. Vol. 1, *Historical Perspectives.* New York: Wiley, 1996. A historical summary, partially based on Gutowsky's 1975 article, "Chemical Aspects of Nuclear Magnetic Resonance," cited above.

OTHER SOURCES

Becker, Edwin D., Cherie Fisk, and C. L. Khetrapal. "The Development of NMR." In *Encyclopedia of Nuclear Magnetic Resonance,* edited by David M. Grant and Robin K. Harris. Vol. 1, *Historical Perspectives.* New York: Wiley, 1996. The standard history of NMR.

Jonas, Jiri, and Charles P. Slichter. "Herbert Sander Gutowsky 1919–2000." *National Academy of Sciences Biographical Memoirs* 88 (2006): 1–17.

Reinhardt, Carsten. "Chemistry in a Physical Mode: Molecular Spectroscopy and the Emergence of NMR." *Annals of Science* 61 (2004): 1–32. Includes an account of Gutowsky's early work at Harvard.

———. *Shifting and Rearranging: Physical Methods and the Transformation of Modern Chemistry.* Sagamore Beach, MA: Science History Publications, 2006. Chapter 2 discusses Gutowsky's major contributions.

Slichter, Charles P. "Some Scientific Contributions of Herbert S. Gutowsky." *Journal of Magnetic Resonance* 17 (1975): 274–280.

Zandvoort, Henk. *Models of Scientific Development and the Case of Nuclear Magnetic Resonance.* Dordrecht, Netherlands: Reidel, 1986. A study of the early history of NMR that is a further development of Imre Lakatos's approach to the philosophy of science.

Carsten Reinhardt

H

HABER, FRITZ (*b.* Breslau, Germany [now Wrocław, Poland], 9 December 1868; *d.* Basel, Switzerland, 29 January 1934), *chemistry.* For the original article on Haber see *DSB,* vol. 5.

From the many new sources that have become available since the first edition of the *DSB,* a much richer, more nuanced portrait of Haber has emerged, revealing a twentieth-century scientist with many faces. These include Haber the academic scientist and industrial pioneer, the benefactor of humanity and creator of destructive weapons, the science organizer and military advisor, and not least the assimilated Jew and German patriot who nevertheless died in exile. To elucidate the complexity that characterized Haber, this postscript will focus on three critical events in Haber's life and their consequences: the ammonia synthesis that made him famous, World War I that made him infamous, and finally the crisis of 1933, which hastened his death. In the process it will at times correct information in the original *DSB* article.

The Path to Synthetic Ammonia. Unlike most of the German physical chemists in the generation after Wilhelm Ostwald, Fritz Haber did not work with Ostwald; indeed, he followed a convoluted path into the field. His first exposure to gas chemistry, which would become a major focus of his research, came from three semesters with Robert Bunsen in Heidelberg, but Bunsen did not supervise doctoral work. Haber took a doctorate in the then-dominant field of organic chemistry from the University of Berlin (the Charlottenburg Technische Hochschule [College of Technology], where he had done his research, could not yet award doctorates in 1891). Organic chemistry did not inspire him, however, either in an academic or an industrial setting (including the business owned by his father, with whom he had a stormy relationship). He tried repeatedly but failed to get a position with Ostwald in Leipzig, and he clashed at times with Ostwald's heir apparent as leader of physical chemistry in Germany, Walther Nernst. Haber did, however, cultivate friendships with other young physical chemists, who helped him work his way into the field.

In 1894 Haber found his first paid assistantship in the Karlsruhe College of Technology chemistry department, then led by two relatively liberal men who were experts in oil (Carl Engler) and gas (Hans Bunte). Bunte encouraged Haber to develop a wide-ranging research program, beginning with hydrocarbon gas combustion analysis and going on to electrochemistry and thermodynamics (see details in the original *DSB* article).

Haber was clearly energized by challenges that had defeated others, particularly technical problems of immense practical significance, whose solution required a sophisticated application of theoretical knowledge as well as tremendous concentration and hard work. This is what drew him to gas reactions, then on the forefront of research in thermodynamics, and eventually to the ammonia synthesis, which Ostwald himself had failed to solve. Despite Nernst's humiliating public criticism of Haber and Robert Le Rossignol's early results in 1907, they went on to perfect the process, while Nernst abandoned it as technically impracticable. By 1908 Haber had a consulting relationship with the BASF (Badische Anilin- & Soda-Fabrik) chemical corporation, which purchased the rights to his high-pressure, catalytic ammonia synthesis in 1909 at the recommendation of Carl Bosch, who directed

Fritz Haber. *Fritz Haber, November 26, 1919.* HULTON ARCHIVE/GETTY IMAGES.

the technical development of what became known as the Haber-Bosch process. Synthetic ammonia—"fixed" nitrogen—would eliminate the threat of mass starvation from the exhaustion of Chilean nitrate deposits as global demand for nitrogen-based fertilizers escalated; it also meant replacing an import by a product made in Germany.

Haber's ammonia synthesis caught the attention of the wealthy Berlin businessman Leopold Koppel, who in 1910 offered to endow a prestigious new Kaiser Wilhelm Institute for research in physical chemistry and electrochemistry, specifying him as director. This brought Haber in 1912 to the Berlin suburb of Dahlem, where his new friend, the organic chemist Richard Willstätter, was senior scientific member (not codirector) of the neighboring Kaiser Wilhelm Institute for Chemistry.

Haber as Military Scientist. After World War I began in 1914 Haber transformed himself with no apparent qualms from benefactor of humanity to weapons scientist and advisor to the Prusso-German Army on chemical questions. His mediation helped initiate a series of major, government-subsidized expansions of BASF's ammonia plants. In 1918 the fixed nitrogen thus produced, about 90,000 tons (of a planned capacity approaching 300,000 tons), would be the principal source of nitric acid for German munitions (whereas fertilizers came from other sources). Haber earned fifteen marks (about $3.50 in 1918 dollars) in royalties per ton, wealth that would, however, shrink in the postwar inflation.

Haber's involvement in chemical warfare began in late 1914, complementing his efforts to expand nitrate production. As an alternative to nitrogen-based explosives, he proposed and directed the first large-scale release of chlorine gas at Ypres on the Western Front on 22 (not 11) April 1915. Although the attack brought only temporary success, gas (with its dramatic effects on unprotected troops) seemed promising; Haber was commissioned a captain with responsibility for the further development of chemical weapons. This led to an office for chemical questions and, in November 1916, the creation of Chemical Section A 10 within the General War Department of the Prussian War Ministry (which effectively served as Imperial War

Ministry until 1918). Haber thus became the first scientist in charge of a section in the War Ministry, and he worked toward the further mobilization of German scientists for military purposes. Continuing to direct his own research institute, Haber converted and expanded it into a research and development center for chemical agents (mainly used in shells rather than clouds after 1916) and protective measures. By 1917 Haber's organization had 9 sections, employing 150 academics and about 1,300 others. Despite his rare ability to focus on, grasp, and quickly deal with a wide variety of scientific and technical problems, he was later criticized for a professorial reluctance to delegate authority, as well as for inadequate field testing of chemical agents developed in his institute. Allied countermeasures eventually neutralized all of Haber's initiatives, and the hoped-for breakthrough never occurred.

As with ammonia, the war's challenges energized Haber, who drove himself relentlessly. Then in his late forties, Haber evidently enjoyed the uniform and rank (which a German Jew could not hold in peacetime) and even the occasional danger at the front, so unlike his previous academic world. Unfortunately the war also heightened his isolation from his family. Since his marriage to Clara Immerwahr in 1901 he had increasingly relegated her to a domestic role (despite her doctorate in chemistry) while neglecting their son. In deepening depression, she saw his scientific successes coming at the cost of his (and her) humanity. The end came soon after his return from Ypres in 1915, when she committed suicide—a tragedy that many have seen as a protest against chemical warfare, despite the lack of conclusive evidence. Two years later Haber remarried, but his much younger bride, Charlotte Nathan, ultimately proved to be too different from him for the marriage to last.

Following Germany's defeat, Haber had a near breakdown, then fled to Switzerland for a few months to escape possible prosecution for his chemical warfare work. An Allied tribunal never materialized, but ironically the same year brought him news that he would receive a Nobel Prize for the ammonia synthesis. Despite criticism, Haber never expressed any regret for his military service; indeed, he continued to serve the military, along with his other postwar activities mentioned in the original *DSB* article, including the initially secret project to extract gold from the sea in the vain hope of paying German reparations. First he briefly administered economic demobilization in chemicals, a task probably too business-oriented and political for him. Until 1926 he also played a mediating and advisory role for the new German Ministry of National Defense (Reichswehr) in covert efforts to evade the Versailles Peace Treaty through chemical warfare projects in Spain and Soviet Russia as well as Germany. After the Allies uncovered and suppressed some of these activities, Haber apparently lost his influence with the military. By then, however, he had helped to create a government-regulated civilian pesticide company staffed by chemical warfare veterans and using a cyanide-based product, Zyklon B, later used for mass murder in Auschwitz. It was derived from a wartime agent developed by Haber's own institute.

Postwar Teaching and Scientific Organizing. Haber was a gifted teacher and scientific leader, much admired by his students and assistants. At Karlsruhe he had become a leading teacher of physical chemistry, but once in Dahlem his teaching role was limited to a few doctoral students, as he had only an honorary professorship at the University of Berlin. After the war he nearly followed the organic chemist Emil Fischer (1852–1919) as director of the Berlin university institute for chemistry, the largest in Germany. Carl Duisberg, influential director of the Bayer corporation, prevented the appointment by threatening the withdrawal of industrial contributions for academic institutes should a physical chemist be given responsibility for training organic chemists. Haber was, however, accorded a greater role in university teaching through his Dahlem institute.

The postwar Haber Colloquium in Dahlem was an unusually "democratic" and interdisciplinary forum within the normally hierarchical, specialized world of German academe. Even doctoral students felt free to speak along with full professors, enhancing the critical discussion of rapidly changing physical theories during the 1920s. This, and the high productivity of his institute, reflects Haber's inspiring leadership.

In 1920 Haber helped organize the Notgemeinschaft der Deutschen Wissenschaft (Emergency Association of German Science, later Deutsche Forschungsgemeinschaft [German Research Association]), which provided the first large-scale national government subsidies to the state university system, primarily through fellowships but also (for physical chemistry) through purchasing equipment to be lent to institutes for specific projects. Haber's policy here was especially effective during the hyperinflation that climaxed in 1923, when monetary grants quickly became worthless.

Haber also played an influential role in the development of the Kaiser Wilhelm Society for the Advancement of the Sciences, to which his institute belonged. In 1928 he took the initiative in organizing an interdisciplinary scientific advisory council for the society, composed of the permanent scientific members and directors of its institutes; Haber was elected head of the section for chemistry, physics, and technology.

Finally, Haber was among those working to reintegrate German scientific organizations into the postwar international structure of science, from which the victorious Allies had excluded them. In 1930 the newly formed Verband Deutscher Chemischer Vereine (Federation of German Chemical Associations), chaired by Haber, entered the International Union of Pure and Applied Chemistry, whose presidium Haber joined in 1931, only to resign in 1933 after the National Socialist takeover in Germany.

1933: The Fatal Crisis. Although born to a Jewish family, Haber had in 1892 converted to Protestantism. This was not unusual among academics at the time, when religion meant little to many scientists and conversion could foster scholarly advancement. The National Socialist "racial" laws forced Haber, like many other assimilated German Jews, to reaffirm an identity he had tried to ignore (notwithstanding that most of his close associates, like Willstätter, were Jewish or of Jewish descent, and both his wives were converts from Judaism). Although Haber's war service exempted him from dismissal in 1933, he chose to resign his directorship, postponing the effective date for a few months in order to help his Jewish subordinates find new positions abroad. His letter of resignation, rejecting the use of "racial character" as a criterion for scientific appointments (the first *DSB* article freely translates this as "on the basis of their grandmothers"), made him anathema to the government. Still proud of serving "humanity in peace, the fatherland in war," as he wrote in his farewell message to his institute in September 1933, Haber departed Germany a broken man, with heart disease so severe that he could hardly work. After suffering two months of bad climate in Cambridge, England, he decided to try Palestine but died on the way, having evidently lost the will to live.

SUPPLEMENTARY BIBLIOGRAPHY

For Haber's published works see the list in the original DSB *article; the most complete bibliography is in Szöllösi-Janze's biography (see below). Archival documents are in the Haber Collection (Haber-Sammlung), Archiv zur Geschichte der Max-Planck-Gesellschaft, Berlin-Dahlem.*

WORKS BY HABER

Fritz Haber, Briefe an Richard Willstätter, 1910–1934. Edited by Petra Werner and Angelika Irmscher. Studien und Quellen zur Geschichte der Chemie, Bd. 6. Berlin: Verlag für Wissenschafts- und Regionalgeschichte Dr. Michael Engel, 1995.

Fritz Haber in seiner Korrespondenz mit Wilhelm Ostwald sowie in Briefen an Svante Arrhenius. Edited by Regine Zott. Berliner Beiträge zur Geschichte der Naturwissenschaften und der Technik 20. Berlin: ERS-Verlag, 1997.

OTHER SOURCES

Charles, Daniel. *Master Mind: The Rise and Fall of Fritz Haber, the Nobel Laureate Who Launched the Age of Chemical Warfare.* New York: HarperCollins, 2005. Pub. in the U.K. as *Between Genius and Genocide: The Tragedy of Fritz Haber, Father of Chemical Warfare.* London: Cape, 2005. Relatively short, directed toward a general audience, with useful discussion of long-term impact of nitrogen fixation.

Haber, L. F. (Ludwig Fritz). *The Poisonous Cloud: Chemical Warfare in the First World War.* Oxford: Clarendon Press, 1986. Thoughtfully evaluates his father's chemical warfare work.

Hahn, Ralf. *Gold aus dem Meer: Die Forschungen des Nobelpreisträgers Fritz Haber in den Jahren 1922–1927.* Berlin and Diepholz, Germany: Verlag für Geschichte der Naturwissenschaften und der Technik, 1999. On the effort to extract gold from the sea.

Stoltzenberg, Dietrich. *Fritz Haber: Chemist, Nobel Laureate, German, Jew.* History of Modern Chemical Sciences series. Philadelphia: Chemical Heritage Foundation, 2004. Translation of the author's abridgment of the original (1994) German edition; good on technical chemistry.

Szöllösi-Janze, Margit. *Fritz Haber 1868–1934: Eine Biographie.* Munich, Germany: C. H. Beck, 1998. Longer and with more critical scholarship than Stoltzenberg; closest we are likely to get to a definitive biography.

Travis, Anthony. "High Pressure Industrial Chemistry: The First Steps, 1909–1913, and the Impact." In *Determinants in the Evolution of the European Chemical Industry, 1900–1939: New Technologies, Political Frameworks, Markets, and Companies,* edited by Anthony S. Travis, et al., 3–21. Dordrecht, Netherlands, and Boston: Kluwer, 1998.

Witschi, Hanspeter R. *Fritz Haber and His Legacy to the Science of Toxicology.* Amsterdam: Elsevier, 2000. A brief account.

Jeffrey Allan Johnson

HAECKEL, ERNST (*b.* Potsdam, Germany, 16 February 1834; *d.* Jena, Germany, 9 August 1919), *zoology, embryology, evolution.* For the original article on Haeckel see *DSB,* vol. 6.

Haeckel scholarship has flourished in the decades since the original *DSB* article was written. Recent assessments have expanded scholars' understanding of Haeckel's personality, his animal morphology, his pioneering visual representations of evolutionary concepts, and his ideas on human evolution. Greater attention to popularization among historians of science and greater attention to science among general historians have yielded new assessments of his place in European culture, though consensus remains elusive.

Personality Development. It is impossible to understand Ernst Haeckel's scientific career without understanding his personality. He was by turns combative and loving, passionate and analytical, and he erected few boundaries between these aspects of his personality. He loved his cousin and first wife, Anna Sethe Haeckel, intensely, and her death on his thirtieth birthday in 1864 deepened his preexisting alienation from traditional Christian beliefs into bitter opposition. His efforts to replace Christian thought and institutions with his own monistic philosophy, which erased the distinctions between spirit and matter, between life and afterlife, and between humans and other animals lent religious and political heat to his evolutionary writings, especially his more popular ones. He became one of the great controversialists of his time; like Thomas Henry Huxley, he embraced battle in public forums, especially over the appropriate roles of science and religion in modern society. Both within and beyond the scientific community, he never missed an opportunity to snipe at those whom he viewed as his enemies, and because he often clung dogmatically to his own ideas, over time he viewed more and more people (including most of his former zoology students) as opponents, or, as he often saw them, betrayers. At the same time, on certain scientific problems he adopted a remarkable analytical flexibility that allowed him to view the same issue (such as organic individuality or evolutionary tree-making) from multiple perspectives and, sometimes, to alter his views in the face of new evidence—an aspect of his thought that has been overshadowed by his dogmatism on philosophical issues.

Morphological Theory. Haeckel is known as one of Europe's greatest apostles of evolution, but his perspective drew as much from German scientific and philosophical roots as from Charles Darwin. The foundation of Haeckel's scientific work is his *Generelle Morphologie* (1866), a difficult, two-volume monograph that sought to establish a new foundation for animal morphology. Although this work was deeply evolutionist and indebted to Darwin in its acceptance of common descent and selection, it also developed ideas that owed little to Darwinian evolution.

Central to Haeckel's morphology was his view of the complex nature of organic individuality, a critical problem for zoologists in the 1850s and early 1860s. Haeckel argued that the scientist should understand organic individuals from three independent perspectives: morphological, physiological, and genealogical. In the vertebrates, with which scientists are most familiar, these three aspects of individuality coincide, but this is not necessary; in many marine invertebrates (such as sponges or siphonophores), a physiological individual is actually formed by a community of morphologically distinct individuals, each of which performs different functions for the common whole, and none of which can survive without the others. Moreover, Haeckel argued, each of these kinds of individuality existed at different levels, with higher levels of individuality (such as the race) subsuming lower ones (such as the nation, the individual human, or the colonial organism), all the way down to the smallest level (the cell). Crucially, in discussing genealogical individuality he posited three levels—the individual as commonly understood, the species, and the phylum, each of which followed the same laws of development. Haeckel's biogenetic law, that ontogeny (individual development) recapitulates phylogeny (development of the species), depends crucially on the concept of levels and kinds of individuality. Although it would rapidly transform into a tool for evolutionary research, in its inception the biogenetic law is best understood as an outgrowth of Haeckel's effort to solve the conundrum of organic individuality, combined with his commitment to the idea of universal development.

The *Generelle Morphologie* also incorporated Haeckel's first efforts to found a new science of "promorphology," which would analyze the geometry of organic forms to establish the fundamental possibilities that constrained their development. This impulse was strongly influenced by his studies of the radiolaria, a group of radially symmetrical but otherwise highly varied marine organisms. It also reveals other debts, both to his early mineralogical studies and to the Romantic tradition, especially as represented by Lorenz Oken and Carl Gustav Carus. Although Haeckel did not succeed in establishing promorphology as a basic biological science, it remained critical to his thinking throughout his life. His interest in nature's symmetries would undergird much of his invertebrate systematics, especially of the radiolaria, and late in his life he would again stress the importance of the promorphological "foundational forms" (*Grundformen*) in his *Systematische Phylogenie* (3 vols., 1894–1896; Systematic phylogeny). Although he failed to gain a substantial following for promorphology among biologists, he did better among artists. His symmetrical images and his naturalistic theory of aesthetics, which resulted in his *Kunstformen der Natur* (1899; *Art Forms in Nature,* 1974), would have a strong influence on the Jugendstil movement in the decorative arts.

Representing Embryos and Ancestors. Haeckel is better known for two visual forms—the comparative embryological grid and the phylogenetic tree—than any particular piece of writing. In developing both, he brought into general usage two of the most important visual representations of evolutionary thought.

Perhaps his most enduring legacy has been a series of illustrations of vertebrate embryos depicting their similarity at the earliest stages of development and their increasing differentiation. The first version appeared in the initial edition of *Natürliche Schöpfungsgeschichte* (1868; *The*

History of Creation, 1875); Haeckel developed it in subsequent editions and in his *Anthropogenie* (1874; *Evolution of Man,* 1883), where it reached its most elaborated expression. This visual codification of comparative embryology has persisted across more than a century of biology textbooks as striking evidence of commonality of form and descent, long after the "biogenetic law" with which it was associated fell out of favor as a theoretical guide to research. In 1997 embryologist Michael K. Richardson, with others, published a series of photographs of embryos of the same species that Haeckel had used at the same developmental stages as those in the latter's illustrations. These revealed that Haeckel must have edited his original forms substantially in order to draw out the similarities—to the point of distorting their truthfulness. Richardson's work revived charges of fraud that had dogged Haeckel from the images' first appearance in the early 1870s.

Recent historical work has situated these illustrations within the conventions of popular and professional illustration. Whereas idealized or schematized images have generally been accepted as having heuristic value in popular and educational forums before and after Haeckel, this approach has been less acceptable for evidentiary claims in professional research work. Haeckel's illustrations attracted criticism not just because they were tendentious but also because his writing (and figures) lay at the boundaries of these two genres, where the rules of evidence were hazy. The controversy over the truthfulness of his pictures has distracted attention from their major achievement (arguably, the one that has made them endure): Haeckel redrew different embryos to the same scale and in the same position, which facilitated direct comparison of embryo types in a way that had never existed before. Thus, even as it typologized embryos more extensively than had been done previously, lending weight to charges of falsification of the visual record, Haeckel's gridlike illustration offered a new step toward rendering comparative embryology practical.

Equally liminally placed between research and popularization were his visually striking phylogenetic trees. Unlike Darwin's famous "branching tree" diagram in *On the Origin of Species* (1859), which looked little like a tree, Haeckel's trees resembled productions of nature. His most famous tree, originally published in the *Anthropogenie,* encapsulated his progressive hierarchy through the thick oaklike trunk running from the ancestral Monera at the base to humans at the top. But like much of Haeckel's thought, this represented just one of his perspectives. In fact, he experimented with numerous forms of trees, ranging from typographically dominated ones connecting taxonomic group names with straight lines to a variety of shrub- and kelp-like images in different efforts to convey simultaneously degrees of taxonomic similarity, levels of complexity, and historical emergence. One phylogenetic tree in the *Generelle Morphologie* places the genus "Homo" on a tiny branch in the upper-right-hand corner—a startling contrast to the more familiar oak tree image. Other trees, working at broader or lower taxonomic levels, do not include humans at all.

Ernst Haeckel. HULTON ARCHIVE/GETTY IMAGES.

Humanity, Race, and Language. Although Haeckel's original scientific investigations were confined to invertebrates, his influence lay in his broader evolutionary claims, especially about humans. Controversially at the time (though in concert with Darwin), he naturalized humans fully, arguing that they were different only in degree from other animals, not in kind. Unlike Darwin, his species criteria did not emphasize interbreeding; using morphological and linguistic criteria, he derived twelve "species" of humans that derived from a single hypothetical prelinguistic Urmensch. In close interaction with the Jena linguist August Schleicher (whose evolutionary trees of language relationships were inspired by his Haeckel-recommended reading of Darwin's *On the Origin of Species*), Haeckel developed the idea of a phylogenetic tree of human racial types in which language differences (along with the physical features of hair texture) played the most critical role as distinguishing criteria. This tree

Haeckel

combined history and progress into a single vertical scale. It both embraced and reinforced the hierarchical racialism of his time, placing the "smooth-haired" Australian aboriginals at the bottom of his scale, followed by the "woolly-haired" Hottentots and Papuans. "Indo-Germans," of course, rested at the top, with "Semites" (later "Hamosemites") just behind them (suggesting that Haeckel, though sharing the ethnocentrism of his class, was not the virulent anti-Semite that some have supposed). Numerous details of this tree changed over time as new evidence appeared, reminding us that it was not purely a figment of preexisting racial assumptions. Yet Haeckel's characterization of races as different "species" lent his authority to post-Darwinian racism.

Haeckel's Influence. Haeckel's magnetic and effusive presence and his passionate dedication to the causes of evolution, morphology, and monism have led recent historians to seek to assess his influence, with differing results. He attracted thousands of students to his lectures at the tiny University of Jena, yet few became zoologists, and nearly all of those who did would later part company with him over major features of his system. In contrast to his close friend and colleague, Carl Gegenbaur, who developed a loyal school, Haeckel was more successful in supporting those in other fields who shared his general evolutionary views than in sustaining a scientific research program. Although he gained an early reputation as a serious invertebrate zoologist and systematist, his massive synthetic theoretical works, the *Generelle Morphologie* and the *Systematische Phylogenie,* attracted far fewer adherents than he had hoped. By contrast, his more popular books went through many editions, which he continually revised, and were translated into other languages. The *Natürliche Schöpfungsgeschichte,* based on his Jena lecture course, went through eleven German editions between 1868 and its final version in 1911, with translations into English, French, Swedish, and Russian; the *Anthropogenie* had six editions (1874–1910), plus translations into English, French, Bulgarian, and Turkish; and *Die Welträthsel* (1899; Riddles of the universe, most unfortunately mistitled *Riddle of the Universe* in its English-language editions, which began in 1900) had at least nine editions (though some were unchanged); as a whole text or as selections, it has been translated into English, Spanish, Chinese, Japanese, Russian, Hungarian, Uighur, Hebrew, and Hindi.

Haeckel's "popular" science did not exactly fall into the better-established popular genres of anecdotal natural history, dialogues for well-bred ladies, or the emerging popular science writings for mass-circulation periodicals (though later in life he would publish some accounts of his travel to exotic places, engaging in one of the most popular nonfiction genres). His most successful books contained often dense scientific and philosophical argumentation and were seeded with neologisms that the serious reader had to track closely to follow the argument—for every new term that gained entry into the common vocabulary, such as ontogeny, phylogeny, and ecology, Haeckel produced a handful that failed to become accepted. Thus, as successful as Haeckel's popular works were, these remained at the technical end of the popular spectrum; indeed, his ideas themselves were subject to further simplification and clarification by mass-audience writers such as Wilhelm Boelsche and Carus Sterne (the pen name of Ernst Krause).

Haeckel's standing as a scientist lent particular weight to his pronouncements in some circles, and some historians have identified him as a leading proponent of eugenics, racism, and anti-Semitism and as the source for both the ideology of Fascism and German National Socialism. There is little doubt that he believed in a hierarchy of human types and found eugenics a logical step for a rational society following evolutionary principles, but he shared these views with many—perhaps most—scientifically educated Europeans of his time, just as he shared his German nationalism with many contemporaries. Scholars divide over the significance of his pronouncements on these issues, and therefore over his role as a shaper of German and European cultural and political attitudes. His primary commitments were always to evolution, morphology, and monism, areas in which his influence is uncontested.

SUPPLEMENTARY BIBLIOGRAPHY

The reunification of Germany has eased access to Haeckel's voluminous notes and correspondence, held at the Ernst-Haeckel-Haus of the University of Jena. No comprehensive bibliography of Haeckel's published writings, including translations and posthumous reprints, exists. The most complete bibliography of his original German writings remains that of Thilo Krumbach (1919), reprinted in Heberer (1968).

Breidbach, Olaf. *Visions of Nature: The Art and Science of Ernst Haeckel.* Munich, Germany; and London: Prestel, 2006.

Di Gregorio, Mario A. *From Here to Eternity: Ernst Haeckel and Scientific Faith.* Göttingen, Germany: Vandenhoeck and Ruprecht, 2005.

Gasman, Daniel. *Haeckel's Monism and the Birth of Fascist Ideology.* New York: P. Lang, 1998.

Heberer, Gerhard, ed., *Der gerechtfertigte Haeckel. Einblicke in seine Schriften aus Anlaß des Erscheinens seines Hauptwerkes "Generelle Morphologie der Organismen" vor 100 Jahren.* Stuttgart, Germany: Gustav Fischer Verlag, 1968. Includes selections from Haeckel's main writings as well as biographical and autobiographical sketches and the most complete bibliography of Haeckel's work, reprinted from Thilo Krumbach 1919 (below).

Hopwood, Nick. "Pictures of Evolution and Charges of Fraud: Ernst Haeckel's Embryological Illustrations." *Isis* 97 (2006): 260–301.

Kockerbeck, Christoph. *Ernst Haeckels "Kunstformen der Natur" und ihr Einfluss auf die deutsche bildende Kunst der Jahrhundertwende.* Frankfurt am Main, Germany: P. Lang, 1986.

Krausse, Erika. *Ernst Haeckel.* 2nd ed. Leipzig, Germany: Teubner, 1987. A brief but thorough biography.

Krumbach, Thilo. "Die Schriften Ernst Haeckels." *Die Naturwissenschaften* 7 (1919): 961–966. The most complete available listing of his works, including popular and newspaper articles.

Lebrun, David. *Proteus: A Nineteenth-Century Vision.* A film by David Lebrun. Brooklyn, NY: First Run-Icarus Films, 2004. An outstanding film on Haeckel's efforts to unify science and art, with particular attention to the radiolaria.

May, Walther. *Ernst Haeckel: Versuch einer Chronik seines Lebens und Wirkens.* Leipzig, Germany: Barth, 1909. Contains a fairly complete bibliography of Haeckel's writings and an invaluable listing of biographical articles and books on Haeckel and "Haeckelismus" up to 1909.

Nyhart, Lynn K. *Biology Takes Form: Animal Morphology and the German Universities, 1800–1900.* Chicago: University of Chicago Press, 1995. Places Haeckel's program of evolutionary morphology in the intellectual, institutional, and disciplinary context of the German universities.

Richards, Robert J. *The Tragic Sense of Life: Ernst Haeckel and the Struggle over Evolutionary Thought.* Chicago: University of Chicago Press, forthcoming.

Richardson, Michael K., and Gerhard Keuck. "Haeckel's ABC of Evolution and Development." *Biological Reviews* 77 (2002): 495–528. Reviews recent scientific and historical assessments of Haeckel's embryological arguments and illustrations and their utility for phylogenetic reasoning. Contains an extensive bibliography.

Rinard, Ruth. "The Problem of the Organic Individual: Ernst Haeckel and the Development of the Biogenetic Law." *Journal of the History of Biology* 14 (1981): 249–276.

Weikart, Richard. *From Darwin to Hitler: Evolutionary Ethics, Eugenics, and Racism in Germany.* New York: Palgrave Macmillan, 2004.

Lynn K. Nyhart

HAHN, OTTO (*b.* Frankfurt am Main, Germany, 8 March 1879, *d.* Göttingen, Germany, 28 July 1968), *radiochemistry.* For the original article on Hahn see *DSB*, vol. 6.

Hahn was an exceptionally prominent public figure in postwar Germany, known for the discovery of nuclear fission, for his principled conduct during National Socialism, and for his leadership in the rehabilitation of German science. For decades he was the subject of admiring media attention and much biographical material, including his own two autobiographies and a posthumously published memoir, but significant aspects of his life and work remained largely exempt from critical historical examination until well after his death. This supplement focuses on the scientific and political context for the fission discovery, Hahn's wartime involvement in the German nuclear fission project, and his postwar advocacy for the German scientific community.

The Discovery of Nuclear Fission: December 1938. Like many conservative academics in the interwar period, Hahn was dismayed by the loss of the imperial monarchy and dismissive of the Weimar Republic. His first reaction to the National Socialist regime was to hope for a national revival, but he was appalled by the purge of Jewish scientists and soon found himself, probably for the first time, in a nonconformist political position. He was concerned for dismissed Jewish colleagues, maintained contact with émigré friends, and at the end tried to intervene on behalf of several Jewish friends who faced deportation. It helped that the Kaiser Wilhelm Institute (KWI) for Chemistry, of which Hahn was director, was privately funded by the chemical industry and therefore was somewhat insulated, at least at first, from direct control by the government. Thus Lise Meitner, Hahn's closest colleague and head of the institute's nuclear physics section, was not dismissed in 1933, although she was of Jewish origin, and Hahn was able to retain Fritz Strassmann, a promising young chemist whose anti-Nazi position made him virtually unemployable outside the institute. From 1934 to 1938 Hahn, Meitner, and Strassmann investigated the radioactive species, thought to be transuranium elements, which were produced by the neutron bombardment of uranium. The work was interdisciplinary, requiring nuclear physics for the reaction processes and chemistry and radiochemistry for analyzing the many radioactive products.

Meitner fled Germany for Sweden in July 1938, but she and Hahn were able to maintain contact by mail. In November 1938 they met secretly in Copenhagen, soon after Hahn and Strassmann found several new activities among the uranium products, which they attributed to isotopes of radium. To Meitner and other physicists it seemed impossible that slow neutrons could cause uranium to lose two alpha particles and form radium, and Meitner pressed Hahn to rigorously reexamine the new activities. Hahn and Strassmann then began a series of fractional crystallization and indicator experiments designed to verify the radium by separating it from the barium that they had used as a carrier. When they could not separate it, the chemists concluded that their "radium" was in fact an isotope of the much lighter element barium—the first indication that uranium nuclei had split. Hahn informed Meitner toward the end of December

Hahn

Otto Hahn. *Otto Hahn in his chemistry laboratory.* © CORBIS.

1938, asking her to find some "fantastic explanation" for the surprising result. She and her physicist nephew Otto Robert Frisch provided the first theoretical interpretation, calculated the energy released, and named the process *nuclear fission.*

In Germany the discovery came at a time of heightened political tension, and Hahn, regarded as politically unreliable, was suddenly threatened with the loss of his institute. When he and Strassmann published the barium finding in early January 1939, physicists worldwide greeted it as sensational news, but for Hahn it was also a "heaven-sent gift" that he urgently hoped would protect him and his institute. Afraid that others would learn that he had continued to collaborate with Meitner in exile and that he had informed her of the barium before publication, he insisted that the discovery resulted solely from chemical experiments that he and Strassmann had done in December, and that physics had played no part. In the end, Hahn and his institute were safe. But historians have come to regard his effort to distance the discovery from physics and himself from Meitner as an injustice to her and a misrepresentation of the interdisciplinary nature of the scientific work. At the very least, this can be seen as an instance in which normal standards of scientific attribution were compromised by the effects of anti-semitism, forced emigration, and fear.

Wartime Fission Research in Germany. In March 1939 Frédéric Joliot and his group in Paris reported that secondary neutrons are released during uranium fission, raising the possibility of an energy-producing chain reaction. The German military took notice, and just after the war began in September 1939 the Army Ordnance unit for high explosives convened a group of leading atomic scientists to explore the military potential of nuclear fission. Hahn, still concerned for his institute, was eager to participate and committed the KWI for Chemistry to the fission project. Hahn later recalled that the first mention of an atomic bomb gave him a "terrible fright" but that he resolved to go on with his research as before.

The field was new, and much fundamental research was indeed necessary, but German scientists, like their Allied counterparts, quickly understood that weapons could in principle be made from two fissile nuclides: the rare isotope of uranium, uranium-235, and the transuranium element 94. Accordingly, the German fission project focused on building a nuclear reactor, for energy and to breed element 94, and on developing methods for separating uranium-235 from natural uranium. Neither goal was met. The German project was active and well supported, but it was far smaller in scale than the corresponding Allied effort.

The KWI for Chemistry was involved in every major aspect of the project and was classified at the highest level of importance to the war effort until the end. Institute physicists investigated neutron reaction processes and the properties of moderators, essential for bomb physics and for the theory and design of the reactor under construction at the nearby KWI for Physics. A sizable group worked on mass spectroscopic methods for isotope separation. Chemists analyzed and purified uranium and its compounds for the reactor, prepared a small amount of element 93 (later named neptunium) and attempted to find element 94 (plutonium). Hahn and Strassmann characterized a large number of fission fragments, data that would have been essential for the operation of a working reactor. With few exceptions, the results were unpublished, circulating as secret reports within the fission project.

After the war Hahn repeatedly stated that he had done only basic research, citing his work on fission fragments, most of which was openly published, and the work on elements 93 and 94. No doubt Hahn preferred to think of himself as a simple scientist engaged in fundamental research, but during the war his primary role was to head an institute that made its scientific expertise available to the state. The institute thrived, and Hahn became one of the Nazi regime's technocratic and military elites, was permitted to travel in occupied Eastern Europe to promote German "cultural influence," and was even allowed to visit neutral Sweden, where he was made a foreign member of the Royal Academy of Sciences, a prelude to the Nobel Prize. In 1943 he received a high-ranking civilian award for his contributions to the war effort. After air raids destroyed the institute buildings in Berlin-

Dahlem in February–March 1944, Hahn and the KWI for Chemistry relocated to southern Germany, where the work continued until the war's end.

Postwar. Hahn dedicated himself to the rebuilding effort, serving as president of the Kaiser Wilhelm Gesellschaft (KWG) and its successor, the Max Planck Gesellschaft, from 1946 to 1960. To an entire generation of German scientists, he was an iconic figure, the prototype of the decent German, a Nobel laureate whose most famous discovery was the result of basic research, a man known for his upright stance during National Socialism. As spokesperson for the KWG and, by extension, for the scientific community, Hahn projected an image of German science as undiminished in excellence and uninvolved in politics or the war. Particularly in the precarious early postwar years, his leadership succeeded in fostering solidarity among scientists and drawing support from the Allied occupation authorities.

As with most Germans of his generation, however, Hahn's advocacy meant rewriting the history of the recent past. In his public statements and autobiographical writings, Hahn described his wartime work as unfettered fundamental research that was unrelated to the war effort, never examining his part in the fission project as a whole, the secret research in his institute, or its ties to industry, government, and the military. Like other fission scientists, he misrepresented the objective of the fission project, claiming that it was never directed toward a bomb but only to a nuclear reactor for energy production. Similarly, Hahn depicted the KWG under National Socialism as a haven for free, independent science, even though he was quite aware of the KWG's ties to the Hitler regime and the military, and its opportunistic expansion into German-occupied Europe.

Hahn's postwar efforts to distance himself and his institutions from National Socialism were typical of the self-portrayals of his generation. With his prominence, reputation, and the sheer quantity of his writings, he created a widely accepted narrative that obscured rather than illuminated the realities of scientific structures in the National Socialist state. It was only after the late twentieth century that historians had the necessary documentation and critical distance to explore the accommodation and collaboration of science in this period.

SUPPLEMENTARY BIBLIOGRAPHY

By far the most important archival source for Otto Hahn is the collection of his personal and professional papers in the Archiv zur Geschichte der Max-Planck-Gesellschaft, Berlin. A list of Hahn's publications and selected secondary literature has been assembled by his grandson and published in Otto Hahn: Erlebnisse und Erkenntnisse, *edited by Dietrich Hahn, Düsseldorf: Econ Verlag, 1975, which includes Hahn's frankest memoir, written in 1945 and published posthumously, together with selected correspondence and postwar writings.*

WORKS BY HAHN

A Scientific Autobiography, translated and edited by Willy Ley. London: MacGibbon & Kee, 1967.

My Life. Translated by Ernst Kaiser and Eithne Wilkins. New York: Herder and Herder, 1968.

OTHER SOURCES

Berninger, Ernst, ed. *Otto Hahn—Eine Bilddokumentation: Persönlichkeit, wissenschaftliche Leistung, Öffentliches Wirken.* Munich: H. Moos Verlag, 1969.

Crawford, Elisabeth, Ruth Lewin Sime, and Mark Walker. "A Nobel Tale of Wartime Injustice." *Nature* 382 (1996): 393–395.

Gerlach, Walther, and Dietrich Hahn, ed. *Otto Hahn: Ein Forscherleben unserer Zeit.* Stuttgart: Wissenschaftliche Verlagsgesellschaft, 1984.

Hahn, Dietrich, ed. *Otto Hahn Begründer des Atomzeitalters, Eine Biographie in Bildern und Dokumenten.* Munich: List Verlag, 1979.

———. *Otto Hahn: Leben und Werken in Texten und Bildern.* Frankfurt/Main: Insel, 1988.

Krafft, Fritz. *Im Schatten der Sensation: Leben und Wirken von Fritz Straßmann.* Weinheim: Verlag Chemie 1981.

Sime, Ruth Lewin. *Lise Meitner: A Life in Physics.* Berkeley: University of California Press, 1996.

———. "The Politics of Memory: Otto Hahn and the Third Reich." *Physics in Perspective* 8 (2006): 3–51.

———. "Otto Hahn and the Kaiser-Wilhelm-Institut für Chemie in World War II." In *Gemeinschaftsforschung, Bevollmächtigte und der Wissenstransfer. Die Organisation kriegsrelevanter Forschung und die Kaiser-Wilhelm-Gesellschaft im NS-System,* edited by Helmut Maier. Wallstein: Göttingen, 2007.

Walker, Mark. *German National Socialism and the Quest for Nuclear Power 1939–1949.* Cambridge, U.K.: Cambridge University Press, 1989.

———. "Otto Hahn: Responsibility and Repression." *Physics in Perspective* 8 (2006): 116–163.

Ruth Lewin Sime

HALL, PHILIP (*b.* London, England, 11 April 1904; *d.* Cambridge, England, 30 December 1982), *mathematics, algebra, group theory.*

Hall was an algebraist who worked in Cambridge for nearly fifty years, beginning in 1927, when he moved smoothly from being a student to becoming a research worker. He was enormously influential both through his writings and through his research students. His main

Hall

work was in group theory, in which he made fundamental discoveries, particularly about soluble groups.

Origins and Education. Hall's parents were George Hall and Mary Laura Sayers (1872–1965). They were not married and the father disappeared soon after Hall's birth. Philip was educated at a local primary school until he won a scholarship to Christ's Hospital, a foundation dedicated to the free education of orphans (which at the time meant fatherless children), which he joined in May 1915. From Christ's Hospital, where his mathematical talents had become evident, he won a scholarship and sufficient financial support to enable him to enter King's College, Cambridge, in October 1922. Hall was one of the Wranglers in the Mathematical Tripos of 1925 and took his BA that same year. As was common at the time, he did not study for a doctorate. The Cambridge undergraduate syllabus of the 1920s was rich in analysis, geometry, and applied mathematics but contained little algebra. There were lectures on group theory by Henry F. Baker and by F. P. White, however, which Hall attended, and he was encouraged by Arthur Berry, an assistant tutor at King's College, to read some of the works of William Burnside, especially the book *Theory of Groups of Finite Order* (2nd ed., Cambridge, 1911) and some of his later papers, and questions on this material were set for him in the Tripos examination.

Career. The first year after graduation Hall remained in Cambridge, learning languages, competing unsuccessfully in the civil service examination and, presumably, thinking about finite abelian groups. He submitted a dissertation on that subject, which, in spite of the fact that it was unfinished, won him a fellowship at King's College and had great influence on later writers. For the first few months of 1927 he worked as a research assistant to Karl Pearson in London, but statistics did not suit him and he returned to Cambridge and to group theory. Some years later, when Hall was elected to the Royal Society in 1942, he wrote:

> The aim of my researches has been to a very considerable extent that of extending and completing in certain directions the work of Burnside. I asked Burnside's advice on topics of group-theory which would be worth investigation & received a postcard in reply containing valuable suggestions as to what would be worth-while problems. This was in 1927 and shortly afterwards Burnside died [on 21 August 1927]. I never met him, but he has been the greatest influence on my ways of thinking. (Gruenberg and Roseblade, 1988, p. 8)

In Cambridge he was appointed university lecturer in 1933, promoted to reader in 1949, and elected Sadleirian Professor in 1953, but his primary allegiance was always to King's College, where he remained a Fellow until his death and taught undergraduates for eight hours per week until he became professor. From September 1941 until the end of the World War II he had leave of absence from Cambridge to work in the Government Code and Cypher School at Bletchley Park, where he contributed to the decoding of Italian and Japanese material.

Hall was an uncommonly successful supervisor of research students. Although a little reclusive, he would offer students as much time and genial companionship—and mathematical guidance and advice—as they wished for. He guided Garrett Birkhoff in universal algebra and lattice theory during the academic year 1932–1933 and three (Bernhard H. [B. H.] Neumann, Paul Cohn, and James A. [J. A.] Green) of the twenty-nine students he supervised were, in due course, elected Fellows of the Royal Society. His influence was enormous, not only on their mathematics but also on their personality: several of his students acquired handwriting that was almost indistinguishable from his; several of them acquired one of the curious characteristics of his lecturing—that, when explaining the mathematics he would often be looking down at the floor to his left while pointing to the relevant formula on the blackboard behind him to his right.

Hall's distinction was recognized in many ways. He was elected Fellow of the Royal Society in 1942 and awarded its Sylvester Medal in 1961. He served as president of the London Mathematical Society from 1955 to 1957 (he had served as one of its honorary secretaries (from 1938 to 1941 and from 1945 to 1948) and was awarded its Senior Berwick Prize in 1958 and its De Morgan Medal, the greatest mark of distinction the Society can offer, in 1965. He was awarded honorary doctorates by the universities of Tübingen (1963) and Warwick (1977), and he was elected to an Honorary Fellowship of Jesus College, Cambridge in 1976.

Mathematics. Hall's major contributions were to five areas of algebra. In 1928 he published a short paper showing how the Sylow Theorems might be significantly extended for finite soluble groups. In 1872 Ludvig Sylow had published theorems guaranteeing *inter alia* that in a finite group G of order $p^a m$, where p is a prime number that does not divide m, any subgroup whose order is a power of p will be contained in a subgroup of order p^a; moreover, all subgroups of order p^a must be conjugate to each other. What Hall proved was that if G is soluble and its order is mn, where m and n are co-prime, then any subgroup whose order divides m is contained in a subgroup of order m (such subgroups were later known as Hall subgroups), and moreover all the subgroups of order m are conjugate to each other.

Nine years later he published an even shorter paper proving a converse: If a finite group *G* has Hall subgroups of all possible orders then it must be soluble. These theorems, together with the theory of Sylow systems and system normalisers that he developed in 1937, became the basis for an extensive theory of finite soluble groups that developed particularly strongly in the 1960s and 1970s. The second theorem, as a characterization theorem for soluble groups, played a major part in the work of John Thompson and others working on the search for simple groups from 1960 to 1980 and beyond. Related, but in many ways very different, work on the *p*-length of *p*-soluble groups, published jointly with Graham Higman in 1956, had a great influence not only in providing tools for the search for finite simple groups but also in attacks on the Burnside Problem about groups of finite exponent. Hall rarely collaborated. In this case what happened was that Higman submitted a paper about groups of exponent 6 to the London Mathematical Society, and Hall, who had been appointed referee, recognized that the methods could be generalized far beyond where Higman had taken them, so they carried out the generalization together.

Hall contributed greatly to the theory of finite *p*-groups, that is, groups of prime-power order. In a long and much-cited article published in 1934, he extended some late work of William Burnside, establishing the modern theory of commutators and the lower central series in these groups. This was later extended to general nilpotent groups in lectures given in Canada in 1957. His theory of isoclinism of *p*-groups provides one of the main tools for classifying them—indeed essentially the only successful tool until the advent of co-class theory in the early 1980s.

Papers published in 1951, 1959, and 1961 opened up the theory of infinite soluble groups. Taking Hilbert's Theorems about Noetherian rings and generalizing them to group-rings of finitely generated nilpotent groups, and treating the last term *L* of the derived series of a soluble group *G* as a module over the group-ring of the quotient group *G/L*, Hall was able to prove that finitely generated abelian-by-nilpotent groups satisfy the ascending chain condition for normal subgroups and are residually finite, and much more besides. Many of his students developed this line of thinking into an extensive area of algebra.

Hall's interest in finite abelian groups, which earned him his fellowship of King's College in 1927, has led to the eponymous Hall Algebra, which plays a large part in representation theory and the modern theory of symmetric functions. Hall's only publication on the subject was a brief survey that summarized lectures given at the Fourth Canadian Mathematical Congress in 1957, but his ideas have been disseminated through lectures and through the exposition and extension of his work by Ian G. Macdonald and others.

This necessarily brief account of Hall's work and influence omits mention of much of his work on aspects of infinite group theory—his studies of locally finite groups, of characteristically simple groups, of simple groups, and much more besides. He published relatively few papers, but every paper made a significant point and was greatly influential in one way or another. He was the most cited group theorist of the twentieth century.

BIBLIOGRAPHY

WORK BY HALL

Gruenberg, K. W. and J. E. Roseblade, eds. *The Collected Works of Philip Hall.* Oxford: Clarendon Press, 1988. Contains Hall's thirty-four research articles.

OTHER SOURCES

Gruenberg, K. W., and J. E. Roseblade. *Group Theory: Essays for Philip Hall.* London: Academic Press, 1984.

Macdonald, I. G. *Symmetric Functions and Hall Polynomials.* 2nd ed. Oxford: Oxford University Press, 1995.

Roseblade, J. E., J. A. Green, and J. G. Thompson. "Philip Hall." *Bulletin of the London Mathematical Society* 16 (1984): 603–626. Obituary. Also published in *Biographical Memoirs of Fellows of the Royal Society* 30 (1984): 603–626, and reprinted in the *Collected Works of Philip Hall,* 1988.

Peter Neumann

HALLER, [VICTOR] ALBRECHT VON

(*b.* Bern, Switzerland, 16 October 1708; *d.* Bern, 12 December 1777), *anatomy, physiology, botany, bibliography.* For the original article on Haller see *DSB,* vol. 6.

In 1970, Haller's scientific achievements and activity had only been studied perfunctorily. After that a lot was learned about his thoughts, concepts, and the spread of his ideas. Scholars have analyzed the unity of his thought, science, and religion; explored his ideals of science and research; investigated his experimental approach; examined the principles and spread of his theory of irritability and sensibility; reassessed his changing views on embryology; registered his vast correspondence; and studied his communication within the Republic of Letters.

Richard Toellner made the first—and as of 2007 the only—modern attempt to grasp the general frame of Haller's thought. He argued that the Christian dualism of creator and creation, the Cartesian dualism of matter and soul, and the Newtonian dualism of force and matter enabled Haller to separate the areas which could be studied (creation, matter) from those which could not (creator, soul, essence of forces). These separations did not, however, tear up his world. It was God who guaranteed its

Haller

Albrecht von Haller. SCIENCE PHOTO LIBRARY.

unity although it was unknown to mankind how the areas were connected. It is in this sense that one has to understand Haller's famous lines: "Into inner nature no created mind penetrates, He is very fortunate when nature shows its outer shell" (*Die Falschheit menschlicher Tugenden,* 1730). It was God who had arranged the structures, laws, and functions in nature, and it was man, or more precisely, the scientist who could try to discover them. However, this was only the outward appearance of nature; the inner nature, the ultimate laws, structures and purposes were known only to God.

Physiology and Methodology. Haller's single contributions to physiology have to be seen as parts of a broader research program already envisaged in the early 1740s: the establishment of a new physiology, based on an experimental foundation. He pursued this project both on the institutional and the methodological level. Haller envisaged the university not only as a place of teaching but also of research. It was the place most suited to contribute to the advancement of science on a steady and long-term basis, not least through the work of the students. Haller's doctoral candidates had to perform experimental studies for their dissertations and were thus important contributors to his research program. Extremely ambitious himself, Haller asked for public reward of scientific achievements as he considered the drive for recognition and fame to be one of the main driving forces behind research.

Research itself—and this is a central element of Haller's methodology—had to focus on a small and well-defined area. It was the continuous performance of specialized research rather than the great theories that added to the advancement of science. The single larger or smaller results, though, should not remain isolated but in their totality would help to construct and extend the single branches of science. In this ongoing process the use of hypotheses linking the various fragments of knowledge was allowed as long as the hypotheses were clearly marked as such. Hypotheses, Haller said, led to novelties and truth, and no discoverer, not even Newton, could do without them. Most importantly, they posed questions which would not have occurred to us and which called for experimental testing.

It is the vast collection of facts and results combined with a cautious use of hypotheses that is characteristic for Haller's works, and notably his opus magnum, the *Elementa physiologiae.* Animal experiments were carried out by many scientists in the seventeenth and early eighteenth centuries, but Haller was the first to perform them in their hundreds, in a systematic manner in order to answer to a well-defined set of questions and considered part of a far-reaching program seeking to establish the basis of a new science. He intended to explore all areas of physiology but did so only in selected subjects. This was partly due to his early leave from the university. His main contribution based on experimental testing was his highly influential, but controversial, concept of irritability and sensibility that stimulated supporters and opponents to perform animal experiments all over Europe, on a scale never seen before.

The results, however, were contradictory, due to contrasting ideological presumptions and due to the lack of standards of procedure. This fostered the perception of animal experimentation as an uncertain method which did not respect the complexity of physiological processes. There was no agreement upon the procedural aspects and heuristic value of this research technique. Animal experiments were performed by several distinguished researchers but not on an institutional basis. Only in the 1820s, when standards of procedure were established, did animal experimentation slowly gain acceptance as a central method in physiological research.

The rejection of Haller's particular findings—which has long been underestimated by historians—allowed for the rejection of his whole concept. Although Haller's description of an innate bodily faculty had a great impact on the evolution of physiological thought and fostered the development of vitalist theories, only a few adopted his definition of the two qualities. The majority regarded irritability as a purely mechanical phenomenon or as a vital faculty extended beyond the muscular fibers and conceived sensibility as an unconscious activity on a local or central nervous level. As a result, most authors did not accept Haller's view of the muscular and the nervous system as entirely independent territories.

Haller's much discussed conversion from epigenesis to preformism has often been regarded as a result of his religious orthodoxy favoring the idea of a fully preformed embryo. Maria Teresa Monti, however, has shown convincingly that although ideological assumptions played a role it was the totality of his many observations which urged him to convert to preformism. Only an explanation based on thorough experimental testing was compatible with his physico-theological belief. What humans saw, Haller thought, could never be against religion. As the visible phenomena could not be denied, it was not science but religion which was endangered by such a confrontation: "Wanting to oppose religion to visible truths is the most dangerous thing one can undertake against it" (*Göttingische Gelehrte Anzeigen* 1760, p. 1356).

Haller's extensive scientific and literary activity (twenty-four monographs in seventy-five volumes, four hundred shorter works, nine-thousand book reviews), his unpublished papers (one-hundred sixty volumes), his well documented library (twenty-three thousand titles) and his large correspondence (seventeen-thousand surviving letters) make him a case exceptionally well-suited to examine how science and the Republic of Letters in the eighteenth century worked. As of 2007, only his correspondence has been studied in some detail. It shows clearly that science and scientific organization was not only dependent on communication by letter but that it was also driven and shaped by it.

SUPPLEMENTARY BIBLIOGRAPHY

WORKS BY HALLER

The Correspondence between Albrecht von Haller and Charles Bonnet. Edited by Otto Sonntag. Bern, Switzerland: Huber, 1983.

The Correspondence between Albrecht von Haller and Horace-Bénédict de Saussure. Edited by Otto Sonntag. Bern, Switzerland: Huber, 1990.

John Pringle's Correspondence with Albrecht von Haller. Edited by Otto Sonntag. Basel: Schwabe, 1999.

Commentarius de formatione cordis in ovo incubato. Edited by Maria Teresa Monti. Basel: Schwabe, 2000. Critical edition, the lengthy introduction (in Italian and English) delivers a thorough analysis of Haller's embryology.

Repertorium zu Albrecht von Hallers Korrespondenz 1724–1777. Edited by Urs Boschung et al. 2 vols. Basel: Schwabe, 2002. Catalogue of 17,000 letters, including summaries of Haller's 1,200 correspondences.

Bibliographia Halleriana. Verzeichnis der Schriften von und über Albrecht von Haller. Edited by Hubert Steinke and Claudia Profos. Basel: Schwabe, 2004. Complete bibliography of primary and secondary literature arranged according to subjects.

OTHER SOURCES

Cherni, Amor. *Epistémologie de la transparence. Sur l'embryologie de A. von Haller.* Paris: Vrin, 1998. Based on a limited knowledge of Haller's writings, to be used with caution.

Duchesneau, François. *La physiologie des lumières. Empirisme, modèles, théories.* The Hague: Martinus Nijhoff, 1982. Thorough epistemological analysis of Haller's physiology and embryology on pp. 126–234, 277–311.

Mazzolini, Renato. "Sugli studi embriologici di Albrecht von Haller negli anni 1755–1758." *Annali dell'Istituto storico italo-germanico in Trento* (1977): 183–242.

Monti, Maria Teresa, ed. *Catalogo del Fondo Haller della Biblioteca Nazionale Braidense di Milano,* 13 vols. Milan, 1983–1994. Catalogue of Haller's massive library (now in Milan) with 13,000 monographs and 10,000 dissertations.

———. *Congettura ed esperienza nella fisiologia di Haller: la riforma dell'anatomia animata e il sistema della generazione.* Florence: Olschki, 1990.

Roe, Shirley A. *Matter, Life and Generation. Eighteenth-Century Embryology and the Haller-Wolff Debate.* Cambridge, U.K.: Cambridge University Press, 1981.

———. "Anatomia Animata: the Newtonian Physiology of Albrecht von Haller." In *Transformation and Tradition in the Sciences,* edited by Everett Mendelsohn. Cambridge: Cambridge University Press, 1984.

Sonntag, Otto. "Albrecht von Haller on the Future of Science." *Journal of the History of Ideas* 35 (1974): 313–322.

———. "The Motivations of the Scientist: The Self-Image of Albrecht von Haller." *Isis* 65 (1974): 336–351.

Steinke, Hubert. *Irritating Experiments: Haller's Concept and the European Controversy on Irritability and Sensibility 1750–1790.* Amsterdam: Rodopi, 2005.

Stuber, Martin et al., eds. *Hallers Netz. Ein europäischer Gelehrtenbriefwechsel zur Zeit der Aufklärung.* Basel: Schwabe, 2005. Analysis of Haller's correpondence, focusing on communication in the Republic of Letters.

Toellner, Richard. *Albrecht von Haller. Über die Einheit im Denken des letzten Universalgelehrten.* Wiesbaden, Germany: Steiner, 1971.

Hubert Steinke

HAMBURGER, VIKTOR (*b.* Landeshut, Silesia [later Poland], 9 July 1900; *d.* St. Louis, Missouri, 12 June 2001), *embryology, neuroembryology.*

Hamburger was one of the most influential neuroembryologists of the twentieth century. A student of Hans Spemann at Frieburg, he was among the first to transfer to the chick embryo the transplantation techniques worked out in Spemann's lab on amphibians. During the early part of his career, he studied the problem of how the vertebrate limb is innervated during embryonic development. This work, carried out from the late 1940s onward in partial collaboration with Rita Levi-Montalcini, led to discovery of nerve growth factor (NGF), a protein that maintains nerve cells as they grow out from the central nervous system to a peripheral target such as a limb bud. For isolating and characterizing NGF Levi-Montalcini and the biochemist Stanley Cohen received the 1976 Nobel Prize in Medicine or Physiology. For the last thirty years of his career Hamburger studied the neurological basis of endogenous pre-hatching behavior patterns in the chick. He also maintained a continuing interest in the history of his field, authoring numerous articles over the course of fifty years and one book, *The Heritage of Experimental Embryology* (1988).

Hamburger was one of two sons born to Max and Else Hamburger, who had moved from Breslau (later Wrocław, Poland) to take over the family textile industry. Max Hamburger was considered a progressive in his day, establishing one of the first organized and planned residential towns (not a "company town" in the U.S. sense) in eastern Europe for workers in his factory. Hamburger's parents were middle-class and well-educated: His father was an avid art collector and friend of many important German artists and his mother an ardent naturalist. Hamburger often said that his mother introduced him to a love of nature, and his father to a love of art. Later in life Hamburger became a modest collector of art himself, and one of his favorite outings was to visit the St. Louis Art Museum; the other was to go on field trips with his colleagues from the Biology Department at Washington University. Although he was primarily a laboratory biologist, field trips into natural areas always remained one of his most satisfying activities.

Hamburger attended the universities of Breslau, Heidelberg, Munich, and Freiburg, obtaining his PhD at the latter in 1925 under the direction of Hans Spemann. He served as a research associate at the University of Göttingen (1925–1926) and at the Kaiser-Wilhelm Institute for Biology in Berlin-Dahlem (1926–1927). In 1927 he returned to Freiburg for five years (1927–1932), when he was awarded a Rockefeller fellowship at the University of Chicago. While he was in Chicago, the National Socialist government came to power in Germany, and Hamburger was dismissed from his post. He remained in Chicago two more years, finally accepting a post as assistant professor of zoology at Washington University in St. Louis, Missouri, where he remained for the rest of his life. He retired officially in 1966, but continued his laboratory work for another twenty years.

In 1928 Hamburger married Martha Fricke, a young biologist whom he had met in Göttingen. They had two daughters, Doris (born in Germany) and Carola (born in the United States). In his scientific and personal life Hamburger was known for his quiet, almost self-effacing manner, his incisive views and his dry wit. He worked intensively and with great concentration, always a hands-on experimentalist, continuing laboratory work into his mid-eighties. Although always well-funded (Rockefeller Institute, NIH), and a nurturing mentor to graduate students and post-docs, he never became a scientific entrepreneur. He accepted only as many people in his laboratory as he could work with directly, and he never lost day-to-day contact with his first love, the embryos, the frog and later the chick.

Background and Education. Hamburger's interest in nature began with early childhood hikes into the mountains and fields around Landeshut and at the family's summer home in the mountains near the Bohemian border, where he often collected frog and salamander eggs that he watched develop to tadpoles and then metamorphose into adults in an aquarium at home. After graduating from gymnasium (secondary school) in June, 1918, Hamburger was inducted into the German army and sent to basic training in Breslau. Had the armistice not been signed in early November, he would undoubtedly have been sent to the front. After being discharged, he remained in Breslau where he took several courses at the university—in zoology, botany, geology and mathematics—while trying to decide how he might pursue a career in science. The turbulent social and economic conditions in Germany immediately after the war did not make such decisions easier. His parents suggested he should get some experience beyond the confines of Silesia. As it happened, his father's first cousin, Clara Hamburger, was assistant to the distinguished protozoologist Otto Bütschli at the University of Heidelberg. So for the academic year 1919–1920 he enrolled as a full-time student. In addition to a philosophy seminar taught by Hans Driesch, the other course that made a considerable impression was a graduate seminar on developmental biology taught by Curt Herbst, Driesch's long-time collaborator from their years together at the Naples Zoological Station. It was in Herbst's seminar that he first had contact with the work of Wilhelm Roux, which stirred his imagination. Reporting on the seminar years later, Hamburger wrote: "It was that seminar that decided my fate—I was to become an experimental embryologist" (Hamburger, 1988, p. 16). However, the sort of experimental embryology that Herbst himself pursued—physiological studies of the effects of calcium, lithium and other ions on patterns of development—

Hamburger

seemed to Hamburger to be too chemical and reductionist. He looked for other possibilities.

The Spemann Laboratory at Freiburg. In the spring of 1920 Hamburger and a friend visited the Black Forest area near Freiburg on a short holiday. He liked the prospects for hiking and skiing in the mountains nearby, and so when he learned from Clara Hamburger that a distinguished zoologist, Hans Spemann, headed the Zoological Institute there Hamburger applied, and was accepted by Spemann as a graduate student at the Institute for the fall of 1920.

The atmosphere at Freiburg was open and relaxed. Students determined their own course of study, which was highly varied and almost wholly self-directed. Most of his time the first year was spent in the *grosse Praktikum*, an all-day laboratory course, in which individual students studied, at their own tempo, representatives of all phyla, from protozoa to mammals, using preserved specimens and microscope slides. It was in Spemann's Institute that Hamburger met what were to become his two closest friends, Johannes Holtfreter and Hilde Proescholdt, who was just then starting her groundbreaking work on transplantation of tissue from the dorsal "lip" of the blastopore (the area of pushing inward of cells in the gastrula stage of embryonic development), that eventually led to the concept of the "Organizer" and Spemann's 1935 Nobel Prize. The laboratory was an exciting and stimulating place. Discussions occurred daily among the students about their own work and every other conceivable subject, from philosophy of art to politics, literature, and of course, science. Holtfreter was to remain a friend and colleague for life. Proescholdt (soon to be married to Otto Mangold) died several years later.

For his PhD dissertation, completed in the spring of 1925, Hamburger undertook to study the role of the nervous system in the development of peripheral organs such as the limbs (using the frog, *Rana fusca*). Earlier work had suggested that ablation of developing eye tissue had resulted in, among others, defects in limb development. In repeating the earlier experiments, Hamburger found no clear relationship between eye and leg development. However, his experiments did suggest a novel idea: innervation was not necessary for normal limb bud differentiation (though it was necessary for later functional development of the limbs). He established this principle unambiguously later, while working at the Kaiser-Wilhelm Institute for Biology in Berlin-Dahlem.

After Freiburg, Hamburger spent several months working at the Stazione Zoologica in Naples before taking up a postdoctoral position in Göttingen with Alfred Kühn, whom Hamburger described as a polymath and the "universal genius among German zoologists" (1988, p. 101). Kühn assigned Hamburger to one of his many ongoing projects, studying color vision in fish, The project never got very far but the stay in Göttingen did help Hamburger establish a number of contacts among leading German biologists who passed through Kühn's laboratory. It was also in Göttingen that he met his future wife, Martha Fricke.

Moving from Göttingen to the Mangold laboratory at the Kaiser-Wilhelm Institute for Biology in 1926, Hamburger found himself in the center of much new, exciting work, especially in the area of developmental genetics. The embryology department was on the first floor of the institute building, while Richard Goldschmidt's genetics department was on the floor above. Hamburger regularly attended the afternoon teas with the genetics group, where he became close friends with Curt Stern, later to become one of the twentieth century's leading geneticists. Goldschmidt fostered a strong interest within his group in the relationship between genetics and development, a connection that had been largely ignored in Spemann's laboratory. Although Hamburger's attempt in collaboration with Stern to carry out some breeding experiments with the fruit fly, *Drosophila*, did not yield any useful results, the relationship between genetics and embryology that this work inspired became a guiding principle for his later work on interspecific crosses among species of salamanders, which involved observing changes in developmental timing (similar to Goldschmidt's work on interspecific crosses in the gypsy moth, *Lymantria*). After arriving in the United States, he also studied the developmental genetics of a mutation in chickens known as "creeper" because they have developmental problems of the limbs that produce creeping-like motion (Hamburger, 1941, 1942).

From Freiburg to Chicago. When Hamburger was recalled by Spemann to Freiburg in 1927 to become a privatdozent, his main teaching assignment was the grosse Prakticum. He succeeded in establishing an atmosphere of excitement among the laboratory students with his constant questioning and discussion of major developments in the field, especially experimental embryology and genetics. Hamburger's position, and eventually ascendancy through the ranks at Freiburg, seemed assured. In 1932 the Rockefeller Foundation invited Spemann to nominate a candidate for a one-year postdoctoral fellowship to the United States (specifically to the laboratory of Frank Rattray Lillie in Chicago). Spemann at first wanted to nominate Otto Mangold, but he was over the age limit of thirty-five stipulated by the foundation, so Spemann nominated Hamburger instead. The main aim was to adapt the methods and techniques of experimental transplantation developed for amphibians in the Freiburg lab to work on chick embryos in Chicago. Leaving his family

Microsurgery on chicken egg. *Techniques for carrying out microsurgery on chicken eggs learned by Hamburger in the Lillie Lab in Chicago. A hole is cut in the egg shell to provide an opening for microsurgery. The glass needle on the right is the sort Hamburger learned to make in Spemann's lab and is the actual surgical instrument. The hair loop on the left is used to manipulate parts of the embryo during surgery. After the surgery is complete, the window is sealed up with a plastic cover and wax.* GARLAND E. ALLEN, HAMBURGER PHOTO COLLECTION, WASHINGTON UNIVERSITY IN ST. LOUIS.

(with a newborn daughter) in Germany, Hamburger came to the Lillie lab in the fall of 1932.

The initial problem on which Hamburger focused grew out of conflicting results obtained in 1909 by one of Lillie's students (Elizabeth Shorey) using the chick, and a decade later (1919) those of one of Ross Harrison's graduate students (Sam Detwiler) at Yale. The question related to the effects of damaging or removing developing chick limb buds on the further development of sensory and motor nerve tracts in the spinal cord. Shorey, using electrocautery, noticed hypoplasia (diminished development) of both motor and sensory nerve columns. By contrast, Detwiler, using limb extirpation and transplantation methods, found that extirpation caused hypoplasia only in sensory nerve columns, and that transplantation of limb buds to other areas of the embryo resulted in hyperplasia primarily of sensory nerve ganglia. Lillie suggested that Hamburger reinvestigate the problem, using the Spemann techniques of microsurgery on the chick, to resolve the discrepancy.

Hamburger learned microsurgical methods for chick embryos from others in the lab, applying the glass needle end hair-loop techniques developed in Freiburg for limb bud extirpation to determine the effects of development of the adjacent nervous system. The results were clear: Shorey's observation that *both* sensory *and* motor neurons responded to extirpation with hypoplasia, was confirmed. In addition to the actual results, Hamburger was immediately impressed with the use of the chick as a model for investigating vertebrate development. In contrast to amphibians, where motor neurons are not organized into the easily-observed motor columns, in the chick embryo, the motor columns are clearly visible, and thus provide favorable material for analyzing changes in their numbers and size in a way that the amphibian embryo does not allow. From this point onward the chick became Hamburger's primary model organism.

In the middle of his year in Chicago, the National Socialist government came to power in Germany, and within months had promulgated the "Law for the Restoration of the Professional Civil Service," removing all civil servants (which included university employees) of Jewish descent from their jobs. Hamburger was dismissed from his post at Freiburg, and Spemann was powerless to alter the decision. With an extension of the Rockefeller grant Hamburger was able to remain in Chicago until 1935. Returning briefly to Germany to bring his family to the United States, he began searching for jobs. There were only three prospects: Odessa (USSR), Sao Paulo (Brazil) and Swarthmore College. He had decided that the best opportunities for research lay in the United States, but Swarthmore was a small liberal arts college where he would have a heavy teaching load. Fortuitously, a position opened up in 1935 at Washington University, and Hamburger jumped at the opportunity. At Washington he advanced from assistant professor (1935–1939), associate professor (1939–1941), and full professor (1941–1966), and after retirement in 1966, he was appointed Edward Malinckrodt Distinguished University Professor (1968) taking *emeritus* status in 1969. He served as department chairman for twenty-six years (1941–1966).

The vast bulk of Hamburger's research work from 1935 onward focused on three major areas in chick development: (1) the relationship between limb bud extirpation (and reimplantation) and its effects on the outgrowth of motor columns in the spinal cord; (2) developmental genetics of the creeper fowl mutation; and (3) the development of chick behavior, especially during the prehatching period.

One of the outcomes of Hamburger's early extirpation work in Chicago was the accidental discovery (based upon his unconscious removal of different amount of limb bud tissue) that there appeared to be a quantitative relationship between the amount of limb bud tissue removed and the degree of hypoplasia in the lateral motor

Hamburger

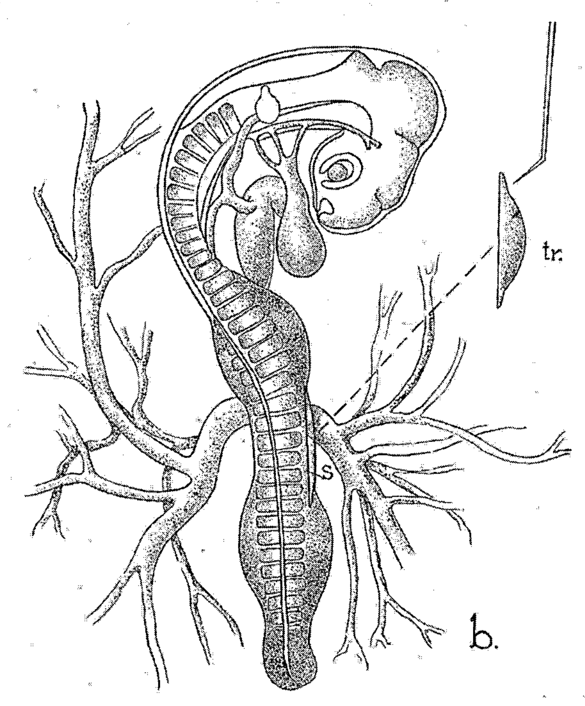

Transplantation of limb bud. *Hamburger's drawing of his innovative experiment, involving transplantation of of a limb bud (labeled tr) from a donor embryo to the flank (the slit in the flank where the transplant will go is labeled s) of a host 3-day-old chick embryo.* GARLAND E. ALLEN, HAMBURGER PHOTO COLLECTION, WASHINGTON UNIVERSITY IN ST. LOUIS.

columns and the related sensory neurons. He also noted that when he transplanted limb bud tissue to other regions of the embryo (flank or belly) that hyperplasia of the motor neurons was enhanced.

In a paper of 1934 Hamburger interpreted this work in the framework of Spemann's induction theory, by putting forward three major conceptual points: (1) The developing peripheral tissue (in this care limb bud) stimulates (by way of an inducer substance) the growth of neurons toward the developing tissue; (2) The inducer substance is transported by retrograde movement from the growing neuron tip back to the cell body to stimulate further growth; and (3) The effect is quantitative: the greater the quantity of inducing tissue, the greater the rate of neuronal growth (and vice-versa, with removal of limb bud tissue).

Discovery of Nerve Growth Factor (NGF). Hamburger had sent a copy of his 1934 paper to an eminent colleague, Giuseppe Levi at the University of Turin Medical Faculty, who eventually passed it on to one of his young post-docs, Rita Levi-Montalcini. During the war, working in exile in the Italian countryside, Levi-Montalcini (who was also Jewish and dismissed from her position in Turin) was intrigued with this paper and had repeated Hamburger's experiments. Publishing her results, along with those of several other Italian workers after the war, Levi-Montalcini came up with a very different interpretation. She had noted something Hamburger had not: After an initial period of proliferation and growth in the non-extirpated side of the chick spinal cord a certain percentage of cells in the motor ganglia began to degenerate, a process she called neuronal death. This was apparently normal, leading Levi-Montalcini to postulate that the limb bud does not have an inductive capacity, but provides a "maintenance factor" that prevents massive neuronal death. When Hamburger read Levi-Montalcini's papers after the war, he was impressed with her work and immediately invited her to St. Louis to work in his lab and try to resolve the discrepancies. With funds provided by the Rockefeller Foundation, Levi-Montalcini came to St. Louis in 1947 for what was intended to be a one-year period. As the work proceeded with exciting results, Hamburger arranged for an extension of the Rockefeller funds, and eventually procured for Levi-Montalcini a faculty position at Washington University that she held for the next thirty years.

In repeating Hamburger's experiments, Levi-Montalcini pointed out the general feature of neuronal death that Hamburger had missed, confirming the hypothesis that the limb bud produces a maintenance rather than an inducing factor. The obvious next step was to isolate and identify the chemical agent responsible, but that was difficult working with chick limb bud tissue, which exists in very small quantities. As it happened, in 1948 Hamburger received a paper from a former student, Elmer Bueker (then at Georgetown University Medical School), detailing an experiment in which he had transplanted a mouse sarcoma into a developing chick egg. Shortly afterward, he noted that the tumor had been thickly invaded by sensory neurons, suggesting that the tumor produced some sort of neuron-stimulating factor.

With Bueker's permission, Hamburger and Levi-Montalcini repeated the experiment and observed a clear quantitative relationship between size of sarcoma and neuronal growth rate. Not being biochemically knowledgeable himself, Hamburger hired a young post-doc from the Washington University Medical School, Stanley Cohen, to identify the active fraction from the tumor. Cohen quickly managed to isolate a nucleo-protein fraction that would stimulate neuronal growth significantly, but it was not clear whether the nucleic acid or protein component was the active agent. Using snake venom as a source of a nucleic-acid digesting enzyme (phosphodiesterase), Cohen showed that the protein fraction had the nerve stimulating property. In fact, the snake venom itself turned out to have a thousandfold greater potency for stimulating neuronal growth than the tumor protein. The

Viktor Hamburger. *Viktor Hamburger and Rita Levi-Montalcini in Hamburger's laboratory at Washington University, 1983.* **GARLAND E. ALLEN, HAMBURGER PHOTO COLLECTION, WASHINGTON UNIVERSITY IN ST. LOUIS.**

system for studying and characterizing the active fraction, which came to be called the nerve growth factor (NGF), was enhanced further by using male mouse salivary glands as a source (which are far easier to obtain than snake venom). Using their system Cohen eventually fully characterized the protein making up NGF.

As the work progressed, Hamburger stepped back from the day-to-day activity, leaving the project in the hands of Levi-Montalcini and Cohen. They were rewarded for their work with receipt of the 1976 Nobel Prize in Physiology or Medicine. Hamburger was not included, a point that disturbed him more than he often let on. His own work admittedly lay in other directions, and he took solace from having started the NGF work and promoted it intellectually and financially during the crucial early years (1934–1954).

The Genetics of Development. In the 1940s and 1950s, while most classically trained embryologists at best paid lip service to the genetics of development, Hamburger's work with the creeper mutant provided one model for how the problem could be approached. The creeper mutant was of interest because in the heterozygous state, the legs are greatly foreshortened due to retardation of growth during embryogenesis, whereas in the homozygous state the eye buds develop a peculiar abnormality known as coloboma (homozygous embryos usually die around the 72-hour stage). Because a single gene appeared to affect these two very different traits, Hamburger realized the creeper system could be used to dissect apart the ways in genes affect developmental pathways. When he transplanted proto limb- and eye-bud tissue from the creeper (heterozygous) strain to the flank of an embryo of a normal strain, the transplant developed the mutant phenotype, as expected (Hamburger, 1942a). But when he transplanted an eye primordium from a homozygous strain to the eye region of a normal embryo, a perfectly normal eye developed. Hamburger's analysis suggested that the effect of the creeper mutation on limb and eye growth must be qualitatively different. The effect on limb

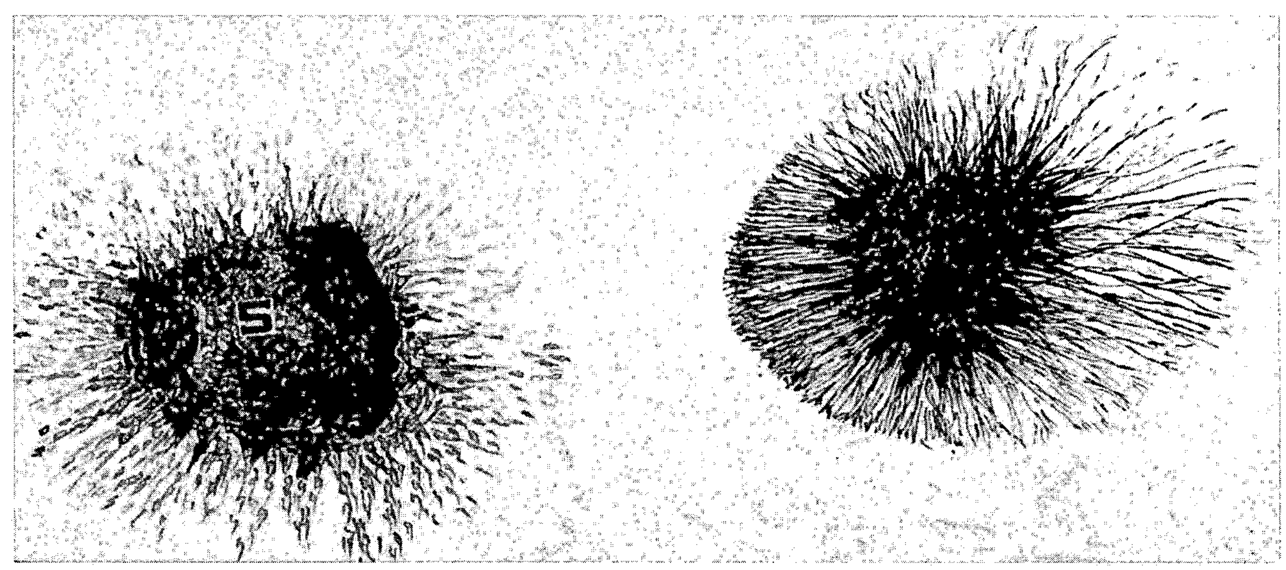

Mouse sarcoma. *Photo of mouse sarcoma 180 (left, labeled S), toward which neurons from a sympathetic ganglion have grown profusely. The mouse sarcoma proved to be a major producer of what came to be known as nerve growth factor (NGF).* **GARLAND E. ALLEN, HAMBURGER PHOTO COLLECTION, WASHINGTON UNIVERSITY IN ST. LOUIS.**

growth was direct, that is, the gene must control some process such as division rate of cells making up the limb tissue, thus affecting (in this case retarding) growth. However, the effect of the creeper gene on eye development must be indirect, altering a secondary process such as development of vasculature of the eye region, rather than a defect in the genetic information for the eye itself.

The outcome of this work suggested that experimental embryology could contribute in at least a small way (for example, by direct and indirect action) to an understanding of the ways in which genes function in development. For the future, he felt "the complete story of the mode of gene action must be written jointly by geneticists, embryologists and physiologists" (Hamburger, 1942a, p. 332). But complex, multicellular organisms were difficult to manipulate for studying the genetics of development, as others, such as Boris Ephrussi and George Beadle, working with *Drosophila* in the 1930s and 1940s, had also discovered. Recognizing the limitations of the creeper fowl work at the time, Hamburger returned to neuroembryology.

The Development of Behavior. Inspired in part by the work of Konrad Lorenz, Hamburger had long been interested in how behavior develops. In the late 1950s and 1960s, at a time when many of his colleagues were thinking about retiring, Hamburger took up a whole new line of experimental work on the neurobiological origin of behavior. Two embryologically-based concepts guided this research: (1) Behavior has an internally guided ontogenesis in the same way as physical organs and systems; and (2) The ontogenesis of behavior and of the structural development of the nervous system are inseparable processes. When he entered this field Hamburger was only dimly aware of the intense debate occurring among developmental psychologists over the issue of the innate or learned quality of even the simplest behavior. This was the period when American behaviorism (stimulated by the work of B. F. Skinner) was in its ascendancy, creating an atmosphere that left little room for ideas about innate factors in the origin of animal behavior. For example, one behaviorist-based theory argued that early movements of the chick head resulted from the embryonic heartbeat, which forced the head up and down repeatedly, leading to adult pecking movements. Recognizing that much of embryogenesis is guided by internal factors, Hamburger decided to investigate the early origin of some simple chick behaviors. The behaviorist view would require, among other things, that the sensory and motor systems in the embryo would develop simultaneously; it would also see embryonic behaviors as coordinated with sensory input and thus nonrandom. Hamburger's approach was to determine how neuronal development correlated with the development of observable behavior in the chick.

Investigating the timing of development, Hamburger noted that the chick motor system began to develop *before* the sensory system, starting at the anterior and proceeding to the posterior region of the spinal chord. Motor neuron development also coincided with the appearance, starting at about 3.5 days, of numerous movements of the head and beak and moving progressively to the wings and hind limbs. Hamburger and his students analyzed these

Hamburger

movements, cataloguing their frequency, duration, and degree of complexity. The movements were found to be random and uncoordinated (one leg or wing would move, the other not) and cycling through periods of activity and quiescence. As embryogenesis progressed, the frequency and complexity of movements increased, while the periods of quiescence decreased.

The next step was to test the hypothesis of spontaneous (non-stimulus-based) movement by removing sections of the afferent (sensory) system leading from a developing limb (they chose the right leg), and nerve tracts from the brain in 2–2.5 day-old embryos. From the initiation of the experiment until around the tenth day, the activity of the leg was identical in the experimental and control (in which afferent nerves had not been removed) groups. To check these observations, Hamburger and several post-docs monitored the electrophysiological discharge of spinal cord motor neurons, finding their activity coincided in frequency and duration with observed spontaneous motility. These findings showed clearly that motor activity *precedes* any sensory input, refuting the orthodox behaviorist explanation. These results were met with considerable opposition, especially within the psychological community. However, with a strong empirical basis, supported by numerous other experiments, Hamburger was able to establish, against opposition from psychologists, the notion of spontaneous motor activity as the beginnings of behavior in vertebrates.

One of Hamburger's most important contributions to the field of embryology was to devise, with Howard Hamilton, a standardized stage series for chick development. A major problem for development of any organism is to have a well-grounded reference system for the stages through which the embryo passes, so that comparisons between experiments can be made at comparable points in the developmental process. The only existing stage series for the chick was a rather loose one drawn up in F. R. Lillie's 1919 *Development of the Chick.* Lillie's series was based on chronology (hours of incubation), a criterion that can be misleading because incubators do not necessarily operate at the same temperature or maintain the same humidity levels, factors that affect growth rate. Hamburger and Hamilton decided early on that what would be most useful would be a stage series based on visible anatomical characteristics. They agreed further that the stages should be chosen on the basis of clear identifiability in external structures, successive stages should be spaced as closely together as possible, and wherever feasible, quantitative measurements such a beak or toe length should be used. Although not as intellectually exciting as some of his other work, according to investigators in the field the Hamburger-Hamilton stage series is likely to be Hamburger's most long-lasting legacy (Hamburger and Hamilton, 1951).

Teaching and Administration. As both a teacher and administrator Hamburger left an important legacy. Serving as Zoology Department chairman at Washington University for twenty-five years, he acquired an outstanding group of faculty (including a number of women, of whose work in science he was a champion). Always a dedicated teacher, he taught at least one course every semester even while serving as department chairman. Two of those courses deserve special mention. One was a year-long, integrated course he developed and co-taught for many years on comparative anatomy and development, accompanied by two two-hour lab sessions per week. The other was a laboratory course in experimental embryology, in which students repeated many of the classic experiments; for this course Hamburger prepared his widely used *Manual of Experimental Embryology,* which went through two editions (Hamburger, 1942b; 1960).

Another of Hamburger's most important educational influences came through his association with the embryology course at the Marine Biological Laboratory in Woods Hole, first as instructor (1936–1941) and then as director of the course (1942–1947). When he took over as director, he converted what had been a traditional, descriptive course into an experimentally-based one, engendering considerable excitement on the part of students. Through this association Hamburger influenced a whole generation of developmental biologists to take up experimental work. It was also through his association with other embryologists at Woods Hole that Hamburger and two other colleagues, Benjamin Willier (Johns Hopkins) and Paul Weiss (University of Chicago) developed the idea of a comprehensive review of the state of developmental biology in the mid-1950s, *The Analysis of Development* (Willier, Weiss, and Hamburger, 1955). Articles were written by specialists on particular processes (gametogenesis, early cleavage, nuclear-cytoplasmic interactions) and on the development of particular animal groups (Hamburger and Holtfreter, for example, wrote the comprehensive chapter on amphibian development). This book became the most influential compendium of experimental embryology of the mid-twentieth century.

Hamburger was a member of many learned societies and institutions, including the American Society of Zoologists (president, 1955), American Association for the Advancement of Science (vice-president, chairman section F, 1960), the American Society of Naturalists, the Society for Developmental Biology (president, 1950–1951), and the International Society for Cell Biology and for Developmental Biologists. He was elected to the National Academy of Sciences (U.S.) in 1953, and the American Academy of Arts and Sciences (1959). He was an honorary member of Sigma Xi and Phi Beta Kappa. In addition, he was awarded a number of prizes in recognition of his work on neuroembryology: The F. O. Schmitt Medal

Hamburger

in Neuroscience (1976), The Ross G. Harrison Prize in Developmental Biology (1981), the Louisa Gross Horwitz Prize in Cell Biology and Developmental Neurobiology (1981), the Ralph Gerard Prize and Medal of the Society for Neuroscience (1985), the Fidia-Georgetown Award in Neuroscience (1987), the National Medal of Science (1989), the Karl Spencer Lashley Award of the American Philosophical Society (1990) and the first Lifetime Achievement Award from the Society of Developmental Biology (1999). He received three honorary degrees: Washington University (1976); the University of Uppsala, Sweden (1984); and the Rockefeller University (1996).

After he closed his laboratory in the mid-1980s, Hamburger devoted his still prodigious energies to historical studies, including the monograph *The Heritage of Experimental Embryology* (Hamburger, 1988) and numerous articles, the last, in his ninety-ninth year, an introduction to and translation of a portion of Spemann's autobiography, focusing on his supposed vitalistic tendencies (Hamburger, 1999). Hamburger died in 2001, at the age of one hundred.

Hamburger's Holistic Philosophy. Hamburger shared with his mentor Spemann and many of his generation an appreciation of biological phenomena in general, and embryology in particular, as dynamic, interconnected, and holistic processes, not reducible simply to chemical and molecular reactions. Unlike Spemann, who had no abiding interest in biochemistry or genetics, Hamburger understood that both were important as complementary ways of understanding the dynamics of development, in particular cellular differentiation. In contrast to the more reductionist philosophy, however, for Hamburger the chemical and molecular basis of ontogenetic changes was the starting point, not the ending point, of investigation. It was necessary to know, but not sufficient to explain development as an interactive and integrated process. He understood clearly that development was not simply a series of mechanical or chemical process, but occurred at a number of organizational levels, from the molecule to the cell, tissue and organ-system.

Hamburger adhered to what might be called (he did not use the term himself) a holistic materialist philosophy. He had no patience with vague or vitalistic ideas, or mystical, immaterial directive forces like the "entelechy" put forward by older biologists such as Hans Driesch. His holistic view was non-mystical and practical. It respected the wholeness, that is, the integrity of the embryo. He once said he made a pact with the embryo: "I promised the embryo that if it would reveal to me some of its secrets I would never homogenize it in a Waring blender." He then added, "I think we have both kept our promises."

BIBLIOGRAPHY

A complete bibliography of Hamburger's published writings can be found in his papers at the Woods Hole Marine Biological Laboratory Library, Special Collections, as well as on the Washington University Library's Internet site, available from http://library.wustl.edu/units/biology/vhl/biblio.html; a few of the most important are listed in Hamburger's autobiographical sketch in History of Neuroscience in Autobiography, *edited by L. R. Squire, Vol. 1 (Washington, DC: Society for Neuroscience, pp. 222–250, and in the Oppenheim paper listed below.*

WORKS BY HAMBURGER

Embryological Writings

"The Effects of Wing Bud Extirpation in Chick Embryos on the Development of the Central Nervous System." *Journal of Experimental Zoology* 68 (1934): 449–494. The first paper in which Hamburger laid out his three-point concept for how limb bud tissue influenced motor neuron growth; this is the paper that also got Levi-Montalcini to start working on the problem of nerve growth during chick development.

"The Larval Development of Reciprocal Species Hybrids of *Triton taeniatus* (and *Tr. palmatus* x *Triton cristatus*." *Journal of Experimental Zoology* 73 (1936): 319–373. One of Hamburger's first attempts to study the effects of different genetic backgrounds (through interspecific hybridization) on developmental processes.

"Motor and Sensory Hyperplasia Following Limb Bud Transplantations in Chick Embryos." *Physiological Zoology* 12 (1939): 268–284.

"Transplantation of Limb Primordia of Homozygous and Heterozygous Chondrodystrophic ("Creeper") Chick Embryos." *Physiological Zoology* 14 (1941): 355–364. In this paper Hamburger showed that limbs from genetically defective embryos (with the "creeper" gene) could develop normally if transplanted to a non-mutant embryo.

"The Developmental Mechanics of Hereditary Abnormalities in the Chick," *Biological Symposia* 6 (1942a): 311–334.

A Manual of Experimental Embryology. Chicago: University of Chicago Press, 1942b; revised 1960.

With Rita Levi-Montalcini. "Proliferation, Differentiation, and Degeneration in the Spinal Ganglia of the Chick Embryo under Normal and Experimental Conditions." *Journal of Experimental Zoology* 111 (1949): 457–502. This paper reports the first results from the authors' collaboration, confirming Levi-Montalcini's observations of neuronal death, and the promotion of the "recruitment" over the "inductive" hypothesis for the effects of limb buds on neuronal growth.

With Rita Levi-Montalcini. "Selective Growth Stimulating Effects of Mouse Sarcoma on the Sensory and Sympathetic Nervous System of the Chick Embryo." *Journal of Experimental Zoology* 116 (1951): 321–362.

With Howard Hamilton. "A Series of Normal Stages in the Development of the Chick Embryo." *Journal of Morphology* 88 (1951): 49–92.

With Rita Levi-Montalcini. "A Diffusible Agent of Mouse Sarcoma, Producing Hyperplasia of Sympathetic Ganglia and Hyperneurotization of Viscera in the Chick Embryo." *Journal of Experimental Zoology* 123 (1953): 233–288.

With Rita Levi-Montalcini and Stanley Cohen. "A Nerve Growth-stimulating Factor Isolated from Sarcomas 37 and 180." *Proceedings of the National Academy of Science USA* 40 (1954): 1014–1018.

With Benjamin Willier and Paul Weiss, eds. *Analysis of Development.* Philadelphia: W. B. Saunders, 1955.

"Some Aspects of the Embryology of Behavior." *Quarterly Review of Biology* 38 (1963): 342–365.

With Elizabeth Wenger and Ron Oppenheim. "Motility in the Chick Embryo in the Absence of Sensory Input." *Journal of Experimental Zoology* 162 (1966): 133–160.

"The Developmental History of the Motor Neuron." *Neuroscience Research Program Bulletin Supplement* 15 (1977): 1–37.

Historical Writings

"Hans Spemann and the Organizer Concept." *Experientia* 25 (1969): 1121–1125.

"Hilde Mangold, Co-Discoverer of the Organizer." *Journal of the History of Biology* 17 (1984): 1–11.

The Heritage of Experimental Embryology. Oxford: Oxford University Press, 1988. A very useful summary of the development of the Freiburg group and the organizer concept. Interspersed with Hamburger's personal commentary (in italics). This very concise and information-filled book provides one of the best examinations of the science coming out of the Spemann lab. Hamburger also devotes a whole chapter to the work of his close friend and colleague, Johannes Holtfreter.

"The Ontogeny of Neuroembryology." *Journal of Neuroscience* 8 (1988): 3535–3540.

"The History of the Discovery of the Nerve Growth Factor." *Journal of Neurobiology* 24 (1993): 893–897.

"Memories of Professor Hans Spemann's Department of Zoology at the University of Freiburg, 1920–1932." *International Journal of Developmental Biology* 40 (1996): 59–62.

"Wilhelm Roux: Visionary with a Blind Spot." *Journal of the History of Biology* 30 (1997): 229–238.

"Hans Spemann on Vitalism in Biology: Translation of a Portion of Spemann's Autobiography." *Journal of the History of Biology* 32 (1999): 231–243.

OTHER SOURCES

Allen, Garland E. "A Pact with the Embryo: Viktor Hamburger, Holistic and Mechanistic Philosophy in the Development of Neuroembryology, 1927–1955." *Journal of the History of Biology* 37 (2004): 421–475. Focuses particularly on the philosophical bases of Hamburger's holistic philosophy and its derivation from Spemann and philosopher Martin Heidegger.

Cowan, W. Maxwell. "Viktor Hamburger's Contribution to Developmental Neurobiology: An Appreciation." In *Studies in Developmental Neurobiology: Essays in Honor of Viktor Hamburger,* edited by W. Maxwell Cowan. New York: Oxford University Press, 1981.

Gluecksohn-Waelsch, Salome. "Viktor Hamburger and Dynamic Concepts of Developmental Genetics." In *Studies in Developmental Neurobiology: Essays in Honor of Viktor Hamburger,* edited by W. Maxwell Cowan. New York: Oxford University Press, 1981.

Kirk, David, and Garland E. Allen. "Viktor Hamburger: A Prepared, Persistent and Deserving Mind Favored by Many Fortuities." *Developmental Dynamics* 222 (2001): 545–551.

Levi-Montalcini, Rita. "One of Hans Spemann's Pupils." In *Studies in Developmental Neurobiology: Essays in Honor of Viktor Hamburger,* edited by W. Maxwell Cowan. New York: Oxford University Press, 1981.

Lillie, Frank R. *The Development of the Chick.* New York: Henry Holt, 1919.

Oppenheim, Ronald W. "Viktor Hamburger (1900–2001): Journey of a Neuroembryologist to the End of the Millennium and Beyond." *Neuron* 31 (2001): 179–190.

———, and Jean Lauder. "Viktor Hamburger at 100: Eight Decades of Neuroembryological Research, 1920–2000." *International Journal of Developmental Neuroscience* 19 (2001): 117–122.

Provine, Robert R. "In the Trenches with Viktor Hamburger and Rita Levi-Montalcini (1965–1974): One Student's Perspective." *International Journal of Developmental Neuroscience* 19 (2001): 143–149.

Garland E. Allen

HAMILTON, WILLIAM DONALD

(*b.* Cairo, Egypt, 1 August 1936; *d.* Oxford, United Kingdom, 7 March 2000) *life sciences, evolutionary biology, sociobiology, population genetics.*

Hamilton, one of the most influential theoretical biologists of the twentieth century, worked in several areas of mathematical evolutionary biology. His theory of inclusive fitness, popularized as kin selection in *The Selfish Gene* by Richard Dawkins (1976), was integral to the foundation of the evolutionary subdiscipline of sociobiology in the 1960s and 1970s. Hamilton ranged widely over questions of evolutionary theory in his career, constellated more or less loosely around two central concerns: the evolution of social behavior, particularly of altruism; and the evolution and maintenance of sexual reproduction.

Early Years. Hamilton was born in Cairo to émigré New Zealand parents and raised largely in the Kent countryside in southern England. Interested in science and natural history from childhood, Hamilton was nearly killed as a boy while experimenting with chemical explosives; less dangerously, he was inspired by a great-aunt's gift of her collection to take up insect collecting. A birthday gift of Edmund Briscoe Ford's *Butterflies* (1945) introduced him to the theories of genetics and evolution, which interested him enough to request a copy of Charles Darwin's *On the Origin of Species* as a school prize. After two years of national service (1955–1957), Hamilton entered St. John's College, Cambridge University, in 1957 on a state scholarship to study natural sciences.

At the time Hamilton went up to Cambridge, molecular genetics, thanks to James D. Watson and Francis Crick, was the avant-garde of biology, but Hamilton made an early decision that his interests lay elsewhere and he would not try to keep up with the field. This independence of intellectual interests and stubbornness in pursuing them—which remained lifelong characteristics—meant that Hamilton's university career, capped by a satisfactory but not outstanding upper second degree, was not evidently brilliant. This was due, Hamilton said in later years, to the time taken from his official studies by his discovery of the book that was to set the course of his scientific life, Ronald A. Fisher's *The Genetical Theory of Natural Selection* (1930), a fundamental text of the so-called modern synthesis uniting Darwinian natural selection with Mendelian genetics. Although Hamilton was studying biology and genetics, none of his professors, who were biologists trained in the interwar period and were more interested in ecology than in questions about the action of natural selection and evolution, assigned Fisher's book. In fact, Hamilton was given to understand by his instructors that Fisher, while sound as a statistician, was suspect as a biologist. Nevertheless, Fisher's book came to the young Hamilton as a revelation. His enthusiasm was roused both by Fisher's rigorous adherence to the principle of natural selection in evolutionary explanation, and by Fisher's lengthy application of his mathematical population genetics to human affairs—the very day he discovered the book, Hamilton wrote to his sister Mary a postcard that was particularly enthusiastic about the final third of the book, devoted to Fisher's analysis of the evolutionary problems facing the human species and his eugenic prescriptions for repair.

In his own autobiographical writings, Hamilton painted his younger student self as an isolated, Romantic hero, burdened with knowledge too great for ordinary minds to bear. Fisher's work provided a focus for Hamilton's lifelong scientific and personal preoccupations, which were the application of the principle of natural selection, as Hamilton strictly understood it, as the key to understanding evolution, and worries about the tenuousness of human society in view of human selfishness and aggression. Hamilton was accustomed from an early age "to believe … that the quickest way to understand what puzzled me was to spend more time thinking about what I already knew, not necessarily collecting more data" (*Narrow Roads of Gene Land,* 1997, vol. 1, p. 12) and the data he had told him that human beings were young Werthers, fundamentally unhappy self-absorbed self-interested creatures—this was what he was himself, he believed, and why would other people be fundamentally different? From gloomy introspection Hamilton turned the tools of population genetics he had learned from Fisher on the problem of explaining why, if fundamental selfishness was the norm, communities could exist at all.

Biologists who had studied the origins of sociality (including of human society), from Darwin through the 1950s, had, in general, considered the evolution of societies to be a more elaborate manifestation of the cooperative tendencies necessarily inherent in all organized life, beginning with the cell and continuing through the organism and the family to societies. Just as the parts of a cell had to function together for life to continue, and as the cells of an individual organism must work together, and as sexual organisms must cooperate to at least a minimal degree to reproduce, so too were the individuals in a society parts of a greater whole whose cooperation was required to maintain life and their species. The questions biologists asked about social evolution, then, had less to do with how societies held together once evolved than with the mechanisms of their original evolution.

Hamilton's principal achievement was to transform the question, "Why do societies exist?" into an individual question, "Why should *I* be part of society?" The first question took the species as the fundamental unit of interest, as had been usual in evolutionary biology until that time, while the second focused on the individual. The answer Hamilton developed lay not in the mechanisms of social interaction, but in the identification of a deeper-lying self-interest that caused societies to evolve under appropriate circumstances of individual advantage.

After university, Hamilton hoped to continue in graduate study of biology, but had a great deal of trouble finding an institution and advisor receptive to his proposed research question, the origins of altruism, and his proposed means of attacking it, mathematical population biology. Potential advisors and institutional homes were put off either by his mathematical bent, or by his interest in the question of altruism, with its clearly implied links to the explanation of human evolution and possible whiff of eugenics. He finally cobbled together a course of study, enrolling for an MSc in human demography at the London School of Economics (LSE), and then for a PhD jointly supervised by John Hajnal, a demographer at the LSE, and Cedric Smith, a geneticist at the Galton Laboratory, University College London. Slowly a mathematical treatment of the evolution of altruistic behavior, defined as behavior actively harmful to the personal reproductive possibilities of its performer, began to take shape.

A Theory of Altruism. Hamilton's theory of inclusive fitness synthesized several different elements and approaches. First were tools drawn from each of the three founding fathers of population genetics, Fisher, the British biologist John Burdon Sanderson Haldane, and the American biologist Sewall Wright. Fisher's mathematical population genetics, with a particular emphasis on the universal applicability of Fisher's "fundamental theorem of natural selection" (natural selection will result in the evolution of organisms equipped to produce a maximum number of offspring given their environmental and other constraints), combined with his concerns about human evolution, provided Hamilton's foundation. Hamilton also drew on an animadversion of Haldane's about the circumstances under which genetically directed self-sacrificial behavior could spread (Haldane had thought it rather unlikely). Finally, after a considerable period of cumbersome ad hoc calculation, Hamilton found and applied to the analysis of altruistic behavior Wright's "coefficient of relatedness," a mathematical expression of the probability that, at a given locus, the alleles present will be identical by descent.

To these three building blocks, Hamilton contributed two major novelties. The first was a rigorous insistence that selective costs and benefits had to be analyzed strictly from the perspective of the individual gene, rather than from the point of view of the species or even of the organism. In this, Hamilton was drawing on the perspectives and techniques of rational choice theory, a school of analysis using the tools of game theory and economic analysis, at first primarily applied in economics and political science. Rational choice theory developed in the years after World War II and aimed to turn decision making into a science and to analyze it according to the principles of economic and game-theoretic logic. Hamilton became interested in the possible applications of rational choice theory to his own biological preoccupations while pursuing his PhD; his coadvisor, Smith, a Quaker interested in applying scientific ideas to promoting world peace, maintained a small library on the subject and hosted a discussion group in peace and conflict studies, an area of rational choice theory associated with pacifist political responses to the Cold War. This mathematized, cost-benefit approach to problems of moral as well as scientific import suited Hamilton's inclinations well. Using the tools of rational choice theory, altruistic behavior could be drained of the troublesomely subjective questions of the motivation of the altruist and the perception of the recipient, to be redefined solely as action conferring reproductive gain to the recipient at a reproductive cost to the altruist.

According to Fisher's fundamental theorem, however, such behaviors could not possibly evolve, as organisms are constantly selected to maximize their own reproduction. The appearance of many such self-sacrifices in nature, then, became a paradox: if natural selection is all-powerful, and acts only to further the reproduction of the individual, no individual could evolve characters that would impede its own reproduction—and yet, examples abound of such characters in nature, including animals that give alarm calls to warn others of predators but thus drawing predators' attention to themselves, and sterile worker castes among social insects. These had presented no problems when the evolution of species and groups had been the primary object of explanation, and when sociality had been a general given; Darwin, for example, had in chapter seven of the *Origin of Species* (1859) dismissed the evolution of sterility in social insects as a problem "of no very great difficulty" for natural selection, as long as it were "profitable to the community" that some individuals should be born "capable of work, but incapable of procreation" (p. 236). Under Fisher's redefinition, however, such cases became problematic indeed.

Hamilton resolved this newly discovered paradox by extending the notion of offspring to cover not only those directly engendered by an organism, but also those related individuals whom the organism caused to exist by its structures, behaviors, or what-have-you. That is, to further the existence and reproduction of siblings, cousins, parents, nieces, or other kin was in a fundamental way the same as furthering the existence of offspring, as doing so perpetuated the share of the organism's own genes that the relative carried, and thus in the organism's own interest just as engendering offspring is. Relatives, however, are not all created equal. Some are genetically closer than others; a diploid organism's children and parents, for example, share exactly one half of its genes, its siblings share one half on average (because of the shuffling of genes that takes place during the formation of sex cells in meiosis, this is an average rather than an exact coefficient), while half siblings and nieces share one quarter on average and first cousins an eighth. Hamilton asserted that the inducement to benefit a relative bearing one's own genes, therefore, had to be discounted by the distance of the relationship (measured by Wright's coefficient of relatedness); he formalized this inducement, denoted k, in what came to be known as Hamilton's rule: $k > 1/r$, a gene causing an organism to benefit relatives at the expense of its own reproduction will be selected and increase in a population if the benefit to the "altruist" outweighs the discounted relationship. As Hamilton himself put it,

> a gene causing altruistic behavior towards brothers and sisters will be selected only if the behavior and the circumstances are generally such that the gain is more than twice the loss; for half-brothers it must be more than four times the loss; and so on. To put the matter more vividly, an animal acting on this principle would sacrifice its life if it could thereby save more than two brothers, but not for less. (1963, p. 355)

An organism's inclusive fitness consisted of all the copies of its own genes it caused to exist, whether by direct

Hamilton

parenthood or by the preservation of relatives containing some fraction. The criterion of fitness was thus broadened from the individual to the family, while at the same time Hamilton shifted the focus of the analysis of natural selection from the organism to the gene, since, he asserted, "despite the principle of 'survival of the fittest' the ultimate criterion which determines whether *G* [a gene causing some theoretical, unspecified kind of altruistic behavior] will spread is not whether the behavior is to the benefit of the behaver but whether it is to the benefit of the gene *G*" (Hamilton, 1963; repr. in *Narrow Roads,* 1997, vol. 1, p. 7).

Hamilton wrote up the theory of inclusive fitness in two versions. One was a lengthy, fully mathematical treatment that unified understanding of a considerable body of case studies of altruistic behaviors that Hamilton drew from the scientific literature, the fruit of his graduate research. The second was a short, mostly verbal abstract of the whole, containing only the mathematical relation of Hamilton's rule and some general, theoretical remarks on its applicability. He met difficulty in publishing both. The first he submitted to the *Journal of Theoretical Biology,* where it spent considerable time in the reviewing process; ultimately the referee (John Maynard Smith, a mathematical biologist of similar interests) asked that it be split into two parts. The second he sent with perhaps naive optimism to *Nature,* which promptly rejected it, the editor suggesting that its specialized topic might be more appropriate to a "psychological or sociological journal." Hamilton was stung by this rejection, which he attributed to his LSE affiliation, but the editor may well have seen that one of Hamilton's objectives was to explain human society, even though his only allusion to the subject in the paper was an oblique concluding reference to Fisher's work on man. On a second submission, to the *American Naturalist,* the paper was accepted and published in 1963.

After the revisions and splitting called for by the referee for the *Journal of Theoretical Biology,* that journal published "The Genetical Evolution of Social Behaviour," parts 1 and 2, in 1964. The first part of the paper contained the mathematical arguments culminating in the derivation of Hamilton's rule; its arguments were almost exclusively cast in the language and methodology of modern population genetics. The second part hearkened back in its methodology to Darwin's, as Hamilton used the theory of inclusive fitness to explain a diverse array of social traits recorded in the biological literature, including alarm calling, mutual grooming, the fusion of colony organisms, and postreproductive behavior in cryptic (camouflaged) moth species compared with that of aposematic species (bad-tasting with vivid warning colors). In each case, Hamilton argued that his theory of inclusive fitness could coherently explain the evolution of phenomena that had been disparate in the literature as aspects of a single principle at work, Fisher's fundamental theorem of natural selection, mandating the maximization of favorable genes under selection.

Like Darwin, Hamilton also turned to the apparently problematic case of the social insects to provide a clinching argument. Where the crux of the problem for Darwin had been the difficulty of evolving castes of differentiated sterile workers that could not directly pass on their sometimes extravagant modifications from the reproductive forms, for Hamilton the difficulty lay in the evolution of sterility itself, for if every individual, and every gene, is, figuratively speaking, attempting to maximize its replication, then evolved sterility would be the ultimate Fisherian impossibility. What possible self-interest could make an organism forgo any chance of reproduction, when reproduction is the very definition of self-interest? Darwin, viewing the community as the object of natural selection in such cases, had, as noted, found no great difficulty in this point, but Hamilton, who did not see communities as meaningful entities, refused to accept Darwin's argument (which had remained the general explanation of the evolution of social behavior since his time), insisting on an argument that acknowledged what he took to be genes' fundamental selfishness. Hamilton pinned his argument on the peculiar genetics of the family Hymenoptera, comprising the wasps, ants, and bees.

Hymenopterans are characterized by an unusual sex-determination system, known as haplodiploidy. Female hymenopterans are, like members of most sexually reproducing species, diploid: they have two sets of chromosomes in each cell, one derived from their mother, one from their father. Males, however, are haploid: they have only one set of chromosomes, from their mother; males hatch from unfertilized eggs and thus, oddly, have no father at all. These facts have interesting consequences for Hamilton's arguments concerning inclusive fitness. A female hymenopteran is related to her mother and to her father by one-half each, likewise to her own daughters and sons by one-half each. But because she shares all of the one-half of her genes derived from her father with all of her sisters (presuming her mother mated only once), she is related to each of her sisters by three-quarters on average (one-half identical in all cases, derived from the father; one-half of the remaining half, derived from the mother, shared on average). By the same calculation, she is related to her brothers by only one-quarter on average. A male is related to his brothers as well as to his sisters by one-quarter on average. Because sisters are more closely related to each other than to any other relatives, including their own parents or potential offspring, the conclusion Hamilton drew is that haplodiploidy, at least in cases where females mated only once, would predispose the Hymenoptera to the evolution of social systems in which sisters furthered each other's success and in which males, relatively little related to their sisters or brothers, would have no incentive to take part. The argument applied only to the haplodiploid hymenoptera, and in its strongest form only to the case in which a fertile female had mated only once (multiple paternity would dilute sisters' relatedness to one another), but it gained particular strength from the long-standing observation that complex social behavior and the evolution of sterile female castes had apparently evolved numerous times in the Hymenoptera from solitary lineages, while, in contrast, complex sociality and sterile castes were known to have evolved only one other time among insects, in the single lineage arising from the cockroaches and leading to the termites (which are fully diploid organisms, and so not subject to the same argument).

The power of inclusive fitness was to make every instance of apparent "altruism" evolutionarily explicable as an act of selfishness. This new view of altruism required a new definition: altruism consisted of promoting another organism's genetic self-interest at the expense of the altruist's own. That is, the individual cost to the altruist became a crucial component of the definition, and analysis of altruistic behavior had correspondingly to focus on the genetic self-interest of the individual, not the colony or the group or the species. In the second part of "The Genetical Evolution of Social Behaviour," Hamilton's rhetorical method also evoked Darwin's in his confrontation of the apparent difficulties for his theory in the form of observations published in the literature that apparently contradicted the evolutionary action of kin selection. Hamilton admitted, for example, that in at least some species of hymenopterans (honeybees, for example) multiple matings by fertile females were well attested, lessening the force of the argument for inclusive fitness as the evolutionary glue holding colonies together. Recorded instances of adoption of unrelated orphan chicks in various bird species likewise provided an apparent counterinstance. Hamilton insisted, however, that in every case, either previous observations must have been misinterpreted, or the behavior in question represented a "biological error," actively maladaptive and thus, by Fisher's principle, doomed. This rigorous insistence on the necessity to analyze behavior as correlated to the genes that promoted it, then to analyze it in terms of the benefits to the reproduction of those genes, was Hamilton's principal contribution in "The Genetical Evolution of Social Behaviour," one that was to help to transform both the language and the theory of evolutionary biology.

Reception of Inclusive Fitness and Further Work on the Evolution of Sociality. Hamilton's papers on inclusive fitness did not at first make much splash. In a letter to *Nature* published in 1964, before the publication of Hamilton's paper in the *Journal of Theoretical Biology,* Maynard Smith, a referee of "The Genetical Evolution of Social Behaviour," coined the phrase *kin selection* to apply to Hamilton's theory, but rather disingenuously equally credited Hamilton's *American Naturalist* article and Haldane's brief remarks of 1951 with the concept (this quasi-breach of the ethics of peer review came between the two men, and Smith came to regret it). The first sustained attention to Hamilton's paper came from students of the Hymenoptera, who specialized in Hamilton's chief case study. Edward O. Wilson, who was at this time emerging as the world's preeminent specialist on ants, read Hamilton's paper in 1965, not expecting to find much of interest in it. By his own account, Wilson was at first hostile to the idea that an unknown graduate student could have "cut the Gordian knot. Anyway, there was no Gordian knot in the first place, was there? I had thought there was probably just a lot of accidental evolution and wonderful natural history.... [But finally] I gave up. I was a convert, and put myself in Hamilton's hands" (Wilson, 1994, p. 320). Wilson contacted Hamilton, and in the fall of 1965 the two men attended a meeting of the Royal Entomological Society of London, where Wilson strongly advocated Hamilton's theory in an invited lecture on the social behavior of insects. Wilson also devoted substantial space to inclusive fitness in his book *The Insect Societies* (1971), the first major synthetic work on the social insects to appear in forty years. However, Wilson, though he played an integral role in publicizing Hamilton's work on inclusive fitness, was never an entire convert to the all-sufficiency of kin selection in explaining the origin of sociality in the social insects. Indeed, although the argument about haplodiploidy provided the catchiest component of Hamilton's 1964 paper, and the only illustration of inclusive fitness that nonbiologists tend to remember, the arguments pro and con as to whether haplodiploidy accounts for the evolution of sociality in the Hymenoptera have never ceased among students of social insects, with no final consensus in sight. Hamilton's work also received favorable mention in George Christopher Williams's *Adaptation and Natural Selection* (1966), an influential manifesto against the arguments for group selection made by Vero Copner Wynne-Edwards and in favor of a rigorously individual-level approach to natural selection.

Hamilton's influence began to grow among evolutionary biologists as the few who had read and understood the import of his papers worked to bring him from his initial scientific and social isolation into the networks of scientists interested in evolution and behavior. Wilson, for example, invited Hamilton to lecture at Harvard University in 1969, en route to a Smithsonian Institution conference on "Man and Beast" that brought together specialists from various fields to discuss the impact of recent biological work on understandings of human nature; it was on this visit to Harvard that Hamilton met Robert Trivers,

Hamilton

then a graduate student there and later an important collaborator and ally in explaining the evolution of altruistic behavior. The two works that brought Hamilton's name and theory before a wider audience of both scientists and the general public, however, were Wilson's *Sociobiology* (1975) and Dawkins's *The Selfish Gene* (1976). While Wilson in *Sociobiology* treated inclusive fitness as just one of a number of motors of social evolution (albeit an extremely important one), Dawkins seized on Hamilton's fundamental vision of the gene as the central locus of natural selection to redefine Darwinism around the idea of the "selfish gene" and to establish a program for biology that made Hamilton's gene-centered cost-benefit theoretical language and apparatus central to the analysis of all evolutionary problems. From about 1974, citations of Hamilton's 1964 papers in the scientific literature began an exponential rise, reaching some four thousand total in the Institute for Scientific Information (ISI) Web of Science database by 2007, making "The Genetical Evolution of Social Behaviour" the most-cited paper ever published in the *Journal of Theoretical Biology*. In concert with Williams, Maynard Smith, Wilson, Dawkins, Trivers, and others, Hamilton's principal achievement was so thoroughly to revise the language of evolutionary biology that it has become nearly impossible to speak in evolutionary explanations except in terms of the self-interest of the organism or gene.

Over the twenty or so years following "The Genetical Evolution of Social Behaviour," Hamilton continued to work on problems connected to the evolution of sociality in both animals and humans. In 1963–1964 he spent time in Brazil at the laboratory of Warwick Kerr, making observations and testing theories of evolution in social insects. After returning to Britain, he was offered a lectureship in genetics at Imperial College, University of London (Hamilton later learned that he had been one of only two applicants for the post, the first of whom had turned it down). This position gave him excellent facilities for observation and natural historical experiment in Silwood Park at the university's field station, an "entomological Mecca." The teaching duties were not especially onerous, fortunately for all concerned: Hamilton began at this period to build a solid lifelong reputation as a dreadful teacher and lecturer (Imperial College students regularly petitioned that marks in Hamilton's courses not be counted toward their degrees, "in view of the nature of the teaching"). Moreover, as Hamilton's professional isolation began to ease in the late 1960s, so too did his personal isolation. In 1966 he married Christine Friess, a student in dentistry; the couple had three daughters.

Hamilton continued in this period to work out problems connected with his thinking on inclusive fitness. The paper that Hamilton claimed to be proudest of in his career, "Extraordinary Sex Ratios," published in *Science* in 1967, treated the evolution in various species of sex ratios deviating from the 50–50 female-male ratio that Fisher had mathematically established to be the evolutionary default in cases of panmixia (where every female has an equal chance of mating with every male). Hamilton took on several different sorts of evolutionary forces that could disturb the force driving the ratio back to 50–50: viscous populations, for example, in which males mated only with the females immediately surrounding them (cases occur often in nature, frequently with sibling mating, as when newly hatched brothers fertilize their sisters from a batch of eggs laid by a parasitic wasp on an insect host). In these cases, Hamilton demonstrated that natural selection would produce a bias toward the production of females, since the return on the investment on sons (which can fertilize many females each) would diminish as they competed among themselves to fertilize females (which would mate only once). Hamilton's paper, however, had larger ends in view than the peculiarities of parasitic insect reproduction. He considered the selective outcomes of the various possibilities that a gene determining sex ratio in a diploid species might be found on either the X (female) chromosome, the Y (male) chromosome, or on an autosome (a chromosome common to both sexes). Again using the gene's-eye perspective, Hamilton argued that different chromosomes would then "want" different sex ratios, because the arguments for inclusive fitness that covered the interactions of one organism with another would equally apply to the interaction of one chromosome with another (given that a diploid organism contains two sets of chromosomes from two different individuals, who may be more or less related to one another). Drawing on the apparatus of mathematical game theory, Hamilton further predicted that sex ratios in populations would, under specified conditions of inheritance and environment, settle at fractions that he called "unbeatable." This idea, viewing organisms as though they were rational, strategic agents seeking to maximize their own inclusive fitness, drew on the same underlying use of game theory and prefigured the more generalized version of the "evolutionarily stable strategy," or ESS, that was proposed in 1973 by Maynard Smith and George Price, whose collaboration was a strong link between Hamilton's and Smith's thinking. Price, a self-taught mathematical population geneticist, had contacted Hamilton in the wake of his papers on inclusive fitness, having subsequently devised an independent mathematical formulation that elegantly covered Hamilton's case. Hamilton and Price subsequently collaborated on a pair of papers published in *Nature* in 1970 covering the evolution of selfish and spiteful behaviors, complementary to the evolution of altruism.

From the very beginning of his systematic thinking on altruism as a Cambridge undergraduate, Hamilton had been motivated to explain the puzzle, as he saw it, of the existence of altruistic behavior not only in the animal world but in human beings as well. In common with Darwin and virtually all evolutionary biologists of the late nineteenth and early twentieth centuries (including, importantly, his idol Fisher), Hamilton believed that evolutionary biology pursued two intertwined aims: the first to explain the history of life on earth, and the second to explain human nature, to explain us to ourselves. While biologizing explanations of human nature, particularly those advancing evolutionary explanations for human racial or individual differences, had fallen out of favor among professional evolutionary biologists in the wake of eugenics and German National Socialist abuses, and as evolutionary biology established itself as an institutional scientific discipline distinct from sociology and anthropology, a number of younger evolutionary biologists in the 1960s, including Hamilton and Wilson, were deeply interested in such questions and preparing to address them directly in their scientific work. Hamilton's first published paper in 1963 had already obliquely alluded to this theme, and in a paper published in 1975 as part of the proceedings of a conference organized by the anthropologist Robin Fox and the primatologist Irven DeVore, "Innate Social Aptitudes of Man: An Approach from Evolutionary Genetics," Hamilton addressed the question of human nature and its evolution directly (in a paper he viewed as an homage to Price, who had died by suicide earlier that year). Hamilton here extended the notion of inclusive fitness, drawing on Price's work, to account for the differential evolution of altruistic behavior among groups. His remarks on the selective advantages of warfare, despite its "gross inefficiency … [as] an alternative to birth control and infanticide," and his speculations about the evolution of intragroup altruism combined with warlike aggressiveness among "barbaric pastoralists" such as the Bantu, drew some heated criticism (including from the anthropologist Sherwood Washburn, one of the volume's dedicatees and coauthor of Hamilton's article's epigraph), criticism that prefigured the storm that was to break out over Wilson's *Sociobiology* and Dawkins's *Selfish Gene* over the next year; Trivers teasingly called it Hamilton's "fascist paper."

In 1978, invited by fellow sociobiologist Richard D. Alexander, Hamilton moved from Britain to the United States, taking up a professorship in the biology department at the University of Michigan, Ann Arbor, where he was to remain until 1984. While at Michigan, Hamilton's longstanding interest in game theory came to the fore in his collaboration with Robert Axelrod, a political scientist who was a colleague at Ann Arbor in the Institute of Public Policy Studies (now the Gerald R. Ford School of Public Policy). Hamilton and Axelrod's collaboration, "The Evolution of Cooperation," published in *Science* in 1981 played, like Maynard Smith and Price's evolutionarily stable strategies, an important role in the reunion of the political and economic roots of rational choice theory with its offshoot in biology. Hamilton had become interested in game theory in general, and in the particular instance known as the Prisoner's Dilemma, in the early 1960s on reading an article in *Scientific American* on John von Neumann's work written by the Russian-American rational choice theorist Anatol Rapoport. The Prisoner's Dilemma is a non-zero-sum game, conventionally described with the following scenario and matrix: two accomplices in a crime, A and B, arrested by the police, are separately interrogated and offered a plea deal to offer state's evidence against the other. If A and B both decline this deal, they will each serve six months. If A takes it, while B remains silent, according to the terms of the deal A will go free while B will serve five years. The reverse will happen if B rats out A. And if each each testifies against the other, both will serve two years.

	Prisoner B remains silent	**Prisoner B testifies**
Prisoner A remains silent	Each serves six months	Prisoner B goes free; Prisoner A serves five years
Prisoner A testifies	Prisoner A goes free; Prisoner B serves five years)	Each serves two years

The source of the game's titular dilemma is that although each prisoner's best strategy is to testify against his accomplice, he knows that this is his accomplice's best strategy too. A rational prisoner would always choose to testify, although this precludes the possibility of a lighter sentence for both, because the penalty for loyalty in the event of his accomplice's treachery is so severe. In its generalized form, the Prisoner's Dilemma stipulates that mutual cooperation has a better outcome than mutual defection, which both have a better outcome than the loser's penalty (the "sucker's payoff") in a situation where one player cooperates and the other defects. Hamilton's initial formulation of "altruism" and its opposite number, "spite," as two choices in a matrix of alternative behaviors (help others at cost to one's own reproduction, hurt others at cost to one's own reproduction) had owed its form to the Prisoner's Dilemma, as Hamilton noted in his paper for the "Man and Beast" colloquium. And in the conclusion to "Innate Social Aptitudes of Man" Hamilton explicitly asserted the relevance of the Prisoner's Dilemma to the evolutionary explication of human evolution and behavior:

"One hears that game theorists, trying to persuade people to play even two-person games like 'Prisoner's Dilemma,' often encounter exasperated remarks like: 'There ought to be a law against such games!' Some of the main points of this paper can be summarized as an answer to this comment: that often, in real life, there is a law, and we can see why, and that sadly we also see the protean nature of this Dilemma, which, when suppressed at one level, gathers its strength at another." (reprinted in *Narrow Roads,* 2001, vol. 2, pp. 347–349)

Axelrod contacted Hamilton, on recommendation from Dawkins, because he was interested in the literature on evolutionarily stable strategies. Hamilton had presumed, as most game theorists did, that continued defection (all-defect or ALL-D) was always the core winning strategy for players of the Prisoner's Dilemma, as it was easily demonstrated to be in the case of a fixed number of games; this perhaps accounted for the melancholy of his conclusion to "Innate Social Aptitudes of Man." Axelrod, however, had run a tournament, open to all comers (fourteen strategies in all, submitted by economists, sociologists, political scientists, and mathematicians, were played against each other in a round-robin), to discover the best strategy for playing an open-ended number of rounds of the game. This tournament was won by Rapoport (Hamilton's first guide in game theory, by happy chance), who submitted the simplest strategy, called TIT FOR TAT: begin by cooperating, then do whatever the opponent has done in the move before, whether cooperate or defect. On a second round of the tournament (sixty-two entries, including evolutionary biologists, physicists, and computer scientists in addition to the earlier entrants), Rapoport's TIT FOR TAT won again. Axelrod and Hamilton argued that Hamilton's kin selection provided a key to understanding how TIT FOR TAT strategies could have won out evolutionarily in the history of life over ALL-D to permit the evolution of sociality, since inclusive fitness gave organisms a genetic incentive to cooperate over defection, even at reproductive cost to themselves. Effectively, this meant that the game's payoff matrix was recalculated, so that apparent losses might in fact conceal a player's part interest in its opponent's gain. In his usual style, Hamilton adduced a number of previously puzzling examples from the published biological literature that might serve as illustrations of the new principle. Axelrod and Hamilton's paper, like Hamilton's original papers on inclusive fitness, gave rise to a veritable industry or subdiscipline within biology, testing examples and attempting to expand or refute the principle; unlike inclusive fitness, however, this work was immediately widely recognized as important, not only published in *Science* but also honored as that prestigious journal's most important paper for the year 1981.

From the late 1970s, Hamilton also began to receive international honors and recognition for his scientific work; among other honors, he was elected a Foreign Honorary Member of the American Academy of Arts and Sciences in 1978 and a Fellow of the Royal Society of London in 1980; in 1988 he received the Darwin Medal of the Royal Society, and in 1993 received both the Crafoord Prize of the Swedish Academy of Sciences and the Kyoto Prize of the Inamori Foundation.

Evolution of Sex. In the late 1970s, Hamilton began investigating the subject that provided the second major focus of his interests in evolutionary theory: the evolution and maintenance of sexual reproduction. Unlike altruism when Hamilton began thinking about it, the evolution of sex was a topic that had since the mid-1960s already been treated by other biologists in his circle (like Williams and Maynard Smith), although Hamilton, in his iconoclastic way, had failed to be convinced by any of them. Although the purpose of sex seems obvious—surely it is for reproduction and to maintain the variability necessary for natural selection to work on to keep a species from going extinct?—from the gene's-eye view it is not. Sexual reproduction not only shuffles an organism's genes, but also eliminates half of them in every offspring, which receives another complementary set from the other parent. In selfish-gene terms, sex inflicts considerable damage on a gene's potential reproduction, unlike asexual reproduction (as by budding or cloning), which replicates all genes. How then could sex have been evolved over this heavy short-term disadvantage, and why should natural selection continue to maintain it?

In a series of papers from 1980 through the mid-1990s, in cooperation with a series of coauthors, including Axelrod, Jon Seger, and Marlene Zuk, Hamilton combined the approaches he had developed since the beginning of his career to tackle this question. The theory he and they developed drew on Hamilton's gene's-eye view, interest in game theory, and broad interests in ecology and natural history. Hamilton believed that it was improbable that inanimate selective forces could maintain sex, because directional selection would not retain variation: eventually alleles would either be fixed in the population or eliminated entirely, but the continued production of variation itself would not be selected. Ecologists, however, had observed that continuous change was fostered in nature in two common situations: predator-prey cycles and host-parasite relations. Ecologists studied the continually varying densities of species rather than of their genes, but Hamilton believed that analogous principles might well apply to foster the continued selection of variability of genotypes within a species, that is, to provide a selective advantage to the continual reshuffling that sexual reproduction provides, over the short-term advantages of asexual reproduction. He focused on parasite-host interactions, because they were universal (every species, even the very smallest bacteria, falls prey at least to viruses) and generally fairly species-specific, which seemed from ecological models to foster the emergence of cycling phenomena. Hosts and parasites would thus be locked in a continuous war of innovation and defense, in which a combination of genes advantageous in one generation might become positively disadvantageous in the next, as parasites and disease organisms evolved to circumvent it. A perverse outcome was the prediction that sexual selection, as studied since Darwin, would prove to have multiple and sometimes conflicting purposes—to distinguish and mate with the healthiest possible individual might make adaptive sense in the short run, but it might also, given that diseases and parasites were always in hot pursuit, make sense to distinguish and mate with the sickest possible individual, whose currently disadvantageous genes might nevertheless be just what was required at the next turn of the cycle.

While straightforward in outline, the working out of such a picture was enormously complicated. Mathematical population genetics models handled well only stable states in simple models, whereas Hamilton needed to create a model in which two or more species were simultaneously accounted for, and in which each species varied at multiple loci, each of which might cycle independently. Eventually, in what Hamilton regarded as his culminating work on the subject, he and his collaborators (Axelrod and Reiko Tanese) proposed a series of individual-based models that argued that under various complex and realistic scenarios, sexual reproduction would be positively selected. This concluding paper and its theory, which Hamilton found satisfyingly in accordance with his finely-honed intuitions about how the natural world worked, contrast strongly in methodology and application with his earlier work on the evolution of sociality. The latter gave rise to two fully generalizable, universal, mathematized predictive theories (inclusive fitness and the TIT FOR TAT resolution of the Prisoner's Dilemma as motors of the evolution of sociality), whereas the former depended for its rhetorical force on the particularity of individual, contingent natural relationships, frequently evoking Hamilton's encyclopedic command of biological and ecological observations, both his own and others'.

Teaching and Research Style. Although the importance of inclusive fitness to the development of the new "neo-Darwinism" of the late 1960s and 1970s brought Hamilton, as observed above, into much greater contact with other scholars (his first coauthored paper, with Robert M. May, was published in 1977), he nevertheless retained throughout his career much of the isolated, contrarian, loner persona of his early, overlooked, graduate-student odyssey through institutions and advisors. To a great degree this was a matter of personal style and choice. Hamilton had little inclination for the kind of institutional empire-building that would have established him in an influential chair, funded by lavish grants, and surrounded by graduate students and postdocs who would further disseminate his power. Moreover, he never ceased to be riven by the deep self-doubts and insecurities that fueled his interest in the origins of sociality and sexual reproduction and his anxieties about where his answers might lead him personally or human society in general. He also positively relished his self-image as a contrarian, who dared to say what few other biologists would (although he never wrote a book accessible to a wider audience than his fellow biologists, and so did not, like Wilson and Dawkins, of whose courage in thus doing he wrote admiringly, put himself in the public line of fire). And he was greatly (self-) handicapped by his inability to communicate with a large audience (whether of students or colleagues). His teaching was notoriously poor, and his colloquia and presentations little better—the technique of using a handheld microphone as a slide pointer, thus rendering his arguments beyond, "Here, as you can see … " inaudible, while his mouth continued visibly to move, was only one of a repertoire that kept him incomprehensible. Hamilton wryly admitted that, on the basis of his lectures, students would have good reason to doubt that he understood even his own ideas.

In 1984 Hamilton left the University of Michigan for a Royal Society Research Professorship at Oxford University, where he remained for the rest of his life. The requirements of the job were tailor-made for Hamilton: it required him to give only one lecture to students per year (which he often forgot to do). Hamilton's contrarian streak also contributed to his decision to leave Ann Arbor, driven out by what he considered the rising tide of insidious (and evolutionarily contraindicated) American political correctness. He was incomprehendingly irate, for example, at the strongly negative reception given (by an acid "lady academic" search committee chair and the student herself) to a letter of recommendation (the strongest, he believed, he had ever written) for a student, in which he praised her mathematical ability as "especially remarkable in view of her sex." Women, in his view, being demonstrably, and almost certainly innately, weaker in mathematics, he had in fact meant the phrase as singling her out for higher regard rather than lower, and could "hardly credit that what [he] wrote could be interpreted in any other way" (*Narrow Roads,* 2001, vol. 2, pp. 307–308).

Hamilton's lifelong determination to follow his evolutionary reasoning out to the logical end, no matter how bitter or pessimistic, led him into other such social fixes. From his earliest thinking about altruism and sociality, under Fisher's tutelage, Hamilton was convinced of the logical imperative underpinning the practice of negative eugenics. In a review of a book on "human diversity" published in 1965, Hamilton asserted that the prevention of the reproduction of unfit people bearing deleterious genes at some stage of their life cycles was necessary, if the "genetic trust built for us by our ancestors" was not to be squandered; he claimed that the most efficient and most merciful means of doing so would be the practice of "humane eugenic infanticide" (Hamilton, 1965, pp. 203–205). Similarly, at a meeting of a Royal Society group for the study of population constituted in the mid-1960s, Hamilton (still a graduate student) advocated that the group should study the biological underpinnings of differential propensities among different human populations, to be met with stony rebuke from the chairman. In the autobiographical essays that Hamilton wrote to accompany the first two volumes of his collected papers, *Narrow Roads of Gene Land* (1997 and 2001), Hamilton enlarged greatly on these related themes, painting a bleak picture of a human future in which individual people, kept alive only by the most pervasive, invasive medical technologies because so many deleterious genes and gene combinations have remained in the pool by the relaxing of human and natural selection, have been reduced by their relationship to technology to mere components in a giant human superorganism, in a dead-end social devolution like that of the social insects.

Hamilton's self-portrait as a disillusioned "crank," doomed to follow the lone Romantic's path, hopelessly out of touch with current social norms and pieties thanks to his rigorous insistence on following evolutionary principles wherever they led him, was, however, at odds with the persona he enjoyed among friends and colleagues. He was greatly revered by colleagues and former students (many of them female), who held him in the highest affection and who attested, particularly after his death, to his great personal kindness and practice of unstinting cooperation, whatever the self-doubts that underlay his practice of them might have been.

Controversies over AIDS; Hamilton's Death. The same contrarian, deeply held intellectual principles that led Hamilton into social and professional difficulties led him to his premature death. In the late 1990s, Hamilton became intrigued by the iatrogenic theory proposed by Edward Hooper of the origin of AIDS: that the virus had been introduced from chimpanzees into human beings by way of polio virus tested by Western doctors on black Africans. Were this to be the case, it would have been the greatest catastrophe in the history of medicine, and Western scientists and pharmaceutical companies would be morally, and possibly legally, liable. Hamilton found the theory plausible, and did his best to help publicize it against what he saw as enormous, scientifically improper suppression of debate by vested interests; he was also worried about the implications for current medicine, as, for example, of xenotransplantation (the transplantation of tissues or organs from other species into humans). He made two expeditions to the Congo to collect samples of chimpanzee feces for analysis; on the second, he contracted a virulent strain of malaria, collapsed soon after returning to Britain, and died a few weeks later at the age of sixty-three. He was interred in Wytham Woods, Oxfordshire, to be given, as he had wished, to burying beetles and fungi and thus returned to the world of living things that had been his life's study.

BIBLIOGRAPHY

Only the principal articles and those quoted in the entry are listed. Hamilton's complete articles have also been collected into three volumes under the title Narrow Roads of Gene Land; *the first two volumes contain original autobiographical essays introducing each article, while the third was published posthumously and includes essays by colleagues and collaborators as well as bibliographical information. Hamilton's personal and professional papers are held by the Manuscripts Division of the British Library, London. Since he died without warning, his papers and other materials remained as he had left them still in mid-career, and his family offered the library the rare opportunity of archiving a working scientist's office, preserving Hamilton's own order and relation among materials.*

WORKS BY HAMILTON

"The Evolution of Altruistic Behavior." *American Naturalist* 97 (1963): 354–356.

"The Genetical Evolution of Social Behaviour, I and II." *Journal of Theoretical Biology* 7 (1964): 1–16, 17–52.

"Human Diversity." *Population Studies* 19, no. 2 (1965): 203–205.

"Extraordinary Sex Ratios." *Science* 156 (1967): 477–488.

"Geometry for the Selfish Herd." *Journal of Theoretical Biology* 31 (1971): 295–311.

"Selection of Selfish and Altruistic Behaviour in Some Extreme Models." In *Man and Beast: Comparative Social Behavior,* edited by J. F. Eisenberg and Wilton S. Dillon. Washington, DC: Smithsonian Institution Press, 1971.

"Altruism and Related Phenomena, Mainly in Social Insects." *Annual Review of Ecology and Systematics* 3 (1972): 193–232.

"Innate Social Aptitudes of Man: An Approach from Evolutionary Genetics." In *Biosocial Anthropology,* edited by Robin Fox, ASA Studies 1. London: Malaby, 1975.

"Sex versus Non-Sex versus Parasites." *Oikos* 35 (1980): 282–290.

With R. Axelrod. "The Evolution of Cooperation." *Science* 211 (1981): 1390–1396.

With Marlene Zuk. "Heritable True Fitness and Bright Birds: A Role for Parasites?" *Science* 218 (1982): 384–387.

With Jon Seger. "Parasites and Sex." In *The Evolution of Sex: An Examination of Current Ideas,* edited by Richard E. Michod and Bruce R. Levin. Sunderland, MA: Sinauer Associates, 1988.

With Robert Axelrod and Reiko Tanese. "Sexual Reproduction as an Adaptation to Resist Parasites (a Review)." *Proceedings of the National Academy of Sciences of the United States of America* 87 (1990): 3566–3573.

Narrow Roads of Gene Land: The Collected Papers of W. D. Hamilton. 3 vols. Oxford: Oxford University Press, 1997–2005.

OTHER SOURCES

Darwin, Charles. *On the Origin of Species, a Facsimile of the First Edition.* Cambridge, MA: Harvard University Press, 1964 [1859].

Grafen, Alan. "William Donald Hamilton." *Biographical Memoirs of the Royal Society* 50 (2004): 109–132.

Wilson, Edward O. *Naturalist.* Washington, DC: Island Press, 1994.

Abigail Lustig

William Hamilton, circa 1860. HULTON ARCHIVE /GETTY IMAGES.

HAMILTON, WILLIAM ROWAN

(*b.* Dublin, Ireland, 4 August 1805; *d.* Dunsink Observatory [near Dublin], 2 September 1865), *mathematics, optics, mechanics.* For the original article on Hamilton see *DSB,* vol. 6.

Hamilton's scientific work was all highly mathematical and abstract. As a result it required mathematicians to do it justice. But because Hamilton is also recognized as Ireland's greatest scientist, he has become a national hero even to those who cannot understand exactly what it was that he accomplished. Hamilton's romanticism, his intuitionist approach to algebra, and his close association with William Wordsworth and Samuel Taylor Coleridge make for fascinating study, but they also make it difficult for historians to fit him into the traditional history of nineteenth-century science. For that reason he will always be a controversial figure.

When the original *DSB* article appeared in the 1970s, historians studying Hamilton had to depend on his published works, the first three volumes of his collected mathematical papers, and the three-volume life and letters written by his friend Robert Perceval Graves. Since 1976, a substantial amount of new material on Hamilton has appeared. In keeping with the change in the history of science since the 1970s, the goal of much of this new material has been to supply a better philosophical and social context for Hamilton's life and work. The purpose of this postscript is to describe how the new work alters our historical understanding of William Rowan Hamilton.

Biographical Studies. After Hamilton's death in 1865, Graves received all of Hamilton's papers and notebooks from which to write a biography. He also wrote to Hamilton's principle correspondents and received many additional letters from them. Upon completion of the biography in 1889 after twenty-four years of labor, Graves returned the mathematical notebooks and correspondence to Trinity College, Dublin, and the personal correspondence to Hamilton's heirs. Because many persons mentioned in the letters were still alive, and because Graves chose to suppress intimate details that might damage his friend's reputation, his biography was incomplete. In the 1970s Hamilton's heirs, the O'Regan family, discovered the family letters in their attic. The letters are now at Trinity College where, along with the mathematical papers and correspondence, they are available for study. Two new biographies by Seán O'Donnell and Thomas L. Hankins exploit this new material. O'Donnell writes from the perspective of an Irishman familiar with Hamilton's surroundings and with local Irish history. Hankins explores the background to Hamilton's philosophy and its significance for Hamilton's mathematical work. The resulting picture is that of an idealist—in philosophy, in mathematics, and in his personal life.

In some ways Hamilton was quite an isolated figure. He never founded a mathematical school, and his theory of algebra as the science of pure time was not accepted by most other mathematicians. Yet he was gregarious in social gatherings. Jack Morrell and Arnold Thackray claim him as one of the "gentlemen of science" who led the British Association. As president of the Royal Irish Academy from 1837 to 1845 he was at the center of scientific activity in Ireland. Through his official positions and his extensive correspondence he helped determine the course of British and Irish science.

The Royal Irish Academy has now completed its project, begun in 1925, of publishing Hamilton's mathematical papers. The fourth and final volume appeared in 2000. The editing was a daunting task because Hamilton was famously disorganized and was by no means the best expositor of his own ideas. This fourth volume lacks the valuable mathematical appendices contained in the first three volumes, but it includes a complete list of Hamilton's works, an index to all four volumes, and a CD of the entire set.

Algebra. Historians since the 1970s have paid most attention to Hamilton's algebra. The work of Helena M. Pycior positions Hamilton in the British debate over symbolical algebra, first as a staunch opponent and then as a reluctant supporter. Peter Øhrstrøm also records this change as it relates to Hamilton's recognition of the properties of an algebraic field. David Bloor argues that Hamilton's intuitive approach to algebra was a product of his conservative political and religious views, a position that is difficult to sustain considering that Hamilton's chief correspondents ranged from Augustus De Morgan to Samuel Taylor Coleridge.

John Hendry argues that Hamilton first adopted his philosophy of algebra as pure time in 1832 and did not conceive of the foundations of algebra in terms of couples until the spring of 1835. The extent to which Immanuel Kant's philosophy influenced Hamilton's algebra will always be a point of debate, because the algebra is not logically dependent on the intuition of time. Hankins argues that Hamilton's reading of Kant largely reaffirmed ideas that Hamilton already held. Kant's philosophy strengthened Hamilton's intuitive approach but could not show him how to create a new science of algebra. Anthony T. Winterbourne argues for a closer relationship with Kant. John O'Neill (1986) uses Hamilton to mount a defense of the intuitionists in their never-ending debate with the algebraic formalists.

Hamilton's discovery of quaternions in 1843 was one of the great "eureka" moments in the history of science (see Figure 1). Quaternions did not turn out to be the key to the universe that Hamilton had hoped for, but they did open up the way to modern algebra. Hamilton saw immediately that quaternions could be used as operators to describe rotations, but as Simon L. Altmann points out, they did not possess the generality that Hamilton claimed. Altmann believes that Hamilton recognized their shortcomings but could not admit that any theory so beautiful could fail in its application. He felt that there must be some way to overcome the contradictions that he encountered. It took another century to resolve the confusion over quaternions as rotators. Teun Koetsier approaches quaternions from a different direction and asks the logical question of what makes a "breakthrough" such as quaternions possible. O'Neill (1993) shows how Hamilton announced and established priority for his discovery.

Optics and Mechanics. Hamilton's optics and mechanics have received less attention from historians than has his algebra, probably because his mechanics left less room for philosophical speculation. Michiyo Nakane and Craig G. Fraser have reviewed the early history of the mechanics of Hamilton and Carl Jacobi, and Nakane has published additional material in Japanese. Hamilton's analogy between optics and mechanics made it possible to carry his methods from classical mechanics into quantum mechanics. On Hamilton's version of the optical-mechanical analogy see the work of James Evans, Kamal K. Nandi, and Anwarul Islam. For the connection between Erwin Schrödinger's wave mechanics and Hamilton's optical-mechanical analogy see Hankins (1981).

Next to quaternions, Hamilton's most surprising discovery was the prediction of conical refraction in 1833. David Attis argues that while Hamilton differed from the Cambridge scientists on the nature of algebra, he wanted to do something to draw their attention to Ireland and the "silent sister," Trinity College, Dublin. His work in geometrical optics had attracted little attention, and so he pursued Augustin-Jean Fresnel's wave theory of light in order to align himself with the Cambridge mathematicians. In contrast to Attis's sociological argument, James G. O'Hara gives a detailed account of the events leading up to Hamilton's prediction of conical refraction and includes the letters between Hamilton and Humphrey Lloyd, who performed the experimental verification. It appears that George Biddell Airy was not as near to the discovery as he later claimed but that Hamilton's colleague James MacCullagh came uncomfortably close to anticipating him.

Hamilton is a good example of how an important scientist can be at the center of scientific activity and on the outside at the same time. He certainly felt himself in that position, ambitious for himself and for Irish science but appreciating his loneliness as a romantic philosopher and an independent thinker.

SUPPLEMENTARY BIBLIOGRAPHY

WORK BY HAMILTON

Mathematical Papers of Sir William Rowan Hamilton. Vol. 4, edited by Brendan Scaife. Cunningham Memoir no. 16. Cambridge, U.K.: Cambridge University Press, 2000.

OTHER SOURCES

Altmann, Simon L. *Icons and Symmetries.* Oxford: Clarendon Press, 1992. Chapter 2.

Attis, David. "The Social Context of W. R. Hamilton's Prediction of Conical Refraction." In *Science and Society in Ireland,* edited by Peter J. Bowler and Nicholas Whyte, 10–35. Belfast, Ireland: Institute of Irish Studies, Queen's University of Belfast, 1997.

Bloor, David. "Hamilton and Peacock on the Essence of Algebra." In *Social History of Nineteenth Century Mathematics,* edited by Herbert Mehrtens, Henk Bos, and Ivo Schneider, 202–232. Boston: Birkhäuser, 1981.

Evans, James, Kamal K. Nandi, and Anwarul Islam. "The Optical-Mechanical Analogy in General Relativity: New Methods for the Paths of Light and of the Planets." *American Journal of Physics* 64, no. 11 (1996): 1404–1415.

Hankins, Thomas L. "Algebra as Pure Time: William Rowan Hamilton and the Foundations of Algebra." In *Motion and Time, Space, and Matter: Interrelations in the History of Philosophy and Science,* edited by Peter K. Machamer and Robert G. Turnbull, 327–359. Columbus: Ohio State University Press, 1976.

———. "Triplets and Triads: Sir William Rowan Hamilton on the Metaphysics of Mathematics." *Isis* 68 (1977): 175–193.

———. *Sir William Rowan Hamilton.* Baltimore, MD: Johns Hopkins University Press, 1980.

———. "How to Get from Hamilton to Schrödinger with the Least Possible Action: Comments on the Optical-Mechanical Analogy." In *Analytic Spirit: Essays in the History of Science in Honor of Henry Guerlac,* edited by Harry Woolf, 295–308. Ithaca, NY: Cornell University Press, 1981.

Hendry, John. "The Evolution of William Rowan Hamilton's View of Algebra as the Science of Pure Time." *Studies in History and Philosophy of Science* 15 (1984): 63–81.

Koetsier, Teun. "Explanation in the Historiography of Mathematics: The Case of Hamilton's Quaternions." *Studies in History and Philosophy of Science* 26 (1995): 593–616.

Mathews, Jerold. "William Rowan Hamilton's Paper of 1837 on the Arithmetization of Analysis." *Archive for History of Exact Science* 19 (1978): 177–200.

Morrell, Jack, and Arnold Thackray. *Gentlemen of Science: Early Years of the British Association for the Advancement of Science.* Oxford: Clarendon Press, 1981.

Nakane, Michiyo, and Craig G. Fraser. "The Early History of Hamilton-Jacobi Dynamics, 1834–1837." *Centaurus* 44 (2002): 161–227.

O'Donnell, Seán. *William Rowan Hamilton: Portrait of a Prodigy.* Dublin, Ireland: Boole Press, 1983.

O'Hara, James G. "The Prediction and Discovery of Conical Refraction by William Rowan Hamilton and Humphrey Lloyd (1832–1833)." *Proceedings of the Royal Irish Academy* 82A (1982): 231–257.

Øhrstrøm, Peter. "W. R. Hamilton's View of Algebra as the Science of Pure Time and His Revision of This View." *Historia Mathematica* 12 (1985): 45–55.

O'Neill, John. "Formalism, Hamilton, and Complex Numbers." *Studies in History and Philosophy of Science* 17 (1986): 351–372.

———. "Intertextual Reference in Nineteenth-Century Mathematics." *Science in Context* 6 (1993): 435–468.

Pickering, Andrew. "Concepts and the Mangle of Practice: Constructing Quaternions." *South Atlantic Quarterly* 94, no. 2 (1995): 417–465.

Pycior, Helena M. *The Role of Sir William Rowan Hamilton in the Development of British Modern Algebra.* PhD diss., Cornell University, 1976.

———. "Early Criticism of the Symbolical Approach to Algebra." *Historia Mathematica* 9 (1982): 392–412.

———. "Internalism, Externalism, and Beyond: 19th-Century British Algebra." *Historia Mathematica* 11 (1984): 424–441.

Richards, Joan L. "The Art and the Science of British Algebra: A Study in the Perception of Mathematical Truth." *Historia Mathematica* 7 (1980): 343–365.

Winterbourne, Anthony T. "Algebra and Pure Time: Hamilton's Affinity with Kant." *Historia Mathematica* 9 (1982): 195–200.

Thomas L. Hankins

HAMMETT, LOUIS PLACK

(*b.* Wilmington, Delaware, 7 April 1894; *d.* Medford, New Jersey, 23 February 1987), *chemistry.*

Hammett is considered one of the founding fathers of physical organic chemistry in the United States. He is best known for his work with strong acids that led to the Hammett acidity function, his work with linear free energy relationships that led to the Hammett equation, and his 1940 book, *Physical Organic Chemistry,* which gave a name to the subdiscipline and provided a research agenda for workers in the field for the next twenty years.

Early Life and Education. Although he was born in Wilmington, Delaware, Hammett—the oldest of three children of Philip and Marie (Plack) Hammett—was raised in Portland, Maine. His father, a Harvard graduate with two additional years at the Massachusetts Institute of Technology (MIT) studying mechanical engineering, was an official of the Maine Central Railroad. Hammett's home was filled with books, and he became an avid reader. His father and an uncle who was an architect introduced him to the use of tools early in life. This early introduction to instruments may account for his willingness to use new technology throughout his research career.

Hammett attended Harvard and was strongly influenced by the organic chemistry lectures of Elmer Peter Kohler. Kohler, in Hammett's words, "inspired his students to be very much interested in problems of structure and reactivity, whatever one could tell about mechanisms without studying reaction rates" (Gortler, 1978, p. 6). This inspiration, along with the belief that reaction rates could provide significant information about the detailed pathways of chemical reactions, was to remain with Hammett throughout his career. James B. Conant, who became one of the country's most eminent organic chemists and later served as president of Harvard, was Hammett's lab instructor in organic chemistry at Harvard. Hammett would have occasion to interact with Conant several times during his career.

After graduation in 1916, Hammett, who had won a Sheldon Traveling Fellowship, spent a year in Zürich at the Eidgenössische Technische Hochschule working with Hermann Staudinger. On his return to the United States, he took a position at the National Bureau of Standards laboratories doing war-related research on cellulose derivatives that were used to coat airplanes. The supervisor for the chemical group was Hal Beans, a physical chemist and a professor at Columbia University, who became a good friend and a mentor.

Shortly after the war, Hammett married Janet Thorpe Marriner of Portland, Maine; they eventually had two children, Philip and Jane. He went to work for the private laboratory of E. C. Worden and S. Isermann in Millburn, New Jersey, where he continued to work on organic materials, primarily dyestuffs and pharmaceuticals.

In 1919 Hammett visited Columbia, was offered a teaching position, and then did his doctoral thesis work (on the hydrogen electrode) with Hal Beans. He credited Beans with teaching him the art of research. After obtaining his PhD in 1923, Hammett was offered an assistant professorship at Columbia. Most of his teaching in the early years was in qualitative analysis; he published a textbook, *Solutions of Electrolytes: With Particular Application to Qualitative Analysis,* in 1929. A second edition of this text appeared in 1936.

The Acidity Function. In 1928 Hammett published an article titled "The Theory of Acidity" in which he advanced several new concepts, one of which concerned the leveling effect of water on acidity. His work in qualitative analysis, his newly developed ideas on acidity, and his reading of the work of J. N. Brønsted and A. Hantzsch led to his first major research contribution, the concept of superacids and the acidity function. This work, a search for a quantitative measure of the acidity of strong acid solutions, began with Alden Deyrup and Nicholas Dietz, his first graduate students. Hammett and Deyrup worked in concentrated sulfuric acid, measuring the ability of the acid to protonate a series of weak neutral bases. The reaction is shown below, where B is a weak base and BH^+ is the protonated form of the base.

$$B + H_2SO_4 \rightleftharpoons BH^+ + HSO_4^-$$

Hammett and Deyrup were constrained in their choice of weak bases by the limitations imposed by the technology of the time. They had to choose compounds (in this case, substituted anilines) that were sufficiently colored in either the protonated or unprotonated state, in order to determine concentrations colorimetrically. After putting a weak base in an acid medium, they would determine the ratio of the protonated and unprotonated species. They would then do the same experiment using more concentrated acid, continuing this process with the same base until the ratio of BH^+/B became too large to measure accurately. Then they would switch to a weaker base and continue the process. It soon became clear that an equation could be written that described the ability of the strong acid to protonate weak bases:

$$H_o = pK_{BH}^+ - \log (BH^+/B)$$

(pK_{BH}^+ is the measured ionization constant of BH^+ in water).

This relationship eventually became known as the Hammett acidity function. Surprisingly, the H_o scale shows that 100 percent sulfuric acid is ten billion times more acidic than 10 percent acid. The rates of many acid-catalyzed reactions demonstrate a linear relationship with H_o, expressed by the equation $H_o + \log k =$ constant (where k is the rate constant for a given reaction). Hammett initially thought that his acidity function was unique, but subsequent work by many chemists, using assorted strong acids and different base systems, has established over four hundred different acidity functions.

Structure-Reactivity Relationships. In 1933 Hammett and his student Helmuth Phluger published a paper describing the reaction of trimethylamine and a series of methyl esters.

$$RCOOCH_3 + N(CH_3)_3 \rightarrow RCOO^- + N(CH_3)_4^+$$

They found a linear relationship between the logarithms of the specific rates of the reactions and the logarithms of the ionization constants (equilibrium constants) of the carboxylic acids

$$RCOOH + H_2O \rightleftharpoons RCOO- + H_3O^+$$

whose methyl esters were being studied, that is, plotting log k (the logarithms of the rate constants) versus log K (the logarithms of the ionization constants) gave a straight line. J. N. Brønsted and K. Pedersen had shown a similar relationship between the rates of some acid-catalyzed reactions and the acidity constants of the catalyzing acids in 1924.

By 1935 Hammett, as well as G. N. Burkhardt in England, had discovered a large number of similar linear free energy relationships in the reactions of substituted benzene derivatives. In a *Chemical Reviews* article that year, Hammett illustrated these relationships with a number of graphs of log k versus log K for a variety of reactions, most of which involve the side-chain reactions of *meta-* and *para-*substituted benzene derivatives.

In a 1937 article Hammett generalized these structure-reactivity relationships with the equation log $k/k_o = \sigma\rho$, or log $K/K_0 = \sigma\rho$, where k and k_0 are the rates of the substituted and unsubstituted benzene derivative, respectively, K and K_0 are equilibrium constants, σ is a substituent constant that measures the effect of replacing H by a given substituent in the *meta-* or *para-* position, and ρ, the reaction constant, is the slope of the line characteristic of the reaction being studied. A reaction that is very sensitive to substituent changes will have a much larger absolute ρ value than a reaction that is only mildly affected by substituent changes.

By defining $\rho = 1$ for the ionization of benzoic acids in water at 25°C, and setting $\sigma = 0$ for X = H, Hammett was able to tabulate fifteen σ values for various substituents (see Figure 1). Using these values and a series of reactions that obey the Hammett equation, he was able to determine additional σ values. In the 1937 paper, Hammett listed twenty-nine σ values and thirty-eight reactions whose rates or equilibria correlated well with the equation.

After the 1937 paper, Hammett did no more work on linear free energy relationships, although there were chapters on the subject in his 1940 and 1970 books. However, work in this area continued in many laboratories throughout the world for several decades and prompted an enormous amount of discussion and research regarding the causes of substituent effects on rate changes.

Hammett continued to study the rates of a variety of organic reactions, mainly nucleophilic substitution reactions, through the late 1930s and the 1940s. He was, of course, looking at organic problems through the eyes of a physical chemist and, in so doing, he was establishing a methodology for others to follow.

The Book: *Physical Organic Chemistry*. In 1940 Hammett published *Physical Organic Chemistry*, a text for an advanced course in chemistry. In its preface, Hammett says that the name he has chosen "implies the investigation of the phenomena of organic chemistry by quantitative and mathematical methods," essentially the methods that Hammett himself had used in the previous twelve years. The book was subtitled *Reaction Rates, Equilibria, and Mechanisms*, reflecting Hammett's primary interests.

In the preface to the book, Hammett wrote of an earlier era, "For a time, it was almost a point of honor with both physical and organic chemists to profess ignorance of the other's field." In the 1966 article "Physical Organic Chemistry in Retrospect," he wrote, "To many physical chemists in the 1920s and early 1930s, the organic chemist was a grubby artisan engaged in an unsystematic search for new compounds, a search which was strongly influenced by the profit motive" (p. 464) Hammett, through his research and his writing, was bridging the gap between these two subdivisions of chemistry.

Hammett was not the only one applying the "methods" of physical chemistry to organic problems. There had been a growing community of such researchers from the late 1920s through the 1930s in England and the United States. Many were organic chemists who were, in a sense, rebelling from classical organic chemistry that had been almost exclusively involved with the preparation of new compounds and the determination of structure. Many were students who had been trained by the first wave that included Christopher Ingold, James Conant, Morris Kharasch, Howard Lucas, William Young, and Hammett. These—mostly young—chemists were seeking to understand the reactions of organic chemistry. Their work had not yet been defined as a subdiscipline, and Hammett's book, if nothing else, provided them with a name, a corporate identity, "physical organic chemists."

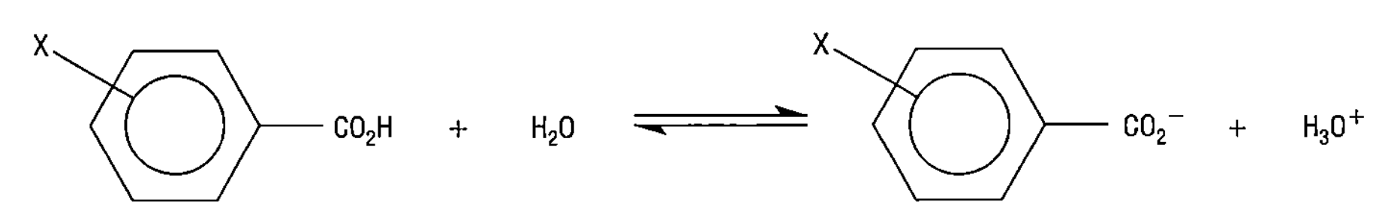

X–C_6H_4–CO_2H + H_2O ⇌ X–C_6H_4–CO_2^- + H_3O^+

Figure 1.

In the book, Hammett described and defined the classic work in physical organic chemistry. The book also set a research agenda for decades. Hammett was not only describing the important problems, he was saying, here is how to look at them and here are some of the difficulties. The book was still being cited in research papers forty years after it was first published.

The War Years. In 1941 Hammett wanted to contribute to the war effort. The United States had not yet entered the war, but research groups were being established, and he asked to join a group being organized by James Conant for work on military explosives. The National Defense Research Committee sent Hammett to England during the summer of 1941 to find out about the British wartime research efforts. When he returned he became the associate research director of the Explosives Research Laboratory in Bruceton, Pennsylvania. When George Kistiakowsky, the laboratory director, moved to Los Alamos, New Mexico, where he was involved with the development of the atomic bomb, Hammett took over as the director of the Bruceton laboratory, which made several important contributions to the war effort.

Postwar Career. After World War II, Hammett returned to Columbia and restarted his research program, investigating, in particular, the hydration of olefins. He also did some work on the use of ion exchange resins in acid catalysis and, finally, he worked with several collaborators on the use of the stirred flow reactor in the study of fast reactions. This use of a new technique was an appropriate career-ending exercise for a chemist who had pioneered in the use of various spectrophotometric techniques.

In 1951 Hammett became chairman of the Chemistry Department at Columbia, a position he held for six years. During his tenure as department chair he hired Cheves Walling, Gilbert Stork, and Ronald Breslow, making the department one of the major organic chemistry centers in the country. Hammett was also active in the American Chemical Society, served a number of years on the board of directors, and was chairman of the board in 1961. He retired from Columbia in 1961 but continued to do some consulting and writing, and lectured at a number of universities. He published the second edition of *Physical Organic Chemistry* in 1970.

Hammett was the recipient of the William H. Nichols Medal in 1957, the James Flack Norris Award for Outstanding Achievement in the Teaching of Chemistry in 1960, the James Flack Norris Award in Physical Organic Chemistry in 1966, the Priestley Medal and the Willard Gibbs Medal in 1961, the G. N. Lewis Medal in 1967, and the Chandler Medal and the National Medal of Science in 1968. He was also a member of the National Academy of Sciences and an Honorary Fellow of the Royal Society of Chemistry.

BIBLIOGRAPHY

A complete list of Hammett's publications, along with autobiographical notes, may be obtained from the American Institute of Physics, Center for History of Physics, College Park, Maryland.

WORKS BY HAMMETT

"The Theory of Acidity." *Journal of the American Chemical Society* 50 (1928): 2666–2673.

With Alden J. Deyrup. "A Series of Simple Basic Indicators. I. The Acidity Functions of Mixtures of Sulfuric and Perchloric Acids with Water." *Journal of the American Chemical Society* 54 (1932): 2721–2739. The parent paper on the acidity function.

With Helmuth Phluger. "The Rate of Addition of Methyl Esters to Trimethylamine." *Journal of the American Chemical Society* 55 (1933): 4079–4089. Hammett's first paper on structure-reactivity relationships.

"Some Relations between Reaction Rates and Equilibrium Constants." *Chemical Reviews* 17 (1935): 125–136.

"The Effect of Structure upon the Reactions of Organic Compounds. Benzene Derivatives." *Journal of the American Chemical Society* 59 (1937): 96–103. The foundation paper for the Hammett equation.

"Physical Organic Chemistry in Retrospect." *Journal of Chemical Education* 43 (1966): 464–469. An autobiographical address on the occasion of his receipt of the James Flack Norris Award in Physical Organic Chemistry.

Physical Organic Chemistry: Reaction Rates, Equilibria, and Mechanisms. New York: McGraw-Hill, 1940; 2nd ed., 1970.

OTHER SOURCES

Gortler, Leon. *Oral Histories with Louis Hammett,* 1 May 1978 and 22 May 1978. American Institute of Physics, Center for History of Physics, College Park, MD.

Shorter, John. "Hammett Memorial Lecture." In *Progress in Physical Organic Chemistry,* vol. 17, edited by Robert W. Taft. New York: John Wiley and Sons, 1990.

———. "The Centenary of the Birth of Louis Hammett." *Pure and Applied Chemistry* 67 (1995): 835–840.

———. "The Prehistory of the Hammett Equation." *Chemické Listy* 94 (2000): 210–214.

Westheimer, Frank H. "Louis Plack Hammett." *Biographical Memoirs of the National Academy of Sciences* 72 (1997): 137–149.

Leon B. Gortler

HARIOT, THOMAS

SEE **Harriot, Thomas**.

HARISH-CHANDRA (*b.* Kanpur, Uttar Pradesh, India, 11 October 1923; *d.* Princeton, New Jersey, 16 October 1983), *mathematics, Lie groups.*

Harish-Chandra was a major figure in the mathematics of the twentieth century. His work linked algebra, analysis, geometry, and group theory in a fundamental and epoch-making manner that subsequently became the foundation on which modern work in a variety of fields, ranging from differential geometry and mathematical physics to numbertheory, is being carried out.

Life and Career Overview. Harish-Chandra's father, Chandra Kishore, was a civil engineer in what was then known as United Provinces, situated in the Gangetic plains of northern India, and his mother, Satyagati Seth Chandrarani, was the daughter of a lawyer. Thus, Harish-Chandra's early years were spent in a comfortable upper-middle-class family. As is often the case, Harish-Chandra's early years were divided between his parents and grandparents. He was deeply influenced in many aspects of his life later by his father who was deeply religious and of great integrity. He was precocious, starting his seventh grade at the age of nine. Although his health was not robust, he was very successful in the formal aspects of education such as examinations, performing brilliantly. He took an MSc degree from the University of Allahabad at Allahabad in 1943. While he was in Allahabad, he came under the influence of Professor K. S. Krishnan, one of India's most outstanding physicists, and so Harish-Chandra's early interests were in theoretical physics. From Allahabad, Harish-Chandra went to Bangalore in southern India, where he worked with Homi Bhabha, also a theoretical physicist, who would later on become the founder-director of the Tata Institute of Fundamental Research in Mumbai. In 1945 he left Bangalore and went to Cambridge, England, to study at Cambridge University with Paul A. M. Dirac, under whom he wrote a thesis on the representations of the Lorentz group. The years in Cambridge convinced him that his talents were more in mathematics than in physics, and he began his lifelong study of representations of semisimple Lie groups.

Harish-Chandra went to the United States in 1947 where he stayed, except for brief visits to India, until the end of his life. In 1950 he went to Columbia University, where he remained until 1963, when he was offered a permanent position at the Institute for Advanced Study in Princeton, New Jersey. Harish-Chandra was named the I.B.M.-von Neumann Professor of Mathematics at the institute in 1968. He was elected a fellow of the Royal Society in 1973 and a member of the National Academy of Sciences of the United States in 1981. He received honorary doctorates from Delhi University in 1973 and Yale University in 1981. Harish-Chandra married Lalitha Kale of Bangalore, India, while he was on a visit to India in 1952. They had two daughters. His health was never very robust, and starting in 1969 he had several heart attacks that diminished his capacity to work intensely. Unfortunately, medical techniques were still not very advanced even in the United States, and the damage to his heart proved irreversible. He died in 1983 while out on a walk in Princeton.

Mathematics of Lie Groups. Harish-Chandra's work was mostly concerned with representations of semisimple Lie groups and harmonic analysis on them. Starting around 1949 he almost single-handedly erected his monumental theory over the course of the next thirty years or so. The depth and beauty of his results suggest that this is one of the most profound works of twentieth-century mathematics by an individual mathematician, and they make a compelling case for regarding him as one of the greatest mathematicians of this era.

The theory of group representations (homomorphisms of the group into the group of invertible linear transformations of a complex vector space) originated in the late nineteenth century with Georg Frobenius. If G is the group and $L(G \to GL(V))$ is the representation with $\dim (V) < \infty$, Frobenius introduced the numerical function $\Theta_L(g) = \mathrm{Tr}(L(g))$ on G, called the character of the representation L, which determined the representation up to equivalence. Then, in the 1920s, Hermann Weyl, building on earlier work of Issai Schur for the orthogonal groups and his own work with F. Peter, developed a complete theory of representations of arbitrary compact groups. Then, in the 1930s, Fourier analysis, which hitherto had been confined to the analysis of functions on a torus (Fourier series) or analysis of functions on $\mathbf{R}^n$ (Fourier integrals), was extended to all locally compact abelian groups by Andrei. Weil and independently by Mark G. Krein, and Israel Gel'fand. All of these developments could be seen in a unified manner as harmonic analysis on the groups in question, and the central question emerged as the expansion of the delta function at the identity element of the group as a linear combination of the characters of irreducible representations of the group. For U^1, the circle group, and $\mathbf{R}$, this expansion takes the familiar form

$$\delta_{U^1}(\theta) = \sum_{n \in Z} e^{in\theta}, \quad 2\pi\delta_{\mathrm{R}}(x) = \int_{\mathbf{R}} e^{i\lambda x} d\lambda,$$

and for a locally compact abelian group G,

$$\delta_G(x) = \int_{\hat{G}} \xi(x)\, d\xi$$

where $\hat{G}$ is the dual group of continuous homomorphisms of G into U^1. This formula, known as the Plancherel formula, takes, for compact G, the form

$$\delta_G(x) = \sum_{\omega \in \hat{G}} dim(\omega)\Theta_\omega(x)$$

where Θ_ω is the character of the representations in the class ω.

From this perspective, the central question for a compact group G is to determine all the functions on the group that are the characters of the irreducible representations, in terms of the structural data of the group. For $G = SU(2)$ of 2×2 unitary matrices of determinant one, let $u_\theta = \begin{pmatrix} e^{i\theta} & 0 \\ 0 & e^{-i\theta} \end{pmatrix}$; then the irreducible characters are given by

$$\Theta_n(u_\theta) = \frac{e^{in\theta} - e^{-in\theta}}{e^{i\theta} - e^{-i\theta}} \quad (n = 1, 2, 3, \ldots) \qquad (1)$$

Since any element of the group is conjugate to some u_θ, this formula determines the character on the full group. Since $\Theta_n(1) = n$, the Plancherel formula becomes

$$\delta_{SU(2)}(x) = \sum_{n \geq 1} n\Theta_n(x) \qquad (2)$$

The formula (1) is a special case of the Weyl character formula valid for any compact connected Lie group G. The elements of G are conjugate to elements of a maximal torus T, the irreducible characters are parametrized by the characters χ of T that are positive in a suitable ordering, and they are given on T by

$$\Theta_\chi(t) = \frac{\sum_{w \in W} \varepsilon(w)\chi(w \cdot t)}{\Delta(t)},$$
$$\Delta(t) = \sum_{w \in W} \varepsilon(w)\rho(\mathrm{w} \cdot t) \qquad (3)$$

where W is the Weyl group acting on T, $\in$, T is generic, and ρ is a special character of T. Weyl also obtained a formula for the dimension of the irreducible representation that has the character Θ_χ.

The growth of quantum mechanics, where symmetries of quantum systems are typically implemented by unitary operators in the Hilbert space of quantum states, gave a great impetus to the theory of infinite dimensional unitary representations of groups. For the Poincaré group, Eugene P. Wigner classified in 1939 all the physically important irreducible unitary representations, leading to the classification of free elementary particles by mass and spin. Then Gel'fand and Dmitri A. Raikov proved in 1943 that any locally compact group has enough irreducible unitary representations to separate points. The theory of representations and harmonic analysis on general locally compact groups began in earnest after this. Valentine Bargmann, following a suggestion of Wolfgang Pauli, developed the theory for the simplest such group, the group SL (2,**R**) of 2×2 real matrices of determinant 1. Independently, Gel'fand and Mark Naimark worked out the theory for the complex classical simple Lie groups of Élie Cartan, especially SL (n,**C**). These works gave a glimpse of a completely new landscape of infinite dimensional unitary representations containing analogs of the Frobenius-Weyl character theory, as well as the Plancherel formula.

Relation between Lie Group and Lie Algebra. This was the situation when Harish-Chandra began his odyssey. In his characteristic manner, he started on a theory of representations and Fourier analysis for all real semisimple Lie groups. His initial papers were dominated by the infinitesimal point of view, where the Lie algebra and its universal enveloping algebra were at the center of the stage. His 1951 paper on the enveloping algebra, "On Some Applications of the Universal Enveloping Algebra of a Semisimple Lie Algebra," for which he received the Cole Prize of the American Mathematical Society in 1954, was perhaps the first one in which representations of infinite dimensional associative algebras were considered. In it he proved the fundamental theorems of semisimple Lie algebras, earlier obtained by Cartan using classification, by general algebraic methods. The techniques and concepts of this paper would play a critical role later in the 1960s in the theory of infinite dimensional (Kac-Moody) Lie algebras, and in the 1980s in the theory of quantum groups.

Harish-Chandra then turned his attention to the study of infinite dimensional representations of real semisimple Lie groups. The method of passing to the Lie algebra, so effective in the finite dimensional case, is a much more subtle one in the infinite dimensional situation. Nevertheless, by a brilliant use of his idea of analytic vectors, Harish-Chandra showed that the correspondence between Lie algebra representations and Lie group representations remained particularly close even in the infinite case. In particular, by such methods he was led to one of his greatest discoveries, namely, that one can associate a character to infinite dimensional irreducible representations also. More precisely, he showed that for any unitary and irreducible representation L, and a smooth function f with compact support on the group G, the operator $L(f) := \int_G f(x)L(x)dx$ is of trace class and its trace $\Theta_L(f)$ is a distribution on G, the distribution character of the representation L. L may even be a Banach space representation satisfying some mild conditions. The distribution Θ_L is invariant (under all inner automorphisms of G) and determines L up to a very sharp equivalence (unitary equivalence when L is unitary, for instance) and is thus the correct generalization of the Frobenius-Weyl character.

In a long series of remarkable papers totaling several hundreds of pages in length, Harish-Chandra answered fundamental questions about the characters and discovered the formulae for the most crucial ones for reaching an explicit Plancherel formula for all real semisimple groups. Because it is not easy to use the condition that the distribution in question is the character of an irreducible unitary representation, Harish-Chandra had the insight to see that almost all of the properties of the character should flow from the fact that it is an eigendistribution of the bi-invariant (i.e., invariant under left and right translations) differential operators on *G*. More precisely, let **3** be the algebra of bi-invariant differential operators. By virtue of the identification of **3** with the center of the universal enveloping algebra of the Lie algebra of *G*, **3** acts on the smooth vectors of the irreducible representation *L* through a homomorphism χ (**3** $\rightarrow$ **C**), and the distribution character Θ_L satisfies the differential equations

$$\partial(z)\Theta_L = \chi(z)\Theta_L \quad (z \in 3)$$

everywhere on the group *G*. He now proved the remarkable theorem (the regularity theorem) that any invariant distribution Θ, which has the property that the space spanned by the derivatives ∂ (*z*) Θ ($z \in$ **3**) is of finite dimension, is a function, that is, there is a function θ, which is locally integrable on *G* and analytic on a dense open set of it, such that

$$\delta(f) = \int_G f(x)\theta(x)dx$$

(*f* smooth and of compact support on *G*).

Other proofs have become available in the early 2000s, but they all have to rely on deep theories of differential operators such as *D*-modules.

Once the regularity theorem is proved, the next step in the Harish-Chandra program became that of writing the formula for the irreducible characters on the group. Very early on he had realized that the irreducible unitary representations of *G* (at least those that would play a role for harmonic analysis on $L^2(G)$) come in several "series" associated to the various conjugacy class of Cartan subgroups of *G*. The Cartan subgroups, the analogs in the noncompact case of the maximal tori of compact groups, are abelian subgroups with the property that a generic point of the group can be conjugated to be in one of them. Up to conjugacy there are only finitely many of these, and at most one can be compact. The work of Bargmann for SL (2,**R**), and his own extensions of it to the case when *G*/*K* is Hermitian symmetric (*K* is the maximal compact subgroup of *G*), led him to the fundamental insight that the series of representations corresponding to a compact Cartan subgroup *B* (when there is one) are parametrized by characters of *B* and have the special property of occurring as discrete direct summands of the regular representation of *G*, hence the name *discrete series* for these, and further that these characters are given on *B* by a very close variant of Weyl's formula in the compact case. If *A* is a non compact Cartan subgroup, one can associate a suitable subgroup *M* of *G* with discrete series and use a very direct procedure to build the series corresponding to this Cartan subgroup. This perspective thus placed the discrete series at the very foundation of the theory and highlighted the fact that they should be constructed before anything can be done.

Harish-Chandra began by constructing the characters of the discrete series, in the first place, as invariant eigendistributions. Because the invariant eigendistributions are functions by his regularity theorem, it is enough to specify them on the Cartan subgroups of *G*. He then proved that if *B* is a compact Cartan subgroup and χ is a generic character of *B*, there is exactly one invariant eigendistribution Θ_χ on the group that is given by Weyl's formula (3) on the compact Cartan subgroup and verifies a suitable boundedness condition on the other Cartan subgroups. The Harish-Chandra formula for Θ_χ on *B* is given by

$$\Theta_\chi(t) = \frac{\sum_{w \in W_G} \varepsilon(w)\chi(w \cdot t)}{\Delta(t)} \qquad (4)$$

where W_G is the subgroup of *W* that arises from elements of *G*. Now *G* = SL (2,**R**) has 2 conjugacy classes of Cartan subgroups whose representatives can be taken to be the compact one *B* of the rotations $r_\theta = \begin{pmatrix} \cos\theta & \sin\theta \\ -\sin\theta & \cos\theta \end{pmatrix}$, and the non compact one *A* of diagonal matrices $h_t = \pm\begin{pmatrix} e^t & 0 \\ 0 & e^{-t} \end{pmatrix}$. In this case the distributions are the Θ_n ($n = \pm 1, \pm 2, \ldots$) with ($\theta \neq 0, \pi, t \neq 0$)

$$\Theta_n(r_\theta) = -\mathrm{sgn}(n)\frac{e^{in\theta}}{e^{i\theta} - e^{-i\theta}}$$

$$\Theta_n(\pm h_t) = (-1)^{\pm(n-1)}\frac{e^{-|n||t|}}{\left|e^t - e^{-t}\right|}.$$

In particular $|\Theta_n(\pm h_t)| \leq |e^t - e^{-t}|^{-1}$ is the boundedness condition. In the general case there is an invariant analytic function *D* (*discriminant*) such that $D = |\Delta|^2$ on any Cartan subgroup, and the boundedness condition is

$$\left|\Theta_\chi(x)\right| \leq \left|\mathrm{D}(x)\right|^{-1/2} \qquad (x \text{ generic in } G) \qquad (5)$$

Note that $W_G = \{1\}$ and so there is no alternating sum as in the case of SU(2). Harish-Chandra's method for continuing the character to the other Cartan subgroups was to use the differential equations satisfied by the distribution at the interfaces of the Cartan subgroups and show that the boundedness condition (5) forced the continuation to be unique. The author will not comment here on the very beautiful but difficult analytic methods Harish-Chandra discovered to prove that the invariant eigendistributions Θ_χ are precisely the characters of the discrete series. In particular, this part of his work implied that the discrete series occurs if and only if one of the Cartan subgroups is compact. The characters of the other series could now be expressed explicitly. For instance, for G = SL (2,**R**), the Cartan subgroup A gives rise to the characters that vanish on B and are given on A by

$$T_\lambda^+(\pm h_t) = \frac{e^{i\lambda t} + e^{-i\lambda t}}{e^t - e^{-t}},$$
$$T_\lambda^-(\pm h_t) = \pm\frac{e^{i\lambda t} + e^{-i\lambda t}}{e^t - e^{-t}} \qquad (6)$$

The third step in the program was then to obtain the Plancherel formula for the group. This involved new ideas, especially in dealing with the continuous part of the decomposition of δ. Harish-Chandra discovered the general principle that the measure that should be used in the Plancherel formula to combine the matrix coefficients can be obtained from the asymptotic expansions of these eigen-functions at infinity on the group. This principle, linking the Plancherel measure with the asymptotics of the matrix coefficients, is a far-reaching generalization of a result of H. Weyl, who had discovered it in his work on the eigenfunction expansions of singular differential operators on a half line. For G = SL (2,**R**), the Plancherel formula becomes

$$2\pi^2\delta_G = \sum_{n\neq 0}|n|\Theta_n + \frac{1}{2}\int_0^\infty \lambda\tanh\frac{\pi\lambda}{2}T_\lambda^+ +$$
$$\frac{1}{2}\int_0^\infty \lambda\coth\frac{\pi\lambda}{2}T_\lambda^- d\lambda$$

The matrix coefficients defined by a suitable vector in the representation corresponding to $T_\lambda^\pm$, say $\varphi_\lambda^\pm$ have the asymptotics

$$e^t\varphi_\lambda^\pm(h_t) \sim c^\pm(\lambda)e^{i\lambda t} + c^\pm(-\lambda)e^{-i\lambda t}$$

where the $c^\pm$ (λ) are rational fractions involving classical Gamma functions, and

$$\frac{2}{\pi}\left|c^+(\lambda)\right|^{-2} = \lambda\tanh\frac{\pi\lambda}{2},\quad \frac{2}{\pi}\left|c^-(\lambda)\right|^{-2} = \lambda\coth\frac{\pi\lambda}{2}$$

Harish-Chandra then turned his attention to the semisimple groups defined over a p-adic field. This was not merely an idle generalization but essential for number theory. In fact, he himself had pioneered some of the most fundamental work on the arithmetic of semisimple groups in his paper with Armand Borel, where they proved that if **G** is a semisimple algebraic matrix group defined over the field **Q** of rational numbers, and $G_{\mathbf{Z}}$ is the sub group of integral matrices, then the space $G_{\mathbf{R}}/G_{\mathbf{Z}}$ has finite volume. For the harmonic analysis of the natural representation of G in $L_2(G_{\mathbf{R}}/G_{\mathbf{Z}})$, which is important in number theory, it turned out to be essential to understand the representation theory and harmonic analysis of the groups $G_{\mathbf{Q}p}$, the groups of p-adic points of the algebraic group **G**.

In his work on the representation theory of the p-adic groups, Harish-Chandra was guided by the same approach that served him so well in the case of real groups. He called this the philosophy of cusp forms. But the discrete series for p-adic groups is much more arithmetic and less accessible than in the real case, although he showed that the main results for the continuous spectrum go through in the p-adic case. Harish-Chandra was very fond of the idea that the representation theory of all the p-adic completions of an algebraic semisimple group defined over **Q** ought to be based on the same set of principles, and he called it the Lefschetz principle. Its full effectiveness can be seen only by constructing the discrete series for the p-adic groups and by going over to the adelic groups. Unfortunately, this was not given to him to accomplish, illness overcoming his ability to work at an intense level in the last years of his life.

Personality. In his creative life, Harish-Chandra opted for intense penetration of a few areas as opposed to extensive knowledge, while in his personal life, his temperament preferred the plain over the ornate. His lifestyle was very simple, even ascetic, involving, especially in his younger years, periods of absolute stillness and concentration stretching for hours at a time; in later years, with the increasing uncertainty of his health, he had to moderate this aspect of his life, but he still had in him the passion for great bursts of work even in later years, one of which was responsible for his fatal heart attack. In his early years he was a good painter, and over the years came to admire intensely Van Gogh and Cezanne. He was conscious of his powers but was modest in a truly deep sense. His personality and achievements compelled others to devote themselves to problems that he considered important. In an age where collaboration and multiple-authorship are the norm, he was a singular figure, working solo to overcome Himalayan obstacles. His work is a faithful reflection of his personality—lofty, intense, uncompromising. It will be a long time before anyone remotely resembling him will arise in the history of mathematics.

BIBLIOGRAPHY

There is no official archive containing Harish-Chadra's unpublished works. The complete bibliography of his works can be found in the Collected Papers *cited here (Vol I).*

WORKS BY HARISH-CHANDRA

"On Some Applications of the Universal Enveloping Algebra of a Semisimple Lie Algebra." *Transactions of the American Mathematical Society* 70 (1951): 28–96.

"Representations of a Semisimple Lie group in a Banach Space." *Transactions of the American Mathematical Society* 75 (1953): 185–243.

With Armand Borel. "Arithmetic Subgroups of Algebraic Groups." *Annals of Mathematics* 75 (1962): 485–535.

"Invariant Eigendistributions on a Semisimple Lie Group." *Transactions of the American Mathematical Society* 119 (1965): 457–508.

"Discrete Series for Semisimple Lie Groups, I: Construction of Invariant Eigendistributions" *Acta Mathematica* 113 (1965): 241–318.

"Discrete Series for Semisimple Lie Groups, II: Explicit Determination of the Characters." *Acta Mathematica* 116 (1966): 1–111.

"Harmonic Analysis on Semisimple Lie Groups." *Bulletin of the American Mathematical Society* 76 (1970): 529–551.

"Harmonicanalysis on Reductive P-adic Groups." In *Harmonic Analysis on Homogeneous Spaces,* edited by Calvin C. Moore. Proceedings of Symposia in Pure Mathematics, XXVI. Providence, RI: American Mathematical Society, 1973.

"Harmonic Analysis on Real Reductive Groups, I: The Theory of the Constant Term." *Journal of Functional Analysis* 19 (1975): 104–204.

"Harmonic Analysis on Real Reductive Groups, II: Wave Packets in the Schwartz Space." *Inventiones Mathematicae* 36 (1976): 1–55.

"Harmonic Analysis on Real Reductive Groups, III: The Maass-Selberg Relations and the Plancherel Formula." *Annals of Mathematics* 104 (1976) 117–201.

Collected Papers/Harish-Chandra. 4 vols. Edited by V. S. Varadarajan. New York: Springer-Verlag, 1984.

OTHER SOURCES

Herb, Rebecca A. "An Elementary Introduction to Harish-Chandra's Work." In *The Mathematical Legacy of Harish-Chandra,* edited by Robert S. Doran and V. S. Varadarajan. Proceedings of Symposia in Pure Mathematics, vol. 68. Providence, RI: American Mathematical Society, 2000.

Howe, Roger. "The Work of Harish-Chandra on Reductive P-adic Groups." In *Collected Papers/Harish-Chandra,* edited by V. S. Varadarajan, vol. 1. New York: Springer-Verlag, 1984.

Langlands, Robert P. "Harish-Chandra (1923–1983)." *Biographical Memoirs of Fellows of the Royal Society* 31 (November 1985): 199–225.

Varadarajan, V. S. "The Theory of Characters and the Discrete Series for Semisimple Lie Groups." In *Harmonic Analysis on Homogeneous Spaces,* edited by Calvin C. Moore. Proceedings of Symposia in Pure Mathematics, vol. 26. Providence, RI: American Mathematical Society, 1973.

———. *Harmonic Analysis on Real Reductive Groups.* Lecture Notes in Mathematics, vol. 576. Berlin: Springer-Verlag, 1977.

———. *An Introduction to Harmonic Analysis on Semisimple Lie Groups.* Cambridge Studies in Advanced Mathematics, no. 16. Cambridge, UK: Cambridge University Press, 1989.

———. "Harish-Chandra, His Work, and Its Legacy." In *The Mathematical Legacy of Harish-Chandra,* edited by Robert S. Doran and V. S. Varadarajan. Proceedings of Symposia in Pure Mathematics, vol. 68. Providence, RI: American Mathematical Society, 2000.

Wallach, Nolan R. "Some Additional Aspects of Harish-Chandra's Work on Real Reductive Groups." In *Collected Papers/Harish-Chandra,* edited by V. S. Varadarajan, vol. 1. New York: Springer-Verlag, 1984.

———. *Real Reductive Groups.* 2 vols. Boston: Academic Press, 1988–1992.

V. S. Varadarajan

HARRIOT (OR HARIOT), THOMAS

(*b.* Oxford, England, c. 1560; *d.* London, England, 2 July 1621), *mathematics, astronomy, physics.* For the original article on Harriot see *DSB,* vol. 6.

Harriot continues to be an important figure in the historical study of early modern science. Recent work has shed light on his ideas about atomism as well as his contributions to astronomy. Harriot's telescopic observations (c. 1609–1612) have been overshadowed by Galilei's rather similar ones, but may have started earlier; he had long-standing personal contacts with the Netherlands, which gave him quicker chances of access to technical developments there than were available to Galileo, and no need to act as if they were his own.

The most important new insights concern his remarkable mathematical achievements. After the death of François Viète (1603), Harriot was the leading mathematician of his time, and a notable scientist and astronomer. He was, in all his various activities, essentially a problem solver; his mathematics made no distinction between pure and applied work (as it is now called). Each arose out of the other, and extended from shipbuilding and optics to the purest geometry and algebra. He was an important part of the chain from Viète to René Descartes and beyond, which made the historic transformation of mathematics from geometric to algebraic formalism that has been the dominant mathematical development since his time, and one whose high points in the seventeenth century were the calculi of Isaac Newton and Gottfried Wilhelm Leibniz.

Harriot himself applied his algebraic notations, almost the same as the modern elementary ones, to geometry, and thence to loci in optics, projectile theory (where the work, if published, would have inaugurated the

Harriot

modern study of ballistics), ship design, cartography, interpolation, and impacts.

J. A. Lohne's original article covers the main areas of Harriot's contributions, but some of his details and emphases are misleading or unreliable. For example, the "ingenious attempts" to rectify and square the equiangular spirals were entirely successful, even extending to the rectification of the loxodromic twisted spiral. These include the first known rectifications, partly repeated by Evangelista Torricelli in the 1640s, and an extension of the classical work of Archimedes and others. Again, the "nearly finished" tables of meridional parts were in fact not only complete, but the most accurate such tables until the 1920s.

Harriot's work would still have been notable done fifty years or more later. Many of his methods and results were rediscovered by others, such as Leibniz, Newton, Isaac Barrow, Willebrord Snel, Descartes, James Gregory, Pierre-Simon Girard, Edmond Halley, Bonaventura Cavalieri, and Thomas Simpson; later some were extended by Johann Lambert and Carl Friedrich Gauss. Particularly notable was his work on conformality and the geometry of the sphere, leading to his directly calculated tables of logarithmic tangents (meridional parts, which solve Mercator's problem, the construction of a conformal plane map of the spherical globe; this logarithmic work was pre-Napierian, and more accurate). The fundamental relation here, equating an exponential of the difference of longitude to a tangent of the colatitude, is identical in form to that of the much later hyperbolic non-Euclidean geometry of Farkas Bolyai and Nikolai Lobachevsky, where the constant surface curvature is negative instead of positive. This relates directly to Harriot's 1603 result on the area of the spherical triangle, and it is intriguing to see how this result, which gradually became known in the seventeenth century, was first modified by Lambert 150 years later for what was (in effect) the hyperbolic geometry, and then extended to more general surfaces by Gauss in the 1820s.

Harriot's numerical methods arose from the general binomial theorem that he derived from working back from finite differences, and which also led him to the limiting exponential series. Harriot's algebraic theory of equations is now available in translation (Steddall's edition of 2003), and was hardly a work for "amateurs." It starts from Viète's work, and includes the key step of associating roots with binomial factors, the derivation of various inequalities, and extensions of Viète's methods of obtaining numerical solutions of polynomial equations, which he applied elsewhere to problems in refraction. Moving on from Viète's positive roots, it recognized both negative and complex roots; he called the latter "noetic," that is, of the mind. It is no longer appropriate to judge Harriot's algebra entirely by the posthumous and incomplete *Artis Analyticae Praxis* of 1631.

Harriot's discovery (or, perhaps, confirmation) of a constant refractive index is dated in his manuscripts to 10:30 A.M. on 21 July 1601 (Old Style). John Shirley, referring to different work, dates the result to before 1597; perhaps both dates are, in some sense, correct. Both amply predate Snel (?1621) and Descartes (1637). Harriot quantified the medieval models in which rainbows were produced by refraction and reflection in spherical raindrops. He found that the maximum value of the exit arc, $2r - i$, occurs when $\tan i = 2 \tan r$. This gave Harriot the "tropical" (i.e., turning) ray, which led him to the height of the primary rainbow. Armed with a constant refractive index, this result can be obtained by elementary infinitesimals, but Harriot's own derivation is unknown.

Harriot's cubic curve solution of Alhazen's problem, mentioned by Lohne, not only anticipated Barrow, but turned out to be the inverse of Christiaan Huygens's hyperbolic solution of 1660. Inversion and its related conformality are a thread in much of Harriot's best work.

Unfortunately, one must mention recent revisionist historical trends ("the new historicism"), as they touch on modern accounts of Harriot's life and work. His 1588 *A Briefe and True Report of the New Found Land of Virginia* (modern North Carolina, in and around the Outer Banks, where he was a senior member of the Roanoke Settlement [1585–1586]), which has long been recognized as a leading source on early American life and settlement, has been seen by some recently as contaminated by racial and class biases. This allegation is then used to ignore or denigrate his scientific work. However, as B. J. Sokol argues forcefully, an unbiased reading of the 1588 text shows that Harriot gave fair, if somewhat optimistic, accounts of the resources, and a sympathetic description of the native population, from whom he learned much, as he himself recognized. Granted that he was part of a settlement, he was perhaps the most open-minded and enlightened of its members. His phonetic system for the local languages, long misunderstood as a "secret code," was a notable contribution to early phonetics.

During his life Harriot was a controversial figure and he continues to provoke lively debate amongst historians.

SUPPLEMENTARY BIBLIOGRAPHY

See also the valuable and continuing series of over forty pamphlets and lectures published by the University of Durham (U.K.) Thomas Harriot Seminar since 1983, covering many and varied aspects of Harriot's life, work, and times. Reference: Prof. G. R. Batho, Harriot Seminar, Durham Miners Hall, Durham, U.K.

WORKS BY HARRIOT

The Greate Invention of Algebra: Thomas Harriot's Treatise on Equations. Edited by Jacqueline A. Steddall. Oxford: Oxford University Press, 2003. An edition in English translation, from the original manuscripts, with introduction and bibliography (pp. 315–320).

OTHER SOURCES

Chapman, Allan. "The Astronomical Work of Thomas Harriot (1560–1621)." *Quarterly Journal of the Royal Astronomical Society* 36 (1995): 97–107.

Fox, Robert, ed. *Thomas Harriot: An Elizabethan Man of Science.* Burlington, VT: Ashgate, 2000. Prints the first ten Thomas Harriot Lectures, Oriel College, Oxford, England, 1990–1999. The next ten are due out in 2010. Also contains a bibliography by Katharine D. Watson (pp. 298–303) of relevant work since the original *DSB* in 1974, and a note by Gordon R. Batho on possible portraits of Harriot (pp. 280–285).

Henry, John. "Thomas Harriot and Atomism: A Reappraisal." *History of Science* 20 (1982): 267–296.

North, J. D. "Thomas Harriot's Papers on the Calendar." In *Light of Nature: Essays in the History and Philosophy of Science Presented to A. C. Crombie,* edited by J. D. North and J. J. Roche. Dordrecht, Netherlands: Nijhoff, 1985.

Shirley, John W. *Thomas Harriot: A Biography.* Oxford: Clarendon Press, 1983. Generally reliable, more complete on life than works; extensive bibliographies, pp. 476–490.

Sokol, B. J. "The Problem of Assessing Thomas Harriot's 'A Briefe and True Report' of His Discoveries in North America." *Annals of Science* 51, no. 1 (January 1994): 1–16.

———. *Invisible Evidence: The Unfounded Attack on Thomas Harriot's Reputation.* Thomas Harriot Seminar Occasional Paper 17. Durham, U.K.: University of Durham, 1995.

Jon V. Pepper

HARSANYI, JOHN CHARLES

(*b.* Budapest, Hungary, 29 May 1920; *d.* Berkeley, California, 9 August 2000), *economics, game theory.*

Harsanyi is best known for providing a decision-theoretic foundation for utilitarianism, for his work on equilibrium selection in noncooperative games, and for developing the conceptual foundations for analyzing games of incomplete information. For the latter research, Harsanyi was awarded the Nobel Prize in Economics in 1994 jointly with John Nash and Reinhard Selten.

Early Life and Education. Harsanyi (born Harsányi János Károly) was the only child of Charles and Alice Gombos Harsanyi. His father, a pharmacist by profession, and mother both converted to Catholicism from Judaism. Harsanyi attended the Lutheran Gymnasium in Budapest, whose graduating class of 1921 included one of the founding fathers of game theory, John von Neumann. In 1937, the year of his graduation, Harsanyi won first prize in the national competition for high school students in mathematics. The next two years were spent working in his father's pharmacy.

Although Harsanyi's own inclination was to study mathematics and philosophy, at his father's urging he went to France in 1939 with the intention of enrolling as a chemical engineering student at the University of Lyons. However, having completed a summer course to improve his French in Grenoble, with the outbreak of World War II his parents summoned Harsanyi back to Budapest, where he studied pharmacology, receiving the diploma in pharmacology from the University of Budapest in 1944. By studying pharmacology, Harsanyi received a military deferment that, because of his Jewish background, would have required that he serve in a forced labor unit. With the Nazi occupation of Hungary, Harsanyi lost this exemption and spent seven months doing forced labor in 1944. When his unit was being deported to work in a mine in Yugoslavia, Harsanyi managed to escape at the Budapest railway station. He found sanctuary in a Jesuit monastery until the end of the Nazi occupation. His mother, an asthmatic whose health deteriorated because of the privations of the war, died later that year.

Following World War II, Harsanyi, then a devout Catholic, studied theology (in Latin) in a Dominican seminary, later joining the Dominicans' lay order. However, he lost his faith in his late twenties and was antireligious for the rest of his life. While at the seminary, Harsanyi simultaneously pursued graduate studies at the University of Budapest, to which he returned in 1946. The following year, after completing his dissertation, "The Logical Structure of Errors in Philosophical Arguments," he was awarded a DrPhil, with minors in sociology and psychology.

Harsanyi spent the academic year 1947–1948 as a faculty member of the university's Institute of Sociology, where he met his future wife, Anne Klauber, who was a student in one of his classes. Forced to resign this position because of his anti-Marxist views, Harsanyi spent the next two years running the family pharmacy, which he now co-owned. In April 1950, when confiscation of the pharmacy by the Communist government was imminent, Harsanyi, his future wife, and her parents escaped to Vienna. At the end of that year, they all immigrated to Sydney, Australia, where Anne and John Harsanyi were married in January 1951, a few days after their arrival. Harsanyi became an Australian citizen in 1956. His father was kept on as a poorly paid state employee after his pharmacy was confiscated and subsequently died of kidney failure in 1954.

John Charles Harsanyi. © FORDEN, PATRICK J. /SYGMA/CORBIS.

In 1951 Harsanyi enrolled as an evening student in economics at the University of Sydney while spending his days working in a series of factory and clerical jobs. He completed his master of arts degree in economics in late 1953 with a dissertation, "Invention and Economic Growth," and then spent two and a half years as a lecturer at the University of Queensland.

Harsanyi then went to Stanford University on a one-year Rockefeller Fellowship in 1956, where he wrote a game theory doctoral dissertation, "A Bargaining Model for the Cooperative *n*-Person Game," supervised by Kenneth Arrow, a 1972 Nobel laureate. Harsanyi's visa permitted him to stay one more year in the United States, which he did, first spending a semester visiting the Cowles Foundation for Research in Economics at Yale University before returning to Stanford as a visiting assistant professor of economics. In 1958 Harsanyi took up a position as a research fellow at the Australian National University a few months before receiving his PhD in economics from Stanford in 1959.

American Career and Later Life. Feeling isolated because of his colleagues' lack of interest in game theory, Harsanyi returned to the United States where, except for visiting positions, he spent the rest of his career, becoming a U.S. citizen in 1990. From 1961 to 1963, he was a professor of economics at Wayne State University in Detroit. Following a year as a visiting professor at the University of California at Berkeley, Harsanyi became a professor of business administration there in 1965, with a secondary appointment as a professor of economics in 1966. In the years from 1966 to 1968, Harsanyi, together with other prominent game theorists, served as consultants to the U.S. Arms Control and Disarmament Agency under contract to Mathematica, the Princeton-based consulting group that included the game theorists Harold Kuhn and Oskar Morgenstern as principals. Harsanyi retired from Berkeley in 1990.

In addition to his Nobel Prize, Harsanyi's many honors included fellowships in the Econometric Society (1968), the American Academy of Arts and Sciences (1984), and the European Academy of Arts, Sciences, and Humanities (1996), as well as a number of honorary doctorates. He was made a Distinguished Fellow of the American Economic Association in 1994 and an honorary member of the Hungarian Academy of Sciences in 1995. Harsanyi was president of the Society for Social Choice and Welfare in 1996–1997. Harsányi János College in Budapest is named after him.

The Harsanyis had one child, a son, Tom, born in 1964 shortly after their arrival in Berkeley. For some time prior to his death in 2000 from a heart attack, Harsanyi had been in poor health, suffering from Alzheimer's disease.

Foundations of Utilitarianism. For utilitarianism to be a well-defined doctrine, individual well-being must be measurable by a cardinal utility function that permits interpersonal comparisons of utility gains and losses. A function is cardinal if any property of this function that is preserved by multiplying the function by an arbitrary positive constant and then adding a second arbitrary constant is meaningful, as is the case with the scales used to measure temperature. Following the ordinalist revolution of the 1930s, it was thought that no cardinal measure of well-being exists. However, in *Theory of Games and Economic Behavior* (1944), John von Neumann and Oskar Morgenstern argued that the preferences of a rational individual evaluating risky alternatives should conform to a set of properties (axioms) that result in these alternatives being ranked by the expected value of a cardinal utility function, what Harsanyi called Bayesian rationality. Subsequent commentators denied that this utility function had any significance for social welfare analysis.

In his first publication, "Cardinal Utility in Welfare Economics and in the Theory of Risk-Taking" (1953), written while still a student in Sydney, Harsanyi set out to refute this claim. For Harsanyi, welfare judgments are the impersonal preferences expressed by an impartial observer who orders social alternatives based on a sympathetic but impartial concern for the interests of everyone in society. Specifically, the impartial observer engages in a thought experiment in which he imagines having an equal chance of being anyone in society, complete with that person's preferences and objective circumstances. Thus, ranking social alternatives is reduced to a problem in individual decision making under risk and therefore, by applying the von Neumann–Morgenstern expected utility theory, Harsanyi argued that different social states should be ranked by the average of the utilities of all the individuals in society, thereby providing a Bayesian decision-theoretic foundation for average utilitarianism.

The hypothetical choice situation utilized in Harsanyi's impartial observer theorem is an example of what the philosopher John Rawls, in his monograph, *A Theory of Justice* (1971), has called an original position. The idea of deriving substantive principles of morality based on rational individual decision making behind a veil of ignorance (to use another Rawlsian expression), in which morally irrelevant information has been withheld, is arguably Harsanyi's most important contribution to ethics. In Rawls's formulation of this idea, less information is permitted behind the veil, with the consequence, or so Rawls argued, that social institutions should be designed so as to maximize the prospects of the worst-off individuals (once priority has been given to ensuring that everyone enjoys equal liberties and fair equality of opportunity). In "Can the Maximin Principle Serve as a Basis for Morality? A Critique of John Rawls's Theory" (1975), Harsanyi defended his Bayesian use of expected utility theory and argued that Rawls's maximin reasoning leads to unsatisfactory outcomes.

Harsanyi's impartial observer must be able to make interpersonal comparisons of utility gains and losses in order to rank the social lotteries he is faced with. In "Cardinal Welfare, Individualistic Ethics, and Interpersonal Comparisons of Utility" (1955), Harsanyi investigated the logical basis for these comparisons. For him, interpersonal utility comparisons are made by empathetic identification; the observer evaluates how well off someone else is in a particular situation by asking how well off he would be if he were put in the place of that individual, complete with that individual's tastes and values. In effect, all interpersonal utility comparisons are reduced to intrapersonal comparisons. Furthermore, these comparisons are empirical statements made on the basis of an a priori principle, Harsanyi's similarity principle, which says that the utility obtained from an alternative by any individual is determined by a function (common to everyone) of the biological and cultural variables that determine tastes and values.

In his 1955 article, Harsanyi also provided an alternative justification for a weighted form of utilitarianism, his social aggregation theorem. In this theorem, alternatives are risky alternatives and all preferences, both individual and social, are assumed to satisfy the von Neumann–Morgenstern expected utility axioms. The individual and social preferences are related to each other by the requirement that if everyone is indifferent between two alternatives, society should be as well. With these assumptions, Harsanyi showed that if von Neumann–Morgenstern utility functions are used to represent the preferences, then alternatives are socially ranked according to a weighted sum of the individual utilities associated with them.

The interpretation of Harsanyi's impartial observer and social aggregation theorems as being theorems about utilitarianism has been controversial. In "Welfare Inequalities and Rawlsian Axiomatics" (1976), Amartya Sen (a 1998 Nobel laureate) argued that, contrary to what many believe, von Neumann–Morgenstern utility functions are not cardinal and, hence, cannot serve as a basis for a defense of utilitarianism. In "A Reconsideration of the Harsanyi-Sen Debate on Utilitarianism" (1991), John Weymark, while endorsing Sen's critique, showed how Harsanyi's utilitarian conclusions could be supported by incorporating ideas from Harsanyi's writings that are not stated explicitly in his theorems.

Harsanyi also wrote extensively about the philosophical issues related to his version of utilitarianism. He was a strong advocate for rule utilitarianism, the doctrine that utilitarian principles should be applied to rules for behavior, not individual acts.

Cooperative Games and Bargaining Theory. Game theory is concerned with the analysis of rational decision making by players (individuals or groups) when the outcome obtained by any player depends not only on the choices he makes, but also on the choices of the other players. In cooperative game theory, binding agreements are possible, whereas in noncooperative game theory, they are not.

In the 1950s, cooperative games dominated the research agenda of game theorists. In John Nash's 1950 article, "The Bargaining Problem," a two-player bargaining problem is described by the set of utility payoffs that are achievable for the players if they can reach an agreement and the payoffs that result if no agreement is reached (the threat point). A solution specifies the payoffs received by the players in each bargaining problem. Proceeding axiomatically, Nash identified a unique solution to all such problems. Earlier, Frederik Zeuthen, in his *Problems of Monopoly and Economic Warfare* (1930), had considered

Harsanyi

a dynamic approach to two-player bargaining in which, at each stage of the bargaining, the player who is less willing to risk a conflict makes the next concession. In "Approaches to the Bargaining Problem before and after the Theory of Games" (1956), Harsanyi showed that Bayesian decision makers would behave as Zeuthen suggested and that the final outcome of Zeuthen's bargaining process is the Nash solution.

In "A Value for *n*-Person Games" (1953), Lloyd Shapley axiomatically characterized a unique solution—the Shapley value—for any *n*-person transferable utility (TU) cooperative game. In a TU game, actions are available that permit the transfer of a unit of utility between any two players. In his Stanford PhD thesis, Harsanyi showed how to extend Shapley's solution to *n*-player cooperative games in which utility is not transferable. Furthermore, his general solution for cooperative games has Nash's bargaining solution for two-player games with variable threat points as a special case. Harsanyi's general solution for cooperative games is supported by a noncooperative threat game in which each coalition of individuals guarantees its members certain payoff levels by announcing a threat strategy that the coalition would implement if it cannot reach agreement with the coalition consisting of the rest of the players.

Games of Incomplete Information. By the early 1960s, Harsanyi had started shifting the focus of his research to noncooperative games. The extensive form of a noncooperative game specifies the order in which the players make decisions (simultaneous moves are not precluded), what actions are available and what information is known to a player about past choices each time he gets to make a decision, and the expected payoffs to each player at the end of the game as a function of the history of these decisions. Exogenous random events are modeled as decisions made by nature. In a game of complete information, the structure of the game is common knowledge, although at any time, players need not know the complete past history of play (in which case, the game is one of imperfect knowledge). A strategy for a player is a contingent plan of action that specifies what choice is to be made each time this player gets to make a decision. A mixed strategy includes nondeterministic choices, whereas a pure strategy does not. In the normal form of a game, the players are regarded as independently and simultaneously choosing these strategies once and for all at the beginning of the game. The decisions specified by these strategies are then implemented as the game unfolds. These strategies are a Nash equilibrium if no individual could change his strategy so as to achieve a higher payoff given the strategy choices of the other players.

The assumption that the payoffs obtained from each history of play is common knowledge in a game of complete information limits the applicability of this theory. In a game of incomplete information, players need not have full knowledge of the extensive form. In particular, a player need not know anyone else's payoff from a given history of play. However, prior to Harsanyi's pathbreaking three-part article, "Games with Incomplete Information Played by 'Bayesian' Players" (1967–1968), little progress had been made in analyzing games of incomplete information. Harsanyi's conceptual breakthrough was to recognize that it is possible to embed a game of incomplete information into a larger game of complete information and use it to determine equilibrium behavior in the original game. He did this by thinking of each player as potentially being one of a number of possible types, with each type corresponding to a different specification of a player's private information about the structure of the game, including this player's beliefs about the other players' types. The augmented game begins with a chance move by nature, made in accordance with a common prior probability distribution on the players' possible types, which determines the types that are to play the rest of the game. Following this chance move, each player learns his own type and updates his beliefs about the other players' types using Bayes's rule. At this point, the original incomplete information game begins. In this way, incomplete information about the other players' types in the original game is transformed into imperfect information about nature's initial decision in the augmented game, which is something that games of complete information were already equipped to handle.

A strategy for a player in the augmented game can be thought of as specifying a conditional plan of action for each possible type of this player. Viewed from this perspective, a Nash equilibrium can be equivalently described using Harsanyi's concept of a Bayesian-Nash equilibrium, which requires each type to choose a strategy so as to maximize its expected payoff, given the beliefs it has about the other players' types and given the strategies of the possible types of the other players. As Harsanyi recognized, this equilibrium concept is well defined even if the type-conditional beliefs are not derivable from a common prior. However, in a way reminiscent of his similarity principle, Harsanyi argued that differences in players' types can be accounted for by differences in their information and that prior to nature's initial move, everyone has the same information, so there should be a common prior. This argument is known as the Harsanyi doctrine.

From the time Harsanyi presented his research on games of incomplete information to the Jerusalem Game Theory workshop in 1965, it has had a major impact. For example, this research helped provide the theoretical basis for the Mathematica arms control project. Harsanyi's formalization of a game of incomplete information and his concept of a Bayesian-Nash equilibrium has become the

Harsanyi

standard way in which games of incomplete information are modeled and analyzed. His insights provided the foundation for much of the subsequent research on problems in which individuals are asymmetrically informed about economically relevant information.

Other Work on Game Theory. In the traditional interpretation of a mixed strategy in a game of complete information, a player chooses the probability that he wishes to assign to each of his pure strategies and then employs a random device to determine which of his pure strategies to implement. In a mixed-strategy Nash equilibrium, a player is indifferent between all of the pure strategies to which he assigns positive probability, but he randomizes so as to hide his intentions from the other players. However, the other players observe only the pure strategy that is actually implemented, which leads one to ask: Why randomize? In "Games with Randomly Disturbed Payoffs: A New Rationale for Mixed Strategy Equilibrium Points" (1973), Harsanyi used his games of incomplete information to provide a reinterpretation of the meaning of a mixed strategy that resolves this paradox. Harsanyi supposed that a player's payoffs are subject to small random perturbations due to factors whose realization is known only to himself. The resulting game of incomplete information has a unique Bayesian-Nash equilibrium in which each type chooses a pure strategy. However, because a player only has probabilistic information about the types of the other players, it actually appears from the perspective of the first player that they are using mixed strategies even though they are behaving deterministically. By letting the size of the payoff perturbations go to zero, a mixed strategy equilibrium of the original game of complete information is obtained.

In "Two-Person Cooperative Games" (1953), John Nash had suggested that the binding agreements that are assumed to be possible in a cooperative game need to be justified by showing that they can arise as equilibrium outcomes in some noncooperative game. The search for noncooperative foundations for cooperative games is known as the Nash program. The noncooperative elements of Harsanyi's general solution for cooperative games can now be seen to be a step toward Harsanyi's full-fledged support of the Nash program. He made a major contribution to this program in "An Equilibrium-Point Interpretation of Stable Sets and a Proposed Alternative Definition" (1974) by providing a noncooperative foundation for the solution for cooperative games proposed by von Neumann and Morgenstern in their *Theory of Games and Economic Behavior.*

A major theme of Harsanyi's work on game theory is that the goal of game theory should be to use Bayesian principles of rationality to determine a unique solution to any game. Games often have multiple equilibria, so in order to achieve this goal, some procedure must be used to select among the equilibria. This research agenda reached its apogee in Harsanyi's *A General Theory of Equilibrium Selection in Games* (1988), with Reinhard Selten, in which the selection is accomplished using an approach in which the tracing procedure introduced by Harsanyi in "The Tracing Procedure: A Bayesian Approach to Defining a Solution for *n*-Person Noncooperative Games" (1975) plays a major role.

The tracing procedure identifies a unique equilibrium in a noncooperative game by analyzing equilibrium behavior in a continuum of auxiliary games that differ from the original game only in the payoffs players receive from the possible strategy combinations. This procedure begins with an auxiliary game in which a probability distribution over a player's pure strategies is given a priori. This distribution represents the initial conjecture on the part of the other players about this player's mixed strategy choice. The payoff to any player from a strategy choice in this auxiliary game is the payoff that would be obtained in the original game if the other players played according to the initially conjectured strategies. In this game, each player has a unique best response to the conjectured strategy choices of the other players, but these best responses are typically not a Nash equilibrium in the original game. Next, for each number t between 0 and 1, a t-auxiliary game is defined in which the payoffs to players are weighted combinations of the payoffs they would obtain in the original game and the initial auxiliary game, with weights t and $1 - t$, respectively, plus a small additional payoff that ensures that the equilibrium in each of the t-auxiliary games is unique. The value $1 - t$ represents the degree of confidence placed in the initial conjecture. The equilibria defined by this procedure converge to a unique equilibrium in the 1-auxiliary game, which is a unique equilibrium in the original game when the values of the small added payoffs go to zero. Harsanyi interpreted the tracing procedure as being a mathematical formalization of the process by which rational players coordinate their choices of strategies.

Harsanyi continued to work on equilibrium selection until his final illness ended his research career. In his 1995 articles on this topic, "A New Theory of Equilibrium Selection for Games with Complete Information" and "A New Theory of Equilibrium Selection for Games with Incomplete Information," Harsanyi's tracing procedure, which for two decades had been an important component of the Harsanyi-Selten theory of equilibrium selection, plays only a minor role.

There is a unity in Harsanyi's research that is quite remarkable when one considers the range of problems that he considered over his lifetime. In his 1977 monograph,

Harsanyi

Rational Behavior and Bargaining Equilibrium in Games and Social Situations, Harsanyi announced that his goal was to provide a systematic account of rational behavior based on Bayesian principles that yields determinate solutions in individual decision making, in games, and in moral decision making. In retrospect, one can see that most of what Harsanyi wrote contributed to the achievement of this objective.

BIBLIOGRAPHY

Some of the information reported here, including corrections to factual errors in other published accounts of Harsanyi's life, was provided by Tom Harsanyi in e-mail correspondence with the author. A transcript and audiotapes of 1999 interviews with Anne and John Harsanyi, conducted by Marion Ross, are available in the Regional Oral History Office, the Bancroft Library, University of California, Berkeley. A slightly edited transcript of a 1996 interview with Harsanyi is in Claude d'Aspremont and Peter J. Hammond, "An Interview with John C. Harsanyi," Social Choice and Welfare *18 (2001): 389–401. A bibliography of Harsanyi's works is in the special John C. Harsanyi memorial issue of* Games and Economic Behavior *36 (2001). Harsanyi's most important research papers have been collected in his* Essays in Ethics, Social Behavior, and Scientific Explanation *(1976) and* Papers in Game Theory *(1982).*

WORKS BY HARSANYI

"Cardinal Utility in Welfare Economics and in the Theory of Risk-Taking." *Journal of Political Economy* 61 (1953): 434–435.

"Cardinal Welfare, Individualistic Ethics, and Interpersonal Comparisons of Utility." *Journal of Political Economy* 63 (1955): 309–321.

"Approaches to the Bargaining Problem before and after the Theory of Games." *Econometrica* 24 (1956): 144–157.

"A Bargaining Model for the *n*-Person Cooperative Game." In *Contributions to the Theory of Games,* edited by Albert W. Tucker and R. Duncan Luce. Vol. 4. Princeton, NJ: Princeton University Press, 1959. An abridged version of Harsanyi's Stanford PhD thesis.

"Games with Incomplete Information Played by 'Bayesian' Players." *Management Science* 14 (1967–1968): 159–182, 320–334, and 486–502.

"Games with Randomly Disturbed Payoffs: A New Rationale for Mixed Strategy Equilibrium Points." *International Journal of Game Theory* 2 (1973): 1–23.

"An Equilibrium-Point Interpretation of Stable Sets and a Proposed Alternative Definition." *Management Science* 20 (1974): 1472–1495.

"Can the Maximin Principle Serve as a Basis for Morality? A Critique of John Rawls's Theory." *American Political Science Review* 69 (1975): 594–606.

"The Tracing Procedure: A Bayesian Approach to Defining a Solution for *n*-Person Noncooperative Games." *International Journal of Game Theory* 4 (1975): 61–94.

Essays in Ethics, Social Behavior, and Scientific Explanation. Dordrecht, Netherlands, and Boston: D. Reidel, 1976.

Rational Behavior and Bargaining Equilibrium in Games and Social Situations. Cambridge, U.K.: Cambridge University Press, 1977.

Papers in Game Theory. Dordrecht, Netherlands, and Boston: D. Reidel, 1982.

With Reinhard Selten. *A General Theory of Equilibrium Selection in Games.* Cambridge, MA: MIT Press, 1988.

"Games of Incomplete Information." *American Economic Review* 85 (1995): 291–303. Harsanyi's Nobel lecture.

"A New Theory of Equilibrium Selection for Games with Complete Information." *Games and Economic Behavior* 8 (1995): 91–122.

"A New Theory of Equilibrium Selection for Games with Incomplete Information." *Games and Economic Behavior* 10 (1995): 318–332.

OTHER SOURCES

Arrow, Kenneth J. "John C. Harsanyi 1920–2000." *Economic Journal* 111 (2001): F747–F752. An obituary by his thesis advisor.

Aumann, Robert J., and Michael B. Maschler. *Repeated Games of Incomplete Information.* Cambridge, MA: MIT Press, 1995. Contains a discussion of the role that Harsanyi and his games of incomplete information played in the Mathematica arms control project.

Breit, William, and Barry T. Hirsch, eds. *Lives of the Laureates: Eighteen Nobel Economists.* 4th ed. Cambridge, MA: MIT Press, 2004. Includes an autobiographical account of Harsanyi's life and work.

Damme, Eric van, and Jörgen W. Weibull. "Equilibrium in Strategic Interaction: The Contributions of John C. Harsanyi, John F. Nash, and Reinhard Selten." *Scandinavian Journal of Economics* 97 (1995): 15–40. An introduction to the contributions to game theory made by Harsanyi and his fellow Nobel laureates.

Games and Economic Behavior 36, no. 1 (2001). This John C. Harsanyi memorial issue contains a number of personal reminiscences of Harsanyi, his portrait, and an overview of Harsanyi's life and work by Reinhard Selten, "John C. Harsanyi, System Builder and Conceptual Innovator."

Nash, John F., Jr. "The Bargaining Problem." *Econometrica* 18 (1950): 155–162.

———. "Two-Person Cooperative Games." *Econometrica* 21 (1953): 128–140.

Neumann, John von, and Oskar Morgenstern. *Theory of Games and Economic Behavior.* Princeton, NJ: Princeton University Press, 1944.

Rawls, John. *A Theory of Justice.* Cambridge, MA: Harvard University Press, 1971.

Sen, Amartya. "Welfare Inequalities and Rawlsian Axiomatics." *Theory and Decision* 7 (1976): 243–262.

Shapley, Lloyd S. "A Value for *n*-Person Games." In *Contributions to the Theory of Games,* edited by Harold W. Kuhn and Albert W. Tucker. Vol. 2. Princeton, NJ: Princeton University Press, 1953.

Weymark, John A. "A Reconsideration of the Harsanyi-Sen Debate on Utilitarianism." In *Interpersonal Comparisons of Well-Being*, edited by Jon Elster and John E. Roemer. Cambridge, U.K.: Cambridge University Press, 1991.

———. "John Harsanyi's Contributions to Social Choice and Welfare Economics." *Social Choice and Welfare* 12 (1995): 313–318. Contains an overview of Harsanyi's research on utilitarianism.

Zeuthen, Frederik. *Problems of Monopoly and Economic Warfare.* London: G. Routledge, 1930.

John A. Weymark

HARTREE, DOUGLAS RAYNER (*b.* Cambridge, England, 27 March 1897, *d.* 12 February 1958), *mathematics, theoretical physics, quantum chemistry, computing, numerical analysis.*

Hartree played a fundamental role in the field of twentieth-century numerical analysis and its application to theoretical physics. He developed practical numerical methods for use with pen and paper, desk calculating machines, differential analyzers, and electronic computers, and he pioneered the application of calculating technologies to scientific problems. In mathematical physics Hartree's most well-known contribution was the invention of the method of the self-consistent field for calculating atomic wave functions, which became known as the Hartree-Fock approximation, following further work on the technique by Vladimir Fock. This and other contributions meant that during the 1920s and 1930s, Hartree played an important role in the development of atomic physics and quantum chemistry, work for which he was elected a Fellow of the Royal Society in 1932.

Hartree specialized in the numerical solution of ordinary and partial differential equations—equations that often described real world problems and therefore needed real world solutions. From his early work on ballistics through research on quantum chemistry, Hartree used the latest computing technology to find practical solutions to differential equations. He was responsible for bringing Vannevar Bush's differential analyzer technology to the United Kingdom and for developing a wide range of scientific and industrial applications for the machine. In the post–World War II period, Hartree was influential in gaining support for the development of electronic computers in England and devising numerical methods for their application to problems in theoretical physics. One of his final contributions was the book *Numerical Analysis,* first published in 1952 and regarded as a classic in the subject.

Origins and Early Career. Hartree was born in Cambridge, England, in 1897. His father, William Hartree, taught in the Engineering Laboratory at Cambridge University until his retirement in 1913 at the age of forty-three. William Hartree was very skilled in numerical computation and continued to undertake scientific work after his retirement from Cambridge, as an assistant to both A. V. Hill and, later, to his son. Hartree's mother, Eva Raynor, was very active in public affairs, working with the Red Cross, the suffragette movement, the League of Nations Union, and the British National Council of Women. She served on the Cambridge Borough Council for twenty years and was the first female mayor of Cambridge in 1925.

Hartree was educated first at a small school in Cambridge and then at Bedales School in Petersfield in Hampshire, from which he won a scholarship to study mathematics at the University of Cambridge in 1915. Hartree completed one year of his undergraduate degree before leaving Cambridge to undertake war work with the Ministry of Munitions. The main role of the Ministry of Munitions was to supply the British Forces with weapons and ammunition throughout World War I. Hartree was invited to join A. V. Hill's Anti-Aircraft Experimental Section of the Munitions Inventions Department of the Ministry of Munitions as a commissioned lieutenant in the Royal Naval Volunteer Reserve, as part of a team made up largely of Cambridge mathematicians and mathematical physicists, including Ralph Fowler, Edward Milne, and Hartree's father. William Hill, a Cambridge physiologist and later pioneer of operations research, had been charged by the Ministry of Munitions with undertaking ballistics research to assist in the development of new anti-aircraft weapons.

The work was a mix of routine ballistics calculations and mathematical research on the ballistics of high-angled fire. Hartree became expert at both pencil and paper calculations and the use of hand-cranked calculating machines, such as the Brunsviga, but he also began to develop new numerical processes to calculate trajectories. His most lasting innovation was the use of time rather than angle of elevation as the independent variable in trajectory calculations, but it was his development and refinement of practical iterative methods for the numerical solution of differential equations that was to shape his future career. After the war Hartree wrote up his work on ballistics calculations for the journal *Nature* (1920) and coauthored a paper with Leonard Bairstow and Ralph Fowler on the pressure distribution on the head of a shell traveling at high velocities, published in the prestigious *Proceedings of the Royal Society,* thereby signaling the start of his career as a mathematical physicist.

Mathematical Physics Research. In 1919, Hartree returned to Cambridge; he completed his undergraduate studies in 1922. Fowler, who had also worked in Hill's group, had also returned to Cambridge as a lecturer, and he continued to influence Hartree. Hartree's experience of working with Fowler during the war made it an easy decision to stay on at Cambridge as a Cavendish Laboratory research student officially supervised by Ernest Rutherford but in practice mentored by Fowler. Inspired, according to his biographers Froese Fischer and Charles Galton Darwin, by the work of Niels Bohr, Hartree began studying the propagation of electromagnetic waves. Undertaken in collaboration with Edward Appleton, the work led to the magneto-ionic theory of the ionosphere and the development of the Appleton-Hartree equation for the refractive index.

The mid- to late 1920s was a time of great change and excitement in theoretical physics, and Hartree was becoming a well-known figure in the field. When news of Erwin Schrödinger's work on wave mechanics reached Cambridge, Hartree was ideally placed to make a contribution, and this is the area of study for which he achieved his PhD in 1926. His experience of numerical integration of differential equations, gained during his ballistics work in World War I, was invaluable. Hartree was able to develop and apply numerical techniques to the solution of increasingly complex atomic structures.

Integral to this work was Hartree's development of the method of the self-consistent field as a way of simplifying the numerical solution of the complex differential equations derived from the Schrödinger equation. Essentially the method enabled an approximation of the wave functions of the electrons of atoms to be described as ordinary differential equations that Hartree could then solve numerically by an iterative process. Hartree collaborated with John Slater, Ivar Waller, and others to continue to develop the method and its application. Later work by Vladimir Fock to further develop the technique resulted in the Hartree-Fock method of calculating molecular orbitals.

In 1929, at the relatively young age of thirty-two, Hartree was appointed Beyer Professor of Applied Mathematics at the University of Manchester. It was here that Hartree began to teach in seriousness and to supervise his own research students. Hartree was to become renowned for the help and support he gave to his students and others who sought his assistance. He continued his research and continued to develop numerical methods using calculating machines. In 1937, Hartree was appointed chairman of Theoretical Physics at the University of Manchester.

Differential Analyzers. In 1931, Vannevar Bush published an article in the *Journal of the Franklin Institute* in which he described the construction at the Massachusetts Institute of Technology (MIT) of a large mechanical device designed to mechanically solve differential equations. The machine, the differential analyzer, consisted of six integrating units connected by means of bus shafts. Each integrating unit was made up of a horizontal disk with a vertical wheel resting on it. The output from the integrating unit was connected to the main bus system through a torque amplifier in order for it to generate sufficient force to drive other components of the machine. Additionally, the differential analyzer had input and output tables and multipliers attached to the bus system.

Hartree learned of Bush's differential analyzer through published accounts and from John Slater, a professor of physics at MIT with whom Hartree often collaborated. Hartree saw how the differential analyzer could be applied to his work on the electron fields of atoms, and he traveled to MIT in the summer of 1932 to see the machine. He again traveled to MIT in 1933, and this time he used the machine to work on the self-consistent field equations for Mercury. Hartree was very impressed by the power of the machine to not only solve differential equations in a fraction of the time it took using pen, paper, and a calculating machine, but also by the way in which solutions could be described by the operation of the differential analyzer. By watching the machine run, the operator obtained a better perspective of how the variables in an equation changed over time and therefore an improved understanding of the phenomena described by the equations.

Hartree's visits to MIT and his use of the differential analyzer on a real problem convinced him of the value of the device and of the potential value of constructing one in England. In order to raise the money to build a differential analyzer at Manchester University, Hartree decided to construct a model machine from the children's construction toy Meccano, and he recruited Arthur Porter, a final-year physics undergraduate at Manchester, to assist him. After graduating, Porter registered as a master's student under Hartree's supervision and built the model differential analyzer in 1934. Porter tested the machine by solving the already known self-consistent field equations for hydrogen before going on to solve the equations for chromium, for which he gained his master's degree.

The model differential analyzer was very much more successful than Hartree had dared hope it would be, and soon Porter was using it to solve a wide variety of problems. The value of a full-sized machine had been more than adequately demonstrated, and Hartree secured a gift of £6,000 from Sir Robert McDougall, the deputy treasurer of the University of Manchester, to build one. Bush supplied both plans and a list of possible improvements, and Hartree placed a contract with the Metropolitan-Vickers Electrical Company to build the machine. The

Hartree

Manchester differential analyzer was installed in the Physics Department at the University of Manchester in March 1935, initially as a four-integrator machine, but it was extended to eight integrators shortly afterward.

A succession of visitors to the both the Meccano model and the full-sized differential analyzer, coupled with Hartree's publications in the popular scientific press describing the machine, meant that the differential analyzer work at Manchester had a considerable influence on the computational landscape of the United Kingdom. In 1935, John Lennard-Jones, Plummer Professor of Theoretical Chemistry at Cambridge, approached Hartree and Porter about the possibility of building a model differential analyzer at Cambridge. Hartree and Porter provided advice and guidance, and the resulting Cambridge Meccano differential analyzer was a more accurate and reliable machine than that at Manchester. As in Manchester, the model machine was a precursor to a funding application to build a full-sized machine that would form the foundation of the Cambridge Mathematical Laboratory. In 1937, Maurice Wilkes joined the Cambridge Mathematical Laboratory to supervise the construction of the full-sized machine. The Cambridge Mathematical Laboratory led by Wilkes was at the forefront of electronic computer development in England in the post–World War II period. In additional to the model at Cambridge, several other model differential analyzers were built in the United Kingdom in the 1930s and 1940s in academic, industrial, and military settings and were found to be useful computing tools, especially in situations where an understanding of the problem was more important than highly accurate numerical solutions.

The original purpose of the Manchester differential analyzer had been to solve self-consistent field equations. However, by the time the machine was installed, Hartree and Fock had refined their methods in ways that no longer required the use of a differential analyzer but were more easily undertaken using desk calculating machines. Hartree therefore applied for and obtained a Department of Scientific and Industrial Research grant to investigate a wide range of problems applicable to the machine.

Using the grant to full effect, Hartree and his students explored many diverse applications for the differential analyzer, including several industrial problems such as the time lag in process control systems. What characterized much of the research was Hartree's ability to work with differential equations and devise practical solutions for them, alongside his ability to teach others how to do the same. While the differential analyzer was applicable only to specific types of problems, it demonstrated the growing need in Britain for large-scale computing resources—a need that was further demonstrated during World War II.

World War II. At the outbreak of World War II, Hartree, along with many other British scientists, immediately became involved in war-related work for the Ministry of Supply, which had a wide-ranging remit relating to the supply and research side of the British Armed Forces. Hartree had several roles throughout the war, some relating very closely to practical work on problems involving differential equations and some rather more on the advisory side. Initially Hartree was assigned to the Projectile Development Establishment to work on anti-aircraft rocket design, a project that had strong links to his work in World War I. This meant that he was no longer in day-to-day contact with the work of the Manchester differential analyzer. However, the differential analyzer was recognized as a valuable computational resource by the Ministry of Supply and was immediately applied to war-related problems, under Hartree's supervision when his other duties would permit. Over the course of the war, the differential analyzer group worked on a very wide range of problems, including ballistics work, control systems for radar and gun control, radio propagation, underwater explosions, motion and stability of aircraft, heat flow problems, and the solution of diffusion and shock wave equations for the British atomic bomb project.

Alongside his advisory role in the Ministry of Supply and his supervision of the differential analyzer group, Hartree was also responsible for the magnetron research group. This group was created with the specific purpose of understanding magnetron theory in order to better inform the design of magnetrons for use in radar. The work required investigating the motions of electrons in the electric field that the electrons themselves had produced—that is, a self-consistent field. Hartree was able to use methods similar to those he had developed in the 1920s for atomic structure calculations. Britain and the United States began to collaborate on aspects of the magnetron work from late 1940 onward, and Hartree and John Slater from MIT found themselves once again working on similar ideas and problems. Much of the work was not suitable for solutions using differential analyzers, so Hartree developed elegant numerical methods for his small team of human computers working with desk calculators.

In addition to his other wartime responsibilities, in 1942, Hartree set up and chaired the influential Interdepartmental Committee on Servomechanisms—usually known as the Servo Panel. The aim of the Servo Panel was to disseminate information about recent advances in servomechanisms and to promote the use of a common terminology. The panel consisted of representatives from the Admiralty, the Ministries of Supply and Aircraft Production, and industry. Under Hartree's leadership the Servo Panel set up a series of lectures and seminars on servomechanisms, which were attended by people from the armed forces, industry, and universities, largely from the United Kingdom but also from the United States and British Commonwealth countries. The Servo Panel addressed the concern that developments in servomechanisms in radar, gun control, aircraft stability, and other applications (such as in the control of power plants and chemical processes) should be shared in order to benefit both military and industrial applications. The influence of the Servo Panel was wide and led to the strong development of the field of control engineering in the postwar period.

Computers and Numerical Analysis. Hartree's wartime advisory experience, coupled with his understanding of practical computation, meant that he was ideally placed to play a significant role in the development and application of electronic computers in the United Kingdom. In addition, his position in the Ministry of Supply and his contacts at MIT allowed him access to and knowledge of electronic computing developments in the United States. In 1945, Hartree paid an official visit to the United States on behalf of the British government, during which he visited the Harvard MARK I and ENIAC projects—both large-scale calculating machine projects. The ENIAC was built at the Moore School of Engineering at the University of Pennsylvania; it led directly to the development of the stored program computer concept, influencing computer design around the world. In 1946, Hartree again visited the ENIAC at the express invitation of the U.S. War Department in order to explore the ENIAC's application to scientific problems, with particular reference to the laminar boundary flow problem. Hartree was thus well placed to understand the advances being made in the United States and to promote computer development in the United Kingdom. It is unclear whether Hartree knew of the top secret Colossus machines built at Bletchley Park for code-breaking purposes, but he certainly moved in social and scientific circles with those who did. Hartree sat on advisory committees and executive groups and gave very positive support to the development of computers. In the late 1940s and early 1950s, electronic computers were developed in three main locations in the United Kingdom—at the University of Manchester, Cambridge University, and the National Physical Laboratory at Teddington. Hartree influenced all three projects, usually acting behind the scenes to promote, enable, or support the work.

The first computer project that Hartree influenced turned out to be the last one to come to fruition. During the war, the need for large-scale, government-sponsored centralized computing facilities had been recognized, and in 1944, Hartree had been asked to join a committee to discuss the matter. The result was the creation of a Mathematical Division at the National Physical Laboratory (NPL) based in Teddington, England, which not only acted as a centralized computing resource for the United Kingdom but also developed the ACE computer designed by Alan Turing. Hartree supported the creation of the NPL Mathematics Division both at the committee stage and in putting plans in place.

On his release from war service, Hartree returned to Manchester University as professor of Engineering Physics. He stayed only a short time before his appointment to the Plummer Chair of Mathematical Physics at Cambridge in 1946, so he was not on site to support the computer developments taking place in the Electrical Engineering Department at Manchester by Frederic ("Freddie") Williams, professor of electrical engineering. However, through the Royal Society, Hartree influenced the financing of a computing laboratory at Manchester run by the mathematician Max Newman to explore the application of electronic computers in pure mathematics.

At Cambridge, Hartree had a more obvious and practical influence. Maurice Wilkes returned from war service to take up the post of director of the Cambridge Mathematical Laboratory, then based around the Cambridge differential analyzer. Hartree described to Wilkes the computer developments taking place in the United States and arranged for Wilkes to attend the now famous series of lectures given by the Moore School of Engineering at the University of Pennsylvania, which effectively disseminated the electronic stored program computer concept worldwide. Wilkes took this information, developed it, and went on to build the EDSAC computer at Cambridge. Hartree contributed to building a library of subroutines for EDSAC and played a role in advising potential EDSAC users.

In addition to helping to initiate computer projects at Cambridge, Manchester, and the NPL, Hartree played an important role in raising awareness of computers and promoting their application to real projects, both by working with machines and by publishing and speaking widely on the topic. On his appointment as Plummer Professor of Mathematical Physics, Hartree gave an inaugural lecture entitled "Calculating Machines: Recent and Prospective Developments and Their Impact on Mathematical Physics." This can be seen as the start of Hartree's work on bringing computers and their potential to the attention of the scientific community. In the summer of 1948, Hartree was invited to spend three months in Los Angeles as acting director of the Institute of Numerical Analysis, which had been set up by the National Bureau of Standards to start work on developing numerical methods applicable to electronic computers; Hartree contributed to the work by identifying numerical processes that needed to be developed in order for scientists to make the best use of the computers then under construction. While in the United

States in 1948, Hartree also gave a series of lectures at the University of Illinois on calculating instruments and machines, later published as a book (*Calculating Instruments and Machines*, 1949), which was influential in shaping opinion during the 1950s.

The EDSAC computer in Cambridge went into operation in May 1949. Hartree was based in the Physics Department but regularly contributed to the work of the Mathematical Laboratory, influencing the programming and applications work of the machine. In particular he supervised an active program of research on atomic structure using EDSAC. More generally, however, he was on hand to give advice when it was needed. He also saw a growing need for those using, or proposing to use, EDSAC to have a good understanding of numerical methods; he developed lecture courses that he titled "Numerical Analysis" and in 1952 published a book of the same name that was regarded as a classic in the subject.

Hartree died suddenly in 1958, of heart failure, survived by his wife Elaine (née Charlton), along with a daughter and three sons. His career had spanned the computing problems of two world wars and saw the art of numerical computation develop from pencil and paper to electronics. While the solution of differential equations was a unifying factor in his work, Hartree had influenced the development of both calculating machines and methods by always focusing on developing numerical methods to further the solution of real life problems.

BIBLIOGRAPHY

A complete list of Hartree's publications can be found in Charlotte Froese Fischer, Douglas Rayner Hartree: His Life in Science and Computing *(River Edge, NJ: World Scientific Publishing, 2003), pp. 213–219. Correspondence and papers are held at Christ College, Cambridge; University of Manchester National Archive for the History of Computing; and the University of Cambridge Library. The American Institute of Physics Niels Bohr Library (College Park, Maryland) holds correspondence with Neils Bohr and interviews with Elaine Hartree, Neville Mott, and John C. Slater; additional correspondence with Bohr resides at the Neils Bohr Archive in Copenhagen.*

WORKS BY HARTREE

With Leonard Bairstow and Ralph Fowler. "The Pressure Distribution on the Head of a Shell Moving at High Velocities." *Proceedings of the Royal Society* Series A 97 (1920): 202–2218.

"Ballistic Calculations." *Nature* 106 (1920): 152–154.

"The Wave Mechanics of an Atom with a Non-coulomb Central Field: Part I, Theory and Methods." *Proceedings of the Cambridge Philosophical Society* 24 (1928): 89–110.

"The Wave Mechanics of an Atom with a Non-coulomb Central Field: Part II, Results and Discussion." *Proceedings of the Cambridge Philosophical Society* 24 (1928): 111–132.

"The Wave Mechanics of an Atom with a Non-coulomb Central Field: Part III, Term Values and Intensities in Series in Optical Spectra." *Proceedings of the Cambridge Philosophical Society* 24 (1928): 426–437.

"The Wave Mechanics of an Atom with a Non-coulomb Central Field: Part IV, Further Results Relating to Terms of the Optical Spectrum." *Proceedings of the Cambridge Philosophical Society* 25 (1929): 310–314.

With Arthur Porter. "The Construction and Operation of a Model Differential Analyzer." *Memoirs of the Manchester Literary and Philosophical Society* 79 (1934–1935): 51–72.

Calculating Instruments and Machines. Urbana: University of Illinois Press, 1949.

Numerical Analysis. Oxford, U.K.: Clarendon Press, 1952.

The Calculation of Atomic Structures. New York: Wiley, 1957.

OTHER SOURCES

Croarken, Mary. *Early Scientific Computing in Britain.* Oxford, U.K.: Clarendon Press, 1990.

Darwin, Charles Galton. "Douglas Rayner Hartree: 1897–1958." *Biographical Memoirs of Fellows of the Royal Society* 4 (1958): 103–116.

Froese Fischer, Charlotte. *Douglas Rayner Hartree: His Life in Science and Computing.* River Edge, NJ: World Scientific Publishing, 2003.

Porter, Arthur. *So Many Hills to Climb.* Silver Spring, MD: Beckham Publications, 2004.

Wilkes, Maurice V. "Introduction." In Douglas Rayner Hartree, *Calculating Machines: Recent and Prospective Developments and Their Impact on Mathematical Physics* and *Calculating Instruments and Machines.* Charles Babbage Institute reprint series in the History of Computing. Cambridge, MA: MIT Press, 1984.

Mary Croarken

HARVEY, HILDEBRAND WOLFE

(*b.* London, United Kingdom, 31 December 1887; *d.* Plymouth, United Kingdom, 26 November 1970), *biological oceanography, marine analytical chemistry, marine ecosystems and production.*

Harvey was one of the guiding spirits of a group of marine scientists at the Plymouth Laboratory of the Marine Biological Association of the United Kingdom who, between the late 1920s and the mid-1950s, established the ways in which marine production is governed by the interplay of the physics of the sea, its chemical composition, and the interactions of the organisms present. Their work involved the development of new techniques for measurement of the nutrient salts necessary for phytoplankton growth; the analysis of how temperature, salinity, light, and organisms were related; and—the crowning achievement of the Plymouth Laboratory during the 1930s—a deductive analysis of the control of marine production by the interplay of environmental factors, plant growth, and grazing by zooplankton. In this, Harvey was the main theoretician as well as a major contributor of new techniques. His books, published in 1928, 1945, and 1955, summarized the state of research in marine plankton production and provided a model of how research in that field could be carried out by impeccable attention to the biology, chemistry, and physics of the ocean.

Background and Training. His parents were Laetitia (née Wolfe), and Henry Allington Harvey, a partner in a manufacturer of high-quality paint. As an undergraduate at the University of Cambridge (1906–1911), Hildebrand Wolfe Harvey studied chemistry. He then went on to postgraduate research under William Hardy in the Cambridge School of Agriculture, working on a series of practical chemical problems, before returning to his family's paint firm in Surrey until the early years of World War I. During the war he served as a navigating officer on a minesweeper in the Barents Sea, developing a love of the ocean that lasted his whole life. After a brief period in naval research after the war, he was hired in October 1921 by the Plymouth Laboratory to carry out surveys of water properties of the English Channel, part of the laboratory's contribution to the scientific program of the International Council for the Exploration of the Sea (ICES), and to do the compilation of temperature observations and analyses of salinity and nutrient salts. At Plymouth, Harvey found himself in the research environment created by the laboratory's director from 1894 to 1936, Edgar Johnson Allen, who had begun to direct the work at Plymouth toward factors controlling marine production and thus underlying coastal fisheries. Equally influential initially was his senior colleague William Ringrose Gelston Atkins, trained in biology, physiology, and chemistry, and appointed to the laboratory only a few months before Harvey, and whose work soon turned toward the analysis of dissolved nutrients essential for plant growth in the sea and to the effects of light and temperature.

The Study of Marine Production. The context into which the work of Harvey and the Plymouth group fitted by the 1930s began in Germany three decades earlier, first in the hands of the physiologist Victor Hensen and then of his younger colleague Karl Brandt, whose research group in the University of Kiel first showed that the production of marine plankton organisms had a seasonal cycle, which could be attributed to changes of light and chemical nutrients, especially phosphorus and nitrogen. By late in the 1920s, the Kiel group had established a theory of plankton production that applied well to seas in temperate latitudes based in large part on applying knowledge of the nitrogen cycle from land to the sea. The group had also developed new analytical techniques for dissolved plant nutrients, and had begun to tackle the problems of how the spring bloom began and why the tropical oceans showed low levels of production. For reasons intrinsic to the German university system, and especially after the devastation of German science by World War I, by the 1920s the German initiative had ceased, and attention to problems of marine production were picked up by E. J. Allen's Plymouth Laboratory, in which Harvey, Atkins, and a few other young researchers began to play increasingly important roles during the late 1920s and early 1930s.

The early survey work on hydrographic and nutrient properties of the English Channel provided the background for Harvey's first book, *Biological Chemistry and Physics of Sea Water* (1928), summarizing what was known of the control of marine plant and animal production, or, as he titled the last section, "Chemical and physical factors controlling the density of population." Atkins and Harvey had found problems with the nutrient analyses developed at Kiel, and as a result both developed new, sensitive, fast, colorimetric techniques for the determination of nutrients that allowed seasonal and geographical differences to be followed with ease. By 1928, Atkins and Harvey's new analytical methods had been incorporated into a standard body of techniques endorsed by ICES. Three years later Harvey joined with European marine chemists to establish standard techniques for analysis of the carbon dioxide system in seawater. Each came to play a role in the synthesis of factors governing marine production that Harvey undertook with his colleagues at Plymouth in the early 1930s, based on the concept that phytoplankton provided the food base for a variety of animals, and that all the organisms provided energy to decomposers; these, in their turn, returned inorganic nutrients to the system. In the early years Harvey and his colleagues examined this scheme in greater and greater detail, concentrating on factors that controlled the rate of phytoplankton production and the regeneration of nutrients.

Plankton Production and Its Control. Harvey's insight by 1928 that the marine system was a closed one, involving producers, grazers, and predators, provided the conceptual background for the Plymouth group's greatest contribution to biological oceanography. Some technical problems, namely the collection and enumeration of phytoplankton cells, had to be overcome first. A skilled instrument maker as well as experimenter and conceptualist, Harvey designed a small metered phytoplankton net, allowing the cells to be captured quantitatively, also a colorimetric method of estimating phytoplankton abundance, which was far faster than enumeration under a microscope. These advances provided him with the ability

Harvey

to quickly follow changes in abundance of plant cells as the spring bloom developed. The first uses of these techniques indicated that phytoplankton populations varied inversely with the abundance of zooplankton, suggesting that grazing by animals limited the growth of phytoplankton populations. The total growth of the phytoplankton population, estimated from the disappearance of their nutrient salts, was less than the number of cells counted, a further indication that grazing was an integral part of the marine production cycle.

With the help of his Plymouth colleagues Leslie Hugh Norman Cooper, a chemist; Marie Lebour, a specialist in phytoplankton; and Frederick Stratten Russell, a zooplankton specialist, in 1934 Harvey organized a year of collaborative research to bring together all the threads of the marine production cycle in the English Channel. The result was one of the most famous of all papers in biological oceanography: Harvey, Cooper, Lebour, and Russell's "Plankton Production and Its Control," published in the *Journal of the Marine Biological Association of the United Kingdom* in 1935. In it they demonstrated, often in deductive fashion, the control of marine phytoplankton abundance by light, vertical water motion, and nutrients, and the role of grazing zooplankton in holding phytoplankton below their potential level of abundance. This accomplishment rapidly came to be regarded as the classic formulation of the causes of the plankton cycle in the sea and the necessary outcome and extension of the work of Harvey's continental European predecessors at Kiel and elsewhere.

Factors Controlling Growth of Phytoplankton. Many problems remained after 1935, including details of the marine nitrogen and phosphorus cycles, and the possibility that trace elements, as well as other major nutrients such as iron and manganese, could play a role in controlling production. His approach was to put his formidable experimental skills to work on the effects of the variation of light, temperature, and a number of trace substances and nonclassical plant nutrients on the growth of the phytoplankton cells. Many of these investigations occupied the last twenty years of his career at Plymouth, up to his retirement in 1958. The larger framework of these investigations was what he had referred to in 1928 as the "mosaic of conditions" controlling plankton abundance and ultimately marine production overall (p. 164). By the time his book *Recent Advances in the Chemistry and Biology of Sea Water* was published in 1945 (the result of enforced "idleness" during World War II, when air raids forced the laboratory to close), Harvey was beginning to think of marine systems as the products of intricate balances among nutrients, plants, and animals. He believed that marine ecosystems were homeostatic, constantly shifting around a maximum level of production that was achieved only when the transfer from one part of the marine production system to another was closely coupled. His last, equally influential book, *The Chemistry and Fertility of Sea Waters* (1955), took up the emerging relations of bacteria in marine ecosystems, along with new ideas on nutrient cycles, emphasizing that marine systems were constantly passing into and out of balance, involving the formation and decomposition of organic matter, and linking what went on in the overlying water and in the sediments below. It was then, in the 1950s, that Harvey began to put together a scheme of marine production that explicitly involved links between inorganic nutrients, plankton, bottom animals, and fish, a subject that had been suggested by E. J. Allen in the 1920s as one of the goals of research at the Plymouth Laboratory. Only with the accumulation of what he regarded as solid observationally and experimentally based knowledge did Harvey believe that such generalizations could be justified.

Harvey's Legacy. His work was recognized by the award of a ScD at Cambridge in 1937, his election as a Fellow of the Royal Society of London in 1945, the award of the Alexander Agassiz Medal of the U.S. National Academy of Sciences in 1952, and by his appointment as a Commander of the Order of the British Empire in 1958. When Harvey retired in 1958, research on marine production and the nature of marine ecosystems was being carried on in many other places outside Plymouth. A great deal of new work, much of it in the United States, extended and amplified the grazing model that Harvey, Cooper, Lebour, and Russell had proposed, as well as the detailed laboratory investigations that Harvey carried out during the late 1940s and 1950s. But Plymouth and Harvey's publications remained the gold standard for work on marine production at least into the 1970s, and the elements of Harvey's contributions are not difficult to detect, although seldom acknowledged and often not recognized, in a great deal of biological oceanographic research in the twenty-first century.

BIBLIOGRAPHY

WORKS BY HARVEY

Biological Chemistry and Physics of Sea Water. Cambridge, U.K.: Cambridge University Press, 1928.

With Leslie Hugh Norman Cooper, Marie Lebour, and Frederick Stratten Russell. "Plankton Production and Its Control." *Journal of the Marine Biological Association of the United Kingdom* 20 (1935): 407–441. One of the great classics of marine science.

"Production of Life in the Sea." *Biological Reviews of the Cambridge Philosophical Society* 17 (1942): 221–246.

Recent Advances in the Chemistry and Biology of Sea Water. Cambridge, U.K.: Cambridge University Press, 1945.

"On the Production of Living Matter in the Sea off Plymouth." *Journal of the Marine Biological Association of the United Kingdom* 29 (1950): 97–137.

The Chemistry and Fertility of Sea Waters. Cambridge, U.K.: Cambridge University Press, 1955.

OTHER SOURCES

Cooper, Leslie Hugh Norman. "Hildebrand Wolfe Harvey 1887–1970." *Biographical Memoirs of the Fellows of the Royal Society* 18 (1972): 331–347. Includes a partial bibliography and significant personal information.

———. "Obituary: Hildebrand Wolfe Harvey." *Journal of the Marine Biological Association of the United Kingdom* 52 (1972): 773–775.

Mills, Eric L. *Biological Oceanography: An Early History, 1870–1960.* Ithaca, NY: Cornell University Press, 1989. See especially chapters 8 and 9 for a detailed account of Harvey's career and work.

Eric L. Mills

HASLER, ARTHUR DAVIS (*b.* Lehi, Utah, 5 January 1908; *d.* Madison, Wisconsin, 23 March 2001), *fish physiology, limnology.*

Hasler was head of the Wisconsin limnological school for about four decades, and he oriented it toward experimental research. He trained forty-one students for MS degrees and fifty-two for PhD degrees. His own research focused primarily on fish ecology, and his most famous discovery of how salmon find their home stream when they swim upriver to spawn was as important for salmon farming as it was for science. He authored or coauthored almost two hundred publications. He was president of three national and one international scientific organizations and received numerous honors for his scientific work.

Early Life. Hasler was the middle of five children born to Walter Thalman Hasler and Ada Elizabeth Broomhead Hasler. He grew up with a fondness for nature and fishing, but when he majored in zoology at Brigham Young University, it was in hopes of following his father into medicine. However, when he graduated in 1932, his father was ill and the country was in the Great Depression, and he could not afford to attend medical school. Instead, he went to the University of Wisconsin Graduate School to continue his zoological studies, since there he could work to defray his expenses. He gravitated to limnology, and he accepted dissertation advisor Chancey Juday's suggestion that he conduct his research on the physiology of digestion in crustacean plankton. In the summer of 1935 he undertook research for the U.S. Fish and Wildlife Service on the effects of a pulp mill's wastes on oysters in the lower York River, Virginia. He transferred sick oysters from that river into the nearby unpolluted Piankatank River and healthy oysters from the Piankatank into the York; undisturbed oysters in both rivers served as controls. He found that sick oysters recovered when moved to the Piankatank and that healthy oysters sickened when moved to the York. This was a harbinger of his later experimental approach to limnological research.

He married Hanna Prüsse Hasler (1908–1969) in 1932 and they had five sons and one daughter. In 1971 he married Hatheway Minton Brooks, who outlived him.

In 1937, after receiving his PhD, he accepted the Wisconsin Zoology Department's invitation to become an instructor in zoology. Juday retired that year from teaching, but remained director of the Trout Lake Limnological Laboratory in northern Wisconsin until 1942. Hasler became assistant professor in 1941, associate professor with tenure in 1945, full professor in 1948, and professor emeritus in 1978. In the spring of 1945 Hasler, who was fluent in German, served as a research analyst with a U.S. Strategic Bombing Survey in Germany, and he took the opportunity to visit Karl von Frisch (who studied the behavior of fish as well as bees) at his Zoologisches Institut in Munich and Wilhelm G. Einsele at the Anstalt für Fischerei near Salzburg, Austria. Later, he reflected on these visits and decided to follow their examples and orient the Wisconsin limnological school toward experimentation and away from the traditional descriptive limnology practiced by Edward A. Birge and Chancey Juday. This decision coincided with a willingness of government to fund scientific research much more heavily than it had before World War II.

Olfactory Homing in Salmon. In summer 1946, Hasler returned to Utah on vacation and repeated two favorite pastimes of his youth—hiking the trails and fishing the streams of the Wasatch Mountains. As he climbed Mount Timpanogos, he wondered how salmon find their way back to their home stream to spawn. A cool breeze from a hidden waterfall brought the fragrance of mosses and columbine to him, and the image of the falls immediately came to his mind, along with childhood associations. If he had such a reaction to a remembered smell, perhaps salmon respond similarly.

Here was one line of research that he and several different graduate students pursued together for the rest of his career. It was a question in pure science, but with enormous practical applications, which made salmon farming practicable. He coauthored a cover story on some initial findings for the August 1955 issue of *Scientific American.* Fortuitously, while this research on salmon was underway, the Michigan Department of Natural Resources

Hasler

introduced Pacific salmon into Lake Michigan to eat the exotic alewife that had become a problem in the Great Lakes. The salmon did control the alewife, though neither species disappeared from the Great Lakes, and the Madison limnologists could then obtain their salmon for research close by. By the 1970s, there were as many as seven coauthors to some of the papers being published by the Madison group working on salmon homing in Lake Michigan.

Hasler synthesized their findings in two books. *Underwater Guideposts* (1966) is divided into three parts: (1) the hypothesis of olfactory location of the river mouth and the natal stream, with the supporting experiments; (2) the hypothesis of Sun orientation in open-sea migration and supporting evidence; and (3) the complete migration hypothesis, which emphasizes the sensory mechanisms and environmental cues. The second, a coauthored book, *Olfactory Imprinting and Homing in Salmon* (1983), delves more deeply into the physiology involved, including the hormones and biochemistry.

Other Research and Leadership. However, salmon migration was only one line of research Hasler and his students pursued. Other early experiments conducted by his students for doctoral dissertations concerned aquatic plant productivity (1947), minnow productivity (1949), and the introduction of hydrated lime into dystrophic lakes (1954, 1958) (Hasler, 1963). In 1953–1954 Hasler and his family moved to Munich on a Fulbright Research Scholarship to study fish sensory abilities with von Frisch. In Munich he found that the European minnow could orient itself toward a lamp (simulating the Sun) in the laboratory to obtain food, while other environmental factors varied randomly. After returning to Madison he wondered if Sun-compass orientation could be demonstrated in fish in both laboratory and in natural environments. He persuaded several doctoral and postdoctoral students to investigate several aspects of this question. Salmon are guided by smell when they swim up their home stream, but they spend up to five years at sea. How do they locate the river up which they swim? A whole different set of experiments demonstrated that Sun-compass navigation is used to find the right river.

As busy as Hasler was doing research and guiding that of his students, he also found time for professional activities. He was able to hire research managers, paid out of research grants, to help his students and free some of his time for other matters. The Limnological Society of America was founded in 1936, and in 1948 it expanded to become the American Society of Limnology and Oceanography. Hasler was its president in 1951. In 1961 he brought in an associate professor from Montana, John C. Wright, to help organize the Fifteenth Congress of the International Association of Limnology—the first one in the United States. Under his chairmanship, it was held in Wisconsin in 1962, and it inspired the encyclopedic volume *Limnology in North America* (Hasler, 1963), written by thirty-two collaborators. Hasler also served as president of the Ecological Society of America in 1961, the American Society of Zoologists in 1971, and the International Association for Ecology, 1967–1974, and presided at the First Congress of the latter association at The Hague in 1974. His achievements also led to memberships in prestigious societies. He was elected a fellow of the Philadelphia Academy of Sciences in 1953, the American Institute of Fisheries Research Biology in 1958, the American Association for the Advancement of Science in 1960, the Animal Behavior Society in 1967, and a member of the National Academy of Sciences in 1969 and the Royal Netherlands Academy of Sciences in 1976.

In 1937, Hasler had for his use only a small two-room laboratory on the shore of Lake Mendota, the lake adjacent to the university campus. As the limnological school grew under Hasler, its needs could not be fully met by the Department of Zoology's budget. In 1962 Hasler obtained from the National Science Foundation funds to build a new Laboratory of Limnology. Hasler chose the location on the shore of Lake Mendota, within the university campus. He also chose the architect, and worked with him in designing the building. Since 1998 it has been enclosed by the Arthur Davis Hasler Lake Laboratory Garden, and in 2006 the laboratory was renamed the Arthur Davis Hasler Laboratory of Limnology. Hasler was its head from the opening in 1963 until his retirement in 1978. The Wisconsin limnological school under Birge and Juday lasted for forty years, and under Hasler for another forty years. They made Lake Mendota the most widely studied lake in the world.

BIBLIOGRAPHY

Hasler authored or coauthored almost two hundred publications.

WORKS BY HASLER

"Wisconsin, 1940–1961." In *Limnology in North America,* edited by David G. Frey. Madison: University of Wisconsin Press, 1963. Hasler describes the Wisconsin limnological school under his guidance during the first two decades.

Underwater Guideposts: Homing of Salmon. Madison: University of Wisconsin Press, 1966.

With Allan T. Scholz and Robert W. Goy. *Olfactory Imprinting and Homing in Salmon: Investigations into the Mechanism of the Imprinting Process.* New York: Springer-Verlag, 1983.

OTHER SOURCES

Beckel, Annamarie L., and Frank N. Egerton, eds. "Breaking New Waters: A Century of Limnology at the University of Wisconsin." Special issue, *Transactions of the Wisconsin*

Academy of Sciences, Arts, and Letters (1983). Describes Hasler's career.

Likens, Gene E. "Arthur Davis Hasler, January 5, 1908–March 23, 2001." *Biographical Memoirs,* vol. 82. Washington, DC: National Academy of Sciences, 2002. Available from http://fermat.nap.edu/html/biomems/. Likens was one of Hasler's doctoral students.

Frank N. Egerton

HAURWITZ, BERNHARD (*b.* Glogau, Germany [later Głogów, Poland], 14 August 1905; *d.* Fort Collins, Colorado, 22 February 1986), *dynamic meteorology, atmospheric tides, wave motions.*

Researcher, educator, and author Bernhard Haurwitz was an archetypical model of scientific success in the twentieth century. Educated in Europe, effectively displaced by the upheaval there in the 1930s, and eventually welcomed to the United States, Haurwitz witnessed and participated in the explosion of interest in the sciences that blossomed in the post–World War II era. Meteorology was no exception to this rule, and Haurwitz made use of the growing supply of data to learn more about the dynamics of the tides in the atmosphere and oceans that are affected and modulated by the Moon and the Sun.

Training. Bernhard Haurwitz was born the son of a merchant father, and had one sister. Having had an interest in science from a young age (particularly astronomy), Haurwitz pursued advanced training in the areas of physical science. He studied at the University of Göttingen, after a period at the University of Breslau, where he had matriculated in 1923. While at the University of Göttingen, his interest in meteorology developed while studying under such luminaries as Richard Courant. In 1925, Haurwitz moved to the Geophysical Institute at the University of Leipzig in order to work with Dr. Ludwig Weickmann, whose paper on atmospheric waves interested him.

While in Leipzig, Haurwitz used data from early radiosonde balloon flights to predict the existence of the level of nondivergence in a hydrostatic atmosphere. This finding was of particular importance in early numerical weather prediction efforts, and remains an important theoretical assumption in many meteorological research efforts to this day. While a doctoral student, Haurwitz paid visits to Oslo, Sweden, and Bergen, Norway, in order to study with scientists who were then the world leaders in theoretical and applied meteorology, respectively. During the 1920s the group at the Bergen School, as it has come to be known, were the progenitors of the Norwegian

Bernard Haurwitz. © 2007 UNIVERSITY CORPORATION FOR ATMOSPHERE RESEARCH.

Cyclone Model, a weather forecasting tool that described how low pressure systems developed and evolved, and dominated operational meteorology throughout the twentieth century. Yet his interests remained in the realm of theoretical meteorology, and while in Norway he worked with such notable contemporaries as Harald Sverdrup, Halvor Solberg, and Carl Størmer. Upon returning to Leipzig, Haurwitz completed his dissertation in 1927. He then focused his attention on wave motions in the atmosphere, in particular the dynamics of billow clouds. Haurwitz completed his second (habilitation) thesis in 1931.

Early Career. In 1932, Haurwitz traveled to the United States to work temporarily at the Massachusetts Institute of Technology (MIT) with Carl-Gustaf Rossby. While at MIT, he was also employed part time at the Blue Hill Observatory near Boston. It was during this time that Haurwitz investigated the height of the typical tropical cyclone. Until then, observations in tropical cyclones at levels above the surface were virtually nonexistent. Consequently, tropical cyclones were thought to be shallow phenomena, specifically in terms of the physical depth of the constituent clouds. Previous investigators had concluded that tropical cyclones must be relatively "thin," based largely on the observed weakening behavior of hurricanes and typhoons near mountains and other topographical features. If tropical cyclones weaken so dramatically when encountering mountains, the reasoning went, then they must not be as deep as their midlatitude cyclone cousins.

Haurwitz

However, Haurwitz also observed that many tropical cyclones regenerated after crossing a mountain range. By extension, he surmised then that the original circulation must have been much deeper than just a few kilometers, and that regeneration was aided by the remnants of the original circulation that persisted aloft. Indeed, it has long been known that warm-core low-pressure systems weaken with height. As such, it is reasonable to expect that at some level over the center of the cyclone, the flow "smoothes out"; this is known as the surface of pressure equalization. Although below the height of the top of the tropical cyclone, this surface of pressure equalization was considered a good index for the cloud depth. Haurwitz's 1935 article "The Height of Tropical Cyclones and of the 'Eye' of the Storm" used the barometric equation to show convincingly that the surface of pressure equalization should be found at 10 kilometers in realistic tropical cyclones. Later observational evidence has shown that tropical cyclones extend over the depth of the troposphere.

In early 1933, Haurwitz had occasion to visit the California Institute of Technology (Caltech) to deliver a set of lectures. While in California, Haurwitz also visited the Scripps Institution of Oceanography at the behest of Horace Byers. It was around this same time that Adolf Hitler became chancellor of Germany, and Haurwitz's ostensibly temporary travels outside his home country became permanent. Haurwitz returned from California and remained employed by MIT until September 1935, when he went to work at the University of Toronto.

While in Canada, Haurwitz did a great deal of teaching for the university, which also had an agreement with the Canadian Meteorological Service for the instruction of its staff. He taught several sections of dynamic meteorology (the subdiscipline that describes mathematically the fundamentals of atmospheric motion) during this period, and developed a collection of lecture notes on the topic that were quite thorough and complete. Given that a satisfactory text for an introduction to the subject did not exist at the time, Haurwitz penned one, and it was published in 1941, as *Dynamic Meteorology.*

The time spent in Canada was some of the most productive of Haurwitz's career. Landmark papers by Haurwitz (1937, 1940a,b) on the motion of large-scale horizontal atmospheric waves emerged from this period. Together, these papers complemented Rossby's work wherein a detailed theoretical description was provided for the motion of horizontal planetary waves in the atmosphere. The earlier (1937) work described the westward motion for planetary scale waves with life spans well in excess of one day. The later (1940a,b) works built upon the earlier paper and included the beta effect (how the coriolis force changes as a function of latitude), the treatment of the wavelength of the system, as well as the influence of friction on planetary waves moving across a rotating, spherical Earth. With the 1940 results, Haurwitz was able to show practical benefit from his work. Specifically he was able to account for much of the motion (or lack thereof) on the part of semipermanent pressure systems in the atmosphere (e.g., the subpolar Icelandic and Aleutian lows as well as the subtropical Pacific and Azore highs). This wave class has come to be known as Rossby-Haurwitz waves.

In addition to an improved understanding of Earth's global circulation, these findings also had broader application to the daily practice of weather forecasting, especially in the early years of numerical weather prediction. Certainly, Haurwitz's work helped to give operational weather forecasting a firm mathematical foundation. Although the Norwegian cyclone model was useful as a conceptual tool to describe the life cycle of extratropical cyclones in the midlatitudes, it was just that: a qualitative graphical description of extratropical cyclone evolution, devoid of mathematical rigor. Throughout the 1930s and 1940s, forecasts of the future state of a cyclone were based upon pattern recognition and extrapolation toward a future state suggested by the Norwegian model. Haurwitz's work treated the atmosphere for what it was, namely, a three-dimensional fluid whose future state could be predicted using the Navier-Stokes equations and adequate initial conditions. His work in this area helped to provide the dynamical, mathematical underpinnings of meteorology in the latter half of the twentieth century.

A Leader in Meteorology. In 1941, Haurwitz returned to the United States to work again for MIT at the invitation of Sverre Petterssen, a towering figure in the subdiscipline of synoptic meteorology. Haurwitz's primary teaching responsibility was the dynamic meteorology course (a cornerstone of the meteorology training of both navy and army air corps personnel at MIT) as well as one devoted to physical climatology, about which he coauthored a text with James Austin in 1944. Also while at MIT, Haurwitz served as the fourteenth president of the American Meteorological Society. These obligations, and the divorce from his wife (the former Eva Schick, with whom Haurwitz had one son, Frank) of twelve years in 1946, appear to have limited Haurwitz's research productivity during his later period at MIT.

From 1947 to 1954 Haurwitz chaired the Department of Meteorology at New York University; this move was made at the behest of Athelstan Spilhaus. During this time, he helped to oversee the assembly of the *Compendium of Meteorology* (1951), a collection of papers and essays on the state of meteorology at the time authored by the world leaders in the field. Haurwitz's contribution

Haurwitz

concerned perturbation equations in meteorology. This was not only a basic treatise on the mathematics of dynamic meteorology, but also a review of his own work and that of Rossby to describe quantitatively the motion of waves on a rotating, spherical platform (e.g., a planet).

In that same year, he returned briefly to the area of tropical meteorology with a paper that addressed the motion of binary tropical cyclones. Known as the Fujiwhara effect after the Japanese scientist who wrote the first paper on the phenomenon, the term refers to the tendency of two tropical cyclones in proximity to one another, and in a weak background flow, to tend to rotate about one another's center in a counterclockwise fashion. Haurwitz extended the work of Fujiwhara by showing mathematically that the motion was a function of the cyclones' intensities as well as the distance between their centers.

Later Pursuits. In the years beyond 1954, Haurwitz made his home in the western United States, enjoying affiliations with the University of Alaska, Colorado State University, and the University of Colorado. Haurwitz settled in Colorado after 1959 and was elected to the National Academy of Sciences in 1960, as well as the Deutsche Akademie der Naturforscher Leopoldina in 1964. Also in 1964, Haurwitz joined the National Center for Atmospheric Research and its Advanced Study Program, which he directed from 1966 to 1969. On the homefront, Haurwitz did remarry in 1961, to Marion Wood of Colorado.

During this period, Haurwitz returned to a topic that had interested him from earlier years, the subject of atmospheric tides. In addition to the daily oscillations in the atmospheric surface pressure due to the passage of transient cyclones and anticyclones, there are also longer-scale pressure oscillations that are ever present in the background. In particular, there is the diurnal pressure tide (known as S_1) and a semidiurnal pressure tide (known as S_2). Moreover, both tides were known to be thermally driven modes and thus clearly related to the Sun's influence. What was troublesome to Haurwitz was the relatively small size of S_1 compared to S_2, and the inconsistency between the diurnal and semidiurnal temperature oscillations. Our own human experience tells us that there is generally only one maximum temperature and one minimum temperature at any given location in a given day. This is another kind of S_1, but for temperature, and it is typically much larger than any other shorter variation. Yet the same is not true for the S_1 of pressure; it is not the dominant mode.

Until the mid-twentieth century, the dominance of S_2 over S_1 had been ascribed to resonance theory, which demanded a free oscillation in the atmosphere with a period of very nearly twelve hours. Yet another unsavory outcome of resonance theory demanded stratospheric temperatures well in excess of what are observed normally. Later, Haurwitz (1965) published a paper that used a spherical-harmonic analysis of a global dataset to document the behaviors of S_1 and S_2 and show that the magnitude of the latter was nearly double the former, thus making another step toward a viable replacement for resonance theory. What his analysis provided was evidence for the weaker signal in the S_1 pressure tide that was later corroborated and explained by contemporaries Richard S. Lindzen and S. Kato (a sequence of events described in detail by Platzman, 1996), who showed that the absorption of solar radiation by water vapor and ozone in the stratosphere excited the S_1 pressure tide.

About a decade later, Haurwitz effectively retired in 1976. For his achievements in meteorology and geophysics, Haurwitz had received the Carl-Gustaf Rossby Award for Extraordinary Scientific Achievement from the American Meteorological Society in 1962, and the Bowie Medal by the American Geophysical Union in 1972. Bernhard Haurwitz was a twentieth-century leader in meteorology, at the forefront of its establishment as a legitimate and distinct scientific discipline. His contributions to the subdiscipline of dynamic meteorology before, during, and immediately after World War II allowed the day-to-day task of operational weather forecasting to assume a more rigorous and quantitative approach, and thus a firmer scientific footing. Because of Haurwitz's work, our understanding of large-scale, long-period, planetary motions in Earth's atmosphere has been altered permanently and for the better.

BIBLIOGRAPHY

WORKS BY HAURWITZ

"The Height of Tropical Cyclones and of the 'Eye' of the Storm." *Monthly Weather Review* 63 (1935): 45–49.

"The Oscillations of the Atmosphere." *Gerlands Beitrage zur Geophysik* 51 (1937): 195–233.

"The Motion of Atmospheric Disturbances." *Journal of Marine Research* 3 (1940a): 35–50.

"The Motion of Atmospheric Disturbances on a Spherical Earth." *Journal of Marine Research* 3 (1940b): 254–267.

Dynamic Meteorology. New York: McGraw-Hill, 1941.

"The Diurnal Surface Pressure Oscillation." *Archiv für Meteorologie, Geophysik und Bioklimatologie* A14 (1965): 361–379.

"Meteorology in the 20th Century—A Participant's View: Part I." *Bulletin of the American Meteorological Society* 66 (1985): 282–291.

"Meteorology in the 20th Century—A Participant's View: Part II." *Bulletin of the American Meteorological Society* 66 (1985): 424–431.

"Meteorology in the 20th Century—A Participant's View: Part III." *Bulletin of the American Meteorological Society* 66 (1985): 498–504.

"Meteorology in the 20th Century—A Participant's View: Part IV." *Bulletin of the American Meteorological Society* 66 (1985): 628–633.

OTHER SOURCES

London, Julius. "Bernhard Haurwitz." *Biographical Memoirs,* vol. 69. Washington, DC: National Academy of Sciences, 1996. Available from http://books.nap.edu/html/biomems/bhaurwitz.html.

Platzman, George W. "The S-1 Chronicle: A Tribute to Bernhard Haurwitz." *Bulletin of the American Meteorological Society* 77 (1996): 1569–1577.

Patrick S. Market

HAUSDORFF, FELIX (*b.* Breslau, Germany, 8 November 1868; *d.* Bonn, Germany, 26 January 1942), *mathematics, philosophy, literature.*

Hausdorff studied at Leipzig, Freiburg, and Berlin between 1887 and 1891 and started research in applied mathematics. After his *habilitation* (1895) he taught at the University of Leipzig and a local commercial school. He moved in a milieu of Leipzig intellectuals and artists, strongly influenced by the early work of Friedrich Nietzsche (1844–1900), striving for a cultural modernization of late-nineteenth-century Germany.

Between 1897 and 1910 Hausdorff published two philosophical books, a poem collection, and a satirical theater play under the pseudonym Paul Mongré. He regularly contributed cultural critical essays to the *Neue Deutsche Rundschau,* a leading German intellectual journal of the time. In his second book, *Das Chaos in kosmischer Auslese* (1898; Chaos in cosmic selection), he radicalized Kantian transcendental idealism by a Nietzschean perspective and attempted to dissolve the belief in any determined a priori form of transcendent reality. In particular he reviewed the contemporary discussion on space and time, employing transformations of increasing generality. In the end he was led to considering transfinite Cantorian sets and their general set transformations as a mathematical expression for a completely unstructured reality, and thus to "transcendent nihilism."

During this period, Hausdorff reoriented his mathematical work toward the new field of transfinite set theory. He gave one of the first lecture courses on this topic in summer 1901 and contributed important results to it, among others the *Hausdorff recursion* for aleph exponentiation (1904) and deep methods for the classification of order structures (confinality, gap types, general ordered products, and eta-alpha sets; 1906–1907). He employed a "naive" concept of set, but even so achieved an exceptionally high precision of argumentation. He contributed crucial insights into foundational questions, most importantly his maximal chain principle (related to but different from Zorn's lemma), a characterization of weakly inaccessible cardinals (in present terminology), and the universality property for order structures of what he called "eta-alpha sets." The latter became one of the roots of *saturated structures* in model theory of the 1960s. Moreover, Hausdorff hit on the importance of the *generalized continuum hypothesis* in these studies.

In summer 1910 Hausdorff started teaching at the University of Bonn and broadened his perspective on set theory as a general basis for mathematics. In early 1912 he found an axiomatic characterization of topological spaces by neighborhood systems and started to compose a monograph on "basic features of set theory" (*Grundzüge der Mengenlehre*). It was finished two years later (1914b), after he was called in 1913 to a full professorship at the University of Greifswald.

In this book, Hausdorff showed how set theory could be used as a working frame for mathematics more broadly. While he introduced set theory in a nonaxiomatic style, although with extraordinary precision, topological spaces and measure theory were given an axiomatic presentation. In part two Hausdorff published his neighborhood axioms found two years earlier, introduced separation and countability axioms, and studied connectivity properties. This part of the book contained the first comprehensive treatment of the theory of metric spaces, initiated by Maurice-René Fréchet in 1906. It laid the basis for an important part of general topology of the twentieth century.

In part three he provided a lucid introduction to measure theory, building on the work of Émile Borel and Henri-Léon Lebesgue. In a paper published shortly before the book (also in an appendix to it) Hausdorff gave a negative answer to Lebesgue's question, whether a (finitely) additive content function invariant under congruences can be defined on *all* subsets of Euclidean three-space (1914a). His peculiar use of the axiom of choice became the starting point for the later paradoxical constructions of measure theory by Stefen Banach and Alfred Tarski.

The *Grundzüge* became influential only after World War I, most strongly in the rising schools of modern mathematics in Poland, around the journal *Fundamenta Mathematicae,* and in the Soviet Union mainly among Nikolai N. Luzin's students around Pavel Alexandrov. The *Grundzüge* became one of the founding documents of mathematical modernism in the 1920 and 1930s.

Already in the *Grundzüge* Hausdorff had started to study Borel sets. In 1916 he, and independently Alexandrov, could show that any infinite Borel set in a separable metrical space is countable or of cardinality of the continuum. That was an important step forward for a strategy proposed by Georg Cantor to clarify the continuum hypothesis. Although this goal could not be achieved along this road, it led to the development of an extended field of investigation on the border region between set theory and analysis, now dealt with in descriptive set theory.

On the other side, Hausdorff took up questions in real analysis, now informed by the new basic features of general set theory. His introduction of what came to be called Hausdorff measure and Hausdorff dimension (1919) became of long-lasting importance in the theory of dynamical systems, geometrical measure theory, and the study of "fractals."

Other important technical contributions dealt with summation methods of infinite divergent series and a generalization of the Riesz-Fischer theorem, which established the well-known relation between function spaces and series of Fourier coefficients (1923). It opened the path for later developments in harmonic analysis on topogical groups. In a lecture course in 1923 Hausdorff introduced an axiomatic basis for probability theory, which anticipated Andrey Kolmogorov's axiomatization of 1933.

When Hausdorff revised his magnum opus for a second edition, he rewrote the parts on descriptive set theory and topological spaces completely, extending the first part considerably and concentrating the second one on metrical spaces. As other books on general set and general topology had appeared in the meantime, he omitted these parts for the so-called second edition, which became essentially a new book (1927).

In 1921 Hausdorff had returned to Bonn, now as a full professor and colleague of Eduard Study and (some years later) Otto Toeplitz. While he was still regularly emeritated in early 1935, general life and working conditions deteriorated drastically for Hausdorff and other people of Jewish origin, after the rise to power of the Nazi regime. His attempt at emigration came too late. When Hausdorff, his wife Charlotte, and a sister of hers were ordered to leave their house for a local internment camp in January 1942, they opted for suicide rather than suffering further persecution. His scientific *Nachlass* was handed over to a local friend. It survived the end of the war with only minor damage.

BIBLIOGRAPHY

Hausdorff's complete works are currently being published under the title Gesammelte Werke: Einschließlich der unter dem Pseudonym Paul Mongré erschienenen philosophischen und literarischen Schriften und ausgewählte Texte aus dem Nachlass, *edited by Egbert Brieskorn, Friedrich Hirzebruch, Walter Purkert, et al. (Berlin: Springer: 2001–). Nine volumes are planned. Volumes, with year of publication, are as follows: vol. 2 (2002), vol. 3 (2007), vol. 4 (2001), vol. 5 (2005), and vol. 7 (2004). Reference is made below to works that have been published in the above volumes (*Werke II, Werke IV, *and so forth).*

WORKS BY HAUSDORFF

(Under pseudonym Paul Mongré.) *Das Chaos in kosmischer Auslese—Ein erkenntniskritischer Versuch.* Leipzig, Germany: Naumann, 1898. In *Werke VII,* pp. 587–807.

"Der Potenzbegriff in der Mengenlehre." *Jahresberichte der Deutschen Mathematiker-Vereinigung* 13 (1904): 569–571. English translation in *Hausdorff on Ordered Sets,* edited by Jacob M. Plotkin, pp. 31–33. Providence, RI: American Mathematical Society, 2005.

"Untersuchungen über Ordnungstypen I–V." *Berichte Verhandlungen Sächsische Gesellschaft der Wissenschaften Leipzig, Math-Phys. Klasse* 58 (1906): 106–169, and 59 (1907): 84–159. English translation in *Hausdorff on Ordered Sets,* edited by Jacob M. Plotkin, pp. 35–171. Providence, RI: American Mathematical Society, 2005.

"Bemerkung über den Inhalt von Punktmengen." *Mathematische Annalen* 75 (1914a): 428–433. In *Werke IV,* pp. 3–10.

Grundzüge der Mengenlehre. Leipzig, Germany: Veit, 1914b. In *Werke II,* pp. 91–576.

"Dimension und äußeres Maß." *Mathematische Annalen* 79 (1919): 157–179. In *Werke IV,* pp. 21–43.

"Eine Ausdehnung des Parsevalschen Satzes über Fourierreihen." *Mathematische Zeitschrift* 16 (1923): 163–169. In *Werke IV,* pp. 173–181.

Vorlesung Wahrscheinlichkeitsrechnung, Bonn 1923, *Nachlass* Fasz. 64. In *Werke V,* pp. 595–723.

Mengenlehre. Berlin: Gruyter, 1927. In *Werke III.*

Nachgelassene Schriften. 2 vols. Edited by Günter Bergmann. Stuttgart, Germany: Teubner, 1969.

"Nachlass." Handschriftenabteilung Universitätsbibliothek Bonn. Findbuch (catalog). Available from http://www.aic.uni-wuppertal.de/fb7/hausdorff/findbuch.asp.

OTHER SOURCES

Brieskorn, Egbert, ed. *Felix Hausdorff zum Gedächtnis.* Braunschweig, Germany: Vieweg, 1996.

Chatterji, Srishti D. "Measure and Integration Theory." In *Werke II,* pp. 788–800.

Eichhorn, Eugen, and Ernst-Jochen Thiele, eds. *Vorlesungen zum Gedenken an Felix Hausdorff.* Berlin: Heldermann, 1994.

Epple, Moritz, Horst Herrlich, Mirek Hušek, et al. "Zum Begriff des topologischen Raumes." In *Werke II,* pp. 675–744. Also available from http://hausdorff-edition.de/media/pdf/Topologischer_Raum.pdf.

Felgner, Ulrich. "Die Hausdorffsche Theorie der eta-alpha-Mengen und ihre Wirkungsgeschichte." In *Werke II,* pp. 645–674. Also available from http://hausdorff-edition.de/media/pdf/Eta_Alpha.pdf.

Koepke, Peter, and Vladimir Kanovei. "Deskriptive Mengenlehre in Hausdorffs Grundzügen der Mengenlehre." In *Werke II,* pp. 773–787.

Moore, Gregory. *Zermelo's Axiom of Choice: Its Origins, Development, and Influence.* New York: Springer, 1982.

Neuenschwander, Erwin. "Felix Hausdorffs letzte Lebensjahre nach Dokumenten aus dem Bessel-Hagen Nachlaß." In *Felix Hausdorff zum Gedächtnis,* edited by Egbert Brieskorn, 253–270. Braunschweig, Germany: Vieweg, 1996.

Plotkin, Jacob M. *Hausdorff on Ordered Sets.* Providence, RI: American Mathematical Society, 2005.

Purkert, Walter. "Grundzüge der Mengenlehre: Historische Einführung." In *Werke II,* pp. 1–90. Also available from http://hausdorff-edition.de/media/pdf/HistEinfuehrung.pdf.

Stegmaier, Walter. "Ein Mathematiker in der Landschaft Zarathustras: Felix Hausdorf als Philosoph." *Nietzsche Studien* 31 (2002): 195–240. Similarly editor's introduction in *Werke VII,* pp. 1–83. Also available from http://hausdorff-edition.de/media/pdf/Einleitung.pdf.

Vollhardt, Friedrich, and Udo Roth. "Die Signifikanz des Außenseiters: Der Mathematiker Felix Hausdorff und die Weltanschauungsliteratur um 1900." In *Literatur und Wissen(schaften), 1890–1935,* edited by Christine Maillard and Michael Titzmann, 213–234. Stuttgart, Germany: Metzler, 2002.

Erhard Scholz

HEBB, DONALD OLDING (*b.* Chester, Nova Scotia, Canada, 22 July 1904; *d.* Halifax, Nova Scotia, 20 August 1985), *psychology, neuropsychology, cognitive psychology, cognitive neuroscience.*

Hebb was one of the preeminent neuropsychologists of the twentieth century. When Hebb arrived on the psychological scene in the 1930s, behavioristic formulations, which typically evaded questions of mind and reference to the nervous system, dominated North American academic psychology. In his major theoretical work, *The Organization of Behavior* (1949), Hebb presented a comprehensive neuropsychological account of behavior, grappling with essential mental events, while also confronting the learning theories of the behaviorists and the perceptual phenomena described by the Gestalt psychologists. By virtue of the ideas presented in *The Organization of Behavior,* the publication of Hebb's unique *Textbook of Psychology* (1958), and the research emerging from McGill University laboratories in the 1950s and early 1960s, Hebb played a major role in sparking the cognitive revolution in psychology and, particularly, the development of cognitive neuroscience.

Early Life, Marriages, and Education. Both of Donald Hebb's parents, Arthur Morrison Hebb and Mary Clara Olding, were physicians. He was the oldest child in the family. One younger brother, Andrew, was trained as a lawyer but subsequently became a businessman. A second brother, Peter, became a physician. Donald Hebb's youngest sibling, Catherine, received her PhD in physiology from McGill University and later achieved international recognition for her work on acetylcholine. As for Hebb, until the age of eight he was educated at home by his mother. At school in Chester, Donald advanced rapidly until the eleventh grade, which he failed. He later stated that "things came too easily, I had never learned to work, I was bored by school from the day I entered to the day I left" (Hebb 1980, p. 277).

After repeating grade 11 in Chester and taking grade 12 at the Halifax Academy in Halifax, Nova Scotia, Hebb entered Dalhousie University, also in Halifax, Nova Scotia, in 1921 and graduated with a BA in English and philosophy in 1925. He intended to become a writer but obtained a teaching certificate from the Nova Scotia Teachers College in Truro, Nova Scotia, and worked for some years as an elementary school teacher and principal in Nova Scotia and Montreal, Quebec. During his recuperation from tuberculosis of the hip in 1931, Hebb married Marion Clark, but after only eighteen months of marriage, his wife died in an automobile accident. Hebb married Elizabeth Donovan in 1937, a union that produced two daughters, Jane and Mary Ellen. Elizabeth died in 1962; Hebb married Margaret Wright in 1966.

Discovering Psychology and Graduate Education. Hebb studied psychology in two philosophy courses at Dalhousie and was introduced to the ideas of Sigmund Freud, which he found interesting but insufficiently rigorous. While he was teaching in Montreal in 1929, Professors Clarke and Chester Kellogg from McGill University conducted IQ tests on his students, and Hebb discovered that children of all abilities were not performing as well as anticipated. To encourage students to study more, Hebb changed the classroom rules, making schoolwork a pleasure rather than a punishment. This educational experiment resulted in Hebb's first published paper (in *Teacher's Magazine* in 1930), demonstrated his unconventional turn of mind, and resulted in Hebb coming a part-time graduate student at McGill, completing his MA thesis under the supervision of Kellogg.

While recuperating from his tubercular hip in 1930–1931, Hebb read works by Charles S. Sherrington and Ivan Pavlov and completed a theoretical MA thesis that considered the possibility that spinal reflexes were influenced by neural activity in utero. A version of what was to become known as the "Hebb synapse" was presented for the first time in this thesis (described in Brown & Milner, 2003). Subsequently, Hebb did hands-on studies of Pavlovian conditioning of the salivary response in dogs with two of Pavlov's students who were on the McGill faculty, Boris Babkin and Leonid Andreyev, but Hebb found fault with Pavlovian methodology.

Searching for a graduate program where he could proceed with the study of neuropsychology, Hebb was offered admission at Yale University by Robert Yerkes, but

Hebb

Babkin persuaded him to go to the University of Chicago to study with Karl Lashley. More than any other single choice, the decision to work with Lashley was to shape the questions that Hebb addressed many years later in *The Organization of Behavior.* In the years preceding Hebb's arrival in Chicago, Lashley had pioneered the experimental study of the brain and behavior, focusing on neocortical localization of visual discrimination and intellectual function in the laboratory rat. Lashley also had worked on Gestalt-like field interpretations of responses to visual stimuli and of the effects of deprivation of early visual experience on discrimination of distance. At Chicago, Hebb took classes from some of the most distinguished professors of the day, including L. L. Thurstone, Harvey A. Carr, Wolfgang Kohler, C. Judson Herrick, and Nathanial Kleitman. When Lashley moved to Harvard University in 1934, Hebb followed and completed his PhD thesis there in 1936. Hebb's dissertation concerned the effects of deprivation of early visual experience on brightness and size discrimination learning. The dissertation was published in three articles, as "The Innate Organization of Visual Activity" in 1937 and 1938 (in the *Journal of Genetic Psychology* and the Journal of *Comparative Psychology*).

However, Hebb's preferred topic involved spatial learning. In an ingenious series of experiments, Hebb demonstrated that rats relied on distal visual cues, rather than intramaze cues, in learning the optimal path from start to goal, and that lesions of the neocortex resulted in a switch from reliance on distal to proximal cues. The results of those experiments were published in the *Journal of Comparative Psychology* in 1938.

Human Neuropsychology. After completing his work at Harvard, Hebb was in an uncomfortable position, job hunting during the Great Depression of the 1930s. However, his sister Catherine, who was just completing her PhD at McGill, wrote with news of a position at the Montreal Neurological Institute (MNI) to study the effects of surgical intervention by Dr. Wilder Penfield on the intellectual capacity of human patients. Hebb was awarded this position and, in the course of studying Penfield's patients, he discovered that removal of a large portion of one frontal lobe sometimes resulted in improved performance on standardized IQ tests. He subsequently postulated that general patterns of response, learned early in life, are dependent on frontal lobe activity, but that once acquired, the information can be processed in other brain areas. Hence, the effects of early brain injury could be more severe than later injury to the same tissue. Finally, Hebb recognized that there was more to cognitive function than IQ, suggesting the possible involvement of the right temporal lobe in human visual perception and developing novel tests of cognitive function.

In 1939 Hebb accepted a position as a lecturer at Queens University in Kingston, Ontario, followed by promotion to assistant professor of psychology for the 1941–1942 academic year. He was to remain at Queens until 1942, publishing papers based on his work at the MNI and pursing the development of a novel test of intellectual function in the rat. The Hebb-Williams maze required that the rat maintain visual orientation in order to choose an optimal route to the goal box when faced with shifting barriers between the start box and a goal box containing food. It was to be used in a variety of innovative studies by Hebb and his graduate students concerned with the effects of early experience and cortical lesions on adult learning.

The Yerkes Years. In 1942 Lashley was appointed director of the Yerkes Laboratories of Primate Biology in Orange Park, Florida, where a large colony of captive chimpanzees was available for study. Lashley proposed that Hebb join him in Florida to study the intellectual and emotional sequelae of brain lesions in chimpanzees. Although Hebb was to work at the Yerkes Labs from 1942 to 1947, the brain lesion research program was never pursued. But Hebb did describe the emotional behavior of chimpanzees, relying on the intuitive recognition of emotional states in the chimpanzee by human observers. In addition, Hebb published a set of innovative papers on the development of fear, the occurrence of spontaneous neuroses, and the assessment of individual differences in temperament. Observing complexity and planning in chimpanzee behavior also encouraged Hebb's conviction that autonomous central processes (i.e., thought) had to be considered in the construction of psychological theories. Later, he would describe the years spent watching chimpanzees at Yerkes as teaching him more about human behavior than any other years—with the exception of the first. And, in the paper on "On the Nature of Fear" (1946), Hebb first used a hypothetical neural construct, the phase sequence, to account for behavior.

Hebb was engaged in much more than animal watching during the Yerkes years. In 1944 he began writing the manuscript that would become *The Organization of Behavior.* His goal, as stated in the preface, was "to bring together a number of different lines of research, in a general theory of behavior that attempts to bridge the gap between neurophysiology and psychology, as well as that between laboratory psychology and the problems of the clinic" (1949, p. vii). In addition to overcoming the theoretical aversion to physiologizing that characterized the psychological theories of the 1930s and 1940s, Hebb also focused on the phenomena of an active mind, not on a stimulus-response automaton. Early in the book, we find Hebb grappling with questions of set, attention, and the interaction between sensory input and an active brain.

Donald Hebb. COURTESY OF PETER M. MILNER.

The existence of spontaneous activity in the central nervous system was a direct inference from Hans Berger's 1929 account of the electroencephalogram (as summarized in Jasper, 1937), while R. Lorente do No's description of reverberatory circuits in 1938 provided a potential mechanism for temporary storage of information.

At the heart of Hebb's system lie two neurophysiological constructs, that is, inferences from behavior that are introduced to account for images and thought: "Any frequently repeated, particular stimulation will lead to the slow development of a 'cell assembly,' a diffuse structure comprising cells in the cortex and diencephalon ... capable of acting briefly as a closed system, delivering facilitation to other such systems.... A series of such events constitutes a 'phase sequence'—the thought process" (*Organization of Behavior,* 1949, p. xix). But the development of the cell assembly, and presumably the linkage of assemblies in a phase sequence, required a permanent, experience-dependent, change in the activity of the nervous system. This was accounted for by introducing what is known in contemporary neuroscience as the Hebb synapse: "When an axon of cell A is near enough to excite a cell B and repeatedly or persistently takes part in firing it, some growth process or metabolic change takes place in one or both cells such that A's efficiency, as one of the cells firing B is increased" (*Organization of Behavior,* 1949, p. 62).

With this hypothetical machinery in place, Hebb developed a single theory to account for learning and memory as studied by the behaviorists as well as the perceptual phenomena emphasized by the Gestalt psychologists. For example, he had to account for the fact that form recognition is a stable, reliable process in an adult mammal, despite widely divergent patterns of stimulation on the retina, as an object is viewed from different perspectives. The Gestalt psychologists had presented this kind of result as posing an impossible obstacle for a connectionist theory of neurological function and proposed that there was an innate isomorphic organization of electrical fields in the brain, where relationships among stimuli were maintained.

Hebb was determined to account for the Gestalt phenomena of perception within the framework of a connectionist nervous system. His solution involved a crucial role for early visual experience, in which the immediate visual "constancies" experienced by an adult mammal were "assembled" during early life through successive fixations on objects from different perspectives. He drew heavily on data collected by Marius von Senden involving accounts of initial perception by congenital cataract patients whose vision had been restored by surgical intervention. In general, these patients had color vision and primitive figure-ground perception immediately following surgery but experienced an initial difficulty with perception of entire forms, often piecing together a percept from successive examinations of edges. In addition, Austin Riesen's description of visual deficits in chimpanzees deprived of visual experience during infancy supported the possibility that the seemingly innate, instantaneous perceptions of the adult were actually dependent on early experience. These results forced Hebb to reexamine his own dissertation data and, for the first time, he noted that, although the discriminative capacities of dark-reared rats were ultimately the same as their normal counterparts, initial learning required many more trials.

The original drafts of *The Organization of Behavior* were critical of behavioristic and Gestalt interpretations of psychological phenomena, and Hebb began to reevaluate the previous work of Kohler, Lashley, and even himself in light of his new ideas. Hebb gave Lashley an early draft for comments and offered him coauthorship, but Lashley declined. Lashley's comments on the manuscript strike the contemporary reader as focused on minor technical issues, never coming to grips with the central themes of the book. Although complimentary to Hebb in a personal letter, Lashley subsequently complained to a group of scientists at a dinner party, claiming that Hebb's book presented a garbled version of ideas that he (Lashley) had developed over the years.

It seems more likely that Hebb, while grappling with the same questions as those raised by Lashley, had reached very different conclusions. For example, where Lashley had minimized the role of early experience in visually guided behavior, Hebb focused on early experience as an essential component in the development of adult visual perception. Another example of divergent conclusions concerned the synapse. In his celebrated address to the Ninth International Congress of Psychology in 1929, Lashley said: "There is no direct evidence for any function of the anatomical synapse; there is no evidence that synapses vary in resistance, or that, if they do, the resistance is altered by passage of the nerve impulse" (Lashley, 1930, p. 1). The synapse had still not been visualized when Hebb wrote *The Organization of Behavior.* But his speculative description of the "Hebb synapse" and its properties, was to prove an enormously generative answer to Lashley's critique.

While in Florida, Hebb reared a group of rats at home and demonstrated that these rats were superior to laboratory-reared rats in learning the Hebb-Williams maze. Subsequent work by Hebb's students at McGill established that early environmental enrichment enhanced later cognitive functioning, and this work was instrumental in the development of animal studies on environmental enrichment and brain function and on programs such as Head Start, which provided impoverished children with early environmental enrichment.

The McGill Years. In 1947 Hebb returned to McGill as professor of psychology, and in 1948 he became chair of the Psychology Department. He was instrumental in creating a graduate program that minimized formal coursework and emphasized the generation of independent research programs by individual graduate students (Glickman, 1996). Hebb's graduate seminar and a statistics course were the only required coursework. The system worked exceptionally well. In "A Neuropsychological Theory" (1959), Hebb described an impressive array of experiments conducted by graduate students and postdoctoral fellows, as the result of his unusual approach to graduate (and postdoctoral) training. In particular, Hebb identified the examination of the effects of enriched infant experience on maze learning in rats, and of early reading experience in humans on adult perceptual tendencies, as significant research that was initiated in response to the theory; on the other hand, he described studies of sensory deprivation on perception and thought, habituation of the arousal reaction, and the discovery of self-stimulation ("pleasure") systems in the brain as filling in gaps in his theorizing. Hebb had created an atmosphere in which attention was directed to problems that would endure, whether or not specific details of his theory proved to be true.

In the studies of sensory deprivation mentioned above, McGill undergraduates were paid to lie in cubicles without patterned visual, auditory, or somesthetic stimulation (for a maximum of one week), which were instigated with support from the Defence Research Board of Canada. There were two goals: to understand the importance of the normal human sensory environment for maintenance of functional thought and perception, and to understand why prisoners of war had "confessed" to things they had not done (during the Korean War) when sensory isolation, but not "conventional" torture, had been the only identifiable tool of the captors. Deprivation-induced disturbances of perception and thought were identified in these students and, in response to listening to self-requested positive lectures on ghosts, student attitudes toward that phenomenon shifted in the direction of increased belief. Although "classified" by the Defence Research Board of Canada for some years, the essential results were published in an article by Hebb's former student, Woodburn Heron (1961), with an introduction by Hebb.

Hebb's *A Textbook of Psychology* was published in 1958. It contains his construction of the essential components of the field. In "Donald Olding Hebb (1904–1985)" (Beach, 1987), an obituary, the distinguished comparative psychologist Frank Beach placed this book alongside *The Organization of Behavior* as one of Hebb's two most significant publications. In the preface, Hebb presented his goal as "to clarify and codify the ideas which make up the main structure of psychological theory" (1958, p. vii). He added that "in doing so I have omitted (or treated very succinctly) matters that have traditionally made up a good proportion of the introductory course; and have included others that are, as far as I know, here stated formally for the first time" (1958, p. vii). He proceeded to state that psychology is fundamentally a biological science and that "the student's approach to either social or applied psychology … is through … theories of learning, perception, emotion … which are biological because they have always been profoundly influenced by neurophysiology, neuroanatomy, and evolutionary and genetic theory" (1958, p. vii). Where Hebb's mentor Lashley once accused his fellow psychologists of including an obligatory chapter on the nervous system in their textbooks "in order to provide an excuse for pictures to an otherwise dry and monotonous text," Hebb used the structure of the nervous system to explain the difference

Hebb

between sense-dominated behavior and behavior involving mediating processes—the latter constituting the phenomena of greatest interest to psychologists—and stated that incorporating relevant neural substrates is essential for understanding these phenomena, not simply added on and, afterwards, dismissed (Lashley, 1930, p. 1).

Following his retirement as professor of psychology in 1970, Hebb was appointed chancellor of McGill University. In 1975 he retired from McGill and returned to his boyhood surroundings in Nova Scotia. Dalhousie University provided an appointment as a professor emeritus and office space, and Hebb continued to attend seminars at the university until his death in 1985.

Awards and Honors. Hebb received many honors in his lifetime, including membership in the Royal Society of Canada and the Royal Society of London, along with election to the presidencies of the Canadian Psychological Association and the American Psychological Associations, and an honorary presidency of the Royal Society of Canada. He was also awarded honorary degrees by fifteen universities. Hebb was nominated for, but did not receive, the Nobel Prize in 1965. The nominators had several problems. First, his primary contribution involved theoretical writing, whereas Nobel Prizes are traditionally awarded for "discoveries." Then, Hebb's name was not on the masthead of the research papers published by his students on enriched environments or sensory deprivation, and these were the highlighted research accomplishments that formed the basis for the Nobel Prize nomination. In contrast to the dominant traditions of contemporary science, Hebb refused to have his name on work done by students, even when the work was clearly inspired by his theorizing and supported by his grants.

Hebb's influence, and the style employed in service of his goals, have been superbly summarized by Ernest Hilgard in his book *Psychology in America: An Historical Survey* (1987):

> Theoretical interest in brain mechanisms lessened among psychologists following Lashley's important work. Lashley … had argued against neurologizing by psychologists; Skinner … had warned against the unjustified fictions of the conceptual nervous system. This flagging interest was reversed by the appearance of a book by Donald O. Hebb.… The qualities of Hebb's *Organization of Behavior* (1949) that appealed were a combination of great originality in both breadth and specificity, a willingness to examine arguments on their merits, and an ability to dispose of them with incisive criticisms that were without polemic. Hebb was considerate of those he was attacking, while always sticking to his guns. The capacity and style required to achieve his results are difficult to define, but they are unusual in revolutionary scientific writing, and Hebb represented them well. (pp. 435–436)

BIBLIOGRAPHY

Hebb's correspondence can be found in the archives of the McGill University library.

WORKS BY HEBB

"The Innate Organization of Visual Activity: I. Perception of Figures by Rats Reared in Total Darkness." *Journal of Genetic Psychology* 51 (1937): 101–126.

"The Innate Organization of Visual Activity. II. Transfer of Response in the Discrimination of Brightness and Size by Rats Reared in Total Darkness." *Journal of Comparative Psychology* 24 (1937): 277–299.

"The Innate Organization of Visual Activity. III. Discrimination of Brightness after Removal of the Striate Cortex in the Rat." *Journal of Comparative Psychology* 25 (1938): 427–437.

"Studies of the Organization of Behavior. I. Behavior of the Rat in a Field Orientation." *Journal of Comparative Psychology* 25 (1938): 333–353.

"Studies of the Organization of Behavior. II. Changes in the Field Orientation of the Rat after Cortical Destruction." *Journal of Comparative Psychology* 26 (1938): 427–441.

"On the Nature of Fear." *Psychological Review* 53 (1946): 259–276.

The Organization of Behavior: A Neuropsychological Theory. New York: Wiley, 1949.

A Textbook of Psychology. Philadelphia: Saunders, 1958.

"A Neuropsychological Theory." In *Psychology: A Study of a Science.* Vol. 1. Edited by Sigmund Koch. New York: McGraw-Hill, 1959.

"D. O. Hebb." In *A History of Psychology in Autobiography.* Vol. 7. Edited by Gardner Lindzey. San Francisco: W.H. Freeman, 1980.

OTHER SOURCES

Beach, Frank A. "Donald Olding Hebb (1904–1985)." *American Psychologist* 42 (1987): 186–187.

Brown, Richard E., and P. M. Milner. "The Legacy of Donald O. Hebb: More than the Hebb Synapse." *Nature Reviews Neuroscience* 4 (2003): 1013–1019.

Glickman, Stephen E. "Donald Olding Hebb: Returning the Nervous System to Psychology." In *Portraits of Pioneers in Psychology.* Vol. 2, edited by G. A. Kimble, C. A. Boneau, and Michael Wertheimer. Washington, DC: American Psychological Association, 1996.

Heron, Woodburn. "Cognitive and Physiological Effects of Perceptual Isolation." In *Sensory Deprivation,* edited by P. Solomon, P. E. Kubzansky, P. H. Leiderman, et al. Cambridge, MA: Harvard University Press, 1961.

Hilgard, Ernest R. *Psychology in America: An Historical Survey.* New York: Harcourt Brace Jovanovich, 1987.

Jasper, H. H. "Electrical Signs of Cortical Activity." *Psychological Bulletin* 34 (1937): 411–481.

Heckel

Lashley, Karl. "Basic Neural Mechanisms in Behavior." *Psychological Review* 37 (1930): 1–24. The first published version of Lashley's address to the Ninth International Congress of Psychology in 1929.

Lorente de No, R. "Analysis of the Activity of the Chains of Internuncial Neurons." *Journal of Neurophysiology* 1 (1938): 207–244.

Milner, Peter M. "The Mind and Donald O. Hebb." *Scientific American* 268 (1993): 124–129.

Stephen Glickman
Richard E. Brown

HECKEL, ÉDOUARD-MARIE

(*b.* Toulon, France, 24 March 1843; *d.* Marseille, France, 20 January 1916), *economic botany, colonial sciences, materia medica.*

Heckel excelled in the applied natural history of exotic floras. Partisan of the French colonial mission, his entrepreneurial and administrative skills found application in Marseille as the city embraced its colonial vocation. His career divides naturally into two periods; the first spent voyaging as a naval pharmacist; the second, dating from the 1870s, spent largely in Marseille.

Heckel's father, Joseph Heckel, was a naval infantry captain. His mother, Elise Breillot Heckel, died shortly after his birth. Heckel, who was reared by a religious confraternity, entered Toulon's naval medical school as a pharmacy student at age sixteen. Two years later, in 1861, he sailed to the Antilles. Heckel regarded this assignment, where he surveyed local flora for potential therapeutic agents, as formative to his scientific career. Promoted at age twenty-two to chief of naval pharmacy for New Caledonia, he found himself characterized by his superiors as an impoverished bachelor of considerable intelligence but his service was considered slow and delivered without enthusiasm. In contrast, Heckel was extremely diligent in preparing for examinations, gaining promotion to pharmacist of the first class with a thesis on the toxicology of mussels (1867) and winning a medical degree (1869) and doctorate in natural sciences (1875), all from Montpellier. A delegate to the Sydney Intercolonial Exposition of 1870, he botanized widely in Australia and undertook additional investigations in Java, Sumatra, Indochina, Ceylon (Sri Lanka), and elsewhere.

Heckel's scientific voyaging ended after service as a physician during the Franco-Prussian War (1870–1871). Taking medical leave from the navy in 1871, he soon married Marie Rosalie Raboisson of Nantes. Their son, Francis, born 31 August 1872, later obtained a medical degree (1897) and collaborated with Émile Roux of the Institut Pasteur. Bouts of anemia, intermittent fevers, and chronic bronchitis, complaints common to naval physicians, wracked the senior Heckel. Also troubled by sciatica, he resigned in 1874.

After transitory posts at the science faculties of Montpellier and Grenoble, and possibly the pharmaceutical school at Nancy, Heckel assumed the chair of botany at the Marseille Faculty of Sciences on 3 November 1877, a post he held until 1913. Heckel, of Alsatian heritage, gained international renown and maintained ties with colleagues in Nancy and Strasbourg after France's defeat in 1870–1871 gave Alsace to Germany. He coauthored more than fifty publications with Charles-Frédéric Schlagdenhauffen of Nancy's École Supérieure de Pharmacie; the two investigated oleaginous plants, antimalarial and other botanical therapies, and soap manufacture. Heckel also translated into French Charles Darwin's *Effects of Cross and Self Fertilization in the Vegetable Kingdom* (1876; trans. 1877), *The Different Forms of Flowers on Plants of the Same Species* (1877; trans. 1878), and *The Power of Movement in Plants* (1880; trans. 1882).

Heckel's best-known research, on African kola plants, merited the Bussy prize from the Association Générale des Pharmaciens de France (1883) and a Barbier prize from the Académie des Sciences (1885). Schlagdenhauffen and Heckel focused on kola's botanical, chemical, and therapeutic potential and identified a physiologically active substance, kola-red, as something additional to caffeine, tannin, and cacao's chief alkaloid, theobromine. Heckel, in a series of ingenious studies linking laboratory and field, championed the efficacy and medicinal specificity of kola-red, later determined to be a kola-tannate of caffeine. Dr. Germain Sée challenged the field study methodology, and conclusions, of Heckel's investigations before the Académie de Médecine. The patriotic Heckel promoted kola cakes to the army as a way to reduce the fatigues of march and campaign. Though the cakes received glowing attestations from horse owners, who administered them to their animals, as well as from members of bicycle clubs, mountain climbers, soldiers, and others who participated in field trials that compared the effects of caffeine with kola cakes, both the military and general public failed to adopt the product.

Heckel led several local scientific institutions. Serving for two years as director of Marseille's museum of natural history, he resigned in 1879 upon being appointed as professor of materia medica at the municipal medical school. Vitally committed to his adopted city, he was also a member of the Council of Hygiene and an administrator for the city's hospices. In 1885 the city council named him director of the municipal botanical garden, where he conducted studies on the acclimatization of exotic plants. His long career also included service on the Marseille city council and on the departmental council for the department of Var.

Though remembered as the founder of Marseille's Institut Colonial and Musée Colonial, both founded in 1893 and inaugurated in 1896, his colleague on the faculty of sciences, the professor of geology Gaston Vasseur, had proposed similar schemes to link science with colonial exploration, commerce, and governance. The Institut Colonial and Musée Colonial undertook scientific evaluation and promotion of products derived from colonial flora and fauna. Until its closure in 1962 the Musée Colonial displayed, interpreted, and promoted colonial products to the larger public, primary school students, and researchers. Heckel's special genius was securing funds from the Chambre de Commerce and mobilizing support for scientific institutions. The Chambre de Commerce, which sponsored many scientific and technological initiatives in the city, funded six teaching chairs on colonial subjects including botany, history, geography, climatology, hygiene, and parasitology. In 1899 the city council allocated funds for an additional five courses on colonial subjects including exotic pathology and bacteriology, a clinical course for tropical diseases, and materia medica. The largess of the Chambre de Commerce and municipality, Heckel's administrative acumen, and the addition in 1905 of the "Pharo," the army's new postgraduate school of colonial medicine, made Marseille the premier city in France for the study of colonial medical and scientific topics.

Heckel also labored for colonial causes as an organizer of the colonial section for the 1900 Universal Exposition at Paris and as one of two coorganizers for the lavish 1906 Marseille Colonial Exposition. Many honors flowed to Heckel, including election to corresponding membership in the rural economy section of the Académie des Sciences on 11 November 1907. Interested in plant geography as well as applied natural history, he served as president of the Société de Géographie de Marseille from 1909 to 1912.

BIBLIOGRAPHY

A partial list of publications may be found in Royal Society of London, Catalogue of Scientific Papers, *vol. 7, p. 932; vol. 10, p. 174; vol. 12, p. 320; vol. 15, pp. 711–713. Manuscript sources include L'Alcazar—Bibliothèque Municipale à Vocation Régionale, Marseilles (Archives of the Société de Géographie de Marseille); Archives départementales des Bouches-du-Rhône, 1 M 104 (Legion of Honor application of 1898); and "Edouard Marie Heckel," Service historique de la défense (Marine), Vincennes, CC 7 Alpha 1160 (information on health, naval service, and marriage).*

WORKS BY HECKEL

"Expériences comparés entre l'action du kola et le la caféine sur la fatigue et l'essoufflement provenant des grandes marches." *Marseille Médicale* 27 (1890): 587–598, 649–665.

Les kolas africains, monographie botanique, chimique, thérapeutique & pharmacologique (Emploi stratégique et alimentaire: Commerce). Paris: Société d'Éditions Scientifiques, 1893.

With others. *L'Institut et le Musée colonial de Marseille.* Paris: Henri Roberge, 1900.

With Cyprien Mandine. *L'enseignement colonial en France et à l'étranger.* Marseille, France: Barlatier, 1907. Reviews pedagogy and courses on the colonial sciences.

OTHER SOURCES

Aillaud, Georges J. "Edouard Heckel, un savant organisateur: De la botanique appliquée à l'Exposition coloniale de 1906." *Provence historique* 43, no. 172 (1993): 153–165.

———. "Le jardin d'essai colonial de Marseille." In *Le jardin entre science et représentation: [actes du 120e Congrès national des sociétés historiques et scientifiques, 23–29 octobre 1995, Aix-en-Provence],* edited by Jean-Louis Fischer, 79–90. Paris: Comité des Travaux Historiques et Scientifiques, 1999.

———. "Édouard Heckel et l'Institut colonial de Marseille." In *Désirs d'ailleurs: Les expositions colonials de Marseille 1906 et 1922, Archives municipals de Marseille,* 45–53. Marseille, France: Éditions alors hors du temps, 2006.

Chevalier, Auguste. "L'oeuvre du Dr. Édouard Heckel." *Bulletin de la Société d'Acclimatation,* no. 5 (1916): 145–151.

Labrude, Pierre. "Le professeur Heckel à Nancy (1873–1876), sa longue et fructueuse collaboration avec le professeur Schlagdenhauffen." *Bulletin de Liaison-Association des Amis du Musée de la Pharmacie* (Montpellier) 22 (1997): 57–65.

Lacroix, Alfred. *Notice historique sur quatre botanistes, membre ou correspondants de l'Académie des sciences, ayant travaillé pour la France d'outre-mer de la fin du siècle dernier à nos jours. Lecture faite en la séance annuelle du 19 décembre, 1938.* Paris: Gauthier-Villars, 1938. Contains biographical materials on Heckel and his protégé and successor, Henri Jumelle.

Michael A. Osborne

HECKMANN, OTTO HERMANN LEOPOLD

(*b.* Opladen, Germany, 23 June 1901; *d.* Regensburg, Germany, 13 May 1983), *astronomy, astrophysics, cosmology.*

Heckmann was a German astronomer and astrophysicist active between 1925 and the 1970s who mastered the roles of observing astronomer, theoretical astrophysicist, and manager for the astronomical community in Europe, even worldwide. He was one of the founding members of the European Southern Observatory (ESO) in Chile, and left a particularly strong imprint. His scientific research covered astrometry (positions and proper motions of stars), photographic photometry of stellar clusters, the application of statistical mechanics to stellar dynamics, optical design, and theoretical cosmology.

Formative Period: Astrometry. Heckmann stemmed from a Catholic family in the Rhineland; his parents were Max

Heckmann, a notary in Opladen, and Agnes Heckmann, née Grüter. He received his schooling at a gymnasium (secondary school) whose teaching was directed more toward the sciences than that of the regular humanistic schools. He studied mathematics, physics, and astronomy at the University of Bonn. Under the guidance of his astronomy teacher Karl Friedrich Küstner he wrote a doctoral thesis in astrometry concerning the precise determination of star positions in the open star cluster Praesepe in Cancer. He used photographic plates obtained at the Bonn Observatory. After graduation in 1925 he became an assistant to Küstner, who was involved in the planning for the star catalog AGK2 of the Northern Hemisphere, with the Bonn part then directed by Ernst Arnold Kohlschütter. (The catalog AGK1 had started in the 1870s and was completed in the 1930s.) Heckmann closely inspected the four-lens optical system of the Bonn telescope with the help of which this new star catalog was to be made. This time spent learning the optical adjustment of telescopes, one of his hobbies, later helped him with instruments in Göttingen, Hamburg, and at the ESO.

Career Steps: Photometry, Stellar Dynamics, Cosmology. Upon becoming, in 1927, an assistant of Hans Kienle, then director of the Göttingen Observatory, Heckmann, with his background in the determination of positions and proper motions of stars, shifted his focus to photographic photometry and its instrumental and observational problems. A program of measuring star colors in the red and blue band was carried through until 1935. Together with his collaborator Hans Haffner he succeeded in reaching an unprecedented astrometric precision for Praesepe by this photographic method. Both astronomers showed that, in the color-luminosity diagram, a sharp main sequence resulted. In 1929, Heckmann obtained his *venia legendi* (habilitation) at the University of Göttingen with an investigation of star positions in the star group Coma Berenices. In 1935, he received the honorary title of professor while remaining Kienle's assistant. His observations in Göttingen were made with a new ASTROgraph in the Hainberg observatory, a telescope that cost Heckmann and Kienle two years of painstaking adjustment until it began working properly. In 1937 this instrument was supplemented by the first commercially built Schmidt telescope (by Zeiss-Jena) with an effective aperture of circa 38 centimeters.

While extending these empirical studies to weak-group stars in Praesepe, some of his theoretical interest went into the stellar statistics of globular clusters. These self-gravitating systems are intrinsically unstable; it is known that a final equilibrium state of maximal entropy cannot be reached. The treatment of clusters by statistical methods is notoriously difficult due to the long-range gravitational force. In a highly idealized model assuming energy conservation, and using the Boltzmann equation, Heckmann and Heinrich Siedentopf (1930) showed that by two-body interactions, that is, the scattering of point-like stars, an approximate isothermal state may be obtained. For this, the cluster must be thought to be embedded in an infinite system. (While this result had been encouraging then, it can at best be used as a solution of lowest approximation. Today, numerical integration of the Fokker-Planck equation is providing reasonable insight into the dynamics of the collapsing core and the postcollapse evolution of a globular cluster.) Heckmann and Siedentopf concluded that for their model of a globular cluster, Albert Einstein's relativistic theory would give more natural results than Isaac Newton's classical theory. (This belief is not backed by present observations restricting relativistic effects to the nuclei of galaxies.)

Also in Göttingen, papers with Hans Strassl (an astronomer also trained as an insurance mathematician) analyzed the detailed properties of the star stream, that is, the distribution of star velocities in our neighborhood in the Milky Way, by applying statistical mechanics (Heckmann and Strassl, 1934, 1935). By use of a Gaussian distribution, the authors succeeded in describing the differential rotation of the galaxy in addition to the effect of solar motion. Such investigations showed Heckmann's interest and expertise in theoretical questions, and his ability to find competent collaborators.

A subject close to Heckmann's heart during all of his scientific life, and understood by him as a "personal pleasure," was cosmological theory. Already during his student days in Bonn he had given a mathematical seminar on Charlier's hierarchical cosmological model. In the 1920s, with Einstein's general relativity becoming the dominant theory of gravitation, Heckmann's interest centered around cosmological models of this theory.

As a consequence of Einstein's first cosmological model of 1917, until the 1930s physicists (Georges Lemaître, Einstein, Willem de Sitter, Arthur Eddington) dealt exclusively with world models with constant positive space curvature. At the time, apart from the introduction of the cosmological constant, this had been the sensational part of Einstein's paper: that three-dimensional space in his cosmological model must be closed, that is, be a space with a finite volume but without boundaries. Up to then, infinitely extended Euclidean space with zero constant curvature had been assumed to describe reality. In addition, Alexander Friedmann had shown in 1924 that expanding homogeneous and isotropic cosmological models with constant negative space curvature do also exist. Provided with the simplest topology, they also are infinitely extended. In 1929 Howard P. Robertson independently rederived the world models with nonpositive curvature.

Heckmann

Heckmann, who had given his first course on general relativity in Göttingen during the winter term 1929–1930, was aware only of de Sitter's and Lemaître's results connected with positive space curvature. Thus in 1931, he again obtained Friedmann's and Robertson's geometries in his world models generated by an ideal fluid (with nonvanishing pressure) and a photon gas, both noninteracting, as their material source. The famous mathematician Hermann Weyl, who had also given contributions to cosmology, handed in this paper to the Göttingen Academy. While Robertson's paper is conceptually very clear, Heckmann's contribution seems more physical by stressing the differential form of the energy conservation law for matter (cf. also North, 1965). In Heckmann's opinion, a decision for one of the three possibilities for positive, negative, or zero space curvature could not yet be made: the measurements of the matter density in the cosmos were too unprecise. He seemed to tend toward negative curvature (Heckmann, 1932, p. 105). De Sitter received a copy of Heckmann's publication and wrote a joint paper with Einstein mentioning Heckmann's name without giving a precise reference. In it, they acknowledged that "at the present time it is possible to represent the facts without assuming a curvature of 3-dimensional space" (Einstein & de Sitter, 1932, p. 214). Today, this particular world model is called Einstein–de Sitter space; the name Robertson–Heckmann solution would be also justified. In 1932, Heckmann gave a complete discussion and classification of the homogeneous and isotropic solutions of Friedmann's equations (with cosmological constant).

Heckmann also was interested in theoretical optics: After Max Born had been fired by the Nazi authorities, Heckmann took over his course on theoretical optics at the University of Göttingen, apparently with Born's encouragement (Heckmann, 1976, p. 30).

Observatory Director: Cosmology, AGK3, and Schmidt Telescope. In 1934, Edward Arthur Milne and William Hunter McCrea had developed what now is named Newtonian cosmology, that is, a cosmological theory based on Newton's theory of gravitation supplemented with the so-called world postulate and a new definition of inertial systems. Heckmann, an astronomer continuously involved in painstaking observational work, was always inclined to test theories against practice. When he learned of Milne's approach to cosmology in 1935, he compared it to Einstein's and slightly expanded on it (Heckmann, 1940).

In 1937 the Hamburg University faculty's call of Heckmann to the Observatory of Bergedorf near Hamburg was obstructed for years by the Government of the Reich, by the Reichsdozentenbund (an association of government lecturers dominated by the Nazis), and by various agencies within the Nazi Party, which, on the other side, ended the academic career of his coworker Strassl altogether. The call materialized only in April 1941, when Heckmann was named substitute director, and in January 1942 when he finally became director and full professor in Hamburg (Hentschel & Renneberg, 1995). In the meantime, since 1939, Heckmann had been administrative director of the Göttingen Observatory.

In his 1942 monograph *Theorien der Kosmologie,* Heckmann cleverly sandwiched his exposition of Einstein's general relativity as applied to cosmology between Milne's dynamical cosmology based on Newton, and Milne's kinematical cosmology resting on the Lorentz group. The empirical material did not force him to take sides, and he left open his predilections (cf. Hentschel & Renneberg, 1995). However, he pointed out that Newtonian cosmology could properly describe light propagation only with difficulty. Werner Heisenberg and Friedrich Hund in Leipzig did a critical reading "of large parts of the manuscript." Twenty years later, Heckmann's conclusion was that Einstein's theory should be preferred: "if we approach limits of velocity or of compression, or if we want to handle large-scale optical problems" (Heckmann, 1962, p. 430).

Heckmann continued to investigate both nonrelativistic and relativistic theories of gravitation after 1945. For some years, with Engelbert Schücking, he was able to maintain a research group for theoretical cosmology paralleling the much larger group of Pascual Jordan at Hamburg University. In a direct collaboration with Jordan and a younger astronomer, Walter Fricke, solutions of a generalization of general relativity, a scalar-tensor-theory of gravitation now called Jordan-Brans-Dicke theory, and corresponding to the Schwarzschild space-time, were obtained (Heckmann, Jordan, & Fricke, 1951). Within Newtonian cosmology, Schücking and Heckmann found cosmological models with rotation as analogs to the Gödel space-time in Einstein's theory, and also more general rotating solutions with expansion and shear (Heckmann & Schücking, 1955, 1956). Heckmann hoped that the existence of rotation (and of shear) in cosmological models would avoid the occurrence of a big bang. With Schücking, he wrote two articles on cosmological theory in the new *Encyclopedia of Physics* (1959). In numerous lectures, contributions to conferences, and book articles, research concerning "world models," both in Newtonian and in relativistic cosmology, remained a constant theme of Heckmann's until the early 1960s. Heckmann's contributions to cosmological modeling, although not pioneering work, are still appreciated by today's cosmologists with an interest in the history of their field.

Heckmann had not been directly involved with observational work for the star catalog AGK2, started around 1930, but when in Hamburg he saw to it that this catalog was carried through to its completion. This was done until 1950 by the observatory's director preceding him, Richard Schorr. Heckmann then initiated a new catalog of star positions comprising 180,000 stars in the Northern Hemisphere: AGK3. His motivation was to increase the precision for the positions of fixed stars in the Northern Hemisphere, and to possibly determine their proper motions since the measurements for AGK2. The work was performed between 1955 and 1975 under the scientific direction of Wilhelm Dieckvoss (Heckmann, 1975) who had already been involved in AGK2.

In the field of photographic photometry, among other investigations, Heckmann identified an assembly of stars around alpha Persei as an open star cluster, and determined proper motions for stars in the neighborhood of Praesepe. Since 1942, observations of the Hyades cluster had been made in Hamburg, from which, through a collaboration with Klaus Lübeck, a precise color-magnitude diagram was obtained.

Still another area of Heckmann's unrelenting activity was the planning and acquisition of new telescopes. In 1931, the inventor Bernhard Schmidt had given the Hamburg Observatory its first Schmidt telescope. As early as 1937 a larger such instrument had been approved but remained unbuilt until the end of World War II. Due to Heckmann's energetic prodding, a Schmidt telescope with an 80-centimeter free opening and a mirror diameter of 100 centimeters could be installed in 1954. It used an objective prism for getting spectra. The optical adjustment was done by Heckmann and his colleague Haffner, in Hamburg since 1937. His experience with this instrument helped Heckmann in the planning of the Schmidt telescope for ESO (100/120 cm) operating since the early 1970s. In the meantime, Heckmann's advice had also been appreciated for the construction of an even larger Schmidt telescope at the Zentralinstitut für Astrophysik in Tautenburg in the German Democratic Republic.

A Powerful Organizer. After his indirect involvement in the star catalog AGK2, he successfully convinced a dozen European observatories to provide positions of reference stars by meridian observations for the new zonal star catalog AGK3. He also supported a similar reference project for the Southern Hemisphere (Southern Reference Stars Project, SRS), and provided the transit circle of the Bergedorf Observatory for astronomers in Perth, Australia. Since the original letter of intent, signed on 26 January 1954 by astronomers from six European countries, the idea of an ESO had taken up an increasing share of Heckmann's many activities. He kept a close relationship with the influential astronomer Walter Baade, who had given an important first impulse to the idea of a joint European project in the Southern Hemisphere. In 1962, Heckmann obtained a leave of absence from Hamburg University in order to fill the first directorship of ESO, then still in its organizational gestation.

In the 1955–1963 period, the search for an appropriate observing site was focused on South Africa. Even before the final site in the Andes Mountains at La Silla (Chile) was formally approved by ESO on 26 May 1964, Heckmann, with the help of Chilean friends, in the fall of 1963 had been able to negotiate with the government of Chile. He had reached an agreement to be endorsed by the ESO Council and the Chilean Parliament. According to Heckmann, this unauthorized and later criticized but accepted move had speeded the project by circumventing lengthy formal debates among European governments. As to the installation of instruments, the time won in setting up the organization was partially lost, again, when the chief construction engineer for the Schmidt telescope chosen by Heckmann did not comply with the specifications.

Heckmann's contributions to the planning of the observatory and the realization of ESO's headquarters in Santiago and Garching is his greatest and lasting organizational achievement. He carried the main burden before full operation could be achieved; his French colleague in the instrumentation committee of ESO, Charles Fehrenbach, called him the "work horse" of the organization (Fehrenbach, 1984, p. 592). Indeed, he took on his responsibilities as the director of ESO until his mandatory retirement from the university in 1969, and continued as a consultant until 1972 (Blaauw, 1991). The period of his ESO directorship was filled with many honors: doctoral degrees from universities in France, Argentina, and the United Kingdom; medals from professional societies in the United States and France; membership in many scientific academies; and the presidency of the International Astronomical Union from 1967 to 1970.

BIBLIOGRAPHY

WORKS BY HECKMANN

With Heinrich Siedentopf. "Zur Dynamik kugelförmiger Sternhaufen." *Zeitschrift für Astrophysik* 1 (1930): 67–97.

"Über die Metrik des sich ausdehnenden Universums." *Nachrichten von der Gesellschaft der Wissenschaften zu Göttingen, Mathematisch-Physikalische Klasse* (1931): 126–130.

"Die Ausdehnung der Welt in ihrer Abhängigkeit von der Zeit." *Nachrichten von der Gesellschaft der Wissenschaften zu Göttingen, Mathematisch-Physikalische Klasse* (1932): 97–106.

With Hans Strassl. "Zur Dynamik des Sternsystems." *Nachrichten von der Gesellschaft der Wissenschaft zu Göttingen, Mathematisch-Physikalische Klasse, Fachgruppe II* (1934): 91–106; also *Veröffentlichungen der Universitätssternwarte Göttingen* no. 41: 191–206.

———. "Zur Dynamik des Sternsystems (Fortsetzung)." *Nachrichten von der Gesellschaft der Wissenschaft zu Göttingen, Mathematisch-Physikalische Klasse, Fachgruppe II* (1935): 153–170; also *Veröffentlichungen der Universitätssternwarte Göttingen,* no. 43: 217–221.

"Zur Kosmologie." *Nachrichten von der Gesellschaft der Wissenschaft zu Göttingen, Mathematisch-Physikalische Klasse, Neue Folge, Fachgruppe II,* 3, no. 15 (1940); also *Veröffentlichungen der Universitätssternwarte Göttingen,* no. 68.

Theorien der Kosmologie. Fortschritte der Astronomie. Edited by P. Ten Bruggencate, vol. 2. Berlin: Springer, 1942. Reprinted Berlin: Springer, 1968, with an additional preface and new comments. The first monograph on cosmological theories in Germany.

With Pascual Jordan and Walter Fricke. "Zur erweiterten Gravitationstheorie. I." *Zeitschrift für Astrophysik* 28 (1951): 113–149. Spherically symmetric solutions of Jordan-Brans-Dicke theory.

"The Value of a Third AG Catalogue." *Astrophysical Journal* 59 (1954): 31–34.

With Engelbert Schücking. "Bemerkungen zur Newtonschen Kosmologie. I." *Zeitschrift für Astrophysik* 38 (1955): 95–109.

———. "Bemerkungen zur Newtonschen Kosmologie. II." *Zeitschrift für Astrophysik* 40 (1956): 81–92.

With Klaus Lübeck. "Helligkeiten und Eigenbewegungen in den Hyaden." *Zeitschrift für Astrophysik* 40 (1956): 1–20. A shorter English version is: "Photographic Photometry of the Hyades." *Vistas of Astronomy* 2 (1956): 1115–1122.

With Engelbert Schücking. "Newtonsche und Einsteinsche Kosmologie" and "Andere kosmologische Theorien." In *Encyclopedia of Physics,* edited by S. Flügge, vol. 53, *Astrophysics IV: Stellar Systems.* Berlin: Springer, 1959.

"General Review of Cosmological Theories." In *Problems of Extra-Galactic Research,* edited by G. C. McVittie. IAU Symposium No. 15 (1961). London: Collier-Macmillan, 1962.

"On the Possible Influence of a General Rotation on the Expansion of the Universe." *Astrophysical Journal* 66 (1961): 599–603.

AGK3: Star Catalogue of Positions and Proper Motions North of –2.5 deg. Declination. 8 vols. Edited by Wilhelm Dieckvoss. Hamburg and Bergedorf, Germany: Sternwarte, 1975. Planned by O. Heckmann; produced and edited by W. Dieckvoss, in collaboration with H. Kox, A. Günther, and E. Brosterhus.

Sterne Kosmos Weltmodelle: Erlebte Astronomie. Munich, Germany: Piper, 1976. An instructive autobiography.

OTHER SOURCES

Blaauw, Adriaan. *ESO's Early History: The European Southern Observatory from Concept to Reality.* Munich, Germany: ESO, 1991.

Einstein, Albert, and Willem de Sitter. "On the Relation between the Expansion and the Mean Density of the Universe." *Proceedings of the National Academy of Sciences of the United States of America* 18 (1932): 213–214.

Fehrenbach, Charles. "La vie et l'oeuvre d'Otto Heckmann." *Comptes rendus,* general series, 1 (1984): 591–593.

Friedmann, Alexander. "Über die Möglichkeit Einer welt mit Konstanter Negativer Krümmung des Raumes." *Zeitschrift für Physik* 21 (1924): 326–332.

Hentschel, Klaus, and Monika Renneberg. "Eine Akademische Karriere: Der Astronom Otto Heckmann im Dritten Reich." *Vierteljahreshefte für Zeitgeschichte* 43 (1995): 581–610. For those interested in political and administrative maneuverings during the Third Reich and the position Heckmann took.

North, John David. *The Measure of the Universe: A History of Modern Cosmology.* Oxford: Clarendon Press, 1965. A general presentation of the field in which Heckmann's contributions to cosmology are evaluated.

Robertson, Howard P. "On the Foundations of Relativistic Cosmology." *Proceedings of the National Academy of Sciences of the United States of America* 15 (1929): 822–829.

Voigt, Hans Heinrich. "Nachruf auf Otto Heckmann." *Jahrbuch der Akademie der Wissenschaften in Göttingen* (1983): 80–87. An obituary written by the former director of the Göttingen Observatory, who was close to Heckmann.

Hubert Goenner

HELMONT, JOHANNES (JOAN) BAPTISTA VAN

(*b.* Brussels, Belgium, 12 January 1579; *d.* Brussels, Belgium, 30 December 1644), *alchemy, chemistry, controlled experimentation, natural philosophy, medicine, mysticism, quantification.* For the original article on Helmont see *DSB,* vol. 6.

The focal points of modern Van Helmont research are twofold: Van Helmont's experimental method, and especially the role of quantification in his experimental practice, has undergone closer scrutiny; and his mysticism, more specifically the original place he occupies in the history of mysticism, has provoked novel interpretations. These two trends are discussed below in more detail. It should be stressed that these two aspects—often delineated from each other as the "scientific" and the "non-scientific" or "extra-scientific" aspects of Van Helmont's work—were two sides of the same coin for Van Helmont. The underlying unity in Van Helmont's *philosophia naturalis* has been emphasized in the works of Van Helmont's main biographer, the German historian Walter Pagel. The study of both trends as well as the insight that they were inseparable for Van Helmont can be seen as fruitful results of Pagel's arduous work, which paved the way for following generations of historians of science to add further nuance to Van Helmont's natural philosophy.

Experimental Method. Research has shown that, although Van Helmont's experimental procedures were

***Johannes Van Helmont.** Engraving of Johannes Van Helmont in his laboratory.* SPL/PHOTO RESEARCHERS, INC.

still far removed from modern experimental practice, he contributed significantly to the emergence of experimental practice and reasoning. In Van Helmont's work, there was not yet a sharp distinction between "an experience" and "an experiment." In contrast to an experience, an experiment presupposes the involvement of a specific question about nature that the experimental outcome is designed to answer. Van Helmont's experimental practice also included a broad variety of argumentative strategies in support of naturalistic theses such as anecdotes, histories, loose observations, questioning by fire (i.e. chemical fire analysis, "*quaerere per ignem*"), and especially mechanical demonstrations (*mechanicae probationes*). Especially the last two strategies contain the most developed features of his experimental practice. The term "mechanical demonstration" is perhaps somewhat misleading, since to Van Helmont's mind it was not directly related to simple machines. The Low-German equivalent "*handtdadelijcke mechanijcke bewesen*," in other words, "hand-on" or "handicraft," better illustrates Van Helmont's notion of a mechanical experiment. Generally, it referred to natural processes that were deliberately manipulated at the hand of the investigator of nature (and is thus not directly connected to simple machines). His scientific practice contained a strong insistence on intervening and manipulating natural processes.

In Van Helmont's work can be seen the gradual emergence of controlled experimentation. Van Helmont frequently set out to control certain variables while varying others. This method is especially striking in several of his famous experiments: in his experiment with the thermoscope, where it is shown that if the thermoscope is kept perfectly shut no water can be transformed into air; in his ice-experiment, where he keeps fixed the absolute weight of water in order to infer that the increase in its specific weight can only be due to an internal action of the water itself; and also in his famous willow experiment, where Van Helmont controlled (or at least thought so) the purity of the administered water and the purity of the earth in which the tree grows—all three examples are from *Ortus Medicinae* (1648). Johann Joachim Becher (1667) and James Woodward (1700) later criticised Van Helmont's experiment on the grounds that the measurements involved were not precise enough and that not enough variables were controlled.

Van Helmont's work did not explicitly appeal to certain social conventions—which were clearly present in Robert Boyle's work—that experimental philosophers should use in dealing with each other and considering knowledge claims. Van Helmont did not engage much in public experimentation. In addition to that, detailed prescriptions, that would allow readers to redo the experiments Van Helmont describes, are also absent in his work. The contrast with Boyle's careful written accounts of his experiments and air-pumps is striking in this respect. Van Helmont did mention replication and reproducibility rather sporadically but did not insist much on them as criteria of valuable scientific knowledge. Correspondingly, he did not give specific information that allowed one to redo certain experiments. For Van Helmont, an experiment was thus a personal testimony that is not necessarily supposed to be redone by different agents in order to qualify as scientifically valuable. The absence of the stress on replication and reproducibility characteristic of Van Helmont's experimental practice separates it from modern approaches.

The view that a modest degree of quantification was essential to Van Helmont's experimental work has gained more support by historians. Van Helmont's critique of mathematics (abundant in *Ortus Medicinae*, 1648) should not be interpreted as a rejection of mathematics *in toto*, only as a careful awareness of the limits of mathematics. According to Van Helmont, mathematics places entities under the *praedicamentum quantitatis*: It does not succeed in penetrating the essence of things ("*wesentheyt*"), which is only provided by knowledge of the *semina*. In similar fashion, Van Helmont argues that because Aristotelian philosophy ignores the *semina*, it is like a sculptor that skilfully imitates the external shape of a man, but does not know its internal structure. Nevertheless, mathematics is useful for the establishment of scientific propositions (he frequently used the term "*demonstratio mathematica*" and "*mathesis*").

The importance of mathematical arguments in Van Helmont's work is mainly restricted to determination of weights and density-ratios. For example, Van Helmont's ordering of the density-ratios of tin (which he used as his standard unit), iron, copper, silver, lead, mercury, and gold differs from the modern ones by only an average of less than 2 percent. Although modern quantitative-like aspects play a role in Van Helmont's experimental procedures and although he often stressed the mathematical component in his arguments, it would be clearly exaggerated to call Van Helmont's experimental procedures as quantified as those of the early twenty-first century, in which both the level of accuracy has become more important (because modern means of measurement have expanded drastically) and the mathematics involved has become more complex (for example, the usage of statistics and formulae). Exact values are rarely provided by Van Helmont and values are mostly determined and presented roughly (at least in the published versions).

In his famous willow experiment, the weights of the earth and the willow are determined and compared only roughly. Van Helmont dried approximately 200 pounds of earth, in which he planted a willow (weighing five pounds), and isolated it from the external world by means of a tin plate with small holes, to guarantee that no other elements than earth could enter the pot. The water Van Helmont administered was equally "pure" (i.e., either distilled water or rainwater), so that again no other elements than water could reside in the pot. In contemporary parlance, it would be said that these variables (earth and water) were controlled. After five years the willow was weighed again (now c. 169 pounds). Van Helmont only weighed the "Wood, Barks, and Roots." Apparently, Van Helmont did not include the weight of the leaves for whatever reason. Notice that Van Helmont is not worried at all by the disappearance of two ounces of earth over the period of time. *Given* that there did not reside any other elements than earth and water in the pot, and *given* that the earth did not diminish significantly, Van Helmont (wrongly) concluded that only the administered water produced the additional gain of 164 pounds. *Quam proxime* was good enough for Van Helmont. He did not have the instrumental means to discover and detect the role of minerals in the growth-process of plants. As Van Helmont strongly believed in the indestructibility of matter, he claimed that the weights of the *reagentia* during chemical reactions are unalterable.

In the establishment of his experimental natural philosophy, Van Helmont succeeded in breaking with the dichotomy between art (*articificialia*) and nature (*naturalia*): In manipulating natural processes nature's *modus operandi* remains the same. Hence, the art of fire is a legitimate source of objective knowledge of nature. It is by manipulating nature (*naturae operationes mutando*) in an experimental way that one succeeds in establishing science.

Mysticism. According to Van Helmont, who explicitly aligned himself with hermetic and Pythagorean philosophies, the world humans experience is but a sign (*signatum*) of the hidden spiritual world behind it. The Aristotelian school stopped at the external façade and therefore reached only superficial knowledge about the external world. Van Helmont believed that there are two ways of obtaining true knowledge about the creation: One was to study nature by experiments, in which the experimenter indirectly communicates with God; the other was mysticism, in which direct communication with God's workings is attained. It should be stressed that Van Helmont saw these ways as intimately connected. Experiments demonstrated the working forces, i.e. the spiritual *archei*, which produce natural phenomena. Mystical experience equally allowed penetrating the deeper spiritual significance of nature. It should be noted that Van Helmont's mysticism is quite different from traditional mysticism (such as that developed by Thomas à Kempis whom Van Helmont highly respected) in which the mystical unity (*unio mystica*) is mostly associated with experiencing the divine being. For Van Helmont, the object of mystical experiences was far more mundane: It involved questions relating to scientific, chemical, and medical phenomena. The objects of Van Helmont's mystical experiences were "mystified" natural phenomena, i.e. substances he manipulated by alchemical operations and contemplated correspondingly. This is a striking aspect of Van Helmont's mysticism. Van Helmont, then, was not only a reformer of natural philosophy, but also a reformer regarding spiritual experience.

SUPPLEMENTARY BIBLIOGRAPHY

Becher, Johann Joachim. *Physica Subterranea*. Edited by Georg Ernst Stahl. Leipzig, Germany: Officina Weidmanniana, 1733 [1667].

Bono, James J. "Essay Review. The Ferment of Van Helmont's Ideas." *Journal of the History of Biology* 27, no. 2 (1984): 291–294.

Browne, Alice. "J. B. Van Helmont's Attack on Aristotle." *Annals of Science* 36, no. 6 (1979): 575–591.

Helmont

———. "From Van Helmont to Boyle. A Study of the Transmission of Helmontian Chemical and Medical Theories in Seventeenth Century England." *British Journal for the History of Science* 26, no. 3 (1993): 303–334.

Clericuzio, Antonio. *Elements, Principles and Corpuscles, A Study of Atomism and Chemistry in the Seventeenth Century.* Dordrecht: Kluwer, 2000.

Coultert, Harris L. *Divided Legacy: A History of the Schism in Medical Thought* Vol. 2 *The Origins of Modern Western Medicine: J.B. Van Helmont to Claude Bernard.* Berkeley, CA: North Atlantic Books, 1988.

Debus, Allen G. "The Chemical Philosophers: Chemical Medicine from Paracelsus to Van Helmont." *History of Science* 12, no. 4 (1974): 235–259.

———. *The Chemical Philosophy. Paracelsian Science and Medicine in the Sixteenth and Seventeenth Centuries.* New York: Science History Publications, 1977.

———. "Chemists, Physicians, and Changing Perspectives on the Scientific Revolution." *Isis* 89, no. 1 (1998): 66–81.

———. *Chemistry and Medical Debate: Van Helmont to Boerhaave.* Nantucket, MA: Science History Publications, 2001.

Duchesneau, F. "The Scientific Revolution and the Problematics of the Living Being with Special Reference to the Theoretical Concepts of William Harvey and J .B. Van Helmont." *Revue Philosophique de Louvain* 94 (4) (1996): 568–598.

Ducheyne Steffen. "J.B. Van Helmont and the Question of Experimental Modernism." *Physis: Rivista Internazionale di Storia della Scienza* 43 (2006): 305–332.

Giacomini, G. " Jean Baptiste Van Helmont and the 'per ignem' Treatment." *Quaderni Storici* 38 (1) (2003): 61–92.

Giglioni, Guido. *Immaginazione e Malattia, Saggio su Jan Baptiste Van Helmont.* Milan: Franco Angeli, 2000.

Halleux, Robert. "Gnosis and Experience in the Chemical Philosophy of Jean Baptiste Van Helmont." *Bulletin de la classe des sciences, Académie Royale de Belgique* 65, no. 5 (1979): 217–227.

———. "Theory and Experiment in the Early Writings of Johan Baptist Van Helmont." In *Theory and Experiment, Recent Insights and New Perspectives on Their Relation,* edited by Diderik Batens and Jean Paul Van Bendegem. Dordrecht, The Netherlands: Reidel, 1988.

———. "Helmontiana." *Mededelingen Van de Koninklijke Academie voor Wetenschappen, Letteren en Schone Kunsten Van België, Academia Analecta, Klasse der Wetenschappen,* 45, no. 3 (1983): 33–63.

Heinecke, Berthold. "The Mysticism and Science of Johann Baptista Van Helmont (1579-1644)." *Ambix* 47, no. 2 (1995): 65–78.

———. *Wissenschaft und Mystik bei J. B. Van Helmont (1579-1644).* Bern, Germany: Deutsche Literatur von den Anfängen bis 1700, 1996.

Hershey, David. "Misconception about Helmont's Willow Experiment." *Plant Science Bulletin* 49, no. 3 (2003): 78–83.

Hirai. Hiro. *Le Concept de Semence dans les Théories de la Matière à la Renaissance, de Marsile Ficin à Pierre Gassendi.* Turnhout, Belgium: Brepols, 2005.

Jensen, William B. "A Previously Unrecognised Portrait of Joan Baptista Van Helmont (1579–1644)." *Ambix* 51, no. 3 (2004): 263–268.

Joly, Bernard. "La réception de la pensée de Van Helmont dans l'oeuvre de Pierre Jean Fabre." *Alchemy Revisited. Proceedings of the International Conference on the History of Alchemy at the University of Groningen,* 17–19 April 1989.

———. "L'alkahest, dissolvent universel ou quand la théorie rend pensable une pratique impossible." *Revue d'histoire des sciences* 49 (1996): 305–1344.

Lofstedt, B. "Notes of a Latinist on the Writings of J.B. van Helmont." *Latomus* 62, no. 3 (2003): 672–675.

López-Piñero, José. M. "Helmont, Johannes Baptista Van (1579–1644)." In *Encyclopedia of the Scientific Revolution, From Copernicus to Newton,* edited by Wilbur Applebaum. New York: Garland Publishing, 2000.

Moran, Bruce T. *Distilling Knowledge, Alchemy, Chemistry, and the Scientific Revolution.* Cambridge, MA: Harvard University Press, 2005.

Newman, William R. and Lawrence Principe. "Van Helmont's Concept of Disease—To Be or Not To Be? The Influence of Paracelsus." *Bulletin of the History of Medicine* 46, no. 5 (1972): 419–454.

———. "The Spectre of J. B. Van Helmont and the Idea of Continuity in the History of Chemistry." In *Changing Perspectives in the History of Science. Essays Dedicated to Joseph Needham,* edited by Mikulas Teich and Robert Young. London: Heinemann, 1973.

———. "Johannes Baptista Van Helmont als Naturmystiker." *Epochen der Naturmystik. Hermetische Tradition im wissenschaftlichen Fortschritt.* Edited by Antoins Faivre. Berlin: Rolf C. Zimmermann, 1979.

Pagel, Walter. *Joan Baptista Van Helmont: Reformer of Science and Medicine.* Cambridge, U.K.: Cambridge University Press, 1982.

———. "The Corpuscular Theory of J. B. Van Helmont and Its Medieval Sources." *Vivarium* 31, no. 1 (1993): 161–191.

———. "The Background the Newton's Chemistry." In *The Cambridge Companion to Newton,* edited by I. Bernard Cohen and George E. Smith. Cambridge, U.K.: Cambridge University Press, 2002.

———. *Alchemy Tried in the Fire: Starkey, Boyle and the Fate of Helmontian Chymistry.* Chicago: Chicago University Press, 2002.

Porto, Paulo A. "The Physician George Thomson and the Early Developments of the Concept of Gas." *Quimica Nova* 24, no. 2 (2001): 286–292.

———. "Early Developments of the Helmontian Concept of Gas—Part II." *Qiumica Nova* 26, no. 2 (2003): 141–146.

Waddell, Mark A. "The Perversion of Nature: Johannes Baptista Van Helmont, the Society of Jesus, and the Magnetic Cure of Wounds." *Canadian Journal of History* 38, no. 2 (2003): 179–197.

Walton, Michael T. "Boyle and Newton on the Transmutation of Water and Air, from the Root of Helmont's Tree." *Ambix* 27, no. 1 (1980): 11–18.

Woodward, John. "Some Thoughts and Experiments Concerning Vegetation." *Philosophical Transactions of the Royal Society* 21 (1699): 193–227.

Steffen Ducheyne

HENNIG, (EMIL HANS) WILLI

(*b.* Dürrhennersdorf, Germany, 20 April 1913; *d.* Ludwigsburg, Germany, 5 November 1976), *evolutionary biology, systematics, taxonomy, phylogenetic systematics, entomology, education.* For the original article on Hennig, see *DSB,* vol. 3.

Hennig was a German entomologist specializing in the systematics of flies and fossil insects. He became the most influential systematist and taxonomist in the twentieth century by developing the philosophy and methodology of phylogenetic systematics (cladistics). His basic philosophy and approach to the analysis of evolutionary relationships of organisms are the dominant paradigms of systematics in the twenty-first century.

Hennig the Biologist. Hennig began his career while still in *Gymnasium* (high school) in Dresden, when he worked as a volunteer at the Zoological Museum. His early interest in systematics dates to an essay written in 1931 on the "state of systematics in zoology." Early papers include works on snakes (at age nineteen, with Wilhelm Meise) and *Draco,* the flying lizards of Asia. His interest in flies (order Diptera) grew from his work with Dresden entomologists Fritz van Emden and Emden's successor, Klaus Günther. After finishing his doctorate in the reproductive anatomy of flies at the University of Leipzig in 1936, he joined the German Entomological Institute (GEI) of the Kaiser Wilhelm Society (later the Max Planck Society) in Berlin. By 1939 he had already published some forty-one papers, many dealing with the morphology of the copulatory organs of flies, but also including papers on classifying higher taxa (groups of many species; genera, families, etc.) and geographic variation.

Hennig served in the German army between 1939 and 1945. In spite of being wounded on the Russian front and later serving in Greece and Italy as a mosquito control specialist, he managed to publish some twenty-five papers dealing with fly systematics as well as mosquito control. As a prisoner of war, he was pressed into mosquito control work by his British captors and also began working on his magnum opus, *Grundzüge einer Theorie der Phylogenetischen Systematik* (Fundamentals of the theory of phylogenetic systematics), published in 1950.

After release, Hennig first served as acting director of the Zoological Institute at the University of Leipzig (1945–1947) and then returned to the GEI in 1947, where he finished his major work on the larvae of flies (1948) and began his studies on fossil insects. Many works followed, including papers on dipteran systematics, phylogenetics, biogeography, and chapters on invertebrates for the *Textbook of Zoology.* By 1961 Hennig had finished a revision of his phylogenetics book, which was sent to the United States to be translated into English, appearing as *Phylogenetic Systematics* in 1966.

Hennig was nominated for the directorship of the GEI. His appointment was delayed due to his open opposition of the East German government. After the erection of the Berlin Wall in 1961, he decided to terminate his appointment because he felt he might be in political danger. This suspicion proved to be well founded, as the documents of the East German Secret Service (Stasi) later confirmed that proceedings had been initiated to imprison him. Hennig briefly held a professorship at the Technical University (West) Berlin (TU Berlin), but moved in 1963 to the State Museum of Natural History, Stuttgart, where he turned his attention to fossil insects preserved in amber (authoring some twenty papers). This renewed interest in fossil insects, coupled with his extensive knowledge of insect diversity and systematics, culminated with the publication of *Die Stammesgeschichte der Insekten* (1969), with an authorized English translation, *Insect Phylogeny,* published in 1981. This monumental work included both the most comprehensive review of Paleozoic and Mesozoic insects to date, and also contributed to his development of phylogenetic systematics.

Hennig's Phylogenetic Systematics. Although Hennig is remembered by entomologists for his fundamental works in dipteran systematics and fossil insects, his influence reached all aspects of evolutionary biology through his works on phylogenetic systematics. Hennig considered himself a reformer rather than a revolutionary, and his goal was to bring studies of the evolutionary relationships and classification of organisms fully into the Darwinian paradigm. Before Hennig's work there were no generally acceptable protocols for reconstructing the evolutionary histories of species, the "Tree of Life."

Hennig provided the basic methods for such protocols, enabling biologists to present their hypotheses of relationship in a rigorous and testable framework. Hennig's proposal was fairly simple. First, *relationship* means "genealogical relationship," the relationship among ancestors and descendants (alternate concepts equated *relationship* with "similarity"). Second, only certain kinds of characters can be used to test a proposed genealogical relationship. Homologous characters (characters whose similarity is due to common ancestry), Hennig argued, may be of two kinds: more ancient (plesiomorphies) and more recent (apomorphies). Ancient homologues may make two species appear similar, but cannot form the basis for uniting these species into a unique common ancestry group.

For example, humans and lizards share the homology of having five toes on each limb, while living horses have a single toe. Is this evidence that humans and lizards share a common ancestor not shared by horses? No, states Hennig; having multiple toes is an ancient evolutionary innovation found in the ancestor of all legged vertebrates, horses included. More recent homologies are evidence of unique common ancestry. For example, humans and horses share the homology of having fur-covered bodies while lizards have scales. Is this evidence that horses share a common ancestor with humans that is not shared with lizards? Yes, states Hennig; having fur is a relatively recent homology not found in the common ancestor of lizards, humans, and horses, but only in the common ancestor of humans and horses (and other mammals). Thus, it is a valid test of the hypothesis that humans are more closely related to horses than humans are to lizards.

The basis for Hennig's methods for testing common ancestry relationships rests on the ability of systematists to distinguish between different kinds of homologous similarities and to distinguish between homologous and nonhomologous similarities (convergent similarities, independently evolved two or more times). The method works for analysis of the evolution of morphology, behavior, DNA sequences, ontogeny, and indeed any heritable characters that evolve. The phylogenetic trees produced from these analyses form the basis for many other studies, including speciation and extinction dynamics, historical biogeography, genomic research, and even disease tracking.

In addition to his method of testing alternative phylogenetic trees, Hennig provided the rationale for modern biological classifications by rigorously defining what constitutes a natural group of organisms (termed a clade or monophyletic group) from unnatural groups, some of which had previously been considered natural. This created the possibility of a taxonomic system that was objective and logical relative to the phylogenies being proposed by the existing, qualitative analytical protocols. It is also a source of continuing controversy, as many familiar groups are identified as unnatural because they formed paraphyletic groups.

Before Hennig, all systematists had agreed that polyphyletic groups were unnatural because the common ancestor was not included in the group. An example is the polyphyletic group Homeothermia, composed of birds and mammals. Paraphyletic groups included the ancestor, but only some of the descendants. An example is Reptilia, which includes the common ancestor but excludes birds and mammals. Hennig argued that natural groups (his monohyletic groups) must include both the ancestor and all descendants. For example, the family of great apes, Pongidae, excludes one of the descendants of the common ancestor, humans, who are placed in another family, Hominidae. By Hennigian logic, the Pongidae, as a paraphyletic group, is unnatural. Humans should either be placed in Pongidae or the great apes in Hominidae to form a natural group that includes the ancestor and all descendants. And, if Reptilia was to be natural, it should include birds and mammals as well as crocodiles and lizards.

It should be noted that Hennig did not work in a vacuum: he was influenced by earlier workers, especially Walter Zimmermann. But his synthesis was the work that convinced others that a rigorous science could be developed for discovering the Tree of Life. Although phylogenetic systematics has undergone many refinements, Hennig's basic philosophy persists as the basis of modern evolutionary analysis of relationships among species and higher groups.

Hennig's contributions to entomology and systematics were widely recognized. He was an elected member of several scientific academies, including the German Academy of Natural Scientists Leopoldina (1963) and the Swedish Royal Academy of Science (1972). He received many honors. He received the Fabricius Medal from the German Entomological Society (1953), and gold medals from the Linnaean Society, London (1974), and the American Museum of Natural History, New York (1975). He was awarded an honorary doctorate from the Free University of Berlin in 1968.

Hennig the Man. Hennig was one of three sons born to Karl (1873–1947) and Marie (1885–1965) Hennig in Dürrhennersdorf, near Dresden. His father was a railroad official. One brother, Karl Herbert (1917–1943?) went missing at Volgograd (then Stalingrad) and his fate remains unknown; the other, Fritz Rudolf (1915–1990), was a minister. Hennig married fellow student Irma Wehnert (1910–1990) in 1939. Her contributions to his career were many. During World War II, Irma Hennig acted as research assistant, editor, and librarian for her husband, enabling him to publish numerous papers even while serving in the military. Hennig served in the German army from 1939 to1945, serving in the infantry in Poland, France, and Russia until wounded in 1942, and thereafter as a medical entomologist. (It should be noted that Hennig was never associated with the Nazi Party of Germany or the Communist Party of East Germany.) Willi and Irma had three sons, Wolfgang (b. 1941, geneticist; four children), Bernd (b. 1943, geneticist; two children), and Gerd (b. 1945, teacher; one child). Hennig's grandchildren adored him. He was a lover of classical music, especially Mozart, and an avid reader of literature as well as science. He eschewed personality cults and refused to the end of his life to use his personal influence to promote phylogenetic systematics, preferring to let the discipline grow or die on its merits. History has proven him correct.

The author would like to thank Dr. Wolfgang Hennig for reviewing this essay and providing helpful comments and critical revisions.

SUPPLEMENTARY BIBLIOGRAPHY

WORKS BY HENNIG

Grundzüge einer Theorie der Phylogenetischen Systematik. Berlin: Deutscher Zentralverlag, 1950.

"Phylogenetic Systematics." *Annual Review of Entomology* 10 (1965): 97–116. A short exposition of Hennig's methods and goals.

Phylogenetic Systematics. Translated by D. Dwight Davis and Rainer Zangerl. Urbana: University of Illinois Press, 1966. Translation of the revised *Theorie der Phylogenetischen Systematik;* a Spanish-language and a Chinese translation also were published.

Die Stammesgeschichte der Insekten. Senckenberg-Buch 49. Frankfurt, Germany: Kramer, 1969. Translated by Adrian C. Pont as *Insect Phylogeny.* Chichester, U.K.: Wiley, 1981.

OTHER SOURCES

Ax, Peter. "Professor Dr. H. C. Willi Hennig." *Zoomorphology* 87 (1977): 1–2.

Hennig, Wolfgang. "In Memoriam: Willi Hennig." *Beiträge zur Entomologie* 28 (1978): 169–177. Written by the son of Willi Hennig. The volume also includes a complete list of Willi Hennig's publications.

Hull, David L. *Science as a Process. An Evolutionary Account of the Social and Conceptual Development of Science.* Chicago: University of Chicago Press, 1988. Places Hennig into the larger context of debates over systematics in the twentieth century.

Schlee, D. "In Memoriam Willi Hennig 1913–1976." *Eine biographische Skizze. Entomologica Germanica* 4 (1978): 377–391. Shortened translation in English available from http://zoo.bio.ufpr.br/diptera/bz023/willi_hennig.htm.

E. O. Wiley

HERO OF ALEXANDRIA

(*fl.* Alexandria, maybe first century CE), *mathematics, optics, pneumatics, mechanics.* For the original article on Hero see *DSB,* vol. 6.

The main points in the present postscript are the problem of Hero's dating, returned to scholarly attention; an updated account of the treatise ascribed to him and known as *De speculis;* the extent, contents and aims of his commentary on Euclid's *Elements*; and his peculiar approach to the procedure of analysis and synthesis. Scholarship is beginning to assess Hero's mathematical works in a way unbiased by his traditional renown as the *mechanician.* It appears that he was a skilled and original author who played a key role in the development of Greek mathematics, not only as a "vital link in a continuous tradition of practical mathematics" (*DSB,* p. 314), but also in mastering and adapting purely theoretical tools.

Hero's Dating. A lunar eclipse was described in *Dioptra* 35 as observable in Alexandria at the fifth hour (and in Rome at the third hour) of the night ten days before the vernal equinox. The eclipse was identified as the one that occurred on 13 March 62 CE, although with some latitude, because the vernal equinox fell on 20 March 62 CE. This provides a *terminus post quem.* The argument was completed by observing that the eclipse must have really been observed by Hero because its proximity to the equinox makes it particularly ill-suited to the graphical solution he is proposing for the analemma-problem solved in *Dioptra* 35. The identification has been challenged by two kinds of arguments. The first argument is a statistical one. References to Hero in Pappus of Alexandria and to Archimedes in Hero leave a span of approximately five hundred years as the one in which Hero must have lived. Within such a time span there is a probability of about three over four that at least one lunar eclipse actually fits the date, and even more if some margin for error is allowed. The probability reduces to about 10 percent if one inserts the time datum, but remains nonnegligible. Therefore, the fact that *one* eclipse fitting Hero's data has been found does not authenticate his description as a reference to a historical eclipse rather than a textbook example. The second argument concerns the identification of the eclipse itself. Two other lunar eclipses fit the temporal data as well as the one of 62, and the date actually better than that. In any of the three cases, however, considerable latitude must be allowed for the determination both of the date of the equinox and of the hours in which the eclipse took place in Alexandria and in Rome: one might well wonder how much can be tolerated for Hero's description to keep the status of an accurate observational report. The argument that the eclipse is ill-suited to a graphical solution does not stand, because it can be shown that the same problem can be solved exactly, and of course also the other two eclipses are ill-suited as well.

To these arguments it can be added that Hero's reference to the eclipse was worded in a very peculiar way. He asserted that if simultaneous observations of a lunar eclipse cannot be found in the almanacs, then the reader can provide one, because they occur at intervals of five or six months. After that, the mere existence of the eclipse and its temporal data are set out, by using imperatives, in

Hero of Alexandria

the typical format of geometrical propositions. This puts the assertions under the hypothetical mode of expression and strengthens the suspicion that the data of the eclipse in *Dioptra* 35 have been invented by Hero. Finally, care should be taken in handling astronomical phenomena for dating purposes. They are easily transformed from *termini post quem* into absolute chronological determinations by a very questionable application of a principle of economy of hypotheses. The same holds for chronological determinations that have been proposed on the basis of other passages in Hero's works. What is more, all of these concur to a year near 62 and are in fact intended to support the dating by means of the eclipse. The search for textual clues is thus biased by the assumption that this is correct and hence they are of no independent value.

The *De speculis*. A new edition led to an improved assessment of this short monograph, preserved only in the Latin translation of William of Moerbeke. The ascription to Ptolemy in the title was long ago recognized as a copyist's mistake: for the late optical author Damianus ascribed to Hero a proof that straight lines reflected at equal angles are minimal among those that inflect on the same (straight) line. This is precisely the proof found in the *De speculis,* even if Damianus's testimony does not guarantee that the short treatise is originally Heronian. It is now clear that the Greek text translated by Moerbeke was a late compilation. A first clue comes from the phrase *in rymis sive in plateis* (in the streets or lanes) in the enunciation of section 22: it transliterates a Greek expression in Luke 14:12 and otherwise found only in Christian writers. This presupposes in the author an acquaintance with Christian literature that suggests a late dating. The very initial portion of the introduction refers to Plato and develops considerations on the harmony of the spheres that are at odds with the typically direct argumentations of Hero's introductions.

The original Heronian work appears, as far as can be discerned from a critical assessment of the extant *De speculis,* to have aimed at providing tighter foundations for the theory of reflection than the ones found in the *Catoptrics* ascribed to Euclid. To this end, the equal-angle rule for reflection is based on a less contrived assumption than the one in the *Catoptrics.* The argument leading to this basic assumption is a combination of mathematical and physical arguments that is typically Heronian. Visual rays move with infinite speed, and what moves with the greatest speed moves along a straight line, for, because of the speed, it tends to move along the shortest path and straight lines realize the shortest path between two fixed points. In case of reflection, direct vision being excluded, the assumption naturally reduces to the requirement of realizing the shortest path through broken straight lines. The compiler completed the original theoretical part, that possibly contained also a proof of the contrived assumption of the *Catoptrics,* with a rather arbitrary choice from an initial segment of the *Catoptrics* itself. The subsequent description of the several mirror devices was shortened to an extent that cannot be determined, as the introduction mentions arrangements that are not found in the extant text. The bad status of many of the excerpted descriptions must more likely be ascribed to accidents in the transmission of the text than to ineptitude of the compiler. An exception is section 23, where a defective trivialization of *Catoptrics* 14 is expounded. Marks of original Heronian conception surface here and there, however: for instance, the proof in section 22 is shaped in the format of analysis and synthesis and a dioptra is employed to perform a part of the construction.

The Commentary to the *Elements*. Extensive and literal quotations from Hero's commentary to Euclid's *Elements* are found in Proclus and in a number of Arabic commentators, most notably in an-Nayrīzī. The title of the commentary as reported in the *Fihrist* and in other Arabic sources is *Book of the Solution of the Difficulties in Euclid.* It appears that Hero was one of the first authors of technical commentaries. He possibly originated the genre by fixing some canonical critical attitudes toward the commented text:

- addition of missing cases, of lemmas and corollaries or of mathematical complements;
- proposal of alternative proofs suited to strengthen the deductive structure or to simplify it;
- replacement of proofs by reduction to impossible with direct proofs or, less frequently, the opposite;
- structural adjustments, such as inversion of the order of certain propositions, suppression or addition of definitions and axioms;
- even rewriting entire segments of the text, such as propositions 2–10 of Book 2.

As is clear, such a commentary was less exegetical and more aggressive than the ones compiled in late antiquity. It speaks for an author concerned with issues of logical coherence and deductive structure, adapting demonstrative techniques from other fields, as in the case of the rewritten proofs of 2.2–10. If a comparison can be made, it is more to the Alexandrian commentaries of the literary genre, where difficult passages of the edited author were explained but on the same grounds substantial modifications to the text were proposed. However, it is unlikely that Hero procured a new text of the *Elements.* Proposals of modifications rather than direct changes are found there and the Arabic title at least suggests that the work

Hero of Alexandria

might have had a format and a circulation independent from the Euclidean treatise. Minor changes in the text cannot be detected with the available critical methods.

What is unquestionable is that Hero's commentary, in the hands of later editors, interfered with the transmission of the *Elements,* producing modifications that affected both the received Greek and Arabic versions, often in independent ways. For instance, the alternative proof to 3.10 proposed by Hero was is now attested as such in the Greek manuscripts of the *Elements,* whereas the case added to 3.11 directly became 3.12. Additional cases of 3.20, 25, and 30 found their way into the text, whereas the proposed displacement of 3.25 affected a part of the Arabic tradition only. It is not clear whether Hero's commentary aimed at didactical purposes, as is usually assumed for any such work. The fact that it belonged to a well-established literary genre appears to provide enough reasons for its existence, and its aims are more properly described as scholarly than as pedagogical.

Analysis and Synthesis. Two heterodox variants of the technique of analysis and synthesis are found in the Heronian corpus. The first occurs in the *Metrica,* the second in the alternative proofs to *Elements* 2.2–10. The proofs in the *Metrica* concern problems that are set out assigning numerical values to the relevant quantities, such as, for instance, the sides of a triangle whose area is sought. Typically, the sought quantity is obtained at the end of an analysis, consisting of a series of steps framed in the language of givens. The analysis is followed by a calculation. The latter is termed *synthesis* by Hero, who overcame in this way any concern about constructions. The synthesis–calculation repeats step by step the chain of the givens. The calculation is performed with specific numbers, but they must be taken as paradigmatic, as always in Hero, and hence the calculation must be read as a description of an algorithm. Proofs similar to those in the *Metrica* can be found in other treatises of applied mathematics, for instance in Ptolemy's *Almagest,* where the format of the chain of givens is employed to show how to single out one magnitude from an expression in which it is involved. The unifying feature of such proofs is that the calculation is legitimated once the analysis has shown that the magnitude in question is uniquely determined by the givens of the problem.

The alternative proofs to *Elements* 2.2–10 are reported by an-Nayrīzī. They form a strict deductive sequence. Each proposition is considered as proved insofar as it is reduced to previous results. Such a feature makes these proofs similar to the kind of analysis of complex deductive chains developed within the framework of Stoic logic. Both analysis and synthesis are framed as reductive sequences, in which two expressions, combining squares and rectangles formed from suitable lines, are transformed until it is manifest that they are equal. As a consequence, the analysis already ends with the proof of the sought equality. No chain of givens is displayed. Analysis and synthesis really become two independent and full-fledged ways of proof, as Hero himself is reported, in the short account preceding the alternative proofs, to have already stressed in his definition of the method. Such an approach can be found also in treatises dealing with number theory, such as Diophantus's *De polygonis numeris.* To the Heronian proofs of 2.2–10 the alternative ones to 13.1–5 attested in the manuscript tradition of the *Elements* are usually but not properly compared.

SUPPLEMENTARY BIBLIOGRAPHY

WORKS BY HERO OF ALEXANDRIA

Jones, Alexander. "Pseudo-Ptolemy *De Speculis.*" *SCIAMVS* 2 (2001): 145–186. This is the new edition of the *De Speculis,* based on a fresh reading of the autograph of William of Moerbeke's translation.

OTHER SOURCES

an-Nayrīzī. *Anaritius' Commentary on Euclid. The Latin Translation I–IV.* Edited by P. M. J. E. Tummers. Nijmegen, Netherlands: Ingenium Publishers, 1994. The Latin version of an-Nayrīzī's commentary is now read in this critical edition, superseding, as far as the first four books are concerned, Ernst Curtze's edition published as a *Supplementum* to Johan l. Heiberg and Heinrich Menge's *Euclidis Opera Omnia.*

Argoud, Gilbert, ed. *Science et vie intellectuelle à Alexandrie (Ier–IIIe siècle après J.-C.).* Saint-Étienne, France: Publications de l'Université de Saint-Étienne, 1994. Much scholarly attention is being paid to the mechanical works of Hero. Besides the entire volume containing Souffrin's note cited below, several contributions specifically dealing with Heronian matters may be found here.

Cambiano, Giuseppe. "Automaton." *Studi Storici* 35 (1994): 613–633. This and the following article investigate the relationships between Hero's mechanics and the philosophical background.

Guillaumin, Jean-Yves. "L'Éloge de la géométrie dans la préface du livre 3 des *Metrika* d'Héron d'Alexandrie." *Revue des etudes anciennes* 99 (1997): 91–99.

Høyrup, Jens. "Hero, Ps.-Hero, and Near Eastern Practical Geometry. An Investigation of *Metrica, Geometrica,* and other Treatises." In *Antike Naturwissenschaft und ihre Rezeption,* edited by Klaus Döring, Bernard Herzhoff, and Georg Wöhrle, 67–93 Band 7. Trier, Germany: Wissenschaftlicher Verlag Trier, 1997. This text focuses on Hero as a link between Babylonian and post-Greek mathematics.

Keyser, Paul. "Suetonius *Nero* 41.2 and the Date of Heron Mechanicus of Alexandria." *Classical Philology* 83 (1988): 218–220. A textual finding that supports (with the reservations expressed in the text) Neugebauer's proposal is found here.

———. "A New Look at Heron's 'Steam Engine.'" *Archive for History of Exact Sciences* 44 (1992): 107–124. The author proposes to interpret a device described by Hero in the *Pneumatics* as an experimental refutation of one Aristotelian thesis on self-motion.

Knorr, Wilbur R. "*Arithmêtikê Stoicheiôsis*: On Diophantus and Hero of Alexandria." *Historia Mathematica* 20 (1993): 180–192. Knorr makes an attempt to challenge the traditional ascription to Hero of the core of the *Definitiones*.

Sidoli, Nathan. "Heron's *Dioptra* 35 and Analemma Methods: An Astronomical Determination of the Distance between Two Cities." *Centaurus* 47 (2005): 236–258. Neugebauer's identification of the eclipse is criticized in this article.

Souffrin, Pierre. "Remarques sur la datation de la Dioptre d'Héron par l'éclipse de lune de 62." In *Autour de la Dioptre d'Héron d'Alexandrie*, edited by Gilbert Argoud and Jean-Yves Guillaumin, 13–17 Saint-Étienne, France: Publications de l'Université de Saint-Étienne, 2000. This short note contains the statistical argument concerning Hero's dates.

Tybjerg, Karin. "Doing Philosophy with Machines: Hero of Alexandria's Rhetoric of Mechanics in Relation to the Contemporary Philosophy." PhD diss., University of Cambridge, 2000. A rich and updated bibliography may be found here.

Vitrac, Bernard. "A Propos des démonstrations alternatives et autres substitutions de preuves dans les *Éléments* d'Euclide." *Archive for History of Exact Sciences* 59 (2004): 1–44. A preliminary assessment of aims and extent of Hero's commentary on the *Elements* is given here.

———. "Peut-on parler d'algèbre dans les mathématiques grecques anciennes?" *Ayene-ye Miras* n.s. 3 (2005): 1–44. The algorithmic character of some proofs in the Heronian corpus is analyzed in this article.

Fabio Acerbi

HERSCHEL, CAROLINE LUCRETIA

(*b.* Hanover, Germany, 16 March 1750; *d.* Hanover, 9 January 1848), *astronomy.*

Herschel spent the middle half-century (1772–1822) of her long life as assistant and, until William's marriage in 1788, housekeeper to the brother who had rescued her in 1772 from domestic drudgery in their native Hanover. In 2003 the two (incomplete) autobiographies that she wrote were edited and published, and although the second was composed when she was in her nineties, her command of facts continued to be extraordinary. As a result we now have a better understanding of her first thirty-eight years. In addition, her observing books have been studied in detail and the objects she saw identified.

When William and Caroline arrived in the fall of 1782 in the neighborhood of Windsor Castle, William provided Caroline with a simple refractor and told her to search for objects of interest, such as comets, nebulae, and double stars. After a year he made her an ingenious reflector to use in place of the refractor, and in the early 1790s, a larger version of the same. From the end of 1783, Caroline's nights were often taken up with acting as amanuensis to William while he was searching for nebulae; but in 1786, when William was away in Germany, Caroline had leisure to observe on her own account and found her first comet. After William married in 1788, she was free of household duties and her brother observed less often, and so she could regularly "sweep" for comets. Between 1788 and 1797, when she made the disastrous and inexplicable decision to leave the cottage next to William's house and move into lodgings (so effectively ending her career as an observer), she found seven more comets. One we know as Encke's, and it returns every 3.3 years. Another returned in 1939 and is expected again in 2092.

Caroline Herschel. *Drawing of Caroline Herschel.* **SPL/PHOTO RESEARCHERS, INC.**

These discoveries brought her fame, but they were to prove less significant than her earliest sweeps with the little refractor. Soon after Caroline first began observing, she came across some of the bright nebulae that the French comet-hunter Charles Messier had listed because they were confusing his searches for comets. Then, on 26 February 1783, she found two nebulae that she and William agreed were unknown to Messier. This was in fact true of only one of the two, but William was left with the conviction that nebulae were present in the heavens in great numbers and could be found even by an inexperienced observer with a telescope that was little more than a toy. The nature of the nebulae—were they all distant star clusters, or were some truly nebulous?—was an unsolved problem in astronomy, and on 4 March William committed himself "to sweep the heaven for Nebulas and Clusters of stars." With Caroline's help, this would lead to his catalogs of 2,507 nebulae and eventually, late in the nineteenth century, to the *New General Catalogue* that astronomers use today. Faced with the need to classify these nebulae, which for a time he believed were all clusters of stars, William took as his criterion the degree of clustering. The implication was that scattered clusters would in time become more condensed as gravity continued to bring the component stars ever closer together: scattered clusters were young, condensed clusters old. In this way William began the transformation of astronomy from the clockwork universe of Isaac Newton and Gottfried Wilhelm Leibniz to the modern view whereby everything, even the universe itself, evolves.

Caroline's contribution to the setting in motion of these momentous developments far outweighed the negligible importance of the nebulae and clusters she herself discovered, fewer than twenty in total. If William later rediscovered one of them in his regular "sweeps," and if it was recognized as one that Caroline had seen earlier, her initials were inserted in the published catalog; if not, it languished in her observing books. Two of her observations, however, defy identification. In the summer of 1783 she twice observed "a rich spot" in neighboring regions of sky, and although she is specific as to the locations, no nebulae are to be found there today. It seems likely that she was observing a comet that is otherwise unknown.

Her own published volume relating to John Flamsteed's great *British Catalogue* of stars is better appreciated today. William and she used the catalog all the time while sweeping, yet occasionally they found that it did not correspond correctly to what was in the sky. The problem was that there was no way of proceeding back, from the stars as listed in the *British Catalogue* (volume 3 of Flamsteed's *Historia coelestis britannica*) to the observations in volume 2 on which the catalog entries were based. Caroline, in a work that was routine but called for endless patience and meticulous accuracy, supplied this need, and in the process found many errors and no fewer than 561 stars that Flamsteed had overlooked when compiling the catalog.

BIBLIOGRAPHY

WORK BY HERSCHEL

Caroline Herschel's Autobiographies. Edited by Michael Hoskin. Cambridge, U.K.: Science History Publications, 2003. Contains the two incomplete autobiographies that Caroline wrote when she was in her seventies and her nineties, respectively.

OTHER SOURCES

Flamsteed, John. *Historia coelestis britannica.* London, 1725. *British Catalogue* is the third volume of this three-volume work.

Hoskin, Michael. *The Herschel Partnership: As Viewed by Caroline.* Cambridge, U.K.: Science History Publications, 2003. A biography of Caroline that focuses on her relationship with William.

———. "Caroline Herschel as Observer." *Journal for the History of Astronomy* 36 (2005): 373–406. Includes an analysis of the objects she observed.

———. "Caroline Herschel's Catalogue of Nebulae." *Journal for the History of Astronomy* 37 (2006): 251–255.

———. *The Herschels of Hanover.* Cambridge, U.K.: Science History Publications, 2007.

Michael Hoskin

HERSCHEL, JOHN (*b.* Slough, Berkshire, Great Britain, 7 March 1792; *d.* Hawkhurst, Kent, United Kingdom, 11 May 1871), *astronomy, meteorology, geomagnetism, scientific method.* For the original article on Herschel see *DSB,* vol. 6.

When Charles Darwin began his introduction to the *On the Origin of Species* (1859) by describing the topic as "that mystery of mysteries, as it has been called by one of our greatest philosophers," he was alluding to a great influence on his work: John Herschel. Herschel's reputation derived from his achievements in diverse areas of natural philosophy and from his insight into scientific methodology, most explicitly addressed in his *Preliminary Discourse on the Study of Natural Philosophy* (1830), a volume that impacted Darwin, John Stuart Mill, Herschel's close friend William Whewell, and many other significant contemporaries. Herschel played important roles in major scientific organizations—including the Royal Society, the Astronomical Society (later the Royal Astronomical Society), and the British Association for the Advancement of Science (BAAS)—became a member of dozens of others throughout Europe, and served as an advisor to numerous national committees and large-scale, data-gathering projects, such as the mapping of Earth's magnetic field and the collecting of meteorological data. By drawing on his own scientific reputation and on the renown of his surname, Herschel was able to cross social classes, political lines, and philosophical divisions, providing a point of contact and enabling cooperation between diverse groups and interests.

Herschel

A Gentleman of Science. Herschel grew up in an unusual household that was regularly visited by local and foreign dignitaries drawn to his father William's accomplishments and to the world's largest telescope. John's inheritance of twenty-five thousand pounds (plus land and properties) enabled him to live the life of a leisured gentleman able to explore whatever natural phenomena piqued his wide interests. The absence of a signature discovery is an important factor in his lasting reputation not reflecting the renown he enjoyed in his lifetime. A complete explanation of that discrepancy, perhaps part of a still much-needed biography, would need to address the manner in which Herschel's life and work manifest the changing contexts and methods of natural philosophy in mid-nineteenth-century England. These broad changes—sometimes summarized as the movement from gentlemen natural philosophers (typically working alone) to professional, specialized scientists (often working collaboratively)—led to the very origins of the word *scientist,* coined by Whewell at the 1833 meeting of the BAAS, with Herschel (among others) in mind. Indeed, it is instructive to note that Herschel was described in the late twentieth century as "an occupied astronomer" or an occupied gentleman (by science historian Allan Chapman) and as "Britain's first modern physical scientist" (by Herschel scholar and astronomy historian Michael Crowe).

In many ways, Herschel remained a gentleman of science. He relied on his own financial resources to fund investigations of his own choosing, never held a paid philosophical position, and refused monetary assistance even with the huge expenses related to the years spent in South Africa from 1883 to 1888 observing the southern skies, the most carefully studied years of his life. Elizabeth Green Musselman has clearly described Herschel's understanding of his own astronomical work in the context of empire and has demonstrated the mutual interaction of science and empire. This interpretation is complemented by Steven Ruskin's analysis of how Herschel's South African voyage was popularly linked to British imperial ambitions, a linkage reinforced by Herschel's elevation to the baronetcy at the coronation of Queen Victoria on 28 June 1838. Herschel was the only man of science to receive this honor on that occasion, which took place immediately upon his return from the Cape of Good Hope and a decade before his astronomical results actually appeared. Despite the analytical skills that led to numerous publications of great depth on narrow topics, Herschel maintained broad interests, resisting the ever-growing tendency toward specialization.

Nonetheless, Herschel was acutely aware of the limitations of gentleman scholarship and of the Royal Society. He therefore played an active role in the founding of the Astronomical Society in 1820 and in its activities for many years; his efforts to reform the Royal Society itself culminated in his barely failed attempt to attain its presidency in 1830. In addition to his active participation in the BAAS, his writings indicate his awareness, acceptance, and participation in the increasingly democratic and popular aspects of science: His *Treatise on Astronomy* (first edition, 1833) and its transformation into *Outlines of Astronomy* (first edition, 1849) each went through numerous editions and translations, and his *Essays from the Edinburgh and Quarterly Reviews* (1857) and *Familiar Lectures on Scientific Subjects* (1867) reached wide audiences.

John Herschel, 1867. HULTON ARCHIVE/GETTY IMAGES.

Methodology. In his methodology, Herschel also bridged scientific styles. He participated in numerous Baconian data-collecting projects: with James South, he surveyed double stars; with assistants, he extended his father's catalog of double stars, clusters, and nebulae to the southern skies, and expended enormous labor in reducing his data, a task he carried out by himself over a decade. He nonetheless recognized that projects for obtaining magnetic, meteorological, and other scientific data involved larger-scale international collaborations. Herschel also emphasized the importance of rigorous mathematical analysis, and as a result of his investigations into crystallography and the nature of light, realized the importance of hypothetical reasoning and the development of theories for investigating and understanding natural phenomena. This notion appears regularly throughout the *Preliminary Discourse,* and most evocatively in a letter to Whewell: "I remember it was a saying often in my Father's mouth 'Hypotheses fingo' in reference to Newton's 'Hypotheses *non* fingo,' ['I frame no hypotheses'] and certainly it is this facility of framing hypotheses if accompanied with an equal facility of abandoning them which is the happiest structure of mind for theoretical speculation" (John Herschel to William Whewill, 20 August 1837).

Diverging from Eminent Scientists. Eventually, Herschel's broad-ranging interests and the decline of his formidable analytical skills did not enable him to keep pace with the increased specialization of natural philosophy. Darwin, who stopped in to visit Herschel at the Cape while on his *Beagle* voyage, expressed great disappointment when, after publication of *On the Origin of Species,* Herschel declared natural selection to be "the law of higgledy piggledy." In his rejection of Darwin's work, his dismissal of the principle of the conservation of energy, and his continued defense of Boscovichian atomism, Herschel's insights and experience led him in directions that diverged from those taken by other leading scientific practitioners. Still, his extensive extant personal correspondence reveals Herschel's activity and importance as a prominent node in the scientific communications network over several decades.

SUPPLEMENTARY BIBLIOGRAPHY

A comprehensive bibliography of Herschel's published works is in Michael J. Crowe, ed., A Calendar of the Correspondence of Sir John Herschel *(Cambridge, U.K.: Cambridge University Press, 1998.) This volume also lists numerous archives housing Herschel's unpublished documents; noteworthy archives include the private collection of John Herschel-Shorland; the Royal Astronomical Society Herschel Archive, London, U.K.; Archives of the Royal Greenwich Observatory, Cambridge University Library, Cambridge, U.K.; Herschel Papers, Royal Society, London, U.K.; St. John's College, Cambridge University, Cambridge, U.K.; Trinity College, Cambridge University, Cambridge, U.K.; Harry Ransom Humanities Center, University of Texas, Austin.*

Bolt, Marvin. "John Herschel's Natural Philosophy: On the Knowing of Nature and the Nature of Knowing in Early-Nineteenth-Century Britain." PhD. diss, University of Notre Dame, 1998.

Carter, Christopher. "Imperialism and Empiricism: Science and State in the Age of Empire." PhD diss., Duke University, 2004. A study of Herschel's roles in geomagnetic and meteorological data-gathering projects and of issues relating to imperial contexts.

Chapman, Allan. "An Occupation for an Independent Gentleman: Astronomy in the Life of John Herschel." *Vistas in Astronomy* 36 (1993): 71–116.

Crowe, Michael J. "John Herschel: Britain's First Modern Physical Scientist." In *John Herschel, 1792–1992: Bicentennial Symposium,* edited by Brian Warner. Royal Society of South Africa, 1994.

———., ed. *A Calendar of the Correspondence of Sir John Herschel.* Cambridge, U.K.: Cambridge University Press, 1998. By far the most important addition to Herschel scholarship in recent years, this massive work provides summaries of nearly fifteen thousand surviving letters and exhaustive bibliographies of Herschel's own publications and of secondary works published up to 1998. It reveals details of Herschel's private life as well as occasional and regular communications between Herschel and others.

———. "Herschel, Sir John Frederick William, First Baronet (1792–1871)." In *Oxford Dictionary of National Biography.* Vol. 26, edited by H. C. G. Matthew and Brian Harrison, 825–831. Oxford: Oxford University Press, 2004.

Evans, David. "Herschel, John Frederick William." In *Biographical Encyclopedia of Astronomers,* edited by Thomas Hockey. New York: Springer, 2006.

Musselman, Elizabeth Green. "Swords into Ploughshares: John Herschel's Progressive View of Astronomical and Imperial Governance." *British Journal for the History of Science* 31 (1998): 419–436.

Ross, Sydney, ed. *Catalogue of the Herschel Library: Being a Catalogue of the Books Owned by Sir William Herschel, Kt. and by His Son Sir John F. W. Herschel, Bart.* Troy, NY: privately printed, 2001.

Ruskin, Steven. *John Herschel's Cape Voyage: Private Science, Public Imagination, and the Ambitions of Empire.* Burlington, VT: Ashgate, 2004.

Marvin Bolt

HERSCHEL, WILLIAM

(*b.* Hanover, Germany, 15 November 1738; *d.* Observatory House, Slough, Berkshire, United Kingdom, 25 August 1822), *astronomy.*

Herschel became a professional astronomer only in the fall of 1782, when he was already forty-three years old. Until then he was a versatile musician who earned his living by performing, conducting, and teaching, and whose ambition in life was to be remembered as a composer. This aspect of his life is now better appreciated. From his time in the north of England (1759–1766) we have his own autobiographical memoranda, his treatises on music and philosophical subjects that took the form of letters to his brother Jacob, and numerous symphonies and other musical compositions. Of his multifarious musical activities during his Bath years (1766–1782) we are still better informed. Not only do we again have his autobiographical memoranda, but from 1772, when his sister Caroline joined him from Hanover, we have her own copious records. In addition, since Bath was a major center of

Herschel

William Herschel. OMIKRON/PHOTO RESEARCHERS, INC.

musical life, detailed studies of the Bath musical scene have shed light on Herschel's sometimes turbulent relationship with his competitors.

Herschel's debt to the selfless devotion of Caroline, who acted as amanuensis at night during the "sweeps" for nebulae (now, we know, left unfinished) and who did all the paperwork connected with his voluminous publications, has always been recognized. The extent of his debt to two of his brothers, Dietrich and Alexander, is only now being appreciated. Dietrich, his youngest brother, spent two years (1777–1779) living in Bath with his siblings before returning to Hanover. Dietrich was an enthusiastic amateur entomologist and he introduced William to butterfly collecting and, more significantly, to the methodology of the natural historian. Hitherto astronomy had been mainly the study of a small number of celestial bodies each with its own proper name—Sun, planets, moons, the brightest stars. William was to collect specimens of double stars by the hundred and nebulae by the thousand, and he classified and dated his specimens, thereby introducing to astronomy the methodology of the natural historian.

Much more extensive was the contribution of Alexander Herschel, who arrived in Bath in 1770 for a short visit and stayed until 1816. Although a musician by profession like all the brothers, Alexander had a remarkable talent for brass work, and was ingenious in finding solutions to the practical problems that arose in telescope construction. Unlike Caroline, he left few written records, and the components he contributed to the telescopes are of course unsigned, but it has become clear that he was the third member of the great partnership. Almost every year, during the summer when Bath was out of season, Alexander stayed some weeks with his siblings, working on gadgetry of all kinds.

William's activities as a telescope maker have come under further scrutiny. Of those he built for his own use, some were precision made while others were huge and designed for the study of distant and faint objects. The 7-foot reflector he made at Bath was an example of the former. Its most important component was the mirror, the accuracy of whose shape he never succeeded in replicating in other instruments. It allowed him (and him alone) to see at a glance that Uranus was no ordinary star; and it was only after great efforts that any other observer was able to confirm that the Pole Star (for example) was double.

It is well known that King George III granted £2,000 for the construction of the 40-foot reflector, and that this was supplemented by a further £2,000 plus other expenses. Only recently has it become evident that the second grant was made in the context of a serious row between monarch and astronomer. Herschel was of course in uncharted territory in attempting the construction of such a monster. The king had understood that the first £2,000 was the total required, and when this proved not to be the case he may well have suspected Herschel of deliberately underestimating the costs involved when making his original application. Although the king acceded—reluctantly—to the second request, from then on Herschel was required to account for every last penny of expenditure, and was told in no uncertain terms that no further grant would be forthcoming.

The 40-foot reflector proved cumbersome and its results did not justify the labor and cost of its construction. What has only recently been appreciated is the extent to which it became a millstone around its creator's neck. From Herschel's point of view, it lost its principal raison d'être in 1790 when an observation with the 20-foot convinced him of the existence of "true nebulosity." But to the king it was an enduring symbol of his patronage of science, and visitors to Windsor Castle were invited to make the short journey to Slough to see the world's biggest telescope. This required Herschel to maintain the monster in some semblance of working order, long after he and Alexander had lost the physical strength necessary to repolish the mirror.

Much more is now known about the wealth that Mary Pitt brought to their marriage in 1788. Her inheritance from her late husband, and subsequent legacies from her mother and other members of her family, rendered Herschel's annual "pension" from the crown insignificant. Why then did he continue to make telescopes for sale? Part of the reason seems to lie in the delight he took at his international eminence in work so far removed from his profession of music—ambassadors were reduced to writing what were, in effect, begging letters, for if Herschel refused them, there was no one else to whom they might turn. But it has been argued that some of his production was destined for fellow observers who might, he hoped, confirm observations that hitherto he alone had been able to make.

BIBLIOGRAPHY

Brown, Frank. *William Herschel, Musician and Composer.* Bath, U.K.: William Herschel Society, 1990.

Caroline Herschel's Autobiographies. Edited by Michael Hoskin. Cambridge, U.K.: Science History Publications, 2003. Contains the two incomplete autobiographies that Caroline wrote when she was in her seventies and her nineties, respectively, and much of the information concerns William.

Hoskin, Michael. "Herschel's 40ft Reflector: Funding and Functions." *Journal for the History of Astronomy* 34 (2003): 1–32.

———. *The Herschel Partnership: As Viewed by Caroline.* Cambridge, U.K.: Science History Publications, 2003. A biography of Caroline that focuses on her relationship with William. Mary Herschel's finances are discussed in pp. 92, 95–96.

———. "Vocations in Conflict: William Herschel in Bath, 1766–1782." *History of Science* 41 (2003): 315–333. Discusses Herschel's musical activities.

———. "Alexander Herschel: The Forgotten Partner." *Journal for the History of Astronomy* 35 (2004): 387–420.

———. "Unfinished Business: William Herschel's Sweeps for Nebulae." *History of Science* 43 (2005): 305–320.

———. *The Herschels of Hanover.* Cambridge, U.K.: Science History Publications, 2007.

James, Kenneth. "Concert Life in 18th Century Bath." PhD diss., University of London, 1987.

Maurer, Andreas. "A Compendium of All Known William Herschel Telescopes." *Journal of the Antique Telescope Society,* no. 14 (1998): 4–15.

Spaight, John Tracy. "'For the Good of Astronomy': The Manufacture, Sale, and Distant Use of William Herschel's Telescopes." *Journal for the History of Astronomy* 35 (2004): 45–69.

Michael Hoskin

HERTZ, HEINRICH RUDOLF

(*b.* Hamburg, Germany, 22 February 1857; *d.* Bonn, Germany, 1 January 1894), *physics, philosophy.* For the original article on Hertz see *DSB,* vol. 6.

The centenaries of Hertz's discovery of radio waves, of his death, and of the publication of *The Principles of Mechanics* served to invigorate scholarship on the life and work of Heinrich Hertz. While it was true until 1994 that there was no book-length study, the next dozen years produced a 600-page biography, two highly focused monographs, and a collection of essays on Hertz as classical physicist and modern philosopher. These books appeared alongside numerous articles and the discovery of new biographical sources, laboratory notes, correspondence, and manuscripts.

Close scrutiny of Hertz's experimental and conceptual procedures produced uncertainty on some biographical questions, new insights on others. In particular, Hertz's "conversion" to a Maxwellian conception of electrodynamics has come to appear as an ever more intriguing problem. The publication of his 1884 lectures on the constitution of matter laid bare the continuity of his philosophical interests. This, in turn, prompted richly nuanced views of the *Principles of Mechanics* and yet another puzzle regarding the ether.

Between Helmholtz and Maxwell. The question of Hertz's "conversion" arises from his 1884 paper "On the Relations between Maxwell's Fundamental Electromagnetic Equations and the Fundamental Equations of the Opposing Electromagnetics." It concluded that "if the choice rests only between the usual system of electromagnetics and Maxwell's, the latter is certainly to be preferred" (1896, p. 289). This statement underwrites the view that in his decisive experiments of 1887 and 1888 Hertz set out to prove Maxwell's theory. However, it is odd not only that Hertz never again referred to this paper but also that he freed himself only very gradually from a Helmholtzian idiom. The publication of his 1884 lectures and 1887 laboratory notes did not settle the issue. On the one hand, they underscore his general distrust of action-at-a-distance theories and thus his sympathy for Maxwell's approach. On the other hand, they indicate that he was exploring the limiting case of Helmholtz's electrodynamics which leads to Maxwell's equations.

In his 1892 introduction to *Electric Waves* Hertz provided several cues as to how this puzzle might be resolved. On his own reconstruction of the course of experimentation, the competing theories of electrodynamics lacked physical meaning until Hertz's experiments. As long as Hertz could say no more about Maxwell's theory than that it is Maxwell's system of equations, all theories that mathematically coincide with Maxwell's equation were

Hertz

equivalent, including that of Helmholtz. In respect to electromagnetic theories, one cannot sensibly ask whether Hertz was a Maxwellian or still a Helmholtzian until the time of the "philosophical … and in a certain sense most important result" of his experiments, namely that they proved the "propagation in time of a supposed action-at-a-distance" (1893, p. 19). This finding simultaneously served to distinguish Helmholtz's and Maxwell's conceptions and to decide in favor of Maxwell's. To fully realize this may have taken Hertz well into 1889. At the same time, that Hertz was a Helmholtzian by training is evident from his laboratory practice, his style of experimentation, and his manner of developing a new phenomenon by literally unfolding and materially transforming a familiar laboratory device (the so-called Rieß spirals) into a sender and receiver of electric waves.

Philosophical Critique. Even before he studied with Helmholtz, Hertz had been exposed in Dresden to lectures on Immanuel Kant, and in January 1878 expressed in a letter to his parents that he was pondering conceptual issues, "and particularly the principles of mechanics (as the very words: force, time, space, motion indicate) can occupy one severely enough" (1977, p. 77). Towards the end of his life, in a letter dated November 23, 1893 Hertz encouraged his publisher to include among the potential readers of *The Principles of Mechanics* "the circle of philosophical readers" (in Fölsing, 1997, p. 509). The publication of his 1884 lectures on the constitution of matter establishes the continuity of Hertz's philosophical interest in conceptual critique. In the case of "force," he rejected it as a fundamental concept of mechanics since it lacked physical meaning but served only as part of its representational apparatus. In the case of "matter," he found the concept indispensable and struggled to determine its physical meaning, showing that on all available definitions it is an indissoluble mixture of a priori and empirical elements. In a highly suggestive passage he therefore compares it to paper money that is issued by the understanding to regulate its relation to things. All this has given rise to an appreciation of Hertz as a philosopher in his own right. He rigorously applies to the conceptual tools of physics a Kantian critique of how scientific experience becomes possible only within clearly specified limits of physical knowledge. He thus offers an original and parsimonious account of the metaphysical foundations of physics.

The Geometrization of Mechanics. In the context of a broadened appreciation of Hertz's concerns, it is no longer possible to divide *The Principles of Mechanics* into two parts, firstly a philosophical introduction that concerns the choice between empirically equivalent but conceptually distinct images of mechanics, and secondly the somewhat tedious articulation of a forceless mechanics.

Heinrich Hertz. © BETTMANN/CORBIS.

Instead, the book appears as a delicate and highly self-conscious exercise to relate physical content and mathematical form. Suspicious that the new mathematics and especially non-Euclidean geometry offer abstractions that are detached from reality, Hertz nevertheless developed a first geometrization of mechanics. The originality of *The Principles of Mechanics* does not consist in the elimination of force, which had been advocated already by one of Hertz's former teachers, Gustav Kirchhoff. Instead it arises from the way in which the new formalism suggests new ways of thinking about physical phenomena. Rather than build up mechanics from the motion of a single mass point, Hertz's geometrization yields a forceless mechanics by beginning with a system of points. Accordingly, forces are replaced by connections within and among systems of points, phenomena that unfold in time are referred to time-independent material systems, causal explanation is reduced to the correspondence between dynamic models, and intentionality is banished along with all phenomena of life from the domain of physics. The domain of physics, however, is to be unified by a single law of mechanics, giving rise to an unsolved biographical and scientific puzzle.

Hertz was clearly aware of the challenge to unify electrodynamics and mechanics and emphasized the need for a theory of the ether in his 1889 lecture on "Electricity and Light." However, while the 1884 lectures express Hertz's skepticism toward any material medium that cannot be isolated and rendered ponderable, *The Principles of Mechanics* hardly mentions the ether at all, except to point out that a clarification of the laws of mechanics is a prerequisite for any theory of the ether. In light of the broadened appreciation of Hertz's intellectual and experimental endeavors, it depends on his active interest or lack thereof in the ether and the unification of physics whether one should view the concern of his final years as primarily empirical or conceptual, as physical or philosophical.

SUPPLEMENTARY BIBLIOGRAPHY

WORKS BY HERTZ

"Annual reviews for the years 1878–1883 of electrostatics, electrochemistry, electrodynamics, thermoelectricity, and related fields." *Die Fortschritte der Physik* 34–39 (1884–1889). Hertz's synoptic reports on altogether 230 papers and books include those of British scientists.

Die Constitution der Materie: Eine Vorlesung über die Grundlagen der Physik aus dem Jahre 1884. Edited by Albrecht Fölsing. Berlin: Springer, 1999. Hertz's 1884 lectures on the constitution of matter.

"An Unpublished Lecture by Heinrich Hertz: 'On the Energy Balance of the Earth.'" Edited by Joseph F. Mulligan and H. Gerhard Hertz. *American Journal of Physics,* 65 (1997): 36–45. Hertz's 1885 inaugural lecture in Karlsruhe.

"Heinrich Hertz's Laboratory Notes of 1887." Edited by H. Gerhard Hertz and Manuel Doncel. *Archive for History of Exact Sciences* 49 (1995): 197–270.

Electric Waves. London: Macmillan, 1893. Reprinted New York: Dover Publications, 1962.

Miscellaneous Papers. London: Macmillan, 1896.

Erinnerungen, Briefe, Tagebücher. Memoirs, Letters, Diaries / Heinrich Hertz. Edited by Johanna Hertz. Second enlarged edition prepared by M. Hertz and C. Susskind. Weinheim/San Francisco: Physik Verlag/San Francisco Press, 1977. This bilingual edition includes roughly a fifth of Hertz's weekly letters to his parents and excerpts from his diary, extensive quotes from the here unpublished material can be found in Fölsing's biography. The first edition appeared in 1927.

OTHER SOURCES

Baird, Davis, R. I. G. Hughes, and Alfred Nordmann, eds. *Heinrich Hertz: Classical Physicist, Modern Philosopher.* Dordrecht, Netherlands; Boston: Kluwer, 1998. Includes contributions by Jed Buchwald, Salvo D'Agostino, Manuel Doncel, Giora Hon, Jesper Lützen, Alfred Nordmann, and Simon Saunders; also a concordance of German and English editions of Hertz's main works; and a comprehensive annotated bibliography of original works and secondary sources.

Buchwald, Jed. *The Creation of Scientific Effects: Heinrich Hertz and Electric Waves.* Chicago: University of Chicago Press, 1994. Reconstructs how a known phenomenon is transformed to yield a novel effect; argues for Hertz's late adoption of a Maxwellian account.

———. "The Scholar's Seeing Eye." In *Reworking the Bench: Research Notebooks in the History of Science,* edited by Frederic Holmes, Jürgen Renn, and Hans-Jörg Rheinberger. Dordrecht, Netherlands; Boston: Kluwer, 2003.

D'Agostino, Salvo. "The Bild-Conception of Physical Theories from Boltzmann to Hertz." In *The Dawn of Cognitive Science: Early European Contributors,* edited by Liliana Albertazzi. Dordrecht, Netherlands; Boston: Kluwer, 2001.

Darrigol, Olivier. "The Electrodynamics of Moving Bodies from Faraday to Hertz." *Centaurus* 36 (1993): 245–360.

Doncel, Manuel. "On the Process of Hertz's Conversion to Hertzian Waves." *Archive for History of Exact Sciences* 43 (1991): 1–27. Includes as evidence for slow conversion a discussion of the differences between the first and final publications of Hertz's papers on electrodynamics.

Fölsing, Albrecht. *Heinrich Hertz: Eine Biographie.* Hamburg: Hoffmann und Campe, 1997. Draws on a vast amount of previously unconsidered source material, for the most part deriving from an otherwise unidentified *Nachlaß Mathilde Hertz,* including laboratory notes for 1886, official and scientific correspondence, documents, manuscripts, and Hertz's diary. Fölsing also identifies some of Hertz's contributions to the Karlsruhe newspaper.

Hon, Giora. "H. Hertz: 'The electrostatic and electromagnetic properties of the cathode rays are either *nil* or very feeble' (1883): A Case-Study of an Experimental Error." *Studies in History and Philosophy of Science* 18 (1987): 367–382.

Hüttemann, Andreas. "Heinrich Hertz and the Concept of a Symbol." In *Symbol and Physical Knowledge,* edited by Massimo Ferrari and I.-O Stamatescu. Berlin and New York: Springer, 2002.

Hyder, David. "Kantian Metaphysics and Hertzian Mechanics." In *The Vienna Circle and Logical Empiricism,* edited by Friedrich Stadler. Dordrecht, Netherlands; Boston: Kluwer, 2003.

Lützen, Jesper. *Mechanistic Images in Geometric Form: Heinrich Hertz's Principles of Mechanics.* Oxford: Oxford University Press, 2005. Establishes the significance of Hertz's geometrization of mechanics; considers the various drafts of the manuscript.

Mulligan, Joseph F., ed. *Heinrich Rudolf Hertz (1857–1894): A Collection of Articles and Addresses.* New York: Garland, 1994. Very useful comprehensive introduction to Hertz; a biographical essay is followed by eight papers from *Electric Waves* and *Miscellaneous Papers,* Hertz's lecture "On the Relations between Electricity and Light," his introductions to *Electric Waves* and the *Principles of Mechanics,* and texts on Hertz by George FitzGerald, Hermann von Helmholtz, Philipp Lenard, and Max Planck.

Nordmann, Alfred. "Heinrich Hertz: Scientific Biography and Experimental Life." *Studies in History and Philosophy of Science* 31 (2000): 537–549.

O'Hara, James, and Willibald Pricha. *Hertz and the Maxwellians: A Study and Documentation of the Discovery of Electromagnetic Wave Radiation, 1873–1894.* London: Peter Peregrinus, 1987. Includes Hertz's correspondence with the Maxwellians, the preamble to his 1879 manuscript on the demonstration of electrical effects in dielectricity, and a series of plates on Hertz's apparatus at the Deutsches Museum in Munich.

Alfred Nordmann

HERTZ, MATHILDE CARMEN (*b.* Bonn, Germany, 14 January 1891; *d.* Cambridge, United Kingdom, 20 November 1975), *Gestalt psychology, comparative psychology, sensory physiology.*

Hertz was a pioneering comparative psychologist. She fused psychological and biological perspectives in her research, and contemporary psychologists and biologists alike held her work in high esteem. She combined innovative experimental techniques and Gestalt principles to examine the visual perception of diverse animal species, including ravens, honeybees, butterflies, and hermit crabs. Time and again facing adversity, Hertz overcame various obstacles to pursue an academic career. She was prolific while her career lasted, but her scholarly work ended abruptly after she emigrated from Germany to England in 1936.

Short Biography. Mathilde Hertz was the youngest daughter of the physicist Heinrich Hertz, who died when Mathilde was three years old. After completing a nonclassical secondary education she began a career as a sculptor. To supplement her income she took a job at the library of the German Museum in Munich, where she drew and sculpted plastic reconstructions of fossilized teeth in the zoological collection. At this time her work came to the attention of Ludwig Döderlein, who was the director of the zoological collection. Overcoming barriers for a scientific career for women at that time, Hertz enrolled at the University of Munich from 1921 to 1922 and later completed her doctoral degree in 1925 with honors on a study about early mammalian jawbones under the supervision of Richard von Hertwig.

By 1925, and inspired by Wolfgang Köhler's research with anthropoid apes, Hertz began work in the field of animal psychology. In 1927 she moved to Berlin and worked in the Department for Genetics and Biology of Animals under the auspices of Richard Goldschmidt. Here she taught and conducted research until her authorization to teach was withdrawn in 1933 due to the implementation of the "Law for the Restoration of Professional Civil Service." According to this law, civil servants who were not of "Aryan descent" were to be retired, and those whose political stance did not guarantee loyalty to the Nazi regime to be dismissed. Hertz was presumably classified as "non-Aryan" according to this law because she had one grandparent, Gustav Ferdinand Hertz, who had been Jewish prior to converting to Christianity.

Mathilde Hertz, 1918. COURTESY OF DR. SIGFRIED JAEGER.

Despite the intervention efforts of Max Planck, the president of the Kaiser Wilhelm Society at that time, she was no longer able to teach, although she continued her research until the end of 1935. Between 1925 and 1935 she published more than thirty articles. In 1936 Hertz immigrated to England, where, after publishing another article on color vision in bees (1939) and an article on vision in migratory locusts (1937b), her empirical work basically came to an abrupt end presumably due to an unfortunate combination of personal and professional factors. Various reasons for this are explored by Regina Siegfried Kressley-Mba and Jaeger (2003), including the fact that Hertz appears to have remained loyal to Germany despite the grave injustices she suffered as a result of Nazi racial policies. Furthermore, the growing popularity of ethology and an emphasis on instinctive behavior may have rendered the phenomenological orientation that was characteristic of Gestalt psychology and Hertz's work obsolete.

Problem-Solving Behavior in Animals. Hertz's first experiments with ravens were explicitly designed and implemented to examine the Gestalt laws of visual perception outlined by Max Wertheimer (1923; Hertz, 1928a,b). Although Gestalt theory offered the theoretical foundation for explaining organization in human perception, thinking, and behavior, Wertheimer viewed Hertz's work as providing indispensable empirical evidence for Gestalt principles of visual perception among animals. Despite their significance for verifying those principles, Hertz's experiments with ravens were valued in yet another light by Gestalt psychologists and zoologists alike, namely as central examples of problem-solving behavior in animals (Duncker, 1945). The methods employed by Hertz with ravens were later implemented in studies examining the problem-solving capacities of primates, for example, by the Gestalt psychologist and Köhler student Johannes von Allesch and the Dutch ethologist Johan Abraham Bierens de Haan.

In her experiments on the visual perception of ravens, Hertz altered the location of food rewards within identical configurations so that she was able to determine, among other things, how jays distinguish between concave and convex stimuli. Based on the assumption that ravens have only a weak sense of smell and that there is no trace of food originating from the hidden object, Hertz reasoned that the birds depend on memory and sensory input to locate the critical area and retrieve bounty by removing debris hiding the food (Hertz, 1928a,b). Based on similar experiments that Köhler had employed with anthropoids, Hertz hid a peanut or hazelnut while the bird was watching and then observed the bird's behavior. This was Hertz's solution for inducing the bird in a laboratory setting to engage in searching behavior that was not necessary for its survival (Hertz, 1928a). Initially the food was covered with a flowerpot as the birds watched. After the birds had learned this exercise, the goal objects and obstacles were modified to match the bird's natural environment, such as using stones, wood, or grass. Hertz (1928a,b) implemented a countless variety of stimulus constellations to detect which variables were essential for finding the hidden food. Figure 1 provides an example of how Hertz tracked flight patterns. In order to rule out the possibility that the birds were responding on the basis of conditioning, Hertz incorporated critical trials in which both the target (food) and intermediate target (object hiding the food) were absent during the search phase.

Significant Findings in Animal Visual Perception. Hertz's findings on visual perception in honeybees—cited by Karl von Frisch (1937)—probably represent her most significant contribution to animal sensory perception. Initially, Hertz worked with birds because their visual systems were similar to those of anthropoids, but later opted for honeybees because of their more primitive visual system. Her research with honeybees served as the basis for her postdoctoral thesis, for which Köhler served as one of the committee members.

Prior to Hertz's work, von Frisch had concluded that bees cannot distinguish between basic geometric forms. Hertz modified von Frisch's method by eliminating the conditioning of the bees prior to the experiments. Hertz (1931) covered a table with black and white figures varying in form and degree of contour and placed bowls of sugar water between the forms. She then observed flight patterns relative to the forms—namely, which sources of food next to which form were frequented by the most bees, most quickly, and most often. Realizing that conditioning to a particular stimulus occurs automatically through preferences developed over the course of a few trials, Hertz then attempted to condition the bees to a different form. The relative resistance of conditioning to a particular stimulus was a further measure of the kind and degree of spontaneous response (Hertz, 1935a).

If bees could not distinguish between triangles and squares as von Frisch had observed, then it was because

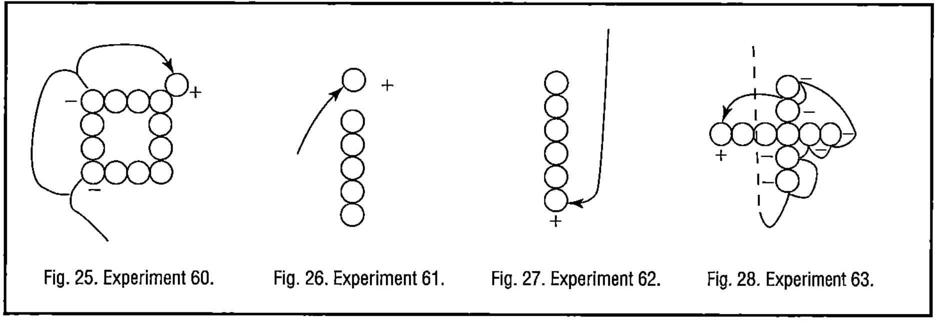

Fig. 25. Experiment 60.
Fig. 26. Experiment 61.
Fig. 27. Experiment 62.
Fig. 28. Experiment 63.

Figure 1. *Shown above are examples of how Hertz tracked the movement of ravens in their attempt to find hidden food among different constellations of stimuli. The arrows indicate the direction of movement, while unsuccessful (–) and successful (+) attempts are designated accordingly.*

Hertz

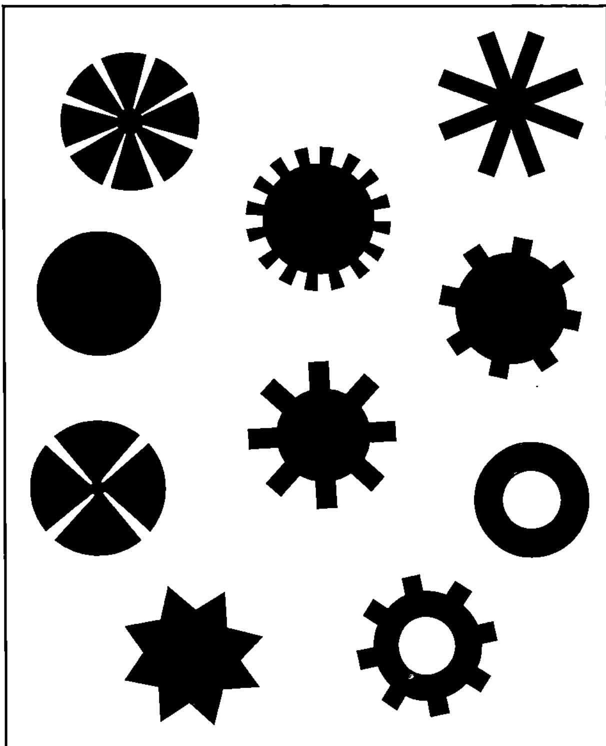

Figure 2. Examples of figures varying in figural quality and intensity are shown above. The shapes with a round outer profile represent shapes with less figural intensity than forms with the prominent pointed or notched outer contours, whereas a circle compared to a star represents a large contrast with respect to figural quality.

they preferred shapes full of contour, which was supported by independent findings that bees could distinguish flowers. Hertz was able to determine visual preferences in bees with regard to patterns (see Figure 2). She coined the term *figural intensity* to designate the visual quality of a figure—the more differentiated and the more pronounced the contours, the greater the bees' preference for those figures. *Figural quality* referred to the basic type of figure (i.e., circle versus star). Hertz (1931) also used variations of forms and patterns to test bees' perception of depth, contrast, and patterns as well as presenting the stimuli at different times of day to study light and shadow effects, particularly during flight approaching a stimulus. These were experimental variations originating from Hertz's earlier work with ravens.

A Compelling Fusion of Biology and Psychology. Hertz's work on the visual perception of ravens exemplifies her conceptual and methodological orientation. Hertz (1928a) had determined that birds picked an object under which the reward was hidden based on the degree of convexity of the object and not on other visual cues in its surroundings. The fact that convexity was an essential visual cue seemed to be consistent with factors in their natural behavioral repertoire, such as jumping or flying from branch to branch and their capacity for depth perception. Hertz's consideration of animals' behaviors in their natural habitats distinguished her from her mentor Köhler.

In a departure from other psychologists working in the field of animal psychology at that time, Hertz did not discount the role of instinct in helping shape behavior. In an essay originally published in French in 1937, Hertz elaborated on the relationship between instinct and intelligence in the animal kingdom. Because the essay appeared so late in her professional career, it reflects the culmination of her views regarding animal behavior in light of her research up to that point in time. She pointed out in the essay that instinct and intelligence were originally thought to be mutually exclusive, but new reports about intelligent behavior in animals had led to questions regarding the relationship between the two (Hertz, 1937a). In this respect, Hertz differed from Köhler in refusing to discount the role of instinct in animal behavior and in her insistence on the "inevitability of the concept of instinct in biology" (Jaeger, 1996, p. 240).

However, contrary to biologists who totally denounced the use of analogy in animal psychology research, Hertz (1933) claimed that although humans and bees have a totally different visual perception of their environment, statements about the perception of experimental animals can be made only by assuming certain fundamental similarities in perceptual processes. Based on this assumption, experiments can be designed to either support or negate the validity of such analogies. By determining the limitations in experimental animals we gain knowledge about the effectiveness of other organisms in comparison with ourselves. Perhaps for this reason she stated dogmatically and unequivocally that, "No sensory physiology is feasible, that would not sooner or later be comparative psychology and nothing but this" (1933, p. 12). Hertz was referring to the fact that both explicit and implicit interspecies comparisons are inevitable in sensory physiology. The defensive tone of Hertz's statement underlines the precarious position of comparative psychologists within animal research at that time and Hertz's identification of herself as a comparative psychologist.

Hertz (1933) stated the imperative for comparative psychology in her article on figural intensities and qualities in the optical perception of bees. Although a stimulus is defined or interpreted as an external event causing changes in behavior, there is the temptation to quickly infer that one particular stimulus elicits a reaction. Hertz pointed out, however, that a stimulus is actually as complex (i.e., has many different qualities) as the ensuing reaction, which is in itself actually a chain of events triggered by the stimulus. For example, the visual perception of a moving stimulus can produce different images on the retina (in other words, the same optical stimulus can trigger different reactions). Hertz claimed that biologists are limited in accounting for these differences presumably because they neglect the phenomenological aspects of animal sensory perception. To this extent, Hertz put an emphasis on discovering laws explaining the relationship between external, objective conditions and events and inner constitution. This stood in stark contrast to more reductionistic or mechanical approaches in biology or comparative psychology at that time, which explained animal behavior, for example, in terms of trial-and-error learning or as being triggered and guided by automatic responses irrespective of peripheral factors in the environment that also play a role in determining behavior.

Although the potential impact of Hertz's work was undoubtedly thwarted by an abrupt end to her experimental work, her research continued to influence—true to her conceptual orientation—work by biologists and psychologists. Some individuals were former students, such as Mercedes Gaffron, who completed her dissertation in 1934 on the stroboscopic vision of invertebrates and fish under Hertz's supervision and immigrated to the United States in 1958 to take a position in the Psychology Department at Duke University where she worked with Karl Zener. Gaffron's (1950a,b) work there focused on the phenomenological attributes and structure of spatial perception in regard to artwork. Another important scientist who was highly impressed by Hertz's early experimental work on bees was Niko Tinbergen, who saw Hertz's work and Frisch's as providing models for his own doctoral dissertation on the homing behavior of the digger wasp.

In other cases they were scholars discovering Hertz's work after her career had ended. The comparative physiologist Bernhard Hassenstein—Otto Koehler's successor as chair at the University of Freiburg and Erich von Holst's doctoral student—completed his dissertation on the physiological consequences of movement as a result of shifted images on the retina, based on Hertz's work regarding the physiology of seen movement (Hertz, 1934, 1935b). Later Hassenstein's research on this topic helped fuel the formation of a new field of research, biocybernetics. These examples show how multifaceted and enduring Hertz's contributions to science were—their impact not yet even fully evaluated.

BIBLIOGRAPHY

WORKS BY HERTZ

"Wahrnehmungspsychologische Untersuchungen am Eichelhäher I" [Perceptual studies with jays I]. *Zeitschrift für vergleichende Physiologie* 7 (1928a): 144–194.

"Wahrnehmungspsychologische Untersuchungen am Eichelhäher II" [Perceptual studies with jays II]. *Zeitschrift für vergleichende Physiologie* 7 (1928b): 617–656.

"Die Organisation des optischen Feldes bei der Biene. III." [The organization of the visual field in the bee. III]. *Zeitschrift für vergleichende Physiologie* 14 (1931): 629–674.

"Über figurale Intensitäten und Qualitäten in der optischen Wahrnehmung der Biene" [On figural intensities and qualities in the visual perception of bees]. *Biologisches Zentralblatt* 53 (1933): 10–40.

"Zur Physiologie der gesehenen Bewegung" [Concerning the physiology of seen movement]. *Biologisches Zentralblatt* 54 (1934): 250–264.

"Die Untersuchungen über den Formensinn der Honigbiene" [The experiments on the sense of shape in honeybees]. *Die Naturwissenschaften* 23 (1935a): 618–624.

"Zur Physiologie des Formen- und Bewegungssehens. II. Auflösungsvermögen des Bienenauges und optomotorische Reaktion" [Concerning the physiology of vision of shape and movement. II. Resolving power of the bee eye and the optomotor reaction]. *Zeitschrift für vergleichende Physiologie* 21 (1935b): 579–603.

"Le rapport de l'instinct et de l'intelligence dans le régne animal" [The relations between instinct and intelligence in the animal kingdom]. *Journal de Psychologie Normale et Pathologique* 34 (1937a): 324–341. (Originally translated into German "Die Beziehungen von Instinkt und Intelligenz im Tierreich" by Gisela Haus and later edited by S. Jaeger.)

With Augustus Daniel Imms. "On the Responses of the African Migratory Locust to Different Types of Background." *Proceedings of the Royal Society of London: Series B, Biological Sciences* 122 (1937b): 281–297.

"New Experiments on Color Vision in Bees." *Journal of Experimental Biology* 16 (1939): 1–8.

OTHER SOURCES

Duncker, Karl. *On Problem-Solving.* Psychological Monographs 58, no. 270. Washington, DC: American Psychological Association, 1945.

Frisch, Karl von. "Psychologie der Bienen" [Psychology of bees]. *Zeitschrift für Tierpsychologie* 1 (1937): 9–21.

Gaffron, Mercedes. *Die Radierungen Rembrandts, Originale und Drucke. Studien über Inhalt und Komposition* [The etchings of Rembrandt, originals and prints: Studies on content and composition]. Mainz, Germany: F. Kupferberg, 1950a.

———. "Right and Left in Pictures." *Art Quarterly* 13 (1950b): 312–331.

Jaeger, Siegfried. "Vom erklärbaren, doch ungeklärten Abbruch einer Karriere—Die Tierpsychologin und Sinnesphysiologin Mathilde Hertz (1891–1975)" [On the accountable, though unaccounted for abrupt end of a career—The animal psychologist and sensory physiologist Mathilde Hertz (1891–1975)]. In *Untersuchungen zur Geschichte der Psychologie und der Psychotechnik,* edited by Horst Gundlach. Munich, Germany: Profil Verlag, 1996.

Kressley-Mba, Regina, and Siegfried Jaeger. "Rediscovering a Missing Link: The Sensory Physiologist and Comparative Psychologist Mathilde Hertz (1891–1975)." *History of*

Herzberg

Psychology 6 (2003): 379–396. Includes a complete bibliography of the scientist's work.

Wertheimer, Max. "Untersuchungen zur Lehre von der Gestalt" [Studies on the theory of Gestalt]. *Psychologische Forschung* 4 (1923): 301–350.

Regina A. Kressley

HERZBERG, GERHARD (*b.* Hamburg, Germany, 25 December 1904; *d.* Ottawa, Ontario, Canada, 3 March 1999), *spectroscopy, chemistry, physics, astrophysics.*

Herzberg was a seminal and prolific spectroscopist active for over sixty years in Germany, the United States, and most importantly, in Canada. His career was dedicated to the elucidation of molecular spectra and structure, focusing on their experimental observation, correlation with theoretical calculations of molecular structure, and identification of molecular species, particularly in astronomical contexts. This lifelong pursuit led to a series of canonical texts, the Nobel Prize in Chemistry in 1971, the mentoring of a generation of junior colleagues, and a significant role in the administration and promotion of Canadian science.

Early Life and Career. Herzberg was one of two sons born to a middle-class Lutheran family. He began his education in 1911 in Hamburg, Germany, first at the Vorschule on Hegenstrasse and, from 1915, as a scholarship student at the Realgymnasium of the Johanneum. There he developed a strong interest in the sciences—particularly astronomy and atomic physics—and enjoyed languages and philosophy.

In 1924, having graduated with the Abitur (needed for university admission) and a high standing in his class, Herzberg began studies at the Technische Hochschule, Darmstadt (THD), with the help of an industrial scholarship and, two years later, with a federal scholarship, graduating at the top of his class with a Diplom Ingenieur degree in 1927. The following year he gained the Doktor Ingenieur degree under Professor Hans Rau, director of the Physics Institute.

Reading, while an undergraduate, one of Erwin Schrödinger's papers, "Quantization as an Eigenvalue Problem," Herzberg's interest in atomic structure was piqued. His own first three papers, dealing with spectra of hydrogen, were published the year of his graduation. The following year, 1928, was the beginning of a prolific scientific period: he published nine more papers. Herzberg's dissertation for his Doktor Ingenieur degree concerned the spectra of the N_2 molecule and N_2^+ ion. This early work on molecular spectroscopy and especially radicals such as H_3 were to be templates for the research over his subsequent career.

The duration of Herzberg's education had been insecure, not least because of the death of his father in 1915 and the emigration of his mother to America in 1922 during the period of rampant inflation in the postwar German economy. Even after his completion of degrees at the THD, Herzberg found that his income remained precarious and that his social class restricted his opportunities for a stable academic career. A series of short but significant posts followed.

In 1928, Herzberg accepted a one-year position as a postdoctoral fellow at the University of Göttingen, working on theoretical problems in the Institute of Theoretical Physics directed by Max Born, and on an experimental investigation of far-ultraviolet molecular absorption spectra at the Second Institute of Experimental Physics of James Franck. This coupling of theoretical and experimental experience, combined with interactions with German physicists and mathematicians actively developing atomic theory and quantum mechanics, provided Herzberg with a solid footing in this rapidly evolving field. Collaborating with Walter H. Heitler at Göttingen on an analysis of the rotational Raman spectrum of N_2, and later contributing to the theory of molecular orbitals originated by Friedrich Hund, Herzberg came to the attention of John E. Lennard-Jones of the University of Bristol, who offered him a research fellowship there.

Herzberg took up this one-year post at the H. H. Wills Physics Laboratory in Bristol, England, in September 1929, and three months later he married Luise Oettinger, another spectroscopist whom he had met at Franck's institute in Nürnberg. Both returned to Bristol and Herzberg acquired and studied (sometimes with the help of Luise) the spectra of molecules such as P_2, C_2H_2, and CH_20 and deepened his understanding of predissociation (an alteration of a molecule in an excited state without the emission or absorption of radiation).

Having completed his habilitation (a postdoctoral qualification in the German academic system that grants access to professorial posts) with a paper on the theory of molecular orbitals, Herzberg returned to Germany in November 1930 to a post as privatdozent (lecturer) at the THD, working from 1931 as an assistant to Professor Hans Rau. As privatdozent, he was able to begin a research program with postdoctoral fellows and the doctoral students he supervised. His work included the use of infrared, visible, and ultraviolet spectrographs to study the spectra of polyatomic molecules, and as at Göttingen, he met and worked with a string of prominent German physicists.

Gerhard Herzberg. SCIENCE PHOTO LIBRARY.

Nevertheless, Herzberg's career remained unsettled. His post as privatdozent did not include remuneration, so he derived his income from special fee-paying lectures, a stipend from the Emergency Association of German Science, and support from Luise's father during his first year; as assistant to Rau, he was later to gain a small stipend. The instability was further constrained by the rise of the National Socialist German Workers' (Nazi) Party. Although not of Jewish background, his surname was commonly misidentified as Jewish. After Adolf Hitler's ascension as chancellor in January 1933, anti-Semitic and anti-Communist tension rapidly rose in Darmstadt. Moreover, Herzberg's wife was Jewish, and university officials gradually implemented a policy of barring suspect academics from university research and academic livelihoods. Herzberg felt compelled in May to post a public notice of his Aryan descent, while recognizing that the sentiments of the majority of THD students effectively blocked any hope of a permanent post at Darmstadt. With the departure that year of Franck and Born and most of their Göttingen assistants with whom Herzberg had collaborated, the fleeing of his best doctoral student, Stephan Gradstein, and the news in April 1934 that, owing to his wife's ancestry, he would no longer be permitted to teach, a future in Germany no longer appeared viable. Rau's support of Herzberg's strong spectroscopic research program could provide only a temporary extension as assistant until October 1935.

Reestablishment in Canada. Some two years, then, after many of his colleagues had begun to leave Germany and its rising oppression, Herzberg began more seriously to seek posts in other countries in 1935. Given the difficult economic climate and the earlier exodus of other German academics, there were few positions available, and Herzberg found his applications rejected repeatedly. His eventual success in finding a post resulted from his collaboration some two years earlier with a Canadian physicist, John W. T. Spinks of the University of Saskatchewan in Saskatoon, Canada, who had spent a year in Rau's lab at Darmstadt. In mid-1935, Spinks was able to arrange a guest professorship at the University of Saskatchewan, supported by a two-year fellowship from the Carnegie Corporation in New York.

Although Saskatoon, located midcontinent in the Canadian prairies, had only a small Physics Department and no suitable research facilities, Herzberg initially seemed to have favored the temporary post as a step toward more appealing possibilities in America. But despite his professional concerns, along with the Great Depression and consequent hesitancy of Canadian immigration officials to accept a permanent immigrant, Herzberg's post as professor of physics was confirmed in 1936. With the prospect of permanence, the Herzbergs had a son and daughter within two years, rapidly adapting to what was an isolated but welcoming small Canadian city, developing an active social life, and adapting to the extreme climate. Over a period of ten years, Herzberg completed two much-praised books, taught numerous undergraduate and ten master's-level graduate students, and established a competent spectroscopy laboratory.

During World War II, however, opportunities for research were limited; Herzberg found himself excluded from some applied research by his national background but eventually contributed to munitions research via investigations of the spectra of explosives. At the close of the war, Herzberg traced links with colleagues and family that had remained in Germany. He did not visit his native country until 1950 and, noting then the gulf between the postwar cultures there and in his adopted home, chose not to renew some acquaintances (whom he judged to have accommodated too readily to Nazi policies) while actively supporting others with food parcels and other aid.

Herzberg

At Yerkes Observatory. Herzberg took advantage of the opportunity of lowered postwar borders to move from Saskatoon in 1945 to a considerably more isolated community in America: the Yerkes Observatory of the University of Chicago, located in the small town of Williams Bay, Wisconsin. He had been introduced to this community of astronomers during a 1938 conference there on the molecular structure of celestial objects, and had been approached about joining the observatory by its director, Otto Struve, in 1943.

The postwar Yerkes Observatory had a large and changing international community of permanent and visiting research staff and graduate students. Productive research—both observational and theoretical—on planets, stars, and interstellar matter was actively pursued, and the staff was relatively unencumbered by teaching responsibilities. At Yerkes, Herzberg supervised two graduate students and two postdoctoral fellows, all of whom went on to successful careers in spectroscopy. With his small research group, which included Luise, Herzberg recorded molecular spectra of CO_2 and CH_4, which also had been observed on Venus and Jupiter, respectively, and thereby determined the gas pressures and depths of planetary atmospheres. Study of the O_2 spectrum proved valuable for upper atmospheric physics, and his detection of the normally rare infrared spectrum of H_2 in the laboratory later allowed astronomers to confirm the existence of hydrogen in the atmospheres of the outer planets.

While Yerkes offered much greater scope for research than did the University of Saskatchewan—in the form of better facilities and equipment, an opportunity to reorient his work toward astrophysics (which had interested him from boyhood), and potential scientific interaction with more colleagues—the new post was in some respects a step downward. Herzberg was not initially offered a full professorship, and interdepartmental rivalries at Chicago and Yerkes soured the atmosphere. Against all expectations, Herzberg—unlike some of his colleagues—did not obtain a research grant from the new Office of Naval Research in 1946. Adding to the Herzbergs' ill ease was the rising rhetoric of anti-Communist sentiment, which suggested parallels with the prewar Germany they had left. In spite of the professional and social drawbacks there, the Herzbergs made close friendships in Williams Bay, notably with the Indian theoretical physicist, Subrahmanyan Chandrasekhar, and his wife.

The National Research Council. When Herzberg was offered a more senior Canadian post in 1948 as principal research officer at the National Research Council of Canada (NRCC) in Ottawa, he quickly accepted. He was to remain at the NRCC for the remaining forty-six years of his career. As he had done at Darmstadt, Saskatoon, and Williams Bay, Herzberg established a spectroscopy laboratory in Ottawa, but this time with considerably more ample funding, facilities, staffing, and opportunities for collaboration. The NRCC supported an active program of postdoctoral fellowships and, situated in Canada's capital city, it was also culturally rich and well placed for international visitors.

Herzberg's prolific research program was tempered only to a degree by increasing administrative work: from 1949, he headed the NRCC Division of Physics for six years, and then its Division of Pure Physics for a further fourteen years after the section was subdivided into applied and pure branches. A regime of long days and routine weekend work extended his research output and, by example, that of his group.

Herzberg's scientific research was characterized by a dogged concentration on molecular spectra and on the nurturing of training and collaborations with junior colleagues. Modeling his attentive and supportive supervisory style on that of his own mentor, Hans Rau, Herzberg developed some prominent students. In Saskatoon in 1941, for example, he observed the spectrum of CH^+ with his master's student, Alex E. Douglas, and confirmed its presence in interstellar space. Douglas was the first and crucial coworker hired by Herzberg to plan and work in his new Spectroscopy Laboratory in Ottawa—a collaboration that continued for the rest of Herzberg's career. Douglas was Herzberg's successor as director of the Physics Division of the NRCC.

The CH^+ spectrum was emblematic of Herzberg's new findings throughout his career. The identification of unknown species in laboratory or astronomical spectra became the trademark of his research group. In 1948, he observed the quadrupole spectrum of the molecular hydrogen; in 1956, the spectrum of CH_3, the free methyl radical; and, three years later, CH_2, the free methylene radical. This productivity continued over the next twenty years and beyond. In 1974, Herzberg and Hin Lew identified the spectrum of the H_2O^+ ion in the comet Kohoutek, confirming that ice was a significant component in its nucleus, and five years later the team observed the rare spectrum of triatomic hydrogen, H_3. In recognition of his research group's particular competence in such domains, Canada's new Herzberg Institute of Astrophysics, which included numerous laboratories and optical and radio observatories, was named after him in 1975.

Books and Recognition. Herzberg had begun his first book, *Atomspektren und Atomstruktur,* while at the University of Göttingen in response to student requests for an introductory text. Published in Germany in 1936, it was translated into English by Spinks as *Atomic Spectra and Atomic Structure* when Herzberg joined him in Saskatoon, and was published in 1937 by Prentice-Hall. Beginning as a 160-page text in German, it was expanded some twenty times in length in six volumes written over four decades. Herzberg's *Spectra of Diatomic Molecules,* the first volume of his *Molecular Spectra and Molecular Structure* series, was published in both German and English in 1939, and in 1945 the second volume, *Infrared and Raman Spectra of Polyatomic Molecules,* was published. The third volume, *Electronic Spectra and Electronic Structure of Polyatomic Molecules,* appeared in 1966, and a final volume, *The Spectra and Structures of Simple Free Radicals*—simple free radicals being chemically unstable and transient molecules in the gas phase—was published in 1971.

These lucid and popular books became standards of the discipline. Combined with some 250 papers over his career and the research of the coworkers that he led, Herzberg had a growing impact on the field of molecular spectroscopy, particularly at the NRCC. But external recognition came even sooner. As early as 1939, Herzberg had been admitted as a Fellow of the Royal Society of Canada and, in 1951, to the Royal Society of London. Acknowledged early not merely as a strong individual researcher but as a builder of research culture in Canada, he was director of the Canadian Association of Physicists in 1956–1957 and president of the Royal Society of Canada in 1966–1967. A string of honors followed up to 1970: honorary membership or fellowship of a dozen scientific societies; medals from some eleven scientific societies or organizations; and twenty-eight honorary degrees.

The defining honor was the Nobel Prize in Chemistry, which Herzberg won in 1971, just months after the death of his wife, Luise. The prize cited his "contributions to the knowledge of electronic structure and geometry of molecules, particularly free radicals," probably the most significant of which were CH_2 and CH_3, the basis of organic chemistry and later observed in interstellar and planetary spectra. The prize, however, recognized an entire lifetime of work in these areas, and his Ottawa laboratory as the center for such research, noting that it played an unusually central role in its field, similar to that of the Cavendish Laboratory in Cambridge, England, and Niels Bohr's institute in Copenhagen. Herzberg's studies of diatomic molecules such as H_2, D_2 (the deuterium, or heavy hydrogen, molecule), HD, and $H_{2>}^+$ had elucidated their dissociation energy, ionization potential, and vibrational and rotational levels in the ground state, and permitted close testing of theoretical predictions. By the time of his prize, Herzberg's NRCC group had studied over sixty such diatomic molecules, providing information about their geometrical structure, electronic structure, and vibrational frequencies in various electronic states.

Equally significant achievements were made on polyatomic molecules, frequently producing spectra of rare chemical species by means of flash photolysis (an excitation and chemical change that follows a brief and intense pulse of light) and, later, flash radiolysis (in which an electron pulse is sent through the absorption cell to produce ions). He and his group had applied such techniques to determine the structures of some thirty short-lived molecular fragments (free radicals), such as free methyl and methylene, that would be difficult to resolve in any other way, and thereby extended understandings of how chemical reactions proceed.

Herzberg relinquished his administrative duties as director of the Division of Pure Physics in 1969 at age sixty-five, but he continued work in a senior role at the NRCC as a distinguished research scientist for a further quarter-century (the last nineteen years being spent at the Herzberg Institute of Astrophysics). In that capacity, he pursued his final and ultimately incomplete quest, the identification of the diffuse bands in interstellar spectra (some one hundred broad spectral absorption lines had been observed by telescope since the 1930s, but not duplicated in laboratory conditions). A further nineteen honorary degrees and twenty-one honorary distinctions followed in the years after his Nobel Prize. Herzberg married Monika Tenthoff in 1972, the niece of his friend Alfred Schulz. He served as chancellor of Ottawa's Carleton University between 1973 and 1980. Herzberg's last mark of honor was his appointment as Member of the Queen's Privy Council for Canada in 1992. After his official retirement from the NRCC in 1994, Gerhard Herzberg's final five years were spent mainly at home, owing to ill health from a series of heart attacks and Parkinson's disease.

BIBLIOGRAPHY

A full bibliography of Gerhard's writings can be found in the microfiche format of Boris P. Stoicheff, "Gerhard Herzberg," Biographical Memoirs of the Royal Society *49 (2003): 179–186.*

WORKS BY HERZBERG

Atomic Spectra and Atomic Structure. Translated by John W. T. Spinks. New York: Prentice-Hall, 1937.

With John W. T. Spinks. *Molecular Spectra and Molecular Structure.* Vol. 1, *Spectra of Diatomic Molecules.* New York: Prentice-Hall, 1939.

Molecular Spectra and Molecular Structure. Vol. 2, *Infrared and Raman Spectra of Polyatomic Molecules.* Princeton, NJ: D. Van Nostrand, 1945.

Molecular Spectra and Molecular Structure. Vol. 3, *Electronic Spectra and Electronic Structure of Polyatomic Molecules.* New York and London: Van Nostrand Reinhold, 1966.

The Spectra and Structures of Simple Free Radicals: An Introduction to Molecular Spectroscopy. Ithaca, NY, and London: Cornell University Press, 1971.

"Spectroscopic Studies of Molecular Structure." In *Les Prix Nobel en 1971,* edited by Wilhelm Odelberg. Stockholm: Nobel Foundation, 1972.

OTHER SOURCES

Claesson, Stig. "The Nobel Prize for Chemistry." In *Les Prix Nobel en 1971,* edited by Wilhelm Odelberg. Stockholm: Nobel Foundation, 1972. The presentation speech for Herzberg's Nobel Prize.

Nobel Committee. "Gerhard Herzberg." In *Les Prix Nobel en 1971,* edited by Wilhelm Odelberg. Stockholm: Nobel Foundation, 1972.

Stoicheff, Boris P. *Gerhard Herzberg: An Illustrious Life in Science.* Ottawa: NRC Press, 2002.

———. "Gerhard Herzberg." *Biographical Memoirs of the Royal Society* 49 (2003): 179–186.

Sean F. Johnston

HESS, WALTER RUDOLF (*b.* Frauenfeld, Switzerland, 17 March 1881; *d.* Locarno, Switzerland, 12 August 1973), *autonomic nervous system, diencephalon, haemodynamics, hypothalamus, ophthalmology, physiology, thalamus.*

In 1949, Hess won the Nobel Prize in Physiology or Medicine for his work in discovering the role certain parts of the brain play in determining and coordinating the functions of internal organs. In particular, Hess was interested in the autonomic nervous system, those nerves extending from the seat of the brain through the spinal cord that control the automatic functions of the body, such as digestion, respiration, and excretion. These nerves can also trigger the activities of a group of organs responding to complex stimuli, such as stress.

An old-fashioned generalist in physiology, Hess studied a wide range of biological phenomena beyond the functional capacities of the diencephalon (interbrain), including the reflex properties of the human circulatory system, the connections between the circulatory and respiratory systems, the brain's links to psychiatric disorders, the mechanisms of sleep, the oculomotor system, how psychotropic drugs affect the brain, and the biological correlates of consciousness.

Early Intellectual Life. Walter Rudolf Hess was born in Frauenfeld, a small German-speaking town on the eastern side of Switzerland, on 17 March 1881. He began attending secondary school there at the age of twelve, graduating in 1900. His father Clemenz Hess, a tremendous influence on Hess's early love of the life sciences, taught physics in the local college. With his father's help, Hess collected and cataloged plants and butterflies from the fields around his home. These experiences fed his interest in the

Walter Hess, 1949. HULTON ARCHIVE/GETTY IMAGES.

functional traits in the biological world around him, and taught him as well the skill of careful observation and documentation. Hess also worked for his father, setting up experiments for his physics students in his classes.

Wanting to explore new traditions and customs, Hess started medical school at the University of Lausanne, in the French-speaking area of Switzerland. He then spent a semester in the capital city of Bern, and finally completed his courses and passed his exams at the University of Zürich in 1905. Hess also studied medicine at the universities in Berlin and Kiel.

It was during his time in Zürich that Hess first published scientific research. During an anatomy class, the instructor pointed out to Hess an anomaly in how the arteries are formed in the foot. Not satisfied with the reason his teacher gave for this anomaly, Hess devised his own explanation based on the relationship between hemodynamics, or blood dynamics, and the morphogenesis of the human arterial system. Hess eventually discussed this idea with Wilhelm Roux, a well-known anatomist at the

Hess

nearby University of Halle, who encouraged Hess to submit this idea as an article to *Archiv für Entwicklungsmechanik,* of which Roux was editor.

Though he would have preferred to study theoretical medicine, which would have entailed an unpaid residency at a university clinic, Hess for financial reasons chose a paid residency in the state hospital of his home canton. There he worked under Dr. Konrad Brunner, a skilled and well-known surgeon. Now being able to see the vascular system in vivo, Hess's fascination with it and hemodynamics intensified.

He became aware that contemporary science paid more attention to the pumping action of the heart than to things such as blood viscosity and resistance. To fill this lacuna, Hess decided to build an apparatus that could measure blood viscosity for clinical use. This device became known as a Hess viscosimeter and soon was found in medical laboratories everywhere. His medical thesis in 1906 outlined how the internal resistance of blood might influence the efficacy of the heart and the circulatory system and argued that scientists would do well to focus more attention on the blood's properties.

Hess wanted to specialize in a branch of medicine that would allow him to pursue basic research on the side. Ophthalmology struck him as the ideal choice. Consequently, Hess became a resident in the department of ophthalmology at the University of Zürich under Professor Otto Haab in 1906. Though Hess was less than taken with the purely morphological approach in his new department, he did learn how to operate with precision, and he did get the chance to study the ocular system dynamically by diagnosing oculomotor disturbances. Through his work with patients with oculomotor pathologies, Hess saw the need to develop a method that would enable doctors to measure eye muscle coordination objectively instead of depending on unreliable verbal reports. The apparatus he devised is still used in modified form under the name Hess screen. Hess's interest in the oculomotor system reemerged later in his life in his study of the general principles behind sensorimotor coordination.

By the time World War I started, Hess had completed his residency in ophthalmology, studied for a brief period in Paris, and had taken over the practice of an ophthalmologist in Rapperswil, a small city near Zürich. In the spring of 1908, Hess married his fiancée, Louise Sandmeier, who had worked as a doctor's aide in the outpatient department of the Zürich Eye Clinic and soon worked in her new husband's office. They had two children, Gertrud (born 1910) and Rudolf Max (born 1913), who followed his father into brain research.

Focus on Research. Hess soon found that a successful practice interfered with his research. He had set up a laboratory to study hemodynamics as they related to blood viscosity and motor coordination, but had little time to spend there. So in 1912, even though it meant a significant cut in pay, Hess accepted a position as an assistant at the Institute of Physiology in Zürich, working under Professor Justus Gaule, a former student of Carl Ludwig. However, Gaule was ill at the time, and as a result Hess was pretty much left to his own devices.

Hess did not lack for research problems to solve. Primary among them was how vascular energy is conserved in circulation. Hess developed an idealized model of optimal vascular performance and then compared it with what he found in a living circulatory system. He presented this work for his *Habilitationsschrift,* a postdoctoral thesis, which was accepted by the medical faculty in 1913, and he was then promoted to privatdozent, or university professor.

World War I interrupted Hess's research and laboratory teaching. Hess, along with everyone else fit for military service, was called to active duty in the Swiss army. As the war continued and the Allies were winning, he was able to return to laboratory research for a few months at a time. In particular, he worked as an assistant in the laboratory of Max Verworn in Bonn. A former student of Ernst Haeckel, Verworn had a lot of experience in general animal physiology, which was the sort of expertise that Hess was looking for. Hess was able to continue his research on hemodynamics with almost complete freedom, this time using dogs as an animal model.

Hess focused on understanding how bodies regulate regional blood flow, and how they adapt blood flow to the changing needs of different organs. At the time, scientists believed that the pulse in part was caused by arterial contractions. Hess investigated whether this notion of a "peripheral heart" was true by looking at a nonbranching section of the carotid artery. Unfortunately, after a year's investigation, Hess only had negative results to report. After that year, Hess had to return both to Zürich and military service, and further research had to wait until after World War I was over.

In 1916 Gaule resigned from his position because of his continuing poor health. Hess was appointed to take his place temporarily until a replacement could be found. In 1917 he was named director of the Physiological Institute at the University of Zürich, though not without considerable opposition. As a newly appointed chief, Hess traveled to a number of British laboratories to learn how the English physiologists ran their programs, including the labs run by Ernest Starling, John Newport Lang, Frederick Hopkins, Henry Dale, and Charles Sherrington. Hess also attended a number of international conferences to learn all he could about cutting-edge research in

Hess

physiology and general medicine so that he could bring this information back to his students.

Hemodynamics remained the focus subject in Hess's institute. It expanded to include the autonomic properties of individual arteries, especially the reflex properties of the arterial rings. Experiments that stimulated arterial sections with salt solutions, adrenalin, acetylcholine, and other substances continued for years. Ultimately this research culminated in his 1930 monograph *Die Regulierung des Blutkreislaufs, gleichzeitig ein Beitrag zur Physiologie des vegetativen Nervensystems* (Regulation of the circulatory system). Hess noticed the close relationship between the circulatory and the respiratory systems and treated the regulation of the respiratory system in the same manner as he did the regulation of the circulatory system. *Die Regulierung der Atmung, gleichzeitig ein Beitrag zur Physiologie des vegetativen Nervensystems* (Regulation of respiration) followed in 1931.

Investigations into the Diencephalon. Hess's shift to studying the regulatory functions of the diencephalon was actually an extension of his earlier interests. In all his earlier work, Hess was seeking to uncover the driving forces and the organizing principles of larger systems, seeking something like Walter B. Cannon's notion of homeostasis. He also sought the meaning behind bodily activities, its "teleology," a controversial stance at the time. Hess was bent on showing that nature optimized performance in context, an idea he first had in his childhood. These overarching goals led Hess to seek the site of the central operational elements, a place where somatomotor and autonomic inputs come together and are correlated with psychological functions. Building on the work of Johann Karplus, Alois Kreidl, and Philip Bard, which connected the sympathetic nervous system with the hypothalamus, Hess selected the diencephalon as the locus of his brain research, for it receives inputs from the visceral, gustatory, and olfactory systems and outputs to the pituitary gland. At the time, S. W. Ranson in Chicago did similar work and got results similar to Hess.

It became clear to Hess that before significant progress could be made, he would have to develop new experimental techniques to stimulate animals electrically while they were free to move about. In addition to working with extremely small electrodes, Hess established the minimum current required for an effect. These new techniques were extremely effective and Hess became quite well known for them.

In addition to new experimental techniques, Hess needed to be able to identify anatomical locations with great precision, which required careful microscopic study of serial histological sections. Hess's experimental team—himself, two assistants (Ewald Weissschedel and Richard Jung), and one secretary/technician (Verena Bucher)—put together three atlases of photomicrographic reproductions of the serial sections cut perpendicular to one another, one for each dimension. By cross-referencing across the atlases, Hess could localize each area of stimulation and functional response precisely.

In 1927 Hess had introduced cinematography in recording, which allowed him to compare the details of experimental results across years. He also developed a filing system, in which data were arranged by functional symptoms. One could look up a symptom and retrieve the protocol, photomicrographic locations results, and the cinematographic documents. An immense collection of functional and morphological data concerning the thalamus, the hypothalamus, and nearby regions of the telencephalon and midbrain was amassed.

Hess published the technical side of this program in 1932 as the monograph *Beiträge zur Physiologie des Hirnstammes. I. Die Methodik der lokalisierten Reizung und Ausschaltung subkortikaler Hirnabschnitte* (The methodology of localized stimulation and destruction of subcortical brain areas). Neither this book, nor the second part, published as *Beiträge zur Physiologie des Hirnstammes. II. Das Zwischenhirn und die Regulation von Kreislauf und Atmung,* in 1938, became well known, largely because of World War II. In addition, only a small number of researchers worked in this area at the time, and Hess published in German, which was unpopular. Switzerland closed itself off to outsiders during the war, and all the type for these editions was destroyed in Leipzig during the war.

Hess continued these experiments, learning little by little how to localize function in the diencephalon. Only after he had collected a huge body of data could he see the functional patterns clearly. Using fine electrodes to stimulate or destroy specific areas of the brain in cats and dogs, Hess found that the seat of autonomous function lies at the base of the brain, in the medulla oblongata and the diencephalon, particularly that part of the interbrain known as the hypothalamus. During the experimental investigations of the diencephalon, he noted both regulatory representations, which control the activity of the internal organs in a coordinated fashion, and somatomotor effects. He focused on understanding the details of these latter symptoms and, in the process, demonstrated a relationship between supporting functions, automatic correcting movements, and the differentiated maintenance of tone in the skeletal musculature. Indeed, he mapped the control centers for each function to such a degree that he could induce the physical behavior pattern of a cat confronted by a dog simply by stimulating the proper points in the animal's hypothalamus. Other studies concerned the control of parts of the forebrain (*area orbitalis*), in which Hess, together with Konrad Akert, uncovered the cortical representation of sight and the oral and pharyngeal regions.

This huge experimental effort was accomplished with only the help of Hess's two assistants, a mechanic, a secretary/technician, and one graduate student. It led to the publication of almost three hundred original articles and two monographs published in 1948 and 1949, *Die funktionelle Organisation des vegetativen Nervensystems,* and *Das Zwischenhirn: Syndrome, Lokalisationen, Funktionen,* respectively. Hess's work was well received, and in 1949, Hess was awarded the Nobel Prize in Physiology or Medicine for his "discovery of the functional organization of the diencephalon and its role in the coordination of the functions of the inner organs." (He shared this award with Egaz Moniz, who had developed the frontal lobotomy as a therapeutic method for psychiatry.)

Other Experimental Results. Regulations required that Hess retire from his professorship and directorship of the Physiological Institute in 1951. Hess had the right to continue his research in other rooms placed at his disposal in the Physiological Institute, and so he continued his work, albeit on a smaller scale.

It was not lost on Hess that the stimulation experiments on the diencephalon occasionally gave rise to various modes of behavior, which suggested the possibility of localizing psychic functions in the brain. He focused his remaining years in research on the biological underpinnings of psychological phenomena. His approach and theories were eventually discussed in Hess's final monographs: *Psychologie in Biologischer Sicht* (1962) and *The Biology of Mind* (1964).

Hess believed that sleep was an active state, not a passive one, as one might find with anesthesia. He concluded this based on careful observations of sleeping cats. He noticed that they experienced changes in their autonomic nervous system: slowed pulse, decreased blood pressure, contracted sphincter muscles, and dark adaptation of the retina. Electrical experimentation in the diencephalon revealed regions that, when stimulated, produced these active symptoms of sleep. The sleep region that Hess identified extended from the medial thalamus almost down to the caudate nucleus. His son, who introduced electroencephalography (EEG) to Switzerland, later demonstrated that Hess's induction of sleep symptoms were accompanied by EEG patterns found in normal sleep. Hess's work on the locus of sleep was controversial at the time, but his basic idea that there is a sleep-inducing projection system deep in the brain is now recognized as largely correct: the cortex receives ascending input from lower brainstem nuclei that modulates brain activity.

In addition to the defensive behaviors he could induce in cats with low-level brain stimulation, Hess also generated other sorts of complex behavioral responses. These included hunger and thirst behaviors, locomotion, cleaning behavior, as well as urination and defecation behaviors. These experiments raised the question of whether the responses were simple autonomic reflexes or required conscious motivational input. Hess was inclined toward the second possibility. It later became known that Hess was probably wrong in this assessment.

Finally, Hess, like many other neuroscientists of the time, was interested in the mind-brain problem. For Hess, psychic functions were an essential part of living organisms, especially for the higher forms of animal life. In particular, he believed that consciousness was a unique and unknown force in nature. These sorts of forces create psychic patterns, which are correlated with patterns found in the nervous system and brain. But beyond identifying correlations between conscious activity and the nervous system, Hess believed that there was little more that could be known about consciousness.

Hess's Legacy. Hess's work has helped bridge the gap that in many ways yawned between physiology and psychiatry. At the same time, Hess advanced hypotheses concerning how psychotropic drugs acted in the brain, the physiological foundations of psychosomatic phenomena, and the type-specific organization of the central nervous system.

Beyond the Nobel Prize, Hess received numerous honors during his life, including being named doctor honoris causa of the University of Bern (1934), the University of Geneva (1944), McGill University (1953), and the University of Freiburg im Breisgau (1959). He was the cofounder and chairman of the board of the Swiss High Altitude Research Laboratory in Jungfraujoch from 1931 to 1937. He was awarded the Marcel Benoist Prize in 1932. He was elected resident of the Sixteenth International Physiological Conference, which was held in Zürich in 1938. That same year, he received the Carl Ludwig Medal of the German Society of Circulation Research.

After retirement, Hess bought a vacation home in Ascona, which had a milder climate, and spent much of his time there, enjoying the weather and his fantastic gardens. Walter Hess died on 12 August 1973 in Locarno, Ascona, Switzerland.

BIBLIOGRAPHY

WORKS BY HESS

"Eine mechanisch bedingte Gesetzmässigkeit im Bau des Blutgefässystems." *Wilhelm Roux Archive für Entwicklungsmechanik der Organismen* 16 (1903): 632–641.

"Ein neuer Apparat zur Bestimmung der Viskosität des Blutes." *Berliner und Munchener Tierarztliche Wochenschrift* 54 (1907): 1590–1591.

"Eine neue Untersuchungsmethode bei Doppelbildern." *Archiv Augenheilkd* 62 (1908): 233–238.

"Das Prinzip des kleinsten Kraftverbrauches im Dienste haemodynamischer Forschung." *Archiv für Physiologie,* no. 1/2 (1914): 1–62.

"Über dieWechselbeziehungen zwischen psychischen und vegetativen Funktionen." *Schweizer Archiv fur Neurologie und Psychiatrie* 15 (1924): 260–277; 16 (1925): 36–55, 285–306.

"The Mechanism of Sleep." *American Journal of Physiology* 90 (1929): 386–387.

Die Regulierung des Blutkreislaufs, gleichzeitig ein Beitrag zur Physiologie des vegetativen Nervensystems. Leipzig, Germany: Thieme, 1930.

Die Regulierung der Atmung, gleichzeitig ein Beitrag zur Physiologie des vegetativen Nervensystems. Leipzig, Germany: Thieme, 1931.

Beiträge zur Physiologie des Hirnstammes. I. Die Methodik der lokalisierten Reizung und Ausschaltung subkortikaler Hirnabschnitte. Leipzig, Germany: Thieme, 1932.

"Der Schlaf." *Klinische Wochenschrift* 12 (1933): 129–134.

Beiträge zur Physiologie des Hirnstammes. II. Das Zwischenhirn und die Regulation von Kreislauf und Atmung. Leipzig, Germany: Thieme, 1938.

"Charakter der im Zwischenhirn ausgelösten Bewegungseffekte." *Pflugers Archiv fur die Gesamte Physiologie des Menschen und der Tiere* 244 (1941): 767–786.

"Die Motorik als Organisationsproblem." *Biologisches Zentralblatt* 61 (1941): 545–572.

"Biomotorik als Organisationsproblem." *Naturwissenschaften* 30 (1942): 441–448, 537–541.

With M. Brügger. "Das subkortikale Zentrum der affektiven Abwehr." *Helvetica Physiologica et Pharmacologica Acta* 1 (1943): 33–52.

"Hypothalamische Adynamie." *Helvetica Physiologica Acta* 2 (1944): 137–147.

Die funktionelle Organisation des vegetativen Nervensystems. Basel, Switzerland: Schwabe, 1948.

Das Zwischenhirn: Syndrome, Lokalisationen, Funktionen. Basel, Switzerland: Schwabe, 1949; 2nd ed., 1954.

"Funktion und nervöse Regulation der innern Organe." *Vierteljahrschr Naturforsch Ges Zürich* 95 (1950): 249–264.

Diencephalon. Autonomic and Extrapyramidal Functions. New York: Grune and Stratton, 1954.

Hypothalamus and Thalamus: Documentary Pictures. Hypothalamus und Thalamus: Experimental-Dokumente. With German and English text. Stuttgart, Germany: Thieme, 1956; 2nd ed., 1969.

Psychologie in Biologischer Sicht. Stuttgart, Germany: Thieme, 1962; 2nd ed., 1968.

"From Medical Practice to Theoretical Medicine. An Autobiographic Sketch." *Perspectives in Biology and Medicine* 6 (1963): 400–423.

The Biology of Mind. Chicago: University of Chicago Press, 1964.

"Walter Rudolf Hess." *Nobel Lectures, Physiology or Medicine, 1942–1962.* Amsterdam: Elsevier Publishing, 1964.

"Causality, Consciousness and Cerebral Organization." *Science* 158 (1967): 1279–1283.

OTHER SOURCES

Akert, Konrad. "Walter Rudolf Hess (1881–1973) and His Contribution to Neuroscience." *Journal of the History of the Neurosciences* 8, no. 3 (1999): 248–263.

Huber, A. "Walter Rudolf Hess as an Ophthalmologist." *Gesnerus* 39, no. 2 (1982): 287–293. In German.

Jung, Richard. "Walter R. Hess (1881–1973)." *Review of Physiology, Biochemistry, and Pharmacology* 88 (1981): 1–21. In German.

Waser, Peter. G. "Walter Rudolf Hess: His Life and Activities at the University of Zürich Medical School Centennial Celebration of His Birth: 14 March 1981." *Gesnerus* 39, no. 2 (1982): 279–286. In German.

Valerie Gray Hardcastle

HILBERT, DAVID (*b.* Königsberg, Germany [now Kaliningrad, Russia], 23 January 1862; *d.* Göttingen, Germany, 14 February 1943), *mathematics.* For the original article on Hilbert see *DSB,* vol. 6.

Scholarship on Hilbert since the 1970s has changed researchers' picture of him in three significant areas: his work on topics in physics including the general theory of relativity, his work on the foundations of geometry, and his work on logic and the foundations of mathematics. There have also been two studies on Hilbert's Paris problems and their impact on the mathematical community.

Hilbert and Physics. Hilbert's education at Königsberg and his close friendship with Hermann Minkowski both stimulated his interest in physics. Inspired by Minkowski, Hilbert studied Heinrich Hertz's ideas about the fundamental principles of physics in 1894, and this seems to have been the catalyst in Hilbert's adoption of the axiomatic approach to mathematical topics. Even at this early stage Hilbert envisaged an axiomatization of geometry leading to a similarly axiomatic treatment of at least the better understood and more traditional branches of physics, such as mechanics. Hilbert held out the hope that as other branches of physics became well understood they too could be formulated in an axiomatic fashion.

When Hilbert moved to Göttingen he began a long series of lectures on many topics. More than one hundred volumes of lecture notes are preserved in the Mathematics Library at Göttingen, and they show that Hilbert lectured on mechanics in 1898 and thereafter on many scientific topics; the last of these lectures was on mathematical models of quantum theory, in 1926–1927. The second

David Hilbert. © BETTMANN/CORBIS.

time he lectured on mechanics, in 1905, he gave an axiomatic account: mechanics is presented as a branch of continuous vector algebra. Axioms are given for a theory of statics and to formalize how space, time, and motion enter the subject. His account of time is, forgivably enough, obscure, but his demonstration of the laws of motion is better than Isaac Newton's, which had been much criticized by Ernst Mach.

Hilbert's introduction of the law of conservation of energy is characteristic of Hilbert's axiomatic approach to physics. He broke with the traditional idea that an axiom is an indemonstrable but obvious truth presented because any explanation must rest ultimately on some undefined terms. Instead, and as he had already done in his foundations of geometry, Hilbert gave as axioms statements that played a decisive role in the theory they underpinned. When presenting scientific subjects, the ones he chose were often conservation laws and variational principles.

Hilbert included thermodynamics in his course. Max Born, who attended these lectures of Hilbert's in Göttingen, suggested that the truly obscure concept of entropy would benefit from a Hilbertian axiomatic presentation; Born's friend Constantin Carathéodory, another Göttingen graduate, took him up on this and published an axiomatization of thermodynamics in 1909. Whatever its merits, Carathéodory's axiomatic presentation did not catch on with physicists, but it was a significant contribution to Hilbert's sixth problem (which called for an axiomatization of physics) all the same.

Probabilistic theories, such as the kinetic theory of gases, also attracted Hilbert's attention. Back in 1899 Hilbert had complained to Gottlob Frege that

> After a concept has been fixed completely and unequivocally, it is in my view completely illicit and illogical to add an axiom—a mistake made very frequently, especially by physicists. By setting up one new axiom after another in the course of their investigations, without confronting them with the assumptions they made earlier, and without showing that they do not contradict a fact that follows from the axioms they set up earlier, physicists often allow sheer nonsense to appear in their investigations. (Corry, 2004a, p. 114)

Hilbert objected that it was not clear when the probabilistic elements of the theory were introduced in order to get results and when they followed from the theory as it stood (or from some simpler theory). One of the successes of Hilbert's theory of integral equations in 1912 was his derivation of Ludwig Eduard Boltzmann's equations.

Hilbert's work on physics shows that his interest in axiomatics was not confined to consistency and independence but extended to considerations about the logical structure of the resulting theory. One could say that he wanted axiom systems that made as clear and as simple as possible what consequences followed from the axioms, not least because such systems were the most robust in the face of unexpected discoveries by experimenters.

Hilbert, Einstein, and the General Theory of Relativity. In 1915 Hilbert's interests swung decisively toward what Albert Einstein was doing in the general theory of relativity. From 1913 to 1915 Einstein was caught in a fundamental confusion about how general it was to be and how this generality was to be expressed. For a while he abandoned his search for a fully covariant theory and looked for a more restricted theory. He found the Göttingen mathematicians, notably Hilbert, Felix Klein, and the young Emmy Noether, a better audience than his colleagues in Berlin, but he may not have realized initially how much he had stimulated their interest. In the event, both Hilbert and Einstein submitted papers to important journals at about the same time, and this has come to be regarded as something of a race, one that Hilbert "won" by publishing first, even though no one disputes that the successful theory was Einstein's. This myth bears only a slight relationship to reality.

In 1913 Hilbert had become interested in the electromagnetic theory of matter, according to which all the fundamental aspects of physics are electromagnetic in nature. Hilbert wanted a unified field theory based on Gustav

Hilbert

Mie's ideas. In late June and early July 1915 Einstein gave talks to the Göttingen Mathematical Society on his ideas about a general theory of relativity, and he reported to Arnold Sommerfeld that the lectures had been a great success. Hilbert seems to have been impressed, but little is known of his research activity until 20 November 1915, when he reported to the Royal Göttingen Scientific Society on his work on a unified field theory. That same November, starting on the 4th, Einstein communicated a series of four weekly papers to the Prussian Academy in Berlin. He sent copies of these to Hilbert, and Hilbert, on 20 November, sent a paper on the "Fundamental Equations of Physics" to the Royal Göttingen Scientific Society. He also sent Einstein a letter on 18 November outlining his ideas. Einstein's fourth and final paper, where for the first time he presented a fully covariant theory of relativity, was given on 25 November. The idea that Hilbert and Einstein were in a race rests entirely on this chronology.

However, Hilbert seems to have revised his note between submitting it and its being printed in March 1916. It has been possible to trace and analyze these revisions, and they show that while the printed formulations of Hilbert's and Einstein's ideas are equivalent (although very different, because Hilbert preferred a variational approach and Einstein used the tensor calculus) the equivalence rests on modifications of Hilbert's approach that were introduced in the revision process. It therefore seems likely that if the question is taken to be who first came up with a fully covariant theory of relativity equivalent to the one formulated in Einstein's equations, the answer is Einstein. To be sure, Einstein's own theory was evolving in 1915, and he did not write down precisely the Einstein equations, but his theory is trivially equivalent. Hilbert's formulation of the energy concept was, however, significantly revised. In the form sent to the Göttingen journal on 21 November it was not equivalent to the final theory, and it became so only on revision, after Hilbert was aware of Einstein's latest ideas.

Hilbert might, perhaps, have been more open about this, and for a time Einstein felt resentful toward him, although he later forgave him. But it is not a mathematician's job to publish work he believes to be wrong; correcting papers at proof stage is not unheard of. There is no element of fraud involved; rather this represents a high-powered attempt to incorporate many ideas into a framework all of Hilbert's own, a characteristic way of working in Göttingen called nostrification by the people there (a made-up word meaning "making it ours"). And it should also be said that fundamental differences remained, notably over the significance of Mie's theory, to which Hilbert was attracted but which Einstein, rightly, found unconvincing. Moreover, Hilbert thought he was presenting general equations governing the structure of matter, whereas gravitation was always a more central issue for Einstein.

Hilbert's Paris Problems. The first International Congress of Mathematicians was held in Zürich in 1897, the second in Paris in 1900. Hilbert, spurred on by his friend Minkowski, took the opportunity to cash in on the excitement generated by the arrival of the new century to propose his list of problems, and while there is no evidence that they immediately captivated their audience, they slowly and steadily came to occupy a major place in the aspirations of many mathematicians. "To solve a Hilbert Problem," said Hermann Weyl, "is to join the Honors class of mathematicians." To some extent this is because Hilbert became the most famous mathematician of his generation, and his university, Göttingen, became the leading university for mathematics before World War I and recovered quickly afterward to regain its lead position, which it held until the Nazi time. But many of the problems were also well chosen, and they were all extremely well presented.

Hilbert opened his address by indicating two fundamental reasons for doing mathematics. One, exemplified by Fermat's last theorem, was the source of many profound ideas in pure mathematics, especially algebra and number theory. The other, exemplified by the brachistochrone problem and the three body problem, was the challenging problems posed to us by nature. Hilbert implied that these were two halves of the same impulse to understand, even though one is the product of the free invention of our minds and the other is forced upon us. Good problems, he suggested, make deep and often unexpected connections with other parts of mathematics and may indeed require the discovery of such connections for their solution.

He then raised the stakes by insisting that rigor in mathematics was the friend, and not the enemy, of simplicity, and that it was the deepest belief of every mathematician that every problem has a solution, although one must allow a rigorous demonstration that a given problem cannot be solved by certain means. Hilbert undoubtedly had Galois theory in mind at this point. The result was that the problems traveled with built-in reasons for their importance. No one who solved a problem need do any work to explain why he or she had bothered.

The first two problems concern set theory and its connection to arithmetic. Hilbert's book *Grundlagen der geometrie* (*The Foundations of Geometry*, 1899) had established the consistency of geometry by reducing it to arithmetic, the consistency of which was assumed. Hilbert held out the possibility that this could be proved, by a simultaneous sophistication of both mathematics and logic. This was not to be, but it was an insight that generated a generation's worth of work, and the work of Kurt Gödel and others founded a new subject, mathematical logic.

The problems on number theory, chiefly but not exclusively algebraic, flow more directly from the work inspired by Fermat's last theorem. Whether solved or not roughly one hundred years later, they all generated a number of deep results, opened interconnections with other branches of mathematics, and generated a surge in mathematical theory-building. This is less true of the next batch of problems, and that is significant, for they are also less well regarded. Hilbert had a knack of picking problems that contributed to and vindicated the development of mathematical theories. There is always a spread of problems in mathematics; what stops them being merely puzzles is their implications. Likewise there are many theories in mathematics, but what makes some more important is the problems they help to solve. Hilbert, as his opening address made clear, got the balance right.

The last five problems relate to mathematical analysis and are the only ones apart from those on foundations that occupied Hilbert himself in later years. These are generally on topics forced upon humans by nature, and three (19, 20, and 23) remain central to any mathematical study of physics and indeed to other more narrowly mathematical questions as well.

Proof Theory, Metamathematics. Since the 1980s renewed attention has been paid to Hilbert's ideas on the foundations of mathematics by philosophers of mathematics. They have not been persuaded that Hans Freudenthal's opinion, as expressed in his *DSB* article, that Hilbert's ideas "look poor and shallow" was sound, or rather, one might say that they find questions to discuss that are not so closely related to the mathematical logic that grew out of the work of Albert Skolem, Gödel, and others and which does indeed considerably surpass Hilbert's. These philosophers recall that Hilbert's ultimate aim was to give reliable foundations for all mathematics, and to this end he and his assistants Paul Bernays and Wilhelm Ackermann offered a finitary formulation of mathematics. They then note that although Gödel, in the paper subsequently taken to have destroyed such hopes, explicitly held the door open for other attempts, none has been successful. Finally, they have concluded that this forces a reconsideration of what Hilbert might actually have meant in his formulation of finitary mathematics.

Gödel's argument shows that any theory *T* that contains enough arithmetic to generate a coding of mathematical statements can express a true statement for which there is no proof. This is the statement (in more formal terms than these) that there is no proof that 0 = 1. Now, if *T* were a provably finitary consistent theory, the proof of its consistency would surely be formalizable and expressible in *T*, but this proof would amount to a proof in *T* that there is no proof that 0 = 1, which is impossible by Gödel's theorem. The difficulty here is that Hilbert gave no precise formulation of a finitary theory. Therefore it is not clear that every finitary theory must be formalizable in theories such as *T*. This was indeed Bernays's reaction to Gödel's results, and it is what Gödel was holding the door open for: a finitary argument not formalizable in the given theory *T*.

A crucial feature of Hilbert's presentation of mathematics was the introduction of what he called ideal elements, by analogy with the ideal elements introduced into arithmetic and geometry by the mathematicians of his time and before. In his case, the ideal elements carried the transfinite part of mathematics. They are adjoined to the elementary theory by axioms (just as complex numbers can be) and are accorded finitary status because every proof in which they appear must be finite. The elementary theory is the decidable part in which all formulas are free of variables and which Hilbert took to be the directly verifiable part of mathematics. The status of these ideal elements is controversial. Some see them as intentionally meaningless, part of a way of rewriting mathematics in an entirely syntactic but finitely checkable way. Others make an analogy with unobservable entities in physics: ideal transfinite propositions have no intuitive meaning but make good sense, just as one does not deal in physics only with objects one can see but also with electrons, quarks, and so forth.

In the absence of a revitalized theory of finitary mathematics, people have turned to following Hilbert's lead but in the area of relative results. This interprets Hilbert's theory of ideal elements as an attempt to show that ideal mathematics would not prove false any proposition known to hold in elementary mathematics. This is expressed in the phrases "ideal mathematics is *conservative over* elementary mathematics" and "ideal mathematics *reduces to* elementary mathematics." It gives modest grounds for accepting ideal mathematics as a legitimate extension of elementary mathematics. In this spirit, Solomon Feferman has shown that a considerable amount of apparently ideal mathematics is reducible to elementary mathematics, including much of what is necessary for modern physics. Others have quarried out other domains of mathematics that have been shown to be reducible to elementary mathematics.

Hilbert has also come to be seen as the leader of a movement that can be called mathematical modernism, one that sees the profound transformations of mathematics in the decades on either side of 1900 as forming a cultural shift akin to the contemporary transformations in the cultural spheres (art, poetry, music, and so on). The historian who did most to present this view was Herbert Mehrtens in his *Moderne Sprache, Mathematik* (1990), who sees the largely German aspects of this story as part of a transition to modernity; for another view see Jeremy Gray's essay "Modern Mathematics as a Cultural Phenomenon," 2006. In this regard Hilbert's *Grundlagen der geometrie* is seen as exemplary of the promotion of abstract, formal mathematics, in which intuition and applicability are played down in favor of rigor and a view of mathematics as a subject done for its own sake. Hilbert's earlier work using non-constructive existence proofs in algebra, his later interests in logic, his confrontation with Luitzen Egbertus Jan Brouwer over intuitionism, his central presence in Göttingen all contribute to this picture of Hilbert as the person who created the modern world of mathematics.

SUPPLEMENTARY BIBLIOGRAPHY

WORKS BY HILBERT

Der Briefwechsel David Hilbert-Felix Klein (1886–1918). Edited by Günther Frei. Göttingen, Germany: Vandenhoeck and Ruprecht, 1985.

Theory of Algebraic Invariants. Translated by Reinhard C. Laubenbacher; edited with an introduction by Bernd Sturmfels. Cambridge, U.K.: Cambridge University Press, 1993.

The Theory of Algebraic Number Fields. A translation of *Theorie der algebraischen Zahlkorper* by Iain T. Adamson; with an introduction from Franz Lemmermeyer and Norbert Schappacher. London: Springer, 1998.

David Hilbert's Lectures on the Foundations of Mathematics and Physics, 1891–1933. Vol. 1, *David Hilbert's Lectures on the Foundations of Geometry, 1891–1902,* edited by Michael Hallett and Ulrich Majer (2004); vol. 2, *David Hilbert's Lectures on the Foundations of Arithmetic and Logic, 1894–1917,* edited by William Ewald, Michael Hallett, Wilfried Sieg, and Ulrich Majer (forthcoming); vol. 3, *David Hilbert's Lectures on the Foundations of Arithmetic and Logic, 1917–1933,* edited by William Ewald, Wilfried Sieg, and Ulrich Majer (forthcoming); vol. 4, *David Hilbert's Lectures on the Foundations of Physics, 1898–1914: Classical, Relativistic, and Statistical Mechanics,* edited by Ulrich Majer, Tilman Sauer, and Klaus Bärwinkel (forthcoming); vol. 5, *David Hilbert's Lectures on the Foundations of Physics, 1915–1927: Relativity, Quantum Theory, and Epistemology,* edited by Ulrich Majer, Tilman Sauer, and Heinz-Jürgen Schmidt (forthcoming); vol. 6, *David Hilbert's Notebooks and General Foundational Lectures,* edited by William Ewald, Michael Hallett, Wilfried Sieg, and Ulrich Majer (forthcoming). Berlin and New York: Springer.

OTHER SOURCES

Corry, Leo. *David Hilbert and the Axiomatization of Physics (1898–1918): From* Grundlagen der Geometrie *to* Grundlagen der Physik. Dordrecht, Netherlands and London: Kluwer Academic, 2004a.

———. *Modern Algebra and the Rise of Mathematical Structures.* 2nd rev. ed. Basel, Switzerland, and Boston: Birkhäuser, 2004b.

Fisher, Charles S. "The Death of Invariant Theory: A Study in the Sociology of Knowledge." *Archive for History of Exact Sciences* 3 (1967): 137–159.

Gray, Jeremy J. *The Hilbert Challenge.* Oxford: Oxford University Press, 2000.

Mehrtens, Herbert. *Moderne Sprache, Mathematik: eine Geschichte des Streits um die Grundlagen der Disziplin und des Subjekts formaler System.* Frankfurt, Germany: Suhrkamp, 1990.

Rüdenberg, Lily, and Hans Zassenhaus, eds. *Hermann Minkowski—Briefe an David Hilbert.* Berlin and New York: Springer, 1973.

Sauer, Tilman. "Einstein Equations and Hilbert Action." *Archive for History of Exact Sciences* 59, no. 6 (2005): 577590.

Thiele, Rüdiger. "Über die Variationsrechnung in Hilberts Werken zur Analysis." *NTM International Journal of History and Ethics of Natural Sciences, Technology and Medicine* 5 (1997): 23–42.

Toepell, Michael-Markus. *Über die Entstehung von David Hilberts. Grundlagen der Geometrie.* Studien zur Wissenschafts-, Sozial-, und Bildungsgeschichte der Mathematik, 2. Göttingen, Germany: Vandenhoeck and Ruprecht, 1986.

Yandell, Benjamin H. *The Honors Class: Hilbert's Problems and Their Solvers.* Natick, MA: A.K. Peters, 2001.

Zach, Richard. "Hilbert's Program." In *The Stanford Encyclopedia of Philosophy,* edited by Edward N. Zalta. 2003. Available from http://plato.stanford.edu/archives/.

Jeremy Gray

HILGARD, ERNEST ROPIEQUET

(*b.* Belleville, Illinois, 25 July 1904, *d.* Palo Alto, California, 22 October 2001), *psychology, education, learning, hypnosis, consciousness.*

Hilgard, commonly known as Jack, enjoyed one of the longest and most productive careers in twentieth-century American psychology. As a scholar who synthesized and advanced important areas of research, a teacher of leading scientists and writer of influential textbooks, an administrator who played key roles in the development of academic and professional organizations, and a strong advocate for the application of psychological knowledge in the improvement of human life, Hilgard left a lasting mark upon the scientific, educational, professional, and social spheres in which he lived and worked. His most notable scientific contributions were his integration of cognitive and motivational factors in the analysis of conditioning and learning, his development of techniques to measure susceptibility to and the effects of hypnosis, and his theoretical speculations about different levels of consciousness.

Overview of Hilgard's Life and Work. Hilgard's father, George Engelmann Hilgard (1876–1918), a physician, was killed in France during World WarI. His mother, Laura Sophie Ropiequet Hilgard (1876–1964), lived a long life, as he himself did. Hilgard considered a career in medicine before receiving a bachelor's degree in chemical engineering from the University of Illinois at Urbana-Champaign in 1924. He then spent a year working at the national headquarters of the Young Men's Christian Association (YMCA) and another year studying social ethics at Yale Divinity School before turning to psychology and earning his PhD in that field at Yale in 1930. He taught and pursued research at Yale from 1929 to 1933, then moved to Stanford University, where he remained for the rest of his career, except during occasional absences, most notably during World War II, when he spent from 1942 to 1944 in the Offices of War Information and Civil Requirements and in the Bureau of Overseas Intelligence in Washington, D.C.. His wartime experiences confirmed his commitment to the development of a scientific psychology that would serve the public good. His presidential address before the American Psychological Association (APA) in 1949, on "Human Motives and the Concept of the Self," was emblematic of this commitment and of his public role in strengthening the connection between scientific and applied psychology—a role that also included major contributions to the rapprochement of scientists and practitioners in the reorganization of APA in the mid-1940s.

Hilgard was promoted to full professor of both psychology and education at Stanford University in 1938. When he returned to Stanford from Washington, D.C., in 1944, he served successively as head of the Department of Psychology and dean of the Graduate Division, contributing significantly to the development of the university. In this period he turned down an offer from Harvard for the position that eventually went to B. F. Skinner, as he had turned down earlier overtures from other leading universities. Among the factors in his consideration of other positions were the opportunities that would be available for his wife, Josephine R. Hilgard, who had earned a PhD in psychology at Yale and an MD from Stanford, received psychoanalytic training as a psychiatrist, and wanted to combine research and clinical practice. They shared many scientific interests and occasional collaboration over the years in the areas of personality, psychodynamic theory, and the use of hypnosis in the relief of pain.

When Hilgard returned to his faculty position in 1951, he shifted the focus of his teaching and research from prior work on learning and conditioning to the scientific investigation of psychodynamic theory, the nature of hypnosis, and the factors and potential benefits of hypnotic susceptibility. Having concluded that hypnosis, though controversial, would provide a means of understanding unconscious processes, he persuaded the Ford Foundation to support his proposed line of research, used a fellowship year at the new Center for Advanced Study in the Behavioral Sciences (which had been located, with his assistance, on Stanford University property) to review the vast and varied literature on this topic, and then, in 1957, opened the Stanford Laboratory of Hypnosis Research. The research produced in this laboratory over the next two decades (1957–1979) brought scientific order and respectability to its subject, just as Hilgard's earlier work and writing had helped to organize the nascent field of conditioning and learning. Hilgard remained active as a scientific researcher, and his laboratory remained a highly visible and influential site for training and research for ten years after his formal retirement in 1969. Many other researchers on hypnosis spent time working under his direction at Stanford.

Blessed with remarkable health and vigor until the final years of his long life, Hilgard continued to write and speak through the 1990s, serving as a living link to psychology's past. Having known many of the early giants in the field, having created some of its major conceptual distinctions, having helped to establish many of the institutional structures that supported its advancement, and having guided that advancement through his own research, teaching, and perceptive judgments of actual and potential developments within the field, Hilgard deserved the frequent plaudits he received for a lifetime of achievements and contributions.

Hilgard's Scientific Contributions. Hilgard's research in the 1930s and early 1940s focused primarily on conditioning. In particular, it focused on experimental studies of eyelid conditioning in dogs, monkeys, and humans. However, Hilgard also explored human learning, especially motor skills and verbal learning, as well as levels of aspiration. Although it may not have been apparent at the time, several themes emerged from these seemingly disparate projects—themes that ran somewhat against the grain of contemporary research and that became characteristic of his later, more innovative contributions to the discipline: His research increasingly demonstrated an interest in voluntary as well as involuntary factors in human learning, and it increasingly revealed an interest in cognition as well as motivation. Specifically, Hilgard showed that conditioned behavior, previously assumed to be unconscious and automatic, could be brought under the control of conscious deliberation. Subjective ideas, in other words, could intervene between objective stimuli and responses. In addition to this incipient focus on cognitive factors in human learning—long before psychology's cognitive revolution in the 1960s—Hilgard's study "The Effects of Personal Heterosuggestion and Two Forms of Autosuggestion upon Postural Movement" (with Joel V. Berreman in 1936) foreshadowed his later research on hypnosis.

It is impossible to separate Hilgard's influence as an experimentalist from his influence as a writer of historically significant textbooks. The first of his major textbooks, *Conditioning and Learning* (coauthored by Donald G. Marquis in 1940 and reissued in revised form by Gregory A. Kimble in 1961), was quickly recognized as a classic. Like his later texts, it pulled together an active but disorganized area of research, established a more common vocabulary, defined a coherent set of issues, and thus gave clearer focus and direction to the field. (Among the distinctions coined in this work was the differentiation between classical conditioning, as represented by Ivan Pavlov, and instrumental conditioning, as advocated by E. L. Thorndike and B. F. Skinner.)

In 1948, Hilgard published *Theories of Learning*, which became and remained a standard reference for psychologists and their students well beyond the publication of its fifth and final edition in 1981. (Gordon H. Bower coauthored the third through fifth editions.) Although this work brought together the research of many others, it conveyed a distinctly Hilgardian spirit of cooperation and synthesis that was not always apparent in the contentious controversies of the time. Noting that "we have not yet reached agreement upon the most appropriate concepts to use in stating our problems and in interpreting our data," Hilgard "approached the task with the desire to be friendly to each of the positions represented, on the assumption that each of them has been proposed by an intelligent and sincere person or group of persons, and that there must be something which each of them can teach us." This might sound like a recipe for uncritical eclecticism, but in fact Hilgard did not shy away from "pointing out such weaknesses as I have detected" after giving each alternative position "a fair hearing" (p. v). His extraordinary ability to extract and relate relevant insights and conclusions, without overlooking relative shortcomings, helped to orient, direct, and advance this important field during a crucial period in the discipline's development. Even in the first edition, Hilgard's openness to cognitive factors and his encouragement of practical applications were readily apparent. "A principle once discovered in a better controlled situation can be validated in a less well-controlled one," he argued (p. 358). While admitting that many theoretical disagreements still awaited resolution, he underscored that "many plain facts about learning, important in practice, have nothing of controversy in them" (p. 359). This emphasis on practical outcomes was typical of Hilgard, who never forgot the real-world needs highlighted by the Depression and World War II.

Accordingly, after spending the first half of the 1940s conducting war-related survey research in Washington, D.C., Hilgard returned to Stanford and turned his teaching and research toward understanding human motivation and dynamics. One of the early manifestations of this turn was a carefully crafted overview of "Experimental Approaches to Psychoanalysis," which appeared in *Psychoanalysis as Science* (edited by E. Pumpian-Mindlin in 1952, based on a lecture series at California Institute of Technology in 1950). With his typical open-minded but critical approach, Hilgard discussed research findings relevant to both psychodynamics and psychotherapy, concluding that "the topics of psychodynamics ... lie at the very heart of psychological subject matter" (p. 24) and that "the obligation is clearly upon experimental, physiological, and clinical psychologists ... to conduct investigations either independently or in collaboration with psychoanalysts" (p. 45). (This was written in a period of considerable controversy and criticism of psychoanalysis.) Hilgard's own subsequent research on hypnosis represented his personal response to this deeply felt obligation.

Hilgard's first publication on hypnosis was "Individual Differences in Susceptibility to Hypnosis," published in 1958 with his important early collaborator's André M. Weitzenhoffer and Philip B. Gough. In the following year, he and Weitzenhoffer published the methodological basis of their research, the *Stanford Hypnotic Susceptibility Scale*. In various forms and adaptations, this performance-based test placed experimental research on hypnosis on a firm basis and made hypnotizability a measurable personality trait. In 1965, after publishing many individual studies, Hilgard summarized what had been learned about hypnosis and hypnotic subjects in *Hypnotic Susceptibility*, a landmark work that included a chapter, "Personality and Hypnotizability: Inferences from Case Studies," by his wife, Josie. This book concluded with a chapter that presented a developmental-interactive theory of hypnotic susceptibility and clarified problems that still had to be addressed.

Over the next decade and a half, many additional studies were conducted by members of Hilgard's lab, including a twin study, a family study, brain-lateralization studies, and studies of the analgesic, or pain-reducing, possibilities of hypnosis. With Josie, in 1975, Hilgard published a groundbreaking monograph, *Hypnosis in the Relief of Pain*, which dealt with the control of pain through hypnotic means in both experimental and clinical conditions. (Josie followed up on this research with *Hypnotherapy of Pain in Children with Cancer*, coauthored by Samuel LeBaron, in 1984. She had published *Personality and Hypnosis: A Study of Imaginative Involvement* in 1970.)

In 1977, Hilgard published his major theoretical work, *Divided Consciousness: Multiple Controls in Human Thought and Action*, which he reissued in an expanded edition in 1986. Because he had closed his lab in 1979, most of the information incorporated into the second edition came from research conducted in other laboratories, much of which would have been impossible without his foregoing contributions. Although the cognitive revolution in psychology was already well under way by 1977, the study of consciousness was not yet a typical part of this revolution. (Information-processing models, based on computer analogs and mathematical formulations, worked without reference to consciousness and unconsciousness.) Pulling together a vast range of phenomena and research not yet integrated into "normal psychology," Hilgard discussed possession states, fugues, multiple personalities, hypnotic age regression, amnesia, dreams, hallucinations, imagination, automatic writing, and divided attention, in addition to hypnotic phenomena. In drawing out commonalities across these disparate mental and behavioral states, he proposed the concept of "the hidden observer" and offered his own "neodissociation interpretation of divided consciousness." This interpretation represented an updated version of Pierre Janet's dissociation theory, which had gone out of favor in the early twentieth century "without effective criticism," Hilgard said, as behaviorism grew on the one hand and psychoanalysis on the other (p. 12). By showing how many psychological phenomena, both normal or abnormal, reflect divided consciousness, in which active and passive, conscious and unconscious, forms of functioning go on at the same time, Hilgard prompted—and helped to set the agenda for—the scientific study of states of consciousness in the 1980s and beyond. (In an important review of "Consciousness in Contemporary Psychology," published in 1980, Hilgard laid out the historical as well as empirical and conceptual context for the reentry of consciousness into psychology.) A clear path can be drawn from Hilgard's proposal of central control processes, which he characterized as executive and monitoring functions, to later theories of conscious, unconscious, and nonconscious cognitive and behavioral activity. His prediction of the increasing relevance of consciousness within the neurosciences, like so many of his predictions, has been amply confirmed.

Associated with his interest in hypnosis and psychodynamics as well as consciousness and unconsciousness was a concern about motivation. In fact, Hilgard himself, in a 1974 autobiographical chapter, said that the "core" running through the "diversity of my research" was "a concern for aspects of human motivation bearing on planning and choice" (pp. 151–152). This central concern was reflected in various ways throughout his career, including his teaching of a graduate course on human motivation in the years following World War II, but it was particularly apparent in his chapter, "Motivation in Learning Theory," which appeared in volume 5 of the monumental *Psychology: A Study of a Science* (edited by Sigmund Koch) in 1963; his chapter, "The Teacher's Role in the Motivation of the Learner" (coauthored by Pauline S. Sears), which appeared in *Theories of Learning and Instruction* (edited by Hilgard) in 1964; and his chapter, "The Motivational Relevance of Hypnosis" in *The Nebraska Symposium on Motivation 1964.* These three chapters summarized the motivational significance of his two major areas of his research, with a special and very sincere nod toward the applied area represented by his secondary appointment as a professor of education at Stanford. Hilgard began the last of these three works with a statement that suggests at least part of his own motivation as a research psychologist: "There is no more important problem for psychology than that of human motivation. The perilous age in which we live would be less hazardous if men understood each other better, and were better able to predict and to avoid the circumstances under which they engage in dangerous and self-destroying actions" (p. 1). Far from concluding that motivation is something that can or should be manipulated by an external agent through behavioral technology, indoctrination, or hypnotic suggestion, Hilgard encouraged research on intrinsic motivation—the kind of self-motivation that had prompted his own career and research.

Hilgard's Other Professional Contributions. Hilgard took his responsibilities as a teacher of undergraduates as well as graduate students very seriously, and he had a significant impact on the field through those whom he influenced in the classroom and laboratory. As already mentioned, his textbooks—an outgrowth of his teaching—were much more than mere expositions of what was known and taken for granted in the field. They elucidated sometimes obscure matters and helped to integrate or at least to bring some coherence to the wide range of topics, methods, and theories in psychology. Even more than his highly regarded and much used *Conditioning and Learning* and *Theories of Learning*, his *Introduction to Psychology*, first published in 1953, was for decades the virtual "Bible" of the discipline. (Revised twelve times up to 2000, the thirteenth edition of *Hilgard's Introduction to Psychology* was published by Rita Atkinson, Richard Atkinson, Edward Smith, Daryl Bem, and Susan Nolen-Hoeksema.) Millions of students, many of whom became active psychologists, were introduced to the discipline through this well-organized, high-level text. (A related educational effort, aimed at practicing scientists as well as advanced students, was his long-term participation as an active contributor, board member, and president of Annual Reviews, the publisher of the *Annual Review of Psychology* as well as annual reviews of a variety of other major disciplines.)

Hilgard's interest in teaching and in student development was apparent from the time of his 1928 publication (with R. H. Edwards) of *Student Counseling*, which explored how vocational dilemmas are resolved, and it

Hilgard

extended through his service on the U.S. Education Commission to Japan in 1946, various publications on human learning and education, his organization and summary of research reports on *Theories of Learning and Instruction* (1964) for the National Society for the Study of Education, and his frequent talks to professional and community groups. The same impulse toward clarifying the past achievements, current situation, and future prospects of psychology spurred his late-career research into the history of psychology. More than a merely avocational interest, his commitment to historical study and understanding spurred his contributions to the establishment of an APA division devoted to the history of psychology as well as the founding and development of the Archives of the History of American Psychology (at the University of Akron), later the major depository of historical records and artifacts pertaining to that history. It also led to a series of publications, including his magisterial history of twentieth-century American psychology, which appeared in 1987 as *Psychology in America: A Historical Survey.* Although the length and comprehensiveness of this work militated against its widespread adoption as a textbook, it was immediately recognized as a valuable addition to the reference shelves of teachers and historians of psychology.

As an academic administrator, both department head and graduate dean, Hilgard played a leading role in bringing Stanford University and its Psychology Department to national prominence in the postwar years. An active participant in professional affairs, he was instrumental in the revision of the bylaws and organization of the APA during World War II, a revision that kept scientists and practitioners under the same umbrella, thus enhancing the possibility of mutually beneficial exchange. He also served among small groups of leading psychologists and scientists who made long-term plans regarding mental health research, the cognitive turn in psychology, and the future of psychology among the other natural and social sciences. The first was sponsored especially by the Ford Foundation; the last by the National Academy of Sciences, of which he was a member.

Committed to public and community service, Hilgard devoted a good deal of time to different cooperative organizations, served on various policy advisory boards, and donated a significant amount of land for environmental protection at the end of his life. In the aftermath of World War II, he helped to organize and managed the Stanford Workshop on Community Leadership, which led to the publication of *Community Planning for Peacetime Living* (which he edited with Louis Wirth and I. James Quillen) in 1946. Though always honorable, forthright, and temperate, his liberal political views led to the most unpleasant experience of his professional life, when he concluded that he had to step down from his graduate deanship because his wartime membership in the League Against War and Fascism and other liberal activities resulted in a cancellation of clearance to serve on certain governmental boards.

For his many contributions to psychology, Hilgard received a wide assortment of honors and awards, including election to the presidencies of many professional organizations (e.g., the American Psychological Association in 1949), the APA's Distinguished Scientific Contribution Award (1969), the American Psychological Foundation's Gold Medal Award (1978), and the APA's Award for Outstanding Lifetime Achievement in Psychology (1994).

BIBLIOGRAPHY

The Ernest R. Hilgard Papers at the Archives of the History of American Psychology, University of Akron, together with other collections at AHAP, provide exceptionally useful information (including an unpublished autobiography) about the context, course, and contributions of Hilgard's career. A listing of Hilgard's scientific publications up to 1967 may be found in the first reference cited under Other Sources, below.

WORKS BY HILGARD

With Donald G. Marquis. *Conditioning and Learning.* New York: Appleton-Century-Crofts, 1940.

Theories of Learning. New York: Appleton-Century-Crofts, 1948.

"Human Motives and the Concept of the Self." *American Psychologist* 4 (September 1949): 374–382.

"Experimental Approaches to Psychoanalysis." In *Psychoanalysis as Science,* edited by Eugene Pumpian-Mindlin. Stanford, CA: Stanford University Press, 1952.

Introduction to Psychology. New York: Harcourt Brace Jovanovich, 1953.

With André M. Weitzenhoffer. *Stanford Hypnotic Susceptibility Scale.* Palo Alto, CA: Consulting Psychologists Press, 1959.

"Motivation in Learning Theory." In *Psychology: A Study of a Science,* vol. 5, edited by Sigmund Koch. New York: McGraw-Hill, 1963.

"The Motivational Relevance of Hypnosis." In *Nebraska Symposium on Motivation 1964,* edited by David Levine. Lincoln: University of Nebraska, 1964.

Theories of Learning and Instruction, edited by Ernest R. Hilgard. Sixty-Third Yearbook of the National Society for the Study of Education. Chicago: University of Chicago Press, 1964. Hilgard authored chapters 3, 8 (with Pauline S. Sears), 17, and the Postscript.

Hypnotic Susceptibility. New York: Harcourt Brace Jovanovich, 1965.

"Ernest Ropiequet Hilgard." In *A History of Psychology in Autobiography,* vol. 7, edited by Gardner Lindzey. Englewood Cliffs, NJ: Prentice-Hall, 1974.

With Josephine R. Hilgard. *Hypnosis in the Relief of Pain.* Los Altos, CA:William Kaufmann, 1975.

Divided Consciousness: Multiple Controls in Human Thought and Action. New York: John Wiley, 1977.

"Consciousness in Contemporary Psychology." *Annual Review of Psychology* 31 (1980): 1–26.

Psychology in America: A Historical Survey. San Diego, CA: Harcourt Brace Jovanovich, 1987.

With James H. Capshew. "The Power of Service: World War II and Professional Reform in the American Psychology Association." In *The American Psychological Association: A Historical Perspective*, edited by Rand B. Evans, Virginia Staudt Sexton, and Thomas C. Cadwallader, pp. 149–175. Washington, DC: American Psychological Association, 1992.

OTHER SOURCES

American Psychological Association Committee on Scientific Awards. "Distinguished Scientific Contribution Award: Ernest Ropiequet Hilgard." *American Psychologist* 22 (December 1967): 1130–1135. Includes a citation, brief biography, and summary listing of Hilgard's scientific publications up to 1967.

American Psychological Foundation. "Gold Medal Award for 1978: Ernest Ropiequet Hilgard." *American Psychologist* 34 (January 1979): 80–85. Includes a citation and biographical sketch.

Bower, Gordon. "Ernest R. Hilgard (1904–2001)." *American Psychologist* (April 2002): 283–285. Provides a general overview, including a list of Hilgard's various professional honors and awards.

Capshew, James H. *Psychologists on the March: Science, Practice, and Professional Identity in America, 1929–1969.* Cambridge, U.K.: Cambridge University Press, 1999. Refers frequently to Hilgard and provides an historical context for understanding his work and career.

Kihlstrom, John F. "In Memoriam: Ernest Ropiequet Hilgard, 1904–2001." *International Journal of Clinical and Experimental Hypnosis* 50 (April 2002): 95–113. Focuses particularly on Hilgard's contributions to the study of hypnosis.

Leary, David E. "Ernest R. Hilgard (1904–2001)." *History of Psychology* 5 (August 2002): 310–314. Focuses particularly on Hilgard's contributions to the history of psychology.

David E. Leary

HILL, DOROTHY (*b.* Brisbane, Queensland, Australia, 10 September 1907; *d.* Brisbane, 23 April 1997), *geology, invertebrate paleontology, reef organisms, Paleozoic corals, and archaeocyathids.*

Throughout most of the twentieth century there were few world-class women paleontologists; outstanding is Dorothy Hill, an Australian who made her mark on the international stage as a geologist, primarily an invertebrate paleontologist contributing especially to the economic growth of her home state. This Queensland woman, who took her first degree in the late 1920s, put Australian paleontology on the international stage. In the second half of the century, she became the world authority on the oldest fossil corals and related organisms, publishing over 150 scientific works and articles mainly on paleontology, stratigraphy, and geology. Her oeuvre on coral faunas and archaeocyathids and especially her work for the *Treatise of Invertebrate Palaeontology* became classics within her lifetime. Her life's work was commemorated with the foundation at the University of Queensland of the Dorothy Hill Chair in Palaeontology and Stratigraphy, established in 1972, and the Dorothy Hill Library, University of Queensland (now subsumed into the Dorothy Hill Physics and Engineering Sciences Library). Although not her main aim, she attained so many firsts in her lifetime that she indirectly promoted the cause of equality for women in science; later in life she advocated university-level education for women. Until the 1960s revolution in geology, she was virtually the only woman working professionally in geology in Queensland and one of the few to achieve high office.

Hill's Work. In the past when women paleontologists made their mark, they seem to have tackled a group, devoting a whole life of zeal and energy to the task to make them their own—Hill epitomized this with fossil corals. Hill was a world authority on Paleozoic corals and her publications remain definitive works in the field. Small in stature, Hill remained fit and active, working well into her eighties, based no doubt on her earlier sporting prowess as a hockey Blue, in rowing and athletics. Malcolm Thomis, the University of Queensland historian, described her as "the most distinguished scholar of all Queensland's graduates" (1985, p. 287) in the first seventy-five years of the university.

Much of Hill's Australian work consisted of interpretation of coral faunas from isolated limestones in thick sequences that had not been properly mapped, and from which other fossils had not been collected. This was frontier paleontology, and she was a pioneer who could not initially apply the closely controlled stratigraphy of the northern hemisphere to her work. Understanding the need to improve geological mapping work in Australia, and the use of a variety of organisms for correlation, enabled her to see why a vast effort had to be put into Australian geology before European standards could be reached. Most European work on corals had been carried out on well-mapped sections with sedimentary facies interpreted into the local stratigraphy. Little work of this kind had been possible in Australia, and Hill early appreciated how much field interpretation was necessary to make her work on corals more effective. This translated into her later emphasis in teaching students about the classical areas of study.

Mentors and Teachers. What influenced her to become a scientist and a geologist? Paleontology was a strange life choice for a young girl in the early twentieth century in Queensland. Certainly her parents supported her education, with her father realizing that his eldest girl had an excellent mind and would have a distinguished career. Born in Brisbane, the state capital, she was the third child (of seven) of Robert Sampson Hill, employee at a large city departmental store, and Sarah Jane Hill (née Kington), of Coorparoo. Hill took to science, probably the first of her family to show any interest and certainly the first to aspire to university education and a higher degree. Her primary schooling was at the local suburban state school; secondary education at the prestigious Brisbane Girls' Grammar School (1920–1924) included mathematics, chemistry, biology, and classics, all relevant to her later cultural life and in her research work.

Gaining awards and an open entrance scholarship to university, her first inclination was to study medicine, with the hope of entering a research laboratory, for she had realized the great gaps in knowledge of the time. The University of Queensland, founded in 1910, had passed its initial basic phase but did not have a medical faculty; students had to go either to Sydney or Melbourne to enroll and Hill's family circumstances precluded this. Fortunately, she won one of the twenty entrance scholarships, choosing to enter the science faculty, to study chemistry but adding geology in an attempt to broaden her education. Like many a freshman, however, she switched emphasis in her first year, finding geology more fascinating. She came under the influence of foundation geology professor, Henry Caselli Richards (1884–1947) who was to be important to her research career. She saw in him a man of integrity, with a strong sense of humor, but what won her to geology were Richards's personality and his interest in developing a wide range of science.

In the fledging department of geology under Richards's guidance, she graduated in 1928 with BSc first-class honors in geology, a Gold Medal "for Outstanding Merit," top graduate of the year, and a scholarship for the Encouragement of Original Research. A second reason for taking geology was the opportunity to work outdoors; Hill enjoyed country (the "bush") life, learned to ride horses, and enjoyed the company of bush people, many of whom she met at the university. During a visit to friends at Mundubbera in southeast Queensland, she first saw fossils and Hill went on to collect specimens that became the subject of her first published Australian coral paper. On an ABC radio program in 1965, Hill reminisced: "as a school girl, I had spent a holiday in the country (near Mundubbera) with a school friend; a farmer showed us some fossil coral in limestone. These corals indicated that part of Queensland had been under the seas at some time and of course we wondered how and why" (Gregory, p. 59). Her subsequent work on the classic Queensland material, first described around 1890 by Robert Logan Jack and Robert Etheridge, and her own fieldwork for her honors studies—done on horseback in the Brisbane Valley to Esk—led to her MSc in June 1930.

Research Training. Few contemporaries in the fledging department of geology who were interested in paleontology continued past the first degree. Hill's undergraduate work was of a sufficiently high standard to gain the university Gold Medal; she was the first woman to be honored, and consequently she won a Foundation Orient Traveling Scholarship to the Sedgwick Museum (Geology Department), in Cambridge, England, to undertake her doctoral studies, not then possible in Australia. Because she had done a year's work on the basic topic of her PhD thesis before she went overseas, Hill convinced her supervisor at Newnham College, Cambridge, Gertrude L. Elles (1872–1960), a specialist on graptolites, that she had already completed preliminary reading; Elles assessed that Hill had already completed one of the three years necessary for doctoral candidature.

Hill obtained her PhD Cantab on "Australian Fossil Corals in Relation to Evolution" in 1932 at the age of twenty-five based on her comparative studies of mid-Paleozoic corals from Queensland, Britain, and continental Europe. This work, started in Brisbane, was on Carboniferous corals from Mundubbera, in the Burnett River Valley of southeast Queensland, compared mainly with the Carboniferous corals of Scotland. Along with Elles, Oliver Meredith Boone Bulman (1902–1974), then a young postdoctoral graptolite worker who became a longstanding correspondent, demonstrated how detailed morphology, based on well-controlled paleontological sequences, could be made to reveal refined biostratigraphic results beyond anything Hill had been led to expect. John S. Jell (1997) revealed "their guidance and methodology in stratigraphic palaeontology laid down valuable lessons for her. Hill was able to compare her fossils with British ones of the same age, discovering that descriptions of these were badly in need of revision" (p. 47). Tim Sherratt noted, "She took on this demanding task herself, but still found time to gain a pilot's license and to indulge in the odd (very odd) game of 'bicycle polo'" (1994, p. 64). Sport was an important part of her early life. While studying she had represented both the University of Queensland and her state in field hockey.

Hill's British work was well appreciated: in 1932 she was awarded the Old Students' Research Fellowship of Newnham College, Cambridge, and in 1934 she won the Daniel Pidgeon Fund from the Geological Society of London. In Britain she had found that only a few people were undertaking seminal work in her research field. Stanley

Smith at Bristol University, whose real interest was in the skeletal structure of corals, also had an understanding of the relationships between the soft and hard tissues; W. D. Lang, an expert taxonomist, and H. Deighton Thomas, both at the British Museum (Natural History) in London, understood the importance of extensive, well-preserved and curated collections for coral research. Their example set a pattern of investigation that Hill followed throughout her career. This made her work, in the words of her students, "stately and meticulous, and left one feeling that she could be followed knowing that she had investigated details carefully"(Campbell & Jell 1998a, p. 209).

Research Prowess. In 1937 Hill decided to return home, and having become a research fellow, she was determined to expand research at her old university. When war intervened she became an officer in the Operations Staff of the Australian Naval Service, working on the codes and ciphers so crucial for the conduct of the Pacific war. Demobbed (demobilized), she returned to the university and was soon made a temporary lecturer in historical geology, then joined the permanent staff, rising through the ranks as lecturer, professor, and professor emeritus.

In her work she tackled problems caused by the different interpretations of earlier workers brought about mainly by misunderstanding the structures being described. She set about defining the structural details of corals in terms of tissue patterns and skeletal deposition, culminating in a paper on the terminology of rugose corals. This was a major advance in the understanding of the group, and most workers accepted her views. She went on to think about the way in which coral structures were the outcome of depositional processes of microscopic features of the skeleton, and how these were formed from the soft tissues of the polyps. She published a series of works on fine skeletal structures and their relationship to the septal invaginations or the basal plates of the polyps. This research, begun in Cambridge, on crystal structure and skeletal features influenced her later studies, and those of her students, reaching fruition after her return to Queensland when she published a paper dealing with the skeletal growth of crystals in hexacorals with Walter H. Bryan (1891–1966), who worked on the processes of crystallization in igneous rocks.

Her research achievements in the next decades proved her earlier promise; in his memorial Bruce Waterhouse noted that she coauthored the first edition on corals for the *International Treatise on Invertebrate Paleontology,* adding that she "then rewrote the two volumes of the second version on her own." Widely involved in regional Queensland geology, she cooperated with the Queensland Geological Survey to produce maps, and coedited the *Geology of Queensland,* published by the Geological Society of Australia in 1960. For many years, she compiled detailed maps of local Brisbane geology. She took on consulting work with oil companies, such as Shell (Qld) Development Pty. Ltd. and strongly supported scientific exploration of the Great Barrier Reef.

A pivotal cooperative relationship began with John West Wells (1907–1994) of Cornell University in the 1950s when Hill had gained her permanent lectureship. Wells had begun work on Devonian fossil fish in Ohio but switched to corals when peers and colleagues emphasized that there was no future in that work (Turner, 1994). He made his mark in the popular scientific press by analyzing the diurnal rhythms of Devonian corals and working out the number of days in a year. He visited Hill on study leave in 1954, to continue preparation of the coral volume for the *Treatise on Invertebrate Paleontology.* Between them they combined expertise from Paleozoic tabulates to younger Mesozoic-Recent scleractinian corals. The interaction of these two preeminent minds, coming from different backgrounds and with markedly different experiences of their science, enhanced the final product, and made real advances in the understanding of coral paleontology. Kenton S. W. Campbell and John S. Jell surmised "This was a very significant move for Hill, because in the 1960–1980 period, many American workers rose to prominence in coral palaeontology" (1998b). In 1971 an International Association for the Study of Fossil Cnidaria and Porifera was inaugurated, promoted by B. S. Sokolov (USSR), J. P. Chevalier (France), and Hill, with Hill elected as the first president. Many American workers were active in this group; foremost was William Oliver Jr., a student of Wells.

Hill notched up many firsts for women, being one of the few postwar female professional scientists in Queensland and also in academe in Australia. She became an Australian Academician and Fellow of the Royal Society of London. Her major influence, however, has been to create an essentially Australian (and maybe even Queensland) school and philosophy of paleontology, in which she encouraged people to take their doctoral degrees within Australia, and in the foundation of the Queensland Palaeontographical Society and then the Australasian Association of Palaeontologists, which publishes the journal *Alcheringa.* Hill also realized the necessity of building a fine geological library, and she created the finest in Australia especially for its foreign paleontological holdings. She maintained a strong interest in the history of collections, geology, and of paleontology, concentrating in later life on these themes.

Hill fostered, nurtured, and inspired a whole generation of paleontologists: her successor as chair, Bruce Waterhouse, explained: "Many of her students are now scattered through the mining industry, the state geological

Dorothy Hill. John Wells and Dorothy Hill. COURTESY OF THE ESTATE OF DOROTHY HILL.

surveys, Bureau of Mineral Resources and successor Australian Geological Survey Organisation, and universities. It must have given great satisfaction to see how well some of them did" (Waterhouse, 1997). Graeme Maxwell discovered an entirely unknown basin, the Yarrol Basin; Ken Campbell made profound contributions in many fossil phyla; Bruce Runnegar (head of the Astrobiology Institute—formerly Exobiology Institute—at the National Aeronautics and Space Administration in 2006) focused first on Permian bivalves and then diversifying into shell ultrastudies; and, pleasingly for her, John Jell assumed the mantle of coral expert. She encouraged them to create their own Australian paleontological style. Her thinking is illustrated by her critical reaction when Waterhouse of New Zealand met her in 1955 and said that he was about to send mid-Triassic ammonoids to Bernard Kummel. She wanted to know why New Zealanders could not attempt to identify the fossils for themselves: "You don't want to remain a colony for ever, do you" (Waterhouse, 1997).

Hill has provided a role model (albeit unconsciously, perhaps) for generations of students, especially women, and the Australian Academy of Science has an annual award in her name for young research women in earth sciences. Bruce Runnegar and Jell (1983) listed most of her publications, with a final tally of around 151 publications in 57 years, as with over ten books, mostly coauthored, she showed her catalytic and cooperative nature. Campbell, her first student, summarized in his memorial: "She never sought publicity for her work, nor did she seek to make an impact on the wider politics of the country. In this respect she did not attract national interest. In her adult life she was never a person for social activity, nor was she out to draw attention to her field of interest through her contribution to the industrial outcome of her work, though this was considerable" (Campbell & Jell, 1998a, p. 222). Despite her fairly pedestrian beginnings, Hill was not afraid to take the lead, and went on to gain distinctions and awards for services to geology and paleontology. A woman of great personal integrity, she is thought of as sacrificing an overseas career because she wanted Australian universities to reach the forefront of academic achievement, but she was quintessentially a Queenslander who preferred her home. Nevertheless, by her brilliance and thorough hard work, she achieved international distinctions at a time when science was a man's world. Her papers are archived at the Australian Academy of Science in Canberra, and the Fryer Library of University of Queensland Archives in St. Lucia.

BIBLIOGRAPHY

The most complete listing of Hill's works can be found in Campbell & Jell, 1998a. Her papers are archived at the Australian Academy of Science in Canberra, and the Fryer Library of University of Queensland Archives in St. Lucia.

WORKS BY HILL

A Monograph on the Carboniferous Rugose Corals of Scotland. 4 vols. London: Palaeontographical Society, 1938–1941.

With John West Wells. *Treatise on Invertebrate Paleontology. Part F, Coelenterata,* edited by Raymond C. Moore. Lawrence: Geological Society of America and University of Kansas Press, 1956, 1981.

With Alan K. Denmead, eds. "The Geology of Queensland." *Journal of the Geological Society of Australia* 7 (1960): 1–474. Queensland centenary production.

With W. G. H. Maxwell. *Elements of the Stratigraphy of Queensland.* Brisbane, Australia: University of Queensland Press, 1962.

"Archaeocyatha from Loose Material at Plunket Point at the Head of Beardmore Glacier." In *Antarctic Geology: Proceedings of the First International Symposium on Antarctic Geology, Capetown, 15–21 September 1963,* edited by R. J. Adie. Amsterdam: North-Holland, 1964.

As editor with others. *Fossils of Queensland.* Brisbane, Australia: Queensland Palaeontographical Society, 1964–1972.

"Devonian of Eastern Australia." In *International Symposium on the Devonian System, Calgary,* vol. 1, edited by D. H. Oswald. Calgary: Alberta Society of Petroleum Geologists (1967): 613–630.

"Phylum Archaeocyatha Vologdin." In *The Fossil Record,* edited by W. Brian Harland, et al. London: Geological Society, 1967.

"The Great Barrier Reef." In *Captain Cook, Navigator and Scientist,* edited by G. M. Badger. Canberra: Australian Academy of Science (1970): 70–86.

"Part E, Vol. I (of 2): Archaeocyatha." In *Treatise on Invertebrate Paleontology,* 2nd ed., edited by Curt Teichert. New York: Geological Society of America, 1972.

"Lower Carboniferous Corals." In *Atlas of Palaeobiogeography,* edited by Anthony Hallam. Amsterdam: Elsevier, 1973.

OTHER SOURCES

Campbell, Kenton S. W., ed. *Stratigraphy and Palaeontology: Essays in Honour of Dorothy Hill.* Canberra: Australian National University Press, 1969.

Campbell, Kenton S. W., and John S. Jell. "Dorothy Hill 1907–1997." *Historical Records of Australian Science* 12, no. 2 (1998a): 205–228. Major source of biography and chronology.

———. "Dorothy Hill 1907–1997." *Biographical Memoirs of the Australian Academy of Science* (1998b). Available from http://www.science.org.au/academy/memoirs/hill.htm.

Denmead, Alan K. "Portrait of a Scientist." *Earth-Science Reviews* 8 (1972): 351–363.

"Dorothy Hill." *Australasian Science* 29 (1988): 39–41. Upon the opening of the Dorothy Hill Geology Library.

"Dorothy Hill. People: In Memoriam." Cambridge University, *Newnham College Roll Letter* X (1998): 112–114. Hill's studies in England.

Flett, Sir John Smith. *The First Hundred Years of the Geological Survey of Great Britain.* London: H.M.S.O., 1937.

Gregory, Helen. "Dorothy Hill CBE Ph.D. D.Sc. Hon. LLD, FRS, FAA. Research Professor of Geology 1959–1972." In *Vivant Professores: Distinguished Members of the University of Queensland 1910–1940,* no. 7. St. Lucia, Australia: Fryer Memorial Library Occasional Publications, 1987.

———. *Great Queensland Women.* Brisbane, Australia: Office for Women, Queensland Government, 2005.

Jell, John S. "Dorothy Hill." In *Brilliant Careers, Women Collectors and Illustrators in Queensland,* edited by Judy McKay. Brisbane, Australia: Queensland Museum, 1997. Written by her first student on fossil corals.

Jell, Peter A. "Dorothy Hill (1907–1997)." *Nature* 388 (17 July 1997): 234. Reflective assessment of her contribution after her death.

Roberts, John, and Peter A. Jell, eds. "Dorothy Hill Jubilee Memoir." *Memoirs of the Association of Australasian Palaeontologists* 1 (1983).

Runnegar, Bruce. "The Message of Alcheringa." *Alcheringa* 1, nos. 1–2 (1975). Hill's achievement in founding a distinctly Australian paleontological journal.

Runnegar, Bruce, and John S. Jell. "Dorothy Hill, C.B.E., Ph.D., D.Sc., LL.D., F.R.S., F.A.A., F.G.S." *Memoirs of the Association of Australasian Palaeontologists* 1 (1983): 9–15. Listed her publications as around 100, with over 10 books.

Sherratt, Tim. "Finding Life in Ancient Corals—Dorothy Hill." *Australasian Science* summer issue (1994): 64.

Simpson, Andrew. "The Work and Type Collections of the Australian Palaeontologist, Professor Dorothy Hill (1907–1997)." *Geological Curator* 7, no. 2 (1999): 51–69. Important source on Hill's specimens for curators.

Thomis, Malcolm I. *A Place of Light & Learning: The University of Queensland's First Seventy-five Years.* St. Lucia, Australia: University of Queensland Press, 1985.

Turner, Susan. "Women in Palaeontology in Australia." In *Useful and Curious Geological Enquiries beyond the World: Pacific-Asia Historical Themes,* edited by David F. Branagan and G. H. McNally. Sydney: 19th Int. INHIGEO Symposium, Sydney, 4–8 July: 248–250, 1994. First recognition of women paleontologists in Australia.

———. "Women in Paleontology in Australia." In *Sciences of the Earth. An Encyclopedia of Events, People, and Phenomena,* edited by Gregory A. Good. New York: Garland, 1998.

———. "Invincible but Mostly Invisible: Australian Women's Contribution to Palaeontology." In *The Role of Women Geologists,* edited by Cynthia Burek. London: Geological Society of London Special Publication, 2006.

Waterhouse, Bruce. "Dorothy Hill AC, CBE (1907–97)." In *Geological Society of New Zealand,* 1997. Available from http://www.gsnz.org.nz/gssuh2.htm.

White, A. H. "Queensland's Contribution to Mining and the Earth Sciences: An Historical Perspective." In *Queensland: The State of Science,* edited by R. W. Johnson and C. R. King. Brisbane, Australia: Royal Society of Queensland, 1995. Mentions Professor Dorothy Hill's treatise on *Coelenterata.*

Susan Turner

HILL TINSLEY, BEATRICE

SEE **Tinsley, Beatrice.**

HIPPARCHUS

HIPPARCHUS (*b.* Nicaea, Bithynia [now İznik, Turkey], first quarter of second century BCE; *d.* Rhodes [?], after 127 BCE), *astronomy, mathematics, geography.* For the original article on Hipparchus see *DSB,* vol. 15.

Hipparchus has continued to be a subject of controversy among historians of astronomy on account of the fragmentary character of much of our evidence for his writings and for Greek astronomy in general before Ptolemy (second century CE). At stake, particularly, is how his work stands in relation on the one hand to Ptolemy's astronomical theories and methods, and on the other to the Babylonian mathematical astronomy of the last three centuries BCE. The prevailing view of Hipparchus's historical place shifted through the great part of the twentieth century away from the assumption that Ptolemy's *Almagest* was substantially a recapitulation and completion of his work. Concepts, conventions, observations, and numerical elements of Babylonian origin have become recognized as pervading his astronomy. More recently, however, scholarship has begun to react against portraying Hipparchus as a user and advocate of the approximative arithmetical methodology characteristic of Babylonian astronomy as opposed to the trigonometrical methods of the *Almagest.*

The original *DSB* article asserted that Hipparchus constructed and used a trigonometrical chord table based on a standard circle of radius 3,438 units. This was, in fact, a hypothesis resting on a reconstruction of Hipparchus's calculations of the eccentricity of the Moon's orbit that its author subsequently repudiated, although it has since been persuasively revived in modified form. That Hipparchus was able to make computations involving plane trigonometry has never been seriously in question. As long ago as 1934 it was shown that a series of terrestrial latitudes that—according to Strabo (64 or 63 BCE–after 23 CE)—Hipparchus associated with specific values for the maximum length of day are in close agreement with

Hipparchus. *Hipparchus in an astronomical observatory.* © BETTMANN/CORBIS.

computation by spherical trigonometry, but this evidence was long disregarded. Analemma techniques could have yielded these latitudes, but they do not seem capable of certain calculations in spherical astronomy reported in the extant *Commentary on Aratus* of Hipparchus. Hence it appears that Hipparchus was in possession of Menelaus's theorem or some equivalent and did not depend on Babylonian-style arithmetical sequences to approximate spherical functions.

Hipparchus's familiarity with Babylonian astronomy has given rise to the attractive conjecture that he might have obtained access to this technical knowledge by visiting Babylon. Remarkably, scholars now have firm evidence that the Babylonian scribes of the late second century BCE knew something of Hipparchus's work on solar theory. The Babylonian cuneiform BM 55555 (published by Neugebauer as ACT No. 210) reports a value for the length of the year that corresponds with high precision to 108,478 days divided by 297. An interval of 297 years turns out to be that between the summer solstice

Hipparchus

observations of Meton in 432 BCE and Hipparchus in 135 BCE that Ptolemy says Hipparchus discussed in his *On the Length of the Year.* Interestingly, the year length in BM 55555 is slightly shorter than the tropical year that Ptolemy took over from Hipparchus, which apparently was derived from comparison of a different pair of solstices.

Fresh studies of the *Commentary on Aratus* necessitate some significant revisions of statements in the original *DSB* article about Hipparchus's data for stellar positions and their relationship to the catalog of stars in Books VII and VIII of the *Almagest.* Heinrich Vogt's 1925 investigation concluding that the *Commentary* data were independent of Ptolemy's positions suffered from serious defects, including limitation of its analysis to the relatively small number of stars for which the *Commentary* appeared to provide sufficient information to allow reconstruction of both ecliptic coordinates. More careful recent analyses of a much larger body of data lead to the conclusion that Ptolemy's coordinates for most of the stars that have positional data in the *Commentary* were derived ultimately from the same measurements as the data in the *Commentary,* and this was presumably a lost catalog by Hipparchus. This does not necessarily mean that Hipparchus's catalog was the source for all Ptolemy's stars, because in particular the *Almagest* catalog is proportionally much more abundant in dim stars than the *Commentary.* Now confirmed is the contention of Jean Baptiste Delambre that, at the time that he wrote the *Commentary,* Hipparchus's regular method of representing stellar positions was by means of equatorial coordinates, so that the dependence of Ptolemy's catalog on Hipparchus must have involved a conversion of coordinates, which may for that matter have occurred during the interval between Hipparchus and Ptolemy.

Combinatorics. That Hipparchus did some work on combinatorics (which has generally not been recognized as having been a distinct mathematical subdiscipline in antiquity) is known from a passage (1047CE) in the *De Stoicorum Repugnantiis* of Plutarch (first and early second centuries CE). The passage asserts that whereas the Stoic Chrysippus (third century BCE) counted "the conjunctions arising from ten assertibles" as exceeding one hundred myriads, Hipparchus proved that "the affirmative yields 103049 conjoined assertibles and the negative 310952." The first light cast on the enigma of what Hipparchus was counting, and how, was the recognition in the 1990s that 103,049 is the tenth of the series of Schröder numbers, while 310,952 differs only in its final digit (2 instead of 4) from half the sum of the tenth and eleventh Schröder numbers—likely reflecting a textual error in antiquity.

The *n*th Schröder number is the number of possible bracketings of a string of *n* symbols. Hipparchus seems to have interpreted Stoic logic as allowing an ordered set of *n* simple affirmative statements to be combined hierarchically by an "and" conjunction according to rules structurally analogous to bracketing, such that any such combination is counted as distinct from any other. A further rule governs the counting of negative conjunctions, understood as a single negation applied to what amounts to the first bracketed section of a set of affirmative statements. (Whether Hipparchus's interpretation of these conjunctions was the same as Chrysippus's is disputable.) From a mathematical point of view, what is most interesting about Hipparchus's computations is that he succeeded in framing and correctly solving a combinatorical problem that was far from trivial and that his method of calculating the Schröder numbers must have had a recursive character.

SUPPLEMENTARY BIBLIOGRAPHY

Acerbi, Fabio. "On the Shoulders of Hipparchus: A Reappraisal of Ancient Greek Combinatorics." *Archive for History of Exact Sciences* 57 (2003): 465–502. Explains the meaning of the numbers reported by Plutarch in relation to Stoic logic and offers a reconstruction of Hipparchus's method of computing them.

Diller, Aubrey. "Geographical Latitudes in Eratosthenes, Hipparchus, and Posidonius." *Klio* 27 (1934): 258–269. On the use of spherical trigonometry in Hipparchus's geographical and astronomical work.

Duke, Dennis W. "Associations between the Ancient Star Catalogues." *Archive for History of Exact Sciences* 56 (2002): 435–450. On the relationship between the Aratus commentary and the *Almagest* star catalog.

———. "Hipparchus' Coordinate System." *Archive for History of Exact Sciences* 56 (2002): 427–433. Shows the equatorial basis of Hipparchus's stellar data.

———. "Hipparchus' Eclipse Trios and Early Trigonometry." *Centaurus* 47 (2005): 163–177. Defends Toomer's reconstruction of the chord table.

Grasshoff, Gerd. *The History of Ptolemy's Star Catalogue.* New York: Springer-Verlag, 1990.

Habsieger, Laurent, Maxim Kazarian, and Sergi Lando. "On the Second Number of Plutarch." *American Mathematical Monthly* 105 (1998): 446. Supplement to Stanley's paper cited below.

Jones, Alexander. "In Order that We Should Not Ourselves Appear to be Adjusting Our Estimates ... to Make Them Fit Some Predetermined Amount." In *Wrong for the Right Reasons,* edited by Jed Z. Buchwald and Allan Franklin. Dordrecht, Netherlands: Springer 2005. A discussion of the implications of the new Hipparchian value for the tropical year in BM 55555 for Hipparchus's and Ptolemy's solar theory.

Rawlins, D. "Hipparchos' Ultimate Solar Orbit & the Babylonian Tropical Year." *Dio* 1 (1991): 49–66. The new

Hipparchian value for the tropical year in BM 55555 is explained.

Sidoli, Nathan. "Hipparchus and the Ancient Metrical Methods on the Sphere." *Journal for the History of Astronomy* 35 (2004): 71–84.

Stanley, Richard P. "Hipparchus, Plutarch, Schröder, and Hough." *American Mathematical Monthly* 104 (1997): 344–350. Original report of Hough's identification of the connection between Hipparchus's combinatorics and Schröder numbers.

Toomer, Gerald J. "Hipparchus and Babylonian Astronomy." In *A Scientific Humanist: Studies in Memory of Abraham Sachs,* edited by Erle Leichty, Maria deJ. Ellis, and Pamela Gerardi. Philadelphia. Occasional Publications of the Samuel Noah Kramer Fund, 9, 1988. Discusses elements of Babylonian astronomy in Hipparchus's work and his conjectural sojourn in Babylon.

Alexander Jones

HIPPOCRATES OF COS (*b.* Cos, 460 BCE; *d.* Larissa, c. 370 BCE), *medicine.* For the original article on Hippocrates of Cos see *DSB,* vol. 6.

Since the middle of the twentieth century, many changes have taken place in the standard picture of Hippocrates, the Father of Medicine, so that in the early twenty-first century even those few details of his life and writings that the majority of scholars once accepted are disputed. Meanwhile, alongside the production of better editions of the texts, and their translation into a range of modern languages, the focus of Hippocratic studies has moved away from identifying which treatises most accurately represent the thinking of Hippocrates toward examining the social context of ancient medicine more generally. As well as trying to gain a better picture of physicians other than Hippocrates who were active in the classical world, this also involves a shift away from individual physicians named in the sources, toward the theories and therapies that patients would encounter. In the process, it has become possible to identify many different versions of "Hippocrates," which have chosen to place their emphasis on different parts of the Hippocratic corpus.

Galen's Construal. Possibly the most significant shift in scholars' understanding of Hippocrates has come about as a result of Wesley Smith's book *The Hippocratic Tradition* (1979), in which the contribution of many ancient as well as modern writers to the construction of "Hippocrates" was demonstrated: above all, that of Galen (129–c. 216). Smith showed how the great nineteenth-century editor of the corpus, Émile Littré, had assembled ancient sources in order to impress the reader with the sheer quantity of evidence for the historicity of Hippocrates, but noted how Littré "seems to mention all suggestions by anyone in antiquity about Hippocrates' reality and importance, with little emphasis on the contradictions in ancient tradition and little emphatic skepticism about the quality of the evidence" (p. 34).

In particular, nineteenth-century editors such as Littré were putting too much credence in Galen, failing to recognize that Galen's account of Hippocratic science and its tradition should instead be recognized as being "in large part his own, a projection of his concerns onto history" (Smith, 1979, p. 175). The quest to identify the "genuine works of Hippocrates," a phrase used in Francis Adams's edition of those works he singled out as by the historical Hippocrates (1849), continues to be based on judgments of literary merit and sufficiently rational content. But Smith showed how Galen created Hippocrates in his own image, by regarding as the "genuine works" of Hippocrates those that most closely approximated to his own views; for example, Galen favored *Nature of Man,* and as a result its four-humor theory came to be seen as genuinely Hippocratic. Nor was this the first construction of Hippocrates, as the rise of empiricism from around 225 BCE had also seen a surge of interest in the Hippocratic writings, in which they were seen as precursors of an approach to medicine that eschews theory.

Since Smith, historians have become far more aware of the need to avoid taking any of the ancient evidence at face value. This even applies to the two short texts that were once claimed as the sole primary sources for the historical Hippocrates, Plato's references to him in the *Protagoras* and the later *Phaedrus.* In *Medical Theories in Hippocrates: Early Texts and the "Epidemics"* (1990), Volker Langholf showed that, despite their chronological proximity to the period in which Hippocrates is supposed to have lived, these should instead be considered as secondary sources, in the sense that they use the image of Hippocrates to make specific points central to Plato's own argument.

In this new climate, in which sources are read with greater attention to their own reasons for mentioning Hippocrates, the "Hippocratic question"—which, if any, of the works in the corpus is by the historical Hippocrates—still continues to hold a fascination for scholars. The best summary of the history of the question remains that by G. E. R. Lloyd (1975; updated 1991). In 1893, when the Anonymus Londinensis papyrus, acquired by the British Museum in 1890, was first published, it caused a stir because it suggested that Aristotle's view was that Hippocrates regarded "breaths" arising from residues in the body as being the origin of disease. Yet the extant medical treatise under the title of *Breaths* had previously been rejected as an inferior work by a "second-rate

Hippocrates of Cos. *Portrait of Hippocrates, circa 400 BCE.* HULTON ARCHIVE/GETTY IMAGES.

Sophist, indeed ... a mere gossipmonger" (Jouanna, 1999, p. 60), and under no circumstances to be linked with the historical Hippocrates. Such a response was also an ancient one: The writer of the papyrus himself disagreed that this theory was Hippocratic, instead looking to *Nature of Man* and *Diseases* 1. *Nutriment,* one of the treatises that Galen considered most genuinely Hippocratic, has been shown conclusively to be from the Hellenistic period, on the grounds of vocabulary and its Stoic roots. The debate is certainly not over yet, as Jaap Mansfeld (1980) has reexamined what Plato meant by attention to "the whole" as a characteristic of Hippocratic medicine, and even Smith (1979) argues that one work of the corpus, *Regimen,* is genuine.

Reading the Texts. Discussions of the vocabulary and dating of the different treatises in the Hippocratic corpus has been facilitated by better editions of many of the texts of the Hippocratic corpus; the manuscripts available to Littré were limited, and improved readings are now possible. In addition, the *Index Hippocraticus,* completed by the Hamburg Thesaurus Linguae Graecae in 1989, allows a far better understanding of variant readings, and provides an insight into the structure and development of the texts. As of 2007 it was being enhanced by a further set of volumes collecting the citations of the Hippocratic corpus in later writers, beginning with Galen. One result of these improved resources, new reference works, and also of computer-based analysis of the vocabulary and syntax of the texts, is a reassessment of what it means to write of "authors" for these materials; this in turn has led to a more detailed awareness of the different strata represented even within a single treatise.

For example, Hermann Grensemann (1975, 1982) has argued for several different stages being represented within the gynecological works. Whatever one thinks of his identification of authors A, B, and C and his arguments for their relative dating, study of the gynecological theories and remedies shows how much of this material was shared, and reworked (King, 1998). Other treatises provide slightly different versions of the same material; *Aphorisms* repeats sections from the gynecological treatises, while some books of the *Epidemics* have material in common with *Diseases of Women* and *On the Nature of Woman.* Papyri have also been discovered which give further variations on the recipes in these texts, showing that this was a developing tradition (Marganne, 1981).

More of the Hippocratic corpus is now available in translation, most notably the Budé French edition, while the Loeb Classical Library translations into English extended to eight volumes by 2007. A series of international conferences under the title "Colloques hippocratiques" has been held, the first at Strasbourg in 1972, whereas another more general conference in Leiden in 1992 led to two volumes of essays under the title *Ancient Medicine in its Socio-Cultural Context* (van der Eijk et al., 1995). The choice of title is significant: Whereas some scholars (most notably James Longrigg, 1993) still emphasize what sets Hippocratic medicine apart from other aspects of Greek thought, regarding the treatises as showing the birth of "rational" medicine, others would now stress how the theories offered are best situated within the specific social and cultural contexts of classical and Hellenistic Greece. In a similar vein, the most recent Colloque hippocratique was entitled "Hippocrates in Context" (proceedings edited by van der Eijk, 2005).

Instead of seeing Hippocratic medicine as being characterized by a rejection of superstition and religion, scholars are now arguing that even a treatise such as *On the Sacred Disease,* which gives a natural explanation for epilepsy, does not represent a complete break with nonmedical accounts of disease and its treatment (van der Eijk, 1991; Laskaris, 2002). Rather than rejecting therapies involving apparently disgusting substances, such as animal dung, as regrettable survivals of pre-Hippocratic ideas, modern scholars look at the pharmacology of the treatises in terms of the relationship with the symbolism of plants, as seen in magic and myth (von Staden, 1992a and 1992b). Rather than measuring Hippocratic medicine

Hippocrates of Cos

against modern Western medicine, it is increasingly compared to medical writing in other literate cultures (Lloyd, 1996; Lloyd and Sivin, 2002; Dean-Jones, 1995) or to other aspects of ancient science (Ferrari and Vegetti, 1983; Nutton, 2004). The context within which Hippocrates worked has been further illuminated by collections of the significant number of fragments of other ancient Greek medical writers, such as Diocles of Carystos and the third-century BCE Herophilos and Erasistratos, as well as by looking at the position of medicine in ancient Near Eastern societies (Horstmanshoff and Stol, 2004). Hippocratic texts have been studied in relation to a wide range of other types of evidence, among them epigraphy (Deichgräber, 1982).

Treatises as Texts. The nature of the treatises as texts has been a particularly fruitful area of study, acknowledging that they were composed for very different audiences: fellow physicians, laypeople, and even for the writer himself. They represent the earliest surviving examples of Greek prose, and the existence of lists, and the practice of grouping together similar items, can be seen as entirely typical of such early literacy (Lonie, 1983). The seven books of case histories known as the *Epidemics,* rather than being understood as evidence of the role of observation in recording case histories, can be reinterpreted as showing "a tendency to present reality in conformity with theory" (Langholf, 1990, p. 210), and as "notes to self" enabling a physician to identify emerging patterns; what they miss may be as significant as what their writers choose to include.

In "Literacy and the Charlatan in Ancient Greek Medicine" (2003), Lesley Dean-Jones has argued that literacy may have led to disputes between those physicians relying on the written word, and others whose training originated in the family. The *Oath* famously sets medical training in a quasi-familial structure in which the person swearing it says that he will treat those who teach him *as if* they were his family. These distinctions are even present in the claims surrounding the education of Hippocrates himself; some later writers suggest that his mother was a midwife, and that his grandfather had written medical treatises, but this biographical tradition may simply reflect a time when medical training normally passed through families, providing a further example of the creation of Hippocrates in the image of those who wrote about him. But alongside this story of "family" education, the sources also name a range of teachers for Hippocrates, among them Gorgias of Leontini, Democritus of Abdera, and the physician Herodicus; however, there is no reliable evidence to link any of them to Hippocrates's training.

Cos and Cnidos? Following Antoine Thivel's study *Cnide et Cos?* (1981), the distinction between Coan and Cnidian medicine was no longer seen as important; even Robert Joly in the original *DSB* came to the conclusion that "the two schools shared essentially the same spirit." Instead of dividing the corpus into "Coan" medicine associated with Hippocrates and his family and students, and inferior "Cnidian"—or even "para-Cnidian"—medicine showing a primitive and more empirical approach, the broad similarities in theories of disease causation and treatment have come to be emphasized, and disagreement is understood to have occurred between individuals rather than "schools." These points have been fruitfully linked to the idea, taken from early modern medical history, of a "medical marketplace" in which not only different types of healer, but also fellow Hippocratics, were in competition for patients. This approach also has the effect of dethroning Hippocrates, looking instead at ancient medicine as a field of equals from which the name of Hippocrates happens to have survived.

But why was there a need for a single founding figure? Some of the impetus may have come from those physicians who continued to be based on Cos, who gave authority to their medical tradition by promoting their "founder." This process may be seen in the Hippocratic pseudepigrapha, part of a wider practice in antiquity of creating letters from famous individuals, and imagining contexts in which they may have met; for Hippocrates, this included encounters with the philosopher Democritos, and the kings of Persia and Macedonia (Smith, 1990; Pinault, 1992). These stories may come from the local traditions of Cos or may have been newly created. In fleshing out the character of Hippocrates, these stories drew attention to his imagined virtues; firstly, patriotism, as he was described as refusing his help to the king of Persia on the grounds that he was an enemy of the Greeks, and secondly his lack of interest in financial rewards—an answer to those who claimed that physicians were only interested in making money out of their patients.

The Afterlife of Hippocrates. The Hippocratic corpus was translated into Latin in sixth-century CE Ravenna, then into Syriac and Arabic; the tenth-century Byzantine encyclopedists added more material to the biographical tradition, while in the twelfth century Joannes Tzetzes traced Hippocrates's ancestors back to the healing god Asklepios. Galen's work remained the basis of Western medicine until the sixteenth century, when a movement back to Hippocrates was triggered by the publication of the full corpus in Latin translation in 1525.

In all periods, subsequent generations continued to create Hippocrates in the image of whatever type of medicine they considered best. Precisely because the corpus is not the work of a single man in a single lifetime, it can supply models and precedents for virtually any medical

Hippocrates of Cos

development. This means that different versions of Hippocrates can be found throughout history, including a chemical Hippocrates, an iatromechanist Hippocrates, a vitalist Hippocrates, a holistic Hippocrates, and so on (Cantor, 2002). This does not only apply to "orthodox" medicine; alternatives such as homeopathy have also claimed Hippocrates as their father. Hippocrates could be the champion of observation, opposed to the dry theories of Galen: or the champion of dogma, with Galen merely as a commentator on his work. In French medicine, Hippocrates was associated with Montpellier, Galen with Paris. Different treatises have moved in and out of fashion according to changes in medicine; for example, Thomas Sydenham (1624–1689), the "English Hippocrates," promoted the value of observation and therefore emphasized the *Epidemics*, while a century later *Airs, Waters, Places* became fashionable because of the rise of climatology. Even the *Oath* is not exempt from use and abuse (Flashar and Jouanna, 1997). Heinrich von Staden (1996) has tried to uncover the original meaning of clauses later interpreted as prohibiting abortion and euthanasia, and protecting patient confidentiality, but it is also clear that many variations on it have existed over time, including its use by National Socialism and at the Nuremberg trials (Leven, 1998).

Rather than Joly's "eminent representative of a significant stage of medicine" (original *DSB*), Hippocrates can thus be seen as a rich resource on which a changing medical science has been able to continue to draw. Yet even while the medical theories of Galen dominated, it was Hippocrates—represented as patriotic, modest, and calm—who remained the model of the ideal physician.

SUPPLEMENTARY BIBLIOGRAPHY

WORKS BY HIPPOCRATES OF COS

The Genuine Works of Hippocrates, Translated from the Greek with a preliminary discourse and annotations by Francis Adams. London: Sydenham Society, 1849.

Hippocrates. Cambridge, MA: Harvard University Press, Loeb Classical Library, 1923–. Volumes continue to be added.

Corpus Medicorum Graecorum. Available from http://www.bbaw.de/bbaw/Forschung/Forschungsprojekte/cmg/de/Publikationen.

Index Hippocraticus. 4 vols. Edited by Josef Hans Kühn and Ulrich Fleischer. Gottingen: Vandenhoeck and Ruprecht, 1986–1999.

OTHER SOURCES

Cantor, David, ed. *Reinventing Hippocrates.* Aldershot, U.K.: Ashgate, 2002. A valuable collection of essays on the different versions of Hippocrates created by medical writers.

Dean-Jones, Lesley. "Autopsia, Historia, and What Women Know: The Authority of Women in Hippocratic Gynaecology." In *Knowledge and the Scholarly Medical Traditions: A Comparative Study,* edited by Don Bates. Cambridge, U.K.: Cambridge University Press, 1995.

———. "Literacy and the Charlatan in Ancient Greek Medicine." In *Written Texts and the Rise of Literate Culture in Ancient Greece,* edited by Harvey Yunis. Cambridge, U.K.: Cambridge University Press, 2003.

Deichgräber, Karl. *Die Patienten des Hippokrates: Historisch-prosopographische Beiträge zu den Epidemien des Corpus Hippocraticum.* Wiesbaden: Franz Steiner, 1982.

Ferrari, Gian A., and Mario Vegetti. "Science, Technology and Medicine in the Classical Tradition." In *Information Sources in the History of Science and Medicine,* edited by Pietro Corsi and Paul Weindling. London: Butterworth Scientific, 1983.

Flashar, Hellmut, and Jacques Jouanna, eds. *Médecine et Morale dans l'Antiquité.* Geneva: Fondation Hardt, 1997.

Garofalo, Ivan. *Erasistrati Fragmenta.* Pisa: Giardini, 1988.

Grensemann, Hermann. *Knidische Medizin,* vol. I. Berlin: de Gruyter, 1975.

———. *Hippokratische Gynäkologie: Die gynäkologischen Texte des Autors C nach den pseudohippokratischen Schriften De muliebribus I, II und De Sterilibus.* Wiesbaden: Franz Steiner, 1982.

Horstmanshoff, H. F. J., and Marten Stol, eds. *Magic and Rationality in Ancient Near Eastern and Graeco-Roman Medicine.* Leiden: Brill, 2004.

Jouanna, Jacques. *Hippocrates,* trans. M.B. DeBevoise. Baltimore, MD: Johns Hopkins University Press, 1999.

King, Helen. *Hippocrates' Woman: Reading the Female Body in Ancient Greece.* London: Routledge, 1998. Study of the context of Hippocratic gynecology and its reception up to the nineteenth century.

Langholf, Volker. *Medical Theories in Hippocrates: Early Texts and the "Epidemics."* Berlin: Walter de Gruyter, 1990.

Laskaris, Julie. *The Art Is Long: On the Sacred Disease and the Scientific Tradition.* Leiden: Brill, 2002.

Leven, Karl-Heinz. "The Invention of Hippocrates: Oath, Letters and Hippocratic Corpus." In *Ethics Codes in Medicine: Foundations and Achievements of Codification since 1947,* edited by Ulrich Tröhler and Stella Reiter-Theil. Aldershot, U.K.: Ashgate, 1998.

Lloyd, G. E. R. *Magic, Reason and Experience: Studies in the Origin and Development of Greek Science.* Cambridge, U.K.: Cambridge University Press, 1979.

———. *Science, Folklore and Ideology: Studies in the Life Sciences in Ancient Greece.* Cambridge, U.K: Cambridge University Press, 1983.

———. "The Hippocratic Question." *Classical Quarterly* 25, no. 2 (1975): 171–192. Reprinted in *Methods and Problems in Greek Science.* Cambridge, U.K.: Cambridge University Press, 1991.

———. *Adversaries and Authorities: Investigations into Ancient Greek and Chinese Science.* Cambridge, U.K.: Cambridge University Press, 1996.

———. "Literacy in Greek and Chinese Science: Some Comparative Issues." In *Written Texts and the Rise of Literate Culture in Ancient Greece,* edited by Harvey Yunis. Cambridge, U.K.: Cambridge University Press, 2003.

Lloyd, Geoffrey, and Nathan Sivin. *The Way and the Word: Science and Medicine in Early China and Greece.* New Haven, CT: Yale University Press, 2002.

Longrigg, James. *Greek Rational Medicine: Philosophy and Medicine from Alcmaeon to the Alexandrians.* London: Routledge, 1993.

Lonie, Iain M. "Literacy and the Development of Hippocratic Medicine." In *Formes de pensée dans la Collection hippocratique: Actes du Colloque hippocratique de Lausanne* 1981, edited by François Lasserre and Philippe Mudry. Geneva: Droz, 1983.

Mansfeld, Jaap. "Plato and the Method of Hippocrates." *Greek, Roman, and Byzantine Studies* 21 (1980): 341–362.

Marganne, Marie-Hélène. *Inventaire analytique des papyrus grecs de médecine.* Geneva: Droz, 1981.

Nutton, Vivian. *Ancient Medicine.* London: Routledge, 2004. A full and detailed survey.

Pinault, Jody Rubin. *Hippocratic Lives and Legends.* Leiden: Brill, 1992.

Smith, Wesley D. *The Hippocratic Tradition.* Ithaca: Cornell University Press, 1979.

———. *Pseudepigraphic Writings.* Leiden: Brill, 1990.

Thivel, Antoine. *Cnide et Cos? Essai sur les doctrines médicales dans la Collection hippocratique.* Paris: Les Belles Lettres, 1981.

Van der Eijk, Philip J., H. F. J. Horstmanshoff, and P. I. Schrijvers, eds. *Ancient Medicine in its Socio-Cultural Context.* 2 vols. Amsterdam: Rodopi, 1995.

Van der Eijk, Philip J. "*Airs, Waters, Places* and *On the Sacred Disease*: Two Different Religiosities?" *Hermes* 119 (1991): 168–176.

———. *Diocles of Carystus. A Collection of the Fragments with Translation and Commentary.* 2 vols. Leiden: Brill, 2000–01.

Van der Eijk, Philip J., ed. *Hippocrates in Context.* Leiden: Brill, 2005.

Von Staden, Heinrich. *Herophilus. The Art of Medicine in Early Alexandria.* Cambridge, U.K.: Cambridge University Press, 1989.

———. "Spiderwoman and the Chaste Tree: The Semantics of Matter." *Configurations* 1 (1992a): 23–56.

———. "Women and Dirt." *Helios* 19 (1992b): 7–30.

———. "'In a Pure and Holy Way:' Personal and Professional Conduct in the Hippocratic Oath?" *Journal of the History of Medicine and Allied Sciences* 51 (1996): 404–37.

Helen King

HIRST, THOMAS ARCHER

(*b.* Heckmondwike, Yorkshire, United Kingdom, 22 April 1830; *d.* London, United Kingdom, 16 February 1892), *mathematics, geometry, education.*

Thomas Hirst was a leading member of London's scientific community during the mid- and late Victorian period. Although his geometrical research proved unimportant, he was a significant reformer of British mathematical education and, as a member of the X-Club, of scientific activity generally. The journals he kept throughout his life are an invaluable source of information and comment on British and European scientific circles in the second half of the nineteenth century.

Early Life and Career. Hirst was born to Thomas Hirst (1797–1842) and Hannah Oates (1804–1849), who headed a family of prosperous wool staplers. After leaving the West Riding Proprietary School in Wakefield at the age of fifteen, he served an apprenticeship surveying the construction of railways in Yorkshire and began a daily journal that he was to keep more or less regularly throughout his life. A fellow surveyor, who also kept a journal, was the much older Irishman, John Tyndall, with whom he formed a lifelong friendship. Both men used their journals to express thoughts on their reading, self-improvement, and the foibles of daily life. Under Tyndall's mentorship, Hirst began to answer mathematical problems in the *Family Herald* and to read Charles Lyell on geology, George Combe on phrenology, Jeremiah Joyce on natural philosophy, and Robert Chambers's *Vestiges of the Natural History of Creation* (1844). He enrolled in evening classes at the Halifax Mechanics Institute, where he read Thomas Carlyle and gained valuable teaching experience. Carlyle's idealism inspired young men like Tyndall and Hirst to develop an inner spirituality linked to a self-consistent naturalistic, integrative view of man, nature, and society that avoided the traditional contradictions of revealed religion.

On the completion of his apprenticeship in 1850, Hirst abandoned the career of civil engineering that was open to him and, inspired by Tyndall's example, he studied chemistry, physics, and mathematics at the University of Marburg in Hesse-Darmstadt. He obtained his doctorate under Friedrich Stegmann on the conjugate diameters of the triaxial ellipsoid in 1852, following which he joined Karl Knoblauch in research on magnetism. He then moved to Berlin where he developed a special friendship with Jakob Steiner, from whom he learned not only pure geometry but also an approach to mathematics teaching that was strongly influenced by the Swiss educational reformer Heinrich Pestalozzi. In 1853 he succeeded Tyndall as a teacher of natural philosophy and surveying at Queenwood College in Hampshire, England, and supplemented his income with French, German, and Italian translations for *Philosophical Magazine,* several of which (notably the translation of Rudolf Clausius's kinetic theory) proved of lasting significance. He married Ann Martin in 1854 but was left a widower after only three years.

A Continental Education. Abandoning teaching, he moved to Paris to devote himself to independent mathematical research and for further studies with Joseph Liouville and Michel Chasles, whose geometry he particularly admired. Moving to Rome in 1858 at the height of the Risorgimento (the movement for Italian unification), he attended the lectures of Barnaba Tortolini and became friendly with other Italian mathematicians, most notably Luigi Cremona, with whom he struck up a correspondence important to both. His experiences with leading continental mathematicians led Hirst to question the absolute, logical, deductive methods of Euclid that dominated English schooling. Although Hirst's commitment to synthetic, rather than analytical, geometry, resulted in a rather special corpus of mathematical research, the educational philosophy he had absorbed during his *Wanderjahre* was to be of considerable importance for English education. Moreover, as one of the few English mathematicians educated in France, Germany, and Italy and through his frequent continental travels and regular correspondence with leading continental mathematicians, he served as a channel through which European work became known in the United Kingdom.

Teaching and Organizational Work. Hirst returned to London in October 1859, intimately acquainted with what was happening in European mathematics. For the next nine years he lodged with Tyndall, under whose wing he soon met a great many of the scientific and literary lions of the day. These savants opened a new world of social and intellectual advantage to him. Materially, he survived on a small inheritance and from teaching mathematics at University College School in London. A giant physically—he was well over six feet tall, with a huge bald head and black beard—he intimidated some of the schoolchildren. While a strict disciplinarian, in practice he proved very adept at explaining complex ideas in a simple manner, and was patient and kind to the hopeless and extremely stimulating to the able. In 1864 he joined with Tyndall, Thomas H. Huxley, Joseph Hooker, Herbert Spencer, and others in the formation of the X-Club, a dining club united by the spirit of political liberalism, scientific materialism, and religious agnosticism. The club's legendary influence upon the organization and image of Victorian science between the 1860s and the 1890s gave a practical focus to Hirst's otherwise lonely life and secured his position in the interlocking directorate of metropolitan science. In 1865, together with other University College associates such as Augustus De Morgan, he became a cofounder of the London Mathematical Society and served as its president between 1872 and 1874. Elected a Fellow of the Royal Society in 1861, Hirst was active on its council during the society's reforming years. His work included management of the society's Government Grant Committee, whose patronage was important for younger research workers. He also acted as secretary of the British Association for the Advancement of Science from 1866 to 1870, a position he regarded as "no joke," that is, it required far more work than he had anticipated.

In 1865, at the age of thirty-five, Hirst moved sideways and upward from school teaching to the chair of physics at University College. Two years later, on De Morgan's retirement, Hirst transferred to the chair of pure mathematics. In 1870 his experience of teaching geometry to the Ladies Educational Association of London (a pioneering organization for women's education) kindled his interest in geometrical reform. In the following year he played an important role in founding the Association for the Improvement of Geometrical Teaching (AIGT; from 1897 the Mathematical Association). He shared the opinion of several progressive teachers that the reform of geometrical teaching in Great Britain was overdue and that the syllogistic system of Euclid should be superseded by more direct and practical methods of demonstration. He was the AIGT's first president, serving from 1871 to 1878.

Geometrical Research. Hirst's own geometrical research was on positive- and negative-derived pedal surfaces and quadratic transformations and inversions of plane curves. Throughout his exceedingly abstract publications in leading British and continental periodicals, three things stand out: Hirst's continual use of analogy and extension of theorems to many dimensions; his ability to generalize the results of other mathematicians (particularly those of Steiner, Chasles, and Cremona) as far as possible; and his concern to show that the work of other mathematicians was derivable from a synthetic geometry that was more intuitively meaningful, logical, and vigorous than analytic geometry.

Hirst was permanently dissatisfied with his meager output of research papers in comparison with his contemporaries—a mere twenty papers over a thirty-year period. He changed positions frequently, hoping that he would gain more time for geometry and freedom from depression and ill health. From 1870 to 1873 Hirst was assistant registrar of the University of London, and from 1873 until 1883 (when he took early retirement) he was director of the new Royal Naval College at Greenwich. The remaining eight years of his life were spent wandering around Europe and socializing in the Athenaeum Club in London. Ironically, his retirement was relatively unproductive, apart from work inspired by Cremona on line congruences. In 1890 he symbolically burned his mathematical notebooks and published nothing more. He died in 1892, a victim of the great influenza epidemic that struck London that winter.

Hirst's death marked the end of a generation of scientists, mathematicians, and educators who had given a particular character to scientific London during the 1860s and 1870s. Through the diaries he left, which Tyndall's widow transcribed in the twentieth century, historians have a clear window through which the social context of mid-Victorian scientific London and other European cities can be viewed.

BIBLIOGRAPHY

WORK BY HIRST

Nurzia, Laura, ed. *La Corrispondenza di Luigi Cremona (1830–1903).* Vol. 4. Palermo, Italy: Universita Bocconi, 1999. Contains Hirst's letters to Cremona.

OTHER SOURCES

Barton, Ruth. "An Influential Set of Chaps: The X Club and Royal Society Politics, 1864–85." *British Journal for the History of Science* 23 (1990): 53–81.

———. "Hirst, Thomas Archer." In *Dictionary of Nineteenth-Century British Scientists,* edited by Bernard Lightman. Vol. 2. London: Thoemmes Continuum, 2004. Offers an excellent analysis of Hirst's position in Victorian society.

Brock, William H. "Geometry and the Universities: Euclid and His Modern Rivals, 1860–1901." *History of Education* 4 (1975): 21–35.

Eve, Arthur S., and C. H. Creasey. *Life and Work of John Tyndall.* London: Macmillan, 1945.

Gardner, Helen J., and Robin J. Wilson. "Thomas Archer Hirst—Mathematician Xtravagant." *American Mathematical Monthly* 100 (1993): 435–441, 531–558, 619–625, 723–731, 827–834, 907–915. Uses Hirst's journals for information on nineteenth-century mathematicians.

MacLeod, Roy M. "The X-Club: A Social Network of Science in Late-Victorian England." *Notes and Records of the Royal Society* 24 (1970): 305–322.

Rice, Adrian, Robin J. Wilson, and Helen J. Gardner. "From Student Club to National Society: The Founding of the London Mathematical Society in 1865." *Historia Mathematica* 22 (1995): 402–421.

Richards, Joan L. *Mathematical Visions: The Pursuit of Geometry in Victorian England.* Boston: Academic Press, 1988. Provides context to the debate over analytic and synthetic geometry.

Secord, James A. *Victorian Sensation: The Extraordinary Publication, Reception, and Secret Authorship of "Vestiges of the Natural History of Creation."* Chicago: University of Chicago Press, 2000. Uses Hirst's journals as a guide to how the Victorians read literature.

Wilson, Robin J. "Hirst, Thomas Archer." In *Oxford Dictionary of National Biography.* Oxford: Oxford University Press. 2004.

William H. Brock

HODGKIN, ALAN

(*b.* Banbury, Oxfordshire, England, 5 February 1914; *d.* Cambridge, England, 20 December 1998), *physiology, the ionic mechanisms of action potentials.*

Hodgkin's most important work, for which he shared the 1963 Nobel Prize in Physiology or Medicine, was on the ionic mechanisms of the action potential. This research and the development of an equation set that fits its electrical characteristics was a keystone of twentieth-century neuroscience and provides the foundation for our current understanding of neuronal conductance. In addition to his research achievements, Hodgkin served the scientific community as a director of research at Trinity College (Cambridge University), president of the Royal Society in London, and finally as master of Trinity College.

Family, Scientific Training, and Initial Discoveries. Born in 1914 to George and Mary Hodgkin, both Quakers, Alan was the oldest of three boys: Alan, Robin, and Keith. His early interest in science was sparked by his Aunt Katie (Catharine; née Wilson). Interestingly, she was related to Alan not only through her marriage to Edward Hodgkin, the elder brother of Alan's father, but also as sister of Alan's maternal grandfather. She encouraged Alan to keep precise records of his ornithological observations—a passion he pursued throughout his youth.

Hodgkin was initially ambivalent about his course of studies. His interests were divided between biology and history, a passion he shared with his grandfather George Hodgkin and his uncle Robin Hodgkin, both historians. His enthusiasm for outdoor explorations eventually tipped him toward natural history, and he decided upon a course of study that pursued this interest. He was accepted at Trinity College in 1932 as a student in botany, zoology, and chemistry.

Hodgkin was surrounded in both his family and professional lives by a cadre of eminent scientists. His cousin, Dorothy Crowfoot Hodgkin, received the 1964 Nobel Prize in Chemistry for "her determinations by x-ray techniques of the structures of important biochemical substances." His wife's father, Peyton Rous, shared the 1966 Nobel Prize in Physiology or Medicine for "his discovery of tumour-inducing viruses." During his first few months at Cambridge, Hodgkin joined the Natural Science Club, a "small elitist organization" (Hodgkin, 1992, p. 51), whose members during Hodgkin's attendance included Edward Bullard, John Pringle, Dick Synge, Maurice Wilkins, and Andrew Huxley—all of whom eventually became fellows of the Royal Society and four of whom won Nobel Prizes. Hodgkin also worked under E. D. (Edgar) Adrian in the physiological laboratory and came into contact with A. V. (Archibald) Hill, both of whom won Nobel Prizes for Physiology or Medicine.

In 1936 Hodgkin became a junior research fellow at Trinity College and spent several months repeating some of his own promising but rudimentary experiments. His results were published in the *Journal of Physiology.* A year

Hodgkin

later he was invited to the Rockefeller Institute by Herbert Gasser, then the institute's director, who later (1944) shared the Nobel Prize in Physiology or Medicine with Joseph Erlanger. This experience proved crucial toward Hodgkin's development of a systematic approach to physiology. By his own account, it transformed him from an "amateur into a professional scientist" (Hodgkin, 1992, p. 95).

While at the Rockefeller Institute, Hodgkin communicated with K. S. (Kacy) Cole, who invited Hodgkin to the Woods Hole Oceanographic Institution in Massachusetts. While there, Cole and Hodgkin conducted a series of experiments to measure resistance-length curves in nervous tissue, hoping that this research would allow them to calculate the resistance of the membrane at rest (Hodgkin & Cole, 1939). However, these experiments did not provide any quantitative data about the resting membrane potential. At the time, Cole and Hodgkin hypothesized that membrane potential could be measured by inserting a miniature electrode into the cell and measuring the potential both at rest and during the action potential. Both continued to carry out these experiments during the following year, with different collaborators.

In the summer of 1939 Hodgkin paired with Andrew Fielding Huxley to test the membrane theory proposed by physiologist Julius Bernstein. According to Bernstein, selective permeability to certain ions was the result of membrane breakdown. On this theory, current flow from a neighboring region makes the inside of the cell less negative, the membrane breaks down, and the resting potential falls, thus generating an action potential. If correct, the action potential should match the potential energy of the cell at rest. Huxley was able to overcome the technical difficulties that ensued from the initial attempts to place an electrode in a neuron, which allowed him and Huxley to record the resting membrane potential. This experimental breakthrough opened the door to studying the action potential. Their experiments yielded the unexpected result of an "overshoot" in the action potential. It was significantly larger than the resting potential: (roughly) +50 millivolts (mV) as compared to -50mV. (Their recorded action potential is displayed in Figure 1.) This finding, along with Howard Curtis and K. S. Cole's (1940), served as disconfirming evidence for Bernstein's idea that the action potential arose merely as the result of a breakdown in the membrane, producing a leak from inside to outside. Instead, they hypothesized that the action potential resulted from a process involving large proteins oriented along the axon. What their hypothesis still required, however, was a mechanism that induced the reversal in the electromagnetic polarity of the membrane.

Hodgkin's initial research on neuronal conductance was halted in late 1939, due to the imminence of World War II. He served for a brief period in an unpaid position with the Royal Aircraft Establishment at Farnborough, but the bulk of his wartime research went toward developing an airborne radar detection system for nocturnal interception. Though Hodgkin and Huxley met occasionally throughout the war years, they did not renew their collaborative efforts researching neurophysiology until 1945.

Subsequent Work on the Action Potential. To appreciate Hodgkin's contribution to scientists' understanding of the action potential, it is useful to consider the basics of the current account. (The following information is rudimentary and can be found in any introductory biology textbook.) The cellular membrane of a neuron is a lipid bi-layer whose resting potential is maintained by a differential charge. This charge results from a differential distribution of ions inside and outside the cell. Potassium (K^+) and organic anions (amino acids, A^-) are found in higher concentration inside the resting cell, while sodium (Na^+) and chlorine (Cl^-) are more abundant in extracellular space. Sodium-potassium pumps, the most prominent transport mechanism in neurons, actively transport Na^+ out and K^+ into the neuron at a rate of three Na^+ ions for every two K^+ ions. Highly concentrated inside the cell, K^+ is driven outward along its concentration gradient, leaving a negative charge inside. Additionally, the negatively charged amino acids are too large to pass through open membrane channels. There is also a greater concentration of Na^+ cations in extracellular space. Overall, the

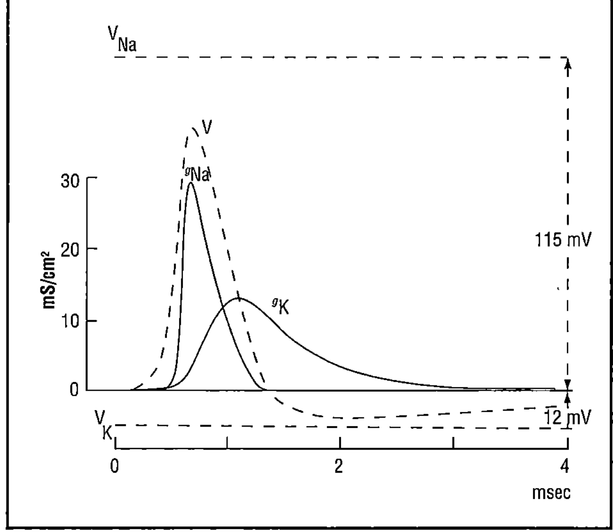

Figure 1. *Record of sodium and potassium current plotted against the resting membrane potential (V). Theoretical solution for propogated action potential and conductances at 18.5° C. Total entry of sodium = 4.33 pmole/cm²; total exit of potassium = 4.26 pmole/cm².*

membrane of a resting neuron is maintained at about -70 mV (with some variation across cell types).

The activity of selectively permeable ion channels permits some ions to flow across the cell membrane. Voltage-gated sodium channels closed at resting membrane potential are opened by a local depolarization, allowing the passage of Na^+ ions into the cell. Na^+ ions, higher in concentration outside the cell, flow inward through the open channels both along their concentration gradient and due to electrostatic pressure. Sodium influx generates a localized increase in positive charge inside the cell, causing additional localized depolarizations at surrounding regions. The result is a sharp change in localized membrane potential, briefly turning from negative to positive. If a critical threshold is reached (when Na^+ inward current is greater than the outward potassium current), depolarization of the membrane becomes irreversible and the cell generates an action potential. Sodium activation is a positive feedback system, propagating the potential down the length of the cell's membrane. This biochemical cascade typically begins at the axon hillock, a structural protrusion at the junction of the cell soma and axon, dense with voltage-gated ion channels predominantly selective for Na^+.

Efflux of K^+ ions through voltage-gated K^+ channels that open at the peak of the action potential—equivalent to the Na^+ equilibrium potential, around +55mV in most types of neurons—stops depolarization. Additionally, within 1 millisecond after reaching the threshold of action potential generation, Na^+ channels begin to close, ceasing Na^+ influx. The electrical potential reverses as a result of the outward movement of K^+, initiating repolarization. The potassium current takes longer than the sodium current to reach its maximum, and the cell membrane, as a result of sustained K^+ efflux in the absence of Na^+ influx, becomes more negative than the resting membrane potential. During this refractory period the cell cannot be brought to threshold to produce an action potential. By the time K^+ channels close, the membrane potential has "overshot" its resting potential and has become hyperpolarized due to the accumulation of K^+ outside the membrane. Resting membrane potential is quickly reestablished by the diffusion of K^+ throughout the extracellular fluid and the active transport of Na^+ ions out of and K^+ ions into the cell by the sodium-potassium pumps.

Hodgkin's Contribution. Initially, Hodgkin worked from Bernstein's account of membrane permeability. Additionally, there was evidence against the sodium theory of the action potential. Curtis and Cole (1940) reported the reversible abolition of the resting potential by increasing the external potassium concentration, equal to the internal concentration. They later (1942) reported a discrepancy between the predicted and observed internal sodium concentrations and found that resting potential was unaffected by the removal of all ions. Based on work by Ernest Overton (1902), who had theorized that the action potential might be the product of sodium and potassium exchange, Hodgkin and Huxley in 1947 provided evidence that potassium leakage occurs during an action potential. After considering several alternatives, Hodgkin proposed an ionic transport mechanism of a lipid-soluble molecule with a large dipole moment—a negatively charged carrier molecule that "ferried" ions across the membrane.

Evidence against Cole and Curtis's (1942) findings was initially provided by Bernard Katz (1947), as well as by Hodgkin's subsequent work after reading Katz's manuscript. Hodgkin placed a nerve fiber in an external sodium-deficient solution to observe the effect on action potential and simultaneously recorded the longitudinal resistance of both the external and internal fluid. He found that reduced external concentration of sodium reduced the action potential by a proportional amount. He repeated these experiments in the spring of 1947 and showed that external solutions of choline chloride yielded an unexcitable nerve fiber.

In the summer of 1948, Hodgkin left for the laboratory of the Marine Biological Association, Plymouth, to be joined by Huxley and Katz that autumn. In a series of experiments that followed, Hodgkin became convinced of the sodium hypothesis. The evidence included the observations that the action potential is both reversibly and rapidly abolished by an external sodium-free solution, and increased by a sodium-rich solution. This increase was proportional to the increase in sodium density, as predicted by the Nernst equation. Finally, the maximum rise in action potential was strongly dependant on the sodium concentration, consistent with Overton's hypothesis.

What was needed was a theory that could predict the potential difference across the membrane, while accounting for features such as the increased sodium permeability over other ions when at rest and its reversal during the action potential. In October 1947, Cole had written to Hodgkin about using a "central outside region with a guard region on each side and [the] use of a feedback circuit to control either the current flow in the central region or the potential difference in that region to the desired value" (Correspondence, 1947, as it appears in *Chance & Design,* 1992, p. 282). This "voltage clamp," as it has come to be termed, for the first time allowed for control over the membrane potential independent of the influence by ionic current. Cole's results seemed to comport with Hodgkin's earlier findings that a membrane suddenly depolarized by 50 mV produced an initial spike in the capacity current, followed by a brief inward current and, finally, an outward current. Though introduced to the technique in March, Hodgkin (working with Huxley) was not able to put it to use until mid-August 1948.

Realizing that two electrodes were necessary in order to measure both voltage and current, Hodgkin and Huxley modified Cole's (and Marmount's) technique to yield both the clamp and a device to measure current. Varying the external ionic concentration and holding the voltage at a predetermined specified step, Hodgkin and Huxley were able to separate the current and determine the relation between ionic permeability and membrane potential. These experiments generated most of the data they analyzed over the next two years and subsequently published in five articles in the *Journal of Physiology* in 1952. These results led them to abandon the carrier mechanism hypothesis of the action potential in favor of a voltage-dependent gating system—the basis of scientists' current understanding.

Hodgkin and Huxley analyzed the action potential into three phases: rising, falling, and refractory. They characterized the early inward current as due to external Na^+ ions moving into the axon, a process that could be reversed if the internal potential were raised beyond the sodium equilibrium or if the external solution were sodium deficient to the point of equilibrium. They characterized the outward current as due to K^+ ion efflux, which was confirmed experimentally by R. D. (Richard) Keynes in 1948 using radioactive tracers to study the leakage of potassium and further confirmed by Hodgkin and Huxley's calculations and indirect measurements (see Figure 2).

Hodgkin, Huxley, and Katz (1952) provided an outline of their methodology and a baseline measure of the relations between current and voltage as a function of time. They sought to measure the resistance of the membrane, the inverse value of which is permeability or conductance. Their methods included using the voltage clamp to step the determined membrane potential to displaced levels. They found that depolarizations of less than 15 mV produced only outward currents, while depolarizations between 15–110mV produced an initial inward current that disappeared at about 110mV and was followed by a sustained outward current. They found a continuous relationship between ionic current and membrane potential.

Hodgkin and Huxley published four other articles in 1952 (a–d). These results revealed the effects of changing the extracellular sodium concentration and resolved the ionic current into sodium and potassium currents. Their experiments included not only varying the voltage of the clamp but also varying the external sodium concentration. This tested for effects on inward and outward current with respect to voltage and time, and permitted them to divide the recorded current into components carried by sodium and potassium, respectively.

The membrane of the squid giant axon, when depolarized by 10mV, produced an initial inward current that was of the right magnitude and location to be capable of "charging the membrane capacity during the rising phase of an action potential" (Hodgkin & Huxley, 1952a, p. 449). This was the phase of the action potential that appeared to be carried by Na^+ ions. When the external sodium concentration was reduced sufficiently, the inward current disappeared, being replaced by "an early hump in the outward current" (1952a, p. 450). This outward current was only slightly altered by the change in external solution. When sodium ions were present, the action potential produced a peak potential above which the ionic current was inward and below which the current flowed outward. This peak varied with external sodium concentration.

These results supported the view that depolarization leads to a rapid increase in permeability, allowing Na^+ ions to flow in either direction toward equilibrium. A delayed outward current, observed during prolonged depolarization, was only marginally affected by replacing Na^+ ions with choline ions. It was here that Hodgkin and Huxley speculated that the reason was that this late current was produced by K^+ ions. Thus, for the first time, it became possible to resolve the inward and outward currents into two distinct currents. Sodium was found to rise rapidly toward a maximum and then decline along an approximately exponential curve. Potassium conductance was found to rise more slowly, along an S-shaped curve, and this increase in permeability was maintained for an appreciably longer period of time (see Figure 2). The effect of stepping from resting level to a new level was a sharp rise in inward current across the membrane, caused by a depolarization of 15mV or greater (up to 100 mV), initiating the cascade of events that constitute the action potential.

Hodgkin and Huxley acknowledged that various molecular mechanisms were consistent with their data. Thus, their 1952 papers aimed at the more modest goal of describing a series of equations that represented the movement of ions across the neural membrane. These equations could be used to determine ionic movement over time, subthreshold phenomena, changes in impedance, and several measurable properties of the action potential, including form, duration, and amplitude. The equation can be presented in several different formulations, but the standard one given by Hodgkin and Huxley (1952d) is:

$$I = C_M\, dV/dt + G_K n^4 (V-V_K) + G_{Na} m^3 h (V-V_{Na}) + G_l (V- V_l)$$

The total current crossing the membrane is represented by I and is the sum of four components: the

Hodgkin

capacity current (C_M dV/dt), the potassium current ($G_K n^4$ (V-V_K)), the sodium current ($G_{Na} m^3 h$ (V-V_{Na})), and the leakage current (G_l (V- V_l)). The capacitance, C_M, is characterized as the ability of the membrane to hold a differential charge across the membrane. G is the maximum conductance value for the indicated ionic current. V_K, V_{Na}, and V_l are the displaced values from equilibrium for each ion, and "V" is the displacement value of the membrane (V_m) from resting (V_{rest}). After dividing the ionic current into two distinct phases, the rising phase controlled by sodium and the falling phase controlled mainly by potassium, each phase was measured and then described, making it possible to predict the properties of the action potential given sufficient conditions to solve the equation.

After the Nobel Prize. Although Hodgkin and Huxley never worked in the same lab after 1952, they continued to consult about their respective research interests. Hodgkin viewed Huxley as a person of "penetrating intelligence" and continued to cherish his friendship. Hodgkin acknowledged that it continued to impact him greatly, even after their scientific interests began to diverge (Hodgkin, 1992).

Subsequent to receiving the Nobel Prize in 1963, Hodgkin shifted away from strictly research toward administration, although he continued to pursue research part time until the end of his life. He continued to investigate ionic mechanisms, including research on sodium-potassium pumps, muscle fibers, and salamander rod cells. He continued to work at Plymouth on squid neurons nearly every autumn until 1970.

In 1969 Hodgkin became a university research chair at Cambridge, obtaining the John Humphrey Plummer Professorship of Biophysics. He became president of the Royal Society in 1970. In 1972 he was knighted, and he received the Order of Merit in the following year. He became master of Trinity College at Cambridge in 1978, the year Trinity first admitted women undergraduates. He held that post until 1984.

Encouraged early in his studies to work on his own, Hodgkin came to view self-directed research as essential and "perhaps the most important thing [learned] at school" (Hodgkin, 1992, p. 30). He never worked toward a PhD degree and never had a formal research supervisor (Hodgkin, 1992). Most of the equipment that he used to address his research questions he either built or borrowed (Detwiler, 1999). These facts reflect his modesty, also found in his writings.

Upon leaving the Trinity College Master's Lodge in 1984, Hodgkin moved with his wife Marion into the British countryside. He continued to pursue the outdoor activities he loved in his youth. He was an avid fisherman and was remembered by family and professional colleagues as a man of "quiet disposition, a good sense of humor, and lively eyes that could express a full range of emotions" (Detwiler, 1999, p. 753). In 1989 he underwent a spinal operation that left him unable to walk and with progressive medical issues. He passed away on 20 December 1998. Alan Hodgkin was survived by his wife and four children, Sarah (S.M.), Deborah (E.D.), Jonathan (J.A.), and Rachel (R.V.).

BIBLIOGRAPHY

WORKS BY HODGKIN

With Kenneth S. Cole. "Membrane and Protoplasm Resistance in the Squid Giant Axon." *Journal of General Physiology* 22 (1939): 671–687.

With Andrew F. Huxley. "Potassium Leakage from an Active Nerve Fibre."*Journal of Physiology* 106 (1947): 341–367.

———. "Currents Carried by Sodium and Potassium Ions through the Membrane of the Giant Axon of Loligo." *Journal of Physiology* 116, no. 4 (1952a): 449–472.

———. "The Components of Membrane Conductance in the Giant Axon of Loligo." *Journal of Physiology* 116, no. 4 (1952b): 473–496.

———. "The Dual Effect of Membrane Potential on Sodium Conductance in the Giant Axon of Loligo." *Journal of Physiology* 116, no. 4 (1952c): 497—506.

———. "A Quantitative Description of Membrane Current and Its Application to Conduction and Excitation in Nerve." *Journal of Physiology* 117, no. 4 (1952d): 500–544.

With Andrew F. Huxley and Bernard Katz. "Measurement of Current-Voltage Relations in the Membrane of the Giant Axon of Loligo." *Journal of Physiology* 116, no. 4 (1952): 424–448.

Chance & Design: Reminiscences of Science in Peace and War. New York: Cambridge University Press, 1992.

OTHER SOURCES

Curtis, Howard J., and Kenneth S. Cole. "Membrane Action Potentials from the Squid Giant Axon." *Journal of Cellular and Comparative Physiology* 15 (1940): 145–157.

———. "Membrane Resting and Action Potentials from the Squid Giant Axon." *Journal of Cellular and Comparative Physiology* 19 (1942): 135–144.

Detwiler, Peter B. "Retrospective: Sir Alan Hodgkin (1914–1998)." *Science* 284 (1999): 753.

Huxley, Andrew F. "Sir Alan Loyd Hodgkin, O.M., K.B.E. 5 February 1914–20 December 1998." *Biographical Memoirs of Fellows of the Royal Society* 46 (2000): 219–241.

———. "From Overshoot to Voltage Clamp." *Trends in Neuroscience* 25 (2002): 553–558.

———. "Hodgkin and the Action Potential, 1935–1952." *Journal of Physiology* 538 (2002): 2. Available from http://jp.physoc.org/cgi.

Katz, Bernard. "The Effect of Electrolyte Deficiency on the Rate of Conduction in a Single Nerve Fibre." *Journal of Physiology* 106 (1947): 411–417.

Hodgkin

Lamb, Trevor. "Obituary: Alan Hodgkin (1914–98)." *Nature* 397 (1999): 112. Available from http://www.nature.com/nature/journal.

Overton, Ernest. "Beiträge zur allgemeinen Muskel- und Nervenphysiologie." *Pflügers Archiv: European Journal of Physiology* 92 (1902): 346–386.

Piccolino, Marco. "Fifty Years of the Hodgkin-Huxley Era." *Trends in Neuroscience* 25 (2002): 552–553.

Sean P. Keating
John Bickle

HODGKIN, DOROTHY MARY CROWFOOT (*b.* Cairo, Egypt, 12 May 1910; *d.* Ilmington, Warwickshire, United Kingdom, 29 July 1994), *crystallography, chemistry.*

Hodgkin pioneered the use of x-ray diffraction techniques to solve the structures of complex organic molecules such as steroids, antibiotics, and proteins. Most notably, her determination of the structure of vitamin B_{12} in 1956 revealed the existence of a hitherto-unsuspected chemical grouping, the corrin nucleus. For her contributions to the x-ray analysis of natural products, Hodgkin was awarded the Nobel Prize in Chemistry for 1964 and in 1965 received Britain's highest civil honor, the Order of Merit.

Early Life. Dorothy Mary Crowfoot was born in Cairo, Egypt, of English parents, in 1910. Her father, John Winter Crowfoot, worked for the Egyptian Educational Service; her mother, the former Grace Mary Hood (known as Molly), was an expert on ancient textiles. Dorothy was the first of four daughters. When World War I broke out in 1914, Dorothy and her sisters were evacuated to England, where they lived for the duration of the war in Worthing, West Sussex, in the care of a nanny and their paternal grandparents. In 1916 John and Molly Crowfoot moved to Khartoum, where John became the director of education for the Sudan. When the war ended, Molly took her daughters to Nettleham, Lincolnshire, while John remained in the Sudan. In 1920 the family moved again, to Beccles in Suffolk. There Dorothy attended the Parents' National Educational Union School, where she first exhibited what was to become a lifelong fascination with chemistry in general and crystals in particular. In the years from 1921 to 1927, she attended the Sir John Leman School at Beccles, where she participated in chemistry classes normally reserved for boys. In 1924 she and her sister Joan spent several months in Khartoum, where a friend of their father's, the chemist Dr. A. F. Joseph, further simulated Dorothy's interest in science by giving her a kit for analyzing minerals.

Dorothy Mary Hodgkin. HULTON ARCHIVE/GETTY IMAGES.

Although there was no family tradition of science, Molly Crowfoot encouraged her eldest daughter's interest in chemistry, buying her copies of William Henry Bragg's books, *Concerning the Nature of Things* (1925) and *Old Trades and New Knowledge* (1926), both of which were based on Christmas lectures for children at the Royal Institution. These books introduced Dorothy to the use of x-rays to solve chemical structures.

Dorothy took the Beccles school leaving certificate exams in 1927, earning distinction in six subjects—not including chemistry. After a year spent studying Latin and botany, she passed the entrance examinations for Oxford University, where her father had earned a degree in classics.

Oxford and Cambridge. From 1928 to 1932, Dorothy Crowfoot read chemistry at Somerville College, Oxford. Part I of the chemistry program normally involved three years of study and led to a BA degree; Part II required a further year spent doing a research project, leading to an honors degree. Crowfoot asked Herbert "Tiny" Powell, the university demonstrator in mineralogy, to act as her research supervisor. Powell assigned her a project involving the use of x-rays to study the structures of thallium dialkyl halide salts. This study was performed in a room in the University Museum. In 1932 Crowfoot became only the third woman to achieve a first-class honors degree in chemistry from Oxford University. She was also awarded half of the Vernon Harcourt Scholarship for 1932–1933.

In October 1932 Crowfoot moved to the Department of Mineralogy at Cambridge University as a PhD student, with John Desmond Bernal as her supervisor. Shortly thereafter she accepted a two-year research fellowship from Somerville College, with the prospect of a permanent fellowship on condition that she spend the first year of the award (1933–1934) at Cambridge. Crowfoot's PhD project was an x-ray diffraction analysis of the sterols and related hydrocarbons. A large number of sterol crystals were characterized in terms of space group (type of three-dimensional lattice), unit cell dimensions, and growth habit. These studies helped discriminate between two proposed ring structures of the sterol nucleus and provided some clues about the stereochemistry of particular compounds. They did not, however, provide unambiguous information about atomic locations.

In her last few months at Cambridge, Crowfoot became involved in a project that profoundly influenced her subsequent career. In April 1934 Bernal acquired some crystals of the enzyme pepsin that had grown by accident in Theodor Svedberg's laboratory at the University of Uppsala in Sweden. Fortunately, these had been brought to England in their mother liquor (the solution in which they formed). When Bernal subjected air-dried crystals of pepsin to x-rays, only a general darkening of the film resulted. However, crystals suspended in mother liquor gave a sharp diffraction pattern including spots corresponding to very small lattice spacings—the first demonstration of atomic regularity in a globular protein.

Crowfoot was not in the laboratory when the pepsin crystals were first analyzed, as she was seeing a consultant about pains in her hands—an early indication of the rheumatoid arthritis that afflicted her for the rest of her life. On her return, she joined in the further analysis of pepsin and coauthored with Bernal the resulting paper, "X-Ray Photographs of Crystalline Pepsin" (1934), published in *Nature.* It was no doubt Bernal who wrote the passage speculating that the pepsin molecule may consist of hexagonal nets rather than a polypeptide chain. Although Crowfoot maintained a close personal and professional relationship with Bernal until his death in 1971, she did not share his approach to research: she was cautious in her interpretations, while Bernal was bold, even foolhardy; she was tenacious in pursuit of a structure, while he was more interested in the next problem than the current one.

Insulin (I). When Crowfoot returned to Oxford in September 1934, she was assigned space adjacent to Powell's area in the University Museum. Robert Robinson, a professor of organic chemistry, helped her to find money to equip an x-ray laboratory. In addition to establishing an independent research program, she continued to work on her PhD thesis, which was successfully defended in 1936. That same year she was awarded a permanent fellowship from Somerville College.

X-ray crystallography was at something of a watershed in the mid-1930s. During his studies on mineral crystals, William Lawrence Bragg, then Langworthy Professor of Physics at Manchester University, had developed what he called the trial-and-error method of x-ray analysis. This involved generating a preliminary model based on crystalline symmetry and the sizes of the atoms present. The theoretical diffraction pattern of the model was then compared with the actual x-ray diffraction pattern of the crystal. Modifications of the model were then made and the comparison repeated until satisfactory agreement was achieved. In practice, the trial-and-error approach was feasible only for crystals with small numbers of parameters (that is, atomic coordinates not dictated by the symmetry of the crystal).

An alternative approach to x-ray analysis had been suggested by Bragg's father. William Henry Bragg, whose books had inspired the young Dorothy Crowfoot, was Fullerian Professor of Chemistry at the Royal Institution. As early as 1915, the elder Bragg had pointed out that the mathematical technique of Fourier analysis could be used to determine the structure of a crystal so long as the amplitudes and phases of the x-rays diffracted by the crystal were known. The amplitudes could easily be determined, but the phases (how the crests and troughs of different x-rays were related in space) could not. The absence of this vital piece of the puzzle became known as the phase problem.

One solution to the phase problem was provided by John Monteath Robertson's 1936 analysis of the plant pigment phthalocyanine. As the phthalocyanine crystal has a symmetry element known as a center of symmetry, all the x-ray beams diffracted by the crystal are either completely in phase (positive) or completely out of phase (negative) with one another. Therefore, one has to consider only the signs rather than the phase angles of the diffracted beams. Robertson showed that the addition of an atom of a heavy metal such as nickel did not change the crystal structure of phthalocyanine—the two crystals are isomorphous. However, the scattering from the nickel atom was so great compared to that from the lighter atoms that the signs of almost all diffracted beams became positive. Knowing the signs, Robertson used Fourier synthesis to construct a map of electron density in the phthalocyanine crystal.

However, the isomorphous replacement method was of limited utility for the vast majority of natural products, as these rarely contain centers of symmetry, and thus the phases of diffracted x-ray beams can have any values between 0° and 180°. Also, the summation of the Fourier series could be prohibitively time-consuming, although tables produced by Arnold Beevers and Henry Lipson greatly simplified the calculations involved.

A means of avoiding, rather than solving, the phase problem was suggested in 1934 by Arthur Lindo Patterson, who had worked with W. H. Bragg. Patterson's idea was to square the amplitudes of the diffracted beams, which would make all values positive. Using the squares of the amplitudes in a Fourier synthesis results in a map of the interatomic vectors present in the crystal. Such Patterson maps could be extremely complicated in crystals with many atoms and, except in the simplest cases, did not have any obvious relationship to the atomic lattice of the crystal.

Svedberg's studies had shown that proteins contain thousands of atoms. Nonetheless, the x-ray diffraction pattern of pepsin contained enough information to describe its structure at atomic resolution—so long as a solution could be found to the phase problem. When Robinson offered Crowfoot crystals of the protein hormone insulin that he had obtained from the Boots Pure Drug Company, she decided that insulin was a suitable molecule for her first independent investigation.

To make crystals large enough for x-ray analysis, Crowfoot used a published method to re-precipitate the insulin in the presence of zinc. These crystals were then air-dried before being subjected to diffraction. From the lengths and angles of the unit cell axes, she concluded that zinc insulin crystals had rhombohedral symmetry, which meant that they possessed a threefold rotation axis. The unit cell therefore contained either one molecule that itself had threefold symmetry or else $3n$ asymmetric molecules. From density measurements, the weight of protein in the unit cell was calculated to be 37,200 daltons.

Crowfoot published a more detailed analysis of zinc insulin in 1938, "The Crystal Structure of Insulin I: The Investigation of Air-Dried Insulin Crystals." The diffraction pattern contained no spots corresponding to lattice spacings of less than 7 Å, suggesting to Crowfoot a lack of order at that level. A recalculation of the unit-cell volume resulted in a slightly revised molecular weight, 37,600. The 1938 paper also included a Patterson analysis of insulin in projection on the plane defined by the a and b axes of the unit cell. The two major sets of peaks were at about 10 Å and 22 Å from the origin of coordinates. The former peaks were reminiscent of atomic spacings found in fibrous proteins by William Astbury of Leeds University.

Although these studies provided almost no insight into the structure of the insulin molecule, at least one of the puzzling features of Crowfoot's analysis was quickly resolved. Investigation of wet insulin crystals showed spots corresponding to lattice spacings as low as 2.4 Å, an indication that the "disorientation" reported earlier was in fact an artifact of drying.

In the late 1930s, Crowfoot also studied lactoglobulin and other proteins for which crystals were available. Thereafter, protein crystallography was set aside in favor of more promising lines of investigation.

Cholesterol and Penicillin. Some of Crowfoot's diffraction of insulin crystals was performed at the Royal Institution, using W. H. Bragg's powerful x-ray tube. While in London she met Thomas Lionel Hodgkin of the Workers' Educational Association, whom she married on 16 December 1937. The Hodgkins had three children: Luke Howard (born 1938), Prudence Elizabeth (born 1941), and Toby (born 1946).

Unlike many scientists, Dorothy Hodgkin was able to work more or less normally during World War II. In fact, she benefited from the evacuation to Oxford of equipment and personnel from Birkbeck College, University of London, where Bernal was now a professor of physics. Hodgkin put Bernal's student Harry Carlisle to work on the analysis of cholesteryl iodide. The approach taken is worth describing in some detail, as it was to form the basis of later studies on more complex organic molecules.

The unit cell of the cholesteryl iodide crystal contains two molecules related by a twofold screw axis (a symmetry element consisting of a 180° rotation plus a translation along the rotation axis). The screw axis is perpendicular to the more-or-less planar sterol molecules. This means that a projection of the crystal structure down the screw axis will have a center of symmetry, even though the crystal itself is not centrosymmetrical.

The strategy began with the use of Patterson maps to determine the positions of the heavy iodine atoms. Next, two-dimensional Fourier maps of a projection onto the ac plane of the unit cell were constructed using the phases calculated from the iodine atoms alone. (As the projection is centrosymmetrical, the phase angles can be only 0° or 180°.) The maps contained peaks corresponding to the approximate positions of atoms along the a and c axes of the unit cell, but provided no information about their positions along the b axis. A three-dimensional Fourier would have given the missing information, but the amount of manual computation required was prohibitive. Instead, Hodgkin and Carlisle constructed one-dimensional Fourier series parallel to the b axis only in the vicinity of the peaks observed in the projection. Because of the center of symmetry, the one-dimensional Fouriers contained peaks corresponding to pairs of real and unreal atoms, related to one another by a mirror plane of symmetry. These could be distinguished by consideration of bond lengths and angles. In a final step, the Fourier analyses were repeated using the phase contributions calculated for the carbon atoms as well as iodine atoms. In the end, approximate values for the *a, b,* and *c* parameters of all twenty-seven carbon atoms were determined. This represented the first three-dimensional analysis of a complex organic molecule.

Later in the war, Hodgkin became heavily involved in a project that was deemed to be of significant military importance: an analysis of the structure of penicillin. This antibiotic, which had been discovered by Alexander Fleming in 1928, was being intensively studied on both sides of the Atlantic. In Britain, the chemical analysis of penicillin was led by a group of Oxford University scientists that included Ernst Chain and Robert Robinson. In 1943, two forms of penicillin were crystallized: benzylpenicillin, or penicillin G, and 2-pentenyl penicillin, or penicillin F. Hodgkin's initial investigations showed that penicillin G had the simpler crystal structure. By April 1944 she had obtained crystals of three salts of penicillin G: those of the potassium and rubidium salts were orthorhombic and isomorphous, while those of the sodium salt were monoclinic.

Patterson analysis located the positions of the metal atoms in the potassium and rubidium salts, but not in the nonisomorphous sodium salt. Hodgkin and her student, Barbara Low, could, therefore, proceed to a two-dimensional Fourier analysis of the rubidium and potassium salts, as had been done for cholesteryl iodide. The sodium salt was turned over to Charles Bunn of Imperial Chemical Industries for analysis using the "fly's eye," an optical device for testing crystal structures that did not require phase information.

The crystallographic analysis of penicillin was hindered by conflicting chemical evidence about whether the molecule existed in the form of an oxazolone or a β-lactam. The conformation of the penicillin molecule represented another unknown, although it was assumed to be approximately linear. By early 1945, Hodgkin's Fourier analyses of the potassium and rubidium salts had incorporated phase information based on proposed positions of several atoms; however, further refinement did not improve the preliminary electron-density maps. Bunn had also generated maps for the sodium salt, but no more progress seemed possible with the fly's eye. However, comparison of the two sets of data enabled Hodgkin to distinguish peaks corresponding to real atoms, which were in the same relationship to one another in both crystals, from peaks corresponding to spurious ones. From this, it appeared that the penicillin molecule was "curled" (roughly semicircular in projection) rather than linear.

New Fourier analyses based on the curled molecule improved the electron-density maps and strongly supported the β-lactam structure. However, the degree of superimposition of atoms in projections of the unit cell made it impossible to determine accurate parameters for all atoms. Therefore, Hodgkin decided to perform a three-dimensional Fourier analysis of the sodium and potassium salts of penicillin G, the first time such an analysis had been attempted. For the potassium salt, this analysis involved summing Fourier series with hundreds of terms at each of 216,000 positions in the unit cell. To carry out the large number of mathematical operations required, Hodgkin used a Hollerith punched-card computer that belonged to the Scientific Computing Service. By 1947, three-dimensional electron-density maps of penicillin G, in the form of contours drawn on stacks of Perspex sheets, confirmed both the β-lactam structure and the curled conformation. Perhaps more importantly, by unambiguously demonstrating the locations of atoms in three dimensions, Hodgkin's studies on penicillin made x-ray crystallography the definitive technique for the structural analysis of organic molecules.

Vitamin B_{12}. Ever since her return to Oxford in 1934, Hodgkin's only position had been her Somerville College fellowship; unlike many fellows, she held no position in the university. In 1945 she applied for a new readership in chemical crystallography, but the post was awarded to Tiny Powell. Instead, Hodgkin was appointed as demonstrator. However, her status as a leading crystallographer was recognized in 1947 when she was elected a Fellow of the Royal Society.

The following year Hodgkin began work on a molecule whose structure was almost entirely unknown: vitamin B_{12}. This substance had been discovered as a cure for pernicious anemia in 1926 and was first crystallized in 1948 by Merck in the United States and Glaxo in the United Kingdom. When Hodgkin found that vitamin B_{12} contained cobalt, she realized that it might be amenable to x-ray analysis. However, the large size of the molecule suggested by elemental analysis—approximately one hundred atoms, not counting hydrogen—and particularly the lack of knowledge about its chemical structure, presented an unprecedented challenge for x-ray crystallography.

In the late 1940s, chemical investigations performed by Alexander Todd at Cambridge University and others provided fragmentary information about the vitamin B_{12} molecule. Acid hydrolysis produced a nucleotide monophosphate-like group, aminopropanol and several amides. In addition, the presence of a cyanide group had been demonstrated spectroscopically. Most atoms in the molecule, including the cobalt, were unaccounted for, although it was speculated that these included a porphyrin (a four-ring structure found in hemoglobin and chlorophyll).

The x-ray analysis of B_{12} began in late 1949, with Hodgkin using crystals from Glaxo and John White of Princeton University using crystals from Merck. The two groups soon combined their efforts, providing independent confirmation (or refutation) at many steps along the way. In initial studies, a three-dimensional Patterson analysis was carried out on air-dried B_{12} crystals. Advances in computing meant that calculation of three-dimensional Fourier series were now easier. Hodgkin used an analogue computer invented by Ray Pepinsky of Auburn University and also purchased a Hollerith machine. The Fourier maps located the cobalt atom within the unit cell and gave indications that it might lie in the middle of a planar group. This was presumably the proposed porphyrin, four nitrogens of which could form coordination bonds with cobalt. A three-dimensional Fourier map was then constructed using the phases of the cobalt atoms alone. In this, the planar group did not look much like a porphyrin, but the nucleotide-like group was tentatively identified as providing a fifth coordination bond to the cobalt atom through one of the nitrogen atoms on its "base." By this time it was believed that the sixth coordination position was occupied by cyanide.

In 1950 analysis began on wet B_{12} crystals; again, the cobalt atom was located by Patterson analysis and a three-dimensional Fourier map was made using the cobalt phases. This map had better resolution than that derived from the dry crystals, but the information about atomic locations provided was largely confirmatory. Two years later Hodgkin's group began to study sulfocyanate and selenocyanate derivatives of B_{12} in the hope that the sulfur and selenium atoms could be used to provide phase information for another Fourier analysis. It turned out that these crystals were not isomorphous, but the analysis did confirm the crystallographers' suspicion that the cyanide group of B_{12} coordinated the cobalt atom on the opposite side of the planar group from the nucleotide-like group. More importantly, the three-dimensional Fourier map of the selenocyanate derivative suggested that the planar group did not consist of four pyrrole rings joined by methylene groups, as in a porphyrin. Rather, it appeared that two of the rings were directly linked.

The final push came in 1953, when Todd's group in Cambridge crystallized a hexacarboxylic acid produced by alkaline hydrolysis of B_{12}. To perform a three-dimensional Fourier on this simpler compound, Hodgkin sent data obtained in her laboratory by Jenny Pickworth and John Robertson to Kenneth Trueblood of the University of California at Los Angeles, who had access to the powerful SWAC computer. The resulting Fourier map confirmed the direct linkage between rings A and D of the planar group and contained much sharper peaks than those from the other crystals. Phase information derived from the positions of another twenty-six atoms was used in a second Fourier analysis. This showed the planar group very clearly, and it also suggested some of the groups attached to it. In general, the hexacarboxylic acid derivative of B_{12} differed from the parent molecule in that the nucleotide-like group was missing, and the sixth coordination of the cobalt atom was provided by a chloride ion.

The next Fourier analysis of B_{12} itself used phase information from almost all atoms in the nucleotide-like, planar, and cyanide groups. This analysis produced a plausible three-dimensional structure of the entire molecule (shown diagrammatically in Figure 1).

The structure of vitamin B_{12}, published in *Nature* in July 1956, represented a giant step forward for x-ray crystallography. The Oxford-Princeton collaboration had provided structural information that was not available from traditional methods of organic analysis, which Hodgkin described in an earlier paper as "for any crystallographer something of a dream-like situation." Even more impressively, the planar group of B_{12} was a novel chemical entity, for which the term *corrin nucleus* was later coined. W. L. Bragg described the B_{12} study as "breaking the sound barrier."

Insulin (II). Hodgkin was promoted to reader in x-ray crystallography in 1955. Five years later she was appointed to the Wolfson Research Professorship of the Royal Society and moved her group from the University Museum at Oxford to the Inorganic Chemistry Laboratory. The Royal Society also honored her with a Royal Medal in 1956 and

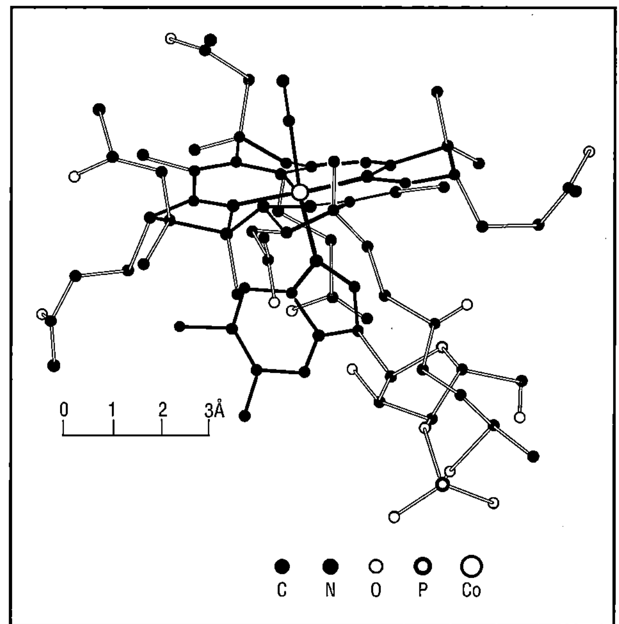

Figure 1. Structure of vitamin B_{12}, viewed parallel to the b axis of the crystal.

the Copley Medal—its highest award—in 1976. In 1964 Hodgkin was awarded the Nobel Prize in Chemistry "for her determinations by X-ray techniques of the structures of important biochemical substances." The following year, she was only the second woman ever to be appointed to the Order of Merit, a group of twenty-five distinguished living citizens selected by the British sovereign.

Despite having achieved the highest scientific and civil honors, Hodgkin still regretted not having pursued the structure of insulin. In the late 1950s, Max Perutz and John Kendrew had successfully used isomorphous replacement to solve the structures of hemoglobin and myoglobin, respectively. Frederick Sanger's determination of the amino acid sequence of insulin had shown that the protein has a molecular weight of approximately 5,800, indicating that the "molecule" Hodgkin had described in 1935 was actually six molecules. This simplified the structural analysis and obviated the need for internal symmetry. In 1956 Hodgkin obtained crystals of pig insulin containing either two or four zinc atoms. However, she was unable to locate the zinc atoms by Patterson analysis and was also unable to make other heavy-atom derivatives. The key breakthrough came in 1964, when Hodgkin learned from visiting Swedish scientists that zinc could be removed from insulin crystals using chelating agents and then replaced with other metals. Guy Dodson, a postdoctoral fellow, made cadmium and lead derivatives; an undergraduate student, Thomas Blundell, made a uranium derivative. Another important step forward was the realization that phase information could be obtained by anomalous scattering effects (slight intensity differences between symmetry-related spots).

The diffraction patterns of the heavy metal derivatives of insulin crystals were analyzed using the linear diffractometer made by Uli Arndt and David Phillips at the Royal Institution; this machine recorded intensities on punched tape that could be fed directly into a computer. By 1969 Hodgkin's group had generated an electron-density map at a resolution of 2.8 Å; using Sanger's data, it was possible to identify the position of each amino acid. A 1.9-Å structure was published in 1971. However, Hodgkin was not satisfied until she achieved a resolution of 1.5 Å, which allowed her to identify the position of every water molecule in the insulin crystal. This structure was published in 1988, when she was seventy-eight years old.

Last Years. In 1966 David Phillips, who had worked with W. L. Bragg at the Royal Institution, moved to Oxford to set up a new Laboratory of Molecular Biophysics in the Zoology Department. Hodgkin's group shared space with Phillips's until her retirement from the Wolfson Professorship in 1977.

In her sixties, Hodgkin left the day-to-day running of her research group to others. She traveled extensively and became involved in the leadership of scientific and nonscientific organizations. She served as the president of the International Union of Crystallography (1972–1975), the president of the British Association for the Advancement of Science (1977–1978), and the chancellor of Bristol University (1970–1988). Long a passionate believer in social justice and peace between nations, she took public stances on many issues, including opposing nuclear weapons and the Vietnam War. From 1975 to 1988 she was president of the Pugwash Conferences on Science and World Affairs. She received the Lenin Peace Prize from the Soviet Union for 1987. Thomas Hodgkin, who (unlike Dorothy) was at one time a member of the Communist Party, had died in 1982.

Hodgkin had never allowed her arthritis to limit her scientific activities or extensive travel. In 1988, however, increasing frailty caused her to resign her remaining positions. A hip fracture in 1990 left her unable to walk. Four years later, a fall fractured Hodgkin's other hip. She died at Crab Mill, a cottage Thomas had inherited from his parents, on 29 July 1994, and was buried in the churchyard at Ilmington. A memorial service was held in March 1995 at the Church of St. Mary the Virgin in Oxford.

Unlike other crystallographers of her generation, Dorothy Hodgkin was not associated with any particular technical breakthrough. She was always at the forefront in the use of computers to carry out crystallographic calculations. However, like others who had cut their teeth on more intuitive approaches, she did not welcome the day when x-ray analysis became automated. Hodgkin's main contribution was in developing an approach to x-ray analysis that filled the gap between the trial-and-error methods used by W. L. Bragg and Linus Pauling in the 1920s and the brute force methods that became feasible in the late 1950s. This approach required profound insights into chemistry and crystallography but was capable of providing unambiguous structural information about organic molecules too complex for more traditional and indirect methods of analysis.

BIBLIOGRAPHY

Hodgkin's papers are in the Bodleian Library at Oxford University. Probably the definitive biography is the microfiche appendix to Dodson's Royal Society memoir (cited below).

WORKS BY HODGKIN

With J. Desmond Bernal. "X-Ray Photographs of Crystalline Pepsin." *Nature* 133 (26 May 1934): 794–795.

"The Crystal Structure of Insulin. I. The Investigation of Air-Dried Insulin Crystals." *Proceedings of the Royal Society of London,* series A, 164 (1938): 580–602.

With J. Desmond Bernal and Isidor Fankuchen. "X-Ray Crystallography and the Chemistry of the Steroids. Part I." *Transactions of the Royal Society,* series A, 239 (1940): 135–182.

With C. H. Carlisle. "The Crystal Structure of Cholesteryl Iodide." *Proceedings of the Royal Society of London,* series A, 184 (1945): 64–83.

With Charles W. Bunn, Barbara W. Rogers-Low, and A. Turner-Jones. "X-Ray Crystallographic Investigation of the Structure of Penicillin." In *Chemistry of Penicillin,* edited by Hans T. Clarke. Princeton, NJ: Princeton University Press, 1949.

With Jennifer Kamper, Maureen MacKay, Jenny Pickworth, et al. "Structure of Vitamin B_{12}." *Nature* 178 (14 July 1956): 64–66.

With Jennifer Kamper, June Lindsey, Maureen MacKay, et al. "The Structure of Vitamin B_{12}. I. An Outline of the Crystallographic Investigation of Vitamin B_{12}." *Proceedings of the Royal Society of London,* series A, 242 (1957): 228–263.

With Margaret J. Adams, Tom L. Blundell, Eleanor J. Dodson, et al. "Structure of Rhombohedral 2 Zinc Insulin Crystals." *Nature* 224 (1 November 1969): 491–495.

With Edward N. Baker, Thomas N. Blundell, John F. Cutfield, et al. "The Structure of 2Zn Pig Insulin Crystals at 1.5 Å Resolution." *Philosophical Transactions of the Royal Society of London,* series B, 319 (1988), 369–456.

The Collected Works of Dorothy Crowfoot Hodgkin. Edited by Guy G. Dodson, Jenny Pickwork Glusker, S. Ramaseshan, et al. 3 vols. Bangalore, India: Interline, 1994.

OTHER SOURCES

Dodson, Guy G. "Dorothy Mary Crowfoot Hodgkin, O.M." *Biographical Memoirs of the Royal Society of London* 48 (2002): 179–219.

Dodson, Guy G., Jenny P. Glusker, and David Sayre, eds. *Structural Studies on Molecules of Biological Interest: A Volume in Honour of Professor Dorothy Hodgkin.* Oxford: Clarendon Press, 1981; New York: Oxford University Press, 1981.

Ferry, Georgina. *Dorothy Hodgkin: A Life.* London: Granta Books, 1998.

Graeme K. Hunter

HOLBROOK, JOHN EDWARDS *(b.* Beaufort, South Carolina, 30 December 1794; *d.* Norfolk, Massachusetts, 8 September 1871), *herpetology, ichthyology.* For the original article on Holbrook see *DSB,* vol. 15.

Holbrook and his monumental *North American Herpetology* continue to hold a place of prestige in the field of herpetology. In recognition of the importance of his classic treatise, the Society for the Study of Amphibians and Reptiles reprinted the volume in 1976. Holbrook's life and work have been more fully discussed in several recent publications, a number of which pay greater attention to his pioneering work on fishes from the waters of the American South.

Revised Information. A recently discovered manuscript of a travel memoir written by Holbrook while he was in the United Kingdom in 1818–1819 reveals previously unknown details about his sojourn there, including his attendance at lectures in medicine and natural history by University of Edinburgh professors.

Although he accepted an appointment as professor of anatomy in the Medical College of South Carolina in 1824, Holbrook relinquished that position in 1834, and became the anatomy professor in a newly formed institution, the Medical College of the State of South Carolina, also located in Charleston. He retired from the latter in 1860.

Upon his marriage to Harriet Pinckney Rutledge in 1827, Holbrook became the joint owner of the numerous slaves she had inherited. During the period 1847–1850 he participated in a debate with his fellow Charleston naturalist John Bachman over the human races, supporting the argument of the polygenists that each race had a separate origin and constituted a distinct species. Although he did not trumpet his position on this issue or on the institution of slavery, Holbrook clearly sanctioned the bondage of blacks and viewed them as a separate and mentally inferior species of humans. In his judgment, then, it was logical that he support the movement for secession of the southern states from the Union in 1861 and aid the Confederacy in its struggle to win the ensuing war for its independence.

Even though he admitted to unorthodoxy in his religious views, Holbrook embraced the conception of natural phenomena as the creations of a divine being. He declined, however, to discuss his notions about religion in any detail. Holbrook was certainly an altruistic man, and supported charitable institutions in Charleston. He was also interested in maintaining an accurate record of the past, and was a founding member of the South Carolina Historical Society. Elected to membership in the National Academy of Sciences in 1868, Holbrook was the first Southern scientist chosen for that honor.

Holbrook and Ichthyology. Although perhaps less well known for his work in ichthyology, Holbrook has recently received wider recognition for his studies of fishes in southern waters. Scholars have sorted through the sometimes confusing profusion of editions and revised plates of his books on fishes, and provided useful guides that help to clarify his contributions to ichthyology. As with his work on herpetology, Holbrook treasured accuracy in illustrating the fishes described in his books, and relied mainly on the talented artist John H. Richard to accomplish the task of providing morphological detail and true representation of color in the plates prepared for these volumes. Twelve taxa, or descriptions, of fishes established by Holbrook as new to science are considered valid today. Although he had evidenced interest in fishes as early as the late 1820s, Holbrook did not begin serious ichthyological research until two decades later, when he was around fifty years of age. His accomplishments in that field are therefore quite remarkable. Some evidence indicates that Holbrook intended to continue his work on fishes, but, given that he devoted four years of his life to serving the Confederate army as a surgeon, that he was nearly seventy-one years old when the American Civil War ended in 1865, and that he lost his entire library as a consequence of the war, it is not surprising that he was unable to resume his research. The value of his meticulous work in herpetology and ichthyology has endured, however, and gained renewed stature during recent years.

SUPPLEMENTARY BIBLIOGRAPHY

WORK BY HOLBROOK

"Manuscript of a Travel Memoir Written from the United Kingdom, 1818–1819." In the South Caroliniana Library, University of South Carolina, Columbia.

OTHER SOURCES

Adler, Kraig. *A Brief History of Herpetology in North America before 1900.* N.p.: Society for the Study of Amphibians and Reptiles, 1979.

Anderson, William D., Jr. "John Edwards Holbrook's Senckenberg Plates and the Fishes They Portray." *Archives of Natural History* 30 (2003): 1–12.

Anderson, William D., Jr., and Lester D. Stephens. "John Edwards Holbrook (1794–1871) and His *Southern Ichthyology.*" *Archives of Natural History* 29 (2002): 317–332.

Blum, Ann Shelby. *Picturing Nature: American Nineteenth-Century Zoological Illustration.* Princeton, NJ: Princeton University Press, 1993.

Sanders, Albert E., and William D. Anderson Jr. *Natural History Investigations in South Carolina: From Colonial Times to the Present.* Columbia: University of South Carolina Press, 1999.

Stephens, Lester D. "John Edwards Holbrook (1794–1871) and Lewis Reeve Gibbes (1810–1894): Exemplary Naturalists in the Old South." In *Collection Building in Ichthyology and Herpetology,* edited by Theodore W. Pietsch and William D. Anderson Jr., 447–458. Lawrence, KS: American Society of Ichthyologists and Herpetologists, 1997.

———. "Holbrook, John Edwards." In *American National Biography,* edited by John A. Garraty and Mark C. Carnes. New York: Oxford University Press, 1999.

———. *Science, Race, and Religion in the American South: John Bachman and the Charleston Circle of Naturalists, 1815–1895.* Chapel Hill: University of North Carolina Press, 2000.

———. "Holbrook, John Edwards." In *South Carolina Encylopedia,* edited by Walter Edgar. Columbia: University of South Carolina Press, 2006.

Worthington, Richard D., and Patricia H. Worthington. "John Edwards Holbrook, Father of American Herpetology." In reprint edition of *North American Herpetology* by John Edwards Holbrook, five volumes in one book, edited by Kraig Adler, xiii–xxvii. N.p.: Society for the Study of Amphibians and Reptiles, 1976.

Lester D. Stephens

HOLLEY, ROBERT WILLIAM

(*b.* Urbana, Illinois, 28 January 1922; *d.* Los Gatos, California, 11 February 1993), *organic chemistry, biochemistry, molecular biology, cell biology.*

Holley was the first to provide the full sequence of an RNA molecule, alanine transfer RNA, and therefore, indirectly, of a gene. He shared the Nobel Prize in Physiology or Medicine with Marshall Warren Nirenberg and Har Gobind Khorana in 1968 for the characterization of the mechanisms by which the genetic code controls the synthesis of proteins.

Early Life and Training. Robert Holley was one of the four sons of Charles and Viola Holley, both educators. He graduated from Urbana High School in 1938, studied chemistry at the University of Illinois, and received his BA degree in 1942. He studied for his PhD in organic chemistry at Cornell University with Professor Alfred T. Blomquist from 1942 to 1947. His graduate work was interrupted for two years during the war (1944–1946) when he participated with Professor Vincent du Vigneaud at Cornell University Medical College in the first chemical synthesis of penicillin. He married Ann Dworkin in 1945, and they had one son, Frederick.

After two years spent as an American Chemical Society Postdoctoral Fellow at Washington State University, he returned as assistant professor of organic chemistry to the Geneva Experiment Station of Cornell University. He was associate professor there from 1950 to 1957.

The work done during this period differed greatly from the subsequent work that would make Holley famous: characterization of the metabolic transformations of 2,4-dichlorophenoxyacetic acid in bean plants, and identification of the plant hormones, auxins, present in cabbage. From his work on penicillin, Holley established a correlation between the chemical reactivity of amides and their spatial structures, and from these observations he proposed in an article published in *Science* a general mechanism of action for enzymes that hydrolyze amides, such as proteases, a mechanism which is no longer tenable. This model was inspired by the model of enzymatic catalysis proposed some years before by Linus Pauling—the stabilization of the transition state of the reaction by the enzyme.

Holley

These early studies were not without influence on the future activities of Holley, even if they did not point to one particular line of research. They already demonstrate the attention paid by Holley to the contributions that organic chemists can make to biochemistry. Most of all, they familiarized him with the purification procedures that would be of a major importance for his future work—in particular, countercurrent distribution.

Sabbatical Year at Caltech. Holley discovered the world of RNA and protein synthesis during a sabbatical year spent studying with James F. Bonner at the California Institute of Technology. It was increasingly obvious at that time that the characterization of the mechanisms of protein synthesis would come from a full description of the components present in the in vitro protein synthesis systems that had been recently developed in various laboratories, in particular by the group of Paul Zamecnik at the Massachusetts General Hospital. The studies had shown that, before being incorporated into proteins, the amino acids were activated as amino acyl-adenylates by a family of enzymes. More recently, the group of Zamecnik and Mahlon Hoagland had made a puzzling observation: the next step was the attachment of amino acids to RNAs; not the RNAs present in the microsomes and considered for that reason as playing a major role in protein synthesis, but to a new family of small RNAs present in another of the subcellular fractions used for the in vitro synthesis system. Because they were present in a supernatant of ultracentrifugation, these RNAs were named soluble RNAs. They were shown to be one hundred nucleotides long, but their precise role in protein synthesis remained unknown.

Holley reached the same conclusion by a different approach—the study of the sensitivity to RNAse, the enzyme which degrades RNAs, of the opposite reaction to that of activation of amino acids. At least as far as the amino acid alanine was concerned, soluble RNAs were involved in amino acid activation and incorporation into proteins.

A relation was progressively established between these soluble RNAs and the adapter nucleic acids, which Francis Crick had hypothesized three years before to make the link between the genetic information contained in the nucleic acids and the amino acids constituting the proteins. It pushed the soluble RNAs to the forefront of research. Their characterization increasingly appeared as a sort of Rosetta stone able to reveal the mechanisms of protein synthesis and, for those who were convinced of its existence, to allow the decipherment of the genetic code.

Purification of Alanine tRNA. When Holley returned to Cornell at the Plant, Soil and Nutrition Laboratory of the U.S. Department of Agriculture, he soon undertook the purification and characterization of tRNA—*t* for transfer, the new name given to soluble RNA to make its function explicit.

Robert Holley. U.S. NATIONAL LIBRARY OF MEDICINE/SCIENCE PHOTO LIBRARY.

The first step in this seven-year study, which occupied most of Holley's time, was the purification of this tRNA from yeast. One hundred fifty kilograms of yeast were necessary to yield two hundred grams of mixed tRNAs and one gram of pure alanine tRNA. Two other tRNAs were purified in parallel, tyrosine tRNA and valine tRNA. The technique that proved essential for this purification was countercurrent distribution, a method based on the differential solubility of a molecule between two solvents, which had been designed at the Rockefeller Institute in the 1940s by Lyman C. Craig and David Craig, with whom Holley had worked, and which he had already used to purify auxins.

It was essential to prepare a pure alanine-tRNA fraction in order to proceed to the second part of the work, the sequencing of tRNA. Holley took a gamble on the purity of the fraction that he had obtained in devoting the next four years to this task. Fortunately for him, the gamble paid off.

Holley

To determine the sequence of the 77-nucleotide molecule, Holley used the same strategy as the one adopted by Fred Sanger for the protein insulin a few years before: to cut the molecule into different fragments by using enzymes acting at different places, and assemble the different fragments thus obtained, like a puzzle, from the overlapping of the fragments. The work on RNA was made more difficult by the fact that there are only four different nucleotides, compared with twenty amino acids, and this created a lot of ambiguities in the relative positioning of the different fragments. Another unexpected difficulty was the existence of bases with a modified structure and unusual properties, such as the lack of absorption of ultraviolet light, the structure of which had to be characterized. These modifications occur after the synthesis of the tRNA from DNA, at a posttranscriptional stage.

Holley used two different nucleases, pancreatic ribonuclease and takadiastase ribonuclease T1, recently characterized by a Japanese group, which cut at different positions in the sequence, and separated the fragments by chromatography on DEAE-cellulose, a recently designed ion-exchange chromatographic technique which Holley adapted to his purpose. It was not sufficient to determine the full sequence, and a lot of additional tricks had to be used to complete it: progressive degradation of the fragments by an exonuclease, snake venom phosphodiesterase, starting at one extremity of these fragments; a limited and preferential cutting of the tRNA molecule into two fragments obtained by working at low temperature; use of the different characteristics of the two extremities of the tRNA molecule and of the modified bases as markers of unique positions, and so forth.

With the help of "platoons" of graduate students, the full sequence was described in 1965. The position of the anticodon, the site of interaction, by base-pairing, with the messenger RNA, and a model for the secondary structure of the molecule were simultaneously proposed.

A Major Discovery. The value of this experimental achievement was immediately recognized. It was the result of intensive work headed by Holley, from his participation in the discovery of soluble RNA to the final characterization of its structure. The race was intense—a half-dozen structures of tRNA were determined in the next two years, and Holley had won it. The importance of the discovery was rapidly acknowledged: Tracy Sonneborn called it a "marvelous achievement" in *Science;* Maxine Singer described it as a "formidable job." Named professor of biochemistry at Cornell University in 1962, Holley became a full professor of biochemistry and molecular biology in 1964 and chairman of the department from 1965 to 1966. He received the Albert Lasker Award in Basic Medical Research in 1965, a first step to the Nobel Prize in 1968, won in conjunction with Marshall Warren Nirenberg and Har Gobind Khorana. He was elected member of the National Academy of Sciences.

The importance of the work was multiple, and the perception of it evolved from its beginnings to its completion. As stated above, tRNAs were first considered as the Rosetta stone leading to the decipherment of the genetic code. But the genetic code was cracked by the use of artificial polynucleotides with a well-determined base composition and sequence from the initial observation made with polyU by Nirenberg. And the anticodon was identified in the tRNA from this previous knowledge. One cause of the degeneracy of the genetic code was explained by the wobble hypothesis proposed by Francis Crick, that is, the imperfect pairing of the third base of the codon with the corresponding one of the anticodon. This hypothesis was proposed from data collected by the use of synthetic polynucleotides, even though it was further supported by observations made on the sequences of tRNAs.

One important result obtained through the sequence of tRNA was the first sequence of a gene. The discovery of Holley was seen as a first step toward knowledge of the full genome. The discourses on what could be expected from this knowledge were not so different from those heard at the end of the twentieth century, when the human genome was sequenced. However, the perception of it as a first step was an illusion: the methodology used for this first study could not provide access to the regulatory sequences that control the expression of genes. In addition, the strategy adopted by Holley could not be easily extended to large RNAs such as messenger RNAs. The technologies for sequencing genes would be invented later, in the mid-1970s, and are of a different nature.

Some of the observations made as Holley's work progressed—such as the abundance of modified bases—are somehow anecdotal: their physiological meaning is still dubious. The cloverleaf secondary structure proposed by Elizabeth Betty Keller and John Penswick and rapidly adopted by Holley was shown to be true for all tRNAs. It was unduly considered by some researchers as a three-dimensional structure until the characterization of crystallized tRNAs by x-ray diffraction studies done by the group of Aaron Klug showed that this was not the case.

This explains why Holley now occupies both an important and a circumscribed place in the historiography of molecular biology. Retrospectively, while the technological exploit is still worthy of acknowledgment, the consequences of this work for later developments in molecular biology are less important than was initially anticipated. Holley's discovery was a milestone for his contemporaries, not for his followers.

Holley

Control of Cell Division and Cancer. In 1968, there were still many questions pending in the field of protein synthesis: the precise three-dimensional structure of tRNAs and ribosomes was ignored, and the different steps in protein synthesis were still fuzzy. Holley followed the same direction for some years, characterizing the structure of other tRNAs, using indirect chemical techniques to try to elucidate the three-dimensional structure of tRNAs, and turning his efforts to the enzymes involved in the modification of the tRNA bases. But he rapidly abandoned tRNAs, and devoted his efforts to the control of cell division in mammalian cells until the end of his academic career.

In 1966–1967, he spent two years at the recently created Salk Institute for Biological Studies as a National Foundation Postdoctoral Fellow. In 1968 he joined the permanent staff of the Salk Institute as a professor in molecular biology. He was also an adjunct professor at the University of California at San Diego.

Holley was not alone in his movement toward complex biological issues. Many of the founders and heroes of molecular biology made a similar move—Francis Crick, Seymour Benzer, and Gunther Stent toward the study of behavior and the brain, François Jacob and Sydney Brenner toward embryogenesis. Holley preferred to focus on the control of cell division in established mammalian cell lines, probably considering it the best system to characterize and isolate the factors involved in this control.

After some experiments on the extensively studied 3T3 cells, Holley focused his work on an epithelial cell line BSC-1, for the reason that most human cancers are of epithelial origin. He demonstrated that the cells secrete a growth inhibitor, the sequence of which he finally characterized in 1988 after more than ten years of effort.

These twenty years of research on the control of cell division and the characterization of growth inhibitors did not consist simply of data generation. A Nobel Prize winner cannot enter a new field of research without expressing new and general views that strongly oppose previous models. Such was Holley's attitude. He never accepted the idea that cell division can be limited by "contact inhibition," signals originating from the physical contact between adjacent cells. For Holley, contact inhibition was only a consequence of a reduced supply of nutrients, due to the fact that their diffusion was limited by the surrounding cells. In a similar way, he was initially reluctant to attribute a major role to growth factors in the control of cell division. In contrast, he emphasized the role of low molecular weight nutrients. In a review article published in 1975 in *Nature,* he admitted the role of polypeptide hormonelike materials, but once again emphasized the importance of the most common molecules, such as metabolites.

Holley was not interested in the internal, intracellular mechanisms controlling cell division. His only attempt in this direction was the characterization of membrane proteins controlling ion exchange. In 1972 he published in the *Proceedings of the National Academy of Sciences* a unifying hypothesis concerning the nature of malignant growth. He believed that the crucial alteration leading to malignancy was an alteration in the cell membrane that resulted in an increased internal concentration of nutrients. Over the following years, with the characterization of oncogenes and tumor suppressor genes, the emphasis in cancer research shifted to transformations occurring inside cells and affecting intracellular signaling pathways and gene regulation, and not to membranes as Holley had anticipated. Because of his well-established opinions on the control of cell division and the origin of tumors, Holley was at odds with mainstream research. This prevented him from making a major breakthrough in his new field of research.

BIBLIOGRAPHY

The Salk Institute has decided to create an archival center at the University of California, San Diego.

WORKS BY HOLLEY

With F. P. Boyle, H. K. Durfee, and A. D. Holley. "A Study of the Auxins in Cabbage Using Countercurrent Distribution." *Archives of Biochemistry and Biophysics* 32 (1951): 192–199.

"Steric Inhibition of Amide Resonance and Its Possible Significance in Enzyme Action." *Science* 117 (1953): 23–25.

"An Alanine-Dependent, Ribonuclease-Inhibited, Conversion of AMP to ATP, and Its Possible Relationship to Protein Synthesis." *Journal of the American Chemical Society* 79 (1957): 658–662.

With Jack Goldstein. "An Alanine-Dependent, Ribonuclease-Inhibited Conversion of Adenosine 5'-Phosphate to Adenosine Triphosphate. II. Reconstruction of the System from Purified Components." *Journal of Biological Chemistry* 234 (1959): 1765–1768.

With John Robert Penswick. "Specific Cleavage of the Yeast Alanine RNA into Two Large Fragments." *Proceedings of the National Academy of Sciences of the United States of America* 53 (1965): 543–546.

With Jean Apgar, George A. Everett, James T. Madison, et al. "Structure of a Ribonucleic Acid." *Science* 147 (1965): 1462–1465.

"The Nucleotide Sequence of a Nucleic Acid." *Scientific American* 214 (February 1966): 30–39.

"Alanine Transfer RNA." Nobel Lecture, 12 December 1968. Available from http://nobelprize.org/nobel_prizes/medicine/laureates/1968/holley-lecture.html.

With Josephine A. Kiernan. "'Contact Inhibition' of Cell Division in 3T3 Cells." *Proceedings of the National Academy of Sciences of the United States of America* 60 (1968): 300–304.

"A Unifying Hypothesis concerning the Nature of Malignant Growth." *Proceedings of the National Academy of Sciences of the United States of America* 69 (1972): 2840–2841.

"Control of Growth of Mammalian Cells in Cell Culture." *Nature* 258 (1975): 487–490.

With Rosemary Armour, Julia H. Baldwin, et al. "Density-Dependent Regulation of Growth of BSC-1 Cells in Cell Culture: Control of Growth by Serum Factors." *Proceedings of the National Academy of Sciences of the United States of America* 74 (1977): 5046–5050.

With Peter Böhlen, Roy Fava, Julia H. Baldwin, et al. "Purification of Kidney Epithelial Cell Growth Inhibitors." *Proceedings of the National Academy of Sciences of the United States of America* 77 (1980): 5989–5992.

With Ronald F. Tucker, Gary D. Shipley, and Harold L. Moses. "Growth Inhibitor from BSC-1 Cells Closely Related to Platelet Type Beta Transforming Growth Factor." *Science* 226 (1984): 705–707.

With Steven K. Hanks, Rosemary Armour, Julia H. Baldwin, et al. "Amino Acid Sequence of the BSC-1 Cell Growth Inhibitor (Polyergin) Deduced from the Nucleotide Sequence of the cDNA." *Proceedings of the National Academy of Sciences of the United States of Amerca* 85 (1988): 79–82.

OTHER SOURCES

Crick, Francis. "Codon-Anticodon Pairing: The Wobble Hypothesis." *Journal of Molecular Biology* 19 (1966): 548–555.

Hoagland, Mahlon. *Toward the Habit of Truth: A Life in Science.* New York: Norton, 1990.

Judson, Horace Freeland. *The Eighth Day of Creation: Makers of the Revolution in Biology.* Plainview, NY: Cold Spring Harbor Laboratory Press, 1996.

Kay, Lily E. *Who Wrote the Book of Life?: A History of the Genetic Code.* Stanford, CA: Stanford University Press, 2000. The most complete historical work on the way that led to the "cracking" of the genetic code.

Portugal, Franklin H., and Jack S. Cohen. *A Century of DNA: A History of the Discovery of the Structure and Function of the Genetic Substance.* Cambridge, MA: MIT Press, 1977.

Rheinberger, Hans-Jörg. *Toward a History of Epistemic Things: Synthesizing Proteins in the Test Tube.* Stanford, CA: Stanford University Press, 1997.

"Robert W. Holley: The Nobel Prize in Physiology or Medicine 1968." Available from http://nobelprize.org/nobel_prizes/medicine/laureates/1968/holley-bio.html.

Singer, Maxine F. "1968 Nobel Laureate in Medicine or Physiology." *Science* 162 (1968): 433–436.

Sonneborn, Tracy M. "Nucleotide Sequence of a Gene: First Complete Specification." *Science* 148 (1965): 1410.

Michel Morange

HOLMES, GORDON MORGAN

(*b.* Dillon House, Castlebellingham, Ireland, 22 February 1876; *d.* Farnham, England, 29 December 1965), *neurology, neuroanatomy, clinical neurophysiology.*

In a generation of gifted neurologists, Holmes was outstanding for his refinements of the clinical examination of the nervous system, which led to his inquisitive searching and original investigations of its functions. His work illuminated and clarified many uncertainties in the functions of the cerebellum, and the sensory and visual pathways in the brain. His rigorous, trenchant approach and inductive reasoning were widely admired and adopted by contemporary neurologists and physicians. In the fields of clinical diagnosis, the deductive reasoning he applied to neurological phenomena shaped clinical techniques and advanced understanding of neurophysiology for his many disciples and their acolytes.

Early Career. Born in Ireland to a Yorkshire Protestant family, Gordon Holmes was a shy, solitary child whose mother, Kathleen (née Morgan) died young. His father's name was also Gordon Holmes. The son qualified in medicine at Trinity College, Dublin, in 1899. As a junior at Richmond Asylum in Dublin he was awarded the Dublin University Travelling Prize in Medicine and the Stewart Scholarship in Nervous and Mental Diseases in 1899. These financed a visit to Frankfurt, Germany, where for two years he studied comparative anatomy with Karl Weigert and Ludwig Edinger. After an arduous start with Edinger, a hard taskmaster, Holmes diligently acquired a remarkably detailed knowledge and experience of neuroanatomy and neurophysiology, which were to be the foundation of much of his subsequent work. When he returned to England in 1902, on Edinger's recommendation he became Resident Medical Officer to Hughlings Jackson at the National Hospital for Paralysis and Epilepsy, Queen Square, London, which became the center of his life and work.

The National Hospital for Paralysis and Epilepsy in London was founded in 1859. Its reputation was based on the work of an unusually celebrated group of physicians, notably Hughlings Jackson and Charles Édouard Brown-Séquard. Its physicians in the early nineteenth century included Sir William Gowers, Sir David Ferrier, Sir Victor Horsley, and William Aldren Turner. Many have come to regard this period as a golden era in neurology.

Holmes obtained the MD in 1903, membership of the Royal College of Physicians, London (MRCP) in 1908, and was elected a Fellow six years later. He quickly mastered the clinical examination and developed it "to a state of well-nigh scientific perfection" (Walshe, 1966). His exhaustive yet rapid examination routine was unprecedented. He became physician to the Royal London Ophthalmic (Moorfields) Hospital and to Charing Cross Hospital. Few now appreciate that physicians of his generation worked as honoraries at their hospitals, receiving no payment for clinical work; teaching and research were likewise vocational and unpaid; their sustenance was supported solely by private practice.

With Sir Henry Head he wrote a classic paper, published in the journal *Brain* in 1911, "Sensory Disturbances from Cerebral Lesions." In it they first described systematically the functions of a deeply placed gray matter nucleus—the thalamus—and its relationship to the cortex. Holmes later emphasized the importance not of showing whether a sensation was impaired or spared by a cortical lesion, but rather inquiring what qualities or aspects of sensory perception relate to the sensory cortex. It was necessary, therefore, for him to refine the sensory examination at the bedside and clinic in an unprecedented fashion, which soon was widely accepted as standard practice. So energetic and industrious was Holmes that by the outbreak of war in 1914 he had published fifty-five papers, seventeen of them in the prestigious journal *Brain.*

Myopia thwarted his volunteering for war service. Frustrated, Holmes joined the staff of a Red Cross hospital just behind the front line in France. His impressive work persuaded the War Office to renegotiate his disqualification. As lieutenant colonel, Holmes became consulting neurologist to the British Expeditionary Force in France. Patients with war injuries of the spinal cord and brain allowed him—in terrible conditions of dirt, cold, and exhaustion—to study the cerebellum and the visual cortex, which were exposed in soldiers whose helmets were incomplete at the back. He had to treat up to three hundred wounded men daily. Holmes performed all the neurological postmortems himself. This work culminated in eighteen published wartime papers, many written at the front in arduous conditions. Spinal injury was the basis of his Goulstonian Lecture to the Royal College of Physicians in 1915. He was twice mentioned in dispatches and was awarded the Order of St. Michael and St. George in 1917 and Commander of the British Empire in 1919.

Clinical Techniques. After World War I, Holmes continued in neurological practice and research. He was thorough and relentlessly precise in his methods of clinical diagnosis, though notoriously impatient with less gifted colleagues. "In teaching," F. M. R. Walshe said in his *Biographical Memoirs of the Royal Society,* "he had the great gift of making clear to his students the thread of his thoughts and the grounds on which he reached his conclusions. He never posed as an oracle or a maker of slick diagnoses. … To be trained by him was a severe but most salutary discipline" (1966, pp. 311–319).

Gordon Holmes developed the foundations of modern neurological examination. He divided the examination into cortical functions, cranial nerves, motor and coordination, sensibility, and reflexes. "He could coax physical signs out of a patient like a Paganini on the violin," observed a colleague, who continued: "every neurologist alive today … is unconsciously utilizing the routine clinical examination propagated, perfected, and perpetuated by Gordon Holmes. It was a sheer delight to watch him evoking one physical sign after another in a patient with say, tabes" (Critchley, 1979, p. 230). (Tabes is caused by syphilis of the nervous system, noted for widespread abnormalities of sensation, pupils, and reflexes.)

Holmes wrote many critical clinical papers, and with W. J. Adie he discovered the myotonic or Holmes-Adie pupil (small asymmetrical pupils that contract very slowly to convergence but not to light stimuli; they can mimic syphilitic pupils). His *Introduction to Clinical Neurology* (1946) was a classic, succinct textbook for students. It was not intended as a description of various diseases, but rather as a discussion of the nature and the significance of the symptoms and abnormal signs that a patient with a nervous disorder may present. It assumed a basic knowledge of anatomy and physiology of the nervous system and subsumed brief accounts of the current views on disordered function. In the foreword he said: "Though tomorrow may disprove some of them, they are put forward in the belief that 'truth comes more readily from error than from confusion.'" With rare exceptions, he deliberately provided no authorities and no references, probably because it was a short textbook for students, who in those days were not encumbered by numerous and tedious references to papers they were unlikely to consult.

The Cerebellum. Among his many contributions. Holmes challenged the accepted theory of the workings of the cerebellum, the "corrugated" lobular structure at the back of the head that controls balance and coordinated movements. With T. Grainger Stewart he described the rebound phenomenon in cerebellar disease, later known as the Stewart-Holmes sign. He also described an inherited degenerative cerebellar ataxia involving the olivary nucleus, known as Holmes' syndrome, and expounded the range of symptoms of cerebellar tumors. He also published a painstaking account of a form of familial degeneration of the cerebellum with a detailed review in which he attempted to classify cerebellar disease. He characterized cerebellar disturbances by asthenia (weakness), ataxia (incoordination), rebound, and adiadochokinesia (inability to perform fine alternating movements). In an excellent biographical review, Caoimhghin S. Breathnach points out how similar was his style and strategy to that of Sir Charles Sherrington, the foremost neurophysiologist of the day. "Holmes," he said, "was as much physiologist as neurologist, a duality which should occasion no surprise when his training, so like his friend Head's in 'basic science' is recalled. Under Ludwig Edinger's guidance he had been initiated into the intricacies of functional neurohistology" (Breathnach, 1975, pp. 194–200).

Holmes

Holmes's notions of the function of the cerebellum were largely original and of major physiological importance. He believed that the cerebellum ensures the regularity and maintenance of muscular contractions and the immediate and effective response of mechanisms to cerebral impulses; it also exerts a regulating and coordinating influence on the motor centers that affect voluntary movements and by this means ensures their harmony, precision, and correct range of movement.

This did not mean, Holmes emphasized, that the cerebellum puts into play the muscles necessary for the accomplishment of complicated movements. It was an organ that had evolved on the sensory, receiving (afferent) side, rather than on the motor side of the central nervous system. But it received and integrated impulses related to position sense from all parts of the body, and by virtue of these it kept the motor mechanisms in such a state of "tone" that they could react promptly and efficiently to voluntary impulses, and it thus ensured the correct cooperation of the separate motor centers that are concerned in individual acts (Holmes, 1927 and 1939).

Visual Disorders. With Henry Head, Holmes investigated both the sensory and visual pathways and the optic thalamus. The results were published in 1911 and were reprinted in Head's *Studies in Neurology* (1920).

Two outstanding problems faced doctors of the day. First, the main central area of vision in the retina lies in the macula (fovea), but its exact representation in the visual cortex was not known. Secondly, there was little understanding of those strange (agnosic) defects of appreciation of size, shape, texture of objects, and the location of the body and of external objects that often result from disease or injury to the parieto-occipital lobes at the back of the brain and which hamper recovery of movement. In his first Montgomery Lecture, in ophthalmology at Trinity College, Dublin, in June 1919, "The Cortical Localisation of Vision," he elucidated macular vision and its sparing in injuries of the occipital lobes:

> the type of blindness that is produced by superficial injuries of both occipital lobes—that is, by wounds that injure the posterior parts of the striate areas. In all such cases we find peripheral vision intact and central vision abolished. They are consequently evidence that central or macular vision is represented in the most posterior parts of the visual areas, and that this region is not concerned with peripheral sight. (p. 194)

The hemianopia (loss of the same half-fields of vision, i.e., to the right or to the left) due to vascular lesions differed from that produced by penetrating gunshot wounds in that the macula is spared. He explained this by observing that at the posterior end of the striate area of the visual cortex, the middle and posterior cerebral arteries meet so that the macula gets the benefit of their overlap. The fovea also gets the larger share of cortical retinal representation. It is probable, he said, that the portion of the striate area that frequently spreads over the occipital pole and on to the outer surface of the brain may be the center of macular sight. The frequency of paracentral scotomata (blind spots near the central visual fields) is consequently accounted for by the more exposed position of this part of the visual area than of that which lies on the inner surfaces of the hemispheres. Not only is each segment of the retinae represented in a definite portion of the visual cortex, but this representation is fixed and immutable, so that if a part of the visual cortex is totally destroyed, there will be a permanent blindness of the corresponding segment of the visual fields.

The second lecture dealt with visuospatial perception. He noted that patients who were unable to recognize the spatial relation between objects and their own bodies were also unable to determine accurately the relative positions of two objects. Patients could not accurately assess size, shape, or length of objects that they saw and could not localize them in space. They also had impaired topographical memory of familiar places, but stereoscopic vision of the thickness and depth in solid objects was often preserved. Holmes said:

> In all my eight cases the condition described above was associated with gunshot wounds of the head which involved the posterior and upper parts of both parietal lobes. (1919b, pp. 230–233)

In two instances of postmortem examination, the outer surfaces were injured while the missiles passed through the inner or mesial surfaces. This was an important contribution to visuospatial function, published in 1918 as "Disturbances of Vision by Cerebral Lesions," which he located by damage of the occipital and parietal lobes of the brain. This work facilitated both clinical analysis in trauma and other pathological conditions and the understanding of the physiological mechanisms of the visual pathways.

Spinal Injuries. Based on work at the front with the surgeon Percy Sargent, at Boulogne, Holmes gave the Goulstonian lectures at the Royal College of Physicians of London in 1915. He had handwritten notes made on site from more than three hundred spinal cord injuries. He described signs of injury to the cord and sympathetic chain, hypothermia, and the unusual occurrence of shingles (herpes zoster) in the upper margin of the sensory loss.

A partial cervical spinal cord lesion that presented with paralysis of the arms but spared the legs was another curiosity that Holmes deduced was caused by "softening," with damage to the gray matter of the cord. Based on his extensive knowledge of pathology, he provided a systematic account of the neuropathological changes after the injury. He observed in some cases that early swelling of nerve fibers distant from the primary site of damage accounted for deterioration days or weeks after injury. Cord hemorrhage and cell death might lead to spinal cord cavities (syringomyelia). Holmes recognized that spinal "concussion," the transient state of paralysis and impaired sensation in the legs (often regarded as nervous or hysterical), was caused by tissue changes without external evidence of injury, such as in troops buried by shell explosions. The diagnosis had to be confirmed by clinical evidence of cord damage.

Honors. In addition to a heavy clinical, teaching, and research workload in the hospital, from 1922 to 1937 Holmes was editor of *Brain,* the most esteemed of neurological journals. His writings on neurology touched on almost every aspect of the subject and were widely regarded as authoritative. Holmes was examiner, councillor, and censor for the Royal College of Physicians. His pre-eminence was recognized by his election as a Fellow of the Royal Society in May 1933.

He received several honorary university degrees: DSc, Dublin, 1933; DSc, National University of Ireland, 1941; the DCL, Durham, 1944; and the LLD, Edinburgh, in 1952. Retirement came in 1941, knighthood, belatedly in 1951. After enduring the London blitz, he moved to a country house in Farnham, where his passions were his garden and golf, which he played with his devoted wife Rosalie. Aged eighty-nine, his quietus came during sleep on 29 December 1965.

Holmes the Man. Words such as *volcanic, tornado-like, brusque,* and *demanding* were sometimes applied to describe him by his pupils. He had boundless energy, but was prone to migraine and duodenal ulcer. Holmes had strong likes and dislikes and no great gift for wit, diplomacy, or compromise. He was an irascible martinet devoted to detailed observation and collection of data. At the front, he disagreed with Harvey Cushing, the celebrated but short-tempered American neurosurgeon, about the treatment of casualties. His notorious feud with Kinnier Wilson, a senior, brilliant clinician and teacher at Queen Square, was related by his house-physician Macdonald Critchley: "Wilson was a vain and touchy man, jealous of Holmes, and he would ostracise anyone who stayed in the other camp. Holmes for his part could not care less, and simply ignored his colleague (Critchley, 1979, pp. 228–235).

Critchley relates the story that whenever Holmes and Wilson made their respective rounds in Queen Square, each with his own retinue of doctors of all ranks, and they met in the passageways, neither of them would budge to make way for the other party. Lengthy blockages ensued. However, despite his manner, he nevertheless inspired affection. And, he warmly entertained many loyal and distinguished medical friends, among them: Godwin Greenfield, Sir Percy Sargent, Charles Beevor, Sir Henry Head, Wilder Penfield, Sir Francis Walshe, William J. Adie, and Sir Charles Symonds. Critchley said of him: "among these [physicians at Queen Square] was that Colossus, physical as well as intellectual, Gordon Holmes who shone brightest among the galaxy of stars surrounding him" (Critchley, 1979, pp. 228–235). Walshe noted Holmes's great gift of making clear to his students the thread of his thoughts and the grounds on which he reached his conclusions. Penfield, the celebrated Canadian surgical pioneer of brain localization, in 1971 noted his softer side, remarking that Holmes was one of the finest teachers he had known; beneath the exterior of a martinet there was an Irish heart of gold.

Holmes was truly modest and could not bear to hear his achievements or formidable reputation discussed in public; on occasion he was so embarrassed that he would leave the room. He eschewed committee meetings and many social engagements whenever possible. Contemporaries thought that Holmes resembled Sir William Gowers more than Hughlings Jackson, his first teacher at Queen Square, showing the same patient, punctilious methods of collecting clinical data, then correlating them with anatomy and pathology. Critchley's obituary notice recorded:

> "many neurologists treasured the memories of their apprenticeship to one of the giants of neurology, and to a staunch, fundamentally warm-hearted counsellor and guide. In his profession, as in his garden, Holmes planted seeds for the profit and wonderment of generations to come. ("Obituary Notice," 1966, p. 111)

Many accounts of Gordon Holmes overlook his leisure activities. He was an enthusiastic if untalented golfer; he spent long summer holidays in his native Ireland, often working on his father's farm, pursuing his avid interest in gardening. He loved to row on the Thames at Foley Bridge. Before appointment to Queen Square he arranged a meeting with Captain Robert Scott, hoping to join his Antarctic expedition; but an Achilles tendon injury forced Holmes reluctantly to withdraw; he was able only to wave farewell at the quayside in 1910. None of Scott's ill-fated party returned. Holmes was devoted to the works of William Shakespeare, and would read passages of poetry each night on retiring.

The life and work of Holmes is the subject of many encomiums and eulogies, which contain details and appraisals of his original, invaluable writings. His wife Rosalie (née Jobson) was an Oxford graduate, an accomplished athlete, and an international hockey player. She and their three daughters provided a close family life at 9 Wimpole Street, London, where they gave unfailing support to him in his demanding work. Gordon Holmes, though at times acidulous, remote, and difficult, exemplified an inspiring, immensely gifted man of an independent spirit and selfless dedication to his science. He left a unique legacy to all those who treat and to those who suffer from diseases of the nervous system.

BIBLIOGRAPHY

WORKS BY HOLMES

With T. Grainger Stewart. "Symptomatology of Cerebellar Tumours: A Study of Forty Cases." *Brain* 27 (1904): 522–591.

"A Form of Familial Degeneration of the Cerebellum." *Brain* 30 (1907): 466–489.

"Review: An Attempt to Classify Cerebellar Disease with a Note on Marie's Hereditary Cerebellar Ataxia." *Brain* 30 (1907): 545–567.

With Henry Head. "Sensory Disturbances from Cerebral Lesions." *Brain* 34 (1911): 102–254. Reprinted in *Studies in Neurology*. Vol. I, edited by Henry Head. London: Oxford University Press, 1920.

———. "A Case of Lesion of the Optic Thalamus with Autopsy." *Brain* 34 (1911): 255–271. Reprinted in *Studies in Neurology*. Vol. I, edited by Henry Head. London: Oxford University Press, 1920.

"Disturbances of Vision by Cerebral Lesions." *Brain* 40 (1918): 461–535.

"The Montgomery Lecture in Ophthalmology. I. The Cortical Localisation of Vision." *British Medical Journal* 2 (1919a): 193–199.

"The Montgomery Lecture in Ophthalmology. II. Disturbances of Visual Space Perception." *British Medical Journal* 2 (1919b): 230–233.

"On the Clinical Symptoms of Cerebellar Disease." Croonian Lectures. *Lancet* I (1922): 1177–1182, 1231–1237; II: 59–65, 111–115.

"A Symposium on the Cerebellum." *Brain* 50 (1927): 385–388.

"Partial Iridoplegia Associated with Symptoms of Other Diseases of the Nervous System." *Trans Ophthalmic Society UK* 51 (1931): 209–228.

"The Cerebellum of Man." *Brain* 62 (1939): 1–30.

Introduction to Clinical Neurology. Edinburgh: Livingstone, 1946.

OTHER SOURCES

Breathnach, Caoimhghin S. "Sir Gordon Holmes." *Medical History* 19 (1975): 194–200. An excellent account of Holmes's work, especially on visual defects.

Critchley, Macdonald. "Gordon Holmes, the Man and the Neurologist." In his *The Divine Banquet of the Brain*, 228–235. New York: Raven Press, 1979. A beautifully written, detailed essay about the man and his professional relations.

Fishman, Ronald S. "Gordon Holmes, the Cortical Retina, and the Wounds of War." *Documenta Ophthalmologica* 93 (1997): 9–28.

Lyons, J. B. "Sir Gordon Holmes: A Centenary Tribute." *Irish Medical Journal* 69 (1974): 300–302. A tribute revealing Holmes's professional prowess and his Irish connections.

Munk's Roll: Lives of the Fellows of the Royal College of Physicians of London. Vol. 5, edited by Richard R. Trail. London: Royal College of Physicians, 1968.

"Obituary Notice: Sir Gordon Holmes." *British Medical Journal* 1 (1966): 111–112. Includes contributions from Macdonald Critchley and Francis M. R. Walshe.

Parsons-Smith, B. Gerald. "Sir Gordon Holmes." In *Historical Aspects of the Neurosciences*, edited by Rose F. Clifford and W. F. Bynum. New York: Raven Press, 1982. A superb essay containing many anecdotes and personal insights.

Pearce, J. M. S. "Sir Gordon Holmes (1876–1965)." *Journal of Neurology, Neurosurgery and Psychiatry* 75 (2004): 1502–1503.

Penfield, Wilder Graves. "Sir Gordon Morgan Holmes (1876–1965)." Obituary. *Journal of Neurological Sciences* 5 (1967): 185–190.

———. "Lights in the Great Darkness." *Journal of Neurosurgery* 35 (1971): 377–383.

Walshe, Francis M. R. "Gordon Morgan Holmes, 1876–1965." In *Biographical Memoirs of Fellows of the Royal Society*. Vol. 12. London: Royal Society, 1966. A typically erudite biography.

J. M. S. Pearce

HOLTFRETER, JOHANNES

(*b.* Richtenberg, Germany, 9 January 1901; *d.* Rochester, New York, 13 November 1992), *experimental embryology, inducers and organizers, tissue affinity.*

Holtfreter was one of the best experimental embryologists of the twentieth century. As a student of Hans Spemann, Holtfreter was trained in a German tradition of experimental embryology. His research defined and addressed issues of fundamental importance in embryology, such as how different embryonic tissues are induced to change, how cells coordinate movement during development, and how tissues recognize each other. With the rise of national socialism in Germany, Holtfreter immigrated to the United States where he continued to develop a reductionist approach to embryology.

Early Years. As the only son in an upper-middle-class family in northeastern Germany, where his father owned a whiskey factory, Johannes Friedrich Karl Holtfreter spent his childhood exploring the countryside not far from the Baltic Sea. His interests in nature developed into an interest in biology in the *Realgymnasium* and then the

University of Rostock and the University of Leipzig, where he studied until 1919, when he transferred to the University of Freiburg. At Freiburg, Holtfreter studied and worked for Hans Spemann, who was quickly becoming established as one of the world's leading embryologists.

In 1924 Holtfreter completed an uninspired thesis on organ development in frog embryos. At the same time, Hilde Mangold performed the foundational experiments on the organizer that would win Spemann the Nobel Prize in 1935.

Spemann was interested in when and how cell fates and structures are determined in the early embryo. Spemann and his group focused on embryos in the blastula stage, when they form a hollow ball of cells, but before gastrulation, when cells move inward through the blastopore to create different germ layers and the basis for the body axis and nervous system. Mangold used Spemann's technique of transplanting groups of cells from one part of the blastula to another in order to determine the developmental potential of those groups of cells. Most of these transplantations had slight effects. When she transplanted cells from the dorsal blastopore lip to the opposite side of the blastopore, however, she discovered that a second body axis began to develop at the transplantation site. Moreover, Mangold and Spemann determined that the transplanted cells had not only continued to develop themselves but had induced the surrounding tissues to change and form part of the new structures. Spemann called this area above the blastopore the organizer, because of its ability to influence or induce changes in surrounding tissue. Spemann and Mangold published their results in 1924 just as Holtfreter was finishing his own graduate research.

Holtfreter was not immediately drawn into organizer research. Spemann, who did not approve of Holtfreter's frequent escapes to hike in the forest, suggested that Holtfreter go to the Naples Zoological Station to study marine biology and embryology there. Using his own funds, Holtfreter traveled to Italy and ended up on the island of Ischia in the Bay of Naples, where he avoided doing any science and instead painted frescoes in the village church in St. Angelo. Holtfreter was a very talented artist, and after two years in Italy he returned to Germany and actually tried to support himself as a portrait painter for awhile.

Job prospects in biology were not good for Holtfreter, especially without Spemann's full support. Holtfreter considered working in a fisheries research station in Helgoland and as a high school teacher. However, in 1928, when he despaired of finding any future in science, Otto Mangold, Spemann's favorite student and Hilde Mangold's spouse, invited Holtfreter to join him as a researcher at the Kaiser Wilhelm Institute for Biology in Berlin-Dahlem. Holtfreter immediately accepted and began one of the most productive periods of his research life soon after.

Kaiser Wilhelm Institute. Spemann's organizer experiments had set off an explosion of research in experimental embryology, and Holtfreter entered the conflagration as a member of Mangold's group. Where Spemann's approach was guided by an idea of the organism as a functional whole, Holtfreter was interested in the developmental potential of the different regions of the gastrula in isolation. Dissecting thousands of embryos into parts and following the development of each part in isolation met with an immediate technical difficulty. Embryos had been cultured in just filtered water and tended to die quickly. Holtfreter needed his embryo sections to grow for a longer period of time in order to determine if any differentiation occurred, so he conducted a series of trials to create a sterile salt solution that allowed cultured embryos to develop much more fully. This solution, which has since become known as "Holtfreter solution," made it possible to carry out much more significant embryological research using amphibians.

One of the key questions raised in organizer research concerned what properties enabled the organizer to induce changes in surrounding tissues. Spemann was sympathetic to the idea that some aspect of the organizer's structure was responsible and in 1931 reported the results of some transplantation experiments using crushed organizers. Holtfreter extended this line of thought with dramatic effect. He killed organizers with heat, cold, and desiccation and then transplanted them into blastula in his solution. The killed organizers induced new neural structures and decisively demonstrated that the inducer was not a property of living tissue, and therefore must be a chemical. In addition, Holtfreter undertook transplantation experiments with adult tissues and tissues from other species and phyla. Many of these were capable of neural induction as well. This very productive period of research in the 1930s raised important new questions about the organizer as it shifted research away from the properties of the organizer as a group of cells to the search for inducing substances. In effect, Holtfreter's induction experiments created biochemical embryology.

The impact of Holtfreter's research was widely appreciated, and in 1934 he was appointed to an associate professorship in the Zoology Department at the University of Munich. After only a year in Munich, Holtfreter took advantage of a Rockefeller Foundation fellowship and a private travel grant to spend a year at Yale University as a member of Ross Harrison's laboratory. Harrison and Spemann were very close friends, and Harrison had been a frequent visitor to Freiburg. Even though Holtfreter knew

Harrison and his research program, he was not deeply interested in the kind of tissue culture research that then dominated Harrison's group at Yale. Instead, after a few months, Holtfreter took his leave to explore the United States. Drawn westward, Holtfreter traveled by train to California and then by steamer to Hawaii and Bali. Captivated by the island and its people, Holtfreter stayed in Bali for several months. Only when his funds ran out did he continue his journey back to Germany.

War Years. The Germany Holtfreter had left was not the same to which he returned. The Nazi Party had continued to consolidate its power in the mid-1930s. To Holtfreter, going from Bali to Nazi Germany was like moving from paradise to hell. Although he was not Jewish or overtly political, he was soon subject to harassment from the Gestapo. In 1938 he presented his research at the Congress of Physics, Chemistry, and Biology at the International Exposition in Paris. As the most notable German participant, he was informed that he was Germany's representative to the congress. Holtfreter nevertheless presented his paper in French and then took the honorarium and explored Algeria before returning to Munich, actions that put him in danger. Once he was back in Germany, he was denounced and imprisoned. An international effort secured his release and emigration in 1939 to England, where he joined Joseph Needham's group at Cambridge University. As the war escalated, however, Holtfreter was classified as an enemy alien and placed in an interment camp in Canada, where he remained until 1942.

Holtfreter later described the two years he spent in a Canadian prison camp as the worst years of his life. Unable to do research and too demoralized to read the scientific literature that was sent to him, he painted landscapes of Bali on wooden shingles. In 1944, with the support of John Berrill, a biologist at McGill University in Montreal, Holtfreter was released from internment and hired at McGill. Old friends such as Ross Harrison rallied around Holtfreter, shipping him amphibian eggs and embryos to restart his research program. After adjusting to his new circumstances, Holtfreter turned to the topic of gastrulation.

Research on Gastrulation. In the 1920s Walter Vogt had used stained living embryos to follow the patterns of cell movement, involution, and germ layer formation. This complex process of gastrulation appeared orderly as the hundreds of cells harmoniously coordinated their movements. Vogt and later Spemann suggested that gastrulation was not merely wandering cells but the result of a superior force that directed the motions of the cells. Holtfreter was skeptical of this approach to gastrulation, just as he had been skeptical of Spemann's account of the organizer. At McGill he applied his techniques of dissection and tissue culture developed in the 1930s to cells involved in gastrulation. As he studied clumps of cells and the movements of individual cells, Holtfreter devised what he thought of as a mechanical explanation for cell movement in gastrulation. Noting that bottle cells tended to elongate, Holtfreter proposed that the invagination of cells at the blastopore was initiated by bottle cell elongation. Other cells on the blastula surface followed the bottle cells into the interior as the result of a coating that bound surface cells together and so produced the apparent coordination of their movement.

Like his earlier work on induction, Holtfreter's research on gastrulation pushed experimental embryology to embrace a more reductionist and analytic understanding of the processes of development. Holtfreter's postwar papers on gastrulation clearly expressed his dissatisfaction with Spemann's and Vogt's view of gastrulation as planned and coordinated by some supercellular agency. In its place, Holtfreter explicitly chose to frame gastrulation as a mechanistic phenomena with cellular and physico-chemical causes.

In the mid-1940s Holtfreter extended his analysis to processes of neural development in early embryos. He wished to understand whether the organizer region was really essential for neuralization. Lester Barth had demonstrated in 1941 that ectoderm could be induced to develop into neural tissue by simply changing the salt concentration of the surrounding solution. Using his earlier technique of culturing isolated amphibian embryonic tissues, Holtfreter subjected ectodermal fragments that would normally form nervous tissues to different concentrations of salt with additional changes in the pH of the solution. By systematically adjusting the chemical conditions, Holtfreter was able to induce ectoderm to form not only neural tissue but sense organs.

Because these salt solutions were presumed to be free of any chemical inducers from the organizer, these experiments demonstrated that ectoderm possessed a capacity to form neural tissues independent of the action of organizer tissues. Holtfreter proposed that the salt solutions he used destroyed the ability of ectoderm to suppress their capacity to form neural tissues, resulting in what he called *autoneuralization.* The observed ability of this tissue to form recognizable neural tissues and structures convinced him that the ectoderm itself was an important source of organization and structure. These experiments on autoneuralization furthered the shift among experimental embryologists away from the organizer as the active determiner of embryonic structures to the inherent capacities of responding tissues.

University of Rochester. In 1946 Curt Stern, a fellow émigré from Germany and an old friend from the Kaiser

Wilhelm Institute for Biology in Berlin-Dahlem, persuaded Holtfreter to leave McGill and join the faculty at the University of Rochester in New York State. Having not been particularly happy in Canada, Holtfreter looked forward to joining other émigrés in the United States. He spent the rest of his life in Rochester, eventually marrying Hiroko Ban, a biologist and former graduate student.

In Rochester, Holtfreter turned again to a series of experiments he had done in Germany in the 1930s. In 1939 Holtfreter had discovered from his long series of isolation experiments that like cells from different structures and germ layers had definite affinities. Mesodermal tissues, for instance, were attracted to both ectodermal and endodermal tissue, while ectoderm and endoderm seemed to avoid each other. This cellular affinity was strongest among older cells that had undergone more differentiation.

At McGill Holtfreter had noted that the cells from isolated embryonic tissues could be separated into an assemblage of free cells. Given a chance under normal conditions, these cells rearranged themselves into tissues very close in structure to those that had existed originally. In the 1950s Holtfreter and his student Philip Townes returned to this research of cellular affinity and the selective adhesion of cells with each other. Using isolated cells, Townes and Holtfreter mixed cells from different germ layers and observed the patterns of reaggregation. They noted both the affinity and movement of different cell types as they sorted themselves into distinct tissue layers. Ectodermal and endodermal cells again demonstrated no affinity for each other but strong affinity for like cells. Mesodermal cells, by contrast, adhered to both endoderm and ectoderm and so resulted in a germ layer arrangement typical of developing embryos with mesoderm sandwiched between the endoderm and ectoderm.

By following the movements of cell types, Townes and Holtfreter demonstrated both preferential movement and association. As with his other embryological work, Holtfreter concluded from these experiments that the organization of germ layers was the result of cellular processes, not higher-level capacities or features of the organism as a whole. Townes and Holtfreter's paper profoundly influenced research on embryonic morphogenesis by refocusing attention away from germ layers to cells and cell types that make up those germ layers. As with his earlier work on induction, this paper marks the starting place for future research on models of cellular adhesion and migration as well as the molecular basis for cell-cell binding.

While Holtfreter and Townes were publishing the results of their experimental program, Holtfreter was also collaborating with his close friend and colleague Viktor Hamburger. Hamburger and Holtfreter had both been students in Spemann's laboratory in Germany. Whereas Holtfreter left Germany for political reasons, Hamburger left as a result of rising anti-Semitism in the 1930s. Hamburger's research in the United States concentrated on developmental genetics and, later, nerve growth using primarily chicken embryos. Nevertheless, Hamburger worked with Holtfreter to craft a landmark chapter on amphibian development for the 1955 book representing the state of the art, *Analysis of Development.* Their chapter documented research stemming from the Spemann tradition and provides an invaluable overview of many of the most important advances in experimental embryology in the twentieth century. Although Holtfreter continued to research cell affinities and movement in the aggregating behavior of slime molds after 1956, his essay with Hamburger was his last major scientific publication and in many ways marked the culmination of his research trajectory from Germany.

Holtfreter was the recipient of numerous awards during his career including two Rockefeller fellowships, a Guggenheim fellowship, and Fulbright fellowship. He was elected to the National Academy of Sciences, the American Academy of Arts and Sciences, and the Swedish Academy of Sciences. In 1968 the American Society of Zoologists meeting and the Hahnemann Symposium were both dedicated to Holtfreter. At the University of Rochester he was named Tracy H. Harris Professor in 1966.

Holtfreter continued as an emeritus professor until 1981. During his retirement he returned to painting and travel until he lost his eyesight. In 1992 Holtfreter died at age ninety-one in Rochester.

BIBLIOGRAPHY

Holtfreter's papers will be donated to the archives at the Marine Biological Laboratories at Woods Hole. His art has been donated to the University of Rochester Art Museum.

WORKS BY HOLTFRETER

With H. Bautzmann, Hans Spemann, and Otto Mangold. "Versuche der Analyse der Induktionsmittel in der Embryonalentwicklung." *Naturwissenschaften* 20 (1932): 971–974.

"Differenzungspotenzen isolierter Teile der Anurengastrula." *Roux' Archive für Entwicklungsmechanik* 138 (1938): 657–738.

"Veränderung der Reaktionsweise im alternden isolierten Gastrulaektoderm." *Roux' Archive für Entwicklungsmechanik* 138 (1938): 163–196.

"A Study of the Mechanics of Gastrulation." Parts 1 and 2. *Journal of Experimental Zoology* 94 (1943): 261–318; 95 (1944): 171–212.

"Neuralization and Epidermization of Gastrula Ectoderm." *Journal of Experimental Zoology* 98 (1945): 169–209.

"Neural Differentiation of Ectoderm through Exposure to Saline Solution." *Journal of Experimental Zoology* 95 (1945): 307–340.

With Viktor Hamburger. "Amphibians." In *Analysis of Development,* edited by Benjamin H. Willier, Paul A. Weiss, and Viktor Hamburger. New York: W. B. Saunders, 1955. A masterful overview of the experimental embryology of amphibians.

With Philip L. Townes. "Directed Movements and Selective Adhesion of Embryonic Amphibian Cells." *Journal of Experimental Zoology* 123 (1955): 53–120.

OTHER SOURCES

Gerhart, John. "Johannes Holtfreter's Contributions to Ongoing Studies of the Organizer." *Developmental Dynamics* 205 (1996): 245–256.

———. "Johannes Holtfreter." *Biographical Memoirs of the National Academy of Science* 73 (1998): 3–22.

Gilbert, Scott, ed. *A Conceptual History of Modern Developmental Biology.* New York: Plenum Press, 1991.

Hamburger, Viktor. *The Heritage of Experimental Embryology: Hans Spemann and the Organizer.* New York: Oxford University Press, 1988.

Keller, Ray. "Holtfreter Revisited: Unsolved Problems in Amphibian Morphogenesis," *Developmental Dynamics* 205 (1996): 257–264.

Steinberg, Malcolm, and Scott Gilbert. "Townes and Holtfreter (1955): Directed Movements and Selective Adhesion of Embryonic Amphibian Cells." *Journal of Experimental Zoology* 301A (2004): 701–706.

Michael R. Dietrich

HOMBERG, WILHELM (*b.* Batavia, Java [later Jakarta, Indonesia], 8 January 1653; *d.* Paris, France, 24 September 1715), *chemistry.* For the original article on Homberg see *DSB,* vol. 6.

Homberg has emerged as a key figure in the history of chemistry. New studies indicate his important innovations in chemical theory and techniques and more accurately situate him in his due context as a major figure of the early eighteenth century.

Essentially all biographical sketches of Homberg, including that of the original *DSB* article, drew uncritically from Bernard de Fontenelle's 1715 *Éloge de Homberg.* But since the publication of the earlier *DSB,* new studies have revealed errors of fact and chronology in that account, and thus it is worth recapitulating his biography in the light of more recent findings.

Life and Travels. Homberg was born in 1653 (not 1652) at the Dutch East Company's settlement at Batavia on the isle of Java. His father, Johann, a native of Quedlinburg in Sachsen-Anhalt, was an officer for the company, and Homberg's mother, Barbara, of Dutch origin, was the widow of Antoni Beer, another company officer. Wilhelm was the fourth of six children and the younger of two sons. The family left Java for Europe in the mid-1660s, settling first in Amsterdam. Wilhelm was sent for a career in law, matriculating at Jena in 1672 and then Leipzig in 1675, where he defended his thesis in March 1676. He then began to practice law at Magdeburg, where he started to develop an interest in natural philosophy and mechanics. These interests were fostered by Otto von Guericke, who apparently shared some of his secrets with the young Homberg.

Homberg then embarked on almost fifteen years of travel, meeting, and trading secrets with notable natural philosophers and visiting natural and industrial sites across Europe. Homberg journeyed first to Italy, studying (without matriculating) at Padua in 1677 and then traveling to Bologna, where he acquired or rediscovered the secret of how to render the celebrated "Bolognian stone" (a native barium sulfate) phosphorescent by means of a careful calcination. Thereafter he worked with the instrument maker Marco Antonio Cellio in Rome, possibly imparting to him the secret of the Bolognian stone in exchange for training. After a possible trip through France, Homberg went to Germany to learn about new phosphorescent materials: Baldwin's "hermetic phosphorus" (phosphorescent calcium nitrate) and Johann Kunckel's white phosphorus. Homberg traded von Guericke's *Wettermännchen,* a kind of a barometer (*not* a hygrometer), for the recipe for the latter. Armed with a letter from Gottfried Wilhelm Leibniz, Homberg journeyed in 1679 to England, where he met Robert Boyle, possibly assisting him with his attempts at that time to prepare phosphorus and receiving alchemical secrets in return. There is no evidence for the claim that Homberg obtained an MD at Wittenberg around this time.

Homberg visited mining operations in eastern Europe (as far down the Danube as Belgrade), then in Sweden, where he may well have associated with Urban Hjärne in 1681. After touring France he settled in Paris in 1682. Here he came to the attention of Jean-Baptiste Colbert and began collaborating with members of the Académie Royale des Sciences, particularly Edme Mariotte, on studies of the air, phosphorus, and the freezing of liquids. In late 1682 Homberg converted to Catholicism (for which his father disowned him) and in January 1683 was naturalized in France. After Colbert's death he was employed by Louis-Armand Bonnin, abbé de Chalucet, on transmutational endeavors. Although this project did not produce precious metal, it did yield a spontaneously inflammable powder (produced initially from roasted human feces) long known as "Homberg's pyrophorus." In 1685 Homberg, his French patronage at an end, went to

Rome, where he associated with the Accademia Fisico-matematica Romana, worked on mechanics and microscopy, wrote a treatise on the generation of animals, and probably practiced medicine. He visited Paris in 1687 in order to demonstrate phosphorus, a new air pump, and the Bolognian stone to the academy, and he may have resettled in Paris shortly thereafter. In late 1691 he was admitted to the academy and spent the rest of his life in Paris as one of the most active academicians of the era.

In 1702 Philippe II, duc d'Orléans and later regent of France, chose Homberg as his tutor in chemistry and built a magnificent laboratory at the Palais Royale where they worked together. In 1704 Homberg became Philippe's first physician. In 1708, at age fifty-five, Homberg married Marguerite-Angélique, the forty-year-old daughter of his recently deceased colleague Denis Dodart; the couple produced no children. In early 1712, following the sudden deaths of the dauphin and dauphine, Homberg was nearly taken to the Bastille for questioning (owing to rumors that they had been poisoned), but this action was forbidden by the king. After a lengthy intestinal malady, Homberg died in 1715 and was buried at Saint-Eustache; his funeral monument was destroyed in the Revolution.

Scientific Work. Homberg worked on many scientific issues during his lifetime. Much of his work before 1700 focused on pneumatics and the vacuum, using an improved air pump of his own design. He examined the sprouting of seeds, the exploding of Prince Rupert's drops, the freezing and evaporation of liquids, and other phenomena in the vacuum. He was the first to propose distillation at reduced pressure to prevent thermal decomposition. He also designed instruments, made botanical, anatomical, and entomological observations, and was called upon by the academy regularly to examine or improve technological and commercial processes.

Homberg's greatest contributions, however, were in chemistry. His work shows a keen interest in weight determinations and the need for pure and standardized reagents. He was the first to attempt to standardize solutions and to measure the various "strengths" of acids and alkalies based on their relative ability to neutralize each other. Throughout his career at the academy he worked to test earlier chemical theories and to determine the constituents of mixed bodies. To this end he examined the vast quantity of plant analyses carried out at the academy since the 1670s and conducted a series of carefully planned experiments that often extended over three or four years. In his own analyses he used a system of weight determinations that has been seen as the foundation for the more celebrated "balance-sheet" method of Antoine-Laurent Lavoisier, who knew and valued Homberg's work.

For the last twenty years of his life he worked on the presentation and illustration of his chemical theory in a textbook. Parts were serially published in the academy's *Mémoires* under the title *Essais de chimie* (1702–1710), and although the full manuscript was complete at the time of his death it remained unpublished. Homberg's *Essais* mark a crucial break in the French didactic tradition; for the first time, pharmaceutical and commercial preparations are absent and the focus is clearly on the derivation of a comprehensive, coherent chemical theory from experimental results. Homberg embraced the five-principle theory of Étienne de Clave and others but also held that these five—mercury, sulfur, salt, water, and earth—were not the ultimate constituents of mixed substances but were instead useful and sensible categories of substances separated by chemical analysis. The centerpiece of Homberg's system is his sulfur principle, the common substance contained in all sulfurous substances. In 1705, after lengthy experiments, he identified this sulfur principle with light. According to Homberg, light can incorporate with the other principles, change their figure and arrangement and add to their weight, and is the sole source of change and activity in matter. The exchange of sulfur/light in different forms explains most chemical reactions. Homberg's theory reflects his lifelong fascination with the interaction of light with matter, exemplified by his work with phosphorescent materials, including his discovery of the piezoluminescence of fused calcium chloride (erroneously called an explosive chlorate in the original *DSB* article). But it was also certainly greatly promoted by the experiments he carried out with the enormous burning lens (not mirror) constructed by Ehrenfried Walther, Graf von Tschirnhaus, and purchased by the duc d'Orléans in early 1702.

Viewing the metals as compound bodies, Homberg also continued to believe in the possibility of metallic transmutation, even while the official stance of the academy increasingly frowned upon it. He knew the traditional chrysopoetic literature very well and was particularly influenced by the writings of Eirenaeus Philalethes (George Starkey). Many of his *Essais* are built around experiments with a specially prepared "philosophical" mercury, the key starting material for the philosopher's stone, and Homberg claims to have had success in transmuting a portion of it into gold by long periods of heating.

Homberg held several posts within the academy—head of the chemical laboratory after 1699, director (1701 and 1707), sous-director (1703 and 1709), and member of various committees. He was the mentor to several younger academicians, most notably Étienne-François Geoffroy. Homberg's work and theory was highly influential in the early eighteenth century; for example, his ideas are often invoked in the writings of Hermann Boerhaave,

Peter Shaw, and Pierre-Joseph Macquer as well as by Georg Ernst Stahl and others.

Contemporaneous accounts of Homberg agree on his friendly, good-natured personality, his generosity, sincere piety, and kindness. Elisabeth Charlotte, duchesse d'Orléans, held him in high regard, writing that "one is unable to get to know Homberg without esteeming him for his honest spirit; he is not at all befuddled as savants usually are, nor ponderous, nor lofty, but instead always merry" (Bodemann, 1891, vol. 2, p. 11). The duc de Saint-Simon avers that Homberg was "one of the greatest chemists of Europe, and one of the most honest men who ever lived; he was the most simple and the most solidly pious" (Saint-Simon, 1985, vol. 5, p. 742).

SUPPLEMENTARY BIBLIOGRAPHY

Bodemann, Eduard, ed. *Aus der Briefe der Herzogin Elisabeth Charlotte von Orléans an die Kurfürstin Sophie von Hannover.* 2 vols. Hannover, Germany, 1891.

Franckowiak, Rémi, and Luc Peterschmitt. "La chimie de Homberg: Une vérité certaine dans une physique contestable." *Early Science and Medicine* 10 (2005): 65–90.

Holmes, Frederic L. "The Communal Context for Étienne-François Geoffroy's *Table des rapports.*" *Science in Context* 9, no. 3 (1996): 289–311.

Principe, Lawrence M. "Wilhelm Homberg: Chymical Corpuscularianism and Chrysopoeia in the Early Eighteenth Century." In *Late Medieval and Early Modern Corpuscular Matter Theories,* edited by Christoph Lüthy, John E. Murdoch, and William R. Newman, 535–556. Leiden, Netherlands, and Boston: Brill, 2001.

———. *Wilhelm Homberg and the Transmutations of Chemistry at the Académie Royale des Sciences.* Forthcoming, 2008.

Saint-Simon, Louis de Rouvroy, duc de. *Mémoires.* 8 vols. Edited by Yves Coirault. Paris: Gallimard, 1985.

Stroup, Alice. "Wilhelm Homberg and the Search for the Constituents of Plants at the 17th-Century Académie Royale des Sciences." *Ambix* 26 (1979): 184–202.

Lawrence M. Principe

HONDIUS, JODOCUS

(*b.* Wakken, West-Vlaanderen, Southern Netherlands [now Belgium], 17 October 1563; *d.* Amsterdam, Netherlands, 12 February 1612), *cartography, engraving, geography.*

Hondius was an illustrious Flemish mapmaker and cartographer. His most important works were the revision of the Mercator Atlas and the Mercator-Hondius Atlas.

Early Years. Jodocus Hondius was born Joost de Hondt on 17 October 1563 in Wakken, West Vlaanderen, Belgium. His father's name was Oliver de Hondt and his mother's Petronella van Havertuyn. When Joost was two, his parents moved to the city of Ghent, where he learned the art of engraving and drawing. When he was older, Joost de Hondt Latinized his name as was the custom among savants in that time. Jodocus became very competent in calligraphy. He also was educated in mathematics and its use.

Hondius was very skillful at engraving copper plates, and the high circles of the elite held him in great esteem. At a young age he made many engravings of very important cities for Alexander Farnese, duke of Parma and governor-general of the Netherlands under Philip II of Spain. But when Ghent was captured by the Spanish in 1584, he fled to London, where he met a number of reformed Protestants. In this milieu of Flemish and Dutch immigrants he met his wife, Colleta van de Keere, the sister of the well-known publisher Petrus Kaerius.

Stay in London. In London he worked for several publishers and writers, such as Richard Hakluyt and Edward Wright. He expanded his knowledge of cartography and geography through his contact with the great English explorers Francis Drake, Thomas Cavendish, and Walter Raleigh. In particular, during 1589 Hondius produced a now-famous map of the cove of New Albion, where Drake briefly established a settlement on the West Coast of North America. Hondius based this map on accounts of the voyage in a journal and eyewitnesses accounts. The map has for centuries fueled speculation about the precise whereabouts of Drake's landing, which even now has not been definitely established by historians.

Back to the Low Countries. In 1593 Hondius moved with his family to Amsterdam, taking with him many mathematical instruments that he had made in London. In the Dutch republic he linked up with the branch of the famous Plantin printing house established in Leiden. There he made several globes that were sold in Antwerp.

In 1602 he moved to Leiden to become a student at the famous University of Leiden, founded in 1575, where he studied mathematics to increase his knowledge of this branch of learning. He intended to apply mathematics in his work. In Leiden, Jodocus became acquainted with Petrus Bertius, the royal cosmographer of the French king Louis XIII. Bertius helped him make a very important decision. In 1604 Hondius was in doubt about whether to purchase the copper plates of the Mercator imperium (a printer business that had ended in that year). Bertius persuaded him to buy these copper plates, which he did on 12 July 1604. From that year on, his life changed as he attained worldwide fame.

Jodocus Hondius. *Copperplate of Flemish cartographers Gerard Mercador and Jodocus Hondius.* SCIENCE SOURCE / PHOTO RESEARCHERS, INC.

The Mercator-Hondius Atlas. In 1578 Gerardus Mercator had published an atlas based on twenty-eight maps of Ptolemy. Mercator had wanted to give a representation of the ancient world. In 1595 he had published his well-known then-current atlas. Hondius bought the plates of both atlases. A couple months later, a remarkable book appeared: *Claudīī Ptolemaeï Alexandrini geographicae libri octo graecog latini,* a reedition of Mercator's *Ptolemaeus atlas.* He published and edited it and had it printed by Jan Theunisz in Amsterdam.

In December of that same year, Hondius bought a house in Amsterdam where he installed his new printing business. He gave the house a name that referred to his birth place: "In De Wackere Hondt" (In the awakening dog).

In 1606 Hondius improved the well-known Mercator Atlas, originally printed in 1595. He augmented it with thirty-six new maps, including several that he himself had produced. Despite his own contributions, Hondius gave Mercator full credit as the author of the work, listing himself as the publisher. The atlas is known under the name the Mercator-Hondius Atlas. It was the first complete atlas: all known continents, regions, seas, and oceans were represented, based on the new discoveries of explorers. The demand for this atlas was enormous; it sold out after a year, and many editions followed, starting in 1607 and 1608.

Jodocus Hondius was a shrewd businessman. He ascertained that smaller atlases were cheaper and easier to use. Therefore, he published a number of those popular, small atlases, and did so in many different languages. Altogether, from 1606 onward, around fifty editions were published in the principal European languages, and as a result of the success of the Mercator-Hondius Atlas, Amsterdam achieved the status of the principal center of cartography until the end of the seventeenth century.

Between 1605 and 1610 he engraved the plates for the maps in John Speed's *The Theatre of the Empire of Great Britain* (1611). In 1611 he published another world map, but in his last years he was occupied with leadership of his business, including negotiations with traders and various correspondences; he had become too busy to produce more maps

Jodocus Hondius died in 1612. The work of the publishing house was carried on by his widow and two sons, Jodocus II and Henricus, and later still in partnership with Jan Jansson, whose name appears on the Mercator-Hondius Atlas as copublisher from 1633.

BIBLIOGRAPHY

Most of Hondius's work is cited in Günter Schilder, Monumenta Cartographica Neerlandica, *Vol. VI,* Nederlandse foliokaarten met decoratieve randen, *1604–60 (Dutch folio-sized single sheet maps with decorative borders, 1604–60). Alphen aan den Rijn, Netherlands: Canaletto, 2000.*

Borchgrave, O. de. "Levensschets van Judocus Hondius." In his *Wakken herdenkt: Wakken.* Tielt, Belgium: Lannoo, 1963.

Heawood, Edward. *The Map of the World on Mercator's Projection by Jodocus Hondius, Amsterdam 1608, … A Memoir.* London: Royal Geographical Society, 1927.

Keuning, Johannes. "The History of an Atlas: Mercator-Hondius." *Imago Mundi* 4 (1947): 37–62.

Krogt, Peter van der. *The Globes of Hondiu: A Most Important Pair of Globes Showing the Results of the Earliest Dutch Exploration Voyages to the East Indies.* Utrecht, Netherlands: Antiquariaat Forum, 1991.

———, comp. *Koeman's tlantes Neerlandici.* 'T Goy-Houten, Netherlands: HES and De Graaf, 1997.

Mercator, Gerard, and Henry Hondius. *L'appendice de l'Atlas de Gérard Mercator et Iudocus Hondius contenant diverses nouvelles tables et descriptions….* Amsterdam: Henry Hondius, 1633.

Mercator, Gerard, J. Janssonius, Raleigh A. Skelton, et al. *Mercator-Hondius-Janssonius Atlas or a Geographicke Description of the World, Amsterdam 1636.* 2 vols. Amsterdam: Theatrum Orbis Terrarum, 1968.

Orenstein, Nadine. *Hendrick Hondius and the Business of Prints in Seventeenth-Century Holland.* Rotterdam, Netherlands: Sound and Vision Interactive, 1996.

De Smet, Antoine. "Gerard Mercator en zijn Westvlaamse voortzetter Jodocus Hondius of Joost de Hondt uit Wakken." In *Album Achivaris Jos. De Smet.* Brugge, Belgium: Westvlaams Verbond van Kringen voor Heemkunde, 1964.

———. *Jodocus Hondius, 1563–1612, kartograaf in het voetspoor van Gerard Mercator.* Brussels: Nationaal Centrum voor de Geschiedenis Centre National d'Histoire des Sciences, 1964.

———. *Album Antoine de Smet.* Brussels: Centre national d'histoire des sciences, 1974.

Steve Philips

HOPPER, GRACE MURRAY

(*b.* New York, New York, 9 December 1906, *d.* Washington, D.C., 1 January 1992), *computer sciences, programming languages, COBOL.*

An admiral who never went to sea, Hopper owed her success in the U.S. Navy, as in civilian life, to her mastery of computers and computing. Entering the field at its very beginnings in the 1940s, she spent the next four decades leading the way in the development of computer languages. In 1969, the Data Processing Management Association named her its first Computer Sciences Man of the Year for her contribution to the development of the widely used programming language, COBOL. Her implementation of Standard COBOL in the Navy revolutionized its management information systems. Often referred to as "Amazing Grace" and "Grandma COBOL" by an admiring press, Hopper gave hundreds of speeches annually in the 1970s and 1980s, becoming a nationally recognized advocate for navy computing and for the computer sciences she had helped to establish.

Origins and Education. The oldest of three children, Hopper was raised in New York City in a family that encouraged intellectual curiosity. An early interest in mathematics was stimulated by both her mother, Mary van Horne Murray, the daughter of a civil engineer, and by her father, Walter Murray, an insurance broker. After attending private girls' schools in New York and New Jersey, Hopper was admitted to Vassar College in September 1924. Vassar, just north of New York City, was a prestigious private college offering a rigorous education to the bright daughters of the affluent. Hopper disregarded the post–World War I trend in women's education toward subjects considered suitable preparation for marriage and motherhood. Instead, she concentrated on mathematics and physics. Henry Sealy White, her most influential mentor, had been trained in Göttingen, Germany, the center of European mathematics. Europe was still well ahead of the United States in mathematics in the 1920s, and many eminent American as well as European mathematicians and physicists trained at Göttingen, among them J. Robert Oppenheimer, Richard Courant, Max Born, Enrico Fermi, John von Neumann, Edward Teller, and Werner Heisenberg.

In 1928, Hopper graduated from Vassar with a Bachelor of Arts degree in mathematics and physics and was elected to Phi Beta Kappa, a preeminent national honor society. She was awarded a Vassar College Fellowship to pursue graduate study at Yale University, not far away in New Haven, Connecticut. Two years later, Hopper received a Master of Arts degree in mathematics from Yale. In June 1930, she married Vincent Foster Hopper, a graduate of Princeton University. Vincent taught English at New York University and soon enrolled in a PhD program in English. Hopper, meanwhile, continued her graduate studies at Yale, one of only two women in the mathematics doctoral program. In 1931, in addition to her own studies, Hopper began teaching mathematics at Vassar. She was a naturally gifted teacher, and for much of the next fifty years she continued to teach, at least a course or two, whenever she could.

In 1934, Hopper was awarded a PhD in mathematics from Yale, the only woman to receive one of seven doctorates in mathematics granted by the university between 1934 and 1937. She had studied under James Pierpont and with algebraist Oystein Ore and wrote her dissertation on "New Types of Irreducibility Criteria." Hopper spent the next nine years teaching at Vassar, advancing from assistant to associate professor. In 1941, she used a Vassar faculty fellowship to study under Richard Courant at New York University. Courant came from the same Göttingen tradition as her mentors at Vassar and Yale, and Hopper worked with him on the calculus of variations and on differential geometry. Her work with him on partial differential equations showed up later on her navy job classification card and was, she believed, the reason for her wartime assignment to the computing program at Harvard University.

World War II and the Navy. World War II changed Hopper's life forever. After Pearl Harbor she was determined to join the navy because, she explained, one of her great grandfathers had been an admiral during the Civil War. Furthermore, she and Vincent had just separated (they were divorced in 1945, and Hopper never remarried), so she was free to serve. In December 1943, at the age of thirty-seven, Hopper was sworn in to the U.S. Navy Reserve. In June 1944, she was commissioned a lieutenant (junior grade) and was sent to the Bureau of Ships Computation Project at Harvard University in Cambridge, Massachusetts.

Between the two world wars the growth of large-scale businesses required dealing with modern calculation and record-keeping needs. Work progressed in several industrial and academic laboratories on improved calculators. One or two early computer designs were also produced. By the early 1930s, Vannevar Bush and his colleagues at MIT had created a differential analyzer, an electromechanical analog computer, copies of which were widely used during World War II. In 1940, George R. Stibitz, of Bell Telephone Laboratories, created an electromechanical digital computer; at Iowa State College, John V. Atanasoff worked on an electronic digital device that some consider the first electronic digital computer in the United States, though it never worked. In Germany, Konrad Zuse developed various generations of computers named for him, and in England, Alan Turing developed a relay-based machine, called a bombe, to decrypt German enigma codes.

In 1937, Howard Aiken began work at Harvard University on an electromechanical relay machine to perform long mathematical calculations automatically. Engineers at IBM built Aiken's device, which he named the Mark I when it was set up at Harvard in the spring of 1944. Desperate for gunnery and ballistics calculations, the navy's Bureau of Ships leased the Mark I from the university for the duration of the war. Aiken, by then a professor of physics and applied mathematics and a naval reserve officer, was assigned to command the Harvard Computation Laboratory for the navy. To run the operation he assembled and trained a small team of mathematicians who, like himself, were serving in the wartime navy. Among them was Grace Hopper.

The Mark I measured 51 feet long, 8 feet tall, and 8 feet deep. It had more than 750,000 parts, used 530 miles of wire, and weighed more than 5 tons. A four-horsepower electric motor and drive shaft drove all the mechanical parts by a system of interlocking gears, counters, switches, and control circuits. Input was entered by punching holes in paper tape that was then fed into the machine. Output was handled automatically by electric typewriters.

What emerged was the first functional, large-scale, automatically sequenced, general-purpose digital computer in the United States. It was electromechanical, destined to dominate the field for only a year or two, briefly bridging the gap between calculators and electronic computers.

The Mark I was reliable, accurate, and speedy—at least one hundred times faster than hand-operated calculators. It was also adaptable and could be set to perform a wide range of different types of numerical calculations. This multipurpose capability of the Mark I set it apart from other contemporary devices, particularly the electronic ENIAC, with which it has been unfavorably compared but which was not fully functional until after the end of the war. Hopper always maintained that the most important thing she learned from Aiken was the notion of a general purpose computer—one that could undertake any task that could be described by a series of logical instructions.

Hopper's task at the Computation Lab was to write the codes that directed the operation of the Mark I. Because the computer was the first of its kind, she had no experience in coding, and she and her colleagues—arguably the first programmers—had to develop ways to express mathematical problems in digital machine code. Each mathematical process had to be broken down into very small steps of addition, subtraction, multiplication, or division, and put into a sequence. After figuring out how to write the machine instructions, Hopper punched them on tape, put the tape in the computer, and hoped it would run. The navy had new rockets but no firing tables for them. They had new magnetic mines but no tables of effective ranges for optimal mine laying. All these things could be computed on the Mark I, but someone had to translate the problems into terms the machine could understand. This was the challenge for Hopper and her colleagues; in learning how to talk to the Mark I, they learned a process that sixty years later was still the essence of programming.

The first problem that Hopper worked on was how to compute rocket trajectories, which involved finding the interpolation coefficients for applications of the arc tangent series. Another problem she worked on concerned the effective range of magnetic mines that were set off by metal ships. Working by trial and error at first, and learning as she went along, Hopper wrote the code for these and many other problems. The Mark I operated twenty-four hours per day, seven days per week, providing information of great practical value to the war effort.

Hopper also worked on creating codes for the Mark II, Aiken's second, and still electro-mechanical, computer, commissioned by the navy. In addition to coding, she wrote a manual of operation for the Mark I. Although she had no engineering background, she taught herself to understand the Mark I's circuits in order to explain its coding procedures and plugging instructions. She compiled 561 pages of detailed descriptions and diagrams of all the computer's parts and how they operated, as well as samples of all kinds of coding.

While at Harvard, Hopper developed the seeds of what, after the war, became her most creative work. Looking for shortcuts to writing programs, Hopper assembled a collection of subroutines—small bits of code for often-repeated functions. These she could copy into new programs, speeding the whole process. Noting that program-stopping errors often crept into her copying, Hopper recognized that if she could make the computer do the copying, she could avoid human copying errors. This insight eventually led to her creation of compilers.

Postwar Work at Harvard. At the end of the war, the Computation Lab was returned to Harvard, with Aiken, a civilian again, retaining control. Vassar College offered Hopper a full professorship, but she preferred to continue working in the innovative new field of computing and never taught full-time again. Instead, she remained at the Computation Lab as a research fellow in engineering systems and applied physics under a three-year, navy-funded contract. As Aiken's deputy she had charge of the operation of the Mark I, which continued to churn out answers to mathematical problems in fields as varied as atomic physics, radio research, optics, electronics, and astronomy. She also worked on Aiken's first electronic computer, the Mark III, commissioned by the navy and equipped with an innovative magnetic storage drum.

Under Aiken's direction, Hopper organized a series of international conferences to promote open discussion of computers and computing. The first of these, the Symposium of Large Scale Digital Calculating Machinery, was held at Harvard in 1947 and attracted many of the big names in computing, including Norbert Wiener, George Stibitz, Jay Forrester, Richard Courant, Wassily Leontief, John Mauchly, Herman Goldstine, and John von Neumann. These conferences introduced Hopper to the growing computer community, as did a number of articles she coauthored with Aiken on their wartime work at the Computation Lab.

After the war, Hopper maintained her naval reserve status and was promoted to lieutenant in 1946. With the passage of the Women's Armed Services Integration Act in 1948, she hoped to transfer to the regular navy, but she was over the age limit and had to settle for remaining in the reserves. With the expiration of her three-year contract at Harvard in 1949, she moved out of academe and into industry.

In Industry. Commercial development of electronic digital computers was in its infancy when Hopper left Harvard. In the late 1940s, even many involved in the design and construction of computers thought that their use was limited to providing mathematical solutions for scientific projects and that a very few would be sufficient to satisfy the world's need. Looking ahead more clearly, Hopper joined the Eckert-Mauchly Computer Corporation (EMCC) in Philadelphia. She chose EMCC because she believed its Universal Automatic Computer (Univac) would be operational before those in development at other fledgling companies, including IBM. Established by J. Presper Eckert and John Mauchly—the creators of the ENIAC—EMCC's high-speed Univac proved very successful. Hopper remained with the Univac division through Eckert-Mauchly's acquisition by Remington

Grace Hopper. *Grace Hopper using an early computer.* © BETTMANN/CORBIS.

Rand in 1950 and then through the merger creating Sperry Rand (later Unisys) in 1955.

Hired as a senior mathematician, Hopper continued her focus on methods to simplify the laborious and labor-intensive task of writing coding instructions. She was one of the original visionaries to recognize that computers could serve as the prime vehicle for their own programming and was a key player in conceiving, developing, and implementing the concept of compilers. In 1951, she began work on her first compiler, and by 1953, she had produced a commercially successful version, the A-2. Many mathematical problems, even with different objectives and results, used some of the same sets of instructions, or subroutines. The subroutines might solve certain classes of equations, or extract roots, and they were identical no matter what program they were inserted into. Yet for each job the programmer had to write pages and pages of duplicate code. Hopper's solution was to design a tape with a three-letter call sign for each set of subroutines. The programmer only had to enter the appropriate call sign for the computer to retrieve the subroutine from its library of instruction tapes. What had previously taken a month of programming time could now be accomplished in five minutes.

By the mid-1950s, as Hopper had predicted, computers were being used by a wide range of businesses. When they began to come off the assembly line, programming—because it was complex and time-consuming—became a bottleneck. Hopper had placed herself in the vanguard of those addressing this problem. She understood that, because it was impossible to teach everyone how to write computer code, there would have to be an interface that would accept what Hopper called "people-oriented" data. This the computer itself would translate into machine code. Pursuing this reasoning, Hopper led the development of a compiled programming language, Flow-Matic, which by the end of 1956 could translate instructions written in a limited vocabulary of English sentences into a computer program ready to run on the Univac.

Contrary to the impression given by some accounts of her accomplishments, Hopper was not the only one working on computer languages. That same year IBM came out with FORTRAN, for use on scientific and mathematical problems, and then developed Comtran, while Honeywell created Fact. And everyone drew on the brilliant early work of British mathematician Alan Turing. Nevertheless, Flow-Matic was a big breakthrough. Apart from a slight difference in terminology, business compilers from that point followed the pattern that it had established, including the use of the imperative form of verbs.

With the proliferation of computers and computing languages came a move among manufacturers to introduce some sort of standardization and portability of languages. Hopper was a key player in this from the very beginning. She was instrumental in the creation of the Committee on Data Systems Languages (CODASYL), tasked with putting together a standard business language. What emerged in 1960 was the first version of COBOL, Common Business Oriented Language, which was frequently updated but not replaced. Although Hopper was only indirectly involved in the work of the committee, the bulk of COBOL, including its format, was based on Hopper's Flow-Matic. When Hopper ran COBOL on a Univac and then on an RCA computer, demonstrating that one data-processing language could be run on different machines produced by different manufacturers, COBOL quickly became the most widely used programming language for mainframe computers.

In 1961, Hopper was named director of research in systems and programming for the Remington Rand division of Sperry Rand, responsible for broad-scale systems and programming research for all Remington Rand divisions. In 1964, she was appointed senior staff scientist at the Univac Division and traveled widely representing Univac interests in Europe and Japan as well as the United States and Canada. She worked on the basic techniques of creating, recording, retrieving, processing, and transmitting information and developed new concepts in systems design and information processing for such computer fields as medical science, language translation, and simulation processes.

During her eighteen years with the Univac Division, Hopper remained active in the naval reserve. Assigned to an ordnance unit in the Philadelphia Navy Yard, she played a part in the extension of computing to different navy tasks, making a name for herself in the navy as she was doing in the civilian world. Finally, in 1967, having reached the mandatory navy retirement age of sixty, Hopper was directed to retire. A few months later the navy recalled her to active duty for six months. She stayed for nineteen years.

Return to the Navy. Taking a military leave of absence from the Univac division, Hopper was assigned to the Pentagon to standardize computer-programming languages for all navy computers not part of weapons systems. She had been handpicked for the job by Norman Ream, special assistant to the Secretary of the Navy, who was tasked with imposing order on the navy's automatic data processing. By 1967, different and incompatible versions of COBOL had been proliferating almost unchecked to accommodate machine-dependent or vendor-unique features as well as the different tasks undertaken at different navy installations. Without a uniform language, there was no portability; programs had to be revised and rewritten every time they were transferred from one machine to another and across generations. Increasing demand for computerized systems in response to the navy's expansion in the Vietnam War made the restructuring of computing essential. Ream turned to Hopper to head an effort mandating the use of Standard COBOL in the navy and developing procedures for validating compliance.

Until 1970, Hopper headed a small group in the Office of Information Systems Planning and Development. Three-quarters of the navy's work was ashore, and COBOL was widely employed for inventory, payroll, personnel, and other management information systems. There were millions of lines of COBOL code to deal with, as well as the usual resistance to change and to the imposition of uniformity that bedevil any bureaucracy. Hopper's task was broad, far-reaching, and difficult, and it required her considerable diplomatic as well as technical skills. Her success in developing Standard Navy COBOL, persuading users throughout the navy to adopt it, creating test routines to check COBOL compilers for compatibility and standards, and providing technical support for its use made her a legend in the navy and beyond. Eventually, Hopper's Standard Navy COBOL was adopted by the entire Department of Defense; it influenced an entire industry as well, because manufactures could not sell their computers to the military unless they were compatible with Hopper's COBOL.

In 1970, Hopper was honored by the American Federation of Information Processing Societies with their prestigious Harry Goode Memorial Award for her leadership in the development of computer software and her influence on the computing profession. Three years later the navy acknowledged her accomplishments, promoting her to the rank of captain. Also in 1973, Hopper became the only woman, and the only American, to be named a Distinguished Fellow of the British Computer Society. She spent her last nine years in the navy as special staff to the commanding admiral of the Naval Data Automation Command. She not only advised him on the state of computing in the navy but became a roving ambassador for navy computing, giving over two hundred speeches annually, across the country and abroad. In 1983, her work was recognized by her promotion to the rank of commodore and, two years later, at the age of seventy-nine, she became a rear admiral.

Life's Work. In 1986, after forty-three years in the navy (and its oldest serving officer), Hopper reluctantly retired. She worked as a consultant for Digital for several years until her health failed. She died in 1992 at the age of eighty-five and was buried with full military honors in Arlington National Cemetery. Tributes poured in from around the world, and the navy named an Aegis guided missile destroyer for her. The USS *Hopper* (DDG 70) was commissioned in San Francisco in 1997. Fittingly, its motto is "Dare and Do."

In addition to her many other awards—including the 1991 National Medal of Technology—Hopper was the recipient of thirty-four honorary degrees. She remained a teacher at heart, influencing generations of students both at work and through the computer courses she taught for many years at various universities. She also published more than fifty papers and articles on computer software and programming languages. Her genius lay in making accessible this new and highly specialized field. In her own person, she represented the entire history of programming languages, from Flow-Matic in the 1950s to COBOL for minicomputers in the 1980s. Yet whenever she gave public addresses, she invariably asked to be introduced simply as one of the programmers on the first large-scale digital computer, the Mark I.

BIBLIOGRAPHY

For a complete list of publications by Grace Hopper, see Charlene W. Billings, Grace Hopper: Navy Admiral and Computer Pioneer *(Hillside, NJ: Enslow Publishers, 1989). Most of Grace Hopper's surviving papers are to be found in the Grace Murray Hopper Collection at the Archives Center, National Museum of American History, Smithsonian Institution.*

WORKS BY HOPPER

A Manual of Operation for the Automatic Sequence Controlled Calculator. Cambridge, MA: Harvard University Press, 1946.

With Howard H. Aiken. "The Automatic Sequence Controlled Calculator, I–III." *Electrical Engineering* 65 (August–September 1946): 384–391, 449–454, 522–528.

"The Education of a Computer." *Symposium of Industrial Applications of Automatic Computing Equipment* (January 1953): 139–44.

"Compiling Routines." *Computers and Automation* (May 1953): 1–5.

With John Mauchly. "Influence of Programming Techniques on the Design of Computers." *Proceedings of the IRE* 41 (October 1953): 1250–1254.

"Standardization and the Future of Computers." *Data Management* (April 1970): 32–35.

With Steve Mandell. *Understanding Computers.* St. Paul. MN: West Publishing, 1984.

OTHER SOURCES

Beyer, Kurt. "Grace Hopper and the Early History of Computer Programming: 1944–1960." PhD diss., University of California, Berkeley, 2002.

Billings, Charlene W. *Grace Hopper: Navy Admiral and Computer Pioneer.* Hillside, NJ: Enslow Publishers, 1989.

Cohen, I. Bernard. New Foreword to *A Manual of Operation for the Automatic Sequence Controlled Calculator.* Cambridge: MIT Press, 1985.

———. *Howard Aiken: Portrait of a Computer Pioneer.* Cambridge, MA: MIT Press, 1999.

———, and Gregory W. Welch, eds. *Makin' Numbers: Howard Aiken and the Computer.* Cambridge, MA: MIT Press, 1999.

"Harvard Computation Laboratory." *Journal of Applied Physics* 17, no. 10 (October 1946): 856.

Light, Jennifer S. "When Computers Were Women." *Technology and Culture* 40, no. 3 (July 1999): 455–483.

Mason, John F. "Grand Lady of Software." *Electronic Design* 22 (25 October 1976): 86.

Mitchell, Carmen Lois. "The Contribution of Grace Murray Hopper to Computer Science and Computer Education." PhD diss., University of North Texas: University Microfilms, 1994.

Prokop, Jan, ed. *Computers in the Navy.* Annapolis, MD: Naval Institute Press, 1976.

Randell, Brian. *The Origin of Digital Computers: Selected Papers.* New York: Springer-Verlag, 1973.

Rodgers, William. *Think: A Biography of the Watsons and IBM.* New York: Stein and Day, 1969.

Spencer, Donald P. *Great Men and Women of Computing.* Ormond Beach, FL: Camelot Publishing Company, 1996.

Stern, Nancy. *From Eniac to Univac: An Appraisal of the Eckert-Mauchly Computers.* Bedford, MA: Digital Press, 1981.

Whitelaw, Nancy. *Grace Hopper: Programming Pioneer.* New York: W. H. Freeman, 1995.

Williams, Kathleen Broome. *Grace Hopper: Admiral of the Cyber Sea.* Annapolis, MD: Naval Institute Press, 2004.

———. *Improbable Warriors: Women Scientists and the U.S. Navy in World War II.* Annapolis, MD: Naval Institute Press, 2001.

Yost, Edna. *Women of Modern Science.* New York: Dodd, Mead, 1959.

Kathleen Broome Williams

HOROWITZ, NORMAN HAROLD

(*b.* Pittsburgh, Pennsylvania, 19 March 1915; *d.* Pasadena, California, 2 June 2005), *genetics, biochemistry of metabolism, prebiotic chemistry, origin of life, astrobiology.*

Horowitz did pioneering work in two main areas: in the biochemical genetics of *Neurospora* and in exobiology (later renamed astrobiology), the search for extraterrestrial life and for the origins of life. In a series of experiments

Horowitz

from 1942 through 1946, Horowitz, along with others in George Beadle's group, worked out much of the detail of the experimental work supporting the "one gene–one enzyme hypothesis." Horowitz was the first to use that expression in print, though he credited Beadle with the concept and with coining the phrase. The pioneering stage of that work was essentially completed by the late 1940s. During the *Neurospora* work, Horowitz had an important insight into the early evolution of multistep metabolic pathways, which he published in 1945.

Because the origin of metabolic pathways pointed backward logically to the origins of life, this was the beginning of his serious involvement in origin-of-life research, and the new discipline of exobiology into which such research was incorporated after 1959. Horowitz was a seminal thinker on the origins of life and an important experimentalist in the other part of exobiology (later astrobiology), the search for extraterrestrial life that began in earnest with the dawn of the space age. This research dominated Horowitz's career from 1960 onward. In his capacity as chief of bioscience at the Jet Propulsion Laboratory (JPL) he supervised the design of experiments, including some of his own, which flew on spacecraft *Mariner 6* and *7* (1969) and on the Viking Mars Landers (1975–1977). He oversaw the design of the gas chromatograph–mass spectrometer and the pyrolytic release experiment (PR) on *Viking 1* and *2*.

Horowitz received a BS in biology from the University of Pittsburgh in 1936 and a PhD in biology from the California Institute of Technology (Caltech) in 1939, where Thomas Hunt Morgan assigned him to work under Albert Tyler on marine animals. As an undergraduate, Horowitz had already published a paper on transplantation of tissue in salamanders in the *Journal of Experimental Zoology.* During 1939 to 1940 he was a National Research Council fellow at Stanford University (at which time he first began work on *Neurospora*), then a research fellow at Caltech from 1940 to 1942. From 1942 to 1946 Horowitz was a research associate in biology with Beadle's group at Stanford. Then he returned to Caltech for the remainder of his career, as associate professor in biology (1947–1953), professor of biology (1953–1982), and professor emeritus from 1982 until his death. He was a Guggenheim Fellow at Boris Ephrussi's lab in Paris from 1954 to 1955. In addition, while continuing as professor at Caltech, from 1965 to 1970 Horowitz simultaneously served as chief of the bioscience section of the National Aeronautics and Space Administration's (NASA) JPL in Pasadena, California. Horowitz was a member of the National Academy of Sciences (NAS) since 1969 and a member since its founding in 1972 of the International Society for the Study of the Origin of Life. He remained active in research and administrative activities until his death.

The One Gene–One Enzyme Hypothesis. Horowitz's interest in the genetics and metabolism of the red bread mold *Neurospora crassa* was piqued by a 1941 talk Beadle gave on his discovery with Edward Tatum that mutants of the mold showed a direct correlation between a single gene mutation and deficiency of the ability to synthesize a single nutrient. The wild-type mold could grow on a very simple growth medium, synthesizing almost every nutrient it needed. Beadle and Tatum irradiated the mold with x-rays to produce mutants, screening them afterward for which single nutrient they could not survive without.

Within a year of the discovery, Horowitz joined Beadle's group at Stanford. Horowitz, David Bonner, and others in this research group sought to systematically demonstrate that each and every nutrient-deficient mutant was altered by only a single-gene mutation and to show what specific enzyme the gene was responsible for. Usually the mutant strain produced some nonfunctional enzyme for a single step in the metabolic pathway to synthesizing some nutrient, such as biotin, another B vitamin, or an amino acid. Horowitz found, for example, that a mutation of the gene for the enzyme tyrosinase was inherited as a simple Mendelian trait; a mutation that produced a tyrosinase molecule having different thermostability characteristics than the wild-type enzyme. The pathway in *Neurospora* for synthesis of the amino acid arginine was found to have seven steps, each controlled by a specific enzyme coded for by a single gene. Horowitz found that some of the biochemical synthetic pathways had branching steps in them, which complicated the attempt to demonstrate a one gene–one enzyme correlation. In the end, however, in eight papers published between 1943 and 1945, the group showed that the one gene–one enzyme correlation was exactly as predicted by the hypothesis.

Horowitz was also involved during the early 1940s in using nutrient-deficient *Neurospora* mutants to assay quantitatively for nutrients in foods, for example, choline and other B vitamins. He also screened for mutants of *Penicillium* that could produce a higher yield of penicillin.

Origin of Multistep Biosynthetic Pathways. Given that multistep synthetic pathways were common in *Neurospora* and that many of the intermediate compounds were not themselves useful nutrients, Horowitz pondered how such a complex pathway could be produced by natural selection, when apparently most of the intermediate, shorter-chain stages would not be functionally adaptive; only the full pathway with all the steps could actually supply the needed nutrient. He reasoned that simple pathways of just a few steps could occasionally arise by chance combinations of mutations. But this would be statistically impossible for pathways such as the seven-step arginine

Horowitz

synthesis, more common in *Neurospora* and most other organisms.

The paradox, however, lent itself to an ingenious solution, which Horowitz was first to recognize. Suppose, he suggested, the essential end product, molecule A, was originally freely available in the external environment. Such an environment abundant in organic molecules had been proposed by Aleksandr Oparin as part of his heterotroph hypothesis for the origin of life. Then the ancestral organism would be under no selective pressure to develop a means to synthesize that nutrient biochemically. However, as the nutrient was gradually depleted once living heterotrophs arose and steadily consumed it, then any mutant that appeared with the capacity to synthesize A with an enzyme that could make it from B + C (two other freely available organic precursors) would be at a substantial selective advantage. So much so that in the continued absence of A soon only those descendants with the new mutation would survive. Eventually B and C would also become depleted, and then selective pressure would favor mutants that by chance arose with the ability to enzymatically synthesize, say, molecule B, from other common precursor molecules D and E.

The process could repeat many times over evolutionary time. "Given a sufficiently complex environment and a proportionately variable germ plasm, long reaction chains can be built up in this way. … This model is thus seen to have potentialities for the rapid evolution of long chain syntheses in response to changes in the environment," said Horowitz (1945, p. 156). Thus an apparently "irreducibly complex" system within cells was not so in fact and could be built up in reverse by simple natural selection. The first organism was, in Horowitz's view, a "self-duplicating nucleoprotein molecule" that originated as a step in Oparin's suggested process of chemical evolution.

> To summarize, the hypothesis presented here suggests that the first living entity was a completely heterotropic [*sic*] unit, reproducing itself at the expense of prefabricated organic molecules in its environment. A depletion of the environment resulted until a point was reached where the supply of specific substrates limited further multiplication. By a process of mutation a means was eventually discovered for utilizing other available substances. With this event the evolution of biosyntheses began. The conditions necessary for the operation of the mechanism ceased to exist with the ultimate destruction of the organic environment [as the initial organics were all consumed]. Further evolution was probably based on the chance combination of genes, resulting to a large extent in the development of short reaction chains utilizing substances whose synthesis had been previously acquired. (p. 157)

Horowitz, then, had not only solved a significant puzzle about early evolution; he had simultaneously been led to stake out a position in agreement with Hermann J. Muller's (1926) claim that a "gene" must have been the first living thing.

Origin of Life: Genes versus Metabolism. Horowitz had stepped into a debate that had been developing for the previous thirty years, over whether a primitive chemical system that counted as "living" needed first to exhibit metabolism, or rather self-duplication (called "replication" after Watson and Crick's 1953 DNA structure made clear that genetic duplication was a much more high-fidelity process than many had previously thought). As mentioned, famed *Drosophila* geneticist H. J. Muller had insisted unequivocally that a naked gene was the first living organism.

Oparin, however, tended to emphasize complex, membrane-bounded metabolizing entities that could only come about through a long, stepwise evolutionary process. He and his supporters were deeply skeptical that any molecule as complex as a gene could possibly develop suddenly, de novo, outside such a preexisting, membrane-bounded, metabolizing structure. They saw this as tantamount to a claim of "spontaneous generation," that is, the old exploded doctrine that a living thing could appear very suddenly in a short time in the right chemical environment.

This debate became only more entangled and complex when molecular biology discovered by the early 1960s that nucleic acids cannot replicate or perform their functions without the assistance of a suite of protein enzymes, usually only found in an enclosed metabolizing cell. Thus a "naked gene" became an oxymoron, and an insoluble "chicken and egg" dilemma emerged. If proteins are absolutely necessary for the functioning of DNA, and DNA is necessary to code for the making of all proteins, then how can such a system have ever come into being without both components? Even assuming the original self-duplicating molecule was much less complex and copied itself with much less fidelity than DNA, it still remains a subject of intense debate in the origin-of-life research community, which of the two probably came first and served as the "scaffolding" upon which the "free-hanging arch" was later created.

When the first International Conference on Origin of Life Research was held, organized by Oparin in 1957 in Moscow at the height of the Cold War, many Western scientists attended, including Horowitz. Some American and British scientists supported the "metabolism-first" view of Oparin (e.g., Sidney Fox, Erwin Chargaff, John Desmond Bernal, H. J. Muller, and Norman Wingate Pirie); nonetheless, the debate about "genes first" became

Horowitz

Norman Horowitz. Norman Horowitz in laboratory. COURTESY OF THE ARCHIVES, CALIFORNIA INSTITUTE OF TECHNOLOGY.

somewhat politicized because of the domination of Soviet biology by Trofim Denisovich Lysenko's anti-Mendelian rhetoric, of which Oparin had been supportive.

Along with Heinz Fraenkel-Conrat and Wendell Stanley, Horowitz forcefully insisted, contrary to Pirie's assertion that "life" is indefinable, that a self-duplicating gene capable of mutability and catalysis of metabolic reactions was a perfectly clear-cut definition. Such living things "arose as individual molecules in a polymolecular environment," Horowitz stated in 1957 (1959, p. 107), much as he had in 1945. In numerous subsequent conferences on the origin of life, Horowitz stuck to this position and was, along with Muller, one of its most steadfast champions. He coauthored a major review of recent origin-of-life research with Stanley Miller (1962). This paper was highly critical of many "test tube" experiments showing possible prebiotic chemistry, because it was common for experimenters to add organic components to their mixture, which were highly unlikely to have ever existed in a realistic prebiotic Earth environment.

Exobiology and Astrobiology. From the earliest attempts by microbiologist Joshua Lederberg to organize the Space Sciences Board of the NAS in support of work on exobiology in 1959, Horowitz was a major helper in this effort. He was an active member of the West Coast branch of the NAS's subpanel on extraterrestrial life (WESTEX), led by Lederberg.

The two men worked together once NASA supported exobiology from 1960 on, to prevent the Cold War politicization of their new science in the way that space exploration had widely become subservient to such interests, especially the human space program. Horowitz and Lederberg both felt that the search for the origin of life and for extraterrestrial life were marginal enough to begin with and that all hope of scientific respectability and high-quality scientific work would be lost if the field of exobiology came to be seen as just one more attempt to "catch up with the Soviets" technologically in the wake of *Sputnik.* They called for high levels of NASA money for research, but in addition they were crucial engineers of an emerging NASA exobiology program that eventually gave half or more of its funds to independent researchers in the academic community (even when it came to design of experiments that would fly on NASA spacecraft), rather than becoming a research effort staffed only by U.S. government employees. Both men became active in early attempts to design life-detection instruments intended to fly on a Mars probe, Horowitz at first when he was asked in 1962 to be a scientific consultant on the "Gulliver" instrument being designed by Gilbert Levin. He was an active participant at a series of meetings sponsored by the NAS (May 1964 through October 1965) on Biology and the Exploration of Mars, cochaired by Colin Pittendrigh and Lederberg.

When *Mariner 4* first successfully made a close flyby of Mars in 1965, however, the photos and other data it returned suggested Mars was much drier, colder, and had a much thinner atmosphere than had been previously thought. The cratered surface of Mars looked much more like the Moon in those photographs than it did Earth. Horowitz had criticized most experimental life-detection designs, which depended upon putting Mars soil into a liquid nutrient broth to see what microbes would grow; no Mars organism could possibly be adapted for life in copious liquid water, he argued, given how dry and cold the planet was. He put more faith than most exobiology scientists in recent Earth-based observations suggesting a very thin and tenuous Martian atmosphere (insufficient pressure for any water to remain in the liquid form on the surface), so he was becoming steadily more skeptical of whether any life could exist on Mars and was less surprised than most by the *Mariner 4* results. But he was surprised to find that most "life on Mars" enthusiasts were still just as optimistic as before about sending their instruments to Mars to look for Earth-like bacteria. (James Lovelock was one of the few scientists involved who was as skeptical as Horowitz in 1965.)

Horowitz had argued from as early as 1960 that concern about contaminating Earth with organisms brought back ("back contamination") from Mars was a waste of time, so unlikely was it that such microbes even existed. He continued to participate in discussions about adequate levels of sterilization for spacecraft before they left Earth, because he thought the possibility of "forward contamination" of other worlds by Earth organisms a scientific problem whose avoidance justified a reasonable level of prudence. Through JPL, Horowitz sponsored research on the microbiology of the dry valleys of Antarctica, showing that these might be the best analogs of Mars-like conditions available on Earth. Ten to 15 percent of the soil samples there contained no bacteria at all, and the rest had very low bacterial counts, confirming Horowitz in his skepticism about Mars soils under much harsher conditions.

Because Horowitz became chief of biosciences at JPL at this time, where the latest Mars spacecraft were being designed and built, he had the opportunity to oversee at close hand the development of the experiments likely to fly on the Viking Mars landers, slated for launch in the early to mid-1970s. In conjunction with Jerry Hubbard and George Hobby, he designed a life-detection device he called the pyrolytic release (PR) experiment, based upon assimilation of a carbon source by microbes in a nonaqueous, cold environment much closer to actual martian conditions. And he was eventually successful in having this chosen as one of the four experiments relevant to life detection that actually flew on the Vikings (Levin's "Gulliver" or Labeled Release [LR] experiment was another). Horowitz's device completely burned (pyrolyzed) the sample after incubation to see if any radioactive carbon-14 from the nutrients had been incorporated into living cells.

In the event, when the experiments reached the surface of Mars on *Viking 1* and *2* in the summer of 1976, they began to collect data immediately. While hypothesized chemical oxidants in the soil at first gave the mistaken impression of microbial activity in both the LR and PR experiments, the gas chromatograph–mass spectrometer showed no organic compounds in the Martian soil at all, leading the majority of Viking researchers to conclude that the experiments had given "false positive" reactions, and that Mars must be sterile, at least at the surface. Levin was the only researcher to continue insisting that the data were best interpreted as indicating microbial life on Mars. Even former Martian-life optimists such as Carl Sagan in the end were converted to Horowitz's view that the Martian surface was lifeless. Subsurface water (and life) remain a possibility, as does fossilized life from a much earlier period in Mars history during which the planet was considerably warmer and wetter.

BIBLIOGRAPHY

WORKS BY HOROWITZ

With Adrian Srb. "The Ornithine Cycle in *Neurospora* and Its Genetic Control." *Journal of Biological Chemistry* 154 (1944): 129–139.

"On the Evolution of Biochemical Syntheses." *Proceedings of the National Academy of Sciences of the United States of America* 31 (1945): 153–157.

With David Bonner, H. K. Mitchell, E. L. Tatum, et al. "Genic Control of Biochemical Reactions in *Neurospora." American Naturalist* 79 (1945): 304–317.

"On Defining 'Life.'" In *Proceedings of the First International Conference on the Origin of Life, Moscow, 19–24 Aug. 1957,* edited by F. Clark and R. L. M. Synge. New York: Pergamon Press, 1959.

With Stanley Miller. "Current Theories on the Origin of Life." *Fortschritte der Chemie Organischer Naturstoffe* [Progress in the chemistry of organic natural products] 20 (1962): 423–459.

"The Design of Martian Biological Experiments." In *Life Sciences and Space Research 2,* edited by Marcel Florkin and A. Dollfus. Amsterdam: North Holland Publishing, 1964.

With Gilbert Levin, A. H. Heim, M. F. Thompson, et al. "'Gulliver': An Experiment for Extraterrestrial Life Detection and Analysis." In *Life Sciences and Space Research 2,* edited by M. Florkin and A. Dollfus. Amsterdam: North Holland Publishing, 1964.

"The Evolution of Biochemical Synthesis—Retrospect and Prospect." In *Evolving Genes and Proteins,* edited by Vernon Bryson and Henry J. Vogel. New York: Academic Press, 1965.

"Impact of Manned Spacecraft on the Exobiology Program." In *Biology and the Exploration of Mars: Report of a Study Held under the Auspices of the Space Science Board, National Academy of Sciences–National Research Council, 1964–1965,* edited by Colin S. Pittendrigh, Wolf Vishnac, and J. P. T. Pearman. National Research Council publication 1296. Washington, DC: National Academy of Sciences, 1966.

"The Search for Extraterrestrial Life." *Science* 151 (18 February 1966): 789–792.

With Robert P. Sharp and Richard W. Davies. "Planetary Contamination I: The Problem and the Agreements." *Science* 155 (24 March 1967): 1501–1505.

With Jerry S. Hubbard and James P. Hardy. "Photocatalytic Production of Organic Compounds from CO and H_2O in a Simulated Martian Atmosphere." *Proceedings of the National Academy of Sciences of the United States of America* 68 (1971): 574–578.

With Roy E. Cameron and Jerry S. Hubbard. "Microbiology of the Dry Valleys of Antarctica." *Science* 176 (21 April 1972): 242–245.

With Jerry S. Hubbard. "The Origin of Life." *Annual Review of Genetics* 8 (1974): 393–410.

With Harold P. Klein, Joshua Lederberg, Alex Rich, et al. "The Viking Mission Search for Life on Mars." *Nature* 262 (July 1976): 24–27.

Hörstadius

With Harold P. Klein, Gilbert Levin, Vance Oyama, et al. "The Viking Biological Investigation: Preliminary Results." *Science* 194 (17 December 1976): 1322–1329.

Oral history interview by Rachel Prud'homme, 9–10 July 1984. Caltech Archives. Available from http://resolver.caltech.edu/CaltechOH:OH_Horowitz_N.

To Utopia and Back: The Search for Life in the Solar System. San Francisco: W. H. Freeman, 1986.

OTHER SOURCES

Beadle, George, and Edward L. Tatum. "Genetic Control of Biochemical Reactions in *Neurospora.*" *Proceedings of the National Academy of Sciences of the United States of America* 27 (1941): 499–506.

Dick, Steven J., and James E. Strick. *The Living Universe: NASA and the Development of Astrobiology.* New Brunswick, NJ: Rutgers University Press, 2004.

Farley, John. Chapter 9 in *The Spontaneous Generation Controversy from Descartes to Oparin.* Baltimore, MD: Johns Hopkins University Press, 1977.

Fry, Iris. *The Emergence of Life on Earth: A Historical and Scientific Overview.* New Brunswick, NJ: Rutgers University Press, 2000.

Kamminga, Harmke. "The Protoplasm and the Gene." In *Clay Minerals and the Origin of Life,* edited by Alexander Graham Cairns-Smith and Hyman Hartman. Cambridge, U.K.: Cambridge University Press, 1986.

Margulis, Lynn, ed. *Origins of Life.* New York: Gordon and Breach, 1970.

———, ed. *Origins of Life, II.* New York: Gordon and Breach, 1971.

Muller, Hermann J. "The Gene as the Basis of Life." [1926]. In *Proceedings of the Fourth International Congress of Plant Biology,* vol. 1. Menasha, WI: Banta Publishing, 1929.

Oparin, Aleksandr. *The Origin of Life.* Translated by Sergius Morgulis. New York: Macmillan, 1938.

James E. Strick

HÖRSTADIUS, SVEN OTTO

(*b.* Stockholm, Sweden, 18 February 1898; *d.* Uppsala, Sweden, 16 June 1996), *developmental biology, experimental embryology.*

Hörstadius was one of the leading experimental embryologists during several decades around the mid-twentieth century. His most important work was on the determination and differentiation of the sea urchin embryo, a topic he studied for half a century. Early work inspired by his teacher John Runnström's double gradient theory showed that gradients of animalness (ectodermal determination) and vegetalness (endodermal determination) existed in the 16- and 32-cell embryos. Hörstadius became famous for his elegant extirpation and transplantation experiments using glass needles, and for his skill in performing microsurgery on the minute embryos of echinoderms. He also made important contributions to the study of cranial neural crest development in the Mexican axolotl, in collaboration with his student Sven Sellman. Hörstadius obtained several honorary doctorates, for example, in the United Kingdom (Cambridge and Bristol) and in France (Sorbonne), and was elected a member of many academies and learned societies, including the Royal Society in London and the Vatican Academy of Sciences.

Short Biography. Sven Hörstadius was born into an upper-class Stockholm family. His father Wilhelm was a judge of appeal, and the family spent their summers in a summer house in the Stockholm Archipelago. Sven showed a keen interest in bird watching already as a schoolboy at the Northern Latin School in Stockholm, and was to remain active as an amateur ornithologist all his life. He went to college in Stockholm and rapidly came to know a zoologist, John Runnström, who was to have a formative influence on his scientific interests and career. Hörstadius obtained a PhD degree in 1928, and married Greta (born Kjellström, 1903–1987). She also had a natural science background and became an important collaborator and assistant to Sven. They published together on protein digestion in gastropods. The marriage produced two children, Göran, who was a physician at Uppsala University Hospital, and Dagmar, who went into banking and married Sven Ågren. Sven Hörstadius remained active as a scientist well into his eighties. The death of his wife in 1987 was difficult to handle, but he remained in good physical shape well into his nineties. In the last decade of his long life, however, his memory often failed him. He died in a nursing home at the age of 98.

The First Experiments. Sven Hörstadius was introduced to experimental embryology as an undergraduate by John Runnström, a young zoologist who would later occupy the chair in zoology at Stockholm University. Runnström and his students did their experimental work at Kristineberg marine station on the Swedish west coast. Kristineberg had been founded by, and was run by, the Royal Swedish Academy of Sciences in Stockholm, and had laboratories where the Runnström group could perform their experiments. Already as an undergraduate, Hörstadius made an important investigation of factors regulating the ripening of the eggs of a polychaete worm, *Pomatoceros triqueter.* He experimented with factors such as temperature, alkalinity, osmotic pressure, and ion concentration, and noted their effects on egg ripening. This led to his first international publication (in 1923) and to a smaller follow-up paper published the following year in a Swedish journal.

Echinoderm Experimental Embryology. Kristineberg was not suitable for experimental work on embryology in the winter, and the north Atlantic echinoderm species did not spawn year-round. Therefore Hörstadius now started a long series of successful stays at the Stazione Zoologica in Naples, Italy. The Stazione became his main winter research station, although he sometimes also visited other marine biology research stations, such as Roscoff in France and Plymouth in England. He first visited Naples in 1922, and then again in 1924. Here he came to work almost exclusively with echinoderms. Much later, when Hörstadius summed up his research on echinoderm experimental embryology in a classic book, he listed the reasons why these animals became so important as experimental objects:

> (a) artificial fertilization is readily achieved and hence desired stages of development can be obtained at any time; (b) the larvae are transparent, as are also the eggs of some species, and thus allow microscopical studies of the living material to be made; (c) eggs can be obtained in large quantities, which facilitates physiological and biochemical investigations; (d) the regular type of cleavage makes possible work with fragments of known size and origin; (e) the egg axis is recognizable by the characteristic 16-cell stage ...; (f) furthermore, ripe ova and sperm are available for long periods from several species, so that by choosing suitable marine stations it is possible to work on the development of sea-urchins at all times of the year. (p. 2)

Hörstadius pointed out repeatedly that in order to even begin to investigate the processes and mechanisms underlying normal development experimentally, one first needs to have a detailed description of cell division, cell movements, and cell fate. In his 1973 book he wrote, "A prerequisite for experimental work is a thorough knowledge of the normal development" (p. 10). Although Hörstadius is known as the great experimentalist, he also made several important descriptive studies of the development of different echinoderm species. A method to keep track of cell divisions and cell movements was to use vital dyes such as Nile blue sulfate to mark selected cells at an early stage. The dye was kept in small blocks of agar-agar, which were put into contact with the target cell or cells. Hörstadius used vital dye staining to determine the fate at gastrulation of ventral cells (see Figure 1), and also in his later studies of neural crest fate (see below). Fate mapping is important for understanding the cellular origin and morphogenesis of the different organs in an organism. By staining the entire vegetal (lower) half of the echinoderm embryo, Hörstadius showed that about a third of the ectoderm (the outer layer of the early embryo, which gives rise to the skin and the nervous system) was derived from the

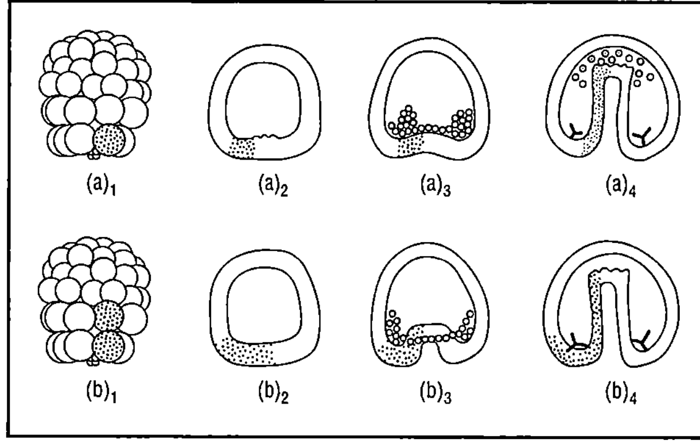

Figure 1. *Vital staining of single blastomeres and their fate during gastrulation. $(a)_1$-$(a)_4$, a veg_2-cell has been stained. $(b)_1$-$(b)_4$, both a veg_1 - and a veg_2-cell has been stained.*

macromeres (the large cells on the underside). When staining only the most ventral cells, veg_2, and micromeres (the small cells on top), Hörstadius could show that their descendants were found in the archenteron (the primitive gut) and in primary mesenchyme. Finally, and most elegantly, he stained single cells at the 64-cell stage using a micropipette. Staining one veg_2-cell resulted in stained cells only in the archenteron (Figure 1[a]$_1$–[a]$_4$) whereas marking both a veg_1- and a veg_2-cell showed that the descendants of the veg_1-cell contribute to the presumptive ectoderm (Figure 1[b]$_1$–[b]$_4$). At the time, this was probably the most detailed fate-mapping study ever undertaken, and served as the basis for Hörstadius's experimental work. Knowing the normal fate of cells makes it possible to interpret experiments in which normal development is altered.

During his first stays at the Stazione Zoologica in Naples, Hörstadius did a number of elegant experiments on determination and induction, the processes by which cells are instructed to develop into a specific cell type. In his first experiments on starfish larvae he used relatively advanced stages such as late gastrulae and did his experiments using glass needles and simple microscopes. He could show that isolated vegetal halves were able to develop into normal-looking older larvae, so-called plutei, while isolated animal (upper) halves were not. Contrary to earlier beliefs, he found that all cells of the early stages had the same potency: isolated vegetal halves of such embryos developed into small but quite normal larvae while animal halves did not (see Figure 2). The logical experiment was then to test how different combinations of cell layers from the 16-cell stage might influence development. The main finding was that even animal halves of the larva developed into normal plutei if they were given influences from the vegetal part, for instance by transplanted micromere cells from the very bottom of the morulae. Other experiments,

Hörstadius

in which he delayed the normal cleavage timetable, showed that differentiation of the embryo is independent of the cleavage scheme. Most of this work was published as his doctoral thesis (1928).

In 1929, Hörstadius's teacher Runnström published an idea he had developed over several years, the double-gradient theory. According to this theory, the animal and vegetal poles of the embryo each set up a gradient of a morphogen, and the cells differentiate according to the levels of these two morphogens that they encounter. Hörstadius was the experimentalist who could put this theory to the test. Already his thesis work had pointed in this direction, and he now followed it up in a range of different experimental setups (see Figure 2).

Another question hotly disputed at the time was whether combining the cytoplasm from one species and the nucleus from another could lead to a zygote that developed normally. This was an important part of the question whether development is determined by the cytoplasm or by the nucleus. Hörstadius published a preliminary report in 1932 and later (1936) a large paper in which he showed convincingly that enucleated eggs from one species with an injected sperm from another could develop to a certain degree, and that the nucleus determines the species-specific development.

Hörstadius stayed in Runnström's research group throughout the 1930s. Runnström was an ambitious leader and needed more modern labs for his group. Government money was hard to come by, but he had contacts with the Swedish businessman Axel Wenner-Gren, and managed to get him interested in supporting his work. Wenner-Gren was the founder of the Electrolux Company, and in the 1930s one of the most influential Swedish industrialists. This contact resulted in the founding of the Wenner-Gren Institute of Experimental Biology in Stockholm, inaugurated in 1939. This institute became important for Swedish physiology, and formed a strong school in developmental biology. Among its members were Per-Erik Lindahl, Tore Hultin, Tryggve Gustafsson, and Björn Afzelius, in addition to Runnström and Hörstadius. The constellation Wenner-Gren Institute–Kristineberg Marine Station has been invaluable for strengthening Swedish developmental biology. Hörstadius became a zoology professor at Uppsala University in 1942, but kept his links with the Wenner-Gren Institute. In collaboration with Runnström and other members of the institute, Hörstadius did important studies of the effects of animalizing and vegetalizing substances on the development of sea urchin larvae. In animalized embryos all cells develop as if they were derived from its animal (upper) part, whereas in vegetalized embryos, all cells differentate into cells of the gut, which normally arise only from the vegetal (lower) part of the embryo. Substances investigated included amino acids

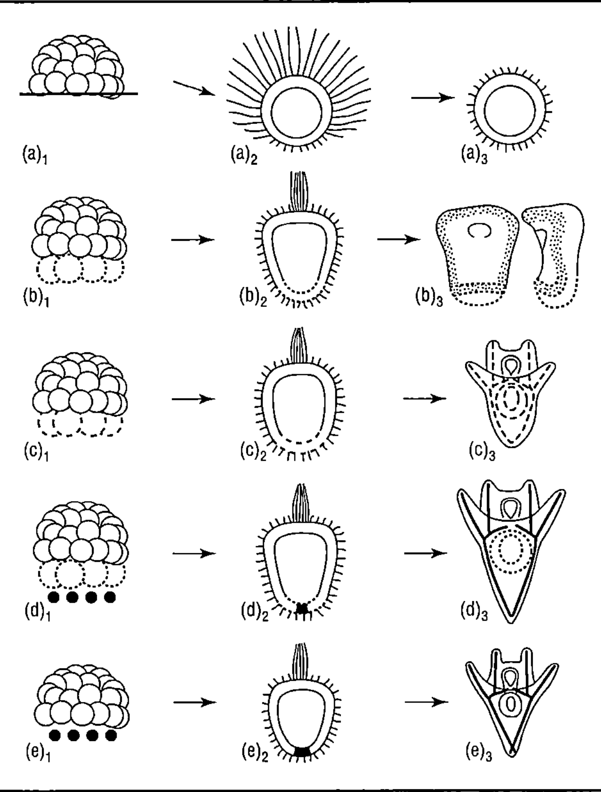

Figure 2. *Hörstadius' classical diagram of the influence of vegetal material from sea urchin blastulae on the differentiation of animal material.*

(1957) and sulfate (1964), but also the vegetalizing effects of dinitrophenol and animalization by trypsin and ficin were documented. Animalized larvae develop an enlarged apical tuft of stereocilia but no intestine, while vegetalized larvae develop an intestine but no ciliary tuft. Together with the biochemist Lars Josefsson in Copenhagen, Hörstadius analyzed the morphogenetic effects of fractions extracted from lyophilized sea urchin eggs (1967). Some of these fractions, which were never clearly defined, were very potent animalizers (1972).

Cranial Neural Crest Development. Toward the end of the 1930s Hörstadius started to work on a new experimental organism and in a new research area: head, in particular cranial neural crest, development in the Mexican axolotl. Head development was a classical subject in morphology and developmental biology, and at the time the origin of cartilage, bone, teeth, and other structures in the head region was a subject receiving renewed scientific attention. Earlier studies had indicated that most of the cranium was derived from the neural crest, but details were largely unknown. The neural crest is an embryonic structure in vertebrates, which develops when the central nervous system is formed at neurulation. Neural crest cells briefly form a crestlike structure on top of the neural tube, and then migrate away to form a large array of different cell types in the embryo, including skeletal, pigment, and nerve cells. There may be more than one explanation for why Hörstadius started to work on the neural crest. He now had a family, and although sea urchin studies could be combined with family life during the summer months, when the Kristineberg station was the ideal place to bring the family, long winter and spring stays in Naples were difficult to combine both with academic teaching and with family life. Carl-Olof Jacobson (2000a,b), however, writes that another factor might have been even more important. In order to be able to obtain a professorship at Swedish universities, it was important to not be seen as too much of a specialist. Usually, candidates who came across as narrowly focused specialists were not chosen, because as a teacher, a zoology professor had to cover a very large area including both invertebrate and vertebrate zoology. Hörstadius might have reasoned that if his skill in invertebrate cell and developmental biology could be supplemented with vertebrate morphology and embryology, his chances of obtaining a chair in zoology would be much better.

Hörstadius had also visited Ross G. Harrison's laboratory at Yale University and the Woods Hole Oceanographic Institute, in Massachusetts, in 1936. From Harrison he learned how to perform microsurgery on amphibian larvae. In the 1930s Harrison was occupied with a series of neural crest experiments and Hörstadius became interested in this remarkable embryonic structure and in the ongoing research on what tissues and organs the neural crest actually gave rise to. He immediately started what would become a thorough analysis of the skeleton-forming capacity of the cranial neural crest in the amphibian genera *Ambystoma* and *Triturus.* These studies were done in collaboration with Sven Sellman, a graduate student from the school of dentistry in Stockholm. Sellman had started an investigation of tooth development in *Triturus,* and the common interest in neural crest biology led to a very fruitful cooperation.

The fate of cranial neural crest cells needed to be mapped, and Hörstadius and Sellman used basically the same technique—vital staining—that had proven so useful in Hörstadius's echinoderm work. Alternating red and blue markers (Nile blue sulfate and neutral red, respectively) were applied to different portions of the neural folds, and the migration of the neural crest cells between the epidermis and the mesoderm could be followed. The main problem was that the stains became more and more diluted with each cell division. In order to learn more about the properties of the neural crest of the head, a vast number of extirpation and transplantation experiments were performed. In this way, they could elucidate both the migration and the normal fate of cranial neural crest cells, as well as the inductive influences from neighboring tissues such as the underlying mesoderm (which gives rise to the axial skeleton and striated muscles) and endoderm (which produces the cells of the digestive tract). Hörstadius and Sellman especially emphasized the role of the endoderm, whereas the overlying ectoderm seemed to have no effect. From 2000 onward the role of the endoderm has received renewed attention.

Other questions addressed in the paper include the importance of the presumptive forebrain for the differentiation of the trabeculae (parts of the neurocranium, which underlie the brain), and the clear evidence that part of the trabeculae, the "ectomesodemal trabeculae" are neural crest derived. Also the neural crest material normally destined to be integrated into the trabeculae was shown to not have the potential to differentiate into visceral arch skeleton, and vice versa. In addition, it was shown that both the neural crest closest to the oral region and the trunk crest do not form cartilage. Finally, new and important observations concerning the development of the ear, teeth, and eyes were also reported.

Another researcher interested in the neural crest, Professor (later Sir) Gavin de Beer, head of the Department of Embryology at University College London, was very impressed by the large (170-page) paper published by Hörstadius and Sellman in 1946. He invited Hörstadius to give a series of lectures on the neural crest in London in the fall of 1947. In his lectures Hörstadius told the full story of how our knowledge of the neural crest has developed, starting with Wilhelm His's first description from 1868 of the neural crest in the chick embryo, and summarizing later work until the mid-1940s. The lectures were later (1950) published as a book, *The Neural Crest,* by Oxford University Press. This book has become a classic and has been reprinted a few times. In 1988 it appeared in facsimile together with a modern treatment of the same topic by Brian K. Hall. Hörstadius always argued that he was an experimentalist and not a theoretician. And perhaps this is exactly why he was able to make such a long-lived summary of a research area. He never went further in his analyses than the results of the experiments allowed him.

Sven Hörstadius the Teacher. Hörstadius gave a lecture series for many years on developmental biology. It ran over two semesters and his lectures are reported to be clear and didactically excellent. Jacobson, who worked together with Hörstadius in undergraduate courses, has given the only eyewitness report:

> [Hörstadius] was a brilliant lecturer and showman, and he loved to perform. It is a pity that his two-semester lecture course on embryology and

Hörstadius

> its research history was never published as a book, even though his lively way of demonstrating form-shaping movements with his whole body would not have appeared in a written version. Especially instructive and entertaining was his elegant way of demonstrating embryogenesis with hand movements, while his face was radiating enthusiasm. (2000b, p. 253)

The only complaint about Hörstadius's lectures noted by Jacobson is that "his wish to be clear in his lectures often led him to oversimplify a scientific problem. As his assistant I often overheard his lectures, and in my mind he too often presented a plausible theory as an established fact" (2000b). Another of Hörstadius's former graduate students, Göran Gezelius, also reports that Hörstadius tended to gloss over problems in his lectures. When asked about this, Gezelius said, "There were never any unsolved problems," whether this was apparent to the undergraduate students is another matter altogether.

Statesman of Science, Bird-watcher, and Environmentalist. Progressively, from the 1930s onward, Hörstadius became more and more involved in academic leadership. When still in Stockholm, he worked as head of department, and in Uppsala, where he got his chair of zoology in 1942, he had to deal with teaching and administration more than before. His zoology professorship made Hörstadius responsible for the teaching of ecology, a new branch of science, both in undergraduate courses and in graduate school. For several years he served as dean of the Faculty of Natural Sciences, and he also organized large conferences. He was a member of the Swedish Natural Science Research Council and the Royal Swedish Academy of Sciences. Hörstadius also took on a number of international responsibilities. He was chairman of the International Union of Biological Sciences for a considerable time and he also served as president of the International Council of Scientific Unions. Hörstadius became a respected statesman of science.

In addition to his academic interests, Hörstadius continued to be interested in bird watching throughout his life. For a while, he was president of the Swedish Ornithological Society. Other hobbies included cross-country skiing and walking tours, and he was an excellent nature photographer. Hörstadius loved to travel, and was a member of the Swedish Tourist Association. Like many biologists, he developed an interest in nature conservation, and was a member of the Swedish Association for Nature Preservation. Hörstadius had considerable social talents, and Jacobson reported that "one of his most cherished accomplishments was to be President of the Uppsala Student Choir called Allmänna Sången.… The duties there and in the Students' Association of Folk Dancers suited his vivid, witty and light personality" (2000b, p. 254).

The Legacy of Sven Hörstadius. Hörstadius had very few graduate students who actually worked on topics close to his own research. Gezelius did a doctoral thesis in 1974 on the effects of sulfate and other ions on echinoderm development, but then became head of the Klubban marine station and did little further research. Jacobson worked on the development of the central nervous system in the Mexican axolotl, a topic that fascinated Hörstadius and which he realized he would not be able to work on himself. Jacobson became a zoology professor in Uppsala, and some of his students, for example, Ted Ebendal and Jan Löfberg, continued the experimental embryology tradition, but with an increasingly molecular emphasis. The transition into the twenty-first century brought an end to the era of experimental embryology in the Hörstadius tradition in Uppsala. Jacobson's student Löfberg retired from his professorship, and his student Lennart Olsson took up a professorship in Jena, Germany. Olsson's research group in Jena continues the fate-mapping and experimental embryology tradition, but with an evolutionary component largely absent from Hörstadius's work. The founder of Entwicklungsmechanik, the experimental embryologist Wilhelm Roux, was born in Jena, so in a way history has come full circle, back to Jena, and the glorious era of experimental embryology started by Runnström and his student Hörstadius when they both worked in Stockholm in the first part of the twentieth century has come to an end, having been replaced by a booming field of model systems developmental biology with medical applications, as well as by a growing interest in the old question of the role of developmental biology for a deeper understanding of evolution.

BIBLIOGRAPHY

Only the most important papers and books by Hörstadius are listed. For a complete bibliography of his scientific works, see Olsson (2000). In 1981, Hörstadius collected reprints from both his scientific works and his writings (mostly in Swedish) on nature photography, nature conservation, and popular science (mainly ornithology). He also made a complete bibliography of his works until then. Hörstadius had the papers and the bibliography bound in five volumes. Only two copies were made: one for the university library in Uppsala, and one for the zoology department in the same city, where he had worked since 1942. Remarkably, no major work about Hörstadius exists, not even a book-length biography. The only sources are two short overviews written by Carl-Olof Jacobson, one of Hörstadius's graduate students, and a few obituaries. As a consequence, this account relies very heavily on Jacobson's papers, and on conversations with him and with Göran Gezelius.

WORKS BY HÖRSTADIUS

"Physiologische Untersuchungen über die Eireifung bei *Pomatoceros triqueter* L." *Archiv für mikroskopische Anatomie und Entwicklungsmechanik* 98 (1923): 1–9. This paper and the next are based on Hörstadius's undergraduate research on factors regulating the ripening of the eggs of a polychaete worm.

"Weitere Studien über die Physiologie der Eireifung bei *Pomatoceros triqueter* L." *Arkiv für Zoologi* 16, no. 11 (1924): 1–4.

"Über die Determination des Keimes bei Echinodermen." *Acta Zoologica* (Stockholm) 9 (1928): 1–191. Hörstadius's doctoral thesis; here he continues investigations of determination and induction in echinoderm embryos, and establishes his experimental techniques of extirpation and recombination of different parts of the embryos using glass needles.

"Über die Determination im Verlaufe der Eiachse bei Seeigeln." *Pubblicazioni della Stazione zoologica di Napoli* 14 (1935): 251–479. A paper the size of a monograph in which many of Hörstadius's classical experiments of determination in sea urchin embryos are detailed and illustrated.

"Studien über heterosperme Seeigelmerogone nebst Bemerkungen über einige Keimblattchimären." *Mémoires du Muséum National d'histoire Naturelle Belgique,* series 2, 3 (1936): 801–880. Hörstadius showed in this paper that sperm nuclei from one species could determine the first steps of development in enucleated eggs from another species, and that the species-specific characters were determined by the nucleus rather than the cytoplasm.

With Sven Sellman. *Experimentelle Untersuchungen über die Determination des Knorpeligen Kopfskelettes bei Urodelen.* Nova acta Regiae societatis scientiarum upsaliensis series 4, vol. 13, no. 8. Uppsala, Sweden: Almqvist & Wiksells, 1946. The major paper emanating from Hörstadius's study of cranial neural crest development in the Mexican axolotl.

The Neural Crest: Its Properties and Derivatives in the Light of Experimental Research. London: Oxford University Press, 1950. The classic book on the neural crest, based on lectures given by Hörstadius at University College London in 1947.

With Tryggve Gustafson. "Changes in the Determination of the Sea Urchin Egg Induced by Amino Acids." *Pubblicazioni della Stazione zoologica di Napoli* 29 (1957): 407–424.

With John Runnström, J. Immers, and M. Fudge-Mastrangelo. "An Analysis of the Role of Sulfate in the Embryonic Differentiation of the Sea Urchin (*Paracentrotus lividus*)." *Revue suisse de zoologie* 71 (1964): 23–54. Two papers in which Hörstadius and collaborators investigate the impact of different substances on sea urchin development.

With Lars Josefsson and John Runnström. "Morphogenetic Agents from Unfertilized Eggs of the Sea Urchin *Paracentrotus lividus.*" *Developmental Biology* 16 (1967): 189–202.

With Lars Josefsson. "Morphogenetic Substances from Sea Urchin Eggs: Isolation of Animalizing Substances from Developing Eggs of *Paracentrotus lividus.*" *Acta embryologiae experimentalis* (1972): 7–25. Two papers with Lars Josefsson, where endogenous substances with vegetalizing and animalizing effects were isolated. Maybe Hörstadius's last important experimental papers.

Experimental Embryology of Echinoderms. Oxford: Clarendon Press, 1973. His legacy in which he summarized fifty years of work on echinoderm development.

With Brian K. Hall. *The Neural Crest: Including a Facsimile Reprint of* The Neural Crest *by Sven Hörstadius.* New York: Oxford University Press, 1988. The latest reprinting of Hörstadius's 1950 book on the neural crest, here preceded by a review on the same topic by the coauthor.

OTHER SOURCES

Jacobson, Carl-Olof. "Sven Hörstadius död." *Upsala Nya Tidning,* 8 July 1996. Obituary in an Uppsala newspaper (in Swedish).

———. "Sven Hörstadius: The Man and His Work." In *Regulatory Processes in Development: The Legacy of Sven Hörstadius (1898–1996),* edited by Lennart Olsson and Carl-Olof Jacobson. Wenner-Gren International Series, vol. 76. London: Portland Press, 2000a. A short overview of Hörstadius's major scientific contributions, and a brief biography.

———. "Sven Otto Hörstadius, 18 February 1898–16 June 1996." *Biographical Memoirs of Fellows of the Royal Society* 46 (2000b): 244–256. Covers the same ground as the biography by the same author in *Regulatory Processes,* but is somewhat longer and more detailed.

Olsson, Lennart. "In Memory: Sven Hörstadius 1898–1996." *SICB Newsletter,* Fall 1996. A short obituary.

———. "The Scientific Publications of Sven Hörstadius—A Bibliography." In *Regulatory Processes in Development: The Legacy of Sven Hörstadius (1898–1996),* edited by Lennart Olsson and Carl-Olof Jacobson. Wenner-Gren International Series, vol. 76. London: Portland Press, 2000. This bibliography covers Hörstadius's scientific works only, and has 100 entries.

Lennart Olsson

HORTON, ROBERT ELMER (*b.* Parma, Michigan, 18 May 1875; *d.* Voorheesville, New York, 22 April 1945), *hydrology, quantitative geomorphology, meteorology, hydraulic engineering.*

Horton is sometimes called the father of American hydrology. His investigations led to important new insights about the relationship between the physical features of drainage basins and water flow on and beneath the surface. He is best known for his theory that relates the infiltration of soils to the generation of floods by surface runoff. Among the first American hydrologists to stress interdisciplinary skills, he emphasized the influence of soils and vegetation on runoff, and his significant contributions to the mechanics of soil erosion contributed to the development of soil conservation techniques. His career culminated in a major landmark paper (1945) in which he analyzed the relationship between the mechanics of slope and channel erosion and runoff processes. The paper's emphasis on quantitative geomorphology for understanding hydrological processes helped turned hydrology from a largely descriptive science into one at once both more theoretical and rational.

Early Development. Horton was the son of Van Rensselaer and Rowena (Rafter) Horton. In 1897 he graduated with a BS degree from Albion College, a small Michigan liberal arts school close to his home. Horton extended by about a year the customary four years for undergraduate work in order to help his father with the family farm and, possibly, to earn money to cover college costs. While in college, Horton devoted the turbulent political summer of 1896 to supporting the Republican presidential candidate William McKinley after concluding that Democratic presidential candidate William Jennings Bryan's pro-silver platform would tighten the money supply and worsen economic conditions. He continued his support of the Republican Party for the rest of his life.

The engineering education Horton received at Albion was rather limited. His scientific courses included geology, physics, astronomy, chemistry, mathematics, and possibly some botany. The mathematics courses comprised algebra, plane and solid geometry, trigonometry, and elementary calculus. Probably these courses did not challenge Horton too much, since he had earlier studied mathematics at home. One story has it that he studied trigonometry while helping his brother haul manure. By working hard and fast, he could fill the wagon faster than his brother could haul the manure away. While waiting for his brother's return, he studied mathematics. At Albion, Horton easily passed an examination that gave him class credit for trigonometry. His record in grammar was equally impressive. After spending two weeks in a grammar class, he was given credit and excused from further attendance. Horton's writing ability largely resulted from the influence of his father, who insisted that his children learn the foundations of good writing. In 1932 Albion College awarded Horton an honorary doctorate.

Horton's uncle on his mother's side was George W. Rafter, a well-known hydrologist who directed his nephew toward the same profession. In 1896, a year before Horton graduated from college, he and Rafter coauthored a paper for the *New York State Engineer* that analyzed rainfall and runoff in the Upper Hudson River Drainage Basin. The authors used probability theory, an approach then in its infancy among hydrologists. Specifically, they applied new ideas about the importance of frequency to determine probable maximum flood stages. Later, Horton worked for his uncle as an assistant engineer for the Board of Engineers on Deep Waterways, which was authorized by Congress to study the possibility of a ship canal from the Great Lakes to the Atlantic seaboard. Horton's own ambition was undeniable. It is reflected in a notebook found in his papers called "Hydraulic Tables and Formulae" (1898). Begun when Horton was still in Michigan, the notebook contains (among some forgettable poetic verse) annotations concerning the formulas of numerous engineers for calculating everything from discharge to coefficients of roughness to mean velocity.

Rafter was a nervous man, caustic and quick to criticize, and Horton occasionally found it difficult to work with him. Yet Rafter effectively opened doors for his nephew. While working on plans for constructing the Great Lakes–Atlantic Ocean ship canal, Rafter had commissioned the hydraulic laboratory at Cornell University, his alma mater, to perform a number of weir studies to identify discharge coefficients for dams of various cross sections. In 1899, he obtained a position for Horton at the laboratory working on the project under the supervision of Professor Gardner Williams, the laboratory's director. He and Horton did not get along. They argued over methodology, and Williams blamed Horton unjustly for some inaccurate readings (the problem lay with the equipment, rather than with Horton) and tried to fire him. Horton appealed to his uncle, who wrote Williams. Subsequently, Williams appeared resigned to Horton's presence.

In the fall of 1899 Horton obtained a per diem appointment with the U.S. Geological Survey (USGS). Again, Rafter's hand is evident. The survey, at Rafter's urging, had recently taken over the gauging stations established by the Deep Waterways Board. A year later, Horton became the survey's resident hydrographer in New York State and obtained full-time civil service status within a few months. With his office established in Utica, New York, Horton oversaw the establishment of gauging stations throughout New York State and Michigan, when that state was added to his district in 1902. His staff included two assistant engineers and from three to five field assistants, including three young college professors. Winter conditions posed special problems. Horton employed "coach candles" to warm current meters during the winter time before lowering them into icy water, where, without being warmed first, they would have frozen. Horton developed his own snow sampler and was among the first to keep a continuous record of snow depth and water equivalent, taking weekly readings for two winters in Utica, from 1903 to 1905. During this time as hydrographer, Horton began to appreciate the significant contribution of groundwater to runoff and began wondering about the process by which surface water reached the aquifer.

Horton's Accomplishments. In May and June 1903, Horton headed a team of researchers at Cornell that performed a variety of experiments on weirs similar to those at USGS gauging stations. This time his dealings with

Professor Williams were evidently more cordial. The conclusions were published by the USGS in 1906 as Water-Supply and Irrigation Paper 150. They were revised the following year in Water-Supply and Irrigation Paper 200, which became a standard reference on the subject of weirs and streamflow.

Horton married Ella H. Young on 19 June 1901. Though the couple was (and remained) childless and a government salary might have satisfied their needs, inadequate government funding for the survey's field offices contributed to Horton's decision to seek new opportunities in the private sector. In 1906 he resigned from the survey and established an office as consulting hydraulic engineer in Albany, New York. He advertised himself as a "Specialist in Hydrology and Critical Reports on Adequacy and Safety of Water Supply and Structures for Power, Public Use and Irrigation." Horton also contributed articles to various engineering journals, including the *Transactions* of the American Society of Civil Engineers and *Engineering News Record.* The articles reflected his broad engineering interest, covering such topics as flood frequency, snow evaporation, and deforestation. His numerous publications following World War I also reflect his increasing interest in meteorology. Just between the years 1919 and 1923, Horton published articles in the *Monthly Weather Review* on such diverse topics as rainfall interception, evaporation observations, areal rainfall estimates, transpiration by forest trees, and rainfall interpolation. In 1918, he moved his residence to Voorheesville, New York, just outside of Albany, where he established a private hydrological (as opposed to hydraulic) laboratory on an 80-acre site complete with an old mill, a stream, and waterfalls.

For a number of years, Horton developed his ideas about *infiltration capacity,* a term he introduced in 1924 to describe the maximum rate at which a given soil surface could absorb falling rain over a specified period of time. In succeeding years, he refined his idea through a number of investigations. He published a major study in 1933 titled "The Role of Infiltration in the Hydrologic Cycle." In this article Horton argued that precipitation reaching the ground divides into either overland flow or infiltrated water. The former becomes storm runoff once it enters a stream. The latter, with net losses to transpiration and evaporation, percolates down to become groundwater and then may slowly seep downhill and eventually enter a stream. Overland flow increases when rainfall intensities or snowmelt rates exceed the infiltration rate. After initial detention in uneven surface areas, it commences to flow uniformly throughout the whole basin, gradually increasing in depth as the water flows to lower elevations. This became known as the theory of infiltration-excess overland flow. One hydrologist, J. A. A. Jones, called this article "the first scientific study of storm runoff" (1997, p. 78).

Subsequent studies showed that Horton's ideas of infiltration and overland flow worked better in semiarid than in humid regions, and that the entire process is more complicated than Horton described. Nevertheless, Horton's contribution provided fundamental insights. In particular, his work showed the critical roles soil type and vegetation had on runoff and soil erosion. One might reasonably argue that showing these impacts and providing a functional vocabulary, thereby increasing the hydrologist's explanatory power, were significant contributions in their own right. The work helped in later computer modeling and provided significant rationale for the acceptance of the unit hydrograph, a method devised by Leroy K. Sherman in 1932 to measure the average shape of storm hydrographs. Unlike earlier hydrographs, which simply plotted stream discharge against time, the unit hydrograph enabled engineers to combine daily precipitation figures with rainfall and runoff data from a 24-hour hydrograph in order to calculate runoff and streamflow for the same or (with somewhat less accuracy) similar watersheds. Sherman did this by calculating the average runoff pattern for a specified unit of rainfall, usually 1 inch or 1 centimeter. Still, without detailed chemical and physical analysis, Horton could not describe in any great detail how the process of runoff actually worked. To do so required more data, more accurate instruments, and numerous techniques. Rather, Horton emphasized what he called hydrophysical relationships; today, it would be called it quantitative geomorphology.

Horton worked on rainfall and runoff throughout his life. The gestation of his ideas from unpublished papers through increasingly sophisticated articles typified Horton's approach on many subjects. His seminal papers reflect years and even decades of thought and investigation. He was often the first to recognize the shortcomings of his own work and was very cautious in advancing his ideas. Only in 1939 did he commit to print a predictive equation for infiltration capacity. More empirical than the work of Henri Darcy and his followers, the equation obtained limited acceptance.

Horton's work on the impact of hydrophysical processes on drainage flow, flood discharge, and other factors culminated in 1945 in a paper that provided new data and theoretical insights, but summarized, with some modifications, many of his earlier ideas. It was Horton's final and most important contribution. In the paper, Horton quantitatively suggested four new laws or principles: the law of steam lengths, the law of stream numbers, limits on infiltration capacity, and the relationship between runoff and detention of water. Horton reversed the European stream order and designated the "fingertip" streams as order one and assigned the main stem stream the highest numerical order. He then used this classification system to compare and contrast the physical features of streams of different orders. With some modification, this approach was commonly used in American hydrology into the mid-1980s. Horton also expanded upon his idea of drainage density, which he had first suggested over a decade before. The term could be defined mathematically:

$$\text{Drainage density, } D_d = \frac{\Sigma L}{A}$$

where ΣL is the total length of streams and A is the drainage basin area, both in units of the same system. Horton's law of stream lengths suggested that "The average lengths of streams of each of the different orders in a drainage basin tend closely to approximate a direct geometric series in which the first term is the average length of streams of the 1st order" (1945, p. 291). In other words, there is a regular relationship between stream lengths of one order and those of other orders of a given stream. Horton demonstrated a constant relationship between the number of streams of different orders within a basin.

Horton's article stimulated a reevaluation of historical and qualitative geomorphology that could be traced to Grove Karl Gilbert and William Morris Davis. Geomorphic typologies that depended on descriptions such as youth, maturity, and old age came under fire as inexact and unscientific. Horton's classification system has been superseded by ecological concepts of energy expenditure and efficiency to understand stream basin organization. Still, Horton deserves credit for helping to put hydrology on a more scientific footing.

Horton's Personality and Professional Involvement. There is little in Horton's papers that reveal much about family or social life. He joined the Cosmos Club in Washington, D.C., in 1934 and remained a member until his death, but even here the record is ambiguous; the Cosmos Club had always attracted a large number of geographers, geologists, and hydrologists (it was founded by John Wesley Powell in 1878), and one can imagine Horton joining colleagues from various federal agencies for lunchtime discussions of professional issues.

In any such discussions, Horton would have adopted a practical and rather hardheaded approach. He had no time for unscientific ruminations. He observed in 1931 that, even though hydrologists did not know the exact maximum rainfall that might fall on Washington, D.C., meteorological research persuasively demonstrated that it could never reach 1,000 inches a month, regardless of what frequency analysis might show. As he put it, "Rock Creek [a small creek in Washington] cannot produce a Mississippi River flood—any more than a barnyard fowl can lay an ostrich egg, and for very much the same reason, namely, it would transcend nature's capabilities under the circumstances" (p. 201). In short, theoretical arguments that fly in the face of empirical evidence must be rejected.

Nor did Horton have much tolerance for moral ambiguities, especially as it applied to his own work. According to Howard L. Cook, one of Horton's protégés, in 1907 Horton complained that John C. Hoyt and Nathan C. Grover, two well-known Geological Survey employees, appropriated without attribution some of the tables Horton had published in Geological Survey Paper 200 in their book *River Discharge.* Arthur Powell Davis, a senior engineer in the Survey, came to the defense of Hoyt and Grover, insisting that these sorts of engineering tables were common property and their use in engineering texts did not constitute plagiarism. The answer did nothing to assuage Horton's outrage. Horton also considered himself a guardian of hydrologic terminology, especially of terms he coined. In 1942, when the Hydrology Committee of the American Society of Agricultural Engineers initiated a project to standardize hydrologic terms, Horton replied with a withering criticism of those who had misused or wrongly defined his term *infiltration capacity.*

Horton contributed to many professional associations. In the late 1920s, he campaigned with other prominent hydrologists for the creation of a hydrology section within the American Geophysical Union (AGU), an effort that needed to overcome some anxiety within the scientific community over whether hydrology was true science or not. In May 1930, the AGU amended its bylaws to create the new section. In the organizational meeting in November, section members elected Horton the vice chairman and Oscar Meinzer, chief of the USGS Division of Ground Water, the chair. In subsequent years, Horton was a major contributor to the AGU *Transactions* on hydrologic issues. He also served as president of the American Meteorological Society in 1939, consultant to the National Resources Commission (1934–1937), and consultant to the Soil Conservation Service (1939–1941). At various times, he advised state and local agencies in New York State.

Horton died of a heart attack on 22 April 1945. He left the bulk of his estate and most of his papers to the AGU. In honor of Horton's contributions, the AGU established the Robert E. Horton Medal, which recognizes outstanding contributions to the geophysical aspects of hydrology. The American Meteorological Society also honored him with the establishment of the Horton Lectureship.

BIBLIOGRAPHY

WORKS BY HORTON

Papers. Record Group 189, 94 Boxes. National Archives and Records Administration, College Park, MD. Includes correspondence, and drafts of reports, articles, and studies.

Weir Experiments, Coefficients and Formulas. U.S. Geological Survey Water-Supply and Irrigation Paper 150. Issued as U.S. Congress. House. 59th Cong., 1st sess. Washington, DC: U.S. Government Printing Office, 1906. H. Doc. 231. Revised and republished as *Weir Experiments, Coefficients and Formulas.* U.S. Geological Survey Water-Supply and Irrigation Paper 200. U.S. Congress. House. 59th Cong., 2nd sess. Washington, DC: U.S. Government Printing Office, 1907. H. Doc. 794.

"The Field, Scope, and Status of the Science of Hydrology." *Transactions of the American Geophysical Union* 12 (1931): 189–202.

"The Role of Infiltration in the Hydrologic Cycle." *Transactions of the American Geophysical Union* 14 (1933): 446–460.

"Erosional Development of Streams and Their Drainage Basins: Hydrophysical Approach to Quantitative Morphology." *Bulletin of the Geological Society of America* 56 (1945): 275–370.

OTHER SOURCES

Bevan, Keith. "Robert E. Horton's Perceptual Model of Infiltration Processes." *Hydrological Processes* 18 (2004): 3447–3460.

Bras, Rafael L. "A Brief History of Hydrology." *Bulletin of the American Meteorological Society* 80 (1999): 1151–1164. Robert E. Horton Lecture.

Cook, Howard L., Papers. Folder 682. Research Collections. Office of History, Headquarters, U.S. Army Corps of Engineers, Alexandria, VA. Contains Cook's handwritten notes pertaining to Horton's childhood and early career.

Hall, Francis R. "Contributions of Robert E. Horton." In *History of Geophysics,* vol. 3, *The History of Hydrology,* edited by Edward R. Landa and Simon Ince. Washington, DC: American Geophysical Union, 1987.

Jones, J. A. A. *Global Hydrology: Processes, Resources and Environmental Management.* Harlow, U.K.: Longman, 1997.

National Research Council, Water Science and Technology Board. *Opportunities in the Hydrologic Sciences.* Washington, DC: National Academy Press, 1991.

Paynter, Henry M. "Robert E. Horton (1875–1945)." American Geophysical Union. Available from http://www.agu.org/inside/awards/horton2.html.

Martin Reuss

HOSPERS, JAN

(*b.* Veendam, Netherlands, 19 June 1925; *d.* Göteborg, Sweden, 17 December 2006), *geocentric axial dipole, geophysics, geomagnetic reversal timescale, geomagnetism, paleomagnetism.*

Hospers made several major contributions to paleomagnetism. He presented significant arguments in support of the sequential reversals in polarity of Earth's magnetic field (field reversals) and argued against the view that reversely magnetized rocks could be explained in terms of self-reversals. He also provided the first extensive empirical support for the geocentric axial dipole (GAD) hypothesis, the hypothesis that the axis of the Earth's magnetic field, a dipole, when averaged over several thousands of years coincides with Earth's axis of rotation. The empirical support he marshaled in favor of GAD, which extended back through the Miocene, provided a firm base on which Kenneth M. Creer, Edward Irving, and Stanley Keith Runcorn at Cambridge, and other paleomagnetists could present arguments favoring mobilism. Hospers also constructed a rudimentary polarity (reversal) timescale, and estimated the time taken for the geomagnetic field to reverse. His work was crucial for the later development of the radiometric polarity (reversal) timescale. He accomplished all of this in just three years (1950–1953) while working on his PhD at Cambridge University.

The Pre-Cambridge Years. Hospers' father, Johannes Hospers, was a teacher; his mother, Marchiena Heilina Slim, a nurse. Hospers had one sister, Hanni Jansen Hospers, who was four years older than he. Hospers received his primary and secondary education at Veendam. He attended the University of Groningen (1945–1948), where he took courses in geology and physics, a somewhat unusual combination at the time. Hospers was most influenced by Philip Henry Kuenen, then head of the Department of Geology at Groningen. Kuenen instilled him with a lifelong interest in sedimentology. Hospers also spent three months in 1946 studying with the geologist Eugene Wegmann at the University of Neuchâtel, Switzerland. After receiving his BSc in geology from Groningen, he began studying at the University of Utrecht, where he worked with four prominent figures: Felix Andries Vening Meinesz (geophysics), Martin G. Rutten (general geology), Reinout Willem van Bemmelen (economic geology), and Wijnand Otto Jan Nieuwenkamp (mineralogy and petrology).

While at Utrecht he was invited on an expedition to Iceland in summer 1950, and was admitted to Cambridge University to work on a PhD in geophysics. Rutten, planning to study Iceland's volcanics and tectonics during summer 1950, invited van Bemmelen to accompany him, and they then invited Hospers to go with them. Icelandic lava flows were notoriously difficult to correlate, and van Bemmelen, who knew a little bit about remanent magnetism, suggested that Hospers should measure the intensity of their remanent magnetization and use it for correlation. Meanwhile, Hospers, an indigent student, needed funding to pursue a PhD. He applied for and was awarded a Royal Dutch/Shell scholarship, which allowed him to study geophysics at Cambridge in the Department of Geodesy and Geophysics.

The Cambridge Years: Hospers's Major Contributions to Paleomagnetism. Receiving the scholarship, Hospers entered Cambridge in fall 1949, still planning to use magnetization intensity as a stratigraphic tool to correlate Icelandic lava flows during summer 1950. He did not plan to study reversal of the geomagnetic field or use paleomagnetistism to test continental drift or polar wandering.

Ben C. Browne, then head of the Department of Geodesy and Geophysics at Cambridge, became and remained Hospers's official dissertation supervisor, even though he never worked in paleomagnetism. Of crucial importance was that, before leaving for Iceland, Hospers became friends with Runcorn. Runcorn was interested in paleomagnetism and had just arrived in January 1950 as assistant director of research in the department; he influenced Hospers most at Cambridge. He encouraged Hospers to return to Iceland in 1951, introduced him to Sir Ronald Aylmer Fisher, and helped with other contacts. In return, Hospers convinced Runcorn of the reality of geomagnetic reversals.

Hospers returned from his first collecting trip to Iceland with twenty-two samples. He found that there were significant groupings and approximately half were reversely magnetized. But there was considerable scattering of directions and he realized that to analyze them he needed a statistical procedure. Runcorn asked Fisher to help. Fisher developed the statistical analysis and even did the calculations for Hospers's first paper (1951). Fisher's statistical method was not published until 1953, but was made available to Cambridge workers in 1950. It is difficult to overestimate the importance of his method for the development of paleomagnetism.

Hospers submitted his first paper in June of 1951. Samples from Quaternary flows were normally magnetized; those from younger Tertiary lava flows were reversely magnetized, and those from older Tertiary lava flows were normally magnetized. He argued for reversals of Earth's magnetic field, proposing the geomagnetic field had been reversed during the later Tertiary. He found no macroscopic and microscopic differences between normal and reversed samples. He eliminated local phenomena such as pressure, reheating, recrystallization, and lightning, because he thought it inconceivable that such processes should affect only the reversed uppermost Tertiary lava flows and not the overlying normal Quaternary flows. He ruled out tectonics; if the reversely magnetized younger Tertiary lava flows had flipped over, the older Tertiary ones would have done so too, but they were normally not reversely magnetized; tectonic inversion was no explanation. Given the estimate that the average time between successive Icelandic lava flows was a thousand years, Hospers proposed that it took five thousand years for a reversal to occur and that the geomagnetic field had been reversed for at least twenty-five thousand years; there were four lava flows between the oldest reversed Tertiary lava flow and youngest normally magnetized Tertiary lava flow, and twenty-six lava flows that had formed while the field was reversed during the later Tertiary. He also found that regardless of polarity the differences between the mean direction of magnetization of his samples and the theoretical dipole field (GAD) were not significant and were closer to the GAD than the present field.

Runcorn encouraged Hospers to return to Iceland in summer 1951 and also to obtain samples from the Eocene Antrim basalts of Northern Ireland. Hospers returned from Iceland with six hundred samples. Using Fisher's statistics, Hospers calculated the mean direction of the magnetization of volcanic units, including several others studied by A. Roche, Stanislaw A. Vincenz, and G. M. Bruckshaw and E. I. Robertson, and compared them with the direction of the present field and that of GAD. Seven out of eight units agreed better with the GAD than with the present field. The eight units, listed from youngest to oldest were Early Quaternary lava flows from western Iceland (Hospers); Plio-Pleistocene, and Mio-Pliocene lava flows from the Plateau Central, France (Roche); Miocene lava flows from northern and southwestern Iceland (Hospers); tholeiite dikes of northern England of Oligocene or Miocene age (Bruckshaw and Robertson); Oligocene dikes, necks, and sills from Plateau Central, France (Roche); Eocene lavas from Northern Ireland (Hospers and H. A. K. Charlesworth); and Eocene lava flows from Scotland (Vincenz). The result that did not fall, within error, along the GAD field was the one from the older Eocene rocks of Northern Ireland. Hospers concluded that the "measurements show that taken over periods of several thousands of years the magnetic pole centres on the geographic pole. This has been so since Miocene times (approximately 20×10^6 years ago)" (1954a, p. 119).

Hospers identified four normal and four reversed periods from the present through the Miocene, and proposed a polarity timescale. He estimated that normal and reversed periods lasted from 250 to 500 thousand years, and that it took 5 to 10 thousand years for a the geomagnetic field to undergo a reversal.

In arguing for field reversals, Hospers had to contend with the possibility that some rocks might become magnetized in a direction opposite to that of the ambient field; they may be self-reversed. The French physicist Louis-Eugène-Félix Néel had been asked in 1949 by John Graham, a paleomagnetist from the United States, if rocks could undergo such a self-reversal; Graham was unhappy about the idea of field reversals. Néel proposed four self-reversing mechanisms, and within a year the Japanese paleomagnetists Takesi Nagata and Seiya Uyeda found a self-reversing rock. Hospers first noted that his normal and reversed samples were each associated with definite stratigraphic levels, precisely what should be expected to give field reversals. He then showed that none of Néel's proposed mechanisms applied to his Icelandic rocks. Obtaining a sample of Nagata and Uyeda's self-reversing rock, he heated it up in the laboratory, and it did become magnetized antiparallel to the ambient field. He then did the same with his Icelandic rocks; none acquired a reversed magnetization; all became magnetized parallel to the ambient field.

The Post-Cambridge Years. Hospers obtained his PhD from Cambridge in 1953, and took a job with Royal Dutch Shell, where he remained until 1963, working in Turkey (1953–1954); Venezuela (1955–1959); Nigeria (1958–1962); and Rijswijk, Netherlands (1962–1963). He returned to academe in 1962, taking a part-time position as an associate professor in geophysics at the University of Utrecht. He then took a position as a full professor for two years in the Department of Physics, University of Alberta, Edmonton, Canada, then moved to the University of Amsterdam in 1965, where he remained as a full professor of solid-earth geophysics until 1975. He then became a full professor of applied geophysics, the first in Norway, at the Norwegian Institute of Technology, University of Trondheim. Much of his work there pertained to the North Sea, studying its basement thickness to help locate oil and gas. Interestingly, Hospers here returned to sedimentary studies, his first love.

Hospers was married to Kerstin Barbro Helga Tunbäck in 1954. They had three sons, Michiel, Martin, and Peter. Hospers was eighty-one when he died on 17 December 2006 after suffering two strokes within fourteen days. He was survived by his wife, sister, and Martin and Peter.

BIBLIOGRAPHY

WORKS BY HOSPERS

"Remanent Magnetism of Rocks and the History of the Geomagnetic Field." *Nature 168* (1951): 1111–1112.

"Reversals of the Main Geomagnetic Field, Part I." *Proceedings of the Royal Netherlands Academy of Sciences, Amsterdam,* ser. B, 56 (1953a): 467–476.

"Reversals of the Main Geomagnetic Field, Part II." *Proceedings of the Royal Netherlands Academy of Sciences, Amsterdam,* ser. B, 56 (1953b): 477–491.

"Reversals of the Main Geomagnetic Field, Part III." *Proceedings of the Royal Netherlands Academy of Sciences, Amsterdam,* ser. B, 57 (1954a): 112–121.

"De Naturlijke Magnetiztie van Ijslandse Gesteenten." *Geologie en Munbouw* 16 (1954b): 48–51.

"Rock Magnetism and Polar Wandering." *Nature* 173 (1954c): 1183–1184.

"Magnetic Correlation in Volcanic Districts." *Geological Magazine* 91 (1954d): 352–360.

"Rock Magnetism and Polar Wandering." *Journal of Geology* 63 (1955): 59–74.

With H. A. K. Charlesworth. "The Natural Permanent Magnetization of the Lower Basalts of Northern Ireland." *Monthly Notices Royal Astronomical Society Geophysical Supplement* 7 (1954): 32–43.

OTHER SOURCES

Frankel, Henry. "Jan Hospers and the Rise of Paleomagnetism." *Eos* 68, no. 24 (1987): 577, 579–581.

Irving, E. "The Paleomagnetic Confirmation of Continental Drift." *Eos* 69, no. 44 (1988): 994–1014.

Langeland, Helge. "Jan Hospers (1925–2006)—Minneord." Department of Petroleum Engineering and Applied Geophysics, Norwegian University of Science and Technology, 2007. Available from http://www.ipt.ntnu.no/hospers.pdf.

Henry Frankel

HOU TE-PANG (DEBANG HOU) (*b.* Fuzhou, Fujian Province, China, 9 August 1890; *d.* Beijing, China, 26 August 1974), *chemistry, applied chemistry, chemical engineering.*

An outstanding Chinese chemist and chemical engineer of the modern period, Hou directed the first successful use in Asia of the Solvay process. He authored *Manufacture of Soda, with Special Reference to the Ammonia Process* (1933), an influential work in which he summarized, from a theoretical perspective, his experience in successfully manufacturing soda. He also overcame the difficulties of wartime to direct the beginnings of a new, dual soda-manufacturing process, one that bears his name: Hou's process. In 1958 he became vice minister of the Ministry of Chemical Industry of the People's Republic of China.

Childhood and Education. Hou Te-pang (also called "Zhiben" and "Debang Hou") was born on 9 August 1890, on the twenty-fourth day of the sixth month in the reign of Emperor Guangxu, and his birth was registered in Fuzhou. His father died young, and Hou was raised by his paternal grandfather, a private tutor. He performed farm chores while studying. At the age of thirteen he entered Yinghua Academy, a former missionary school in Fuzhou. After three years he entered a middle school, where his grades placed him at the head of his class. As a result he was recommended for study at the Fujian-Anhui Railroad College in Shanghai. After graduating in 1908, he was sent to the Tianjin-Puzhou (Pukou) Railroad Company to work as an engineer. To further his education, he successfully passed a test for the Boxer indemnity scholarship and entered Tsinghua (Qinghua) School in Beijing to prepare himself to study abroad. During his period of study there, the school suspended classes because of the outbreak of the Revolution of 1911.

In 1912 Hou graduated with honors from Tsinghua School and, supported by the boxer scholarship, he studied chemical engineering at the Massachusetts Institute of Technology in Cambridge, Massachusetts, from which he received a bachelor's degree in 1917. He then went to Pratt Institute in New York City to study tanning. In 1918 he entered Columbia University, also in New York City, from which he received a master's degree in 1919 and a PhD in chemical engineering in 1921, with a thesis on iron tannage.

In the Soda Industry. After receiving his PhD, Hou received an invitation from Fan Xudong, general manager of Yong Li Soda Plant in Tianjin, to be technical manager of the plant. Hou had had contact with Yong Li Soda Plant before. He deeply respected Fan Xudong's ambition to save China through industrialization, and Fan Xudong admired Hou's knowledge.

After World War I, Fan Xudong and other entrepreneurs were goaded into action by the inflationary effect of the war on markets. After trying to establish themselves as salt manufacturers, they realized the importance of soda manufacturing in a modern industrial system and decided to produce it. To this end they sought to use the rich lime and salt deposits near Tanggu (Tianjin) and to take advantage of the tax exemption for the industrial use of salt that they had acquired from the warlord government of the time. Planning to build a soda plant in three years, they ultimately took nearly ten. Several times they were on the brink of bankruptcy, the primary cause being the cost of overcoming technical difficulties.

At the time, the primary technique for manufacturing soda was the Solvay technique of applying the ammonia process. Around 1900 the Solvay patent rights expired, and many independent factories cropped up. When the Yong Li Soda Plant was set up in 1917, the technology was controlled primarily by the Solvay group and a few independent companies. Fan Xudong and his partners first contacted a Belgian company that had stopped production because of World War I and whose plant was for sale, but because they could not accept the Belgians' stringent conditions, negotiations fell through. They then turned to the United States, where, after much trouble, they were able to commission a retired soda-plant manager to design a factory. The numerous difficulties encountered indicate a flawed design, a major factor in which seems to have been a lack of consideration given to differences between China and the United States regarding the availability of resources.

In 1921, when Hou arrived at the Yong Li Soda Plant, the factory was in the process of installing equipment. After installation came the testing stage, starting in 1922, during which all sorts of technical problems cropped up, one after another, many of which could not have been anticipated. The factory could not yet produce soda, mainly because impure raw materials were used—sea brine instead of rock salt and ammonium sulfate instead of ammonia. Hou, using the theoretical training he had acquired abroad, modified and improved every link in the technology, devised new methods to purify the raw materials, redesigned some key pieces of equipment, and learned from many failures. Regular production began slowly in 1924; in June 1926, he finally achieved lasting success in continuously producing high-grade sodium carbonate. At the Sesquicentennial International Exhibition in Philadelphia in the same year, soda from the company received a gold medal. In 1927 production was up to fourteen thousand tons, and in 1937 to fifty thousand tons. This success in producing soda became, for technical experts who studied in the West, a model for solving the problems that arise in introducing western technology into the uncertainties of the Chinese market. It also planted within Chinese industrial circles confidence in applying science in China's industry.

Writer of International Handbooks. Throughout his career, Hou was an assiduous writer. He wrote in both Chinese and English, publishing ten technical treatises and over seventy papers. His most influential work was *Manufacture of Soda* (1933), written in English and published in New York. For this work the author received a grant from the China Foundation for the Promotion of Education and Culture to travel to the United States to research soda manufacturing. The book attracted much attention in both the chemical industry and academic circles. *Manufacture of Soda* draws on the author's records of, and knowledge gained from, his more than ten years experience in the operation of a soda plant. Though Hou considered the manufacture of soda from a practical point of view, he provided sufficient theoretical exposition to ensure that his points were consistent with the scientific reasoning of the time. He hoped that the fields of physics and chemistry would publish data on gases and liquids so that other chemical industries might benefit from it.

In *Manufacture of Soda,* Hou put forth the complete process of the Solvay method. Recognized throughout the world, the book was considered the primary work on the ammonia process for making sodium carbonate and the best work on the Solvay method. In 1942 a revised edition was published in New York, and in 1948 the State

Chemical Literature Press in the Soviet Union published a Russian translation of the revised edition. In 1942 Hou contributed the chapter titled "Soda and Chlorine Products" to the sixth edition of *Rogers' Industrial Chemistry.*

Production of Nitrogen Fertilizers. In 1934 Yong Li Co. received a large loan from the Republican government in Nanjing in order to become an integrated chemical corporation for the production of ammonia, nitric acid, sulfuric acid, and ammonium sulfate fertilizer. Fan Xudong changed the name of his corporation to the Yong Li Chemical Industry Corp. to reflect its broader scope. A new site was purchased for the erection of the Yong Li Ammonia Plant. In the meantime, Hou went abroad to select appropriate technology, organize the design, select and purchase equipment, organize technical training, and hire foreign experts. He signed a contract with the American Cyanamid Company, which would supervise construction. Within China he organized, built, installed, and tested all the systems. The construction project was done well and completed quickly. In January 1937 Yong Li Ammonia Plant at Xiejiadian in Nanjing had its first successful trial run and began regular production. The Xiejiadian complex was the most modern and complete chemical plant in China before World War II.

The Hou Soda Process. At this point, thanks to Hou, China had acquired the two basic components of the chemical industry, acids and bases. Not long after the Yong Li Ammonia Plant began production, the Japanese Imperial Army captured Nanjing in 1937. Hou evacuated at the last moment, carrying with him only designs and taking with him plant personnel. After passing through many places, they ended up at Wutongqiao, Leshan County, Sichuan Province, where they hoped to reconstruct a base of chemical operations using resources of the area. Even under the trying conditions of war, Hou and his colleagues again greatly improved soda-manufacturing technology.

In Wutongqiao, salt was both cheap and of acceptable quality. Because the Solvay technique for applying the ammonia process has a low salt-utilization rate and requires pure sodium chloride, which could be produced from crude local salt only at enormous cost, this technique is not suited to the Wutongqiao area. At that time Hou became aware of the German patent for the Zahn process, which has a high salt-utilization rate. He went to Germany to negotiate the lease of this patent. He did not succeed, however, because the Germans, due to their close ties to Japan, refused to transfer patents to China. Hou then decided to develop independently a new soda-manufacturing technique with a higher rate of utilization of the raw materials.

Toward the end of 1938, Hou formulated a plan in New York and had teams in Hong Kong and Shanghai carry out experiments. In the fall of 1939 he had enough knowledge of all the technical requirements of the Zahn process. By 1941 he had developed a manufacturing process that, though not perfect, was superior to the Zahn process and that came to be called the Hou soda process. By the end of 1943, after many semi-industrial chemical experiments, he had developed a process entirely different from the Zahn process that could be put into continuous production.

Hou's process has the advantages of both the Solvay and Zahn processes. It uses the carbon dioxide produced by the ammonia plant and also employs the chlorine salt produced by the soda plant. It increases the rate of utilization of the raw materials and avoids the waste liquids produced in the Solvay process. Moreover, it greatly reduces the investment in equipment and costs. Hou's process combines the Solvay soda-manufacturing and the Haber ammonia-production processes and thus is an important development in soda-manufacturing technology. Its final products are soda and ammonium chloride, which can be used as fertilizer. Hou's work built up morale in China's industrial circles during the second Sino-Japanese War, from 1937 to 1945.

Large-scale industrial use of the Hou soda process was achieved only after the establishment of the People's Republic in 1949. In 1964, when it was appraised by China's National Science Council, Hou himself suggested that his process be formally named the dual process rather than Hou's process. At the end of the twentieth century, Hou's process was one of the primary processes used to manufacture sodium carbonate in China, which produces more sodium carbonate than any other country.

On the international stage, Hou helped Brazil build a soda plant, and he helped an Indian soda plant improve its technology and equipment. After Japan's surrender in 1945, he played a major role in negotiations with Japan for the return of equipment removed from China during the war.

Honors and Political Career. For his outstanding contributions, Hou received many honors both at home and abroad. In 1930 he was awarded first-class honors with a university medal from Columbia University. In 1933 he received an honorary gold medal from the chair of the China Association of Engineers. In 1935 he was among the first members of the newly established National Research Council, set up by the Nanking government. In 1943 he was named an honorary member of the British Royal Society of Chemistry in London.

Prior to 1949, Hou held the positions of chief engineer, plant manager, and general manager at Yong Li Co., serving in both a technical and administrative capacity. In 1948 he was elected a member of the Academia Sinica (Chinese Academy) in Taipei. After the establishment of the People's Republic in 1949, Hou was elected as a member of the Academic Division of the Chinese Academy of Sciences in Beijing in 1955. He was appointed as vice minister of the Ministry of Chemical Industry in 1958 and served society in many other capacities. In whatever capacity he served, no matter how high, Hou went down to the shop floor to give lectures, present reports, have personal conversations, gain direct experience, and introduce new technology and knowledge. After 1972, although he suffered from several illnesses and had difficulty getting around, he continued to inspect factories frequently, helped solve technical problems, and invited technical personnel to his house to discuss how to improve and develop Hou's process. In August 1974 Hou died of a cerebral hemorrhage in Beijing.

BIBLIOGRAPHY

WORKS BY HOU

Iron Tannage. New York, 1921.

Manufacture of Soda, with Special Reference to the Ammonia Process: A Practical Treatise. New York: Chemical Catalog, 1933.

"Jianye zhi xingqi" (The rise of the soda industry). *Haiwang* 11, no. 2 (1938): 7.

"Soda and Chlorine Products." In *Rogers' Industrial Chemistry: A Manual for the Student and Manufacturer,* 6th ed., edited by Allen Rogers. New York: D. Van Nostrand, 1942.

Cong huaxuejia guandian tan yuanzi neng. Beijing: Huaxue Gongye Chubanshe, 1957.

Zhijian gongxue (The science of manufacturing soda). Beijing: Huaxue Gongye Chubanshe, 1959–1960.

With Wei Yunchang. *Zhijian gongye gongzuozhe shouce* (Manual for workers in the soda-manufacturing industry). Beijing: Zhongguo Gongye Chubanshe, 1962.

With Hu Xian'geng. *Si suan san jian* (Four acids and three bases). Beijing: Kexue Puji Chubanshe, 1966.

With Hu Xian'geng. *Suan he jian* (Acids and bases). Beijing: Kexue Chubanshe, 1980.

Hou Debang xuanji (Selected papers of Hou Debang). Edited by Li Zhichuan and Chen Xinwen. Beijing: Yejin Gongye Chubanshe, 1990.

OTHER SOURCES

Boorman, Howard L., ed. *Biographical Dictionary of Republican China.* Vol. 2. New York: Columbia University Press, 1968.

Li, Zhichuan, and Chen Xinwen. *Hou Debang.* Tianjin, China: Nankai Daxue Chubanshe, 1986.

Reardon-Anderson, James. *The Study of Change: Chemistry in China, 1840–1949.* New York; Cambridge, U.K.: Cambridge University Press, 1991.

Shijie Guo

HOUDRY, EUGÈNE JULES (*b.* Domont, France, 18 April, 1892; *d.* Upper Darby, Pennsylvania, 18 July 1962), *chemical engineering, catalytic cracking of petroleum, catalysis.*

In the 1930s, Houdry became a successful inventor in the field of oil refining, an industry dominated by large firms with their own research laboratories. Houdry pioneered in the use of catalysts to "crack" the large hydrocarbon molecules in petroleum into smaller ones that could be used in gasoline. Not only did Houdry's process increase the quantity of gasoline, but in addition its quality was superior to all existing gasolines. By 1942, fourteen Houdry units were operating to provide 100-octane aviation fuel for the Allied war effort in World War II. In many of its aspects, Houdry's approach to research resembled that of Thomas Edison. His major area of concentration, catalysts—he became known as Mr. Catalysis—was a field that lacked useful scientific theory to guide research. Therefore, his approach was largely empirical, involving large numbers of experiments. Like Edison, Houdry combined intense labor, often going for days without sleep, with his experience and intuition to develop catalysts and processes that employed them. He surrounded himself with outstanding assistants whom he exhorted to maintain their focus on the goal and to overcome apparent roadblocks. As one longtime associate put it, "Houdry had one remarkable characteristic, and it was not inventiveness, it was … the courage to make a total commitment to his convictions" (Mills, 1986, p. 75). In a forty-year research career, he obtained more than one hundred patents, including one for an automobile catalytic converter shortly before his death.

Childhood and Education. Houdry was born in the Paris suburb of Domont, France, on 18 April 1892, the only son of Jules Houdry, owner of a successful structural steel business, and Émilie Thias Jule Lemaire. To prepare himself to join his father's firm, he studied mechanical engineering at the École des arts et métiers (School of arts and engineering) at Châlons-sur-Marne. He was a halfback and captain of the soccer team that won the French national championship in 1910. A year later he graduated first in his class and went to work as an engineer in his father's plant. With the outbreak of World War I three years later, Houdry joined the French army as a lieutenant in the field artillery but was later transferred into the new secret tank corps. He took part in the first battle that used tanks as an assault weapon. At the battle of Juvincourt in 1917, he was wounded and awarded the Croix de Guerre for having organized the repair of disabled vehicles under heavy fire.

After rejoining the family business after the war, Houdry became increasingly interested in automobiles and served on the board of several automotive companies. His association with one parts manufacturer brought him into contact with engineers who were attempting to improve the performance of automobile engines. One limiting factor was engine knock, a phenomenon he had personally experienced while driving his Bugatti. In 1922 he attended the Indianapolis 500 and toured the Ford assembly plant in Detroit. Upon his return to France, he married Geneviève Marie Quilleret with whom he would have two children.

Petroleum from Coal. In 1922 Houdry combined his passion for automobiles and his French patriotism by becoming involved in developing processes for making gasoline from coal, an abundant resource in petroleum poor France. Houdry learned that in Nice, Eugene A. Prudhomme was generating carbon monoxide and hydrogen from lignite and then using a series of catalyzed and uncatalyzed reactions to create gasoline. After an initial visit to Prudhomme's laboratory, Houdry invested in the enterprise and organized a group of experts to investigate the process. In spite of its many shortcomings, especially a low yield of gasoline and a general lack of understanding of the chemical reactions that were occurring, Houdry decided to form a company to continue the development of the process. He began to study the chemistry of hydrocarbons and set up a laboratory at Beauchamp, near Paris. Within a few months Houdry, assisted by several engineers, built a larger unit that, however, refused to yield any gasoline. Word soon came of similar results obtained by an Italian group. At this point Houdry made a fundamental change to the process: He distilled the lignite to create tars that were upgraded to gasoline using the same hydrotreating steps employed in the Prudhomme process. After months of intense effort, gasoline was obtained. Particularly encouraging was its quality, because at this point in automotive history engine knock was becoming a major problem that limited engine performance.

In 1924 Houdry incorporated what would become the Houdry Process Company of France (Société Anonyme Française pour la Fabrication d'Essences et Pétroles). Over the next three years he continued to improve his process, although much of his time was spent as a promoter rather than as an experimenter. In 1927 it was officially recognized (i.e., sanctioned) by the French government, which directed that a larger pilot plant be constructed (though no subsidies were provided). This plant, which processed sixty tons of lignite per day, started up in June 1929; the gasoline output, however, was 30 percent lower than expected. Although the plant worked, and produced high quality gasoline, the cost was high and the French government decided not to continue the expensive development effort. After a year of operation the plant shut down. By this time, though, Houdry's efforts had shifted to a new area—catalytic cracking of heavy petroleum fractions.

Catalytic Cracking. As the number of automobiles increased rapidly in the 1920s, there was widespread concern about the future supply of gasoline. One response to this expected crisis was the development of processes to make gasoline from coal, especially in countries such as Great Britain, France, and Germany that did not have major domestic sources of petroleum. Another approach was to get more gasoline out of a barrel of crude oil. Crude oil is a mixture of hydrocarbon molecules containing from five to forty carbon atoms. Gasoline consists of relatively volatile or "light" hydrocarbons containing from five to twelve carbon atoms. The gasoline fraction accounts for only about 20 percent of crude oil. More gasoline could be produced if some way could be found to break up, or crack, the larger hydrocarbon molecules. Particularly amenable to cracking were the thirteen to twenty-three carbon atom-range molecules, constituting gas oil that accounted for 40 percent of crude oil. In 1913 William Burton, at Standard Oil of Indiana, developed a process that cracked nearly half of gas oil into gasoline using high temperature and high pressure. During the 1920s so-called thermal cracking had spread throughout the U.S. refining industry.

While he was working on lignite tars, Houdry realized that his process might also work on heavy petroleum fractions. His research focused on finding an efficient catalyst, which required careful experiment design to give meaningful comparisons among catalytic materials. At the time the conventional catalyst was a metal supported by porous materials such as kaolin, fuller's earth, and clays. He had learned earlier, when working with lignite tars, that a major problem with catalytic cracking was that a carbon or coke layer quickly coated the catalyst surface, thereby greatly reducing its effectiveness. What Houdry was looking for was an effective catalyst that would not be destroyed by burning off the coke, a process he called regeneration. After many unsatisfactory experiments with metals, he decided to try the support material without the metal. The results were encouraging and led to a systematic canvassing of claylike materials. In April 1927 he tried an activated clay, used as an adsorbent to purify lubricating oils, which worked well. To test this gasoline cracked from a heavy crude, he tried it out in his Bugatti racer. When his speedometer hit 90 miles (145 km) per hour with the engine still running smoothly, he realized that he had succeeded in turning low-grade crude oil into high-quality gasoline. Just how good the gasoline was could not be determined for a few more years, until the modern octane-rating system was developed.

Houdry

Houdry realized that commercial development would require large sums of money and specialized engineering expertise, so he sought to interest oil companies in his process. He publicized his findings and as early as November 1928 began to demonstrate it for companies such as the Anglo-Iranian Oil Company (now British Petroleum), Royal Dutch Shell, and Standard Oil of New Jersey. However, these companies did not show much interest in the process because many new and difficult engineering problems would have to be solved to make a commercial-scale facility, and the companies were more interested in a competing technology, hydrogenation, which had been developed by the giant German chemical company I. G. Farben.

In 1930 Houdry made contact with the Paris office of Vacuum Oil Company and arranged for the company's European representative, Harold F. Sheets, to visit his laboratory. After seeing Houdry's operation and examining his portfolio of more than fifty patents, Sheets proposed that Vacuum construct a pilot plant if Houdry would bring his apparatus to the United States and operate it continuously for fifteen days. In the fall of 1930, Houdry came to Vacuum's refinery on the Delaware River in Paulsboro, New Jersey, and successfully demonstrated his process. Analysis of the gasoline showed that it was of high quality and had good stability. By May 1931 Vacuum had constructed a sixty-barrel-per-day pilot plant to crack gas oil. About this time the Houdry Process Corporation was organized, with Vacuum having one-third interest and Houdry and his associates the other two-thirds. Soon afterwards, though, the project lost considerable momentum, a victim of the deepening economic depression, and Vacuum's merger with Socony Oil Company. In the spring of 1933, Socony-Vacuum decided to discontinue its support of the project.

The Houdry Process. Houdry next looked across the Delaware River to the Sun Oil Company, whose refinery was located at Marcus Hook, Pennsylvania. He was able to convince Arthur E. Pew Jr. (son of the founder and brother of the president) and chief engineer Clarence H. Thayer to take half of Houdry's interest, making Vacuum, Houdry, and Sun equal partners. Sun had been a lubricating oil company that moved into gasoline during the automobile boom of the 1920s. Sun produced a high quality gasoline that did not need tetraethyllead (TEL) to boost its anti-knock capability. TEL had been commercialized in the late 1920s by General Motors and Standard Oil of New Jersey. Sun was looking for ways to stay ahead in the octane race without having to pay royalties to these corporate giants.

Although the Houdry process produced high quality gasoline, the process was complex and cumbersome. The main problem was the buildup of coke on the catalyst that eventually stopped it from functioning. Houdry's solution to this problem was to burn the coke off the catalyst with air. This required that the process include three reactors, only one of which would be making gasoline. A second would be vacuum purging residual oil vapors from the reactor, which was necessary to avoid an explosion during the third step, burning coke off the catalyst. In April 1936 a two-thousand-barrel-per-day semi-commercial unit was started up at Paulsboro. A year later a much larger, fifteen-thousand-barrel-per-day unit, began operation at Marcus Hook. Size was not the only difference between the plants: Whereas the first plant cracked the relatively light gas oil, the later one attacked very heavy crude oil, a cheaper but more difficult to process feedstock. Also, Sun had made some major modifications to the process. Studies of the cracking process revealed that coke built up so rapidly on the catalyst that after fifteen minutes of operation, little additional gasoline was produced. At this time the plants had been running on cycles that were hours long. Switching to very short cycles created a number of challenging engineering problems. First, they required automated process control, a relatively new technology in the 1930s, to switch the functions of the three reactors. To burn off coke quickly, Sun engineers had to use a turbo-compressor to supply the large volume of air required. Removing the tremendous amount of heat generated during regeneration led to the substitution of molten salt heat transfer agents for water.

While Sun engineers worked out the process, Houdry spent much of his time working on improving the catalyst that had to meet activity, selectivity, and life specifications and needed to be mechanically strong and survive under process conditions. To supply catalyst materials, Houdry relied on the Filtrol Corporation, which used a wide variety of clays for the purification of oils, fats, and waxes. After extensive experimentation, a bentonite-type clay consisting of silica and alumina was chosen. In 1940 Houdry shifted over to a synthetic silica-alumina catalyst that eliminated the variability inherent in natural materials.

Commercial Success. Arthur Pew Jr. announced the commercialization of the Houdry process at an American Petroleum Institute meeting in November 1938. Although the Houdry process generated about as much gasoline as did existing thermal cracking units, the catalytic product had a octane number of 88 compared to 72 for the noncatalytic product. In addition, the Houdry process created higher value by-products that could be burned as fuel oil. In the next few years, Socony-Vacuum and Sun, along with a few other oil companies, made major investments in Houdry units. By 1944, twenty-four units had been built, accounting for 10 percent of the nation's cracking capacity. No new fixed-bed Houdry units were built after that date as catalytic cracking shifted to continuous processes that moved the catalyst through the reactor with the petroleum gases. After exiting the reactor, the catalyst was separated from the gases and sent to a separate regeneration reactor. Early-moving catalyst processes, including one developed by the Houdry organization, used mechanical means to convey the catalyst, but the eventually dominant process, developed by Warren K. Lewis and his co-workers at the Massachusetts Institute of Technology in Cambridge, Massachusetts, and Standard Oil of New Jersey was based on fluidized bed technology. In this process, the catalyst particles are fluidized by the petroleum gases and move through the reactor either upward with the gases or downward by gravity.

The Houdry process, though short-lived, played a critical role in contributing high-octane gasoline that could serve as the base for 100-octane aviation fuel. During World War II this fuel helped give the Allies the edge in the air because the Germans could not get their octane number above 90. During the war's first two years, Houdry units produced 90 percent of the catalytically cracked gasoline.

During the 1930s the Germans tried to get access to Houdry's process, but concerns over Nazi intentions led Houdry to break off negotiations in 1937. Two years later he visited France to advise the government on gasoline issues but could not get much support for his process. After the fall of France in June 1940, Houdry helped to organize the committee France Forever to support the Free French in their efforts to defeat the Nazis. He later became president of that organization and in 1943 had to defend it from charges that it was committed to supporting Charles de Gaulle as the leader of postwar France. In 1942 Houdry became an American citizen.

Butadiene and Catalytic Theory. Eugene Houdry continued to work on the improvement of his process until 1941, when he shifted over to working on catalytic methods to make butadiene, one of the two chemicals needed to produce synthetic rubber—Japanese expansion into Southeast Asia late that year cut off the United States from is sole source of natural rubber. Houdry developed a catalyst that would convert a widely available refinery byproduct, butane, into butadiene in one reaction step. The process was similar in design to the original Houdry process, requiring three reactors simultaneously reacting, purging, and regenerating. Two rather small plants used this process during World War II, but it did not become a major process for butadiene manufacture.

Between 1944 and 1948 Houdry, while president of the Houdry Process Corporation, directed special research and development projects primarily for Sun. In 1948 he left the active management of his company and returned to independent investigation, using a stable behind his home in Ardmore, Pennsylvania, as his laboratory. Houdry had developed some general ideas about catalysis that served as the basis for his research. He asserted that catalysis was the fundamental mechanism of life, referring to humans as *catalytic machines.* He thought that industrial catalysts could be improved by studying enzymes and that industrial catalytic concepts could be applied to medicine. As an example of the latter, he speculated that cancer was caused by catalyst malfunction in cells and that a cure might come from either regenerating or replacing cellular catalysts. Another, more specific, project was using catalysts to promote flameless combustion in applications from extracting heat from waste gases to flameless cooking devices. He organized a new company, Oxy-Catalyst, in 1950 to develop applications of oxidizing catalysts. Several of his ideas coalesced into Houdry's development of an automobile catalytic converter in the 1950s.

In the late 1940s, air pollution in cities such as Los Angeles was becoming worse and scientists connected it with smog caused in part by automobile emissions. At the same time the incidence of lung cancer was rising. Houdry became convinced that the two were causally linked. He pointed out that since 1915 the amount of gasoline burned in the United States had increased twenty-five times, exactly the multiple of lung cancer cases. Cigarette consumption, another suspected cause, had only increased three times over the same time span. Publicly connecting automobile exhaust with lung cancer must not have made him very popular with the oil and automobile companies. In the early 1950s he developed a catalytic converter that consisted of porcelain rods coated with a film of alumina and platinum. The major challenges he faced were those that would confront future designers of catalytic converters. One was that the devices had to operate effectively over a wide range of operating conditions, from starting on cold days to rapid acceleration at high temperatures. Another big problem was the poisoning of the catalyst by the lead in the gasoline. Houdry never completely solved these problems, but he did put his converters on forklift trucks that operated indoors and on unleaded gasoline.

In the postwar decades, numerous catalyst innovations revolutionized the chemical processing industries, but most of these developments came from well-funded laboratories staffed with PhD scientists and engineers. In recognition of his pioneering efforts in the field, Houdry was awarded the Howard N. Potts Medal of the Franklin Institute in 1948, the Perkin Medal of the Society of Chemical Industry in 1959, and the Industrial Engineering Award of the American Chemical Society in 1962. Posthumously—he died after a short illness on July 18, 1962—he was inducted into the National Inventors Hall of Fame in 1990.

BIBLIOGRAPHY

There are materials relating to Houdry and his process in the Sun Oil Company papers (accession 1317) at the Hagley Museum and Library, Wilmington, Delaware. There are two other small collections of Houdry materials: the Eugene Jules Houdry Collection, 1938–1996, at the Chemical Heritage Foundation in Philadelphia and the papers of Eugene Jules Houdry, 1931–1980, in the Library of Congress manuscript collection.

WORKS BY HOUDRY

With Wilber F. Burt, Arthur E. Pew Jr., and W. A. Peters Jr. "Catalytic Processing of Petroleum Hydrocarbons by the Houdry Process." *Proceedings of the American Petroleum Institute* 19, no. 3 (1938): 133–148.

"Practical Catalysis and Its Impact on Our Generation." In *Advances in Catalysis*, vol. 9, edited by Adalbert Farkas. New York: Academic Press, 1957.

"Développements et Tendances de la Catalyse Industrielle." In *Actes du Deuxième Congres International de Catalyse.* Paris: Technip, 1960.

OTHER SOURCES

Enos, John Lawrence. *Petroleum Progress and Profits: A History of Process Innovation.* Cambridge, MA: MIT Press, 1962. See chapter 4.

McEvoy, James E. "Citizen Houdry." *CHEMTECH* 26 (February 1996): 6–10.

Mills, G. Alex. "Catalysis: The Craft according to Houdry." *CHEMTECH* 16 (February 1986): 72–75.

Moseley, Charles G. "Eugene Houdry, Catalytic Cracking, and World War II Aviation Gasoline." *Journal of Chemical Education* 61 (August 1984): 65–66.

Oblad, Alex G. "The Contributions of Eugene J. Houdry to the Development of Catalytic Cracking." In *Heterogeneous Catalysis: Selected American Histories*, edited by Burton H. Davis and William P. Hettinger Jr. Washington, DC: American Chemical Society, 1983.

Spitz, Peter H. *Petrochemicals: The Rise of an Industry.* New York: Wiley, 1988.

John K. Smith

HOWARD, HENRY ELIOT (*b.* Kidderminster, Worcestershire, United Kingdom, 13 November 1873; *d.* Stourport-on-Severn, Worcestershire, 26 December 1940), *ornithology, ethology, animal psychology.*

Howard was an amateur British field ornithologist whose major contribution to science was his theory of the role of "territory" in bird life. He sought through painstaking observations of the life of common birds to understand the emotional and mental lives of birds.

Howard was not a professional scientist but instead a wealthy amateur. Educated at Eton and then at Mason Science College (the forerunner of the University of Birmingham), his primary occupation was that of director of a major steelworks in Worcester. The responsibilities of his job tended to keep him close to home, but he did not need to go any farther abroad to be a passionate observer of birds. In the immediate vicinity of Clareland, his home near Stourport-on-Severn in the Worcestershire countryside, were ponds, moorlands, and marshes where birds could breed and where Howard could watch them. He did so with extraordinary dedication, rising before dawn every morning over the course of many breeding seasons to study in detail the courtship habits of common, native birds.

British field natural history in the early twentieth century was inevitably shaped by the ideas of Charles Darwin. Howard for his part was convinced of the importance of natural selection as a factor in evolution, but his early observations on bird courtship led him to question certain features of Darwin's theory of sexual selection. Darwin had called upon sexual selection to account for "secondary sexual characters," the differences exhibited by males and females of the same species with respect to coloration, "ornaments," weapons used in fighting rivals, vocalization, scent organs, and so forth. He explained that such characters were related not so much to the survival of the organism as to its success in securing a mate and leaving progeny. He proposed that these characters had been developed through "male combat" or "female choice" in those animals sufficiently advanced in their mental powers to feel rivalry or to appreciate beauty.

Among the critics of Darwin's theory was Alfred Russel Wallace. Wallace balked at Darwin's idea of female choice, specifically as it related to the development of sexual differences in the colors of birds. Wallace maintained that the bright colors of the males and the dull colors of the females were the respective results of "male vigor" and natural selection acting to produce protective coloration. As Darwin saw it, however, one had only to consider how male birds displayed themselves to the females of their species to recognize that female choice played a key role in developing such characters.

Howard, who was interested in the mechanisms of evolution, the nature of the bird mind, and the details of bird display, was not satisfied with what either Darwin or Wallace had to say on sexual selection. He first expressed his doubts in one of his earliest papers, published in 1903. His complaints became more specific with the appearance in 1907 of the first installment of what was to be a large, two-volume treatise, *The British Warblers: A History with Problems of Their Lives* (1907–1914). Discussing the courtship of the grasshopper warbler, he stated that females do not usually have the chance to compare the displays of two or more males, nor, for that matter, do they seem much interested in the males' displays at all.

Howard's major contribution to the study of bird behavior was the concept of territory, the idea that males compete with each other for breeding territories, not for females. He first mentioned territory in 1908 in his article on the chiffchaff in *The British Warblers*. The males, he said, have protracted struggles with each other as they compete for the same area. Six years later, as he reached the end of his warbler study, he offered additional observations on the subject. But *The British Warblers* was a cumbersome and expensive work and thus not well suited for making Howard's ideas widely known. Fortunately, Howard was persuaded by Britain's leading authority on animal psychology, Conwy Lloyd Morgan, to write a small book in which Howard spelled out his ideas on territory and bird courtship in a more concentrated fashion. This Howard did in *Territory in Bird Life* (1920). He elaborated further on his observations and ideas in his 1929 book, *An Introduction to the Study of Bird Behaviour*.

Howard explained territory in the following terms. Birds in nature, he said, space themselves out in a way that serves to ensure a sufficient food supply for their offspring. This spacing out is achieved through male pugnacity. Upon arriving at their breeding grounds in the spring, males fight with other males. They fight primarily over territory, not over females, who do not arrive on the scene until days or even weeks after the males do. The male's pugnacity depends upon the area he occupies: when his territory is trespassed upon, he has a strong impulse to fight; but when he crosses the boundary of his territory, this impulse to fight diminishes dramatically. As for the male's bright colors and song, these serve in the first place as a warning to other males and only after that to produce an emotional response in the female. The arrival of the female leads to a heightening of the emotional states of male and female alike, thus furthering the biological goal of mating and reproduction.

The concept of territoriality was not new. In the latter half of the nineteenth century the German ornithologist Bernard Altum had expressed much the same idea, but without attracting attention. As it was, even after Howard published his *Territory in Bird Life* in 1920, it took the vigorous promotion of Howard's thesis by Edward Max Nicholson to capture the imagination of contemporary ornithologists. This was achieved through Nicholson's widely read book, *How Birds Live* (1927).

When it came to thinking about the mechanisms of evolution, Howard believed that natural selection was a key factor, but not the only factor, in the evolutionary process. He doubted that all the various details of bird courtship could have been developed by natural selection on the basis of their utility. From his own observations he knew that different species of birds exhibit small but nonetheless distinctive differences in the gestures or "attitudes" they display when fighting, defending territory, or courting. Some raise their wings a little more or a little less than others do. Some flap their wings slowly while others flutter them quickly. Some utter their songs flying upward while others utter them in descending. Howard could not believe that these small, organic differences were produced simply by the natural selection of fluctuating variations or mutations. But neither was he attracted to the idea of the inheritance of acquired characters. He called upon Morgan's hypothesis of "coincident variations" to explain how individual experience could modify an instinctive behavior pattern and how this modification, though not itself inheritable, could then serve as a kind of "foster-parent" for congenital variations in the same direction.

The topic that continued to intrigue Howard the most, however, was the nature of the bird mind. He hoped that field naturalists, by devoting themselves to the study of a limited number of bird species, would be able to detect mental differences between individuals, and that this would shed light on the genesis of mind and on the relation between animal minds and human minds. His last two books, *The Nature of a Bird's World* (1935) and *A Waterhen's Worlds* (1940), represented his best efforts to comprehend the bird's "viewpoint." However, as the ornithologist David Lack noted in 1959, asking such questions as whether birds had a "world" or "viewpoint" led Howard "into exalted metaphysical regions where, as yet at least, he has had no followers" (p. 74). Quite unlike Howard, the ethologists of the generation that followed him, most notably Niko Tinbergen, were resolute in directing their attention to the observable behavior of animals and in eschewing altogether such topics as the animal mind or animal subjective experience.

Howard, like Edmund Selous, the other major pioneer of British field ornithology in the first quarter of the twentieth century, was a rather reclusive individual, at least in relation to the broader ornithological community. Howard appears to have been happy residing at home with his own family, receiving occasional guests, taking some fishing trips, and devoting himself to his detailed studies of bird life. He was a member of the British Ornithologists' Union for forty-five years, but few of the other members knew him well. His closest scientific contacts were with Morgan and, to a lesser extent, with Julian Huxley. He also interacted briefly with Konrad Lorenz just as Lorenz was beginning his meteoric rise to prominence as the main founder of the new discipline of ethology.

Howard's primary legacy was the concept of territory and the impetus he gave to behavioral field studies through his careful observations of the lives of common birds.

BIBLIOGRAPHY

The Howard papers, including a large collection of letters written to Howard by Conwy Lloyd Morgan, are at the Edward Grey Library, Oxford University.

WORKS BY HOWARD

"On Sexual Selection and the Aesthetic Sense in Birds." *Zoologist,* 4th series, 7 (1903): 407–417.

The British Warblers: A History with Problems of Their Lives. 2 vols. London: R. H. Porter, 1907–1914.

Territory in Bird Life. London: John Murray, 1920.

An Introduction to the Study of Bird Behaviour. Cambridge, U.K.: Cambridge University Press, 1929.

The Nature of a Bird's World. Cambridge, U.K.: Cambridge University Press, 1935.

A Waterhen's Worlds. Cambridge, U.K.: Cambridge University Press, 1940.

OTHER SOURCES

Burkhardt, Richard W., Jr. *Patterns of Behavior: Konrad Lorenz, Niko Tinbergen, and the Founding of Ethology.* Chicago: University of Chicago Press, 2005. The most extended account of Howard's contributions to British field studies of behavior.

Lack, David. "Some British Pioneers in Ornithological Research, 1859–1939." *Ibis* 101 (1959): 71–81.

Lowe, Percy R. "Henry Eliot Howard. An Appreciation." *British Birds* 34 (1941): 195–197.

Nice, Margaret Morse. "The Role of Territory in Bird Life." *American Midland Naturalist* 26 (1941): 441–487.

Nicholson, Edward Max. *How Birds Live: A Brief Account of Bird-Life in the Light of Modern Observation.* London: Williams & Norgate, 1927.

Richard W. Burkhardt Jr.

HOWARD, LUKE

(*b.* Cripplegate, London, United Kingdom, 28 November 1772; *d.* Tottenham, London, United Kingdom, 21 March 1864), *meteorology, pharmacy.*

Howard was a pharmacist by profession, but a meteorologist by inclination, whose amateur (and very British) fascination with the weather led him to devise the classification and nomenclature of clouds that remains in international use today. He also became a pioneer in the study of urban climate, and his twenty-year statistical record of London's weather formed the heart of his landmark publication *The Climate of London* (1818–1820), for which he was elected a Fellow of the Royal Society in 1821.

The son of a devout and commercially successful Quaker tinsmith, Robert Howard (1738–1812) and his wife Elizabeth Leatham (1742–1816), Luke Howard was dispatched at the age of eight to a strict Quaker boarding school in Burford, Oxfordshire, where the rote learning of Latin grammar dominated the curriculum to the exclusion of science and mathematics. "My pretensions as a man of science are consequently but slender," as he wrote in an autobiographical essay in 1822, but his lifelong habit of keeping daily weather notes was already in place by the time he left school in 1787 to begin a seven-year apprenticeship with a Quaker pharmacist in Stockport, Lancashire (Scott, 1976, p. 2).

It was during this formative period that Howard began to spend his evenings studying French, chemistry, and the natural sciences, describing the impact of the works of Antoine Lavoisier as "like the Sun's rising after a night of moonshine" (Scott, 1976, p. 2). Upon his return to London in 1794 Howard intensified his autodidactic regime, attending regular lectures and evening classes, as well as joining a small scientific debating club, the Askesian Society, which was founded in 1796 by William Allen, a fellow Quaker pharmacist with whom Howard had gone into business. In 1797 Howard, now married to Mariabella Eliot (1769–1852), took charge of Allen & Howard's research and manufacturing laboratories at Plaistow, Essex, 8 miles east of the City.

At Plaistow, Howard began to work up some of his meteorological notes, framing them in the light of recent atmospheric theories, particularly those advanced by John Dalton in his *Meteorological Observations* (1793). Dalton's contention that cloud droplets do not "float," but fall continually under the influence of gravity, was instrumental in shaping Howard's conviction that clouds, far from being "airy nothings," were subject to "the same fixed Laws which pervade every other department of Nature" (Howard, 1854, p. 85).

At a meeting of the Askesian Society in December 1802 Howard delivered a paper, "On the Modifications of Clouds," in which he proposed that every cloud belonged to one of three principal families, to which he had given the Latin names: cirrus (meaning "fiber" or "hair"), cumulus ("heap" or "pile"), and stratus ("layer" or "sheet"). In recognition of the essential instability of clouds, Howard also introduced a sequence of intermediate and compound modifications, such as cirrostratus and stratocumulus, in order to accommodate the regular transitions occurring between the cloud types.

Howard was not the first to attempt a classification of clouds—only the previous year Jean-Baptiste Lamarck had proposed a list of descriptive terms in French—but the success of Howard's system was due to his use of universal Latin, as well as to his emphasis on the mutability of clouds. By adopting Linnaean principles of natural history classification—in which objects are grouped into families according to shared external characteristics—and applying them to phenomena as short-lived and changeable as clouds, Howard had arrived at an elegant solution to the problem of naming transitional forms in nature.

Once published, the cloud classification was soon in use around the world, and in 1896 it was officially adopted (with minor amendments) by the World Meteorological Organization. Howard's scientific reputation was secured, and although he remained a full-time pharmacist, establishing his own firm, Howard & Co., in 1807, he continued his meteorological activities, contributing weather columns to a variety of journals, while continuing to keep a daily meteorological register. In 1818, Howard published the first volume of *The Climate of London,* a pioneering work of urban climatology (the second volume appeared in 1820), for which he was elected a Fellow of the Royal Society. In this work, the first to suggest that built environments have a noticeable impact on weather and climate, Howard made the first identification of a now familiar effect—the Urban Heat Island, in which a city's nighttime temperature remains higher than that of the surrounding areas, a phenomenon that he ascribed to the burning of fossil fuels. In 1822, a German translation of his essay on clouds led to a brief correspondence with the poet Johann Wolfgang von Goethe, who wrote a series of cloud poems in Howard's honor, and at whose request Howard wrote the autobiographical essay cited above. In 1823 he became a founding member of the Meteorological Society of London, but the following year Howard and his wife moved to Ackworth, Yorkshire, leaving the flourishing pharmaceutical business in the hands of their two eldest sons, one of whom, John Eliot Howard, (1807–1883) went on to become a celebrated expert on quinine.

Although Howard continued with his meteorological research, his life in Yorkshire became increasingly devoted to charitable and educational work as well as to a series of doctrinal controversies within the Quaker movement, which culminated in his defection to the Plymouth Brethren in 1836. In 1842 he published an unconvincing treatise identifying an eighteen-year cycle in British weather, comprised of a seven-year rise followed by a ten-year fall in average temperature and rainfall; this was followed by his *Barometrographia* (1847), a visually impressive folio volume in which annual fluctuations of the weather were plotted against the phases of the Moon, using large circular diagrams traced by a self-recording barograph, in an attempt to determine the extent of lunar influence on climate.

Following the death of his wife Mariabella in 1852, Howard returned to London to live with his eldest son Robert, at 7 Bruce Grove, Tottenham, where he died, aged ninety-one, in 1864. He was buried in the grounds of the Quaker meetinghouse at nearby Winchmore Hill, the earlier disputes apparently resolved.

Howard lived just long enough to see the advent of the professionalization of modern meteorology, while being one of the last of the amateur observers to make a major contribution to the field. "Never, probably, was Science wooed more entirely for her own sake," as his obituary in the *Friend* (1864) concluded, "never was there a more thorough 'labour of love' than that which he bestowed."

BIBLIOGRAPHY

Luke Howard manuscript collections can be found at: London Metropolitan Archives (business/family papers); Library of the Religious Society of Friends in Britain (family papers); Wellcome Institute for the History of Medicine (personal/scientific letters); and Science Museum, London (personal letters). A collection of Howard's cloud watercolors can be found at the Science Museum, London.

WORKS BY HOWARD

On the Modifications of Clouds. London: J. Taylor, 1804.

"The Natural History of Clouds." *Journal of Natural Philosophy, Chemistry, and the Arts* 30 (1812): 35–62.

The Climate of London, Deduced from Meteorological Observations, Made at Different Places in the Neighbourhood of the Metropolis. 2 vols. London: W. Phillips, 1818–1820. Rev. ed., 1833.

Seven Lectures on Meteorology. Pontefract, U.K.: James Lucas, 1837.

"Luke Howard's Autobiography; with His Own Additions and Corrections down to an Unascertained Date. Probably circ. 1840." MS. Box 5.2. Unpublished manuscript in The Library of the Religious Society of Friends in Britain, Friends House, Euston Road, London.

A Cycle of Eighteen Years in the Seasons of Britain; Deduced from Meteorological Observations Made at Ackworth, in the West Riding of Yorkshire, from 1824 to 1841. London: J. Ridgway, 1842.

Barometrographia: Twenty Years' Variation of the Barometer in the Climate of Britain, Exhibited in Autographic Curves, with the Attendant Winds and Weather. London: R. and J. Taylor, 1847.

Papers on Meteorology, Relating Especially to the Climate of Britain, and to the Variations of the Barometer. London: Taylor and Francis, 1854.

My Ledger; or, A Compromise with Prudence. Written in 1808. London: Taylor and Francis, 1856.

OTHER SOURCES

Dalton, John. *Meteorological Observations and Essays.* London: J. Phillips, 1793.

Day, John A., and Frank H. Ludlam. "Luke Howard and His Clouds: A Contribution to the Early History of Cloud Physics." *Weather* 27 (1972): 448–461.

Hamblyn, Richard. *The Invention of Clouds: How an Amateur Meteorologist Forged the Language of the Skies.* London: Picador, 2001.

Howard, Bernard. "A Luke Howard Miscellany: Compiled by his Great Grandson." Unpublished typescript. 1959. The Library of the Religious Society of Friends in Britain, Friends House, Euston Road, London.

Kington, J. A. "A Century of Cloud Classification." *Weather* 24 (1969): 84–89.

Obituary in *The Friend: A Religious, Literary and Miscellaneous Journal* 4 (1864): 100.

Scott, D. F. S. *Luke Howard (1772–1864): His Correspondence with Goethe and His Continental Journey of 1816.* York, U.K.: William Sessions, 1976.

Slater, A. W. "Luke Howard, F.R.S. (1772–1864) and His Relations with Goethe." *Notes and Records of the Royal Society* 27 (1972): 119–140.

Webb, Nicholas. "Representations of the Seasons in Early-Nineteenth-Century England." PhD diss., University of York, 1998.

Richard Hamblyn

HOYLE, FRED (*b.* Gilstead, Bingley, West Yorkshire, United Kingdom, 24 June 1915; *d.* Bournemouth, Dorset, United Kingdom, 20 August 2001), *cosmology, nuclear astrophysics, astrobiology, science fiction, science journalism.*

Hoyle was an outstanding British cosmologist and astrophysicist whose penchant for controversial theories meant he was seldom out of the public eye between 1950 and 1980. Uniquely he combined a sharp and creative scientific intellect with superb communication skills, which brought his controversial ideas to a wide audience. Publicly, Hoyle was best known as the leading proponent of the steady state theory of cosmology. His greatest achievement was showing how the chemical elements heavier than helium have been created by thermonuclear reactions inside stars. In the latter part of his career he moved away from mainstream astronomy, courting controversy with his enthusiasm for panspermia, or the seeding of life on Earth from space.

Family and Education. Fred Hoyle's father was a wool merchant, and his mother a talented pianist who had trained as a teacher. After Hoyle's birth, his father enlisted as a machine gunner in the army, and spent three years (1915–1918) in the valley of the Somme, France, fighting on the front line. He returned in 1919, physically unscathed but mentally shattered, with a deep contempt of politics, public life, and the establishment, a trait that his son adopted. In the 1920s Hoyle's parents had very little money. He learned arithmetic and reading from his mother: he did not regularly attend school until he was about eight years of age. Evidently he was a star pupil at the rural elementary school he attended because he was the only child to win a place at Bingley Grammar School, which awarded him a clothing allowance. His parents strongly encouraged his schooling, allowing him to perform dangerous chemical experiments at home and rewarding him with a telescope when they noticed his strong interest in the stars.

Hoyle's performance at the grammar school secured him a place at Emmanuel College, Cambridge, where he read mathematics. From the moment he arrived in Cambridge, in October 1933, Hoyle was an outsider. His impoverished background, old clothes, and marked regional accent set him apart from the polished members of the aristocracy and the privileged elite from England's major private schools. He immersed himself in his studies, with stunning success. The university graded him first class at the end of his freshman year. He skipped the second-year curriculum entirely, and moved onto graduate-level courses for his third year. He graduated as the top-ranked applied mathematician of his year.

His undergraduate achievement assured him a place as a research student in the Cavendish Laboratory, the birthplace of nuclear physics, where the electron, isotopes, and the neutron had been discovered, resulting in a string of Nobel Prizes. Hoyle's first supervisor was the German-Jewish émigré Rudolf Peierls and, second, Paul Dirac (Nobel Prize in Physics 1933), then at the height of his fame as a founder of modern quantum theory. In 1938, as a research student, Hoyle wrote a paper on the theory of beta decay (a radioactive process in which a neutron decays to a proton and an electron). This won him the prestigious Smith's Prize, an award at Cambridge for the best performance by a research student in mathematics. The following year two papers on quantum electrodynamics secured him two fellowships, one at St. John's College, Cambridge, and the other from a private foundation. At this stage, with World War II just weeks away, Hoyle decided to switch his interest to astronomy, instead of nuclear physics, which he felt was then already on the path to the production of weapons of mass destruction.

Wartime Research. His first collaborator in astrophysics was Raymond Lyttleton, with whom he wrote papers on the accretion of interstellar matter by stars. The Royal Astronomical Society, to which they submitted their papers, was reluctant to publish what they felt were speculative hypotheses, which led to the first clash between the youthful Hoyle and the British research establishment.

In 1940 Hoyle and Lyttleton were both drafted into defense research. Despite physical separation, they kept up their collaboration, mainly through a voluminous correspondence in which Lyttleton took every opportunity to complain to the then-impressionable Hoyle about the incompetence of the British government and the obstacles to publication of their papers. Lyttleton communicated a disdain for officialdom, conservative procedures, and the British class structure that would remain with Hoyle for the rest of his life.

The Admiralty (the government department responsible for the Royal Navy) recruited Hoyle for theoretical research on radar. Major ships had defensive radar, which could determine the direction and distance of an attacking aircraft, but not its height. This meant that fighter aircraft were virtually flying blind when a ship was threatened. A theoretical analysis enabled Hoyle to devise a method by which a radar operator could deduce the altitude by studying the way in which the radar echo strengthened and faded as an attacking aircraft closed in. His ingenious solution undoubtedly aided the Royal Navy in the early sea battles in the eastern Mediterranean Sea, but, for reasons of secrecy, Hoyle never received public recognition for this significant contribution to Britain's wartime defense.

In 1944 Hoyle participated in a conference held in Washington, D.C., at the Naval Research Laboratory. He took the opportunity to visit three of the most distinguished astronomers in the United States: Henry Norris Russell at Princeton, Harlow Shapley at Harvard, and Walter Baade of the Mount Wilson Observatory, Pasadena. These encounters, which marked the beginning of Hoyle's long and productive relationship with colleagues in the United States, would profoundly guide his research program immediately after the war.

As director of the theory division at the radar establishment, Hoyle recruited in June 1942 a deputy, Hermann Bondi, another Cambridge mathematician. On Bondi's advice, in October 1942 Hoyle brought in Thomas Gold, a Cambridge graduate in engineering science. Bondi and Gold were originally from Vienna, Austria, but they left Austria shortly before the *Anschluss.*

Bondi, Gold, and Hoyle shared a small rented house close to their place of work. They spent their evenings and weekends debating problems in astrophysics. Hoyle directed Bondi toward the accretion work he had done with Lyttleton. Bondi improved the theory considerably, which led to his winning a research fellowship at Trinity College. Hoyle and Bondi published the work in 1947. For many years astrophysicists ignored their ideas until, in the 1970s, it was discovered that there are circumstances under which compact neutron stars can accrete interstellar gas, which creates x-rays. So their 1947 accretion paper is now widely cited, for reasons that were unimaginable when they published the theory.

Cosmology. All three returned to Cambridge in 1945. Hoyle and Gold had jobs as university lecturers, but no workplace in the faculty of mathematics. Consequently all three worked in practice in Bondi's spacious rooms in Trinity College. In 1947 they started to work together on cosmology, then a very difficult subject, which they had previously ignored. There were problems with the observations: from the expansion of the universe, Edwin Hubble gave 1.8 billion years as the Hubble time, about half the age of Earth. This had led theoretical astronomers to propose several conflicting models of the universe, none of which could be tested using the telescopes of the time. The expansion of the universe appeared to imply a singular origin at some point in the past.

In 1942 the cosmologist George Gamow spoke in Washington in favor of an explosive origin for the universe. Four years later he suggested that a primordial explosion in the young universe could have made the chemical elements by nuclear processes. The Cambridge trio were not, however, aware of this work. Baade had privately suggested to Hoyle that the chemical elements were made in red giant stars, an idea he worked on alone from 1946 (Bondi and Gold were not well versed in nuclear physics).

In 1947 Gold suggested that the universe could have had no beginning and would have no end: it had always existed. Bondi and Hoyle seized on this idea, known as steady state cosmology, immediately. Hoyle always felt that an important question in cosmology is whether or not there is a relationship between the structure of the universe and the laws of physics. Dirac, in 1938, had argued that a universe in motion requires laws of physics that change with time. Scientific ideas about the creation of matter in the universe can be traced back to the 1880s. In the steady state cosmology the important feature was that the voids left by the expansion of the universe would be filled by the spontaneous creation of matter, so that the physical appearance of the universe and the laws of physics would be the same for all observers and all epochs. This continuous creation aspect greatly appealed to all three of them.

Unlike the physicists who had earlier toyed with matter creation, Hoyle immediately felt the need for finding a mechanism to create the matter, and he quickly settled on a field theory. The journal *Nature,* and then the Physical Society, rejected his paper on the mechanism. By the time the Royal Astronomical Society eventually published his paper, Bondi and Gold had already published a rival paper on the steady state theory. All three pressed the merits of the theory at scientific conferences. However, in the competition between the steady state theory, and what Hoyle termed the big bang universe, it was clear from the outset that most of the astronomical community and its leaders preferred the big bang. Outside Britain, the steady state theory received no attention.

Hoyle

Fred Hoyle, 1958. HULTON ARCHIVE/GETTY IMAGES.

BBC radio provided Hoyle with a platform for the promotion of continuous creation. On 28 March 1949, he gave a 20-minute talk about his new cosmological ideas. For the first time he referred to the explosive origin of the universe as a big bang. Early the following year the BBC commissioned five lengthy talks from Hoyle, and this gave him another opportunity to bring his ideas to a wide public. The talks were published as a best-selling book, *The Nature of the Universe.* Almost overnight, it seemed, Hoyle had become the most famous astronomer in Britain. Simultaneously, he courted controversy by adding to his hypothesis a naive theological interpretation, critical of Christian belief.

By the 1950s, the emerging discipline of radio astronomy provided a tool for testing the rival theories of cosmology. In the big bang picture the distant parts of the universe will not have exactly the same properties as the local universe because they are being seen at an earlier epoch, when the universe was denser. In the steady state universe no evolution is discernable. Cambridge radio astronomers, led by Martin Ryle, made an early claim to have detected evolution. Their original results were deeply flawed, and naturally Hoyle rejected them. Disagreements between Hoyle and Ryle soon became aired in public, with both sides using the mass media to convey their findings. Ultimately Ryle's observations did show evidence for evolution. Then, in 1965, Arno Penzias and Robert Wilson announced the serendipitous discovery of the cosmic microwave background radiation, immediately interpreted as fossil evidence for a hot dense phase, or big bang, in the early universe. From that point Hoyle's steady state hypothesis was doomed, although he never accepted the confident statements of his rivals in cosmology.

Origin of the Chemical Elements. When Hoyle had arrived in Cambridge, the theoretical astronomer Arthur S. Eddington was at the height of his career, a world expert on the structure and evolution of stars; by observations made at a total eclipse in 1919, Eddington had confirmed a prediction of Einstein's general theory of relativity. Hoyle always looked up to Eddington, whose example he followed in working on the composition of stars. Once the nuclear sources of stellar energy were understood, Hoyle reformulated Eddington's early work on homogeneous stars, discovering that red giant stars must have an inhomogeneous structure. Hoyle was a pioneer in the use of digital computers for modeling stars. He produced the first models of stars that are primarily composed of hydrogen. He visited Princeton in 1954, where he and Martin Schwarzschild gave the first complete account of the evolution of a low-mass star once it has exhausted the hydrogen fuel in the nuclear core.

Hoyle's greatest achievement, a theory of nucleosynthesis in stars, also began in the immediate postwar period. Working alone, Hoyle found the nuclear chain reaction responsible for building the chemical elements from carbon to iron at a temperature of 3 billion degrees (3×10^9 K) in the interiors of red giant stars. He concluded that practically all of the chemical elements had been synthesized in stellar interiors, under a variety of physical conditions. At this point he was still unable to account for the presence of carbon, his starting point.

On his visit in 1953 to the Kellogg Radiation Laboratory at the California Institute of Technology (Caltech), Hoyle solved the carbon puzzle in a spectacular fashion. In effect he discovered the physical mechanism that would allow three helium nuclei to coalesce and form a stable carbon nucleus. For this to happen, Hoyle predicted that the carbon nucleus must have an excited energy state above its normal ground state. The Kellogg lab had the equipment to test this hypothesis, and indeed they found an excited state at precisely the energy level predicted by Hoyle. This result, predicted purely from astrophysics, greatly impressed the nuclear physics community, who now believed in nucleosynthesis in stars.

During his annual visits to Caltech, Hoyle collaborated with the astrophysicists Margaret and Geoffrey Burbidge, and the experimental nuclear physicist William

Fowler, on the origin of the chemical elements. This led to Hoyle's greatest masterpiece, a lengthy paper published in 1957 in *Reviews of Modern Physics.* This paper, authored by the Burbidges, Fowler, and Hoyle, is universally referred to as B2FH by astrophysicists. It is Hoyle's most widely quoted paper, in which an account is given of the origin and abundance of all the isotopes apart from those of the five lightest elements. The basic physical mechanisms for forging the chemical elements in stars remain essentially unchanged. Hoyle's contribution to the paper was huge: it was he who carried out most of the calculations in nuclear physics. Many commentators were deeply shocked when the 1983 Nobel Prize for Physics was awarded to Fowler and Subrahmanyan Chandrasekhar for contributions to nucleosynthesis and stellar structure, respectively, areas in which Hoyle's achievement exceeded that of the two laureates.

Interstellar Matter. Hoyle's early work on accretion led to an interest in interstellar matter that lasted throughout his career. An early paper attributed climate change and ice ages to the cooling effects of the Sun passing through an interstellar dust cloud, which became the theme of his best work of science fiction, *The Black Cloud* (1957). He speculated thirty years before anyone else that hydrogen molecules are an important source of cooling in interstellar clouds. During the 1950s he modeled the fragmentation of gas clouds into galaxies and stars. He filled the gaps in his knowledge in a highly intuitive manner that turned out to be correct.

With his research student N. Chandra Wickramasinghe, Hoyle investigated the composition of interstellar grains from 1960. They suggested that carbon is a major constituent of grains. Data from space observatories in the late 1970s enabled them to explain that complex hydrocarbons must be the main ingredients. They then extended the scope of their investigations, claiming that very complex organic compounds are present in comets and interstellar matter.

Hoyle believed strongly that life could not have originated spontaneously on Earth. He frequently asserted that the probability of life self-assembling from inanimate material is too small. He and Wickramasinghe speculated that life on Earth had arrived as bacteria borne by comets. This assertion was ridiculed by molecular biologists; professional astronomers too began to ignore Hoyle's research from the late 1970s onward. Nevertheless, some of his ideas, such as the suggestion that comets delivered inanimate organic material and water to the early Earth, are now regarded as plausible by astrobiologists. Hoyle, with Lyttleton, was the first to suggest (1939) that astronomical events, including cometary impacts, could cause ecological disaster on Earth. They speculated that the boundary between the Cretaceous and Tertiary periods in the fossil record was due to species extinctions triggered by a cometary impact 65 million years ago.

Hoyle's approach to theoretical research differed markedly from the masters who preceded him. Whereas they had spent a lifetime in just one or two areas (Eddington working on stellar evolution, for example), Hoyle regarded the entire celestial realm as being within the compass of his inquiries. While he intrigued and entertained the public with a copious stream of new, but sometimes weakly supported, ideas, some professionals felt he was the noisy upstart who had invaded their special areas of inquiry.

Administration. In the three decades 1945–1975 Hoyle transformed theoretical astronomy and cosmology in Britain. Wartime defense research had drained the young talent from Britain's universities. Astronomy in the United States was far ahead; the 200-inch Palomar telescope had commenced observations in 1948. Britain had nothing to compete with it. Hoyle led a despondent research community of applied mathematicians away from the fading traditions of dynamical and positional astronomy. He directed his research students toward the richness and diversity of the new astrophysics that began to emerge in the 1960s. Unfortunately he treated his Cambridge colleagues with disdain and failed to develop a fruitful relationship with the astronomically minded members of the faculties of mathematics and physics. Instead he concentrated on his own research students, Stephen Hawking among them, and his rich collaborations with colleagues in the United States, particularly those in Pasadena, California. By the mid-1960s he assembled a world-class team of theorists in Cambridge, which once again became the greatest school of astronomy in Europe.

From 1967 to 1972 Hoyle directed the new Institute of Theoretical Astronomy in Cambridge. He had been instrumental in founding it, securing its initial funding, and obtaining the most powerful computer in the world for his theorists. He ran a vigorous program of summer visiting fellowships, which were used to bring the brightest theorists from North America to the institute. This annual infusion played a significant part in developing theoretical astronomy in the United Kingdom, at a time when British observational astronomers still tended to regard their North American colleagues as competitors rather than collaborators.

Although Hoyle generally found committee work repellent, he served with distinction on the U.K. Science Research Council from 1967 to 1972. As chairman of its astronomy, space, and radio board he was active in the assessment of the astronomical facilities in the Southern Hemisphere, which led to the creation of the 150-inch

Anglo-Australian Telescope. He served as president of the Royal Astronomical Society from 1971 to 1973.

In 1972 he made a dramatic resignation from his professorship at Cambridge, citing as the reason for his departure irreconcilable differences of opinion with the university on the future management of astronomy at Cambridge. He felt that political moves by his Cambridge rivals had made his position untenable.

Hoyle married, in 1939, Barbara Clark, who intensely supported him for more than sixty years during a close and happy marriage. She served as personal assistant, diary secretary, and literary agent, as well as raising their two children, Geoffrey and Elizabeth, and running an open house for graduate students and academic visitors. Hoyle's interests, apart from research and family, extended to hill climbing and classical music. His scientific output encompassed almost four hundred papers. His corpus extended to six research monographs, twenty-seven textbooks and popular science books, and fifteen science-fiction works.

He received many honors, among them Fellow of the Royal Society (1957), associate member of the U.S. National Academy of Sciences (1969), knighted for services to astronomy by Queen Elizabeth II (1972), and gold medalist of the Royal Astronomical Society (1968). The Royal Swedish Academy of Sciences made him joint recipient of the 1997 Crafoord Prize, equal in monetary value to the Nobel Prize.

BIBLIOGRAPHY

A complete bibliography is available on request from the library of the Royal Society, London. A bibliography of papers is given at http://www.fredhoyle.com. Most of his research papers are available to download at Harvard College Observatory by searching under his name at http://adsabs.harvard.edu/abstract_service.html.

WORKS BY HOYLE

"The Synthesis of the Elements from Hydrogen." *Monthly Notices of the Royal Astronomical Society* 106 (1946): 343–383. First paper on the origin of the elements.

"A New Model for the Expanding Universe." *Monthly Notices of the Royal Astronomical Society* 108 (1948): 372–382.

The Nature of the Universe. Oxford: Basil Blackwell, 1950. First popular science book, a best-seller.

Frontiers of Astronomy. New York: Harper, 1955. First textbook, a model of clarity, and a source of inspiration to students.

With Martin Schwarzschild. "The Evolution of Type II Stars." *Astrophysical Journal Supplement* 2 (1955): 1–40. A major contribution to the theory of stellar evolution.

The Black Cloud. New York: Harper, 1957. His first, and arguably his best, science-fiction novel.

With Margaret Burbidge, Geoffrey Burbidge, and William Fowler. "Synthesis of the Elements in Stars." *Reviews of Modern Physics* 29 (1957): 547–650. Definitive account of the creation of all of the chemical elements by nuclear processes in stars.

Home Is Where the Wind Blows. Mill Valley, CA: University Science Books, 1994. This autobiography is an objective and accurate source.

With Geoffrey Burbidge and Jayant Narlikar. *A Different Approach to Cosmology: From a Static Universe through the Big Bang towards Reality.* Cambridge, U.K.: Cambridge University Press, 2000. A research monograph that fully sets out Hoyle's objections to conventional cosmology and his alternative model.

OTHER SOURCES

Burbidge, Geoffrey. "Sir Fred Hoyle." *Biographical Memoirs of Fellows of the Royal Society London* 49 (2003): 213–247. Definitive official biographical summary of Hoyle's major scientific achievements.

Gough, D., ed. *The Scientific Legacy of Fred Hoyle.* Cambridge, U.K.: Cambridge University Press, 2005. Collective work in which associates of Hoyle evaluate his scientific legacy in context.

Gregory, J. *Fred Hoyle's Universe.* Oxford: Oxford University Press, 2005. Biography.

Mitton, Simon. *Conflict in the Cosmos: Fred Hoyle's Life in Science.* Washington, DC: Joseph Henry Press, 2005. Scientific biography.

Wickramasinghe, Chandra. *A Journey with Fred Hoyle.* Singapore: World Scientific, 2005. Autobiographical reminiscences of a major collaborator, with the emphasis on the search for cosmic life.

Wickramasinghe, Chandra, Geoffrey Burbidge, and Jayant Narlikar, eds. *Fred Hoyle's Universe.* Dordrecht, Netherlands: Kluwer Academic Publishers, 2003. Collective work with contributions on all aspects of Hoyle's research.

Simon Mitton

HUANG JIQING (TE-KAN)

(*b.* Renshou County, Sichuan, China, 30 March 1904; *d.* Beijing, China, 22 March 1995), *geotectonic geology, stratigraphy, petroleum geology.*

Huang Jiqing was one of the pioneers and founders of modern geology in China. His contributions covered many fields, such as regional mapping, tectonics, biostratigraphy, and the geology of oil and gas. He was elected an academician of the Academia Sinica (1948), and of the Chinese Academy of Sciences (1955). Huang was not only a versatile geologist but also an important figure in geological administration.

Huang was born into an intellectual family. His father was Huang Ruci, who ran a school with new ideas; his mother's family name is Jiang. Huang received his early education in his father's school. In 1924 he enrolled in the Department of Geology, Peking University, where he trained under the distinguished geologists A. W. Grabau, Weng Wenhao, and J. S. Lee. After graduating in 1928, he joined the staff of the National Geological Survey. From 1933 to 1935 Huang pursued doctoral studies at the University of Neuchâtel under the geotectonist Emil Argand. His DSc dissertation was titled *Étude géologique de la Région Weissmies-Portjengrat,* about which geologist Maurice Lugeon remarked: "Your account of your time spent in the Alps will forever be remembered." Huang's first-rate training laid the foundation for his later distinguished career. In 1936 he returned to China and was employed as chief geologist at the National Geological Survey. On 12 December that year, he married Chen Chuanjun (1908–1999). They subsequently had three children.

Huang was director of the National Geological Survey (1937–1940), president of the Geological Society of China (1938, 1979–1982), director of the Southwest Geological Bureau, China (1952), deputy director of the Academic Division of Earth Sciences of the Chinese Academy of Sciences (1954–1967), deputy president of the Chinese Academy of Geological Sciences (1980–1985), and its honorary president (1985–1995).

Survey Work. Huang made geological surveys of many parts of China, such as Shaanxi, Sichuan (Szechuan), Yunnan, Qinghai, and Xinjiang (Sinkiang), and the results of this work laid the foundation for the geological mapping of the country. One of the best monographs of regional geology, Huang's *Geology of Tsinlingshan and Szechuan,* accompanying the *Geological Map of Tsinling* (1:1,000,000), was published in 1931. From the 1930s, Huang served as chief, or one of the chiefs, of several mapping programs. Under his guidance, fourteen geological maps (1:1,000,000) were compiled (1947–1951), and the first *Geological Map of China* (1:3,000,000) was issued in 1951. From 1960 to 1965, he supervised the editing of a set of maps (1:1,000,000), including geological maps, metallogenic maps, maps of mineral resources distribution, and geotectonic maps. In 1979 the *Geotectonic Map of China* (1:4,000,000) was compiled under his supervision. In 1982 he was awarded a National Scientific Award (Grade 1) for his achievement in geological mapping.

Huang's most notable achievement in biostratigraphy was his study of the Permian. In the early 1930s he published a series of memoirs on the Permian corals and brachiopods of southern China, and used them to subdivide the Permian into the Leping, Yangxin, and Chuanshan Series, in place of the previous twofold division (1932). In the earlier classification, the lower boundary was higher than that used elsewhere in the world. But in Huang's opinion, the so-called Chuanshan Limestone, with its characteristic fossil *Pseudoschwagerina,* should be placed in the Permian, not the Carboniferous. Moreover, a tripartite division of the Permian in China assisted correlation with Permian strata elsewhere, such as in Russia and North America.

Huang's work was the first systematic study of a single geological system in China. Permian research in China subsequently made great progress, and the Leping Series (with the Changhsingian Stage at its top) is now taken as the stratotype of the Upper Permian, and the top of the Changhsingian Stage in the Meishan of Changxing (Changhsing), Zhejiang, in South China serves as the type section for the Permian-Triassic boundary (Jin et al., 2000).

Prospecting. Most oil deposits occur in marine beds. Some people thought that, because China has few Mesozoic and Quaternary marine deposits, and oil would be unlikely in Paleozoic rocks because of their strong deformation everywhere except in the west and the northwest, the country probably did not have much oil. Some investigators, including Pan Zhongxiang (1941), nevertheless pursued the idea that there might be oil deposits in continental or nonmarine source beds in China. In 1942–1943, Huang led a group of geologists to Xinjiang to make a reconnaissance survey for oil. In a report submitted to the National Geological Survey (1947), they elaborated the idea that oil might occur in continental or nonmarine beds. In 1939 Huang discovered the first natural gas field at Shengdeng Shan, Sichuan Province. In addition, as an organizer, he contributed to the discovery of the Laochunmiao oil-bearing anticline, later the famous Yumen oilfield.

In 1954 Huang was appointed a member of the Standing Commission of the National Mineral Resources Survey, Ministry of Geology. After 1955 the survey undertook petroleum prospecting as its main task by order of the Central Government, and a strategic decision was made to carry on with the petroleum reconnaissance, not only in the west and the northwest, but also in the east. Huang called for reconnaissance work in a number of large- and medium-sized sediment basins, among which were the Ordos, Sichuan, North China Plain, and Songliao Basins. In accordance with Huang's instruction, the first prospecting for oil in the Songliao Basin was carried on and had some promising discoveries. In 1956 a newly founded Bureau of Petroleum Geology took over from the survey, and Huang acted as engineer-in-chief. The same year, a strategic reconnaissance investigation for oil was carried out on a large scale. In 1957 a *Map of Prospective Area of Oil Distribution* (1:3,000,000) was completed under his guidance. In 1959 the first well in the Songliao Basin produced oil. Later, the field was named Daqing. Huang was one of the major contributors to the discovery of the Daqing Oilfield, for which he was awarded a National Scientific Award (Grade I) in 1982.

Geotectonics. Huang's best-known achievements were in geotectonics. In 1945 he published his classic monograph, "On the Major Tectonic Forms of China," in which he classified and illustrated the major tectonic features of China in the light of his "polycyclic theory." In contrast to the idea that a geosynclinal system usually ended its development after only one cycle, Huang supposed that geosynclinal systems experience more than one cycle of orogenic movement. For example, the Tianshan fold-belts resulted from the movements of the Caledonian, Hercynian, and Alpine cycles. He further divided the Alpine Orogeny into three subcycles: Indosinian, Yanshan, and Himalayan. Huang's idea about an Indosinian movement has received universal acceptance in China.

The above is a discussion of the polycyclic development of a single geosynclinal fold system in the narrow sense of Huang's theory. More broadly, he envisaged the polycyclic development of the crust as being worldwide and throughout the greater part of geological history.

When Huang discussed the formation of fold systems, he placed emphasis on lateral forces and proposed three types of fold systems in China and contiguous areas: (1) Pacific type; (2) Pal-Asia type, which gave rise to the continent of Pal-Asia; and (3) the "Tethyan-Himalayan" type (1945). The Great Mongolian arc was supposedly formed in the Hercynian Orogeny, as a result of the southward movement of the Siberian Platform. Meanwhile, "Pal-Asia" was formed owing to interaction between the Tarim and Sino-Korean Massifs, and the interaction of these two massifs with the mid-Asian geosyncline. During the Mesozoic, when Pal-Asia was moving toward the Pacific, the Pacific region "resisted" and the circum-Pacific folds resulted. As Pal-Asia drove southward, it met the strong resistance of Gondwanaland (if Alfred Wegener was right), which was moving northward. Thus a strong tangential compression was produced and the thick sediments of the Tethys became the Tethyan-Himalayan fold system, forming the world's greatest mountains.

In addition, Huang suggested that the formation of the Pamir-Himalayan Syntaxis was due to a powerful underthrust, which was caused by a protruding portion of the Gondwanaland. "The strongly arcuate fold systems are developed out of geosynclinal and parageosynclinal sediments. … [T]he overthrusting of the fold is directed towards the foreland" (1945, pp. 114–115).

After the advent of plate tectonics, Huang combined that theory with his polycyclic theory (Yang and Oldroyd, 1989). Huang's group was the first to plot plate suture zones on the *Geotectonic Map of China* (1980), and, considering the evidence from the viewpoint of global dynamics, the three types of fold systems, mentioned above, became three tectonic domains: the Pal-Asian, the Circum-Pacific, and the Tethyan (1980). In the 1980s Huang made a monographic study of the evolution of the Tethys in China and contiguous regions. Moreover, he tried to use plate tectonics to expound the mechanism of polycyclical movements of the crust. In 1983 Huang likened the separation and closure of plates (or tensional and compressional movements) to a kind of "accordion movement," from which he and others developed the concept of "opening and closing" tectonics from the late 1980s on (Jiang, 2004), which has some similarity to the idea of John Tuzo Wilson's cycle. Huang's polycyclic theory was one of the most influential tectonic theories in China and is part of the mainstream of world tectonic theory.

Theory should be able to make predictions. In Huang's view, folding belts have experienced repeated orogenic movements, with associated sedimentation, magmatic activity, metamorphism, and metallogeny. Huang predicted that oil source beds and oil reservoirs would be polygenetic. One of the most telling examples was the prediction of oil in the Junggar Basin, where the chemical properties of the Jurassic and Triassic oils were found to be different from those of the Carboniferous, implying that the oil was formed at different times and horizons in polycyclical development, and was not the result of Carboniferous oil moving upward.

Huang's outstanding contributions to geotectonics won him renown in geological circles and he was awarded the National Scientific Award (Grade II) in 1982. Huang's achievements were also recognized abroad. He was an honorary DSc of *L'École Polytechnique Fédérale de Zurich* (1980), an honorary member of the Geological Society of America (1985), and a foreign academician of the USSR Academy of Sciences (1988).

The author is grateful to David Oldroyd for his encouragement and assistance in the preparation of this article.

BIBLIOGRAPHY

WORKS BY HUANG

"The Permian Formations of Southern China." *Geological Memoirs* (of the Geological Survey of China), Series A, 10 (1932): 1–140. In English.

"On the Major Tectonic Forms of China." *Geological Memoirs* (of the Geological Survey of China), Series A, 20 (1945): 1–165. In English.

With C. C. Young, Y. C. Cheng, M. N. Bien, et al. "Report on Geological Investigation of Some Oil-Fields in Sinkiang."

Geological Memoirs (of the Geological Survey of China) Series A, 21 (1947): 1–118. In English.

Director. *Geotectonics of China and Its Evolution: A Brief Illustration of the Geotectonic Map of China (1:4,000,000).* Beijing: Science Publishing House, 1980. In Chinese.

Selected Works of Huang Jiqing. Vol. 2, edited by Ren Jishun and Xie Guanglian. Beijing: Geological Publishing House, 1992. In English.

Selected Works on Petroleum Geology of Huang Jiqing. Edited by Zhang Qing. Beijing: Science Press, 1993. In Chinese.

OTHER SOURCES

Chinese Academy of Geological Sciences, ed. *Papers in Memory of Huang Jiqing.* Beijing: Geological Press, 1998. In Chinese.

Geological Society of China, ed. *A Chronicle of Huang Jiqing's Life.* Beijing: Geological Press, 2004. In Chinese.

Jiang, Ch. F. "An Accordion Movement and 'Opening and Closing' Tectonics." *Geological Review* 3 (2004): 267–269. In Chinese.

Jin, Y. G., Shang Q. H., and Cao C. Q. "A Review of Permian Stratigraphy." *Journal of Stratigraphy* 24, no. 2 (2000): 99–108. In Chinese.

Li Tingdong. "Professor Huang Jiqing, a Pioneer in Compilation of Geological Maps of China." *Geological Review* 3 (2004): 240–242. In Chinese.

Li, X. X., and J. Zh. Sheng. "Professor Huang Jiqing's Important Contributions to the Study of the Permian of China." *Geological Review* 3 (2004): 230–234. In Chinese.

Ren, J. Sh. "'On the Major Tectonic Forms of China'—A Classic Work of Chinese Geotectonics." *Geological Review* 3 (2004): 235–240. In Chinese.

Yang, J.-Y., and D. R. Oldroyd. "The Introduction and Development of Continental Drift Theory and Plate Tectonics in China: A Case Study in the Transference of Scientific Ideas from West to East." *Annals of Science* 46 (1989): 21–43.

Yang Jing-Yi

HUBBERT, MARION KING

(*b.* San Saba, Texas, 5 October 1903; *d.* Bethesda, Maryland, 11 October 1989), *experimental and theoretical geophysics, modeling, natural resources.*

Hubbert's scientific contributions fell into several key areas: understanding the strength of the Earth, determining the fundamental physics of fluid flow through porous media (critical for groundwater hydrology and petroleum exploration), and finding geophysical explanations for previously perplexing geological phenomena, particularly the mechanism responsible for overthrust faulting. He became best known for developing geophysical methods for calculating the total volume of oil and natural gas reserves in the United States and around the globe, introducing a graphical method for representing the exploitation of crucial minerals over time (the bell-shaped curve for oil, known today as peak oil or Hubbert's peak). One of the most broadly educated geologists of his generation, Hubbert was also deeply involved in efforts to reform the discipline of geology, seeking to rebuild its foundations on physical principles. Driven by concern over natural resources, Hubbert analyzed available energy sources, campaigned for rational planning involving energy production, and backed population control efforts.

Youth on the Texas Frontier. Marion King Hubbert (he became M. King by high school) was born in San Saba, Texas, a flat farmlands area. His father, William B. Hubbert, descended from pioneer stock, was a rancher, and his mother, née Cora Virginia Lee, was a schoolteacher. He attended local schools, including the Methodist-run Cherokee Junior College (where he became valedictorian) and Weatherford College, graduating in 1923. Weatherford classmates described the then nineteen-year-old Hubbert as "a typical Horatio Alger type of schoolboy," with strong intellectual interests (*The Oak Leaf* [published by the Student Association of Weatherford College], June 1922, in Box 80, folder "personal-education," M. King Hubbert papers, American Heritage Center, Laramie, Wyoming).

Early in his college education Hubbert underwent a momentous shift, rejecting the religious fundamentalism of his parents and community as well as his own active involvement in Methodist youth activities. Having "turned heretic," as he later wrote (to Morris W. Leighton, head of Illinois Geological Survey, June 23, 1931, Hubbert file 856–156, Illinois Geological Survey records), and determined to seek a secular education, he left his native Texas for the first time. In January 1924, with money saved from various jobs, including working on railroad track-laying crews, Hubbert arrived unannounced at the University of Chicago and requested admittance. After a probationary period, he became a full-time student, earning a BSc degree in geology and physics with a minor in mathematics in June 1926.

Immediately thereafter, Hubbert enrolled as a graduate student in Chicago's Department of Geology. At the time the University of Chicago had one of the strongest geology departments in the nation, and Hubbert initially addressed problems involving structural geology, working particularly with J Harlen Bretz. His interests soon turned to geophysics, however. Hubbert's decision to pursue geophysics came partly because he trained far more broadly than most of his peers: He studied chemical thermodynamics, physics and electricity, electrodynamics, and theoretical engineering chemistry in addition to petrography and geology. It also came from Hubbert's conviction that

Hubbert

a thorough grounding in these fields would help him resolve outstanding challenges in geology. Even before receiving a 1928 MS for a theoretical study on how thermodynamic processes contributed to producing geologic faults, Hubbert began publishing on a range of problems that intrigued him, including a well-received study of isostasy. He also gained experience in applied geophysics through summer work as an assistant geologist for the Amerada Petroleum Corporation, then (while on leave from Chicago) as a seismographic party member for Amerada's newly formed Geophysical Research Corporation.

Geological Rebel. Hubbert left Chicago before finishing his doctorate (not until 1937 did he submit a set of papers that qualified him for the PhD). In 1931 he began teaching at Columbia University as an instructor in geophysics. Already by the 1930s, Hubbert embraced two firm convictions that would guide his research and professional career for the remainder of his life. The first was his strong belief that the discipline of geology, by pursuing efforts to codify unique laws of geology—and by failing to train students about fundamental principles in physics and chemistry—had made itself parochial and scientifically sterile. While at Columbia, Hubbert championed efforts to introduce new courses in geophysics into the curriculum. He also took on leadership roles in national campaigns by the American Institute of Mining and Metallurgical Engineers and other professional societies to review the state of geophysics training in universities, and campaigned to bring the emerging earth sciences fully within the domain of traditional departments of geology.

The second conviction that Hubbert nurtured during the 1930s was that many mineral and energy resources vital for contemporary civilization, including petroleum and natural gas, were more limited and already more exploited than widely realized, requiring a fundamental reengineering of society's means of production and social governance. In 1932 Hubbert met Howard Scott, the brilliant but didactic engineer and utopian thinker who that summer had convinced the Columbia University engineering faculty to initiate a major hundred-year survey tracing U.S. industrial and agricultural development in terms of production, employment, and energy. Impressed by Scott's knowledge of physical science, and loyal to Scott even after journalists revealed Scott's exaggerated credentials, Hubbert cofounded with him the modern Technocracy movement, serving as Technocracy's director of education through the 1930s. Understanding societal dynamics and uncovering the physical laws governing geological phenomena were, for Hubbert, interwoven and mutually dependent concerns.

While studying mineral economics for his Technocracy associates and teaching courses in basic geology and geophysics at Columbia, Hubbert also continued to apply physics to outstanding geological problems. In 1937 he resolved a standing paradox regarding the apparent strength of materials in the crust of the Earth, for such rocks, despite their evident strength, often show signs of plastic flow. Hubbert demonstrated mathematically that even the hardest of rocks at the Earth's surface, subject to the immense pressures occurring across large areas, will respond in a manner similar to soft muds or clays. While serving during summer breaks as a geophysicist at the Illinois Geological Survey in the early 1930s, Hubbert also pioneered using electrical methods to map faults and to locate groundwater aquifers.

In 1940 Hubbert left Columbia University after failing to secure an appointment as an assistant professor following the awarding of his doctorate. He nevertheless made a final major geophysical contribution while in New York. After spending an intensive year examining the theory of groundwater flow, Hubbert published a book-length study that, drawing from his work on electrical conductivity and a new derivation of the Navier-Stokes equations, showed that the flow is governed jointly by fluid pressure and gravity, challenging prevailing ideas that groundwater invariably flowed from higher to lower pressures. This was a significant achievement, one that provided a physical interpretation of Darcy's law, placed hydrology on a more rigorously theoretical basis, and changed the ways that petroleum corporations and geophysical engineers thought about the transport of fluids through porous media.

Beginning in April 1942, Hubbert spent eighteen months with the Board of Economic Warfare in Washington, D.C. Serving as senior analyst and chief of the Mineral Resources Unit, he supervised assessments of natural resources around the globe critical for the Allied war effort. After joining the board, Hubbert was accused by the U.S. Civil Service Commission of being unsuited for government employment because of his extensive involvement with Technocracy, which commission members deemed a fascist organization for promoting government-run industries and decision-making by educated engineers and planners. Testifying before the commission in 1943, Hubbert boldly reiterated his sympathies for combining "U.S. government powers" with those "held by the big corporations" to effectively manage employment and energy resources (transcript available from www.hubbertpeak.org). While Hubbert retained his wartime Washington appointment, as well as his deep interest in natural resources, he never again advertised his former association with Technocracy.

Career at Shell. In October 1943, Hubbert was hired by Shell Petroleum Company in Houston, Texas. Realizing

Hubbert

that U.S. oil reserves would be substantially diminished following World War II, petroleum companies sought to increase their ability to use geophysical instruments and theories to more accurately predict undiscovered oil reserves and to better exploit existing wells. At Shell—where he became associate director of the newly established Shell Exploration and Production Research Laboratory—Hubbert served two roles. He helped formulate Shell's postwar strategy for locating and exploiting oil deposits, running training programs for colleagues and for new recruits to the industry. Increasingly, as Shell managers came to regard Hubbert as a leading figure in petroleum geology and geophysics, he was also given a far-reaching mandate of doing open-ended research to improve geophysical theory and its applications to natural resource extraction. It was a rare opportunity in the petroleum industry, roughly equivalent to the intellectual freedom that the physicist Irving Langmuir had enjoyed at General Electric Research Labs in the early twentieth century.

Hubbert's achievements at Shell were both institutional and scientific. By the mid-1950s Hubbert had made Shell's research lab—by then known as the Bellaire Research Center—one of the strongest research facilities in the industry. Through his selection as a distinguished lecturer of the American Association of Petroleum Geologists (AAPG) in 1945 and again in 1952, allowing him to visit many university departments associated with the AAPG, Hubbert spoke widely about applied and theoretical geophysics, finding this an effective means to stimulate theoretical physics approaches within traditional departments of geology.

While at Shell, Hubbert also continued his research into theoretical geophysics. In 1953 he extended his fundamental 1940 work on groundwater flow to petroleum entrapment, and in 1957 demonstrated that most hydraulic fractures are vertical, an important insight that led to a major reassessment of techniques employed to locate oil and natural gas deposits. Two years later, in collaboration with William W. Rubey, a geologist at the U.S. Geological Survey (USGS), Hubbert explained the puzzling displacement of enormous blocks of material, known to geologists as overthrust faults, as a consequence of fluid pressure between such blocks and underlying materials.

A prodigious worker who enjoyed considerable research assistance at the Bellaire facility, Hubbert was appointed consultant in general geology at Shell in the mid-1950s, providing him additional time for research. He published widely on issues relating to natural resources and accepted numerous outside tasks, including editorship of the journal *Geophysics* from 1947 to 1949 and the presidency of the Geological Society of America in 1962.

Predicting Oil and Natural Gas Reserves. The most enduring and controversial of Hubbert's scientific contributions were the geophysical methods he devised to estimate the total volume of oil and natural gas in the

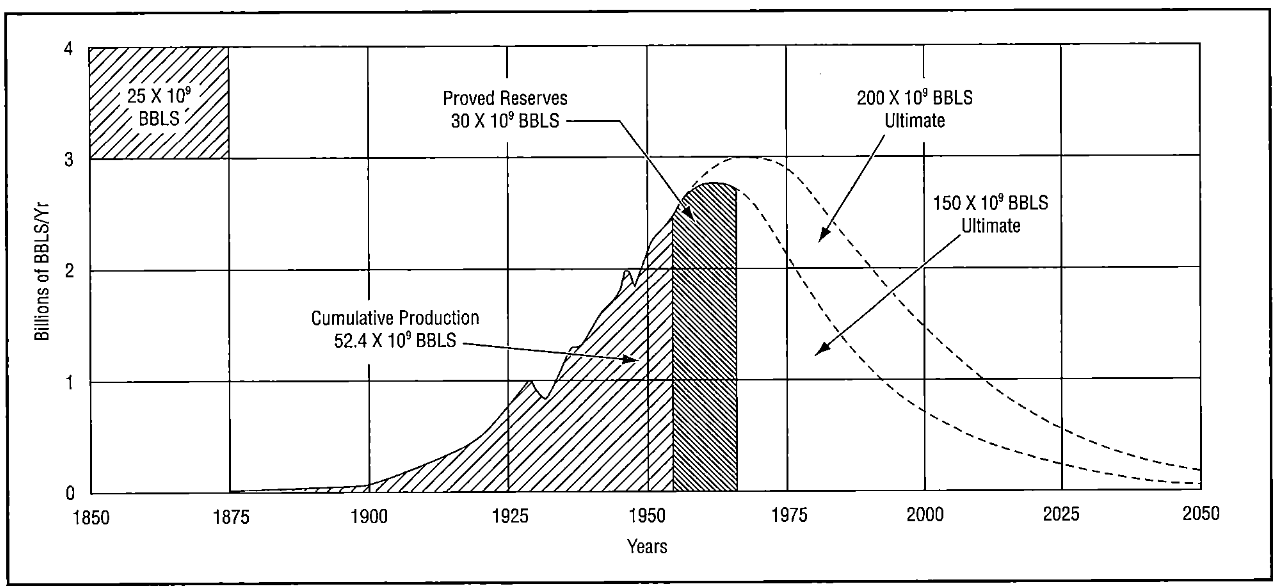

Figure 1. *Graph from Hubbert's 1956 study of natural resources, showing ultimate continental United States crude oil production (based on assumed initial reserves of 150 and 200 billion barrels).*

continental United States and also worldwide, and his concurrent efforts to convince colleagues and political leaders that exponential growth in energy use threatened civilization, because a significant percentage of these resources had already been utilized. His interest in estimating global supplies of critical minerals dated back to his graduate studies at Chicago in the 1920s and his involvement in Technocracy, but was further stimulated by his work at Shell.

In 1956, at a regional meeting of the American Petroleum Institute, Hubbert predicted that total oil reserves in the lower forty-eight states was between 150 and 200 billion barrels (bbl). Hubbert based his calculation on an extrapolation of past drilling and discovery as well as production rates, arguing that the probability of oil discovery was directly proportional to the fraction of yet-undiscovered oil: Over time, both new oil field sizes and total oil production would decrease. For the first time, he also presented his results using a bell curve diagram (see Figure 1), which represented the total volume of petroleum in the continental United States; the apex of the curve, or peak, indicated the point at which half of this natural resource would be produced. Peak oil production in the United States, by his prediction, would occur between 1966 and 1971. In developing this methodology, Hubbert drew on the work of economic geologists such as Donnel Foster Hewett, his insider's knowledge of expected petroleum reserves, and his conviction that the rate of discovery in a mature industry, coupled with firm geologic knowledge, would provide a far more accurate understanding of resources than rosy cornucopian projections made by economists unfamiliar with geology and physics.

Hubbert's 1956 study, expanding research he first presented in 1948, was the first rigorous attempt to graphically predict oil and gas reserves production and remaining reserves. Although industry leaders at the time widely accepted continental U.S. oil reserves of 150 to 200 bbl, Hubbert's prediction that peak domestic oil production would occur within fifteen years was staggering to many, sparking immediate controversy and heated public discussion. Responding to Hubbert's 1956 work, geologists at the USGS, tasked with assessing national mineral resources, developed what became known as volumetric yield methods. In 1961 the USGS geologist Alfred D. Zapp, extrapolating average oil-production yields from already explored regions to less-well-explored parts of the country, calculated that the lower forty-eight states could hold a total of 590 bbl, nearly four times the amount Hubbert believed existed. Several petroleum company leaders joined USGS leaders, including its future director Vincent E. McKelvey, in quickly backing these higher estimates, urging policymakers to eschew figures that suggested an imminent energy crisis.

Simmering tensions between Hubbert and volumetric-yield advocates escalated in 1962, after the National Academy of Sciences asked Hubbert to prepare the energy section of a major report on natural resources requested by President John F. Kennedy. For his 1962 study, Hubbert combined his review of past discovery and production rates with industry figures for proven oil reserves, yielding an estimate of 170 bbl for the continental United States. Hubbert's conclusions were disputed by USGS officials, although an effort to limit distribution of Hubbert's energy report failed after Hubbert intervened with allies in the federal government. Responding to McKelvey, Hubbert wrote, "I submit that if the Zapp estimate were to be accepted as a basis for present policy, and if it should prove to be as erroneous as I think it is, the results in terms of national welfare could be embarrassing" (17 August 1962, p. 8, Box 153, NAS/NRC Resource Committee files, Hubbert papers, American Heritage Center, Laramie, Wyoming).

The rapidly escalating energy crisis in the early 1970s and subsequent gas rationing sparked renewed interest in total U.S. oil reserves, and Hubbert became a regular witness at congressional hearings on energy issues. After new studies validated Hubbert's prediction that peak U.S. oil production had indeed occurred around 1971, incoming President Jimmy Carter in 1977 challenged national policies based on plentiful oil by forcing the resignation of then USGS director McKelvey. Through the 1970s and 1980s Hubbert continued to refine his predictions for peak oil, incorporating additional methodological approaches. By the end of the twentieth century most petroleum experts accepted Hubbert's contention that historical discovery rates produce more accurate resource estimates than volumetric yield methods, although Hubbert's particular methodology was found to work better for the continental United States than for global reserves. Already in his lifetime Hubbert gained folk hero status among conservationists who believed looming near-term exhaustion of oil supplies would deeply challenge technological civilization. An advocate of nuclear power in the 1950s and 1960s, Hubbert came to emphasize solar power as a viable solution to human energy needs late in his career.

Awards and Later Career. After reaching Shell's mandatory retirement age of sixty in 1963, Hubbert joined the USGS as a supergrade research employee, allowing him to further pursue his wide-ranging interests in geophysics, particularly estimates of total oil and gas reserves. He also accepted another long-standing offer to serve as a visiting professor of geology and geophysics at Stanford University, where he taught advanced seminars for one academic quarter each year until 1968; in 1973 he also served as a regents professor at the University of California at

Berkeley. While not directly responsible for training graduate students, he did mentor several established young researchers, including David G. Willis.

Hubbert's scientific activism broadened later in his life, along with his influence on science policy issues. In 1963, increasingly concerned that U.S. academic science was growing more receptive to the desires of patrons than to the pursuit of challenging problems, Hubbert wrote a widely noticed article in *Science*, "Are We Retrogressing in Science?" Echoing critiques of the military-industrial-academic complex, his piece also reflected emerging criticism of military funding for science in the Vietnam War era. He also continued to warn that available natural resources would not allow unchecked exponential growth of the human population, an issue that had first concerned him while involved in the Technocracy movement.

Throughout the end of his life, Hubbert continued to critique the intellectual foundations and practices of geology. With geologist Claude C. Albritton, a fellow Texan who like Hubbert had abandoned a fundamentalist, Biblical-literalism upbringing through exposure to science, Hubbert addressed emerging evidence for catastrophic processes in geology in 1967. Although his criticisms focused primarily on continued adherence to the principle of uniformity, Hubbert's arguments provided support for neocatastrophists who by the late twentieth century declared catastrophic processes, including celestial impacts, to be fundamental geological processes. One of very few prominent mid-twentieth-century geophysicists with no ties to military research programs, Hubbert also advocated broader working definitions of the environmental sciences in graduate training than many of his colleagues, stressing biological as well as solid earth and atmospheric phenomena.

Hubbert received several honors and won significant prizes throughout his career. In addition to his election to the National Academy of Sciences in 1955, and the American Academy of Arts and Sciences two years later, Hubbert received the Anthony F. Lucas Medal from the American Institute of Mining, Metallurgical, and Petroleum Engineers in 1971. In 1977 he was awarded the Rockefeller Public Service Award from Princeton University, followed in 1978 by the William Smith Medal from the Geological Society of London. His later awards included the Elliott Cresson Medal from the Franklin Institute and the Vetlesen Prize from Columbia University (both 1981).

In 1931 Hubbert married Yelena Paulinova; this marriage ended in divorce in 1936. He married Miriam Berry Heath in 1950. No children resulted from these marriages. While raised Methodist, Hubbert moved ever further from formal religious practice as an adult. Politically liberal, late in life Hubbert became an active supporter of Democratic politicians who endorsed resource conservation measures, including Stewart L. Udall and Morris K. Udall. Acerbic and sharp-tongued, he remained loyal to friends and associates but showed little tolerance for those he considered misinformed or inattentive to scientific principles. Hubbert died in Bethesda, Maryland, of complications from a pulmonary embolism, on 11 October 1989.

BIBLIOGRAPHY

Comprehensive bibliographies of Hubbert's primary works, as well as an extensive oral history interview conducted by Ronald E. Doel in 1989, are available at the Niels Bohr Library of the American Institute of Physics, College Park, Maryland, and the American Heritage Center of the University of Wyoming, Laramie, Wyoming, where Hubbert's papers are kept.

WORKS BY HUBBERT

"Theory of Scale Models as Applied to Study of Geological Structures." *Geological Society of America Bulletin* 48 (1937): 1459–1520.

"The Theory of Ground-Water Motion." *Journal of Geology* 48 (1940): 785–944.

"Strength of the Earth." *Bulletin of the American Association of Petroleum Geologists* 29, no. 11 (1945): 1630–1653.

"Energy from Fossil Fuels." *Science* 109, no. 2823 (1949): 103–109.

"Nuclear Energy and the Fossil Fuels." Publication 95, Shell Development Company, 1956.

With William W. Rubey. "Role of Fluid Pressure in Mechanics of Overthrust Faulting." Parts I and II. *Geological Society of America Bulletin* 70 (1959): 115–205.

Energy Resources—A Report to the Committee on Natural Resources. Washington, DC: National Academy of Sciences-National Research Council, 1962. Reprinted by National Technical Information Service, U.S. Department of Commerce, Springfield, Virginia, 1973.

"Are We Retrogressing in Science?" *Science* 139 (1963): 884–890.

OTHER SOURCES

Bowden, Gary. "The Social Construction of Validity in Estimates of US Crude Oil Reserves." *Social Studies of Science* 15, no. 2 (1985): 207–240.

Clark, Robert Dean. "King Hubbert: Science's Don Quixote." *Geophysics, the Leading Edge of Exploration* 2, no. 2 (1983): 16–24.

Deffeyes, Kenneth S. *Hubbert's Peak: The Impending World Oil Shortage.* Princeton, NJ: Princeton University Press, 2001.

Doel, Ronald E. "Hubbert, Marion King." *The Handbook of Texas Online.* Available from http://www.tsha.utexas.edu/handbook/online/articles/HH/fhu85.html.

National Academy of Sciences. "Tribute to M. King Hubbert." *Letters to Members* (National Academy of Sciences) 19, no. 4 (April 1990).

Priest, Tyler. *The Offshore Imperative: Shell Oil's Search for Petroleum in Postwar America.* College Station, TX: Texas A&M University Press, 2007.

Ronald E. Doel

HÜCKEL, ERICH ARMAND ARTHUR

(*b.* Charlottenburg, Germany, 9 August 1896; *d.* Marburg, Germany, 16 February 1980), *physical chemistry, quantum chemistry, chemical bond, molecular orbitals, aromaticity.*

Hückel was born in a suburb of Berlin on 9 August 1896, the second of three sons of Marie and Armand Hückel. The intellectual development of the young Hückel was strongly influenced by his father, who was a physician with interests in the natural sciences. In the cellar of their family home in Göttingen, Hückel's father had built a chemical laboratory. There he introduced his sons to the world of science, and together they conducted experiments in the laboratory while studying books on physics and chemistry, such as Wilhelm Ostwald's *Die Schule der Chemie* (Hückel, 1975). It was thus at home that the Hückel brothers experienced their first contacts with chemistry. Whereas the one-year-older Walter decided to study chemistry in 1914, Erich entered Göttingen University shortly before the outbreak of World War I to study physics and mathematics. There he came under the active influence of the mathematician David Hilbert.

Assistant to David Hilbert, Max Born, and Peter Debye. Hückel attended several of Hilbert's lecture courses. He was particularly influenced by the course "Denkmethoden der exakten Wissenschaften," (Methods of thinking in the exact sciences), which Hilbert gave during the winter semester 1919–1920 and which offered a rich blend of mathematical and physical ideas. Hückel's notes from this course can be found in his papers preserved at the *Staatsbibliothek zu Berlin—Preussischer Kulturbesitz, Handschriftensammlung* (see also Bernays, 1992).

After the course, Hückel served for one year as Hilbert's assistant. Hückel's main activity consisted in helping him as interlocutor in preparing Hilbert's lecture course on the theory of special and general relativity. Hilbert emphasized in his series of one-hour lectures that Albert Einstein's theory of relativity demanded a special intellectual effort because it set forth how the conceptions of space and time from classical mechanics had to be replaced by a far subtler physical conception that could only be grasped by thinking abstractly or by means of analogy. Thus Hückel learned from Hilbert's lecture course that thought structures more abstract than the classical conceptions of space and time were necessary if one wanted to arrive at a deeper insight into the laws of nature. Hilbert also presented the importance of relativity theory in other sciences beyond physics. A repercussion of Hilbert's message was that Hückel was sensitized to approaching critically the foundations of other sciences as well. In an indirect way, Hilbert's axiomatic thinking and methodological approach were to influence Hückel's theoretical ideas, including possibly his quantum mechanical treatment of unsaturated and aromatic compounds during the early thirties.

In 1921 Hückel presented his thesis, written under the supervision of Peter Debye. This was an experimental study of the scattering of x-rays in substances then thought of as liquid crystals. One year later he became assistant to Max Born. Born provided him with his first theoretical task, namely, to assist him in developing a quantum theory of the molecular spectra of molecules consisting of two or more atoms. In 1923 Hückel went to Zürich to work as Debye's assistant until 1927. In this period Hückel made his first important contribution to theoretical chemistry in the form of the theory of strong electrolytes, known in the early twenty-first century as the Debye-Hückel theory. During these years, Hückel learned to use mathematics and physical intuition in the form of models, from which he tried to understand physical and chemical phenomena. This process was accompanied by a comparison between the results of his calculations and experimental data.

Quantum-Mechanical Interpretation of Double Bonding. With this training and methodological background, Hückel spent the following two years, from 1928 to 1930, on a Rockefeller Foundation scholarship that took him to Frederick Donnan in London, Paul Dirac in Cambridge, and Niels Bohr in Copenhagen. Under Bohr's guidance, he began to learn the new quantum mechanics. In his autobiography, Hückel implies that it was the stimulus given to him by Bohr that led him to his work on unsaturated molecules in the summer of 1929. The following year, supported by a scholarship from the Deutsche Notgemeinschaft, Hückel was in Leipzig working with Werner Heisenberg and Friedrich Hund. There he finished his first landmark paper in the new field of quantum chemistry, "Zur Quantentheorie der Doppelbindung" (1930).

In this paper, Hückel undertook to solve a deep problem of classical organic chemistry: the restricted rotation of double bonds and the stability of cis-, trans-, syn-, and anti-isomers. The persistence of stereochemical configurations about C=C or C=N bonds was well known to organic chemists. J. H. van 't Hoff had provided a classical explanation fifty-six years earlier: He imagined the carbon-carbon double bond to be formed by joining two nearby edges of two tetrahedrally disposed valences of each atom. The four remaining valences were conceived as lying in the same plane as the carbon atoms. Hückel attempted to give a quantum theoretical explanation for the hypothesis that valency forces in an unsaturated molecule have a definite direction. He argued that this phenomenon could not arise from forces of a classical nature between the substituted groups; rather it must depend on features of the structure of the double bond that were amenable to treatment only by quantum theory. In his paper Hückel emphasized that the explanation of the chemical facts—in agreement with the conception of the chemists—can only be found in the nature of the double bond (1930, pp. 432–433). According to Hückel's model, in ethylene the two C=C bonds (σ and π) were nonequivalent. In his view, the pair of electrons that corresponds to the second valency bond (π bond) has a positional eigenfunction whose nodal plane coincides with that of the molecule and which is symmetrical in relation to the two carbon atoms. The corresponding statistical charge distribution stabilizes the planar arrangement of the two carbon and four hydrogen atoms. At the same time, the eigenfunction of the remaining electron pair (σ bond) associated with the double bond is nearly axially symmetrical about the C-C axis and has no stabilizing effect for the planarity of the molecule.

Hückel wanted to show that the quantum mechanical treatment of the restricted rotation of double bonds led to a different interpretation from the classical model. This treatment led him to conclude that the direction of the four valency lines in space has no real meaning. According to Hückel, quantum theory can assign a meaning only to the plane in which van 't Hoff's four C-H valency lines lie. Hückel showed that, contrary to van 't Hoff's assumption, two planes must be taken into consideration to account for the restricted rotation of double bonds. The first is the plane with the four C-H valency lines and the C-C bond. The second, perpendicular to the first, is the plane with the charge distribution of the π bond. Hückel remarked that the reason for the restricted rotation had to do with the electrostatic energy between the charge distributions in the two planes. The formation of this charge distribution, according to Hückel, is a quantum mechanical effect without any classical analogues (1930, pp. 454–455).

Thus Hückel opened the way for a critical revision of the classical system of valency and overcame its inability to account for the case of unsaturated molecules and especially for the length of the double bond. His critique of the conventional interpretation of van 't Hoff represented a decisive step away from a naive picture of directed valence lines and toward a new abstract understanding of chemical properties based on quantum mechanics.

Quantum Theory of Aromaticity. In the meantime, through Debye's intervention and with the support of Paul Ewald and Erich Regener, Hückel obtained a position at the Technische Hochschule in Stuttgart teaching "Chemische Physik" from 1930 to 1937. This period was the most fruitful for his scientific production. In the 1931–1932 period, Hückel published three long papers on aromatic and unsaturated molecules, the first providing a quantum theoretical description of benzene (1931, 1932). This was his habilitation thesis leading to the *venia legendi* (right to teach) in theoretical physics at the Technische Hochschule Stuttgart. In this paper Hückel gave two descriptions of benzene: his first method, which eventually came to be known as the valence bond method, and a second, which involved the application of molecular orbital methods. Hückel believed that the experimental data gave him good reasons for preferring the second approach, which was utilized by John Lennard-Jones, Hund, and Robert Mulliken. This second approach is widely known as the HMO method (Hückel's molecular orbital method).

Hückel's second method was essentially adopted from a theory developed by Felix Bloch in a 1928 article to explain phenomena such as the electric conductivity of a metal lattice. Ignoring the mutual interactions, Bloch treated the motion of the electrons in a crystal lattice not as free but rather as influenced by a field of force of the same periodicity as the crystal's lattice structure. Hückel retraced Bloch's considerations in his analysis of the quantum states of a single p_h electron in a field of force of the same periodicity as the structure of the cyclic compound. This field of force is caused by the structure and the p_h electrons other than the one under consideration. One could thus imagine Hückel's benzene lattice as composed of regular hexagons of p_h electrons of carbon. The procedure Hückel used was to set up such a lattice for benzene, calculate the eigenvalues and eigenfunctions in terms of two parameters by solving the Schröndiger equation.

For the calculation of the eigenvalues and eigenfunctions, Hückel employed an approximative procedure indicated by Bloch in which the overlapping fields of potential of the individual atoms are treated as perturbations. Bloch's method yielded the following result for eigenvalue *W*:

$$W^k = \alpha + 2\beta cos\left(\frac{2\pi k}{n}\right)$$

where α and β are two parameters resulting from integrals over the values contributed by the individual atoms. The quantity α represents the potential energy of the unperturbed charge distribution of the $[p]_h$ electron located with the individual atom in the fields of the neighboring atoms. Since α describes an electron bound to an atom, α is negative. The quantity β describes the quantum-mechanical "resonance interaction" between the two neighboring atomic eigenfunctions (ψ^{o}_{f} and ψ^{o}_{f+1}). This is the stabilizing energy of an electron relative to α, when two such entities are interacting within a certain distance. Hückel showed that β is likewise negative for p_h electrons. The eigenfunction for eigenvalue W^k is:

$$\chi^k(r,z,\varphi)=\frac{1}{\sqrt{n}}\sum_{f=0}^{n-1}\varepsilon_n^{fk}\,\Psi_f^0(\varphi)$$

The eigenvalues and eigenfunctions are characterized by the following values for *k*: $k = 0, \pm1, \pm2, \ldots, \pm n/2$, where *n* is even. Such "quantum numbers" characterize the electron states in their energetic sequence. Hückel then plugged in the electron states, taking resonance effects and Wolfgang Pauli's exclusion principle into account, in a manner similar to the molecular orbital (MO) method employed by Hund and Mulliken for diatomic molecules. Drastic negligence of the "interactions between the spins and electronic motions," the energy exchanges between electrons in *k* states, and skillful use of molecular symmetry led Hückel to the following general finding:

> There consequently results for an *n* ring the electronic states characterized by the *k* "quantum numbers." *k* = 0 yields (without spin) one state, *k* = 1 is doubly degenerate and yields (without spin) two states, *k* = 2 likewise, etc. [...] Because, according to the Pauli principle, each state can only be occupied doubly, one obtains a first complete electron shell for 2 electrons, a second for 4 additional electrons (2 + 4 = 6) and another for 4 more electrons (2 + 4 + 4 = 10). (1931, p. 255)

These results, derived from Schrödinger's differential equation, led Hückel to a quantum-theoretical interpretation of aromaticity: The numbers 2, 6, and 10 describe "complete electron shells," which endow monocyclic aromatic molecules with particular stability. The occurrence of the numbers 2, 6, and 10 for "complete electron shells" in a quantum-mechanical analysis of cyclic compounds is characteristic of such compounds. They resulted only from the second method, not from the first. This is based on the fact that Hückel's second method (HMO) yields from *k* = 0 the state of lowest energy, which is not degenerate, whereas for *k* = 1 the corresponding state is doubly degenerate—that is, it appears as a pair of equal energy. Hückel's first method yielded fewer states than the second method. Chemists in the twenty-first century still employ the "Hückel rule" of the form: "$4n + 2$," where $n = 0, 1, 2, 3$, etc., to determine whether a given organic cyclic compound with $4n + 2$ π-electrons is classifiable among the aromatic compounds.

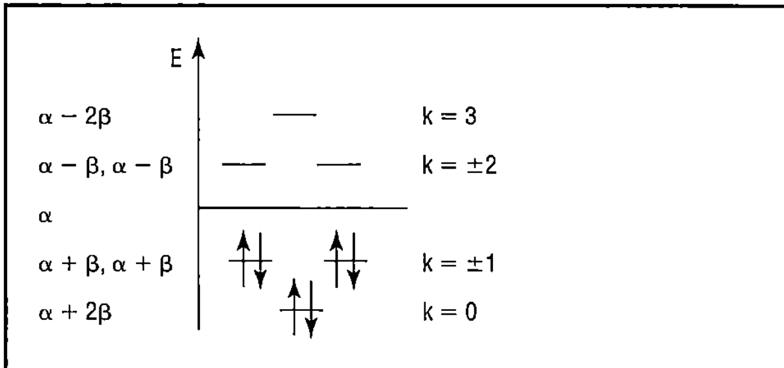

***Figure 1.** The 6 one-electron states of benzene and how they are occupied in the ground state.*

According to Hückel's description, the electron states of benzene are occupied as shown in Figure 1. Hückel emphasized that it was not the number of atoms forming the ring but the number of electrons forming a "complete electron shell" that determined aromaticity. Such "complete electron shells" explained the chemical stability of aromatic cyclic systems—in particular, their strong resistance to chemical addition. Among the aromatic species, that is those with "complete electron shells," only the lowest energy states are occupied. That is why they are particularly low in energy and as a consequence stable and especially chemically resilient. In Hückel's mind, the aromatic molecule constituted the model example of a chemically stable species. Hückel appealed to the analogy between the atomic stability of the noble gases and aromatic molecules. The unusual stability of both species is caused by the possession of "complete electron shells." In the case of the noble gases, the valence electron octet performs the key role. He extended his theory for benzene to other aromatic species and was able to predict the existence of other forms.

Hückel thus offered a chemical explanation, not a physical one, for a molecule's energetic stability. Complete electron shells imply, speaking quantum-theoretically, that the total angular momentum of the electrons equals zero, and that all states are occupied by two electrons of antiparallel spins. Hückel explicates these facts in his paper:

> As already mentioned, the energy content furthermore does not by any means alone govern *the stability of a compound in a chemical sense.* In this the reactivity of a compound is also decisive. This reactivity depends, among other things, on how the energy responds to a disturbance in the atomic arrangement (changes in the separating distances), how easily the molecule is excited, how easily it takes on electrons, and so on. In general, much experimental data has been gathered about the correspondence between the constitution and reactivity of organic molecules. Yet only a very modest number of satisfactory theoretical conceptions

about it exist. We now believe we can contribute a new aspect in the case of cyclic compounds considered here. The introduction alluded to the importance ascribed to the number 6 for "double-bond electrons" in chemistry and stated that *in a certain sense, this number 6* corresponded to *a complete electron shell.* (1931, pp. 254–255; emphasis added)

Hückel extended his theory for benzene to other aromatic species and was able to predict the existence of other forms. In fact, for $n = 6$ members to a ring corresponding to benzene, Hückel obtained 6 electron states in the ground state with a complete electron shell formed of 6 electrons (Figure 1).

For $n = 4$ and $n = 8$ members of a ring, such as for cyclobutadiene (at that time yet to be synthesized) or cycloalkene, Hückel did not obtain complete electron shells from his second method, because their electron states are occupied as shown in Figure 2.

According to Hückel's interpretation, this signified that these cyclic systems are not aromatic in character and are more reactive than benzene, as R. Willstätter and E. Waster had already demonstrated in their contribution "Über Cyclo-octatetraen" published 1911 in *Berichte der Deutschen Chemischen Gesellschaft.* This, Hückel emphasized, was only valid under the condition that the nonplanar arrangement of the ring was unable to have a major influence on its stability and chemical properties. Thus Hückel managed to solve the enigma for classical structural theory in organic chemistry posed by the differing chemical behaviors of benzene, cyclobutadiene and cycloalkene. Moreover, Hückel's quantum-mechanical approach to aromaticity was able to predict the existence of a 10-membered ring (10-annulene) of low reactivity from its closed electron shell. His explicit prediction inspired its eventual synthesis: "It would therefore be interesting to try to produce this compound, and if it worked, to watch whether, unlike the 8-membered ring, it manifests a more aromatic character" (1931, pp. 255–256). Experimental confirmation of Hückel's prediction in fact had to await the end of World War II, after which 10-annulene and other cyclic polyenes (annulenes) of the same aromatic character were synthesized. Hückel's preliminary results on the stability of then-unknown aromatic compounds triggered research specifically focusing on the synthesis of new substances of that class (Garratt, 1986).

Symmetry plays as fundamental a role as does the principle of complete electron shells in Hückel's theory of aromaticity. Andrew Streitwieser, one of Hückel's postwar advocates in America, emphasizes in his autobiographical notes: "The real value of Hückel Theory is that it gives the correct nodal properties of MOs, and these alone can lead to important predictions and understanding of chemistry" (Streitwieser, 1997).

Hückel regarded Friedrich August Kekulé's valence line diagram as a symbolic representation that failed to do adequate justice to the quantum-mechanical forces and resonance interactions between the electrons and carbon atoms. For this reason, a full understanding of the valence line diagram was not possible without appealing to the more fundamental conceptions of quantum theory in which abstract configurational space afforded a better description of the experimentally confirmed equivalence of the six carbon atoms.

Hückel did not limit the application of his second method to cyclic systems in which "the number of electrons is not assignable to simple pairs of bonds" agreeing with the number of atoms on the ring. He also applied it to charged monocyclic polyenes (monocyclic ions). He was able to explain, for example, why cyclopentadiene (C_5H_6)—unlike cycloheptatriene (C_7H_8)— forms a stable potassium salt thereby demonstrating that the $C_5H_6^-$ ion had to be quite stable. Thus one finds a 5-membered ring

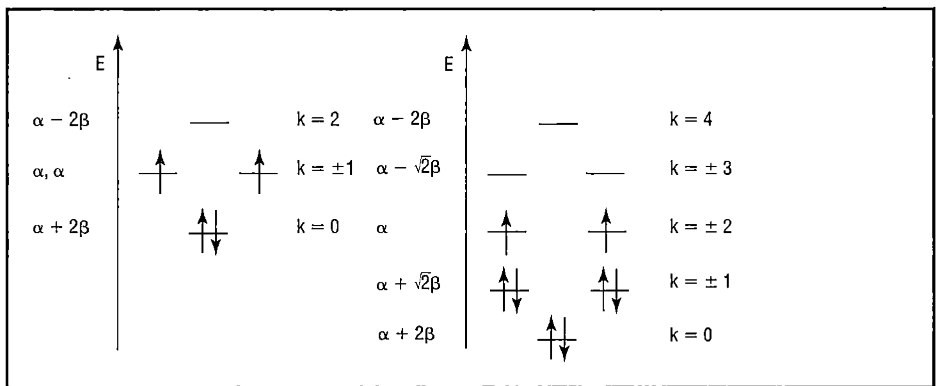

Figure 2. *Electron states of cyclobutadiene and cycloalkene (cyclooctatetraene).*

with 6 electrons occupied, like the 6-membered ring of benzene. Hückel interpreted this "as a tendency toward completion of the closed 6-membered electron shell" (1931, pp. 257–258). By contrast, the $C_7H_7^-$ ion would be occupied in the same way as cyclooctatetraene, which lacks a complete outer electron shell. Hückel again expected cyclononatetraene (C_9H_{10}) to form a stable $C_9H_9^-$ ion because it could form a complete electron group of 10 electrons.

Hückel's theory thus clarified many long-familiar peculiarities of aromatic compounds observed in organic chemistry, even explaining the anomalous properties of annulenes and monocyclic charged polyenes with $4n + 2$ $[p]_h$-electrons. Cyclobutadienes, benzenes, and cyclooctatetraenes (cycloalkenes) were regarded after 1945 as members of a homologous series of conjugate, monocyclic carbon atoms of the general form $(C_2H_2)_n$, where the index n denotes the size of the ring. Such systems were called "annulenes." According to this general nomenclature, benzene is referred to as a 6-annulene and cyclooctatetraene as an 8-annulene. Hückel's theoretical considerations about the molecular stability of as yet unknown compounds also served as a starting point for research concentrating on the synthesis of new substances. Until the end of World War II, the main advances in the field of aromaticity were of a rather theoretical nature. It was only afterward that various research teams synthesized the monocyclic aromatic compounds predicted by Hückel's theory.

The team of researchers led by Franz Sondheimer is a prime example. They started working on the synthesis of a series of aromatic annulenes in 1956. As Jerome Berson pointed out, the most persuasive proof of acknowledgment of Hückel's ideas about aromaticity appears to be the carbocations tropeoline and cyclopropenyl, synthesized in the 1950s and 1960s (1999, p. 53). After much effort and using great synthetic resourcefulness, in 1962 Ronald Breslow was able to confirm the Hückel rule for $n = 0$ by producing the cyclopropenyl cation (Figure 3). This is a three-membered monocyclic ring with a cyclic bond between the three centers and with one delocalized positive charge on the three carbon atoms.

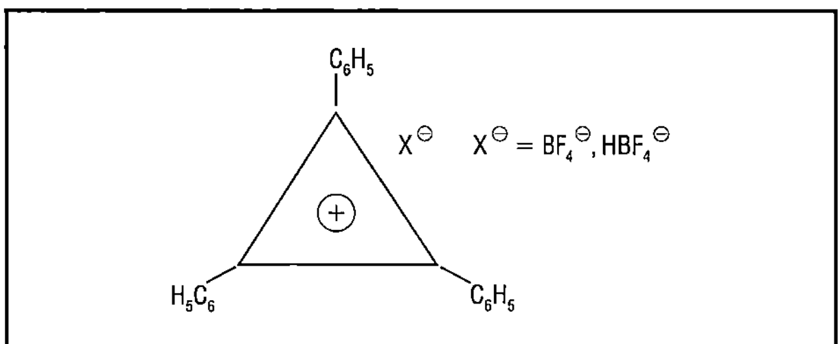

***Figure 3.** Cyclopropenyl cation.*

Aside from a few rare exceptions, the overwhelming majority of chemists apparently did not understand Hückel's theoretical considerations. Hückel's efforts to promote his theory among chemists and chemical physicists in various talks and survey articles could not change this state of affairs. The reason for this failure lay in the experimental and heuristic mentality predominating among chemists in Germany. Traditional training impeded the chemist's ability to adjust conceptually to an unintuitive and purely mathematical treatment of problems in their field. Moreover, Hückel's clumsy communication skills, especially when set against Linus Pauling's persuasive charm, had negative consequences for the general acceptance of his pioneering results. Besides traditionalist tendencies among German chemists, there were other institutional and ideological factors at work during the National Socialist regime that had negative consequences—not just on Hückel's theories but also on the further development of quantum chemistry as a whole inside Germany. In 1965, during the centennial celebration of Kekulé's formula for benzene, Hückel was awarded the Otto Hahn Prize for chemistry and physics for his theory on aromatic compounds. One year later, the Stuttgart polytechnic conferred upon him the honorary degree of Doctor of Natural Sciences—"probably as compensation for the seven years of shame," was Hückel's characteristically wry comment. Hückel was awarded a number of other distinctions for his accomplishments in the field of quantum chemistry before his death on 16 February 1980.

BIBLIOGRAPHY

WORKS BY HÜCKEL

With Peter Debye. "Zur Theorie der Elektrolyte: I. Gefrierpunkterniedrigung und verwandte Erscheinungen; II. Das Grenzgesetz für die elektrische Leitfähigkeit." *Physikalische Zeitschrift* 24 (1923): 185–206, 305–325.

"Zur Theorie der Elektrolyte." *Ergebnisse der exakten Naturwissenschaften* 3 (1924): 199–276.

"Zur Theorie konzentrierter wässeriger Lösungen starker Elektrolyten." *Physikalische Zeitschrift* 26 (1925): 93–147.

"Zur Quantentheorie der Doppelbindung." *Zeitschrift für Physik* 60 (1930): 423–456.

"Quantentheoretische Beiträge zum Benzolproblem. I. Die Elektronenkonfiguration des Benzols und verwandter Verbindungen." *Zeitschrift für Physik* 70 (1931): 204–286.

"Quantentheoretische Beiträge zum Benzolproblem. II. Quantentheorie der induzierten Polaritäten." *Zeitschrift für Physik* 72 (1931): 310–337.

"Quantentheoretische Beiträge zum Problem der aromatischen und ungesättigten Verbindungen, III." *Zeitschrift für Physik* 76 (1932): 628–654.

"Die freien Radikale der organischen Chemie. Quatentheoretische Beiträge zum Problem der aromatischen und ungesättigten Verbindungen, IV." *Zeitschrift für Physik* 83 (1933): 632–668.

"Die Bedeutung der neuen Quantentheorie für die Chemie." *Zeitschrift für Elektrochemie und angewandte physikalische Chemie* 42 (1936): 657–662.

"Grundzüge der Theorie ungesättigter und aromatischer Verbindungen." *Chemie* 43 (1937): 752–788, 827–849.

"Zur modernen Theorie ungesättigter und aromatischer Verbindungen." *Chemie* 61 (1957): 866–890.

Ein Gelehrtenleben: Ernst und Satire. Weinheim, Germany: Verlag Chemie, 1975.

OTHER SOURCES

Bernays, Paul. *Natur und mathematisches Erkennen: Vorlesungen, gehalten 1919–1920 in Göttingen.* Edited by D.E. Rowe. Basel: Birkhäuser, 1992. Transcript of David Hilbert's lectures for the course "Denkmethoden der exacten Wissenschaften."

Berson, Jerome A. "Erich Hückel, Pioneer of Organic Quantum Chemistry: Reflections on Theory and Experiment." *Angewandte Chemie International Edition in English* 108 (1996): 2922–2937.

———. *Chemical Creativity: Ideas from the Work of Woodward, Hückel, Meerwein, and Others.* New York: Wiley-VCH, 1999.

Bloch, Felix. "Über die Quantenmechanik der Elektronen in Kristallgittern." *Zeitschrift für Physik* 52 (1929).

Garratt, Peter J. *Aromaticity.* New York: Wiley, 1986.

Heilbronner, Edgar, and Hans Bock. *Das HMO-Modell und seine Anwendung.* Weinheim, Germany: Verlag Chemie, GmbH, 1968.

Karachalios, Andreas. "On the Making of Quantum Chemistry in Germany." *Studies in the History and Philosophy of Modern Physics,* 31B (2000): 493–510.

———. "Erich Hückel (1896–1980): Von der Physik zur Quantenchemie." Diss., Johannes Gutenberg-Universität, Mainz, Germany, 2003.

Kragh, Helge. "Before Quantum Chemistry: Erich Hückel and the Physics-Chemistry Interface." *Centaurus* 43 (2001): 1–16.

Streitwieser, Andrew. *A Lifetime of Synergy with Theory and Experiment.* Washington, DC: American Chemical Society, 1996.

Woodward, Robert B., and Roald Hoffmann. *Die Erhaltung der Orbitalsymmetrie.* Weinheim: Verlag Chemie, 1970.

Yates, Keith. *Hückel Molecular Orbital Theory.* New York: Academic Press, 1978.

Andreas Karachalios

HULL, CLARK LEONARD (*b.* Akron, New York, 24 May 1884; *d.* New Haven, Connecticut, 10 May 1952), *psychology, behavior theory, animal learning, aptitude testing, hypnotism, concept formation.*

Hull was one of the most influential American psychologists during the period from 1930 to 1950. His main contribution is to be found in his neobehavioristic theory of behavior, which gave new impetus to animal learning research. In addition, he made important contributions to the fields of aptitude testing and hypnosis, and he is the author of a doctoral thesis on the development of concepts that was widely quoted in the psychological literature of the time.

Education. Hull was born in a log farmhouse near Akron, New York. He was the son of Leander Gilday Hull, an ill-tempered farmer who had little schooling because he was required to work as a boy, and Florence Trask, a gentle Connecticut woman who helped her husband to improve his reading after their marriage. When Hull was three or four years old, the family moved to Sickles, Michigan, and his formal education began in the one-room school of this tiny village. At seventeen, he passed a teacher's examination and later taught at the same school for one year. He then attended West Saginaw High School for another year, where he experienced the conveniences of urban living for the first time in his life.

In 1903 Hull continued his studies in Michigan at the Academy of Alma College. There he became fascinated by geometrical reasoning and by the power of the deductive method to generate new knowledge. He wrote in his autobiography: "The study of geometry proved to be the most important event of my intellectual life; it opened to me an entirely new world—the fact that thought itself could generate and really prove new relationships from previously possessed elements" (1952a, p. 144).

At the end of his second year at the Academy, he suffered a severe bout of typhoid fever, which left him with a poor memory for names and delayed his entrance to college for a year. After his recovery, Hull enrolled in Alma College in 1906 as a freshman and took courses in mathematics, physics, and chemistry in order to prepare himself for a career as a mining engineer. Two years later, when working in the Oliver iron mines of Hibbing, Minnesota, he fell victim to an epidemic of poliomyelitis, which left him partially crippled and ended his early hopes for a career in engineering. Looking for a new occupation, he chose psychology; this new field of science was allied to philosophy in that it involved theory, and it would provide him an opportunity to design and work with technical laboratory equipment. As a preliminary survey for the subject, during his convalescence he studied the two volumes of William James's *Principles of Psychology,* a book that made a deep and lasting impression on him. James's functional psychology was one of the main influences on his psychological thought.

Once recovered from the polio attack, Hull entered the University of Michigan at Ann Arbor, where he received his BA degree in 1913. The head of the Department of Psychology, Walter B. Pillsbury, had just published his *Psychology of Reasoning* (1910), which probably reawakened Hull's early interest in higher mental processes. More important, however, was the influence of John P. Shepard, a learning psychologist who introduced him to the rigorous methodology of experimental research and gave him a small Chinese-English dictionary containing the characters and common radicals that Hull would later use in his doctoral dissertation experiments.

In October 1914, after teaching for one year at a small normal school in Richmond, Kentucky, Hull began his graduate training at the University of Wisconsin in Madison. His hope was to contribute to a new experimental science of the higher mental processes. However, the practical atmosphere of the laboratory headed by Joseph Jastrow, a psychologist deeply committed to clinical psychology, led him into the field of applied psychology. During his second year, Hull began his practice in the technique of hypnosis as preparation for teaching an introductory course in medical psychology, which Jastrow had turned over to him. At about the same time, he was asked to teach a course in psychological tests and measurements, and he became involved in the field of psychometrics.

The Evolution of Concepts. In 1918 Hull obtained his PhD in psychology with a dissertation on the "Quantitative Aspects of the Evolution of Concepts" (1920), which was the first study on the subject made with a rigorous experimental methodology. Although the emphasis lay on the measurement of the efficacy of various methods of developing concepts, he included a final "qualitative experiment" designed to observe and determine the nature of the generalizing abstraction that mediates in concept formation.

Hull performed the quantitative experiments with a technique inspired by Hermann Ebbinghaus's memory experiments. The material consisted of a series of Chinese characters with a common radical, which had to be discriminated and then associated to a nonsense syllable playing the role of the concept. The guiding principle for this experimental setting came from William James's notion that the perception of similarity is the essence of reasoning. From the drawings of the common radical made by the subjects at different stages in the qualitative experiment, he reached the conclusion that concept formation was a trial-and-error learning process regulated by Edward L. Thorndike's laws of effect and exercise.

Concept formation was only the first step for Hull on the way to a scientific explanation of reasoning and intelligence. On 5 March 1916 he wrote in his diary: "it seems almost certain now that I shall be a pure psychologist, and that my career will be in the free atmosphere of a great university.... I must set myself a limited task and try by everything in my power to become the supreme authority in that phase of the science.... *The subject shall be the psychology of abstraction and concept formation,* and perhaps, ultimately, of reasoning" (Hull, 1962, p. 814).

After getting his PhD degree, Hull became an assistant professor at the University of Wisconsin and began his work on aptitude testing. Concerned with the chaotic nature of the available material, he worked to improve the instruments and tried to build up a body of scientific knowledge with the help of statistics. For example, he conceived a "universal" assessment battery that might predict the probable vocational aptitude of a youth in each occupation. As this necessitated the computation of large numbers of correlations, he invented a correlation machine that performed nearly all of the arithmetical work automatically (Hull, 1925), which is now housed in the Smithsonian Institution in Washington, D.C. He also wrote *Aptitude Testing* (1928), a book that, according to his disciple Kenneth Spence, "did much to encourage the construction and validation of batteries of aptitude tests so as to yield a maximum of prediction in guidance" (Spence, 1952, p. 641).

In 1922 Hull was promoted to the rank of associate professor and was named director of the Laboratory of Psychology. He then began the research program that eventually led to the wealth of experiments reported in *Hypnosis and Suggestibility: An Experimental Approach,* published in 1933. Dissatisfied with the existing state of knowledge in a field so subjective and prone to deception, Hull planned a research program in which conditioned reflex techniques and physiological response records were used to get objective indexes of the hypnotic trance phenomena. He concluded from his data that hypnosis was a state of hypersuggestiblity or relatively heightened susceptibility to prestige suggestion, and that suggestion was a habit phenomenon. His explanation of suggestion was practically the same as that of Hyppolite Bernheim and other nineteenth-century psychologists, who considered it a kind of "ideomotor action," or action produced by the thought processes. In the hypnotic trance, the subject reacts very easily to the ideas transmitted to him by the hypnotist. As Hull concluded, "a continuous stimulation by words associated with a particular act will bring the act, whether these words are those of the subject himself or of some other person.... The present hypothesis recognizes very fully the rôle played by ideomotor action in the field of hypnosis and suggestibility" (1933, p. 398).

From Reasoning to Learning. In February 1924, when the development of the correlation machine was well underway, Hull instituted a seminar on "reasoning" in order to isolate problems that could be made the object of experimental attack. A year later, in 1925, he studied John B. Watson's behaviorism in another seminar for the purpose of determining "stimulus-response" definitions for the concepts of the "old" psychology of consciousness. By the end of the seminar, he had decided to attempt a neobehavioristic explanation of higher mental processes that would be more sophisticated than Watson's.

According to Hull's own account (1952), it was the attack of Kurt Koffka, the Gestaltist, on the inadequacies of classical behaviorism that confirmed him in this decision. Having tried unsuccessfully to study in Germany with Koffka, he managed to bring him to Wisconsin. In January 1925, in a talk given at Madison, Koffka spent most of his time criticizing behaviorism; this critique left a poor impression on Hull. Instead of being converted to the Gestalt theory, he reached the conclusion "that Watson had not made out as clear a case for behaviorism as the facts warranted" (Hull, 1952, p. 154). Consequently, he decided to improve on Watson's naive associationism with a theory of thinking that would be deductive and at the same time quite materialistic and totally reliant on the principles of mechanics.

Koffka's objections were the catalysts that set in motion Hull's approach to behavior theory, but probably more important was the impact of Wolfgang Köhler's *Mentality of Apes,* a book that was translated into English in 1925. Köhler's experiments on the use and making of instruments indicated that the chimpanzees did not learn punctual stimulus-response connections but rather the relationships between the different objects in their perceptual field. Their behaviors had a definite direction, coherence, and unity that was quite different from the blind trials and errors of the rats in the maze, and indicated some insight or understanding of the problem.

In the following years, Hull delineated the associative mechanisms of his new theory, such as the persisting stimulus of drive, the common response to different stimuli, the fractional anticipatory goal reaction, and the habit-family hierarchy, which later he would publish in separate articles. The persisting stimulus explained purpose because, since it is present in all the stimulus complexes of the habit sequence, it becomes conditioned to all the reactions taking place in it, and later is able to evoke the final act of the original series even in the absence of the external stimuli (Hull, 1930).

The common response to different stimuli mediated conceptual abstraction when there were no identical elements. Suppose, for instance, that R is a response conditioned to three stimuli—*a, b, c*—which are quite different from an objective point of view and have nothing in common. After the conditioning, they will be equivalent in eliciting R, and the kinesthetic stimulus produced by this response will be the element identical to all of them that explains the process of generalizing abstraction.

Hull drafted the mechanism of the fractional anticipatory goal reaction after observing the phenomenon of the antedating movements in the learning experiments. When a rat is approaching the food box in a maze, it tends to make mouth movements before reaching the food; these tiny fractions of the goal reaction guide the animal toward more specific goals than the drive stimulus, because the same drive can be satisfied with many goal reactions. They were the behaviorist equivalent to ideomotor action, and their propioceptive stimulus played the role of guiding ideas.

The family-habit hierarchies were Hull's answer to the Gestalt attacks on the atomistic theories of learning. In the natural environment there are typically multiple routes between a starting point and a goal, and therefore the organism learns alternative ways of moving from a common starting point to a common goal-position, where the reinforcing agent is placed. These alternatives constitute a "family" of equivalent responses because they are united by the fractional anticipatory goal response, which is the same in all of them. They also explain the detour experiments in which the straight line between the learner and the goal is blocked. In Köhler's experiments, the monkey takes an alternate path, such as the stick, in order to grasp the banana that is beyond his reach, because this manipulative habit belongs to the same family as the habit of reaching food with the hands.

By the end of 1927, Hull decided to make these mechanisms known in a series of articles that he would later gather in a magnum opus whose possible titles were: "Psychology of the Thinking Processes, Mechanisms of Thought, Mechanisms of Mind, Mental Mechanisms ..." (Hull, 1962, pp. 824–825). However, in January 1928, after reading Ivan P. Pavlov's *Conditioned Reflexes,* he changed his plans and made the conditioned reflex the subject of his first theoretical article (1929). This marked the beginning of the process that eventually led him to the theory of learning.

In September 1929, Hull moved to Yale University as a research professor at the Institute of Human Relations, where he remained until his death. Although he was supposed to work on aptitude testing, his main goal was the construction of a system that integrated the learning theories of Thorndike and Pavlov. In 1935, when the director, Mark May, gave new impetus to the unification of social sciences, Hull played an increasingly prominent role at the institute. With May's support, he organized a series of seminars and established contacts with the logical

Clark Leonard Hull. **PSYCHOLOGY ARCHIVES, THE UNIVERSITY OF AKRON. REPRODUCED BY PERMISSION.**

positivists of the Vienna Circle. The alliance with this influential group gave prestige to his formal models and was instrumental in his rising to the forefront of American psychology. In this way, Hull's projected magnum opus on thinking became a systematic theory of behavior.

In the summer of 1930, while teaching a summer course in the School of Education at Harvard University, Hull experienced considerable general opposition to his materialistic theory of knowledge. At the same time, however, discussions with the philosophers Clarence I. Lewis and Alfred N. Whitehead strengthened his interest in theory building. He read Isaac Newton's *Principia* thoroughly, finding in this book a powerful scientific theory expressed in the mode of Euclidean geometry. From that point, Newton's set of postulates and theorems would be the model that Hull would follow in his own theorizing.

Hull's Behavior System. Hull developed his system in a piecemeal fashion. During the late 1930s he elaborated the key concepts in "miniature systems," such as the *Mathematico-Deductive Theory of Rote Learning* (1940). A little later, in 1943, he offered the first complete set of sixteen postulates in the *Principles of Behavior*, his most widely known book. This volume was intended to present only the basic theoretical framework, which would eventually be used to explain more complicated behavioral phenomena. Explanation of such phenomena was then to be the subject of two further volumes focusing on individual and social behavior, respectively. However, as time passed, Hull became progressively more engrossed in the quantification of the system. A coronary attack in 1948 convinced him that he would not live long enough to complete this ambitious program. Nevertheless, he was able to publish a final revision in *Essentials of Behavior* (1951), and to finish the manuscript on the single organism's behavior, which was published after his death under the title *A Behavior System* (1952).

Hull's theory of behavior can be considered the best example of hypothetico-deductive system-making in psychology. Taking the biological adaptation of the organism to its environment as a frame of reference, it assumes that survival depends upon optimal conditions of food, water, and so on, as was demonstrated in Walter B. Cannon's physiological research. When one of these conditions deviates from the optimum, the organism enters a state of need, which will be eliminated only through a particular sequence of movements called adaptive behavior.

It was the primary task of psychology to isolate the basic laws by which the stimulation arising from needs on the one hand, and from the external environment on the other, brings about such adaptive behavior. To fulfill this task, the use of unobservable logical constructs, or intervening variables, was permissible, provided that such constructs were functionally related to directly observable environmental events. The central postulates of Hull's system were concerned with learning or "habit," as he termed it. Being the highest and most significant phenomenon produced by the organic evolution, habit consisted in the strengthening of certain receptor-effector connections, or in the setting up of new connections, according to the principle of reinforcement.

In *Principles of Behavior* Hull put aside the associative mechanisms of his earlier theoretical articles and explained reinforcement in terms of drive reduction. For learning to take place, the contiguity of stimulus and response had to be closely associated with a diminution in the drive generated by a need, the Strength of Habit (${}_SH_R$) depending on the number of times it was reinforced. The construct Drive (D) made reference to a general tendency to action generated by the state of need. For instance, in the need of food, the hunger drive will set organisms into a state of general restlessness.

The behavior's concrete direction depended upon another hypothetical entity, the Drive Stimulus (S_D), or stimuli produced by the drive, such as, for example, "hunger pangs," the stomach contractions aroused by hunger. These persistent stimuli become conditioned to all the responses of the habit leading to the food, and in this way they play a leading role in behavior. Without their distinctiveness there could be no way for the animal to learn to go to one place for food when hungry and to another place for water when thirsty.

Drive (D) played a critical part not only in reinforcement, but also in Reaction Potential ($_{S}E_{R}$), the construct expressing the strength of the tendencies determining the vigor and persistency of the activity. The reaction potential equation is based on the assumption that Drive (D) interacts with Habit Strength ($_{S}H_{R}$) in a multiplicative fashion to yield a value for the Reaction Potential ($_{S}E_{R}={}_{S}H_{R} \times D$).

Hull's Legacy. In the final revision of *Essentials of Behavior* (1951), Hull introduced substantial changes in the system to the point that, according to Sigmund Koch, it "defines a set of assumptions so radically different from those of *Principles of Behavior* as to constitute an essentially new theory" (1954, p.2).

The first change is in the conception of primary reinforcement. While in the 1943 postulates it depended upon physiological drive reduction, it came in 1951 to depend chiefly on the reduction of drive-produced stimuli (S_D), or on the decrease of the goal stimulus produced by the fractional anticipatory goal response. This change, due in part to the fact that a nonnutritive substance such as saccharine acted as a powerful reinforcing agent, indicates that Hull was moving in the direction of a contiguity position, although he avoided any clear pronouncement on the critical factor of reinforcement and left the question open until new empirical evidence was available.

The second important change is that the quantitative aspects of reinforcement exert no influence upon habit strength; what counts is only the frequency with which reinforced trials have occurred. This was basically a contiguity theory of association formation, although he never renounced the reinforcement principle.

Hull's last major work, *A Behavior System* (1952), is devoted to applying the principles to a variety of more complex behaviors, such as trial-and-error learning, discrimination learning, maze learning and problem solving. Hull returns to the old mechanism of the "fractional anticipatory goal response" to explain latent learning and Edward C. Tolman's cognitive expectancies. In the chapter on problem solving, Hull considers insight basically in the same way as in his article on "The Mechanism of the Assembly of Behavior Segments in Novel Combinations Suitable for Problem Solution" (1935). Therefore, in a sense the book is the continuation of the projected magnum opus on thinking processes. But Hull limited himself to animal learning, leaving the treatment of abstract thinking to the third volume on social behavior, which he never completed. As a result of his premature death, caused by a heart disease, his system remained unfinished. He married to Bertha E. Iutzi; they had two children: Ruth T. and Richard T. Hull.

Hull's behavior theory has been subject to scathing criticisms since the early 1950s. Some of his theoretical formulations were not as tight as advertised and depended upon very weak empirical evidence. Psychology since the 1950s has progressed in a direction at variance with the premises of Hullian behaviorism. The fall of logical positivism in the philosophy of science and the advent of modern cognitive psychology have put in evidence the weaknesses of the stimulus-response schema.

Hull's influence, however, cannot be minimized. Judging by the number of experimental studies engendered by his theory, he was the most influential of the American neobehaviorists between 1930 and 1950. He also trained a raft of psychologists at Yale. A member of the National Academy of Sciences, he was honored by the presidency of the American Psychological Association in 1936, and in 1945 received the Warren Medal from the Society of Experimental Psychologists. He was a powerful leader in the discipline, and the precision of his theorizing made a deep impression on his disciples, including Kenneth W. Spence. Spence, working at the University of Iowa, developed Hull's system into what came to be called the Hull-Spence theory and trained many who would become leading American experimental psychologists of the 1950s and 1960s.

BIBLIOGRAPHY

Mainly to compensate for his bad memory, Hull recorded in a notebook his ideas concerning all sorts of psychological subjects during the period from October 1902 to April 1952. The notebooks, which he called his "idea books," are held in the archives of the University of Yale. Together with the mimeographed IHR seminar notes and "memoranda," they offer a detailed record of the development of his theory. Extensive excerpts from the "idea books" were published by Robert B. Ammons in the 1962 monograph of Perceptual and Motor Skills *mentioned below.*

WORKS BY HULL

"Quantitative Aspects of the Evolution of Concepts." *Psychological Monographs* 28 (1920): 1–123.

"An Automatic Correlation Calculating Machine." *Journal of the American Statistical Association* 20 (1925): 522–531.

Aptitude Testing. Yonkers-on-Hudson, NY: World Book, 1928.

"A Functional Interpretation of the Conditioned Reflex." *Psychological Review* 36 (1929): 498–511.

"Knowledge and Purpose as Habit Mechanisms." *Psychological Review* 37 (1930): 511–525.

"Goal Attraction and Directing Ideas Conceived as Habit Phenomena." *Psychological Review* 38 (1931): 487–506.

Hypnosis and Suggestibility: An Experimental Approach. New York: Appleton, 1933.

"The Concept of the Habit-Family Hierarchy and the Maze Learning." *Psychological Review* 41 (1934): 33–52, 134–152.

"The Mechanism of the Assembly of Behavior Segments in Novel Combinations Suitable for Problem Solution." *Psychological Review* 42 (1935): 219–245.

"Mind, Mechanism and Adaptive Behavior." *Psychological Review* 44 (1937): 1–32. APA Presidential Address delivered in Hanover, New Hampshire, on 4 September 1937. Hull's first miniature system on adaptive behavior.

With Carl I. Hovland, Robert T. Ross, et al. *Mathematico-Deductive Theory of Rote Learning: A Study in Scientific Methodology.* New Haven, CT: Yale University Press, 1940.

Principles of Behavior: An Introduction to Behavior Theory. New York: Appleton, 1943.

"Behavior Postulates and Corollaries: 1949." *Psychological Review* 57 (1950): 173–180.

Essentials of Behavior. New Haven, CT: Yale University Press. 1951.

"Clark L. Hull." In *A History of Psychology in Autobiography.* Vol. 4, edited by Edwin G. Boring et al., 143–162. Worcester, MA: Clark University, 1952a.

A Behavior System: An Introduction to Behavior Theory Concerning the Individual Organism. New Haven, CT: Yale University Press, 1952b.

"Psychology of the Scientist: IV. Passages from the 'Idea Books' of Clark L. Hull." *Perceptual and Motor Skills* 15 (1962): 807–882.

Mechanisms of Adaptive Behavior: Clark L. Hull's Theoretical Papers, with Commentary. Edited by Abram Amsel and Michael E. Rashotee. New York: Columbia University Press, 1984. A collection of the papers published in the *Psychological Review* from 1929 to 1950.

OTHER SOURCES

Beach, Frank. "Clark Leonard Hull." In *Biographical Memoirs.* vol. 33, edited by the National Academy of Sciences, 125–141. New York: Columbia University, 1959. With a complete bibliography of Hull's published writings.

Gondra, José M. "Clark Hull's Cognitive Articles: A New Perspective on His Behavior System." *Revista de Historia de la Psicología* 22 (2001): 113–134.

———. *Mecanismos Asociativos del Pensamiento: La "Obra Magna" Inacabada de Clark L. Hull.* Bilbao, Spain: Desclée de Brouwer, 2007.

Kimble, Gregory A. "Psychology from the Standpoint of a Mechanist: An Appreciation of Clark L. Hull." In *Portraits of Pioneers in Psychology.* Vol. 1, edited by Gregory A. Kimble et al., 209–225. Washington, DC: American Psychological Association, 1991.

Koch, Sigmund. "Clark L. Hull." In *Modern Learning Theory,* edited by William K. Estes et al., 1–176. New York: Appleton, 1954.

Logan, Frank A. "The Hull-Spence Approach." In *Psychology: A Study of a Science.* Vol. 1, edited by Sigmund Koch, 293–358. New York: McGraw-Hill, 1959.

Smith, Lawrence D. *Behaviorism and Logical Positivism.* Stanford, CA: Stanford University Press, 1986.

Spence, Kenneth W. "Clark L. Hull: 1884–1952." *American Journal of Psychology* 65 (1952): 639–646.

Triplet, Rodney G. "The Relationship of C. L. Hull's Hypnosis Research to His Later Learning Theory." *Journal of the History of the Behavioral Sciences* 18 (1982): 22–31.

José María Gondra

HUTCHINSON, G. EVELYN (*b.* Cambridge, England, 30 January 1903; *d.* London, England, 17 May 1991), *population and theoretical ecology, limnology, biogeochemistry.*

Hutchinson pioneered modern ecology, limnology, and biogeochemistry in the United States. He was the leading developer of theoretical ecology in the middle years of the twentieth century. In addition, he provided superb graduate training for many of the next generation of leading ecologists. Although Hutchinson was born and educated in England, and did research in South Africa, India, and Italy as well as in the United States, he worked and taught at Yale University for most of his long scientific career.

Origins and Education. Cambridge, England, influenced many of Hutchinson's views of science and the teaching of science. Hutchinson himself wrote in his partial autobiography, *The Kindly Fruits of the Earth* (1979), that throughout his early years Cambridge was inhabited by genius, much of which he was exposed to by his family. His father, Arthur Hutchinson, was a mineralogist who taught at Cambridge University, and was later the master of a Cambridge college. His mother, Evaline Shipley Hutchinson, was a feminist and writer.

He attended Gresham's, a public school (in the English sense) in Norfolk, which emphasized science and mathematics. While there, Hutchinson belonged to every science club and conducted his own studies of the taxonomy and behavior of aquatic insects. He published his first paper, about a swimming grasshopper, at age fifteen, launching his seventy-year publishing career.

Hutchinson entered Cambridge University in 1921 to study zoology, but was already well trained in chemistry, physics, and mathematics. This background in physical sciences influenced his future ecological research. He took advantage of the university's open-ended graduate program, particularly the opportunity to choose among its many famous professors—including F. Gowland Hopkins, Joseph Needham, and J. B. S. Haldane, all at that time in biochemistry. In zoology, G. P. Bidder influenced him the most.

While at Cambridge, Hutchinson became an expert on several groups of aquatic insects, particularly the Corixidae or water boatmen and their sound-producing organs. His observations were published in Edward A. Butler's *A Biology of the British Hemiptera-Heteroptera* (London: Witherby, 1923). Henceforth his depth of knowledge on corixids and other groups of water bugs served him well, both in his limnological research and in his more theoretical ecological studies.

Early Postgraduate Research. Although Hutchinson received a "first," the highest grade, in Parts I and II of the Zoology Tripos (final exams), he chose not to stay on for further graduate work at Cambridge University, but to accept a Rockefeller Higher Education Fellowship to do research at the Stazione Zoologica in Naples. His studies of the endocrine system of the octopus were largely unsuccessful, but Italian culture became an important part of his life; he returned later to do important research on Italian lakes—and even to give limnological lectures in Italian.

Hutchinson began his first professional teaching and research position in 1926, at the University of the Witwatersrand in Johannesburg, South Africa. While there he married his fellow Cambridge zoology student, Grace E. Pickford, who became a well-known fish endocrinologist and Yale professor. Together they carried out, and later published, extensive limnological research on the pans or dry lakes of South Africa. This was not only seminal work, including both physical and biological parameters, but also involved ecological questions. As a result of this work, Hutchinson discovered his new research field: limnology, the study of lakes and other freshwater systems. Lancelot Hogben, then professor of zoology at the University of Cape Town, who sponsored their limnology research, informed Hutchinson of a fellowship open at Yale University. He applied late, by cable. The fellowships were all taken, but he received a newly vacated instructorship instead. This unlikely event proved to be the beginning of his long and extremely productive career at Yale.

Beginnings at Yale. Evelyn Hutchinson and Pickford arrived at Yale in 1928. He taught many undergraduate courses, including embryology. This was the field of Yale's most eminent scientist, Ross Granville Harrison, who became Hutchinson's supporter in these early years and to whose encouragement he credited his eventually highly successful research career. Ordinarily a young professor in the United States would try to make his research name in one particular field. Hutchinson never did this. His publications in the first five years after arriving at Yale were in a bewildering variety of fields: the taxonomy of water bugs (Neonectidae and Corixidae); the branchial gland of the octopus; the limnology of South African pans (with Pickford); evidence from cores of climatic change in high altitude lakes in (Indian) Tibet (with Hellmut de Terra); South African Onychophora (a phylum-linking invertebrate group that fascinated him); and the relation between oxygen deficit and productivity of lakes. He also did a major project on arid lakes in Nevada while waiting for his divorce from Pickford in 1933. Hutchinson always credited department head Harrison for encouraging him in his various research endeavors instead of insisting on one area of research. Importantly, Harrison supported him when the question of his tenure at Yale arose. Not all of his colleagues were equally impressed by his early research in so many areas.

Later Hutchinson did the same with his own graduate students' choice of research projects; there were many paths to follow in Hutchinsonian ecology. His graduate students worked on a great number of organisms, as distinct from Harrison's Research School, which did so much definitive work on salamander development. In the fifties alone, Willard Hartman's dissertation was on sponges, Larry Slobodkin's on *Daphnia,* Thomas Goreau's on coral, Peter Klopfer's on Anatidae (ducks and geese), Alan Kohn worked on Hawaiian cone shells, and Robert MacArthur on birds, the wood warblers of Maine. Some graduate students did research on biogeochemistry or on more theoretical aspects of ecology.

Hutchinson's graduate students, right from the start, worked on many different problems. They used a variety of techniques, some invented by the graduate students themselves. Although Hutchinson certainly discussed and influenced their research, he rarely put his names on their papers, not even the famous seminal paper in systems ecology by his postdoctoral student Ray Lindeman. He was never the "Herr professor"; most of his graduate students called him Hutch or Evelyn. The graduate students who arrived in the 1930s, Gordon A. Riley, Edward S. Deevey, W. T. Edmondson, and Maxwell J. Dunbar, worked on diverse research problems; all had outstanding scientific careers. Riley and Deevey were both Yale professors before moving to other universities and starting their own research groups. The next generation, those of the 1940s, also included two future Yale professors, John L. Brooks and Willard Hartman, as well as other very well-known ecologists including Fred Smith, Slobodkin, and Klopfer.

Thus, in spite of the great number of Hutchinson graduate students over four decades, Hutchinson's was a research group rather than a classic Research School like Harrison's in embryology at Yale. Hutchinson and his research students were connected by a research philosophy, not by particular tools, organisms, one set of problems, or only one aspect of ecology.

The Yale North India Expedition. In 1932 an opportunity arose for Hutchinson to go on the Yale North India Expedition, which traveled to Kashmir and to present-day Ladakh in the Himalayas. German geologist Hellmut de Terra led the expedition; Hutchinson was the head biologist. He collected all kinds of insects, aquatic life, animals, plants, and fossils and recruited specialists from all over the world to identify those specimens not belonging to his own special groups. A Yale undergraduate student, W. T. (Tommy) Edmondson, who already knew rotifers, worked and published with Hutchinson on the North Indian collections of that group. He later became a Hutchinson graduate student and an influential limnologist. Hutchinson also arranged for the publication of all this taxonomic data.

Hutchinson's own interests on this expedition, however, were largely ecological. For example, how could all the lake biota live at the very high elevations of Ladakh? He studied lakes at more than 5,000 meters. He took physical and chemical measurements, conducted experiments, and made much of the needed equipment himself en route, all of which he described in many letters to Pickford. He wrote to her that he was "pushing on with experimental ecology … because that is where the results will come from that are really exciting now." His research provided new insights into biogeography and paleolimnology, as well as much new data on high elevation ecology. A crustacean, for example, was often the top predator; many of these lakes did not support fish. Long before he published his famous ecological niche model, Hutchinson was searching for niche dimensions important in the lives of these lake organisms. For example, did ultraviolet light levels correlate with the lake levels at which different planktonic crustaceans were found? He was continually testing such hypotheses.

The Yale North India Expedition proved to be a milestone in Hutchinson's life in a different respect as well: it was the beginning of his literary career. He wrote a book about his experiences, *The Clear Mirror* (1936). It got excellent reviews. The back cover of a later edition reads, "In 1932 a young biologist … recorded his observations with the eye of a trained scientist and the style and sensitivity of a novelist." The book contains strikingly beautiful descriptions of the colors of the landscape, the lakes and their inhabitants.

Limnology and Hutchinson's First Graduate Students. Not yet thirty, Hutchinson had already conducted research on four continents: Europe, Africa, Asia, and North America. Back in the United States he worked on a lake close to Yale, Linsley Pond, as did several of his first graduate students, Deevey, Edmondson, and Riley. All of them eventually started long-lasting research groups of their own. Edmondson arrived first, but Riley was Hutchinson's first official graduate student. Riley came to Yale in 1935 to work with Ross Harrison, but found Harrison's group of graduate students too large and new problems too scarce. By that time Hutchinson was teaching a graduate course in limnology. Riley wrote, "One lecture was enough to make me sit up straight and bright-eyed and to struggle to assimilate every word of his thick British accent. He was dynamic and obviously very bright. … Within a week I knew where I wanted to be. Unsolved problems stuck out all over the place" (1984).

Hutchinson was heavily involved in the biogeochemistry of lakes at that time, studying nitrogen, phosphorus, carbon, and other cycles. Riley's research problem involved copper cycling in Linsley Pond and other Connecticut lakes. In those early years Hutchinson was in the field with his students, working on the lake and in the laboratory. As Riley described it, the two of them took to the lake as soon as it was ice-free in the same inflatable rubber boat Hutchinson had used in Ladakh. It leaked and they both got cold and wet. The best part, Riley remembered, was the talk: "a rare opportunity to further my education … with a man whom I have always regarded as having the keenest and best informed mind of any scientist I have known" (1984).

Riley's research later turned from limnology to biological oceanography. He did research in that field as a faculty member at Yale and later headed a large department at Dalhousie University in Halifax, Nova Scotia. Riley made a trenchant comment in his memoir about Hutchinson's philosophy of doing ecology that permeated all of his own plankton work: "He maintained that populations needed to be studied in terms of dynamic processes—rates of production and consumption and ways these are affected by ecological factors" (1984).

Deevey also participated in this lake research and scientific discussions with Hutchinson. He, however, was initiating a new field of ecology in the United States, paleoecology, including the history of human impacts on lake environments. He was taking cores from Linsley Pond to study the fossil pollen and macrofossils that had been deposited there over a long period. He left the Botany Department and went to zoology to work with Hutchinson, who encouraged Deevey's attempt to integrate botany, zoology, paleoanthropology, and paleolimnology. Such a comprehensive study had never been done before. When Carbon 14 dating became available just after World War II, this provided an independent method for determining the chronology of such lake cores. Paleoecology became Deevey's major research field. He and Hutchinson worked together on a core Hutchinson had

Hutchinson

collected on the North India expedition. Hutchinson and his later research associates, particularly Ursula M. Cowgill, continued to work in this field in other parts of the world as well.

Edmondson was the third of the early graduate students. He had a desk in Hutchinson's laboratory as an undergraduate and became an expert on rotifers, microscopic but complex aquatic invertebrates with interesting behavior and life cycles. As a graduate student Edmondson studied growth rates and population biology of lake rotifers, making several important discoveries. He was the first Hutchinson student to bring limnology to a West Coast university. Edmondson and a large group of graduate students at the University of Washington were responsible for the ecological studies of Lake Washington that made possible the reversal of pollution in that large Seattle lake.

Dunbar also came to work with Hutchinson in the 1930s, on a fellowship from Oxford University. Later he completed a PhD at McGill University in Montreal, working in the Canadian Arctic but keeping in touch with Hutchinson about his plankton studies. He had a distinguished career in arctic research. Dunbar related, in an interview with this author, that once when Hutchinson was visiting Oxford, he and Charles Elton were seen "plotting together on the Broad … two people responsible for most of ecology." Elton's 1927 book on animal ecology had greatly influenced Hutchinson, but this was the first time they had actually met.

Hutchinson wrote many more papers concerning lake biota. He is known as the source of modern ecological ideas in American limnology and as the synthesizer of his own work and that of many others in this field. His four-volume *Treatise on Limnology* is the bible of this field in English. The first volume, published in 1957, covered the geography, physics, and chemistry of lakes; the following volumes included plankton and other lake biota, including plants (Volume III). The fourth volume was published posthumously, but Hutchinson had finished the text. The *Treatise* is also a superb guide to the worldwide literature in limnology, which has become part of the broader field of ecology. Hutchinson never really left limnology. Many of Hutchinson's later theoretical papers concern the population and community ecology of lake biota. The American Society of Limnology and Oceanography gives out the G. Evelyn Hutchinson Award every year.

Research in Biogeochemistry. The field of biogeochemistry is one that Hutchinson was instrumental in bringing to the United States. He was very much impressed by the scientific work of the Russian scientist V. I. Vernadsky. Hutchinson had his work translated to make his ideas about the biosphere and about the chemistry of organisms available in English. Hutchinson and his graduate students in the 1940s and 1950s did a great deal of work in this field. Probably the best known of them is Howard T. Odum, who studied the biogeochemistry of strontium. He went on to become an important innovator in the new field of systems ecology. Hutchinson himself wrote papers about the biogeochemistry of phosphorus, nitrogen, carbon, aluminum, and thiamine. He was probably the first to discuss carbon dioxide in the atmosphere; he wrote a major paper on the biochemistry of the terrestrial atmosphere. His study of aluminum in many species of *Lycopodium* (club mosses) was his only major research on higher plants.

Two well-known Hutchinson papers were published in 1948: "On Living in the Biosphere," a general approach to the significance of nutrient cycles on this planet, and "Circular Causal Systems in Ecology." The latter was closely related to cybernetics, a major subject of the Macy Conferences in New York in the 1940s. Hutchinson was a participant in these conferences, together with Margaret Mead, Gregory Bateson, Norbert Wiener and other notable social and biological scientists from a variety of fields.

Hutchinson was in charge of the Survey of Contemporary Knowledge of Biogeochemistry. As part of that survey he published a 550-page article titled "The Biogeochemistry of Vertebrate Excretion" (1950), largely about guano and guano islands and also bat caves in many parts of the world. It is quite a Darwinian book in terms of data and letters collected from sea captains and guano workers and from obscure published sources. He reworked the data in many cases and added his own ideas. It is a fascinating book, quite different from his other works.

By 1948 Hutchinson was well known in both limnology and ecology, but probably best known for his research in biogeochemistry. At this time he was offered a high position by the U.S. Geological Survey to do research on biogeochemistry or whatever he wished. He was tempted by this offer, but it did not include graduate students. He turned it down because he felt that his graduate teaching had succeeded in turning out outstanding young ecologists who were rapidly becoming leaders in their fields. He wanted to stay at Yale to continue his teaching; seven of his graduate students had already completed PhDs by that time. Thirteen more, in addition to postdoctoral students, arrived in the 1950s, and an additional eighteen completed their PhDs in the 1960s and early 1970s. The later years included women graduate students, several of whom, including Karen Glaus Porter, Maxine Watson, Donna Haraway, and Alison Jolly, went on to important academic and research careers. Hutchinson turned down at least six other academic positions as well, and remained at Yale until he was eighty-eight.

The Beginnings of Systems and Radiation Ecology. In the 1940s, work by Hutchinson and his students was responsible for the initiation of two new fields in ecology, systems ecology and radiation ecology. In 1942 his postdoctoral student Raymond Lindeman had written "The Trophic Dynamic Aspect of Ecology," the acknowledged seminal paper in the field that became ecosystem or systems ecology. Hutchinson contributed ideas and quantitative methods to Lindeman's paper. He was also instrumental in getting it published in *Ecology* after it was originally turned down as too theoretical by two reviewers, both established leaders in the field of limnology at that time. The paper was published, with an addendum by Hutchinson, after Lindeman's death in early 1942. Systems ecology became a major area of research, particularly in the 1950s and 1960s. It included the International Biological Program, which studied productivity and related ecological topics in many different ecosystems.

The first experiments on the use of radioactive isotopes in ecological research were published in 1947 by Hutchinson and his graduate student, Vaughan T. Bowen: "A Direct Demonstration of the Phosphorous Cycle in a Small Lake."

Radiation ecology also became a major research area involving diverse ecosystems, many workers, and Atomic Energy Commission funding. His former graduate student Odum did important large research projects in this field, but Hutchinson himself, who preferred smaller projects and other types of funding, moved on.

G. Evelyn Hutchinson. © BETTMANN/CORBIS.

Experimental and Mathematical Ecology; Population Growth. What about experimental and theoretical ecology, the field in which Hutchinson was most influential? Recall his comment to Pickford about the importance of ecological experiments during the 1932 Yale North India Expedition. Hutchinson was already working in this field, however, even before that expedition. He published a 1932 paper titled "Experimental Studies in Ecology: I. The Magnesium Tolerance of Daphnidae and its Ecological Significance." Most of Hutchinson's early papers were published in European hydrobiology journals. There was little work of this kind being carried out in the United States at the time.

Hutchinson had been reasonably well trained in mathematics and was long an advocate for its use in ecology. He made this clear in a 1940 review he had written of *Bio-ecology,* a book in which the plant ecologist Frederic Clements and the animal ecologist Victor Shelford had tried to synthesize the field. Hutchinson was critical of this attempt, particularly because mathematical methods of analysis of ecological processes were completely omitted. Clements and Shelford expressed grave doubts that mathematical and statistical methods could be applied to the complex processes studied in ecology.

Mathematics became important in Hutchinson's own research group, in terms of population growth. Lawrence B. (Larry) Slobodkin (PhD 1951) did innovative experiments and studied population dynamics of the water flea, the microscopic cladoceran crustacean *Daphnia.* F. E. (Fred) Smith (PhD 1950), who studied benthos populations, also did experiments on *Daphnia* and later worked out equations for its population growth in relation to population density.

Hutchinson and his students had predecessors, particularly George F. Gause and Raymond Pearl, on the study of population growth (and decline). Gause had produced a population (logistic) growth curve for *Paramecium* and Pearl had studied population growth in *Drosophila,* both in the 1930s. Pearl also worked on human population growth curves. Hutchinson, always interested in the history of his sciences, thoroughly reviewed the earlier work in *An Introduction to Population*

Ecology (1978.) He wrote here about the logistic curve of population growth:

> The important thing about any simple and easily understood formulation such as the logistic is that it can provide a stepping stone to a number of other, less simple, less general, but more accurate theories. This is in fact one of the significant uses of general theories in science. (p. 31)

By the 1950s mathematics had become an essential part of experimental ecology in Hutchinson's group. Hutchinson himself introduced the concept of the time lag, a complication to the logistic equation. For example, the process of reproduction may not be instantaneous, as in *Daphnia* when the parthenogenic female liberates newly hatched babies from her brood pouch. Hutchinson credited the original equation including a time lag in population growth to economists, but he brought it into ecology in his 1948 Macy Conference paper, "Circular Causal Systems in Ecology."

Competition was becoming a central concern of ecologists. Garrett Hardin published his competitive exclusion principle in 1960, but it too had its predecessors. Many experiments had been done in the laboratory using two closely related species of flour beetle, *Paramecium,* and other organisms, showing that, depending on the set-up of the experiment, one species would outcompete the other. The type of food or some sort of refuge might be a deciding factor in such experiments. In Hardin's dictum, complete competitors cannot coexist (in laboratory experiments or in nature).

The mathematical biologist to whom competition equations are usually attributed is Vito Volterra; his work goes back to 1926. Gause carried out laboratory experiments on competing organisms using Volterra's work as a mathematical basis. Alfred J. Lotka was also involved in the early 1920s in the development of competition equations. They are often referred to as the Lotka-Volterra equations, although the two worked independently.

American ecologists paid little attention to this early work, perhaps because the more complete account of Gause's experiments was published in French. It was only the 1940s and thereafter that competition in mathematical terms was again taken up, in large part due to Hutchinson's amazing knowledge of the literature of ecology and limnology. He himself read French, German, and Italian, and found others to translate the important Russian work.

Much of this early work was done in the laboratory, using protozoans—particularly related *Paramecium* species—and species of flour beetles, *Tribolium.* All of these reproduce rapidly in the laboratory, and the environmental conditions of these small organisms were easy to regulate. The outcome of competition varied with these external conditions, and could be measured mathematically. Hutchinson was well aware of these studies; he, however, was most interested in competition and competitive exclusion—or coexistence—not in the laboratory but in the field.

Population Ecology in Nature. Slobodkin brought Robert MacArthur, whose previous training was in mathematics, into Hutchinson's group of graduate students. When MacArthur and, later, another graduate student, Egbert Leigh, came to work with Hutchinson, he had first-rate mathematicians in his research group. Hutchinson and MacArthur published two joint papers about competition in birds and other animals in 1959.

MacArthur's dissertation research (PhD 1958), known to every first-year ecology student, concerned the population ecology of the brightly colored warbler species that breed in the coniferous forests of northern New England. MacArthur took many hours of data on the feeding habits of five closely related warblers of the genus *Dendroica* in the spruce trees of Maine. Thousands of birdwatchers follow these species' migrations every spring, but no one had conducted a quantitative study of their feeding or breeding habits.

The question MacArthur asked was a very Hutchinsonian one: how can so many closely related species coexist without competitive exclusion? MacArthur's study answered this question. The warblers search for their food in different zones of the spruce trees; MacArthur was able to quantify the amount of time each species spent in each zone, as well as the overlap between different species. He also recorded the number of breeding pairs per 5 acres, and was able to write competition equations for four of these warbler species. The environment in which these warblers were feeding was sufficiently coarse-grained to allow for their continuing coexistence.

Many ecologists have since worked on similar problems in nature, working on a variety of organisms, aquatic and terrestrial, animals and plants. Among Hutchinson students, Alan J. Kohn worked on the many species of the mollusk genus *Conus* in Hawaii, and in the 1970s, Maxine Watson worked on competition and niche diversification among the members of the moss family Polytrichaceae, the haircap mosses.

The Multidimensional Niche. In 1957 Hutchinson published his most influential paper, in which he introduced his own niche concept. Its title, "Concluding Remarks," came from his role in summing up a Cold Spring Harbor Symposium. Hutchinson later wrote pages of footnotes on the history of niche concepts in his population ecology book, but the quantitative aspects of niche study in ecology are not very old. Hutchinson presented a timely new niche concept that enabled many ecologists to evaluate niche relationships quantitatively.

Hutchinson called it the "*n*-dimensional niche" but pointed out that it would probably not be possible to quantify all the *n* dimensions of any particular species' niche, in other words all the tolerances and needs of a particular species. Two or three niche factors, whether biotic or abiotic, may be enough to separate the niches of two interacting species. He gave a hypothetical example of temperature, food size, and branch density delimiting a three-dimensional niche of one species of squirrel; such a niche can be diagramed in terms of measured variables. Hutchinson made a very useful distinction between a species' fundamental niche in the absence of competition, and its realized (postinteractive) niche in the presence of a competitor, in this case a second species of squirrel. Competitive exclusion could occur where the fundamental niches of two species overlapped, or the overlap area could be divided, producing separate realized niches for each species. These differences can be measured and expressed in terms of competition coefficients; species that have contiguous niches will show high values of these coefficients; for those whose *n*-dimensional niches hardly overlap, the value will approach 0. Niche breadth and niche overlap can also be mathematically determined.

Rachel Carson brought the term *ecology* to the attention of the American public. But it was Hutchinson's view of ecological niches that could be quantified, and his concept of niche diversification in a great variety of organisms and ecosystems, that spawned so much PhD research, so many ecological papers, new mathematical and statistical methods, and eventually experimental manipulations in organisms from birds to wood rats to protozoa to pond weeds and mosses. MacArthur, Richard Levins, and many other ecologists have written theoretical papers and books using Hutchinson's and later related niche concepts.

As is the case with much theoretical ecology, Hutchinson's niche concept and particularly the importance of competition as a major factor in structuring ecological communities, have been subject to criticism and rival theories, but ecological research using these concepts continues.

Biodiversity and Biogeography. For Hutchinson, a related major puzzle was the whole question of animal diversity. "Homage to Santa Rosalia" (1959), another of his very influential papers, explored this question and spurred the interest in and funding for biodiversity studies. Both the understanding and the preservation of biodiversity of organisms on this planet were a longtime concern of Hutchinson, and also, notably, of Edward O. Wilson. Both have paid attention to the remarkable, and still largely unknown, diversity of insects, particularly in the tropics. As Hutchinson concluded, the great diversification of animals, including insects, is highly dependent on the great variety of plants and their interactions with the animal world.

Hutchinson considered MacArthur his most brilliant student and was devastated at his early death at age forty-two. He was MacArthur's mentor while he was a student as well as his codeveloper of ecological theory. MacArthur went beyond Hutchinson in the development of mathematical theory, in both population ecology and in biogeography, a field that Hutchinson had contributed to since his North India studies in 1932. Wilson and Hutchinson in their *Biographical Memoir* about MacArthur for the National Academy of Sciences wrote that as a "mathematician naturalist," he had eventually formed many of the "parameters of ecology, biogeography and genetics into a common framework of fundamental theory." The ideas and research of the 1950s and 1960s changed ecology from a descriptive science to a "structured predictive science that combined powerful quantitative theories with the recognition of widespread patterns in nature."

Hutchinson and his earlier students, including Lindeman, Slobodkin, and Odum, initiated this change in large part. According to Martin Cody and Jared Diamond, the "revolution in ecology" was carried further by MacArthur's work in the 1960s. Hutchinson's 1975 paper in the book by these two authors is titled "Variations on a Theme by Robert MacArthur," whom he quoted as writing

> Scientists are perennially aware that it is best not to trust theory until it is confirmed by evidence. It is equally true, as Arthur S. Eddington [and also Hutchinson] pointed out, that it is best not to put much stock in facts until they have been confirmed by theory. (p. 492)

MacArthur had written that both the ecological theories and the facts had serious inadequacies, which provided stumbling blocks to progress in ecology. Hutchinson illustrated these problems in his paper. In the area of competitive exclusion, he concluded, facts and theories had worked out well, but in the study of population cycles, that had not yet happened. The theoretical ecologist might consider "all possible models," but it was the field or experimental ecologist's responsibility to find out which of these models were realized in nature. In order for this to happen in the future, Hutchinson wrote that ecologists must be trained to have "a deep understanding of organisms" (1975, p. 515). Hutchinson's classic remark about his mathematical theorist student follows: "MacArthur really knew his warblers." At the beginning of the twenty-first century, experimental field ecologists are busy testing ecological theory with real data.

Writings and Prizes. In 1943 Hutchinson began a series of "Marginalia," essays and reviews on a great many scientific subjects, constituting a special column in the *American Scientist* from that date until 1957. It was revived in the 1970s and thereafter. Many of these columns were reprinted elsewhere. Several books, *The Itinerant Ivory Tower* (1953), *The Enchanted Voyage, and Other Studies* (1962), and *The Ecological Theater and the Evolutionary Play* (1965), consisted of Marginalia as well as some new essays. Through the original articles in a journal intended for scientists in many fields, and through his books, Hutchinson became well known as an excellent science writer, and to some extent even as a literary figure. He was very much interested in literature, as was his second wife, Margaret Seal Hutchinson. The writer Rebecca West was a close friend of Hutchinson's. They first met as a result of her reading one of his Marginalia articles. They exchanged hundreds of letters (now at the Beinecke Library at Yale and at the University of Tulsa). When West died in 1983, Hutchinson became her literary executer. Margaret Mead was also a good friend; he helped to edit one of her later books.

Hutchinson received all the honors and prizes available to him, throughout the many decades of his career; there is no Nobel Prize in Ecology. These included many honorary doctorates, including one from Cambridge University in his old age. He could almost certainly have sent his published papers to Cambridge and received an earned doctorate. Early in his career he was afraid of being turned down, as one of his fellow students had been; later, already famous in at least two fields of ecology, he was rather proud not to have one. He enjoyed the pomp of his 1981 Cambridge honorary degree, however, parading in the company of molecular biologist Max Perutz and other notable honorees.

Hutchinson received the Benjamin Franklin Medal in 1979 for "developing the scientific basis of ecology." He was both proud and humbled to be in the company of previous winners who included Thomas Edison, Max Planck, and Albert Einstein. He was a member of the National Academy of Sciences (NAS) and a foreign member of the Royal Society. He put both memberships to good use when, as a NAS spokesman, he flew to London to talk to the Royal Society in the successful battle to preserve the remarkable biodiversity of the island of Aldabra.

Hutchinson had a serious though usually quiet role as an environmentalist, primarily through his research, throughout his career. He wrote in the *American Scientist* in 1943 as reprinted in his 1953 book:

> The writer believes that the most practical lasting benefit science can now offer is to teach man how to avoid destruction of his own environment, and how … to find ways to avoid injuries that at present he inflicts on himself with such devastating energy. (p. 270)

His contribution to public awareness of these issues resulted in the NAS Cottrell Award for Environment. When he won the Daniel Giraud Elliot Medal in 1984, the citation read: "Hutchinson was admired as limnologist, biochemist, ecologist, evolutionist, art historian and ranks among our zoological giants."

Hutchinson is perhaps the only scientist to have been awarded the U.S. National Medal of Science twice. Hutchinson turned it down for political reasons when it was offered during the Nixon administration. It was offered again in 1991 after Hutchinson's death. His nephew, Francis Hutchinson, came to Washington, D.C., from London to accept the award. Hutchinson's final award during his lifetime was the 1986 Kyoto Prize in Basic Science, sometimes called the Japanese Nobel Prize. He was over eighty at that time. His third wife, Anne Twitty Goldsby Hutchinson, whom he married after Margaret's death, accompanied him to Japan.

Renowned as the major inventor of modern ecology in the United States, and for his research in and synthesis of limnology, Hutchinson himself always cited his role in the education of graduate students as equally important. He officially retired from Yale in 1971 but still had graduate students thereafter, and he continued his work there until 1990. The 1971 intellectual family tree of his students and their students to three and even four generations created by Yvette Edmondson includes a great many of the best-known American ecologists. By the time of Hutchinson's death there were six generations.

Hutchinson moved back to England after his wife Anne's death in 1990 and died in London in 1991. Yale held a 100th birthday celebration of his life and work in 2003.

BIBLIOGRAPHY

WORKS BY HUTCHINSON

With Grace E. Pickford and J. F. M. Schuurman. "The Inland Waters of South Africa." *Nature* 123 (1929): 832–834.

Letters from the Yale North India Expedition (1932). G. E. Hutchinson archives, Yale University Library. Written to Grace E. Pickford.

"Experimental Studies in Ecology: I. The Magnesium Tolerance of Daphnidae and its Ecological Significance." *Internationale Revue der gesamten Hydrobiologie und Hydrographie* 28, no. 11–12 (1932): 90–108.

The Clear Mirror: A Pattern of Life in Goa and in Indian Tibet. Cambridge, U.K.: Cambridge University Press, 1936.

Hutchinson

Review of F. E. Clements and V. E. Shelford's *Bio-ecology. Ecology* 21, no. 2 (1940): 267–268.

"Limnological Studies in Connecticut: IV. Mechanisms of Intermediary Metabolism in Stratified Lakes." *Ecological Monographs* 11, no. 1 (1941): 21–60.

"The Biogeochemistry of Aluminum and Certain Related Elements." *Quarterly Review of Biology* 18 (1943): 1–29.

With Vaughan T. Bowen. "A Direct Demonstration of the Phosphorous Cycle in a Small Lake." *Proceedings of the National Academy of Sciences of the United States of America* 33, no. 5 (1947): 148–153.

"Circular Causal Systems in Ecology." *Annals of the New York Academy of Science* 50 (1948): 221–246.

"On Living in the Biosphere." *The Scientific Monthly* 67, no. 6 (1948): 393–397.

"Survey of Existing Knowledge of Biogeochemistry: 3. The Biogeochemistry of Vertebrate Excretion." *Bulletin of the American Museum Natural History* 96 (1950): 1–554.

"Copepodology for the Ornithologist." *Ecology* 32 (1951): 571–577.

The Itinerant Ivory Tower: Scientific and Literary Essays. New Haven, CT: Yale University Press, 1953. Reprints from "Marginalia," *American Scientist,* and one unpublished article.

"Concluding Remarks." *Cold Spring Harbor Symposium Quantitative Biology* 22 (1957): 415–427.

A Treatise on Limnology. Vol. 1, *Geography, Physics, and Chemistry.* New York: Wiley, 1957.

"Homage to Santa Rosalia, or Why Are There So Many Kinds of Animals?" *American Naturalist* 93, no. 870 (1959): 145–159.

With Robert H. MacArthur. "A Theoretical Ecological Model of Size Distributions among Species of Animals." *American Naturalist* 93, no. 869 (1959): 117–125.

"The Paradox of the Plankton." *American Naturalist* 95 (1961): 137–147.

The Enchanted Voyage, and Other Studies. New Haven, CT: Yale University Press, 1962. Reprinted articles and three unpublished essays.

With Ursula M. Cowgill. "Chemical Examination of a Core from Lake Zeribar, Iran." *Science* 140, no. 5 (1963): 67–69. Hutchinson and Cowgill published on lake cores from all over the world. This is an early example.

"The Lacustrine Microcosm Reconsidered." *American Scientist* 52 (1964): 334–341.

The Ecological Theater and the Evolutionary Play. New Haven, CT: Yale University Press, 1965.

"To Save [Lake] Baikal." *New York Times,* 23 June 1966. One of many such letters to the editor about environmental issues.

A Treatise on Limnology. Vol. 2, *Introduction to Lake Biology and the Limnoplankton.* New York: Wiley, 1967.

"When Are Species Necessary?" In *Population Biology and Evolution,* edited by Richard Lewontin. Syracuse, NY: Syracuse University Press, 1968.

"The Biosphere." *Scientific American* 223, no. 3 (1970): 45–53. A good introduction for students and general readers.

"G. Evelyn Hutchinson Celebratory Issue." Edited by Yvette H. Edmondson. *Limnology and Oceanography* 16, no. 2 (1971). Includes a complete Hutchinson bibliography from 1918 to 1971.

A Treatise on Limnology. Vol. 3, *Limnological Botany.* New York: Wiley, 1973.

"Variations on a Theme by Robert MacArthur." In *Ecology and Evolution of Communities,* edited by Martin T. Cody and Jared M. Diamond. Cambridge, MA: Belknap Press, Harvard University, 1975.

An Introduction to Population Ecology. New Haven, CT: Yale University Press, 1978. A very useful book for both biologists and historians.

The Kindly Fruits of the Earth: Recollections of an Embryo Ecologist. New Haven, CT: Yale University Press, 1979. A partial autobiography through the early days at Yale.

"Marginalia: What Is Science For?" *American Scientist* 71, no. 6 (1983): 639–644.

"Keep Walking." *Physiological Ecology Japan* 24 (Special number, 1987): s81–s87. Lecture of the 1986 Kyoto Prize in Basic Science.

With Edward O. Wilson. "Robert Helmer MacArthur." *Biographical Memoirs* 58 (1989): 318–327.

A Treatise on Limnology. Vol. 4, *The Zoobenthos,* edited by Yvette H. Edmondson. New York: Wiley, 1993.

OTHER SOURCES

Hagen, Joel B. *An Entangled Bank: The Origins of Ecosystem Ecology.* New Brunswick, NJ: Rutgers University Press, 1992.

Kingsland, Sharon. *Modeling Nature: Episodes in the History of Population Ecology.* Chicago: Chicago University Press, 1985.

Levin, Simon A. *Fragile Dominion: Complexity and the Commons.* Reading, MA: Perseus Books, 1999.

MacIntosh, Robert P. *The Background of Ecology: Concept and Theory.* Cambridge, U.K.: Cambridge University Press, 1985. Hutchinson and his work appear in nearly every chapter of this book.

Mills, Eric L. *Biological Oceanography: An Early History, 1870–1960.* Ithaca, NY: Cornell University Press, 1989.

Riley, Gordon A. *Reminiscences of an Oceanographer.* 1984, 166 pages. Unpublished; in possession of author.

Slack, Nancy G. "Botanical and Ecological Couples: A Continuum of Relationships." In *Creative Couples in the Sciences,* edited by Helen M. Pycior, Nancy G. Slack, and Pnina G. Abir-Am. New Brunswick, NJ: Rutgers University Press, 1995.

———. *G. Evelyn Hutchinson and the Invention of Modern Ecology.* New Haven, CT: Yale University Press, forthcoming.

———. "G. Evelyn Hutchinson: From Cambridge, England School Boy to America's Foremost Ecologist." In *The Beauty of the World: The Writings of G. Evelyn Hutchinson,* edited by David Skelly. New Haven, CT: Yale University Press, forthcoming.

Slobodkin, Lawrence B., and Nancy G. Slack. "George Evelyn Hutchinson: 20th-Century Ecologist." *Endeavour* 23, no. 1 (1999): 24–30.

Nancy G. Slack

HUTTON, JAMES (*b.* Edinburgh, Scotland, United Kingdom 3 June 1726; *d.* Edinburgh, 26 March 1797), *geology, agriculture, physical sciences, philosophy.* For the original article on Hutton see *DSB*, vol. 6.

Since the publication of Eyles's article, several of Hutton's major works have been reissued, including his doctoral dissertation (Donovan and Prentiss, 1980), the *Abstract* (1785/1987) (which Eyles drew on extensively), his *Investigation of the Principles of Knowledge* (1794/1999), and some of Hutton's correspondence (Jones et al., 1994, 1995). A collection of colored drawings illustrating Hutton's geotheory has been located and published (Craig et al., 1978). These were due to John Clerk of Eldin, Jr., or his father John Clerk of Eldin, also an artist friend of Hutton, who accompanied him on some of his geological excursions. They include a section by John Clerk Jr. showing Hutton's idea of the likely structure of the large mass of granite in the Isle of Arran (Scotland), with a subterranean magma chamber and the strata adjacent to the granite upheaved by the igneous mass. Also, there are pictures of granitic veins penetrating the country rock at Glen Tilt, Perthshire, which supported Hutton's theory. Dean's republication of volume 3 of Hutton's *Theory of the Earth* (1899/1997) provides access to his accounts of his fieldwork in the latter part of his career.

The secondary literature has emphasized the cyclic aspects of Hutton's theory, his matter theory and its relationship to his geological theory, his economic interests, his agricultural interests and ideas on natural selection, his philosophical/methodological notions, and his religious views. Hutton has been the subject of an excellent intellectual biography (Dean, 1992). Drake (1981) has suggested that Hutton's geotheory was significantly influenced by Robert Hooke, without acknowledgement.

Cyclic Theory and Unconformities; Geological Time. Hutton's dissertation on the circulation of the blood (1749) contained the following passage:

> Being about to treat of blood and bodily fluids, I shall, as far as possible, ignore solid materials in order to avoid digressions from the main subject-matter, although there exists so close a connection between those related items … that it is not easy to determine which of them has prior existence, both advancing in step, one refashioning the other and one modifying the other; and thus they display the glorious cycle of life and a very beautiful instance of perpetual moving—an instance in which matter moves without a material cause, in which it seeks its own special aims on the fertile earth, and in which it reconstitutes its daily diminutions by means of the very cause of its destruction; and before yielding its life-producing movement to the fatal necessity of material machines, it produces new offshoots, which will complete its role in the microcosmic grove. (Donovan and Prentiss, 1980, p. 30)

This early work suggests that Hutton was already thinking (teleologically) about cyclic processes, both in humans and in terrestrial cycles that sustain the Earth's fertility. The hint of interest in agriculture and the machine analogy may also be remarked. Davies (1969) emphasized the importance of the steam engine (seen by Hutton when in Birmingham with James Watt in 1774, with all the movements generated by the action of a fire—almost as a perpetual motion machine!) as an analogical source for Hutton's geotheory.

A remarkable feature of Hutton's theory was that it was initially developed as a model or hypothesis, largely relying on the evidence of hand-specimens, and it was only after he had presented his ideas in 1785 that he embarked on a series of geological excursions specifically to find evidence that might support his theory. In particular, his journeys took him to the Isle of Arran near Glasgow (1787), where he saw the granite mountain, Goat Fell, with the surrounding sediments forming an eroded domed structure, and also a structural phenomenon at Lochranza that was later called an unconformity by Robert Jameson (one of Hutton's opponents in Edinburgh). But a clearer example of an unconformity was observed and figured by the River Jed near Jedburgh, in the Scottish Border country, on Hutton's return journey to Edinburgh. The river cutting showed horizontal layers of Old Red Sandstone, overlying vertical gritty sandstone—called "schistus" by Hutton (see Figure 1).

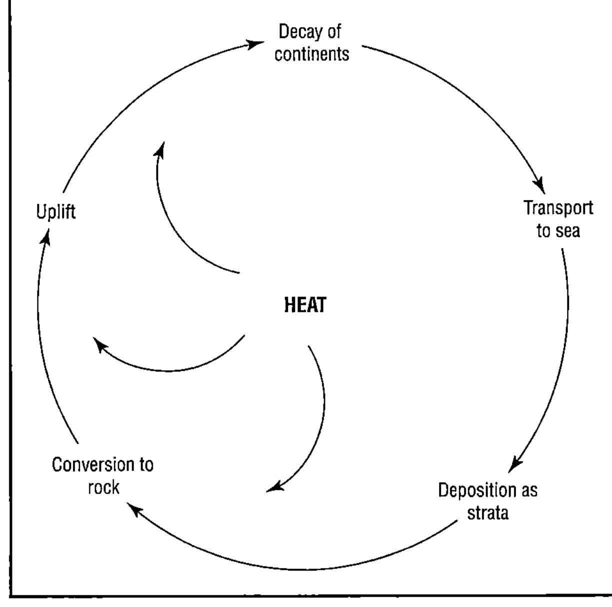

Figure 1. *James Hutton's first vision of the rock cycle.*

The events leading to the formation of such a structure could be construed according to Hutton's theory as follows: deposition of sediments in the ocean; their compaction and consolidation, aided by subterranean heat, to form "schistus"; elevation and folding of strata by expansive subterranean forces; erosion of the now almost vertical strata of "schistus" to an approximately level surface; subsidence followed by deposition and consolidation of the sandstone strata now called Old Red Sandstone. The upward and downward movements were not fully explained, but the production of the sediments would have occurred by the erosion and weathering of neighboring higher ground. The contact between the vertical schistus and the horizontal Old Red Sandstone was the plane of unconformity and represented a large time-gap and break in the sedimentation. Given the slow processes of weathering, erosion, etc., the rocks obviously represented a huge amount of time, in human terms. Hutton's overall theory may be summarized diagrammatically, as shown in Figure 2.

Later (1788) Hutton and two friends, John Playfair and Sir James Hall, sailed along the Berwickshire coast, looking for a contact similar to that at Jedburgh. Hutton knew that such rocks were in the vicinity, as his nearby upland farm was located on schistus while his lower farm was situated on Old Red Sandstone. The contact was found at a locality called Siccar Point, now famous in the annals of geology. Playfair (1805, p. 73) described his feelings on the occasion thus:

> Revolutions still more remote appeared in the distance of this extraordinary perspective. The mind seemed to grow giddy by looking so far into the abyss of time; and while we listened with earnestness and admiration to the philosopher … unfolding to us the order and series of these wonderful events, we became sensible how much farther reason may sometimes go than imagination can venture to follow.

Thus theory and observations yielded a reasoned argument for the Earth's antiquity. Evidence of two cycles of sedimentation could be seen directly. But there could or would have been untold earlier cycles. Time was needed for unconformities.

Chemical and Physical Aspects. But the source of terrestrial heat was mysterious. Hutton knew that plants required the Sun. Its light and warmth are called forms of radiant energy in the early twenty-first century. Hutton, however, talked about "solar substance." Thus solar energy was regarded as a weightless "substance," perhaps analogous to "caloric." This "solar substance" might take various forms: "sensible" (or "specific") heat, such as people feel when they touch a hot object; "latent" heat or the principle of fluidity, as discussed by Hutton's friend Joseph Black; phlogiston; or electricity. Gerstner (1968) has suggested how, in his post–Siccar Point work, Hutton tried in his *Dissertations on Different Subjects in Natural Philosophy* (1792) to account for episodes of subsidence and consolidation of strata, and then expansion.

Hutton accepted Newtonian theory, particles being mutually attracted according to the inverse square law. But there could also be expansive forces, as exhibited in steam engines. So he imagined that if particles were pushed very close together, repulsive forces (a form of "solar substance"), acting according to some higher law than the square law, could begin to prevail, causing melting, expansion, and elevation of strata. There could be heat without fire. So Hutton sought to explain cycles of compression/heating, and expansion/elevation. His matter theory also supposedly allowed for the intrusion of subterranean matter, either as liquid or vapor. It is historically interesting that he tried to develop a physical theory to support his geological theory; but it led nowhere.

Hutton and Agriculture. Hutton spent a considerable time studying modern farming practices, and successfully improved his two farms in Berwickshire. Jones (1985) has pointed out how his experiences as a farmer would have shown the constant erosion of land and transport of sediments to the sea. Decayed plants helped renew the soil. Thus Hutton's agricultural experience formed a background to his cyclic geotheory. Eyles mentioned that Hutton's unpublished *Principles of Agriculture* contained ideas that foreshadowed Darwinian natural selection. Pearson (2003) has pointed out that such ideas also occurred in chapter 3 of the little-read 2,138-page, three-volume *Investigation of the Principles of Knowledge.* The following quotation illustrates:

> if an organised body is not in the situation and circumstances best adapted to its sustenance and propagation, then, in conceiving an indefinite variety among the individuals of that species, >> those which depart most from the best adapted constitution, will be most liable to perish, while, … those organised bodies, which most approach to the best constitution for the present circumstances, will be best adapted to continue, in preserving themselves and multiplying … their race. (2:501)

Hutton went on to talk about artificial selection (of dogs), the influence of the environment; and to all intents and purposes he entertained speciation. His words might well have been written by Darwin (which raises the question of whether Darwin picked up such ideas when he was studying in Edinburgh). Of course, Hutton's geotheory would have allowed ample time for Darwinian evolution.

Hutton's Philosophy and Method in Science. It is well known that Immanuel Kant developed a form of philosophical idealism, whereby the mind is regarded as an active agent in the acquisition of knowledge. It necessarily sees things in (Euclidean) space and (Newtonian) time and constructs and filters sensory information in terms of certain categories of the understanding. He proposed such ideas in response to problems raised by David Hume's empiricism (e.g., the problem of induction).

It is striking that Hutton's *Principles of Knowledge* (1794) developed a response to Hume somewhat analogous to Kant's, though almost certainly independently of him. For Hutton, like Kant, space and time are mere conceptions of the mind. Hume had offered an implausible account of human understanding of causal connections: It depended on habit. For example, one sees a billiard ball move whenever struck by another one, and one comes to suppose that it will *always* happen thus. Human understanding of causes and effects is, for Hume, simply a probabilistic extrapolation from empirically known instances. But Hutton wrote, in a Kantian manner:

> [T]he knowledge of cause and effect, or the relation of things existing in succession, is discerned in the mind, where, without any form of an argument, a judgment is formed, or a new species of knowledge is produced, in an operation called reason. (1794, 2:188)

Observation per se does not discover cause. Ideas of necessary causal connection are the product of *reasoning.* Hutton, then, saw a radical difference between humans and "brutes" as regards wisdom. Insofar as an animal can reason, it does so without general principles. Also, only humans, not animals, can have moral principles inculcated.

Significantly, Hutton maintained that there had to be a first cause for everything, which he regarded as absolute, self-existing, efficient, and final. Knowledge of this was found by exercise of reason, not by the "superstitions" of religion. But while humans could recognize the existence of a first cause, they could not properly apprehend its nature:

> [I]n the contemplation of this world, so beautiful is the order and arrangement of things, so plain and simple are the means, so deep and complicated the design, so secret every cause, and so certain the effect, we must conclude that nothing but a wisdom without defect had been employed, and that such wisdom is infinite or incomprehensible to man. (1794, 3: 645)

So, for Hutton, the universe was, as he put it, ordained in perfect wisdom. He was a teleologist and a deist.

These ideas were formally expressed in Hutton's technical philosophy after his geological fieldwork ended, but they underpinned his geology, and probably derived in part from his agricultural experience. Erosion was continuous, spoiling the farmer's circumstances. But the world—supposedly designed in wisdom—had its soils naturally replenished. Hutton's geotheory explained how the design was maintained. This avoided what has been called the "denudation dilemma" (Davies, 1969, p. 160) or the "paradox of the soil" (Gould, 1987, p. 76). There was a wise adaptation of means to ends.

Although Hutton's philosophy had quasi-Kantian features, in fact, it stood essentially within the British empiricism tradition of John Locke, George Berkeley, and Hume. He was not saying (à la Kant) that notions of space and time are *intrinsic* faculties of the mind—necessary conditions for experience. They were, rather, abstracted from experience. But having acquired the notion of time experientially, the geologist could look into the past and try to understand it. With a cyclic geotheory, there was a nice interplay of contemporary experiences (e.g., soil erosion) and past changes on the Earth. So Hutton had a philosophical warrant for what was later known as actualism or methodological uniformitarianism ("the present is the key to the past," Geikie [1962, p. 299]).

There has, then, been discussion as to whether Hutton's geology was a priori and teleological or had an empirical base. Was he a hypothetico-deductivist or an inductivist/empiricist? Which came first: the philosophy or the observations? The former alternative has been advocated particularly by Gould (1987, p. 76), who stated that "Hutton present[ed] his theory as the *a priori* solution to a problem in causation, not as an induction from the field evidence." That is, philosophy and theory came first, and only then was the theory tested in the field. Dean (1992), however, has argued, against Gould, that there was a *development* of Hutton's ideas over time, so that he did not simply invent his theory a priori in his early years and then spend the rest of his time seeking to test it by observation. The two interpretations have been examined by Leveson (1996), who concluded that Hutton's inductivism was not without foundation but needed to be interpreted with caution. Hutton was, in fact, a hypothetico-deductivist. To which one might add that it did not matter pragmatically whether the theory came from Hutton's epistemology, his deism, the Aristotelian notion of final causes, or acceptance of the world as manifesting divine wisdom, or whatever. The theory did lead to certain observational expectations, and these were mostly fulfilled.

Hutton's Religious Views. Şengör (2001) has suggested that Hutton was an atheist, but that in the context of eighteenth-century Edinburgh he did not choose to reveal

Hutton

James Hutton. SPL/PHOTO RESEARCHERS, INC.

this. It is certainly accepted that Hutton lost any conventional Christian faith early, having encountered deism while a student via the mathematics lecturer Colin Maclaurin. It is hard to agree with Şengör's suggestion, however, given the *enormous* effort involved in writing the *Principles of Knowledge*, according to which humankind could derive delight from contemplating the universe "so beautifully calculated." And such limited wisdom as humans possess derives from a higher cause: "we do not exist independent of our author, who is the cause of us, and of the faculties in which we exist; and it is only in knowing this, that we know there is, in God, both intellect and truth" (1794, 3:198–199). Hutton evidently had a reasoned faith.

Founder of Modern Geology? Hutton has often been regarded as the "founder of modern geology" (e.g., Dean, 1992, p. 1). But in his examination of the origins of geology as a historical science, Martin Rudwick (2005) suggests that Hutton's work came at the end—perhaps the culmination—of the older tradition of theories of the Earth, or "geotheory," to use Rudwick's preferred term. Rudwick sees the emergence of geology as involving "bursting the limits of time" (which Hutton surely did) and the study of the Earth as an object with a *contingent* history, which could be unraveled chiefly with the help of biostratigraphy. Hutton's doctrine of unlimited repetitive cycles, lacking any direction, was not, for Rudwick, the stuff of the new geology at the turn of the nineteenth century, with Cuvier as the leading light. Certainly, Hutton was not a stratigrapher, and his cyclism gave less scope for historical contingencies than did Cuvier's unidirectional geohistory. But in his *Theory of the Earth* (1795, 1:363) he wrote:

> [N]ature, forming strata, is subject to vicissitudes; and … [there] is not always the same regular operation with respect to the materials, although always forming strata upon the same principles. Consequently, upon the same spot in the sea, different materials may be accumulated at different periods of time, and, conversely, the same or similar materials may be collected in different places at the same time.

This implies that things would not necessarily be the same from one geocycle to the next; therefore, even if one *defines* geology to be a historical science, requiring the examination of different contingent states of affairs through time, Hutton's geology would be compatible with that definition. And his cyclic theory, for all its problems, gave investigators a basic understanding of the Earth that has survived to the present—alongside biostratigraphy and much else besides. It seems reasonable to regard Hutton as at least *a* founder of modern geology, his eighteenth-century metaphysical basis notwithstanding.

SUPPLEMENTARY BIBLIOGRAPHY

WORKS BY HUTTON

James Hutton's Theory of the Earth: The Lost Drawings, edited by Gordon Y. Craig, Donald B. McIntyre, and Charles D. Waterston. Edinburgh: Scottish Academic Press, 1978.

James Hutton's Medical Dissertation, edited by Arthur Donovan and Joseph Prentiss. Transactions of the American Philosophical Society, vol. 70, part 6. Philadelphia: American Philosophical Society, 1980.

The 1785 Abstract of James Hutton's Theory of the Earth, introduction by G. Y. Craig. Edinburgh: Scottish Academic Press, 1987.

Dissertations on Different Subjects in Natural Philosophy. Edinburgh: A. Strahan and T. Cadell, 1792.

An Investigation of the Principles of Knowledge and of the Progress of Reason, from Sense to Science and Philosophy, with a new Introduction by Jean Jones and Peter Jones. 3 vols. Bristol: Thoemmes Press, 1999. Facsimile reprint of the 1794 edition of Strahan and Cadell.

Theory of the Earth: With Proofs and Illustrations. 3 vols. Edinburgh: Cadell, Davies, and Creech, 1795–1899.

James Hutton in the Field and in the Study: Being an Augmented Reprinting of Vol. III of Hutton's Theory of the Earth *(I, II, 1795), as First Published by Sir Archibald Geikie (1899); A Bicentenary Tribute to the Father of Modern Geology,* edited by Dennis R. Dean. Delmar, NY: Scholars' Facsimiles and Reprints, 1997.

OTHER SOURCES

Allchin, Douglas. "James Hutton and Phlogiston." *Annals of Science* 51 (1994): 615–635.

Davies, Gordon L. "The Huttonian Earth-Machine 1785–1802." In *The Earth in Decay: A History of British Geomorphology, 1578–1878,* by Gordon L. Davies. London: Macdonald Technical and Scientific, 1969.

Dean, Dennis R. *James Hutton and the History of Geology.* Ithaca, NY: Cornell University Press, 1992.

———. "Hutton Scholarship, 1992–1997." In *James Hutton—Present and Future,* edited by Gordon Y. Craig and John H. Hull. London: The Geological Society, 1999.

Drake, Ellen Tan. "The Hooke Imprint on the Huttonian Theory." *American Journal of Science* 281 (September 1981): 963–973.

Donovan, Arthur L. "James Hutton, Joseph Black, and the Chemical Theory of Heat." *Ambix* 25 (1978): 176–180.

Geikie, Sir Archibald. *The Founders of Geology.* 2nd edition. New York: Dover Publications, 1962 (reprint of Macmillan, 1905).

Gerstner, Patsy A. "James Hutton's Theory of the Earth and His Theory of Matter." *Isis* 59 (1968): 26–31.

Gould, Stephen J. *Time's Arrow, Time's Cycle.* Cambridge, MA: Harvard University Press, 1987.

Jones, Jean. "James Hutton's Agricultural Research and His Life as a Farmer." *Annals of Science* 42 (1985): 574–601.

———, Eric Robinson, and Hugh S. Torrens. "The Correspondence between James Hutton (1726–1797) and James Watt (1736–1819) with Two Letters from Hutton to George Clerk-Maxwell (1715–1784)." *Annals of Science* 51 (1994): 637–653; 52 (1995): 357–382.

Jones, Peter. "An Outline of the Philosophy of James Hutton (1726–97)." In *Philosophers of the Scottish Enlightenment,* edited by Vincent Hope. Edinburgh: Edinburgh University Press, 1984.

Leveson, David J. "What Was Hutton's Methodology?" *Archives of Natural History* 23 (1996): 61–77.

McIntyre, Donald B. "James Hutton's Edinburgh: The Historical, Social, and Political Background." *Earth Sciences History* 16 (1997): 100–157.

O'Rourke, Joseph. "A Comparison of James Hutton's *Principles of Knowledge* and *Theory of the Earth.*" *Isis* 69 (1978): 5–20.

Pearson, Paul N. "In Retrospect: *An Investigation of the Principles of Knowledge and the Progress of Reason, from Sense to Science and Philosophy* by James Hutton 1794." *Nature* 425 (2003): 665.

Playfair, John. "Biographical Account of the Late Dr James Hutton, F. R. S. Edin." *Transactions of the Royal Society of Edinburgh* 5, part 3 (1805): 39–99.

Rudwick, Martin J. S. *Bursting the Limits of Time: The Reconstruction of Geohistory in the Age of Revolution.* Chicago: University of Chicago Press, 2005.

Şengör, A. M. Celâl. *Is the Present the Key to the Past or Is the Past the Key to the Present? James Hutton and Adam Smith versus Abraham Gottlob Werner and Karl Marx in Interpreting History.* Geological Society of America Special Paper 355. Boulder, CO: Geological Society of America, 2001.

David Oldroyd

HUXLEY, JULIAN

HUXLEY, JULIAN (*b.* London, England, 22 June 1887; *d.* London, England, 14 February 1975), *embryology, ethology, evolution, eugenics, secular humanism, popularization of science.*

Huxley developed grand syntheses through scientific research and the popularization of scientific ideas. He is remembered for his contributions to ethology, evolutionary biology, and embryology. Huxley also promoted the use of scientific knowledge to improve the human condition. He advanced evolutionary humanism and actively participated in the eugenics movement. He pushed for the inclusion of science when the United Nations' Education and Cultural Organization was formed and served as the first director-general of the United Nations Educational, Scientific, and Cultural Organization (UNESCO) from 1946–1948.

Huxley was a scientist of many talents and prodigious intellectual output. His life consisted of a chain of intense periods—stints of brilliant laboratory and field research, episodes of self-doubt and clinical depression, intervals of writing ambitious synthetic works, and periods of public administration and global politicking. He was part of an elite intellectual family descending from his famous grandfathers, Thomas Henry Huxley (the biologist sometimes called "Darwin's Bulldog") and Thomas Arnold, headmaster of Rugby School. Huxley's family included his aunt, the novelist Mrs. Humphrey Ward (Mary Augusta Ward); his brother, the writer Aldous Huxley; and his half-brother, Andrew Huxley, who won the Nobel Prize for his research in physiology. While the focus of Julian Huxley's professional activities was never fixed for long, the motivation and interests underlying his work remained fairly constant. He sought to develop grand syntheses in biology, to create a religion of evolutionary humanism based on biology, and to bring these efforts to fruition through both popularization of science and liberal political action.

As a research biologist, Huxley covered an extraordinary range of topics, though in general his laboratory work was related to the development of individual organisms and his fieldwork concerned evolution—in particular the evolution of ritualized behavior exhibited by birds. In addition to dozens of specialized articles, Huxley wrote three major scientific books in which he attempted to synthesize broad ranges of biological findings concerning relative growth, embryology, and evolution. Although Huxley's work on evolutionary theory is typically cited as his greatest contribution to biology (he coined many terms of contemporary evolutionary biology including "cline" and gave the name to the evolutionary synthesis), the bulk of his original research was devoted to issues of individual development.

Early Years. During his childhood, which was spent mostly in the English countryside, Huxley showed a keen interest in observing nature, an interest that was encouraged by his family. In later years, he was especially proud of the letter in which his grandfather, T. H. Huxley, predicted of the precocious five-year-old: "There are some people who see a great deal and some who see very little in the same things. When you grow up I dare say you will be one of the great-deal seers and see things more wonderful than water babies where other folks can see nothing" (Huxley, 1970, pp. 24–25).

Huxley started his formal education at Hillside Preparatory School in 1897. Three years later, he entered Eton College, where his grandfather Huxley had formerly been governor. After finishing at Eton, Huxley went on to Balliol College, Oxford. In 1908 he won the Naples biological scholarship to conduct research at the Naples Stazione Zoologica (which his grandfather had helped rescue from financial difficulty thirty years before). He visited the research station after finishing his degree at Oxford and performed experiments on the development of sponges by separating them into their individual cells and observing the ways in which they reformed and developed. The results of his laboratory work were published, but when he returned to Oxford in 1910 as lecturer at Balliol College and demonstrator in the Department of Zoology and Comparative Anatomy, he directed much of his attention to natural history—and especially to ornithology. During his first vacation from Oxford, Huxley began a series of studies on the evolution of bird courtship rituals.

Bird Courtship. Huxley's most famous paper, "The Courtship Habits of the Great Crested Grebe" (1914), was written on the basis of observations he made on a two-week holiday from his duties at Oxford. Influenced by the work of Eliot Howard, an English amateur, Huxley argued that the courtship behavior must have evolved by natural selection, not by artificial (human-directed), as previously supposed. He observed that the courtship displays did not contribute to mate selection or stimulate coition. He concluded that the behavior, which occurs after birds pair, functions to preserve the couples by keeping the paired birds constantly together. As Richard W. Burkhardt Jr. notes, Huxley's paper, in addition to exploring relations between artificial and natural selection, emphasizes the emotional side of bird life.

Huxley left Oxford in 1913 to become assistant professor and founding head of the Department of Biology at Rice Institute in Houston, Texas. While traveling to Houston, he visited Thomas Hunt Morgan's famous fly room at Columbia, where he met Morgan's student, Hermann Joseph Muller. He quickly hired Muller to be his assistant at Rice Institute. (Muller later won a Nobel Prize for his work in genetics.) In Texas, Huxley conducted research with Muller on genetics, studied relative growth of the fiddler crab, and pursued his ornithological studies by observing an egret colony in Louisiana. He also designed and implemented an innovative biology curriculum, which emphasized laboratory and field instruction. At the outbreak of World War I, he returned home to join the war effort. When Huxley left Rice in 1916, he gave a series of public lectures entitled "Biology and Man," presenting his highly controversial views on science and religion, which he referred to as "scientific humanism" (and in later years as "evolutionary humanism").

Huxley first served the war effort in the censor's office, but was bored and soon enlisted in the Army Service Corps. During the war, he met Juliette Baillot, a French-Swiss woman ten years his junior, whom he married in the spring of 1919.

After the war Huxley returned to Oxford, this time as fellow of New College and senior demonstrator in the Department of Zoology and Comparative Anatomy. During his postwar years at Oxford, Huxley taught a number of promising students, including John Baker, Gavin de Beer, Charles Elton, Edmund Brisco Ford, and Alister Hardy. Huxley's research interests remained diverse during these six years at Oxford (1917–1925). He resumed his ornithological studies, describing the courtship behavior of different bird species and theorizing about the evolutionary origins of their rituals. In addition, he embarked on laboratory studies that continued through the 1920s and well into the 1930s. Most of them focused on embryology, and he published a number of articles on differentiation, morphogenesis, the hormonal control of growth and development, and rate genes.

Allometry. Huxley's most important and long-lasting contribution to laboratory research was his simple allometry formula that related the growth of different parts of an organism. Huxley first used the formula to relate the growth of the large claw in a fiddler crab to the growth of the rest of its body. He let x = the weight of a crab's large claw and y = the weight of the crab minus the weight of its large claw, and showed that the formula $y = bx^k$ is satisfied throughout development. In *Problems of Relative Growth* (1932), he showed that this formula can be used to relate the growth of key organs in many species, including tails in mice, skulls in baboon, and roots in plants. Subsequently it was shown to relate the growth of key organs to one another as well.

Huxley's first claim to public fame, however, came with a short article in *Nature*, which was misinterpreted in the popular press. He was credited with discovering the "Elixir of Life." Huxley's attempt to clarify his work on the axolotl marked his entry into science popularization. During his postwar years at Oxford he wrote a number of articles on popular science. His first book on biology for public consumption, *Essays of a Biologist*, was published in 1923. This was followed by nearly twenty more books of popular science. He also pursued his interests in issues of wider concern, for instance the ramifications of biological knowledge for the humanities and public policy. His early views on these issues can be traced in his popular writings, though most of his major contributions to these areas were yet to come.

During their postwar years at Oxford, Huxley and his wife started a family. They had two sons, both of whom developed the family interest in nature. Anthony, born in 1920, became a botanist. Francis, born in 1923, took up social anthropology. The Huxley family seems to have been reasonably happy during the Oxford years, and Juliette supported her husband's work in numerous ways, including tending his laboratory experiments while he was away conducting field research.

In 1925, with little prospect of promotion at Oxford, Huxley accepted a chair in zoology at King's College at the University of London. Although his field studies were drawing to a close, he continued his experimental research at King's. He also began to write an encyclopedic work on biology with Herbert George Wells and Wells's son, George Wells, then a zoologist at University College in London. The project became burdensome, and in 1927, after just two years at King's College, Huxley resigned his chair in order to devote greater attention to *The Science of Life*. Huxley did most of the original writing of this three-volume work, which was completed in 1930 and was his greatest popular success.

Move to London. Huxley maintained a frantic pace during the eight years beginning with his resignation from King's College in 1927 and ending with his appointment as secretary of the Zoological Society of London in 1935. He continued to use his laboratories at King's College during this period and published at least nine substantive articles and two original books on experimental biology, *Problems of Relative Growth* (1932) and *The Elements of Experimental Embryology* (with Gavin Rylands de Beer, 1934). In addition to these substantive works, which were written for professional biologists, he continued to popularize science and pursued a career in broadcasting. He gave many radio talks and held debates over the air with Hyman Levy on topics concerning science and society. Huxley also supported the call to bring scientific education to the world community and visited East and Central Africa at the invitation of the Colonial Office's committee on education.

In addition to his laboratory work, lecturing, scientific and popular writing, trips overseas, and broadcasting, the enterprising Huxley joined the film industry. In the early 1930s, he edited *Cosmos, the Story of Evolution* and prepared the Eugenics Society's *Heredity in Man*. He also served as general supervisor of biological films for G. B. Instructional Ltd. His greatest achievement in film was his making of *The Private Life of the Gannet* with John Grierson and Ronald M. Lockley. The film documented the nesting and feeding habits of the great white sea birds, capturing their elaborate display behavior as well as their spectacular aerial dives. The film won an Oscar for best documentary of the year and clinched Huxley's candidacy for the head administrative post of the Zoological Society of London.

In 1935, when Huxley was appointed secretary of the Zoological Society, he was a well-known public figure. He had already written several popular books on science, regularly contributed articles to magazines such as *The Spectator*, and appeared frequently for the British Broadcasting Corporation (BBC). Soon after the outbreak of World War II, Huxley joined a new radio program, "The Brains Trust," which was aired by the BBC.

Huxley's experience as a practicing scientist put him in an excellent position to advise the Zoological Society on how to sponsor pure research, though the society supported little scientific research during his reign. His experience and flair as a science educator and popularizer, however, were fully utilized. He brought about important innovations—regular public lectures for children (given by Huxley and the curators), special exhibits designed to illustrate scientific principles, Pet's Corner (a children's zoo), *Zoo Magazine*, numerous films, and the Studio of Animal Art.

Huxley had always been interested in evolution, and the theoretical import of his fieldwork on birds concerned the selective mechanism behind the evolutionary origin of their behavior. But the bulk of Huxley's research publications, if not his popular writings, had thus far stemmed from his work in the laboratory. This changed when Huxley went to the zoo. He abandoned his laboratory at

Julian Huxley. *Julian Huxley with Jacqueline the chimp.* © HULTON-DEUTSCH COLLECTION/CORBIS.

King's College and redirected his research attention to evolution.

From 1936 to 1941, Huxley wrote several articles on evolutionary theory, coined key terms, and wrote the book that gave the name to the consensus emerging in evolutionary biology: *Evolution, the Modern Synthesis* (1942). The central neo-Darwinian theme of this work, which combined elements of the new genetics with Darwin's mechanism of natural selection, was anticipated in several of Huxley's popular writings. But he did not present his synthetic, neo-Darwinian account of evolution to professional biologists until he gave the presidential address to the zoological section of the British Association for the Advancement of Science in 1936.

Work on Eugenics. Throughout his lifetime but especially in the 1930s, Huxley pursued a keen interest in eugenics, the highly controversial "science" of "improving" the genetic makeup of the human species. He published a number of articles on eugenics throughout his career, some intended for the public, others for professional scientists. He was also an active member of the movement's leading professional society, the Eugenics Society, serving as its president from 1959 until 1962.

Huxley played a key role in the transformation of what has been called "old" eugenics into "new," or "reform" eugenics. "Old style" eugenics, advanced by a previous generation of Darwinians, including Karl Pearson and Charles Davenport, reportedly emphasized heredity to the near exclusion of environmental influences and included overt race and class biases associated with conservative politics. Huxley was part of a generation of eugenicists, including John Burdon Sanderson Haldane, Muller, and Frederick Osborn, who shared a more sophisticated understanding of genetics and evolution. These "reform eugenicists" reportedly appreciated the importance of the environment, were more sensitive to race and class biases, and had liberal political outlooks. Huxley argued that eugenics would not succeed without the "leveling up" of the environment, contended that "population thinking" showed that races did not exist, and rejected the idea that the upper classes should be encouraged to reproduce and lower classes discouraged. Nevertheless, his eugenical speeches and writing, as well as his support of sterilization and birth control practices, reveals that he did not escape racial, ethnic, and class biases.

After resigning from the zoo in 1942, Huxley earned his living by giving lectures and talks on the BBC, and kept busy meeting with various groups and committees on higher education and planning. One of these groups was involved with the preliminary plans for forming a United Nations agency concerned with education and culture. Huxley and Joseph Needham led the drive for the inclusion of science as an area of concern, and they have been credited with putting the "S" in UNESCO (the United Nations Educational, Scientific, and Cultural Organization). Huxley replaced the ailing Sir Alfred Zimmern as full-time secretary of the UNESCO Preparatory Commission, which was charged with drawing up a charter and defining the scope of the future United Nations agency. He quickly wrote a pamphlet, *UNESCO: Its Purpose and Its Philosophy*, which announced that the future UN organization could not rely on religious doctrines or any of the conflicting systems of academic philosophy. Instead, the organization was to carry out its work within the framework of a humanism that seeks to treat "all peoples and all individuals within each people as equals in terms of human dignity, mutual respect, and educational opportunity." He stated that it "must also be a scientific humanism, in the sense that the application of science provides most of the material basis for human culture, and also that the practice and the understanding of science need be integrated with that of other human activities" (1947, p. 5). After conceding that the humanism must "embrace the spiritual and mental," he went on to contend that the humanism must be evolutionary because evolutionary theory

> shows us man's place in nature and his relations to the rest of the phenomenal universe. ... [It] not only gives us a description of various types of evolution and the various trends and directions within them, but it allows us to distinguish desirable and undesirable trends, and to demonstrate the existence of progress in the cosmos. And finally it shows us man as now the sole trustee of further evolutionary progress, and gives us important guidance as to the courses he should avoid and those he should pursue if he is to achieve that progress. (1947, p. 6)

The mission of UNESCO, he stated, was to facilitate further advances by supporting the spread of scientific ideas, and facilitating cultural exchange. Huxley's views were attacked as atheism in disguise, and the members of the commission decided not to endorse his document. Nevertheless, Huxley was elected UNESCO's first director-general, though he was offered a term of just two years, rather than the constitutional six.

After Huxley left UNESCO at the age of sixty-one, he never took another regular position. The remaining twenty-seven years of his life were spent giving lectures, writing, and traveling. During this period, he wrote hundreds of articles and chapters as well as over half a dozen new books. Many of his writings were on general topics, including conditions in various countries, social problems, international organizations, evolutionary ethics, and eugenics. Huxley continued to play an important role in the scientific profession and was called on to give key lectures at scientific meetings, to organize scientific conferences, and to support professional societies, including the Ecological Society, the Society for the Study of Evolution, and the Association for the Study of Animal Behavior, the latter two of which he helped found. He continued to work for the causes he advanced as director-general of UNESCO and remained active in many of the agency's affiliated international commissions.

BIBLIOGRAPHY

WORKS BY HUXLEY

"The Courtship Habits of the Great Crested Grebe (Podiceps cristatus); with an Addition to the Theory Of Sexual Selection." *Proceedings of the Zoological Society of London* 35 (1914): 491–562.

"Metamorphosis of Axolotl Caused by Thyroid Feeding." *Nature* 104 (1920): 435.

Essays of a Biologist. New York: Knopf, 1923.

Huxley

Essays in Popular Science. London: Chatto & Windus, 1926.

With Herbert G. Wells and G. P. Wells. *The Science of Life: A Summary of Contemporary Knowledge about Life and Its Possibilities.* 3 vols. London: Amalgamated Press, 1929–1930; Garden City, NY: Doubleday, Doran, 1931.

"Eugenic Sterilisation." *Nature* 126 (1930): 503.

Problems of Relative Growth. London: Methuen, 1932.

"Sterilisation: A Social Problem." *New Chronicle*, 21 January 1934, p. 2.

With Gavin Rylands de Beer. *The Elements of Experimental Embryology.* Cambridge, U.K.: Cambridge University Press, 1934.

"The Concept of Race: In the Light of Modern Genetics." *Harper's Monthly Magazine* 170 (1935): 689–698.

"Eugenics and Society." *Eugenics Review* 28 (1936): 11–31.

"The Concept of Race: In the Light of Modern Genetics." In *The Uniqueness of Man.* London: Chatto & Windus, 1941. (Published in the United States as *Man Stands Alone* [New York: Harper, 1941]).

Evolution, the Modern Synthesis. London and New York: Harper, 1942.

UNESCO: Its Purpose and Its Philosophy. Washington, DC: Public Affairs Press, 1947.

"Eugenics in Evolutionary Perspective." *The Eugenics Review* 54 (1962): 123–141.

Memories. 2 vols. London: Allen & Unwin, 1970–1973.

If I Am to Be Remembered: The Life and Work of Julian Huxley with Selected Correspondence. Edited by Krishna R. Dronamraju. Singapore and River Edge, NJ: World Scientific, 1993.

OTHER SOURCES

Armytage, W. H. G. "The First Director-General of UNESCO." In *Evolutionary Studies: A Centenary Celebration of the Life of Julian Huxley; Proceedings of the Twenty-fourth Annual Symposium of the Eugenics Society, London, 1987*, edited by Milo Keynes and G. Ainsworth Harrison. Basingstoke, U.K.: and London: Macmillan, 1989.

Baker, John Randall. "Julian Sorrell Huxley, 22 June 1887–14 February 1975, elected F. R. S. 1938." *Biographical Memoirs of Fellows of the Royal Society* 22 (1976): 207–238.

———. *Julian Huxley, Scientist and World Citizen, 1887–1975: A Biographical Memoir.* Paris: UNESCO, 1978. Includes a bibliography prepared by Jens-Peter Green.

Bartley, Mary M. "Courtship and Continued Progress: Julian Huxley's Studies on Bird Behavior." *Journal of the History of Biology* 28, no. 1 (1995): 91–108.

Bates, Sarah C., Marjorie G. Winkler, and Christina Riquelmi. *A Guide to the Papers of Julian Sorell Huxley.* Houston, TX: Woodson Research Center, Rice University Press, 1984.

Beatty, John. "Julian Huxley and the Evolutionary Synthesis." In *Julian Huxley: Biologist and Statesman of Science*, edited by Albert Van Helden and C. Kenneth Waters. Houston, TX: Rice University Press, 1992.

Boothe, Nancy L. "The Julian Sorell Huxley Papers, Rice University Library." In *Julian Huxley: Biologist and Statesman of Science*, edited by Albert Van Helden and C. Kenneth Waters. Houston, TX: Rice University Press, 1992.

Burkhardt, Richard W., Jr. "Huxley and the Rise of Ethology." In *Julian Huxley: Biologist and Statesman of Science*, edited by C. Kenneth Waters and Albert Van Helden. Houston, TX: Rice University Press, 1992.

Churchill, Frederick B. "On the Road to the k Constant: A Historical Introduction." In *Problems of Relative Growth*, by Julian S. Huxley. Baltimore, MD: Johns Hopkins University Press, reprint edition 1993.

Clark, Ronald William. *The Huxleys.* New York: McGraw-Hill, 1968.

Divall, Colin. "Capitalising on 'Science': Philosophical Ambiguity in Julian Huxley's Politics, 1920–1950." PhD diss., Manchester University, 1985.

Durant, John R. "Julian Huxley and the Development of Evolutionary Studies." In *Evolutionary Studies: A Centenary Celebration of the Life of Julian Huxley; Proceedings of the Twenty-fourth Annual Symposium of the Eugenics Society, London, 1987*, edited by Milo. Keynes and G. Ainsworth. Harrison. Basingstoke, U.K.: and London: Macmillan, 1989.

Ford, Edmund Briscoe. "Some Recollections Pertaining to the Evolutionary Synthesis." In *The Evolutionary Synthesis: Perspectives on the Unification of Biology*, edited by Ernst Mayr and William B. Provine. Cambridge, MA: Harvard University Press, 1980.

Gascoigne, Robert M. "Julian Huxley and Biological Progress." *Journal of the History of Biology* 24, no. 3 (1991): 433–455.

Green, Jens-Peter. "Bibliography." In *Julian Huxley, Scientist and World Citizen 1887–1975: A Biographical Memoir*, by John Randall Baker. Paris: UNESCO, 1978.

Greene, John C. "The Interaction of Science and World View in Sir Julian Huxley's Evolutionary Biology." *Journal of the History of Biology* 23, no. 1 (March 1990): 39–55.

Hubback, David "Julian Huxley and Eugenics." In *Evolutionary Studies: A Centenary Celebration of the Life of Julian Huxley; Proceedings of the Twenty-fourth Annual Symposium of the Eugenics Society, London, 1987*, edited by Milo. Keynes and G. Ainsworth. Harrison. Basingstoke, U.K. and London: Macmillan, 1989.

Huxley, Juliette. *Leaves of the Tulip Tree.* London: John Murray Ltd., 1986.

Keynes, Milo, and G. Ainsworth Harrison, eds. *Evolutionary Studies: A Centenary Celebration of the Life of Julian Huxley; Proceedings of the Twenty-fourth Annual Symposium of the Eugenics Society, London, 1987.* Basingstoke, U.K.: Macmillan, 1989.

Medawar, Peter B. "Obituary of Julian Huxley." *Nature* 254 (1975): 4.

Muller, Hermann Joseph. "A Biographical Appreciation of Sir Julian Huxley." *The Humanist* nos. 2–3 (1962): 51–55.

Olby, Robert. "Huxley's Place in Twentieth-century Biology." In *Julian Huxley: Biologist and Statesman of Science*, edited by Albert Van Helden and C. Kenneth Waters. Houston, TX: Rice University Press, 1992.

Patten, Robert L. "The British Context of Huxley's Popularization." In *Julian Huxley: Biologist and Statesman of*

Science, edited by Albert Van Helden and C. Kenneth Waters. Houston, TX: Rice University Press, 1992.

Rugina, Anghel N. "How a Natural Scientist Sees Socio-Economic Problems and Their Solution: A Dialogue with Sir Julian Huxley." *International Journal of Social Economics* 27, nos. 7–10 (2000): 720–738.

Smith, Roger. "Biology and Values in Interwar Britain: C. S. Sherrington, Julian Huxley, and the Vision of Progress." *Past and Present* 178, no. 1 (February 2003): 210–242.

Swetlitz, Marc. "Julian Huxley and the End of Evolution." *Journal of the History of Biology* 28, no. 2 (1995): 181–217.

Waters, C. Kenneth. "Introduction: Revising Our Picture of Julian Huxley." In *Julian Huxley: Biologist and Statesman of Science,* edited by Albert Van Helden and C. Kenneth Waters. Houston, TX: Rice University Press, 1992.

Waters, C. Kenneth, and Albert Van Helden, eds. *Julian Huxley: Biologist and Statesman of Science.* Houston, TX: Rice University Press, 1992.

C. Kenneth Waters

HUXLEY, THOMAS HENRY (*b.* Ealing, Middlesex, England, 4 May 1825; *d.* Hodeslea, Eastbourne, Sussex, England, 29 June 1895), *zoology, evolution, paleontology, ethnology, popularization, professionalization.* For the original article on Huxley see *DSB,* vol. 6.

Huxley studies underwent a transformation in the later twentieth century. From his "science versus religion" metaphor to his Darwinian propaganda, from his cultural context to his biology training-programs, little remained untouched. The *Life and Letters of Thomas Henry Huxley* (1900), which informed much of the original *DSB* entry, was superseded by culturally embedded studies that show how Dissenting, industrializing, and scientific currents sustained Huxley and how he in turn reframed the great questions of duty, morality, and the value of science.

Medical Education. Huxley's trajectory away from Anglicanism began in the 1835–1840 period in Coventry, where he mixed with Dissenting ribbon masters. In this industrial heartland, with its sectarian politics, he began questioning the duality of matter and soul and the legitimacy of the established church.

More has become known about Huxley's education. His two medical brothers-in-law were John Charles Cooke, who apprenticed him in Coventry (1839), and John Godwin Salt—not "Scott" (an alias taken when he fled to the United States). In January 1841 Huxley's apprenticeship continued under the reformer Thomas Chandler in East London, where Huxley experienced the privations of the poor, then later that year under Salt. In 1841–1842 he studied at Sydenham College, a cheap medical school where Cooke taught (and where Marshall Hall was developing his reflex arc). Huxley took the botany prize and was awarded a silver medal by the Worshipful Company of Apothecaries. On finishing at Charing Cross Hospital (1845), he passed part one of the London University Bachelor of Medicine exam, but his debts forced him to forego part two. He had no degree. Too young to obtain a Royal College of Surgeons' license to practice, he joined the navy as assistant surgeon.

***Rattlesnake* Voyage and Oceanic Hydrozoa.** A spate of studies on HMS *Rattlesnake's* voyage to Australia's Great Barrier Reef appeared in the 1960s and 1970s, to coincide with Australia's bicentenary celebrations. They exploited the numerous journals kept by the captain and crew and threw fresh light on Huxley's circumnavigation.

Huxley specialized in the jellyfish and sea nettles (Siphonophora). He was deeply versed in European invertebrate anatomy, as was shown by his later London disagreements with Christian Gottfried Ehrenberg on the organelle content of protozoa, with Richard Owen on "Alternation of Generations," and with the Schleiden-Schwann cell theory. Huxley dissected widely, especially ascidians (he discovered two new orders), but it was his studies on his forty new genera of jellyfish and siphonophores that made his name. Mary P. Winsor (1976) has elucidated Huxley's work on the siphonophore archetype with its two "foundation membranes," the basis of his new class, *Nematophora* (Heinrich Frey and Rudolf Leuckart preempted him with the term *Coelenterata*). Huxley's views on jellyfish and ascidians as single organisms (rather than colonies) were also anticipated by Leuckart's polymorphism theory. Huxley further fragmented Georges Cuvier's *embranchement,* the *Radiata,* in 1851, when he unsuccessfully combined rotifers, flatworms, and starfish in a new group, the *Annuloida.*

The School of Mines and Fossil Work. In Sydney, Huxley became engaged to Henrietta Heathorn, a brewer's daughter. Paul White has analyzed their touching correspondence to show how Huxley's ideal of the selfless man of science emerged out his engagement with Henrietta's domestic qualities of self-sacrifice and feminine virtue. They were married in London in 1855 and had eight children: Noel (1856–1860), Jessie Oriana (1858–1926), Marian (1859–1887), Leonard (1860–1933), Rachel (1862–1934), Henrietta (1863–1940), Henry (1865–1946), and Ethel Gladys (1866–1941).

In London, Huxley penetrated the *Westminster Review* heart of literary radicalism. His column in the *Review* (1854–1857) bolstered what the English novelist George Eliot (pseudonym of Marian Evans) called his haughty scientific persona. But his predicament as a freelancer trapped in a commercial science nexus showed in his savagery toward Robert Chambers's *Vestiges of the Natural History of Creation.* The book was not denounced because of Huxley's "critical skepticism of all theories," as the original *DSB* article has it. With the antithetical categories of professional/amateur and elite/popular knowledge still forming, Huxley was using his scientific reportage to gain audience recognition of his expertise. He took shares in the *Westminster,* and in the *Reader* in 1864, and carried his goals through into *Nature* in 1869. Secular London science was seeking a distinct literary niche; and its birth pangs became evident when Huxley's slashing "Science and 'Church Policy'" editorial (1864) split the *Reader* consensus, alienating its Christian Socialist backers.

In 1854 he was appointed lecturer in natural history and paleontology at the Government School of Mines (a seeding institution training industrialists, surveyors, and teachers). Joining the Geological Survey, which, as James A. Secord (1986) shows, encouraged paleoecological research, Huxley was pushed increasingly into paleontology. He established that the coelacanths were relicts of Devonian Crossopterygian fish. And in proving that the Elgin sandstone reptiles were Triassic, not Devonian, he removed the last evidence for Charles Lyell's nonprogressionist paleontology.

Huxley's early paleontological views were idiosyncratic. Himself influenced by Lyell's nonprogressionism, he harped on the unchanging nature of fossil lineages (his "Persistent Types"). In 1859 he believed that the major taxa had appeared before the Silurian period, after which they persisted little changed (so people might yet see Paleozoic pottery). This has been interpreted as a reaction to Owen's archetypal progressionism in part. While Huxley's *Life and Letters* castigated Owen as an aggressor, revisionists have investigated Owen's and Huxley's contrasting Oxford-Anglican and industrial-Dissenting patronage strings and their career rivalry in a confined field. Contemporaries called Huxley's personality reactive. And Dov Ospovat illustrated the point: Where Owen's archetype was made flesh through a specializing series of forms (illustrated by toe loss in fossil horses), Huxley—before Charles Darwin published *On the Origin of Species* (1859)—placed his abstract archetypes at the center of William Sharp MacLeay's quinarian circles. The living types were situated equidistantly about the archetype, so there could be no specializing fossil series. Nor could humans result from a fossil ascent (Huxley, as an anonymous *Westminster* columnist, called humanity an "aberrant modification").

Evolution. After visiting Darwin in 1856, Huxley found his secular needs better served by Darwinian naturalism and began his piecemeal reorientation. In January 1859 he declared that humans must have evolved from animals, pushing ahead of Darwin, who avoided humankind in the *Origin of Species.* Huxley's campaign against the clergy was recast as a Manichean "Evolution versus Creation" dichotomy. In class he caricatured "Creation" as atoms flashing together into elephants, and Darwin ended the *Origin* with this straw-man alternative to evolution.

The original *DSB* article dwells on Owen's antitransmutationist claim that humans alone possess a neuroanatomical ridge, the *Hippocampus minor.* Huxley's rebuttal has generated a large literature. Christopher Cosans (1994) looks at Huxley's Cartesianism and the Kantian Owen's neuropsychological understanding; C. U. M. [Christopher Upham Murray] Smith (1997) too sees deeper contrasting philosophies but is more sympathetic to an accompanying social explanation; as is Charles G. Gross (1993), who has examined the neuroanatomy (and shown how Huxley detected new sulci during his dissections).

The *DSB* on the 1860 Huxley–Samuel Wilberforce repartee typifies an older warfare historiography (since deconstructed by James R. Moore, 1979). Subsequent revisionism includes Frank M. Turner's 1993 territorial conflict thesis—which sees London's men of science undercutting the spiritual sanction of a rival profession. This can itself be wrapped within Sheridan Gilley's 1981 study of the contemporary splits within Anglicanism and a rising industrial Dissent, represented by the Puritan Huxley. (His zoological Calvinism, which emphasized stoicism in the face of hardship, could discipline a new industrial workforce, and his educational campaigns were backed by the manufacturers Joseph Whitworth and William Armstrong.) But note that Oxford's liberal clergy, including the vice-chancellor Francis Jeune, were also sympathetic to Huxley's rebuke of Wilberforce. This liberal Anglican alliance was reflected inside Huxley's home, where Henrietta's vicar, the Christian Socialist Llewelyn Davies, was welcomed.

Also problematic is the *DSB*'s summary of Huxley's understanding of Darwinism. He was a morphologist where Darwin was a field naturalist, so Huxley was not particularly well acquainted with all of Darwin's evidence. And it is untrue that "[f]or Huxley and others natural selection provided a method of organizing their own facts." Both James G. Paradis (1978) and Turner foreground Huxley's Carlylean Romanticism, which left him out of step with Darwin's utilitarian approach. Huxley rarely mentioned natural selection: He does so only once in his *Encyclopedia Britannica* entry "Evolution" (1878), then negates with talk of the proclivity of organisms to vary.

Huxley also differed from Darwin on the completeness of the analogy between artificial and natural

Huxley

Thomas Henry Huxley. © HULTON-DEUTSCH COLLECTION/CORBIS.

selection, on saltationism, and on drowned continents. Evolutionary naturalism at times seemed their sole point of contact. For Huxley the *Origin* stretched "the domination of Science": It authorized the man of science to talk on morality and origins. Indeed the book's meritocratic Malthusianism made it a "Whitworth gun in the armoury of liberalism" (Huxley, 1860, p. 23).

Descriptive morphology remained Huxley's forte, and only latterly did his monographs broach ancestry—of partridges (1868), crocodiles (1875), and crayfish (1880). While tentative family trees sometimes adorned his later notes, they were heuristic devices (illustrations are published in Desmond, 1997). His changing approach was stimulated by the concept of phylogeny in Ernst Haeckel's *Generelle Morphologie* (1866). Whereas in his 1863–1864 lectures Huxley had united reptiles and birds in the "Sauropsida," only after reading Haeckel and finding the avianlike ilium of the dinosaur *Euskelesaurus* in Oxford University Museum in 1867 did he make dinosaurs actual bird ancestors.

Huxley was a persuasive publicist. As his audiences varied from jam factory workers to Eton toffs, so did his presentation. His provocative workingmen's talks, such as those on human-ape relationships, secured this disenfranchised constituency by picturing evolution as a bottom-up system of self-betterment.

Education and Scientific Administration. Huxley held three chairs simultaneously in the 1860s: at the School of Mines, the College of Surgeons (1862–1869), and the Royal Institution (1866–1869). And, despite the Tory grandees trying to engineer one of their own as president of the British Association for the Advancement of Science (BAAS) in 1870, this too fell to Huxley: a sign of the nobility's prestige in administrative affairs passing to the careerists. He was president of the Royal Society in 1883–1885. Of all his coteries, it was the informal "X Club" (formed in 1864), which met before Royal Society meetings, that has attracted most attention. X-Clubbers had been viewed as establishment outsiders on a professionalizing bent, but Ruth Barton (1981) shows this coalition of gentlemen and careerists to have been more concerned with employment, expertise, and recognition than professional accreditation.

Evelleen Richards (1989) has exposed Huxley's attitudes toward women and race, particularly at the Ethnological Society. Here Huxley recast the human populations as persistent "stocks"—meeting the Anthropological Society ultraracists (who viewed the races as separate species) halfway before merging with them. Seeing a free society as the most efficient, he was against chattel and domestic slavery. As such he supported the North in the American Civil War (even though his brother-in-law Dr. "Scott" was a Confederate surgeon). He believed that women should not suffer educational discrimination, whatever their biological limitations. And Richards assesses how far Victorian women acquiesced in Huxley's views of their limitations. Of course events overtook him: The only schoolmistress in his first South Kensington summer course in 1871 finished first in the class. Such successes eroded patrician prejudices, and Huxley had a woman demonstrator by 1874. In the 1880s women routinely attended his academic lectures.

Scholars now understand the context of Huxley's biological Type-system. The 1870 Education Act led to the establishment of school boards. Huxley—a Chamberlainite interventionist—was elected for London's Marylebone ward, and his education committee published a blueprint for London's schooling. Huxley helped supply the necessary textbooks, with his *Physiography* (1877) and *Introductory Science Primer* (1880). New teacher-training techniques were also needed. The Science Schools at South Kensington (later the Royal College of Science) was established, and here Huxley devised a simplified school biology, whittled down to a few laboratory types. This became the standard school biology course for a century.

He helped to establish the vocational City and Guilds Institute in 1884. Although ironically, as Barton notes, by emphasizing the moral discipline of pure science (to make it rival the classics in forming the character, and to put his science teachers on a par with the dons), he increased the theoretical bent of technical education. His claim that science's ethical obligations toward truth made it better than the classics for ushering in a moral reformation led to a dialogue with Matthew Arnold.

The exegesis of Huxley agnosticism has proceeded apace. Adrian Desmond (1994) documents Huxley's early skepticism and the way he stretched the Dissenters' "sin of conformity" into a "sin of faith." The timing of Huxley's neologism, appearing as the spiritualist Alfred Russel Wallace and the Catholic St. George Mivart fragmented the Darwinian coalition, is examined by Moore (1991). Huxley tied agnosticism to middle-class values, and Bernard Lightman (1989) recounts his faltering control as agnosticism was appropriated by radical groups.

Huxley's agnostic ideological slate was never blank: His naturalism assumed axioms of the uniformity of nature and correlation of forces. He returned in the 1870s to the reflex arcs (pioneered in his student days) to discuss Cartesian brutes as self-adjusting machines and the mechanical equivalent of consciousness. His naturalism was polemically displayed in debates with William Ewart Gladstone on Genesis, the socialists on equality, and the bishops on their realist views of natural law.

His last major speech, "Evolution and Ethics," at Oxford in 1893, has been reevaluated to show how he detached a brutal Malthusian nature from a pure human ethics after the death of his daughter Marian. Michael S. Helfand (1977) has him staking his Liberal political ethics midway between socialist demands for natural rights and Spencer's laissez-faire alternative. The justice he had once seen in nature was gone: He now portrayed ethical man revolting against a morally indifferent cosmos.

Huxley and History. Huxley's *Collected Essays* provide a propagandist insight into an emerging evolutionary worldview. He reinterpreted duty and morality for a secularizing, industrializing culture. His was a winner's history, with its denigration of clergy and pre-Darwinian biology. In the later twentieth century this partisan image was transcended by historiographical approaches based on an understanding of the religious, industrial, and scientific currents that swept Huxley along, approaches that no less recognized his achievements in education, administration, and the assimilation of science. The centenary of his death was marked by new biographies, book-length studies, and a symposium at Imperial College, London, where the Huxley Archives are housed.

BIBLIOGRAPHY

WORKS BY HUXLEY

On the Educational Value of the Natural History Sciences. London: Van Voorst, 1854.

The Oceanic Hydrozoa: *A Description of the* Calycophoridae *and* Psysophoridae *Observed During the Voyage of H.M.S. "Rattlesnake," in the Years 1846-1850.* London: Printed for the Ray Society, 1859.

"On the Theory of the Vertebrate Skull." *Proceedings of the Royal Society of London* 9 (1859): 381-487.

Evidence as to Man's Place in Nature. London & Edinburgh: Williams & Norgate, 1863; New York: Appleton, 1863.

Lectures on the Elements of Comparative Anatomy. London: Churchill, 1864.

Lessons in Elementary Physiology. London: Macmillan, 1866; London & New York: Macmillan, 1871.

Lay Sermons, Addresses and Reviews. London: Macmillan, 1870; New York: Appleton, 1870.

A Manual of the Anatomy of Vertebrated Animals. London: Churchill, 1871; New York: Appleton, 1872.

Critiques and Addresses. London: Macmillan, 1873; New York: Appleton, 1873.

A Course of Practical Instruction in Elementary Biology, by Huxley with the assistance of H. N. Martin. London: Macmillan, 1875.

The Evidence of the Miracle of Resurrection .London: Printed for the Metaphysical Society, 1876.

American Addresses, with a Lecture in the Study of Biology. London: Macmillan, 1877; New York: Appleton, 1877.

A Manual of the Anatomy of Invertebrated Animals. London: Churchill, 1877; New York: Appleton, 1878.

Physiography: An Introduction to the Study of Nature. London: Macmillan, 1877; New York: Appleton, 1882.

Hume. London: Macmillan, 1878.

Introductory [science primer] London: Macmillan, 1880; New York: Appleton, 1882.

Science and Culture, and Other Essays. London: Macmillan, 1881; New York: Appleton, 1882.

An Introduction to the Study of Zoology, Illustrated by the Crayfish. New York: Appleton, 1884.

The Advance of Science in the Last Half-Century. New York: Appleton, 1887.

"Autobiography," in *From Handel to Hallé: Biographical Sketches with Autobiographies of Professor Huxley and Professor Herkomer,* edited by Louis Engel. London: Sonnenschein, 1890.

Social Diseases and Worse Remedies. London: Macmillan, 1891.

Essays on Some Controverted Questions. London & New York: Macmillan, 1892; New York: Appleton, 1892.

Evolution and Ethics. London & New York: Macmillan, 1893.

Collected Essays, 9 volumes. London: Macmillan, 1893-1894; New York: Appleton, 1894.

The Scientific Memoirs of T. H. Huxley, 5 volumes, edited by Michael Foster, and E. Ray Lankester. London: Macmillan/New York: Appleton, 1898-1903.

T. H. Huxley's Diary of the Voyage of H.M.S. Rattlesnake, edited by Julian Huxley. London: Chatto & Windus, 1935; Garden City: Doubleday, Doran, 1936.

Thomas Henry Huxley: List of His Correspondence with Miss Henrietta Anne Heathorn, Later Mrs. Huxley, 1847-54, edited by Jeanne Pingree. London: Imperial College of Science and Technology, 1969.

OTHER SOURCES

Barr, Alan P., ed. *Thomas Henry Huxley's Place in Science and Letters: Centenary Essays.* Athens: University of Georgia Press, 1997.

Bartholomew, Michael. "Huxley's Defence of Darwin." *Annals of Science* 32 (1975): 525–535.

Barton, Ruth. "Scientific Opposition to Technical Education." In *Scientific and Technical Education in Early Industrial Britain,* edited by Michael D. Stephens and Gordon W. Roderick. Nottingham, U.K.: Department of Adult Education, University of Nottingham, 1981.

———. "'Huxley, Lubbock, and Half a Dozen Others': Professionals and Gentlemen in the Formation of the X Club, 1851–1864." *Isis* 89 (1998): 410–444.

Collie, Michael. *Huxley at Work: With the Scientific Correspondence of T. H. Huxley and the Rev. Dr. George Gordon of Birnie, Near Elgin.* Basingstoke, U.K.: Macmillan, 1991.

Cosans, Christopher. "Anatomy, Metaphysics, and Values: The Ape Brain Debate Reconsidered." *Biology and Philosophy* 9 (1994): 129–165.

Darwin, Angela, and Adrian Desmond, eds. *The Thomas Henry Huxley Family Correspondence.* 4 vols. Chicago: University of Chicago Press (Forthcoming).

Desmond, Adrian. *Archetypes and Ancestors: Palaeontology in Victorian London, 1850–1875.* London: Blond & Briggs, 1982.

———. *Huxley: The Devil's Disciple.* London: Michael Joseph, 1994.

———. *Huxley: Evolution's High Priest.* London: Michael Joseph, 1997. These two volumes were combined as *Huxley: From Devil's Disciple to Evolution's High Priest.* Reading, MA: Addison-Wesley, 1997; Harmondsworth, U.K.: Penguin, 1998.

———. "Redefining the X Axis: 'Professionals,' 'Amateurs,' and the Making of Mid-Victorian Biology—A Progress Report." *Journal of the History of Biology* 34 (2001): 3–50.

Di Gregorio, Mario A. *T. H. Huxley's Place in Natural Science.* New Haven, CT: Yale University Press, 1984.

Forgan, Sophie, and Graeme Gooday. "Constructing South Kensington: The Buildings and Politics of T. H. Huxley's Working Environment." *British Journal for the History of Science* 29 (1996): 435–468.

Gilley, Sheridan. "The Huxley-Wilberforce Debate: A Reconsideration." In *Religion and Humanism: Papers Read at the Eighteenth Summer Meeting and the Nineteenth Winter Meeting of the Ecclesiastical History Society,* edited by Keith Robbins. Oxford: Blackwell, 1981.

Gilley, Sheridan, and Ann Loades. "Thomas Henry Huxley: The War between Science and Religion." *Journal of Religion* 61 (1981): 285–308.

Gross, Charles G. "Hippocampus Minor and Man's Place in Nature: A Case Study in the Social Construction of Neuroanatomy." *Hippocampus* 3 (1993): 403–416.

Helfand, Michael S. "T. H. Huxley's 'Evolution and Ethics.'" *Victorian Studies* 20 (1977): 159–177.

Huxley, Thomas Henry. "The Origin of Species [1860]. In *Darwiniana: Essays by Thomas H. Huxley.* London: Macmillan, 1893.

Lightman, Bernard. "Ideology, Evolution, and Late-Victorian Agnostic Popularizers." In *History, Humanity, and Evolution: Essays for John C. Greene,* edited by James R. Moore. Cambridge, U.K.: Cambridge University Press, 1989.

———. "Huxley and Scientific Agnosticism: The Strange History of a Failed Rhetorical Strategy." *British Journal for the History of Science* 35 (2002): 271–289.

Lyons, Sherrie L. *Thomas Henry Huxley: The Evolution of a Scientist.* Amherst, NY: Prometheus, 1999.

MacLeod, Roy M. *The "Creed of Science" in Victorian England.* Aldershot, U.K.: Ashgate/Variorum, 2000.

Moore, James R. *The Post-Darwinian Controversies: A Study of the Protestant Struggle to Come to Terms with Darwin in Great Britain and America, 1870–1900.* Cambridge, U.K.: Cambridge University Press, 1979.

———. "Deconstructing Darwinism: The Politics of Evolution in the 1860s." *Journal of the History of Biology* 24 (1991): 353–408.

Ospovat, Dov. "The Influence of Karl Ernst von Baer's Embryology, 1828–1859: A Reappraisal in Light of Richard Owen's and William B. Carpenter's 'Palaeontological Application of "Von Baer's Law."'" *Journal of the History of Biology* 9 (1976): 1–28.

Paradis, James G. *T. H. Huxley: Man's Place in Nature.* Lincoln: University of Nebraska Press, 1978.

———. "*Evolution and Ethics* in Its Victorian Context." In *Evolution and Ethics: T. H. Huxley's Evolution and Ethics; With New Essays on its Victorian and Sociobiological Context,* edited by James G. Paradis and George C. Williams. Princeton, NJ: Princeton University Press, 1989.

Richards, Evelleen. "Huxley and Woman's Place in Science: The 'Woman Question' and the Control of Victorian Anthropology." In *History, Humanity, and Evolution: Essays for John C. Greene,* edited by James R. Moore. Cambridge, U.K.: Cambridge University Press, 1989.

———. "The 'Moral Anatomy' of Robert Knox: The Interplay between Biological and Social Thought in Victorian Scientific Naturalism." *Journal of the History of Biology* 22 (1989): 373–436.

Richmond, Marsha L. "T. H. Huxley's Criticism of German Cell Theory: An Epigenetic and Physiological Interpretation of Cell Structure." *Journal of the History of Biology* 33 (2000): 247–289.

Roos, David A. "Neglected Bibliographical Aspects of the Works of Thomas Henry Huxley." *Journal of the Society for the Bibliography of Natural History* 8 (1978): 401–420.

Secord, James A. "The Geological Survey of Great Britain as a Research School, 1839–1855." *History of Science* 24 (1986): 223–275.

Smith, C. U. M. [Christopher Upham Murray]. "Worlds in Collision: Owen and Huxley on the Brain." *Science in Context* 10 (1997): 343–365.

Smith, Roger. "The Background of Physiological Psychology in Natural Philosophy." *British Journal for the History of Science* 6 (1973): 75–123.

Turner, Frank M. *Contesting Cultural Authority: Essays in Victorian Intellectual Life.* Cambridge, U.K.: Cambridge University Press, 1993.

White, Paul. *Thomas Huxley: Making the "Man of Science."* Cambridge, U.K.: Cambridge University Press, 2003.

Winsor, Mary P. *Starfish, Jellyfish, and the Order of Life: Issues in Nineteenth-Century Science.* New Haven, CT: Yale University Press, 1976.

Adrian Desmond

HYMAN, LIBBIE HENRIETTA

(*b.* Des Moines, Iowa, 6 December 1888; *d.* New York, New York, 3 August 1969), *invertebrate zoology.* For the original article on Hyman see *DSB,* vol. 17, Supplement II.

The final decade of the twentieth century saw new interest among zoologists in the history and development of their discipline over the course of the century. Hyman's life and work were the subjects of a symposium held at the 1991 meeting of the American Society of Zoologists and were a part of a symposium on twentieth-century zoology at the Eighteenth International Congress of Zoology, 2000. Evaluations of her scientific contributions by participants in those events firmly established her as a major contributor in the following areas:

Laboratory Manuals. Libbie Hyman's earliest contributions to zoology as a whole came in graduate school, when she developed laboratory manuals for the zoology and vertebrate anatomy classes at the University of Chicago. The Zoology Department was switching the emphasis of its student laboratories from the old typological approach to the newer comparative method, and no suitable laboratory manuals were available. Those Hyman created as a graduate student assistant were so useful to Chicago students that they were published by the University of Chicago Press (1919 and 1922) and remained in print for many years, her efforts instructing and influencing generations of zoology students.

Libbie Hyman. THE LIBRARY OF CONGRESS.

Experimental Work. Hyman's second contribution was the body of experimental work she produced during her sixteen years as Charles Manning Child's assistant in the Zoology Department at Chicago. The physiological papers she published, while contributing to Child's gradient concept of the regulation of development, also placed her work in a broader context of morphology, natural history, and systematics.

Flatworm Taxonomy. The third contribution was her work on flatworm taxonomy, studies she continued through most of her life. Her publications put the taxonomy of the group on a solid basis by incorporating the histology of body structures and copulatory apparatus in taxonomic descriptions. Hyman described twenty-seven new species and two new genera of land planarians and, perhaps even more importantly, encouraged young workers to study and publish in the field. She also produced a large body of work on other marine and freshwater Turbellaria, more than sixty papers in all. The phylogenetic framework she presented in the second volume of *The Invertebrates* has been improved, but not abandoned, by incorporation of new ultrastructural and molecular characters and by application of cladistic paradigms.

Role Model. Because of her publications, her position, even though unpaid, at the American Museum of Natural History, and her teaching in the Marine Biological Laboratory (Woods Hole) summer courses, Hyman became a model for young women interested in invertebrate zoology at a time when there were few women professors to serve as role models. As early as 1943 her biography appeared in a book intended to interest girls in careers in science, *American Women of Science,* by Edna Yost. Although sometimes abrupt with adult visitors who interrupted her work, Hyman always responded to queries from students. In addition, she supported some deserving students financially.

The Invertebrates. Her most important contribution was undoubtedly *The Invertebrates.* The six volumes' abundant illustrations and uniform format, incorporating historical background, general characteristics, classification, morphology, physiology, development, ecology, and phylogeny for each group, ensured their value to zoologists. Monolingual North American zoologists appreciated her work for its summary and interpretation of the European zoological literature. But zoologists worldwide, even those who could read French or German, relied on her interpretation of that literature. *The Invertebrates* was not merely a compilation: each volume included new observations and drawings of living organisms made by Hyman herself during summer stays at marine laboratories, new information obtained from experts on each group, and the author's own synthesis of phylogenetic relationships. Hyman's zoological education at Chicago under the direction of Child and Charles Otis Whitman, both educated at Leipzig, had rooted her firmly in the comparative tradition begun in the 1860s in Germany and culminated in the transformation of morphology by evolutionism in the late nineteenth century. Her opus carried this approach, the "Chicago Style" of biology, with its emphasis on functional and evolutionary morphology and whole organism research, forward into the era of the evolutionary developmental and systematic studies of the second half of the twentieth century.

The Invertebrates has become outdated because of the enormous amount of new information based on studies using scanning and transmission electron microscopy, molecular genetics, and other approaches unknown when the books were published. In the twenty-first century it is unlikely that one person could even attempt to accomplish such a review, but Hyman's enthusiasm, intelligence, and tenacity in pursuing her goals continue to inspire biologists.

SUPPLEMENTARY BIBLIOGRAPHY

Jenner, Ronald A. "Libbie Henrietta Hyman (1888–1969): From Developmental Mechanics to the Evolution of Animal Body Plans." *Journal of Experimental Zoology* 302B (2004): 413–423.

Winston, Judith E. "Libbie Henrietta Hyman: Life and Contributions." *American Museum Novitates* 3277 (1999): 1–66. Available from http://library.amnh.org/resources/ejournals.html.

———. "Libbie Hyman and Invertebrate Zoology in the 20th Century." In *The New Panorama of Animal Evolution,* edited by Anastasio Legakis, et al. Proceedings of the Eighteenth International Congress of Zoology, Athens, Greece. Sofia, Bulgaria: Pensoft, 2003.

Yost, Edna. *American Women of Science.* New York: Stokes, 1943.

Judith E. Winston

HYPATIA (*d.* Alexandria, 415), *mathematical commentaries, philosophy.*

For the original article on Hypatia, see *DSB,* vol. 6.

Hypatia was the daughter of Theon of Alexandria and the only woman in antiquity for whom historians have some positive evidence of her mathematical activities. However, the information about her achievements in this and other fields is particularly scanty, and comes either from authors, such as Christian writers, that were overtly hostile to her or from sources not favorably oriented. The latter is the case of Damascius' testimony, making up the bulk of the entry of the *Suidas* lexicon. Such biased reports have exposed even the reasons and the oft-repeated circumstances of her murder to scholarly romancing.

Hypatia was renowned as a philosopher, but only conjectures can be made about her philosophical allegiances and her teaching. The former have been characterized either as Cynic, on the basis of tendentious and caricatural remarks by Damascius, or Neoplatonic with a strong Iamblichean tinge, mainly because of analogous doctrines embraced in the works of her pupil Synesius of Cyrene. No testimony about her philosophical writings has survived, and it is reasonable to doubt that any such writings ever existed. It seems sufficiently established that a circle of pupils of remarkable intellectual level gathered around her, but it is not clear whether her teaching was a public or a private one, whether formal or informal, and there is not the slightest hint that she held an official chair. She was never the head of the Neoplatonic school in Alexandria.

Damascius asserts that his master Isidorus was superior to Hypatia as a philosopher is to a mathematician. At best this suggests that Hypatia was probably no first-rank philosopher, and Isidorus was definitely a very bad mathematician. To be sure, it is no great virtue to be a good mathematician in a period in which this meant being able

Hypatia of Alexandria *Conte Crayon drawing of Hypatia.* © BETTMANN/CORBIS.

to understand and expound the mathematical proofs in the treatises of the canonical authors.

In fact, the only two sources mentioning Hypatia's mathematical achievements attest that she was engaged in composing commentaries. The *Suidas*, drawing from Hesychius, reports that she "Here wrote a commentary on Diophantus, the astronomical table, a commentary on Apollonius' *Conics* " (Adler, 1935, 644.3-5). The inscription of Theon's commentary on *Almagest III* reads "Commentary of Theon of Alexandria on the third of Ptolemy's *Mathematical Syntaxis*, the edition having been proof-read by the philosopher Hypatia, my daughter" (Rome, 1943, p. 807). Both testimonies raise serious problems. The wording of the former probably requires emendations and does not allow the reader to decide whether Hypatia wrote an astronomical table or a commentary on such a work (in this case almost surely Ptolemy's *Handy Tables*). The latter option can be doubted, because Theon already had written two commentaries on the same work. However, writing an astronomical table is not the same as editing the text of the *Handy Tables* and the latter proposal too should be dismissed. Even more implausible is the hypothesis that Hypatia compiled new tables of which nothing has survived.

As for the second testimony, one interpretation pictures Hypatia as proofreading the text of the *Almagest* itself in assistance to her father's effort as a commentator, thereby procuring a reliable edition of Ptolemy's treatise. Yet, the minimal interpretation that Hypatia simply checked the final version of Theon's commentary on book III appears by far the most plausible one. Theon's exegeses were first performed as lectures and then redacted in due form, and a checking was necessary-given the presence of non-trivial calculations. Such an authorized copy was the edition alluded to by the inscription. Parallel passages in Eutocius' commentaries confirm that this was the current practice. There have been attempts to detect stylistic differences between the third and the other books of Theon's commentary, but the result is that no differences subsist. A recent and thorough search for Hypatia's own contributions to book III itself rests on arbitrary assumptions about her style and is at bottom circular. Attempts, based on the same stylistic criteria, at assigning Hypatia a role in the very complex tradition of Archimedes' *Dimensio circuli* and at singling out relics from her commentary in the extant commentary by Eutocius on Apollonius' *Conics*, must be regarded as highly hypothetical speculations as well.

Many of the above proposals rest on the questionable assumption that a wide-ranging enterprise of editing and commenting on mathematical texts was undertaken by Theon and his circle. On the contrary, Theon apparently wrote no commentaries on the only two works historians can be reasonably sure he edited, the *Elements* and the *Data*, whereas he commented on treatises that researchers have not the slightest reason to suspect he edited. An analogous net of conjectures has been built upon Hypatia's alleged commentary on Diophantus' *Arithmetica*. The Greek text is incomplete. To explain this, it can be surmised that Hypatia procured a revised and commented text; her commentary arrived as far as the sixth book only and this entailed that the remaining seventh book got lost. The discovery of an Arabic version, containing four more books, disproves such a hypothesis. In its turn, the Arabic text, fairly different in its format, has led to conjecture that it is the translation of a text commented by Hypatia. Difficulties with this proposal are that the Arabic version is a new recension of the treatise, not a commentary, and normally a commentary does not interfere with the text in such a way. Moreover, the modifications with respect to the format of the Greek text are extensive but of no mathematical relevance. It is more charitable to deny than to affirm any Hypatian authorship to such worthless and pedantic additions.

In a letter to a certain Paeonius, Synesius provides a rather clumsy description of a plane astrolabe. As Theon is reported to have written a treatise on the construction of the astrolabe, it is likely that Synesius directly drew from that work, even if he mentions Hypatia as his teacher

Hypatia

on the matter. A reference to a hydroscope in a letter of Synesius to Hypatia is too obscure to be explained except arbitrarily. Such a quantity of entirely conjectural reconstructions is self-perpetuating, as any new hypothesis is allegedly supported by all the others taken as established facts, and very often they consist in questionable projections of doctrines and textual formats typical of some of the works of Hypatia's pupils or relatives.

SUPPLEMENTARY BIBLIOGRAPHY

Adler, A. ed. *Lexicographi Graeci.* Vol. I. *Suidae Lexicon A-W. Index. Pars 4: P-Y.* Leipzig: B.G. Teubner, 1935, 644–646. The entry in *Suidae Lexicon,* vol. IV: 644–646 is the main source on Hypatia. Adler draws in part from Damascius (hence a portion of the entry is edited as fragments 102–105 of Damascius, *Vita Isidori* (see following citation).

Damascius. *Vita Isidori.* Edidit Adnotationibusque Instruxit C. Zintzen. Hildesheim: Georg Olms Verlag, 1967, fragments. 102–105. A part of the *Suidas* entry on Hypatia comes from this work and is here re-edited in the form of fragments.

Cameron, Alan. "Isidore of Miletus and Hypatia: On the Editing of Mathematical Texts." *Greek, Roman and Byzantine Studies* 31 (1990): 103–127. This article contains the analysis of the inscription to Theon's *Commentary, Book III* and the proposal that Hypatia edited the *Almagest.*

Cameron, Alan, and Jacqueline Long. *Barbarians and Politics at the Court of Arcadius.* Berkeley: University of California Press, 1993, 39–62. The authors present a detailed discussion of the extant evidence, still over-optimistic in its assessment of the sources.

Charles, R.H. (trans.), *The Chronicle of John, Bishop of Nikiu.* Oxford: Oxford University Press, 1916, 100–102. A further source on Hypatia. The text is currently available only as an English translation of an Ethiopian version of a (lost) Arabic translation.

Dzielska, Maria. *Hypatia of Alexandria.* Cambridge, MA: Harvard University Press, 1996. Presents an extensive discussion of the extant evidence and contains a very rich bibliography.

Jones, Alexander. "Uses and Users of Astronomical Commentaries in Antiquity." In *Commentaries – Kommentare,* edited by Glenn W. Most. Aporemata: Kritische Studien zur Philologiegeschichte, Band 4. Göttingen: Vandenhoeck und Ruprecht, 1999, 149–172. Alan Cameron's conclusions are criticized in this article.

Knorr, Wilbur R. *Textual Studies in Ancient and Medieval Geometry.* Boston: Birkhäuser, 1989, 753–84. Hypatia's contributions to several extant commentaries and edited works are here singled out.

Rome, Adolphe. *Commentaires de Pappus et de Théon d'Alexandrie sur l'Almageste. Tome III: "Théon d'Alexandrie," Commentaire sur les livres 3 et 4 de l'Almageste.* Texte établi et annoté par A. Rome. Città del Vaticano: Biblioteca Apostolica Vaticana, 1943: cxvi-cxxi. The introduction contains the first stylistic analysis of Theon's *Commentary.*

Saffrey, Henri D. "Hypatie d'Alexandrie." In *Dictionnaire des Philosophes Antiques,* edited by Richard Goulet. Paris: CNRS Editions, 2000. A first orientation, with bibliography, on Hypatia's possible philosophical affiliations.

Sesiano, Jacques, trans. *Books IV to VII of Diophantus' Arithmetica.* Attributed to Qustâ ibn Lûqâ. New York: Springer-Verlag, 1982, 68–75. Hypatia's role in the tradition of *Diophantus'* Arithmetica is discussed here.

Socrates. *Historia Ecclesiastica.* In *Patrologiae Cursus Completus, Accurante J.-P. Migne. Patrologiae Graecae Tomus 67.* Paris: 1864, VII.13–15. A well-balanced exposition of Hypatia's life by a her contemporary.

Synésios de Cyrène, *Tome II: Correspondance: Lettres I-LXIII; Tome III: Correspondance: Lettres LXIV–CLVI.* Texte établi par A. Garzya, traduit par D. Roques. Paris: Les Belles Lettres, 2000.

Tannery, Paul. "L'article de Suidas sur Hypatia." *Annales de la Faculté des Lettres de Bordeaux,* 2 (1880): 197–201, reprinted in *Mémoires Scientifiques,* tome I (1912), no. 7: 74–79. This first critical discussion of the *Suidas* entry was valuable into the early 2000s.

Fabio Acerbi